Standard Catalog of®

World Paper Money

12th OFFICIAL Edition

Modern Issues • 1961-Present

Edited by George S. Cuhaj

Data Entry Coordinator
Lori Anderson

Book Designer
Sally Olson

Cover/Color Section Designers
Kara Grundman, Marilyn McGrane

Special Contributors
Colin R. Bruce II, Ricardo Faillace,
Flemming Lyngbeck Hansen, Art Matz,
Juozas Minikevicius, Jon Morowitz, Tony Pisciotta,
Kavan Ratnatunga, Neil Shafer

©2006 KP Books

Published by

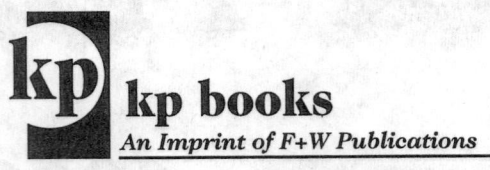

kp books
An Imprint of F+W Publications

700 East State Street • Iola, WI 54990-0001
715-445-2214 • 888-457-2873

Our toll-free number to place an order or obtain
a free catalog is (800) 258-0929.

Library of Congress Catalog Number: 1538-2028

ISBN: 978-0-89689-356-6
ISBN: 0-89689-356-6-1

Printed in the United States of America

INTRODUCTION

Welcome to the 12th edition of the Standard Catalog of World Paper Money, Modern Issues.

For those of you already familiar with this volume, you will note numerous enhancements and additions to the text as well as illustrations. Extensive specimen varieties continue to be added throughout

In our constant endeavor to provide as much detail as possible, we have added illustrations and more detailed text and signature information. Extensive price analysis has been performed to provide timely insight to the ever-changing world paper money marketplace. Renumbering has been held to an absolute minimum, except for Fiji which received extensive review.

For the ease of identification, notes are listed under their historic country identification (British Honduras is no longer hidden within Belize). Notes of a particular bank are listed in release date order, and then grouped in ascending denomination order. In the cases of countries where more than one issuing authority is in effect at a single time, follow the bank headings in the listings and it will become apparent if that country's listing is by date or alphabetical by issuing authority. In the cases where a country has changed from a kingdom to a republic all the banknotes of the kingdom's era would be listed before that of the republic.

An Invitation

Users of this catalog may find a helpful adjunct to be the Bank Note Reporter, the only monthly newspaper devoted exclusively to North American and world paper money. Each issue presents up-to-date news, feature articles and valuable information. All purchasers of this catalog are invited to subscribe to the Bank Note Reporter. Requests for a sample copy should be addressed to Bank Note Reporter, 700 East State Street, Iola, WI, 54990-0001.

A review of modern paper money collecting

Paper money collecting is as old as paper money itself. This segment of the numismatic hobby did not begin to reach a popularity approaching that of coin collecting until the latter half of the 1970's. While coins and paper money are alike in that both served as legal obligations to facilitate commerce, long-time paper money enthusiasts know the similarity ends there.

Coins were historically guaranteed by the intrinsic value of their metallic content - at least until recent years when virtually all circulating coins have become little more than legal tender tokens, containing little or no precious metal - while paper money possesses a value only when it is accepted for debts or converted into bullion or precious metals. With many note issues, this conversion privilege was limited and ultimately negated by the imposition of redemption cutoff dates.

The development of widespread collector interest in paper money of most nations was inhibited by a near total absence of adequate documentation. No more than three and a half decades ago collectors could refer to only a few catalogs and dealer price lists of limited scope, most of which were difficult to acquire, or

they could build their own knowledge through personal collecting pursuits and contact with fellow collectors.

The early catalogs authored by Albert Pick chronicled issues of Europe and the Americas and were assembled as stepping-stones to the ultimate objective, which became reality with publication of the first Standard Catalog of World Paper Money in 1975. That work provided collectors with fairly complete listings and up-to-date valuations of all recorded government note issues of the 20th century, incorporating Pick's previously unpublished manuscripts on Africa, Asia and Oceania, plus many earlier issues.

This completely revised and updated 11th Edition of Volume III, Modern Issues, along with the companion 10th Edition Volume II General Issues, presents a substantial extension of the cataloging effort initiated in 1975 and revised in succeeding editions. As the most comprehensive world paper money references ever assembled, they fully document the many and varied legal tender paper currencies issued and circulated by over 380 past and current government issuing authorities of the world from 1300's to present.

George S. Cuhaj
Editor

TABLE OF CONTENTS

ADVERTISER INDEX

COUNTRY INDEX

— 12th EDITION —
ACKNOWLEDGMENTS

Over time contributor enhancements to this catalog have been many and varied, and to recognize them all would be a volume in itself. Accordingly, we wish to acknowledge these invaluable collectors, scholars and dealers in the world paper money field, both past and present, for their specific contributions to this work through the submission of notes for illustration, improved descriptive information and market valuations.

Emmanuel K. Aboagye
Dundar Acikalin
Jim Adams
Esko Ahlroth
Jan Alexandersson
Paulo Almeida
Milan Alusic
Carl A. Anderson
Dr. Jorge E. Arbelaez
Donald Arnone
David B. August
Thomas Augustsson
Keith Austin
Cem Barlok
Adriaan C. F. Beck
Dan Bellan
Daniel Bena
Abdullah Beydoun
Milt Blackburn
Ed Bohannon
Joseph E. Boling
Arthur John Boyko
Wilfried A. Bracke
Jean Bricaud
Alejandro Brill
Robert J. Brooks
Mahdi Bseiso
Christopher J. Budesa
Weldon D. Burson
Doru Calin
Lance K. Campbell
David Carew
Arthur Chadwick
Arthur D. Cohen
George Conrad
Scott E. Cordry
Guido Crapanzano
Ray Czahor
Thomas Dallmann
Howard A. Daniel III
C. M. Desai
Jacques Desbordes
Bruce Donahue
Duane Douglas
Michel Dufour

James A. Downey
Arnoldo Efron
Wilhelm Eglseer
Jos F. M. Eijsermans
Esko Ekman
Wilfred Faroh
Ricardo Faillace
Edward Feltcorn
Mark Fox
W. A. Frick
Brian Giese
Vanjo Grobljar
Edmund Hakimian
Murray Hanewich
Flemming Lyngbeck Hansen
Len Harsel
Mark Hartford
Allan Hauck
William G. Henderson
Robert W. Holbrook
Victor S. Holden
Anton Holt
Armen Hovsepian
Yu Jian Hua
Mikhail Istomin
Jaya Hari Jha
A. J. Jacobs
Edouard Jean-Pierre
Kishore Jhunjhunwalla
Erik Johansen
William M. Judd
Alex Kaglyan
Olaf Kiemer
Josef Klaus
Ladislav Klaus
Michael E. Knabe
Tristan Kolm
Lazare Kouami
David C. Kranz
Chester L. Krause
Michael Kvasnica
Samson K.C. Lai
Michael Lang
Morris Lawing
Akos Ledai

Dr. Edmund Lee
C. K. Leong
Raymond Lloyd
Claire Lobel
Don Ludwig
Alan Luedeking
Stu Lumsden
Dr. Dennis Lutz
Martin MacDaid
Ma Tak Wo
Ranko Mandic
Claudio Marana
Rolf Marklin
Ian Marshall
John T. Martin
Arthur C. Matz
William McNatt
Ali Mehilba
Marvin E. Mericle
Daniel Meyer
Juozas Minikevicius
Arthur Morowitz
Jon Morowitz
Michael Morris
Rene Muller
Richard Murdoch
Wiliam J. Myers
Quoc Nguyen
Andrew Oberbillig
Fred O'Connell
Geoffrey P. Oldham
Frank Passic
Antonio E. Pedraza
Juan Pena
Tony Pisciotta
Laurence Pope
Savo Popovic
Richard Puls
Yahya J. Qureshi
Nazir Rahemtulla
Kavan Ratnatunga
Rudolph Richter
Mircea Raicopol
Bob Reis
John Rishel

William Rosenblum
Alan Sadd
Karl Saethre
Robert Sayre
Walter Schmidt
Wolfgang Schuster
Harmut Schoewa
Christian Selvais
Victor C. Seper
Joel Shafer
Neil Shafer
Ladislav Sin
Lee Sing Song
Evzen Sknouril
Gary F. Snover
Mauricio Soto
Jimmie C. Steelman
Herbert Stein
Jeremy Steinberg
Mel Steinberg
Tim Steiner
Georg H. Stocker
Zeljko Stojanovic
Alim A. Sumana
Peter Symes
Imre Szatmari
Steven Tan
Frank Tesson
Reinhardt Tetting
Anthony Tumonis
W. J. van der Drift
Jan Vandersade
Norbert von Euw
Michael Vort-Ronald
Ludek Vostal
Evangelos Vyzas
Wakim Wakim
Stewart Westdal
Trevor Wilkin
Peter L. Willems
Dr. Heinz Wirz
Joseph Zaffern
Christof Zellweger

ASSOCIATION & CENTRAL BANKS

American Numismatic Association
International Bank Note Society

American Numismatic Society
L.A.N.S.A.

Smithsonian Institution
East Midland Chapter, I.B.N.S.

Le Change des Monnaies Etrangers
by R. L. Martin. 12, rue Poincaré, F 55800 Revigny, France.
(Illustrated guide of current world bank notes.)

MRI Bankers' Guide to Foreign Currency
by Arnoldo Efron, Monetary Research Institute, P.O. Box 3174, Houston, Texas, U.S.A., 77253-3174.
(Quarterly illustrated guide of current world bank notes and travelers checks.)

ISSUER & BANK INDEX

HOW TO USE THIS CATALOG

Catalog listings consist of all regular and provisional notes attaining wide circulation in their respective countries for the period covered. Notes have been listed under the historical country name. Thus Dahomey is not under Benin, and so on, as had been the case in some past catalogs. Where catalog numbers have changed, and you may find some renumbering in this edition, the old catalog numbers appear in parentheses directly below the new number. The listings continue to be grouped by issue range rather than by denomination, and a slight change in the listing format should make the bank name, issue dates as well as catalog numbers and denominations easier to locate. These changes have been made to make the catalog as easy to use as possible for you.

The editors and publisher make no claim to absolute completeness, just as they acknowledge that some errors and pricing inequities will appear. Correspondence is invited with interested persons who have notes previously unlisted or who have information to enhance the presentation of existing listings in succeeding editions of this catalog.

Catalog Format

Listings proceed generally according to the following sequence: country, geographic or political, chronology, bank name and sometimes alphabetically or by date of first issue. Release within the bank, most often in date order, but sometimes by printer first.

Catalog number — The basic reference number at the beginning of each listing for each note. For this Modern Issues volume the regular listings require no prefix letters except when 'A' or 'B' appear within the catalog number. (Military and Regional prefixes are explained later in this section.)

Denomination — the value as shown on the note, in western numerals. When denominations are only spelled out, consult the numerics chart.

Date — the actual issue date as printed on the note in day-month-year order. Where more than one date appears on a note, only the latest is used. Where the note has no date, the designation ND is used,.followed by a year date in parentheses when it is known. If a note is dated by the law or decree of authorization, the date appears with an L or D and is italicized.

Descriptions of the note are broken up into one or more items as follows:

Color — the main color(s) of the face, and the underprint are given first. If the colors of the back are different, then they follow the face design description.

Design — The identification and location of the main design elements if known. Back design elements identified if known.

If design elements and or signatures are the same for an issue group then they are printed only once at the heading of the issue, and apply for the group that follows.

Printer — often a local printer has the name shown in full. Abbreviations are used for the most prolific printers. Refer to the list of printer abbreviations elsewhere in this introduction. In these listings the use of the term "imprint" refers to the logo or the printer's name as usually appearing in the bottom frame or below in the margin of the note.

Valuations — are generally given under the grade headings of Good, Fine and Extremely Fine for early notes; and Very Good, Very Fine and Uncirculated for the later issues. Listings that do not follow these two patterns are clearly indicated. UNC followed by a value is used usually for specimens and proofs when lower grade headings are used for a particular series of issued notes.

Catalog prefix or suffix letters

A catalog number preceded by a capital 'A' indicated the incorporation of an earlier listing as required by type or date; a capital letter following the catalog number usually shows the addition of a later issue. Both may indicate newly discovered lower or higher denominations to a series. Listings of notes for regional circulation are distinguished from regular national issues with the prefix letter 'R'; military issues use a 'M' prefix; foreign exchange certificates are assigned a 'FX' prefix. Varieties, specific date or signature listings are shown with small letters 'a' following a number within their respective entries. Some standard variety letters include: 'p' for proof notes, 'r' for remainder notes, 's' for specimen notes and 'x' for errors.

Denominations

The denomination as indicated on many notes issued by a string of countries stretching from eastern Asia, through western Asia and on across northern Africa, often appears only in unfamiliar non-Western numeral styles. With the listings that follow, denominations are always indicated in Western numerals.

A comprehensive chart keying Western numerals to their non-Western counterparts is included elsewhere in this introduction as an aid to the identification of note types. This compilation features not only the basic numeral systems such as Arabic, Japanese and Indian, but also the more restricted systems such as Burmese, Ethiopian, Siamese, Tibetan, Hebrew, Mongolian and Korean. Additionally, the list includes other localized variations that have been applied to some paper money issues.

In consulting the numeral systems chart to determine the denomination of a note, one should remember that the actual numerals styles employed in any given area, or at a particular time, may vary significantly from these basic representations. Such variations can be deceptive to the untrained eye, just as variations from Western numeral styles can prove deceptive to individuals not acquainted with the particular style employed.

Dates and Date Listing Policy

In previous editions of this work it was the goal to provide a sampling of the many date varieties that were believed to exist. In recent times, as particular dates (and usually signature combinations) were known to be scarcer, that particular series was expanded to include listings of individual dates. At times this idea has been fully incorporated, but with some series it is not practicable, especially when just about every day in a given month could have been an issue date for the notes.

Accordingly, where it seems justifiable that date spans can be realistically filled with individual dates, this has been done. In order to accommodate the many new dates, the idea of providing variety letters to break them up into narrower spans of years has been used. If it appears that there are too many dates for a series, with no major differences in value, then a general inclusive date span is used (beginning and ending) and individual dates within this span are not shown.

For those notes showing only a general date span, the only important dates become those that expand the range of years, months or days earlier or later. But even they would have no impact on the values shown.

Because a specific date is not listed does not necessarily mean it is rare. It may be just that it has not been reported. Those date varieties known to be scarcer are cataloged separately. Newly reported dates in a wide variety of listings are constantly being reported. This indicates that research into the whole area is very active, and a steady flow of new dates is fully expected upon publication of this edition.

Abbreviations

Certain abbreviations have been adopted for words occurring frequently in note descriptions. Following is a list of these:

#	-	number (catalog or serial)
bldg.	-	building
ctr.	-	center
dk.	-	dark
FV	-	face value
Gen.	-	General
govt.	-	government
Kg.	-	king
l.	-	left
lg.	-	large
lt.	-	light
m/c	-	multicolored
ND	-	no date
ovpt.	-	overprint
portr.	-	portrait
Qn.	-	queen
r.	-	right
sign.	-	signature or signatures
sm.	-	small
unpt.	-	underprint (background printing)
wmk.	-	watermark
w/	-	with
w/o	-	without

Valuations

Valuations are given for most notes in three grades. Earlier issues are usually valued in the grade headings of Good, Fine and Extremely Fine; later issues take the grade headings of Very Good, Very Fine and Uncirculated. While it is true that some early notes cannot be valued in Extremely Fine and some later notes have no premium value in Very Good, it is felt that this coverage provides the best uniformity of value data to the collecting community. There are exceptional cases where headings are adjusted for either single notes or a series that really needs special treatment.

Valuations are determined generally from a consensus of individuals submitting prices for evaluation. Some notes have NO values; this does not necessarily mean they are expensive or even rare, but it shows that no pricing information was forthcoming. A number of notes have a 'Rare' designation, and no values. Such notes are generally not available on the market, and when they do appear the price is a matter between buyer and seller. No book can provide guidance in these instances except to indicate rarity.

Valuations used in this book are based on the IBNS grading standards and are stated in U.S. dollars. They serve only as aids in evaluating paper money since actual market conditions throughout the worldwide collector community are constantly changing. In addition, particularly choice examples of many issues listed often bring higher premiums than values listed. Users should remember that a catalog such as this is only a guide to values.

FV (for Face Value) is used as a value designation on new issues as well as older but still redeemable legal tender notes in lower conditions. FV may appear in one or both condition columns before Uncirculated, depending on the relative age and availability of the note in question.

Collection care

The proper preservation of a collection should be of paramount importance to all in the hobby - dealers, collectors and scholars. Only a person who has housed notes in a manner giving pleasure to him or herself and others will keep alive the pleasure of collecting for future generations. The same applies to the way of housing as to the choice of the collecting specialty: it is chiefly a question of what most pleases the individual collector.

Arrangement and sorting of a collection is most certainly a basic requirement. Storing the notes in safe paper envelopes and filing boxes should, perhaps, be considered only when building a new section of a collection, for accommodating varieties or for reasons of saving space when the collection has grown quickly.

Many paper money collections are probably housed in some form of plastic-pocketed album, which are today manufactured in many different sizes and styles to accommodate many types of world paper money. Because the number of bank note collectors has grown continually over the past thirty-five years, some specialty manufacturers of albums have developed a paper money selection. The notes, housed in clear plastic pockets, individually or in groups, can be viewed and exchanged without difficulty. These albums are not cheap, but the notes displayed in this manner do make a lasting impression on the viewer.

A word of concern: certain types of plastic and all vinyl used for housing notes may cause notes to become brittle over time, or cause an irreversible and harmful transfer of oils from the vinyl onto the bank notes.

The high demand for quality that stamp collectors make on their products cannot be transferred to the paper money collecting fraternity. A postage stamp is intended for a single use, then is relegated to a collection. With paper money, it is nearly impossible to acquire uncirculated specimens from a number of countries because of export laws or internal bank procedures. Bends from excessive counting, or even staple holes, are commonplace. Once acquiring a circulated note, the collector must endeavor to maintain its state of preservation.

The fact that there is a classification and value difference between notes with greater use or even damage is a matter of course. It is part of the opinion and personal taste of the individual collector to decide what is considered worthy of collecting and what to pay for such items.

For the purposed of strengthening and mending torn paper money, under no circumstances should one use plain cellophane tape or a similar material. These tapes warp easily, with sealing marks forming at the edges, and the tape frequently discolors. Only with the greatest of difficulty (and often not at all) can these tapes be removed, and damage to the note or the printing is almost unavoidable. The best material for mending tears is an archival tape recommended for the treatment and repair of documents.

There are collectors who, with great skill, remove unsightly spots, repair badly damaged notes, replace missing pieces and otherwise restore or clean a note. There is a question of morality by tampering with a note to improve its condition, either by repairing, starching, ironing, pressing or other methods to possibly deceive a potential future buyer. Such a question must, in the final analysis, be left to the individual collector.

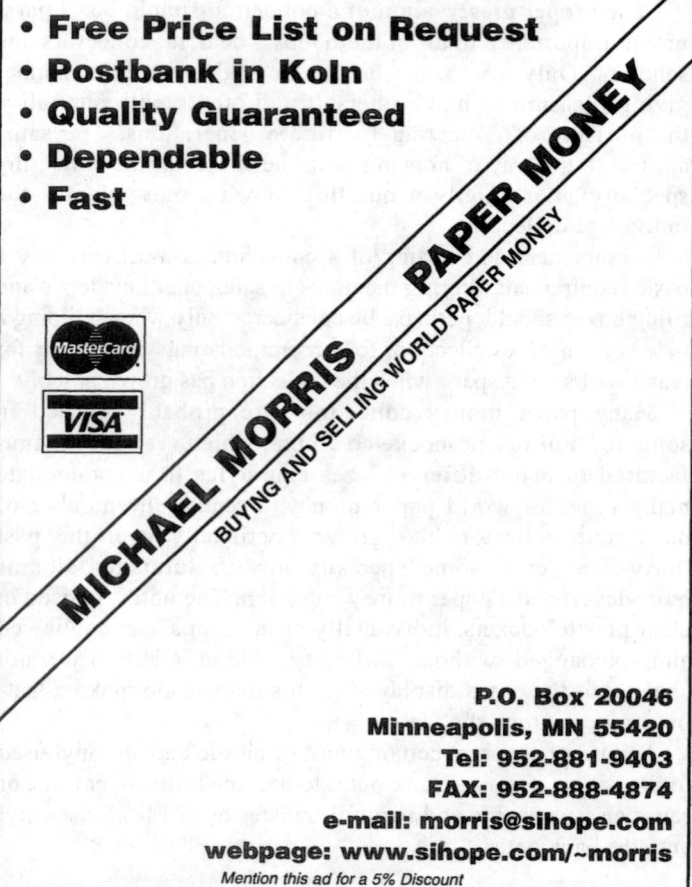

IBNS GRADING STANDARDS FOR WORLD PAPER MONEY

The following introduction and Grading Guide is the result of work prepared under the guidance of the Grading Committee of the International Bank Note Society (IBNS). It has been adopted as the official grading standards of that society.

Introduction

Grading is the most controversial component of paper money collecting today. Small differences in grade can mean significant Vdifferences in value. The process of grading is so subjective and dependent on external influences such as lighting, that even a very experienced individual may well grade the same note differently on separate occasions.

To facilitate communication between sellers and buyers, it is essential that grading terms and their meanings be as standardized and as widely used as possible. This standardization should reflect common usage as much as practicable. One difficulty with grading is that even the actual grades themselves are not used everywhere by everyone. For example, in Europe the grade 'About Uncirculated' (AU) is not in general use, yet in North America it is widespread. The European term 'Good VF' may roughly correspond to what individuals in North America call 'Extremely Fine' (EF).

The grades and definitions as set forth below cannot reconcile all the various systems and grading terminology variants. Rather, the attempt is made here to try and diminish the controversy with some common-sense grades and definitions that aim to give more precise meaning to the grading language of paper money.

How to look at a banknote

In order to ascertain the grade of a note, it is essential to examine it out of a holder and under a good light. Move the note around so that light bounces off of it at different angles. Try holding the note obliquely, so the note is even with your eye as you look up at the light. Hard-to-see folds or slight creases will show up under such examination. Some individuals also lightly feel along the surface of the note to detect creasing.

Cleaning, Washing, Pressing of Banknotes

a) Cleaning, washing or pressing paper money is generally harmful and reduces both the grade and the value of a note. At the very least, a washed or pressed note may lose its original sheen and its surface may become lifeless and dull. The defects a note had, such as folds and creases, may not necessarily be completely eliminated and their telltale marks can be detected under a good light. Carelessly washed notes may also have white streaks where the folds or creases were (or still are).

b) Processing of a note which started out as Extremely Fine will automatically reduce it at least one full grade.

Unnatural Defects

Glue, tape or pencil marks may sometimes be successfuly removed. While such removal will leave a cleaned surface, it will improve the overall appearance of the note without concealing any of its defects. Under such circumstances, the grade of that note may also be improved.

The words "pinholes", "staple holes", "trimmed", "graffiti", "writing on face", "tape marks" etc. should always be added to the description of a note. It is realized that certain countries routinely staple their notes together in groups before issue. In such cases, the description can include a comment such as "usual staple holes" or something similar. After all, not everyone knows that certain notes cannot be found otherwise.

The major point of this section is that one cannot lower the overall grade of a note with defects simply because of the defects. The value will reflect the lowered worth of a defective note, but the description must always include the specific defects.

GRADING
Definitions of Terms

UNCIRCULATED: A perfectly preserved note, never mishandled by the issuing authority, a bank teller, the public or a collector.

Paper is clean and firm, without discoloration. Corners are sharp and square without any evidence of rounding. (Rounded corners are often a tell-tale sign of a cleaned or "doctored" note.)

NOTE: Some note issuers are most often available with slight evidence of very light counting folds which do not "break" the paper. Also, French-printed notes usually have a slight ripple in the paper. Many collectors and dealers refer to such notes as AU-UNC.

ABOUT UNCIRCULATED: A virtually perfect note, with some minor handling. May show very slight evidence of bank counting folds at a corner or one light fold through the center, but not both. An AU note canot be creased, a crease being a hard fold which has usually "broken" the surface of the note.

Paper is clean and bright with original sheen. Corners are not rounded.

NOTE: Europeans will refer to an About Uncirculated or AU note as "EF-Unc" or as just "EF". The Extremely Fine note described below will often be referred to as "GVF" or "Good Very Fine".

EXTREMELY FINE: A very attractive note, with light handling. May have a maximum of three light folds or one strong crease.

Paper is clean and firm, without discoloration. Corners are sharp and square without any evidence of rounding. (Rounded corners are often a tell-tale sign of a cleaned or "doctored" note.)

VERY FINE: An attractive note, but with more evidence of handling and wear. May have several folds both vertically and horizontally.

Paper may have minimal dirt, or possible color smudging. Paper itself is still relatively crisp and not floppy.

There are no tears into the border area, although the edges do show slight wear. Corners also show wear but not full rounding.

FINE: A note that shows consideralble circulation, with many folds, creases and wrinkling.

Paper is not excessively dirty but may have some softness.

Edges may show much handling, with minor tears in the border area. Tears may not extend into the design. There will be no center hole because of excessive folding.

Colors are clear but not very bright. A staple hole or two would would not be considered unusual wear in a Fine note. Overall appearance is still on the desirable side.

VERY GOOD: A well used note, abused but still intact.

Corners may have much wear and rounding, tiny nicks, tears may extend into the design, some discoloration may be prsent, staining may have occurred, and a small hole may sometimes be seen at center from excessive folding.

Staple and pinholes are usually present, and the note itself is quite limp but NQ pieces of the note can be missing. A note in VG condition may still have an overall not unattractive appearance.

GOOD: A well worn and heavily used note. Normal damage from prolonged circulation will include strong multiple folds and creases, stains, pinholes and/or staple holes, dirt, discoloration, edge tears, center hole, rounded corners and an overall unattractive appearance. No large pieces of the note may be missing. Graffiti is commonly seen on notes in G condition.

FAIR: A totally limp, dirty and very well used note. Larger pieces may be half torn off or missing besides the defects mentioned under the Good category. Tears will be larger, obscured portions of the note will be bigger.

POOR: A "rag" with severe damage because of wear, staining, pieces missing, graffiti, larger holes. May have tape holding pieces of the note together. Trimming may have taken place to remove rough edges. A Poor note is desiralble only as a "filler" or when such a note is the only one known of that particular issue.

A word on crimps to otherwise uncirculated notes. Due to inclusion of wide security foils, crimps appear at the top and bottom edge during production or counting. Thus notes which are uncirculated have a crimp. Examples without these crimps are beginning to command a premium.

STANDARD INTERNATIONAL GRADING TERMINOLOGY AND ABBREVIATIONS

U.S. and ENGLISH SPEAKING LANDS	UNCIRCULATED	EXTREMELY FINE	VERY FINE	FINE	VERY GOOD	GOOD	POOR
Abbreviation	UNC	EF or XF	VF	FF	VG	G	PR
BRAZIL	(1) DW	(3) S	(5) MBC	(7) BC	(8)	(9) R	UTGeG
DENMARK	O	O1	1+	1	1+	2	3
FINLAND	0	01	1+	1	1?	2	3
FRANCE	NEUF	SUP	TTB or TB	TB or TB	B	TBC	BC
GERMANY	KFR	II / VZGL	III / SS	IV / S	V / S.g.E.	VI / G.e.	G.e.s.
ITALY	FdS	SPL	BB	MB	B	M	—
JAPAN	未使用	極美品	美品	並品	—	—	—
NETHERLANDS	FDC	Pr.	Z.F.	Fr.	Z.g.	G	—
NORWAY	0	01	1+	1	1+	2	3
PORTUGAL	Novo	Soberbo	Muito bo	—	—	—	—
SPAIN	Lujo	SC, IC or EBC	MBC	BC	—	RC	MC
SWEDEN	0	01	1+	1	1?	2	—

STANDARD INTERNATIONAL NUMERAL SYSTEMS

PREPARED ESPECIALLY FOR THE **STANDARD CATALOG OF WORLD PAPER MONEY**© 2006 BY KP Books

WESTERN	0	½	1	2	3	4	5	6	7	8	9	10	50	100	500	1000
ROMAN			I	II	III	IV	V	VI	VII	VIII	IX	X	L	C	D	M
ARABIC-TURKISH	•	۱/۲	١	٢	٣	٤	٥	٦	٧	٨	٩	١٠	٥٠	١٠٠	٥٠٠	١٠٠٠
MALAY-PERSIAN	•	۱/۲	١	٢	٣	٤	٥	٦ or ۷	٧	٨	٩	١٠	٥٠	١٠٠	٥٠٠	١٠٠٠
EASTERN ARABIC	0	½	١	٢	٣	٤	٥	٦	٧	٩	9	١٠	٤١٠	١٠٠	٤١٠٠	١٠٠٠
HYDERABAD ARABIC	0	۱/۲	١	٢	٣	٤	٥	٤	‹	٨	٩	10	٥٠	100	٥٠٠	1000
INDIAN (Sanskrit)	०	½	१	२	३	४	५	६	७	८	९	१०	४०	१००	४००	१०००
ASSAMESE	০	৹/২	১	২	৩	৪	৫	৬	৭	৮	৯	১০	50	১০০	500	১০০০
BENGALI	০	৷৴২	১	২	৩	৪	৫	৬	৭	৮	৯	১০	৫০	১০০	৫০০	১০০০
GUJARATI	૦	૧/૨	૧	૨	૩	૪	૫	૬	૭	૮	૯	૧૦	૪૦	૧૦૦	૪૦૦	૧૦૦૦
KUTCH	०	⅓	૧	ર	૩	૪	૫	૬	૭	૮	૮	10	૪૦	100	૪૦૦	1000
DEVAVNAGRI	०	૧/૨	૧	૨	३	४	५	६	૭	८	९	९०	४०	९००	४००	९०००
NEPALESE	०	⅓	૧૧	૨	૩	४	૪૫	६	७	८	९	10	४०	100	४००	१०००
TIBETAN	०	༠/༢	༡	༢	༣	༤	༥	༦	༧	༨	༩	༧༠	༤༠	༧༠༠	༤༠༠	༧༠༠༠
MONGOLIAN	᠐	½	᠑	᠒	᠓	᠔	᠕	᠖	᠗	᠘	᠙	᠑᠐	᠕᠐	᠑᠐᠐	᠕᠐᠐	᠑᠐᠐᠐
BURMESE	၀	⅔	၁	၂	၃	၄	၅	၆	၇	၈	၉	၁၀	၅၀	၁၀၀	၅၀၀	၁၀၀၀
THAI-LAO	๐	⅚	๑	๒	๓	๔	๕	๖	๗	๘	๙	๑๐	๕๐	๑๐๐	๕๐๐	๑๐๐๐
JAVANESE	꧐		꧑	꧒	꧓	꧔	꧕	꧖	꧗	꧘	꧙	꧑꧐	꧕꧐	꧑꧐꧐	꧕꧐꧐	꧑꧐꧐꧐
ORDINARY CHINESE JAPANESE-KOREAN	零	半	一	二	三	四	五	六	七	八	九	十	十五	百	百五	千
OFFICIAL CHINESE			壹	貳	叁	肆	伍	陸	柒	捌	玖	拾	拾伍	佰	佰伍	仟
COMMERCIAL CHINESE			〡	〢	〣	乂	〥	〦	〧	〨	〩	十	〥十	百	〥百	十千
KOREAN		반	일	이	삼	사	오	육	칠	팔	구	십	오십	백	오백	천

GEORGIAN			ა	ბ	გ	დ	ე	ვ	ზ	თ	ი	კ	ლ	მ	ნ	ჟ
			[11]	[20]	[30]	[40]	[50]	[60]	[70]	[80]	[90]	[100]	[200]	[300]	[400]	[600] [700] [800]
			ჲ	ჳ	ჴ	ჵ	ჶ	ჷ	ჸ	ჹ	ჺ	ჼ	ჽ	ჾ	ჿ	

ETHIOPIAN	◆		፩	፪	፫	፬	፭	፮	፯	፰	፱	፲	፶	፻		
			[20] ፳	[30] ፴	[40] ፵		[60] ፷	[70] ፸	[80] ፹	[90] ፺						

HEBREW			א	ב	ג	ד	ה	ו	ז	ח	ט	י	נ	ק	תק	
			[20] כ	[30] ל	[40] מ		[60] ס	[70] ע	[80] פ	[90] צ		[200] ר	[300] ש	[400] ת	[600] תר [700] תש [800] תת	

GREEK			Α	Β	Γ	Δ	Ε	ΣΤ	Ζ	Η	Θ	Ι	Ν	Ρ	Φ	Α
			[20] Κ	[30] Λ	[40] Μ		[60] Ξ	[70] Ο	[80] Π		[200] Σ	[300] Τ	[400] Υ	[600] Χ	[700] Ψ	[800] Ω

Foreign Exchange Table

The latest foreign exchange fixed rates below apply to trade with banks in the country of origin. The left column shows the number of units per U.S. dollar at the official rate. The right column shows the number of units per dollar at the free market rate.

Country	Official #/$	Market #/$
Afghanistan (New Afghani)	42.8	–
Albania (Lek)	95.5	–
Algeria (Dinar)	72	–
Andorra uses Euro	.76	–
Angola (Readjust Kwanza)	87	–
Anguilla uses E.C.Dollar	2.67	–
Antigua uses E.C.Dollar	2.67	–
Argentina (Peso)	2.93	–
Armenia (Dram)	470	–
Aruba (Florin)	1.79	–
Australia (Dollar)	1.264	–
Austria (Euro)	.76	–
Azerbaijan (Manat)	4,900	–
Bahamas (Dollar)	1.0	–
Bahrain Is.(Dinar)	.377	–
Bangladesh (Taka)	63	–
Barbados (Dollar)	1.99	–
Belarus (Ruble)	2,160	–
Belgium (Euro)	.76	–
Belize (Dollar)	1.97	–
Benin uses CFA Franc West	495	–
Bermuda (Dollar)	.99	–
Bhutan (Ngultrum)	43.6	–
Bolivia (Boliviano)	8.07	–
Bosnia-Herzegovina (Deutschmark)	1.49	–
Botswana (Pula)	4.46	–
British Virgin Islands uses U.S.Dollar	1.00	–
Brazil (Real)	2.66	–
Brunei (Dollar)	1.63	–
Bulgaria (Lev)	1.48	–
Burkina Faso uses CFA Fr.West	495	–
Burma (Kyat)	6.42	1,250
Burundi (Franc)	1,080	–
Cambodia (Riel)	3,850	–
Cameroon uses CFA Franc Central	495	–
Canada (Dollar)	1.23	–
Cape Verde (Escudo)	83	–
Cayman Is.(Dollar)	0.82	–
Central African Rep.	495	–
CFA Franc Central	495	–
CFA Franc West	495	–
CFP Franc	90.5	–
Chad uses CFA Franc Central	495	–
Chile (Peso)	585	–
China, P.R. (Renminbi Yuan)	8.276	–
Colombia (Peso)	2,330	–
Comoros (Franc)	375	–
Congo uses CFA Franc Central	495	–
Congo-Dem.Rep. (Congolese Franc)	495	–
Cook Islands (Dollar)	1.73	–
Costa Rica (Colon)	466	–
Croatia (Kuna)	5.63	–
Cuba (Peso)	1.00	27
Cyprus (Pound)	.44	–
Czech Republic (Koruna)	23.4	–
Denmark (Danish Krone)	5.62	–
Djibouti (Franc)	172	–
Dominica uses E.C.Dollar	2.67	–
Dominican Republic (Peso)	27.5	–
East Caribbean (Dollar)	2.67	–
Ecuador uses U.S. Dollar	1.00	–
Egypt (Pound)	5.81	–
El Salvador uses U.S. Dollar	1.00	–
Equatorial Guinea uses CFA Franc Central	495	–
Eritrea (Nafka)	15	–
Estonia (Kroon)	11.8	–
Ethiopia (Birr)	8.6	–
Euro	.76	–
Falkland Is. (Pound)	.52	–
Faroe Islands (Krona)	5.62	–
Fiji Islands (Dollar)	1.64	–
Finland (Euro)	.76	–
France (Euro)	.76	–
French Polynesia uses CFP Franc	90.5	–
Gabon (CFA Franc)	495	–
Gambia (Dalasi)	29.5	–
Georgia (Lari)	1.84	–
Germany (Euro)	.76	–
Ghana (Cedi)	9,020	–
Gibraltar (Pound)	.52	–
Greece (Euro)	.76	–
Greenland uses Danish Krone	5.96	–
Grenada uses E.C.Dollar	2.67	–
Guatemala (Quetzal)	7.65	–
Guernsey (Pound Sterling)	.52	–
Guinea Bissau (CFA Franc)	495	–
Guinea Conakry (Franc)	2,850	–
Guyana (Dollar)	180	–
Haiti (Gourde)	36.3	–
Honduras (Lempira)	18.8	–
Hong Kong (Dollar)	7.80	–
Hungary (Forint)	180	–
Iceland (Krona)	60.4	–
India (Rupee)	43.6	–
Indonesia (Rupiah)	9,350	–
Iran (Rial)	8,860	–
Iraq (Dinar)	1,460	1,930
Ireland (Euro)	.76	–
Isle of Man (Pound Sterling)	.52	–
Israel (New Sheqalim)	4.33	–
Italy (Euro)	.76	–
Ivory Coast uses CFA Franc West	495	–
Jamaica (Dollar)	61.2	–
Japan (Yen)	105	–
Jersey (Pound Sterling)	.52	–
Jordan (Dinar)	.71	–
Kazakhstan (Tenge)	130	–
Kenya (Shilling)	76	–
Kiribati uses Australian Dollar	1.264	–
Korea-PDR (Won)	2.2	500
Korea-Rep. (Won)	1,010	–
Kuwait (Dinar)	.292	–
Kyrgyzstan (Som)	40.7	–
Laos (Kip)	7,840	–
Latvia (Lat)	.53	–
Lebanon (Pound)	1,515	–
Lesotho (Maloti)	5.93	–
Liberia (Dollar) "JJ"	1.00	20.00
"Liberty"	–	40.00
Libya (Dinar)	1.3	–
Liechtenstein uses Swiss Franc	1.17	–
Lithuania (Litas)	2.61	–
Luxembourg (Euro)	.76	–
Macao (Pataca)	8.01	–
Macedonia (New Denar)	47.2	–
Madagascar (Franc)	1,900	–
Malawi (Kwacha)	108	–
Malaysia (Ringgit)	3.8	–
Maldives (Rufiya)	12.97	–
Mali uses CFA Franc West	495	–
Malta (Lira)	.33	–
Marshall Islands uses U.S.Dollar	1.00	–
Mauritania (Ouguiya)	260	–
Mauritius (Rupee)	28.7	–
Mexico (Peso)	11.03	–
Moldova (Leu)	12.61	–
Monaco uses Euro	.76	–
Mongolia (Tugrik)	1,205	–
Montenegro uses Euro	.76	–
Montserrat uses E.C.Dollar	2.67	–
Morocco (Dirham)	8.42	–
Mozambique (Metical)	18,750	–
Myanmar (Burma) (Kyat)	6.42	1,250
Namibia (Rand)	5.96	–
Nauru uses Australian Dollar	1.264	–
Nepal (Rupee)	72	–
Netherlands (Euro)	.76	–
Netherlands Antilles (Gulden)	1.78	–
New Caledonia uses CFP Franc	90.5	–
New Zealand (Dollar)	1.365	–
Nicaragua (Cordoba Oro)	16.2	–
Niger uses CFA Franc West	495	–
Nigeria (Naira)	130	–
Northern Ireland (Pound Sterling)	.52	–
Norway (Krone)	6.22	–
Oman (Rial)	.385	–
Pakistan (Rupee)	59.3	–
Palau uses U.S.Dollar	1.00	–
Panama (Balboa) uses U.S.Dollar	1.00	–
Papua New Guinea (Kina)	3.05	–
Paraguay (Guarani)	6,365	–
Peru (Nuevo Sol)	3.26	–
Philippines (Peso)	55	–
Poland (Zloty)	2.94	–
Portugal (Euro)	.76	–
Qatar (Riyal)	3.64	–
Romania (Leu)	27,600	–
Russia (New Ruble)	27.7	–
Rwanda (Franc)	550	–
St.Helena (Pound)	.52	–
St.Kitts uses E.C.Dollar	2.67	–
St.Lucia uses E.C.Dollar	2.67	–
St.Vincent uses E.C.Dollar	2.67	–
San Marino uses Euro	.76	–
Sao Tome e Principe (Dobra)	9,050	–
Saudi Arabia (Riyal)	3.751	–
Scotland (Pound Sterling)	.52	–
Senegal uses CFA Franc West	495	–
Serbia (Dinar)	61.3	–
Seychelles (Rupee)	5.42	6.4
Sierra Leone (Leone)	2,450	–
Singapore (Dollar)	1.63	–
Slovakia (Sk. Koruna)	28.5	–
Slovenia (Tolar)	180	–
Solomon Is.(Dollar)	7.27	–
Somalia (Shilling)	3,100	–
Somaliland (Somali Shilling)	1,800	4,00
South Africa (Rand)	5.84	–
Spain (Euro)	.76	–
Sri Lanka (Rupee)	99.7	–
Sudan (Dinar)	250	30
Surinam (Guilder)	2,515	–
Swaziland (Lilangeni)	5.93	–
Sweden (Krona)	6.83	–
Switzerland (Franc)	1.17	–
Syria (Pound)	52.2	–
Taiwan (NT Dollar)	30.8	–
Tajikistan (Somoni)	3.04	–
Tanzania (Shilling)	1,110	–
Thailand (Baht)	38.4	–
Togo uses CFAFranc West	495	–
Tonga (Paánga)	1.88	–
Transdniestra (Ruble)	6.51	–
Trinidad & Tobago (Dollar)	6.28	–
Tunisia (Dinar)	1.23	–
Turkey (New Lira)	1.26	–
Turkmenistan (Manat)	5,150	–
Turks & Caicos uses U.S.Dollar	1.00	–
Tuvalu uses Australian Dollar	1.264	–
Uganda (Shilling)	1,700	–
Ukraine (Hryvnia)	5.29	–
United Arab Emirates (Dirham)	3.673	–
United Kingdom (Pound Sterling)	.52	–
Uruguay (Peso Uruguayo)	25.71	–
Uzbekistan (Som)	1,070	–
Vanuatu (Vatu)	105	–
Vatican City uses Euro	.76	–
Venezuela (Bolivar)	2,150	2,00
Vietnam (Dong)	15,800	–
Western Samoa (Tala)	2.59	–
Yemen (Rial)	183	–
Zambia (Kwacha)	4,735	–
Zimbabwe (Dollar)	6,060	–

Dating

Determining the date of issue of a note is a basic consideration of attribution. As the reading of dates is subject not only to the vagaries of numeric styling, but to variations in dating roots caused by the observation of differing religious eras or regal periods from country to country, making this determination can sometimes be quite difficult. Most countries outside the North African and Oriental spheres rely on Western date numerals and the Christian (AD) reckoning, although in a few instances note dating has been tied to the year of a reign or government.

Countries of the Arabic sphere generally date their issues to the Muslim calendar that commenced on July 16, 622 AD when the prophet Mohammed fled from Mecca to Medina. As this calendar is reckoned by the lunar year of 354, its is about three percent (precisely 3.3 percent) shorter than the Christian year. A conversion formula requires you to subtract that percent from the AH date, and then add 621 to gain the AD date.

A degree of confusion arises here because the Muslim calendar is not always based on the lunar year (AH). Afghanistan and Iran (Persia) used a calendar based on a solar year (SH) introduced around 1920. These dates can be converted to AD by simply adding 621. In 1976, Iran implemented a solar calendar based on the founding of the Iranian monarchy in 559 BC. The first year observed on this new system was 2535(MS) which commenced on March 20, 1976.

Several different eras of reckoning, including the Christian (AD) and Muslim (AH), have been used to date paper money of the Indian subcontinent. The two basic systems are the Vikrama Samvat (VS) era that dates from October 18, 58 BC,. and the Saka (SE) era, the origin of which is reckoned from March 3, 78 AD. Dating according to both eras appears on notes of several native states and countries of the area.

Thailand (Siam) has observed three different eras for dating. The most predôminant is the Buddhist (BE) era originating in 543 BC. Next is the Bangkok or Ratanakosind-sok (RS) era dating from 1781 AD (and consisting of only 3 numerals), followed by the Chula-Sakarat (CS) era dating from 638 AD, with the latter also observed in Burma.

Other calendars include that of the Ethiopian (EE) era that commenced 7 years, 8 months after AD dating, and that of the Hebrew nation beginning on October 7, 3761 BC. Korea claims a dating from 2333 BC which is acknowledged on some note issues.

The following table indicates the years dating from the various eras that correspond to 2003 by Christian (AD) calendar reckoning. It must be remembered that there are overlaps between the eras in some instances:

Christian Era (AD)	—	2003
Mohammedan era (AH)	—	AH1424
Solar year (SH)	—	SH1382
Monarchic Solar era (MS)	—	MS2562
Vikrama Samvat era (VS)	—	SE2060
Saka era (SE)	—	Saka 1925
Buddhist era (BE)	—	BE2546
Bangkok era (RS)	—	RS222
Chula-Sakarat era (CS)	—	CS1365
Ethiopian era (EE)	—	EE1995
Jewish era	—	5763
Korean era	—	4336

Paper money of Oriental origin - principally Japan, Korea, China, Turkestan and Tibet - generally date to the year of the government, dynastic, regnal or cyclical eras, with the dates indicated in Oriental characters usually reading from right to left. In recent years some dating has been according to the Christian calendar and in Western numerals reading from left to right.

More detailed guides to the application of the less prevalent dating systems than those described, and others of strictly local nature, along with the numeral designations employed, are presented in conjunction with the appropriate listings.

Some notes carry dating according to both the locally observed and Christian eras. This is particularly true in the Arabic sphere, where the Muslim date may be indicated in Arabic numerals and the Christian date in Western numerals.

In general the date actually shown on a given paper money issue is indicated in some manner. Notes issued by special Law or Decree will have L or D preceding the date. Dates listed within parentheses may differ from the date appearing on the note; they have been documented by other means. Undated notes are listed with ND, followed by a year only when the year of actual issue is known.

Timing differentials between the 354-day Muslim and the 365-day Christian year cause situations whereby notes bearing dates of both eras have two date combinations that may overlap from one or the other calendar system.

China – Republic 9th year, 1st month, 15th day (15.1.1920), read r. to l.

Thailand (Siam) – 1 December 2456

Poland – 28 February 1919

Israel – 1973, 5733

Egypt – 1967 December 2

Russia – 1 October 1920

Korea – 4288 (1955)

Afghanistan – Solar year 1356

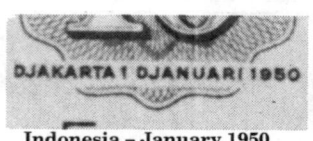

Indonesia – January 1950

Greece – 5 March 1943

HEJIRA DATE CONVERSION CHART

HEJIRA (Hijira, Hegira), the name of the Muslim era (A.H. = Anno Hegirae) dates back to the Christian year 622 when Mohammed "fled" from Mecca, escaping to Medina to avoid persecution from the Koreish tribemen. Based on a lunar year the Muslim year is 11 days shorter.

*=Leap Year (Christian Calendar)

AH Hejira	AD Christian Date
1010	1601, July 2
1011	1602, June 21
1012	1603, June 11
1013	1604, May 30
1014	1605, May 19
1015	1606, May 19
1016	1607, May 9
1017	1608, April 28
1018	1609, April 6
1017	1608, April 28
1018	1609, April 6
1019	1610, March 26
1020	1611, March 16
1021	1612, March 4
1022	1613, February 21
1023	1614, February 11
1024	1615, January 31
1025	1616, January 20
1026	1617, January 9
1027	1617, December 29
1028	1618, December 19
1029	1619, December 8
1030	1620, November 26
1031	1621, November 16
1032	1622, November 5
1033	1623, October 25
1034	1624, October 14
1035	1625, October 3
1036	1626, September 22
1037	1627, Septembe 12
1038	1628, August 31
1039	1629, August 21
1040	1630, July 10
1041	1631, July 30
1042	1632, July 19
1043	1633, July 8
1044	1634, June 27
1045	1635, June 17
1046	1636, June 5
1047	1637, May 26
1048	1638, May 15
1049	1639, May 4
1050	1640, April 23
1051	1641, April 12
1052	1642, April 1
1053	1643, March 22
1054	1644, March 10
1055	1645, February 27
1056	1646, February 17
1057	1647, February 6
1058	1648, January 27
1059	1649, January 15
1060	1650, January 4
1061	1650, December 25
1062	1651, December 14
1063	1652, December 2
1064	1653, November 22
1065	1654, November 11
1066	1655, October 31
1067	1656, October 20
1068	1657, October 9
1069	1658, September 29
1070	1659, September 18
1071	1660, September 6
1072	1661, August 27
1073	1662, August 16
1074	1663, August 5
1075	1664, July 25
1076	1665, July 14
1077	1666, July 4
1078	1667, June 23
1079	1668, June 11
1080	1669, June 1
1081	1670, May 21
1082	1671, May 10

AH Hejira	AD Christian Date
1083	1672, April 29
1084	1673, April 18
1085	1674, April 7
1086	1675, March 28
1087	1676, March 16*
1088	1677, March 6
1089	1678, February 23
1090	1679, February 12
1091	1680, February 2*
1092	1681, January 21
1093	1682, January 10
1094	1682, December 31
1095	1683, December 20
1096	1684, December 8*
1097	1685, November 28
1098	1686, November 17
1099	1687, November 7
1100	1688, October 26*
1101	1689, October 15
1102	1690, October 5
1103	1691, September 24
1104	1692, September 12*
1105	1693, September 2
1106	1694, August 22
1107	1695, August 12
1108	1696, July 31*
1109	1697, July 20
1110	1698, July 10
1111	1699, June 29
1112	1700, June 18
1113	1701, June 8
1114	1702, May 28
1115	1703, May 17
1116	1704, May 6*
1117	1705, April 25
1118	1706, April 15
1119	1707, April 4
1120	1708, March 23*
1121	1709, March 13
1122	1710, March 2
1123	1711, February 19
1124	1712, Feburary 9*
1125	1713, January 28
1126	1714, January 17
1127	1715, January 7
1128	1715, December 27
1129	1716, December 16*
1130	1717, December 5
1131	1718, November 24
1132	1719, November 14
1133	1720, November 2*
1134	1721, October 22
1135	1722, October 12
1136	1723, October 1
1137	1724, September 19
1138	1725, September 9
1139	1726, August 29
1140	1727, August 19
1141	1728, August 7*
1142	1729, July 27
1143	1730, July 17
1144	1731, July 6
1145	1732, June 24*
1146	1733, June 14
1147	1734, June 3
1148	1735, May 24
1149	1736, May 12*
1150	1737, May 1
1151	1738, April 21
1152	1739, April 10
1153	1740, March 29*
1154	1741, March 19
1155	1742, March 8
1156	1743, Feburary 25
1157	1744, February 15*
1158	1745, February 3
1159	1746, January 24
1160	1747, January 13
1161	1748, January 2
1162	1748, December 22*
1163	1749, December 11
1164	1750, November 30
1165	1751, November 20
1166	1752, November 8*
1167	1753, October 29
1168	1754, October 18
1169	1755, October 7
1170	1756, September 26*
1171	1757, September 15
1172	1758, September 4
1173	1759, August 25
1174	1760, August 13*

AH Hejira	AD Christian Date
1175	1761, August 2
1176	1762, July 23
1177	1763, July 12
1178	1764, July 1*
1179	1765, June 20
1180	1766, June 9
1181	1767, May 30
1182	1768, May 18*
1183	1769, May 7
1184	1770, April 27
1185	1771, April 16
1186	1772, April 4*
1187	1773, March 25
1188	1774, March 14
1189	1775, March 4
1190	1776, February 21*
1191	1777, February 9
1192	1778, January 30
1193	1779, January 19
1194	1780, January 8*
1195	1780, December 28*
1196	1781, December 17
1197	1782, December 7
1198	1783, November 26
1199	1784, November 14*
1200	1785, November 4
1201	1786, October 24
1202	1787, October 13
1203	1788, October 2*
1204	1789, September 21
1205	1790, September 10
1206	1791, August 31
1207	1792, August 19*
1208	1793, August 9
1209	1794, July 29
1210	1795, July 18
1211	1796, July 7*
1212	1797, June 26
1213	1798, June 15
1214	1799, June 5
1215	1800, May 25
1216	1801, May 14
1217	1802, May 4
1218	1803, April 23
1219	1804, April 12*
1220	1805, April 1
1221	1806, March 21
1222	1807, March 11
1223	1808, February 28*
1224	1809, February 16
1225	1810, February 6
1226	1811, January 26
1227	1812, January 16*
1228	1813, January 5
1229	1813, December 24
1230	1814, December 14
1231	1815, December 3
1232	1816, November 21*
1233	1817, November 11
1234	1818, October 31
1235	1819, October 20
1236	1820, October 9*
1237	1821, September 28
1238	1822, September 18
1239	1823, September 8
1240	1824, August 26*
1241	1825, August 16
1242	1826, August 5
1243	1827, July 25
1244	1828, July 14*
1245	1829, July 3
1246	1830, June 22
1247	1831, June 12
1248	1832, May 31*
1249	1833, May 21
1250	1834, May 10
1251	1835, April 29
1252	1836, April 18*
1253	1837, April 7
1254	1838, March 27
1255	1839, March 17
1256	1840, March 5*
1257	1841, February 23
1258	1842, February 12
1259	1843, February 1
1260	1844, January 22*
1261	1845, January 10
1262	1845, December 30
1263	1846, December 20
1264	1847, December 9
1265	1848, November 27*
1266	1849, November 17

AH Hejira	AD Christian Date
1267	1850, November 6
1268	1851, October 27
1269	1852, October 15*
1270	1853, October 4
1271	1854, September 24
1272	1855, September 13
1273	1856, September 1*
1274	1857, August 22
1275	1858, August 11
1276	1859, July 31
1277	1860, July 20*
1278	1861, July 9
1279	1862, June 29
1280	1863, June 18
1281	1864, June 6*
1282	1865, May 27
1283	1866, May 16
1284	1867, May 5
1285	1868, April 24*
1286	1869, April 13
1287	1870, April 3
1288	1871, March 23
1289	1872, March 11*
1290	1873, March 1
1291	1874, February 18
1292	1875, Febuary 7
1293	1876, January 28*
1294	1877, January 16
1295	1878, January 5
1296	1878, December 26
1297	1879, December 15
1298	1880, December 4*
1299	1881, November 23
1300	1882, November 12
1301	1883, November 2
1302	1884, October 21*
1303	1885, October 10
1304	1886, September 30
1305	1887, September 19
1306	1888, September 7*
1307	1889, August 28
1308	1890, August 17
1309	1891, August 7
1310	1892, July 26*
1311	1893, July 15
1312	1894, July 5
1313	1895, June 24
1314	1896, June 12*
1315	1897, June 2
1316	1898, May 22
1317	1899, May 12
1318	1900, May 1
1319	1901, April 20
1320	1902, april 10
1321	1903, March 30
1322	1904, March 18*
1323	1905, March 8
1324	1906, February 25
1325	1907, February 14
1326	1908, February 4*
1327	1909, January 23
1328	1910, January 13
1329	1911, January 2
1330	1911, December 22
1331	1912, December 11
1332	1913, November 30
1333	1914, November 19
1334	1915, November 9
1335	1916, October 28*
1336	1917, October 17
1337	1918, October 7
1338	1919, September 26
1339	1920, September 15*
1340	1921, September 4
1341	1922, August 24
1342	1923, August 14
1343	1924, August 2*
1344	1925, July 22
1345	1926, July 12
1346	1927, July 1
1347	1928, June 20*
1348	1929, June 9
1349	1930, May 29
1350	1931, May 19
1351	1932, May 7*
1352	1933, April 26
1353	1934, April 16
1354	1935, April 5
1355	1936, March 24*
1356	1937, March 14
1357	1938, March 3
1358	1939, February 21
1359	1940, February 10*

AH Hejira	AD Christian Date
1360	1941, January 29
1361	1942, January 19
1362	1943, January 8
1363	1943, December 28
1364	1944, December 17*
1365	1945, December 6
1366	1946, November 25
1367	1947, November 15
1368	1948, November 3*
1369	1949, October 24
1370	1950, October 13
1371	1951, October 2
1372	1952, September 21*
1373	1953, September 10
1374	1954, August 30
1375	1955, August 20
1376	1956, August 8*
1377	1957, July 29
1378	1958, July 18
1379	1959, July 7
1380	1960, June 25*
1381	1961, June 14
1382	1962, June 4
1383	1963, May 25
1384	1964, May 13*
1385	1965, May 2
1386	1966, April 22
1387	1967, April 11
1388	1968, March 31*
1389	1969, march 20
1390	1970, March 9
1391	1971, February 27
1392	1972, February 16*
1393	1973, February 4
1394	1974, January 25
1395	1975, January 14
1396	1976, January 3*
1397	1976, December 23*
1398	1977, December 12
1399	1978, December 2
1400	1979, November 21
1401	1980, November 9*
1402	1981, October 30
1403	1982, October 19
1404	1984, October 8
1405	1984, September 27*
1406	1985, September 16
1407	1986, September 6
1408	1987, August 26
1409	1988, August 14*
1409	1989, August 3
1410	1990, July 24
1411	1991, July 13
1412	1992, July 2*
1413	1993, June 21
1414	1994, June 10
1415	1995, May 31
1416	1996, May 19*
1417	1997, May 9
1418	1998, April 28
1419	1999, April 17
1420	2000, April 6*
1421	2001, March 26
1422	2002, March 15
1423	2003, March 5
1424	2004, February 22*
1425	2005, February 10
1426	2006, January 31
1427	2007, January 20
1428	2008, January 10*
1429	2008, December 29
1430	2009, December 18
1431	2010, December 8
1432	2011, November 27*
1433	2012, November 15
1434	2013, November 5
1435	2014, October 25
1436	2015, October 15*
1437	2016, October 3
1438	2017, September 22
1439	2018, September 12
1440	2019, September 11*
1441	2020, August 20
1442	2021, August 10
1443	2022, July 30
1444	2023, July 19*
1445	2024, July 8
1446	2025, June 27
1447	2026, June 17
1448	2027, June 6*
1450	2028, May 25

Algeria, 10 Dinars, #123

Armenia, 5000 Dram, # 51

Aruba, 100 Florin, #14

Azerbaijan, 1000 Manat, #23

Barbados, 50 Dollars, #64

Belgium, 1000 Francs, #144

Bermuda, 50 Dollars, #56

Bhutan, 20 Ngultrum, #22

Brunei, 10 Ringgit, #24

Cambodia, 50 Reils, #52

Cape Verde, 200 Escudos, #63

Central African States, Congo, 5000 Francs, #110T

Chad, 5000 Francs, #8

China (Taiwan), 2000 Yuan, #1995

Croatia, 10 Kuna, #45

Cyprus, 10 Pounds, #59

Denmark, 2000 Kroner, #57

Egypt, 5 Pounds, #66

Equatorial Guinea, 5000 Francs, #22

Faeroes, 50 Kronur, #24

France, 50 Francs, #152

Gibraltar, 5 Pounds, #29

Ghana, 20,000 Cedis, #36

Hong Kong, 500 Dollars, #210

Honduras, 500 Lempiras, #78

Hungary, 2000 Forint, #186

Ireland, 50 Pounds, #73

Jordan, 20 Dinars, #37

Kazakhstan, 10000 Tenge, #25

Lao, 10 Kip, #15s

Luxembourg, 100 Francs, #14As

Macau, 1000 Patacas, #75

Malawi, 20 Kwacha, #17s

Malawi, 500 Kwacha, #48

Malaysia, 10 Ringgit, #49

Mexico, 10,000 Pesos, #78e

Mongolia, 10000 Tugrik, #69

Morocco, 100 Dirhams, #68

Mozambique, 500,000 Meticais, #142

Norway, 500 Kroner, #51

Papua New Guinea, 20 Kina, #27

Portugal, 100 Escudos, #165s

Portuguese Guinea, 100 Escudos, #45s

Qatar, 500 Dinars, #25

Romania, 50,000 Lei, #113

Russia, Military use note, 50 Ruble, #M21

Rwanda, 1000 Francs, #31

Samoa, 20 Tala, #28

Saudi Arabia, 100 Riyals, #29

Scotland, 5 Pounds, #363

Seychelles, 100 Rupees, #27s

Sierra Leone, 1000 Leones, #20

Singapore, 10000 Dollars, #8

St. Helena, 10 Pounds #8G

Sudan, 2000 Pounds, #63

Suriname, 25,000 Gulden, #64

Turkmenistan, 10000 Manat, #13

Uganda, 50000 Shilingi, #45

Ukraine, 1 Hryvnia, #108

United Arab Emirates, 50 Dirhams, #27

United States, 20 Dollars, #522

Uruguay, 2000 Pesos, #86

Viet Nam, 50000 Dong, #119

West African States, Ivory Coast 5000 Francs, #117A

AFGHANISTAN

The Islamic Republic of Afghanistan, which occupies a mountainous region of Southwest Asia, has an area of 251,773 sq. mi. (652,090 sq. km.) and a population of 25.59 million. Presently about a fifth of the total population reside mostly in Pakistan in exile as refugees. Capital: Kabul. It is bordered by Iran, Pakistan, Tajikistan, Turkmenistan, Uzbekistan and Peoples Republic of China's Sinkiang Province. Agriculture and herding are the principal industries; textile mills and cement factories are recent additions to the industrial sector. Cotton, wool, fruits, nuts, sheepskin coats and hand-woven carpets are exported but foreign trade has been sporadic since 1979.

Because of its strategic position astride the ancient land route to India, Afghanistan - formerly known as Aryana and Khorasan - was conquered by Darius I, Alexander the Great, various Scythian tribes, the Arabs, the Turks, Genghis Khan, Tamerlane, the Mughals, the Persians, and in more recent times by Great Britain.

It was a powerful empire under the Kushans, Hephthalites, Ghaznavids and Ghorids. The name Afghanistan, *Land of* the Afghans, came into use in the eighteenth and nineteenth centuries to describe the realm of the Afghan kings. Previously this mountainous region was the easternmost frontier of the Iranian world, with strong cultural influences from the Turks and Mongols to the north and India to the south.

The first Afghan king, Ahmad Shah Abdali, founder of the Durrani dynasty, established his rule at Qandahar in 1747. He conquered large territories in India and eastern Iran, which were lost by his grandson Zaman Shah. A new family, the Barakzays, drove the Durrani king out of Kabul in 1819, but the Durranis were not eliminated completely until 1858. Further conflicts among the Barakzays prevented full unity until the reign of 'Abd al-Rahman in 1880. In 1929 a commoner, Baccha-i-Saqao, *Son of the Water-Carrier*, drove King Amanullah from the throne and ruled as Habibullah Ghazi for less than a year before he was defeated by Muhammad Nadir Shah. The last king, Muhammad Zahir Shah, became a constitutional, though still autocratic, monarch in 1964. In 1973 a *coup d'etat* displaced him and created the Republic of Afghanistan. A subsequent military *coup* established the pro-Soviet Khalq Democratic Republic of Afghanistan under Nur Muhammad Taraqi in 1978. Mounting resistance and violence led to the Soviet invasion of late 1979 and the installation of Babrak Kamal as prime minister. A brutal civil war ensued, even after Soviet forces withdrew in 1989 and Kamal's government was defeated in 1992. An unstable coalition of former *Mujahideen* (Freedom Fighters) factions attempted to govern for several years but were gradually overcome by the Taliban, a Muslim fundamentalist force supported from Pakistan. On Sept. 26, 1996 Taliban forces captured Kabul and set up a government under Mohammed Rabbani. Afghanistan was declared a complete Islamic state under Sharia law.

In the Fall of 2001 the continuing revolution came to a head and by December the Taliban government was overthrown with the assistance of the U.S. military and a grand council endorsed the Transitional Authority, which continues to govern the country and is preparing for elections to take place in late 2004.

RULERS:
Muhammad Zahir Shah, SH1312-1352/1933-1973AD

MONETARY SYSTEM:
1 Afghani = 100 Pul

KINGDOM

BANK OF AFGHANISTAN

1961-63 ISSUES

#37-42 Kg. Muhammad Zahir (third portrait) at l. and as wmk. Printer: TDLR.

37	10 AFGHANIS	VG	VF	UNC
	SH1340 (1961). Brown on m/c unpt. Mosque of Khwajeh Mohammad Abu-Nasr Parsa in Balkh at ctr. on back.	0.25	1.00	5.00

38	20 AFGHANIS	VG	VF	UNC
	SH1340 (1961). Blue on m/c unpt. Independence monument in Kabul at ctr. on back.	0.25	1.00	7.00

39	50 AFGHANIS	VG	VF	UNC
	SH1340 (1961). Green on m/c unpt. Mausoleum of Kg. Nadir Shah in Kabul at ctr. on back.	0.50	1.50	12.50

40	100 AFGHANIS	VG	VF	UNC
	SH1340 (1961). Red on m/c unpt.	1.25	7.50	32.50

40A	500 AFGHANIS	VG	VF	UNC
	SH1340 (1961). Orange on m/c unpt.	5.00	25.00	100.00

41	500 AFGHANIS	VG	VF	UNC
	SH1340 (1961); SH1342 (1963). Olive-brown on m/c unpt.			
	a. 8 digit serial #. SH1340.	5.00	25.00	100.00
	b. Serial # w/prefix. SH1342.	3.50	15.00	75.00

44	100 AFGHANIS	VG	VF	UNC
	SH1346 (1967). Lilac on m/c unpt. Mosque in Kabul at ctr. r. on back.	0.75	2.50	9.00

45	500 AFGHANIS	VG	VF	UNC
	SH1346 (1967). Black and dk. blue on m/c unpt. Qandahar Airport at r. on back.	1.50	17.50	50.00

42	1000 AFGHANIS	VG	VF	UNC
	SH1340 (1961); SH1342 (1963). Blue-gray on m/c unpt. Arch of Qila'-e Bost in Lashkargah at r. on back.			
	a. 8 digit serial #. SH1340.	4.00	32.50	175.00
	b. Prefix serial #. SH1342.	4.00	25.00	150.00

1967 ISSUE

#43-46 Kg. Muhammad Zahir at l. and as wmk. W/o imprint.

46	1000 AFGHANIS	VG	VF	UNC
	SH1346 (1967). Brown on m/c unpt.	3.50	15.00	75.00

REPUBLIC
SH1352-1358/1973-1979 AD

BANK OF AFGHANISTAN

1973-78 ISSUE

#47-53 Pres. Muhammad Daud at l. and as wmk.

Note: It is possible that all notes #47-53 dated SH1354 are replacements.

43	50 AFGHANIS	VG	VF	UNC
	SH1346 (1967). Green on m/c unpt. Arg-e Shahi, King's palace at ctr. r. on back.			
	a. Issued note.	0.50	1.50	6.00
	s. Specimen.	—	—	—

47	10 AFGHANIS	VG	VF	UNC
	SH1352 (1973); SH1354 (1975); SH1356 (1977). Green on m/c unpt. Arch of Qila'-e Bost in Lashkargah at ctr. r. on back.			
	a. Issued note.	0.10	0.50	2.25
	s. Specimen.	—	—	—

51	500 AFGHANIS	VG	VF	UNC
	SH1352 (1973); SH1354 (1975). Blue on m/c unpt. Fortified tribal village at ctr. r. on back.			
	a. Issued note.	0.50	3.00	20.00
	s. Specimen.	—	—	—

48	20 AFGHANIS	VG	VF	UNC
	SH1352 (1973); SH1354 (1975); SH1356 (1977). Purple on m/c unpt. Canal at r. on back.			
	a. Issued note.	0.10	0.50	3.00
	s. Specimen.	—	—	—

52	500 AFGHANIS	VG	VF	UNC
	SH1356 (1977). Brown on m/c unpt. Like #51.			
	a. Issued note.	1.00	5.00	25.00
	s. Specimen.	—	—	—

49	50 AFGHANIS	VG	VF	UNC
	SH1352 (1973); SH1354 (1975); SH1356 (1977). Green on m/c unpt. Men riding yaks at ctr. on back.			
	a. Issued note.	0.20	1.00	4.50
	s. Specimen.	—	—	—

53	1000 AFGHANIS	VG	VF	UNC
	SH1352 (1973); SH1354 (1975); SH1356 (1977). Brown on m/c unpt. Mosque of Mazâr-e Sharîf, the Noble Shrine at ctr. r. on back.	0.75	3.50	20.00

KHALQ DEMOCRATIC REPUBLIC

SH1357-1370/1978-1992 AD

DA AFGHANISTAN BANK

1978 ISSUE

#53A and 54 w/Khalq Government emblem from flag at top l. or r. ctr.

50	100 AFGHANIS	VG	VF	UNC
	SH1352 (1973); SH1354 (1975); SH1356 (1977). Brown-lilac on m/c unpt. Friday Mosque in Herât at ctr. r. on back.			
	a. Issued note.	0.25	2.00	10.00
	s. Specimen.	—	—	—

53A	20 AFGHANIS	VG	VF	UNC
	AH1357 (1978). Purple on m/c unpt. Fortress at ctr. on back. Specimen, punched hole cancelled.	—	—	175.00

54	**50 AFGHANIS**	VG	VF	UNC
	SH1357 (1978). Blue-green on m/c unpt. Dar-al-Aman Palace in Kabul on back.	0.50	3.00	20.00

DEMOCRATIC REPUBLIC

DA AFGHANISTAN BANK

1979 ISSUE

#55-61 bank arms w/horseman at top ctr. or ctr. r. on face.

55	**10 AFGHANIS**	VG	VF	UNC
	SH1358 (1979). Green and blue on m/c unpt. Mountain road scene at ctr. on back.			
	a. Issued note.	0.10	0.20	0.60
	s. Specimen. Punch hole cancelled, ovpt: *SPECIMEN*.	—	—	8.00

56	**20 AFGHANIS**	VG	VF	UNC
	SH1358 (1979). Purple on m/c unpt. Bldg. and mountains at ctr. on back. Sign. varieties.			
	a. Issued note.	0.10	0.25	1.00
	s. Specimen. Punch hole cancelled, ovpt *SPECIMEN*.	—	—	20.00

57	**50 AFGHANIS**	VG	VF	UNC
	SH1358-70 (1979-91). Greenish black with black text on m/c unpt. Similar to #54.			
	a. SH1358 (1979). 2 sign. varieties.	0.10	0.20	0.75
	b. SH1370 (1991).	0.10	0.25	1.00
	s. Specimen. As a. Punch hole cancelled. Ovpt: *SPECIMEN*.	—	—	40.00

58	**100 AFGHANIS**	VG	VF	UNC
	SH1358-70 1979-91). Deep red-violet on m/c unpt. Farm worker in wheat field at r. Hydroelectric dam in mountains at ctr. on back.			
	a. SH1358 (1979). 2 sign. varieties.	0.10	0.50	2.00
	b. SH1369 (1990).	0.10	0.50	2.50
	c. SH1370 (1991).	0.10	0.25	1.00

59	**500 AFGHANIS**	VG	VF	UNC
	SH1358 (1979). Violet and dk. blue on m/c unpt. Horsemen competing in Buzkashi at r. Fortress at Kabul at l. ctr. on back.	0.50	2.00	12.50

60	**500 AFGHANIS**	VG	VF	UNC
	SH1358-70 (1979-91). Reddish-brown, deep green and deep brown on m/c unpt. Like #59. Back deep green on m/c unpt.			
	a. SH1358 (1979).	0.20	0.75	2.50
	b. SH1369 (1990).	0.25	1.00	4.00
	c. SH1370 (1991).	0.10	0.25	1.50

61 1000 AFGHANIS
SH1358-70 (1979-91). Dk. brown and deep red-violet on m/c unpt.
Mosque at Mazar-e-Sharif at r. Victory Arch near Kabul at l. ctr. on
back.

	VG	VF	UNC
a. SH1358 (1979).	0.50	2.50	7.50
b. SH1369 (1990).	0.10	0.50	2.50
c. SH1370 (1991).	0.10	0.25	1.50

1993 ISSUE

#62-64 bank arms w/horseman at top l. ctr. Wmk: Bank arms.

62 5000 AFGHANIS
SH1372 (1993). Violet and blue-black on m/c unpt. Mosque
w/minaret at r. Tomb of Kg. Habibullah, Jalalabad at ctr. on back.

VG	VF	UNC
0.20	0.50	2.00

63 10,000 AFGHANIS
SH1372 (1993). Black, deep olive-green and deep blue-green on
m/c unpt. Gateway between minarets at r. Arched gateway at Bost
in ctr. on back.

	VG	VF	UNC
a. W/o small space between *Da* and *Afghanistan* on back.	0.20	0.75	3.00
b. W/small space between *Da* and *Afghanistan* on back.	0.15	0.50	2.00

REPUBLIC (2001)

DA AFGHANISTAN BANK

2002 ISSUE

1000 'old' afghani = 1 'new' afghani.

64 1 AFGHANI
SH1381 (2002). Purple on m/c unpt. Bank name around ancient coin,
cornucopia pair below. Mosque at Mazar-i Sharif at center on back.

VG	VF	UNC
FV	FV	0.50

65 2 AFGHANIS
SH 1381 (2002). Slate blue on m/c unpt. Bank name around
ancient coin, cornucopia pair below. Victory Arch near Kabul on
back.

VG	VF	UNC
FV	FV	0.50

66 5 AFGHANIS
SH 1381 (2002). Olive on m/c unpt. Bank name around ancient
coin, cornucopia pair below. Fortress at Kabul at ctr. on back.

VG	VF	UNC
FV	FV	0.75

67 10 AFGHANIS
SH 1381 (2002). Green and brown on m/c unpt. Mosque at r.
Victory Arch near Kabul at ctr. on back. Segmented security thread.

VG	VF	UNC
FV	FV	1.25

68 20 AFGHANIS
SH 1381 (2002). Green and purple on m/c unpt. Tomb at r. Arg-e
Shahi, King's Palace at ctr. on back.

VG	VF	UNC
FV	FV	1.50

69	**50 AFGHANIS**	VG	VF	UNC
	SH 1381 (2002). Green and brown on m/c unpt. Salang Pass at ctr. on back.	FV	FV	3.00
70	**100 AFGHANIS**	VG	VF	UNC
	SH 1381 (2002). Arch at Qila'-e Bost on back.	FV	FV	6.00

71	**500 AFGHANIS**	VG	VF	UNC
	SH 1381 (2002). Violet and blue on m/c unpt. Airport tower on back.	FV	FV	25.00

72	**1000 AFGHANIS**	VG	VF	UNC
	SH 1381 (2002). Orange and brown on yellow and m/c unpt. Tomb on back.	FV	FV	50.00

ALBANIA

The Republic of Albania, a Balkan republic bounded by the rump Yugoslav state of Montenegro and Serbia, Macedonia, Greece and the Adriatic Sea, has an area of 11,100 sq. mi. (28,748 sq. km.) and a population of 3.5 million. Capital: Tirana. The country is mostly agricultural, although recent progress has been made in the manufacturing and mining sectors. Petroleum, chrome, iron, copper, cotton textiles, tobacco and wood products are exported.

Since it had been part of the Greek and Roman Empires, little is known of the early history of Albania. After the disintegration of the Roman Empire, Albania was overrun by Goths, Byzantines, Venetians and Turks. Skanderbeg, the national hero, resisted the Turks and established an independent Albania in 1443, but in 1468 the country again fell to the Turks and remained part of the Ottoman Empire for more than 400 years.

Independence was re-established by revolt in 1912, and the present borders established in 1913 by a conference of European powers which, in 1914, placed Prince William of Wied on the throne; popular discontent forced his abdication within months. In 1920, following World War I occupancy by several nations, a republic was set up. Ahmet Zogu seized the presidency in 1925, and in 1928 proclaimed himself king with the title of Zog I. King Zog fled when Italy occupied Albania in 1939 and enthroned King Victor Emanuel of Italy. Upon the surrender of Italy to the Allies in 1943, German troops occupied the country. They withdrew in 1944, and communist partisans seized power, naming Gen. Enver Hoxha provisional president. In 1946, following a victory by the communist front in the 1945 elections, a new constitution modeled on that of the USSR was adopted. In accordance with the constitution of Dec. 28, 1976, the official name of Albania was changed from the People's Republic of Albania to the People's Socialist Republic of Albania. A general strike by trade unions in 1991 forced the communist government to resign. A new government was elected in March 1992. In 1997 Albania had a major financial crisis which caused civil disturbances and the fall of the administration.

MONETARY SYSTEM:
   1 Lek = 100 Qindarka 1948-1965
   1 "heavy" Lek = 10 old Leke, 1965-1992
   1 Lek Valute = 50 Leke, 1992-1993
   Established by the French in 1917.

PEOPLES REPUBLIC

BANKA E SHTETIT SHQIPTAR

1964 ISSUE

#33-39 arms at upper r. on back. Wmk: Curved *BSHSH* repeated.

33	**1 LEK**	VG	VF	UNC
	1964. Green and deep blue on m/c unpt. Peasant couple at ctr. Shkoder fortress at l. ctr. on back.			
	a. Issued note.	0.15	0.50	1.50
	s. Specimen ovpt: *MODEL* or *SPECIMEN*.	—	—	3.00

34	**3 LEKË**	VG	VF	UNC
	1964. Brown and lilac on m/c unpt. Woman w/basket of grapes at l. Saranda view at l. ctr. on back.			
	a. Issued note.	0.20	0.65	2.25
	s. Specimen ovpt: *MODEL* or *SPECIMEN*.	—	—	4.00

35 **5 LEKË**
1964. Purple and dk. blue on m/c unpt. Truck and steam passenger
train crossing viaduct at l. ctr. Ship at l. on back.

	VG	VF	UNC
a. Issued note.	0.25	0.90	3.00
s. Specimen ovpt: *MODEL* or *SPECIMEN*.	—	—	5.00

36 **10 LEKË**
1964. Dk. green on m/c unpt. Woman working w/cotton spinning
frame. People at l. ctr., male portr. at upper r. on back.

	VG	VF	UNC
a. Issued note.	0.35	1.20	4.00
s. Specimen ovpt: *MODEL* or *SPECIMEN*.	—	—	6.00

37 **25 LEKË**
1964. Blue-black on m/c unpt. Peasant woman w/sheaf at l.,
combine and truck at ctr. Farm tractor at l. ctr. on back.

	VG	VF	UNC
a. Issued note.	0.60	2.00	7.00
s. Specimen ovpt: *MODEL* or *SPECIMEN*.	—	—	7.50

38 **50 LEKË**
1964. Red-brown on m/c unpt. Soldiers on parade at l. ctr., bust of
Skanderbeg at upper r. Rifle and pick axe at l., modern bldg. under
construction at l. ctr. on back.

	VG	VF	UNC
a. Issued note.	1.00	3.50	12.00
s. Specimen ovpt: *MODEL* or *SPECIMEN*.	—	—	8.50

39 **100 LEKË**
1964. Brown-lilac. Worker and boy at coffer dam at l. ctr. Steel
worker and well rigger at ctr. on back.

	VG	VF	UNC
a. Issued note.	2.25	7.50	25.00
s. Specimen ovpt: *MODEL* or *SPECIMEN*.	—	—	10.00

PEOPLES SOCIALIST REPUBLIC

BANKA E SHTETIT SHQIPTAR

1976 ISSUE

#40-46 like #33-39. Arms at upper r. on back. Wmk: Bank name around radiant star, repeated.

40 **1 LEK**
1976. Green and deep blue on m/c unpt.

	VG	VF	UNC
a. Issued note.	0.05	0.15	0.50
s1. Red ovpt: *SPECIMEN* w/all zeros serial #.	—	—	3.50
s2. Red ovpt: *SPECIMEN* w/normal serial #.	—	—	0.50
s3. Lg. blue ovpt: *SPECIMEN* on face. Black ovpt: *E PRANUESHME* on back.			

Note: #40 w/lg. blue ovpt: *SPECIMEN* on face and black rectangular ovpt. for bank 25th anniversary on back
is a private issue.

41 **3 LEKË**
1976. Brown and lilac on m/c unpt.

	VG	VF	UNC
a. Issued note.	0.10	0.25	0.75
s1. Red ovpt: *SPECIMEN* w/all zeros serial #.	—	—	4.00
s2. Red ovpt: *SPECIMEN* w/normal serial #.	—	—	0.75

42	5 LEKË	VG	VF	UNC
	1976. Lilac and blue on m/c unpt.			
	a. Issued note.	0.10	0.35	1.25
	s1. Red ovpt: *SPECIMEN* w/all zeros serial #.	—	—	4.50
	s2. Red ovpt: *SPECIMEN* w/normal serial #.	—	—	1.00
	s3. Lg. blue ovpt: *SPECIMEN* on face. Black ovpt: *E PRANUESHME* on back.	—	—	

Note: #42 w/lg. blue ovpt: *SPECIMEN* on face and black rectangular ovpt. for bank 25th anniversary on back is a private issue.

43	10 LEKË	VG	VF	UNC
	1976. Dk. green on m/c unpt.			
	a. Issued note.	0.10	0.40	1.50
	s1. Red ovpt: *SPECIMEN* w/all zeros serial #.	—	—	5.50
	s2. Red ovpt: *SPECIMEN* w/normal serial #.	—	—	1.25

44	25 LEKË	VG	VF	UNC
	1976. Blue-black on m/c unpt.			
	a. Issued note.	0.15	0.50	3.50
	s1. Red ovpt: *SPECIMEN* w/all zeros serial #.	—	—	6.50
	s2. Red ovpt: *SPECIMEN* w/normal serial #.	—	—	1.75

45	50 LEKË	VG	VF	UNC
	1976. Red-brown on m/c unpt.			
	a. Serial # prefix w/o serifs. Chinese printing.	0.30	1.00	6.00
	b. Serial # prefix w/serifs. Crossbar of 4 is thicker than bottom serif. (1st European printing).	0.45	1.25	8.00
	c. Serial # prefix w/serifs. Crossbar of 4 is same thickness as bottom serif. (2nd European printing).	0.25	0.75	5.00
	s1. Red ovpt: *SPECIMEN* w/all zeros serial #.	—	—	7.50
	s2. Red ovpt: *SPECIMEN* w/normal serial #.	—	—	2.50
	s3. Lg. blue ovpt: *SPECIMEN* on face. Black ovpt: *E PRANUESHME* on back.	—	—	

Note: #45 w/lg. blue ovpt: *SPECIMEN* on face and black rectangular ovpt. for bank 25th anniversary on back is a private issue.

46	100 LEKË	VG	VF	UNC
	1976. Brown-lilac on m/c unpt.			
	a. Issued note.	0.30	1.50	10.00
	s1. Red ovpt: *SPECIMEN* w/all zeros serial #.	—	—	8.50
	s2. Red ovpt: *SPECIMEN* w/normal serial #.	—	—	3.00

ND ISSUE

46A	100 LEKË	VG	VF	UNC
	ND. Steel worker at l., steel mill at ctr. Oil well derricks at l. ctr., arms at upper r. on back. Specimen only.			
	a. Blue and dull red on lt. green and lt. yellow unpt.	—	—	200.00
	b. Brown and dull red on lt. green and lt. yellow unpt.	—	—	200.00

1991 ISSUE

#47 and 48 arms at upper r. on back. Wmk: Bank name around radiant star, repeated.

47	100 LEKË	VG	VF	UNC
	1991. Deep brown and deep purple on pale orange and m/c unpt. Steel workers at l., steel mill at r. Refinery at l. ctr. on back.			
	a. Issued note.	0.50	2.00	6.00
	s. Specimen.	—	—	5.00

48	500 LEKË	VG	VF	UNC
	1991; 1996. Purple, red and blue-green on lt. blue and lt. orange unpt. Peasant woman by sunflowers at l. ctr. Evergreen trees, mountains at l. ctr. on back.			
	a. 1991.	FV	FV	14.00
	b. Enhanced UV printing. 1996.	FV	FV	10.00

1992 ND ISSUE

#48A-50 steelworker at ctr. Electrical transmission towers at l., arms at upper ctr., hydroelectric generator at r. on back. Wmk: *B.SH.SH.* below star, repeated.

48A	1 LEK VALUTË (= 50 LEKË)	VG	VF	UNC
	ND (1992). Purple and gray-green on m/c unpt. (Not issued).	—	—	35.00

49	10 LEK VALUTË (= 500 LEKË)	VG	VF	UNC
	ND (1992). Deep green and purple on m/c unpt.			
	a. W/serial #.	2.00	5.00	15.00
	b. W/o serial #.	2.00	5.00	15.00
	s. Specimen.	—	—	—

Note: Many examples of #49 have mismatched serial #'s. No additional premium is given for such.

50	50 LEK VALUTË (= 2500 LEKË)	VG	VF	UNC
	ND (1992). Deep brown-violet and gray-green on m/c unpt.			
	a. W/serial #.	8.00	18.00	60.00
	b. W/o serial #.	2.00	6.00	15.00
	s. Specimen.	—	—	25.00

#51 not assigned.

REPUBLIC

BANKA E SHQIPERISE

1992 ISSUE

#52-54 wmk: Repeated ring of letters *B.SH.SH.*

52	200 LEKË	VG	VF	UNC
	1992. Deep reddish-brown on m/c unpt. Ismail Qemali at l. Citizens portrayed in double-headed eagle outline on back.			
	a. Issued note.	FV	FV	6.00
	s. Specimen.			

53	500 LEKË	VG	VF	UNC
	1992. Deep blue on blue and m/c unpt. Naim Frasheri at l. Rural mountains at l., candle at ctr. on back.			
	a. Issued note.	FV	FV	14.00
	s. Specimen.			

54	1000 LEKË	VG	VF	UNC
	1992. Deep green and green on m/c unpt. Skanderbeg at l. Kruja Castle at l., crowned arms at ctr. on back.			
	a. Issued note.	FV	FV	25.00
	s. Specimen.	—	—	12.00

1993-94 ISSUE

55	**100 LEKË**		VG	VF	UNC
	1993-96. Purple on m/c unpt. L. Kombetar at l. Mountain peaks at				
	l. ctr., Lanner Falcon at ctr. on back.				
	a. 1993.		FV	FV	6.00
	b. 1994.		FV	FV	4.00
	c. Enhanced U-V printing. 1996.		FV	FV	3.00
	s. Specimen.		—	—	2.50

58	**1000 LEKË**		VG	VF	UNC
	1994. Deep green on green and m/c unpt. Like #54.				
	a. Issued note.		FV	FV	20.00
	s. Specimen.		—	—	12.50

1995-96 ISSUE

#59-61 like #56-58 but w/segmented foil over security thread.

56	**200 LEKË**		VG	VF	UNC
	1994. Deep reddish brown on m/c unpt. Like #52.				
	a. Issued note.		FV	FV	4.50
	s. Specimen.		—	—	4.00

59	**200 LEKË**		VG	VF	UNC
	1996. Deep reddish brown on m/c unpt. Like #56.		FV	FV	5.00

57	**500 LEKË**		VG	VF	UNC
	1994. Deep blue on blue and m/c unpt. Like #53.				
	a. Issued note.		FV	FV	10.00
	s. Specimen.		—	—	6.50

60	**500 LEKË**		VG	VF	UNC
	1996. Deep blue on blue and m/c unpt. Like #57.		FV	FV	10.00

61 1000 LEKË
1995-96. Deep green and green on m/c unpt.

		VG	VF	UNC
a. 1995. Olive-green sign.		FV	FV	25.00
b. 1995. Black sign.		FV	FV	20.00
c. 1996. Black sign.		FV	FV	20.00

1996 ISSUE

62 100 LEKË
1996 (1997). Purple, dk. brown and orange on m/c unpt. Fan S. Noli at l. and as wmk. First Albanian parliament bldg. at upper r. on back.

VG	VF	UNC
FV	FV	2.50

63 200 LEKË
1996 (1997). Brown and brown-orange on m/c unpt. Niam Frasheri at l. and as wmk. Frasheri's birthplace at upper r. on back.

VG	VF	UNC
FV	FV	4.50

NOTICE
Readers with unlisted dates, signature varieties, etc. are invited to submit photocopies of their notes to: Standard Catalog of World Paper Money, 700 East State St. Iola, WI 54990-0001, E-Mail: george.cuhaj@fwpubs.com.

64 500 LEKË
1996 (1997). Dk. blue, purple and brown on m/c unpt. Ismail Qemali at l. and as wmk. Independence house in Vlora at upper r. on back.

VG	VF	UNC
FV	FV	8.50

65 1000 LEKË
1996 (1997); 1999. Green and dk. green on m/c unpt. Pjeter Bogdani at l. and as wmk. Church of Vau i Dejes at upper r. on back.

VG	VF	UNC
FV	FV	17.50

66 5000 LEKË
1996 (1999). Olive green and m/c. Skanderbeg at l. and as wmk. Kruja castle, equestrian statue, crown on back.

VG	VF	UNC
FV	FV	110.00

2001 ISSUE

#68-70 like #63-65 but with new sign. and enhanced security features.

		VG	VF	UNC
67	**200 LEKË** 2001. Brown and brown-orange on m/c unpt. N. Frasheri at l. and as wmk. Frasheri's birthplace at upper r. on back.	FV	FV	3.50
68	**500 LEKË** 2001. Dk. blue, purple and brown on m/c unpt. I. Qemali at l. and as wmk. House at upper r. on back.	FV	FV	7.50
69	**1000 LEKË** 2001. Green and dk. green on m/c unpt. P. Bogadani at l. and as wmk. Church of Vau i Dejes at upper r. on back.	FV	FV	15.00
70	**5000 LEKË** 2001 (2004). Olive green and m/c. Skanderbeg at l. and as wmk. Kruja castle, equestrian statue, crown on back.	FV	FV	95.00

FOREIGN EXCHANGE CERTIFICATES

BANKA E SHTETIT SHQIPTAR

1965 ISSUE

#FX21-FX27 arms at r. Bank arms at ctr. on back.

FX21	.05 LEK		VG	VF	UNC
	1965. Deep blue-green on pink and pale yellow-orange unpt.		—	—	40.00

FX22	.10 LEK		VG	VF	UNC
	1965. Deep olive-brown on pink and pale blue unpt.		—	—	40.00

FX23	1/2 LEK		VG	VF	UNC
	1965. Deep purple on pink and lilac unpt.		—	—	40.00

FX24	1 LEK		VG	VF	UNC
	1965. Blackish green on pale yellow and pale yellow-orange unpt.		—	—	40.00

FX25	5 LEK		VG	VF	UNC
	1965. Blue-black on pale yellow-green unpt.		—	—	110.00

FX26	10 LEK		VG	VF	UNC
	1965. Blue-green on pale yellow and pale grayish green unpt.		—	—	110.00

FX27	50 LEK		VG	VF	UNC
	1965. Deep red-brown on pink and pale yellow unpt.		—	—	110.00

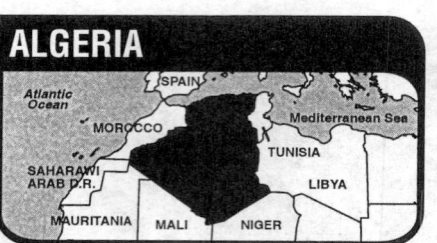

The Democratic and Popular Republic of Algeria, a North African country fronting on the Mediterranean Sea between Tunisia and Morocco, has an area of 919,595 sq. mi. (2,381,741 sq. km.) and a population of 28.6 million. Capital: Algiers (Alger). Most of the country's working population is engaged in agriculture although a recent industrial diversification, financed by oil revenues, is making steady progress. Wines, fruits, iron and zinc ores, phosphates, tobacco products, liquified natural gas, and petroleum are exported.

Algiers, the capital and chief seaport of Algeria, was the site of Phoenician and Roman settlements before the present Moslem city was founded about 950. Nominally part of the sultanate of Tlemcen, Algiers had a large measure of independence under the amirs of its own. In 1492 the Jews and Moors who had been expelled from Spain settled in Algiers and enjoyed an increasing influence until the imposition of Turkish control in 1518. For the following three centuries Algiers was the headquarters of the notorious Barbary pirates. The French took Algiers in 1830, and after a long and wearisome war completed the conquest of Algeria and annexed it to France, 1848. Following the armistice signed by France and Nazi Germany on June 22, 1940, Algeria fell under Vichy Government control until liberated by the Allied invasion forces under the command of Gen. Dwight D. Eisenhower on Nov. 8, 1942. The inability to obtain equal rights with Frenchmen led to an organized revolt which began on Nov. 1, 1954 and lasted until a ceasefire was signed on July 1, 1962. Independence was proclaimed on July 5, 1962, following a self-determination referendum.

RULERS:
French to 1962

MONETARY SYSTEM:
1 Franc = 100 Centimes to 1960
1 Nouveau Franc = 100 Old Francs, 1959-64
1 Dinar = 100 Centimes, 1964-

FRENCH ADMINISTRATION - POST WWII

BANQUE DE L'ALGÉRIE

1959 ISSUE

118	5 NOUVEAUX FRANCS	VG	VF	UNC
	1959. Green and m/c. Ram at bottom ctr., Bacchus at r. Like #106.			
	a. 31.7.1959; 18.12.1959.	12.50	75.00	300.00
	s. Specimen. 31.7.1959.	—	—	160.00

119   **10 NOUVEAUX FRANCS**

		VG	VF	UNC
1959-61. Brown and yellow. Isis at r. Like #104.				
a. 31.7.1959-2.6.1961.		12.50	85.00	325.00
s. Specimen. 31.7.1959.		—	—	165.00

120   **50 NOUVEAUX FRANCS**

		VG	VF	UNC
1959. M/c. Pythian Apollo at l. Like #109.				
a. 31.7.1959; 18.12.1959.		32.50	165.00	500.00
s. Specimen. 31.7.1959.		—	—	375.00

121   **100 NOUVEAUX FRANCS**

		VG	VF	UNC
1959-61. Blue and m/c. Seagulls w/city of Algiers in background. Like #110.				
a. 31.7.1959; 18.12.1959.		60.00	200.00	550.00
b. 3.6.1960; 25.11.1960; 10.2.1961; 29.9.1961.		20.00	100.00	375.00
s. Specimen. 31.7.1959.		—	—	175.00

REPUBLIC

BANQUE CENTRALE D'ALGÉRIE

1964 ISSUE

#122-125 wmk: Amir Abd el-Kader.

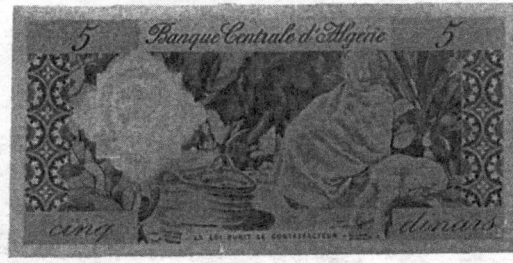

122   **5 DINARS**

		VG	VF	UNC
1.1.1964. Purple and lilac. Griffon vulture, tawny eagle perched on rocks at l. ctr. Native objects on back. 2 styles of numerals in date and serial #.				
a. Issued note.		5.00	40.00	200.00
s. Specimen.		—	—	—

123   **10 DINARS**

		VG	VF	UNC
1.1.1964. Lilac and m/c. Pair of storks and minaret. Native craft on back. 2 styles of numerals in date and serial #.				
a. Issued note.		2.50	20.00	65.00
s. Specimen.		—	—	—

124	**50 DINARS**	VG	VF	UNC
	1.1.1964. Lt. brown and m/c. 2 mountain sheep. Camel caravan on back.			
	a. Issued note.	4.00	25.00	85.00
	s. Specimen.	—	—	—

127	**10 DINARS**	VG	VF	UNC
	1.11.1970. Red-brown and m/c. Sheep at l., peacock at r. Seated elderly man at l., ornate bldg. at r. on back. Minor plate varieties in French text on back.			
	a. Issued note.	1.50	6.00	25.00
	s. Specimen.	—	—	30.00

125	**100 DINARS**	VG	VF	UNC
	1.1.1964. M/c. Harbor scene. Modern bldg. complex at l. ctr. on back. 2 styles of numerals in date and serial #.			
	a. Issued note.	3.00	10.00	50.00
	s. Specimen.	—	—	—

128	**100 DINARS**	VG	VF	UNC
	1.11.1970. Brown, brown-orange, blue-gray and pale yellow-orange. 2 men at at l., airport at ctr., wheat ears at r. Scenery w/edmi gazelle at r. on back.			
	a. Deep brown.	2.50	12.50	55.00
	b. Lt. brown.	2.50	10.00	45.00
	s. Specimen.	—	—	30.00

1970 ISSUE

#126 and 127 wmk: Amir Abd el-Kader.

126	**5 DINARS**	VG	VF	UNC
	1.11.1970. Blue and m/c. Warrior w/shield and sword at ctr. r. Ruppel's sand fox at l. ctr., village in background at ctr. r. on back. Sign. varieties.			
	a. Issued note.	0.50	6.00	20.00
	s. Specimen.	—	—	30.00

129	**500 DINARS**	VG	VF	UNC
	1.11.1970. Purple. View of city. Galleon, fortress on back.			
	a. Issued note.	6.00	30.00	75.00
	s. Specimen.	—	—	50.00

1977; 1981 ISSUE

#130 and 131 wmk: Amir Abd el-Kader.

		VG	VF	UNC
130	**50 DINARS**			
	1.11.1977. Dk. green on m/c unpt. Shepherd w/flock at lower l. ctr. Farm tractor on back. Sign. varieties.			
	a. Issued note.	1.00	2.00	7.50
	s. Specimen.	—	—	—

		VG	VF	UNC
131	**100 DINARS**			
	1.11.1981. Dk. blue and aqua on lt. blue unpt. Village w/minarets at l. Man working w/plants at ctr. on back.			
	a. Issued note.	1.50	4.00	12.50
	s. Specimen.	—	—	—

1982-83 ISSUE

#132-135 wmk: Amir Abd el-Kader.

		VG	VF	UNC
132	**10 DINARS**			
	2.12.1983. Black on brown and blue-green unpt. Diesel passenger train at ctr. Back blue, blue-green and brown; mountain village at ctr.			
	a. Issued note.	FV	0.40	2.50
	s. Specimen.	—	—	—

		VG	VF	UNC
133	**20 DINARS**			
	2.1.1983. Red-brown on ochre unpt. Vase at l. ctr., handcrafts at r. Tower at ctr. on back.			
	a. Issued note.	FV	0.50	3.50
	s. Specimen.	—	—	—

		VG	VF	UNC
134	**100 DINARS**			
	8.6.1982. Pale blue and gray. Similar to #131 but w/o bird at upper r. on face.			
	a. Issued note.	FV	17.50	50.00
	s. Specimen.	—	—	—

		VG	VF	UNC
135	**200 DINARS**			
	23.3.1983. Brown and dk. green on m/c unpt. Monument to the Algerian martyrs at l., bridge over canyon at, ctr., amphora at r. on back.			
	a. Issued note.	FV	4.00	15.00
	s. Specimen.	—	—	—

#136 not assigned.

BANQUE D'ALGÉRIE

1992 DATED (1995; 1996) ISSUE

		VG	VF	UNC
137	**100 DINARS**	FV	FV	6.00
	21.5.1992 (1996). Dk. blue w/black text on pale blue and m/c unpt. Army charging at r. Seal w/horsemen charging at l., ancient galley at ctr. on back. Wmk: Horse's head.			

138   200 DINARS
21.5.1992 (1996). Dk. brown and red-brown on m/c unpt. Koranic
school at ctr. r., bldg. at ctr. on back. Wmk: Horse's head.

	VG	VF	UNC
	FV	FV	12.50

139   500 DINARS
21.5.1992 (1996). Deep purple, violet and red-violet on m/c unpt.
Hannibal's troops and elephants engaging the Romans at ctr. r.
Waterfalls at l., tomb ruins of Numid Kg. Massinissa at l. ctr.,
elephant mounted troops at ctr. r. on back. Wmk: Elephan

	VG	VF	UNC
	FV	FV	25.00

140   1000 DINARS
21.5.1992 (1995). Red-brown and orange on m/c unpt. Tassili cave
carvings of animals at lower ctr., water buffalo's head at r. and as
wmk. Hoggar cave painting of antelope at l., ruins at ctr. on back.

	VG	VF	UNC
	FV	FV	35.00

1998 DATED (2000) ISSUE

Similar to #139-140 but with holographic band at l.

141   500 DINARS
10.6.1998. Deep purple, violet and red-violet on m/c unpt. Similar
to #139. holographic band at l. ctr.

	VG	VF	UNC
	FV	FV	20.00

142   1000 DINARS
21.5.1992; 10.6.1998. Red-brown and orange on m/c unpt. Similar
to #140. holographic band at l. ctr.

		VG	VF	UNC
a. 21.5.1992.		FV	FV	35.00
b. 6.10.1998.		FV	FV	25.00

2005 COMMEMORATIVE ISSUE

143   1000 DINARS
22.3.2005. Red-brown and orange on m/c unpt. Arab League's
60th Anniversary seal and holographic band added.

	VG	VF	UNC
	—	—	27.50

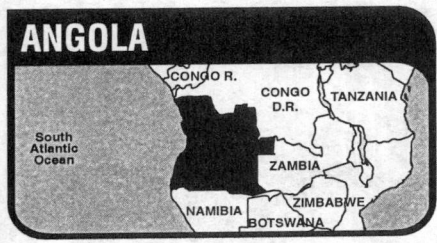

ANGOLA

The Peoples Republic of Angola, a country on the west coast of southern Africa bounded by Zaïre, Zambia and Namibia (South-West Africa), has an area of 481,354 sq. mi. (1,246,700 sq. km.) and a population of 12.78 million, predominantly Bantu in origin. Capital: Luanda. Most of the people are engaged in subsistence agriculture. However, important oil and mineral deposits make Angola potentially one of the richest countries in Africa. Iron and diamonds are exported.

Angola was discovered by Portuguese navigator Diogo Cao in 1482. Portuguese settlers arrived in 1491, and established Angola as a major slaving center which sent about 3 million slaves to the New World.

A revolt against Portuguese rule, characterized by guerrilla warfare, began in 1961 and continued until 1974, when a new regime in Portugal offered independence. The independence movement was actively supported by three groups, the National Front, based in Zaïre, the Soviet-backed Popular Movement, and the moderate National Union. Independence was proclaimed on Nov. 11, 1975.

RULERS:
Portuguese to 1975

MONETARY SYSTEM:
1 Escudo = 100 Centavos, 1954-77
1 Kwanza = 100 Lwei, 1977-95
1 Kwanza Reajustado = 1,000 "old" Kwanzas, 1995-

	SIGNATURE VARIETIES	
	Governor	Administrator
1		
	Governor	Administrator
2		
	Governor	Administrator
3		
	Governor	Vice-Governor
4		
	Governor	Vice-Governor
5		
	Governor	Vice-Governor
6		
	Governor	Administrator
7		
	Governor	Administrator
8		
	Governor	Administrator
9		
	Governor	Administrator
10		
	Governor	Vice-Governor
11		

	SIGNATURE VARIETIES	
	Governor	Administrator
12		
	Governor	Administrator
13		
	Governor	Vice-Governor
14		
	Governor	Vice-Governor
15		
	Governor	Vice-Governor
16		
	Governor	Vice-Governor
17		
	Governor	Vice-Governor
18		
	Governor	Vice-Governor
19		
	Governor	Administrator
20		

PORTUGUESE ADMINISTRATION

BANCO DE ANGOLA

1962 ISSUE

Escudo System

#92-96 portr. Americo Tomas. at l. or r. Printer: TDLR.

92	20 ESCUDOS	VG	VF	UNC
	10.6.1962. Black on m/c unpt. Dock at l. Gazelles running on back. Sign. 1.	1.25	6.50	32.50

93	**50 ESCUDOS**	VG	VF	UNC
	10.6.1962. Lt. blue on m/c unpt. Airport at l. ctr. Various animals at water hole on back. Sign. 2.	2.50	12.50	50.00

94	**100 ESCUDOS**	VG	VF	UNC
	10.6.1962. Lilac on m/c unpt. Salazar bridge at l. Elephants at watering hole on back. Sign. 3.	4.00	30.00	125.00
95	**500 ESCUDOS**			
	10.6.1962. Red on m/c unpt. Port of Luanda at ctr. 2 black rhinoceros on back. Sign. 4.	9.50	50.00	325.00
96	**1000 ESCUDOS**			
	10.6.1962. Blue on m/c unpt. Dam at ctr. Herd on back. Sign. 4.	8.00	45.00	260.00

100	**50 ESCUDOS**	VG	VF	UNC
	24.11.1972. Green and brown on m/c unpt. Plants on back. Sign. 8.	0.30	1.25	6.50

1970 ISSUE

#97-98 portr. Americo Tomas at l. or r. Printer: TDLR.

101	**100 ESCUDOS**	VG	VF	UNC
	24.11.1972. Lt. and dk. brown on m/c unpt. Tree and plants on back. Sign. 7.	0.50	1.50	6.50

97	**500 ESCUDOS**	VG	VF	UNC
	10.6.1970. Red on m/c unpt. Like #95. Sign. 5.	10.00	40.00	215.00
98	**1000 ESCUDOS**			
	10.6.1970. Blue on m/c unpt. Like #96. Sign. 5.	12.50	45.00	225.00

1972 ISSUE

#99-103 Arms at l., M. Carmona at ctr. r. and as wmk. Printer: TDLR.

102	**500 ESCUDOS**	VG	VF	UNC
	24.11.1972. Blue on m/c unpt. Rock formation at Pungo Andongo at ctr. r. on back. Sign. 6.	1.00	5.00	20.00

99	**20 ESCUDOS**	VG	VF	UNC
	24.11.1972. Red and brown on m/c unpt. Flowers on back. Sign. 7.	0.30	1.25	6.50

103	**1000 ESCUDOS**	VG	VF	UNC
	24.11.1972. Purple on m/c unpt. Waterfalls on back. Sign. 5.	1.75	6.00	37.50

1973 ISSUE

#104-108 Luiz de Camoes at r. and as wmk.

104	20 ESCUDOS 10.6.1973. Blue, purple and green on m/c unpt. Cotton plant on back. Sign. 10.	VG	VF	UNC
	a. Issued note.	1.00	5.00	22.50
	ct. Color trial.	—	—	225.00

105	50 ESCUDOS 10.6.1973. Blue and brown on m/c unpt. Plant on back. Sign. 9.	VG	VF	UNC
	a. Issued note.	0.25	1.00	3.75
	ct. Color trial. Blue, purple and green on m/c unpt.	—	—	225.00

106	100 ESCUDOS 10.6.1973. Brown, black and maroon on m/c unpt. Back dk. green and maroon on m/c unpt. Tree at l. Sign. 10.	VG	VF	UNC
		0.50	1.50	5.00

107	500 ESCUDOS 10.6.1973. Dk. brown, violet and purple on m/c unpt. High rock formation on back. Sign. 11.	VG	VF	UNC
		1.50	4.50	20.00

108	1000 ESCUDOS 10.6.1973. Olive and blue on m/c unpt. Waterfalls on back. Sign. 11.	VG	VF	UNC
		2.00	9.00	37.50

PEOPLES REPUBLIC

BANCO NACIONAL DE ANGOLA

1976 ISSUE

Kwanza System

#109-113 Antonio Agostinho Neto at r. Arms at lower l. on back.

109	20 KWANZAS 11.11.1976. Brown, green and orange. Soldiers in field on back. Sign. 12.	VG	VF	UNC
	a. Issued note.	0.50	3.50	12.75
	s. Specimen.	—	—	

110	50 KWANZAS 11.11.1976. Purple, brown and black. Field workers on back. Sign. 12.	VG	VF	UNC
	a. Issued note.	0.50	2.00	9.50
	s. Specimen.	—	—	

111   100 KWANZAS
    11.11.1976. Green on m/c unpt. Textile factory workers on back.
    Sign. 12.

	VG	VF	UNC
a. Issued note.	0.50	1.50	6.25
s. Specimen.	—	—	—

112   500 KWANZAS
    11.11.1976. Blue on m/c unpt. Cargo ships dockside on back.
    Sign. 12.

	VG	VF	UNC
a. Issued note.	2.00	6.00	25.00
s. Specimen.	—	—	—

113   1000 KWANZAS
    11.11.1976. Red on m/c unpt. School class on back. Sign. 12.

	VG	VF	UNC
a. Issued note.	2.00	9.50	40.00
s. Specimen.	—	—	—

1979 Issue

#114-117 w/2 serial #. Sign. titles, date of independence added under bank name on face. Arms at lower l. on back.

114   50 KWANZAS
    14.8.1979. Purple, brown and black. Like #110. Sign. 13.

VG	VF	UNC
0.40	2.50	10.00

		VG	VF	UNC
115	**100 KWANZAS** 14.8.1979. Green on m/c unpt. Like #111. Sign. 13.	0.30	1.75	7.50
116	**500 KWANZAS** 14.8.1979. Blue on m/c unpt. Like #112. Sign. 13.	2.75	17.50	75.00

117   1000 KWANZAS
    14.8.1979. Red on m/c unpt. Like #113. Sign. 13.

	VG	VF	UNC
a. Issued note.	2.50	10.00	47.50
s. Specimen.	—	—	—

1984-87 Issue

#118-125 conjoined busts of José Eduardo dos Santos and Antonio Agostinho Neto at r. Arms at lower l. on back. Wmk: bird (weak).

Replacement notes: Serial # prefixes *ZA, ZB, ZC,* etc.

118   50 KWANZAS
    7.1.1984. Deep brown and green on lt. green and tan unpt.
    Classroom and teacher on back. Sign. 14.

VG	VF	UNC
0.25	1.25	5.00

Note: #118 dated 11.11.1987 may exist (see #122).

119   100 KWANZAS
    7.1.1984; 11.11.1987. Deep blue, violet and brown on lt. blue and
    m/c unpt. Picking cotton on back. Sign. 14.

VG	VF	UNC
2.00	10.00	25.00

Note: #119 dated 1987 was issued only w/ovpt. (see #125).

120	500 KWANZAS	VG	VF	UNC
	1984; 1987. Brown, red-brown and red on lilac and m/c unpt. Offshore oil platform at l., worker at r. on back.			
	a. Sign. 14. 7.1.1984.	2.50	11.00	50.00
	b. Sign. 15. 11.11.1987.	2.25	10.00	45.00

121	1000 KWANZAS	VG	VF	UNC
	1984; 1987. Purple, blue-black and blue on lt. blue and m/c unpt. Soldiers embarking dockside at l. ctr. and soldier at r. on back.			
	a. Sign. 14. 7.1.1984.	2.75	12.50	65.00
	b. Sign. 15. 11.11.1987.	2.50	11.00	57.50

1991 PROVISIONAL ISSUE

#121-125 portr. conjoined bust of José Eduardo dos Santos and Antonio Agostinho Neto at r. and as wmk. Arms at lower l. on back.

122	50 NOVO KWANZA ON 50 KWANZAS	Good	Fine	XF
	ND (-old date 11.11.1987). Ovpt: *NOVO KWANZA* on unissued date of #118. Sign. 15.	Reported Not Confirmed		

123	500 NOVO KWANZA ON 500 KWANZAS	VG	VF	UNC
	ND (-old date 11.11.1987). Ovpt: *NOVO KWANZA* in lt. green on #120b.	2.50	13.00	65.00

124	1000 NOVO KWANZA ON 1000 KWANZAS	VG	VF	UNC
	ND (-old date 11.11.1987). Ovpt: *NOVO KWANZA* in red on #121b.	3.00	13.00	65.00

125	5000 NOVO KWANZA ON 100 KWANZAS	VG	VF	UNC
	ND (-old date 11.11.1987). Ovpt: *NOVO KWANZA 5000* in brown on unissued date of #119. Sign. 15.	25.00	100.00	285.00

1991 ISSUE

#126-134 portr. conjoined busts of Jose Eduardo dos Santos and Antonio Agostinho Neto at r. and as wmk. Arms at lower l. on back.

#126-131 replacement notes: Serial # prefixes *AZ, BZ, CZ, DZ, EZ.*

126	100 KWANZAS	VG	VF	UNC
	4.2.1991. Purple, green and brown. Rock formation at Pungo Andongo at l. ctr. Tribal mask at r. on back. Sign. 16.	0.30	1.25	5.75
127	500 KWANZAS			
	4.2.1991. Blue and violet. Back blue, violet, green and brown. Like #126. Specimen.	—	—	—

128	500 KWANZAS	VG	VF	UNC
	4.2.1991. Purple and deep blue-green on m/c unpt. Serra da Leba at l. ctr., native pot at r. on back.			
	a. Sign. 16.	0.75	5.00	25.00
	b. Sign. 17.	0.50	2.50	10.00
	c. Sign. 18.	0.60	3.25	12.50

129	1000 KWANZAS	VG	VF	UNC
	4.2.1991. Brown, orange, purple and red-violet on m/c unpt. Banco Nacional at l. ctr., native doll at r. on back.			
	a. Sign. 16.	1.25	7.50	37.50
	b. Sign. 17.	0.40	2.75	12.75
	c. Sign. 18.	0.75	5.00	16.00

133	100,000 KWANZAS	VG	VF	UNC
	4.2.1991 (1993). Orange and aqua on emerald green and m/c unpt. Like #131 except for value. Sign. 18.			
	a. Microprint around wmk area reads: *100000 BNA*, latent print: *100000 CEM MIL*. Wmk: *100000*.	1.00	5.00	9.50
	x. Microprint around wmk. area reads: *10000 BNA*, latent print: *10000 DEZ MIL*. Wmk: *10,000*. (error).	2.00	15.00	57.50

130	5000 KWANZAS	VG	VF	UNC
	4.2.1991. Dk. green, blue-green and dk. brown on m/c unpt. Waterfalls and stylized statue of "The Thinker" on back.			
	a. Sign. 16.	2.25	15.00	50.00
	b. Sign. 17.	1.00	5.00	20.00
	c. Sign. 18.	1.50	7.50	22.50

134	500,000 KWANZAS	VG	VF	UNC
	4.2.1991 (1994). Red, brown and violet on m/c unpt. Rhinoceros at l. on back. Sign. 19.	0.50	2.00	6.50
134A	1,000,000 KWANZAS			
	4.2.1991.			Reported Not Confirmed

1995 ISSUE

Kwanza Reajustado System

#135-142 portr. conjoined busts of José Eduardo dos Santos and Antonio Agostinho Neto at r. Arms at lower l., mask at upper r. on back. Wmk: Sculpture.

131	10,000 KWANZAS	VG	VF	UNC
	4.2.1991. Red, olive-green and purple on m/c unpt. Sable antelope herd and shell on back.			
	a. Sign. 17.	2.00	15.00	80.00
	b. Sign. 18.	0.60	3.25	12.50

135	1000 KWANZAS REAJUSTADOS	VG	VF	UNC
	1.5.1995. Black and blue on m/c unpt. Sable antelope at l. on back. Sign. 20.	0.50	1.50	3.75

132	50,000 KWANZAS	VG	VF	UNC
	4.2.1991. Bright green, yellow-green and dk. brown on m/c unpt. Like #130. Sign. 18.	0.50	2.50	9.50

		VG	**VF**	**UNC**
136	**5000 KWANZAS REAJUSTADOS**	0.50	2.25	9.00
	1.5.1995. Green and brown on m/c unpt. Banco Nacional at l. on back. Sign. 20.			

		VG	**VF**	**UNC**
137	**10,000 KWANZAS REAJUSTADOS**	0.50	2.25	9.50
	1.5.1995. Red and purple on m/c unpt. Off shore oil platform at l. on back. Sign. 20.			

		VG	**VF**	**UNC**
138	**50,000 KWANZAS REAJUSTADOS**	0.50	2.50	9.00
	1.5.1995. Orange and green on m/c unpt. Telecommunications station in Luanda at l. ctr. on back. Sign. 20.			

		VG	**VF**	**UNC**
139	**100,000 KWANZAS REAJUSTADOS**	0.50	2.75	6.50
	1.5.1995. Dk. blue and brown-violet on m/c unpt. Mask and pottery at l. ctr. on back. Sign. 20.			

		VG	**VF**	**UNC**
140	**500,000 KWANZAS REAJUSTADOS**	1.00	3.00	7.50
	1.5.1995. Dk. brown and red-brown on m/c unpt. Matala dam at l. ctr. on back. Sign. 20.			

		VG	**VF**	**UNC**
141	**1,000,000 KWANZAS REAJUSTADOS**	1.00	3.50	9.50
	1.5.1995. Bright blue and red-brown on m/c unpt. School girl at l. ctr. on back. Sign. 20.			

		VG	**VF**	**UNC**
142	**5,000,000 KWANZAS REAJUSTADOS**	1.50	7.50	50.00
	1.5.1995. Violet and red-brown on m/c unpt. Serra da Leba at l. ctr. on back. Sign. 20.			

1999; 2003 ISSUE

1 Kwanza = 1,000,000 reajustados Kwanzas.

#143-146 portr. conjoined busts of Jose Eduardo dos Santos and Antonio Agostinho Neto at r. Arms at lower l., mask at at upper r. on back. Wmk: Sculpture. Printer: FCO.

143 **1 KWANZA**
10.1999. Dk. brown, pink and light blue on m/c unpt. Women
picking cotton on back. Sign. 21

	VG	VF	UNC
	FV	FV	0.25

147 **100 KWANZAS**
10.1999. Olive and m/c unpt. Banco Nacional bldg. on back.

	VG	VF	UNC
	FV	FV	6.00

144 **5 KWANZAS**
10.1999. Purple, light-blue and dk. blue on m/c unpt. Mountain
pass on back. Sign. 21.

	VG	VF	UNC
	FV	FV	0.50

148 **200 KWANZAS**
11.2003. Mauve, aqua, pink and orange on m/c unpt. Aerial view of
Luanda's coastline boulevard on back. Sign. 22.

	VG	VF	UNC
	FV	FV	11.00

145 **10 KWANZAS**
10.1999. Brown, orange and purple on m/c unpt. Two antelope on
back. Sign. 21.

	VG	VF	UNC
	FV	FV	0.75

149 **500 KWANZAS**
11.2003. Mauve, yellow and green on m/c unpt. Cotton harvesting
scene on back. Sign. 22.

	VG	VF	UNC
	FV	FV	26.00

146 **50 KWANZAS**
10.1999. Off-shore oil rig on back.

	VG	VF	UNC
	FV	FV	3.00

150 **1000 KWANZAS**
11.2003. Red, oragne, blue and purple on m/c unpt. Coffee
plantation on back. Sign. 22.

	VG	VF	UNC
	FV	FV	50.00

151	2000 KWANZAS	VG	VF	UNC
	11.2003. Lt. and dk. green on m/c unpt.	FV	FV	75.00

ARGENTINA

The Argentine Republic, located in South America, has an area of 1,068,301 sq. mi. (2,766,889 sq. km.) and a population of 37.03 million. Capital: Buenos Aires. Its varied topography ranges from the subtropical lowlands of the north to the towering Andean Mountains in the west and the windswept Patagonian steppe in the south. The rolling, fertile pampas of central Argentina are ideal for agriculture and grazing, and support most of the republic's population. Meat packing, flour milling, textiles, sugar refining and dairy products are the principal industries. Oil is found in Patagonia, but most of the mineral requirements must be imported.

Argentina was discovered in 1516 by the Spanish navigator Juan de Solis. A permanent Spanish colony was established at Buenos Aires in 1580, but the colony developed slowly. When Napoleon conquered Spain, the Argentines set up their own government in the name of the Spanish king on May 25, 1810. Independence was formally declared on July 9, 1816.

MONETARY SYSTEM:
  1 Peso (m/n) = 100 Centavos to 1970
  1 'New' Peso (Ley 18.188) = 100 'Old' Pesos (m/n), 1970-83
  1 Peso Argentino = 10,000 Pesos, (Ley 18.188) 1983-85
  1 Austral = 100 Centavos = 1000 Pesos Argentinos, 1985-92
  1 Peso = 10,000 Australes, 1992-

REPLACEMENT NOTES:
  #260d onward: R prefix before serial #.

REPUBLIC

BANCO CENTRAL

Signature Titles:

A - *GERENTE GENERAL*

B - *SUBGERENTE GENERAL*

C - *GERENTE GENERAL* and *PRESIDENTE*

D - *SUBGERENTE GENERAL* and *VICE-PRESIDENTE*

E - *SUBGERENTE GENERAL* and *PRESIDENTE*

F - *VICE PRESIDENTE* and *PRESIDENTE*

G - *PRESIDENTE B.C.R.A.* and *PRESIDENTE H.C. SENADORES*

H - *PRESIDENTE B.C.R.A.* and *PRESIDENTE H.C. DIPUTADOS*

I - *VICE PRESIDENTE* and *GERENTE GENERAL*

1960-69 ND ISSUE

W/o Ley- Moneda Nacional

#275-277, 279-280 Portr. Gen. José de San Martín in uniform at r. Sign. varieties.

Notes begin with *SERIE A* unless noted.

275	5 PESOS	VG	VF	UNC
	ND (1960-62). Brown on yellow unpt. People gathering before bldg. on back. Printer: CMN. 3 sign. varieties. Serie A.			
	a. Sign. titles: D.	0.30	1.50	6.00
	b. Sign. titles: C.	0.75	3.00	12.50
	c. Sign. titles: E.	0.40	1.75	5.50

276	50 PESOS	VG	VF	UNC
	ND (1968-69). Green. Army in mountains on back. *SERIE D.* Sign. titles: C.	0.35	1.25	5.00

277	100 PESOS	VG	VF	UNC
	ND (1967-69). Red-brown. Spanish and Indians on back. *SERIE E, F, G.* 2 sign. varieties. Sign. titles: C.	0.25	1.25	4.00

278	500 PESOS	VG	VF	UNC
	ND (1964-69). Blue on blue and gold unpt. Portr. elderly Gen J. de San Martín not in uniform at r. Grand Bourg House in France on back. 4 sign. varieties. Serie A.			
	a. Sign. titles: E.	3.00	10.00	17.50
	b. Sign. titles: C.	1.50	4.00	10.00

279	1000 PESOS	VG	VF	UNC
	ND (1966-69). Purple. Portr. young Gen J. de San Martín in uniform at r. Sailing ship on back. *SERIE C, D.* 3 sign. varieties.			
	a. Sign. titles: E.	1.00	3.75	15.00
	b. Sign. titles: C.	0.75	3.25	10.00
280	5000 PESOS			
	ND (1962-69). Brown on yellow-green unpt. Portr. young Gen. J. de San Martín in uniform. Capitol on back. 6 sign. varieties. Serie A.			
	a. Sign. titles: E.	4.50	15.00	50.00
	b. Sign. titles: C.	3.50	12.50	37.50
	s. As a. Specimen.	—	—	200.00

281	10,000 PESOS	VG	VF	UNC
	ND (1961-69). Deep red on blue and yellow unpt. Portr. elderly Gen J. de San Martín not in uniform at r. Armies in the field on back. *SERIE A, B.* 5 sign. varieties.			
	a. Sign. titles: E. Serie A, B.	4.50	15.00	50.00
	b. Sign. titles: C. Serie B.	2.50	12.50	35.00
	s. As a. Specimen.	—	—	200.00

1969 ND PROVISIONAL ISSUE

Ley 18.188.

#282-286 Overprint in wmk. area on face. Sign. titles: C.

282	1 PESO ON 100 PESOS	VG	VF	UNC
	ND (1969-71). Red-brown. Ovpt: New denomination on #277. *SERIE G.*	0.50	3.00	10.00

283 5 PESOS ON 500 PESOS
ND (1969-71). Blue on blue and gold unpt. Ovpt: New denomination on #278. 2 sign. varieties. *Serie A.*

	VG	VF	UNC
	1.50	7.50	22.50

284 10 PESOS ON 1000 PESOS
ND (1969-71). Purple. Ovpt: New denomination on #279. *SERIE D, E.*

	VG	VF	UNC
	1.50	7.50	22.50

285 50 PESOS ON 5000 PESOS
ND (1969-71). Brown on yellow green unpt. Ovpt: New denomination on #280. *SERIE A.*

	VG	VF	UNC
	2.25	12.50	37.50

286 100 PESOS ON 10,000 PESOS
ND (1969-71). Deep red on blue and yellow unpt. Ovpt: New denomination on #281. *SERIE B.* 2 sign. varieties.

	VG	VF	UNC
	10.00	22.50	75.00

LEY 18.188; 1970-73 ND ISSUE

#287-289 Gen. Manuel Belgrano at r. Printer: CMN. Many sign. varieties. W/o colored threads in white or grayish tint paper. Wmk. varieties.

#287-292 replacement notes: Serial # prefix *R*.

287 1 PESO
ND (1970-73). Orange on m/c unpt. Scene of Bariloche-Llao-Llao at ctr. on back. *SERIE A-E.* 5 sign. varieties.

	VG	VF	UNC
	0.15	0.40	1.50

288 5 PESOS
ND (1971-73). Blue on m/c unpt. Monument to the Flag at Rosario at ctr. on back. 2 sign. varieties.

	VG	VF	UNC
	0.25	1.00	4.50

289 10 PESOS
ND (1970-73). Purple on m/c unpt. Waterfalls at Iguazu at ctr. on back. *SERIE A, B.* 6 sign. varieties.

	VG	VF	UNC
	0.10	0.30	2.00

#290-292 Gen. José de San Martín at r. Colored threads in paper. Wmk: Arms.

290 50 PESOS
ND (1972-73). Black and brown on m/c unpt. Hot springs at Jujuy at ctr. on back. 3 sign. varieties.

	VG	VF	UNC
	0.50	3.00	15.00

291 100 PESOS
ND (1971-73). Red on m/c unpt. Coastline at Ushuaia at ctr. on back. *SERIE A, B.* 4 sign. varieties.

	VG	VF	UNC
	1.00	5.00	20.00

292 500 PESOS
ND (1972-73). Green on m/c unpt. Army monument at Mendoza at ctr. on back. 2 sign. varieties.

	VG	VF	UNC
	1.50	10.00	30.00

DECRETO-LEY 18.188/69; 1973-76 ND ISSUE

#293-295 Gen. Manuel Belgrano at r. Sign. varieties. W/o colored threads in paper (varieties). Wmk: Arms. Wmk. varieties.

#293-299 replacement notes: Serial # prefix *R*.

#296-299 Gen. José de San Martín at r. Sign. varieties. Colored threads in paper. Wmk: Arms.

		VG	VF	UNC
293	**1 PESO**			
	ND (1974). Orange on m/c unpt. Like #287. Scene of Bariloche-Llao-Llao at ctr. on back. *SERIE E, F.*	0.15	0.50	1.50

		VG	VF	UNC
296	**50 PESOS**			
	ND (1974-75). Black and brown on m/c unpt. Like #290. Hot springs at Jujuy at ctr. on back. *SERIE A, B.* 2 sign. varieties.	0.15	0.50	1.50

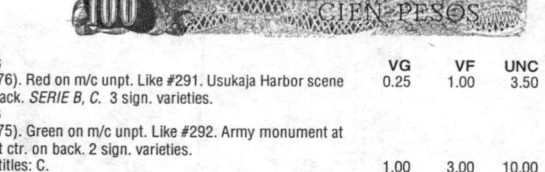

		VG	VF	UNC
297	**100 PESOS**			
	ND (1973-76). Red on m/c unpt. Like #291. Usukaja Harbor scene at ctr. on back. *SERIE B, C.* 3 sign. varieties.	0.25	1.00	3.50
298	**500 PESOS**			
	ND (1974-75). Green on m/c unpt. Like #292. Army monument at Mendoza at ctr. on back. 2 sign. varieties.			
	a. Sign. titles: C.	1.00	3.00	10.00
	b. Sign. titles: F.	0.50	2.00	7.50
	c. Sign. titles :I.	1.00	3.00	10.00

		VG	VF	UNC
294	**5 PESOS**			
	ND (1974-76). Blue on m/c unpt. Like #288. Monument to the Flag at Rosario at ctr. on back. *SERIE A, B.* 2 sign. varieties.	0.10	0.40	1.25

		VG	VF	UNC
295	**10 PESOS**			
	ND (1973-76). Purple on m/c unpt. Like # 289. Waterfalls at Iguazu at ctr. on back. *SERIE C, D.* 4 sign. varieties.	0.15	0.50	2.50

		VG	VF	UNC
299	**1000 PESOS**			
	ND (1973-76). Brown on m/c unpt. *Plaza de Mayo* in Buenos Aires at ctr. on back. *SERIE A-C.* 3 sign. varieties.	1.25	5.00	12.50

1976-83 ND ISSUE

W/o Decreto or Ley

#301-310 Replacement notes: Serial # prefix *R*.

#300-302 wmk: Arms.

300	10 PESOS	VG	VF	UNC
	ND (1976). Purple on m/c unpt. Like #289. Gen. M. Belgrano at r. Waterfalls at Iguazu at ctr. on back. *SERIE D, E.*	0.10	0.20	1.00

#301-310 Gen José de San Martín at r. Sign. and wmk. varieties.

301	50 PESOS	VG	VF	UNC
	ND (1976-78). Black on m/c unpt. Like #290. Hot springs at Jujuy at ctr. on back. *SERIE B, C.* 2 sign. varieties. Engraved or lithographed back.			
	a. W/o colored threads in paper.	1.25	5.00	10.00
	b. Colored threads in paper.	0.10	0.20	0.75

302	100 PESOS	VG	VF	UNC
	ND (1976-78). Red on m/c unpt. Like #291. Coastline at Ushuaia at ctr. on back. *SERIE C-E.*			
	a. W/o colored threads in paper. 2 sign. varieties.	0.15	0.50	2.50
	b. Colored threads in paper. 2 sign. varieties.	0.10	0.30	1.00

303	500 PESOS	VG	VF	UNC
	ND (1977-82). Green on m/c unpt. Like #292. Army monument at Mendoza at ctr. on back. *SERIE A-D.* 4 sign. varieties.			
	a. Wmk: Arms. W/o colored threads in paper.	0.10	0.20	1.50
	b. Wmk: Arms. Colored threads in paper.	0.15	0.50	2.50
	c. Wmk: Multiple sunbursts. Colored threads. Back lithographed. *SERIE C, D.*	0.05	0.20	0.75

#304-305 Color varieties in underprint: yellow or green, maroon or ochre.

304	1000 PESOS	VG	VF	UNC
	ND (1976-83). Brown on m/c unpt. Like #299. *Plaza de Mayo* in Buenos Aires at ctr. on back. *SERIE C-I.* 5 sign. varieties.			
	a. Wmk: Arms. W/o colored threads in paper.	0.10	0.30	2.00
	b. Wmk: Arms. Colored threads in paper. 2 sign. varieties.	0.05	0.20	1.50
	c. Wmk: Multiple sunbursts. Back engraved.	0.05	0.20	1.00
	d. Wmk: Multiple sunbursts. Back lithographed. *SERIE I.*	0.05	0.15	0.75

#305-310 w/colored threads.

305	5000 PESOS	VG	VF	UNC
	ND (1977-83). Blue and olive-green on m/c unpt. Coastline of Mar del Plata on back.			
	a. Wmk: Arms. 2 sign. varieties. *SERIE A, B.*	0.20	0.40	2.00
	b. Wmk: Multiple sunbursts. 2 sign. varieties. *SERIE B.*	0.10	0.20	1.00

		VG	**VF**	**UNC**
306	**10,000 PESOS**			
	ND (1976-83). Orange and red on m/c unpt. National park on back. 4 sign. varieties.			
	a. Wmk: Arms. 3 sign. varieties. *SERIE A-G.*	0.25	0.75	3.00
	b. Wmk: Multiple sunbursts. *SERIE G.*	0.20	0.50	1.50

		VG	**VF**	**UNC**
309	**500,000 PESOS**	0.25	1.00	5.00
	ND (1980-83). Green, brown and blue on m/c unpt. Founding of Buenos Aires at l. ctr. on back. Wmk: Multiple sunbursts. 2 sign. varieties.			

		VG	**VF**	**UNC**
307	**50,000 PESOS**	0.25	1.00	3.00
	ND (1979-83). Brown on m/c unpt. Banco Central bldg. at l. ctr. on back. Wmk: Arms. 2 sign. varieties.			

		VG	**VF**	**UNC**
310	**1,000,000 PESOS**	1.50	7.50	17.50
	ND (1981-83). Blue and pink on m/c unpt. Independence Declaration w/*25 de Mayo* at l. ctr. on back. Wmk: Multiple sunbursts. *SERIE A, B.* 3 sign. varieties.			

1983-85 ND Issue

Peso Argentino System

#311-319 w/colored threads. Watermark varieties. Replacement notes: Serial # prefix *R.*

#311-317 face design w/San Martín at r.

#311-316 wmk: Multiple sunbursts. Printer: CdM.

		VG	**VF**	**UNC**
308	**100,000 PESOS**			
	ND (1979-83). Gray and red on m/c unpt. Mint bldg. at l. ctr. on back.			
	a. Wmk: Arms. *SERIE A, B.*	0.25	2.00	10.00
	b. Wmk: Multiple sunbursts. *SERIE B.*	0.25	1.00	3.00

		VG	**VF**	**UNC**
311	**1 PESO ARGENTINO**			
	ND (1983-84). Red-orange and purple on blue and m/c unpt. Like #287. Scene of Bariloche-Llao-Llao at ctr. on back. *SERIE A, B.* 2 sign. varieties.			
	a. Issued note.	0.05	0.15	0.75
	s. Specimen.	—	—	25.00

312	5 PESOS ARGENTINOS	VG	VF	UNC
	ND (1983-84). Brown-violet and black on m/c unpt. Like #288. Monument to the Flag at Rosario at ctr. on back. 2 sign. varieties. White or grayish tint paper.			
	a. Issued note.	0.05	0.15	0.75
	s. Specimen.	—	—	25.00

315	100 PESOS ARGENTINOS	VG	VF	UNC
	ND (1983-85). Blue on m/c unpt. Like #291. Coastline at Ushuaia at ctr. on back. *SERIE A, B*. 2 sign. varieties.			
	a. Issued note.	0.15	0.50	1.50
	s. Specimen.	—	—	25.00

313	10 PESOS ARGENTINOS	VG	VF	UNC
	ND (1983-84). Black and red on green and m/c unpt. Like #289. Waterfalls at Iguazu at ctr. on back. *SERIE A, B*. 2 sign. varieties. White or grayish tint paper.			
	a. Issued note.	0.05	0.15	0.75
	s. Specimen.	—	—	25.00

316	500 PESOS ARGENTINOS	VG	VF	UNC
	ND (1984). Purple on m/c unpt. Town meeting of May 22, 1810 on back. White or grayish tint paper.			
	a. Issued note.	0.15	0.50	1.50
	s. Specimen.	—	—	25.00

317	1000 PESOS ARGENTINOS	VG	VF	UNC
	ND (1983-85). Blue-green and brown on m/c unpt. *El Paso de los Andes* battle scene on back.			
	a. Wmk: San Martín. (1983). *SERIE A, B*. 2 sign. varieties.	0.25	1.50	7.00
	b. Wmk: Multiple sunbursts (1984). *SERIE C, D*.	0.15	0.50	1.50
	s1. As a. Specimen. Ovpt: *MUESTRA*.	—	—	25.00
	s2. As b. Specimen. Ovpt.: *MUESTRA*.	—	—	25.00

314	50 PESOS ARGENTINOS	VG	VF	UNC
	ND (1983-85). Brown on green and m/c unpt. Like #290. Hot springs at Jujuy at ctr. on back. 2 sign. varieties.			
	a. Issued note.	0.05	0.15	0.75
	s. Specimen.	—	—	25.00

		VG	VF	UNC
318	**5000 PESOS ARGENTINOS**			
	ND (1984-85). Red-brown on m/c unpt. J. B. Alberdi at r. Constitutional meeting of 1853 on back. Wmk: Young San Martín. *SERIE A, B.*			
	a. Issued note.	0.50	2.00	10.00
	s. Specimen.	—	—	25.00

		VG	VF	UNC
319	**10,000 PESOS ARGENTINOS**			
	ND (1985). Blue-violet on m/c unpt. M. Belgrano at r. Creation of Argentine flag on back. Wmk: Young San Martín.			
	a. Issued note.	0.75	3.50	15.00
	s. Specimen.	—	—	25.00

1985 ND Provisional Issue

Austral System

#320-322 ovpt. on Peso Argentino notes. Rectangle on wmk. area on face.

		VG	VF	UNC
320	**1 AUSTRAL**			
	ND (1985). New denomination ovpt. in numeral and wording in box, green on face and blue on back of #317b. Series D. Wmk: sunburst.	0.15	0.50	2.50

		VG	VF	UNC
321	**5 AUSTRALES**			
	ND (1985). New denomination ovpt. as #320, purple on face and brown on back of #318, Series B. Wmk: San Martín.	0.50	2.00	5.00

		VG	VF	UNC
322	**10 AUSTRALES**			
	ND (1985). New denomination ovpt. as #320 on #319.			
	a. Blue ovpt. on face and back. Wmk: San Martín. Series A; B.	0.50	4.00	9.00
	b. Like a. but wmk: Multiple sunbursts. Series A-C.	0.25	1.75	6.00
	c. Blue ovpt on face, lt. olive-green ovpt. on back. Series B; C.	0.25	1.75	5.00
	d. Series B w/o ovpt.	7.50	30.00	60.00
	s. As b. Specimen.	—	—	25.00

1985-91 ND Issue

#323-330 latent image "BCRA" on face. Liberty (Progreso) w/torch and shield seated at l. ctr. on back. Printer: CdM. Sign. varieties.

Replacement notes: Serial # prefix *R*.

		VG	VF	UNC
323	**1 AUSTRAL**			
	ND (1985-89). Blue-green and purple on m/c unpt. B. Rivadavia at ctr. Wmk: Multiple sunbursts.			
	a. Sign. titles E. Series A.	0.10	0.75	3.00
	b. Sign. titles C. Series B; C. 2 sign. varieties.	0.05	0.15	0.40
	s. Sign. titles C. Series A. Specimen.	—	—	25.00

324   5 AUSTRALES

	VG	VF	UNC
ND (1986-89). Brown and deep olive-green on m/c unpt. J. J. de Urquiza at ctr. Wmk: Multiple sunbursts.			
a. Sign. titles E. Series A.	0.10	0.25	2.00
b. Sign. titles C. Series A.	0.05	0.15	0.40

325   10 AUSTRALES

	VG	VF	UNC
ND (1985-89). Dk. blue and purple on m/c unpt. S. Derqui at ctr. Wmk: Multiple sunbursts.			
a. Coarse portrait in heavy horizontal wavy lines. Sign. titles E. Series A.	0.25	0.75	3.50
b. Modified portrait in finer horizontal wavy lines. Sign. titles C. Series A; B; C.	0.05	0.15	0.40

326   50 AUSTRALES

	VG	VF	UNC
ND (1986-89). Purple and deep brown on m/c unpt. B. Mitre at ctr. Wmk: Multiple sunbursts.			
a. Sign. titles E. Series A.	0.50	6.00	20.00
b. Sign. titles C. Series A. 3 sign. varieties.	0.10	0.15	0.50
s. As b. Specimen.	—	—	25.00

327   100 AUSTRALES

	VG	VF	UNC
ND (1985-90). Dk. red and purple on m/c unpt. D. F. Sarmiento at ctr. Wmk: Multiple sunbursts.			
a. Sign. titles E. Series A.	0.50	4.00	15.00
b. Sign. titles C. Engraved back. Series A; B. 3 sign. varieties.	0.10	0.20	0.75
c. Sign. titles C. Back pink and lithographed; w/o purple and blue. Series C; D.	0.05	0.15	0.50
s. As b. Specimen.	—	—	25.00

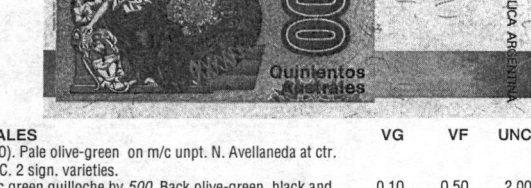

328   500 AUSTRALES

	VG	VF	UNC
ND (1988-90). Pale olive-green on m/c unpt. N. Avellaneda at ctr. Sign. titles: C. 2 sign. varieties.			
a. Metallic green guilloche by *500*. Back olive-green, black and m/c. Wmk: Liberty. Series A. (1988).	0.10	0.50	2.00
b. Dk. olive-green guilloche by *500*. Back pale olive-green and m/c; lithographed (w/o black). Wmk: Multiple sunbursts. Series A. (1990).	0.05	0.20	0.75
s. As a. Specimen.	—	—	25.00

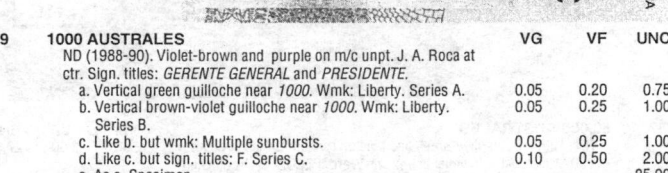

329   1000 AUSTRALES

	VG	VF	UNC
ND (1988-90). Violet-brown and purple on m/c unpt. J. A. Roca at ctr. Sign. titles: *GERENTE GENERAL* and *PRESIDENTE*.			
a. Vertical green guilloche near *1000*. Wmk: Liberty. Series A.	0.05	0.20	0.75
b. Vertical brown-violet guilloche near *1000*. Wmk: Liberty. Series B.	0.05	0.25	1.00
c. Like b. but wmk: Multiple sunbursts.	0.05	0.25	1.00
d. Like c. but sign. titles: F. Series C.	0.10	0.50	2.00
s. As a. Specimen.	—	—	25.00

330   5000 AUSTRALES

	VG	VF	UNC
ND (1989-91). Dk. brown and red-brown on m/c unpt. M. Juarez at ctr.			
a. Green shield design at upper ctr. r. Sign titles: E. Wmk: Liberty. Series A.	0.50	3.00	12.50
b. Green shield design at upper ctr. r. Sign titles: C. Wmk: Liberty. Series A.	0.75	5.00	17.50
c. Dk. brown shield design at upper ctr. r. Sign. titles: E. Wmk: Liberty. Series B.	0.50	2.50	8.00

330	5000 AUSTRALES	VG	VF	UNC
	d. Dk. brown shield design. Sign. titles: C. Wmk: Liberty. Series B.	0.50	2.00	7.00
	e. Dk. brown shield design. Sign. titles: F. Lithographed back. Wmk: Multiple sunbursts. Series C.	0.20	1.00	4.00
	f. Series D (1991).	20.00	60.00	125.00

1989; 1991 ND PROVISIONAL ISSUE

#331-333 use modified face plates from earlier issue. Wmk: Multiple sunbursts. Series M. Printer: CdM-A. Replacement notes: Serial # prefix R.

331	10,000 AUSTRALES	VG	VF	UNC
	ND (1989). Black-blue, deep blue-green and brown on m/c unpt. Face similar to #306. Ovpt. value in olive-green in box at l. Word "PESOS" at ctr. blocked out. Denomination repeated in lines of text and ovpt. value at r. on back. Sign. titles: C.	2.00	7.50	25.00

332	50,000 AUSTRALES	VG	VF	UNC
	ND (1989). Deep olive-green and blue on m/c unpt. Face similar to #307. Ovpt. value in violet in box at l. Word "PESOS" at ctr. blocked out. Back similar to #331. Value in lt. brown at r. Sign. titles: E.	2.00	8.00	27.50
333	500,000 AUSTRALES			
	ND (1990). Black, purple and red on m/c unpt. Face similar to #309. Ovpt. value in box at l. Word "PESOS" at bottom r. blocked out. Back similar to #331. Value at r. Sign. titles: F.	7.50	30.00	75.00

1989-91 ND ISSUE

#334-338 Liberty (Progreso) w/torch and shield seated at l. ctr. on back. Wmk: Liberty head. Printer: CdM-A. Replacement notes: Serial # prefix R.

334	10,000 AUSTRALES	VG	VF	UNC
	ND (1989-91). Black on deep blue, brown and m/c unpt. w/brown diamond design at upper ctr. R. C. Pellegrini at ctr.			
	a. Sign. titles: C. Series A; B.	0.25	1.25	3.50
	b. Sign. titles: F. Series C. Wmk: sunbursts.	0.50	1.50	6.00

335	50,000 AUSTRALES	VG	VF	UNC
	ND (1989-91). Black on ochre, olive-green and m/c unpt. w/black flower design at upper ctr. r. L. Saenz Peña at ctr. Sign. titles: C. Series A; B.	1.00	6.00	25.00

336	100,000 AUSTRALES	VG	VF	UNC
	ND (1990-91). Dk. brown and reddish brown on pale brown and m/c unpt. Coarsely engraved portr. of J. Evaristo Uriburu at ctr. Black sign. titles: F. Series A; B.	2.00	10.00	45.00

337	100,000 AUSTRALES	VG	VF	UNC
	ND (1991). Dk. brown and reddish brown on brown and m/c unpt. Finely engraved portr. of J. Evaristo Uriburu at ctr. Brown sign. titles. Series B.	1.50	8.00	50.00

338	500,000 AUSTRALES	VG	VF	UNC
	ND (1991). Black-violet, red and blue on m/c unpt. M. Quintana at ctr. Series A, B. 2 sign. varieties.	4.00	25.00	75.00

1991-92 ND Issue

Peso System

#339-341 wmk: Multiple sunbursts. Printer: CdM-A.

#339-345 replacement notes: Serial # prefix *R*.

339	1 PESO	VG	VF	UNC
	ND (1992-94). Dk. blue and violet-brown on m/c unpt. C. Pelligrini at r. Back gray on m/c unpt; National Congress bldg. at l. ctr.			
	a. Sign. titles: F. (1992). Series A, B.	FV	FV	3.00
	b. Sign. titles: G. (1993). Series B, C, D.	FV	FV	2.50
	c. Sign. titles as a. Serial # prefix L. (1994).	FV	FV	5.00

340	2 PESOS	VG	VF	UNC
	ND (1992-97). Deep blue and red-violet on m/c unpt. B. Mitre at r. Back lt. blue on m/c unpt; Mitre Museum at l. ctr.			
	a. Sign. titles: F. (1992). Series A.	FV	FV	5.00
	b. Sign. titles: H. (1993). Series A-C.	FV	FV	4.00

341	5 PESOS	VG	VF	UNC
	ND (1992-97). Deep olive-green and red-orange on m/c unpt. Gen. J. de San Martín at r. Back lt. olive-gray on m/c unpt; monument to the Glory of Mendoza at l. ctr.			
	a. Sign. titles: F. (1992). Series A.	FV	FV	8.00
	b. Sign. titles: G. (1993). Series A-C.	FV	FV	9.00
	c. Sign. titles as a. Serial # prefix L. (1994).	FV	FV	10.00

#342-343 wmk: Liberty head. Printer: CdM-A.

342	10 PESOS	VG	VF	UNC
	ND (1992-97). Deep brown and dk. green on m/c unpt. M. Belgrano at r. Monument to the Flag at Rosario w/city in background at l. ctr. on back.			
	a. Sign. titles: F. (1992). Series A-B.	FV	FV	20.00
	b. Sign. titles: H. (1993). Series C-E.	FV	FV	17.50

343	20 PESOS	VG	VF	UNC
	ND (1992-97). Carmine and deep blue on m/c unpt. J. Manuel de Rosas at r. *Vuelta de Obligado* battle scene at l. ctr. on back.			
	a. Sign. titles: F. (1992). Series A.	FV	FV	35.00
	b. Sign. titles: G. (1993). Series A-B.	FV	FV	30.00

344	50 PESOS	VG	VF	UNC
	ND (1992-97). Black and red on m/c unpt. D. Faustino Sarmiento at r. and as wmk. Plaza de Mayo in Buenos Aires at l. ctr. on back.			
	a. Sign. titles: F. (1992). Series A.	FV	FV	75.00
	b. Sign. titles: H. (1993). Series A-B.	FV	FV	70.00

345   100 PESOS

	VG	VF	UNC
ND (1992-97). Violet, lilac and green on m/c unpt. J. A. Roca at r. and as wmk. Back violet and m/c; *La Conquista del Desierto* scene at l. ctr.			
a. Sign. titles: F. (1992). Series A.	FV	FV	125.00
b. Sign. titles: G. (1993). Series A-D.	FV	FV	110.00

1997-2000 ND ISSUE

#346-351 ascending size serial # at upper r. Printer: CdM-A. Replacement notes: Serial # prefix R.

346   2 PESOS

	VG	VF	UNC
ND (1997-2002). Deep blue and brown-violet on m/c unpt. B. Mitre at r. and as wmk., ornate gate at ctr. Mitre Museum at l. ctr. on back. Sign. titles: H. 2 sign. varieties. Series A-D.	FV	FV	3.00

347   5 PESOS

	VG	VF	UNC
ND (1998-2003). Deep olive-green and purple on m/c unpt. Gen. J. de. San Martín at r. and as wmk., Gen. San Martín on horseback w/troops at ctr. Monument to the Glory at Mendoza at l. ctr. on back. Sign. titles: G. 2 sign. varieties. Series A-C.	FV	FV	7.00

348   10 PESOS

	VG	VF	UNC
ND (1998-2003). Deep brown and dk. green on m/c unpt. M. Belgrano at r. and as wmk., Liberty w/flag at ctr. Monument to the Flag at Rosario w/city in background at l. ctr. on back. Sign. titles: H. 3 sign. varieties. Series A-E.	FV	FV	15.00

349   20 PESOS

	VG	VF	UNC
ND (1999-2003). Red-brown and purple on m/c unpt. J. Manuel de Rosas at r. and as wmk. *Vuelta de Obligado* battle scene at l. ctr. on back. Sign. titles: G. 2 sign. varieties. Series A, B.	FV	FV	30.00

350   50 PESOS

	VG	VF	UNC
ND (1999-2003). M/c. D. Faustino Sarmiento at r. and as wmk. Government office w/monuments, palm trees in foreground at l. ctr. on back. Sign. titles: H. 3 sign. varieties. Series A.	FV	FV	65.00

351   100 PESOS

	VG	VF	UNC
ND (1999-2002). M/c. J. A. Roca at r. and as wmk. *La Conquista del Desierto* scene at l. ctr. on back. Sign. titles: G. 4 sign. varieties. Series A, B.	FV	FV	120.00

2002 ND ISSUE

#352-357 similar to #346-351 but no clause: *CONVERTIBLES DE CURSO LEGAL*.

		VG	VF	UNC
352	**2 PESOS**			
	ND (2002). Similar to #346. Series D-E. 3 sign. varieties.	FV	FV	3.00
353	**5 PESOS**			
	ND (2002-03). Similar to #347. Series C-D. 2 sign. varieties.	FV	FV	7.00
354	**10 PESOS**			
	ND (2002-03). Similar to #348. Series E-G. 2 sign. varieties.	FV	FV	15.00
355	**20 PESOS**			
	ND (2002-03). Similar to #349. Series B. 2 sign. varieties.	FV	FV	30.00
356	**50 PESOS**			
	ND (2002-03). Similar to #350. Series A-B. 2 sign. varieties.	FV	FV	65.00
357	**100 PESOS**			
	ND (2002-03). Similar to #351. Series B-D. 2 sign. varieties.	FV	FV	120.00

ARMENIA

The Republic of Armenia (formerly the Armenian S.S.R.) is bounded to the north by Georgia, to the east by Azerbaijan and to the south and west by Turkey and Iran. It has an area of 11,490 sq. mi. (29,800 sq. km) and a population of 3.7 million. Capital: Yerevan. Agriculture including cotton, vineyards and orchards, hydroelectricity, chemicals - primarily synthetic rubber and fertilizers, and vast mineral deposits of copper, zinc and aluminum and production of steel and paper are major industries.

The earliest history of Armenia records continuous struggles with Babylonia and later Assyria. In the sixth century B.C. it was called Armina. Later under under the Persian empire it was a vassal state. Conquered by Macedonia, it later defeated the Seleucids and thus Greater Armenia was founded under the Artaxis dynasty. Christianity was established in 303 A.D. which led to religious wars with the Persians and Romans who then divided it into two zones of influence. The Arabs succeeded the Sassanids. In 862 A.D. Ashot V was recognized as the "prince of princes" and established a throne recognized by Baghdad and Constantinople in 886 A.D. The Seljuks overran the whole country and united with Kurdistan whic eventually ran the new government. From 1240 A.D. onward the Mongols occupied almost all of western Asia until their downfall in 1375 A.D. when various Kurdish, Armenian and Turkoman independent principalities arose. After the defeat of the Persians in 1516 A.D. the Ottoman Turks gradually took control with Kurdish tribes settling within Armenian lands. In 1605 A.D, the Persians relocated thousands of Armenians as far as India to develop colonies. Persia and the Ottoman Turks were again at war, with the Ottomans once again prevailing. The Ottomans later gave absolute civil authority to a Christian bishop allowing the Armenians free enjoyment of their religion and traditions.

Russia occupied Armenia in 1801 until the Russo-Turkish war of 1878. British intervention excluded either side from remaining although the Armenian remained more loyal to the Ottoman Turks. In 1894 the Ottoman Turks sent in an expeditionary force of Kurds fearing a revolutionary movement. Large massacres were followed by retaliations, an amnesty was proclaimed which continued to 1916, when Armenia was occupied by Russian forces. From 1917-1918 the Georgians, Armenians and Azerbaijanis formed the short-lived Transcaucasian Federal Republic which split into three independent republics on May 26, 1918. Communism developed and in Sept. 1920 the Turks attacked the Armenian Republic; the Russians soon followed suit, routing the Turks. On Nov. 29, 1920 Armenia was proclaimed a Soviet Socialist Republic. On March 12, 1922, Armenia, Georgia and Azerbaijan were combined to form the Transcaucasian Soviet Federated Socialist republic, which on Dec. 30, 1922, became a part of U.S.S.R. On Dec. 5, 1936, the Transcaucasian federation was dissolved and Armenia became a constituent republic of the U.S.S.R.

A new constitution was adopted in April 1978. Elections took place on May 20, 1990. The Supreme Soviet adopted a declaration of sovereignty in Aug. 1991, voting to unite Armenia with Nagorno-Karabakh. This newly constituted Republic of Armenia became independent by popular vote in Sept. 1991. It joined the CIS in Dec.1991.

Fighting between Christians in Armenia and Muslim forces of Azerbaijan escalated in 1992 and continued through early 1994. Each country claimed the Nagorno-Karabakh, an Armenian ethnic enclave in Azerbaijan. A temporary cease-fire was announced in May 1994.

MONETARY SYSTEM:
1 Dram = 100 Lumma

ARMENIAN REPUBLIC BANK

1993-95 ISSUE

#33-38 wmk: Crude outlined coat, or refined coat. Printer: G&D (w/o imprint).

33	10 DRAM	VG	VF	UNC
	1993. Dk. brown, lt. blue and pale orange on m/c unpt. Statue of David from Sasoun at upper ctr. r., main railway station in Yerevan at upper l. ctr. Mt. Ararat at upper ctr. r. on back.	0.05	0.25	0.75

34	25 DRAM	VG	VF	UNC
	1993. Brown and lt. red on m/c unpt. Frieze w/lion from Erebuni Castle at ctr. r., cuneiform tablet at upper l. ctr. Arched ornament at upper ctr. r. on back.	0.10	0.25	1.00

35	50 DRAM	VG	VF	UNC
	1993. Dk. blue on pink and m/c unpt. State Museum of History and National Gallery at upper l. ctr. Parliament bldg. at upper ctr. r. on back.	0.10	0.25	1.25

36	100 DRAM	VG	VF	UNC
	1993. Purple, lt. blue and lt. red on m/c unpt. Mt. Ararat at upper l. ctr., Church of Zvarnots at ctr. r. Opera and ballet theater in Yerevan at upper ctr. r. on back.			
	a. Wmk: Crude outline arms.	0.10	0.25	1.75
	b. Wmk: Refined arms.	0.10	0.25	1.50

37	200 DRAM	VG	VF	UNC
	1993. Brown, green and red on m/c unpt. Church of St. Hripsime in Echmiadzin at ctr. r. Circular design at upper ctr. r. on back.			
	a. Wmk: Crude outline arms.	0.10	0.50	3.00
	b. Wmk: Refined arms.	0.10	0.50	3.00

38	500 DRAM	VG	VF	UNC
	1993. Dk. green and red-brown on m/c unpt. Tetradrachm of Kg. Tigran II the Great at ctr. r., Mt. Ararat at upper l. ctr. Open book and quill pen at upper ctr. r. on back.			
	a. Wmk: Crude outline arms.	0.10	0.50	3.00
	b. Wmk: Refined arms.	0.10	0.50	3.00

39 **1000 DRAM**

	VG	VF	UNC
1994. Dk. brown and brown on m/c unpt. Statue of Mesrop Mashtotz at l. Matenadaran facade at r. on back. Wmk: Arms.	0.25	1.00	5.00

40 **5000 DRAM**

	VG	VF	UNC
1995. Brown-violet on m/c unpt. Temple of Garni at ctr. Goddess Anahit on back.	0.50	1.00	8.00

CENTRAL BANK OF THE REPUBLIC OF ARMENIA

1998-99 ISSUE

#41-45, 48 printer: (T)DLR (w/o imprint.) Wmk. is portr. #41, 42, 44 replacement notes serial # first digit is 9.

41 **50 DRAM**

	VG	VF	UNC
1998. Brownish pink and slate blue on m/c unpt. Aram Khachaturian at l., opera house at r. Scene from *Gayaneh* Ballet and Mt. Ararat on back.	0.15	0.50	1.25

42 **100 DRAM**

	VG	VF	UNC
1998. Lt. and dk. blue on m/c unpt. Victor Hambartsumyan at l., solar system map at r. Byurakan Observatory on Mt. Arakadz on back.	0.15	0.50	1.50

43 **200 DRAM**

1999.   Expected New Issue

44 **500 DRAM**

	VG	VF	UNC
1999 (2000). Black on red and m/c unpt. Alexander Tamanyan and city plan. House of the Government in Yerevan at l. ctr. on back.	0.15	0.75	4.00

45 **1000 DRAM**

	VG	VF	UNC
1999. Aqua and green on m/c unpt. Yeghishe Charents at l., lines of poetry at r. Old Yerevan city scene on back.	0.75	2.50	8.00

46 **5000 DRAM**

	VG	VF	UNC
1999 (2000).Dk and lt. brown on green, gold and m/c unpt. H. Tumanyan at l. Saryan's picture of Lory mountains on back. Printer: JEZ.	1.00	4.00	17.50

47 **20,000 DRAM**

	VG	VF	UNC
1999. Brown and yellow on m/c unpt. Martiros Saryan, painter at l., abstract painting in ctr. Hologram at r. Saryan painting *Armenia* on back.	2.00	7.50	30.00

2001 COMMEMORATIVE ISSUE
#48, 1700 years of Christianity in Armenia

		VG	VF	UNC
48	**50,000 DRAM** 2001. Brown and m/c. Cathedral of Holy Echmiatzin at ctr., holographic strip at l. w/commemorative text vertically. St Gregory and Kg. Tiridat holding church on back.	—	—	200.00

2001; 2003 ISSUE

		VG	VF	UNC
50	**1000 DRAM** 2001 (2002). Aqua and green on m/c unpt. Like #45 but with additional security features.	1.00	3.00	10.00

		VG	VF	UNC
51	**5000 DRAM** 2003.	FV	10.00	20.00

		VG	VF	UNC
52	**10,000 DRAM** 2003. Avetik Isahakyan Gyumri at l.	FV	20.00	40.00

Aruba, formerly a part of the Netherlands Antilles, achieved on Jan. 1, 1986 a special status "status aparte" as the third state under the Dutch crown, together with the Netherlands and the remaining five islands of the Netherlands Antilles. On Dec. 15, 1954 the Netherlands Antilles were given complete domestic autonomy and granted equality within the Kingdom of the Netherlands.

Aruba was the second-largest island of the Netherlands Antilles and is situated near the Venezuelan coast. The island has an area of 74-1/2 sq. mi. (193 sq. km.) and a population of 68,000. Capital: Oranjestad, named after the Dutch royal family. Chief industry is tourism. For earlier issues see Curaçao and the Netherlands Antilles. During Jan. 1986 the banknotes of the Netherlands Antilles were redeemed at a ratio of 1 to 1.

MONETARY SYSTEM:
1 Florin = 100 Cents

DUTCH ADMINISTRATION

BANCO CENTRAL DI ARUBA

1986 ISSUE

#1-5 flag at l., coastal hotels at ctr. Arms of Aruba at ctr. on back. Printer: JEZ.

		VG	VF	UNC
1	**5 FLORIN** 1.1.1986. Green.	FV	FV	17.50

		VG	VF	UNC
2	**10 FLORIN** 1.1.1986. Green.	FV	FV	27.50

		VG	VF	UNC
3	**25 FLORIN** 1.1.1986. Green.	FV	FV	37.50

				VG	VF	UNC
4	50 FLORIN			FV	FV	60.00
	1.1.1986. Green.					

				VG	VF	UNC
5	100 FLORIN			FV	FV	125.00
	1.1.1986. Green.					

CENTRALE BANK VAN ARUBA

1990 ISSUE

#6-10 geometric forms with pre-Columbian Aruban art on back. Wmk: Stylized tree. Printer: JEZ.

				VG	VF	UNC
6	5 FLORIN			FV	FV	17.50
	1.1.1990. Purple and m/c. Tortuga Blanco (sea turtle) at ctr. r.					

				VG	VF	UNC
7	10 FLORIN			FV	FV	17.50
	1.1.1990. Blue and m/c. Calco Indian conch at ctr. r.					

				VG	VF	UNC
8	25 FLORIN			FV	FV	32.50
	1.1.1990. Brown and m/c. Rattlesnake at r.					

				VG	VF	UNC
9	50 FLORIN			FV	FV	60.00
	1.1.1990. Red-brown and m/c. Burrowing owl at ctr. r.					

				VG	VF	UNC
10	100 FLORIN			FV	FV	185.00
	1.1.1990. Olive-green and m/c. Frog at ctr. r.					

1993 ISSUE

#11-15 like #7-10 but w/text: *Wettig Betaalmiddel* (legal tender). Wmk: Stylized tree. Printer: JEZ.

				VG	VF	UNC
11	10 FLORIN			FV	FV	15.00
	16.7.1993 (1996). Blue and m/c. Like #7.					
12	25 FLORIN			FV	FV	30.00
	16.7.1993 (1996). Brown and m/c. Like #8.					
13	50 FLORIN			FV	FV	57.50
	16.7.1993 (1996). Red-brown and m/c. Like #9.					

14	100 FLORIN		VG	VF	UNC
	16.7.1993 (1996). Olive-green and m/c. Like #10.		FV	FV	110.00

18	50 FLORIN		VG	VF	UNC
	1.12.2003. Red-brown and m/c. Like #13.		FV	FV	52.50

15	500 FLORIN		VG	VF	UNC
	16.7.1993. Blue and m/c. Grouper fish at ctr r.		FV	FV	450.00

2003 ISSUE

#16-20 like #11-15 but w/additional security features and different signatures. Printer:JEZ.

19	100 FLORIN		VG	VF	UNC
	1.12.2003. Olive-green and m/c. Like #14.		FV	FV	105.00
20	500 FLORIN				
	1.12.2003. Blue and m/c. Like #15.		FV	FV	400.00

COLLECTOR SERIES

CENTRALE BANK VAN ARUBA

1990 ISSUE

CS1	1990 5-100 FLORIN	Issue Price	Mkt.	Value
	#6-10 w/low matched serial # in six page special presentation folder. 200 sets produced.	—		450.00

16	10 FLORIN		VG	VF	UNC
	1.12.2003. Blue and m/c. Like #11.		FV	FV	12.50

17	25 FLORIN		VG	VF	UNC
	1.12.2003. Brown and m/c. Like #12.		FV	FV	27.50

AUSTRALIA

The Commonwealth of Australia, the smallest continent and largest island in the world, is located south of Indonesia between the Indian and Pacific oceans. It has an area of 2,967,909 sq. mi. (7,686,849 sq. km.) and a population of 18.84 million. Capital: Canberra. Due to its early and sustained isolation, Australia is the habitat of such curious and unique fauna as the kangaroo, koala, platypus, wombat and barking lizard. The continent possesses extensive mineral deposits, the most important of which are gold, coal, silver, nickel, uranium, lead and zinc. Livestock raising, mining and manufacturing are the principal industries. Chief exports are wool, meat, wheat, iron ore, coal and nonferrous metals.

The first caucasians to see Australia probably were Portuguese and Spanish navigators of the late 16th century. In 1770, Captain James Cook explored the east coast and annexed it for Great Britain. The Colony of New South Wales was founded by Captain Arthur Phillip on Jan. 26, 1788, a date now celebrated as Australia Day. Dates of creation of six colonies that now comprise the states of the Australian Commonwealth are: New South Wales, 1823; Tasmania, 1825; Western Australia, 1838; South Australia, 1842; Victoria, 1851; Queensland, 1859. A constitution providing for federation of the colonies was approved by the British Parliament in 1900; the Commonwealth of Australia came into being in 1901. Australia passed the Statute of Westminster Adoption Act on Oct. 9, 1942, which officially established Australia's complete autonomy in external and internal affairs, thereby formalizing a situation that had existed for years.

During WWII Australia was the primary supply and staging area for Allied forces in the South Pacific Theatre.

Australia is a member of the Commonwealth of Nations. Elizabeth II is Head of State as Queen of Australia.

RULERS:
British

MONETARY SYSTEM:
1 Shilling = 12 Pence
1 Pound = 20 Shillings; to 1966
1 Dollar = 100 Cents, 1966-

RESERVE BANK

1960-61 ND ISSUE

#33-36 like #29-32. Sign. H. C. Coombs w/title: *GOVERNOR/RESERVE BANK of AUSTRALIA* below lower l. sign. R. Wilson. Wmk: Capt. James Cook. Replacement notes: Serial # suffix *.

33	10 SHILLINGS	VG	VF	UNC
	ND (1961-65). Dk. brown on orange and green unpt. Arms at lower l., portr. Matthew Flinders at r. Old Parliament House in Canberra on back. Like #29.			
	a. Issued note.	8.00	25.00	150.00
	r. Serial # suffix *, replacement.	250.00	3000.00	19000.00
	s. Specimen.	—	6500.00	25000.00

34	1 POUND	VG	VF	UNC
	ND (1961-65). Black on green and yellow unpt. Arms at upper ctr., cameo portr. Qn. Elizabeth II at r. Back green; facing portr. Charles Sturt and Hamilton Hume. Like #30.			
	a. Issued note.	6.00	25.00	150.00
	r. Serial # suffix *, replacement.	500.00	4000.00	25000.00
	s. Specimen.	—	7500.00	30000.00

35	5 POUNDS	VG	VF	UNC
	ND (1960-65). Black on blue unpt. Arms at upper l., portr. Sir John Franklin at r. Back blue; cattle, sheep and agricultural products across ctr. Like #31.			
	a. Issued note.	20.00	45.00	400.00
	r. Serial # suffix *, replacement.	750.00	7500.00	30000.00
	s. Specimen.	—	8500.00	35000.00

36	10 POUNDS	VG	VF	UNC
	ND (1960-65). Black on red unpt. Arms at top ctr., portr. Gov. Arthur Philip at l. Symbols of science and industry on back. Like #32.			
	a. Issued note.	40.00	100.00	1200.00
	s. Specimen.	—	9000.00	38000.00

1966-67 ND Issue

#37-41 w/text: *COMMONWEALTH OF* in heading. Wmk: Capt. James Cook. Replacement notes: Serial # prefixes *ZAA-ZXA* w/suffix *.

37	1 DOLLAR	VG	VF	UNC
	ND (1966-72). Dk. brown on orange and m/c unpt. Arms at ctr., Qn. Elizabeth II at r. Stylized aboriginal figures and animals on back.			
	a. Sign. H. C. Coombs and R. Wilson. (1966).	2.00	7.00	40.00
	ar. As a, serial # suffix *, replacement.	100.00	500.00	3000.00
	b. Sign. H. C. Coombs and R. J. Randall. (1968).	25.00	75.00	500.00
	br. As b, serial # suffix *, replacement.	400.00	1250.00	6000.00
	c. Sign. J. G. Phillips and R. J. Randall. (1969).	2.00	5.00	35.00
	cr. As c, serial # suffix *, replacement.	75.00	350.00	2750.00
	d. Sign. J. G. Phillips and F. H. Wheeler. (1972).	2.00	5.00	35.00
	s1. Specimen in oval on each side.	—	2500.00	8000.00
	s2. Specimen eight times each side.	—	4200.00	15000.00
	s3. Specimen twice diagonally each side.	—	3000.00	12000.00

38	2 DOLLARS	VG	VF	UNC
	ND (1966-72). Black on green, blue and yellow m/c unpt. John MacArthur at r., sheep at ctr. William Farrer at l., wheat at ctr. on back.			
	a. Sign. H. C. Coombs and R. Wilson. (1966).	2.00	5.00	25.00
	ar. As a, serial # suffix *, replacement.	85.00	325.00	1600.00
	as. As a. Specimen.	—	—	—
	b. Sign. H. C. Coombs and R. J. Randall. (1967).	7.50	15.00	60.00
	br. As b, serial # suffix *, replacement.	200.00	700.00	3500.00
	c. Sign. J. G. Phillips and R. J. Randall. (1968).	1.00	4.00	25.00
	cr. As c, serial # suffix *, replacement.	75.00	450.00	2200.00
	d. Sign. J. G. Phillips and F. H. Wheeler. (1972).	1.00	4.00	25.00

39	5 DOLLARS	VG	VF	UNC
	ND (1967-72). Deep purple on m/c unpt. Sir Joseph Banks at r., plants at ctr. Caroline Chisholm, ship, bldgs., and women on back.			
	a. Sign. H. C. Coombs and R. J. Randall. (1967).	3.00	10.00	80.00
	ar. As a, serial # suffix *, replacement.	300.00	900.00	4750.00
	b. Sign. J. G. Phillips and R. J. Randall. (1969).	3.00	10.00	75.00
	br. As b, serial # suffix *, replacement.	650.00	1800.00	8500.00
	c. Sign. J. G. Phillips and F. H. Wheeler. (1972).	3.00	8.00	75.00

40	10 DOLLARS	VG	VF	UNC
	ND (1966-72). Black on blue, orange and m/c unpt. Francis Greenway at r., village scene at ctr. Henry Lawson and bldgs. on back.			
	a. Sign. H. C. Coombs and R. Wilson. (1966).	7.00	10.00	37.50
	ar. As a, serial # suffix *, replacement.	90.00	375.00	2150.00
	b. Sign. H. G. Coombs and R. J. Randall. (1967).	12.50	30.00	200.00
	br. As b, serial # suffix *, replacement.	250.00	1100.00	8000.00
	c. Sign. J. G. Phillips and R. J. Randall. (1968).	7.00	10.00	35.00
	cr. As c, serial # suffix *, replacement.	100.00	400.00	3500.00
	d. Sign. J. G. Phillips and F. H. Wheeler. (1972).	7.00	10.00	35.00

41	20 DOLLARS	VG	VF	UNC
	ND (1966-72). Black on red, yellow and m/c unpt. Sir Charles Kingsford-Smith at r. Lawrence Hargrave at l., aeronautical devices on back.			
	a. Sign. H. C. Coombs and R. Wilson. (1966).	15.00	20.00	45.00
	b. Sign. H. G. Coombs and R. J. Randall. (1968).	37.50	250.00	3150.00
	c. Sign. J. G. Phillips and R. J. Randall. (1968).	15.00	20.00	125.00
	cr. As c, serial # suffix *, replacement.	150.00	975.00	9250.00
	d. Sign. J. G. Phillips and F. H. Wheeler. (1972).	15.00	20.00	160.00

AUSTRALIA, RESERVE BANK

1973; 1984 ND Issue

#42-48 w/o text: *COMMONWEALTH OF* in heading.

#42-46 like #37-41. Wmk: Capt. James Cook.

42	1 DOLLAR	VG	VF	UNC
	ND (1974-83). Dk. brown on orange and m/c unpt. Like #37.			
	a. Sign. J. G. Phillips and F. H. Wheeler. (1974).	FV	3.00	25.00
	as. As a. Specimen.	—	—	—
	b1. Sign. H. M. Knight and F. H. Wheeler. (1976). Center security thread.	FV	2.00	12.50
	b2. As b1. Side security thread.	FV	1.00	2.00
	c. Sign. H. M. Knight and J. Stone. (1979).	FV	1.00	2.00
	d. Sign. R. A. Johnston and J. Stone. (1983).	FV	FV	1.25

43	**2 DOLLARS**	VG	VF	UNC
	ND (1974-85). Black on green, blue and yellow unpt. Like #38.			
	a. Sign. J. G. Phillips and F. H. Wheeler. (1974).	FV	5.00	25.00
	as. As a. Specimen.	—	—	—
	b. Sign. H. M. Knight and F. H. Wheeler. (1976). 2 serial # varieties.	FV	2.00	10.00
	c. Sign. H. M. Knight and J. Stone. (1979).	FV	FV	6.00
	d. Sign. R. A. Johnston and J. Stone. (1983).	FV	FV	6.00
	e. Sign. R. A. Johnston and B. W. Fraser. (1985).	FV	FV	3.00

46	**20 DOLLARS**	VG	VF	UNC
	ND (1974-94). Black on red, yellow and m/c unpt. Like #41.			
	a. Sign. J. G. Phillips and F. H. Wheeler. (1974).	FV	25.00	150.00
	as. As a. Specimen.	—	—	—
	b. Sign. H. M. Knight and F. H. Wheeler. (1975).	FV	FV	110.00
	c. Sign. H. M. Knight and J. Stone. (1979). 2 serial # varieties.	FV	FV	65.00
	d. Sign. R. A. Johnston and J. Stone. (1983).	FV	FV	65.00
	e. Sign. R. A. Johnston and B. W. Fraser. (1985) 2 serial # varieties.	FV	FV	80.00
	f. Sign. M. J. Phillips and B. W. Fraser. (1989).	FV	FV	45.00
	g. Sign. B. W. Fraser and C. I. Higgins. (1989).	FV	FV	50.00
	h. Sign. B. W. Fraser and A. S. Cole. (1991).	FV	FV	40.00
	i. Sign. B. W. Fraser and E. A. Evans. (1994).	FV	FV	35.00

44	**5 DOLLARS**	VG	VF	UNC
	ND (1974-91). Deep purple on m/c unpt. Like #39.			
	a. Sign. J. G. Phillips and F. H. Wheeler. (1974).	FV	12.50	80.00
	as. As a. Specimen.	—	—	—
	b. Sign. H. M. Knight and F. H. Wheeler. (1976). 2 serial # varieties.	FV	8.00	30.00
	c. Sign. H. M. Knight and J. Stone. (1979).	FV	FV	15.00
	d. Sign. R. A. Johnston and J. Stone. (1983).	FV	FV	15.00
	e. Sign. R. A. Johnston and B. W. Fraser. (1985). 2 serial # varieties.	FV	FV	12.50
	f. Sign. B. W. Fraser and C. I. Higgins. (1990).	FV	FV	12.50
	g. Sign. B. W. Fraser and A. S. Cole. (1991).	FV	FV	10.00

47	**50 DOLLARS**	VG	VF	UNC
	ND (1973-94). Dk. brown and black on m/c unpt. Teaching implements at ctr., Lord Howard Walker Florey at r., Ian Clunies-Ross at l., space research at ctr. on back.			
	a. Sign. J. G. Phillips and F. H. Wheeler. (1973).	FV	45.00	150.00
	b. Sign. H. M. Knight and F. H. Wheeler. (1975).	FV	40.00	160.00
	c. Sign. H. M. Knight and J. Stone. (1979).	FV	FV	110.00
	d. Sign. R. A. Johnston and J. Stone. (1983).	FV	FV	115.00
	e. Sign. R. A. Johnston and B. W. Fraser. (1985). 2 serial # varieties.	FV	FV	115.00
	f. Sign. M. J. Phillips and B. W. Fraser. (1989).	FV	FV	80.00
	g. Sign. B. W. Fraser and C. I. Higgins. (1989).	FV	FV	130.00
	h. Sign. B. W. Fraser and A. S. Cole. (1991).	FV	FV	70.00
	i. Sign. B. W. Fraser and E. A. Evans. (1994).	FV	FV	65.00

45	**10 DOLLARS**	VG	VF	UNC
	ND (1974-91). Black on blue and orange unpt. Like #40.			
	a. Sign. J. G. Phillips and F. H. Wheeler. (1974).	7.50	20.00	125.00
	as. As a. Specimen.	—	—	—
	b. Sign. H. M. Knight and F. H. Wheeler. (1976).	FV	12.50	35.00
	c. Sign. H. M. Knight and J. Stone. (1979). 2 serial # varieties.	FV	FV	55.00
	d. Sign. R. A. Johnston and J. Stone. (1983).	FV	FV	40.00
	e. Sign. R. A. Johnston and B. W. Fraser. (1985).	FV	FV	20.00
	f. Sign. B. W. Fraser and C. I. Higgins. (1990).	FV	FV	20.00
	g. Sign. B. W. Fraser and A. S. Cole. (1991).	FV	FV	17.50

48	**100 DOLLARS**	VG	VF	UNC
	ND (1984-92). Blue and gray on m/c unpt. Sir Douglas Mawson at ctr. J. Tebbutt at l. ctr. on back.			
	a. Sign. R. A. Johnston and J. Stone. (1984).	FV	FV	135.00
	b. Sign. R. A. Johnston and B. W. Fraser. (1985).	FV	FV	135.00
	c. Sign. B. W. Fraser and C. I. Higgins. (1990).	FV	FV	135.00
	d. Sign. B. W. Fraser and A. S. Cole. (1992).	FV	FV	130.00

Note: See also "Collector Series" following note listings.

1988 ND Commemorative Issue

#49, Bicentennial of British Settlement

Polymer plastic. Printer: NPA.

49	**10 DOLLARS**	VG	VF	UNC
	1988; ND. Brown and green on m/c unpt. Capt. Cook OVD at upper l., colonists across background; Cook's ship *Supply* at lower r. shoreline. Aboriginal youth, rock painting and ceremonial *Morning Star* pole at ctr. on back. Sign. R. A. John			
	a. Serial # prefix AA. 26.1.1988. Issued in folder.	—	—	25.00
	b. Issued note. Serial # prefix AB. ND.	FV	FV	20.00

1992-2001 Issues

#50-56 Dates are indicated by the first two digits of the serial #. Printer: NPA.

50	**5 DOLLARS**	VG	VF	UNC
	ND (1992); (19)93. Black, red and blue on m/c unpt. Branch at l., Qn. Elizabeth II at ctr. r. Back black on lilac and m/c unpt., the old and the new Parliament Houses in Canberra at ctr., gum flower OVD at lower r.			
	a. Sign. B. W. Fraser and A. S. Cole.	FV	FV	12.50
	b. Sign. B. W. Fraser and E. A. Evans.	FV	FV	8.00

51	**5 DOLLARS**	VG	VF	UNC
	(19)95-(20)01. Black, red and bright purple. Like #50 but w/orientation bands in upper and lower margins, gum flower OVD at lower r. Back w/darker unpt. colors.			
	a. W/4 diagonal white lines in orientation band at lower l. Sign. B. W. Fraser and E. A. Evans.	FV	FV	10.00
	b. As a, but w/11 diagonal white lines in orientation band at lower l. Plate error.	FV	FV	17.50
	c. Sign. I. Macfarlane and E. A. Evans.	FV	FV	8.00

52	**10 DOLLARS**	VG	VF	UNC
	(19)93-(20)01. Dk. blue and purple on m/c unpt. Man on horseback at l., A. B. "Banjo" Paterson at ctr., windmill OVD in transparent window at lower r. Dame Mary Gilmore at ctr. r. on back.			
	a. Sign. B. W. Fraser and E. A. Evans.	FV	FV	25.00
	b. Sign. I. Macfarlane and E. A. Evans.	FV	FV	20.00

53	**20 DOLLARS**	VG	VF	UNC
	(19)94-(20)01. Black and red on orange and pale green unpt. Mary Reiby at ctr., sailing ship at l. Compass OVD in transparent window at lower r. Biplane at l., Rev. John Flynn at ctr. r., camel at r. on back.			
	a. Sign. B. W. Fraser and E. A. Evans.	FV	FV	35.00
	b. Sign. I. Macfarlane and E. A. Evans.	FV	FV	27.50

54	**50 DOLLARS**	VG	VF	UNC
	(19)95-(20)01. Black and deep purple on yellow-brown, green and m/c unpt. David Unaipon at l. ctr., Mission Church at Point McLeay at lower l., patent drawings at upper ctr. r., Southern Cross constellation OVD in transparent window at lower r. Edith			
	a. Sign. B. W. Fraser and E. A. Evans.	FV	FV	65.00
	b. Sign. I. Macfarlane and E. A. Evans.	FV	FV	50.00
55	**100 DOLLARS**			
	(19)96-(20)01. Black and green on orange and m/c unpt. Opera stage at l., Dame Nellie Melba at ctr., stylized peacock OVD in transparent window at lower r. Sir John Monash and WWI battle scenes and insignia on back.			
	a. Sign. B. W. Fraser and E. A. Evans.	FV	FV	125.00
	b. Sign. I. Macfarlane and E. A. Evans.	FV	FV	115.00

2001 COMMEMORATIVE ISSUE

#56, Centennial of the Commonwealth

56	**5 DOLLARS**	VG	VF	UNC
	1.1.2001. Black, violet and blue on m/c unpt. Sir Henry Parkes at ctr. Catherine Helen Spence at ctr. on back.	FV	FV	8.00

2002-03 ISSUE

#57-61 as previous issue but w/names added below portrait.

57	**5 DOLLARS**	VG	VF	UNC
	(20)03.			Expected New Issue
58	**10 DOLLARS**			
	(20)02. Dk. blue and purple on m/c unpt. Like #52.	FV	FV	10.00

59	**20 DOLLARS**	VG	VF	UNC
	(20)02. Black and red on orange and pale green unpt. Like #53.	FV	FV	17.50
60	**50 DOLLARS**			
	(20)03.			Expected New Issue
61	**100 DOLLAR**			
	(20)03.			Expected New Issue

COLLECTOR SERIES

AUSTRALIA, RESERVE BANK

Many varieties of products have been produced for collectors in the form of uncut sheets, special serial # prefixes, various coin fair ovpts., souvenir folders including coin and bank note sets too numerous to list. These are documented occasionally in *Australian Coin Review* by Michael Vort-Ronald.

1994 DATED ISSUE

CS50	**5 DOLLARS**	Issue Price	Mkt.	Value
	1992; 1994. Ovpt. on #50.			
	a. 7.7.1992.	—		10.00
	b. Sign. B. W. Fraser and E. A. Evans. Red serial #. (900). 1994.	32.00		50.00
	c. As a. Black serial #. (9,000). 1994.	10.50		12.50

The Republic of Austria (Oesterreich), a parliamentary democracy located in mountainous central Europe, has an area of 32,374 sq. mi. (83,849 sq. km.) and a population of 8.1 million. Capital: Vienna. Austria is primarily an industrial country. Machinery, iron and steel, textiles, yarns and timber are exported.

The territories later to be known as Austria were overrun in pre-Roman times by various tribes, including the Celts. Upon the fall of the Roman Empire, the country became a margravate of Charlemagne's Empire. Premysl 2 Otakar, King of Bohemia, gained possession in 1252, only to lose the territory to Rudolf of Habsburg in 1276. Thereafter, until World War I, the story of Austria was that of the ruling Habsburgs, Holy Roman emperors from 1438-1806. From 1815-1867 it was a member of the *Deutsche Bund* (German Union).

During World War I, the Austro-Hungarian Empire was one of the Central Powers with Germany, Bulgaria and Turkey. At the end of the war, the empire was dissolved and Austria established as an independent republic. In March 1938, Austria was incorporated into Germany's Third Reich. Allied forces of both East and West liberated Austria in April 1945, and subsequently divided it into four zones of military occupation. On May 15, 1955, the four powers formally recognized Austria as a sovereign independent democratic state.

MONETARY SYSTEM:
 1 Schilling = 100 Groschen, 1924-1938, 1945-2002
 1 Euro = 100 Cents, 2002-

REPUBLIC

OESTERREICHISCHE NATIONALBANK

AUSTRIAN NATIONAL BANK

1956-65 ISSUES

136	**20 SCHILLING**	VG	VF	UNC
	2.7.1956. Brown on red-brown and m/c unpt. Carl Auer Freiherr von Welsbach at r., arms at l. Village Maria Rain, church and Karawanken mountains on back.			
	a. Issued note.	0.75	7.50	15.00
	s. Specimen.	—	—	50.00

137	**50 SCHILLING**	VG	VF	UNC
	2.7.1962 (1963). Purple on m/c unpt. Richard Wettstein at r., arms at bottom ctr. Mauterndorf castle in Salzburg on back.			
	a. Issued note.	1.50	9.00	20.00
	s. Specimen.	—	—	50.00

1966-70 ISSUES

138   100 SCHILLING
1.7.1960 (1961). Dk. green on m/c unpt. Violin and music at lower
l., Johann Strauss at r., arms at l. Schönbrunn Castle on back.

	VG	VF	UNC
a. Issued note.	3.00	10.00	40.00
s. Specimen.	—	—	50.00

139   500 SCHILLING
1.7.1965 (1966). Red-brown on m/c unpt. Josef Ressel at r. Steam
powered screw propeller ship *Civetta* at l., arms at lower r. on back.

VG	VF	UNC
20.00	50.00	120.00

140   1000 SCHILLING
2.1.1961 (1962). Dk. blue on m/c unpt. Viktor Kaplan at r. Dam
and Persenburg Castle, arms at r. on back. 148 x 75mm.

	VG	VF	UNC
a. Issued note.	—	Rare	
s. Specimen.	—	400.00	800.00

Note: #140 was in use for only 11 weeks.

141   1000 SCHILLING
2.1.1961 (1962). Dk. blue on m/c unpt. Like #140 but w/blue lined
unpt. up to margin. 158 x 85mm.

	VG	VF	UNC
a. Issued note.	35.00	90.00	185.00
s. Specimen. Ovpt. and perforated: *Muster*.	—	—	1500.00

142   20 SCHILLING
2.7.1967 (1968). Brown on olive and lilac unpt. Carl Ritter von
Ghega at r., arms at lower ctr. Semmering Railway bridge over the
Semmering Pass (986 meters) on back.

VG	VF	UNC
1.00	2.50	4.50

143   50 SCHILLING
2.1.1970 (1972). Purple on m/c unpt. Ferdinand Raimund at r.,
arms at l. Burg Theater in Vienna at l. ctr. on back.

	VG	VF	UNC
a. Issued note.	3.00	6.00	12.00
s. Specimen. Ovpt: *Muster*.	—	—	500.00

144   50 SCHILLING
2.1.1970 (1983). Like #143 but w/ovpt. *2. AUFLAGE* (2nd issue) at
lower l. ctr.

VG	VF	UNC
3.00	6.00	12.00

145	100 SCHILLING	VG	VF	UNC
	2.1.1969 (1970). Dk. green on m/c unpt. Angelika Kauffmann at r. Large house on back.			
	a. Issued note.	FV	10.00	22.50
	s. Specimen. Ovpt: *Muster*.	—	—	750.00

146	100 SCHILLING	VG	VF	UNC
	2.1.1969 (1981). Like #145 but w/ovpt: *2 AUFLAGE* (2nd issue) at upper l.	FV	12.00	22.50

147	1000 SCHILLING	VG	VF	UNC
	1.7.1966 (1970). Blue-violet on m/c unpt. Bertha von Suttner at ctr. r., arms at r. Leopoldskron Castle and Hohensalzburg Fortress on back.			
	a. Issued note.	FV	90.00	150.00
	s. Specimen. Ovpt: *Muster*.	—	—	1250.00

1983-88 ISSUE

#148-153 Federal arms at upper l. Wmk: Federal arms and parallel vertical lines.

148	20 SCHILLING	VG	VF	UNC
	1.10.1986 (1988). Dk. brown and brown on m/c unpt. Moritz Daffinger at r. Vienna's Albertina Museum at l. ctr. on back.	FV	FV	3.25

149	50 SCHILLING	VG	VF	UNC
	2.1.1986 (1987). Purple and violet on m/c unpt. Sigmund Freud at r. Vienna's *Josephinum* Medical School at l. ctr. on back.	FV	FV	7.00

150	100 SCHILLING	VG	VF	UNC
	2.1.1984 (1985). Dk. green, gray and dk. brown on m/c unpt. Eugen Böhm v. Bawerk at r. Wissenschaften Academy in Vienna at l. ctr. on back. 3 serial # varieties.	FV	FV	15.00

151	500 SCHILLING	VG	VF	UNC
	1.7.1985 (1986). Dk. brown, deep violet and orange-brown on m/c unpt. Architect Otto Wagner at r. Post Office Savings Bank in Vienna at l. ctr. on back.	FV	FV	65.00

152	1000 SCHILLING	VG	VF	UNC
	3.1.1983. Dk. blue and purple on m/c unpt. Erwin Schrödinger at r. Vienna University at l. ctr. on back.	FV	FV	135.00

153	**5000 SCHILLING**	VG	VF	UNC
	4.1.1988 (1989). Lt. brown and purple on m/c unpt. Woflang	FV	FV	575.00

Amadeus Mozart at r., kinegram of Mozart's head at lower l. Vienna
Opera House at ctr. on back.

1997 ISSUE

154	**500 SCHILLING**	VG	VF	UNC
	1.1.1997. Brown on m/c unpt. Rosa Mayreder at l. Rosa and Karl	FV	FV	60.00

Mayreder w/group at r. on back.

155	**1000 SCHILLING**	VG	VF	UNC
	1.1.1997. Blue on m/c unpt. Karl Landsteiner at l. Landsteiner	FV	FV	125.00

working in his laboratory in Licenter at r. on back.

Note: For later issues used in Austria, see European Union listings.

AZERBAIJAN 49

The Republic of Azerbaijan includes the Nakhichevan Autonomous Republic and Nagorno-Karabakh Autonomous Region (which was abolished in 1991). Situated in the eastern area of Transcaucasia, it is bordered in the west by Armenia, in the north by Georgia and the Russian Federation of Dagestan, to the east by the Caspian Sea and to the south by Iran. It has an area of 33,430 sq. mi. (86,600 sq. km.) and a population of 7.83 million. Capital: Baku. The area is rich in mineral deposits of aluminum, copper, iron, lead, salt and zinc, with oil as its leading industry. Agriculture and livestock follow in importance.

In ancient times home of Scythian tribes and known under the Romans as Albania and to the Arabs as Arran, the country of Azerbaijan formed at the time of its invasion by Seljuk Turks a prosperous state under Persian suzerainty. From the 16th century the country was a theatre of fighting and political rivalry between Turkey, Persia and later Russia. Baku was first annexed to Russia by Czar Peter I in 1723. After the Russian retreat in 1735, the whole of Azerbaijan north of the Aras River became a khanate under Persian control until 1813 when annexed by Czar Alexander I into the Russian empire.

Until the Russian Revolution of 1905 there was no political life in Azerbaijan. A Mussavat (Equality) party was formed in 1911. After the Russian Revolution of March 1917, the party started a campaign for independence, but Baku, the capital, with its mixed population, constituted an alien enclave in the country. While a national Azerbaijani government was established at Gandzha (Elizavetpol), a Communist-controlled council assumed power at Baku. The Gandzha government joined first, on Sept. 20, 1917, a Transcaucasian federal republic, but on May 28, 1918, proclaimed the independence of Azerbaijan. On June 4, 1918, at Batum, a peace treaty was signed with Turkey and a Turko-Azerbaijani force started an offensive against Baku, but it was occupied on Aug. 17, 1918 by 1,400 British troops coming by sea from Anzali, Persia. On Sept. 14 the British evacuated Baku, returning to Anzali, and three days later the Azerbaijan government, headed by Fath Ali Khan Khoysky, established itself at Baku.

After the collapse of the Ottoman empire the British returned to Baku, at first ignoring the Azerbaijan government. A general election with universal suffrage for the Azerbaijan constituent assembly took place on Dec. 7, 1918 and out of 120 members there were 84 Mussavat supporters; Ali Marden Topchibashev was elected speaker, and Nasib Usubekov formed a new government. On Jan. 15, 1920, the Allied powers recognized Azerbaijan de facto but on April 27 of the same year the Red army invaded the country and a Soviet Republic of Azerbaijan was proclaimed the next day.

The Azerbaijan Communist party held its first congress at Baku in Feb. 1920. From 1921 to 1925 its first secretary was a Russian, S.M. Kirov, who directed a mass deportation to Siberia of about 120,000 Azerbaijani "nationalist deviationists," among them the country's first two premiers. Later it became a member of the Transcaucasian Federation joining the U.S.S.R. on Dec. 30, 1922. It became a self-constituent republic in 1936.

In 1990 it adopted a declaration of republican sovereignty, and in Aug. 1991 declared itself formally independent; this was approved by a vote of referendum in Jan. 1992.

The Armed forces of Azerbaijan and the Armenian separatists of the Armenian ethnic enclave of Nagurno-Karabakh supported in all spheres by Armenia fought over the control of the enclave in 1992-94. A cease-fire was declared in May 1994 with Azerbaijan actually losing control over the territory. A Treaty of Friendship and Cooperation w/Russia was signed on 3 July 1997.

REPUBLIC

AZERBAYCAN MILLI BANKI

1992 ND ISSUE

In 1993, due to a cash crisis, bonds of the State Loan of Azerbaijan Republic were officially used as currency; however, they were not freely accepted in the local bazaars. The acceptance term of these bonds in the branches of the State Savings Bank was until 1 June 2000.

11	**1 MANAT**	VG	VF	UNC
	ND (1992). Deep olive-green on m/c unpt.	0.10	0.25	3.00

12	**10 MANAT**	VG	VF	UNC
	ND (1992). Deep brown-violet on m/c unpt.	0.20	0.50	7.50

13	**250 MANAT**	VG	VF	UNC
	ND (1992). Deep blue-gray on m/c unpt.			
	a. Original issue w/fraction prefix.	1.50	10.00	50.00
	b. Reissue w/2 prefix letters.	0.25	0.75	2.50

16	**10 MANAT**	VG	VF	UNC
	ND (1993). Deep grayish blue-green on pale blue and m/c unpt.	FV	FV	7.00

AZERBAYCAN REPUBLIC STATE LOAN BONDS

1993 ISSUE

#13A-13C printer: Goznak.

13A	**250 MANAT**	VG	VF	UNC
	1993. Olive-green on m/c unpt.	—	—	—
13B	**500 MANAT**			
	1993. Pinkish-red on m/c unpt.	—	—	—
13C	**1000 MANAT**			
	1993. Steel-blue on m/c unpt.	—	—	—

AZERBAYCAN MILLI BANKI

1993 ND; 1994-95 ISSUE

#14-20 ornate "value" backs. Wmk: 3 flames.

#14-18 different view Maiden Tower ruins at ctr.

#13b, 17b, 18b, 19b, 20b replacement notes: Serial # prefix *BZ*.

17	**50 MANAT**	VG	VF	UNC
	ND (1993). Red on ochre and m/c unpt.			
	a. Original issue w/fraction prefix.	FV	FV	10.00
	b. Reissue w/2 prefix letters.	FV	FV	1.00

14	**1 MANAT**	VG	VF	UNC
	ND (1993). Deep blue on tan, dull orange and green unpt.	FV	FV	3.00

18	**100 MANAT**	VG	VF	UNC
	ND (1993). Red-violet on pale blue and m/c unpt.			
	a. Original issue w/fraction prefix.	FV	FV	12.50
	b. Reissue w/2 prefix letters.	FV	FV	1.75

15	**5 MANAT**	VG	VF	UNC
	ND (1993). Deep brown on lilac and m/c unpt.	FV	FV	5.00

19	**500 MANAT**	VG	VF	UNC
	ND (1993). Deep brown on pale blue, pink and m/c unpt. Portr. N. Gencevi at r.			
	a. Original issue w/fraction prefix.	FV	FV	15.00
	b. Reissue w/2 prefix letters.	FV	FV	3.00

20　1000 MANAT
ND (1993). Dk. brown and blue on pink and m/c unpt. M. E.
Resulzado at r.

	VG	VF	UNC
a. Original issue w/fraction prefix.	FV	FV	9.00
b. Reissue w/2 prefix letters.	FV	FV	3.00

21　10,000 MANAT
1994. Dull dk. brown and pale violet on m/c unpt. Shirvansha's
Palace at ctr. r. Wmk: AMB repeated.

	VG	VF	UNC
a. Security thread.	5.00	20.00	60.00
b. Segmented foil over security thread.	FV	FV	10.00

22　50,000 MANAT
1995. Blue-green and lt. brown on m/c unpt. Mausoleum in
Nachziban at ctr. r. Carpet design at l. on back. Segmented foil over
security thread.

	VG	VF	UNC
	FV	FV	40.00

2001 ISSUE

23　1000 MANAT
2001. Slate blue on lt. blue and m/c unpt. Oil rigs and pumps at ctr.
r. Value on back.

	VG	VF	UNC
	FV	FV	4.00

BAHAMAS

The Commonwealth of The Bahamas is an archipelago of about 3,000 islands, cays and rocks located in the Atlantic Ocean east of Florida and north of Cuba. The total land area of the 800-mile (1.287 km.) long chain of islands is 5,380 sq. mi. (13,935 sq. km.). They have a population of 302,000. Capital: Nassau. The Bahamas imports most of their food and manufactured products and exports cement, refined oil, pulpwood and lobsters. Tourism is the principal industry.

The Bahamas were discovered by Columbus in October, 1492, but Spain made no attempt to settle them. British influence began in 1626 when Charles I granted them to the lord proprietors of Carolina. They continued under British proprietors until 1717, when the civil and military governments were surrendered to the King and the islands designated a British Crown Colony. The Bahamas obtained complete internal self-government under the constitution of Jan. 7, 1964. Full independence was achieved on July 10, 1973. The Bahamas is a member of the Commonwealth of Nations. Elizabeth II is Head of State, as Queen of Bahamas.

RULERS:
British

MONETARY SYSTEM:
1 Shilling = 12 Pence
1 Pound = 20 Shillings to 1966
1 Dollar = 100 Cents 1966-

COMMONWEALTH

GOVERNMENT OF THE BAHAMAS

1965 CURRENCY NOTE ACT

#17-25 Qn. Elizabeth II at l. Sign. varieties. Arms at r. on back. Wmk: Shellfish. Printer: TDLR. Replacement notes: Serial # prefix Z.

17　1/2 DOLLAR
L.1965. Purple on m/c unpt. Straw market on back.

	VG	VF	UNC
	0.75	2.00	8.50

18　1 DOLLAR
L.1965. Green on m/c unpt. Sea garden on back.

	VG	VF	UNC
a. 2 sign.	1.25	3.00	32.50
b. 3 sign.	1.50	5.00	45.00
s. As b. Specimen.	—	—	—

19 **3 DOLLARS**

		VG	VF	UNC
L.1965. Red on m/c unpt. Paradise Beach on back.				
a. Sign. Sands and Higgs.		4.00	7.50	25.00
b. Sign. Francis and Higgs. Specimen.		—	—	300.00

20 **5 DOLLARS**

		VG	VF	UNC
L.1965. Green on m/c unpt. Government House on back.				
a. Issued note.		8.00	20.00	100.00
s. Specimen.		—	—	—

21 **5 DOLLARS**

		VG	VF	UNC
L.1965. Orange on m/c unpt. Like #20.				
a. 2 sign.		10.00	35.00	325.00
b. 3 sign.		25.00	250.00	775.00

22 **10 DOLLARS**

		VG	VF	UNC
L.1965. Dk. blue on m/c unpt. Flamingos on back.				
a. 2 sign.		15.00	60.00	650.00
b. 3 sign.		35.00	350.00	1200.00

23 **20 DOLLARS**

		VG	VF	UNC
L.1965. Dk. brown on m/c unpt. Surrey on back.				
a. 2 sign.		50.00	200.00	900.00
b. 3 sign.		200.00	400.00	1750.00
s. Specimen. 3 sign.		—	—	100.00

24 **50 DOLLARS**

		VG	VF	UNC
L.1965. Brown on m/c unpt. Produce market on back.				
a. Issued note.		100.00	300.00	1650.00
s. Specimen. 3 sign.		—	—	200.00

25 **100 DOLLARS**

		VG	VF	UNC
L.1965. Blue on m/c unpt. Deep sea fishing on back.				
a. 2 sign.		200.00	600.00	2750.00
b. 3 sign.		450.00	—	—
s. Specimen. 3 sign.		—	—	300.00

BAHAMAS MONETARY AUTHORITY

1968 MONETARY AUTHORITY ACT

#26-33 Qn. Elizabeth II at I. Back designs like #17-25. Wmk: Shellfish. Printer: TDLR. Replacement notes: Serial # prefix Z.

26 **1/2 DOLLAR**

		VG	VF	UNC
L.1968. Purple on m/c unpt. Back like #17.				
a. Issued note.		0.65	1.50	6.50
s. Specimen.		—	—	20.00

27 **1 DOLLAR**

		VG	VF	UNC
L.1968. Green on m/c unpt. Back like #18.				
a. Issued note.		1.25	2.25	15.00
s. Specimen.		—	—	20.00

28 **3 DOLLARS**

		VG	VF	UNC
L.1968. Red on m/c unpt. Back like #19.				
a. Issued note.		3.50	7.50	25.00
s. Specimen.		—	—	25.00

29 **5 DOLLARS**

		VG	VF	UNC
L.1968. Orange on m/c unpt. Back like #20.				
a. Issued note.		7.00	50.00	200.00
s. Specimen.		—	—	50.00

30 **10 DOLLARS**

		VG	VF	UNC
L.1968. Dk. blue on m/c unpt. Back like #22.				
a. Issued note.		25.00	150.00	750.00
s. Specimen.		—	—	50.00

31	20 DOLLARS	VG	VF	UNC
	L.1968. Dk. brown on m/c unpt. Back like #23.			
	a. Issued note.	60.00	300.00	1350.00
	s. Specimen.	—	—	100.00

37	5 DOLLARS	VG	VF	UNC
	L.1974. Orange on m/c unpt. Back like #20.			
	a. Sign. T. B. Donaldson.	6.50	18.50	90.00
	b. Sign. W. C. Allen.	10.00	50.00	225.00

32	50 DOLLARS	VG	VF	UNC
	L.1968. Brown on m/c unpt. Back like #24.			
	a. Issued note.	150.00	450.00	2000.00
	s. Specimen.	—	—	200.00

38	10 DOLLARS	VG	VF	UNC
	L.1974. Dk. blue on m/c unpt. Back like #22.			
	a. Sign. T. B. Donaldson.	11.00	40.00	350.00
	b. Sign. W. C. Allen.	20.00	150.00	550.00

33	100 DOLLARS	VG	VF	UNC
	L.1968. Blue on m/c unpt. Back like #25.			
	a. Issued note.	300.00	700.00	3250.00
	s. Specimen.	—	—	300.00

#34 not assigned.

CENTRAL BANK OF THE BAHAMAS

1974 CENTRAL BANK ACT

#35-41 Qn. Elizabeth II at l. Back designs like #18-25 and #27-33. Wmk: Shellfish. Printer: TDLR. Replacement notes: Serial # prefix Z.

39	20 DOLLARS	VG	VF	UNC
	L.1974. Dk. brown on m/c unpt. Back like #23.			
	a. Sign. T. B. Donaldson.	27.50	85.00	450.00
	b. Sign. W. C. Allen.	42.50	185.00	750.00
40	50 DOLLARS			
	L.1974. Brown on m/c unpt. Back like #24.			
	a. Sign. T. B. Donaldson.	75.00	250.00	1200.00
	b. Sign. W. C. Allen.	85.00	350.00	1750.00
41	100 DOLLARS			
	L.1974. Blue on m/c unpt. Back like #25.			
	a. Sign. T. B. Donaldson.	135.00	400.00	2000.00
	b. Sign. W. C. Allen.	200.00	600.00	3000.00

1974 CENTRAL BANK ACT; 1984 ND ISSUE

#42-49 map at l., mature portr. Qn. Elizabeth II at ctr. r. Arms at r. on back. Wmk: Sailing ship. Printer: TDLR. Replacement notes: Serial # prefix Z.

35	1 DOLLAR	VG	VF	UNC
	L.1974. Dk. blue-green on m/c unpt. Back like #18.			
	a. Sign. T. B. Donaldson.	1.25	2.00	12.50
	b. Sign. W. C. Allen.	1.50	7.50	25.00

#36 not assigned.

42   1/2 DOLLAR

L.1974 (1984). Green on m/c unpt. Baskets at l. Sister Sarah in
Nassau market on back. Sign. W. C. Allen.

	VG	VF	UNC
	FV	FV	1.50
a. Issued note.	FV	FV	1.50
s. Specimen.	—	—	—

43   1 DOLLAR

L.1974 (1984). Deep green on m/c unpt. Fish at l. Royal Bahamas
Police band at ctr. on back.

	VG	VF	UNC
a. Sign. W. C. Allen.	FV	FV	4.00
b. Sign. F. H. Smith. 2 horizontal serial #.	FV	FV	5.00

44   3 DOLLARS

L.1974 (1984). Red-violet on m/c unpt. Paradise Beach at l. Family
Island sailing regatta on back. Sign. W. C. Allen.

	VG	VF	UNC
	FV	FV	7.00

45   5 DOLLARS

L.1974 (1984). Orange on m/c unpt. Statue at l. Local dancers
Junkanoo at ctr.

	VG	VF	UNC
a. Sign. W. C. Allen.	FV	9.50	55.00
b. Sign. F. H. Smith. 2 horizontal serial #.	FV	9.00	45.00

46   10 DOLLARS

L.1974 (1984). Pale blue on m/c unpt. 2 flamingos at l. Lighthouse
and Abaco Settlement on back.

	VG	VF	UNC
a. Sign. W. C. Allen.	FV	15.00	95.00
b. Sign. F. H. Smith. 2 horizontal serial #.	FV	40.00	150.00

47   20 DOLLARS

L.1974 (1984). Red and black on m/c unpt. Horse and carriage at
l. Nassau harbor on back.

	VG	VF	UNC
a. Sign. W. C. Allen.	FV	30.00	150.00
b. Sign. F. H. Smith. 2 horizontal serial #.	FV	22.50	60.00

48   50 DOLLARS

L.1974 (1984). Purple, orange and green on m/c unpt. Lighthouse
at l. Central Bank on back.

	VG	VF	UNC
a. Sign. W. C. Allen.	65.00	150.00	475.00
b. Sign. F. H. Smith. 2 horizontal serial #.	100.00	300.00	1250.00

NOTICE
Readers with unlisted dates, signature varieties, etc. are invited to
submit photocopies of their notes to: Standard Catalog of World
Paper Money, 700 East State St. Iola, WI 54990-0001, E-Mail:
george.cuhaj@fwpubs.com.

49	100 DOLLARS	VG	VF	UNC
	L.1974 (1984). Purple, deep blue and red-violet on m/c unpt. Sailboat at l. Blue marlin on back. Sign. W. C. Allen.	FV	200.00	750.00

1992 COMMEMORATIVE ISSUE

#50, Quincentennial of First Landfall by Christopher Columbus

53	10 DOLLARS	VG	VF	UNC
	L.1974 (1992). Pale blue on m/c unpt. Like #46b but w/serial # vertical and horizontal. Printer: BABN.	FV	20.00	90.00

#54-56 printer: TDLR.

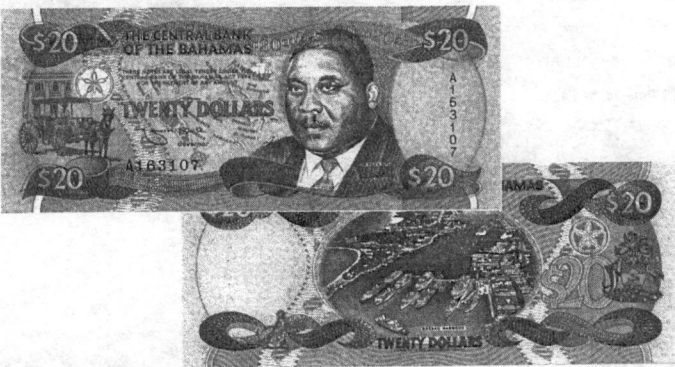

54	20 DOLLARS	VG	VF	UNC
	L.1974 (1993). Black and red on m/c unpt. Sir Milo B. Butler at r., horse drawn surrey at l. Aerial view of ships in Nassau's harbor at ctr.	FV	25.00	55.00

50	1 DOLLAR	VG	VF	UNC
	ND (1992). Dk. blue and deep violet on m/c unpt. Commercial seal at l., bust of C. Columbus r. w/compass face behind. Flamingos, rose-throated parrots, lizard, islands, ships across back w/arms at lower r. Printer: CBNC.			
	a. Issued note.	FV	FV	—
	s. Specimen.	—	—	—

55	50 DOLLARS	VG	VF	UNC
	L.1974 (1992). Brown, blue-green and orange on m/c unpt. Like #48b but w/serial # vertical and horizontal.	FV	70.00	175.00

1974 CENTRAL BANK ACT; 1992-95 ND ISSUE

#51-56 arms at r. on back. Wmk: Caravel sailing ship. Sign. F.H. Smith.

51	1 DOLLAR	VG	VF	UNC
	L.1974 (1992). Deep green on m/c unpt. Like #43b but w/serial # vertical and horizontal. Printer: BABN.	FV	FV	4.00

52	5 DOLLARS	VG	VF	UNC
	L.1974 (1995). Dk. brown, brown and orange on m/c unpt. Statue of Columbus at l., Wallace-Whitfield at r. Back like #45. Printer: TDLR.	FV	FV	15.00

56	100 DOLLARS	VG	VF	UNC
	L.1974 (1992). Purple, deep blue and red-violet on m/c unpt. Like #49 but w/serial # vertical and horizontal.	FV	125.00	385.00

1974 CENTRAL BANK ACT; 1996 ISSUE

#57, 59, 61, and 62 mature bust of Qn. Elizabeth II. Ascending size serial # at lower l. Arms at r. on back. Sign. F. H. Smith.

57	1 DOLLAR	VG	VF	UNC
	1996. Deep green on m/c unpt. Like #51. Printer: BABN.	FV	FV	3.50

#58 *Deleted.* See #63.

59	10 DOLLARS	VG	VF	UNC
	1996. Deep blue-green, green and violet on m/c unpt. Like #53. Printer: TDLR.	FV	FV	25.00

#60 not assigned.

61	50 DOLLARS	VG	VF	UNC
	1996. Red-brown and deep green on m/c unpt. Like #55. Printer: TDLR.	FV	FV	100.00

Note: The following notes were stolen and are not redeemable. Serial # G101,001-103,000; G104,001-G105,000; G108,001-G109,000.

62	100 DOLLARS	VG	VF	UNC
	1996. Purple, deep blue and violet on m/c unpt. Like #56. Printer: BABN.	FV	FV	185.00

Note: The following notes were stolen and are not redeemable. Serial # G541,001-G548,000.

1974 CENTRAL BANK ACT; 1997; 2000 ISSUE

Serial #'s vertical and ascending size horizontal.

63	5 DOLLARS	VG	VF	UNC
	1997. Dk. brown, brown and orange on m/c unpt. Like #52. Printer: TDLR. 2 sign. varieties.			
	a. 1997. *GOVERNOR* title in orange.	FV	FV	15.00
	b. 2002. *GOVERNOR* in black.	FV	FV	15.00

64	10 DOLLARS	VG	VF	UNC
	2000. Deep blue-green, green and violet on m/c unpt. Sir Stafford Sands and OVD at r., pair of flamingos at l.	FV	FV	20.00
65	20 DOLLARS			
	1997; 2000. M/c.			
	a. 1997. 2 sign. varieties.	FV	FV	45.00
	b. 2000. Modified security features.	FV	FV	42.50

66	50 DOLLARS	VG	VF	UNC
	2000. Sir Roland Symonette and OVD at r., lighthouse at l.	FV	FV	85.00

67	**100 DOLLARS**	**VG**	**VF**	**UNC**
	2000. M/c. Qn. Elizabeth II, OVD at r.	FV	FV	175.00

2000 CENTRAL BANK ACT; 2001 ISSUE

68	**1/2 DOLLAR**	**VG**	**VF**	**UNC**
	2001. Slate blue and green on tan and m/c unpt. Qn. Elizabeth II at r., baskets at l. Sister Sarah in Nassau market on back.	FV	FV	2.75

69	**1 DOLLAR**	**VG**	**VF**	**UNC**
	2001. Green, brown and m/c. Sir. Lynden O. Pindling at r. Police band on back. Printer: TDLR.	FV	FV	4.00
70	**5 DOLLARS**			
	2001. Brown and rose on m/c unpt. Sir Cecil Wallace-Whitefield at r., statue at l. Junkandoo dancers on back.	FV	FV	15.00

2002 SERIES

71	**1 DOLLAR**	**VG**	**VF**	**UNC**
	2002. Deep green on m/c unpt. Like #43. Segemnted foil security strip added. Printer TDLR.	FV	FV	4.00

2005 SERIES

72	**10 DOLLARS**	**VG**	**VF**	**UNC**
	2005. Blue and m/c. Qn. Elizabeth II at r. Serial # prefix A, B, C.	FV	FV	30.00

COLLECTOR SERIES

BAHAMAS GOVERNMENT

1965 ISSUE

		Issue Price	Mkt.	Value
CS1	**1/2-100 DOLLARS**	—		2500.00
	L.1965. #17-25 ovpt: SPECIMEN. (100 sets).			

BAHAMAS MONETARY AUTHORITY

1968 ISSUES

		Issue Price	Mkt.	Value
CS2	**1/2-100 DOLLARS**	—		500.00
	L.1968. #26-33 ovpt: SPECIMEN.			
CS3	**1/2-100 DOLLARS**	90.00		250.00
	L.1968. #26-33 ovpt: SPECIMEN, punched hole cancelled.			

BAHRAIN

KUWAIT

IRAN

OMAN

Persian
Gulf

SAUDI ARABIA   QATAR

Gulf of Oman

UNITED ARAB
EMIRATES   OMAN

The State of Bahrain, a group of islands in the Persian Gulf off Saudi Arabia, has an area of 258 sq. mi. (622 sq. km.) and a population of 618,000. Capital: Manama. Prior to the depression of the 1930s, the economy was based on pearl fishing. Petroleum and aluminum industries and transit trade are the vital factors in the economy today.

The Portuguese occupied the islands in 1507 but were driven out in 1602 by Arab subjects of Persia. They in turn were ejected by Arabs of the Ataiba tribe from the Arabian mainland who have maintained possession up to the present time. The ruling sheikh of Bahrain entered into relations with Great Britain in 1805 and concluded a binding treaty of protection in 1861. In 1968 Great Britain decided to terminate treaty relations with the Persian Gulf sheikhdoms. Unable to agree on terms of union with the other sheikhdoms, Bahrain decided to seek independence as a separate entity and became fully independent on August 15, 1971.

A new constitution establishing Bahrain as a kingdom was published on December 14, 2002.

RULERS:
Isa Bin Sulman al-Khalifa, 1961-

MONETARY SYSTEM:
1 Dinar = 1000 Fils

KINGDOM

BAHRAIN CURRENCY BOARD

AUTHORIZATION 6/1964

#1-6 dhow at l., arms at r. Wmk: Falcon's head. For specimen notes with a maltese cross serial # prefix, see CS1 at the end of the country listing.

1	100 FILS	VG	VF	UNC
	L.1964. Ochre on m/c unpt. Back green and orange; palm trees at ctr.			
	a. Issued note.	FV	1.25	7.00
	s. Specimen.	—	—	35.00

2	1/4 DINAR	VG	VF	UNC
	L.1964. Brown on m/c unpt. Oil derricks on back.			
	a. Issued note.	FV	2.00	10.00
	s. Specimen.	—	—	35.00

3	1/2 DINAR	VG	VF	UNC
	L.1964. Purple on m/c unpt. Ships at the Mina Sulman Jetty on back.			
	a. Issued note.	FV	2.25	12.50
	s. Specimen.	—	—	40.00

4	1 DINAR	VG	VF	UNC
	L.1964. Brownish red on m/c unpt. Ruins of the Suq al-Khamis mosque, dominated by two minarets, on back.			
	a. Issued note.	FV	5.00	15.00
	s. Specimen.	—	—	40.00

5	5 DINARS	VG	VF	UNC
	L.1964. Blue-black on m/c unpt. Two pearling dhows on back.			
	a. Issued note.	FV	75.00	300.00
	s. Specimen.	—	—	200.00

6	10 DINARS	VG	VF	UNC
	L.1964. Green on m/c unpt. Aerial view of the town of Isa on back.			
	a. Issued note.	FV	50.00	125.00
	s. Specimen.	—	—	150.00

BAHRAIN MONETARY AGENCY

AUTHORIZATION 23/1973

#7-11 map at l., dhow at ctr., arms at r. Wmk: Falcon's head.

7	1/2 DINAR	VG	VF	UNC
	L.1973. Brown on m/c unpt. Cast copper head of bull at lower l. Smelting works of Aluminium Bahrain at l. on back.	FV	2.50	5.00

8　1 DINAR

	VG	VF	UNC
L.1973. Red on m/c unpt. Minaret of the Manama Mosque at l. Headquarters of Bahrain Monetary Agency at l. on back.	FV	4.00	5.00

8A　5 DINARS

	VG	VF	UNC
L.1973. Dark blue on m/c unpt. Minaret of the Suq al-Khamis mosque at l. Pearling dhows at l. on back.	FV	10.00	40.00

9　10 DINARS

	VG	VF	UNC
L.1973. Green on m/c unpt. Wind tower at l. Dry dock at l. on back.			
a. 2 horizontal serial #.	FV	30.00	60.00
b. Serial # vertical and horizontal.	FV	35.00	60.00

10　20 DINARS

	VG	VF	UNC
L.1973. Reddish-brown on m/c unpt. Minaret of the al-Fadhel mosque at l. Government House at l. on back.			
a. Issued note.	FV	75.00	175.00
s. Specimen.	—	—	—

11　20 DINARS

	VG	VF	UNC
L.1973. Face like #10, but w/symbol changed at r. of map. Silvering added at lower l. denomination. Back has open frame and symbol around wmk. area. Also various color differences.			
a. 2 horizontal serial #.	FV	60.00	110.00
b. Serial # vertical and horizontal.	FV	65.00	125.00

AUTHORIZATION 23/1973; 1993 ND ISSUE

#12-16 arms at ctr., outline map at l. Wmk: Antelope's head.

12　1/2 DINAR

	VG	VF	UNC
L.1973 (1986). Dk. brown and violet on violet on m/c unpt. Red shield at ctr. Man weaving at r. Back brown and violet on m/c unpt. "Aluminum Bahrain" facility at l. ctr.	FV	1.50	4.00

13　1 DINAR

	VG	VF	UNC
L.1973 (1993). Violet and red-orange on m/c unpt. Ancient Dilmun seal at r. Bahrain Monetary Agency bldg. at l. ctr. on back. Narrow security thread.	FV	3.00	7.50

14　5 DINARS

	VG	VF	UNC
L.1973 (1993). Dk. blue and deep blue-green on m/c unpt. Riffa Fortress at r. Bahrain International Airport at l. ctr. on back.	FV	12.50	45.00

15	10 DINARS	VG	VF	UNC
	L.1973 (1993). Deep olive-green and green on m/c unpt. Dhow at r. Aerial view of Kg. Fahad Causeway at l. ctr. on back.	FV	40.00	75.00

16	20 DINARS	VG	VF	UNC
	L.1973 (1993). Purple and violet m/c unpt. Bab al-Bahrain gate at r. Ahmed al-Fateh Islamic Center at l. ctr. on back.	—	60.00	140.00

Note: A second printing was ordered using a false authorization. These are easily distinguished by a space between the 2 Arabic letters in the serial # prefix and are not redeemable. Collector value is approximately $10.00.

AUTHORIZATION 23/1973; 1996 ND ISSUE

17	1/2 DINAR	VG	VF	UNC
	L.1973 (1996). Deep brown, violet and brown w/deep brown shield at ctr. Like #12. Narrow security thread.	FV	FV	5.00

AUTHORIZATION 23/1973; 1998 ND ISSUE

#18-20 arms at lower ctr., wide security thread.

#20-23 with hologram at lower l.

18	1/2 DINAR	VG	VF	UNC
	L.1973 (1998). Similar to #17.			
	a. W/microprinting.	FV	FV	3.50
	b. W/o microprinting.	FV	FV	3.50

19	1 DINAR	VG	VF	UNC
	L.1973 1998. Similar to #13.			
	a. W/*BMA* microprinting on security thread.	FV	FV	7.50
	b. W/o microprinting on security thread.	FV	FV	5.00

20	5 DINARS	VG	VF	UNC
	L.1973 (1998). Blue on m/c unpt. Like #14.			
	a. W/*BMA* microprinting on security thread.	FV	40.00	60.00
	b. W/o microprinting on security thread.	FV	FV	30.00

21	10 DINARS	VG	VF	UNC
	L.1973 (1998). Green on m/c unpt. Like #15.			
	a. W/*BMA* microprinting on security thread.	FV	60.00	125.00
	b. W/o microprinting on security thread.	FV	FV	45.00

22	20 DINARS	VG	VF	UNC
	L.1973 (1998). Purple on m/c unpt. Like #16 but with hologram and wide micro-printed security thread.	50.00	200.00	500.00

23   20 DINARS
L. 1973 (1998). Orange and black on m/c unpt. Like #16.

	VG	VF	UNC
	FV	75.00	150.00

AUTHORIZATION 23/1973; 2001 ND ISSUE

24   20 DINARS
ND (2001). Orange on m/c unpt. Shaikh Hamad bin Issa al Khalifa, King of Bahrain at r.

	VG	VF	UNC
	FV	FV	100.00

2001 ND SECOND ISSUE

25   5 DINARS
ND (2002). Blue on m/c unpt. Hologram added to #20.

	VG	VF	UNC
	FV	FV	30.00

COLLECTOR SERIES

COLLECTOR SERIES

AUTHORIZATION 23/1973

#7-11 map at l., dhow at ctr., arms at r. Wmk: Falcon's head.

CS1   100 FILS - 20 DINARS
ND (1978). #1-6 and 10 w/ovpt: *SPECIMEN* and Maltese cross serial # prefix.

	Issue Price	Mkt.	Value
	14.00		80.00

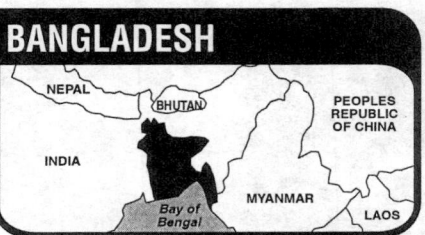

The Peoples Republic of Bangladesh (formerly East Pakistan), a parliamentary democracy located on the Bay of Bengal bordered by India and Burma, has an area of 55,598 sq. mi. (143,998 sq. km.) and a population of 128.31 million. Capital: Dhaka (Dacca). The economy is predominantly agricultural. Jute products and tea are exported.

British rule over the vast Indian sub-continent ended in 1947 when British India attained independence and was partitioned into the two successor states of India and Pakistan. Pakistan consisted of East and West Pakistan, two areas united by the Moslem religion but separated by culture and 1,000 miles of Indian territory. Restive under the de facto rule of the militant but fewer West Pakistanis, the East Pakistanis unsuccessfully demanded greater economic benefits and political reforms. The inability of the leaders of East and West Pakistan to resolve a political breakdown occasioned by the East Pakistan success in the general elections of 1970 precipitated massive civil disobedience in East Pakistan which West Pakistan sought to suppress militarily. East Pakistan seceded from Pakistan, March 26, 1971, and with the support of India declared an independent Peoples Republic of Bangladesh led by Mujibur Rahman who was later assassinated on Aug. 15, 1975. Bangladesh is a member of the Commonwealth of Nations. The president is the Head of State and of Government.

MONETARY SYSTEM:
   1 Rupee = 100 Paise to 1972
   1 Taka = 100 Paisas 1972-

REPUBLIC

PEOPLES REPUBLIC OF BANGLADESH

1971 ND PROVISIONAL ISSUE

#1-3 w/*BANGLADESH* ovpt. in English or Bengali on Pakistan notes. The Bangladesh Bank never officially issued any Pakistan notes w/ovpt. These are considered locally issued by some authorities.

1   1 RUPEE
ND (1971). Blue. Purple ovpt. *BANGLADESH* on Pakistan #9. Four different overprints are documented.

	VG	VF	UNC
	7.50	30.00	90.00

1A   1 RUPEE
ND (1971). Blue. Purple Bengali ovpt. on Pakistan #9. Two different overprints are documented.

	VG	VF	UNC
	7.50	30.00	90.00

		VG	VF	UNC
2	**5 RUPEES**			
	ND (1971). Brown-violet. Purple Bengali ovpt. on Pakistan #15.	10.00	32.50	100.00
2A	**5 RUPEES**			
	ND (1971). English ovpt. on Pakistan #15.	10.00	32.50	100.00

		VG	VF	UNC
3	**10 RUPEES**			
	ND (1971). Brown. Purple Bengali ovpt. on Pakistan #13.	10.00	35.00	120.00
3A	**5 RUPEES**			
	ND (1971). English ovpt. on Pakistan #18.	20.00	75.00	175.00
3B	**10 RUPEES**			
	ND (1971). English ovpt. on Pakistan #19.	25.00	125.00	225.00

1972-89 ND ISSUES

		VG	VF	UNC
4	**1 TAKA**			
	ND (1972). Brown on orange and blue unpt. Map of Bangladesh at l.	0.20	0.75	6.00

		VG	VF	UNC
5	**1 TAKA**			
	ND (1973). Purple and ochre. Hand holding rice plants at l. Arms at r. on back.			
	a. W/wmk: Tiger's head.	0.20	0.75	5.00
	b. W/o wmk. (2 sign. varieties).	0.20	0.75	5.00

		VG	VF	UNC
6	**1 TAKA**			
	ND (1973). Purple on ochre and blue unpt. Woman preparing grain at l. Hand holding rice plants at ctr., arms at r. on back. Wmk: Tiger's head.			
	a. Issued note.	0.20	0.60	7.00

	s. Specimen.	—	—	100.00

		VG	VF	UNC
6A	**1 TAKA**			
	ND (1979). Purple on m/c. unpt. Arms at r. Deer at l. ctr. on back. Wmk: Tiger's head.	0.10	0.50	2.00

		VG	VF	UNC
6B	**1 TAKA**			
	ND (1982). Purple on m/c unpt. Similar to #6A but no printing on wmk. area at l. Modified tiger wmk.			
	a. Sign. title in Bengali: *FINANCE SECRETARY*. Solid security thread. Six sign. varieties.	0.05	0.10	0.75
	b. Sign. title in Bengali: *PRINCIPAL FINANCE SECRETARY*. Solid security thread. 1 sign. variety.	0.05	0.10	0.50
	c. Sign. title in Bengali: *FINANCE SECRETARY*. Micro-printed security thread. One sign. variety.	0.05	0.10	0.50

		VG	VF	UNC
6C	**2 TAKA**			
	ND (1988). Gray-green on orange and green unpt. Monument at r. Dhyal or Magpie-robin at l. on back. 6 sign. varieties. Wmk: Tiger's head.			
	a. Solid security thread. Four sign. varieties.	FV	FV	0.75
	b. Security thread reads: *BANGLADESH BANK* in Bengali.	FV	FV	0.50
	c. Security thread reads: *GOVERNMENT OF BANGLADESH* in Bengali. One sign.	FV	FV	0.50
	d. As c, but smaller wmk.	FV	FV	0.50
	e. Dated 2002 on back.	FV	FV	0.50
	f. Dated 2003 on back.	FV	FV	0.50

BANGLADESH BANK

1972 ND ISSUE

#7-9 map of Bangladesh at l., portr. Mujibur Rahman at r.

		VG	VF	UNC
7	**5 TAKA**			
	ND (1972). Purple on m/c unpt.	0.50	3.00	17.50

		VG	VF	UNC
8	**10 TAKA**			
	ND (1972). Blue on m/c unpt.	1.00	5.00	27.50

1974 ND Issue

#13-14 Mujibur Rahman at r. Wmk: Tiger's head.

9	100 TAKA	VG	VF	UNC
	ND (1972). Green on m/c unpt.	2.00	8.00	75.00

1973 ND Issue

#10-12 Mujibur Rahman at l. Wmk: Tiger's head.

13	5 TAKA	VG	VF	UNC
	ND (1973). Red on m/c unpt. Aerial view of factory on back. 2 sign. varieties.			
	a. Issued note.	0.25	1.50	12.50
	s. Specimen.	—	—	110.00

10	5 TAKA	VG	VF	UNC
	ND (1972). Red on m/c unpt. Lotus plants at ctr. r. on back.			
	a. Issued note.	0.25	1.50	10.00
	s. Specimen.	—	—	

14	10 TAKA	VG	VF	UNC
	ND (1973). Green on m/c unpt. Rice harvesting scene at l. ctr. on back. 2 sign. varieties.			
	a. Issued note.	0.25	1.00	10.00
	s. Specimen.	—	—	110.00

1976; 1977 ND Issue

#15-17, 19 Star mosque in Dhaka at r. Wmk: Tiger's head.

11	10 TAKA	VG	VF	UNC
	ND (1972). Green on m/c unpt. River scene on back.			
	a. Serial # in Western numerals.	0.50	4.00	17.50
	b. Serial # in Bengali numerals.	2.00	7.50	25.00
	s. Specimen.	—	—	

15	5 TAKA	VG	VF	UNC
	ND (1977). Lt. brown on m/c unpt. Back like #13.			
	a. Issued note.	0.10	0.25	5.00
	s. Specimen.	—	—	100.00

12	100 TAKA	VG	VF	UNC
	ND (1972). Brown on m/c unpt. River scene on back.			
	a. Serial # in western numerals.	0.75	3.00	17.50
	b. Serial # in Bengali numerals.	25.00	50.00	100.00

16	**10 TAKA**	VG	VF	UNC
	ND (1977). Violet on m/c unpt. Back like #14.			
	a. Issued note.	0.25	0.75	7.50
	s. Specimen.	—	—	110.00

17	**50 TAKA**	VG	VF	UNC
	ND (1976). Orange on m/c unpt. Harvesting scene on back.			
	a. Issued note.	0.25	1.00	15.00
	s. Specimen.	—	—	100.00

18	**100 TAKA**	VG	VF	UNC
	ND (1976). Blue-violet on m/c unpt. Back like #12. Wmk: Tiger's head.	1.00	7.50	50.00

19	**500 TAKA**	VG	VF	UNC
	ND (1976). Blue and lilac on m/c unpt. High Court in Dhaka on back.	25.00	90.00	250.00

Note: For similar 500 Taka but w/o printing on wmk. area, see #30.

1978-82 ND Issue

#20-24 wmk: Tiger's head.

20	**5 TAKA**	VG	VF	UNC
	ND (1978). Brown on m/c unpt. Mihrab in *Kushumba* mosque at r. Back like #13.			
	a. Issued note.	0.20	0.50	4.00
	s. Specimen.	—	—	100.00

21	**10 TAKA**	VG	VF	UNC
	ND (1978). Violet on m/c unpt. *Atiya Jam-e* mosque in Tangali at r. Back like #14.			
	a. Issued note.	0.25	0.50	6.00
	s. Specimen.	—	—	110.00

22	**20 TAKA**	VG	VF	UNC
	ND (1979). Dk. blue-green on m/c unpt. *Chote Sona* mosque at r. Harvesting scene on back. Unpt. over wmk. area at l. Micro-printed security thread.	0.25	0.75	6.00

23	**50 TAKA**	VG	VF	UNC
	ND (1979). Orange on m/c unpt. Sat Gamnbuj Mosque in Dhaka at r. Women harvesting tea on back.	0.25	1.00	8.00

24	**100 TAKA**	VG	VF	UNC
	ND (1977). Blue-violet, deep brown and orange on m/c unpt. Star mosque in Dhaka at r. Unpt. throughout wmk. area at l. Ruins of Lalbagh Fort at l. ctr. on back.	0.50	3.00	20.00

1982-88 ND ISSUE

#25-32 wmk: Modified tiger's head. Sign. varieties.

27	**20 TAKA**	VG	VF	UNC
	ND (1988); 2002. Blue-green on m/c unpt. Similar to #22 but w/o printing on wmk. area. 3 sign. varieties.			
	a. Black sign. Lg. serial #. 2 sign. varieties.	FV	FV	4.00
	b. Green sign. Sm. serial #. 2 sign. varieties.	FV	FV	3.50
	c. Foil security thread. Green sign. small serial #.	FV	FV	3.50

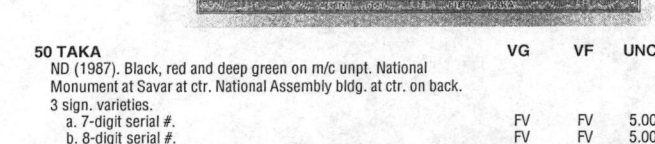

25	**5 TAKA**	VG	VF	UNC
	ND (1981). Similar to #20 but w/o printing on wmk. area at l. on face.			
	a. Solid security thread. Black sign. Lg. serial #. 1 sign. variety.	0.10	0.25	1.50
	b. Micro-printed security thread. Black sign. Sm. serial #. 2 sign. varieties.	FV	0.15	1.00
	c. Micro-printed security thread. Brown sign. Sm. serial #. 3 sign. varieties.	FV	FV	0.75
	s. Specimen.	—	—	—

28	**50 TAKA**	VG	VF	UNC
	ND (1987). Black, red and deep green on m/c unpt. National Monument at Savar at ctr. National Assembly bldg. at ctr. on back. 3 sign. varieties.			
	a. 7-digit serial #.	FV	FV	5.00
	b. 8-digit serial #.	FV	FV	5.00
	c. Different tiger in wmk. Clouds on back have been re-engraved. Unpt. colors changed.	FV	FV	5.00

26	**10 TAKA**	VG	VF	UNC
	ND (1982). Violet and red-violet on m/c unpt. *Atiya Jam-e* mosque in Tangali at r. Hydroelectric dam at l. ctr. on back.			
	a. W/curved line of text above and below mosque. Solid security thread.	0.10	0.25	2.50
	b. W/o curved line of text above mosque. Solid security thread. 2 sign. varieties.	FV	0.40	1.25
	c. Micro-printed security thread. 3 sign. varieties.	FV	FV	1.25

29	**100 TAKA**	VG	VF	UNC
	ND (1981). Blue-violet, deep brown and orange on m/c unpt. Similar to #24, but w/o printing on wmk. area at l.	FV	FV	10.00

30 **500 TAKA**

		VG	VF	UNC
ND (1982). Gray, blue and violet on m/c unpt. Similar to #19 but w/o printing on wmk. area at l. on face.				
a. W/o segmented foil. 2 sign. varieties.		FV	FV	55.00
b. W/segmented foil over security thread. 2 sign. varieties.		FV	FV	30.00
c. Eight numerals in serial #.		FV	FV	30.00

31 **100 TAKA**

		VG	VF	UNC
ND (1983). Like #29 but w/circular toothed border added around wmk. area on face and back.				
a. Solid security thread. 2 sign. varieties.		FV	FV	6.50
b. Micro-printed security thread. 2 sign. varieties.		FV	FV	6.00
c. Segmented foil security thread. 2 sign. varieties.		FV	FV	6.00
d. Segmented foil thread w/micro-printing. 1 sign. variety.		FV	FV	6.00
e. Solid foil thread w/micro-printing.		FV	FV	6.00

1997 ND ISSUE

32 **10 TAKA**

	VG	VF	UNC
ND (1997). Dk. brown and deep blue-green on m/c unpt. M. Rahman at r. and as wmk. Arms at l., Lalbagh Fort mosque at l. ctr. on back. 2 sign. varieties.	FV	FV	2.50

1996 ND COMMEMORATIVE ISSUE

#35, Victory Day. Ovpt: *VICTORY DAY SILVER JUBILEE '96* in lower l. wmk. area.

33 **10 TAKA**

	VG	VF	UNC
ND (1996). Violet on m/c unpt. Commemorative ovpt. on #26b at lower l. in wmk. area.	FV	FV	3.00

1998 ND ISSUE

34 **500 TAKA**

	VG	VF	UNC
ND (1998). Brown, blue, purple and red on m/c unpt. National Monument in Savar at ctr. r. Black slate blue; High Court building in Dhaka.	FV	FV	30.00

2000-01 ISSUE

35 **10 TAKA**

	VG	VF	UNC
2000. Brown, red and m/c. Mujibur Rahman at l. National Assembly bldg. on back. Polymer plastic.	FV	FV	2.00

36 **50 TAKA**

	VG	VF	UNC
ND (2000). Brown and blue on m/c unpt. National Assembly bldg. at l. Bagha Mosque of Rajshahi at r. on back.	FV	FV	3.00

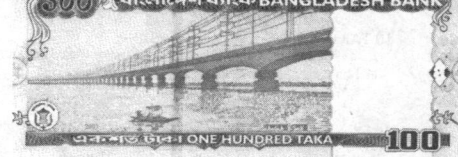

37 **100 TAKA**

	VG	VF	UNC
2001. Dk. blue on lt. red-brown unpt. Mujibur Rahman at l., Sixty Dome Mosque at r. Bangabandhu Bridge on back.	FV	FV	5.00

38 500 TAKA
2000. Brownish purple on m/c unpt. Mujibur Rahman at r., Sat
Gambuj Mosque in ctr. High Court bldg. in Dhaka on back.
VG FV   VF FV.   UNC 22.50

2002 ISSUE

39 10 TAKA
2002; 2003; 2004; 2005. Brown, red and m/c. National emblem at
l. bldg. at lower r. National Assembly bldg. on back.
VG FV   VF FV   UNC 2.00

40 20 TAKA
2002; 2003; 2004. Blue-green on m/c unpt. Similar to #27 but
reduced size. Enhanced security features.
VG FV   VF FV   UNC 3.50

41 50 TAKA
2003; 2004; 2005. Brown and blue on m/c unpt. Similar to #36 but
reduced size. Iridescent security thread, sight impaired features.
VG FV   VF FV   UNC 4.00

42 100 TAKA
2002; 2003; 2004. Dk. blue on lt. red-brown unpt. National
monument at Savar at ctr. Bangabandhu Bridge on back.
VG FV   VF FV   UNC 5.00

43 500 TAKA
2002; 2003. Brownish purple on m/c unpt. National Monument at
Savar at right, Sat Gambuj Mosque in ctr. High Court bldg. in Dhaka
on back.
VG FV   VF FV   UNC 22.50

2004-05 ISSUE

44 100 TAKA
2005. M/c like #42. But value in upper left is a solid color.
VG FV   VF FV   UNC 5.00

45 500 TAKA
2003; 2004. Like # 43. Value at upper left is in solid color. Value in
text is in color shifting ink.
VG FV   VF FV   UNC 22.50

BARBADOS

DOMINICA

MARTINIQUE

ST. LUCIA

ST. VINCENT AND
THE GRENADINES

GRENADA

Barbados, an independent state within the British Commonwealth, is located in the Windward Islands of the West Indies east of St. Vincent. The coral island has an area of 166 sq. mi. (431 sq. km) and a population of 269,000. Capital: Bridgetown. The economy is based on sugar and tourism. Sugar, petroleum products, molasses and rum are exported.

Barbados was named by the Portuguese who achieved the first landing on the island in 1563. British sailors landed at the site of present-day Holetown in 1624. Barbados was under uninterrupted British control from the time of the first British settlement in 1627 until it obtained independence on Nov. 30, 1966. It is a member of the Commonwealth of Nations. Elizabeth II is Head of State, as Queen of Barbados.

Barbados was included in the issues of the British Caribbean Territories - Eastern Group and later the East Caribbean Currency Authority until 1973.

RULERS:
British to 1966

MONETARY SYSTEM:
1 Dollar = 100 Cents, 1950-

STATE

CENTRAL BANK OF BARBADOS

1973 ND ISSUE

#29-35 arms at l. ctr. Trafalgar Square in Bridgetown on back. Sign. C. Blackman. Wmk: Map of Barbados. Printer: (T)DLR. Replacement notes: serial # prefix *Z1*.

			VG	VF	UNC
29	1 DOLLAR				
	ND (1973). Red on m/c unpt. Portr. S. J. Prescod at r.				
	a. Issued note.		FV	1.00	10.00
	s. Specimen.		—	—	50.00

			VG	VF	UNC
30	2 DOLLARS				
	ND (1980). Blue on m/c unpt. Portr. J. R. Bovell at r.		FV	3.00	16.00

			VG	VF	UNC
31	5 DOLLARS				
	ND (1973). Green on m/c unpt. Portr. S. J. Prescod at r.				
	a. Issued note.		FV	8.00	30.00
	s. As a. Specimen.		—	—	50.00

			VG	VF	UNC
32	5 DOLLARS				
	ND (1975). Dk. green on m/c unpt. Portr. Sir. F. Worrell at r.		FV	8.00	25.00

			VG	VF	UNC
33	10 DOLLARS				
	ND (1973). Dk. brown on m/c unpt. Portr. C. D. O'Neal at r.		FV	10.00	37.50

			VG	VF	UNC
34	20 DOLLARS				
	ND (1973). Purple on m/c unpt. Portr. S. J. Prescod at r.		FV	17.50	52.50

35 **100 DOLLARS** | VG | VF | UNC
ND (1973). Gray and blue on m/c unpt. Portr. Sir. G. H. Adams at r. Treetops are grayish blue on back. Serial # to E3200000. | FV | 80.00 | 190.00

1986 ND Issue

35A **10 DOLLARS** | VG | VF | UNC
ND. Dk. Brown and green on m/c unpt. Like #38 but w/o seahorse at l. Sign. King. | FV | 15.00 | 40.00

35B **100 DOLLARS** | VG | VF | UNC
ND. Brown, purple and gray-blue on m/c unpt. Like #41, but Sign. Blackman | FV | 75.00 | 185.00

1986-89 ND Issue

#36-41 sign. K. King. Printer: (T)DLR. Replacement notes: serial # prefix *Z1*.

36 **2 DOLLARS** | VG | VF | UNC
ND (1986). Blue on m/c unpt. Portr. J. R. Bovell at r. | FV | 3.00 | 15.00

37 **5 DOLLARS** | VG | VF | UNC
ND (1986). Dk. green on m/c unpt. Portr. Sir. F. Worrell at r. | FV | 6.00 | 22.50

---

38 **10 DOLLARS** | VG | VF | UNC
ND (1986). Dk. Brown and green on m/c unpt. Like #33 but seahorse in rectangle at l. on face and at r. on back. | FV | 7.00 | 27.50
39 **20 DOLLARS** | | |
ND (1988). Purple on m/c unpt. Like #34 but bird emblem in rectangle at l. on face and at r. on back. | FV | 15.00 | 45.00

40 **50 DOLLARS** | VG | VF | UNC
ND (1989). Orange, blue and gray on m/c unpt. Portr. Prime Minister E. W. Barrow at r. Trident emblem at l. on face and r. on back. | FV | 40.00 | 105.00

41 **100 DOLLARS** | VG | VF | UNC
ND (1986). Brown, purple and gray-blue on m/c unpt. Like #35 but seahorse emblem at r. on face and l. on back. Treetops are green. Serial # above E3200000. | FV | 65.00 | 155.00

1993-94 ND Issue

#42-45 arms at l. ctr. Trafalgar Square in Bridgetown on back. Sign. C. M. Springer. Wmk: Map of Barbados. Printer: (T)DLR. Replacement notes: serial # prefix *Z1*.

42 **2 DOLLARS** | VG | VF | UNC
ND (1993). Blue on m/c unpt. Portr. J. R. Bovell at r. | FV | FV | 12.50
43 **5 DOLLARS** | | |
ND (1993). Dk. green on m/c unpt. Portr. Sir. F. Worrell at r. | FV | FV | 17.50
44 **20 DOLLARS** | | |
ND (1993). Purple on m/c unpt. Portr. S. J. Prescod at r. | FV | FV | 40.00

45 **100 DOLLARS** | VG | VF | UNC
ND (1994). Brown, purple and gray-blue m/c unpt. Portr. Sir. G. H. Adams at l. | FV | FV | 145.00

NOTICE

Readers with unlisted dates, signature varieties, etc. are invited to submit photocopies of their notes to: Standard Catalog of World Paper Money, 700 East State St. Iola, WI 54990-0001, E-Mail: george.cuhaj@fwpubs.com.

1995-96 ND ISSUE

#46-49 ascending size serial # at upper l. Enhanced security features. Printer (T)DLR. Replacement notes: serial # prefix *Z1*.

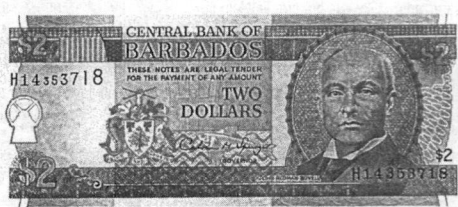

46	2 DOLLARS		VG	VF	UNC
	ND (1995). Blue on m/c unpt. Similar to #42.		FV	FV	11.00

47	5 DOLLARS		VG	VF	UNC
	ND (1996). Dk. green on m/c unpt. Similar to #43.		FV	FV	15.00

48	10 DOLLARS		VG	VF	UNC
	ND (1995). Dk. brown and green on m/c unpt. Similar to #38.		FV	FV	22.50

49	20 DOLLARS		VG	VF	UNC
	ND (1996). Red-violet and purple on m/c unpt. Similar to #39.		FV	FV	37.50

1996-97 ND ISSUE

#50-52 w/enlarged denomination numerals at upper l. Sign. C. M. Springer. Printer: (T)DLR. Replacement notes: serial # prefix *Z1*.

50	20 DOLLARS		VG	VF	UNC
	ND (1997). Red-violet and purple on m/c unpt. Similar to #49.		FV	FV	35.00

51	50 DOLLARS		VG	VF	UNC
	ND (1997). Orange, blue and gray on m/c unpt. Similar to #40.		FV	FV	80.00
52	100 DOLLARS				
	ND (1996). Brown, purple and blue-gray on m/c unpt. Similar to #45.		FV	FV	130.00

1997 ND COMMEMORATIVE ISSUE

#53, 25th Anniversary Central Bank

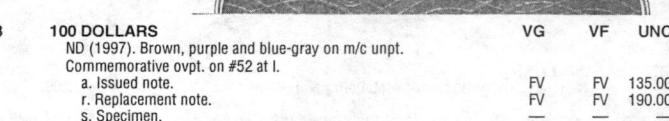

53	100 DOLLARS		VG	VF	UNC
	ND (1997). Brown, purple and blue-gray on m/c unpt. Commemorative ovpt. on #52 at l.				
	a. Issued note.		FV	FV	135.00
	r. Replacement note.		FV	FV	190.00
	s. Specimen.		—	—	—

1998 ND ISSUE

#54-59 enhanced security features. Sign. W. Cox. Printer: (T)DLR. Replacement notes: serial # prefix *Z1*.

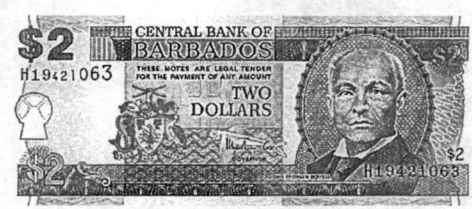

54	2 DOLLARS	VG	VF	UNC
	ND (1998). Blue on m/c unpt. Similar to #46.			
	a. ND (1998). Face-to-back register device of windmill with blades dark.	FV	FV	8.50
	b. ND (1999). Face-to-back register device of windmill with two quarters filled in.	FV	FV	7.50

55	5 DOLLARS	VG	VF	UNC
	ND (1999). Dk. green on m/c unpt. Similar to #47.	FV	FV	12.50

56	10 DOLLARS	VG	VF	UNC
	ND (1999). Dk. brown and green on m/c unpt. Similar to #48.	FV	FV	17.50
57	20 DOLLARS			
	ND (1999). Red-violet and purple on m/c unpt. Similar to #50.	FV	FV	27.50

58	50 DOLLARS	VG	VF	UNC
	ND (1999). Orange, blue and gray on m/c unpt. Similar to #51.	FV	FV	75.00

59	100 DOLLARS	VG	VF	UNC
	ND (1999). Brown, purple and blue-gray on m/c unpt. Similar to #52.	FV	FV	125.00

2000 ND Issue

#60-65 similar to #54-59 but with enhanced security features. Sign. M. Williams. Printer: (T)DLR. Replacement notes: Serial # prefix *Z1*.

60	2 DOLLARS	VG	VF	UNC
	ND (2000). Blue on m/c unpt. Similar to #54.	FV	FV	6.50

61	5 DOLLARS	VG	VF	UNC
	ND (2000). Dk. green on m/c unpt. Similar to #55.	FV	FV	10.00

62	10 DOLLARS	VG	VF	UNC
	ND (2000). Dk. brown and green on m/c unpt. Similar to #56.	FV	FV	15.00

63	20 DOLLARS	VG	VF	UNC
	ND (2000). Red-violet and purple on m/c unpt. Similar to #57.	FV	FV	25.00

64	50 DOLLARS		VG	VF	UNC
	ND (2000). Orange, blue and gray on m/c unpt. Similar to #58.		FV	FV	62.50

65	100 DOLLARS		VG	VF	UNC
	ND (2000). Brown, purple and blue-gray on m/c unpt. Similar to #59.		FV	FV	110.00

Belarus (Byelorussia, Belorussia, or White Russia) is bounded in the west by Poland, to the north by Latvia and Lithuania, to the east by Russia and the south by the Ukraine. It has an area of 80,134 sq. mi. (207,600 sq. km.) and a population of 10.3 million. Capital: Minsk. Peat, salt, agriculture including flax, fodder and grasses for cattle breeding and dairy products, along with general manufacturing industries comprise the economy.

An independent state of Byelorussia never existed. When Kiev was the center of Rus, there were a few feudal principalities in the Byelorussian lands, those of Polotsk, Smolensk and Turov being the most important. The principalities, protected by the Pripet marshes, escaped invasion until, in the first half of the 13th century, the Tatars destroyed the Kievan Rus. The area was soon incorporated into the Grand Duchy of Lithuania. They respected the Christianity of the conquered and gradually Byelorussian became the official language of the grand duchy. When Lithuania was absorbed by Poland in the 16th century, Polish replaced Byelorussian as the official language of the country. Until the partitions of Poland at the end of the 18th century, the history of Byelorussia is identical with that of Lithuania.

When Russia incorporated the whole of Byelorussia into its territories in 1795, it claimed to be recovering old Russian lands and denied that the Byelorussians were a separate nation. The country was named Northwestern territory and in 1839 Byelorussian Roman Catholics of the Uniate rite were forced to accept Orthodoxy. A minority remained faithful to the Latin rite. The German occupation of western Byelorussia in 1915 created an opportunity for Byelorussian leaders to formulate, in December 1917 their desire for an independent Byelorussia. On February 25, 1918, Minsk was occupied by the Germans, and in the Brest-Litovsk peace treaty of March 3rd between the Central Powers and Soviet Russia the existence of Byelorussia was ignored. Nevertheless, on March 25, the National council proclaimed an independent republic. After the collapse of Germany, the Soviet government repudiated the Brest treaties and on January 1, 1919, proclaimed a Byelorussian S.S.R. The Red army occupied the lands evacuated by the Germans, and by February all Byelorussia was in Communist hands. The Polish army started an eastward offensive, however, and on August 8th entered Minsk. The peace treaty between Poland and the U.S.S.R. in March 1921, partitioned Byelorussia. In its eastern and larger part a Soviet republic was formed, which in 1922 became a founder member of the U.S.S.R. The eastern frontier was identical with the corresponding section of the Polish-Russian frontier before 1772. The first premier of the Byelorussian S.S.R., The Moscow treaty of August 16, 1945, fixed the Polish-Soviet frontier, and left Bialystok to Poland. From January 1, 1955, the republic was divided into seven oblasti or provinces: Minsk, Brest, Grodno, Molodechno, Mohylev (Mogilev), Homel (Gomel) and Vitebsk. On August 25, 1991, following an unsuccessful coup, the Supreme Soviet adopted a declaration of independence, and the "Republic of Belarus" was proclaimed in September. In December it became a founding member of the Commonweath of Independent States.

MONETARY SYSTEM:
1 Ruble = 100 Kapeek

REPUBLIC

НАЦЫЯНАЛЬНАГА БАНКА БЕЛАРУСІ

BELARUS REPUBLIC

1991 FIRST RUBLE CONTROL COUPON ISSUE

A1	RUBLEI - VARIOUS AMOUNTS		VG	VF	UNC
	ND (1991).		0.25	1.50	6.00

Note: The 50, 75, and 100 Rublei denominations were issued in various colors on a sheet of 28 coupons. Uniface.

1991 SECOND RUBLE CONTROL COUPON ISSUE

A3	20 RUBLEI	VG	VF	UNC
	ND (1991).	0.50	0.75	2.50

Note: The 20 Rublei denomination was issued on a sheet of 12 coupons. Uniface.

A4	RUBLEI - VARIOUS AMOUNTS	VG	VF	UNC
	ND (1991).	0.50	1.50	5.00

Note: The 50, 75, 100, 200, 300, and 500 Rublei denominations were issued in various colors on a sheet of 28 coupons. Uniface.

BELARUS NATIONAL BANK

1992-96 РАЗЛІКОВЫ БІЛЕТ - EXCHANGE NOTE ISSUE

#1-10 "Pagonya," a defending warrior wielding sword on horseback at ctr. Wmk. paper.

1	50 KAPEEK	VG	VF	UNC
	1992. Red and brown-orange on pink unpt. Squirrel at ctr. on back.	0.05	0.10	0.30

2	1 RUBLE	VG	VF	UNC
	1992. Blue-green and blue. Back brown on m/c unpt. rabbit at ctr. r. on back.	0.05	0.25	0.50

3	3 RUBLEI	VG	VF	UNC
	1992. Green, red-orange and pale olive-green on m/c unpt. 2 beavers at ctr. r. on back.	0.05	0.25	0.50

4	5 RUBLEI	VG	VF	UNC
	1992. Deep blue on lt. blue, lilac, violet and m/c unpt. 2 wolves at ctr. r. on back.	0.05	0.10	0.50

5	10 RUBLEI	VG	VF	UNC
	1992. Deep green on lt. green, orange and m/c unpt. Lynx w/kitten at ctr. r. on back.	0.05	0.10	0.50

6	25 RUBLEI	VG	VF	UNC
	1992. Violet on red, green and m/c unpt. Moose at ctr. r. on back.	0.05	0.10	0.50

7	50 RUBLEI	VG	VF	UNC
	1992. Deep purple on red and green unpt. Bear at ctr. r. on back.	0.05	0.10	0.50

8	100 RUBLEI	VG	VF	UNC
	1992. Brown, gray and tan on m/c unpt. Wisent (European Bison) at ctr. on back.	0.05	0.10	0.50

9	200 RUBLEI	VG	VF	UNC
	1992. Deep brown-violet, orange, green and ochre on m/c unpt. City view at ctr. r. on back.	0.10	0.25	0.75

10   500 RUBLEI
    1992. Violet, tan, lt. blue and orange on m/c unpt. Victory Plaza in
    Minsk at ctr. r. on back.

	VG	VF	UNC
	0.10	0.50	1.00

11   1000 RUBLEI
    1992 (1993). Lt. blue, pale olive-green and pink. Back dk. blue and
    dk. green on m/c unpt.; Academy of Sciences bldg. at ctr. r. on back.

	VG	VF	UNC
	0.10	0.50	1.50

12   5000 RUBLEI
    1992 (1993). Purple and red-violet on m/c unpt. Back brown-violet
    and olive-green on m/c unpt. Bldgs. in Minsk lower city at ctr. r.

	VG	VF	UNC
	0.10	0.50	2.50

1994-96 ISSUE

13   20,000 RUBLEI
    1994. Dk. brown on m/c unpt. National Bank bldg. at l. ctr.,
    Pagonya (National emblem) on back. Wmk: Tower and tree.

	VG	VF	UNC
	0.50	1.00	5.00

14   50,000 RUBLEI
    1995. Dk. brown on m/c unpt. Yellow paper. Brest's tower,
    Holmsky Gate at l., tapestry at ctr. r. Star shaped war memorial
    gateway at ctr. r. on back.

	VG	VF	UNC
	0.75	2.50	8.00

15   100,000 RUBLEI
    1996. Deep blue and violet on m/c unpt. Bolshoi Opera and Ballet
    Theatre at ctr., tapestry at l. Scene from Glebov's ballet *Vibrannitsa*
    at ctr. on back.

	VG	VF	UNC
	1.00	3.00	12.50

1998 ISSUE

16   1000 RUBLEI
    1998. Lt. blue, pale olive-green and pink. Similar to #11 but single
    value moved to oval replacing *Pagonya*, warrior on horseback at l.
    ctr. Wmk. paper.

	VG	VF	UNC
	0.05	0.10	0.50

1998-99 ISSUE

17   5000 RUBLEI
    1998. M/c. Back like #12.

	VG	VF	UNC
	0.05	0.10	0.60

18   500,000 RUBLEI
    1998. Lt. red and green on yellow unpt. Palace of Culture bldg. at
    ctr. façade fragment on back.

	VG	VF	UNC
	1.00	3.00	10.00

19   1,000,000 RUBLEI
    1999. Green on m/c unpt. National Museum of Art at ctr. Artwork:
    Wife's Portrait w/Flowers and Fruits on back.

	VG	VF	UNC
	1.00	3.50	10.00

20 5,000,000 RUBLEI
1999. Purple and green on m/c unpt. Minsk sports complex at ctr.
Winter sports complex on back.

	VG	VF	UNC
	2.00	4.50	15.00

24 20 RUBLEI
2000. Brown on m/c unpt. National Bank bldg. at l. ctr. Interior view
on back.

	VG	VF	UNC
	—	0.20	1.00

2000 ISSUE

21 1 RUBLE
2000. Green on m/c unpt. Back similar to #11.

	VG	VF	UNC
	—	0.15	0.50

22 5 RUBLEI
2000. Pale red and violet on m/c unpt. Back similar to #17.

	VG	VF	UNC
	—	0.15	0.75

25 50 RUBLEI
2000. Red-borwn on m/c unpt. Similar to #14. Holmsky Gate at l.
ctr. War memorial gateway on back.

	VG	VF	UNC
	—	0.20	1.50

23 10 RUBLEI
2000. Lilac on m/c unpt. National Library at r. on back.

	VG	VF	UNC
	—	0.15	0.75

26 100 RUBLEI
2000. Green on m/c unpt. Similar to #15. Bolshoi Opera and Ballet
Theater. Scene from ballet *Vibrannitsa* on back. Wmk: Ballerina.

	VG	VF	UNC
	—	0.25	3.00

27 500 RUBLEI
2000. Brown and green on tan unpt. Palace of Culture. Façade
fragment on back.

	VG	VF	UNC
	0.20	1.50	6.00

28   1000 RUBLEI

	VG	VF	UNC
2000. Blue on yellow unpt. National Museum of Art at l. ctr. Flowers and fruits still-life on back.	0.50	2.50	8.00

29   5000 RUBLEI

	VG	VF	UNC
2000. Purple and slate gray on m/c unpt. Minsk Sports complex at ctr. Winter sports complex (three ski jump hills) on back.	1.00	3.00	12.50

30   10,000 RUBLEI

	VG	VF	UNC
2000 (2001). Orange and blue on m/c unpt. Vitebsk city view. Amphitheater on back.	1.00	3.00	17.50

31   20,000 RUBLEI

	VG	VF	UNC
2000 (2001). Olive on m/c unpt. Palaces in Gomel at ctr. Mountaintop palace on back.	1.00	4.50	25.00

32   50,000 RUBLEI

	VG	VF	UNC
2000 (2002). Blue, gray, lilac on m/c unpt. Mirski Zanak castle at l. ctr. Details of Mirski Zanak on back. Printer: Goznak.	2.00	6.00	50.00

2001 COMMEMORATIVE ISSUE

#33, 10th Anniversary National Bank of Belarus

33   20 RUBLEI

	VG	VF	UNC
2001. Brown on m/c unpt. #24 w/OVD denomination at upper ctr. r. and gold-stamped dates *1991-2001* with bank initials at r. Issued in a special folder.	0.75	1.50	6.00

2005 ISSUE

34   100,000 RUBLEI

	VG	VF	UNC
ND (2005). Brown on rose and m/c unpt. Building at ctr. Castle on back.	FV	FV	80.00

КУПОН РЭСПУБЛIКА БЕЛАРУСЬ

1991 FIRST RUBLE CONTROL COUPON ISSUE

AA1   20 RUBLEI

	VG	VF	UNC
ND (1991).	0.25	2.00	6.00

Note: The 20 Rublei denomination was issued on a sheet of 14 coupons. Uniface.

COLLECTOR SERIES

BELARUS NATIONAL BANK

2000 COMMEMORATIVE

CS1   RUBLEI - VARIOUS AMOUNTS

	Issue Price	Mkt.	Value
10-piece set of notes in blue folder. Set consists of #21-30 dated 2000 and with matching serial #. The 20 Rublei and higher include an ovpt: *MILLENNIUM* at the lower left on the back.	—		25.00

BELGIUM

The Kingdom of Belgium, a constitutional monarchy in northwest Europe, has an area of 11,779 sq. mi. (30,513 sq. km.) and a population of 10.26 million, chiefly Dutch-speaking Flemish and French-speaking Walloons. Capital: Brussels. Agriculture, dairy farming, and the processing of raw materials for re-export are the principal industries. "Beurs voor Diamant" in Antwerp is the world's largest diamond trading center. Iron and steel, machinery, motor vehicles, chemicals, textile yarns and fabrics comprise the principal exports.

The Celtic tribe called "Belgae," from which Belgium derived its name, was described by Caesar as the most courageous of all the tribes of Gaul. The Belgae eventually capitulated to Rome and the area remained for centuries as a part of the Roman Empire known as Belgica.

As Rome began its decline, Frankish tribes migrated westward and established the Merovingian, and subsequently, the Carolingian empires. At the death of Charlemagne, Europe was divided among his three sons Karl, Lothar and Ludwig. The eastern part of today's Belgium lay in the Duchy of Lower Lorraine while much of the western parts eventually became the County of Flanders. After further divisions, the area was absorbed into the Duchy of Burgundy from whence it passed into Hapsburg control when Marie of Burgundy married Maximilian of Austria. Phillip I (the Fair), son of Maximilian and Marie, then added Spain to the Hapsburg empire by marrying Johanna, daughter of Ferdinand and Isabella. Charles and Ferdinand, sons of Phillip and Johanna, began the separate Spanish and Austrian lines of the Hapsburg family. The Burgundian lands, along with the northern provinces which make up present day Netherlands, became the Spanish Netherlands. The northern provinces successfully rebelled and broke away from Hapsburg rule in the late 16th century and early 17th century. The southern provinces along with the Duchy of Luxembourg remained under the influence of Spain until the year 1700 when Charles II, last of the Spanish Hapsburg line, died without leaving an heir and the Spanish crown went to the Bourbon family of France. The Spanish Netherlands then reverted to the control of the Austrian line of Hapsburgs and became the Austrian Netherlands. The Austrian Netherlands along with the Bishopric of Liege fell to the French Republic in 1794.

At the Congress of Vienna in 1815 the area was united with the Netherlands but in 1830 independence was gained and the constitutional monarchy of Belgium was established. A large part of the Duchy of Luxembourg was incorporated into Belgium and the first king was Leopold I of Saxe-Coburg-Gotha. It was invaded by the German army in Aug. 1914 and the German forces carried on a devastating occupation of most of the territory until the Armistice. Belgium joined the League of Nations. On May 10, 1940 it was invaded again by Nazi German armies. The Belgian and Allied forces were quickly overwhelmed and were evacuated through Dunkirk. Allied troops reached Belgium again in Sept. 1944. Prince Charles, Count of Flanders assumed King Leopold's responsibilities until his liberation by the U.S. army in Austria on May 8, 1945. From 1920-1940 and since 1944 Eupen-Malmedy went from Germany to Belgium.

RULERS:
Baudouin I, 1952-93
Albert II, 1993-

MONETARY SYSTEM:
1 Franc = 100 Centimes to 2001
1 Euro = 100 Cents, 2002-

KINGDOM - 1944-PRESENT

BANQUE NATIONALE DE BELGIQUE

NATIONALE BANK VAN BELGIE

1961-71 ISSUE

#134-137 wmk: Kg. Baudouin I.

	100 FRANCS	VG	VF	UNC
134	1.2.1962-2.6.1977. Violet on m/c unpt. Lambert Lombard at l. Allegorical figure at ctr. on back. 4 sign. varieties.			
	a. Serial # 00001 A 001 to 10000 Z 999. Sign (1 and 7), (1 and 8).	3.00	5.00	10.00
	b. Serial # 1001 A 0001 to 2350 Z 999. Sign. (1 and 8), (2 and 8) and (3 and 8).	3.00	5.00	10.00
	c. Series 3000. Coated with plastic. Sign. (2 and 8).	15.00	25.00	50.00

NOTICE
Readers with unlisted dates, signature varieties, etc. are invited to submit photocopies of their notes to: Standard Catalog of World Paper Money, 700 East State St. Iola, WI 54990-0001, E-Mail: george.cuhaj@fwpubs.com.

#135-137 replacement notes: Serial # prefix Z/1.

	500 FRANCS	VG	VF	UNC
135	2.5.1961-28.4.1975. Blue-gray and m/c. Bernard Van Orley at ctr. Margaret of Austria and Malines Palace façade at r. 4 sign. varieties.			
	a. Serial # 0001 A 001 to 2500 Z 999. Sign. (1 and 7) and (1 and 8).	20.00	25.00	60.00
	b. Serial # 251 A 0001 to 556 Z 9999. Sign. (1 and 8), (2 and 8) and (3 and 8).	15.00	20.00	50.00

	1000 FRANCS	VG	VF	UNC
136	2.1.1961-8.12.1975. Brown and blue. Gérard Kremer (called Mercator) at l. Atlas holding globe on back. 4 sign. varieties.			
	a. Serial # 0001 A 001 to 10400 Z 999. Sign. (1 and 7).	35.00	50.00	80.00
	b. Serial # 1041 A 0001 to 1877 Z 999. Sign. (1 and 8), (2 and 8) and (3 and 8).	30.00	40.00	60.00

	5000 FRANCS	VG	VF	UNC
137	6.1.1971-15.9.1977. Green. André Vesalius at ctr. Escapelus statue and temple of Epidaure on back. Sign. (1 and 8), (2 and 8), (3 and 8) and (3 and 9).	200.00	275.00	400.00

KINGDOM

ROYAUME DE BELGIQUE - KONINKRIJK BELGIE

TRÉSORERIE - THESAURIE (TREASURY NOTES)

1964-66 ISSUE

#138 and 139 replacement notes: Serial # prefix Z/1.

	20 FRANCS	VG	VF	UNC
138	15.6.1964. Black on blue, orange and m/c unpt. Kg. Baudouin I at l. and as wmk., arms at lower r. Atomium complex in Brussels at r. on back. Sign. 18, 19, 20.	0.25	0.50	2.00

139   50 FRANCS

	VG	VF	UNC
16.5.1966. Brown-violet and orange-brown on m/c unpt. Arms at lower l. ctr., Kg. Baudouin I and Qn. Fabiola at r. Parliament bldg. in Brussels on back. Wmk: Baudouin I. Sign. 18, 19, 20, 21.	1.00	2.00	4.00

BANQUE NATIONALE DE BELGIQUE - CONTINUED

1978; 1980 ND ISSUE

#140-142 wmk: Kg. Baudouin I. Sign. only on face side.

140   100 FRANCS

	VG	VF	UNC
ND (1978-81). Maroon, blue and olive-green on m/c unpt. Hendrik Beyaert at ctr. r. Architectural view and plan at l. Geometric design on back. Sign. (3 and 9), (3 and 10).	15.00	20.00	30.00

141   500 FRANCS

	VG	VF	UNC
ND (1980-81). Deep blue-violet and deep green on blue and m/c unpt. Constantin Meunier at l. ctr. Unpt. of 2 coal miners and mine conveyor tower at ctr. r. 5 circular designs on back. Sign. (3 and 8).	35.00	50.00	75.00

1981-82 ND ISSUE

#142-145 wmk: K. Baudouin I.

142   100 FRANCS

	VG	VF	UNC
ND (1982-94). Like #140 but w/sign. on face and back. Sign. (3 and 10), (4 and 10), (4 and 11), (4 and 12), (4 and 13), (5 and 14), (5 and 15).	4.00	6.00	10.00

143   500 FRANCS

	VG	VF	UNC
ND (1982-98). Like #141 but w/sign. on face and back. Sign. (3 and 10), (4 and 10), (4 and 11), (4 and 12), (4 and 13), (5 and 14), (5 and 15).	15.00	20.00	40.00

144   1000 FRANCS

	VG	VF	UNC
ND (1980-96). Brown and green on m/c unpt. André Gretry at l. ctr., bass violin ctr. r. in background. Tuning forks and view of inner ear on back. Sign. (3 and 10), (4 and 10), (4 and 11), (4 and 12), (4 and 13), (5 and 14), (5 and 15).			
a. Name as: *ANDRÉ ERNEST MODESTE GRETRY. 1741-1813.*	40.00	60.00	90.00
x1. Name as: *ERNEST • MODESTE.*	50.00	120.00	300.00
x2. Name as: *ANDRÉ ERNEST MODESTE TRY.*	60.00	75.00	120.00

145   5000 FRANCS

	VG	VF	UNC
ND (1982-92). Green on m/c unpt. Guido Gezelle at l. ctr. Tree and stained glass window behind. Back green, red and brown; dragonfly and leaf at ctr. Sign. (4 and 10), (4 and 11), (4 and 12), (4 and 13), (5 and 14).	175.00	225.00	350.00

1992 ND ISSUE

146 **10,000 FRANCS**

	VG	VF	UNC
	350.00	475.00	600.00

ND (1992-97). Grayish purple on m/c unpt. Kg. Baudouin I and Qn. Fabiola at l. and as wmk., aerial map as unpt. Flora and greenhouses at Laeken (royal residence) at ctr. on back. Sign. (5 and 15).

1994-97 ND Issue

147 **100 FRANCS**

	VG	VF	UNC
	3.00	5.00	7.50

ND (1995-2001). Red-violet and black on m/c unpt. James Ensor at l. and as wmk., masks at lower ctr. and at r. Beach scene at l. on back. Sign. (5 and 15), (6 and 16).

148 **200 FRANCS**

	VG	VF	UNC
	6.00	10.00	15.00

ND (1995). Black and brown on yellow and orange unpt. Adolphe Sax at l. and as wmk., saxophone at r. Saxophone players outlined at l., church, houses in Dinant outlined at lower r. on back. Sign. (5 and 15).

149 **500 FRANCS**

	VG	VF	UNC
	15.00	25.00	35.00

ND (1998). Blue-black, purple and blue-green on m/c unpt. René Magritte at l. and as wmk., birds in plants at lower ctr., tree at r. 6 men, chair at l., men at ctr. r. on back. Sign. (5 and 15).

150 **1000 FRANCS**

	VG	VF	UNC
	30.00	40.00	60.00

ND (1997). Dk. brown on m/c unpt. Constant Permeke at l. and as wmk., sailboat at ctr. *Sleeping Farmer* painting at l. on back. Sign. (5 and 15).

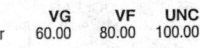

151 **2000 FRANCS**

	VG	VF	UNC
	60.00	80.00	100.00

ND (1994-2001). Purple and blue-green on m/c unpt. Baron Victor Horta at l. and as wmk. Flora and *Art Nouveau* design at l. on back. Sign. (5 and 15).

152 **10,000 FRANCS**

	VG	VF	UNC
	300.00	350.00	400.00

ND (1997). Deep purple on m/c unpt. Kg. Albert II and Queen Paola at l., aerial view of Parliamentary chamber at r. Greenhouses at Laeken (royal residence) on back. Wmk: Kg. Albert II. Sign. (5 and 15).

Note: For later issues used in Belgium, see European Union listings.

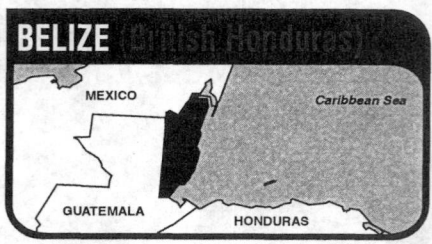

Belize (formerly British Honduras) is situated in Central America south of Mexico and east and north of Guatemala. It has an area of 8,867 sq. mi. (22,965 sq. km.) and a population of 242,000. Capital: Belmopan. Sugar, citrus fruits, chicle and hard woods are exported.

The area, site of the ancient Mayan civilization, was sighted by Columbus in 1502, and settled by shipwrecked English seamen in 1638. British buccaneers settled the former capital of Belize in the 17th Century. Britian claimed administrative right over the area after the emancipation of Central America from Spain, and declared it a dependency of the Colony of Jamaica in 1862. It was established as the separate Crown Colony of British Honduras in 1884. The anti-British People's United Party, which attained power in 1954, won a constitution, effective in 1964 which established self-government under a British appointed Governor. British Honduras became Belize on June 1, 1973, following the passage of a surprise bill by the People's United Party, but the consititutional relationship with Britain remained unchanged.

In Dec. 1975, the U.N. General Assembly adopted a resolution supporting the right of the people of Belize to self-determination, and asked Britian and Guatemala to renew their negotiations on the future of Belize. They obtained independence on Sept. 21, 1981. Elizabeth II is Head of State, as Queen of Belize.

For earlier bank notes, see British Honduras.

MONETARY SYSTEM:
1 Dollar = 100 Cents

BELIZE

GOVERNMENT OF BELIZE

1974-75 ISSUE

#33-37 arms at l., portr. Qn. Elizabeth II at r.

33	**1 DOLLAR**	VG	VF	UNC
	1974-76. Green on m/c unpt.			
	a. 1.1.1974.	1.50	10.00	60.00
	b. 1.6.1975.	1.00	6.00	50.00
	c. 1.1.1976.	1.00	5.00	45.00
	ct. Color trial. Blue, green and pale orange.	—	—	200.00
	s. Specimen.	—	—	100.00

34	**2 DOLLARS**	VG	VF	UNC
	1974-76. Violet on lilac and m/c unpt.			
	a. 1.1.1974.	4.00	20.00	85.00
	b. 1.6.1975.	3.00	10.00	75.00
	c. 1.1.1976.	2.50	9.00	70.00
	ct. Color trial. Brown, orange and red.	—	—	225.00
	s. Specimen.	—	—	125.00

35	**5 DOLLARS**	VG	VF	UNC
	1975; 1976. Red on m/c unpt.			
	a. 1.6.1975.	7.50	30.00	165.00
	b. 1.1.1976.	5.00	25.00	135.00
	ct. Color trial. Red on m/c unpt.	—	—	200.00
	s. Specimen.	—	—	150.00

36	**10 DOLLARS**	VG	VF	UNC
	1974-76. Black on m/c unpt.			
	a. 1.1.1974.	20.00	75.00	600.00
	b. 1.6.1975.	17.50	60.00	450.00
	c. 1.1.1976.	15.00	50.00	375.00
	ct. Color trial. Green and orange.	—	—	725.00
	s. Specimen.	—	—	375.00

37	**20 DOLLARS**	VG	VF	UNC
	1974-76. Brown on m/c unpt.			
	a. 1.1.1974.	40.00	175.00	1100.00
	b. 1.6.1975.	25.00	95.00	625.00
	c. 1.1.1976.	25.00	85.00	575.00
	ct. Color trial. Blue, green and pale yellow.	—	—	1200.00
	s. Specimen.	—	—	650.00

MONETARY AUTHORITY OF BELIZE

ORDINANCE NO. 9 OF 1976; 1980 ISSUE

#38-42 linear border on arms in upper l. corner, Qn. Elizabeth II at ctr. r. 3/4 looking l., underwater scene w/reef and fish in ctr. background. House of Representatives at ctr. Jabiu stork at r. on back. Wmk: Carved head of the "sleeping giant." Replacement notes: Serial # prefix Z/1; Z/2; Z/3; Z/4; Z/5.

38	**1 DOLLAR**	VG	VF	UNC
	1.6.1980. Green on m/c unpt.			
	a. Issued note.	1.00	5.00	25.00
	s. Specimen.	—	—	—

39	**5 DOLLARS**	VG	VF	UNC
	1.6.1980. Red on m/c unpt.			
	a. Issued note.	2.50	7.50	65.00
	s. Specimen.	—	—	—

40	10 DOLLARS	VG	VF	UNC
	1.6.1980. Violet on m/c unpt.			
	a. Issued note.	7.50	25.00	125.00
	s. Specimen.	—	—	—

41	20 DOLLARS	VG	VF	UNC
	1.6.1980. Brown on m/c unpt.	15.00	45.00	300.00

42	100 DOLLARS	VG	VF	UNC
	1.6.1980. Blue on m/c unpt.	65.00	200.00	1200.00

CENTRAL BANK OF BELIZE

ACT 1982; 1983 ISSUE

#43-45 similar to #38, 40 and 41. Wreath border on arms at upper l. Replacement notes: Serial # prefix Z/1; Z/3; Z/4.

43	1 DOLLAR	VG	VF	UNC
	1.7.1983. Green on m/c unpt. Like #38.	1.00	3.00	20.00

44	10 DOLLARS	VG	VF	UNC
	1.7.1983. Black on red and m/c unpt. Like #40.			
	a. Issued note.	6.00	15.00	75.00
	s. Specimen.	—	—	—

45	20 DOLLARS	VG	VF	UNC
	1.7.1983. Brown on m/c unpt. Like #41.	12.50	40.00	385.00

ACT 1982; 1983-87 ISSUE

#46-50 like #38-42. Lg. tree behind arms at upper l. Sign. varieties. Replacement notes: Serial # prefix Z/1; Z/2; Z/3; Z/4; Z/5.

46	1 DOLLAR	VG	VF	UNC
	1983-87. Green on m/c unpt. Like #38.			
	a. 1.11.1983.	FV	4.00	20.00
	b. 1.1.1986.	FV	2.25	17.50
	c. 1.1.1987.	FV	FV	15.00
	s. Specimen.	—	—	—

47	5 DOLLARS	VG	VF	UNC
	1987; 1989. Red on m/c unpt. Like #39.			
	a. 1.1.1987.	3.50	25.00	200.00
	b. 1.1.1989.	FV	5.00	35.00

48	10 DOLLARS	VG	VF	UNC
	1987; 1989. Black on red and m/c unpt. Like #40.			
	a. 1.1.1987.	6.00	10.00	75.00
	b. 1.1.1989.	10.00	40.00	350.00

49	20 DOLLARS	VG	VF	UNC
	1986; 1987. Brown on m/c unpt. Like #41.			
	a. 1.1.1986.	FV	25.00	150.00
	b. 1.1.1987.	FV	15.00	65.00

50	100 DOLLARS	VG	VF	UNC
	1983; 1989. Blue on m/c unpt. Like #42.			
	a. 1.11.1983.	FV	125.00	650.00
	b. 1.1.1989.	FV	150.00	750.00

ACT 1982; 1990 ISSUE

#51-57 older facing portr. of Qn. Elizabeth II at r. Wmk: Carved head of the "sleeping giant." Printer: TDLR.

51	1 DOLLAR	VG	VF	UNC
	1.5.1990. Green on lt. brown, blue and m/c unpt. Lobster at l. Back green and red; marine life of Belize across ctr.	FV	1.25	11.50

52	2 DOLLARS	VG	VF	UNC
	1990; 1991. Purple on lt. green, blue and m/c unpt. Carved stone pillar at l. Mayan ruins of Belize on back.			
	a. 1.5.1990.	FV	1.50	15.00
	b. 1.6.1991.	FV	1.50	12.50

53	5 DOLLARS	VG	VF	UNC
	1990; 1991. Red-orange, orange and violet on m/c unpt. C. Columbus medallion at l, silver tiger fish below. St. George's Caye, coffin, outline map and bldg. on back.			
	a. 1.5.1990.	FV	3.50	30.00
	b. 1.6.1991.	FV	3.50	25.00

54	10 DOLLARS	VG	VF	UNC
	1990; 1991. Black, olive-brown and deep blue-green on m/c unpt. Court House clock tower at l. Government House, Court House and St. John's Cathedral on back.			
	a. 1.5.1990.	FV	7.50	45.00
	b. 1.6.1991.	FV	7.50	35.00

55	20 DOLLARS	VG	VF	UNC
	1.5.1990. Dk. brown on m/c unpt. Upper l. Dog-like Bat; lower l. Kinkajou; upper ctr. Black Howler Monkey; lower ctr. l. Collared Peccary; upper ctr. r. Northern Tamandua; lower ctr. r. Red Brocket; upper r. Ringtail; lower r. Jaguar. Fauna of Belize	FV	17.50	55.00

56	50 DOLLARS	VG	VF	UNC
	1990; 1991. Purple, brown and red on m/c unpt. Boats at l. Bridges of Belize on back.			
	a. 1.5.1990.	FV	35.00	105.00
	b. 1.6.1991.	FV	30.00	95.00

57	100 DOLLARS	VG	VF	UNC
	1990-94. Blue-violet, orange and red on m/c unpt. Keel-billed toucan at l. Birds of Belize - jabiru stork, brown pelican, red-footed booby, magnificent frigate bird, yellow-headed parrot and king vulture on back.			
	a. 1.5.1990.	FV	75.00	275.00
	b. 1.6.1991.	FV	75.00	300.00
	c. 1.5.1994.	FV	70.00	225.00

ACT 1982; 1996 ISSUE

#58-59 like #53-54 but w/segmented foil over security strip and ascending size serial # at upper r. Printer: TDLR.

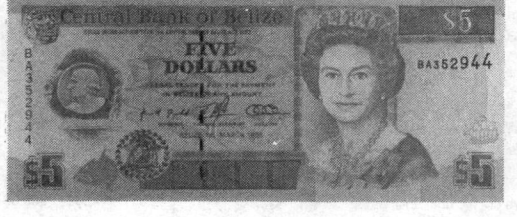

58	**5 DOLLARS**	VG	VF	UNC
	1.3.1996. Red-orange, orange and violet on m/c unpt. Like #53.	FV	3.50	22.50
59	**10 DOLLARS**			
	1.3.1996. Black, olive brown and deep blue-green on m/c unpt. Like #54.	FV	6.00	32.50

1997-2002 ISSUES

#60-65 reduced size.

60	**2 DOLLARS**	VG	VF	UNC
	1999; 2002. Purple on lt. green, blue and m/c unpt. Like #52.			
	a. 1.1.1999.	FV	FV	11.00
	b. 1.1.2002.	FV	FV	9.00

61	**5 DOLLARS**	VG	VF	UNC
	1999; 2002. Red-orange, orange and violet on m/c unpt. Like #53.			
	a. 1.1.1999.	FV	FV	20.00
	b. 1.1.2002.	FV	FV	15.00

62	**10 DOLLARS**	VG	VF	UNC
	1997; 2001. Black, olive-brown and deep blue-green on m/c unpt. Like #59.			
	a. 1.6.1997.	FV	FV	30.00
	b. 1.2001. (no day)	FV	FV	25.00

63	**20 DOLLARS**	VG	VF	UNC
	1997; 2000. Dk. Brown on m/c unpt. Like #55.			
	a. 1.6.1997.	FV	FV	45.00
	b. 1.10.2000.	FV	FV	37.50

64	**50 DOLLARS**	VG	VF	UNC
	1997; 2000. Purple, brown and red on m/c unpt. Like #56.			
	a. 1.6.1997.	FV	FV	90.00
	b. 1.9.2000.	FV	FV	85.00

65	**100 DOLLARS**	VG	VF	UNC
	1.6.1997. Blue-violet, orange and red on m/c unpt. Like #57.	FV	FV	165.00

2003 ISSUE

#66-71 like #60-65 but additional security features. Printer: TDLR.

66	**2 DOLLARS**	VG	VF	UNC
	1.6.2003.	FV	FV	7.50
67	**5 DOLLARS**			
	2003-05.			
	a. 1.6.2003.	FV	FV	15.00
	b. 1.1.2005.	FV	FV	12.50

68	**10 DOLLARS**	VG	VF	UNC
	1.3.2003; 1.1.2005.	FV	FV	22.50
69	**20 DOLLARS**			
	2003-05.			
	a. 1.1.2003.	FV	FV	32.50
	b. 1.1.2005.	FV	FV	30.00

		VG	VF	UNC
70	50 DOLLARS 1.3.2003.	FV	FV	75.00

		VG	VF	UNC
71	100 DOLLARS 1.1.2003.	FV	FV	145.00

COLLECTOR SERIES

CENTRAL BANK OF BELIZE

1984 ND ISSUE

Note: The Central Bank of Belize will no longer exchange these notes for regular currency. (It is illegal to export the currency afterwards). Value is thus speculative.

		Issue Price	Mkt.	Value
CS1	ND (1984) COLLECTION Stamped from paper bonded within gold foil. Denominations: $1 (1 pc.), $2 (2 pcs.) $5 (3 pcs.) $10 (4 pcs.), $20 (2 pcs.), $25 (6 pcs.), $50 (7 pcs.), $75 (5 pcs.), $100 (6 pcs.). Total 36 pcs. All have QE II and bldg. on face, different animals, ships on back.	—	325.00	

BERMUDA

Atlantic Ocean

The Parliamentary British Colony of Bermuda, situated in the western Atlantic Ocean 660 miles (1,062 km.) east of North Carolina, has an area of 20.6 sq. mi. (53 sq. km.) and a population of 60,100. Capital: Hamilton. Concentrated essences, beauty preparations, and cut flowers are exported. Most Bermudians derive their livelihood from tourism.

Bermuda was discovered by Juan de Bermudez, a Spanish navigator, in 1503. British influence dates from 1609 when a group of Virginia-bound British colonists under the command of Sir George Somers was shipwrecked on the islands for 10 months. The islands were settled in 1612 by 60 British colonists from the Virginia Colony and became a crown colony in 1684. Internal autonomy was obtained by the constitution of June 8, 1968.

In February, 1970, Bermuda converted from its former currency, the British pound, to a decimal currency, termed a dollar, On July 31, 1972, Bermuda severed its monetary link with the British pound and pegged its dollar to be the same value as the U.S. dollar.

RULERS:
British

MONETARY SYSTEM:
1 Shilling = 12 Pence
1 Pound = 20 Shillings, to 1970
1 Dollar = 100 Cents, 1970-

BRITISH ADMINISTRATION

BERMUDA GOVERNMENT

1952 ISSUE

Royal crest on back. Printer: BWC.

		VG	VF	UNC
18	5 SHILLINGS 1952; 1957. Brown on m/c unpt. Portr. Qn. Elizabeth II at upper ctr. Hamilton Harbor in frame at bottom ctr.			
	a. 20.10.1952.	10.00	35.00	135.00
	b. 1.5.1957.	8.00	30.00	100.00
	s. As b. Specimen.	—	—	—

1952-66 ISSUE

#18-22 arms at ctr. on back. Printer: BWC.

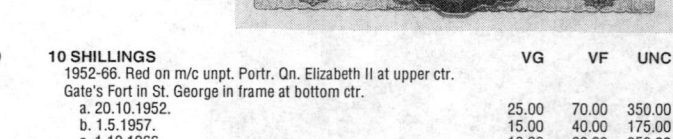

		VG	VF	UNC
19	10 SHILLINGS 1952-66. Red on m/c unpt. Portr. Qn. Elizabeth II at upper ctr. Gate's Fort in St. George in frame at bottom ctr.			
	a. 20.10.1952.	25.00	70.00	350.00
	b. 1.5.1957.	15.00	40.00	175.00
	c. 1.10.1966.	18.00	60.00	250.00
	s. As b. Specimen.	—	—	—

20   1 POUND
1952-66. Blue on m/c unpt. Qn. Elizabeth II at r. Bridge at l.

	VG	VF	UNC
a. 20.10.1952.	30.00	90.00	450.00
b. 1.5.1957. W/o security strip.	25.00	70.00	375.00
c. 1.5.1957. W/security strip.	22.50	70.00	350.00
d. 1.10.1966.	20.00	60.00	275.00
s. As d. Specimen.	—		

21   5 POUNDS
1952-66. Orange on m/c unpt. Portr. Qn. Elizabeth II at r., lg. value at l. ship entering Hamilton Harbor at l. Back orange and green.

	VG	VF	UNC
a. 20.10.1952.	100.00	300.00	1400.00
b. 1.5.1957. W/o security strip.	110.00	325.00	1600.00
c. 1.5.1957. W/security strip.	65.00	200.00	1250.00
d. 1.10.1966.	60.00	200.00	950.00

22   10 POUNDS
28.7.1964. Purple on m/c unpt. Portr. Qn. Elizabeth II at r.   150.00   500.00   2000.00

1970 ISSUE

#23-27 Qn. Elizabeth II at r. looking 3/4 to l., arms at l. ctr. Wmk: Tuna fish.

23   1 DOLLAR
6.2.1970. Dk. blue on tan and aqua unpt. Bermuda petrel or cahow at ctr. Sailboats at l. ctr., bldgs. at upper r. on back.

	VG	VF	UNC
a. Issued note.	1.50	4.00	27.50
s. Specimen.	—	—	25.00

24   5 DOLLARS
6.2.1970. Red-violet on aqua and m/c unpt. Lighthouse at l., bldgs. at ctr. r. on back.

	VG	VF	UNC
a. Issued note.	6.50	10.00	45.00
s. Specimen.	—	—	25.00

25   10 DOLLARS
6.2.1970. Purple on brown and m/c unpt. Bermuda petrel and seashell at ctr., beach at l. on back.

	VG	VF	UNC
a. Issued note.	FV	15.00	95.00
s. Specimen.	—	—	25.00

26   20 DOLLARS
6.2.1970. Green on m/c unpt. Bldg., sailboat and bridge at l. ctr. on back.

	VG	VF	UNC
a. Issued note.	FV	30.00	135.00
s. Specimen.	—	—	35.00

27   50 DOLLARS
6.2.1970. Brown on m/c unpt. Lighthouse at l., map at upper r. on back.

	VG	VF	UNC
a. Issued note.	FV	80.00	300.00
s. Specimen.	—	—	60.00

NOTICE

Readers with unlisted dates, signature varieties, etc. are invited to submit photocopies of their notes to: Standard Catalog of World Paper Money, 700 East State St. Iola, WI 54990-0001, E-Mail: george.cuhaj@fwpubs.com.

BERMUDA MONETARY AUTHORITY

1974-82 ISSUE

#28-33 Qn. Elizabeth II at r. looking 3/4 to l. Wmk: Tuna fish. Replacement notes: Serial # prefix *Z/1*.
#28-32 like #23-27.

28	1 DOLLAR	VG	VF	UNC
	1975-88. Dk. blue on tan and aqua unpt. Like #23.			
	a. Sign. titles: *CHAIRMAN* and *MANAGING DIRECTOR*.	1.00	5.00	30.00
	1.7.1975; 1.12.1976.			
	b. 1.4.1978; 1.9.1979; 2.1.1982; 1.5.1984.	1.00	3.00	15.00
	c. Sign. titles: *CHAIRMAN* and *GENERAL MANAGER*. 1.1.1986.	1.00	3.50	17.50
	d. Sign. titles: *CHAIRMAN* and *DIRECTOR*. 1.1.1988.	1.00	3.00	15.00
	s. Specimen, punch hole cancelled.	—	—	—

29	5 DOLLARS	VG	VF	UNC
	1978-88. Red-violet on aqua and m/c unpt. Like #24.			
	a. Sign. titles: *CHAIRMAN* and *MANAGING DIRECTOR*.	FV	8.00	37.50
	1.4.1978.			
	b. 2.1.1981.	FV	7.50	35.00
	c. Sign. titles: *CHAIRMAN* and *GENERAL MANAGER*. 1.1.1986.	FV	7.50	35.00
	d. Sign. titles: *CHAIRMAN* and *DIRECTOR*. 1.1.1988.	FV	7.50	30.00
	s. Specimen, punch hole cancelled.	—	—	—

30	10 DOLLARS	VG	VF	UNC
	1978; 1982. Purple on brown and m/c unpt. Like #25.			
	a. 1.4.1978.	FV	30.00	125.00
	b. 2.1.1982.	FV	25.00	100.00
	s. Specimen, punch hole cancelled.	—	—	—

31	20 DOLLARS	VG	VF	UNC
	1974-86. Green on m/c unpt. Like #26.			
	a. 1.4.1974.	25.00	100.00	475.00
	b. 1.3.1976.	FV	45.00	185.00
	c. 2.1.1981; 1.5.1984.	FV	25.00	90.00
	d. Sign. title: *GENERAL MANAGER* at r. 1.1.1986.	FV	25.00	95.00
	s. Specimen, punch hole cancelled.	—	—	—

32	50 DOLLARS	VG	VF	UNC
	1974-82. Brown on m/c unpt. Like #27.			
	a. 1.5.1974.	75.00	300.00	1500.00
	b. 1.4.1978; 2.1.1982.	FV	85.00	400.00
	s. Specimen, punch hole cancelled.	—	—	—

33	100 DOLLARS	VG	VF	UNC
	1982-86. Orange and brown on m/c unpt. House of Assembly at l., Camden bldg. at upper ctr. r. on back.			
	a. 2.1.1982.	FV	FV	385.00
	b. Sign. title: *GENERAL MANAGER* ovpt. at r. 14.11.1984.	FV	FV	350.00
	c. Sign. title: *GENERAL MANAGER* at r. 1.1.1986.	FV	FV	325.00
	s. Specimen, punch hole cancelled.	—	—	—

1988-89 ISSUE

#34-39 mature bust of Qn. Elizabeth II at r. Back similar to #29-33 but w/stylistic changes; arms added at upper l. Sign. titles: *CHAIRMAN* and *DIRECTOR*. Wmk.: Tuna fish. Replacement notes: Serial # prefix *Z/1, Z/2*.

34	2 DOLLARS	VG	VF	UNC
	1988; 1989. Blue-green on green and m/c unpt. Dockyards clock tower bldg. at upper l., map at ctr., arms at ctr. r. on back.			
	a. Serial # prefix: *B/1*. 1.10.1988.	FV	FV	9.00
	b. Serial # prefix: *B/2*. 1.8.1989.	FV	FV	8.50

1992 COMMEMORATIVE ISSUE; ACT 1969

#40, Quincentenary of Christopher Columbus

35	5 DOLLARS		VG	VF	UNC
	20.2.1989. Red-violet and purple on m/c unpt. Similar to #29.				
	a. Sign. title: *DIRECTOR* on silver background at bottom ctr. Serial # prefix: *B/1*.		FV	7.00	25.00
	b. Sign. title: *DIRECTOR* w/o silver background. Serial # prefix: *B/1, B/2*.		FV	FV	12.50

40	50 DOLLARS	VG	VF	UNC
	12.10.1992. Dk. blue, brown and red on m/c unpt. Face like #38 but w/commemorative details. Maltese cross as serial # prefix at upper l., c/c fractional prefix at r., and ovpt: *Christopher Columbus / Quincentenary / 1492-1992* at l. Scuba diver	FV	FV	120.00

ACT 1969; 1992-96 ISSUE

#40A-45 issued under Bermuda Monetary Authority Act 1969. Like #34-39 but w/Authorization text in 3 lines at ctr. Wmk: Tuna fish.

36	10 DOLLARS	VG	VF	UNC
	20.2.1989. Purple, blue and ochre on m/c unpt. Similar to #30.	FV	FV	25.00

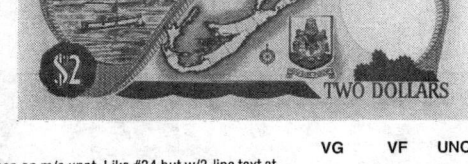

40A	2 DOLLARS	VG	VF	UNC
	1996-97. Blue and green on m/c unpt. Like #34 but w/3-line text at ctr.			
	a. 29.2.1996.	FV	FV	9.00
	b. 6.6.1997.	FV	FV	5.00

37	20 DOLLARS		VG	VF	UNC
	20.2.1989. Green and red on m/c unpt. Similar to #31.				
	a. Serial # prefix: *B/1*.		FV	FV	42.50
	b. Serial # prefix: *B/2*.		FV	FV	40.00

38	50 DOLLARS	VG	VF	UNC
	20.2.1989. Brown and olive on m/c unpt. Similar to #32.	FV	FV	100.00

39	100 DOLLARS	VG	VF	UNC
	20.2.1989. Orange, brown and violet on m/c unpt. Similar to $33.	FV	FV	185.00

NOTICE
Readers with unlisted dates, signature varieties, etc. are invited to submit photocopies of their notes to: Standard Catalog of World Paper Money, 700 East State St. Iola, WI 54990-0001, E-Mail: george.cuhaj@fwpubs.com.

41	5 DOLLARS	VG	VF	UNC
	1992-97. Red-violet and purple on m/c unpt. Like #35 but w/3-line text at ctr.			
	a. 12.11.1992.	FV	FV	12.50
	b. 25.3.1995.	FV	FV	11.00
	c. 20.2.1996.	FV	FV	10.00
	d. 10.6.1997.	FV	FV	8.00

45	**100 DOLLARS**		VG	VF	UNC
	14.2.1996. Orange, brown and violet on m/c unpt. Like #39 but w/3-line text at ctr.		FV	FV	175.00

1994 COMMEMORATIVE ISSUE

#46, 25th Anniversary Bermuda Monetary Authority

46	**100 DOLLARS**		VG	VF	UNC
	20.2.1994. Orange, brown and violet on m/c unpt. Like #45 but w/ovpt: *25th Anniversary*....		FV	FV	170.00

1997 COMMEMORATIVE ISSUE

#47, Opening of Burnaby House

42	**10 DOLLARS**		VG	VF	UNC
	1993-99. Purple, deep blue and orange on m/c unpt. Like #36 but w/3-line text at ctr.				
	a. 4.1.1993.		FV	FV	22.50
	b. 15.3.1996.		FV	FV	20.00
	c. 17.6.1997.		FV	FV	20.00
	d. 31.5.1999. W/security strip.		FV	FV	20.00

43	**20 DOLLARS**		VG	VF	UNC
	1996; 1999. Green and red on m/c unpt. Like #37 but w/3-line text at ctr.				
	a. 27.2.1996.		FV	FV	40.00
	b. 13.5.1999. W/security strip.		FV	FV	37.50

47	**20 DOLLARS**		VG	VF	UNC
	17.1.1997. Green and red on m/c unpt. Ovpt. on #43. *To commemorate the opening of Burnaby House*... in wmk. area at l.		FV	FV	35.00

1997 REGULAR ISSUE

44	**50 DOLLARS**		VG	VF	UNC
	1992-96. Dk. blue, brown and red on m/c unpt. Similar to #40 but w/o commemorative details.				
	a. 12.10.1992.		FV	FV	100.00
	b. 25.3.1995.		FV	FV	90.00
	c. 23.2.1996.		FV	FV	85.00

48	**50 DOLLARS**		VG	VF	UNC
	6.6.1997. Dk. blue, brown and red on m/c ovpt. Like #44 but w/segmented foil over security thread.		FV	FV	87.50

49	**100 DOLLARS**	VG	VF	UNC
	30.6.1997. Orange and brown on m/c unpt. Like #45 but w/segmented foil over security thread.	FV	FV	165.00

2000 ISSUE

Mature portr. Qn. Elizabeth II at r. Backs like #40A-45. Replacement notes: Serial # prefix *Z/I.*

53	**20 DOLLARS**	VG	VF	UNC
	24.5.2000. Green and red on m/c unpt. Bldg. at ctr. Bridge and harbor scene on back.			
	a. Issued note.	FV	FV	37.50
	s. Specimen.	—		

50	**2 DOLLARS**	VG	VF	UNC
	24.5.2000. Blue and green on m/c unpt. Sea horse at ctr. Boats and bldg. at l., island map at ctr. on back.			
	a. Issued note.	FV	FV	4.00
	s. Specimen, punch hole cancelled.	—		

54	**50 DOLLARS**	VG	VF	UNC
	24.5.2000. Bluish black, red and brown on m/c unpt. Bldg. at ctr. Scuba divers and wreck at l. map at upper ctr. on back.			
	a. Issued note.	FV	FV	85.00
	s. Specimen.	—		

51	**5 DOLLARS**	VG	VF	UNC
	24.5.2000. Purple and burgundy on m/c unpt. Shell and fish at ctr. Lighthouse at l., bay view at ctr. on back.			
	a. Issued note.	FV	FV	8.50
	s. Specimen.	—		

55	**100 DOLLARS**	VG	VF	UNC
	24.5.2000. Red-orange and brown on m/c unpt. Flowers and shell at ctr. House of Assembly at l. on back.			
	a. Issued note.	FV	FV	165.00
	s. Specimen.	—		

2003 COMMEMORATIVE ISSUE

52	**10 DOLLARS**	VG	VF	UNC
	24.5.2000. Dk. blue and mauve on m/c unpt. Flower and Bermuda Petrel at ctr. Bay scene, Bermuda Petrel and shell on back.			
	a. Issued note.	FV	FV	17.00
	s. Specimen.	—		

56	**50 DOLLARS**	VG	VF	UNC
	2.6.2003. Similar to #54 but with golden crown at right with overprint: *TO COMMEMORATE THE CORONATION OF QUEEN ELIZABETH II 1953-2003."*	FV	FV	85.00

COLLECTOR SERIES

BERMUDA MONETARY AUTHORITY

1978-84 DATED ISSUE (1985)

CS1	1978-84 1-100 DOLLARS	Issue Price	Mkt.	Value
	#22-33 w/normal serial #, punched hole cancelled, ovpt: *SPECIMEN* (1985).	—		65.00

1981-82 ISSUE (1985)

CS2	1981-82 1-100 DOLLARS	Issue Price	Mkt.	Value
	#28-33 w/all zero serial #, punched hole cancelled in all 4 corners, ovpt: *SPECIMEN* (1985).	—		65.00

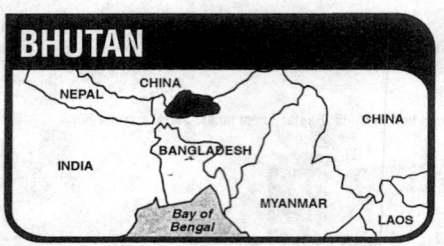

The Kingdom of Bhutan, a landlocked Himalayan country bordered by Tibet, India, and Sikkim, has an area of 18,147 sq. mi. (47,000 sq. km.) and a population of 2.03 million. Capital: Thimphu; Paro is the administrative capital. Virtually the entire population is engaged in agricultural and pastoral activities. Rice, wheat, barley, and yak butter are produced in sufficient quantity to make the country self-sufficient in food. The economy of Bhutan is primitive and many transactions are conducted on a barter basis.

Bhutan's early history is obscure, but is thought to have resembled that of rural medieval Europe. The country was conquered by Tibet, which still claims sovereignty over Bhutan, in the 9th century, and subjected to a dual temporal and spiritual rule until the mid-19th century, when the southern part of the country was occupied by the British and annexed to British India. Bhutan was established as a hereditary monarchy in 1907, and in 1910 agreed to British control of its external affairs. In 1949, India and Bhutan concluded a treaty whereby India assumed Britain's role in subsidizing Bhutan and conducting its foreign affairs.

RULERS:
Jigme Singye Wangchuk, 1972-

MONETARY SYSTEM:
1 Ngultrum (= 1 Indian Rupee) = 100 Chetrums, 1974-

	SIGNATURE CHART				
1	Chairman *(signature)* **Ashi Sonam Wangchuck**		2	Bank of Bhutan *(signature)* **Yeshe Dorji**	
3	Chairman *(signature)* **Dorji Tsering**				

KINGDOM

ROYAL GOVERNMENT OF BHUTAN

1974-78 ND ISSUE

#1-4 wmk: 4-petaled symbol, called a *dorje*, the Buddhist version of a thunderbolt, symbol of a "flash" of enlightenment.

1	1 NGULTRUM	VG	VF	UNC
	ND (1974). Blue on m/c unpt. Dragon design at l. and r.	0.50	2.50	6.00

2	5 NGULTRUM	VG	VF	UNC
	ND (1974). Red-brown on m/c unpt. Portr. J. Singye Wangchuk at ctr. Simtokha Dzong palace ctr. r. on back.	1.50	15.00	50.00

3	10 NGULTRUM	VG	VF	UNC
	ND (1974). Blue-violet on m/c unpt. Portr. J. Dorji Wangchuk at top ctr. Paro Dzong palace ctr. r. on back.	3.50	30.00	200.00

4	100 NGULTRUM	VG	VF	UNC
	ND (1978). Green and brown on m/c unpt. Portr. J. Singye Wangchuk at ctr., circle w/8 good luck symbols at r. Tashichho Dzong palace at l. ctr. on back.	300.00	1000.00	—

1981 ND ISSUE

#5-11 serial # at upper l. and r.

5	1 NGULTRUM	VG	VF	UNC
	ND (1981). Blue on m/c unpt. Royal emblem between facing dragons at ctr. Simtokha Dzong palace at ctr. on back.	0.10	0.25	3.00

6	2 NGULTRUM	VG	VF	UNC
	ND (1981). Brown and green on m/c unpt. Like #5. Royal emblem between facing dragons at ctr. Simtokha Dzong palace at ctr. on back.	0.15	0.50	4.50

7	5 NGULTRUM	VG	VF	UNC
	ND (1981). Brown on m/c unpt. Royal emblem between facing birds at ctr. Paro Dzong palace at ctr. on back.	0.50	2.50	10.00

#8-11 royal emblem at l.

8	10 NGULTRUM	VG	VF	UNC
	ND (1981). Purple on m/c unpt. Royal emblem at l., Portr. J. Singye Wangchuk at r. Paro Dzong palace at ctr. on back.	0.75	5.00	17.50

9	20 NGULTRUM	VG	VF	UNC
	ND (1981). Olive on m/c unpt. Facing portr. Jigme Dorji Wangchuk at r. Punakha Dzong palace at ctr. on back.	1.25	7.50	30.00

10	50 NGULTRUM	VG	VF	UNC
	ND (1981). Purple, violet and brown on m/c unpt. Face like #9. Tongsa Dzong palace at ctr. on back.	3.00	15.00	75.00

11 **100 NGULTRUM**
ND (1981). Dk. green, olive-green and brown-violet on m/c unpt.
Bird at ctr., portr. J. Singye Wangchuk at r. Tashichho Dzong
palace at ctr. on back.

	VG	VF	UNC
	5.00	27.50	150.00

ROYAL MONETARY AUTHORITY OF BHUTAN

1985-92 ND ISSUE

#12-18 similar to #5-11. Serial # at lower l. and upper r. #12-15 reduced size.

12 **1 NGULTRUM**
ND (1986). Blue on m/c unpt. 2 sign. varieties. Similar to #5.

	VG	VF	UNC
	FV	FV	0.50

13 **2 NGULTRUM**
ND (1986). Brown and green on m/c unpt. Similar to #6.

	VG	VF	UNC
	FV	FV	0.75

14 **5 NGULTRUM**
ND (1985). Brown on m/c unpt. Similar to #7.

	VG	VF	UNC
	FV	FV	1.50

15 **10 NGULTRUM**
ND (1986; 1992). Purple on m/c unpt. Similar to #8.
  a. Serial # prefix fractional style. (1986).
  b. Serial # prefix 2 lg. letters (printed in China.) (1992).

	VG	VF	UNC
a.	FV	FV	1.75
b.	FV	FV	2.00

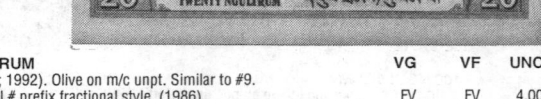

16 **20 NGULTRUM**
ND (1986; 1992). Olive on m/c unpt. Similar to #9.
  a. Serial # prefix fractional style. (1986).
  b. Serial # prefix 2 lg. letters (printed in China.) (1992).

	VG	VF	UNC
a.	FV	FV	4.00
b.	FV	FV	3.50

17 **50 NGULTRUM**
ND (1985; 1992). Violet and brown on m/c unpt. Similar to #10.
  a. Serial # prefix fractional style. (1986).
  b. Serial # prefix letters 2 lg. letters (printed in China.) (1992).

	VG	VF	UNC
a.	FV	3.00	15.00
b.	FV	2.00	6.50

18 **100 NGULTRUM**
ND (1986; 1992). Green and brown on m/c unpt. Similar to #11.
  a. Serial # prefix fractional style. (1986).
  b. Serial # prefix 2 lg. letters (printed in China.) (1992).

	VG	VF	UNC
a.	FV	5.00	25.00
b.	FV	4.00	17.50

1994 ND Issue

#19 and 20 similar to #17 and 18 but with modified unpt. including floral diamond shaped registry design at upper ctr. Wmk: Wavy *ROYAL MONETARY AUTHORITY* repeated.

19	50 NGULTRUM	VG	VF	UNC
	ND (1994). Purple, violet and brown on m/c unpt. Similar to #17.	FV	FV	6.00

20	100 NGULTRUM	VG	VF	UNC
	ND (1994). Green and brown on m/c unpt. Similar to #18.	FV	FV	9.00

1994 ND Commemorative Issue

#21, National Day

21	500 NGULTRUM	VG	VF	UNC
	ND (1994). Red-orange on m/c unpt. Portr. Kg. Jigme Singye Wangchuk in headdress at r. Punakha Dzong palace on back. Both serial #s ascending size. Wmk: 4-petaled symbol.	FV	FV	40.00

2000-01 ND Issue

22	10 NGULTRUM	VG	VF	UNC
	ND (2000). Purple and blue on m/c unpt. Royal emblem at l., portr. Kg. Jigme Singye Wangchuk at r. Back like #15.	FV	FV	1.75
23	20 NGULTRUM			
	ND (2000). Olive on m/c unpt. Like #16 but w/sign. 3.	FV	FV	4.00

24	50 NGULTRUM	VG	VF	UNC
	ND (2000). Violet and brown on m/c unpt. Like #19.	FV	FV	6.50

25	100 NGULTRUM	VG	VF	UNC
	ND (2000). Green and brown on m/c unpt. Portr. Kg. Jigme Singye Wangchuk at r., vertical serial # at r., both ascending size. Back similar to #18. Wmk: 4-petaled symbol.	FV	FV	17.50

26	500 NGULTRUM	VG	VF	UNC
	ND (2000). Red-orange on m/c unpt. Portr. Kg. Jigme Singye Wangchuk in headdress at r. Punakha Dzong palace on back.	FV	FV	32.50

On May 27, 1967, Gen. Yakubu Gowon, head of the Federal Military Government of Nigeria, created three states from the Eastern Region of the country. Separation of the region, undertaken to achieve better regional and ethnic balance, caused Lt. Col. E. O. Ojukwu, Military Governor of the Eastern Region, to proclaim on May 30, 1967, the independence of the Eastern Region as the "Republic of Biafra." Fighting broke out between the Federal Military Government and the forces of Lt. Col. Ojukwu and continued until Biafra surrendered on Jan. 15, 1970. Biafra was then reintegrated into the Republic of Nigeria as three states: East-Central, Rivers, and South-Eastern.

For additional history, see Nigeria.

MONETARY SYSTEM:
1 Shilling = 12 Pence
1 Pound = 20 Shillings

BANK OF BIAFRA

1967 ND ISSUE

#1-2 palm tree, lg. rising sun at l.

		VG	VF	UNC
1	**5 SHILLINGS** ND (1967). Blue on lilac unpt. (Color varies from orange to yellow for rising sun.) Back brown on lt. blue unpt.; four girls at r.	0.50	3.00	12.50

		VG	VF	UNC
2	**1 POUND** ND (1967). Blue and orange. Back brown on lt. blue unpt., arms at r.	1.00	25.00	100.00

1968 ND ISSUE

#3-7 palm tree and small rising sun at l. to ctr.

		VG	VF	UNC
3	**5 SHILLINGS** ND (1968-69). Blue on green and orange unpt. Back similar to #1.			
	a. Issued note.	0.50	5.00	15.00
	b. W/o serial #.	1.00	12.50	35.00

		VG	VF	UNC
4	**10 SHILLINGS** ND (1968-69). Dk. green on blue and and orange unpt. Bldgs. at r. on back.	0.25	1.50	4.50

		VG	VF	UNC
5	**1 POUND** ND (1968-69). Dk. brown on green, brown and orange unpt. Back similar to #2.			
	a. Issued note.	0.10	0.25	1.00
	b. W/o serial #.	0.50	5.00	20.00

		VG	VF	UNC
6	**5 POUNDS** ND (1968-69). Purple on green and orange unpt. Arms at l., weaving at l. ctr. on back.			
	a. Issued note.	4.00	17.50	65.00
	b. W/o serial #.	2.00	6.00	27.50

		VG	VF	UNC
7	**10 POUNDS** ND (1968-69). Black on blue, brown and orange unpt. Arms at l., carver at l. ctr. on back.			
	a. Issued note.	4.00	15.00	75.00
	b. W/o serial #.	2.50	7.50	35.00

BOLIVIA

The Republic of Bolivia, a landlocked country in west central South America, has an area of 424,165 sq. mi. (1,098,581 sq. km.) and a population of 8.33 million. Capitals: La Paz (administrative); Sucre (constitutional). Mining is the principal industry and tin the most important metal. Minerals, petroleum, natural gas, cotton and coffee are exported.

The Incas, who ruled one of the world's greatest dynasties, incorporated the area that is now western Bolivia into their empire about 1200AD. Their control was maintained until the Spaniards arrived in 1535 and reduced the predominantly Indian population to slavery. When Napoleon occupied Madrid in 1808 and placed his brother Joseph on the Spanish throne, a fervor of revolutionary activity quickened in Bolivia, culminating with the 1809 proclamation of independence. Sixteen years of struggle ensued before the republic, named for the famed liberator General Simón Bolívar, was established on August 6, 1825. Since then, Bolivia has had more than 60 revolutions, 70 presidents and 11 constitutions.

RULERS:
Spanish to 1825
1 Boliviano = 100 (Centavos) to 1965
1 Bolivar = 100 Centavos, 1945-1962
1 Peso Boliviano = 100 Centavos, 1962-1987
1 Boliviano = 100 Centavos, 1987-

SPECIMEN NOTES:

All *SPECIMEN, MUESTRA, MUESTRA SIN VALOR* and *ESPECIMEN* notes always have serial #'s of zero.

BANCO CENTRAL DE BOLIVIA

LEY DE 13 DE JULIO DE 1962 - FIRST ISSUE

Peso Boliviano System

#152-157 old and new denomination on back at bottom. Arms at l. Sign. varieties. Printer: TDLR.

152	1 PESO BOLIVIANO	VG	VF	UNC
	L.1962. Black on m/c unpt. Portr. Campesino at r. Agricultural scene at ctr. r. on back. Series A-E.			
	a. Issued note.	2.00	7.50	20.00
	s. Specimen w/red ovpt: *SPECIMEN.* Series A.	—	—	20.00

153	5 PESOS BOLIVIANOS	VG	VF	UNC
	L.1962. Blue on m/c unpt. Portr. Mayor Gualberto Villarroel Lopez at r. Petroleum refinery on back. Series A-B1. 11 sign. varieties.			
	a. Issued note.	1.00	3.00	12.00
	b. Uncut sheet of 4 signed notes.	—	—	100.00
	s. Specimen w/red ovpt: *SPECIMEN.* Series A; T; Z.	—	—	40.00

154	10 PESOS BOLIVIANOS	VG	VF	UNC
	L.1962. Olive-green on m/c unpt. Portr. Colonel Germán Busch Becerra at r. Mountain of Potosí on back. Series A-U3. 18 sign. varieties.			
	a. Issued note.	0.05	0.20	0.75
	b. Uncut sheet of 4 signed notes. Series U2.	—	—	30.00
	s1. Specimen w/red ovpt: *SPECIMEN.* Series A.	—	—	—
	s2. As s1 but w/punched hole cancellation and TDLR oval stamp. Series A.	—	—	—
	s3. Specimen ovpt: *SPECIMEN.* Series A.	—	—	8.00
	s4. Uncut sheet of 4 specimen notes. Series U2.	—	—	25.00

155	20 PESOS BOLIVIANOS	VG	VF	UNC
	L.1962. Purple on m/c unpt. Portr. Pedro Domingo Murillo at r. La Paz mountain on back. Series A.			
	a. Issued note.	1.00	15.00	50.00
	s. Specimen w/red ovpt: *SPECIMEN.* Series A.	—	—	20.00

156	50 PESOS BOLIVIANOS	VG	VF	UNC
	L.1962. Orange on m/c unpt. Portr. Antonio Jose de Sucre at r. Puerta del Sol on back. Series A.			
	a. Issued note.	30.00	85.00	225.00
	s. Specimen w/red ovpt: *SPECIMEN.* Series A.	—	—	20.00

157	100 PESOS BOLIVIANOS	VG	VF	UNC
	L.1962. Red on m/c unpt. Unpt. w/green at l., blue at r. Portr. Simón Bolívar at r. Red serial #, and security thread at l. ctr. Back darker red; engraved, scene of the declaration of the Bolivian Republic. Series A.			
	a. Issued note. Large, wide, dark signatures.	30.00	85.00	225.00
	b. Issued note. Small, thin, light signatures.	30.00	75.00	185.00
	s. Specimen w/red ovpt: *SPECIMEN*. Series A.	—	—	20.00

LEY DE 13 DE JULIO DE 1962 - SECOND ISSUE

#158, 161-164A only new denomination on back. Sign. varieties. Printer: TDLR.

158	1 PESO BOLIVIANO	VG	VF	UNC
	L.1962. Like #152. Series F-F1. 7 sign. varieties.			
	a. Issued note.	0.25	0.75	8.00
	s. Specimen w/red ovpt: *SPECIMEN*. Series Y.	—	—	—

#159, 160 not assigned.

161	20 PESOS BOLIVIANOS	VG	VF	UNC
	L.1962. Like #155. Series B-H. 4 sign. varieties.			
	a. Issued note.	0.25	1.00	10.00
	s. Specimen w/red ovpt: *SPECIMEN*. Series E.	—	—	—

#162-164 replacement notes: Serial # prefixes: ZX; ZY; ZZ.

162	50 PESOS BOLIVIANOS	VG	VF	UNC
	L.1962. Like #156. Series A-W7. 22 sign. varieties.			
	a. Issued note.	0.10	0.25	1.00
	b. Uncut sheet of 4 signed notes. Series L2, Y2.	—	—	10.00
	bx. Uncut sheet of 4 notes w/sign. at top of notes. Series L2; Y2. (error).	—	—	10.00
	r. Uncut sheet of 4 unsigned notes. Series AZ.	—	—	20.00
	s1. Specimen w/red ovpt: *SPECIMEN*. Series F; X; D1.	—	—	—
	s2. As s1 but w/punched hole cancellation (in l. sign. area) and TDLR oval stamp. Series C.	—	—	125.00

163	100 PESOS BOLIVIANOS	VG	VF	UNC
	L.1962. Red on m/c unpt. Like #157. Brighter red back, engraved. Lower # prefixes (from B to T9). 19 sign. varieties.			
	a. Issued note. Prefix Z2.	0.10	0.25	1.00
	b. Uncut sheet of 4 signed notes. Series X4; D5; U5.	—	—	40.00
	r. Uncut sheet of 4 unsigned notes. Series AZ.	—	—	—
	s. Specimen w/red ovpt: *SPECIMEN*. Series G.	—	—	—

164	100 PESOS BOLIVIANOS	VG	VF	UNC
	L.1962 (1983). Red on m/c unpt. Like #163.			
	a. Back dull red, lithographed w/poor detail. Black serial #. W/o security thread. Prefixes #10E-13D. 2 sign. varieties.	0.25	0.75	4.00
	b. As a. but w/solid black security thread.	0.25	0.75	5.00
	c. As a. but w/segmented security thread.	0.50	2.00	8.00
	r. Unsigned remainder. Prefix #12H.	—	—	17.50
	s. Specimen w/red ovpt: *SPECIMEN*. Prefix #10E.	—	—	—
164A	100 PESOS BOLIVIANOS	0.10	0.25	2.00
	L.1962. Red on m/c unpt. Like #163 including engraved back, security thread and red serial #. Higher # prefixes (13E-19T) than for 164a. 2 sign. varieties.			

1981-84 VARIOUS DECREES ND ISSUE

#165-171 replacement notes: Serial # prefixes: Z; ZY; ZZ.

165	500 PESOS BOLIVIANOS	VG	VF	UNC
	D. 1.6.1981. Deep blue, blue-green and black on m/c unpt. Arms at ctr., portr. Eduardo Avaroa at r. and as wmk at l. Back blue on m/c unpt. View of Puerto de Antofagasta, ca. 1879 at ctr. Series A. Printer: ABNC.			
	a. Issued note. 2 sign. varieties.	0.10	0.25	2.00
	r. Remainder w/o series, decreto or sign. printing.	20.00	45.00	75.00
	s. Specimen w/red ovpt: *MUESTRA*.	—	—	—
166	500 PESOS BOLIVIANOS			
	D. 1.6.1981. Like #165 but Series B; C. Printer: TDLR.			
	a. Issued note.	0.25	0.30	1.25
	b. Specimen w/red ovpt: *SPECIMEN*. Series B.	—	—	50.00

167   1000 PESOS BOLIVIANOS

D. 25.6.1982. Black on m/c unpt. Arms at ctr., portr. Juana
Azurday de Padilla at r. and as wmk. at l. House of Liberty on back.
Sign. varieties. Series A1-Z9; (6 digits) A-L; (8 digits) each only to
49,999,999). Printer: TDLR. 3 sign. variet

	VG	VF	UNC
a. Issued note.	0.25	0.30	1.00
s. Specimen w/red ovpt: *SPECIMEN*. Series A1.			

168   5000 PESOS BOLIVIANOS

D. 10.2.1984. Deep brown on m/c unpt. Arms at ctr., Marshal J.
Ballivian y Segurola at r. and as wmk. at l. Stylized condor and
leopard on back. Printer: BDDK. Series A.

	VG	VF	UNC
a. Issued note. Sign. varieties.	0.50	1.00	2.00
s1. Specimen w/red ovpt: *MUESTRA SIN VALOR*. Series A.	—	—	—
s2. Specimen pin-holed cancelled: *SPECIMEN*.			

169   10,000 PESOS BOLIVIANOS

D. 10.2.1984. Blackish purple and purple w/dk. green arms on m/c
unpt. Arms at ctr. Portr. Marshal Andres de Santa Cruz at r. and as
wmk. at l. Back brown, bluish purple and green; Legislative palace
at ctr. Printer: BDDK. Series A.

	VG	VF	UNC
a. Issued note.	0.05	0.20	0.75
s. Specimen w/red ovpt: *MUESTRA SIN VALOR*. Series A.	—	—	—

170   50,000 PESOS BOLIVIANOS

D. 5.6.1984. Deep green on m/c unpt. Arms at l., portr. Gualberto
Villarroel Lopez at ctr. Petroleum refinery on back. Printer: TDLR.
Series A; B.

	VG	VF	UNC
a. Issued note. 2 sign. varieties.	0.05	0.25	1.00
s. Specimen w/red ovpt: *MUESTRA SIN VALOR*. Series A.			

171   100,000 PESOS BOLIVIANOS

D. 5.6.1984. Brown-violet on m/c unpt. Arms at l., Portr.
Campesino at r. Agricultural scene at ctr. r. on back. Printer: TDLR.
Series A; B.

	VG	VF	UNC
a. Issued note. 2 sign. varieties.	0.15	0.50	2.00
s. Specimen w/red ovpt: *MUESTRA SIN VALOR*. Series A.			

1982-86 MONETARY EMERGENCY

BANCO CENTRAL DE BOLIVIA

DECRETO SUPREMO No. 19078, 28 JULIO 1982

CHEQUE DE GERENCIA ISSUE

172   5000 PESOS BOLIVIANOS

D.1982.

	VG	VF	UNC
a. Stub w/text attached at r.	—	—	8.00
b. W/o stub at r.	—	—	7.00

173   10,000 PESOS BOLIVIANOS

D.1982.

	VG	VF	UNC
a. Stub w/text attached at r.	—	—	10.00
b. W/o stub at r.	—	—	9.00

NOTICE

Readers with unlisted dates, signature varieties, etc. are invited to
submit photocopies of their notes to: Standard Catalog of World
Paper Money, 700 East State St. Iola, WI 54990-0001, E-Mail:
george.cuhaj@fwpubs.com.

#174 and 175 not assigned.

176	50,000 PESOS BOLIVIANOS	Good	Fine	XF
	4.6.1984; 7.6.1984.			
	a. Issued note.	—	—	—
	b. Ovpt: *ANULADO* (cancelled) across face.	40.00	90.00	200.00

#177 not assigned.

178	1,000,000 PESOS BOLIVIANOS			
	4.6.1984; 7.6.1984.			
	a. Issued note.	—	—	—
	b. Ovpt: *ANULADO* across face.	60.00	100.00	250.00

#179 not assigned.

180	100,000 PESOS BOLIVIANOS	Good	Fine	XF
	18.6.1984. Olive-green text on pale green unpt. Black text on back.			
	a. Issued note.	—	—	—
	b. Ovpt: *ANULADO* across face.	50.00	100.00	210.00
	c. Paid. Punched hole cancelled.	70.00	150.00	275.00

181	500,000 PESOS BOLIVIANOS	Good	Fine	XF
	4.6.1984; 18.6.1984.			
	a. Issued note.	—	—	—
	b. Ovpt: *ANULADO* across face.	60.00	110.00	225.00
	c. Paid. Punched hole cancelled.	60.00	175.00	300.00

182	1,000,000 PESOS BOLIVIANOS	Good	Fine	XF
	18.6.1984.			
	a. Issued note.	—	—	—
	b. Ovpt: *ANULADO* across face.	70.00	120.00	240.00
	c. Paid. Punched hole cancelled.	100.00	210.00	425.00

DECRETO SUPREMO No. 20272, 5 JUNIO 1984, FIRST ISSUE

#183-185 brown on pink unpt. Mercury at upper l. Series A. Printer: JBNC. Usable for 90 days after date of issue (Spanish text at lower r. on back).

Note: Unpt. of "B.C.B." and denom. boxes easily fade from pink to lt. tan to pale yellow.

183	10,000 PESOS BOLIVIANOS	VG	VF	UNC
	D.1984.	3.00	7.00	20.00

184	20,000 PESOS BOLIVIANOS	VG	VF	UNC
	D.1984.	15.00	50.00	125.00

185	50,000 PESOS BOLIVIANOS	VG	VF	UNC
	D.1984.	1.00	5.00	17.50

DECRETO SUPREMO No. 20272, 5 JUNIO 1984, SECOND ISSUE

#186-187 like #183-184 but w/o 90 day use restriction text on back.

186	10,000 PESOS BOLIVIANOS	VG	VF	UNC
	D.1984. Lt. blue on pink unpt. Series A.	1.00	2.50	8.00

187	20,000 PESOS BOLIVIANOS	VG	VF	UNC
	D.1984. Green on pink unpt. Series A.	1.00	2.50	8.50

#188 has 90-day use restriction clause similar to #183-185.

188	100,000 PESOS BOLIVIANOS	VG	VF	UNC
	21.12.1984. Reddish brown on lt. blue and lt. reddish brown unpt. 90 day usage clause at lower r. on back. Series A. Imprint and wmk: CdMB.	0.20	0.75	3.00

DECRETO SUPREMO No. 20272, DE 5 DE JUNIO DE 1984

189	500,000 PESOS BOLIVIANOS	VG	VF	UNC
	D.1984. Deep green on green and peach unpt. No 90-day clause on back. Wmk: CdMB. W/o imprint.	0.20	0.75	3.50

DECRETO SUPREMO No. 20732, 8 MARZO 1985; FIRST ISSUE

190	1 MILLION PESOS BOLIVIANOS	VG	VF	UNC
	D.1985. Blue on yellow and pale blue unpt. Similar to previous issue. No 90-day restriction clause at lower r. on back. Series A. Wmk: CdMB. W/o imprint.			
	a. Issued note.	0.25	1.00	5.50
	s. Specimen perforated: SPECIMEN.			

#191 and 192 Series A. Printer: G&D.

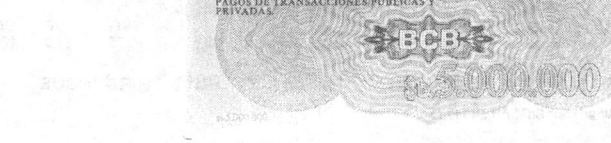

191	5 MILLION PESOS BOLIVIANOS	VG	VF	UNC
	D.1985. Brown-orange and red-brown on m/c unpt. Similar to previous issues but higher quality printing and appearance. M/c back; bank initials in ornate guilloche at ctr. No 90-day restriction clause. Series A.			
	a. Issued note.	0.30	1.50	8.00
	s. Specimen ovpt: SPECIMEN.	—	—	—

192	10 MILLION PESOS BOLIVIANOS	VG	VF	UNC
	D.1985. Rose, violet and purple on m/c unpt. Similar to #191. Series A.			
	a. Issued note.	2.00	8.00	20.00
	s. Specimen ovpt: SPECIMEN.	—	—	35.00-

NOTICE

Readers with unlisted dates, signature varieties, etc. are invited to submit photocopies of their notes to: Standard Catalog of World Paper Money, 700 East State St. Iola, WI 54990-0001, E-Mail: george.cuhaj@fwpubs.com.

DECRETO SUPREMO No. 20732, 8 MARZO 1985; SECOND ISSUE

#192A and 192B similar to #191 and 192. Printer: CdM-Brazil.

		VG	VF	UNC
192A	**5 MILLION PESOS BOLIVIANOS** D.1985. Similar to #191. Series B.	0.50	2.00	7.50

		VG	VF	UNC
192B	**10 MILLION PESOS BOLIVIANOS** D.1985. Rose, violet and purple on m/c unpt. Similar to #192. Series B.	0.75	3.50	10.00

DECRETO SUPREMO No. 20732, 8 MARZO 1985; THIRD ISSUE

#192C-194 printer: CdM-Argentina.

		VG	VF	UNC
192C	**1 MILLION PESOS BOLIVIANOS** D.1985. Blue and m/c. Lg. guilloche at l., Mercury head in unpt. at r. Series L.			
	a. Issued note.	0.20	0.75	3.25
	s. Specimen w/black ovpt: *MUESTRA*.	—	—	15.00

		VG	VF	UNC
193	**5 MILLION PESOS BOLIVIANOS** D.1985. Brown w/reddish brown text on m/c unpt. Similar to #192C. Series N.			
	a. Issued note.	0.75	3.25	7.50
	s. Specimen w/black ovpt: *MUESTRA*.	—	—	30.00

		VG	VF	UNC
194	**10 MILLION PESOS BOLIVIANOS** D.1985. Violet w/lilac text on m/c unpt. Similar to #192C. Series M.			
	a. Issued note.	1.00	4.00	20.00
	s. Specimen w/black ovpt: *MUESTRA*.	—	—	40.00

REPUBLIC, 1986-

BANCO CENTRAL DE BOLIVIA

1987 ND PROVISIONAL ISSUE

		VG	VF	UNC
195	**1 CENTAVO ON 10,000 PESOS BOLIVIANOS** ND (1987). Ovpt. at r. on back of #169.	0.10	0.25	1.00

		VG	VF	UNC
196	**5 CENTAVOS ON 50,000 PESOS BOLIVIANOS** ND (1987). Ovpt. at r. on back of #170.	0.15	0.50	2.25
196A	**10 CENTAVOS ON 100,000 PESOS BOLIVIANOS** ND (1987). Ovpt. at r. on back of #171.	0.50	1.50	7.00

197   10 CENTAVOS ON 100,000 PESOS BOLIVIANOS
ND (1987). Ovpt. at r. on back of #188.

	VG	VF	UNC
	0.15	0.50	3.00

198   50 CENTAVOS ON 500,000 PESOS BOLIVIANOS
ND (1987). Ovpt. at r. on back of #189.

	VG	VF	UNC
	0.20	0.75	3.25

199   1 BOLIVIANO ON 1,000,000 PESOS BOLIVIANOS
ND (1987). Ovpt. at r. on back of #192C.

	VG	VF	UNC
	0.25	0.50	2.50

**200   5 BOLIVIANOS ON 5,000,000 PESOS BOLIVI-
ANOS**
ND (1987). Ovpt. at l. on back of #192A.

	VG	VF	UNC
a. Issued note.	0.30	1.25	6.00
x1. Error. Inverted ovpt. on left end.	1.00	6.00	15.00
x2. Error. Ovpt. on r. end.	—	—	—

Note: Several varieties of "errors" have been reported and all should be looked upon as suspect.

**201   10 BOLIVIANOS ON 10,000,000 PESOS BOLIVI-
ANOS**
ND (1987). Ovpt. at l. on back of #192B.

	VG	VF	UNC
	1.00	4.00	20.00

LEY 901 DE 28.11.1986; 1987-2001 ND ISSUES

#202-208 arms at lower l., ctr. or r. Wmk: S. Bolívar, unless otherwise noted. Printer: F-CO.
Series A sign. titles: *PRESIDENTE BCB* and *MINISTRO DE FINANZAS*. Serial # suffix *A*.
Series B sign. titles: *PRESIDENTE DEL B.C.B.* and *GERENTE GENERAL B.C.B.* Serial # suffix *B*.
Series E sign. titles: *PRESIDENTE BCB* and *GERENTE GENERAL BCB*. Serial # suffix *E*.

202   2 BOLIVIANOS
L.1986. (1987; 1990). Black on m/c unpt. Antonio Vaca Diez at r., arms at lower ctr. Trees and bldgs. at ctr. on back.

	VG	VF	UNC
a. Series A (1987). W/control #.	FV	FV	3.50
b. Series B (1990). W/control #.	FV	FV	4.00
s. As a. Specimen w/red ovpt: *ESPECIMEN*.	—	—	—

203   5 BOLIVIANOS
L.1986. (1987; 1990; 1998). Olive-green on m/c unpt. Adela Zamudio at r., arms at lower l. Religious shrine at l. ctr. on back.

	VG	VF	UNC
a. Series A (1987). W/control #.	FV	FV	6.00
b. Series B (1990). W/control #.	FV	FV	6.50
c. Series E (1998). W/o control #.	FV	FV	4.00
s. As a. Specimen w/red ovpt: *ESPECIMEN*.	—	—	—

204   10 BOLIVIANOS
L.1986. (1987-97). Blue-black on m/c unpt. Cecilio Guzman de
Rojas at r., arms at lower l. Figures overlooking city view on back.

	VG	VF	UNC
a. Series A (1987). W/control #.	FV	FV	9.50
b. Series B (1990). W/control #.	FV	FV	12.50
c. Series E (1997). W/o control #.	FV	FV	5.00
s. As a. Specimen w/red ovpt: *ESPECIMEN*.	—	—	—

205   20 BOLIVIANOS
L.1986. (1987; 1990). Orange on m/c unpt. Pantaleon Dalence at
r., arms at lower ctr. Bldg. at ctr. on back.

	VG	VF	UNC
a. Series A (1987). W/control #.	FV	FV	20.00
b. Series B (1990). W/control #.	FV	FV	25.00
c. Series E (1997). W/o control #.	FV	FV	8.50
s. As a. Specimen w/red ovpt: *ESPECIMEN*.	—	—	—

206   50 BOLIVIANOS
L.1986. (1987; 1997). Purple on m/c unpt. Melchor Perez de
Holguin at r., arms at lower ctr. Tall bldg. at ctr. on back.

	VG	VF	UNC
a. Series A (1987). W/control #.	FV	FV	50.00
b. Series E (1997). W/o control #.	FV	FV	17.50
s. As a. Specimen w/red ovpt: *ESPECIMEN*.	—	—	—

207   100 BOLIVIANOS
L.1986 (1987; 1997). Red-violet and orange on m/c unpt. Gabriel
Rene Moreno at r., arms at lower r. University bldg. at ctr. on back.

	VG	VF	UNC
a. Series A (1987). W/control #. Wmk: Simon Bolívar.	FV	FV	110.00
b. Series E (1997). W/o control #. Wmk: Gabriel Rene Moreno.	FV	FV	35.00
s. As a. Specimen w/red ovpt: *ESPECIMEN*.	—	—	—

208   200 BOLIVIANOS
L.1986 (1987; 1997). Brown and dk. brown on m/c unpt. Franz
Tamayo at r., arms at lower ctr. Ancient statuary on back.

	VG	VF	UNC
a. Series A (1987). W/control #. Wmk: Simon Bolívar.	FV	FV	225.00
b. Series E (1997). W/o control #. Wmk: F. Tamayo.	FV	FV	60.00
s. As a. Specimen w/red ovpt: *ESPECIMEN*.	—	—	—

Ley 901 de 28.11.1986; 1993 ND Issue

#209-214 similar to #203-208 but many stylistic differences. Sign. titles: *PRESIDENTE BCB* and *GERENTE
GENERAL BCB*. Serial # suffix *C*. Printer: FNMT.

#209-212 wmk: S. Bolívar.

209   5 BOLIVIANOS

	VG	VF	UNC
L.1986 (1993). Olive-green on m/c unpt. Series C. Similar to #203.	FV	FV	17.50

210   10 BOLIVIANOS

	VG	VF	UNC
L.1986 (1993). Blue-black on m/c unpt. Series C. Similar to #204.	FV	FV	6.50

#215 and 216 like #209 and 210 but w/many stylistic differences including sign. titles. Wmk: S. Bolívar. Printer: TDLR.

			VG	VF	UNC
211	20 BOLIVIANOS				
	L.1986 (1993). Orange on m/c unpt. Series C. Similar to #205.		FV	FV	10.00

			VG	VF	UNC
215	5 BOLIVIANOS				
	L.1986 (1995). Olive-green on m/c unpt. Series C. Like #209.				
	a. Issued note.		FV	FV	6.00
	s. Specimen w/red ovpt: *MUESTRA SIN VALOR.*		—	—	

			VG	VF	UNC
212	50 BOLIVIANOS				
	L.1986 (1993). Purple on m/c unpt. Series C. Similar to #206.		FV	FV	22.50

			VG	VF	UNC
216	10 BOLIVIANOS				
	L.1986 (1995). Blue-black on m/c unpt. Series C. Like #210.				
	a. Issued note.		FV	FV	12.00
	s. Specimen w/red ovpt: *MUESTRA SIN VALOR.*		—	—	

#217-222 like #209-214 but w/many stylistic differences and sign. titles: *PRESIDENTE BCB* and *GERENTE GENERAL BCB.* W/o 4 control #'s. Printer: TDLR.

#217-220 wmk: S. Bolívar.

			VG	VF	UNC
213	100 BOLIVIANOS				
	L.1986 (1993). Red and orange on m/c unpt. Series C. Similar to #207.		FV	FV	45.00

			VG	VF	UNC
217	5 BOLIVIANOS				
	L.1986 (1995). Olive-green on m/c unpt. Series D. Like #209.		FV	FV	3.50

			VG	VF	UNC
214	200 BOLIVIANOS				
	L.1986 (1993). Brown and dk. brown on m/c unpt. Series C. Similar to #208.		FV	FV	90.00

218	10 BOLIVIANOS	VG	VF	UNC
	L.1986 (1995). Blue-black on m/c unpt. Series D. Like #210.	FV	FV	5.00

219	20 BOLIVIANOS	VG	VF	UNC
	L.1986 (1995). Orange on m/c unpt. Series D. Like #211.	FV	FV	9.00

220	50 BOLIVIANOS	VG	VF	UNC
	L.1986 (1995). Purple on m/c unpt. Series D. Like #212.			
	a. Issued note.	FV	FV	20.00
	s. Specimen w/red ovpt: *MUESTRA SIN VALOR.*	—	—	—
221	100 BOLIVIANOS			
	L.1986 (1996). Red and orange on m/c unpt. Wmk: Gabriel Rene Moreno. Series D. Like #213.	FV	FV	35.00
222	200 BOLIVIANOS			
	L.1986 (1996). Brown and dk. brown on m/c unpt. Wmk: F. Tamayo. Series D. Like #214.	FV	FV	65.00

Note: For Series E, see #203a-208a.

Ley 901 de 28.11.1986; 2001 ND Issue

#223-227, like #207b, 208b, 210-212 but w/ addition of raised marks for the blind and narrow clear text security thread. Printer: F-CO. Sign. titles: PRESIDENTE BCB and GERENTE GENERAL BCB. W/o 4 control #'s. Wmk. Simon Bolívar or as noted.

223	10 BOLIVIANOS	VG	VF	UNC
	L. 1986 (2001). Blue-black on m/c unpt. Series F. Like #210.	FV	FV	4.00

224	20 BOLIVIANOS	VG	VF	UNC
	L.1986 (2001). Orange and brown-orange on m/c unpt. Series F. Like #211.	FV	FV	7.00
225	50 BOLIVIANOS			
	L.1986 (2001). Purple on m/c unpt. Series F. Like #212.	FV	FV	15.00
226	100 BOLIVIANOS			
	L.1986 (2001). Red-violet and orange on m/c unpt. Series F. Like #207b.	FV	FV	30.00
227	200 BOLIVIANOS			
	L.1986 (2001). Brown and dk. brown on m/c unpt. Series F. Like #208b.	FV	FV	60.00

Ley 901 de 28.11.1986; 2005 ND Issue

#228-232 like #223-227. Wide clear text security thread. Printer: F-CO. Sign. titles: *PRESIDENTE BCB* and *GENENTE GENERAL BCB.* W/o 4 control #s. Wmk: as portr., with value in numerals vertically.

228	10 BOLIVIANOS	VG	VF	UNC
	L.1986 (2005). Blue-black on m/c unpt. Like #223. W/o security thread. Series G.	FV	FV	4.00
229	20 BOLIVIANOS			
	L.1986 (2005). Orange and brown-orange on m/c unpt. Like #224. Narrow security thread. Series G.	FV	FV	7.00
230	50 BOLIVIANOS			
	L.1986. (2005). Purple on m/c unpt. Like #225. Wide security thread. Series G.	FV	FV	15.00
231	100 BOLIVIANOS			
	L.1986. (2005). Red-violet and orange on m/c unpt. Like #226. Wide security thread. Series G.	FV	FV	30.00
232	200 BOLIVIANOS			
	L.1986. (2005). Brown and dk. brown on m/c unpt. Like #227. Wide security thread. Series G.	FV	FV	60.00

BOSNIA AND HERZEGOVINA

The Republic of Bosnia-Herzegovina borders Croatia to the north and west, Serbia to the east and Montenegro in the southeast with only 12.4 miles of coastline. The total land area is 19,735 sq. mi. (51,129 sq. km.). It has a population of 4.34 million. Capital: Sarajevo. Electricity, mining and agriculture are leading industries.

Bosnia's first ruler of importance was the Ban Kulin, 1180-1204. Stephen Kotromanió was invested with Bosnia, held loyalty to Hungary and extended his rule to the principality of Hum or Zahumlje, the future Herzegovina. His daughter Elisabeth married Louis the Great and he died in the same year. His nephew Tvrtko succeeded and during the weakening of Serbian power he assumed the title *Stephen Tvrtko, in* Christ God King of the Serbs and Bosnia and the Coastland. Later he assumed the title of *King of* Dalmatia and Croatia, but died before he could consolidate power. Successors also asserted their right to the Serbian throne.

In 1459 the Turks invaded Serbia. Bosnia was invaded in 1463 and Herzegovina in 1483. During Turkish rule Islam was accepted rather than Catholicism. During the 16th and 17th centuries Bosnia was an important Turkish outpost in continuing warfare with the Habsburgs and Venice. When Hungary was freed of the Turkish yoke, the imperialists penetrated Bosnia, and in 1697 Prince Eugene captured Sarajevo. Later, by the Treaty of Karlowitz in 1699, the northern boundary of Bosnia became the northernmost limit of the Turkish empire while the eastern area was ceded to Austria, but later restored to Turkey in 1739 lasting until 1878 following revolts of 1821, 1828, 1831 and 1862. On June 30, 1871 Serbia and Montenegro declared war on Turkey and were quickly defeated. The Turkish war with Russia led to the occupation by Austria-Hungary. Insurgents attempted armed resistance and Austria-Hungary invaded, quelling the uprising in 1878. The Austrian occupation provided a period of prosperity while at the same time prevented relations with Serbia and Croatia. Strengthening political and religious movements from within forced the annexation by Austria on Oct. 7, 1908. Hungary's establishment of a dictatorship in Croatia following the victories of Serbian forces in the Balkan War roused the whole Yugoslav population of Austria-Hungary to feverish excitement. The Bosnian group, mainly students, devoted its efforts to revolutionary ideas. After Austria's Balkan front collapsed in Oct. 1918 the union with Yugoslavia developed and on Dec. 1, 1918 the former Kingdom of the Serbs, Croats and Slovenes was proclaimed (later to become the Kingdom of Yugoslavia on Oct. 3, 1929).

After the defeat of Germany in WWII during which Bosnia was under the control of Pavelic of Croatia, a new Socialist Republic was formed under Marshal Tito having six constituent republics all subservient, quite similar to the constitution of the U.S.S.R. Military and civil loyalty was with Tito. In Jan. 1990 the Yugoslav government announced a rewriting of the constitution, abolishing the Communist Party's monopoly of power. Opposition parties were legalized in July 1990. On Oct. 15, 1991 the National Assembly adopted a Memorandum on Sovereignty that envisaged Bosnian autonomy within a Yugoslav Federation. In March 1992 an agreement was reached under EC auspices by Moslems, Serbs and Croats to set up 3 autonomous ethnic communities under a central Bosnian authority. Independence was declared on April 5, 1992. The 2 Serbian members of government resigned and fighting broke out between all 3 ethnic communities. The Dayton (Ohio, USA) Peace Accord was signed in 1995 which recognized the Federation of Bosnia-Herzegovina and the Srpska (Serbian) Republic. Both governments maintain separate military forces, schools, etc., providing humanitarian aid while a treaty allowed NATO "Peace Keeping" forces to be deployed in Dec. 1995 replacing the United Nations troops previously acting in a similar role.

RULERS:
Ottoman, until 1878
Austrian, 1878-1918
Yugoslavian, 1918-1941

MONETARY SYSTEM:
1 Dinar = 100 Para 1992-1998
1 Convertible Marka = 1 Deutschemark
1 Convertible Marka = 100 Convertible Pfeniga, 1998-

REPUBLIKA BOSNA I HERCEGOVINA

MOSLEM REPUBLIC

НАРОДНА БАНКА БОСНЕ И ХЕРЦЕГОВИНЕ

NARODNA BANKA BOSNE I HERCEGOVINE

Bank was transformed into the Central Bank of Bosnia and Herzegovina on August 11, 1997.

1992 FIRST PROVISIONAL ISSUE

#1-2 violet handstamp: *NARODNA BANKA BOSNE I HERCEGOVINE,* also in Cyrillic around Yugoslav arms, on Yugoslav regular issues. Handstamp varieties exist.

		Good	Fine	XF
1	**500 DINARA**			
	ND (1992). 27mm or 31mm handstamp on Yugoslavia #109.			
	a. Handstamp w/o numeral.	10.00	30.00	100.00
	b. Handstamp w/numeral: *1.*	10.00	30.00	100.00
	c. Handstamp w/numeral: *2.*	10.00	30.00	100.00

		Good	Fine	XF
2	**1000 DINARA**			
	ND (1992). 48mm handstamp on Yugoslavia #110.			
	a. Handstamp w/o numeral.	8.00	25.00	125.00
	b. Handstamp w/numeral 1.	8.00	25.00	125.00
	c. Handstamp w/numeral 2.	8.00	25.00	125.00

#3 and 4 not assigned.

1992 SECOND PROVISIONAL NOVCANI BON ISSUE

#6-9 issued in various Central Bosnian cities. Peace dove at upper l. ctr. Example w/o indication of city of issue are remainders.

		Good	Fine	XF
6	**100 DINARA**			
	1992. Deep pink on gray and yellow unpt.			
	a. Handstamped: *BREZA* on back.	7.50	25.00	100.00
	b. Circular red handstamp: *FOJNICA* on back.	3.00	10.00	50.00
	c. Rectangular purple handstamp on face, circular purple handstamp: *KRESEVO* on back.	6.50	20.00	80.00
	d. Handstamped: *TESANJ* on back.	5.50	20.00	80.00
	e. Handstamped: *VARES* on back.	10.00	35.00	110.00
	f1. Handstamped: *VISOKO* 31mm on back.	2.00	6.00	30.00
	f2. Handstamped: *VISOKO* 20mm on back.	3.00	10.00	55.00
	g. Circular red ovpt: *ZENICA,* 11.5.1992. on back r. W/printed sign. at either side.	1.00	3.00	9.00
	r. Remainder, w/o handstamp or ovpt.	1.00	3.00	10.00

		Good	Fine	XF
7	**500 DINARA**			
	1992. Pale greenish-gray on gray and yellow unpt.			
	a. Handstamped: *BREZA* on back.	5.00	17.50	70.00
	b. Circular red handstamp: *FOJNICA* on back.	5.00	17.50	70.00
	c. Handstamped: *KRESEVO* on back.	12.50	45.00	120.00
	d. Handstamped: *TESANJ* on back.	2.00	7.50	35.00
	e. Handstamped: *VARES* on back.	5.00	17.50	70.00
	f. Circular red handstamp: *VISOKO* on back.	3.00	12.50	40.00
	g. Circular red handstamp on back, details as #6g: *ZENICA* (small or large), 11.5.1992.	0.50	2.00	7.00

8 1000 DINARA
1992. Blue on gray unpt.

	Good	Fine	XF
a. Handstamped: *BREZA* on back.	5.00	15.00	65.00
b. Handstamped: *FOJNICA* on back.	5.00	15.00	65.00
c. Handstamped: *KRESEVO* on back.	8.00	30.00	90.00
d. Handstamped: *TESANJ* on back.	6.50	20.00	75.00
e. Handstamped: *VARES* on back.	6.50	20.00	75.00
f1. Handstamped: *VISOKO* 31mm on back.	2.00	9.00	35.00
f2. Handstamped: *VISOKO* 20mm on back.	9.00	30.00	100.00
g. Handstamped: *ZENICA* on face, no date on stamping.	8.00	25.00	75.00
h. Circular red ovpt. on back, details as 6g: *ZENICA*, 11.5.1992.	0.50	2.00	10.00

9 5000 DINARA
1992. Dull brown on gray and yellow unpt.

	Good	Fine	XF
a. Handstamped: *BREZA* on back.	3.00	10.00	35.00
b. Circular red handstamp: *FOJNICA* on back.	2.00	8.00	30.00
c. Handstamped: *KRESEVO* on back.	12.50	50.00	125.00
d. Handstamped: *TESANJ* on back.	25.00	85.00	350.00
e. Handstamped: *VARES* on back.	7.00	20.00	75.00
f1. Handstamped: *VISOKO* on back.	2.00	6.00	18.00
f2. Handstamped: *VISOKO* 32mm on back.	7.50	30.00	90.00
f3. Handstamped: *VISOKO* 20mm on back.	3.00	10.00	35.00
g. Handstamped: *ZENICA* on face, w/o date in stamping.	7.00	22.50	65.00
h. Circular violet ovpt. on back, details as 6g: *ZENICA*, 11.5.1992.	0.50	2.00	7.50
r. Remainder, w/o handstamp or ovpt.	1.00	5.00	20.00

1992-93 ISSUES

#10-15 guilloche at l. ctr. 145x73mm. Wmk: Repeated diamonds. Printer: Cetis (Celje, Slovenia).

#10-18 serial # varieties.

10 10 DINARA
1.7.1992. Purple on pink unpt. Mostar stone arch bridge at r. on back.

	VG	VF	UNC
a. Issued note.	0.10	0.25	1.00
s. Specimen.	—	—	30.00

11 25 DINARA
1.7.1992. Blue-black on lt. blue unpt. Crowned arms at ctr. r. on back.

	VG	VF	UNC
a. Issued note.	0.10	0.20	1.25
s. Specimen.	—	—	30.00

12 50 DINARA
1.7.1992. Blue-black on red-violet unpt. Mostar stone arch bridge at r. on back.

	VG	VF	UNC
a. Issued note.	0.10	0.50	1.50
s. Specimen.	—	—	30.00

13 100 DINARA
1.7.1992. Dull black on olive-green unpt. Crowned arms at ctr. r. on back.

	VG	VF	UNC
a. Issued note.	0.10	0.50	1.75
s. Specimen.	—	—	30.00

14 500 DINARA
1.7.1992. Dull violet-brown on pink and ochre unpt. Crowned arms at ctr. r. on back.

	VG	VF	UNC
a. Issued note.	0.20	0.75	3.50
s. Specimen.	—	—	30.00

15 1000 DINARA
1.7.1992. Deep purple on lt. green and lilac unpt. Mostar stone arch bridge at r. on back.

	VG	VF	UNC
a. Issued note.	0.25	1.00	4.50
s. Specimen.	—	—	30.00

#16 and 17 grayish blue shield w/fleur-de-lis replaces crowned shield w/raised scimitar on back. Reduced size notes. Printed in Zenica.

		VG	VF	UNC
16	**5000 DINARA**			
	25.1.1993. Pale olive-green on yellow-orange unpt. Arms at ctr. r. on back.			
	a. Issued note.	1.00	3.00	7.50
	b. W/ovpt: *SDK...ZENICA* on back w/ handstamp or machine printing.	1.75	5.00	15.00

		VG	VF	UNC
17	**10,000 DINARA**			
	25.1.1993. Brown on pink unpt. Arms at ctr. r. on back.			
	a. Issued note.	1.25	3.50	8.50
	b. W/ovpt: *SDK...ZENICA* on back w/handstamp or machine printing.	1.75	5.00	15.00

1992-94 Bon Issue

#21-33 shield at l. on back. Issued during the seige of Sarajevo. Grayish green or yellow unpt. on back.

		VG	VF	UNC
21	**10 DINARA**			
	1.8.1992. Violet.			
	a. Issued note.	2.00	6.00	35.00
	s. Specimen.	—	—	30.00

		VG	VF	UNC
22	**20 DINARA**			
	1.8.1992. Blue-violet.			
	a. Issued note.	1.50	5.00	30.00
	s. Specimen.	—	—	30.00

		VG	VF	UNC
23	**50 DINARA**			
	1.8.1992. Pink.			
	a. Issued note.	2.00	6.00	35.00
	s. Specimen.	—	—	30.00

		VG	VF	UNC
24	**100 DINARA**			
	1.8.1992. Green.			
	a. Issued note.	5.00	25.00	125.00
	s. Specimen.	—	—	30.00

		VG	VF	UNC
25	**500 DINARA**			
	1.8.1992. Orange. Back red-orange on pale purple and grayish green unpt.			
	a. Issued note.	3.00	8.00	40.00
	s. Specimen.	—	—	30.00

		VG	VF	UNC
26	**1000 DINARA**			
	1.8.1992. Brown.			
	a. Issued note.	1.50	6.00	35.00
	s. Specimen.	—	—	30.00

		VG	VF	UNC
27	**5000 DINARA**			
	1.8.1992. Violet.			
	a. Issued note.	1.50	6.00	35.00
	s. Specimen.	—	—	30.00

		VG	VF	UNC
28	**10,000 DINARA**			
	6.4.1993. Lt. Blue.	1.50	6.00	35.00

		VG	**VF**	**UNC**
29	**50,000 DINARA** 1.5.1993. Pink.	2.50	10.00	40.00

		VG	**VF**	**UNC**
30	**100,000 DINARA** 1.8.1993. Green on m/c unpt. Back green on gray unpt.	1.50	5.00	30.00

		VG	**VF**	**UNC**
31	**100,000 DINARA** 1.8.1993. Green. Back green on yellow unpt.	1.50	5.00	30.00

		VG	**VF**	**UNC**
32	**500,000 DINARA** 1.1.1994. Brown. Back brown on pale yellow-green unpt.	1.50	5.00	25.00

		VG	**VF**	**UNC**
33	**1,000,000 DINARA** 1.1.1994. Red.	1.50	5.00	25.00

1993 NOVCANI BON EMERGENCY ISSUE

		VG	**VF**	**UNC**
34	**100,000 DINARA** 1993 (-old date 1.7.1992). Rectangular crenalated framed ovpt: *NOVCANI BON 100,000...*on face and back of #10. a. Purple ovpt. 1.9.1993. b. Blue ovpt. and sign. ovpt. 10.11.1993.	 2.00 2.00	 7.50 7.50	 17.50 17.50

		VG	**VF**	**UNC**
35	**1,000,000 DINARA** 10.11.1993 (old date-1.7.1992). Blue-violet ovpt. on #11. (Not issued) a. Purple ovpt. 1.9.1993. b. Blue ovpt. and sign. ovpt. 10.11.1993.	 0.50 0.50	 8.00 3.50	 20.00 9.00

		VG	**VF**	**UNC**
36	**10,000,000 DINARA** 10.11.1993 (old date-1.7.1992). Blue-violet ovpt. on #12. (Not issued)	—	4.00	12.50

		VG	**VF**	**UNC**
37	**100,000,000 DINARA** 10.11.1993 (old date-1.7.1992). Blue-violet ovpt. on #13. (Not issued)	—	4.00	12.50

1994 ISSUE

Currency Reform, 1994

1 New Dinar = 10,000 Old Dinara

#39-46 alternate with shield or Mostar stone bridge at ctr. r. on back. Wmk: block design. Printer: DD "Dom Stampe" Zenica.

39	1 DINAR	VG	VF	UNC
	15.8.1994. Purplish gray on red-violet and pale green unpt.			
	a. Issued note.	0.05	0.15	0.75
	s. Specimen.	—	—	—

40	5 DINARA	VG	VF	UNC
	15.8.1994. Purplish gray on lilac, red and orange unpt.			
	a. Issued note.	0.05	0.15	0.75
	s. Specimen.	—	—	—

41	10 DINARA	VG	VF	UNC
	15.8.1994. Purple on red, orange and red-violet unpt.			
	a. Issued note.	0.10	0.25	1.00
	s. Specimen.	—	—	—

42	20 DINARA	VG	VF	UNC
	15.8.1994. Brown on violet, red and yellow unpt.			
	a. Issued note.	0.15	0.50	1.50
	s. Specimen.	—	—	—

43	50 DINARA	VG	VF	UNC
	15.8.1994. Purplish gray on red-violet and pale purple unpt.			
	a. Issued note.	0.15	0.50	2.00
	s. Specimen.	—	—	—

44	100 DINARA	VG	VF	UNC
	15.8.1994. Dull black on aqua, yellow and olive-green unpt.			
	a. Issued note.	0.15	0.50	2.25
	s. Specimen.	—	—	—

45	500 DINARA	VG	VF	UNC
	15.8.1994. Dull brown on lilac and yellow unpt.			
	a. Large #'s.	0.25	1.50	6.00
	b. Small #'s.	0.25	1.50	6.00
	s. Specimen.	—	—	—

46	1000 DINARA	VG	VF	UNC
	15.8.1994. Blue-gray on gray-green, red-violet and lt. green unpt.			
	a. Large #'s.	1.00	4.50	12.50
	b. Small #'s.	1.00	4.50	12.50
	s. Specimen.	—	—	—

1995 ND ISSUE

#47-47C Printed in London but unable to be delivered.

47	50 DINARA	VG	VF	UNC
	ND (1995). Purple on pink and ochre unpt. Bridge at r. Wmk: Lis.	1.00	6.00	20.00
47A	100 DINARA			
	ND (1995). Design as #47. (Not issued).	—	—	—
47B	500 DINARA			
	ND (1995). Design as #47. (Not issued).	—	—	—

NOTICE

Readers with unlisted dates, signature varieties, etc. are invited to submit photocopies of their notes to: Standard Catalog of World Paper Money, 700 East State St. Iola, WI 54990-0001, E-Mail: george.cuhaj@fwpubs.com.

47C   1000 DINARA
ND (1995). Design as #47. (Not issued).

	VG	VF	UNC
	—	—	—

1992 ND NOVCANI BON ISSUE

#48-52 plain design w/value at ctr. w/Travnik, Novi Travnik or Vitez Branch handstamps.

48   200 DINARA
ND (1992). Orange.

	VG	VF	UNC
a. Handstamped: *TRAVNIK.*	2.50	10.00	40.00
b. Handstamped: *NOVI TRAVNIK.*	5.00	20.00	80.00
c. Handstamped: *VITEZ.*	7.50	35.00	110.00

49   500 DINARA
ND (1992). Brown.

	VG	VF	UNC
a. Handstamped: *TRAVNIK.*	2.50	15.00	55.00
b. Handstamped: *NOVI TRAVNIK.*	7.50	30.00	95.00
c. Handstamped: *VITEZ.*	10.00	45.00	120.00

50   1000 DINARA
ND (1992). Lilac.

	VG	VF	UNC
a. Handstamped: *TRAVNIK.*	2.50	8.00	30.00
b. Handstamped: *NOVI TRAVNIK.*	4.00	18.00	70.00
c. Handstamped: *VITEZ.*	5.00	25.00	95.00

51   5000 DINARA
ND (1992). Lt. blue.

	VG	VF	UNC
a. Handstamped: *TRAVNIK.*	10.00	70.00	500.00
b. Handstamped: *NOVI TRAVNIK.*		Rare	
c. Handstamped: *VITEZ.*		Rare	

52   10,000 DINARA
ND (1992). Red on blue unpt.

	VG	VF	UNC
a. Handstamped: *TRAVNIK.*	2.50	15.00	45.00
b. Handstamped: *NOVI TRAVNIK.*	5.00	25.00	95.00
c. Handstamped: *VITEZ.*	7.50	35.00	110.00

1993 EMERGENCY ISSUE

#53-56 like #10-13 w/additional 3 solid zeroes printed after large value on face w/Travnik Branch dated handstamp.

53   10,000 DINARA
1993. Red on yellow unpt.

	VG	VF	UNC
a. 15.10.1993. Short green zeroes.	1.00	2.50	7.50
b. 15.10.1993. Short red zeroes.	1.00	2.50	7.50
c. 24.12.1993. Tall green zeroes.	1.00	2.50	7.50
d. 24.12.1993. Tall red zeroes.	1.00	2.50	7.50

54   25,000 DINARA
1993. Green on blue unpt.

	VG	VF	UNC
a. 15.10.1993. Short green zeroes.	1.00	2.50	7.50
b. 15.10.1993. Short red zeroes.	1.00	2.50	7.50
c. 24.12.1993. Tall green zeroes.	1.00	2.50	7.50
d. 24.12.1993. Tall red zeroes.	1.00	2.50	7.50

55   50,000 DINARA
1993. Red.

	VG	VF	UNC
a. 15.10.1993. Short green zeroes.	1.00	2.50	7.50
b. 15.10.1993. Short red zeroes.	1.00	2.50	7.50
c. 24.12.1993. Tall green zeroes.	1.00	2.50	7.50
d. 24.12.1993. Tall red zeroes.	1.00	2.50	7.50

56   100,000 DINARA
1993. Green.

	VG	VF	UNC
a. 15.10.1993. Short green zeroes.	1.00	2.50	7.50
b. 15.10.1993. Short red zeroes.	1.00	2.50	7.50
c. 24.12.1993. Tall green zeroes.	1.00	2.50	7.50
d. 24.12.1993. Tall red zeroes.	1.00	2.50	7.50

ЦЕНТРАЛНА БАНКА БОСНЕ И ХЕРЦЕГОВИНЕ

CENTRALNA BANKA BOSNE I HERCEGOVINE

Established in Sarajevo on Aug. 11, 1997.

1998 ND ISSUE

#57-70 w/alternating texts of bank name and denominations. Wmk: Central bank monogram repeated vertically. Printer: F-CO (w/o imprint).

57   50 CONVERTIBLE PFENIGA
ND (1998). Dk. blue on blue and lilac unpt. Portr. S. Kulenovic at r.
Stecak Zgosca fragment at l. ctr. on back.

	VG	VF	UNC
a. Issued note.	FV	FV	0.75
s. Specimen.	—	—	—

58   50 CONVERTIBLE PFENIGA
ND (1998). Dk. blue on blue and lilac unpt. Portr. B. Copic at r.
Open book, cabin at l. ctr. on back.

	VG	VF	UNC
a. Issued note.	FV	FV	0.75
s. Specimen.	—	—	—

59   1 CONVERTIBLE MARKA
ND (1998). Dk. green on green and yellow-green unpt. I. F. Jukic at
r. *Stecak Stolac* fragment at l. ctr. on back.

	VG	VF	UNC
a. Issued note.	FV	FV	1.50
s. Specimen.	—	—	—

60   1 CONVERTIBLE MARKA
ND (1998). Dk. green on green and yellow-green unpt. I. Andric at
r. Bridge at l. ctr. on back. (Not issued).

Note: Some examples of #60 were stolen and have been offered on the market at about $80.00-100.00.

61   5 CONVERTIBLE MARAKA
ND (1998). Violet on m/c unpt. M. Selimovic at r. Trees at l. ctr. on
back. English letters in bank name as top line.

	VG	VF	UNC
a. Issued note.	FV	FV	7.50
s. Specimen.	—	—	—

62   5 CONVERTIBLE MARAKA
ND (1998). Violet on m/c unpt. Like #61 but Cyrillic bank name and
denomination as top line.

	VG	VF	UNC
a. Issued note.	FV	FV	7.50
s. Specimen.	—	—	—

63   10 CONVERTIBLE MARAKA
ND (1998). Orange-brown on dull purple and orange-brown unpt.
M. M. Dizdar at r. *Stecak Radimlja* fragment at l. ctr. on back.

	VG	VF	UNC
a. Issued note.	FV	FV	12.50
s. Specimen.	—	—	—

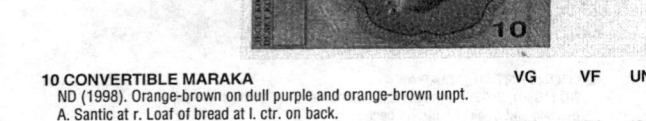

64   10 CONVERTIBLE MARAKA
ND (1998). Orange-brown on dull purple and orange-brown unpt.
A. Santic at r. Loaf of bread at l. ctr. on back.

	VG	VF	UNC
a. Issued note.	FV	FV	12.50
s. Specimen.	—	—	—

#65-70 variable optical device at upper l. ctr.

	20 CONVERTIBLE MARAKA	VG	VF	UNC
65	ND (1998). Dk. brown on m/c unpt. A. B. Simic at r. *Stecak Radimilja* fragment at l. ctr. on back.			
	a. Issued note.	FV	FV	20.00
	s. Specimen.	—	—	—

	20 CONVERTIBLE MARAKA	VG	VF	UNC
66	ND (1998). Dk. brown on m/c unpt. F. Visjic at r. "Gusle" musical instrument at l. ctr. on back.			
	a. Issued note.	FV	FV	20.00
	s. Specimen.	—	—	—

	50 CONVERTIBLE MARAKA	VG	VF	UNC
67	ND (1998). Purple on lilac and m/c unpt. M. C. Catic at r. Stone relief at l. ctr. on back.			
	a. Issued note.	FV	FV	55.00
	s. Specimen.	—	—	—

	50 CONVERTIBLE MARAKA	VG	VF	UNC
68	ND (1998); 2002. Purple on lilac and m/c unpt. I. Ducic at r. Pen, glasses and book at l. ctr. on back.			
	a. Issued note.	FV	FV	55.00
	s. Specimen.	—	—	—

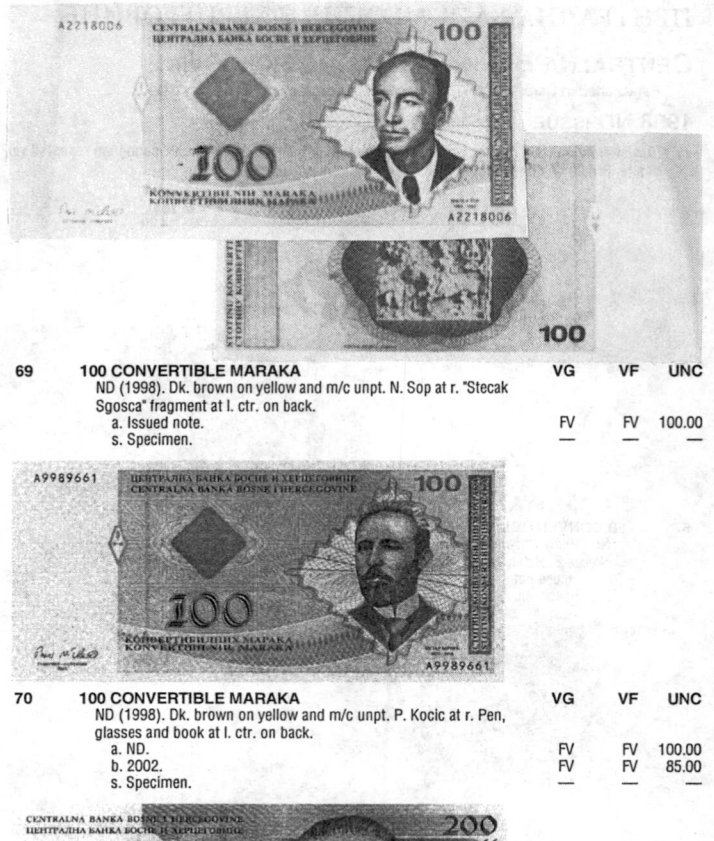

	100 CONVERTIBLE MARAKA	VG	VF	UNC
69	ND (1998). Dk. brown on yellow and m/c unpt. N. Sop at r. "Stecak Sgosca" fragment at l. ctr. on back.			
	a. Issued note.	FV	FV	100.00
	s. Specimen.	—	—	—

	100 CONVERTIBLE MARAKA	VG	VF	UNC
70	ND (1998). Dk. brown on yellow and m/c unpt. P. Kocic at r. Pen, glasses and book at l. ctr. on back.			
	a. ND.	FV	FV	100.00
	b. 2002.	FV	FV	85.00
	s. Specimen.	—	—	—

	200 CONVERTIBLE MARAKA	VG	VF	UNC
71	ND (2002). Blue.	FV	FV	165.00

Srpska (Serbian) Republic

Народна Банка Српскерепублике Босне и Херцеговине

Narodna Banka Srpske Republike Bosne i Hercegovine

National Bank of the Serbian Republic of Bosnia-Herzegovina

Ceased operations in August 1997.

1992-93 Banja Luka Issue

#133-139 arms at l., numerals in heart-shaped design below guilloche at ctr. r. Curved artistic design at l. ctr., arms at r. on back.

#133-135 wmk: Portr. of a young girl.

133	10 DINARA	VG	VF	UNC
	1992. Deep brown or orange and silver unpt. Back with ochre unpt.			
	a. Issued note.	0.10	0.50	1.50
	s. Specimen.	—	—	5.00

134	50 DINARA	VG	VF	UNC
	1992. Deep olive-gray on ochre and m/c unpt.			
	a. Issued note.	0.15	0.50	1.50
	s. Specimen.	—	—	5.00

135	100 DINARA	VG	VF	UNC
	1992. Dk. blue on lilac and silver unpt.			
	a. Issued note.	0.25	1.00	3.00
	s. Specimen.	—	—	5.00

#136-140 wmk: Portr. of a young boy.

136	500 DINARA	VG	VF	UNC
	1992. Dk. blue on pink and m/c unpt.			
	a. Issued note.	0.50	1.50	4.50
	s. Specimen.	—	—	5.00

137	1000 DINARA	VG	VF	UNC
	1992. Slate gray on peach and tan unpt. Back with orange unpt.			
	a. Issued note.	0.50	1.25	3.75
	s. Specimen.	—	—	5.00
138	5000 DINARA			
	1992. Violet on lilac and lt. blue unpt.			
	a. Issued note.	0.50	2.50	10.00
	s. Specimen.	—	—	5.00
139	10,000 DINARA			
	1992. Gray on tan and lt. blue unpt.			
	a. Issued note.	0.50	2.50	10.00
	s. Specimen.	—	—	5.00
140	50,000 DINARA			
	1993. Brown on olive-green and m/c unpt.			
	a. Issued note.	2.00	8.00	30.00
	s. Specimen.	—	—	7.50

Note: For similar notes to #136-140 but differing only in text at top, sign., and Knin as place of issue, see Croatia-Regional.

141	100,000 DINARA	VG	VF	UNC
	1993. Purple on brown and m/c unpt. Wmk: Portr. of young woman w/head covering.			
	a. Issued note.	0.50	1.50	4.00
	s. Specimen.	—	—	7.50

#142-144 wmk: Portr. of a young girl.

			VG	VF	UNC
142	**1 MILLION DINARA**				
	1993. Dp. purple on pink, yellow and m/c unpt.				
	a. Issued note.		2.00	8.00	40.00
	s. Specimen.		—	—	7.50
143	**5 MILLION DINARA**				
	1993. Dk. brown on lt. blue and yellow-orange unpt.				
	a. Issued note.		0.25	1.00	3.00
	s. Specimen.		—	—	7.50

			VG	VF	UNC
144	**10 MILLION DINARA**				
	1993. Dk. blue-violet on olive-green and yellow-orange unpt.				
	a. Issued note.		0.50	1.50	4.50
	s. Specimen.		—	—	7.50

НАРОДНА БАНКА РЕПУБЛИКЕСРПСКЕ

NARODNA BANKA REPUBLIKE SRPSKE

NATIONAL BANK OF THE SERBIAN REPUBLIC

1993 BANJA LUKA FIRST ISSUE

			VG	VF	UNC
145	**50 MILLION DINARA**				
	1993. Dk. brown on pink and gray unpt.				
	a. Issued note.		0.75	2.50	7.50
	s. Specimen.		—	—	5.00

			VG	VF	UNC
146	**100 MILLION DINARA**				
	1993. Pale blue-gray on lt. blue and gray unpt.				
	a. Issued note.		0.50	1.50	4.00
	s. Specimen.		—	—	5.00

			VG	VF	UNC
147	**1 MILLIARD DINARA**				
	1993. Orange on pale blue and lt. orange unpt.				
	a. Issued note.		0.50	1.50	5.00
	s. Specimen.		—	—	5.00

			VG	VF	UNC
148	**10 MILLIARD DINARA**				
	1993. Black on pink and pale orange unpt.				
	a. Issued note.		0.50	1.50	5.00
	s. Specimen.		—	—	5.00

1993 BANJA LUKA SECOND ISSUE

#149-155 P. Kocic at l. Serbian arms at ctr. r. on back. Wmk: Greek design repeated.

			VG	VF	UNC
149	**5000 DINARA**				
	1993. Red-violet and purple on pale blue-gray unpt.				
	a. Issued note.		0.25	1.00	3.00
	s. Specimen.		—	—	7.50

			VG	VF	UNC
150	**50,000 DINARA**				
	1993. Brown and dull red on ochre unpt.				
	a. Issued note.		0.25	1.00	3.00
	s. Specimen.		—	—	7.50

151 100,000 DINARA

1993. Violet and blue-gray on pink unpt.

	VG	VF	UNC
a. Issued note.	0.25	1.00	3.00
s. Specimen.	—	—	7.50

155 500,000,000 DINARA

1993. Brown-violet and grayish green on pale olive-brown unpt.

	VG	VF	UNC
a. Issued note.	0.50	1.50	5.00
s. Specimen.	—	—	7.50

152 1,000,000 DINARA

1993. Black and blue-gray on pale purple unpt.

	VG	VF	UNC
a. Issued note.	0.50	1.50	5.00
s. Specimen.	—	—	7.50

156 10,000,000,000 DINARA

1993. Blue and red. (Not issued.)

	VG	VF	UNC
	—	—	150.00

157 50,000,000,000 DINARA

1993. Brown. (Not issued.)

	VG	VF	UNC
	—	—	150.00

153 5,000,000 DINARA

1993. Orange and gray-blue on pale orange unpt.

	VG	VF	UNC
a. Issued note.	0.50	1.50	5.00
s. Specimen.	—	—	7.50

154 100,000,000 DINARA

1993. Dull grayish green and pale olive-brown on lt. blue unpt.

	VG	VF	UNC
a. Issued note.	0.50	1.50	5.00
s. Specimen.	—	—	7.50

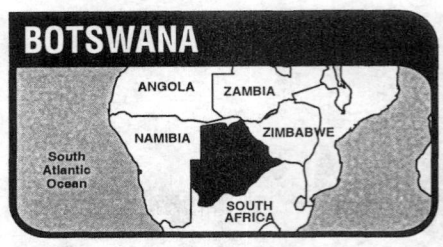

The Republic of Botswana (formerly Bechuanaland), located in south central Africa between Southwest Africa, (Namibia) and Zimbabwe has an area of 231,805 sq. km.) and a population of 1.62 million. Capital: Gaborone. Botswana is a member of a Customs Union with South Africa, Lesotho, and Swaziland. The economy is primarily pastoral with a rapidly developing mining industry, of which diamonds, copper and nickel are the chief elements. Meat products and diamonds comprise 85 percent of the exports.

Little is known of the origin of the peoples of Botswana. The early inhabitants, the Bushmen, did not develop a recorded history and are now dying out. The ancesters of the present Botswana probably arrived about 1600 AD in Bantu migrations from the north and east. Bechuanaland was first united early in the 19th century under Chief Khama III to more effectively resist incursions by the Boer trekkers from Transvaal and by the neighboring Matabeles. As the Boer threat intensified, appeals for protection were made to the British Government, which proclaimed the whole of Bechuanaland a British protectorate in 1885. In 1895, the southern part of the protectorate was annexed to Cape Province. The northern part, known as the Bechuanaland Protectorate, remained under British administration until it became the independent Republic of Botswana on Sept. 30, 1966. Botswana is a member of the Commonwealth of Nations. The president is Chief of State and Head of Government.

MONETARY SYSTEM:
1 Pula (Rand) = 100 Thebe (Cents)

	MINISTER OF FINANCE	GOVERNOR
1	Sir Q.K.J. Masire	Q. Hermans
2	Sir Q.K.J. Masire	B.C. Leavitt
3	P.S. Mmusi	F.G. Mogae
4	P.S. Mmusi	C. Kilonyogo
5	P.S. Mmusi	Q. Hermans
6a	F.G. Mogae	Q. Hermans
6b	F.G. Mogae	Q. Hermans
7a	P.H.K. Kedikilwe	B. Gaolatlhe
7b	P.H.K. Kedikilwe	B. Gaolatlhe
8a	B. Gaolatlhe	Mrs. L.K. Mohohlo
8b	B. Gaolatlhe	Mrs. L.K. Mohohlo

REPUBLIC

BANK OF BOTSWANA

1976-79 ND ISSUE

#1-5 Pres. Sir Seretse Khama at l., arms at upper r. Wmk: Rearing zebra. Printer: TDLR. Replacement notes: Serial # prefixes Z/1, X/1, Y/1 for 1, 10, and 20 respectively. For specimen notes with a maltese cross serial # prefix see the CS1 listing at the end of the country.

1	1 PULA		VG	VF	UNC
	ND (1976). Brown on m/c unpt. Bird at ctr. Farmer milking cow at ctr. r. on back.				
		a. Issued note.	0.60	1.75	6.00
		s. Specimen. Serial # prefix: A/1.	—	—	95.00

2	2 PULA		VG	VF	UNC
	ND (1976). Blue on m/c unpt. Bird at ctr. Various workers at ctr. r. on back.				
		a. Issued note.	FV	3.00	14.00
		s. Specimen. Serial # prefix: B/1.	—	—	95.00

3	5 PULA		VG	VF	UNC
	ND (1976). Purple on m/c unpt. Bird at ctr. Gemsbok antelope at ctr. r. on back.				
		a. Issued note.	FV	6.00	35.00
		s. Specimen. Serial # prefix: C/1.	—	—	90.00

4	10 PULA		VG	VF	UNC
	ND (1976). Green on m/c unpt. Bird at ctr. Lg. bldg. at ctr. r. on back.				
		a. Sign. 1.	7.50	30.00	150.00
		b. Sign. 2.	12.50	45.00	300.00
		s1. As a. Specimen. Serial # prefix: D/1.	—	—	95.00
		s2. As b. Specimen. Serial # prefix: D/4.	—	—	95.00

5 **20 PULA**
ND (1979). Red, purple and brown on m/c unpt. Bird at ctr. Mining
conveyors at ctr. r. on back.

		VG	VF	UNC
	a. Sign. 1.	15.00	50.00	300.00
	b. Sign. 2.	17.50	55.00	400.00
	s1. As a. Specimen. Serial # prefix *E/1*.	—	—	95.00
	s2. As b. Specimen. Serial # prefix *E/2*.	—	—	95.00

1982-83 ND Issue

#6-10 Pres. Q.K.J. Masire at l. wearing coarser pin-stripe suit. Printer: TDLR. Replacement notes: Serial #
prefix *Z/1, X/1, Y/1* for 1, 10 and 20 respectively.

6 **1 PULA**
ND (1983). Dk. brown. Cattle, arms and plants on back. Sign. 4.

		VG	VF	UNC
	a. Issued note.	FV	0.75	4.00
	s. Specimen. Serial # prefix: *A/1*.	—	—	70.00

#7-10 Pres. Q.K.J. Masire at l., arms at upper r. Wmk: Rearing zebra.

7 **2 PULA**
ND (1982). Blue on m/c unpt. Grey lourie at ctr. Various workers at
ctr. r. on back.

		VG	VF	UNC
	a. Sign. 3.	1.00	2.50	16.00
	b. Sign. 4.	FV	1.00	8.50
	c. Sign. 5.	FV	1.50	13.00
	d. Sign. 6a.	—	1.00	7.00
	s1. As a. Specimen. Serial # prefix *B/6*.	—	—	70.00
	s2. As b. Specimen. Serial # prefix *B/7*.	—	—	70.00
	s3. As c. Specimen. Serial # prefix *B/16*.	—	—	70.00
	s4. As d. Specimen. Serial # prefix *B/21*.	—	—	70.00

8 **5 PULA**
ND (1982). Deep violet on m/c unpt. Helmeted guinea fowl at ctr.
Gemsbok antelope at ctr. r. on back.

		VG	VF	UNC
	a. Sign. 3.	1.50	5.00	35.00
	b. Sign. 4.	FV	2.00	19.00
	c. Sign. 5.	FV	1.50	15.00
	s1. As a. Specimen. Serial # prefix *C/5*.	—	—	70.00
	s2. As b. Specimen. Serial # prefix *C/6*.	—	—	70.00
	s3. As c. Specimen. Serial # prefix *C/10*.	—	—	70.00

9 **10 PULA**
ND (1982). Green on m/c unpt. Crowned hornbill at ctr. Lg. bldg. at
ctr. r. on back.

		VG	VF	UNC
	a. Sign. 3.	2.50	10.00	50.00
	b. Sign. 4.	FV	3.50	28.50
	c. Sign. 5.	FV	4.00	35.00
	d. Sign. 6a.	FV	3.00	22.50
	s1. As a. Specimen. Serial # prefix: *D/7*.	—	—	70.00
	s2. As b. Specimen. Serial # prefix: *D/12*.	—	—	70.00
	s3. As c. Specimen. Serial # prefix: *D/21*.	—	—	70.00
	s4. As d. Specimen. Serial # prefix: *D/26*.	—	—	70.00

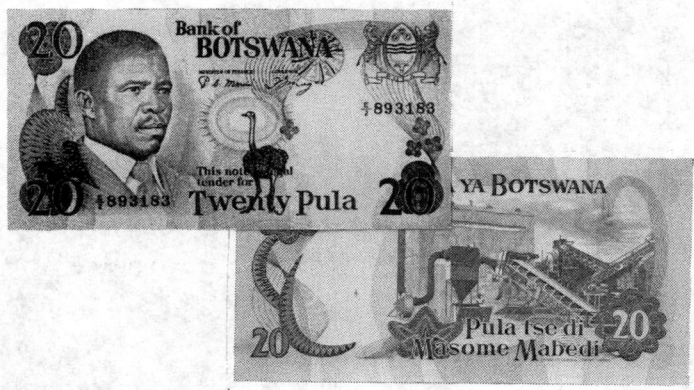

10 **20 PULA**
ND (1982). Red, purple and brown on m/c unpt. Ostrich at ctr.
Mining conveyors at ctr. r. on back.

		VG	VF	UNC
	a. Sign. 3.	6.00	17.50	70.00
	b. Sign. 4.	FV	7.50	58.00
	c. Sign. 5.	FV	8.50	60.00
	d. Sign. 6a.	FV	5.00	37.50
	s1. As a. Specimen. Serial # prefix: *E/2*.	—	—	70.00
	s2. As b. Specimen. Serial # prefix: *E/5*.	—	—	70.00
	s3. As c. Specimen. Serial # prefix: *E/9*.	—	—	70.00
	s4. As d. Specimen. Serial # prefix: *E/13*.	—	—	70.00

1992-95 ND Issue

#11-15 Pres. Q.K.J. Masire at l., arms at upper r. Wmk: Rearing zebra.

#11-13 printer: Harrison.

		VG	VF	UNC
11	**5 PULA** ND (1992). Deep violet on m/c unpt. Similar to #8; sm. stylistic differences. Sign. 6a.			
	a. Issued note.	FV	1.50	6.00
	s. Specimen. Serial # prefix C/18, C/19, C/27.	—	—	125.00
12	**10 PULA** ND (1992). Green on m/c unpt. Similar to #9; sm. stylistic differences. Sign. 6a.			
	a. Issued note.	FV	2.50	10.00
	s. Specimen. Serial # prefix: D/45, D/46.	—	—	135.00

		VG	VF	UNC
13	**20 PULA** ND (1993). Red, purple and brown on m/c unpt. Similar to #10; sm. stylistic differences. Sign. 6a.			
	a. Issued note.	FV	6.00	20.00
	s. Specimen. Serial # prefix: E/21, E/29.	—	—	150.00

		VG	VF	UNC
14	**50 PULA** ND (ca. 1992). Dk. brown and dk. green on m/c unpt. Malachite kingfisher at ctr. Man in canoe and African fish eagle at ctr. r. on back. W/o imprint. Sign. 6b. Printer: Fidelity Printers (Zimbabwe - Harare).			
	a. Issued note.	FV	15.00	65.00
	s1. Specimen. Serial # F000000A.	—	—	60.00
	s2. Specimen. Serial # F0000000A. Punch-hole cancelled.	—	—	60.00
15	**50 PULA** ND(1995). Similar to #14. Printer: TDLR.			
	a. Issued note.	FV	12.50	52.50
	s. Specimen. Serial # prefix: F...C. (suffix)	—	—	60.00

		VG	VF	UNC
16	**100 PULA** ND (1993). Blue-violet and ochre on m/c unpt. Diamond and fish eagle at ctr. Worker sorting rough diamonds at ctr. r. on back. Sign. 6. Printer: TDLR.			
	a. Issued note.	FV	FV	75.00
	b. Specimen. Serial # prefix: G/1, G/6.	—	—	60.00

1997 ND ISSUE

#17-19 President Q.K.J. Masire at l. wearing finer stripped pin suit, arms at upper r. Wmk: Rearing zebra. Printer as: ...RUE, LIMITED.

		VG	VF	UNC
17	**10 PULA** ND(1997). Similar to #12.			
	a. Issued note. Sign. 6a.	FV	3.00	17.50
	s. Specimen. Serial # prefix: D/54.	—	—	60.00
18	**20 PULA** ND(1997). Similar to #13.			
	a. Issued note. Sign. 6a.	FV	5.00	22.50
	s. Specimen. Serial # prefix: E/33.	—	—	60.00
19	**50 PULA** ND(1997). Similar to #14.			
	a. Issued note. Sign. 6b.	FV	12.50	42.50
	s. Specimen. Serial # prefix: F/13.	—	—	60.00

1999-2000 ND ISSUE

#20-23 Wmk: Rearing zebra.

		VG	VF	UNC
20	**10 PULA** ND(1999). Green on m/c unpt. Pres. F. Mogae at l., arms at upper r., Hornbill at ctr. Parliament on back. Printer: F-CO.			
	a. Sign. 7a.	FV	FV	11.00
	b. Sign 8a.	FV	FV	6.50
	s1. As a. Specimen. Serial # prefix D/62.	—	—	60.00
	s2. As b. Specimen. Serial # prefix D/72.	—	—	60.00

		VG	VF	UNC
21	**20 PULA** ND (1999). Red, purple and brown on m/c unpt. K. Motsete at l., arms at upper r. Ostrich ctr. Mining conveyors at ctr. r. on back. Printer: SABN.			
	a. Sign 7b.	FV	FV	16.00
	s1. As a. Specimen. Serial # prefix E/42.	—	—	60.00

25	20 PULA	VG	VF	UNC
	2002. Red, purple and brown on m/c unpt. Printer: DLR.			
	a. Sign 8b.	FV	FV	9.50
	s. As a. Specimen. Serial # prefix E/52.	—	—	60.00

2005 ND ISSUE

22	50 PULA	VG	VF	UNC
	ND (2000). Dk. brown and dk. green on m/c unpt. Sir Seretse Khama at l., malachite kingfisher at ctr., Arms on r. Optical variable ink star at r. Man in canoe and fish eagle at ctr. r. on back. Printer: F-CO.			
	a. Sign. 8a.	FV	FV	22.50
	s. As a. Specimen. Serial # prefix F/18.	—	—	60.00

26	100 PULA	VG	VF	UNC
	ND. Like #23a but w/circular Kinegram added at lower r.	FV	FV	52.50

COLLECTOR SERIES

BANK OF BOTSWANA

1979 ND ISSUE

23	100 PULA	VG	VF	UNC
	ND (2000). Blue-violet and ochre on m/c unpt. Three chiefs: Sebeli I, Bathoen I and Khama III at l., fisheagle at ctr., arms and optical variable ink diamond at r. Worker sorting rough diamonds at ctr. on back. Printer: F-CO.			
	a. Sign. 8a.	FV	FV	52.50
	s. As a. Specimen. Serial # prefix G/11.	—	—	60.00

2002 ND ISSUE

#24-25 wide security thread added.

CS1	ND (1979) 1-20 PULA	Issue Price	Mkt.	Value
	#1-3, 4a, 5a. Ovpt: *SPECIMEN* and Maltese cross serial # prefix.	14.00		40.00

24	10 PULA	VG	VF	UNC
	2002. Green on m/c unpt. Printer: DLR.			
	a. Sign. 8b.	FV	FV	6.50
	s. As a. Specimen. Serial # prefix D/82.	—	—	60.00

BRAZIL

The Federative Republic of Brazil, which comprises half the continent of South America, is the only Latin American country deriving its culture and language from Portugal. It has an area of 3,286,470 sq. mi. (8,511,965 sq. km.) and a population of 169.2 million. Capital: Brasília. The economy of Brazil is as varied and complex as any in the developing world. Agriculture is a mainstay of the economy, although but 4 percent of the area is under cultivation. Known mineral resources are almost unlimited in variety and size of reserves. A large, relatively sophisticated industry ranges from basic steel and chemical production to finished consumer goods. Coffee, cotton, iron ore and cocoa are the chief exports.

Brazil was discovered and claimed for Portugal by Admiral Pedro Alvares Cabral in 1500. Portugal established a settlement in 1532 and proclaimed the area a royal colony in 1549. During the Napoleonic Wars, Dom João VI established the seat of Portuguese government in Rio de Janeiro. When he returned to Portugal, his son Dom Pedro I declared Brazil's independence on Sept. 7, 1822, and became emperor of Brazil. The Empire of Brazil was maintained until 1889 when a republic was established. The Federative Republic was established in 1946 by terms of a constitution drawn up by a constituent assembly. Following a coup in 1964, the armed forces retained overall control under dictatorship until a civilian government was restored on March 15, 1985. The current constitution was adopted in 1988.

MONETARY SYSTEM:
- 1 Cruzeiro = 100 Centavos, 1942-1967
- 1 Cruzeiro Novo = 1000 Old Cruzeiros, 1966-1985
- 1 Cruzado = 1000 Cruzeiros Novos, 1986-1989
- 1 Cruzado Novo = 1000 Cruzados, 1989-1990
- 1 Cruzeiro = 1 Cruzado Novo, 1990-1993
- 1 Cruzeiro Real (pl. Reais) = 1000 Cruzeiros, 1993-1994
- 1 Real (pl. Reais) = 100 Centavos, 1994-

SIGNATURE VARIETIES

8	Sebastião P. Almeida	Carlos Augusto Camilho
9	Clemente Mariani	Carlos A. Carrílho
10	Walter M. Salles	Reginaldo F. Nunes
11	Reginaldo F. Nunes, 1962	Walter M. Salles
12	Reginaldo F. Nunes, 1963	Miguel Calmon
13	Reginaldo F. Nunes, 1964	Otávio Gouvex Bulhões
14	Sérgio A. Ribeiro, 1964-66	Otávio Gouvex Bulhões
15	Dénio Nogueira, 1966-67	Otávio Gouvex Bulhões
16	Ruy Leme, 1967	Antônio Delfim Netto

SIGNATURE VARIETIES

17	Ername Galveas, 1967-72	Antônio Delfim Netto
18	Mário Henrique Simonsen, 1974-79	Paulo H.P. Lira
19	Karlos Rischbieter, 1979-80	Ernane Galvêas
20	Ernane Galvêas, 1980-81	Carlos P. Langoni
21	Ernane Galvêas, 1983-85	Alfonso C. Pastore
22	Francisco Dornélles, 1985	Antonio Lengruber
23	Dilson Funaro, 1985-86	Fernao C.B. Bracher
24	Dilson Funaro, 1987	Francisco Gross
25	Luiz Carlos Bresser Pereira, 1987	Fernando M. Oliveira
26	Maílson Ferreira Da Nóbrega, 1988-89	Elmo Camões
27	Maílson Ferreira Da Nóbrega, 1989-90	Wadico Bucchi
28	Zélia Cardoso De Mello, 1990	Ibrahim Éris
29	Marcílio M. Moreira, 1991-92	Francisco Gross
30	Paulo R. Haddad, 1993	Gustavo Loyola
31	Elizeu Resende, 1993	Paulo Ximenes
32	Fernando H. Cardoso, 1993	Paulo Ximenes
33	Fernando H. Cardoso, 1993-94	Pedro Malan

SIGNATURE VARIETIES

34	Rubens Ricúpero, 1994	Pedro Malan
35	Ciro Gomes, 1994	Pedro Malan
36	Pedro Malan, 1995	Pérsio Arida
37	Pedro Malan, 1995-97	Gustavo Loyola
38	Pedro Malan, 1998	Gustavo Franco
39	Pedro Malan, 1999-	Arminia Fraganeto
40	Antonio Palocci Filho, 2003-	Henrique De Campos Meirelles

REPUBLIC

TESOURO NACIONAL, VALOR RECEBIDO

ESTAMPA 3; 1961 ND ISSUE

166	5 CRUZEIROS		VG	VF	UNC
	ND (1961-62). Dk. brown and brown. Raft w/sail at l., male Indian at r. Flower on back. Printer: CdM-B.				
	a. Sign. 8. Series #1-75.		0.10	0.50	2.00
	b. Sign. 10. Series #76-111.		0.10	0.25	1.25

TESOURO NACIONAL, VALOR LEGAL

ESTAMPA 1A; 1961 ND ISSUE

#167-173 dk. blue on m/c unpt. 2 printed sign. Printer: ABNC.

167	10 CRUZEIROS		VG	VF	UNC
	ND (1961-63). Portr. G. Vargas at ctr. Back green; allegory of "Industry" at ctr.				
	a. Sign. 9. Series #331-630. (1961).		0.15	0.50	2.00
	b. Sign. 12. Series #631-930. (1963).		0.15	0.50	1.75
	s. As a or b. Specimen.		—	—	110.00

168	20 CRUZEIROS		VG	VF	UNC
	ND (1961-63). Portr. D. da Fonseca at ctr. Back red; allegory of "the Republic" at ctr.				
	a. Sign. 9. Series #461-960. (1961).		0.15	0.50	2.25
	b. Sign. 12. Series #961-1260. (1963).		0.15	0.50	2.00
	s. As a or b. Specimen.		—	—	115.00

169	50 CRUZEIROS		VG	VF	UNC
	ND (1961). Portr. Princess Isabel at ctr. Back purple; allegory of "Law" at ctr. Sign. 9. Series #721-1220.				
	a. Issued note.		0.15	1.50	7.50
	s. Specimen.		—	—	115.00

170	100 CRUZEIROS		VG	VF	UNC
	ND (1961-64). Portr. D. Pedro at ctr. Back red-brown; allegory of "National Culture" at ctr.				
	a. Sign. 9. Series #761-1160. (1961).		0.25	2.25	9.00
	b. Sign. 13. Series #1161-1360. (1964).		0.25	1.00	4.50
	c. Sign. 14. Series #1361-1560. (1964).		0.25	2.00	8.00
	s. As a, b or c. Specimen.		—	—	125.00

171	200 CRUZEIROS	VG	VF	UNC
	ND (1961-64). Portr. D. Pedro at ctr. Back olive-green; battle scene at ctr.			
	a. Sign. 9. Series #671-1070. (1961).	0.50	3.50	15.00
	b. Sign. 13. Series #1071-1370. (1964).	0.50	3.00	12.00
	c. Sign. 14. Series #1371-1570. (1964).	0.50	3.00	12.00
	s. As a, b or c. Specimen.	—	—	125.00

172	500 CRUZEIROS	VG	VF	UNC
	ND (1961-62). Portr. D. Joao VI at ctr. Back blue-black; allegory of "Maritime Industry" at ctr.			
	a. Sign. 9. Series #261-660. (1961).	1.00	5.00	25.00
	b. Sign. 11. Series #661-1460. (1962).	0.75	4.00	20.00
	s. As a, b. Specimen.	—	—	125.00
173	1000 CRUZEIROS			
	ND (1961-63). Portr. P. Alvares Cabral at ctr. Back orange; scene of the "First Mass" at ctr.			
	a. Sign. 9. Series #1331-1730. (1961).	0.75	8.00	50.00
	b. Sign. 11. Series #1731-3030. (1962).	0.75	6.00	40.00
	c. Sign. 12. Series #3031-3830. (1963).	1.00	7.00	45.00
	s. As a, b or c. Specimen.	—	—	135.00

174	5000 CRUZEIROS	VG	VF	UNC
	ND (1963-64). Blue-gray on m/c unpt. Portr. Tiradentes at r. Back red; Tiradentes in historical scene at ctr. Printer: ABNC.			
	a. Sign. 12. Series #1-400. (1963).	1.00	5.00	35.00
	b. Sign. 13. Series #401-1400. (1964).	1.00	4.50	30.00
	c. Sign. 14. Series #1401-1650. (1965).	1.75	8.00	50.00
	s. As a, b or c. Specimen.	—	—	150.00

ESTAMPA 2A; 1962-63 ND ISSUE

#175 *Deleted, see #182B.*

#176-182 2 printed sign. Printer: TDLR.

176	5 CRUZEIROS	VG	VF	UNC
	ND (1962-64). Brown on m/c unpt. Portr. Barao do Rio Branco at ctr.			
	a. Sign. 11. Series #2301-3500. (1962).	0.10	0.25	1.00
	b. Sign. 12. Series #3501-3700. (1963).	0.10	0.25	2.50
	c. Sign. 13. Series #3701-3748; 4149-4180; 4201-4232. (1964).	0.10	0.25	5.00
	d. Sign. 14. Series #3749-4148; 4181-4200; 4233-4700. (1964).	0.10	0.25	0.75
177	10 CRUZEIROS			
	ND (1962). Green on m/c unpt. Like #167.			
	a. Sign. 10. Series #2365-3055.	0.10	0.25	1.50
	b. Sign. 11. Series 2394A.	0.10	0.25	1.50

178	20 CRUZEIROS	VG	VF	UNC
	ND (1962). Red-brown on m/c unpt. Like #168. Sign. 11. Series #1576-2275.	0.15	0.50	2.25

179	50 CRUZEIROS	VG	VF	UNC
	ND (1963.) Purple on m/c unpt. Like #169. Sign. 12. Series #586-785.	0.25	1.00	4.00
180	100 CRUZEIROS			
	ND (1963). Red on m/c unpt. Like #170. Sign. 12. Series #216-415.	0.25	2.00	9.00

181	1000 CRUZEIROS	VG	VF	UNC
	ND (1963). Orange on m/c unpt. Like #173. Sign. 12. Series #791-1590.	0.50	3.00	15.00

182	5000 CRUZEIROS	VG	VF	UNC
	ND (1963-64). Red on m/c unpt. Like #174. Sign. at l. w/*Director Caixa de Amortizacao.*			
	a. Sign. 12. Series #1-400. (1963).	1.00	4.50	30.00
	b. Sign. 13. Series #401-1400. (1964).	0.75	4.00	25.00
	c. Sign. 14. Series #1401-1700. (1964).	1.50	6.00	40.00

BANCO CENTRAL DO BRASIL
1965; 1966 ND ISSUE

182A 5000 CRUZEIROS
ND (1965). Red on m/c unpt. Like #174. Sign. D. Nogueira w/title: *Presidente do Banco Central* and O. Gouvea de Bulhões. Sign 15. Series #1701-2200.

	VG	VF	UNC
	1.00	5.00	35.00

182B 10,000 CRUZEIROS
ND (1966). Gray on m/c unpt. Portr. S. Dumont at r. Back blue; early airplane at r. Sign. 15. Printer: ABNC.

	VG	VF	UNC
a. Series #1-493.	4.00	17.50	70.00
b. Series #561-590.	45.00	175.00	350.00
s. As a. Specimen.	—	—	175.00

1966; 1967 ND PROVISIONAL ISSUE

Feb. 1967 Monetary Reform: 1 Cruzeiro Novo = 1,000 Cruzeiros

#183-190 black circular ovpt: *BANCO CENTRAL* and new currency unit in black circle on Tesouro Nacional notes.

183 1 CENTAVO ON 10 CRUZEIROS
ND (1966-67). Green on m/c unpt. Ovpt. on #177. Sign. 15.

	VG	VF	UNC
a. Error: *Minstro* below r. sign. (2 types of 1 in ovpt.) (1966). Series #3056-3151.	0.10	0.20	1.00
b. *Ministro* below r. sign. (1967). Series #3152-4055.	0.10	0.20	1.00
s. As b. Specimen ovpt: *MODELO*.	—	—	—

184 5 CENTAVOS ON 50 CRUZEIROS
ND (1966-67). Purple on m/c unpt. Ovpt. on #179. Sign. 15.

	VG	VF	UNC
a. Type of #183a. Series #786-1313.	0.10	0.25	1.50
b. Type of #183b. Series #1314-1885.	0.10	0.25	1.50

185 10 CENTAVOS ON 100 CRUZEIROS
ND (1966-67). Red on m/c unpt. Ovpt. on #180. Sign. 15.

	VG	VF	UNC
a. Type of #183a. Series #416-911.	0.10	0.25	2.00
b. Type of #183b. Series #912-1515.	0.10	0.25	1.75

186 50 CENTAVOS ON 500 CRUZEIROS
ND (1967). Blue on m/c unpt. Ovpt. on #172. Sign. 15. Series #1461-2360.

	VG	VF	UNC
a. Issued note.	0.75	2.00	4.50
s. Specimen.	—	—	100.00

187 1 CRUZEIRO NOVO ON 1000 CRUZEIROS
ND (1966-67). Blue on m/c unpt. Ovpt. on #173.

	VG	VF	UNC
a. Sign. 14. Series #3831-3930.	2.00	7.50	22.50
b. Sign. 15. Series #3931-4830.	1.50	2.50	7.50
s. As b. Specimen.	—	—	115.00

188 5 CRUZEIROS NOVOS ON 5000 CRUZEIROS
ND (1966-67). Blue-green on m/c unpt. Ovpt. on #174.

	VG	VF	UNC
a. Sign. 14. Series #1651-1700.	10.00	30.00	60.00
b. Sign. 15. Series #1701-2900.	2.00	8.00	22.50
s. As b. Specimen.	—	—	115.00

189 10 CRUZEIROS NOVOS ON 10,000 CRUZEIROS
ND (1966-67). Gray on m/c unpt. Bold or semi-bold ovpt. on #182B. Printer: ABNC.

	VG	VF	UNC
a. Sign. 15. Series #494-560 and 591-700. (1966).	2.50	25.00	85.00
b. Sign. 16. Series #701-1700. (1967).	1.00	6.00	25.00
c. Sign. 17. Series #1701-2700. (1967).	1.00	5.00	20.00
s. As b. Specimen.	—	—	150.00

190 10 CRUZEIROS NOVOS ON 10,000 CRUZEIROS
ND (1967). Brown on pink and m/c unpt. Like #182B. Printer: TDLR.

	VG	VF	UNC
a. Sign. 16. Series #1-1000.	1.00	3.50	15.00
b. Sign. 17. Series #1001-2100.	0.75	2.25	10.00

1970 ND ISSUES

#191-195 portr. as wmk. Sign. varieties. 5 digit series # above serial #.

#191-194, 195A printer: CdM-B.

191   1 CRUZEIRO

		VG	VF	UNC
ND (1970-72). Dk. green and blue on ochre and green unpt. w/medallic Liberty head at r. in brown. Banco Central bldg. at l. on back. Series # prefix A. Sign. 17.				
a. Series #1-3000.		0.20	0.50	2.00
s. Specimen. Ovpt: *MODELO*.		—	—	25.00

191A   1 CRUZEIRO

		VG	VF	UNC
ND (1972-80). Dk. green and blue w/medallic Liberty head in green. Series # prefix B.				
a. Sign. 17. Series #1-3781 (1972).		0.10	0.25	1.00
b. Sign. 18. Series #3782-13194 (1975).		0.05	0.15	0.75
c. Sign. 20. Series #13195-18094 (1980).		0.05	0.10	0.50
s. As a. Specimen ovpt. and perforated: *MODELO*.		—	—	25.00

192   5 CRUZEIROS

		VG	VF	UNC
ND (1970-80). Blue on orange and green unpt. Portr. D. Pedro I at r. Back maroon; parade square at l.				
a. Back darkly printed. Sign. 17. Series # prefix A. Series #1-107 (1970-71).		0.25	5.00	20.00
b. Back lightly printed. Sign. 17. Series # prefix B. Series #1-2467 (1973).		0.10	0.25	1.25
c. Sign. 18. Series #2468-6050 (1974).		0.10	0.25	1.50
d. Sign. 19. Series #6051-6841 (1979).		0.10	0.25	2.00
s. As a. Specimen ovpt: *SEM VALOR*, perforated: *MODELO*.		—	—	25.00

193   10 CRUZEIROS

		VG	VF	UNC
ND (1970-80). Grayish purple and dk. brown on orange-brown blue-green and m/c unpt. Portr. D. Pedro II at r. Back green, violet and brown; statue of the Prophet Daniel.				
a. Back darkly printed. Sign. 17. Series # prefix A. Series #1-1429 (1970).		0.50	2.50	15.00
b. As a. Sign. 18. Series #1430-7745 (1974).		0.15	0.50	1.75
c. Back lightly printed. Sign. 18. Series # prefix B. Series #1-2394 (1979).		0.25	1.00	5.00
d. As c. Sign. 19. Series #2395-2870 (1980).		0.15	0.50	2.50
e. As d. Sign. 20. Series #2871-5131 (1980).		0.10	0.50	2.00
s. Specimen.		—	—	25.00

194   50 CRUZEIROS

		VG	VF	UNC
ND (1970-81). Black, purple, blue-black and violet on lilac and m/c unpt. Portr. D. da Fonseca at r. Back brown, lilac and blue; coffee loading at l.				
a. Sign. 17. Series #1-1250 (1970).		1.00	3.00	20.00
b. Sign. 18. Series #1251-3841 (1974).		0.20	0.50	3.00
c. Sign. 20. Series #3842-5233 (1980).		0.15	0.50	2.50
s. Specimen.		—	—	25.00

195   100 CRUZEIROS

		VG	VF	UNC
ND (1970-81). Purple and violet on pink and m/c unpt. Portr. Marshal F. Peixoto at r. Back blue, brown and violet; National Congress at l. Printer: TDLR. Sign. 17 (w/imprint CdM-B). Series #1-01358.				
a. Issued note.		1.50	6.00	35.00
s. Specimen.		—	—	—

195A	100 CRUZEIROS	VG	VF	UNC
	ND (1974-81). Purple and violet on pink and m/c unpt. Like #195. Printer: CdM-B.			
	a. Sign. 18. Series #01359-10455 (1974).	0.25	0.75	6.00
	b. Sign. 20. Series #10456-12681 (1981).	0.25	0.75	6.00
	s. Specimen.	—	—	25.00

Note: The difference between #195 and 195A is in the wmk.

1972 COMMEMORATIVE ISSUE

#196, 196A, 150th Anniversary of Brazilian Independence

196	500 CRUZEIROS	VG	VF	UNC
	1972 (1972-74). Dk. olive-green and brown on violet and m/c unpt. Portr. of 5 men of differing racial groups. Wmk: Dates *1822 1972* in clear area at l. 5 different historical maps of Brazil on back. Printer: CdM-B.			
	a. Sign. 17. Series # prefix A. #1-90 (1972).	35.00	100.00	300.00
	b. As a. Sign. 18. Series #91-2636 (1974).	1.00	5.00	35.00
	s1. Specimen. Sign. 17. Ovpt: *MODELO*.	—	—	70.00
	s2. Specimen. Sign. 18. Ovpt: *MODELO*.	—	—	50.00

196A	500 CRUZEIROS	VG	VF	UNC
	1972 (1979-80). Like #196 but wmk. area has vertical lines printed on face and back.			
	a. Sign. 18. Series # prefix B. #1-1401 (1979).	1.00	4.00	25.00
	b. As a. Sign. 19. Series #1402-1959 (1979).	1.00	4.00	25.00
	c. As a. Sign. 20. Series #1960-2763 (1980).	1.00	4.00	25.00
	s. Specimen.	—	—	50.00

1978 ND ISSUE

#197, the first 4 digits of the serial # represent the series #.

197	1000 CRUZEIROS	VG	VF	UNC
	ND (1978-80). Green and brown. Double portr. B. do Rio Branco and as wmk. *BANCO CENTRAL DO BRASIL* in 2 lines. Double view of machinery on back. Also, small plate modification on back.			
	a. Sign. 18. Series #1-665 (1978).	1.50	8.00	50.00
	b. Sign. 19. Series #666-2072 (1979).	1.75	6.00	32.50
	c. Sign. 20. Series #2073-3297 (1980).	0.75	6.00	35.00

1981-85 ND ISSUE

#198-205 portr. as wmk. Sign. varieties. Printer: CdM-B. The first 4 digits of the serial # represent the series #.

#198-202 double portr. and vignettes.

198	100 CRUZEIROS	VG	VF	UNC
	ND (1981-84). Red and purple on m/c unpt. D. de Caxias at ctr. Back gray-blue and red; battle scene and sword at ctr.			
	a. Sign. 20. Series #1-4081 (1981).	0.05	0.15	0.50
	b. Sign. 21. Series #4082-8176 (1984).	0.05	0.15	0.50

199	200 CRUZEIROS	VG	VF	UNC
	ND (1981-84). Green and violet on m/c unpt. Princess Isabel at ctr. Back brown and green; 2 women cooking outdoors.			
	a. Sign. 20. Series #1-2996 (1981).	0.05	0.15	0.50
	b. Sign. 21. Series #2997-4960 (1984).	0.05	0.15	0.50

200 500 CRUZEIROS
ND (1981-85). Blue and brown on m/c unpt. D. da Fonseca at ctr.
Back pink, brown and purple; group of legislators.

	VG	VF	UNC
a. Sign. 20. Series #1-3510 (1981).	0.05	0.20	1.00
b. Sign. 21. Series #3511-4238 (1985).	0.05	0.15	0.75

201 1000 CRUZEIROS
ND (1981-86). Brown and dk. olive on m/c unpt. Similar to #197,
but bank name in 1 line. Back tan and blue.

	VG	VF	UNC
a. Sign. 20. Series # prefix A, #1-5733 (1981).	0.10	0.50	2.50
b. As a. Sign. 21. Series #5734-7019 (1984).	0.05	0.15	0.75
c. As b. Sign. 22. Series #7020-9999 (1985).	0.05	0.15	0.75
d. Sign. 22. Series # prefix B, #1-788 (1986).	0.05	0.15	0.75

202 5000 CRUZEIROS
ND (1981-85). Purple and brown on m/c unpt. C. Branco at ctr.
Back brown, purple and blue; antennas.

	VG	VF	UNC
a. Sign. 20. Series # prefix A, #1-9205 (1981).	0.15	0.75	6.50
b. As a. Sign. 21. Series #9206-9999 (1983).	0.10	0.25	1.50
c. Sign. 21. Series # prefix B, #1-2118 (1984).	0.10	0.25	1.00
d. As c. Sign. 22. Series #2119-2342 (1985).	0.25	0.50	2.00

203 10,000 CRUZEIROS
ND (1984-85). Brown on m/c unpt. Desk top at ctr., Rui Barbosa at
ctr. r. Conference scene on back.

	VG	VF	UNC
a. Sign. 21. Series #1-3619 (1984).	0.25	1.25	4.50
b. Sign. 22. Series #3620-3696 (1985).	0.75	4.00	22.50

204 50,000 CRUZEIROS
ND (1984-86). Purple on m/c unpt. Microscope at ctr., O. Cruz at r.
Cruz Institute at ctr. on back.

	VG	VF	UNC
a. Sign. 21. Series #1-1673 (1984).	0.50	3.75	20.00
b. Sign. 22 (reversed). Series #1674-2170 (1985).	1.00	5.00	15.00
c. Sign. 22 (corrected). Series #2171-3248 (1985).	0.25	1.75	7.00
d. Sign. 23. Series #3249-3290 (1986).	0.50	2.00	12.50

205 100,000 CRUZEIROS
ND (1985). Black on blue, gold and m/c unpt. Electric power station
at ctr., Pres. J. Kubitschek at r. Old and modern bldgs. at ctr. on
back. Sign. 23. Series #1-4347.

VG	VF	UNC
0.50	2.50	5.50

1986 ND PROVISIONAL ISSUE

Feb. 1986 Monetary Reform: 1 Cruzado = 1,000 Cruzeiros

#206-208 black circular ovpt: *Banco Central Do Brasil* and new currency unit on #203-205.

		VG	VF	UNC
206	**10 CRUZADOS ON 10,000 CRUZEIROS**			
	ND (1986). Ovpt. on #203. Sign. 23. Series #3697-5124.	0.10	0.20	1.50

		VG	VF	UNC
207	**50 CRUZADOS ON 50,000 CRUZEIROS**			
	ND (1986). Ovpt. on #204. Sign. 23. Series #3291-4592.	0.20	0.75	2.50

		VG	VF	UNC
208	**100 CRUZADOS ON 100,000 CRUZEIROS**			
	ND (1986). Ovpt. on #205. Sign. 23. Series #4348-6209.	0.20	0.75	5.00

1986 ND ISSUE

#209-211 printer: CdM-B.

		VG	VF	UNC
209	**10 CRUZADOS**			
	ND (1986-87). Similar to #203 except for denomination.			
	a. Sign. 23. Series #1-1155 (1986).	0.05	0.20	1.00
	b. Sign. 25. Series #1156-1505 (1987).	0.05	0.15	0.50

		VG	VF	UNC
210	**50 CRUZADOS**			
	ND (1986-88). Similar to #204 except for denomination.			
	a. Sign. 23. Series #1-1617 (1986).	0.05	0.20	0.75
	b. Sign. 25. Series #1618-2044 (1987).	0.05	0.20	0.75
	c. Sign. 26. Series #2045-2051 (1988).	2.50	15.00	100.00

		VG	VF	UNC
211	**100 CRUZADOS**			
	ND (1986-88). Similar to #205 except for denomination.			
	a. Sign. 23. Series #1-1176 (1986).	0.10	0.40	2.00
	b. Sign. 24. Series #1177-1582 (1987).	0.10	0.40	2.00
	c. Sign. 25. Series #1583-3045 (1987).	0.05	0.15	0.50
	d. Sign. 26. Series #3046-3059 (1988).	0.50	3.00	17.50

1986 ND COMMEMORATIVE ISSUE

#212, Birth Centennial of H. Villa-Lobos

		VG	VF	UNC
212	**500 CRUZADOS**			
	ND (1986). Blue-green on green and m/c unpt. H. Villa-Lobos at ctr. r. and as wmk. Villa-Lobos conducting at l. ctr. on back. Printer: CdM-B.			
	a. Sign. 23. Series #1-2352 (1986).	0.10	0.50	3.00
	b. Sign. 24. Series #2353-2842 (1987).	0.10	0.50	2.50
	c. Sign. 25. Series #2843-7504 (1987).	0.05	0.15	0.50
	d. Sign. 26. Series #7505-8309 (1988).	0.05	0.20	1.00

1987 ND REGULAR ISSUE

#213-215 portr. as wmk. Printer: CdM-B. Series # are first 4 digits of serial #.

213	1000 CRUZADOS	VG	VF	UNC
	ND (1987-88). Purple and brown-violet on m/c unpt. J. Machado at r. Street scene from old Rio de Janeiro on back.			
	a. Sign. 25. Series #1-2744 (1987).	0.20	1.00	6.00
	b. Sign. 26. Series #2745-9919 (1988)	0.05	0.15	0.75

214	5000 CRUZADOS	VG	VF	UNC
	ND (1988). Blue on m/c unpt. Portion of mural at l. ctr., C. Portinari at r. C. Portinari painting at ctr. on back. Sign. 26. Series #1-1757.	0.25	1.00	4.00

215	10,000 CRUZADOS	VG	VF	UNC
	ND (1989). Red and brown on m/c unpt. C. Chagas at r. Chagas w/lab instruments on back. Sign. 26. Series #1-1841.	0.25	1.00	7.00

1989 ND PROVISIONAL ISSUE

Jan. 1989 Monetary Reform: 1 Cruzado Novo = 1,000 Cruzados

#216-218 black triangular ovpt. of new currency unit on #213-215.

216	1 CRUZADO NOVO ON 1000 CRUZADOS	VG	VF	UNC
	ND (1989). Purple and brown-violet on m/c unpt. Ovpt. on #213.			
	a. Sign. 26. Series # prefix A, #9920-9999 (1989).	0.10	0.50	2.00
	b. Sign. 26. Series # prefix B, #1-1617 (1989).	0.10	0.15	0.50
	c. As b. Sign. 27. Series #1618-1792 (1989).	0.10	0.25	1.25

217	5 CRUZADOS NOVOS ON 5000 CRUZADOS	VG	VF	UNC
	ND (1989). Blue on m/c unpt. Ovpt. on #214.			
	a. Sign. 26. Series #1758-3531 (1989).	0.10	0.50	1.75
	b. Sign. 27. Series #3532-3818 (1989).	0.10	0.50	1.75

218	10 CRUZADOS NOVOS ON 10,000 CRUZADOS	VG	VF	UNC
	ND (1989-90). Red and brown on m/c unpt. Ovpt. on #215.			
	a. Sign. 26. Series #1842-4171 (1989).	0.10	0.25	1.50
	b. Sign. 27. Series #4172-4502 (1990).	0.10	0.50	2.50

1989 ND ISSUE

#219 and 220 printer: CdM-B. Wmk: Liberty head.

219	50 CRUZADOS NOVOS	VG	VF	UNC
	ND (1989-90). Brown and black on m/c unpt. C. Drummond de Andrade at r. Back black, red-brown and blue; de Andrade writing poetry.			
	a. Sign. 26. Series #1-3340 (1989).	0.10	0.25	1.50
	b. Sign. 27. Series #3341-3358 (1990).	0.25	2.00	15.00

220	100 CRUZADOS NOVOS	VG	VF	UNC
	ND (1989). Orange, purple and green on m/c unpt. C. Meireles at r. Back brown, black and m/c; child reading and people dancing.			
	a. Sign. 26. Series #1-6772.	0.15	0.75	1.50
	b. Sign. 27. Series #6773-8794.	0.20	1.00	5.00

1989 ND COMMEMORATIVE ISSUE

#221, Centenary of the Republic

221	200 CRUZADOS NOVOS	VG	VF	UNC
	ND (1989). Blue and black on m/c unpt. Political leaders at ctr., sculpture of the Republic at ctr. r., arms at r. Oil painting "Patria" by P. Bruno w/flag being embroidered by a family on back. Wmk: Liberty head. Printer: CdM-B. Sign. 27. Series #1	0.20	1.00	5.00

1990 ND ISSUE

222	500 CRUZADOS NOVOS	VG	VF	UNC
	ND (1990). Green and purple on m/c unpt. Orchids at ctr., A. Ruschi at r. Back lt. orange, purple and blue; swalow-tailed hummingbird, orchids and A. Ruschi at ctr. Wmk: Liberty head. Sign. 27. Series #1-3700.	0.75	2.00	7.50

1990 ND PROVISIONAL ISSUE

March 1990 Monetary Reform: 1 Cruzeiro = 1 Cruzado Novo

#223-226 black rectangular ovpt. of new currency unit on #219-222. Sign. 27.

223	50 CRUZEIROS ON 50 CRUZADOS NOVOS	VG	VF	UNC
	ND (1990). Brown and black on m/c unpt. Ovpt. on #219. Series #3359-5338.	0.10	0.15	0.50

224	100 CRUZEIROS ON 100 CRUZADOS NOVOS	VG	VF	UNC
	ND (1990). Orange, purple and green on m/c unpt. Ovpt. on #220.			
	a. Series #8601.	10.00	50.00	140.00
	b. Series #8795-9447.	0.10	0.40	1.50

225	200 CRUZEIROS ON 200 CRUZADOS NOVOS	VG	VF	UNC
	ND (1990). Blue and black on m/c unpt. Ovpt. on #221.			
	a. Series #1725.	20.00	75.00	175.00
	b. Series #1965-2668.	0.10	0.50	1.00

226	500 CRUZEIROS ON 500 CRUZADOS NOVOS	VG	VF	UNC
	ND (1990). Green and purple on m/c unpt. Ovpt. on #222.			
	a. Series #3111.	10.00	35.00	100.00
	b. Series #3701-7700.	0.10	0.25	0.75

1992 ND EMERGENCY ISSUE

227	5000 CRUZEIROS	VG	VF	UNC
	ND (1990). Deep olive-green and deep brown on m/c unpt. Liberty head in green at r. and as wmk. Arms at l. on back. Printer: CdM-B. Provisional type. Sign. 28. Series #1-1520.	0.20	0.75	2.00

1990-93 ND REGULAR ISSUE

#228-236 printer: CdM-B.

#228-231 similar to #220-223 but w/new currency unit and new sign. titles.

228	100 CRUZEIROS	VG	VF	UNC
	ND (1990). Like #220. Sign. 28. Series #1-1045.	0.10	0.20	0.50

229   200 CRUZEIROS
ND (1990). Like #221. Sign. 28. Series #1-1646.

	VG	VF	UNC
	0.05	0.15	0.50

230   500 CRUZEIROS
ND (1990). Like #222. Sign. 28. Series #1-0210.

	VG	VF	UNC
	0.30	0.75	3.00

231   1000 CRUZEIROS
ND (1990-91). Dk. brown, brown, violet and black on m/c unpt. C. Rondon at r., native hut at ctr., map of Brazil in background. 2 Indian children and local food from Amazonia on back. Wmk: Liberty head.

	VG	VF	UNC
a. Sign. 28. Upper sign. title: *MINISTRO DA ECONOMIA,*... Series #1-4268 (1990).	0.10	0.40	2.50
b. Upper sign. title: *MINISTRA DA ECONOMIA,*... Series #4269-6796 (1990).	0.10	0.30	2.00
c. Sign. 29. Series #6797-8453 (1991).	0.05	0.15	0.50

232   5000 CRUZEIROS
ND (1990-93). Blue-black, black, and deep brown on lt. blue and m/c unpt. C. Gomes at ctr. r., Brazilian youths at ctr. Statue of Gomes seated, grand piano in background at ctr. on back.

	VG	VF	UNC
a. Sign. 28. Series #1-4489 (1990).	0.10	0.50	2.00
b. Sign. 29. Series #4490-5501 (1992).	0.10	0.25	1.50
c. Sign. 30. Series #5502-6041 (1993).	0.10	0.20	1.00

233   10,000 CRUZEIROS
ND (1991-93). Black and brown-violet on m/c unpt. V. Brazil at r. and as wmk. Extracting poisonous venom at ctr. One snake swallowing another at ctr. on back.

	VG	VF	UNC
a. Sign. 28. Series #1-3136 (1991).	0.10	0.50	3.00
b. Sign. 29. Series #3137-6937 (1992).	0.10	0.25	1.25
c. Sign. 30. Series #6938-7365 (1993).	0.05	0.15	1.00

234   50,000 CRUZEIROS
ND (1992). Dk. brown and red-orange on m/c unpt. C. Cascudo at ctr. r. and as wmk. 2 men on raft in background at l. ctr. Folklore dancers at l. ctr. on back. Sign. 29. Series #1-6289.

	VG	VF	UNC
	0.10	0.25	1.25

#235 and 236 wmk: Sculptured head of *Brasilia*.

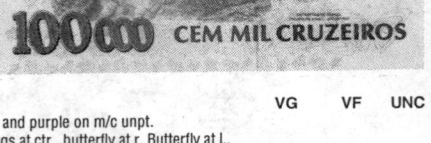

235   100,000 CRUZEIROS
ND (1992-93). Brown, green and purple on m/c unpt. Hummingbird feeding nestlings at ctr., butterfly at r. Butterfly at l., Iguaçú cataract at ctr. on back.

	VG	VF	UNC
a. Sign. 29. Series #1-6052 (1992).	0.15	0.50	6.00
b. Sign. 30. Series #6053-6226 (1993).	0.15	0.50	5.00
c. Sign. 31. Series #6227-6290 (1993).	0.15	0.50	5.00
d. Sign. 32. Series #6291-6733 (1993).	0.10	0.25	1.25

236	500,000 CRUZEIROS	VG	VF	UNC

ND (1993). Red-violet, brown and deep purple on m/c unpt. M. de Andrade at r., native Indian art in unpt. Bldg., de Andrade teaching children at ctr. on back.

	a. Sign. 30. Series #1-3410 (1993).	0.50	2.50	12.00
	b. Sign. 31. Series #3411-4404 (1993).	0.50	2.00	10.00
	c. Sign. 32. Series #4405-8291 (1993).	0.20	0.50	4.00

1993 ND PROVISIONAL ISSUE

August 1993 Monetary Reform: 1 Cruzeiro Real = 1,000 Cruzeiros

#237-239 black circular ovpt. of new value on #234-236. Sign. 32.

237	50 CRUZEIROS REAIS ON 50,000 CRUZEIROS	VG	VF	UNC
	ND (1993). Dk. brown and red-orange on m/c unpt. Ovpt. on #234. Series #6290-6591.	0.05	0.20	1.00

238	100 CRUZEIROS REAIS ON 100,000 CRUZEIROS	VG	VF	UNC
	ND (1993). Brown, green and purple on m/c unpt. Ovpt. on #235d. Series #6734-7144.	0.10	0.20	1.00

239	500 CRUZEIROS REAIS ON 500,000 CRUZEIROS	VG	VF	UNC

ND (1993). Red-violet, brown and deep purple on m/c unpt. Ovpt. on #236c.

| | a. Series prefix A, #8292-9999. | 0.10 | 0.50 | 3.00 |
| | b. Series prefix B, #1-717. | 0.10 | 0.25 | 2.25 |

1993-94 ND ISSUE

#240-242 wmk: Sculptured head of "Brasilia." Printer: CdM-B. Sign. 33.

240	1000 CRUZEIROS REAIS	VG	VF	UNC
	ND (1993). Black, dk. blue and brown on m/c unpt. A. Teixeira at ctr. r. "Parque" school at l. ctr. Children and workers on back. Series #1-2515.	0.10	0.50	2.00

NOTICE

Readers with unlisted dates, signature varieties, etc. are invited to submit photocopies of their notes to:
Standard Catalog of World Paper Money,
700 East State St. Iola, WI 54990-0001,
E-Mail: george.cuhaj@fwpubs.com.

241	5000 CRUZEIROS REAIS	VG	VF	UNC
	ND (1993). Black, red-brown and dk. olive-green on m/c unpt. Gaucho at ctr. r., ruins of São Miguel das Missões at l. ctr. Back vertical format; gaucho on horseback roping steer at ctr. Series #1-9999.	0.50	2.50	12.50

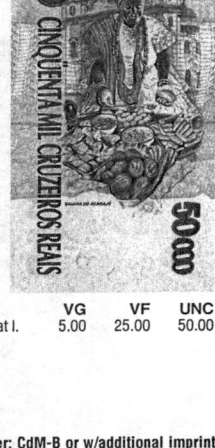

242	50,000 CRUZEIROS REAIS	VG	VF	UNC
	ND (1994). Deep purple and brown-violet on m/c unpt. Dancer at l. ctr., Baiana at ctr. r. Back vertical format; Baiana do Acarajé preparing food at ctr. Series #1-1200.	5.00	25.00	50.00

1994 ND ISSUE

July 1994 Monetary Reform: 1 Real = 2750 Cruzeiros Reais

#243-247 sculpture of the Republic at ctr. r. Back vertical format. Printer: CdM-B or w/additional imprint of secondary printer. Series # is first 4 digits of serial #. Sign. varieties.

243	1 REAL	VG	VF	UNC

ND (1994-97). Black, olive-green and blue-green on aqua and pale green unpt. White-necked jacobin hummingbirds at ctr. on back.

	a. Sign. 33. W/o text DEUS SEJA LOUVADO, Series #1-2409 (1994). Serial #A-A.	0.50	1.00	6.00
	b. Sign. 34. Series 2410-3833 (1994).	0.50	1.00	6.00
	c. Sign. 34. W/text: DEUS SEJA LOUVADO at lower l. Series #3834-6568.	0.50	1.00	6.00
	d. Sign. 35. Series 6569-7019.	0.50	1.00	9.00
	e. Sign. 37. Series 7020-9999.	0.50	1.00	5.00
	f. Sign. 37. Series 0001-0072, serial #A-B.	0.50	2.00	17.50

243A	**1 REAL**	VG	VF	UNC
	ND (1997). Black, olive-green and blue-green on aqua and pale green unpt. Similar to #243 but wmk: Flag. Serial #A-B, B-B or C-B.			
	a. Sign. 37. Series #0001-3247.	0.50	1.00	4.00
	b. Sign. 38. Series #3248-7561.	0.50	1.00	4.00
	c. Sign. 39. Series #7562-8948.	0.50	1.00	6.00
	d. Sign. 39. Series #8949-9999.	0.50	1.00	4.00
	e. Sign. 39. Series #0001-9999, series B-B.	FV	FV	3.00
	f. Sign. 39. Serial C-B. Series #0001-3382.	FV	FV	2.00
	g. Sign. 40. Series 3383-.	FV	FV	2.00

244	**5 REAIS**	VG	VF	UNC
	ND (1994-97). Violet, dk. brown and blue on lilac unpt. Great egret at ctr. on back. Serial #A-A. Wmk: Republic.			
	a. Sign. 33. W/o text: *DEUS SEJA LOUVADO*. Series #0001-1411.	2.00	5.00	22.50
	b. Sign. 33. W/o text. Printer: G & D. Series A-B,#1-1000.	5.00	20.00	55.00
	c. Sign. 34. W/o text. Series A-A: #1412-1609.	10.00	50.00	130.00
	d. Sign. 34. W/text: *DEUS SEJA LOUVADO. Series #1610-4093.*	2.00	5.00	17.50
	e. Sign. 35. W/text. Series 4094-5378.	2.00	5.00	17.50
	f. Sign. 36. W/text. Series 5379-5798.	2.00	5.00	22.50
	g. Sign. 37. W/text. Series #5799-8232.	2.00	5.00	17.50
244A	**5 REAIS**			
	ND (1997-). Violet, dk. brown and blue on lilac unpt. Similar to #244 but wmk: Flag and series A-C.			
	a. Sign. 37. Series #0001-1504.	2.00	5.00	17.50
	b. Sign. 38. Series #1505-3034.	2.00	5.00	17.50
	c. Sign. 39. Series #3035-3196.	2.00	7.50	22.50
	d. Sign. 39. Series #3197-8817.	FV	2.00	6.00
	e. Sign. 40. Series #8818-.	FV	FV	5.00

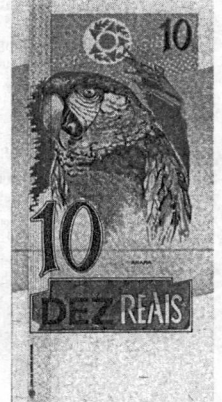

245	**10 REAIS**	VG	VF	UNC
	ND (1994). Dk. brown, brown-violet and brown-orange on lilac and pale orange unpt. Macaw at ctr. on back. Wmk: Republic.			
	a. Sign. 33. W/o text: *DEUS SEJA LOUVADO*. Series A-A: #1-0713.	5.00	10.00	45.00
	b. Sign. 33. Printer: TDLR. Series #A-B: #0001-1200.	5.00	15.00	55.00
	c. Sign. 34. W/o text: *DEUS SEJA LOUVADO* at lower l. Series #0714-1817.	5.00	10.00	30.00
	d. Sign. 34. W/text at lower l. Series #1818-3403.	5.00	10.00	30.00
	e. Sign. 35. Series #3404-6102.	5.00	10.00	30.00
	f. Sign. 36. Series 6103-6714.	5.00	15.00	55.00
	g. Sign. 37. Series 6715-9999.	5.00	10.00	30.00
	h. Sign. 37. Series #0001-4844. Serial A-B.	5.00	15.00	55.00
245A	**10 REAIS**			
	ND (1997-). Dk. brown, brown-violet and brown-orange on lilac and pale orange unpt. Similar to #245. Wmk. Flag.			
	a. Sign. 37. Series #0001-4571. Serial A-C.	4.00	7.00	22.50
	b. Sign. 38. Series #4572-9179.	4.00	7.00	22.50
	c. Sign. 39. Series #9180-9999.	4.00	7.00	22.50
	d. Sign. 39. Series #0001-0075. Serial B-C.	4.00	10.00	27.50
	e. Sign. 39. Series #0076-9999.	4.00	5.00	12.50
	f. Sign. 39. Serial C-C. Series #0001-1136.	FV	FV	8.00
	g. Sign. 40. Series #1136-.	FV	FV	8.00

246	**50 REAIS**	VG	VF	UNC
	ND (1994-). Dk. brown and red-brown on m/c unpt. Jaguar on back.			
	a. Sign. 33. W/o text: *DEUS SEJA LOUVADO.* Series A-A: #0001-1249.	25.00	50.00	115.00
	b. Sign. 33. W/o text. Printer: F-CO. Series A-B: #0001-0400.	25.00	50.00	165.00
	c. Sing. 34. W/o text. Series #1250-1338.	20.00	40.00	135.00
	d. Sign. 34. W/text. Series #1339-1438.	25.00	50.00	165.00
	e. Sign. 36. Series #1439-1636.	50.00	100.00	550.00
	f. Sign. 37. Series #1637-8405.	25.00	50.00	120.00
	g. Sign. 38. Series #8406-9999.	20.00	40.00	135.00
	h. Sign. 38. Series #0001-1004. Serial #B-A.	20.00	40.00	135.00
	i. Sign. 39. Series #1005-1483. Serial #B-A.	20.00	40.00	135.00
	j. Sign. 39. Series #1484-9057.	20.00	25.00	60.00
	k. Sign. 40. Series #9058-.	FV	FV	30.00

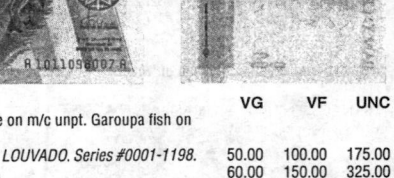

247	**100 REAIS**	VG	VF	UNC
	ND (1994-). Blue-green and purple on m/c unpt. Garoupa fish on back.			
	a. Sign. 33. W/o text: *DEIS SEJA LOUVADO. Series #0001-1198.*	50.00	100.00	175.00
	b. Sign. 34. Series #1199-1201.	60.00	150.00	325.00
	c. W/text: *DEUS SEJA LOUVADO* at lower l. Sign. 34. Series #1202-1300.	50.00	125.00	225.00

2000 COMMEMORATIVE ISSUE

#248, 500th Anniversary of the Discovery of Brazil

248	**10 REAIS**	VG	VF	UNC
	ND (2000). Dk. Blue, blue and orange. Pedro Alvares Cabral at ctr. compass to l. Map and many portraits on back. Polymer plastic.			
	a. Name as: *PEDRO A. CABRAL.* Series #0001-0586.	FV	FV	25.00
	b. Name as: *PEDRO ALVARES CABRAL.* Series #0587-2536.	FV	FV	15.00

#248 Series #0001 was also available in a special folder, value $20.00.

2001-02 ISSUE

249	2 REAIS	VG	VF	UNC
	ND (2001-). Blue-green and black on m/c unpt. Tartaruga Marinha turtles on back.			
	a. Sign. 39. Series #0001-2798.	FV	FV	2.50
	b. Sign. 40. Series #2799-.	FV	FV	2.50

250	20 REAIS	VG	VF	UNC
	ND (2002-). Yellow and rose on m/c unpt. Lion monkey on back.			
	a. Sign. 39. Series #0001-2125.	FV	FV	12.50
	b. Sign. 40. Series #2126-.	FV	FV	15.00

REPUBLICA FEDERATIVA DO BRAZIL

BANCO CENTRAL DO BRAZIL

2003 ISSUE

251	1 REAL	VG	VF	UNC
	ND (2003-). Serial #A-C. Similar to #243A.			
	a. Sign. 40. Series 0001-.	FV	FV	2.00
252	5 REAIS			
	ND (2005). Violet.	FV	FV	3.50
253	10 REAIS			
	ND (2005). Dk. brown.	FV	FV	6.00
254	20 REAIS			
	ND (2005).	FV	FV	12.50
255	50 REAIS			
	ND (2005). Dk. brown.	FV	FV	25.00

The British Caribbean Territories (Eastern Group), a currency board formed in 1950, comprised the British West Indies territories of Trinidad and Tobago; Barbados; the Leeward Islands of Anguilla, Saba, St. Christopher, Nevis and Antigua; the Windward Islands of St. Lucia, Dominica, St. Vincent and Grenada; British Guiana and the British Virgin Islands.

As time progressed, the members of this Eastern Group varied.

For later issues see East Caribbean States listings in Volume 3, Modern issues.

RULERS:
British

MONETARY SYSTEM:
1 Dollar = 100 Cents

BRITISH ADMINISTRATION

BRITISH CARIBBEAN TERRITORIES, EASTERN GROUP

1953 ISSUE

#7-12 map at lower l., portr. Qn. Elizabeth II at r. Arms in all 4 corners on back. Printer: BWC.

7	1 DOLLAR	VG	VF	UNC
	1953-64. Red on m/c unpt.			
	a. Wmk: Sailing ship. 5.1.1953.	15.00	75.00	325.00
	b. Wmk: Qn. Elizabeth II. 1.3.1954-2.1.1957.	8.00	30.00	225.00
	c. 2.1.1958-2.1.1964.	7.00	25.00	185.00

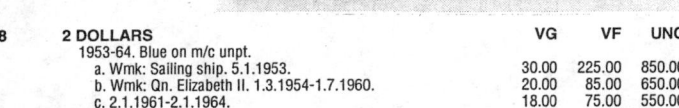

8	2 DOLLARS	VG	VF	UNC
	1953-64. Blue on m/c unpt.			
	a. Wmk: Sailing ship. 5.1.1953.	30.00	225.00	850.00
	b. Wmk: Qn. Elizabeth II. 1.3.1954-1.7.1960.	20.00	85.00	650.00
	c. 2.1.1961-2.1.1964.	18.00	75.00	550.00

9	**5 DOLLARS**	VG	VF	UNC
	1953-64. Green on m/c unpt.			
	a. Wmk: Sailing ship. 5.1.1953.	35.00	275.00	1100.00
	b. Wmk: Qn. Elizabeth II. 3.1.1955-2.1.1959.	25.00	100.00	925.00
	c. 2.1.1961-2.1.1964.	22.50	90.00	850.00

10	**10 DOLLARS**	VG	VF	UNC
	1953-64. Brown on m/c unpt.			
	a. Wmk: Sailing ship. 5.1.1953.	60.00	400.00	—
	b. Wmk: Qn. Elizabeth II. 3.1.1955-2.1.1959.	40.00	250.00	1750.00
	c. 2.1.1961; 2.1.1962; 2.1.1964.	37.50	200.00	1500.00

11	**20 DOLLARS**	VG	VF	UNC
	1953-64. Purple on m/c unpt.			
	a. Wmk: Sailing ship. 5.1.1953.	90.00	600.00	—
	b. Wmk: Qn. Elizabeth II. 2.1.1957-2.1.1964.	45.00	300.00	—
12	**100 DOLLARS**			
	1953-63. Black on m/c unpt.			
	a. Wmk: Sailing ship. 5.1.1953.	500.00	2000.00	—
	b. Wmk: Qn. Elizabeth II. 1.3.1954; 2.1.1957; 2.1.1963.	300.00	1350.00	—
	s. As b. Specimen.	—	—	2500.00

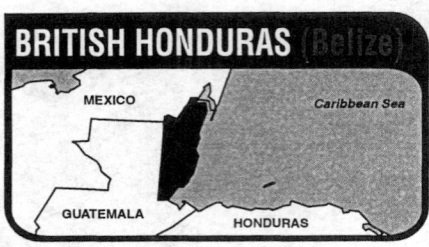

The former British colony of British Honduras is now Belize, a self-governing dependency of the United Kingdom situated in Central America south of Mexico and east and north of Guatemala, has an area of 8,867 sq. mi. (22,965 sq. km.) and a population of 209,000. Capital: Belmopan. Sugar, citrus fruits, chicle and hard woods are exported.

The area, site of the ancient Mayan civilization, was sighted by Columbus in 1502, and settled by shipwrecked English seamen in 1638. British buccaneers settled the former capital of Belize in the 17th century. Britain claimed administrative right over the area after the emancipation of Central America from Spain, and declared it a colony subordinate to Jamaica in 1862. It established as the separate Crown Colony of British Honduras in 1884. The anti-British People's United Party, which attained power in 1954, won a constitution, effective in 1964 which established self-government under a British appointed governor. British Honduras became Belize on June 1, 1973, following the passage of a surprise bill by the Peoples United Party, but the constitutional relationship with Britain remained unchanged.

In Dec. 1975, the U.N. General Assembly adopted a resolution supporting the right of the people of Belize to self-determination, and asking Britain and Guatemala to renew their negotiations on the future of Belize. Belize obtained independence on Sept. 21, 1981.

RULERS:
British

MONETARY SYSTEM:
1 Dollar = 100 Cents

GOVERNMENT OF BRITISH HONDURAS

1952-53 ISSUE

#28-32 arms at l., portr. Qn. Elizabeth II at r.

28	**1 DOLLAR**	VG	VF	UNC
	1953-73. Green on m/c unpt.			
	a. 15.4.1953-1.10.1958.	6.00	30.00	225.00
	b. 1.1.1961-1.5.1969.	5.00	15.00	100.00
	c. 1.6.1970-1.1.1973.	5.00	10.00	80.00
	s. As a, b, c. Specimen.	—	—	75.00

29	**2 DOLLARS**	VG	VF	UNC
	1953-73. Purple on m/c unpt.			
	a. 15.4.1953-1.10.1958.	10.00	65.00	550.00
	b. 1.10.1960-1.5.1965.	7.50	30.00	200.00
	c. 1.1.1971-1.1.1973.	5.00	20.00	150.00
	s. As a, b, c. Specimen.	—	—	50.00

30	**5 DOLLARS**	**VG**	**VF**	**UNC**
	1953-73. Red on m/c unpt.			
	a. 15.4.1953-1.10.1958.	15.00	85.00	700.00
	b. 1.3.1960-1.5.1965.	10.00	45.00	450.00
	c. 1.1.1970-1.1.1973.	10.00	35.00	250.00
	s. As a, c. Specimen.	—	—	75.00

31	**10 DOLLARS**	**VG**	**VF**	**UNC**
	1958-73. Black on m/c unpt.			
	a. 1.10.1958-1.11.1961.	35.00	200.00	—
	b. 1.4.1964-1.5.1969.	20.00	100.00	900.00
	c. 1.1.1971-1.1.1973.	15.00	75.00	700.00
	s. As a, c. Specimen.	—	—	150.00

32	**20 DOLLARS**	**VG**	**VF**	**UNC**
	1952-73. Brown on m/c unpt.			
	a. 1.12.1952-1.10.1958.	50.00	285.00	—
	b. 1.3.1960-1.5.1969.	37.50	200.00	1650.00
	c. 1.1.1970-1.1.1973.	30.00	175.00	1500.00
	s. As a, c. Specimen.	—	—	200.00

Note: For similar notes but w/BELIZE heading, see Belize listings.

Negara Brunei Darussalam (The State of Brunei), a member of the British Commonwealth is located on the northwest coast of the island of Borneo, has an area of 2,226 sq. mi. (5,765 sq. km.) and a population of 326,000. Capital: Bandar Seri Begawan. Crude oil and rubber are exported.

Magellan was the first European to visit Brunei in 1521. It was a powerful state, ruling over Northern Borneo and adjacent islands from the 16th to the 19th century. Brunei became a British protectorate in 1888 and a British dependency in 1905. The Constitution of 1959 restored control over internal affairs to the sultan, while delegating responsibility for defense and foreign affairs to Britain.

On Jan. 1, 1984, Brunei became a fully independent member of the Commonwealth.

RULERS:
Sultan Sir Omar Ali Saifuddin III, 1950-1967
Sultan Hassanal Bolkiah I, 1967-

MONETARY SYSTEM:
1 Dollar = 100 Sen to 1967
1 Ringgit (Dollar) = 100 Sen, 1967-

STATE

KERAJAAN BRUNEI

GOVERNMENT OF BRUNEI

1967 ISSUE

#1-5 Sultan Omar Ali Saifuddin III w/military cap at r. and as wmk. Mosque on back. Printer: BWC.

1	**1 RINGGIT**	**VG**	**VF**	**UNC**
	1967. Dk. blue on m/c unpt. Back gray and lavender on pink unpt.			
	a. Issued note.	6.00	20.00	50.00
	s. Specimen.	—		

2	**5 RINGGIT**	**VG**	**VF**	**UNC**
	1967. Dk. green on m/c unpt. Back green on pink unpt.			
	a. Issued note.	10.00	30.00	125.00
	s. Specimen.	—		

3	**10 RINGGIT**	**VG**	**VF**	**UNC**
	1967. Red on m/c unpt. Back red.			
	a. Issued note.	20.00	50.00	175.00
	s. Specimen.	—		

4	50 RINGGIT	VG	VF	UNC
	1967. Dk. brown on m/c unpt. Back olive.	75.00	125.00	300.00

5	100 RINGGIT	VG	VF	UNC
	1967. Blue on m/c unpt. Back purple.	175.00	300.00	550.00

1972-79 ISSUE

#6-10 Sultan Hassanal Bolkiah I in military uniform at r. and as wmk. Mosque on back. Printer: BWC.

6	1 RINGGIT	VG	VF	UNC
	1972-88. Blue on m/c unpt.			
	a. 1972; 1976; 1978.	FV	3.00	12.50
	b. 1980; 1982.	FV	1.50	10.00
	c. 1983-1986.	FV	1.25	8.00
	d. 1988.	FV	FV	7.50
	s. Specimen.	—	—	130.00

7	5 RINGGIT	VG	VF	UNC
	1979-86. Green on m/c unpt.			
	a. 1979; 1981.	1.50	6.00	35.00
	b. 1983; 1984; 1986.	1.50	6.00	32.50
	s. Specimen.	—	—	150.00

8	10 RINGGIT	VG	VF	UNC
	1976-86. Red on m/c unpt.			
	a. 1976; 1981.	3.00	15.00	60.00
	b. 1983; 1986.	3.00	12.50	50.00
	s. Issued note.	—	—	175.00

9	50 RINGGIT	VG	VF	UNC
	1973-86. Dk. brown on m/c unpt.			
	a. 1973.	FV	60.00	150.00
	b. 1977; 1982.	FV	45.00	125.00
	c. 1981.	FV	75.00	100.00
	d. 1986.	FV	45.00	120.00
	s. Specimen.	—	—	250.00

10	100 RINGGIT	VG	VF	UNC
	1972-88. Blue on m/c unpt.			
	a. 1972; 1976.	FV	100.00	300.00
	b. 1978; 1980.	FV	90.00	225.00
	c. 1982; 1983; 1988.	FV	80.00	225.00
	s. Specimen.	—	—	400.00

1979; 1987 ISSUE

#11 and 12 Sultan Hassanal Bolkiah I in royal uniform at r. and as wmk. Printer: BWC.

11	500 RINGGIT	VG	VF	UNC
	1979; 1987. Orange on m/c unpt. Mosque at ctr. on back.			
	a. 1979.	FV	450.00	1000.00
	b. 1987.	FV	425.00	900.00
	s. Specimen.	—	—	1100.00

12	1000 RINGGIT	VG	VF	UNC
	1979; 1986; 1987. Gray, brown and greenish blue. Brunei Museum on back.			
	a. 1979.	FV	900.00	1500.00
	b. 1986-87.	FV	850.00	1350.00
	s. Specimen.	—	—	1750.00

NEGARA BRUNEI DARUSSALAM

1989 ISSUE

#13-20 Sultan Hassanal Bolkiah I at r. and as wmk.

13	1 RINGGIT	VG	VF	UNC
	1989-95. Purple on m/c unpt. Aerial view on back.			
	a. 1989; 1991.	FV	2.00	4.00
	b. 1994-95.	FV	FV	3.50

14	5 RINGGIT	VG	VF	UNC
	1989-91; 1993; 1995. Blue-gray and deep green on m/c unpt. Houses and boats on back.	FV	FV	12.50

15	10 RINGGIT	VG	VF	UNC
	1989-92; 1995. Purple and red-orange on m/c unpt. Waterfront village w/mosque on back.	FV	FV	18.00

16	50 RINGGIT	VG	VF	UNC
	1989-91; 1994; 1995. Brown, olive-green, and orange on m/c unpt. People in power launch on back.	FV	FV	75.00

17	100 RINGGIT	VG	VF	UNC
	1989-92; 1994. Blue and violet on m/c unpt. River scene on back.	FV	FV	150.00

18   500 RINGGIT

1989-92. Red-orange, purple, olive and black on m/c unpt. Houses at l. ctr. Padian woman paddling her boat in Kampong Ayer on back.

	VG	VF	UNC
	FV	FV	650.00

19   1000 RINGGIT

1989-91. Red-violet, purple, olive and blue-green on m/c unpt. Waterfront village of Kampong Ayer and Istana Nurul Iman.

	VG	VF	UNC
	FV	FV	1000.00

20   10,000 RINGGIT

1989. Dk. brown and dk. green on m/c unpt. Aerial view of Bandar Seri Begawan harbor on back.

	VG	VF	UNC
a. Issued note.	FV	FV	8500.00
s. Specimen. Ovpt: *CONTOH SPECIMEN* in two lines.	—	—	4500.00

1992 COMMEMORATIVE ISSUE

#21, 25th Anniversary of Accession

21   25 RINGGIT

1992. Brown, lilac, green and m/c. Royal procession at ctr., Sultan at r. and as wmk. at l. Crown at l., coronation at ctr. on back. Dates *1967* and *1992* w/text at top.

	VG	VF	UNC
	FV	FV	40.00

1996 ISSUE

#22-27 Sultan Jam'Asr Hassan Bolkiah I at r.

#22-24 arms at upper l. Polymer plastic. Printer: NPA (w/o imprint).

22   1 RINGGIT

1996. Blue-black and deep green on m/c unpt. Riverside simpur plant at l. ctr. Back blue and m/c; rain forest waterfall at l. ctr.

	VG	VF	UNC
	FV	FV	2.50

23   5 RINGGIT

1996; 2002. Black on green and m/c unpt. Pitcher plant at l. ctr. Rain forest floor on back.

	VG	VF	UNC
	FV	FV	8.00

24	10 RINGGIT	VG	VF	UNC
	1996; 1998. Dk. brown and brown on red and m/c unpt. Purple-leafed forest yam at l. ctr. Rain forest canopy on back.	FV	FV	14.00

#25-27 are paper issues.

25	50 RINGGIT	VG	VF	UNC
	1996. Brown, blue and purple on m/c unpt. Offshore oil rig on back.	FV	FV	55.00

26	100 RINGGIT	VG	VF	UNC
	1996. Brown and orange on m/c unpt. Brunei International Airport on back.	FV	FV	90.00

27	500 RINGGIT	VG	VF	UNC
	2000. Deep orange and brown on m/c unpt. Bolkiah Mosque on back.	FV	FV	500.00

2004 COMMEMORATIVE ISSUE

28	50 RINGGIT	VG	VF	UNC
	15.7.2004. Brown, green and blue on m/c unpt. Kantan medicinial flower at ctr. Polymer plastic.	FV	FV	50.00

29	100 RINGGIT	VG	VF	UNC
	15.7.2004. Brown, orange and yellow on m/c unpt. Kjojk medicinial flower at ctr. Polymer plastic.	FV	FV	90.00

BULGARIA

The Republic of Bulgaria (formerly the Peoples Republic of Bulgaria), a Balkan country on the Black Sea in southeastern Europe, has an area of 42,855 sq. mi. (110,993 sq. km.) and a population of 8.31 million. Capital: Sofia. Agriculture remains a key component of the economy but industrialization, particularly he- avy industry, has been emphasized since the late 1940's. Machinery, tobacco and cigarettes, wines and spirits, clothing and metals are the chief exports.

The area now occupied by Bulgaria was conquered by the Bulgars, an Asiatic tribe, in the 7th century. Bulgarian kingdoms continued to exist on the peninsula until it came under Turkish rule in 1395. In 1878, after nearly 500 years of Turkish rule, Bulgaria was made a principality under Turkish suzerainty. Union seven years later with Eastern Rumelia created a Balkan state with borders approximating those of present-day Bulgaria. A Bulgarian kingdom fully independent of Turkey was proclaimed Sept. 22, 1908.

During WWI Bulgaria had been aligned with Germany. After the Armistice certain land concessions were granted to Greece and Romania. In 1934 King Boris III suspended all political parties and established a dictatorial monarchy. In 1938 the military began rearming through the aid of the Anglo-French loan. As WWII developed Bulgaria again supported the Germans but Boris protected its Jewish community. Boris died mysteriously in 1943 and Simeon II became king at the age of six. The country was then ruled by a pro-Nazi regency until it was invaded by Soviet forces in 1944. The monarchy was abolished and Simeon was ousted by plebiscite in 1946, and Bulgaria became a People's Republic in the Soviet pattern. Following demonstrations and a general strike, the communist government resigned in Nov. 1990. A new government was elected in Oct. 1991.

TITLES:
Bulgarian People's Republic:
НАРОДНА РЕПУБЛИКА БЪЛГАРИЯ
Bulgarian National Bank:
БЪЛГАРСКА НАРОДНА БАНКА

MONETARY SYSTEM:
1 Lev ЛЕВ = 100 Stotinki СТОТИНКИ
until 1999
1 Lev = 1,000 "Old" Lev, 1999

PEOPLES REPUBLIC

БЪЛГАРСКА НАРОДНА БАНКА

BULGARIAN NATIONAL BANK

1962 ISSUE

#88-92 arms at l.

88	1 LEV	VG	VF	UNC
	1962. Brown-lilac on m/c unpt. Monument for the Battle of Shipka Pass (1877) at l. ctr. on back.			
	a. Issued note.	0.10	0.25	1.75
	s. Specimen.	—	—	17.50

89	2 LEVA	VG	VF	UNC
	1962. Black and blue on green unpt. Woman picking grapes in vineyard at r. on back.			
	a. Issued note.	0.20	0.40	2.50
	s. Specimen.	—	—	17.50

90	5 LEVA	VG	VF	UNC
	1962. Red on blue and m/c unpt. Coastline village.			
	a. Issued note.	0.25	0.50	4.50
	s. Specimen.	—	—	20.00

91	10 LEVA	VG	VF	UNC
	1962. Black on blue and m/c unpt. G. Dimitrov at l. on back.			
	a. Issued note.	0.25	0.50	7.50
	s. Specimen.	—	—	22.50

92	20 LEVA	VG	VF	UNC
	1962. Brown-lilac on m/c unpt. Factory. G. Dimitrov at l. on back.			
	a. Issued note.	0.25	0.50	12.50
	s. Specimen.	—	—	25.00

1974 ISSUE

#93-97 modified arms w/dates *681-1944* at l.

#93-95 wmk: Decorative design.

93	1 LEV	VG	VF	UNC
	1974. Brown on m/c unpt. Like #88.			
	a. Issued note.	0.10	0.20	1.00
	s. Specimen.	—	—	15.00

94	2 LEVA	VG	VF	UNC
	1974. Black and blue on green unpt. Like #89.			
	a. Issued note.	0.10	0.25	1.75
	s. Specimen.	—	—	15.00

95	5 LEVA	VG	VF	UNC
	1974. Red on blue and m/c unpt. Like #90.			
	a. Issued note.	0.15	0.50	1.75
	s. Specimen.	—	—	17.50

#96 and 97 wmk: Hands holding hammer and sickle.

REPUBLIC

БЪЛГАРСКА НАРОДНА БАНКА

BULGARIAN NATIONAL BANK

1991-94 ISSUE

#100-103 wmk: Arms (lion).

		VG	VF	UNC
96	**10 LEVA**			
	1974. Black on blue and m/c unpt. Like #91.			
	a. Issued note.	0.15	0.50	4.50
	s. Specimen.	—	—	20.00

		VG	VF	UNC
100	**20 LEVA**	FV	FV	0.25
	1991. Blue-black and blue-green on m/c unpt. Dutchess Sevastokrat Oritza Desislava at l. ctr. Boyana Church at r. on back.			

		VG	VF	UNC
97	**20 LEVA**			
	1974. Brown-lilac on m/c unpt. Like #92.			
	a. Issued note.	0.50	1.00	8.50
	s. Specimen.	—	—	22.50

		VG	VF	UNC
101	**50 LEVA**	FV	FV	0.40
	1992. Purple and violet on m/c unpt. Khristo G. Danov at l. Platen printing press at r. on back.			

1989; 1990 ISSUES

		VG	VF	UNC
98	**50 LEVA**			
	1990. Brown and dk. blue on m/c unpt. Arms at l. ctr. Back brown and dk. green; castle ruins at ctr. r. on back. Wmk: Hands holding hammer and sickle.			
	a. Issued note.	0.50	1.00	6.00
	s. Specimen.	—	—	120.00

#98 was withdrawn from circulation shortly after its release.

		VG	VF	UNC
102	**100 LEVA**			
	1991; 1993. Dk. brown and maroon on m/c unpt. Zhary Zograf (artist) at l. ctr. Wheel of Life at r. on back.			
	a. 1991.	FV	FV	1.25
	b. 1993.	FV	FV	0.40

		VG	VF	UNC
99	**100 LEVA**			
	1989. Purple on lilac unpt. Arms at l. ctr. Horseman w/2 dogs at ctr.	—	—	150.00

#99 carries the name of the Bulgarian Peoples Republic, probably the reason it was not released. An esti-mated 500-600 pieces were "liberated" from the recycling process.

		VG	VF	UNC
103	**200 LEVA**	FV	FV	0.60
	1992. Deep violet and brown-orange on m/c unpt. Ivan Vazov at l., village in unpt. Lyre w/laurel wreath at r. on back.			

104	**500 LEVA** 1993. Dk. green and black on m/c unpt. D. Christov at l. and as wmk. Opera house in Varna at ctr. r., herring gulls at lower r. on back.	**VG** FV	**VF** FV	**UNC** 1.00

108	**5000 LEVA** 1996. Violet on m/c unpt. Z. Stoyanov at l. and as wmk. quill pen at ctr. r. Monument (2 views) at ctr., and *1885 Proclamation to the* *Bulgarian People* at r. on back.	**VG** FV	**VF** 4.00	**UNC** 9.00

105	**1000 LEVA** 1994; 1997. Dk. green and olive-brown on m/c unpt. V. Levski at l. and as wmk., Liberty w/flag, sword and lion at upper ctr. r. Monument and writings of Levski at ctr. r. on back.	**VG** FV	**VF** FV	**UNC** 1.50

109	**10,000 LEVA** 1996. Brown and purple on m/c unpt. V. Dimitrov at l. and as wmk., palette, brushes, Academy of the Arts at ctr. Sketches at ctr., "Bulgarian Madonna" at r. on back.	**VG** FV	**VF** 6.00	**UNC** 17.50

#110 Deleted, see #105.

1994-96 ISSUE

#106-109 w/wide hologram foil strip at l.

1997 ISSUE

111	**5000 LEVA** 1997. Violet on m/c unpt. Like #108. W/o wide holographic foil strip at l.	**VG** FV	**VF** 4.00	**UNC** 9.00

#112 and 113 w/wide hologram foil strip at l. Reduced size.

106	**1000 LEVA** 1996. Dk. green and olive-brown on m/c unpt. Like #105 but w/wide hologram foil strip at l.	**VG** FV	**VF** FV	**UNC** 1.50

112	**10,000 LEVA** 1997. M/c. Dr. P. Beron at l. Telescope at r. on back.	**VG** FV	**VF** 6.00	**UNC** 18.00

107	**2000 LEVA** 1994; 1996. Black and dk. blue on m/c unpt. N. Ficev at l. and as wmk., bldg. outlines at ctr., wide hologram foil strip at l. Steeple, bldg. plans at ctr. r. on back.	**VG** FV	**VF** 1.00	**UNC** 3.50

113	**50,000 LEVA** 1997. Purple on m/c unpt. St. Cyril at l., St. Methodius at ctr. r. Architectural monuments of the ancient Bulgarian capitals of Pliska and Preslav on back.	**VG** FV	**VF** 25.00	**UNC** 50.00

1999-2003 Issue

Monetary Reform: 1 Lev = 1000 "Old" Leva.

#114-119 w/holographic strip at l.

114	1 LEV	VG	VF	UNC
	1999. Red and blue on yellow unpt. Icon of St. John of Rila at l. Rila Monastery on back.	FV	FV	0.85

115	2 LEVA	VG	VF	UNC
	1999. Violet and pink on lt. blue unpt. Paisii Hilendarski at l. Heraldic lion on back.	FV	FV	1.75

116	5 LEVA	VG	VF	UNC
	1999. Red, brown and green on m/c unpt. Ivan Milev at l. Parts of paintings on back.	FV	FV	4.50

117	10 LEVA	VG	VF	UNC
	1999. Dk. green on ochre unpt. Dr. Peter Beron at l. Astronomy sketches and telescope on back.	FV	FV	9.00

118	20 LEVA	VG	VF	UNC
	1999. Blue on m/c unpt. S. Stambolov at l. National Assembly bldg. and Eagles' and Lions' Bridges in Sofia on back.	FV	FV	17.50

119	50 LEVA	VG	VF	UNC
	1999. Brown and yellow on m/c unpt. Pencho Slaveykov at l. Illustrations from his poetry works on back.	FV	FV	45.00

120	100 LEVA	VG	VF	UNC
	2003. Green on m/c unpt. Aleka Konstantinov at r. His character "Uncle Ganyo" on back.	FV	FV	85.00

FOREIGN EXCHANGE CERTIFICATES

CORECOM

1966 ND Issue

		VG	VF	UNC
FX1	**1 LEV**			
	ND (1966). Lt. brown on yellow unpt.	3.00	10.00	15.00
FX2	**2 LEVA**			
	ND (1966). Lt. brown on yellow unpt.	5.00	12.50	20.00
FX3	**5 LEVA**			
	ND (1966). Lt. brown on yellow unpt.	10.00	20.00	30.00
FX4	**10 LEVA**			
	ND (1966). Lt. brown on yellow unpt.	12.50	25.00	40.00
FX5	**20 LEVA**			
	ND (1966). Lt. brown on yellow unpt.	20.00	40.00	60.00
FX6	**50 LEVA**			
	ND (1966). Lt. brown on yellow unpt.	22.50	60.00	100.00
FX7	**100 LEVA**			
	ND (1966). Lt. brown on yellow unpt.	40.00	75.00	150.00

1968 ND Issue

			VG	VF	UNC
FX8	**1 LEV**				
	ND (1968). Brown on lt. green unpt.		3.00	10.00	15.00
FX9	**2 LEVA**				
	ND (1968). Brown on lt. green unpt.		5.00	12.50	20.00

			VG	VF	UNC
FX10	**5 LEVA**				
	ND (1968). Brown on lt. green unpt.		7.50	15.00	25.00
FX11	**10 LEVA**				
	ND (1968). Brown on lt. green unpt.		10.00	20.00	30.00
FX12	**20 LEVA**				
	ND (1968). Brown on lt. green unpt.		15.00	30.00	40.00
FX13	**50 LEVA**				
	ND (1968). Brown on lt. green unpt.		22.50	50.00	80.00
FX14	**100 LEVA**				
	ND (1968). Brown on lt. green unpt.		30.00	60.00	100.00

1975 ND Issue

			VG	VF	UNC
FX14A	**.05 LEV**				
	ND (1975).		2.00	5.00	9.00

			VG	VF	UNC
FX15	**1 LEV**				
	ND (1975). Brown on lt. pink unpt.		3.00	6.00	10.00

			VG	VF	UNC
FX16	**2 LEVA**				
	ND (1975).		5.00	10.00	15.00

			VG	VF	UNC
FX17	**5 LEVA**				
	ND (1975).		7.50	12.50	20.00
FX18	**10 LEVA**				
	ND (1975).		10.00	20.00	30.00
FX19	**20 LEVA**				
	ND (1975).		15.00	30.00	40.00
FX20	**50 LEVA**				
	ND (1975).		20.00	40.00	60.00
FX21	**100 LEVA**				
	ND (1975).		22.50	50.00	80.00

1978 ND Issue

#FX22-28 Wmk: Wavy lines.

			VG	VF	UNC
FX22	**1 LEV**				
	ND (1978). Red on lt. blue unpt.		1.00	3.00	5.00
FX23	**2 LEVA**				
	ND (1978).		2.00	5.00	10.00
FX24	**5 LEVA**				
	ND (1978).		3.00	7.50	15.00
FX25	**10 LEVA**				
	ND (1978).		7.50	12.50	20.00
FX26	**20 LEVA**				
	ND (1978).		15.00	30.00	40.00

			VG	VF	UNC
FX27	**50 LEVA**				
	ND (1978).		30.00	40.00	50.00
FX28	**100 LEVA**				
	ND (1978).		35.00	50.00	60.00

BULGARIAN NATIONAL BANK

1981 Issue

#FX29-35 Wmk: BNB in oval, repeated. Specimens exist.

			VG	VF	UNC
FX29	**1 LEV**				
	1981. Lt. brown on pale red unpt.		1.00	3.00	5.00
	a. Issued note.				
	s. Specimen.		—	—	—

			VG	VF	UNC
FX30	**2 LEVA**				
	1981.				
	a. Issued note.		2.00	5.00	10.00
	s. Specimen.		—	—	—

			VG	VF	UNC
FX31	**5 LEVA**				
	1981. Green-blue on yellow unpt.				
	a. Issued note.		3.00	8.00	15.00
	s. Specimen.		—	—	—

			VG	VF	UNC
FX32	**10 LEVA**				
	1981.				
	a. Issued note.		5.00	12.50	20.00
	s. Specimen.		—	—	—
FX33	**20 LEVA**				
	1981.		15.00	30.00	40.00
FX34	**50 LEVA**				
	1981.		25.00	50.00	80.00
FX35	**100 LEVA**				
	1981.		30.00	100.00	125.00

1986 Issue

#FX36-FX42 specimens exist.

			VG	VF	UNC
FX36	**1 LEV**				
	(19)86. Red on ochre unpt.				
	a. Issued note.		1.00	3.00	5.00
	s. Specimen.		—	—	—

FX37 2 LEVA
  (19)86. Blue on grey unpt.
    a. Issued note.
    s. Specimen.

	VG	VF	UNC
a.	2.00	6.00	10.00
s.	—	—	—

FX38 5 LEVA
  (19)86.
    s. Specimen.

	VG	VF	UNC
s.	—	—	—

FX39 10 LEVA
  (19)86.
    a. Issued note.
    s. Specimen.

	VG	VF	UNC
a.	5.00	12.50	20.00
s.	—	—	—

FX40 20 LEVA
  (19)86.
    a. Issued note.
    s. Specimen.

	VG	VF	UNC
a.	10.00	20.00	30.00

FX41 50 LEVA
  (19)86.

	VG	VF	UNC
	20.00	35.00	50.00

FX42 100 LEVA
  (19)86. Olive on lt. brown unpt.

	VG	VF	UNC
	30.00	50.00	100.00

Note: A 1988 dated issue is not confirmed.

BURMA

The Socialist Republic of the Union of Burma (now called Myanmar), a country of Southeast Asia fronting on the Bay of Bengal and the Andaman Sea, has an area of 261,228 sq. mi. (676,577 sq. km.) and a population of 49.34 million. Capital: Rangoon. Myanmar is an agricultural country heavily dependent on its leading product (rice) which embodies two-thirds of the cultivated area and accounts for 40 percent of the value of exports. Petroleum, lead, tin, silver, zinc, nickel, cobalt and precious stones are exported.

The first European to reach Burma, about 1435, was Nicolo Di Conti, a merchant of Venice. During the beginning of the reign of Bodawpaya (1782-1819AD) the kingdom comprised most of the same area as it does today including Arakan which was taken over in 1784-85. The British East India Company, while unsuccessful in its 1612 effort to establish posts along the Bay of Bengal, was enabled by the Anglo-Burmese Wars of 1824-86 to expand to the whole of Burma and to secure its annexation to British India. In 1937, Burma was separated from India, becoming a separate British colony with limited self-government. The Japanese occupied Burma in 1942, and on Aug. 1, 1943 Burma became an "independent and sovereign state" under Dr. Ba Maw who was appointed the Adipadi (head of state). This puppet state later collapsed with the surrender of Japanese forces. Burma became an independent nation outside the British Commonwealth on Jan. 4, 1948. the constitution of 1948 providing for a parliamentary democracy and the nationalization of certain industries. However, political and economic problems persisted, and on March 2, 1962, Gen. Ne Win took over the government, suspended the constitution, installed himself as chief of state, and pursued a socialistic program with nationalization of nearly all industry and trade. On Jan. 4, 1974, a new constitution adopted by referendum established Burma as a "socialist republic" under one-party rule. The country name was changed formally to the Union of Myanmar in 1989.

For later issues refer to Myanmar.

MONETARY SYSTEM:
  1 Kyat = 100 Pya, 1943-45, 1952-89

REPUBLIC

PEOPLES BANK OF BURMA

1965 ND ISSUE

#52-55 portr. Gen. Aung San at ctr. Arms at upper l. on back. Wmk: pattern throughout paper. Printed in East Berlin. Replacement notes have special Burmese characters w/serial #.

52 1 KYAT
  ND (1965). Purple and blue-gray on m/c unpt. Fisherman at ctr. on back. Serial # varieties.

	VG	VF	UNC
	0.15	0.30	1.00

53 5 KYATS
  ND (1965). Green and lt. blue. Back green; man w/ox at ctr.

	VG	VF	UNC
	0.25	1.00	2.50

54	10 KYATS		VG	VF	UNC
	ND (1965). Red-brown and violet. Back red-brown, woman picking cotton at r.		0.50	1.50	5.00

58	10 KYATS		VG	VF	UNC
	ND (1973). Red and violet on m/c unpt. Native ornaments at l. ctr. on back.		0.15	0.50	1.00

55	20 KYATS		VG	VF	UNC
	ND (1965). Brown and tan. Farmer on tractor at ctr. r. on back.		0.75	2.50	8.00

UNION OF BURMA BANK

1972-79 ND ISSUE

#56-61 various military portrs. of Gen. Aung San at l. and as wmk.

59	25 KYATS		VG	VF	UNC
	ND (1972). Brown and tan on m/c unpt. Mythical winged creature at ctr. on back.		0.25	0.75	1.50

56	1 KYAT		VG	VF	UNC
	ND (1972). Green and blue on m/c unpt. Ornate native wheel assembly at r. on back.		0.10	0.15	0.40

57	5 KYATS		VG	VF	UNC
	ND (1973). Blue and purple on m/c unpt. Palm tree at l. ctr. on back.		0.15	0.25	1.00

60	50 KYATS		VG	VF	UNC
	ND (1979). Brown and violet on m/c unpt. Mythical dancer at l. ctr. on back.		3.00	10.00	25.00

64   45 KYATS
ND (1987). Blue-gray and blue on m/c unpt. Po Hla Gyi at r. 2
workers w/rope and bucket at l. ctr., oil field at ctr. on back.

VG	VF	UNC
FV	FV	4.00

61   100 KYATS
ND (1976). Blue and green on m/c unpt. Native wheel and musical
string instrument at l. ctr. on back.

VG	VF	UNC
1.50	4.00	15.00

1985-87 ND Issue

#62-66 reduced size notes. Various portrs. Gen. Aung San as wmk.

65   75 KYATS
ND (1985). Brown on m/c unpt. Gen. Aung San at l. ctr. Dancer at
l. on back.

VG	VF	UNC
0.20	0.75	2.75

62   15 KYATS
ND (1986). Blue-gray and green on m/c unpt. Gen. Aung San at l.
ctr. Mythical dancer at l. on back.

VG	VF	UNC
FV	FV	2.00

66   90 KYATS
ND (1987). Brown, green and blue on m/c unpt. Seya San at r.
Farmer plowing w/oxen at l. ctr., rice planting at upper r. on back.

VG	VF	UNC
FV	FV	6.00

Note: For later issues see Myanmar.

63   35 KYATS
ND (1986). Brown-violet and purple on m/c unpt. Gen. Aung San in
military hat at l. ctr. Mythical dancer at l. on back.

VG	VF	UNC
0.20	0.50	1.50

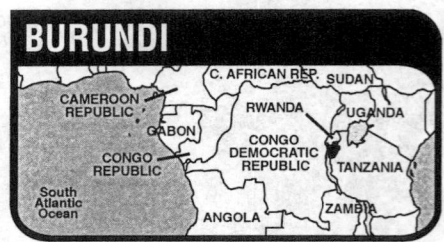

The Republic of Burundi, a landlocked country in central Africa, east of Lake Taganyila has an area of 10,759 sq. mi. (27,834 sq. km.) and a population of 6.97 million. Capital: Bujumbura. Burundi has a predominantly agricultural economy. Coffee, tea and cotton are exported.

The original inhabitants of Burundi are believed to be the Twa (pygmy); they were there when the Hutu (Bantu) arrived in the 14th century, imposing their language and customs. The development of the state structure began in the 15th centruy when migrating Tutsi, imposed themselves as feudal rulers over the Hutu. Burundi had a caste system and was ruled by a monarch, so-called the *Mwami;* however, the political and social structures were not rigid, the marriages between the two communites were common, and the Hutu enjoyed greater economic independence.

Since 1820, the caravans of Zanzibar traversed the country, but the Islamic infulence was minimal. In 1858 the first British travelers arrived in the country, and in 1871 the explorer Livingstone and journalist Stanley. As a result of Bismark's continuing interest in Africa, Burundi (then called Urundi) was occupied in the 1880s and the German Protectorate established in 1890. The country was incorporated with Rwanda (called Ruanda), into German East Africa.

During World War I, Belgium occupied Ruanda-Urundi and later the League of Nations gave the mandate area as part of Belgian Congo. After World War II, it was made a UN trust territory administrated by Belgium. The indigenous social structures were maintained in Urundi, including the presence of a local monarch, King Mwambutsa IV Bangiricenge The UN supervised election of 1961 established limited self-government. Burundi became a constitutional monarchy on July 1, 1962 and was admitted to the UN. Political rivalry between the Hutu and Tutsi intensified. The monarchy was overthrown in a military *coup* in 1966, A 1972 Hutu uprising lead to widespread massacres. Additional *coups* occured in 1976, 1987 and 1992. Since elections of 1993, there has been continual civil unrest.

RULERS:
Mwambutsa IV, 1962-1966
Ntare V, 1966

MONETARY SYSTEM:
1 Franc = 100 Centimes

KINGDOM

BANQUE DU ROYAUME DU BURUNDI

1964 ND PROVISIONAL ISSUE

#1-7 lg. *BURUNDI* ovpt. on face only of Banque d'Emission du Rwanda et du Burundi notes.

1	5 FRANCS	Good	Fine	XF
	ND (1964 - old dates 15.5.1961; 15.4.1963). Lt. brown. Black ovpt. on Rwanda-Burundi #1.	10.00	45.00	200.00

2	10 FRANCS	Good	Fine	XF
	ND (1964 - old date 5.10.1960). Gray. Red ovpt. on Rwanda-Burundi #2.	15.00	75.00	250.00

3	20 FRANCS	Good	Fine	XF
	ND (1964 - old date 5.10.1960). Green. Black ovpt. on Rwanda-Burundi #3.	20.00	75.00	250.00

4	50 FRANCS	Good	Fine	XF
	ND (1964 - old dates 15.9.1960-1.10.1960). Red. Black ovpt. on Rwanda-Burundi #4.	20.00	75.00	250.00

5	100 FRANCS	Good	Fine	XF
	ND (1964 - old dates 1.10.1960; 31.7.1962). Blue. Red ovpt. on Rwanda-Burundi #5.	15.00	65.00	235.00
6	500 FRANCS			
	ND (1964 - old dates 15.9.1960-15.5.1961). Lilac brown. Black ovpt. on Rwanda-Burundi #6.	150.00	650.00	1150.00

7	1000 FRANCS	Good	Fine	XF
	ND (1964 - old date 31.7.1962). Green. Black ovpt. on Rwanda-Burundi #7.	100.00	400.00	1250.00

1964; 1965 REGULAR ISSUE

#8-14 arms at ctr. on back.

8	5 FRANCS	VG	VF	UNC
	1.10.1964; 1.12.1964; 1.5.1965. Lt. brown on gray-green unpt. 2 young men picking coffee beans at l.	2.00	10.00	30.00

9	10 FRANCS	VG	VF	UNC
	20.11.1964; 25.2.1965; 20.3.1965; 31.12.1965. Dk. brown on lilac-brown unpt. Cattle at ctr.	2.00	10.00	35.00

10	20 FRANCS	VG	VF	UNC
	20.11.1964; 25.2.1965; 20.3.1965. Blue-green. Dancer at ctr.	7.50	35.00	125.00

11 50 FRANCS

	VG	VF	UNC
1964-66. Red-orange. View of Bujumbura.			
a. Sign. titles: *LE VICE-PRESIDENT* and *LE PRESIDENT*.	15.00	65.00	200.00
1.10.1964-31.12.1965.			
b. Sign. titles: *L'ADMINISTRATEUR* and *LE PRESIDENT*. 1.7.1966.	—	—	—

Note: #11b was prepared but apparently not released w/o ovpt. See #16b.

12 100 FRANCS

	VG	VF	UNC
1964-66. Bluish purple. Prince Rwagasore at ctr.			
a. Sign. titles: *LE VICE-PRESIDENT* and *LE PRESIDENT*.	6.00	65.00	200.00
1.10.1964; 1.12.1964; 1.5.1965.			
b. Sign. titles: *L'ADMINISTRATEUR* and *LE PRESIDENT*. 1.7.1966.	—	—	—

13 500 FRANCS

	VG	VF	UNC
5.12.1964; 1.8.1966. Brown on yellow unpt. Bank at r.	45.00	175.00	—

14 1000 FRANCS

	VG	VF	UNC
1.2.1965. Green on m/c unpt. Kg. Mwami Mwambutsa IV at r.	150.00	625.00	—

REPUBLIC

BANQUE DE LA RÉPUBLIQUE DU BURUNDI

1966 ND PROVISIONAL ISSUE

#15-19 black ovpt: *DE LA REPUBLIQUE* and *YA REPUBLIKA* on face only of Banque du Royaume du Burundi notes.

15 20 FRANCS

	VG	VF	UNC
ND (1966 - old date 20.3.1965). Ovpt. on #10.	15.00	55.00	200.00

16 50 FRANCS

	VG	VF	UNC
ND (1966 - old dates 1.5.1965; 31.12.1965; 1.7.1966).			
a. Ovpt. on #11a.	17.50	75.00	250.00
b. Ovpt. on #11b.	22.50	85.00	275.00

Note: Ovpt. on #16 has letters either 3.2 or 2.6mm high.

17 100 FRANCS

	VG	VF	UNC
ND (1966).			
a. Ovpt. on #12a. (- old date 1.5.1965).	10.00	55.00	200.00
b. Ovpt. on #12b. (- old date 1.7.1966).	10.00	55.00	200.00

Note: Ovpt. on #17 has letters either 3.2 or 2.6mm high.

18 500 FRANCS

	VG	VF	UNC
ND (1966 - old dates 5.12.1964; 1.8.1966). Ovpt. on #13.	85.00	250.00	—

19 1000 FRANCS

	VG	VF	UNC
ND (1966 - old date 1.2.1965). Ovpt. on #14.	225.00	725.00	—

1968-75 ISSUES

Sign. varieties.

20 10 FRANCS

	VG	VF	UNC
1968; 1970. Red on green and blue unpt. "Place De La Revolution" monument at r. Sign. titles: *L'ADMINISTRATEUR* and *LE PRESIDENT*.			
a. 1.11.1968.	1.00	4.00	12.50
b. 1.4.1970.	0.50	1.25	4.00

21 20 FRANCS

	VG	VF	UNC
1968-73. Blue on green and violet unpt. Dancer at ctr. Text on back.			
a. Sign. titles: *LE PRESIDENT* and *LE VICE-PRESIDENT*. 1.11.1968.	3.00	10.00	40.00
b. Sign. titles: *LE PRESIDENT* and *L'ADMINISTRATEUR*.	2.00	7.00	30.00
1.4.1970; 1.11.1971; 1.7.1973.			

22 **50 FRANCS**
1968-73. Pale red on m/c unpt. Drummer at l. ctr.

	VG	VF	UNC
a. Sign. titles: *LE VICE-PRESIDENT* and *LE PRESIDENT.* 15.5.1968; 1.10.1968.	3.50	25.00	100.00
b. Sign. titles: *ADMINISTRATEUR* and *PRESIDENT.* 1.2.1970; 1.8.1971; 1.7.1973.	2.50	15.00	40.00
s. Specimen.	—	—	200.00

22A **50 FRANCS**
1.6.1975. Brown on m/c unpt. Like #22b.

	VG	VF	UNC
a. Issued note.	4.00	35.00	115.00
s. Specimen.	—	—	

23 **100 FRANCS**
1968-75. Brown on pale orange, lilac and blue unpt. Prince Rwagasore at r.

	VG	VF	UNC
a. Sign. titles: *LE VICE-PRESIDENT* and *LE PRESIDENT.* 15.5.1968; 1.10.1968.	4.00	50.00	150.00
b. Sign. titles: *ADMINISTRATEUR* and *LE PRESIDENT.* 1.2.1970; 1.8.1971; 1.7.1973; 1.6.1975.	3.00	30.00	100.00
s. Specimen.	—	—	200.00

24 **500 FRANCS**
1968-75. Brown. Bank bldg. at r.

	VG	VF	UNC
a. Sign. titles: *LE PRESIDENT* and *LE VICE-PRESIDENT.*1.8.1968.	75.00	250.00	900.00
b. Sign. titles: *LE PRESIDENT* and *L'ADMINISTRATEUR.* 1.4.1970; 1.8.1971.	75.00	200.00	750.00
c. Sign. titles: *LE PRESIDENT* and *LE VICE-PRESIDENT.* 1.7.1973; 1.6.1975.	75.00	200.00	750.00

25 **1000 FRANCS**
1968-75. Blue and m/c. Paradise whydah and flowers. Back blue and lt. brown; cattle at ctr.

25 **1000 FRANCS**

	VG	VF	UNC
a. Sign. titles: *L'ADMINISTRATEUR* and *LE PRESIDENT.* 1.4.1968; 1.5.1971; 1.2.1973.	45.00	175.00	550.00
b. Sign. title: *LE VICE-PRESIDENT* 1.6.1975; 1.9.1976.	35.00	150.00	500.00
s. Specimen.	—	—	850.00

26 **5000 FRANCS**
1968; 1971; 1973. Blue. Pres. Micombero in military uniform at r. Loading at dockside on back.

	VG	VF	UNC
a. Sign. titles: *LE VICE-PRESIDENT* and *LE PRESIDENT.* 1.4.1968; 1.7.1973.	200.00	500.00	1500.00
b. Sign. title: *L'ADMINISTRATEUR.* 1.5.1971.	200.00	500.00	1750.00

1975-78 ISSUE
#27-31 face like #20-26. Arms at ctr. on back.

27 **20 FRANCS**
1977-2005. Red on m/c unpt. Face design like #21. Sign. titles: *LE GOUVERNEUR* and *L'ADMINISTRATEUR.*

	VG	VF	UNC
a. 1.7.1977; 1.6.1979; 1.12.1981.	FV	0.50	2.00
b. 1.12.1983; 1.12.1986; 1.5.1988; 1.10.1989.	FV	0.40	1.25
c. 1.10.1991; 25.5.1995.	FV	FV	0.75
d. Sign. titles: *LE GOUVERNEUR* and *LE 2e VICE-GOUVERNEUR.* 5.2.1997; 1.8.2001; 1.7.2003; 5.2.2005.	FV	FV	0.75
s. Specimen.	—	—	100.00

28 **50 FRANCS**
1977-93. Brown on m/c unpt. Face like #22.

	VG	VF	UNC
a. 1.7.1977; 1.5.1979.	0.15	0.75	3.00
b. 1.12.1981; 1.12.1983.	FV	0.50	2.00
c. 1.5.1988; 1.10.1989; 1.10.1991; 1.5.1993.	FV	FV	1.25
s. Specimen.	—	—	100.00

29 **100 FRANCS**
1977-93. Purple on m/c unpt. Face design like #23. Sign. titles: *L'ADMINISTRATEUR* and *LE GOUVERNEUR.*

	VG	VF	UNC

29	100 FRANCS	VG	VF	UNC
	a. 1.7.1977; 1.5.1979.	FV	1.00	3.50
	b. 1.1.1981; 1.7.1982; 1.11.1984; 1.11.1986.	FV	0.75	3.00
	c. 1.5.1988; 1.7.1990; 1.5.1993.	FV	FV	2.00
	s. Specimen.	—	—	100.00

30	500 FRANCS	VG	VF	UNC
	1977-88. Dk. blue on m/c unpt. Face design like #24. Numeral and date style varieties. Sign. titles: *LE GOUVERNEUR* and *LE VICE-GOUVERNEUR.*			
	a. 1.7.1977; 1.9.1981.	FV	10.00	40.00
	b. 1.7.1985; 1.9.1986.	FV	7.00	20.00
	c. 1.5.1988.	FV	5.00	12.50
	s. Specimen. 1.1.1980; 1.7.1985.	—	—	175.00

31	1000 FRANCS	VG	VF	UNC
	1977-91. Dk. green on m/c unpt. Like #25.			
	a. Sign. titles: *LE VICE-GOUVERNEUR* and *LE GOUVERNEUR.*1.7.1977; 1.1.1978; 1.5.1979; 1.1.1980.	FV	15.00	50.00
	b. 1.1.1981; 1.5.1982; 1.1.1984; 1.12.1986.	FV	12.50	35.00
	c. Sign. titles: *L'ADMINISTRATEUR* and *LE VICE-GOUVERNEUR.* 1.6.1987.	FV	20.00	65.00
	d. Sign. titles: *LE VICE-GOUVERNEUR* and *LE GOUVERNEUR.* 1.5.1988; 1.10.1989; 1.10.1991.	FV	7.50	12.50
	s. Specimen.	—	—	175.00

32	5000 FRANCS	VG	VF	UNC
	1978-95. Dk. brown and grayish purple on m/c unpt. Arms at upper ctr.; bldg. at lower r. Ship dockside on back.			
	a. 1.7.1978; 1.10.1981.	30.00	60.00	200.00
	b. 1.1.1984; 1.9.1986.	FV	30.00	100.00
	c. 1.10.1989; 1.10.1991.	FV	20.00	80.00
	d. Sign titles: *LE 1ER VICE-GOUVERNEUR* and *LE GOUVERNEUR.* 19.5.1994; 25.5.1995.	FV	FV	62.50

1979-81 Issues

#33 and 34 replacement notes: Serial # prefix Z.

33	10 FRANCS	VG	VF	UNC
	1981-2005. Blue-green on tan unpt. Map of Burundi w/arms superimposed at ctr. Text on back.			
	a. Sign. titles: *LE GOUVERNEUR* and *ADMINISTRATEUR.* 1.6.1981; 1.12.1983.	FV	FV	1.00
	b. 1.12.1986; 1.5.1988; 1.10.1989; 1.10.1991.	FV	FV	0.75
	c. 25.5.1995.	FV	FV	0.50
	d. Sign. titles: *LE GOUVERNEUR* and *LE 2E GOUVERNEUR.* 5.2.1997; 1.8.2001; 1.7.2003; 5.2.2005.	FV	FV	0.50

34	500 FRANCS	VG	VF	UNC
	1.6.1979; 1.1.1980; Tan, blue-black, purple and green on m/c unpt. Back purple on m/c unpt. Similar to #30. Sign. titles: *LE GOUVERNEUR* and *LE VICE-GOUVERNEUR.*	5.00	12.50	50.00

1993-97 Issue

#35 not assigned.

36	50 FRANCS	VG	VF	UNC
	19.5.1994; 5.2.1999; 1.8.2001; 1.7.2003; 5.2.2005. Dull brown-violet on m/c unpt. Man in dugout canoe at l., arms at lower ctr. Four men w/canoe at ctr., hippopotamus at lower r. on back.	FV	FV	2.00

37 **100 FRANCS**
1.10.1993; 1.12.1997; 1.8.2001; 1.5.2004. Dull purple on m/c
unpt. Archway at l. ctr., Prince Rwagasore at r. Arms lower l., home
construction at ctr. on back. Sign. titles: *LE 2eme VICE-
GOUVERNEUR* and *LE GOUVERNEUR*.

	VG	VF	UNC
a. Issued note.	FV	FV	3.00
s. Specimen.	—	—	125.00

38 **500 FRANCS**
1997-2003. Gray and violet on m/c unpt. Native painting at l. Back
blue on m/c unpt.; bank bldg. at ctr., arms at r. Wmk: Ox.

	VG	VF	UNC
a. 1.5.1997.	FV	FV	7.50
b. 5.2.1999.	FV	FV	6.00
c. 5.2.1999.	FV	FV	6.00
d. 1.7.2003.	FV	FV	6.00

39 **1000 FRANCS**
1994; 1997; 2000. Greenish black and brown-violet on m/c unpt.
Cattle at l., arms at lower ctr. Monument at ctr. on back. Sign. titles:
LE GOUVERNEUR and *LE 1ER VICE-GOUVERNEUR*. Wmk: Pres.
Micombero.

	VG	VF	UNC
a. 19.5.1994.	FV	FV	17.50
b. 1.12.1997.	FV	FV	9.00
c. 1.7.2000.	FV	FV	9.00

40 **5000 FRANCS**
5.2.1997. Olive-green and dk. green on m/c unpt. Like #32 but
w/date moved to l. and segmented foil over security thread.

VG	VF	UNC
FV	FV	55.00

1999-2001 ISSUE

41 **2000 FRANCS**
25.6.2001. Blue and green on m/c unpt. Harvest scene at r. Lake
and dam on back.

VG	VF	UNC
FV	FV	15.00

42 **5000 FRANCS**
Green, olive and 1999; 2003. lt. red on m/c unpt. Like #40, but
printed bull's head w/OVD ink at lower l. ctr. on face.

	VG	VF	UNC
a. 5.2.1999.	FV	FV	40.00
b. 1.7.2003.	FV	FV	25.00
c. 5.2.2005.	FV	FV	25.00

43 **10,000 FRANCS**
25.10.2004. M/c. Two men at lower l. Three students at ctr. on
back.

VG	VF	UNC
FV	FV	60.00

CAMBODIA

Cambodia, formerly known as Democratic Kampuchea and the Khmer Republic, a land of paddy fields and forest-clad hills located on the Indo-Chinese peninsula fronting on the Gulf of Thailand, has an area of 69,898 sq. mi. (181,035 sq. km.) and a population of 9.86 million. Capital: Phnom Penh. Agriculture is the basis of the economy, with rice the chief crop. Native industries include cattle breeding, weaving and rice milling. Rubber, cattle, corn, and timber are exported.

The region was the nucleus of the Khmer empire which flourished from the 5th to the 12th century and attained an excellence in art and architecture still evident in the magnificent ruins at Angkor. The Khmer empire once ruled over much of Southeast Asia, but began to decline in the 13th century as the Thai and Vietnamese invaded the region and attached its territories. At the request of the Cambodian king, a French protectorate attached to Cochin-China was established over the country in 1863, saving it from dissolution, and in 1885, Cambodia was included in the French Union of Indo-China. France established a constitutional monarchy for Cambodia within the French Union in 1949. The 1954 Geneva Convention resulted in full independence for the Kingdom of Cambodia. King Sihanouk abdicated to his father and won the office of Prime Minister.

Prince Sihanouk was toppled by a bloodless coup led by Lon Nol in March of 1970. Sihanouk moved to Peking to head a government-in-exile. On Oct. 9, 1970, Cambodia became the Khmer Republic, and Lon Nol its President. The government of Lon Nol was in turn toppled, April 17, 1975, by the Khmer Rouge insurgents who took control of the government and renamed the country Democratic Kampuchea.

The Khmer Rouge completely eliminated the economy and created a state without money, exchange or barter. Everyone worked for the state and was taken care of by the state. The Vietnamese supported People's Republic of Kampuchea was installed in accordance with the constitution of January 5, 1976. The name of the country was changed from Democratic Cambodia to Democratic Kampuchea, afterwards reverting to Cambodia.

In the early 1990's the UN supervised a ceasefire and in 1992 Norodom Sihanouk returned as Chief of State. He was crowned king in 1993, and in 2004 abdicated in favor of one of his sons.

RULERS:
Norodom Sihanouk (as Chief of State), 1960-1970
Lon Nol, 1970-1975
Pol Pot, 1975-1979
Heng Samrin, 1979-1985
Hun Sen, 1985-1991
Norodom Sihanouk (as Chairman, Supreme National Council), 1991-1993
Norodom Sihanouk (as King), 1993-2002
Boromneath Norodom Sihamoni, 2004-

MONETARY SYSTEM:
1 Riel = 100 Sen

SIGNATURE CHART			
	Governor	Chief Inspector	Advisor	Date
1				28.10.1955
2				1956
3				1956
4				Late 1961
5				Mid 1962
6				1963
7				1965
8				1968
9				1968

SIGNATURE CHART				
10				1969
11				1970
12				1972
13				1972
14				1974
15				March, 1975 (printed 1974)
16	Le Gouverneur — Thor Peng Leath (08-07-93/23-03-98)		Le Caissier General — Tieng Seng, 1995-	
17	Le Gouverneur — Chea Chanto 23-03-98-		Le Caissier General — Tieng Seng, 1995-	

CAMBODIA - KINGDOM

BANQUE NATIONALE DU CAMBODGE
1956; 1958 ND SECOND ISSUE

	1 RIEL		VG	VF	UNC
4	ND (1956-75). Grayish green on m/c unpt. Boats dockside in port of Phnom-Penh. Royal palace throne room on back. Printer: BWC (w/o imprint).				
	a. Sign. 1; 2.		0.50	3.00	15.00
	b. Sign. 6; 7; 8; 10; 11.		0.15	0.25	3.00
	c. Sign. 12.		0.10	0.15	1.00
	s. Specimen. Sign. 1. Perforated and printed: *SPECIMEN*.		—	—	150.00

5   20 RIELS
ND (1956-75). Brown on m/c unpt. Combine harvester at r. Phnom
Penh pagoda on back. Wmk: Buddha. Printer: BWC (w/o imprint).

	VG	VF	UNC
a. Sign. 3.	0.25	1.00	6.00
b. Sign. 6.	0.25	0.75	4.00
c. Sign. 7; 8; 10.	0.20	0.50	2.00
d. Sign. 12.	0.10	0.25	1.00

#6 not assigned.

7   50 RIELS
ND (1956-75). Blue and orange. Fishermen fishing from boats
w/lg. nets in Lake Tonle Sap at l. and r. Back blue and brown;
Angkor Wat. Wmk: Buddha. Printer: TDLR (w/o imprint).

	VG	VF	UNC
a. Western numeral in plate block designator. Sign. 3.	0.50	3.00	20.00
b. Cambodian numeral in plate block designator. 5-digit serial #. Sign. 7; 10.	0.25	1.00	3.00
c. As b. Sign. 12.	0.25	0.50	1.00
d. Cambodian serial # 6-digits. Sign. 12.	0.10	0.20	1.00
s. As c. Specimen.	—	—	100.00

8   100 RIELS
ND (1957-75). Brown and green on m/c unpt. Statue of Lokecvara
at l. Long boat on back. Wmk: Buddha.

	VG	VF	UNC
a. Imprint: *Giesecke & Devrient AG, Munchen.* Sign. 3.	0.50	3.00	20.00
b. As a. Sign. 7; 8; 11.	0.50	1.00	4.00
c. Imprint: *Giesecke & Devrient-Munchen.* Sign. 12; 13.	0.20	0.50	2.00
s. Specimen. As a. Sign. 3. Perforated *Specimen. Uniface printings.*	—	—	200.00

9   500 RIELS
ND (1958-70). Green and brown on m/c unpt. Sculpture of 2 royal
women dancers - *Devatas* at l. 2 royal dancers in ceremonial
costumes on back. Wmk: Buddha. Printer: G&D.

	VG	VF	UNC
a. Sign. 3.	3.00	20.00	75.00
b. Sign. 6.	2.00	17.50	55.00
c. Sign. 9.	1.00	3.00	12.50
s. Specimen.			

Note: This banknote was withdrawn in March 1970 because of counterfeiting.

1962-63 ND THIRD ISSUE

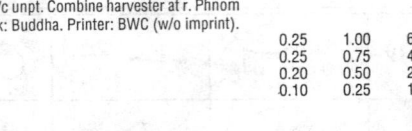

10   5 RIELS
ND (1962-75). Red on m/c unpt. Bayon stone 4 faces of
Avalokitesvara at l. Royal Palace Entrance - Chanchhaya at r. on
back. Wmk: Buddha. Printer: BWC (w/o imprint).

	VG	VF	UNC
a. Sign. 4; 6.	0.50	3.00	20.00
b. Sign. 7; 8; 11.	0.20	0.50	4.00
c. Sign. 12.	0.10	0.25	1.00
s. Specimen. Sign. 4, 8. Perforated *SPECIMEN.*	—	—	200.00

11   10 RIELS
ND (1962-75). Red-brown on m/c unpt. Temple of Banteay Srei at
r. Central Market bldg. at Phnom-Penh at l. on back. Wmk: Buddha.
Printer: TDLR (w/o imprint).

	VG	VF	UNC
a. Sign. 5; 6.	0.50	3.00	20.00
b. Sign. 7; 8; 11.	0.20	0.50	3.00
c. Sign. 12. 5 digit serial #.	0.10	0.25	1.00
d. As c. 6 digit serial #.	0.20	0.50	2.00
s. Specimen. Sign. 6, 8.	—	—	125.00

12   100 RIELS
ND (1963-72). Blue-black, dk. green and dk. brown on m/c unpt.
Sun rising behind Temple of Preah Vihear at l. Back blue, green and
brown; aerial view of the Temple of Preah Vihear. Wmk: Buddha.
Printer: G&D.

	VG	VF	UNC
a. Sign. 6.	0.50	3.00	20.00
b. Sign. 13. (Not issued).	0.10	0.20	1.00
s. Specimen. Sign. 6.	—	—	200.00

15	**100 RIELS**	VG	VF	UNC
	ND. Purple and violet on m/c unpt. Carpet weaving. Angkor Wat on back. Wmk: Man's head. Printer: TDLR (w/o imprint). (Not issued).			
	a. Sign. 13.	0.10	0.35	2.00
	b. Sign. 14.	0.25	1.25	7.50

16	**500 RIELS**	VG	VF	UNC
	ND(1973-75). Green and black on m/c unpt. Girl w/vessel on head at l. Rice paddy scene on back. Wmk: Man's head. Printer: TDLR (w/o imprint).			
	a. Sign. 13; 14.	0.25	2.00	10.00
	b. Sign. 15.	0.10	0.20	1.00
	s. As a. Specimen.	—	—	

13	**100 RIELS**	VG	VF	UNC
	ND (1956-1972). Blue on lt. blue unpt. 2 oxen at r. 3 ceremonial women on back.			
	a. Printer: ABNC w/ imprint on lower margins, face and back. Sign. 3.	3.00	20.00	100.00
	b. W/o imprint on either side. Sign. 12.	0.10	0.25	2.00
	p. Uniface proofs.	FV	FV	75.00
	s. As a. Specimen. Sign. 3.	—	—	200.00

17	**1000 RIELS**	VG	VF	UNC
	ND. Green on m/c unpt. School children. Head of Lokecvara at Ta Som on back. Wmk: School girl. Sign. 13. Printer: BWC. (Not issued).	0.10	0.20	1.00

KAMPUCHEA

BANK OF KAMPUCHEA

1975 ISSUE

#18-24 prepared by the Khmer Rouge but not issued. New regime under Pol Pot instituted an "agrarian moneyless society." All notes dated 1975.

#20-24 wmk: Angkor Wat.

14	**500 RIELS**	VG	VF	UNC
	ND (1958-1970). M/c. Farmer plowing w/2 water buffalo. Pagoda at r., doorway of Preah Vihear at l. on back. Wmk: Buddha. Printer: BdF (w/o imprint).			
	a. Sign. 3.	0.50	4.00	30.00
	b. Sign. 5; 7.	0.50	2.00	10.00
	c. Sign. 9.	0.50	1.50	9.00
	d. Sign. 12.	0.15	1.00	5.00
	x1. Lithograph counterfeit; wmk. barely visible. Sign. 3; 5.	30.00	80.00	130.00
	x2. As x1. Sign 7; 9.	20.00	60.00	110.00
	x3. As x1. Sign. 12.	10.00	30.00	75.00

18	**0.1 RIEL (1 KAK)**	VG	VF	UNC
	1975. Purple and green on orange and m/c unpt. Mortar crew l. Threshing rice on back.			
	a. Issued note.	0.20	0.50	3.00
	s. Specimen.	—	—	200.00

KHMER REPUBLIC

BANQUE NATIONALE DU CAMBODGE

1973 ND ISSUE

#15 and 16 replacement notes: Series #90.

19	**0.5 RIEL (5 KAK)**	VG	VF	UNC
	1975. Red on lt. green and m/c unpt. Troops marching at l. ctr. Bayon sculpture at l., machine and worker at r. on back.			
	a. Issued note.	0.20	0.50	3.00
	s. Specimen.	—	—	200.00

20   1 RIEL
1975. Red-violet and red on m/c unpt. Women farm workers at l.
ctr. Woman operating machine on back.

	VG	VF	UNC
a. Issued note.	0.20	0.50	3.00
s. Specimen.	—	—	200.00

21   5 RIELS
1975. Deep green on m/c unpt. Ancient temples of Angkor Wat at
ctr. r. Landscaping crew on back.

	VG	VF	UNC
a. Issued note.	0.20	0.40	3.50
s. Specimen.	—	—	200.00

22   10 RIELS
1975. Brown and red on m/c unpt. Soldiers (Machine gun crew) at
ctr. r. Rice harvesting on back.

	VG	VF	UNC
a. Issued note.	0.20	0.75	6.00
s. Specimen.	—	—	200.00

23   50 RIELS
1975. Purple on m/c unpt. Planting rice at l., Bayon sculpture at r.
Woman's militia at ctr. r. on back.

	VG	VF	UNC
a. Issued note.	0.50	2.00	12.00
s. Specimen.	—	—	200.00

24   100 RIELS
1975. Deep green on m/c unpt. Factory workers at l. ctr. Back black;
harvesting rice.

	VG	VF	UNC
a. Issued note.	0.75	4.00	17.50
s. Specimen.	—	—	200.00

STATE BANK OF DEMOCRATIC KAMPUCHEA

1979 ISSUE

#25-32 issued 20.3.1980 by the Vietnamese-backed regime of Heng Samrin which overthrew Pol Pot in 1979.

25   0.1 RIEL (1 KAK)
1979. Olive-green on lt. blue unpt. Arms at ctr. Water buffalos on
back.

	VG	VF	UNC
a. Issued note.	0.05	0.15	0.50
s. Specimen.	—	—	15.00

26   0.2 RIEL (2 KAK)
1979. Grayish green on tan unpt. Arms at ctr. Rice workers on
back.

	VG	VF	UNC
a. Issued note.	0.10	0.20	0.50
s. Specimen.	—	—	15.00

27   0.5 RIEL (5 KAK)
1979. Red-orange on tan and gray unpt. Arms at l., modern
passenger train at r. Men fishing from boats w/nets on back.

	VG	VF	UNC
a. Issued note.	0.10	0.20	1.00
s. Specimen.	—	—	15.00

28   1 RIEL
1979. Brown on yellow and m/c unpt. Arms at ctr. Women
harvesting rice on back.

	VG	VF	UNC
a. Issued note.	0.10	0.20	0.50
s. Specimen. 2 serial # var.	—	—	15.00

29   5 RIELS
1979. Dk. brown on lt. green and m/c unpt. 4 people at l., arms at
r. Independence from France (now Victory) monument on back.

	VG	VF	UNC
a. Issued note.	0.10	0.30	2.00
s. Specimen.	—	—	15.00
x. Counterfeit (contemporary).	—	1.00	3.00

34	10 RIELS	VG	VF	UNC
	1987. Like #30 but green on lt. blue and m/c unpt. Back deep green and lilac on lt. blue unpt.	0.10	0.35	2.00

CAMBODIA

PEOPLES NATIONAL BANK OF CAMBODIA

1990-92 ISSUE

#35-37 wmk: Stylized lotus flowers.

35	50 RIELS	VG	VF	UNC
	1992. Dull brown on m/c unpt. Arms at ctr., male portrait at r. Ships dockside on back. Printer: NBC (w/o imprint).			
	a. Issued note.	0.10	0.25	2.00
	s. Specimen.	—	—	35.00

30	10 RIELS	VG	VF	UNC
	1979. Dk. gray on lilac and m/c unpt. Arms at l., harvesting fruit trees at r. School on back.			
	a. Issued note.	0.20	0.50	4.00
	s. Specimen.	—	—	15.00

31	20 RIELS	VG	VF	UNC
	1979. Purple on pink and m/c unpt. Arms at l. Water buffalos hauling logs on back. Wmk: Arms.			
	a. Issued note.	0.10	0.35	5.00
	s. Specimen.	—	—	20.00
	x. Counterfeit (contemporary).	1.00	2.00	4.00

36	100 RIELS	VG	VF	UNC
	1990. Dk. green and brown on lt. blue and lilac unpt. Independence from France (now Victory) monument at l. ctr., male portrait at r. Rubber trees on back.			
	a. Issued note.	0.10	0.50	3.00
	s. Specimen.	—	—	50.00

32	50 RIELS	VG	VF	UNC
	1979. Deep red on yellow-green and m/c unpt. Arms at l., Bayon stone head at ctr. Angkor Wat on back. Wmk: Arms.			
	a. Issued note.	0.10	0.35	7.50
	s. Specimen.	—	—	20.00

1987 ISSUE

33	5 RIELS	VG	VF	UNC
	1987. Like #29 but red and brown on lt. yellow and lt. green unpt. Back red on pale yellow unpt.	0.10	0.35	2.00

37	200 RIELS	VG	VF	UNC
	1992. Dull olive-green and tan on m/c unpt. Floodgates at r. Bayon sculpture in Angkor Wat ctr. on back. Printer: NBC.			
	a. Issued note.	0.15	0.50	2.00
	s. Specimen. 1993.	—	—	125.00

38   500 RIELS

	VG	VF	UNC
1991. Red, purple and brown-violet on m/c unpt. Arms above Angkor Wat at ctr. Animal statue at l., cultivating with tractors at ctr. on back. Wmk: Sculptured heads.			
a. Issued note.	0.25	0.50	3.00
s. Specimen. (two different serial # varieties.)	—	—	50.00

39   1000 RIELS

	VG	VF	UNC
1992. Dk. green, brown and black on m/c unpt. Bayon Temple ruins in Angkor Wat. Fishermen fishing in boats w/lg. nets in Lake Tonle Sap on back. Wmk: Chinze. (Not released).	—	—	10.00

40   2000 RIELS

	VG	VF	UNC
1992. Black, dp. blue and violet-brown on m/c unpt. King N. Sihanouk at l. and as wmk., Temple portal at Preah Vihear at r. (Not released).	—	—	10.00

NATIONAL BANK OF CAMBODIA
1995 ISSUE

	SIGNATURE VARIETIES	
	Le Gouverneur	Le Caissier Général
16	Thor Peng Leath,	Tieng Seng, 1999-
17	Chea Chanto, 1999-	Tieng Seng, 1999-

#41-43 arms at upper l. Wmk: Stylized lotus flowers. Printer: NBC. Sign. 16 or 17.

41   100 RIELS

	VG	VF	UNC
1995; 1998. Grayish green and brown on m/c unpt. Chinze, Independence from France (Now Victory) monument at r. Tapping rubber trees on back.			
a. 1995. Sign. 16.	0.10	0.20	1.00
b. 1998. Sign. 16; 17.	0.10	0.20	0.50
s. Specimen. 1995.	—	—	35.00

42   200 RIELS

	VG	VF	UNC
1995; 1998. Dk. olive-green and brown on m/c unpt. Similar to #37 but smaller size. Sign. 16.			
a. 1995.	FV	FV	2.00
b. 1998.	FV	FV	0.35
s. Specimen. 1995.	—	—	25.00

43   500 RIELS

	VG	VF	UNC
1996, 1998. Red and purple on m/c unpt. Angkor Wot at r. Mythical animal at l., rice fields at ctr. on back.			
a. 1996. Sign. 16.	FV	FV	1.00
b. 1998. Sign. 16; 17.	FV	FV	1.00
s. Specimen. 1996.	—	—	25.00

#44-50 Replacement notes have an *0* at the end of the serial # prefix, eg. *A0.*

Printer: F-CO.

#44 and 45 wmk: Cube design.

44   1000 RIELS

	VG	VF	UNC
ND (1995). Blue-green on gold and m/c unpt. Bayon stone 4 faces of Avalokitesvara at l. Prasat Chan Chaya at r. on back.			
a. ND (1995).	FV	FV	2.00
s. Specimen.	—	—	30.00

48 20,000 RIELS

	VG	VF	UNC
ND (1995). Violet and red on m/c unpt. Boats dockside in Port of Phnom-Penh at ctr. Throne Room in National Palace on back. Sign. 16.			
a. Issued note.	FV	FV	20.00
s. Specimen.	—	—	30.00

45 2000 RIELS

	VG	VF	UNC
ND (1995). Reddish brown on m/c unpt. Fishermen fishing from boats w/nets in Lake Tonie Sap at l. and r. Temple ruins at Angkor Wat on back.			
a. Issued note.	FV	FV	3.50
s. Specimen.	—	—	30.00

#46-49 Kg. N. Sihanouk at r. and as wmk.

46 5000 RIELS

	VG	VF	UNC
ND (1995); 1998. Deep purple and blue-black w/black text on m/c unpt. Temple of Banteai Srei at lower l. ctr. Central market in Phnom-Penh on back.			
a. ND (1995). Sign. 16.	FV	FV	10.00
b. 1998. Sign. 16, 17.	FV	FV	6.50
s. Specimen. ND (1995); 1998.	—	—	30.00

49 50,000 RIELS

	VG	VF	UNC
ND (1995); 1998. Dk. brown, brown and deep olive-green on m/c unpt. Preah Vihear Temple at ctr. Road to Preah Vihear Temple on back.			
a. ND (1995). Sign. 16.	FV	FV	52.50
b. 1998. Sign. 16, 17.	FV	FV	50.00
s. Specimen. ND (1995); 1998.	—	—	35.00

50 100,000 RIELS

	VG	VF	UNC
ND (1995). Green, blue-green and black on m/c unpt. Chief and First Lady at r. and as wmk. Chief and First Lady receiving homage of people at ctr. r. on back. Sign. 16.			
a. Issued note.	FV	FV	95.00
s. Specimen. Ovpt. *SPECIMEN*.	—	—	40.00

47 10,000 RIELS

	VG	VF	UNC
ND (1995); 1998. Blue-black, black and dk. green on m/c unpt. Statue of Lokecvara at lower l. ctr. People rowing long boat during the water festival at lower ctr. on back.			
a. ND (1995). Sign. 16.	FV	FV	12.50
b. 1998. Sign. 16, 17.	FV	FV	12.00
s. Specimen. ND(1995); 1998.	—	—	30.00

1999 ISSUE

51 1000 RIELS

	VG	VF	UNC
1999. Dk. brown and dk. olive-green on m/c unpt. Temples at ctr. r. Back brown and slate blue; construction site at ctr. Sign. 17.			
a. Issued note.	FV	FV	1.25
s. Specimen.	—	—	30.00

NOTICE

Readers with unlisted dates, signature varieties, etc. are invited to submit photocopies of their notes to: Standard Catalog of World Paper Money, 700 East State St. Iola, WI 54990-0001, E-Mail: george.cuhaj@fwpubs.com.

2001-02 ISSUE

#52-54 naga heads sculpture at lower l. ctr. Wmk: Bayon sculpture in Angkor Wat.

52	50 RIELS	VG	VF	UNC
	2002. Dk. brown and tan on m/c unpt. Preah Vihear temple at ctr. Dam at ctr. on back. Sign. 17.			
	a. Issued note.	FV	FV	0.35
	s. Specimen.	—	—	25.00

53	100 RIELS	VG	VF	UNC
	2001. Purple, brown and green. Independence Monument at r. ctr. Students and school on back. Wmk: multiple lines of text. Sign. 17.			
	a. Issued note.	FV	FV	0.50
	s. Specimen.	—	—	15.00

#53-56 Kg. Norodom Sihanouk at r.

54	500 RIELS	VG	VF	UNC
	2002; 2004. Red and purple on m/c unpt. Angkor Wat temple at ctr. Bridge spanning Mekong river at Kampong Cham at ctr. on back. Sign. 17.			
	a. 2002.	FV	FV	1.50
	b. 2004.	FV	FV	1.00
	s. Specimen.	FV	FV	15.00

55	5000 RIELS	VG	VF	UNC
	2001; 2004. Green and gray. Bridge of Kampong Kdei in Siemreap Province on back. Sign. 17.			
	a. 2001.	FV	FV	6.00
	b. 2004.	FV	FV	5.00
	s. Specimen.	—	—	15.00

56	10,000 RIELS	VG	VF	UNC
	2001. Violet, brown and blue. Water festival before Royal Palace on back. Sign. 17.			
	a. Issued note.	FV	FV	8.00
	s. Specimen.	—	—	15.00

57	50,000 RIELS	VG	VF	UNC
	2001. Violet, brown and blue. Angkor Wat temple on back. Sign. 17.			
	a. Issued note.	FV	FV	40.00
	s. Specimen.	—	—	30.00

COLLECTOR SERIES

NATIONAL BANK OF CAMBODIA

1995 ND ISSUE

CS1	1000 - 100,000 RIELS	Issue Price	Mkt.	Value
	ND (1995). #44-50. Specimen.	—		250.00

Note: Issued in a special folder w/notes laminated in plastic including 50, 100, 200 and 500 Riels coins dated BE2538 (1994).

FOREIGN EXCHANGE CERTIFICATES

MINISTERE DU TOURISME DU CAMBODGE

1960's BON TOURISTIQUE ISSUE

#FX1-FX5 black text. Shoreline at l. ctr., royal dancer at r. Black text on back. Perforated along l. edge.

FX1	1 RIEL	VG	VF	UNC
	ca. 1960's. Pink and tan.	7.00	30.00	100.00

FX2	2 RIELS	VG	VF	UNC
	1961. Lt. green and violet.	7.00	30.00	100.00

FX3	5 RIELS	VG	VF	UNC
	ca. 1960's. Dk. purple and orange.	7.00	30.00	100.00
FX4	10 RIELS			
	ca. 1960's. Yellow and lt. green.	7.00	30.00	100.00
FX5	20 RIELS			
	ca. 1960's. Brown and pale green.	7.00	30.00	100.00

REGIONAL

KHMER ROUGE INFLUENCE

Issued for circulation in Khmer Rouge occupied areas in exchange for Thailand Baht. Printed in Thailand. The issue was ordered destroyed, but examples have recently become available in the market. Deceptive forgeries (copies) of these notes exist.

1993 ND ISSUE

#R1-R5 w/sign. of Pres. Khieu Samphan.

R1	5 RIELS	VG	VF	UNC
	ND (1993-99). M/c. Children harvesting vegetables at ctr., temple carvings at l. and r. Caravan of ox carts at ctr., temple carvings at l. on back.	0.50	3.00	10.00

R2	10 RIELS	VG	VF	UNC
	ND (1993-99). M/c. Village at ctr. r., temple carvings at l. and r. Fishing village, boats at ctr., temple carvings at l. and r. on back.	0.50	3.00	10.00

R3	20 RIELS	VG	VF	UNC
	ND (1993-99). M/c. Villagers leading cattle along road at ctr., temple carvings at l. and r. Street scene at ctr., temple carvings at l. and r. on back.	1.00	4.00	15.00
R4	50 RIELS			
	ND (1993-99). M/c. Planting rice at ctr. Ox-drawn carts at l. ctr. Temple carvings at l. and r. on back.	1.00	4.00	15.00

R5	100 RIELS	VG	VF	UNC
	ND (1993-99). M/c. Field workers at ctr., temple carvings at l. Temples of Angkor Wat at ctr., temple carvings at l. and r. on back.	2.00	10.00	55.00

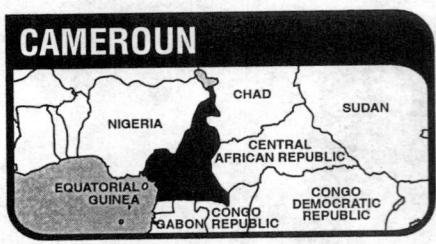

CAMEROUN

The United Republic of Cameroun, located in west-central Africa on the Gulf of Guinea, has an area of 185,568 sq. mi. (475,440 sq. km.) and a population of 15.13 million. Capital: Yaounde. About 90 percent of the labor force is employed on the land; cash crops account for 80 percent of the country's export revenue. Cocoa, coffee, aluminum, cotton, rubber and timber are exported.

European contact with what is now the United Republic of Cameroun began in the 16th century with the voyage of Portuguese navigator Fernando Po. The following three centuries saw continuous activity by Spanish, Dutch and British traders and missionaries. The land was spared colonial rule until 1884, when treaties with tribal chiefs brought German domination. After Germany's defeat in WWI, the League of Nations in 1919 divided the Cameroons between Great Britain and France, with the larger eastern area going to France. The French and British mandates were converted into United Nations trusteeships in 1946. French Cameroon became the independent Cameroon Republic on Jan. 1, 1960. The federation of East (French) and West (British) Cameroon was established in 1961 when the southern part of British Cameroon voted for reunification with the Cameroun Republic, and the northern part for union with Nigeria. On Nov. 1, 1995 the Republic of Cameroon joined the Commonwealth. Issues continue under Central African States.

MONETARY SYSTEM:
1 Franc = 100 Centimes

SIGNATURE VARIETIES:
Refer to introduction of Central African States.

RÉPUBLIQUE DU CAMEROUN

BANQUE CENTRALE

1961 ND ISSUE

#7-9 denominations in French only, or French and English.

		Good	Fine	XF
7	**1000 FRANCS** ND (1961). M/c. Man w/basket harvesting cocoa. Sign. 1A.	150.00	600.00	1750.00
8	**5000 FRANCS** ND (1961). M/c. Pres. A. Ahidjo at r. Sign. 1A.	75.00	300.00	1500.00

		Good	Fine	XF
9	**5000 FRANCS** ND. Like #8 but denomination also in English words at lower l. ctr. Sign. 1A.	150.00	600.00	1900.00

RÉPUBLIQUE FÉDÉRALE DU CAMEROUN

BANQUE CENTRALE

1962 ND ISSUE

#10-13 denominations in French and English.

		VG	VF	UNC
10	**100 FRANCS** ND (1962). M/c. Pres. of the Republic at l. Ships on back. Sign. 1A. Wmk: Antelope's head.	5.00	30.00	125.00

		VG	VF	UNC
11	**500 FRANCS** ND (1962). M/c. Man w/2 oxen. Man w/bananas at l., truck on road at ctr. r., 2 ships in background at upper r. on back. Sign. 1A.	15.00	125.00	450.00

Note: Engraved (intaglio) and lithographic varieties.

		VG	VF	UNC
12	**1000 FRANCS** ND (1962). M/c. Like #7 but w/title: *RÉPUBLIQUE FÉDÉRALE . . .* on back. Sign. 1A.	25.00	125.00	600.00

Note: Engraved (intaglio) and lithographic varieties.

13	**5000 FRANCS** ND (1962). M/c. Like #9 but w/title: *RÉPUBLIQUE FÉDÉRALE . . .* on back. Sign. 1A.	100.00	400.00	1300.00

1972 ND Issue

14 **10,000 FRANCS**

	VG	VF	UNC
ND (1972). M/c. Pres. A. Ahidjo at l., fruit at ctr., wood carving at r. Statue at l. and r., tractor plowing at ctr. on back. Sign. 2.	40.00	125.00	375.00

RÉPUBLIQUE UNIE DU CAMEROUN

BANQUE DES ÉTATS DE L'AFRIQUE CENTRALE

1974 ND Issue

15 **500 FRANCS**

ND (1974; 1984); 1978-83. Red-brown and m/c. Woman wearing hat at l., aerial view of modern bldgs. at ctr. Mask at l., students and chemical testing at ctr., statue at r. on back.

	VG	VF	UNC
a. Sign. titles: *LE DIRECTEUR GÉNÉRAL* and *UN CENSEUR*. Engraved. Wmk: Antelope in half profile. Sign. 3. ND (1974).	20.00	75.00	250.00
b. As a. Sign. 5.	FV	7.00	27.50
c. Sign. titles: *LE GOUVERNEUR* and *UN CENSEUR*. Wmk: Antelope in profile. Sign. 10. 1.4.1978.	FV	5.00	20.00
d. Sign. 12. 1.6.1981; 1.1.1983.	FV	3.00	10.00
e. Sign. 12. 1.1.1982.	5.00	25.00	75.00

16 **1000 FRANCS**

ND (1974); 1978-83. Blue and m/c. Hut at ctr., girl w/plaits at r. Mask at l., trains, planes and bridge at ctr., statue at r. on back.

	VG	VF	UNC
a. Sign. titles: *LE DIRECTEUR GÉNÉRAL* and *UN CENSEUR*. Engraved. Wmk: Antelope in half profile. Sign. 5. ND (1974).	FV	10.00	40.00
b. Sign. titles like a. Lithographed. Wmk: like c. Sign. 8. ND (1978).	20.00	55.00	175.00
c. Sign. titles: *LE GOUVERNEUR* and *UN CENSEUR*. Lithographed. Wmk: Antelope in profile. Sign. 10. 1.4.1978, 1.7.1980.	FV	7.50	25.00
d. Sign. 12. 1.6.1981; 1.1.1982; 2; 1.1.1983.	FV	4.50	17.50
s. As a. Specimen.	—	—	—

17 **5000 FRANCS**

ND (1974). Brown and m/c. Pres. A. Ahidjo at l., railway loading equipment at r. Mask at l., industrial college at ctr., statue at r. on back.

	VG	VF	UNC
a. Sign. titles: *LE DIRECTEUR GÉNÉRAL* and *UN CENSEUR*. Engraved. Sign. 3. ND (1974).	50.00	175.00	550.00
b. Like a. Sign. 5.	30.00	100.00	350.00
c. Sign. titles: *LE GOUVERNEUR* and *UN CENSEUR*. Sign. 11; 12.	10.00	75.00	350.00

18 **10,000 FRANCS**

ND (1974; 1978; 1981). M/c. Pres. A. Ahidjo at l. Similar to #14 except for new bank name on back.

	VG	VF	UNC
a. Sign. titles: *LE DIRECTEUR GÉNÉRAL* and *UN CENSEUR*. Sign. 5. ND (1974).	15.00	75.00	350.00
b. Sign. titles: *LE GOUVERNEUR* and *UN CENSEUR*. Sign. 11; 12. ND (1978; 1981).	10.00	50.00	250.00

1981 ND Issue

19 **5000 FRANCS**

	VG	VF	UNC
ND (1981). Brown and m/c. Mask at l., woman carrying bundle of fronds at r. Plowing and mine ore conveyor on back. Sign. 12.	FV	20.00	75.00

20	**10,000 FRANCS**	VG	VF	UNC
	ND (1981). Brown, green and m/c. Stylized antelope heads at l., woman at r. Loading of fruit onto truck at l. on back. Sign. 12.	FV	35.00	125.00

RÉPUBLIQUE DU CAMEROUN

BANQUE DES ÉTATS DE L'AFRIQUE CENTRALE

1984 ND ISSUE

25	**1000 FRANCS**	VG	VF	UNC
	1.1.1985. Dk. blue on m/c unpt. Carving at l., small figurines at ctr., man at r. Incomplete map of Chad at top. Elephant at l., carving at r. on back.	FV	5.00	25.00

26	**1000 FRANCS**	VG	VF	UNC
	1986-92. Like #25 but w/completed outline map of Chad at top ctr.			
	a. Sign. 12. 1.1.1986-1.1.1989.	FV	4.00	12.50
	b. Sign. 13. 1.1.1990.	FV	4.50	15.00
	c. Sign. 15.1.1.1992.	FV	3.75	12.00

21	**1000 FRANCS**	VG	VF	UNC
	1.6.1984. Blue and m/c. Like #16 except for new country name. Sign. 12.	2.50	7.50	25.00
22	**5000 FRANCS**			
	ND (1984; 1990; 1992). Brown and m/c. Like #19 except for new country name. Sign. 12; 13; 15.	FV	15.00	60.00
23	**10,000 FRANCS**			
	ND (1984; 1990). Brown, green and m/c. Like #20 except for new country name. Sign. 12; 13.	FV	30.00	110.00

1985-86 ISSUE

#24-26 wmk: Carving (as on notes).

24	**500 FRANCS**	VG	VF	UNC
	1985-90. Brown on m/c unpt. Carving and jug at ctr. Man carving mask at l. ctr. on back.			
	a. Sign. 12. 1.1.1985-1.1.1988.	FV	2.50	7.00
	b. Sign. 13. 1.1.1990.	FV	FV	6.00

CANADA

Canada is located to the north of the United States, and spans the full breadth of the northern portion of North America from Atlantic to Pacific oceans, except for the State of Alaska. It has a total area of 3,850,000 sq. mi. (9,970,610 sq. km.) and a population of 30.68 million. Capital: Ottawa.

Jacques Cartier, a French explorer, took possession of Canada for France in 1534, and for more than a century the history of Canada was that of a French colony. Samuel de Champlain helped to establish the first permanent colony in North America, in 1604 at Port Royal, Acadia - now Annapolis Royal, Nova Scotia. Four years later he founded the settlement of Quebec.

The British settled along the coast to the south while the French, motivated by a grand design, pushed into the interior. France's plan for a great American empire was to occupy the Mississippi heartland of the country, and from there to press in upon the narrow strip of English coastal settlements from the rear. Inevitably, armed conflict erupted between the French and the British; consequently, Britain acquired Hudson Bay, Newfoundland and Nova Scotia from the French in 1713. British control of the rest of New France was secured in 1763, largely because of James Wolfe's great victory over Montcalm near Quebec in 1759.

During the American Revolution, Canada became a refuge for great numbers of American Royalists, most of whom settled in Ontario, thereby creating an English majority west of the Ottawa River. The ethnic imbalance contravened the effectiveness of the prevailing French type of government, and in 1791 the Constitutional act was passed by the British parliament, dividing Canada at the Ottawa River into two parts, each with its own government: Upper Canada, chiefly English and consisting of the southern section of what is now Ontario; and Lower Canada, chiefly French and consisting principally of the southern section of Quebec. Subsequent revolt by dissidents in both sections caused the British government to pass the Union act, July 23, 1840, which united Lower and Upper Canada (as Canada East and Canada West) to form the Province of Canada, with one council and one assembly in which the two sections had equal numbers.

The union of the two provinces did not encourage political stability; the equal strength of the French and British made the task of government all but impossible. A further change was made with the passage of the British North American act, which took effect on July 1, 1867, and established Canada as the first federal union in the British Empire. Four provinces entered the union at first: Upper Canada as Ontario, Lower Canada as Quebec, Nova Scotia and New Brunswick. The Hudson's Bay Company's territories were acquired in 1869 out of which were formed the provinces of Manitoba, Saskatchewan and Alberta. British Columbia joined in 1871 and Prince Edward Island in 1873. Canada took over the Arctic Archipelago in 1895. In 1949 Newfoundland came into the confederation. Canada is a member of the Commonwealth. Elizabeth II is Head of State as Queen of Canada.

RULERS:
British 1763-

MONETARY SYSTEM:
12 Pence = 1 Shilling
20 Shillings = 1 Pound
100 Cents = 1 Dollar

DOMINION

BANQUE DU CANADA / BANK OF CANADA

1954 MODIFIED HAIR STYLE ISSUE

74	1 DOLLAR	VG	VF	UNC
	1954 (1955-72). Black on green unpt. Like #66 but Queen's hair in modified style. Back green; western prairie scene. Printer: CBNC.			
	a. Sign. Beattie-Coyne. (1955-61).	1.00	2.50	15.00
	b. Sign. Beattie-Rasminsky. (1961-72).	1.00	2.00	12.50
75	1 DOLLAR			
	1954 (1955-74). Like #74. Printer: BABNC.			
	a. Sign. Beattie-Coyne. (1955-61).	1.00	2.50	20.00
	b. Sign. Beattie-Rasminsky. (1961-72).	1.00	1.50	7.50
	c. Sign. Bouey-Rasminsky. (1972-73).	1.00	1.50	8.50
	d. Sign. Lawson-Bouey. (1973-74).	1.00	1.50	7.50

76	2 DOLLARS	VG	VF	UNC
	1954 (1955-75). Black on red-brown unpt. Like #67 but Queen's hair in modified style. Back red-brown. Quebec scenery. Printer: BABNC.			
	a. Sign. Beattie-Coyne. (1955-61).	1.75	4.00	30.00
	b. Sign. Beattie-Rasminsky. (1961-72).	1.75	3.00	20.00
	c. Sign. Bouey-Rasminsky. (1972-73).	1.75	3.00	15.00
	d. Sign. Lawson-Bouey. (1973-75).	1.75	3.00	15.00
77	5 DOLLARS			
	1954 (1955-72). Black on blue unpt. Like #68 but Queen's hair in modified style. Back blue; river in the north country. Printer: CBNC.			
	a. Sign. Beattie-Coyne. (1955-61).	5.00	10.00	65.00
	b. Sign. Beattie-Rasminsky. (1961-72).	4.50	7.50	35.00
	c. Sign. Bouey-Rasminsky. (1972).	4.50	7.50	30.00
78	5 DOLLARS			
	1954 (1955-61). Like #77. Sign. Beattie-Coyne. Printer: BABNC.	4.50	10.00	65.00

79	10 DOLLARS	VG	VF	UNC
	1954 (1955-71). Black on purple unpt. Like #69 but Queen's hair in modified style. Back purple; Rocky Mountain scene. Printer: BABNC.			
	a. Sign. Beattie-Coyne. (1955-61).	9.00	12.50	55.00
	b. Sign. Beattie-Rasminsky. (1961-71).	9.00	12.50	45.00

80	20 DOLLARS	VG	VF	UNC
	1954 (1955-70). Black on olive olive-green unpt. Like #70 but Queen's hair in modified style. Back olive green; Laurentian hills in winter. Printer: CBNC.			
	a. Sign. Beattie-Coyne. (1955-61).	17.50	25.00	100.00
	b. Sign. Beattie-Rasminsky. (1961-70).	FV	20.00	65.00

81   50 DOLLARS

	VG	VF	UNC
1954 (1955-75). Black on orange unpt. Like #71 but Queen's hair in modified style. Back orange; Atlantic coastline. Printer: CBNC.			
a. Sign. Beattie-Coyne. (1955-61).	FV	50.00	175.00
b. Sign. Beattie-Rasminsky. (1961-72).	FV	50.00	150.00
c. Sign. Lawson-Bouey. (1973-75).	FV	65.00	200.00

82   100 DOLLARS

	VG	VF	UNC
1954 (1955-76). Black on brown unpt. Queen's hair in modified style. Back brown; mountain lake. Printer: CBNC.			
a. Sign. Beattie-Coyne. (1955-61).	FV	100.00	275.00
b. Sign. Beattie-Rasminsky. (1961-72).	FV	100.00	225.00
c. Sign. Lawson-Bouey. (1973-76).	FV	100.00	250.00

83   1000 DOLLARS

	VG	VF	UNC
1954 (1955-87). Black on rose unpt. Like #73 but Queen's hair in modified style. Back rose; central Canadian landscape.			
a. Sign. Beattie-Coyne. (1955-61).	800.00	1250.00	2500.00
b. Sign. Beattie-Rasminsky. (1961-72).	FV	950.00	1750.00
c. Sign. Bouey-Rasminsky. (1972).	FV	950.00	1700.00
d. Sign. Lawson-Bouey. (1973-84).	FV	FV	1250.00
e. Sign. Thiessen-Crow. (1987).	FV	1000.00	1500.00

1967 COMMEMORATIVE ISSUE

#84, Centennial of Canadian Confederation

84   1 DOLLAR

	VG	VF	UNC
1967. Black on green unpt. Qn. Elizabeth II at r. Back green; First Parliament Building. Sign. Beattie-Rasminsky.			
a. Centennial dates: *1867-1967* replaces serial #.	1.00	1.50	3.50
b. Regular serial #'s.	1.00	1.50	5.00

1969-75 ISSUE

#85-91 arms at l.

85   1 DOLLAR

	VG	VF	UNC
1973. Black on lt. green and m/c unpt. Qn. Elizabeth II at r. Parliament Building as seen from across the Ottawa River on back.			
a. Engraved back. Sign. Lawson-Bouey.	FV	1.00	5.00
b. Lithographed back. Sign. as a. Serial # prefix: *AFF-*.	FV	1.00	5.50
c. Sign. Crow-Bouey.	FV	1.00	3.50

Note: Two formats of uncut 40-note sheets of #85b were sold to collectors in 1988 (BABN) and again in 1989 (CBNC). BABN format: 5x8 notes regular serial # prefixes *BFD, BFK, BFL* and replacement prefix *BAX*. CBNC format: 4x10 notes regular serial # prefixes *ECP, ECR, ECV, ECW* and replacement prefix *EAX*.

86   2 DOLLARS

	VG	VF	UNC
1974. Red-brown on m/c unpt. Qn. Elizabeth II at r. Inuits preparing for hunt on back.			
a. Sign. Lawson-Bouey.	FV	2.00	10.00
b. Sign. Crow-Bouey.	FV	2.00	10.00

Note: Two formats of uncut 40-note sheets of #86b were sold to collectors in 1995-96. BABN format: 5x8 notes. CBNC format: 4x10 notes.

87	5 DOLLARS	VG	VF	UNC
	1972. Blue on m/c unpt. Sir Wilfred Laurier at r. Serial # on face. Salmon fishing boat at Vancouver Island on back.			
	a. Sign. Bouey-Rasminsky.	FV	6.00	37.50
	b. Sign. Lawson-Bouey.	FV	6.00	35.00

88	10 DOLLARS	VG	VF	UNC
	1971. Purple on m/c unpt. Sir John A. MacDonald at r. Oil refinery at Sarnia, Ontario, on back.			
	a. Sign. Beattie-Rasminsky.	FV	12.50	60.00
	b. Sign. Bouey-Rasminsky.	FV	12.50	65.00
	c. Sign. Lawson-Bouey.	FV	FV	40.00
	d. Sign. Crow-Bouey.	FV	FV	40.00
	e. Sign. Thiessen-Crow.	FV	FV	40.00

89	20 DOLLARS	VG	VF	UNC
	1969. Green on m/c unpt. Arms at l. Qn. Elizabeth II at r. Serial # on face. Alberta's Lake Moraine and Rocky Mountains on back.			
	a. Sign. Beattie-Rasminsky.	FV	25.00	95.00
	b. Sign. Lawson-Bouey.	FV	22.50	80.00

90	50 DOLLARS	VG	VF	UNC
	1975. Red on m/c unpt. William Lyon MacKenzie King at r. Mounted Police in *Dome* formation (from their Musical Ride program) on back.			
	a. Sign. Lawson-Bouey.	FV	55.00	195.00
	b. Sign. Crow-Bouey.	FV	50.00	175.00

91	100 DOLLARS	VG	VF	UNC
	1975. Brown on m/c unpt. Sir Robert Borden at r. Lunenburg, Nova Scotia harbor scene on back.			
	a. Sign. Lawson-Bouey.	FV	105.00	250.00
	b. Sign. Crow-Bouey.	FV	100.00	225.00

1979 ISSUE

#92 and 93 arms at l.

92	5 DOLLARS	VG	VF	UNC
	1979. Blue on m/c unpt. Similar to #87, but different design element at upper ctr. Serial # on back.			
	a. Sign. Lawson-Bouey.	FV	FV	30.00
	b. Sign. Crow-Bouey.	FV	FV	32.50

93	20 DOLLARS	VG	VF	UNC
	1979. Deep olive-green on m/c unpt. Similar to #89, but different guilloches on face. Serial # on back.			
	a. Sign. Lawson-Bouey.	FV	FV	75.00
	b. Sign. Crow-Bouey.	FV	FV	70.00
	c. Sign. Thiessen-Crow.	FV	FV	55.00

1986-91 ISSUE

#94-100 arms at upper l. ctr. Replacement notes: Third letter of serial # prefix is *X*.

94	2 DOLLARS	VG	VF	UNC
	1986. Brown on m/c unpt. Qn. Elizabeth II, Parliament Bldg. at r. Pair of robins on back.			
	a. Sign. Crow-Bouey.	FV	FV	8.50
	b. Sign. Thiessen-Crow.	FV	FV	3.50
	c. Sign. Bonin-Thiessen.	FV	FV	3.00

95	5 DOLLARS	VG	VF	UNC
	1986. Blue-gray on m/c unpt. Sir Wilfrid Laurier, Parliament bldgs. at r. Kingfisher on back.			
	a1. Sign. Crow-Bouey. W/yellow plate # on back.	FV	5.50	30.00
	a2. Sign. Crow-Bouey. W/blue plate # on back.	FV	FV	17.50
	b. Sign. Thiessen-Crow.	FV	FV	10.00
	c. Sign. Bonin-Thiessen.	FV	FV	10.00
	d. Sign. Knight-Thiessen.	FV	FV	8.50
	e. Sign. Knight-Dodge.	FV	FV	7.50

96	10 DOLLARS	VG	VF	UNC
	1989. Purple on m/c unpt. Sir John A. Macdonald, Parliament bldgs. at r. Osprey in flight on back.			
	a. Sign. Thiessen-Crow.	FV	FV	14.00
	b. Sign. Bonin-Thiessen.	FV	FV	15.00
	c. Sign. Knight-Thiessen.	FV	FV	13.50

97	20 DOLLARS	VG	VF	UNC
	1991. Deep olive-green and olive-green on m/c unpt. Green foil optical device w/denomination at upper l. Qn. Elizabeth II, Parliament library at r. Common loon on back.			
	a. Sign. Thiessen-Crow.	FV	FV	30.00
	b. Sign. Bonin-Thiessen.	FV	FV	27.50
	c. Sign. Knight-Thiessen.	FV	FV	25.00
	d. Sign. Knight-Dodge.	FV	FV	22.50

Note: The letter "I" in prefix exists serif and sans-serif.

98	50 DOLLARS	VG	VF	UNC
	1988. Red on m/c unpt. William Lyon MacKenzie King, Parliament bldg. at r., gold optical device w/denomination at upper l. Snowy owl on back.			
	a. Sign. Thiessen-Crow.	FV	FV	75.00
	b. Sign. Bonin-Thiessen.	FV	FV	85.00
	c. Sign. Knight-Thiessen.	FV	FV	65.00
	d. Sign. Knight-Dodge.	FV	FV	60.00

99	100 DOLLARS	VG	VF	UNC
	1988. Dk. brown on m/c unpt. Sir Robert Bordon, Parliament bldg. at r., green optical device w/denomination at upper l. Canadian geese on back.			
	a. Sign. Thiessen-Crow.	FV	FV	150.00
	b. Sign. Bonin-Thiessen.	FV	FV	185.00
	c. Sign. Knight-Thiessen.	FV	FV	125.00
	d. Sign. Knight-Dodge.	FV	FV	120.00

100	1000 DOLLARS	VG	VF	UNC
	1988. Pink on m/c unpt. Qn. Elizabeth II, Parliament library at r. Optical device w/denomination at upper l. Pine grosbeak pair on branch at r. on back.			
	a. Sign. Thiessen-Crow.	FV	FV	1250.00
	b. Sign. Bonin-Thiessen.	FV	FV	1100.00

2001-03 ISSUE

#101-105 redesigned portraits, new back designs. The "Canadian Journey" series.

101	5 DOLLARS	VG	VF	UNC
	2002. Blue and tan-yellow. Sir Wilfrid Laurier at l., west block of Parliament at ctr. Winter sports - children skating, tobogganing, and playing hockey on back. Sign. Knight-Dodge.	FV	FV	7.00

NOTICE

Readers with unlisted dates, signature varieties, etc. are invited to submit photocopies of their notes to: Standard Catalog of World Paper Money, 700 East State St. Iola, WI 54990-0001, E-Mail: george.cuhaj@fwpubs.com.

102 10 DOLLARS
2001. Purple and tan on m/c. Sir John A. Macdonald at l.,
Parliament Library at ctr. Veteran and children at memorial at r.,
peacekeeper w/binoculars at ctr., poppies, doves and and the first
verse of *In Flanders Fields* at r. on back.

		VG	VF	UNC
a. Sign. Knight-Thiessen.		FV	FV	12.50
b. Sign. Knight-Dodge.		FV	FV	10.00

102A 10 DOLLARS
2005. Purple and tan on m/c unpt. As #102 but w/holographic strip
at l. Sign. Jenkins-Dodge. — FV FV 10.00

103 20 DOLLARS
2004. Green and tan on m/c unpt. Qn. Elizabeth II at l. Bill Reid
sculpture, westcoast native art theme on back. Sign. Jenkins-
Dodge. — FV FV 22.50

104 50 DOLLARS
2004. Red-orange and tan on m/c unpt. William Lyon Mackenzie
King at l. Accomplishments of the Famous Five and Thérèse
Casgrain on back. Sign. Jenkins-Dodge. — FV FV 55.00

105 100 DOLLARS
2004. Brown and green on m/c unpt. Sir Robert Borden at r.
Historic and satellite maps of Canada on back. Sign. Jenkins-
Dodge.

	VG	VF	UNC
	FV	FV	110.00

CAPE VERDE

MAURITANIA

SENEGAL

GAMBIA

GUINEA BISSAU

GUINEA

The Republic of Cape Verde, is
located in the Atlantic Ocean,
about 370 miles (595 km.) west
of Dakar, Senegal off the coast
of Africa. The 14-island republic
has an area of 1,557 sq. mi.
(4,033 sq. km.) and a population
of 437,000. Capital: Praia. The
refueling of ships and aircraft is
the chief economic function of
the country. Fishing is important
and agriculture is widely
practiced, but the Cape Verdes
are not self-sufficient in food.
Fish products, salt, bananas,
coffee, peanuts and shellfish are exported.

The date of discovery of the islands is uncertain. Possibly they were visited by Venetian
Captain Alvise Cadamosto in 1456. Portuguese navigator Diogo Gomes claimed them for Portugal
in May of 1460. Settlement began two years later. The early importance and wealth of the islands,
which caused them to be attacked by Sir Francis Drake and the Dutch, resulted from the monopoly
of the Guinea slave trade granted the inhabitants in 1466. Poverty and famine occasioned by
frequent periods of severe drought have marked the history of the country since abolition of the
slave trade in 1876.

After 500 years of Portuguese rule, the Cape Verdes became independent on July 5, 1975.

RULERS:
Portuguese to 1975

MONETARY SYSTEM:
1 Escudo = 100 Centavos, 1911-

PORTUGUESE ADMINISTRATION

BANCO NACIONAL ULTRAMARINO

CABO VERDE

1971; 1972 ISSUE

Decreto Lei 39221 and 44891

#52 and 53 portr. S. Pinto at r., bank seal at l., arms at lower ctr. Allegorical woman w/ships on back.
W/security thread. Sign. titles: *ADMINISTRADOR* and *VICE-GOVERNADOR*.

52 20 ESCUDOS
4.4.1972. Green on m/c unpt. 2 sign. varieties.

	VG	VF	UNC
a. Issued note.	6.00	25.00	90.00
s. Specimen.	—	—	150.00

53 50 ESCUDOS
4.4.1972. Blue on m/c unpt.

	VG	VF	UNC
a. Issued note.	10.00	40.00	120.00
s. Specimen.	—	—	175.00

		VG	VF	UNC
53A	**500 ESCUDOS**			
	16.6.1971; 29.6.1971. Olive-green on m/c unpt. Infante D. Henrique at r.			
	a. Issued note.	25.00	100.00	300.00
	ct. Color trial. Blue on m/c unpt.	—	—	450.00
	s. Specimen.	—	—	350.00

REPUBLIC

BANCO DE CABO VERDE

1977 ISSUE

#54-56 A. Cabral w/native hat at r. and as wmk. Printer: BWC.

		VG	VF	UNC
54	**100 ESCUDOS**			
	20.1.1977. Red and m/c. Bow and musical instruments at l. Mountain at l. ctr. on back.			
	a. Issued note.	1.25	2.50	15.00
	s. Specimen.	—	—	75.00

		VG	VF	UNC
55	**500 ESCUDOS**			
	20.1.1977. Blue and m/c. Shark at l. Harbor at Praia on back.			
	a. Issued note.	6.00	12.50	25.00
	s. Specimen.	—	—	100.00

		VG	VF	UNC
56	**1000 ESCUDOS**			
	20.1.1977. Brown and m/c. Electrical appliance at l. Workers at quarry at l. ctr., banana stalk at r. on back.			
	a. Issued note.	12.50	25.00	50.00
	s. Specimen.	—	—	135.00

1989 ISSUE

#57-61 A. Cabral at r. and as wmk. Serial # black at l., red at r. Printer: TDLR.

		VG	VF	UNC
57	**100 ESCUDOS**			
	20.1.1989. Red and dk. purple on m/c unpt. Festival at l. ctr. on back.			
	a. Issued note.	FV	FV	5.00
	s. Specimen.	—	—	30.00

		VG	VF	UNC
58	**200 ESCUDOS**			
	20.1.1989. Green and black on m/c unpt. Modern airport collage in vertical format on back.			
	a. Issued note.	FV	FV	8.00
	s. Specimen.	—	—	35.00

59	500 ESCUDOS	VG	VF	UNC
	20.1.1989. Blue on m/c unpt. Shipyard on back.			
	a. Issued note.	FV	FV	17.50
	s. Specimen.	—	—	40.00

64	500 ESCUDOS	VG	VF	UNC
	23.4.1992. Purple, blue and dk. brown on m/c unpt. Dr. B. Lopes da Silva at ctr. r. Back like #59.	FV	FV	12.50

60	1000 ESCUDOS	VG	VF	UNC
	20.1.1989. Brown and red-brown on m/c unpt. Insects at l. ctr. on back.			
	a. Issued note.	FV	FV	35.00
	s. Specimen.	—	—	50.00

65	1000 ESCUDOS	VG	VF	UNC
	5.6.1992. Dk. brown, red-orange and purple on m/c unpt. Cape Verde warbler at ctr. r. Insects at l. ctr. on back.	FV	FV	22.50

1999-2000 ISSUE

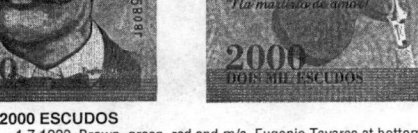

61	2500 ESCUDOS	VG	VF	UNC
	20.1.1989. Violet on m/c unpt. Palace of National Assembly on back.			
	a. Issued note.	FV	FV	67.50
	s. Specimen.	—	—	75.00

66	2000 ESCUDOS	VG	VF	UNC
	1.7.1999. Brown, green, red and m/c. Eugenio Tavares at bottom. Cardeal flower and stanza from poem Morna de Aguada on back.	FV	FV	30.00

1992 ISSUE

#63-64 wmk: A. Cabral. Printer: TDLR.

63	200 ESCUDOS	VG	VF	UNC
	8.8.1992. Black and blue-green on m/c unpt. Sailing ship Ernestina at ctr. r. Back like #58.	FV	FV	6.00

67	5000 ESCUDOS	VG	VF	UNC
	5.7.2000. Orange, red and m/c. Woman carrying stones. Fortress details on back.	FV	FV	65.00

CAYMAN ISLANDS

The Cayman Islands, a British Crown Colony situated about 180 miles (290 km.) northwest of Jamaica, consists of three islands: Grand Cayman, Little Cayman and Cayman Brac. The islands have an area of 102 sq. mi. (259 sq. km.) and a population of 41,000. Capital: Georgetown. Seafaring, commerce, banking and tourism are the principal industries. Rope, turtle shells and shark skins are exported.

The islands were discovered by Columbus in 1503, and were named by him, Tortugas (Spanish for "turtles") because of the great number of turtles in the nearby waters. The Cayman Islands were colonized from Jamaica by the British and remained dependencies of Jamaica until 1959, when they became a unit territory within the West Indies Federation. They became a separate colony when the Federation was dissolved in 1962.

RULERS:
British

MONETARY SYSTEM:
1 Dollar = 100 Cents

BRITISH ADMINISTRATION

CAYMAN ISLANDS CURRENCY BOARD

1971 CURRENCY LAW

#1-4 arms at upper ctr., Qn. Elizabeth II at r. Wmk: Tortoise. Printer: TDLR. Replacement notes: Serial # prefix Z/1.

1	1 DOLLAR	VG	VF	UNC
	L.1971 (1972). Blue on m/c unpt. Fish, coral at ctr. on back.			
	a. Issued note.	2.00	3.50	17.50
	r. Replacement. Serial # Prefix Z/1.	—	—	70.00
	s. Specimen.	—	—	—

2	5 DOLLARS	VG	VF	UNC
	L.1971 (1972). Green on m/c unpt. Sailboat at ctr. on back.			
	a. Issued note.	9.00	11.00	60.00
	r. Replacement. Serial # prefix Z/l.	—	—	140.00
	s. Specimen.	—	—	—

3	10 DOLLARS	VG	VF	UNC
	L.1971 (1972). Red on m/c unpt. Beach scene at ctr. on back.	15.00	30.00	190.00

4	25 DOLLARS	VG	VF	UNC
	L.1971 (1972). Brown on m/c unpt. Compass and map at ctr. on back.	40.00	100.00	625.00

1974 CURRENCY LAW

#5-11 arms at upper ctr., Qn. Elizabeth II at r. Wmk: Tortoise. Printer: TDLR. Replacement notes: Serial # prefix Z/1.

5	1 DOLLAR	VG	VF	UNC
	L.1974 (1985). Blue on m/c unpt. Like #1.			
	a. Sign. as #1 illustration.	2.00	3.00	15.00
	b. Sign. Jefferson.	1.50	2.00	11.00
	r1. Replacement. As a. Serial # prefix Z/1.	—	—	60.00
	r2. Replacement. As b. Serial # prefix Z/1.	—	—	55.00

6	5 DOLLARS	VG	VF	UNC
	L.1974. Green on m/c unpt. Like #2.			
	a. Issued note.	9.00	12.00	35.00
	r. Replacement. Serial # prefix Z/1.	—	—	95.00

7	10 DOLLARS	VG	VF	UNC
	L.1974. Red on m/c unpt. Like #3.			
	a. Issued note.	20.00	50.00	165.00
	r. Replacement. Serial # prefix Z/1.	—	—	265.00

8	25 DOLLARS	VG	VF	UNC
	L.1974. Brown on m/c unpt. Like #4.			
	a. Issued note.	35.00	45.00	135.00
	r. Replacement. Serial # prefix Z/1.	—	—	245.00

9 40 DOLLARS

	VG	VF	UNC
L.1974 (1981). Purple on m/c unpt. Pirates Week Festival (crowd on beach) at ctr. on back.			
a. Issued note.	60.00	90.00	165.00
r. Replacement. Serial # prefix *Z/1*.	80.00	125.00	260.00

10 50 DOLLARS

	VG	VF	UNC
L.1974 (1987). Blue on m/c unpt. Govt. house at ctr. on back.			
a. Issued note.	75.00	110.00	185.00
r. Replacement. Serial # prefix *Z/1*.	125.00	250.00	625.00

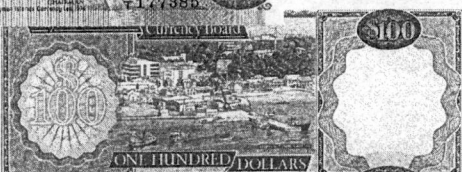

11 100 DOLLARS

	VG	VF	UNC
L.1974 (1982). Deep orange on m/c unpt. Seacoast view of George Town at ctr. on back.	125.00	175.00	300.00

1991 ISSUE

#12-15 arms at upper ctr., Qn. Elizabeth II at r., treasure chest at lower l. ctr. Red coral at l. on back. Wmk: Tortoise. Printer: TDLR. Replacement notes: Serial # prefix *Z/1*.

12 5 DOLLARS

	VG	VF	UNC
1991. Dk. green, blue-green and olive-brown on m/c unpt. Sailboat in harbor waters at ctr. on back.			
a. Issued note.	6.00	10.00	20.00
r. Replacement. Serial # prefix *Z/1*.	20.00	35.00	60.00

13 10 DOLLARS

	VG	VF	UNC
1991. Red and purple on m/c unpt. Open chest, palm tree along coastline at ctr. on back. (2 varieties in color of conch shell at upper ctr. on back.)	FV	FV	90.00

14 25 DOLLARS

	VG	VF	UNC
1991. Deep brown, tan and orange on m/c unpt. Island outlines and compass at ctr. on back.	FV	FV	65.00

15 100 DOLLARS

	VG	VF	UNC
1991. Orange and dk. brown on m/c unpt. Harbor view at ctr. on back.	FV	FV	240.00

1996 ISSUE

#16-20 Qn. Elizabeth at r. Wmk: Tortoise. Printer: TDLR.

16 1 DOLLAR

	VG	VF	UNC
1996. Purple, orange and deep blue on m/c unpt. Back similar to #1.	FV	3.00	11.00

NOTICE

Readers with unlisted dates, signature varieties, etc. are invited to submit photocopies of their notes to: Standard Catalog of World Paper Money, 700 East State St. Iola, WI 54990-0001, E-Mail: george.cuhaj@fwpubs.com.

17   5 DOLLARS

	VG	VF	UNC
1996. Dk. green, blue-green and olive-brown on m/c unpt. Back similar to #12.	FV	FV	17.50

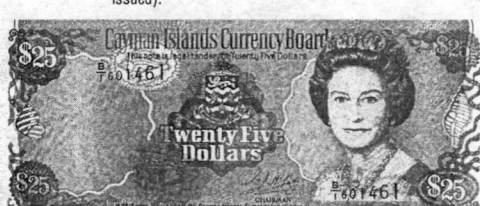

18   10 DOLLARS

	VG	VF	UNC
1996. Red and purple on m/c unpt. Back similar to #13.			
a. Serial # prefix B/l.	FV	FV	30.00
b. Serial # prefix X/l. Experimental paper. (100,000 pieces issued).	125.00	600.00	—

19   25 DOLLARS

	VG	VF	UNC
1996. Deep brown, tan and orange on m/c unpt. Back similar to #14.	FV	FV	75.00

20   100 DOLLARS

	VG	VF	UNC
1996. Orange and brown on m/c unpt. Back similar to #15.	FV	150.00	225.00

CAYMAN ISLANDS MONETARY AUTHORITY

1998 ISSUE; 1996 LAW

#21-25 Qn. Elizabeth at r. Segmented foil over security thread. Wmk: Tortoise. Printer: (T)DLR.

21   1 DOLLAR

	VG	VF	UNC
1998. Purple, orange and deep blue on m/c unpt. Like #16.			
a. Issued note.	FV	3.50	8.50
r. Replacement. Serial # prefix Z/1.	7.50	15.00	55.00

22   5 DOLLARS

	VG	VF	UNC
1998. Olive-green and blue-green on m/c unpt. Like #17.			
a. Issued note.	FV	12.00	22.50
r. Replacement. Serial # prefix Z/l	12.50	25.00	65.00

23   10 DOLLARS

	VG	VF	UNC
1998. Red and purple on m/c unpt. Like #18.	FV	22.50	30.00

24   25 DOLLARS

	VG	VF	UNC
1998. Deep brown, tan and orange on m/c unpt. Like #19.	FV	FV	60.00

25 100 DOLLARS
1998. Orange and brown on m/c unpt. Like #20.

	VG	VF	UNC
	FV	FV	200.00

2001 ISSUE, 2001 LAW REVISION

#26-29 Qn. Elizabeth at r. Segmented foil over security thread. Wmk: Tortoise and CIMA. Printer: (T)DLR.

26 1 DOLLAR
2001. M/c. Like #21.

	VG	VF	UNC
a. Issued note.	FV	FV	7.50
r. Replacement. Serial # prefix *Z/1*.	FV	7.50	50.00
s. Specimen.	—	—	—

27 5 DOLLARS
2001. M/c. Like #22.

	VG	VF	UNC
a. Issued note.	FV	FV	15.00
s. Specimen.	—	—	—

28 10 DOLLARS
2001. M/c. Like #23.

	VG	VF	UNC
a. Issued note.	FV	FV	27.50
s. Specimen.	—	—	—

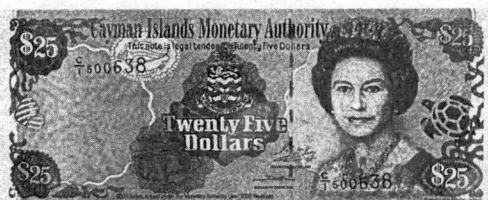

29 50 DOLLARS
2001. M/c.

	VG	VF	UNC
a. Issued note.	FV	FV	120.00
r. Replacement. Serial # prefix *Z/1*.	50.00	100.00	275.00
s. Specimen.			

2003 COMMEMORATIVE ISSUE

500th Anniversary of discovery.

30 1 DOLLAR
2003. M/c.

	VG	VF	UNC
a. Issued note.	FV	6.00	12.50
b. Issued note in presentation folder (4000 made).	—	—	45.00
s. Specimen.	—	—	—

2003 ISSUE

31 25 DOLLARS
2003. M/c.

	VG	VF	UNC
a. Issued note.	FV	FV	57.50
s. Specimen.	—	—	—

32	50 DOLLARS	VG	VF	UNC
	2003. M/c.			
	a. Issued note.	FV	FV	110.00
	s. Specimen.	—	FV	—

2005 ISSUE

33	10 DOLLARS	VG	VF	UNC
	2005.	FV	FV	25.00

COLLECTOR SERIES

CAYMAN ISLANDS CURRENCY BOARD

1974 CURRENCY LAW ISSUE

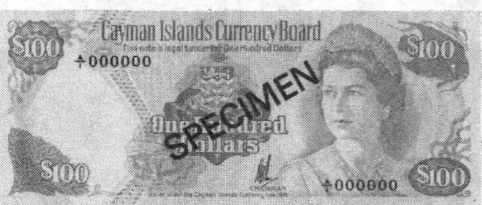

CS1	1974. 1-100 DOLLARS	Issue Price	Mkt.	Value
	#5-11 ovpt: SPECIMEN. (300 sets.)	61.35		600.00

1991 ISSUE

CS2	1991 5-100 DOLLARS	Issue Price	Mkt.	Value
	#12-15 ovpt: SPECIMEN. (300 sets.)	61.35		325.00

1996 ISSUE

CS3	1996 1-100 DOLLARS	Issue Price	Mkt.	Value
	#16-20 ovpt: SPECIMEN. (300 sets.)	61.35		300.00

1998 ISSUE

CS4	1998 1-100 DOLLARS	Issue Price	Mkt.	Value
	#21-25 ovpt: SPECIMEN. (Only 100 complete sets exist.)	61.35		550.00

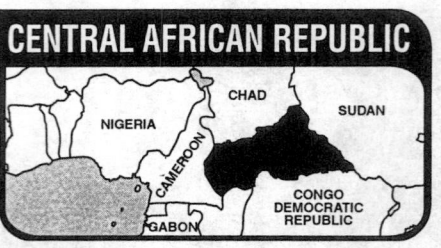

CENTRAL AFRICAN REPUBLIC

The Central African Republic, a landlocked country in Central Africa, bounded by Chad on the north, Cameroon on the west, Democratice Republic of the Congo and the Republic of the Congo on the south, and The Sudan on the east, has an area of 240,535 sq. mi. (622,984 sq. km.) and a population of 3.64 million. Capital: Bangui. Deposits of uranium, iron ore, manganese and copper remain to be developed. Diamonds, cotton, timber and coffee are exported.

The area that is now the Central African Republic was constituted as the French territory of Ubangi-Shari in 1894. It was united with Chad in 1905 and joined with Middle Congo and Gabon in 1910, becoming one of the four territories of French Equatorial Africa. Upon dissolution of the federation on Dec. 1, 1958, the constituent territories became full autonomous members of the French Community. Ubangi-Shari proclaimed its complete independence as the Central African Republic on Aug. 13, 1960.

On Jan. 1, 1966, Col. Jean-Bedel Bokassa, Chief of Staff of the Armed Forces, overthrew the government of President David Dacko and assumed power as president of the republic. President Bokassa abolished the constitution of 1959 and dissolved the National Assembly. In 1972 the Congress of the sole political party appointed Bokassa president for life. The republic became a constitutional monarchy on Dec. 4, 1976; President Bokassa was named Emperor Bokassa I. Bokassa was ousted as Central African emperor in a bloodless takeover of the government led by former president David Dacko on Sept. 20, 1979, and the African nation was proclaimed once again a republic. In 1996-97 a mutiny of army personnel created great tensions. It is a member of the "Union Monetaire des Etats de l'Afrique Centrale."

See also Central African States, Equatorial African States, and French African States.

RULERS:
Emperor J. B. Bokassa I, 1976-79

MONETARY SYSTEM:
1 Franc = 100 Centimes

SIGNATURE VARIETIES:
Refer to introduction to Central African States.

RÉPUBLIQUE CENTRAFRICAINE

BANQUE DES ÉTATS DE L'AFRIQUE CENTRALE

1974-76 ND ISSUE

#1-4 Pres. J. B. Bokassa at r. Wmk: Antelope's head.

1	500 FRANCS	VG	VF	UNC
	ND (1974). Lilac-brown and m/c. Landscape at ctr. Mask at l., students and chemical testing at ctr., statue at r. on back. Sign. 6.	10.00	40.00	175.00

2	1000 FRANCS	VG	VF	UNC
	ND (1974). Blue and m/c. Rhinoceros at l., water buffalo at ctr. Mask at l., trains, planes and bridge at ctr., statue at r. on back. Sign. 6.	20.00	60.00	250.00

		VG	VF	UNC
7	**5000 FRANCS** ND (1979). Similar to #3. Sign. 9.	50.00	225.00	900.00

		VG	VF	UNC

3	**5000 FRANCS**
	ND (1974). Brown and m/c. Field workers hoeing at l., combine at
	ctr. Mask at l., bldgs. at ctr., statue at r. on back.
	  a. Sign. 4.
	  b. Sign. 6.
		
		35.00
		30.00
			
			150.00
			125.00
				
				600.00
				550.00

		VG	VF	UNC
8	**10,000 FRANCS** ND (1978). Similar to #4. Sign. 6.	50.00	200.00	800.00

RÉPUBLIQUE CENTRAFRICAINE

BANQUE DES ÉTATS DE L'AFRIQUE CENTRALE

Note: For notes with similar back designs see Cameroon Republic, Chad, Congo (Brazzaville)
and Gabon. #9-10 wmk: Antelope's head.

1980 ISSUE

		VG	VF	UNC
4	**10,000 FRANCS** ND (1976). M/c. Sword hilts at l. and ctr. Mask at l., tractor cultivating at ctr., statue at r. on back. Sign. 6.	75.00	300.00	900.00

EMPIRE CENTRAFRICAIN

BANQUE DES ÉTATS DE L'AFRIQUE CENTRALE

1978-79 ISSUE

#5-8 Emp. J. B. Bokassa I at r. Wmk: Antelope's head.

		VG	VF	UNC
5	**500 FRANCS** 1.4.1978. Similar to #1. Specimen.	—	—	2000.00

		VG	VF	UNC
9	**500 FRANCS** 1.1.1980; 1.7.1980; 1.6.1981. Red and m/c. Woman weaving basket at r. Back like #1. Lithographed. Sign. 9.	1.50	4.00	15.00

		VG	VF	UNC
6	**1000 FRANCS** 1.4.1978. Similar to #2. Sign. 9.	50.00	200.00	800.00

10	**1000 FRANCS**		**VG**	**VF**	**UNC**
	1.1.1980; 1.7.1980; 1.6.1981; 1.1.1982; 1.6.1984. Blue and m/c. Butterfly at l., waterfalls at ctr., water buffalo at r. Back like #2. Lithographed. Sign. 9.		4.50	8.00	25.00

11	**5000 FRANCS**		**VG**	**VF**	**UNC**
	1.1.1980. Brown and m/c. Girl at l., village scene at ctr. Carving at l., airplane, train crossing bridge and tractor hauling logs at ctr., man smoking a pipe at r. Similar to Equatorial African States #6. Sign. 9.		12.50	50.00	250.00

1983-84 ND Issue

12	**5000 FRANCS**		**VG**	**VF**	**UNC**
	ND (1984). Brown and m/c. Mask at l., woman w/bundle of fronds at r. Plowing and mine ore conveyor on back.				
	a. Sign. 9.		12.50	22.50	80.00
	b. Sign. 14.		10.00	20.00	70.00

13	**10,000 FRANCS**		**VG**	**VF**	**UNC**
	ND (1983). Brown, green and m/c. Stylized antelope heads at l., woman at r. Loading fruit onto truck at l. on back. Sign. 9.		22.50	35.00	100.00

1985 Issue

#14-16 wmk: Carving (as printed on notes). Sign. 9.

14	**500 FRANCS**		**VG**	**VF**	**UNC**
	1985-91. Brown on orange and m/c unpt. Carving and jug at ctr. Man carving mark at l. ctr. on back.				
	a. 1.1.1985.		2.00	4.00	12.50
	b. 1.1.1986.		1.75	3.50	8.00
	c. 1.1.1987.		1.75	3.25	7.00
	d. 1.1.1989; 1.1.1991.		1.75	3.25	7.00

15	**1000 FRANCS**		**VG**	**VF**	**UNC**
	1.1.1985. Dull blue-violet on m/c unpt. Carving at l., map at ctr., Gen. Kolingba at r. Incomplete map of Chad at top ctr. Elephant at l., animals at ctr., carving at r. on back.		3.50	7.50	20.00

1986 Issue

16	**1000 FRANCS**		**VG**	**VF**	**UNC**
	1.1.1986-1.1.1990. Dull blue-violet on m/c unpt. Like #15 but complete outline map of Chad at top ctr. Wmk: Carving. Sign. 9.		2.75	5.00	12.50

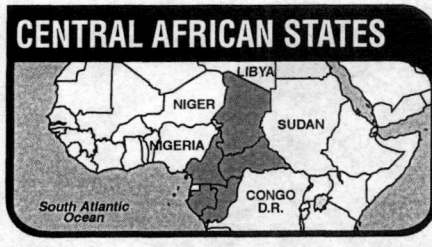

The Bank of the Central African States (BEAC) is a regional central bank for the monetary and customs union formed by Cameroun, Central African Republic, Chad, Congo (Brazzaville), Gabon, and (since 1985) Equatorial Guinea. It succeeded the Equatorial African States Bank in 1972-73 when the latter was reorganized and renamed to provide greater African control over its operations. The seat of the BEAC was transferred from Paris to Yaounde in 1977 and an African governor assumed responsibility for direction of the bank in 1978. The BEAC is a member of the franc zone with its currency denominated in CFA francs and pegged to the French franc at a rate of 50-1.

BEAC notes carry country names on the face and the central bank name on the back. The 1974-84 series had common back designs but were face-different. A new series begun in 1983-85 uses common designs also on the face except for some 1000 franc notes. The notes carry the signatures of *LE GOUVERNEUR* (LE DIRECTEUR GENERAL prior to 1-4-78) and *UN CENSEUR* (since 1972). Cameroun, Gabon, and France each appoint one censeur and one alternate. Cameroon and Congo notes carry the Cameroun censeur signature. Central African Republic, Equatorial Guinea, and Gabon notes carry the Gabon censeur signature. Chad notes have been divided between the two.

Prior to 1978, all BEAC notes were printed by the Bank of France. Since 1978, the 500 and 1000 franc notes have been printed by the private French firm F. C. Oberthur. The Bank of France notes are engraved and usually undated. The F. C. Oberthur notes are lithographed and most carry dates.

See individual member countries for additional note listings. Also see Equatorial African States and French Equatorial Africa.

CONTROL LETTER or CODE

Country	1993-2001	1993 Onward
Cameroun	E	U
Central African Republic	F	M
Chad	P	C
Congo	C	T
Equatorial Guinea	N	F
Gabon	L	A

SIGNATURE VARIETIES

	Le Directeur-Genera	Le President	
1	Panouillot	Gautier	1955-72
1a	Panouillot	Duouedi (Un Censeur)	1961-72
2	Panouillot	Koulla (Un Censeur)	1972-73
3	Joudiou	Koulla (Un Censeur)	1974
4	Joudiou	Renombo (Un Censeur)	1974
5	Joudiou	Ntang (Un Censeur)	1974-77
6	Joudiou	Ntoutoume (Un Censeur)	1974-78

SIGNATURE VARIETIES

	Le Directeur-Genera / Le Gouvemeur	Un Censeur	
7	Joudiou	Beke Bihege	1977
8	Joudiou	Kamgu	1978
9	Oye Mba	Ntoutoume	1979-90
10	Oye Mba	Kamgueu	1978-86
11	Oye Mba	Kamgueu	1978-80
12	Oye Mba	Tchepannou	1981-89
13	Oye Mba	Dang	1990
14	Mamalepot	Ntoutoume	1991
15	Mamalepot	Mebara	1991-93
16	Mamalepot	Ognagna	1994
17	Mamalepot	Kaltjob	1994-2000
18	Mamalepot		1998-99
19	Mamalepot		2000-03
20	Mamalepot		2000

BANQUE DES ÉTATS DE L'AFRIQUE CENTRALE(1993-2001)

C FOR CONGO

1993; 1994 ISSUE

#101C-103C map of Central African States at lower l. ctr. First 2 digits of serial # are year of issue.

		VG	VF	UNC
101C	**500 FRANCS**			
	(19)93-(20)00. Dk. brown and gray on m/c unpt. Shepherd at r. and as wmk., zebus at ctr. Baobab, antelopes and Kota mask on back.			
	a. Sign. 15. (19)93.	FV	FV	5.00
	b. Sign. 16. (19)94.	FV	FV	4.50
	c. Sign. 16. (19)95.	FV	FV	4.50
	d. Sign. 16. (19)97.	FV	FV	4.00
	e. Sign. 16. (19)98.	FV	FV	4.00
	f. Sign. 16. (19)99.	FV	FV	4.00
	g. Sign. 19. (20)00.	FV	FV	4.00
	h. Sign. 19. (20)02.	FV	FV	4.00
102C	**1000 FRANCS**			
	(19)93-(20)00. Dk. brown and red w/black text on m/c unpt. Young man at r. and as wmk., harvesting coffee beans at ctr. Forest harvesting, Okoume raft and Bakele wood mask on back.			
	b. Sign. 16. (19)94.	FV	FV	9.00
	c. Sign. 16. (19)95.	FV	FV	8.00
	d. Sign. 16. (19)97.	FV	FV	8.00
	e. Sign. 16. (19)98.	FV	FV	7.50
	f. Sign. 16. (19)99.	FV	FV	7.50
	g. Sign. 19. (20)00.	FV	FV	7.50
	h. Sign. 19. (20)02.	FV	FV	7.00
		FV	FV	7.50
103C	**2000 FRANCS**			
	(19)93-(19)99. Dk. brown and green w/black text on orange and m/c unpt. Woman's head at r. and as wmk. surrounded by tropical fruit. Exchange of passengers and produce w/ship at l. ctr. on back.			
	a. Sign. 15. (19)93.	FV	FV	14.00
	b. Sign. 16. (19)94.	FV	FV	12.50
	c. Sign. 16. (19)95.	FV	FV	12.00
	d. Sign. 16. (19)97.	FV	FV	12.00
	e. Sign. 16. (19)98.	FV	FV	12.00
	f. Sign. 16. (19)99.	FV	FV	12.00
	g. Sign. 19. (20)00.	FV	FV	9.00
	h. Sign. 19. (20)02.	FV	FV	10.00
104C	**5000 FRANCS**			
	(19)94-(20)00. Dk. brown, brown and blue w/violet text on m/c unpt. Laborer wearing hard hat at ctr. r., riggers w/well drill at r. Woman w/head basket at lower l., gathering cotton at ctr. on back.			
	a. Sign. 16. (19)94.	FV	FV	27.50
	b. Sign. 16. (19)95.	FV	FV	27.50
	c. Sign. 16. (19)97.	FV	FV	25.00
	d. Sign. 16. (19)98.	FV	FV	25.00
	e. Sign. 16. (19)99.	FV	FV	25.00
	f. Sign. 16. (20)00.	FV	FV	25.00
105C	**10,000 FRANCS**			
	(19)94-(20)00. Dk. brown and blue w/blue-black text on m/c unpt. Modern bldg. at ctr., young woman at r. Fisherman, boats and villagers along shoreline at l. ctr. on back.			
	a. Sign. 16. (19)94.	FV	FV	47.50
	b. Sign. 16. (19)95.	FV	FV	45.00
	c. Sign. 16. (19)97.	FV	FV	42.50
	d. Sign. 16. (19)98.	FV	FV	45.00
	e. Sign. 16. (19)99.	FV	FV	45.00
	f. Sign. 19. (20)00.	FV	FV	45.00
	g. Sign. 19. (20)02.	FV	FV	45.00

BANQUE DES ÉTATS DE L'AFRIQUE CENTRALE (2003-)

T FOR CONGO

2002 ISSUE

		VG	VF	UNC
106T	**500 FRANCS**			
	2002 Sign. 19.	FV	FV	4.00
107T	**1000 FRANCS**			
	2002 Sign. 19.	FV	FV	7.00
108T	**2000 FRANCS**			
	2002. Sign. 19.	FV	FV	10.00
109T	**5000 FRANCS**			
	2002. Sign. 19.	FV	FV	25.00
110T	**10,000 FRANCS**			
	2002. Sign. 19.	FV	FV	45.00

BANQUE DES ÉTATS DE L'AFRIQUE CENTRALE(1993-2001)

E FOR CAMEROUN

1993; 1994 ISSUE

		VG	VF	UNC
201E	**500 FRANCS**			
	(19)93-(20)02. Dk. brown and gray on m/c unpt. Like #101C.			
	a. Sign. 15. (19)93.	FV	FV	5.00
	b. Sign. 17. (19)94.	FV	FV	4.50
	c. Sign. 17. (19)95.	FV	FV	4.50
	d. Sign. 17. (19)97.	FV	FV	4.50
	e. Sign. 18. (19)98.	FV	FV	4.50
	f. Sign. 18. (19)99.	FV	FV	4.50
	g. Sign. 20. (20)00.	FV	FV	4.00
	h. Sign. 20. (20)02.	FV	FV	4.00

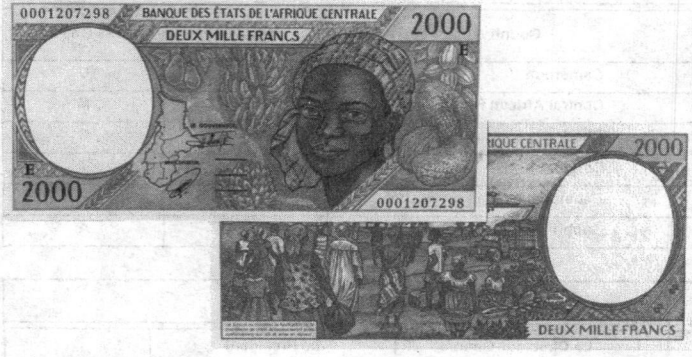

		VG	VF	UNC
202E	**1000 FRANCS**			
	(19)93-(20)02. Dk. brown and red w/black text on green and m/c unpt. Like #102C.			
	a. Sign. 15. (19)93.	FV	FV	9.00
	b. Sign. 17. (19)94.	FV	FV	8.00
	c. Sign. 17. (19)95.	FV	FV	8.00
	d. Sign. 17. (19)97.	FV	FV	8.00
	f. Sign. 18. (19)99.	FV	FV	7.00
	g. Sign. 20. (20)00.	FV	FV	6.50
	h. Sign. 20. (20)02.	FV	FV	6.50
203E	**2000 FRANCS**			
	(19)93-(20)02. Dk. brown and green w/black text on orange and m/c unpt. Like #103C.			
	a. Sign. 15. (19)93.	FV	FV	15.00
	b. Sign. 17. (19)94.	FV	FV	12.50
	c. Sign. 17. (19)95.	FV	FV	12.50
	d. Sign. 17. (19)97.	FV	FV	12.00
	e. Sign. 18. (19)98.	FV	FV	11.00
	f. Sign. 18. (19)99.	FV	FV	12.00
	g. Sign. 20. (20)00.	FV	FV	12.00
	h. Sign. 20. (20)02.	FV	FV	12.00
204E	**5000 FRANCS**			
	(19)94-(20)02. Dk. brown, brown and blue w/violet text on m/c unpt. Like #104C.			
	a. Sign. 17. (19)94.	FV	FV	27.50
	b. Sign. 17. (19)95.	FV	FV	27.50
	c. Sign. 17. (19)97.	FV	FV	25.00
	d. Sign. 18. (19)98.	FV	FV	25.00
	e. Sign. 18. (19)99.	FV	FV	25.00
	f. Sign. 20. (20)00.	FV	FV	22.00
	g. Sign. 20. (20)02.	FV	FV	22.00
205E	**10,000 FRANCS**			
	(19)94-(20)00. Dk. brown and blue w/blue-black text on m/c unpt. Like #105C.			
	a. Sign. 17. (19)94.	FV	FV	45.00
	b. Sign. 17. (19)95.	FV	FV	45.00
	c. Sign. 17. (19)97.	FV	FV	45.00
	d. Sign. 18. (19)98.	FV	FV	45.00
	e. Sign. 18. (19)99.	FV	FV	45.00
	f. Sign. 20. (20)00.	FV	FV	45.00
	h. Sign. 20. (20)02.	FV	FV	45.00

BANQUE DES ÉTATS DE L'AFRIQUE CENTRALE (2003-)

U FOR CAMEROUN

2002 ISSUE

		VG	VF	UNC
206U	**500 FRANCS**			
	2002. Sign. 20.	FV	FV	4.00
207U	**1000 FRANCS**			
	2002. Sign. 20.	FV	FV	7.00
208U	**2000 FRANCS**			
	2002. Sign. 20.	FV	FV	10.00
209U	**5000 FRANCS**			
	2002. Sign. 20.	FV	FV	25.00
210U	**10,000 FRANCS**			
	2002. Sign. 20.	FV	FV	45.00

BANQUE DES ÉTATS DE L'AFRIQUE CENTRALE(1993-2001)

F FOR CENTRAL AFRICAN REPUBLIC

1993; 1994 ISSUE

		VG	VF	UNC
301F	**500 FRANCS**			
	(19)93-(19)99. Dk. brown and gray on m/c unpt. Like #101C.			
	a. Sign. 15. (19)93.	FV	FV	6.00
	b. Sign. 16. (19)94.	FV	FV	5.00
	c. Sign. 16. (19)95.	FV	FV	5.00
	d. Sign. 16. (19)97.	FV	FV	4.00
	e. Sign. 16. (19)98.	FV	FV	4.00
	f. Sign. 16. (19)99.	FV	FV	4.00
	g. Sign. 19. (20)00.	FV	FV	4.00
302F	**1000 FRANCS**			
	(19)93-(19)99. Dk. brown and red w/black text on green and m/c unpt. Like #102C.			
	a. Sign. 15. (19)93.	FV	FV	9.00
	b. Sign. 16. (19)94.	FV	FV	8.50
	c. Sign. 16. (19)95.	FV	FV	8.00
	d. Sign. 16. (19)97.	FV	FV	7.50
	e. Sign. 16. (19)98.	FV	FV	7.00
	f. Sign. 16. (19)99.	FV	FV	7.00
303F	**2000 FRANCS**			
	(19)93-(19)99. Dk. brown and green w/black text on orange and m/c unpt. Like #103C.			
	a. Sign. 15. (19)93.	FV	FV	17.50
	b. Sign. 16. (19)94.	FV	FV	15.00
	c. Sign. 16. (19)95.	FV	FV	13.00
	d. Sign. 16. (19)97.	FV	FV	13.00
	e. Sign. 16. (19)98.	FV	FV	13.00
	f. Sign. 16. (19)99.	FV	FV	12.00
304F	**5000 FRANCS**			
	(19)94-(19)99. Dk. brown, brown and blue w/violet text on m/c unpt. Like #104C.			
	a. Sign. 16. (19)94.	FV	FV	32.50
	b. Sign. 16. (19)95.	FV	FV	30.00
	c. Sign. 16. (19)97.	FV	FV	25.00
	d. Sign. 16. (19)98.	FV	FV	25.00
	e. Sign. 16. (19)99.	FV	FV	25.00
305F	**10,000 FRANCS**			
	(19)94-(19)99. Dk. brown and blue w/blue-black text on m/c unpt. Like #105C.			
	a. Sign. 16. (19)94.	FV	FV	55.00
	b. Sign. 16. (19)95.	FV	FV	50.00
	c. Sign. 16. (19)97.	FV	FV	45.00
	d. Sign. 16. (19)98.	FV	FV	45.00
	e. Sign. 16. (19)99.	FV	FV	45.00
	f. Sign. 19. (20)00.	FV	FV	45.00

BANQUE DES ÉTATS DE L'AFRIQUE CENTRALE (2003-)

M FOR CENTRAL AFRICAN REPUBLIC

2002 ISSUE

		VG	VF	UNC
306M	**500 FRANCS**			
	2002. Sign. 19.	FV	FV	4.00
307M	**1000 FRANCS**			
	2002. Sign. 19.	FV	FV	7.00
308M	**2000 FRANCS**			
	2002. Sign. 19.	FV	FV	10.00
309M	**5000 FRANCS**			
	2002. Sign. 19.	FV	FV	25.00
310M	**10,000 FRANCS**			
	2002. Sign. 19.	FV	FV	45.00

BANQUE DES ÉTATS DE L'AFRIQUE CENTRALE(1993-2001)

L FOR GABON

1993; 1994 ISSUE

		VG	VF	UNC
401L	**500 FRANCS**			
	(19)93-(20)00. Dk. brown and gray on m/c unpt. Like #101C.			
	a. Sign. 15. (19)93.	FV	FV	5.00
	b. Sign. 16. (19)94.	FV	FV	4.50
	c. Sign. 16. (19)95.	FV	FV	4.50
	g. Sign. 16. (20)00.	FV	FV	4.50

		VG	VF	UNC
402L	**1000 FRANCS**			
	(19)93-(20)00. Dk. brown and red w/black text on green and m/c unpt. Like #102C.			
	a. Sign. 15. (19)93.	FV	FV	8.50
	b. Sign. 16. (19)94.	FV	FV	8.00
	c. Sign. 16. (19)95.	FV	FV	7.50
	d. Sign. 16. (19)97.	FV	FV	7.50
	e. Sign. 16. (19)98.	FV	FV	7.50
	f. Sign. 16. (19)99.	FV	FV	7.50
	g. Sign. 19. (20)00.	FV	FV	7.50
	h. Sign. 19. (20)02.	FV	FV	7.50
403L	**2000 FRANCS**			
	(19)93-(20)00. Dk. brown and green w/black text on orange and m/c unpt. Like #103C.			
	a. Sign. 15. (19)93.	FV	FV	15.00
	b. Sign. 16. (19)94.	FV	FV	15.00
	c. Sign. 16. (19)95.	FV	FV	15.00
	d. Sign. 16. (19)97.	FV	FV	12.50
	e. Sign. 16. (19)98.	FV	FV	12.50
	f. Sign. 16. (19)99.	FV	FV	12.50
	g. Sign. 19. (20)00.	FV	FV	12.50
	h. Sign. 19. (20)02.	FV	FV	7.50
404L	**5000 FRANCS**			
	(19)94-(20)00. Dk. brown, brown and blue w/violet text on m/c unpt. Like #104C.			
	a. Sign. 16. (19)94.	FV	FV	25.00
	b. Sign. 16. (19)95.	FV	FV	25.00
	c. Sign. 16. (19)97.	FV	FV	25.00
	d. Sign. 16. (19)98.	FV	FV	25.00
	e. Sign. 16. (19)99.	FV	FV	25.00
	f. Sign. 16. (20)00.	FV	FV	25.00
405L	**10,000 FRANCS**			
	(19)94-(20)00. Dk. brown and blue w/blue-black text on m/c unpt. Like #105C.			
	a. Sign. 16. (19)94.	FV	FV	52.50
	b. Sign. 16. (19)95.	FV	FV	47.50
	c. Sign. 16. (19)97.	FV	FV	45.00
	d. Sign. 16. (19)98.	FV	FV	45.00
	e. Sign. 16. (19)99.	FV	FV	45.00
	f. Sign. 19. (20)00.	FV	FV	45.00
	g. Sign. 19 (20)02.	FV	FV	45.00

BANQUE DES ÉTATS DE L'AFRIQUE CENTRALE (2003-)

A FOR GABON

2002 ISSUE

		VG	VF	UNC
406A	**500 FRANCS**			
	2002. Sign. 19.	FV	FV	4.00
407A	**1000 FRANCS**			
	2002. Sign. 19.	FV	FV	7.00
408A	**2000 FRANCS**			
	2002. Sign. 19.	FV	FV	10.00
409A	**5000 FRANCS**			
	2002. Sign. 19.	FV	FV	25.00
410A	**10,000 FRANCS**			
	2002. Sign. 19.	FV	FV	45.00

BANQUE DES ÉTATS DE L'AFRIQUE CENTRALE(1993-2001)

N FOR EQUATORIAL GUINEA

1993; 1994 ISSUE

		VG	VF	UNC
501N	**500 FRANCS**			
	(19)93-(20)00. Dk. brown and gray on m/c unpt. Like #101C.			
	a. Sign. 15. (19)93.	FV	FV	6.00
	b. Sign. 16. (19)94.	FV	FV	6.00
	c. Sign. 16. (19)95.	FV	FV	6.00
	d. Sign. 16. (19)97.	FV	FV	4.50
	f. Sign. 16. (19)99.	FV	FV	4.50
	g. Sign. 19. (20)00.	FV	FV	4.50
502N	**1000 FRANCS**			
	(19)93-(20)00. Dk. brown and red w/black text on m/c unpt. Like #102C.			
	a. Sign. 15. (19)93.	FV	FV	9.00
	b. Sign. 16. (19)94.	FV	FV	8.00
	c. Sign. 16. (19)95.	FV	FV	7.50
	d. Sign. 16. (19)97.	FV	FV	7.50
	e. Sign. 16. (19)98.	FV	FV	7.50
	f. Sign. 16. (19)99.	FV	FV	7.50
	g. Sign. 16. (20)00.	FV	FV	7.00
	h. Sign. 19. (20)00.	FV	FV	7.50

		VG	VF	UNC
503N	**2000 FRANCS**			
	(19)93-(20)00. Dk. brown and green w/black text on m/c unpt. Like #103C.			
	a. Sign. 15. (19)93.	FV	FV	15.00
	b. Sign. 16. (19)94.	FV	FV	15.00
	c. Sign. 16. (19)95.	FV	FV	15.00
	d. Sign. 16. (19)97.	FV	FV	12.50
	g. Sign. 19. (20)00.	FV	FV	12.50
504N	**5000 FRANCS**			
	(19)94-(20)00. Dk. brown, brown and blue w/violet text on m/c unpt. Like 104C.			
	a. Sign. 16. (19)94.	FV	FV	25.00
	b. Sign. 16. (19)95.	FV	FV	25.00
	d. Sign. 16. (19)98.	FV	FV	25.00
	e. Sign. 16. (19)99.	FV	FV	25.00
	f. Sign. 19. (20)00.	FV	FV	25.00
505N	**10,000 FRANCS**			
	(19)94-(20)00. Dk. brown and blue w/blue-black text on m/c unpt. Like #105C.			
	a. Sign. 16. (19)94.	FV	FV	47.50
	b. Sign. 16. (19)95.	FV	FV	47.50
	c. Sign. 16. (19)97.	FV	FV	45.00
	d. Sign. 16. (19)98.	FV	FV	47.50
	e. Sign. 16. (19)99.	FV	FV	45.00
	f. Sign. 19. (20)00.	FV	FV	45.00

BANQUE DES ÉTATS DE L'AFRIQUE CENTRALE (2003-)

F FOR EQUATORIAL GUINEA

2002 ISSUE

		VG	VF	UNC
506F	**500 FRANCS**			
	2002. Sign. 19.	FV	FV	4.00
507F	**1000 FRANCS**			
	2002. Sign. 19.	FV	FV	7.00
508F	**2000 FRANCS**			
	2002. Sign. 19.	FV	FV	10.00
509F	**5000 FRANCS**			
	2002. Sign. 19.	FV	FV	25.00
510F	**10,000 FRANCS**			
	2002. Sign. 19.	FV	FV	45.00

BANQUE DES ÉTATS DE L'AFRIQUE CENTRALE(1993-2001)

P FOR CHAD

1993; 1994 ISSUE

		VG	VF	UNC
601P	**500 FRANCS**			
	(19)93-(20)00. Dk. brown and gray on m/c unpt. Like #101C.			
	a. Sign. 15. (19)93.	FV	FV	6.00
	b. Sign. 16. (19)94.	FV	FV	5.00
	c. Sign. 16. (19)95.	FV	FV	5.00
	d. Sign. 16. (19)97.	FV	FV	5.00

	VG	VF	UNC
e. Sign. 16. (19)98.	FV	FV	4.50
f. Sign. 16. (19)99.	FV	FV	4.50
g. Sign. 19. (20)00.	FV	FV	4.50

		VG	VF	UNC
602P	**1000 FRANCS**			
	(19)93-(20)00. Dk. brown and red w/black text on green and m/c unpt. Like #102C.			
	a. Sign. 15. (19)93.	FV	FV	8.50
	b. Sign. 16. (19)94.	FV	FV	7.50
	c. Sign. 16. (19)95.	FV	FV	7.00
	d. Sign. 16. (19)97.	FV	FV	7.00
	e. Sign. 16. (19)98.	FV	FV	7.50
	f. Sign. 16. (19)99.	FV	FV	7.50
	g. Sign. 19. (20)00.	FV	FV	7.50
603P	**2000 FRANCS**			
	(19)93-(20)00. Dk. brown and green w/black text on orange and m/c unpt. Like #103C.			
	a. Sign. 15. (19)93.	FV	FV	15.00
	b. Sign. 16. (19)94.	FV	FV	15.00
	c. Sign. 16. (19)95.	FV	FV	12.50
	d. Sign. 16. (19)97.	FV	FV	12.50
	e. Sign. 16. (19)98.	FV	FV	12.50
	f. Sign. 16. (19)99.	FV	FV	12.50

		VG	VF	UNC
604P	**5000 FRANCS**			
	(19)94-(20)00. Dk. brown, brown and blue w/violet text on m/c unpt. Like #104C.			
	a. Sign. 16. (19)94.	FV	FV	30.00
	b. Sign. 16. (19)95.	FV	FV	27.50
	c. Sign. 16. (19)97.	FV	FV	27.50
	d. Sign. 16. (19)98.	FV	FV	25.00
	e. Sign. 16. (19)99.	FV	FV	25.00
	f. Sign. 19. (20)00.	FV	FV	25.00

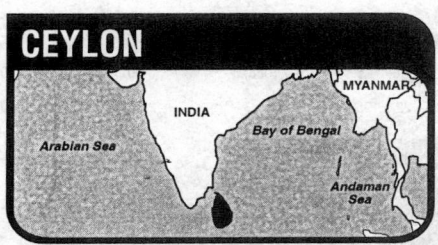

605P	**10,000 FRANCS**		VG	VF	UNC
	(19)94-(20)00. Dk. brown and blue w/blue-black text on m/c unpt. Like #105C.				
	a. Sign. 16. (19)94.		FV	FV	50.00
	b. Sign. 16. (19)95.		FV	FV	50.00
	c. Sign. 16. (19)97.		FV	FV	47.50
	d. Sign. 16. (19)98.		FV	FV	45.00
	e. Sign. 16. (19)99.		FV	FV	45.00
	f. Sign. 19. (20)00.		FV	FV	45.00

BANQUE DES ÉTATS DE L'AFRIQUE CENTRALE (2003-)

C FOR CHAD

2002 ISSUE

606C	**500 FRANCS**	VG	VF	UNC
	2002. Sign. 19.	FV	FV	4.00
607C	**1000 FRANCS**			
	2002. Sign. 19.	FV	FV	7.00
608C	**2000 FRANCS**			
	2002. Sign. 19.	FV	FV	10.00
609C	**5000 FRANCS**			
	2002. Sign. 19.	FV	FV	25.00
610C	**10,000 FRANCS**			
	2002. Sign. 19.	FV	FV	45.00

Ceylon (later to become the Democratic Socialist Republic of Sri Lanka), situated in the Indian Ocean 18 miles (29 km.) southeast of India, has an area of 25,332 sq. mi. (65,610 sq. km.) and a population of 18.82 million. Capital: Colombo. The economy is chiefly agricultural. Tea, coconut products and rubber are exported.

The earliest known inhabitants of Ceylon, the Veddahs, were subjugated by the Sinhalese from northern India in the 6th century BC. Sinhalese rule was maintained until 1498, after which the island was controlled by China for 30 years. The Portuguese came to Ceylon in 1505 and maintained control of the coastal area for 150 years. They were supplanted by the Dutch in 1658, who were in turn supplanted by the British who seized the Dutch colonies in 1796, and made them a Crown Colony in 1802. In 1815, the British conquered the independent Kingdom of Kandy in the central part of the island. Constitutional changes in 1931 and 1946 granted the Ceylonese a measure of autonomy and a parliamentary form of government. Ceylon became a self-governing dominion of the British Commonwealth on February 4, 1948. On May 22, 1972, the Ceylonese adopted a new constitution which declared Ceylon to be the Republic of Sri Lanka - "Resplendent Island." Sri Lanka is a member of the Commonwealth of Nations. The president is Chief of State. The prime minister is Head of Government.

For later issues, see Sri Lanka.

RULERS:
Dutch to 1796
British, 1796-1972

MONETARY SYSTEM:
1 Rupee = 100 Cents

STATE

CENTRAL BANK OF CEYLON

1956 ISSUE

#56-61 arms of Ceylon at l. W/o bank name in English. Various date and sign. varieties. Wmk: Chinze. Printer: BWC.

56	**1 RUPEE**	VG	VF	UNC
	1956-63. Blue on orange, green and brown unpt. Ornate stairway on back.			
	a. W/o security strip. 30.7.1956.	1.00	5.00	22.50
	b. W/o security strip. 31.5.1957; 9.4.1958; 7.11.1958; 11.9.1959.	0.75	2.00	10.00
	c. W/security strip. 18.8.1960; 29.1.1962; 5.6.1963.	0.50	1.50	7.50

57	**2 RUPEES**	VG	VF	UNC
	1956-62. Brown and lilac on blue and green unpt. Pavilion on back.			
	a. W/o security strip. 30.7.1956-11.9.1959.	2.00	6.00	27.50
	b. Security strip. 18.8.1960; 29.1.1962.	2.00	6.00	22.50

58 5 RUPEES
1956-62. Orange on aqua, green and brown unpt. Standing figure on back.

	VG	VF	UNC
a. W/o security-strip. 30.7.1956; 31.5.1957; 10.6.1958; 1.7.1959.	3.00	7.50	50.00
b. Security strip. 18.8.1960; 29.1.1962.	2.50	6.00	40.00

64 10 RUPEES
12.6.1964; 28.8.1964; 19.9.1964. Green and purple on orange and blue unpt. Ceremonial figures on back.

	VG	VF	UNC
	2.50	8.00	30.00

59 10 RUPEES
1956-63. Green on violet, brown and blue unpt. Ceremonial figures on back.

	VG	VF	UNC
a. W/o security strip. 30.7.1956; 7.11.1958; 11.9.1959.	3.00	8.00	50.00
b. Security strip. 18.8.1960; 7.4.1961; 5.6.1963.	2.00	7.00	45.00

60 50 RUPEES
30.7.1956; 7.11.1958; 11.9.1959. Blue and violet on m/c unpt. Ornate stairway on back.

	VG	VF	UNC
	22.50	60.00	250.00

61 100 RUPEES
24.10.1956. Brown on m/c unpt. 2 women in national dress on back.

	VG	VF	UNC
	25.00	80.00	300.00

Note: For later issues see Ceylon and Sri Lanka listings in Volume 3, Modern Issues.

1962-64 ISSUE

#62-66 S. Bandaranaike at r. Wmk: Chinze. Printer: BWC.

62 2 RUPEES
1962-65. Lt. brown on lilac, green and blue unpt. Pavilion at l. ctr. on back.

	VG	VF	UNC
a. Sign. P. B. G. Kaluga and D. W. Rajapatirana. 8.11.1962.	2.50	6.00	15.00
b. Sign. T. B. Illangaratue and D. W. Rajapatirana. 11.4.1964; 12.6.1964.	2.50	5.00	12.50
c. Sign. U. B. Wanninayake and D. W. Rajapatirana. 6.4.1965.	2.00	5.00	10.00

65 50 RUPEES
1961-65. Blue and purple on m/c unpt. Back blue; ornate stairway.

	VG	VF	UNC
a. Sign. F. R. D. Bandaranaike and D. W. Rajapatirana. 2.11.1961.	5.00	20.00	100.00
b. Sign. T. B. Illangaratne and D. W. Rajapatirana. 5.6.1963.	4.50	17.50	80.00
c. Sign. U. B. Wanninayake and D. W. Rajapatirana. 6.4.1965.	3.75	15.00	70.00

Note: An issue was prepared dated 12.6.1964 which was later destroyed.

66 100 RUPEES
5.6.1963. Brown and blue on m/c unpt. 2 women in national dress on back.

	VG	VF	UNC
	12.50	30.00	100.00

1965-68 ISSUE

#67-71 statue of Kg. Parakkrama at r. W/o bank name in English. Back designs like #57-61. Various date and sign. varieties. Wmk.: Chinze. Printer: BWC.

63 5 RUPEES
1962; 1964. Orange and brown on m/c unpt. Back green and orange; standing figure at ctr. on back.

	VG	VF	UNC
a. Sign. P. B. G. Kalugalla and D. W. Rajapatirana. 8.11.1962.	2.50	7.50	20.00
b. Sign. N. M. Perera and D. W. Rajapatirana. 12.6.1964.	2.00	7.00	15.00

67 2 RUPEES
1965-68. Lt. brown on lilac, lt. green and blue unpt.

	VG	VF	UNC
a. Sign. U. B. Wanninayake and D. W. Rajapatirana. 9.9.1965; 15.7.1967.	1.00	2.50	7.00
b. Sign. U. B. Wanninayake and W. Tennekoon. 10.1.1968.	1.00	2.50	6.00

68 5 RUPEES
1965-68. Orange and brown on m/c unpt. Back green and orange.

	VG	VF	UNC
a. Sign. U. B. Wanninayake and D. W. Rajapatirana. 9.9.1965; 15.7.1967.	1.00	3.00	12.00
b. Sign. U. B. Wanninayake and W. Tennekoon. 1.9.1967; 10.1.1968.	1.00	2.00	10.00

69 10 RUPEES
10.1.1968. Green and purple on orange and blue unpt.

	VG	VF	UNC
	1.50	4.00	20.00

70 50 RUPEES
1967; 1968. Blue and purple on m/c unpt.

	VG	VF	UNC
a. Sign. U. W. Wanninayake and D. W. Rajapatirana. 7.3.1967.	10.00	40.00	125.00
b. Sign. U. B. Wanninayake and W. Tennekoon. 10.1.1968.	10.00	35.00	110.00

71 100 RUPEES
1966-68. Brown and blue on m/c unpt.

	VG	VF	UNC
a. Sign. U. W. Wanninayake and D. W. Rajapatirana. 28.5.1966; 22.11.1966.	7.50	40.00	200.00
b. Sign. U. B. Wanninayake and W. Tennekoon. 10.1.1968.	5.00	35.00	175.00

1968-69 ISSUE

#72-76 w/bank name in English on both sides. Various date and sign. varieties. Wmk.: Chinze. Printer: BWC.

76	100 RUPEES	VG	VF	UNC
	10.5.1969. Brown and blue on m/c unpt. Like #71.	7.50	30.00	95.00

1970 ISSUE

#58 and 59 Smiling Pres. Bandaranaike w/raised hand. Wmk.: Chinze. Printer: TDLR. Replacement notes serial # prefix *W/1* and *V/1*.

72	2 RUPEES	VG	VF	UNC
	1969-77. Lt. brown on lilac, lt. green and blue unpt. Like #67.			
	a. Sign. U. B. Wanninayake and W. Tennekoon. 10.5.1969.	0.50	1.50	6.00
	b. Sign. N. M. Perera and W. Tennekoon. 1.6.1970; 1.2.1971; 7.6.1971; 12.5.1972; 21.8.1973; 27.8.1974.	0.25	1.25	5.00
	c. Sign. R. J. G. de Mel and H. E. Tennekoon. 26.8.1977.	0.25	1.00	4.00

73	5 RUPEES	VG	VF	UNC
	1969-77. Orange and brown on m/c unpt. Back green and orange. Like #68.			
	a. Sign. U. B. Wanninayake and W. Tennekoon. 10.5.1969.	0.50	2.00	8.00
	b. Sign. N. M. Perera and W. Tennekoon. 1.6.1970; 1.2.1971; 21.8.1973; 16.7.1974; 27.8.1974.	1.00	3.50	7.00
	c. Sign. F. R. D. Bandaranaike and H. E. Tennekoon. 26.8.1977.	0.40	1.50	6.00
	ct. Color trial.	—	—	150.00

77	50 RUPEES	VG	VF	UNC
	26.10.1970; 29.12.1970. Blue on lilac, yellow and brown unpt. Monument on back.	3.00	15.00	75.00
78	100 RUPEES			
	26.10.1970; 9.12.1970. Red-violet on m/c unpt. Female dancers on back.	5.00	25.00	100.00

1971-72 ISSUE

#79 and 80 smiling Pres. Bandaranaike w/o hand raised. Wmk.: Chinze. Printer: BWC.

79	50 RUPEES	VG	VF	UNC
	28.12.1972; 27.8.1974. Purple and m/c. Landscape on back.	3.00	12.00	60.00
	a. Issued note.	3.00	12.50	60.00
	s. Specimen.	—	—	175.00

74	10 RUPEES	VG	VF	UNC
	1969-77. Green and purple on orange and blue unpt. Like #69.			
	a. Sign. U. B. Wanninayake and W. Tennekoon. 20.10.1969.	2.00	7.00	20.00
	b. Sign. N. M. Perera and W. Tennekoon. 1.6.1970; 1.2.1971; 7.6.1971; 21.8.1973; 16.7.1974.	0.50	2.50	10.00
	c. Sign. F. R. D. Bandaranaike and H. E. Tennekoon. 6.10.1975.	0.50	2.25	9.00
	ct. Color trial.	—	—	175.00
	d. Sign. R. J. G. de Mel and H. E. Tennekoon. 26.8.1977.	0.50	2.00	8.00
75	50 RUPEES			
	20.10.1969. Blue and purple on m/c unpt. Like #70.	10.00	40.00	125.00

80	100 RUPEES	VG	VF	UNC
	1971-75. Brown and purple on m/c unpt. Ornate stairway on back.			
	a. Sign. N. M. Perera and H. E. Tennekoon. 18.12.1971; 16.7.1974; 27.8.1974.	4.00	17.50	85.00
	b. Sign. F. R. D. Bandaranaike and H. E. Tennekoon. 6.10.1975.	3.75	15.00	75.00

Note: For later issues see Sri Lanka.

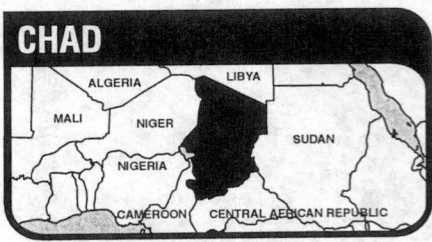

The Republic of Chad, a landlocked country of central Africa, is the largest country of former French Equatorial Africa. It has an area of 495,755 sq. mi. (1,284,000 sq. km.) and a population of 7.27 million. Capital, N'Djaména. An expanding livestock industry produces camels, cattle and sheep. Cotton (the chief product), ivory and palm oil are important exports.

Although supposedly known to Ptolemy, the Chad area was first visited by europeans in 1823. Exaggerated estimates of its economic importance led to a race for its possession (1890-93) which resulted in territory being divided by treaty between Great Britain, France and Germany. As a consequence of World War I, the German area was mandated to France in 1919. Chad was absorbed into the colony of French Equatorial Africa, as a part of Ubangi-Shari, in 1910 and became a separate colony in 1920. Upon dissolution of French Equatorial Africa in 1959, the component states became autonomous members of the French Union. Chad became an independent republic on Aug. 11, 1960.

Conflicts between the government and secessionists began in 1965 and developed into civil war. A ceasefire in 1987 was followed by an attempted coup. In 1990, Idress Déby declared himself president.

For later issues, see Central African States.

MONETARY SYSTEM:
1 Franc = 100 Centimes

SIGNATURE VARIETIES:
Refer to introduction to Central African States.

RÉPUBLIQUE DU TCHAD

BANQUE CENTRALE

1971 ISSUE

		VG	VF	UNC
1	**10,000 FRANCS** ND (1971). M/c. Pres. Tombalbaye at l., cattle watering at ctr. r. Mask at l., tractor plowing at ctr., statue at r. on back. Sign. 1.	150.00	750.00	2250.00

BANQUE DES ÉTATS DE L'AFRIQUE CENTRALE

1974-78; ND ISSUE

		VG	VF	UNC
2	**500 FRANCS** ND (1974); 1978. Brown and red on m/c unpt. Woman at l., Flamingos, crowned cranes, abdim's stork at ctr. and at r. Mask at l., students and chemical testing at ctr., statue at r. on back.			
	a. Sign. titles and wmk. like #3a. Sign. 6. (1974).	2.50	12.50	40.00
	b. Sign. titles, wmk. and date like #3c. Sign. 10. 1.4.1978.	20.00	75.00	200.00

		VG	VF	UNC
3	**1000 FRANCS** ND; 1.4.1978. Blue and brown on m/c unpt. Woman at r. Mask at l., trains, planes and bridge at ctr., statue at r. on back.			
	a. Sign. titles: *LE DIRECTEUR GÉNÉRAL* and *UN CENSEUR*. Engraved. Wmk: Antelope. in half profile. Sign. 5; 7.	4.00	15.00	90.00
	b. Sign. titles: *LE DIRECTEUR GÉNÉRAL* and *UN CENSEUR*. Lithographed. Wmk: Antelope in profile. Sign. 8.	3.00	12.50	50.00
	c. Sign. titles: *LE GOUVERNEUR* and *UN CENSEUR*. Sign. 10. 1.4.1978.	FV	8.00	30.00

		VG	VF	UNC
4	**5000 FRANCS** ND (1974). Brown-orange on m/c unpt. Pres. Tombalbaye at l. Mask at l., industrial collage at ctr., statue at r. on back. Sign. 4.	100.00	250.00	650.00

		VG	VF	UNC
5	**5000 FRANCS** ND. Brown on m/c unpt. Woman at l. Like #4 on back.			
	a. Sign. 6. (1976).	25.00	75.00	275.00
	b. Sign. 9. (1978).	20.00	50.00	200.00

NOTICE

Readers with unlisted dates, signature varieties, etc. are invited to submit photocopies of their notes to: Standard Catalog of World Paper Money, 700 East State St. Iola, WI 54990-0001, E-Mail: george.cuhaj@fwpubs.com.

1980 ISSUE

6   500 FRANCS
1.6.1980; 1.6.1984. Red and brown on m/c unpt. Woman weaving
basket at r. Like #2 on back. Sign. 10.

	VG	VF	UNC
	1.50	3.00	20.00

7   1000 FRANCS
1.6.1980; 1.6.1984. Blue and dull purple on m/c unpt. Water
buffalo at r. Back like #3. Sign. 9; 10.

	VG	VF	UNC
	3.00	8.50	30.00

8   5000 FRANCS
1.1.1980. Brown and m/c. Girl at lower l., village scene at ctr. Back
w/carving, airplane, train, tractor and man smoking pipe. Similar to
Central African Republic #11 and others. Sign. 9.

	VG	VF	UNC
	15.00	40.00	200.00

1984-85; ND ISSUE

9   500 FRANCS
1985-92. Brown on m/c unpt. Carved statue and jug at ctr. Man
carving mask at l. ctr. on back. Wmk: Carving.

	VG	VF	UNC
a. Sign. 10. 1.1.1985; 1.1.1986.	FV	FV	8.00
b. Sign. 12. 1.1.1987.	FV	FV	7.00
c. Sign. 13. 1.1.1990.	FV	FV	7.00
d. Sign. 15. 1.1.1991.	FV	FV	6.50
e. Sign. 15. 1.1.1992.	FV	FV	6.00

10   1000 FRANCS
1.1.1985. Dull blue-violet on m/c unpt. Animal carving at lower l.,
map at ctr., starburst at lower r. Incomplete outline map of Chad at
top ctr. Elephants at l., statue at r. on back. Wmk: Animal carving.
Sign. 9.

	VG	VF	UNC
	15.00	40.00	100.00

#10 was withdrawn shortly after issue because of the incompleteness of the map at top.

10A   1000 FRANCS
1985-92. Like #10 but complete outline map of Chad at top ctr.

	VG	VF	UNC
a. Sign. 9. 1.1.1985; 1.1.1988; 1.1.1989; 1.1.1990.	FV	FV	12.50
b. Sign. 15. 1.1.1991.	3.50	15.00	35.00
c. Sign. 15. 1.1.1992.	FV	FV	12.50

11	5000 FRANCS	VG	VF	UNC
	ND (1984-91). Brown on m/c unpt. Mask at l., woman w/bundle of fronds at r. Plowing and mine ore conveyor on back. Sign. 9; 15.	FV	15.00	75.00

12	10,000 FRANCS	VG	VF	UNC
	ND (1984-91). Black, brown and dk. green on m/c unpt. Stylized antelope heads at l., woman at r. and as wmk. Loading fruit onto truck at l. on back.			
	a. Sign. 9.	FV	25.00	100.00
	b. Sign. 15.	FV	20.00	90.00

Note: For notes with similar back designs see Cameroun Republic, Central African Republic, Congo (Brazzaville) and Gabon.

CHILE

The Republic of Chile, a ribbonlike country on the Pacific coast of southern South America, has an area of 292,258 sq. mi. (756,945 sq. km.) and a population of 15.21 million. Capital: Santiago. Historically, the economic base of Chile has been the rich mineral deposits of its northern provinces. Copper, of which Chile has about 25 percent of the world's reserves, has accounted for more than 75 per cent of Chile's export earnings in recent years. Other important exports are iron ore, iodine, fruit and nitrate of soda.

Diego de Almargo was the first Spaniard to attempt to wrest Chile from the Incas and Araucanian tribes, 1536. He failed, and was followed by Pedro de Valdivia, a favorite of Pizarro, who founded Santiago in 1541. When the Napoleonic Wars involved Spain, leaving the constituent parts of the Spanish Empire to their own devices, Chilean patriots formed a national government and proclaimed the country's independence, Sept. 18, 1810. Independence, however, was not secured until Feb. 12, 1818, after a bitter struggle led by Generals Bernardo O'Higgins and José de San Martín.

In 1925, the constitution was ratified to strengthen the Executive branch at the expense of the Legislature.

MONETARY SYSTEM:
1 Escudo = 100 Centesimos, 1960-75
1 Peso = 100 "old" Escudos, 1975-

REPLACEMENT NOTES:
#140, 143, 145-148 w/R next to serial #.
#149-158 w/R near to plate position #.

BANCO CENTRAL DE CHILE

1960 ND PROVISIONAL ISSUE

1 Escudo = 1000 Pesos (= 100 Centesimos)

#124-133 Escudo denominations in red as part of new plates overprinted in wmk. area on back. Wmk: D. Diego Portales. Sign. titles: *PRESIDENTE* and *GERENTE GENERAL*. Sign. varieties. Printer: CdM-Chile.

124	1/2 CENTESIMO ON 5 PESOS	Good	Fine	XF
	ND (1960-61). Blue. Portr. Bernard O'Higgins at l. Ovpt. on #119.		Rare	

125	1 CENTESIMO ON 10 PESOS	VG	VF	UNC
	ND (1960-61). Red-brown. Portr. Manuel Bulnes at l. Series F. Ovpt. on #120.	1.00	2.50	12.50

126	5 CENTESIMOS ON 50 PESOS	VG	VF	UNC
	ND (1960-61). Green. Portr. Anibal Pinto at l. Series C. Ovpt. on #121. 3 sign. varieties.			
	a. Imprint on face 25mm wide.	0.25	1.00	2.50
	b. Imprint on face 22mm wide.	0.10	0.20	2.00
	s. Specimen.	—	—	12.50

134A **1/2 ESCUDO**

	VG	VF	UNC
ND. Like #134, but tan unpt. Black serial #.			
a. Paper of #121. Series B-G.	0.10	0.25	1.50
s. Specimen.	—	—	17.50

127 **10 CENTESIMOS ON 100 PESOS**

	VG	VF	UNC
ND (1960-61). Red. Portr. Arturo Prat at l. Ovpt. on #122. 3 sign. varieties. Light and dark back varieties. Series C-K.			
a. Issued note.	0.25	1.00	2.50
s. Specimen.	—	—	12.50

128 **50 CENTESIMOS ON 500 PESOS**

	VG	VF	UNC
ND (1960-61). Blue. Portr. Manuel Montt at r. Ovpt. on #115. Series A.	0.50	2.50	15.00

135 **1 ESCUDO**

	VG	VF	UNC
ND. Brown-violet w/lilac guilloche on tan unpt. Portr. Arturo Prat at ctr. Red-brown arms w/founding of Santiago on back. Engraved. Wmk: Balmaceda.			
a. Lg. and sm. brown serial #. Wmk: *1000* at r. Series A.	0.50	3.00	10.00
b. Lg. and sm. black serial #. Wmk: *500* at r. Series A.	1.00	5.00	20.00
c. W/o wmk. at r. Series J; B.	0.50	1.50	5.00
d. Sm. black serial #. W/o wmk. at r. Arms in red-brown at l. on back.	0.20	0.50	2.00
s. As c. Specimen.	—	—	17.50

135A **1 ESCUDO**

	VG	VF	UNC
ND. Like #135c but w/arms in olive at l. on back. 2 sign. varieties.			
a. Series G-I. W/o wmk. at r.	0.10	0.20	1.00
b. W/V under portr. Paper of #121. Series J-N.	0.10	0.20	1.00

129 **1 ESCUDO ON 1000 PESOS**

	VG	VF	UNC
ND (1960-61). Dk. brown. Portr. Manuel Blanco Encalada at l. Ovpt. on #116. Series A.	0.50	2.00	12.50

130 **5 ESCUDOS ON 5000 PESOS**

	VG	VF	UNC
ND (1960-61). Brown-violet. Portr. Manuel Antonio Tocornal at l. Ovpt. on #117. 2 sign. varieties. Series J.	1.00	5.00	25.00

131 **10 ESCUDOS ON 10,000 PESOS**

	VG	VF	UNC
ND (1960-61). Purple on lt. blue unpt. Portr. Jose Manuel Balmaceda at l. Ovpt. on #118. Dual wmk: Head at l., words *DIEZ MIL* at r. Series F.	2.00	10.00	40.00

132 **10 ESCUDOS ON 10,000 PESOS**

	VG	VF	UNC
ND (1960-61). Red-brown. Portr. Jose Manuel Balmaceda at l. Similar to #131 but w/o wmk. at r. Series F.	2.00	15.00	55.00

133 **50 ESCUDOS ON 50,000 PESOS**

	VG	VF	UNC
ND (1960-61). Blue-green Portr. Arturo Alessandri at l. and brown on m/c unpt. Ovpt. on #123. Series A.	4.50	25.00	75.00

1962-75 ND Issue

#134-141 sign. varieties. Wmk: D. Diego Portales P. at l. Printer: CdM-Chile.

136 **1 ESCUDO**

	VG	VF	UNC
ND (1964). Dull violet on tan unpt. Portr. Arturo Prat. Like #135 but arms on back in lt. olive. Lithographed. 3 sign. varieties. 6 or 7 digit serial #. Series N; P; Q.	0.10	0.25	0.75

134 **1/2 ESCUDO**

	VG	VF	UNC
ND. Dk. blue on pale orange and lt. blue unpt. Portr. Gen. Bernardo O'Higgins at ctr. Explorer on horseback at l. ctr. on back. Red serial #.			
a. Paper of #122. Series A. 3 sign. varieties.	0.15	0.50	3.00
b. Paper of #121. Series B. 2 sign. varieties.	0.15	0.50	3.00
s. Specimen.	—	—	15.00

137	5 ESCUDOS	VG	VF	UNC
	ND. Reddish brown on m/c unpt. Portr. Manuel Bulnes at ctr. Battle of Rancagua at ctr., yellow-orange arms at l. on back.			
	a. Series A.	0.75	2.00	12.50
	s. Specimen.	—	—	17.50
138	5 ESCUDOS	0.10	0.25	2.00
	ND (1964). Red and brown-violet on m/c unpt. Like #137. Red-brown arms at l. on back. 4 sign. varieties. 6 or 7 digit serial #. Series A-E.			

139	10 ESCUDOS	VG	VF	UNC
	ND. Violet, blue-gray and dull purple on m/c unpt. Portr. Jose Manuel Balmaceda at ctr. Dk. or lt. brown arms at l., soldiers meeting at ctr. on back. 3 sign. varieties.			
	a. Series A-G.	0.25	0.75	5.00
	s. Specimen.	—	—	25.00

140	50 ESCUDOS	VG	VF	UNC
	ND. Dk. green and olive-brown on m/c unpt. Porr. Arturo Alessandri at ctr. Back brown and green; Banco Central bldg. 5 sign. varieties.			
	a. Series A-D.	1.00	1.75	8.00
	b. Series E-F.	0.10	0.25	2.00
	s. Specimen.	—	—	25.00

141	100 ESCUDOS	VG	VF	UNC
	ND. Blue-gray and violet-brown on tan unpt. Portr. Manuel Regifo at r. Sailing ships at ctr. arms at l. on back. 2 sign. varieties.			
	a. Series A-G.	0.25	0.75	4.00
	s. Specimen.	—	—	25.00

1967-76 ND ISSUES

#142-148 sign. varieties. Wmk: D. Diego Portales P. at l. Printer: CdM-Chile. Replacement notes: Serial # suffix *R* or *R* in area of sheet position #.

142	10 ESCUDOS	VG	VF	UNC
	ND (1970). Gray-green, violet-brown and blue-gray on m/c unpt. Portr. Jose Manuel Balmaceda at r. Red-brown lower margin on back. Engraved. Series A. 2 sign. varieties.	0.20	0.50	2.00

142A	10 ESCUDOS	VG	VF	UNC
	ND. Like #142 but w/green lower margin on back. Lithographed.			
	a. Series B.	0.20	0.50	2.00
	s. Specimen.	—	—	20.00
143	10 ESCUDOS	0.10	0.25	1.50
	ND. Grayish brown on tan unpt. Like #142. Lithographed. 3 sign. varieties. Series A.			
144	500 ESCUDOS		Rare	
	1971. Red-brown on m/c unpt. Copper worker at l. Strip mining at ctr. r. on back. W/o 3-line text: *NO DEBEMOS CONSENTIR...* at bottom.			

145	500 ESCUDOS	VG	VF	UNC
	1971. Like #144 but w/3-line text: *NO DEBEMOS CONSENTIR...*at bottom on back. 2 sign. varieties. Series A; B.	0.15	0.50	2.50

Note: #144 and 145 commemorate the nationalization of iron and copper mines.

146	1000 ESCUDOS	VG	VF	UNC
	ND. Purple and violet on m/c unpt. Jose Miguel Carrera at l. Back like #147. 2 sign. varieties. Series A; B.	0.15	0.50	3.00

147 5000 ESCUDOS
ND. Dk. green and brown on m/c unpt. Jose Miguel Carrera at l. Carrera House at ctr. r. on back.

	VG	VF	UNC
a. Back w/deep green vignette. Lithographed. Series A.	0.50	1.50	5.00
b. Back w/dk. olive-green vignette. Partially engraved. Series B. 2 sign. varieties.	0.25	0.75	3.00

150 10 PESOS
1975-76. Red on m/c unpt. Gen. Bernardo O'Higgins at r. and as wmk. Back similar to #148.

	VG	VF	UNC
a. B. O'HIGGINS under portr. 1975.	0.75	1.75	8.00
b. LIBERTADOR B. O'HIGGINS under portr. 1975; 1976.	0.50	1.00	6.00
s. As a. Specimen.	—	—	25.00

148 10,000 ESCUDOS
ND. Orange-brown on m/c unpt. Gen. Bernardo O'Higgins at l. Blue serial #. Battle of Rancagua on back. Series A. 2 sign. varieties.

VG	VF	UNC
1.00	3.50	6.00

151 50 PESOS
1975-81. Dk. blue and aqua on green and lt. blue unpt. Portr. Capt. Arturo Prat at r. Sailing ships at ctr. on back. 3 sign. varieties.

	VG	VF	UNC
a. 1975; 1976; 1977; 1978.	0.20	0.50	3.00
b. 1980; 1981 (2 sign. varieties.)	0.15	0.25	2.00
s. Specimen. 1975.	—	—	25.00

1975-89 ISSUES

#149-152 wmk: D. Diego Portales P. Sign. varieties. Replacement notes: R serial # suffix. #149-156 printer: CdM-Chile.

152 100 PESOS
1976-84. Purple and red-violet on m/c unpt. Diego Portales at r. 1837 meeting at l. ctr. on back. 6 sign. varieties.

	VG	VF	UNC
a. Normal serial # w/o prefix letter. Series A. 1976.	1.50	4.00	10.00
b. Electronic sorting serial # w/prefix letter. 1976-77, 1979-84. 6 sign. varieties (2 for 1981).	0.30	0.50	3.00
s. Specimen. 1976.	—	—	25.00

149 5 PESOS
1975-76. Green on olive unpt. Jose Miguel Carrera at r. Back similar to #147.

	VG	VF	UNC
a. 1975.	0.50	1.50	5.00
b. 1976.	10.00	25.00	55.00
s. As a. Specimen.	—	—	25.00

153	**500 PESOS**	VG	VF	UNC
	1977-2000. Dk. brown and brown-violet w/black text on m/c unpt. Pedro de Valdivia at r. Wmk: Carrera. Founding of Santiago at ctr. on back. 11 sign. varieties.			
	a. 1977; 1978.	FV	1.50	7.50
	b. 1980-82; 1985-90.	FV	FV	4.50
	c. Sign. titles: *PRESIDENTE* and *GERENTE GENERAL INTERINO.* 1991.	FV	2.00	7.50
	d. 1991-93.	FV	FV	4.00
	e. 1994-2000. (1999 w/o imprint).	FV	FV	3.00
	s. Specimen. 1977.	—	—	25.00

154	**1000 PESOS**	VG	VF	UNC
	1978-. Deep blue-green, dk. olive-brown on m/c unpt. Ignacio Carrera Pinto at r. and as wmk., military arms at ctr. Monument to Chilean heroes on back. 12 sign. varieties.			
	a. Sign. titles: *PRESIDENTE* and *GERENTE GENERAL.* 1978-80.	FV	4.00	25.00
	b. 1982.	FV	FV	10.00
	c. 1984-90.	FV	FV	9.50
	d. Sign. titles: *PRESIDENTE* and *GERENTE GENERAL INTERINO.* 1990.	FV	FV	9.00
	e. Sign. titles as a. 1991-94. (2 sign. var. in 1994).	FV	FV	7.50
	f. Designer's names omitted from lower l. and r. 1995-2004. (w/o imprint 1999; 2001-).	FV	FV	5.00
	s. Specimen. 1978. Ovpt. *Especimen.*	—	—	50.00

155	**5000 PESOS**	VG	VF	UNC
	1981-. Brown and red-violet on m/c unpt. Allegorical woman w/musical instrument, seated male at ctr. Statue of woman w/children at l. ctr., Gabriela Mistral at r. on back and as wmk. 9 sign. varieties.			
	a. Sign. titles: *PRESIDENTE* and *GERENTE GENERAL.* 1981. Plain security thread.	FV	FV	70.00
	b. 1986-90.	FV	FV	50.00
	c. Sign. titles: *PRESIDENTE* and *GERENTE GENERAL INTERINO.* 1991.	FV	FV	35.00
	d. Sign. titles: *PRESIDENTE* and *GERENTE GENERAL.* 1991-94.	FV	FV	27.50
	e. As d but w/segmented foil security thread. 1994-2003. (w/o imprint, 2002-).	FV	FV	20.00
	s. Specimen. 1981; 1993.	—	—	100.00

156	**10,000 PESOS**	VG	VF	UNC
	1989-95. Dk. blue and dk. olive-green on m/c unpt. Capt. Arturo Prat at r. and as wmk. Statue of Liberty at l., Hacienda San Agustin de Punual Cuna at l. ctr. on back. 5 sign. varieties.			
	a. Plain security thread. 1989-93.	FV	FV	60.00
	b. As a. 1994.	FV	FV	50.00
	c. W/imprint. Segmented foil over security thread. 1994-95.	FV	FV	45.00
	s. Specimen. 1994.	—	—	100.00

1994 ISSUE

157	**10,000 PESOS**	VG	VF	UNC
	1994-99; 2001-04. Dk. blue and deep olive-green on m/c unpt. Like #156c. Printer: TDLR (w/o imprint). 2 sign. varieties.	FV	FV	35.00

1997 ISSUE

158	**2000 PESOS**	VG	VF	UNC
	1997; 1999 (w/imprint); 2001-03 (w/o imprint). Purple and dk. brown on m/c unpt. Manuel Rodriguez E. at r. and as wmk., statue of Manuel Rodriguez on horseback at ctr. Iglesia de los Dominicos (church) at ctr. on back. Printer: CdM-C.	FV	FV	9.00

1998 ISSUE

159	**20,000 PESOS**	VG	VF	UNC
	1998-2001. Lilac brown, green and m/c. Don Andres Bello at r. University bldg. on back. Printer: CdM-C.	FV	FV	60.00

2004 POLYMER ISSUE

160	**2000 PESOS**		VG	VF	UNC
	2004. Lilac and brown on m/c unpt. Manuel Rodríguez E. at r. and as statue on horseback. Polymer plastic. Similar to #158.		FV	FV	7.50

CHINA / Peoples Republic

The Peoples Republic of China, located in eastern Asia, has an area of 3,696,100 sq. mi. (9,572,900 sq. km.), including Manchuria and Tibet, and a population of 1.276 billion. Capital: Beijing. The economy is based on agriculture, mining and manufacturing. Textiles, clothing, metal ores, tea and rice are exported.

In the fall of 1911, the middle business class of China and Chinese students educated in Western universities started a general uprising against the Manchu dynasty which forced the abdication on Feb. 12, 1912, of the boy emperor Hsuan T'ung (Pu-yi), thus bringing to an end the dynasty that had ruled China since 1644. Five days later, China formally became a republic with physician and revolutionist Sun Yat-sen as first provisional president.

Dr. Sun and his supporters founded a new party called the Kuomintang, and planned a Chinese republic based upon the Three Principles of Nationalism, Democracy and People's Livelihood. They failed, however, to win control over all of China, and Dr. Sun resigned the presidency in favor of Yuan Shih Kai, the most powerful of the Chinese Army generals. Yuan ignored the constitution of the new republic and tried to make himself emperor.

After the death of Yuan in 1917, Sun Yat-sen and the Kuomintang established a republic in Canton. It failed to achieve the unification of China, and in 1923 Dr. Sun entered into an agreement with the Soviet Union known as the Canton-Moscow Entente. The Kuomintang agreed to admit Chinese communists to the party. The Soviet Union agreed to furnish military advisers to train the army of the Canton Republic. Dr. Sun died in 1925 and was succeeded by one of his supporters, General Chiang Kai-shek.

Chiang Kai-shek launched a vigorous campaign to educate the Chinese and modernize their industries and agriculture. Under his command, the armies of the Kuomintang captured Nanking (1927) and Peking (1928). In 1928, Chiang was made president of the Chinese Republic. His government was recognized by most of the great powers, but he soon began to exercise dictatorial powers. Prodded by the conservative members of the Kuomintang, he initiated a break between these members and the Chinese Communists which, once again, prevented the unification of China.

Persuaded that China would fare better under the leadership of its businessmen in alliance with the capitalist countries than under the guidance of the Chinese Communists in alliance with the Soviet Union, Chiang expelled all Communists from the Kuomintang, sent the Russian advisers home, and hired German generals to train his army.

The Communists responded by setting up a government and raising an army that during the period of 1930-34 acquired control over large parts of Kiangsi, Fukien, Hunan, Hupeh and other provinces.

When his army was sufficiently trained and equipped, Chiang Kai-shek led several military expeditions against the Communist Chinese which, while unable to subdue them, dislodged them south of the Yangtze, forcing them to undertake in 1935 a celebrated "Long March" of 6,000 miles (9,654 km.) from Hunan northwest to a refuge in Shensi province just south of Inner Mongolia from which Chiang was unable to displace them.

The Japanese had now assumed warlike proportions. Chiang rejected a Japanese offer of cooperation against the Communists, but agreed to suppress the movement himself. His generals, however, persuaded him to negotiate a truce with the Communists to permit united action against the greater of Japanese aggression. Under the terms of the truce, Communists were again admitted to the Kuomintang. They, in turn, promised to dissolve the Soviet Republic of China and to cease issuing their own currency.

The war with Japan all but extinguished the appeal of the Kuomintang, appreciably increased the power of the Communists, and divided China into three parts. The east coast and its principal cities - Peking, Tientsin, Nanking, Shanghai and Canton - were in Japanese-controlled, puppet-ruled states. The Communists controlled the countryside in the north where they were the de facto rulers of 100 million peasants. Chiang and the Kuomintang were driven toward the west, from where they returned with their prestige seriously damaged by their wartime performance.

At the end of World War II, the United States tried to bring the Chinese factions together in a coalition government. American mediation failed, and within weeks the civil war resumed.

By the fall of 1947, most of northeast China was under Communist control. During the following year, the war turned wholly in favor of the Communists. The Kuomintang armies in the northeast surrendered, two provincial capitals in the north were captured, a large Kuomintang army in the Huai river basin surrendered. Four Communist armies converged upon the demoralized Kuomintang forces. The Communists crossed the Yangtse in April 1949. Nanking, the Nationalist capital, fell. The civil war on the mainland was virtually over.

Chiang Kai-shek relinquished the presidency to Li Tsung-jen, his deputy, and after moving to Canton, to Chungking and Chengtu, retreated from the mainland to Taiwan (Formosa) where he resumed the presidency.

The Communist Peoples Republic of China was proclaimed on September 21, 1949. Thereafter relations between the Peoples Republic and the Soviet Union steadily deteriorated. China emerged as an independent center of Communist power in 1958.

MONETARY SYSTEM:
   1 Yüan = 10 Chiao
   1 Chiao = 10 Fen

MONETARY UNITS	
Yuan	圓 *or* 圜
Pan Yuan	圓半
5 Jiao	角伍
1 Jiao	角壹
1 Fen	分壹

NUMERICAL CHARACTERS

No.	CONVENTIONAL			FORMAL	
1	一	正	元	壹	弌
2	二			弍	貳
3	三			弎	叁
4	四			肆	
5	五			伍	
6	六			陸	
7	七			柒	
8	八			捌	
9	九			玖	
10	十			拾	什
20	十二	廿		拾貳	念
25	五十二	五廿		伍拾貳	
30	十三	卅		拾叁	
100	百一			佰壹	
1,000	千一			仟壹	
10,000	萬一			萬壹	
100,000	萬十	億一		萬拾	億壹
1,000,000	萬百一			萬佰壹	

COMPANION CATALOGS

Volume 1 - Specialized Issues
Volume 2 - General Issues, 1368-1960

The Companion Catalogs in the Standard Catalog of World Paper Money series include a volume on Specialized Issues of the World - listed are those banknotes which were issued on a limited circulation basis rather than the central monetary authority note issues detailed in this work. The Specialized volume is currently in its 10th edition, and it is updated periodically. The General Issues volume lists national notes dated and issued, before 1960. The 11th edition is due out in Fall 2006. Inquiries about the availability of both these volumes are invited to contact Book Department, Krause Publications, 700 East State Street, Iola, WI 54990-0001 or you may call 1-800-258-0929 or www.fwpubs.com.

PEOPLES BANK OF CHINA

行銀民人國中
Chung Kuo Jen Min Yin Hang

中國人民銀行
Zhong Guo Ren Min Yin Hang

1953 SECOND ISSUE

#860-870 arms at ctr. on back.

		VG	VF	UNC
860	**1 FEN**			
	1953. Brown on yellow-orange unpt. Produce truck at r.			
	a. Roman control numerals and serial #.	0.25	0.75	2.50
	b. 3 Roman control numerals only.	FV	0.10	0.25
	c. 2 Roman control numerals.	FV	FV	0.20

		VG	VF	UNC
861	**2 FEN**			
	1953. Dk. blue on lt. blue unpt. Airplane at r.			
	a. Roman control numerals and serial #.	0.25	1.00	3.00
	b. Roman control numerals only.	FV	0.10	0.25

		VG	VF	UNC
862	**5 FEN**			
	1953. Dk. green on green unpt. Cargo ship at r.			
	a. Roman control numerals and serial #.	1.00	4.00	15.00
	b. Roman control numerals only.	FV	0.10	0.30

1962; 1965 ISSUE

#877-879 arms at r. on back.

		VG	VF	UNC
877	**1 JIAO**			
	1962. Brown on m/c unpt. Workers at l.			
	a. Back brown on green and lt. orange unpt. W/o wmk.	3.00	12.50	45.00
	b. As a. Wmk: stars.	20.00	60.00	180.00
	c. Serial # prefix: 3 blue Roman numerals. Back brown. W/o wmk.	FV	0.20	1.00
	d. Like c, serial # prefix: 2 blue Roman numerals.	FV	0.30	1.50
	e. Like b, partially engraved. Serial # prefix: 2 red Roman numerals. Wmk: Stars.	FV	0.20	0.50
	f. Like c but lithographed, serial # prefix: 2 red Roman numerals. W/o wmk.	FV	0.15	0.50

		VG	VF	UNC
878	**2 JIAO**			
	1962. Green. Bridge over Yangtze River at l.			
	a. Engraved face. Serial # prefix: 3 Roman numerals.	FV	0.50	2.00
	b. Lithographed face. Serial # prefix: 3 Roman numerals.	FV	0.20	0.50
	c. As b. Serial # prefix: 2 Roman numerals.	FV	0.15	0.50
	x. As b. Red back. Post production chemical alteration.	FV	1.00	3.50

879 10 YÜAN
1965. Black on m/c unpt. Representatives of the National Assembly
at ctr. Palace gate at l. on back. Wmk: Great Hall w/rays.

	VG	VF	UNC
a. Serial # prefix: 3 Roman numerals.	FV	2.00	8.00
b. Serial # prefix: 2 Roman numerals.	FV	1.50	6.00

1972 ISSUE

880 5 JIAO
1972. Purple and m/c. Women working in textile factory. Arms at r.
on back.

	VG	VF	UNC
a. Engraved bank title and denomination. Serial # prefix: 3 Roman numerals. Wmk: Stars.	FV	0.40	1.50
b. As a. but lithographed face. W/wmk.	FV	0.50	2.00
c. Lithographed face. W/o wmk.	FV	0.20	0.75

1980 ISSUE

#881-888 illustrate 14 persons of various minorities.

#881-883 arms at ctr. on back.

881 1 JIAO
1980. Brown and dk. brown on m/c unpt. 2 Taiwanese men at l.

	VG	VF	UNC
	FV	FV	0.50

882 2 JIAO
1980. Grayish olive-green on m/c unpt. Native *Pu Yi* and Korean
youth at l.

	VG	VF	UNC
	FV	FV	0.50

883 5 JIAO
1980. Purple and red-violet on m/c unpt. *Miao* and *Zhuang*
children at l. Back: brown-violet on m/c unpt.

	VG	VF	UNC
	FV	FV	0.75

#884-889 arms at upper l., stylized birds in unpt. at ctr., dot patterns for poor of sight at lower l. or r.

884 1 YÜAN
1980; 1990; 1996. Brown-violet on m/c unpt. *Dong* and *Yao* youths
at r. Great Wall at ctr. on back.

	VG	VF	UNC
a. Engraved. Dk. blue serial #. Wmk: Ancient *Pu* (pants) coin repeated. 1980.	FV	FV	1.50
b. Partially engraved. Wmk. as a. Black serial #. 1990.	FV	FV	0.75
c. Litho. Wmk: Stars. Black serial #. 1996.	FV	FV	0.50

885 2 YÜAN
1980; 1990. Dk. olive-green on m/c unpt. *Hyger* and *Ye Yien* youths
at r. Rocky shoreline of South Sea on back. Wmk: Ancient *Pu*
(pants) coin repeated.

	VG	VF	UNC
a. Engraved back. 1980.	FV	FV	3.00
b. Litho. back. 1990.	FV	FV	0.75

886 5 YÜAN
1980. Dk. brown on m/c unpt. Old Tibetan man and young Islamic
woman at r. Yangtze Gorges on back. Wmk: Ancient *Pu* (pants)
coin repeated.

	VG	VF	UNC
	FV	FV	2.50

887   **10 YÜAN**
1980. Black on blue and m/c unpt. Elder Han and youthful
Mongolian man at r. Mountains on back. Wmk: Young Mongolian
man.

	VG	VF	UNC
	FV	FV	4.00

888   **50 YÜAN**
1980; 1990. Black on lt. green and m/c unpt. Intellectual, farm girl
and industrial male worker at ctr. Waterfalls of Yellow River on
back. Wmk: Industrial male worker.

	VG	VF	UNC
a. 1980.	FV	FV	18.00
b. Security thread at r. 1990.	FV	FV	12.50

889   **100 YÜAN**
1980; 1990. Black on m/c unpt. 4 great leaders at ctr. Mountains at
Ding Gang Sha (starting point of the "Long March") on back. Wmk:
Bust of Mao Tse-tung.

	VG	VF	UNC
a. 1980.	FV	FV	30.00
b. Security thread at r. 1990.	FV	FV	20.00

890   **500 YÜAN**
1990. Black on m/c unpt.

	VG	VF	UNC
	—	—	—

Note: #890 was used for inter-bank transfers only.

1999 COMMEMORATIVE ISSUE

891, 50th Anniversary of Revolution

891   **50 YÜAN**
1999. Red on m/c unpt. Mao Tse-tung delivering speech. 5 pigeons
in flight, carvings to l. and r. on back.

	VG	VF	UNC
	FV	FV	15.00

1999 REGULAR ISSUE

#892-901 Mao Tse-tung at r., flora at lower ctr. and as wmk.

		VG	VF	UNC
892	**1 JIAO** 1999.			Expected New Issue
893	**2 JIAO** 1999.			Expected New Issue
894	**5 JIAO** 1999.			Expected New Issue

		VG	VF	UNC
895	**1 YÜAN** 1999.	FV	FV	0.50
896	**2 YÜAN** 1999.			Expected New Issue

897   **5 YÜAN**
1999 (2002). Purple on m/c unpt. Mountain valley veiw on back.

	VG	VF	UNC
	FV	FV	1.00

898   **10 YÜAN**
1999 (2000). Slate blue and m/c. Three gorges of Yangtze river on
back.

	VG	VF	UNC
	FV	FV	2.50

899   **20 YÜAN**
1999. Brown on m/c unpt. River scene on back.

	VG	VF	UNC
	FV	FV	4.50

900   50 YÜAN
1999 (2001). Green and m/c. Potala of Tibet on back.

	VG	VF	UNC
	FV	FV	10.00

901   100 YÜAN
1999. Red and m/c. Hall of the People on back.

	VG	VF	UNC
	FV	FV	20.00

2000 COMMEMORATIVE ISSUE

#902, Year 2000 commemorative

902   100 YÜAN
2000. Orange, red and green. Polymer plastic. Dragon at center,
clear window w/image at lower l., OVD at upper r. Scientific bldg.
on back.

	VG	VF	UNC
	FV	FV	32.50

2005 ISSUE

No.	Denom.			
		VG	VF	UNC
903	**5 YÜAN** 2005. M/c.			Expected New Issue
904	**10 YÜAN** 2005. M/c.			Expected New Issue
905	**20 YÜAN** 2005. M/c.			Expected New Issue
906	**50 YÜAN** 2005. M/c.			Expected New Issue
907	**100 YÜAN** 2005. M/c.			Expected New Issue

FOREIGN EXCHANGE CERTIFICATES

BANK OF CHINA

This series has been discontinued and is no longer redeemable.

中國銀行

Chung Kuo Yin Hang

1979 ISSUE

#FX1-FX7 only uncirculated examples command a premium.

FX1   10 FEN
1979. Brown on m/c unpt. waterfalls at ctr.

	VG	VF	UNC
a. Wmk: 1 lg. and 4 sm. stars.	—	—	0.50
b. Wmk: Star and torch.	—	—	1.00

#FX2-FX4 wmk: Star and Torch.

FX2   50 FEN
1979. Purple on m/c unpt. Temple of Heaven at l. ctr.

	VG	VF	UNC
	—	—	1.50

FX3   1 YÜAN
1979. Deep green on m/c unpt. Pleasure boats in lake w/mountains
behind at ctr.

	VG	VF	UNC
	—	—	1.00

FX4   5 YÜAN
1979. Deep brown on m/c unpt. Mountain scenery at ctr.

	VG	VF	UNC
	—	—	2.00

FX5   10 YÜAN
1979. Deep blue on m/c/ unpt. Yangtze Gorges at ctr.

	VG	VF	UNC
	—	—	2.50

#FX6-FX9 wmk: National badge.

FX6	50 YÜAN	VG	VF	UNC
	1979. Purple and red on m/c unpt. Mountain lake at Kweilin at ctr.	—	—	20.00

FX7	100 YÜAN	VG	VF	UNC
	1979. Black and blue on m/c unpt. Great Wall at ctr.	—	—	25.00

1988 ISSUE

#FX8-FX9 only uncirculated examples command a premium.

FX8	50 YÜAN	VG	VF	UNC
	1988. Black, orange-brown and green on m/c unpt. Shoreline rock formations at ctr.	—	—	15.00
FX9	100 YÜAN			
	1988. Olive-green on m/c unpt. Great Wall at ctr.	—	—	20.00

PEOPLES REPUBLIC - MILITARY

MILITARY PAYMENT CERTIFICATES

军用代金券

Chün Yung Tai Chin Ch'üa n

1965 ISSUE

M41	1 FEN	VG	VF	UNC
	1965. Greenish brown. Airplane at l. ctr.	5.00	15.00	60.00

M42	5 FEN	VG	VF	UNC
	1965. Red. Airplane at ctr.	6.00	30.00	90.00

M43	1 CHIAO	VG	VF	UNC
	1965. Purple. Steam passenger train at ctr. r.	15.00	60.00	175.00

#M44 Held in reserve.

M45	1 YÜAN	VG	VF	UNC
	1965. Green. Truck convoy at l.	15.00	75.00	300.00
M46	5 YÜAN			
	1965. Truck convoy at l.	25.00	125.00	500.00

CHINESE ADMINISTRATION OF TAIWAN

The Republic of China, comprising Taiwan (an island located 90 miles off the southeastern coast of mainland China), the islands of Quemoy and Matsu and nearby islets of the Pescadores chain, has an area of 14,000 sq. mi. (35,981 sq. km.) and a population of 20.2 million. Capital: Taipei. In recent years, manufacturing has replaced agriculture in importance. Fruits, vegetables, plywood, textile yarns, fabrics and clothing are exported.

Chinese migration to Taiwan began as early as the sixth century. The Dutch established a base on the island in 1624 and held it until 1661, when they were driven out by supporters of the Ming dynasty who used it as a stage for their unsuccessful attempt to displace the ruling Manchu dynasty on the mainland. Manchu forces occupied the island in 1683 and remained under the suzerainty of China until its cession to Japan in 1895. Following World War II Taiwan was returned to China, and on December 8, 1949 it became the last remnant of Dr. Sun Yat-sen's Republic of China when Chiang Kai-shek moved his army and government from the mainland to the islands following his defeat by the Communist forces of Mao Tse-tung.

BANK OF TAIWAN

行銀灣臺

T'ai Wan Yin Hang

CIRIULATING BANK CASHIER'S CHECKS

PORTRAIT ABBREVIATIONS

SYS = Dr. Sun Yat-sen, 1867-1925
President of Canton Government,
1917-25
Taiwan, 1949-1975

CKS = Chiang Kai-shek, 1886-1975
President in Nanking, 1927-31
Head of Formosa Government,

Note: Because of the frequency of the above appearing in the following listings, their initials are used only in reference to their portraits.

PRINTERS

CPF:
(Central Printing Factory)   廠製印央中

CPFT:
(Central Printing Factory, Taipei)   廠北台廠製印央中

FPFT:
(First Printing Factory)   廠刷印一第

PFBT:
(Printing Factory of Taiwan Bank)   所刷印行銀灣臺

1961 ISSUE

#1971-1975 portr. SYS at l. Printer: CPF.

1971	1 YÜAN		VG	VF	UNC
	1961. Dk. blue-green and purple on m/c unpt. Steep coastline at r. Printer: PFBT.				
	a. Engraved.		0.20	0.75	5.00
	b. Lithographed. (1972).		0.10	1.50	3.00

1972	5 YÜAN	VG	VF	UNC
	1961. Red on m/c unpt. House w/tower at r.	0.20	0.75	4.00

1973	5 YÜAN	VG	VF	UNC
	1961. Brown on m/c unpt. Similar to #972.	0.25	1.50	10.00
1974	50 YÜAN			
	1961. Purple on m/c unpt.	FV	3.00	20.00
1975	100 YÜAN			
	1961. Green on m/c unpt. SYS at l.	FV	3.25	22.00

1964 ISSUE

#1976 and 1977 portr. SYS at l. Printer: CPF.

1976	50 YÜAN	VG	VF	UNC
	1964. Purple on m/c unpt. Similar to #1974.	FV	2.00	15.00

1977	100 YÜAN	VG	VF	UNC
	1964. Green on m/c unpt. Similar to #1975.	FV	3.00	20.00

REPUBLIC OF CHINA-TAIWAN BANK

行銀灣臺 國民華中

Chung Hua Min Kuo-T'ai Wan Yin Hang

1969 ISSUE

#1978 and 1979 portr. SYS at l. Printer: CPF.

1978	5 YÜAN	VG	VF	UNC
	1969. Blue on m/c unpt.			
	a. Issued note.	0.15	0.40	3.00
	s. Specimen. Uniface impression of each side.	—	—	150.00

1979	10 YÜAN	VG	VF	UNC
	1969. Red on m/c unpt. Similar to #1978.			
	a. W/o plate letter.	0.20	0.50	3.00
	b. Plate letter A at lower r. on face.	0.15	0.35	2.50
	s. As a. Specimen. Uniface printing of each side.	—	—	150.00

1970 ISSUE

#1980-1983 SYS at l. Printer: CPF.

1980	50 YÜAN	VG	VF	UNC
	1970. Purple on m/c unpt.	FV	2.25	10.00
1981	100 YÜAN			
	1970. Green on m/c unpt.	FV	4.50	15.00

1972 ISSUE

			VG	VF	UNC
1982	**50 YÜAN**				
	1972. Purple and lt. blue on m/c unpt. Chungshan bldg. on back. Wide margin w/guilloche at r.				
	a. Issued note.		FV	2.00	6.00
	s. Specimen. Uniface printing of each side.		—	—	150.00

			VG	VF	UNC
1983	**100 YÜAN**				
	1972. Dk. green, lt. green and orange on m/c unpt. Palace on back.				
	a. Issued note.		FV	3.50	8.00
	s. Specimen. Uniface printing of each side.		—	—	150.00

1976 ISSUE

#1984-1986 printer: CPF.

			VG	VF	UNC
1984	**10 YÜAN**				
	1976. Red on m/c unpt. SYS at I. Bank on back.		FV	0.50	2.00
1985	**500 YÜAN**				
	1976. Olive, purple and m/c. CKS at I. Chungshan bldg. on back. W/o wmk. at r.		FV	20.00	45.00

			VG	VF	UNC
1986	**1000 YÜAN**				
	1976. Blue-black, olive-brown and violet on m/c. unpt. CKS at I. Presidential Office bldg. on back. W/o wmk. at r.		FV	40.00	120.00

1981 ISSUE

#1987 and 1988 CKS at I. Printer: CPF.

			VG	VF	UNC
1987	**500 YÜAN**		FV	FV	40.00
	1981. Brown and red-brown on m/c unpt. Similar to #1985 but wmk. of CKS at r.				

			VG	VF	UNC
1988	**1000 YÜAN**		FV	FV	80.00
	1981. Blue-black on m/c unpt. Similar to #1986 but wmk: CKS at r.				

1987 ISSUE

			VG	VF	UNC
1989	**100 YÜAN**		FV	FV	7.00
	1987 (1988). Red, red-brown and brown-violet on m/c unpt. SYS at I. and as wmk. Chungshan bldg. on back.				

1999 COMMEMORATIVE ISSUE

#1990, 50th Anniversary of Taiwan

			VG	VF	UNC
1990	**50 YÜAN**		FV	FV	4.00
	Red on m/c unpt. Currency and high-speed train at I. Bank bldg. on back. Polymer plastic.				

1999; 2001 ISSUE

1991	100 YÜAN		VG	VF	UNC
	2001. M/c.		FV	FV	7.50

1992	200 YÜAN		VG	VF	UNC
	2001. Green.		FV	FV	8.50

1993	500 YÜAN		VG	VF	UNC
	1999; 2001. Brown and rose on m/c unpt. Boy's baseball team at ctr., Professional Pitcher at r. Formosan Sika Deer family on back.		FV	FV	25.00

1994	1000 YÜAN		VG	VF	UNC
	1999. Lt. and dk. blue on lt. green unpt. Schoolchildren studying globe at ctr. Two Mikado Pheasant and mountian vista on back.		FV	FV	40.00

1995	2000 YÜAN		VG	VF	UNC
	2002. Purple and lilac on m/c unpt. Satellite Dishes and rocket. Two salmon and Mt. Nanhu on back.		FV	FV	80.00

OFF-SHORE ISLAND CURRENCY
BANK OF TAIWAN

行銀灣臺

T'ai Wan Yin Hang

Notes of the Bank of Taiwan and later notes of the Republic of China/Bank of Taiwan w/ovpt:

門金

KINMEN (QUEMOY) BRANCH
1949-51 (1963; 1967) ISSUE

用通門金限

Hsien Chin Men T'ung Yung

#R101-R109 portr. SYS at upper ctr. Vertical format.
#R101, R106 and R107 portr. SYS at upper ctr. Vertical format.

R101	1 YÜAN		VG	VF	UNC
	1949 (1963). Green on m/c unpt. Printer: CPF.		0.25	2.00	10.00

1950-51 ISSUES

R106	10 YÜAN		VG	VF	UNC
	1950 (1963). Blue. Printer: CPF.		0.50	1.50	18.00

R107	50 YÜAN		VG	VF	UNC
	1951 (1967). Green. Printer: FPFT.		3.00	20.00	120.00

1955-72 ISSUES

R109	5 YÜAN		VG	VF	UNC
	1966. Violet-brown. Printer: CPF.		0.75	3.00	20.00

R110	10 YÜAN		VG	VF	UNC
	1969 (1975). Red on m/c unpt. Red ovpt. on #1979a.		1.00	2.00	10.00

R111	50 YÜAN	VG	VF	UNC
	1969 (1970). Dk. blue on m/c unpt. SYS at r.	2.00	3.50	25.00

R112	100 YÜAN	VG	VF	UNC
	1972 (1975). Green ovpt. on #1983.	4.00	7.50	40.00

1976; 1981 ISSUE

R112A	10 YÜAN	VG	VF	UNC
	1976. Ovpt. on #1984.	0.25	0.75	10.00
R112B	100 YÜAN			
	1981. Ovpt. on #1988.	5.00	8.00	30.00
R112C	1000 YÜAN			
	1981. Ovpt. on #1988.	35.00	50.00	200.00

1950-51 DATED (1964; 1967) ISSUE

#R113-R115 horizontal format.

#R117 and 118 portr. SYS at upper ctr. Vertical format.

R117	10 YÜAN	VG	VF	UNC
	1950 (1964). Blue on m/c unpt. Printer: CPF.	1.00	3.00	25.00

R118	50 YÜAN	VG	VF	UNC
	1951 (1967). Green on m/c unpt. Printer: FPDT.	3.00	8.00	80.00

1969; 1972 ISSUE

R122	10 YÜAN	VG	VF	UNC
	1969 (1975). Red on m/c unpt. Ovpt. on #1979a. Printer: CPF.	0.50	1.00	10.00

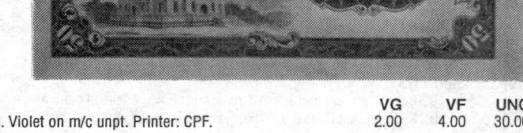

R123	50 YÜAN	VG	VF	UNC
	1969 (1970). Violet on m/c unpt. Printer: CPF.	2.00	4.00	30.00
R124	100 YÜAN			
	1972 (1975). Dk. green, lt. green and orange on m/c unpt. Green ovpt. on #1983. Printer: CPF.	4.00	10.00	80.00

1976; 1981 ISSUE

R125	10 YÜAN	VG	VF	UNC
	1976. Red on m/c unpt. Ovpt. on #1984.	0.40	1.00	8.00
R126	500 YÜAN			
	1981. Brown and red-brown on m/c unpt. Ovpt. on #1987.	FV	20.00	80.00
R127	1000 YÜAN			
	1981. Blue-black on m/c unpt. Ovpt. on #1988.	FV	37.50	200.00

COLOMBIA

The Republic of Colombia, located in the northwestern corner of South America, has an area of 439,737 sq. mi. (1,138,914 sq. km.) and a population of 42.3 million. Capital: Bogotá. The economy is primarily agricultural with a mild, rich coffee the chief crop. Colombia has the world's largest platinum deposits and important reserves of coal, iron ore, petroleum and limestone; precious metals and emeralds are also mined. Coffee, crude oil, bananas, sugar, coal and flowers are exported.

The northern coast of present Colombia was one of the first parts of the American continent to be visited by Spanish navigators, and the site, at Darien in Panama, of the first permanent European settlement on the American mainland in 1510. New Granada, as Colombia was known until 1861, stemmed from the settlement of Santa Maria in 1525. New Granada was established as a Spanish Colony in 1549. Independence was declared in 1810, and secured in 1824. In 1819, Simón Bolívar united Colombia, Venezuela, Panama and Ecuador as the Republic of Greater Colombia. Venezuela withdrew from the Republic in 1829; Ecuador in 1830; and Panama in 1903.

MONETARY SYSTEM:
    1 Peso = 100 Centavos 1993
    1 Peso Oro = 100 Centavos to 1993

REPLACEMENT NOTES:
Earlier issues, small *R* just below and between signatures. Larger *R* used later. Some TDLR printings have *R* preceding serial number. Later Colombian-printed notes use circled asterisk usually close to sign. or a star at r. of upper serial #. Known replacements: #389-407, 409, 413-15, 417-19, 421-22, 425-29, 431-433, 436-41, 443, 445-48.

REPUBLIC

BANCO DE LA REPÚBLICA

1943 PESOS ORO ISSUE

			VG	VF	UNC
392	20 PESOS ORO				
	1943-63. Purple and m/c. Bust of Francisco José de Caldas at l., bust of Simon Bolívar at r. Liberty at ctr. on back. Printer: ABNC.				
	a. Series U in red. 20.7.1943.		20.00	200.00	500.00
	b. Series U in purple. 20.7.1944; 1.1.1945.		10.00	60.00	200.00
	c. Series U. Prefix A. 7.8.1947.		3.00	15.00	80.00
	d. Series DD. 1.1.1950; 1.1.1951.		1.50	7.50	50.00
	e. Series DD. 2.1.1963.		1.50	7.50	50.00
	s. Specimen.		—	—	65.00

1953 PESOS ORO ISSUE
#400-401 printer: TDLR.

			VG	VF	UNC
400	10 PESOS ORO				
	1953-61. Blue on m/c unpt. Similar to #377, but palm trees at r. instead of wmk. Portr. General Antonio Nariño w/Mercury alongside at l. Bank bldg. at Cali on back. Series N.				
	a. 1.1.1953.		1.00	7.50	35.00
	b. 1.1.1958; 1.1.1960.		1.00	7.50	35.00
	c. 2.1.1961.		1.00	7.50	35.00
	s. Specimen. W/red TDLR and *SPECIMEN* ovpt. Punched hole cancelled.		—	—	100.00

			VG	VF	UNC
401	20 PESOS ORO				
	1953-65. Red-brown on m/c unpt. Similar to #378, but Liberty in circle at r. instead of wmk. Portr. Francisco José de Caldas and allegory at l. Newer bank bldg. at Barranquilla on back. Series O.				
	a. 1.1.1953.		1.00	7.50	35.00
	b. 1.1.1960.		1.00	7.50	35.00
	c. 2.1.1961; 2.1.1965.		1.00	6.00	30.00
	s1. Specimen. W/ red TDLR ovpt. and *SPECIMEN*. Punched hole cancelled.		—	—	100.00
	s2. Specimen. Red ovpt: *SPECIMEN*. Punched hole cancelled.		—	—	65.00

1958 PESOS ORO ISSUE
#402-403 printer: ABNC.

			VG	VF	UNC
402	50 PESOS ORO				
	1958-67. Lt. brown on m/c unpt. Portr. Antonio José de Sucre at lower l. Back olive-green; Liberty at ctr. Series Z.				
	a. 20.7.1958; 7.8.1960.		1.00	10.00	60.00
	b. 1.1.1964; 12.10.1967.		1.00	8.00	50.00
	s1. Specimen.		—	—	135.00
	s2. Specimen. Red ovpt: *SPECIMEN*. Punched hole cancelled.		—	—	135.00

			VG	VF	UNC
403	100 PESOS ORO				
	1958-67. Gray on m/c unpt. Portr. Gen. Francisco de Paula Santander at r. Back green; like #402. Series Y.				
	a. 7.8.1958.		1.00	8.00	60.00
	b. 1.1.1960; 1.1.1964.		1.00	6.00	40.00
	c. 20.7.1965; 20.7.1967.		1.00	6.00	40.00
	p1. Face proof. W/o date, signatures, series or serial #. Punched hole cancelled.		—	—	150.00
	s. Specimen.		—	—	75.00

1959-60 PESOS ORO ISSUE
Printer: Imprenta de Billets - Bogota.

			VG	VF	UNC
404	1 PESO ORO				
	1959-77. Blue on m/c unpt. Portr. Simón Bolívar at l., portr. General Francisco de Paula Santander at r. Liberty head and condor w/waterfall and mountain at ctr. on back.				
	a. Security thread. 12.10.1959.		0.25	2.50	10.00
	b. Security thread. 2.1.1961; 7.8.1962; 2.1.1963; 12.10.1963; 2.1.1964; 12.10.1964.		0.20	2.00	7.50

404	1 PESO ORO	VG	VF	UNC
	1959-77. Blue on m/c unpt. Portr. Simón Bolívar at l., portr. General Francisco de Paula Santander at r. Liberty head and condor w/waterfall and mountain at ctr. on back.			
	a. Security thread. 12.10.1959.	0.25	2.50	10.00
	b. Security thread. 2.1.1961; 7.8.1962; 2.1.1963; 12.10.1963; 2.1.1964; 12.10.1964.	0.20	2.00	7.50
	c. As b. 20.7.1966.	1.25	10.00	40.00
	d. W/o security thread. 20.7.1966; 20.7.1967; 1.2.1968; 2.1.1969.	0.15	1.25	5.00
	e. W/o security thread. 1.5.1970; 12.10.1970; 7.8.1971; 20.7.1972; 7.8.1973; 7.8.1974.	0.10	0.50	3.00
	f. As e. 1.1.1977.	0.75	5.00	30.00
	s1. Specimen.	—	—	50.00
	s2. Specimen. Red ovpt: *ESPECIMEN*.	—	—	50.00

1961-64 ISSUE

#406-407 replacement notes: Serial # prefix *R* or *.

406	5 PESOS ORO	VG	VF	UNC
	1961-81. Deep greenish black and deep brown on m/c unpt. Condor at l., José María Córdoba at r. Fortress at Cartagena at ctr. on back.			
	a. Security thread. 2.1.1961; 1.5.1963; 2.1.1964.	1.00	6.00	30.00
	b. Security thread. 11.11.1965; 12.10.1967; 20.7.1968.	0.50	3.00	15.00
	c. Security thread. 20.7.1971.	0.25	2.50	10.00
	d. As c. 1.1.1973.	10.00	50.00	200.00
	e. W/o security thread. 1.1.1973; 20.7.1974; 20.7.1975; 20.7.1976; 20.7.1977.	0.15	1.00	4.00
	f. W/o security thread. 1.10.1978; 1.4.1979; 1.1.1980; 1.1.1981.	0.10	0.75	2.50
	s. Specimen.	—	—	40.00

407	10 PESOS ORO	VG	VF	UNC
	1963-80. Lilac and slate blue on green and m/c unpt. General Antonio Nariño at l., condor at r. Back red-brown and slate blue; archaeological site w/monoliths.			
	a. Security thread. 20.7.1963.	1.50	10.00	40.00
	b. As a. 20.7.1964.	0.75	4.00	25.00
	c. 20.7.1965; 20.7.1967; 2.1.1969.	0.50	4.00	17.50
	d. As c. W/segmented security thread. 12.10.1970; 1.1.1973.	0.50	2.00	10.00
	e. As d. 20.7.1974.	15.00	75.00	300.00
	f. W/o security thread. 20.7.1974; 1.1.1975; 20.7.1976; 1.1.1978.	0.25	0.75	5.00
	g. As f. 7.8.1979; 7.8.1980.	0.05	0.35	3.00
	h. Like f., but *SERIE AZ* at l. ctr. and upper r. on face. 7.8.1980. *Serie AZ*.	0.10	0.50	4.00
	s. Specimen.	—	—	40.00

408	500 PESOS ORO	VG	VF	UNC
	20.7.1964. Olive-green on m/c unpt. Portr. Simon Bolivar at r. Back has no open space under Liberty head. Printer: ABNC. Series *AA*. 6 or 7 digit serial #.			
	a. Issued note.	10.00	50.00	150.00
	s. Specimen. Ovpt. *MUESTRA* and punched hole cancelled.	—	—	150.00

1966-68 ISSUE

#409 replacement note: Serial # prefix *R* or *.

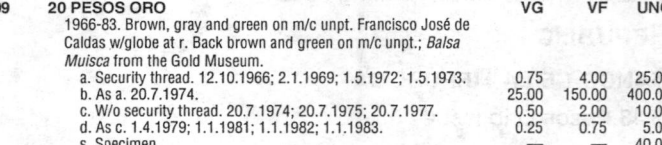

409	20 PESOS ORO	VG	VF	UNC
	1966-83. Brown, gray and green on m/c unpt. Francisco José de Caldas w/globe at r. Back brown and green on m/c unpt.; *Balsa Muisca* from the Gold Museum.			
	a. Security thread. 12.10.1966; 2.1.1969; 1.5.1972; 1.5.1973.	0.75	4.00	25.00
	b. As a. 20.7.1974.	25.00	150.00	400.00
	c. W/o security thread. 20.7.1974; 20.7.1975; 20.7.1977.	0.50	2.00	10.00
	d. As c. 1.4.1979; 1.1.1981; 1.1.1982; 1.1.1983.	0.25	0.75	5.00
	s. Specimen.	—	—	40.00

410	100 PESOS ORO	VG	VF	UNC
	1968-71. Blue on m/c unpt. General Francisco de Paula Santander at r. Capitol at Bogotá on back. Wmk: Simon Bolivar. Series Y. Printer: TDLR.			
	a. 1.1.1968.	1.25	10.00	45.00
	b. 2.1.1969.	1.50	6.00	35.00
	c. 1.5.1970; 20.7.1971.	1.25	4.00	22.50
	s. Specimen.	—	—	50.00

411	500 PESOS ORO	VG	VF	UNC
	1968; 1971. Green on m/c unpt. Simón Bolívar at r. Zipaquirá subterranean salt cathedral Wmk: Liberty head. Series A. Printer: ABNC.			
	a. 1.1.1968.	7.50	30.00	100.00
	b. 12.10.1971.	12.50	40.00	100.00
	s. Specimen.	—	—	125.00

1969 ISSUE

412   50 PESOS ORO
1969-70. Purple on pale blue, lilac and pink unpt. Blue design w/o
border at l., Camilo Torres at r. and as wmk. Arms and flowers on
back. Printer: TDLR.

	VG	VF	UNC
a. 2.1.1969.	1.00	6.00	35.00
b. 12.10.1970.	0.75	4.00	25.00
s. Specimen. Punched hole cancelled.	—	—	100.00

1972-73 ISSUE

#413-415 replacement notes: Serial # prefix *R* or *.

413   2 PESOS ORO
1972-77. Purple on m/c unpt. Policarpa Salavarietta at l. Back
brown; *El Dorado* from the Gold Museum.

	VG	VF	UNC
a. Lg. size serial #, and # at r. near upper border. 1.1.1972; 20.7.1972; 1.1.1973.	0.25	1.00	5.00
b. Sm. size serial #, and # at r. far from upper border. 20.7.1976; 1.1.1977; 20.7.1977.	0.25	1.00	4.00
s. Specimen.	—	—	50.00

414   50 PESOS ORO
20.7.1973; 20.7.1974. Purple on pale blue, lilac and pink unpt.
Similar to #412, but curved dk. border added at l. and r., also at r.
on back. Printer: TDLR.

VG	VF	UNC
0.75	3.00	17.50

415   100 PESOS ORO
20.7.1973; 20.7.1974. Similar to #410 but curved dk. border added
at l. and r., also at r. on back. Series Y. Printer: TDLR.

VG	VF	UNC
1.00	4.00	25.00

416   500 PESOS ORO
7.8.1973. Red on m/c unpt. Like #411. Series A. Printer: ABNC.

	VG	VF	UNC
a. Issued note.	12.50	40.00	80.00
s. Specimen.	—	—	100.00

1974 ISSUE

#417 replacement note: Serial # prefix *R*.

417   200 PESOS ORO
1974; 1975. Green on m/c unpt. Simón Bolívar at ctr. r. and as
wmk., church at r. *BOGOTÁ COLOMBIA* at lower l. ctr. Man picking
coffee beans on back. Printer: TDLR.

	VG	VF	UNC
a. 20.7.1974.	2.50	12.50	45.00
b. 7.8.1975.	1.00	5.00	20.00

1977-79 ISSUE

#418-420 replacement notes: Serial # prefix *R* or *.

418   100 PESOS ORO
1977-80. Purple and black on m/c unpt. General Francisco de Paula
Santander at ctr. r. Capitol at Bogotá on back. Wmk: Liberty head.
Printer: TDLR.

	VG	VF	UNC
a. 1.1.1977.	0.25	1.50	8.00
b. 1.1.1980.	0.25	1.25	6.00
c. Serial # prefix *A-C*. 1.1.1980.	0.25	1.25	6.00
s1. Specimen.	—	—	75.00
s2. Specimen. Red ovpt: *SPECIMEN*. Punch hole cancelled.	—	—	50.00

Note: Numerals at upper ctr. and upper r. are darker on 1980 dated notes, also the word *CIEN*.

419	200 PESOS ORO	VG	VF	UNC
	20.7.1978; 1.1.1979; 1.1.1980. Like #417 but w/only *COLOMBIA* at lower l. ctr. Printer: TDLR.	0.50	1.50	8.00

420	500 PESOS ORO	VG	VF	UNC
	1977-79. Olive and m/c. Gen. Francisco de Paula Santander at l. and in profile as wmk. Back gray; subterranean church and Liberty head. Printer: ABNC.			
	a. 20.7.1977.	1.50	6.00	30.00
	b. 1.4.1979.	1.00	4.50	20.00
	s. Specimen.	—	—	100.00

421	1000 PESOS ORO	VG	VF	UNC
	1.4.1979. Black and m/c. José Antonio Galan at r. and as wmk. Nariño Palace on back. Printer: ABNC.			
	a. Issued note.	1.00	7.50	30.00
	s. Specimen.	—	—	150.00

1980-82 Issues

#422 replacement note: Serial # prefix *.

422	50 PESOS ORO	VG	VF	UNC
	1980-83. Purple on pale blue, lilac and pink unpt. *COLOMBIA* added near border at upper l. ctr. Printer: TDLR (w/o imprint). *			
	a. 1.1.1980; 7.8.1981.	FV	1.00	4.00
	b. 1.1.1983.	FV	0.50	2.00
	s. Specimen.	—	—	50.00

423	500 PESOS ORO	VG	VF	UNC
	1981-86. Brown, dk. green and red-brown on m/c unpt. General Francisco de Paula Santander at l. and in profile as wmk., Bogotá on back; screw coinage press at lower r. Printer: TDLR.			
	a. 20.7.1981.	FV	4.00	20.00
	b. 20.7.1984; 20.7.1985.	FV	2.00	10.00
	c. 12.10.1985; 20.7.1986.	FV	1.00	6.00
	s. Specimen.	—	—	50.00

424	1000 PESOS ORO	VG	VF	UNC
	1982-87. Deep blue and olive-brown on m/c unpt. Simón Bolívar at l. and as wmk. Scene honoring 1819 battle heroes on back. Printer: TDLR.			
	a. 1.1.1982.	FV	5.00	20.00
	b. 7.8.1984.	FV	3.00	10.00
	c. 1.1.1986; 1.1.1987.	FV	2.00	7.00
	s. Specimen.	—	—	75.00

1982-84 Issues

#425-430 replacement notes: Serial # prefix circled-*.

425	50 PESOS ORO	VG	VF	UNC
	1984-86. Purple on pale blue, lilac and pink unpt. Similar to #414. W/o wmk. Printer: IBB.			
	a. 12.10.1984; 1.1.1985.	FV	1.00	3.00
	b. 1.1.1986.	FV	FV	2.00
	s. Specimen.	—	—	50.00

426	**100 PESOS ORO**	VG	VF	UNC
	1983-91. Violet, brown, orange and dk. red on m/c unpt. General Antonio Nariño at l. and as wmk. Villa de Leyva on back; flat bed printing press at lower r. Printer: IBB.			
	a. 1.1.1983; 12.10.1984.	FV	FV	3.00
	b. 12.10.1985; 1.1.1986; 12.10.1986.	FV	FV	2.50
	c. Larger stylized serial #. 1.1.1987; 12.10.1988.	FV	FV	2.50
	d. Back colors slightly off shade from earlier issues. 7.8.1989.	FV	FV	2.25
	e. Sign. titles: *GERENTE* and *SECRETARIO*. 1.1.1990; 1.1.1991.	FV	FV	1.50
	s. Specimen. Ovpt. *MUESTRA SIN VALOR.*	—	—	50.00
426A	**100 PESOS ORO**			
	7.8.1991. Like #426 but red omitted from back. Printer: IBSFB.	FV	FV	1.00
427	**200 PESOS ORO**			
	1.1.1982. Like #419 but printer: IBB.	FV	FV	5.00

428	**200 PESOS ORO**	VG	VF	UNC
	1.4.1983. Deep green and black on m/c unpt. Church and Fr. José Celestino Mutis at l. and as wmk., arms at upper r. Bogota Observatory *Observatorio Astronomico Nacional* at r. on back. Printer: TDLR.			
	a. Issued note.	FV	1.50	10.00
	s. Specimen.	—	—	50.00
429	**200 PESOS ORO**			
	1983-91. Deep green and black on m/c unpt. Like #428.			
	a. Printer: IBB. 1.4.1983; 20.7.1984.	FV	5.00	25.00
	b. 20.7.1984; 1.11.1984; 1.4.1985.	FV	FV	10.00
	c. 1.11.1985.	FV	FV	7.00
	d. Larger stylized and bold serial #. 1.4.1987; 1.4.1988; 1.11.1988; 1.4.1989; 1.11.1989; 1.4.1991.	FV	FV	4.00
	s. Specimen. Red ovpt *MUESTRA SIN VALOR.* Punch hole cancelled.	—	—	50.00
429A	**200 PESOS ORO**			
	10.8.1992. Like #439. Printer: IBSFB.	FV	FV	1.25

430	**2000 PESOS ORO**	VG	VF	UNC
	1983-86. Dk. brown and brown-orange on m/c unpt. Simón Bolívar at l. and as wmk. Scene at *Paso del Paramo de Pisba* at ctr. r. on back. Printer: TDLR.			
	a. 24.7.1983.	FV	5.00	35.00
	b. 24.7.1984.	FV	4.00	20.00
	c. 17.12.1985.	FV	3.00	15.00
	d. 17.12.1986.	FV	3.00	10.00
	s. Specimen. Some punched hole cancelled.	—	—	50.00

1986-87 ISSUE

#431-433 replacement notes: Serial # prefix *.

431	**500 PESOS ORO**	VG	VF	UNC
	20.7.1986; 12.10.1987; 20.7.1989; 12.10.1990. Like #423. Printer: IBB.	FV	FV	3.00
431A	**500 PESOS ORO**			
	2.3.1992; 4.1.1993. Like #431, but green omitted from back. Printer: IBSFB.	FV	FV	2.50
432	**1000 PESOS ORO**			
	1.1.1987; 1.1.1990; 1.1.1991. Black, blue-green and deep olive-brown on m/c unpt. Like #424. Printer: IBB.	FV	FV	7.50
432A	**1000 PESOS ORO**			
	31.1.1992; 1.4.1992; 4.1.1993. Like #432. Printer: IBSFB.	FV	FV	4.50
433	**2000 PESOS ORO**			
	17.12.1986; 17.12.1988; 17.12.1990. Dk. brown and brown-orange on m/c unpt. Like #430 but w/redesigned *2's* in denomination. Printer: IBB.	FV	FV	9.00
433A	**2000 PESOS ORO**			
	1992. Like #433. Printer: IBSFB.			
	a. 2.3.1992; 1.4.1992.	FV	FV	5.00
	b. 3.8.1992.	5.00	10.00	50.00

1986 COMMEMORATIVE ISSUE

#434, Centennial of the Constitution

434	**5000 PESOS ORO**	VG	VF	UNC
	5.8.1986. Deep violet and red-violet on m/c unpt. Rafael Nuñez at l. and as wmk. Statue of Miguel Antonio Caro at ctr. r. on back. Printer: BDDK.			
	a. Issued note.	FV	FV	50.00
	s. Specimen w/red serial # at upper r.	—	—	75.00

1987 ISSUE

435	**5000 PESOS ORO**	VG	VF	UNC
	5.8.1987; 5.8.1988. Deep violet and red-violet on m/c unpt. Similar to #434 but printer: IPS-Roma.	FV	FV	35.00

1990 ISSUE

#436 replacement note: Serial # prefix *.

436	**5000 PESOS ORO**	VG	VF	UNC
	1.1.1990. Deep violet and red-violet on m/c unpt. Like #435. Printer: IBB.	FV	FV	25.00
436A	**5000 PESOS ORO**			
	31.1.1992. 4.1.1993. Like #436. Printer: IBSFB.	FV	FV	25.00

NOTICE

Readers with unlisted dates, signature varieties, etc. are invited to submit photocopies of their notes to: Standard Catalog of World Paper Money, 700 East State St. Iola, WI 54990-0001, E-Mail: george.cuhaj@fwpubs.com.

1992 COMMEMORATIVE ISSUE

#437, Quincentennial of Columbus' Voyage, 12.10.1492

		VG	VF	UNC
437	**10,000 PESOS ORO**			
	1992. Lt. and dk. brown on m/c unpt. Early sailing ships at ctr., youthful woman *Mujer Embera* at ctr. r. and as wmk, native gold statue at r. Native birds around antique world map at l. ctr., Santa Maria sailing ship at lower r. on back.			
	a. Issued note.	FV	FV	60.00
	s. Specimen.	—	—	100.00

1993 ISSUE

		VG	VF	UNC
437A	**10,000 PESOS ORO**			
	1993; 1994. Deep brown and black on m/c unpt. Like #437. Printer: IBSFB.	FV	FV	40.00

Note: 1,000,000 pieces of #437A dated 1993 were stolen in 1994.

1993-95 ISSUES

Peso System

#437A-441 printer: IBSFB.

		VG	VF	UNC
438	**1000 PESOS**			
	3.1.1994; 1.11.1994; 1.7.1995; 2.8.1995; 2.10.1995. Like #432 but *EL* omitted from title and *ORO* omitted from value. Black omitted on back.	FV	FV	5.00

#439-443 portr. as wmk.

		VG	VF	UNC
439	**2000 PESOS**			
	1993-94. Dk. brown and brown-orange on m/c unpt. Like #433 but *EL* omitted from title, *ORO* deleted from value.			
	a. 1.7.1993.	FV	FV	10.00
	b. Orange omitted from back. 1.7.1994; 1.11.1994; 17.12.1994.	FV	FV	8.00

Note: 1,700,000 pieces of #439a were stolen.

		VG	VF	UNC
440	**5000 PESOS**			
	3.1.1994; 4.7.1994; 2.1.1995. Deep violet and red-violet on m/c unpt. Like #434-436 but *EL* deleted from the title, *ORO* deleted from the value.	FV	FV	20.00

Note: 2,200,000 pieces of #440 dated 3.1.1994 were stolen in 1994.

		VG	VF	UNC
441	**5000 PESOS**			
	1.3.1995; 1.3.1996. Dk. brown, brown and deep blue-green on m/c unpt. José Asunción Silva and bug at upper r., trees at l. and ctr. Wmk: Asunción Silva. Woman, trees and monument at ctr. on back. Printer: IBSFB.			
	a. Issued note.	FV	FV	20.00
	s. Specimen.	—	—	75.00
442	**5000 PESOS**			
	1.7.1995. Dk. brown, brown and deep blue-green on m/c unpt. Like #441. Printer: TDLR.			
	a. Issued note.	FV	FV	25.00
	s. Specimen.	—	—	75.00
443	**10,000 PESOS**			
	1.3.1995; 1.8.1996; 23.7.1997; 6.1.1998; 23.7.1998; 23.7.1999; 17.12.1999; 1.6.2001. Deep brown and black on m/c unpt. Like #442, but *EL* omitted from title, *ORO* omitted from value, diff. sign. and titles. Printer: IBSFB.			
	a. Issued note.	FV	FV	20.00
	s. Specimen.	—	—	75.00

1995 COMMEMORATIVE ISSUE

#444, 200th Anniversary of Policarpa Salavarrieta *"La Pola"*

Replacement note: Serial # prefix *.

		VG	VF	UNC
444	**10,000 PESOS**			
	1.7.1995; 1.8.1995. Red-brown and green on m/c unpt. Policarpa Salavarrieta at r., Village of Guaduas (ca. 1846) at l. ctr. on back. Printer: TDLR.			
	a. Issued note.	FV	FV	30.00
	s. Specimen.	—	—	75.00

1996-97, 2000 ISSUE

#445-449 printer: IBSFB. New arms used afer 1999.

		VG	VF	UNC
445	**2000 PESOS**			
	2.4.1996; 6.5.1997; 6.1.1998; 7.8.1998; 9.4.1999; 12.10.1999. Dk. olive-green, red-brown and dk. brown on m/c unpt. General Francisco de Paula Santander at r. and as wmk. Casa de Moneda bldg., entrance at l. ctr. on back.			
	a. Issued note.	FV	FV	4.00
	s. Specimen.	—	—	50.00

		VG	VF	UNC
446	**5000 PESOS**			
	2.1.1997. Dk. brown and deep blue-green on m/c unpt. Like #442.			
	a. Issued note.	FV	FV	10.00
	s. Specimen.	—	—	75.00

		VG	VF	UNC
447	**5000 PESOS**			
	12.10.1997; 2.4.1998; 23.7.1999; 12.10.1999. Deep violet and red-violet on m/c unpt. Like #442 but w/bank seal at ctr.			
	a. Issued note.	FV	FV	8.00
	s. Specimen.	—	—	75.00

NOTICE

Readers with unlisted dates, signature varieties, etc. are invited to submit photocopies of their notes to: Standard Catalog of World Paper Money, 700 East State St. Iola, WI 54990-0001, E-Mail: george.cuhaj@fwpubs.com.

		VG	VF	UNC
448	**20,000 PESOS**			
	23.7.1996; 6.1.1998; 7.8.1998; 6.5.1999, 1.5.2000; 12.10.2000. Black, deep green and dk. blue on m/c unpt. Julio Garavito Armero at r. and as wmk. View of the moon at ctr. Satellite view of earth at ctr. r., moon's surface along bottom, geometric for			
	a. Issued note.	FV	FV	22.50
	s. Specimen.	—	—	60.00

		VG	VF	UNC
449	**50,000 PESOS**			
	7.8.2000. Purple, green and lt. orange on m/c unpt. Jorge Isaacs at lower ctr. Maria, character from book at ctr. *Hacienda el Paraiso* on back. Vertical format.			
	a. Issued note.	FV	FV	45.00
	s. Specimen.	—	—	100.00

2001 ISSUE

#450-455 printer: IBBR.

		VG	VF	UNC
450	**1000 PESOS**			
	7.8.2001; 27.9.2001; 17.12.2001; 7.5.2002; 30.5.2003; 10.2.2004. Brown and orange on m/c unpt. Crowd at ctr., Jorge Eliecer Gaitán at r. and as wmk. Gaitán w/right arm raised, crowd behind at ctr. on back.			
	a. Issued note.	FV	FV	1.00
	s. Specimen.	—	—	50.00
451	**2000 PESOS**			
	12.10.2000; 23.7.2001; 12.10.2001; 11.11.2001; 8.5.2002; 13.5.2002; 2.6.2003; 18.2.2004. Dk. olive-green, red-brown and dk. brown on m/c unpt. Like #445.			
	a. Issued note.	FV	FV	2.00
	s. Specimen.	—	—	50.00
452	**5000 PESOS**			
	11.11.2001; 17.12.2001; 9.5.2002; 6.6.2003. Deep violet and red-violet on m/c unpt. Like #447.			
	a. Issued note.	FV	FV	6.00
	s. Specimen.	—	—	50.00
453	**10,000 PESOS**			
	20.7.2001; 10.5.2002; 20.11.2002; 25.11.2002. Deep brown and black on m/c unpt. Like #443.			
	a. Issued note.	FV	FV	11.00
	s. Specimen.	—	—	75.00
454	**20,000 PESOS**			
	1.6.2001; 23.7.2001; 7.8.2001; 14.5.2002; 20.11.2002; 13.6.2003. Black, deep green and dk. blue on m/c unpt. Like #448.			
	a. Issued note.	FV	FV	20.00
	s. Specimen.	—	—	75.00
455	**50,000 PESOS**			
	1.5.2001; 23.7.2001; 15.5.2002; 20.7.2003. Purple, green and lt. orange on m/c unpt. Like #449.			
	a. Issued note.	FV	FV	45.00
	s. Specimen.	—	—	100.00

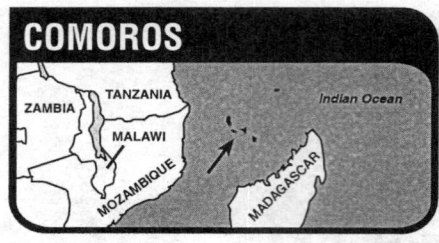

The Federal Islamic Republic of the Comoros, a volcanic archipelago located in the Mozambique Channel of the Indian Ocean 300 miles (483 km.) northwest of Madagascar, has an area of 838 sq. mi. (1,797 sq. km.) and a population of 714,000. Capital: Moroni. The economy of the islands is based on agriculture. There are practically no mineral resources. Vanilla, essence for perfumes, copra and sisal are exported.

Ancient Phoenician traders were probably the first visitors to the Comoros Islands, but the first detailed knowledge of the area was gathered by Arab sailors. Arab dominion and culture were firmly established when the Portuguese, Dutch and French arrived in the 16th century. In 1843 a Malagasy ruler ceded the island of Mayotte to France; the other three principal islands of the archipelago - Anjouan, Moheli and Grand Comore - came under French protection in 1886. The islands were joined administratively with Madagascar in 1912. The Comoros became partially autonomous, with the status of a French overseas territory in 1946 and achieved complete internal autonomy in 1961. On Dec. 31, 1975, after 133 years of French association, the Comoros Islands became the independent Republic of the Comoros.

Mayotte retained the option of determining its future ties and in 1976 voted to remain French. Its present status is that of a French Territorial Collectivity. Euro coinage and currency circulates there.

RULERS:
French to 1975

MONETARY SYSTEM:
· 1 Franc = 100 Centimes

REPUBLIC

BANQUE DE MADAGASCAR ET DES COMORES

1960 ND PROVISIONAL ISSUE

#2-6 additional red ovpt: *COMORES*.

2	50 FRANCS	VG	VF	UNC
	ND (1960-63). Brown and m/c. Woman w/hat at r. Man on back. Ovpt. on Madagascar #45.			
	a. Sign. titles: *LE CONTROLEUR GAL.* and *LE DIRECTEUR GAL.* ND (1960).	—	—	—
	b. Sign. titles: *LE DIRECTEUR GAL. ADJOINT* and *LE PRESIDENT DIRECTEUR GAL.* ND (1963). 2 sign varieties.	5.00	25.00	100.00
	s. Specimen.	—	—	—

3	100 FRANCS	VG	VF	UNC
	ND (1960-63). M/c. Woman at r., palace of the Qn. of Tananariva in background. Woman, boats and animals on back. Ovpt. on Madagascar #46.			
	a. Sign. titles: *LE CONTROLEUR GAL.* and *LE DIRECTEUR GAL.* ND (1960).	8.00	45.00	150.00
	b. Sign. titles: *LE DIRECTEUR GAL. ADJOINT* and *LE PRESIDENT DIRECTEUR GAL.* ND (1963).	3.00	15.00	55.00
	s. Specimen.	—	—	—

#4-6 dated through 1952 have titles "a", those dated 1955 or ND have titles "b".

4	500 FRANCS	VG	VF	UNC
	ND (1960-63). M/c. Man w/fruit at ctr. Ovpt. on Madagascar #47.			
	a. Sign. titles: *LE CONTROLEUR GAL.* and *LE DIRECTEUR GAL.* - old date 30.6.1950; 9.10.1952 (1960).	25.00	150.00	450.00
	b. Sign. titles: *LE DIRECTEUR GAL. ADJOINT* and *LE PRESIDENT DIRECTEUR GAL.* ND (1963).	12.50	100.00	350.00
5	1000 FRANCS			
	ND (1960-63). M/c. Woman and man at l. ctr. Ox cart on back. Ovpt. on Madagascar #48.			
	a. Sign. titles: *LE CONTROLEUR GAL.* and *LE DIRECTEUR GAL.* - old date 1950-52; 9.10.1952 (1960).	35.00	200.00	550.00
	b. Sign. titles: *LE DIRECTEUR GAL. ADJOINT* and *LE PRESIDENT DIRECTEUR GAL.* ND (1963).	20.00	125.00	400.00

6	5000 FRANCS	VG	VF	UNC
	ND (1960-63). M/c. Portr. Gallieni at upper l., young woman at r. Huts at l., woman w/baby at r. on back. Ovpt. on Madagascar #49.			
	a. Sign. titles: *LE CONTROLEUR GAL.* and *LE DIRECTEUR GAL.* - old date 30.6.1950 (1960).	150.00	425.00	925.00
	b. Sign. titles: *LE DIRECTEUR GAL. ADJOINT* and *LE PRESIDENT DIRECTEUR GAL.* ND (1963).	100.00	325.00	800.00
	c. Sign. titles: *LE DIRECTEUR GÉNÉRAL* and *LE PRÉSIDENT DIRECTEUR GAL.*	125.00	350.00	800.00

INSTITUT D'ÉMISSION DES COMORES

1976 ND ISSUE

#7-9 wmk: Crescent on Maltese cross.

NOTICE

Readers with unlisted dates, signature varieties, etc. are invited to submit photocopies of their notes to: Standard Catalog of World Paper Money, 700 East State St. Iola, WI 54990-0001, E-Mail: george.cuhaj@fwpubs.com.

7   500 FRANCS

		VG	VF	UNC
ND (1976). Blue-gray, brown and red on m/c unpt. Bldg. at ctr., young woman wearing a hood at r. 2 women at l., boat at r. on back. 2 sign. varieties.
a. Issued note. | | FV | 3.00 | 10.00 |
s. Specimen. | | — | | 50.00 |

8   1000 FRANCS

		VG	VF	UNC
ND (1976). Blue-gray, brown and green on m/c unpt. Woman at r., palm trees at water's edge in background. Women on back.
a. Issued note. | | FV | 6.00 | 20.00 |
s. Specimen. | | — | — | 50.00 |

9   5000 FRANCS

		VG	VF	UNC
ND (1976). Green on m/c unpt. Man and woman at ctr., boats and bldg. in l. background. Pres. Djohr at ctr. on back.
a. Issued note. | | FV | 35.00 | 100.00 |
s. Specimen. | | — | — | 100.00 |

BANQUE CENTRALE DES COMORES

1984-86 ND ISSUE

#10-12 like to #7-9 but w/new bank name. Wmk: Maltese cross w/crescent.

10   500 FRANCS

		VG	VF	UNC
ND (1986-). Blue-gray, brown and red on m/c unpt. Like #7.
a. Partially engraved. Sign. titles: *LE DIRECTEUR GÉNÉRAL* and *LE PRÉSIDENT DU CONSEIL D'ADMINISTRATION* (1986). | | FV | 2.25 | 7.50 |
b. Offset. Sign. titles: *LE GOUVERNEUR* and *PRÉSIDENT DU...* (1994). (2 sign. varieties.) | | FV | FV | 5.00 |

11   1000 FRANCS

		VG	VF	UNC
ND (1984-). Blue-gray, brown and green on m/c unpt. Like #8.
a. Partially engraved. Sign. titles: *LE DIRECTEUR GÉNÉRAL* and *LE PRÉSIDENT DU CONSEIL D'ADMINISTRATION.* (1986). | | FV | 4.00 | 15.00 |
b. Offset. Sign. titles: *LE GOUVERNEUR* and *PRÉSIDENT DU....* (1994). (2 sign. varieties.) | | FV | 3.25 | 10.00 |

12   5000 FRANCS

		VG	VF	UNC
ND (1984-). Green on m/c unpt. Like #9. Engraved.
a. Sign. titles: *LE DIRECTEUR GÉNÉRAL* and *LE PRÉSIDENT DU CONSEIL D'ADMINISTRATION.* | | FV | 17.50 | 50.00 |
b. Sign. titles: *LE GOVERNEUR* and *LE PRESIDENT...* | | FV | FV | 40.00 |

1997 ND ISSUE

#13 and 14 wmk: 4 stars below crescent (arms).

13   2500 FRANCS

		VG	VF	UNC
ND (1997). Purple and blue on m/c unpt. Woman wearing colorful scarf at l. Sea turtle at lower l. ctr. on back. | | FV | FV | 25.00 |

14 10,000 FRANCS
ND (1997). Yellow, brown and blue on m/c unpt. 2 seated women weaving baskets at ctr. Al-Habib Seyyid O. Bin Sumeit at l., mosque at ctr. on back.

	VG	VF	UNC
	FV	FV	70.00

CONGO DEMOCRATIC REPUBLIC

The Congo Democratic Republic (formerly Zaïre), located in the south-central part of Africa, has an area of 905,568 sq. mi. (2,345,409 sq. km.) and a population of 51.75 million. Capital: Kinshasa. The mineral-rich country produces copper, tin, diamonds, gold, zinc, cobalt and uranium.

In ancient times the territory comprising Zaïre was occupied by Negrito peoples (Pygmies) pushed into the mountains by Bantu and Nilotic invaders. The interior was first explored by the American correspondent Henry Stanley, who was subsequently commissioned by King Leopold II of Belgium to conclude development treaties with the local chiefs. The Berlin conference of 1885 awarded the area to Leopold, who administered and exploited it as his private property until it was annexed to Belgium in 1908. Following the eruption of bloody independence riots in 1959, Belgium granted the Belgian Congo independence as the Republic of the Congo on June 30, 1960. The Belgian Congo attained independence with the distinction of being the most ill-prepared country to ever undertake self-government. Without a single doctor, lawyer or engineer, with no organized unit capable of maintaining law and order, independence disintegrated into an orgy of anarchy. Provinces seceded. Intertribal warfare erupted. Belgian troops intervened to protect Belgian citizens from retributive massacre. By 1961, four groups were fighting for political dominance. The most serious threat to the viability of the country was posed by the secession of mineral-rich Katanga province on July 11, 1960.

After two and one-half years of sporadic warfare with a U.N. military force, Katanga's leaders capitulated, Jan. 14, 1963 and the rebellious province was partitioned into three provinces. The nation officially changed its name to Zaïre on Oct. 27, 1971. In May 1997, the dictator was overthrown after a three year rebellion. The country changed its name to the Democratic Republic of the Congo. A change to a Francs-Congolese currency has been considered, but meanwhile "hard" currency such as U.S.A. dollars circulate freely.

See also Rwanda, Rwanda-Burundi, and Zaïre.

MONETARY SYSTEM:
1 Franc = 100 Centimes to 1967
1 Zaïre = 100 Makuta, 1967-71
1 Franc = 100 Centimes, 1997-

SIGNATURE VARIETIES		
Conseil Monétaire de la République du Congo (1962-1963)		
	President	**Vice President**
1	Walter Jansen	Jean N'sele

CONGO (KINSHASA)

CONSEIL MONÉTAIRE DE LA RÉPUBLIQUE DU CONGO

1962-63 ISSUE

#1-3 various date and sign varieties.

1 100 FRANCS
1.6.1963-8.7.1963. Green and m/c. Dam at l. Dredging at r. on back.

	VG	VF	UNC
a. Issued note.	5.00	40.00	160.00
ct. Color trial. Blue on m/c unpt.	—	—	175.00
s. Specimen.	—	85.00	145.00

2 1000 FRANCS

	VG	VF	UNC
15.2.1962. Purple on m/c unpt. Portr. African man at l. Text: *EMISSION DU CONSEIL MONÉTAIRE DE LA RÉPUBLIQUE DU CONGO* in place of wmk. Back deep violet on pink unpt; waterbuck drinking in stream.
a. Issued note.	25.00	100.00	525.00
s. Specimen.	—	—	385.00

3 5000 FRANCS

	VG	VF	UNC
1.12.1963. Gray-green. Portr. African woman at l. Oarsmen on back.
a. Issued note.	500.00	1750.00	—
ct. Color trial. Blue on m/c unpt.	—	—	4500.00
s. Specimen.	—	—	4000.00

BANQUE NATIONALE DU CONGO

	SIGNATURE VARIETIES		
2	Le Gouverneur Albert Ndele	3	Le Gouverneur Sambwa Pida Nbangui

1961 ISSUE
#4-8 sign. 1.

4 20 FRANCS

	VG	VF	UNC
15.11.1961-15.9.1962. Green, blue and brown. Girl seated at r. and as wmk. Stylized tree at ctr. on back. Printer: JEZ.
a. Issued note.	3.50	15.00	60.00
s. Specimen.	—	—	75.00

#5-8 long bldg. at bottom on back.

5 50 FRANCS

	VG	VF	UNC
1.9.1961-1.7.1962. Green. Lion at l., bridge and lake at ctr. r. in background.
a. Issued note.	6.00	30.00	145.00
ct. Color trial. Brown on m/c unpt.	—	—	150.00
s. Specimen.	—	—	85.00

6 100 FRANCS

	VG	VF	UNC
1.9.1961-1.8.1964. Dk. brown on m/c unpt. J. Kasavubu at l., two crowned cranes at r. Printer: TDLR.
a. Issued note.	5.00	25.00	120.00
s. Specimen.	—	—	95.00

7 500 FRANCS

	VG	VF	UNC
15.10.1961; 1.12.1961; 1.1.1962; 1.8.1964. Lilac. Mask at l. Wmk: Bird.
a. Issued note.	15.00	55.00	265.00
s. Specimen.	—	—	145.00

8	**1000 FRANCS**	VG	VF	UNC
	15.10.1961; 15.12.1961; 1.8.1964. Dk. blue on m/c unpt. J. Kasavubu at l., carving at r. Wmk: Antelope's head. Printer: TDLR.			
	a. Issued note.	12.00	50.00	200.00
	s. Specimen.	—	—	120.00

1967 ISSUE

#9-13 various date and sign. varieties. Printer: TDLR. Replacement notes: Serial # prefix ZZ.

9	**10 MAKUTA**	VG	VF	UNC
	2.1.1967; 1.9.1968; 14.1.1970; 21.1.1970. Blue on olive-green and m/c unpt. Stadium at l., Mobutu at r. Long bldg. on back. Sign. 1.			
	a. Issued note.	3.00	12.50	60.00
	s. Specimen.	—	—	35.00

10	**20 MAKUTA**	VG	VF	UNC
	1967-70. Black on green, blue and m/c unpt. Man w/flag at ctr., P. Lumumba at r. People in long boat at l. ctr. on back. Wmk: Antelope's head.			
	a. Sign. 1. 24.11.1967; 21.1.1970.	6.00	32.50	130.00
	b. Sign. 2. 1.10.1970.	5.50	30.00	120.00
	s. Specimen. 21.1.1970.	—	—	100.00

11	**50 MAKUTA**	VG	VF	UNC
	1967-70. Red on olive-green and m/c unpt. Stadium at ctr. l., Mobutu at r. Gathering coconuts on back.			
	a. Sign. 1. 2.1.1967; 1.9.1968; 21.1.1970.	6.50	35.00	145.00
	b. Sign. 2. 1.10.1970.	6.50	35.00	145.00
	s. Specimen. 1.9.1968.	—	—	125.00

12	**1 ZAÏRE = 100 MAKUTA**	VG	VF	UNC
	1967-70. Brown and green on m/c unpt. Stadium at l., Mobutu at r. Mobutu's "time to work" to gathering of people at l. ctr. on back. Wmk: Antelope's head.			
	a. Sign. 1. 2.1.1967; 24.11.1967; 1.9.1968.	5.50	30.00	120.00
	b. Sign. 2. 21.1.1970; 1.10.1970.	5.50	30.00	120.00
	s1. Specimen. 24.11.1967.	—	—	125.00
	s2. Specimen. 1.10.1970.	—	—	125.00

13	**5 ZAÏRES = 500 MAKUTA**	VG	VF	UNC
	1967-70. Green and m/c. Mobutu at r. Long bldg. at l. ctr. on back. Wmk: Antelope's head.			
	a. Sign. 1 above title: *LE GOUVERNEUR*. Green date. 2.1.1967; 24.6.1967.	20.00	95.00	385.00
	b. Sign. 2 below title: *LE GOUVERNEUR*. Black date. 2.1.1967; 24.11.1967; 1.9.1968; 21.1.1970.	15.00	75.00	285.00
	s1. Specimen. 2.1.1967.	—	—	275.00
	s2. Specimen. 21.1.1970.	—	225.00	275.00

1971 ISSUE

#14 and 15 portr. Mobutu at l. and as wmk., leopard at lower r. facing r. Sign. 2. Printer: G&D. Replacement notes: Serial # suffix Z.

14	**5 ZAÏRES**	VG	VF	UNC
	24.11.1971. Green, black and m/c. Carving at l. ctr., hydroelectric dam at ctr. r. on back.			
	a. Issued note.	20.00	80.00	325.00
	s. Specimen.	—	—	250.00

15	**10 ZAÏRES**	VG	VF	UNC
	30.6.1971. Blue, brown and m/c. Arms on back w/yellow star.			
	a. Issued note.	20.00	90.00	355.00
	s. Specimen.	—	—	250.00

DEMOCRATIC REPUBLIC

BANQUE CENTRALE DU CONGO

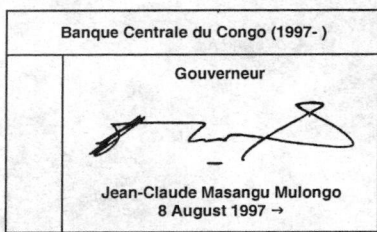

Banque Centrale du Congo (1997-)
Gouverneur
(signature)
—
Jean-Claude Masangu Mulongo
8 August 1997 →

1997 ISSUE

#80-90 bank monogram at ctr. Wmk: Single Okapi head or multiple heads repeated vertically.

#80-84 printer imprint is very light.

80 1 CENTIME
1.11.1997. Deep olive-green, violet and dk. brown on m/c unpt.
Woman harvesting coffee beans at l. Nyiragongo volcano erupting
at r. on back. Printer: ATB.

	VG	VF	UNC
a. Issued note.	FV	FV	1.00
s. Specimen.	—	—	3.00

81 5 CENTIMES
1.11.1997. Purple on m/c unpt. Suku mask at l. Zande Harp at ctr.
r. on back. Printer: G&D.

	VG	VF	UNC
a. Issued note.	FV	FV	1.00
s. Specimen.	—	—	10.00

82 10 CENTIMES
1.11.1997. Red-violet and dk. brown on m/c unpt. Pende mask at
l. Pende dancers at ctr. r. on back. Printer: ATB.

	VG	VF	UNC
a. Issued note.	FV	FV	1.25
s. Specimen.	—	—	3.00

83 20 CENTIMES
1.11.1997. Blue-green and black on m/c unpt. Waterbuck at l.
Waterbuck herd by lg. tree at ctr. r. on back. Printer: ATB.

	VG	VF	UNC
a. Issued note.	FV	FV	1.25
s. Specimen.	—	—	4.00

84 50 CENTIMES
1.11.1997. Dk. brown and brown on m/c unpt. Okapi's head at l.
Family of Okapis at l. ctr. on back. Printer: G&D.

	VG	VF	UNC
a. Issued note.	FV	FV	1.75
s. Specimen.	—	—	5.00

84A 50 CENTIMES
1.11.1997. As #84. Printer: ATB. Serial # prefix: E; suffix: A-E, T.

	VG	VF	UNC
	FV	FV	1.75

85 1 FRANC
1.11.1997 (1998). Deep purple and blue-violet on m/c unpt. Lg.
mining complex at l. Prisoners Lumumba and 2 companions at ctr.
r. on back. Printer: G&D.

	VG	VF	UNC
a. Issued note.	FV	FV	4.00
s. Specimen.	—	—	6.00

86 5 FRANCS
1.11.1997 (1998). Purple and black on m/c unpt. White rhinoceros
at l. Kamwanga Falls at ctr. r. on back. Printer: NBBPW.

	VG	VF	UNC
a. Issued note.	FV	FV	5.00
s. Specimen.	—	—	12.50

86A 5 FRANCS
1.11.1997 (1998). As #86. Printer: HdM.

	VG	VF	UNC
	FV	FV	5.00

		VG	VF	UNC
87	**10 FRANCS**			
	1.11.1997 (1998). Olive-brown, olive-green and deep blue-green on m/c unpt. "Apui-tete Chef Luba" carving of a couple at l. "Coupe en Bois Luba" carving at r. on back. Printer: NBBPW. Serial # prefix: H, suffix: A.			
	a. Issued note.	FV	4.00	15.00
	s. Specimen.	—	—	15.00
87A	**10 FRANCS**			
	1.11.1997. As 87 but printer G&D. Serial # prefix: H; suffix: B-E.	FV	5.00	17.50
87B	**10 FRANCS**			
	1.11.1997. As #87. Printer: HdM.	FV	FV	15.00

		VG	VF	UNC
88	**20 FRANCS**			
	1.11.1997 (1998). Brown-orange and red-orange on m/c unpt. Male lion's head at l. Lioness lying w/2 cubs at ctr. r. on back. Printer: NBBPW.			
	a. Issued note.	FV	5.00	20.00
	s. Specimen.	—	—	17.50
88A	**20 FRANCS**			
	1.11.1997 (1998). As #88. Printer: HdM.	FV	4.00	15.00

		VG	VF	UNC
89	**50 FRANCS**			
	1.11.1997 (1998). Olive-green. Head at l. Village scene on back. Printer: NBBPW.			
	a. Issued note.	FV	10.00	45.00
	s. Specimen.	—	—	25.00

		VG	VF	UNC
90	**100 FRANCS**			
	1.11.1997 (1998). Brown. Elephant at l. Dam on back. Printer: NBBPW.			
	a. Issued note.	FV	17.50	75.00
	s. Specimen.	—	—	30.00

2000 ISSUE

		VG	VF	UNC
91	**50 FRANCS**	FV	FV	45.00
	4.1.2000. Lilac brown. Like #89.			

		VG	VF	UNC
92	**100 FRANCS**	FV	FV	75.00
	4.1.2000. Slate blue. Like #90.			

2003 ISSUE

		VG	VF	UNC
93	**10 FRANCS**	FV	FV	0.25
	30.6.2003. Brown and red on orange and blue m/c unpt. Like #87. Printer G&D.			

		VG	VF	UNC
94	**20 FRANCS**	FV	FV	0.50
	30.6.2003. Blue-green on green m/c unpt. Male lion's head at l. Lioness lying w/2 cubs at ctr. r. on back. Printer: HdM-B.O.C.			
95	**50 FRANCS**	FV	FV	0.75
	30.6.2000 (2003). Lilac and olive green on m/c unpt. Two farmers at l. Four men working on logs.			

The Republic of the Congo (formerly the Peoples Republic of the Congo), located on the equator in west-central Africa, has an area of 132,047 sq. mi. (342,000 sq. km.) and a population of 2.98 million. Capital: Brazzaville. Agriculture forestry, mining, and food processing are the principal industries. Timber, industrial diamonds, potash, peanuts, and cocoa beans are exported.

The Portuguese were the first Europeans to explore the Congo (Brazzaville) area, 14th century. They conducted a slave trade with the tribal kingdoms of Teke, Loango, and Kongo without attempting developmental colonization. French influence was established in 1883 when the King of Teke signed a treaty with Savorgnan de Brazza, thereby placing his kingdom under the protection of France. While a French protectorate, the area was known as Middle Congo. In 1910 Middle Congo became a part of French Equatorial Africa, which also included Gabon, Ubangi-Shari (now the Central African Republic), and Chad. Following World War II, during which it was an important center of Free French activities, the Middle Congo was given a large measure of internal autonomy, and its inhabitants were made French citizens. Upon approval of the constitution of the Fifth French Republic, 1958, it became a member of the new French Community. On Aug. 15, 1960, Middle Congo became the independent Republic of the Congo-Brazzaville. In Jan. 1970 the country's name was changed to Peoples Republic of the Congo. A new constitution which asserts the government's advocacy of socialism was adopted in 1973. In June and July of 1992, a new 125-member National Assembly was elected. Later that year a new president, Pascal Lissouba, was elected. In November, President Lissouba dismissed the previous government and dissolved the National Assembly. A new 23-member government, including members of the opposition, was formed in December 1992 and the name was changed to République du Congo.

Violence erupted in 1997 nearly emptying the capitol.

RULERS:
    French to 1960

MONETARY SYSTEM:
    1 Franc = 100 Centimes

SIGNATURE VARIETIES:
    Refer to introduction of Central African States.

RÉPUBLIQUE POPULAIRE DU CONGO

BANQUE CENTRALE

1971 ISSUE

	500 FRANCS		VG	VF	UNC
96	4.1.2002 (2004). Blue on m/c unpt. Miners and diamond at l.		FV	FV	3.25

	10,000 FRANCS	VG	VF	UNC
1	ND (1971). M/c. Young Congolese woman at l., people marching w/sign at ctr. Statue at l. and r., tractor plowing at ctr. on back. Sign. 1.	150.00	800.00	2250.00

BANQUE DES ÉTATS DE L'AFRIQUE CENTRALE

1974 ND ISSUE

2	**500 FRANCS**	**VG**	**VF**	**UNC**
	ND (1974)-1983. Lilac-brown and m/c. Woman at l., river scene at ctr. Mask at l., students and chemical testing at ctr., statue at r. on back.			
	a. Sign. titles: *LE DIRECTEUR GENERAL* and *UN CENSEUR*. Engraved. Sign. 5. ND (1974).	2.50	15.00	50.00
	b. Sign. titles: *LE GOUVERNEUR* and *UN CENSEUR*. Lithographed. Sign. 10. 1.4.1978.	5.00	25.00	90.00
	c. Titles as b. Sign. 10; 1.7.1980.	1.50	7.50	25.00
	d. Titles as b. Sign. 12. 1.6.1981; 1.1.1982; 1.1.1983; 1.6.1984.	1.50	4.00	20.00

3	**1000 FRANCS**	**VG**	**VF**	**UNC**
	ND (1974)-1984. Blue and m/c. Industrial plant at ctr., man at r. Mask at l., trains, planes and bridge at ctr., statue at r. on back.			
	a. Sign. titles: *LE DIRECTEUR GENERAL* and *UN CENSEUR*. Engraved. Wmk: Antelope head in half profile. Sign. 3. ND (1974).	10.00	40.00	200.00
	b. Like a. Sign. 5.	4.00	12.50	75.00
	c. Sign. titles: *LE DIRECTEUR GENERAL* and *UN CENSEUR*. Lithographed. Wmk: Antelope head in profile. Sign. 8. ND (1978).	3.00	8.50	35.00
	d. Sign. titles: *LE GOUVERNEUR* and *UN CENSEUR*. Lithographed. Wmk: like b. Sign. 10. 1.4.1978.	2.75	7.50	30.00
	e. Titles as d. Sign. 12; 1.6.1981; 1.1.1982; 1.1.1983; 1.6.1984.	2.25	6.50	22.50

4	**5000 FRANCS**	**VG**	**VF**	**UNC**
	ND (1974; 1978). Brown. Man at l. Mask at l., bldgs. at ctr., statue at r. on back.			
	a. Sign. titles: *LE DIRECTEUR GENERAL* and *UN CENSEUR*. Sign. 3. ND (1974).	35.00	100.00	450.00
	b. Like a. Sign. 5.	15.00	75.00	250.00
	c. Sign. titles: *LE GOUVERNEUR* and *UN CENSEUR*. Sign. 11; 12. ND (1978).	13.50	35.00	200.00

5	**10,000 FRANCS**	**VG**	**VF**	**UNC**
	ND (1974-81). M/c. Like #1 except for new bank name on back.			
	a. Sign. titles: *LE DIRECTEUR GENERAL* and *UN CENSEUR*. Sign. 5; 7. ND (1974; 1977).	30.00	65.00	275.00
	b. Sign. titles: *LE GOUVERNEUR* and *UN CENSEUR*. Sign. 11; 12. ND (1978; 1981).	25.00	75.00	225.00

1983-84 ND Issue

6	**5000 FRANCS**	**VG**	**VF**	**UNC**
	ND (1984; 1991). Brown and m/c. Mask at l., woman w/bundle of fronds at r. Plowing and mine ore conveyor on back.			
	a. Sign. 12. (1984).	15.00	35.00	125.00
	b. Sign. 15. (1991).	15.00	30.00	100.00

7	**10,000 FRANCS**	**VG**	**VF**	**UNC**
	ND (1983). Brown, green and m/c. Stylized antelope heads at l., woman at r. Loading fruit onto truck at l. on back. Sign. 12.	25.00	40.00	150.00

1985-87 ISSUES

Note: For issues w/similar back designs see Cameroun Republic, Central African Republic, Chad and Gabon.

#8-10 sign. titles: *LE GOUVERNEUR* and *UN CENSEUR*.

8	500 FRANCS	VG	VF	UNC
	1985-91. Brown on m/c unpt. Statue at l. ctr. and as wmk., jug at ctr. Man carving mask at l. ctr. on back.			
	a. Sign. 12. 1.1.1985; 1.1.1987; 1.1.1989.	FV	1.00	7.00
	b. Sign. 12. 1.1.1988.	50.00	—	—
	c. Sign. 13. 1.1.1990.	FV	1.00	6.00
	d. Sign. 15. 1.1.1991.	FV	1.00	6.00

9	1000 FRANCS	VG	VF	UNC
	1.1.1985. Dull blue-violet on m/c unpt. Animal carving at lower l., map of 6 member states at ctr. Unfinished map of Chad at upper ctr. Elephant at l., animals at ctr., carving at r. on back. Wmk: Animal carving. Sign. 12.	1.25	7.50	20.00

10	1000 FRANCS	VG	VF	UNC
	1987-91. Dull blue-violet on m/c unpt. Like #9 but completed map of Chad at top on face.			
	a. Sign. 12. 1.1.1987; 1.1.1988; 1.1.1989.	1.00	4.50	15.00
	b. Sign. 13. 1.1.1990.	0.75	4.00	12.00
	c. Sign. 15. 1.1.1991.	0.75	3.50	10.00

RÉPUBLIQUE DU CONGO

BANQUE DES ÉTATS DE L'AFRIQUE CENTRALE

1992 ISSUE

11	1000 FRANCS	VG	VF	UNC
	1.1.1992. Dull blue-violet on m/c unpt. Like #10, but w/new country name. Sign. 15.	FV	FV	11.00

1992 ND ISSUE

12	5000 FRANCS	VG	VF	UNC
	ND (1992). Black text and brown on pale yellow and m/c unpt. African mask at l. and as wmk., woman carrying bundle of cane at r. African string instrument at far l., farm tractor plowing at l. ctr., mineshaft cable ore bucket lift at r. on back. Sign	5.00	15.00	45.00

13	10,000 FRANCS	VG	VF	UNC
	ND (1992). Greenish-black text, brown on pale green and m/c unpt. Artistic antelope masks at l., woman's head at r. and as wmk. Loading produce truck w/bananas at l. on back. Sign. 15.	5.00	15.00	75.00

Note: For later issues see Central African States.

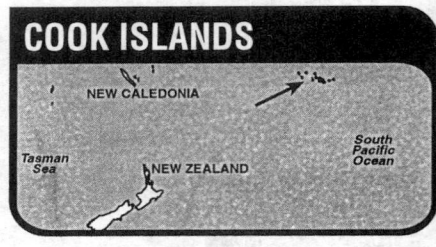

Cook Islands, a political dependency of New Zealand consisting of 15 islands located in the South Pacific Ocean about 2,000 miles (3,218 km.) northeast of New Zealand, has an area of 93 sq. mi. (234 sq. km.) and a population of 20,000. Capital: Avarua. The United States claims the islands of Danger, Manahiki, Penrhyn and Rakahanga atolls. Citrus, canned fruits and juices, copra, clothing, jewelry and mother-of-pearl shell are exported.

The islands were first sighted by Spanish navigator Alvaro de Mendada in 1595. Portuguese navigator Pedro Fernandes de Quieros landed on Rakahanga in 1606. English navigator Capt. James Cook sailed to the islands on three occasions: 1773, 1774 and 1777. He named them Hervey Islands, in honor of Augustus John Hervey, a lord of the Admiralty. The islands were declared a British protectorate in 1888, and were annexed to New Zealand in 1901. They were granted internal self-government in 1965. New Zealand provides an annual subsidy and retains responsibility for defense and foreign affairs.

As a territory of New Zealand, the Cook Islands are considered to be within the Commonwealth of Nations.

Note: In June 1995 the Government of the Cook Islands began redeeming all 10, 20 and 50 dollar notes in exchange for New Zealand currency while most coins originally intended for circulation along with their 3 dollar notes will remain in use.

RULERS:
New Zealand, 1901-

MONETARY SYSTEM:
1 Shilling = 12 Pence
1 Pound = 20 Shillings, to 1967
1 Dollar = 100 Cents, 1967-

NEW ZEALAND ADMINISTRATION

GOVERNMENT OF THE COOK ISLANDS

1987 ND ISSUE

#3-5 Ina and the shark at l.

	3 DOLLARS	VG	VF	UNC
3	ND (1987). Deep green, blue and black on m/c unpt. Fishing canoe and statue of the god of Te-Rongo on back.			
	a. Issued note.	FV	4.75	4.50
	s. Specimen.	—	—	25.00

	10 DOLLARS	VG	VF	UNC
4	ND (1987). Violet-brown, blue and black on m/c unpt. Pantheon of gods on back.			
	a. Issued note.	FV	8.50	17.50
	s. Specimen.	—	—	17.50

	20 DOLLARS	VG	VF	UNC
5	ND (1987). Blue, black and purple on m/c unpt. Conch shell, turtle shell and drum on back.			
	a. Sign. T. Davis.	FV	17.50	32.50
	b. Sign. M. J. Fleming.	FV	17.50	30.00
	s. Specimen.	—	—	20.00

1992 COMMEMORATIVE ISSUE

#6, 6th Festival of Pacific Arts, Rarotonga, Oct. 16-27, 1992

	3 DOLLARS	VG	VF	UNC
6	Oct. 1992. Black commemorative text ovpt. at l. on back of #3.	FV	3.00	5.00

1992 ND ISSUE

#7-10 worshippers at church w/cemetery at ctr. Wmk: Sea turtle.

	3 DOLLARS	VG	VF	UNC
7	ND (1992). Lilac and green on m/c unpt. Back purple, orange and m/c. *AITUTAKI* at upper ctr., local drummers at l., dancers at ctr., Blue lorikeet and fish at r.			
	a. Issued note.	FV	FV	4.50
	s. Specimen.	—	—	20.00

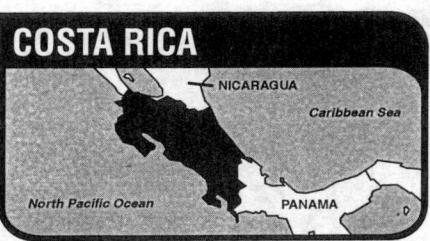

The Republic of Costa Rica, located in southern Central America between Nicaragua and Panama, has an area of 19,575 sq. mi. (50,700 sq. km.) and a population of 3.8 million. Capital: San Jose. Agriculture predominates; coffee, bananas, beef and sugar contribute heavily to the country's export earnings.

Costa Rica was discovered by Christopher Columbus in 1502, during his last voyage to the new world, and was a colony of Spain from 1522 until independence in 1821. Columbus named the territory Nueva Cartago; the name Costa Rica wasn't generally employed until 1540. Bartholomew Columbus attempted to found the first settlement but was driven off by Indian attacks and the country wasn't pacified until 1530. Costa Rica was absorbed for two years (1821-23) into the Mexican Empire of Agustin de Iturbide. From 1823 to 1848 it was a constituent state of the Central American Republic (q.v.). It was established as a republic in 1848.

Constitution revisions followed in 1871 and 1948. In the early 1990's, Costa Rica was beset with economic problems.

MONETARY SYSTEM:
1 Colon = 100 Centimos

		VG	VF	UNC
8	**10 DOLLARS**			
	ND (1992). Green and olive on m/c unpt. Cook Islands Fruit Dove. *RAROTONGA* above hillside gathering on back.			
	a. Issued note.	FV	FV	12.50
	s. Specimen.	—	—	25.00

REPUBLIC

BANCO CENTRAL DE COSTA RICA

1951; 1952 ISSUE - SERIES A

		VG	VF	UNC
9	**20 DOLLARS**			
	ND (1992). Brown-orange and olive on m/c unpt. *NGAPUTORU & MANGAIA* above two islanders w/canoe at ctr., Mangaia kingfisher at r. on back.			
	a. Issued note.	FV	FV	22.50
	s. Specimen.	—	—	20.00

		VG	VF	UNC
220	**5 COLONES**			
	1951-58. Green on m/c unpt. Portr. B. Carillo at r. Back green; coffee worker. Printer: ABNC.			
	a. *POR* (for) added to l. of sign. title at r. 20.11.1952.	3.00	15.00	50.00
	b. W/o sign. title changes. 2.7.1952-6.8.1958.	3.00	15.00	50.00
	c. Sign. title: *SUB-GERENTE* ovpt. at r. 11.7.1956.	3.00	15.00	50.00
	d. *POR* added to l. of sign. title at l. 12.9.1951; 26.5.1954.	3.00	15.00	50.00
	s. Specimen.	—	—	

#221-223 printer: W&S.

		VG	VF	UNC
10	**50 DOLLARS**			
	ND (1992). Blue and green on m/c unpt. 3 islanders in canoe at l., *NORTHERN GROUP* above two seated women weaving at ctr., sooty tern at r. on back.			
	a. Issued note.	FV	FV	55.00
	s. Specimen.	—	—	25.00

COLLECTOR SERIES

GOVERNMENT OF THE COOK ISLANDS

1987 ND ISSUE

		Issue Price	Mkt.	Value
CS1	**ND (1987) 3-20 DOLLARS**			
	#3-5 w/matched serial # in special pack.	55.00		60.00

		VG	VF	UNC
221	**10 COLONES**			
	1951-62. Blue on m/c unpt. Portr. A. Echeverria at ctr. Back blue; ox-cart at ctr.			
	a. *POR* added to l. of sign .title at l. 24.10.1951; 8.11.1951; 19.11.1951; 5.12.1951; 29.10.1952.	6.00	25.00	100.00
	b. *POR* added to both sign. titles. 28.11.1951.	6.00	25.00	100.00
	c. W/o *POR* title changes. 2.7.1952; 28.10.1953-27.6.1962.	6.00	25.00	100.00
	d. *POR* added to l. of sign. title at r. 20.11.1952.	6.00	25.00	100.00

222   20 COLONES

		VG	VF	UNC
1952-64. Red on m/c unpt. Portr. C. Picado at ctr. Back red; university bldg. at ctr.				
a. Date at l. ctr., w/o sign. title changes. 26.2.1952; 11.6.1952; 11.8.1954; 14.10.1955; 13.2.1957; 10.12.62.		15.00	50.00	185.00
b. Sign. title: *SUB-GERENTE* ovpt. at r. 20.4.1955.		15.00	50.00	175.00
c. Date at lower l. 7.11.1957-9.9.1964.		15.00	50.00	175.00
d. *POR* added at l. of sign. title at l. 25.3.1953; 25.2.1954.		15.00	50.00	175.00

223   50 COLONES

		VG	VF	UNC
1952-64. Olive on m/c unpt. Portr. R. F. Guardia at ctr. Back olive; National Library at ctr.				
a. 10.6.1952-25.11.1959.		15.00	50.00	225.00
b. 14.9.1960-9.9.1964.		12.50	45.00	200.00

224   100 COLONES

		VG	VF	UNC
1952-60. Black on m/c unpt. Portr. J. R. Mora at ctr. Back black; statue of J. Santamaría at ctr.				
a. W/o sign. title changes: 11.6.1952-29.4.1960.		15.00	35.00	200.00
b. Sign. title: *SUB-GERENTE* ovpt. at r. 27.3.1957.		15.00	35.00	200.00

#225-226 printer: ABNC.

225   500 COLONES

		VG	VF	UNC
1951-77. Purple on m/c unpt. Portr. M. M. Gutiérrez at r. Back purple; National Theater at ctr.				
a. 10.10.1951-6.5.1969.		60.00	300.00	850.00
b. 7.4.1970-26.4.1977.		50.00	250.00	650.00
s. Specimen.		—	—	650.00

226   1000 COLONES

		VG	VF	UNC
1952-74. Red on m/c unpt. Portr. J. Pena at l. Back red; Central and National Bank at ctr.				
a. 11.6.1952-6.10.1959.		125.00	500.00	1350.00
b. 25.4.1962-6.5.1969.		100.00	350.00	850.00
c. 7.4.1970-12.6.1974.		60.00	150.00	400.00
s. Specimen.		—	—	550.00

1958 ISSUE

227   5 COLONES

	VG	VF	UNC
29.10.1958-8.11.1962. Green on m/c unpt. Portr. B. Carrillo at ctr. Back green; coffee worker at ctr. Series B. Printer: W&S.	3.50	15.00	50.00

1963-70 ISSUES

#228 and 229 printer: TDLR.

228   5 COLONES

		VG	VF	UNC
3.10.1963-29.5.1967. Green on m/c unpt. Portr. B. Carrillo at ctr. Back green; coffee worker at ctr. Series C.				
a. Issued note.		2.50	10.00	45.00
s. Specimen.		—	—	—

232 50 COLONES
9.6.1965-30.6.1970. Greenish-brown on m/c unpt. Portr. Guardia
at ctr. Back greenish brown; National Library at ctr. Series B.

	VG	VF	UNC
	7.50	30.00	125.00

229 10 COLONES
19.9.1962-9.10.1967. Blue on m/c unpt. Portr. Echeverría at ctr.
Back blue; ox-cart at ctr. Series B.

	VG	VF	UNC
	5.00	20.00	80.00

233 100 COLONES
1961-66. Black on m/c unpt. Portr. J. R. Mora at ctr. Statue of J.
Santamaría at ctr. on back. Series B.

	VG	VF	UNC
a. Brown unpt. 18.10.1961-3.12.1964.	10.00	40.00	150.00
b. Olive unpt. and w/security thread. 9.6.1965; 14.12.1965; 27.4.1966.	7.50	30.00	150.00

230 10 COLONES
1969-70; ND. Blue on m/c unpt. Portr. R. Facio Brenes at r. Back
blue; Banco Central bldg. at ctr. Series C. Printer: ABNC.

	VG	VF	UNC
a. 4.3.1969; 17.6.1969.	1.50	8.50	35.00
b. 30.6.1970.	1.00	6.00	25.00
s. Specimen. Ovpt. *MUESTRA.* Punch hole cancelled.	—	—	—
x. W/o date or sign.	—	—	—

Note: It is reported that 10,000 pieces of #230x mistakenly reached circulation.

#231-234 printer: TDLR.

234 100 COLONES
29.8.1966-27.8.1968. Black on m/c unpt. Portr. Mora at ctr., w/o *C*
in corners or at r. Back black; statue of J. Santamaría at ctr. Series
C.

	VG	VF	UNC
a. Issued note.	7.50	30.00	135.00
s. Specimen. Ovpt. *MUESTRA.*	—	125.00-	500.00

1967 PROVISIONAL ISSUE

#235 ovpt: *BANCO CENTRAL DE COSTA RICA/SERIE PROVISIONAL* on Banco Nacional notes.

231 20 COLONES
11.11.1964-30.6.1970. Brown on m/c unpt. Portr. Picado at ctr.
Back brown; University bldg. at ctr. Series B.

	VG	VF	UNC
a. Issued note.	4.00	15.00	60.00
s. Specimen.			

235 2 COLONES
5.12.1967. Black ovpt. on #203 (Vol. 2). Series F.

	VG	VF	UNC
	3.00	12.50	45.00

1968-72 ISSUES

236	5 COLONES	VG	VF	UNC

1968-92. Deep green and lilac on m/c unpt. Rafael Yglesias Castro at l., flowers at r. Back green on m/c unpt; National Theater scene. Series D. Printer: TDLR.

		VG	VF	UNC
a.	Date at ctr. Wmk: *BCCR CINCO.* Security thread. Error name *T. VILLA* on back. 20.8.1968; 11.12.1968.	1.50	5.00	20.00
b.	Date at ctr. r. w/wmk. and security thread. Error name *T. VILLA* on back. 1.4.1969; 30.6.1970; 24.5.1971; 8.5.1972.	0.50	1.25	9.00
c.	Date at ctr. r. wmk. and security thread. Corrected name *J. VILLA* on back. 4.5.1973-4.5.1976.	FV	0.75	6.00
d.	W/o wmk. or security thread. Changed sign. titles. 28.6.1977-4.10.1989.	FV	FV	3.00
e.	As d. 24.1.1990-15.1.1992.	FV	FV	2.00
s.	As d. Specimen. Ovpt: *MUESTRA.*	—	—	50.00
x.	As d. but w/error date: 7.4.1933 (instead of 1983).	5.00	10.00	30.00

237	10 COLONES	VG	VF	UNC

1972-87. Dk. blue on m/c unpt. University bldg. at l., Rodrigo Facio Brenes at r. Central Bank on back. Wmk: *BCCR 10.* Printer: ABNC (w/o imprint). Series D.

		VG	VF	UNC
a.	Security thread. 6.9.1972-1977.	0.75	3.00	10.00
b.	W/o security thread. 26.4.1977-18.2.1987.	0.50	1.00	6.50
s.	As a. Specimen. Ovpt: *MUESTRA.*	—	—	60.00

238	20 COLONES	VG	VF	UNC

1972-83. Dk. brown on m/c unpt. Pres. Cleto González Viquez at l., bldgs. and trees at r. Allegorical scene of Justice on back. Printer: ABNC (w/o imprint). Series C.

		VG	VF	UNC
a.	Wmk: *BCCR 20.* (error). *BARBA* - etc. text under bldgs. at ctr. Sign. titles: *EL PRESIDENTE DE LA JUNTA DIRECTIVA* and *EL GERENTE DEL BANCO.* Date at upper r., w/security strip. 10.7.1972; 6.9.1972.	1.50	5.00	22.50
b.	Wmk. as a. Text and sign. as a., date position at upper ctr., w/security strip. 13.11.1972-26.4.1977.	1.00	3.00	15.00
c.	W/o wmk. Lt. brown. Sign. titles: *PRESIDENTE EJECUTIVO* and *GERENTE.* W/o security thread. (corrected). *BARVA...* etc. text under bldgs. at ctr. Date at upper ctr. r. or upper ctr. 1.6.1978-7.4.1983.	0.50	1.00	8.50
s1.	Specimen. Ovpt: *MUESTRA.* 1.6.1978.	—	—	80.00
s2.	Specimen. ND.	—	—	80.00

Note: For 20 Colones dated 28.6.1983 Series Z, printed on Tyvek, see #252.

NOTICE

Readers with unlisted dates, signature varieties, etc. are invited to submit photocopies of their notes to: Standard Catalog of World Paper Money, 700 East State St. Iola, WI 54990-0001, E-Mail: george.cuhaj@fwpubs.com.

239	50 COLONES	VG	VF	UNC
	6.9.1972-26.4.1977. Olive-green m/c unpt. Meeting scene at l., M. M. de Peralta y Alfaro at r. Casa *Amarilla* (Yellow House) on back. Printer: TDLR (w/o imprint). Series C.	2.00	7.50	30.00

240	100 COLONES	VG	VF	UNC

26.8.1969-26.4.1977. Black on m/c unpt. Ricardo Jimenez O. at l., cows and mountains at ctr. Supreme Court at l. ctr., figures at r. on back. Printer: TDLR. Series D.

		VG	VF	UNC
a.	Issued note.	3.50	12.50	45.00
s.	Specimen. Ovpt: *MUESTRA.*			

1971 COMMEMORATIVE ISSUE

#241-246 circular ovpt: 150 *AÑOS DE INDEPENDENCIA* 1821-1971

241	5 COLONES	VG	VF	UNC
	24.5.1971. Ovpt. on #236b. Series D.	2.00	8.50	35.00

242	10 COLONES	VG	VF	UNC
	24.5.1971. Ovpt. on #230. Series C.	5.00	25.00	100.00

243	50 COLONES	VG	VF	UNC
	24.5.1971. Ovpt. on #232. Series B.	20.00	75.00	300.00

244	100 COLONES	VG	VF	UNC
	24.5.1971; 13.12.1971. Ovpt. on #240. Series D.	30.00	100.00	500.00

245	500 COLONES	VG	VF	UNC
	24.5.1971. Ovpt. on #225. Series A.	125.00	500.00	1000.00

246	1000 COLONES	VG	VF	UNC
	24.5.1971. Ovpt. on #226. Series A.	200.00	650.00	1500.00

1975 COMMEMORATIVE ISSUE

#247, circular ovpt: *XXV ANIVERSARIO BANCO CENTRAL DE COSTA RICA*

247	5 COLONES	VG	VF	UNC
	20.3.1975. Ovpt. on #236. Series D.	1.50	12.50	40.00

1975-79 ISSUE

248	100 COLONES	VG	VF	UNC
	1977-88. Black on m/c unpt. Ricardo Jimenez O. at l. Series E. Printer: TDLR.			
	a. 26.4.1977-24.12.1981.	1.00	4.00	20.00
	b. 18.5.1982-9.11.1988.	0.75	3.00	15.00

249	500 COLONES	VG	VF	UNC
	1979-85. Purple on m/c unpt. M. M. Gutiérrez at r. National Theatre at ctr. r. on back. Series B. Printer: TDLR.			
	a. Red serial #. 4.6.1979-12.3.1981.	3.50	15.00	75.00
	b. Black serial #. 17.9.1981; 24.12.1981; 18.5.1982; 7.8.1984; 20.3.1985.	2.50	12.50	40.00

250	1000 COLONES	VG	VF	UNC
	9.6.1975; 13.11.1978; 24.12.1981; 8.7.1982; 4.11.1982; 7.4.1983; 2.10.1984; 20.3.1985. Red on m/c unpt. T. Soley Guell at l. National Insurance Institute at ctr. r. on back. Series B. Printer: ABNC.	FV	10.00	50.00

1978 COMMEMORATIVE ISSUE

#251, Centennial - Bank of Costa Rica 1877-1977

251	50 COLONES	VG	VF	UNC
	1978-86. Olive-green and m/c. Obverse of 1866-dated 50 Centimos coin at l., Gaspar Ortuno y Ors at r. Old bank, reverse of 50 Centimos coin and commemorative text: *1877-CENTENARIO...* on back. Series D. Printer: TDLR.			
	a. 30.10.1978; 30.4.1979; 18.3.1980; 2.4.1981.	1.50	6.00	22.50
	b. 18.5.1982; 28.8.1984; 22.11.1984; 20.3.1985; 2.4.1986.	1.00	4.00	20.00

1983-88 ISSUE

252	20 COLONES	VG	VF	UNC
	28.6.1983. Design like #238c, but Series Z. Printed on Tyvek (plastic).	1.00	5.00	20.00

253	50 COLONES	VG	VF	UNC
	15.7.1987; 26.4.1988. Olive-green on m/c unpt. Similar to 251 but text: *ANTIGUO EDIFICIO...* on back. Wmk: *BCCR 50* w/security thread. Series E. Printer: CdM-Brazil.	FV	2.00	10.00

1986; 1987 ISSUE

254	100 COLONES	VG	VF	UNC
	30.11.1988; 4.10.1989; 5.10.1990. Black on m/c unpt. Similar to #248. Series F. Printer: ABNC.	0.50	2.50	15.00

255	500 COLONES	VG	VF	UNC
	21.1.1987; 14.6.1989. Brown-orange, brown and olive-brown on m/c unpt. Similar to #249, but clear wmk. area at l. Series C. Printer: TDLR.	FV	4.00	20.00

256	1000 COLONES	VG	VF	UNC
	19.11.1986; 17.6.1987; 6.1.1988; 17.1.1989. Red on m/c unpt. Similar to #250. Series C. Printer: ABNC.			
	a. Issued note.	FV	7.50	40.00
	s. Specimen.	—	—	100.00

1990-92 ISSUE

257	50 COLONES	VG	VF	UNC
	19.6.1991; 28.8.1991; 29.7.1992; 2.6.1993; 7.7.1993. Olive-green on m/c unpt. Similar to #253. Series E. W/o security thread. Printer: TDLR.			
	a. Issued note.	FV	0.50	5.00
	s. Specimen. Ovpt: *MUESTRA.*	—	—	120.00

258	100 COLONES	VG	VF	UNC
	17.6.1992. Black on m/c unpt. Like #254. Series G. Printer: CdM-Brazil.	FV	1.00	8.00

259	1000 COLONES	VG	VF	UNC
	1990-94. Red on m/c unpt. Similar to #250 and #256. Series C. Printer: USBN.			
	a. 24.4.1990; 3.10.1990; 23.10.1991.	FV	4.00	20.00
	b. 2.2.1994; 20.4.1994; 15.6.1994; 10.10.1994.	FV	FV	15.00

260   5000 COLONES

			VG	VF	UNC
1991-95. Dk. blue, blue and dk. brown on m/c unpt. Local sculpture at l. ctr. Toucan, leopard, local carving, foliage and sphere on back. Series A. Printer: TDLR.					
a. 28.8.1991;11.3.1992; 29.7.1992.			FV	20.00	70.00
b. 4.5.1994; 18.1.1995.			FV	FV	55.00

1993-97 ISSUE

261   100 COLONES

			VG	VF	UNC
28.9.1993. Black on m/c unpt. Like #258. Wmk: *BCCR-100* (repeated). Series H. Printer: ABNC.					
a. Issued note.			FV	0.75	5.00
s. Specimen. Ovpt: *MUESTRA.* 28.9.1993.			—		125.00

262   500 COLONES

			VG	VF	UNC
6.7.1994. Brown-orange, brown and olive-brown on m/c unpt. Similar to #255 but w/printing in wmk. area at l. Ascending size serial # at lower l. Series D. Printer: TDLR.					
a. Issued note.			FV	FV	12.50
s. Specimen. Ovpt: *MUESTRA.* 6.7.1994.			—		150.00

#263 *Deleted.* **See #259.**

#264-267 printer: F-CO.

---

264   1000 COLONES

			VG	VF	UNC
23.7.1997; 23.9.1998. Red on m/c unpt. Like #263 but w/ascending size serial # at upper r. Series D.					
a. Issued note.			FV	FV	15.00
s. Specimen. Ovpt. *MUESTRA.* 23.7.1997.			—		200.00

265   2000 COLONES

			VG	VF	UNC
30.7.1997 (1998). Brown-orange and dk. brown on m/c unpt. C. Picado T. at ctr. r. and as wmk., Coco Island in unpt. at ctr. Hammerhead shark at l., dolphin at lower ctr. on back. Series A.					
a. Issued note.			FV	FV	25.00
s. Specimen. Ovpt: *MUESTRA* or *MUESTRA SIN VALOR.*			—		250.00

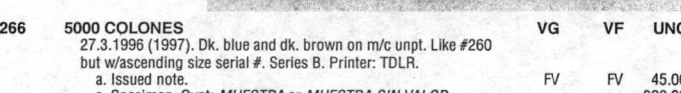

266   5000 COLONES

			VG	VF	UNC
27.3.1996 (1997). Dk. blue and dk. brown on m/c unpt. Like #260 but w/ascending size serial #. Series B. Printer: TDLR.					
a. Issued note.			FV	FV	45.00
s. Specimen. Ovpt: *MUESTRA* or *MUESTRA SIN VALOR.*			—		300.00

267   10,000 COLONES

			VG	VF	UNC
30.7.1997 (1998). Dk. blue and deep blue-green on m/c unpt. E. Gamboa A. at ctr. r. and as wmk., volcanoes in unpt. at ctr. Puma at upper ctr. on back. Series A.					
a. Issued note.			FV	FV	85.00
s. Specimen. Ovpt: *MUESTRA.* 30.7.1997.			—		500.00

1999 ISSUE

267A   1000 COLONES

		VG	VF	UNC
1999. M/c.		FV	FV	10.00

		VG	VF	UNC
268	**5000 COLONES**			
	24.2.1999. Dk. blue and dk. brown on m/c unpt. Like #266 but w/microprinting and security thread added. Series C.			
	a. Issued note.	FV	FV	35.00
	s. Specimen. Ovpt: *MUESTRA* or *MUESTRA SIN VALOR*.	—	—	400.00

2000 COMMEMORATIVE ISSUE

50th Anniversary Banco Central

#269-273 as #262-267 but w/commemorative ovpt. *50 BCCR ANIVERSARIO* added at lower r. 10,000 notes of each denomination were overprinted, but not all on uncirculated notes. All of #269-271 were sold as collectors' Items; however, approximately 1/3 of #272-73 were put into general circulation.

		VG	VF	UNC
272	**5000 COLONES**	VG	VF	UNC
	24.2.1999. Dk. blue and dk. brown on m/c unpt. As #266 but w/commemorative ovpt.	FV	FV	70.00
273	**10,000 COLONES**	VG	VF	UNC
	30.7.1997. Dk. blue and deep blue-green on m/c unpt. As #267 but w/commmemorative ovpt.			
	a. Issued note.	FV	FV	140.00
	s. Specimen.	—	—	

		VG	VF	UNC
269	**500 COLONES**	VG	VF	UNC
	6.7.1994. Brown-orange, brown on m/c unpt. As #262 but w/commemorative ovpt.	FV	FV	10.00

		VG	VF	UNC
270	**1000 COLONES**	VG	VF	UNC
	23.9.1998. Red on m/c unpt. As #264 but w/commemorative ovpt.	FV	FV	15.00

		VG	VF	UNC
271	**2000 COLONES**	VG	VF	UNC
	30.7.1997. Brown-orange and dk. brown on m/c unpt. As #265 but w/commemorative ovpt.	FV	FV	30.00

CROATIA

The Republic of Croatia (Hrvatska), formerly a federal republic of the Socialist Federal Republic of Yugoslavia, has an area of 21,829 sq. mi. (56,538 sq. km.) and a population of 4.48 million. Capital: Zagreb.

Countless archeological sites witness the rich history of the area dating from Greek and Roman times, continuing uninterruptedly through the Middle Ages until today. An Independent state under the first Count Borna (about 800 AD), Croatia was proclaimed a kingdom under Tomislav in 925. In 1102 the country joined the personal union with Hungary, and by 1527 all Croatian lands were included in the Habsburg kingdom, staying in the union until 1918, when Croatia became part of the Yugoslav kingdom together with Slovenia and Serbia. In the past, Croats played a leading role in the wars against the Turks, the Antemuralis Christianitatis, and were renown soldiers in the Napoleonic army. From 1941 to 1945 Croatia was an independent military puppet state; from 1945 to 1991 it was part of the Socialist state of Yugoslavia. Croatia proclaimed its independence from Yugoslavia on Oct. 8, 1991.

Local Serbian forces supported by the Yugoslav Federal Army had developed a military stronghold and proclaimed an independent "SRPSKE KRAJINA" state in the area around Knin, located in southern Croatia. In August 1995 Croat forces overran this political-military enclave.

MONETARY SYSTEM:
1 Dinar = 100 Para

REPUBLIC

REPUBLIKA HRVATSKA

REPUBLIC OF CROATIA

1991-93 ISSUE

#16-27 R. Boskovic at ctr., geometric calculations at upper r. (Printed in Sweden).

#16-22 vertical back with Zagreb cathedral and artistic rendition of city buildings behind.

16	**1 DINAR**	VG	VF	UNC
	8.10.1991. Dull orange-brown on m/c unpt. 4.5mm serial #. Wmk: Lozenges.			
	a. Issued note.	—	0.05	0.10
	s. Specimen.	—	—	20.00

17	**5 DINARA**	VG	VF	UNC
	8.10.1991. Pale purple on m/c unpt. 4mm serial #. Wmk: Lozenges.			
	a. Issued note.	—	0.05	0.15
	s. Specimen.	—	—	20.00

18	**10 DINARA**	VG	VF	UNC
	8.10.1991. Pale red-brown on m/c unpt. 4.5mm serial #. Wmk: Lozenges.			
	a. Issued note.	0.05	0.15	0.30
	s. Specimen.	—	—	20.00

19	**25 DINARA**	VG	VF	UNC
	8.10.1991. Dull purple on m/c unpt. Buff paper w/2.8mm serial #. Wmk: 5's in crossed wavy lines.			
	a. Issued note.	0.10	0.25	0.50
	b. Inverted wmk.	6.50	15.00	32.50
	s. Specimen.	—	—	30.00

Note: The wmk. paper actually used in the production for #19 was originally prepared for printing Sweden 5 Kroner, #51.

20	**100 DINARA**	VG	VF	UNC
	8.10.1991. Pale green on m/c unpt. W/o wmk.			
	a. Issued note.	0.10	0.40	1.00
	s. Specimen.	—	—	40.00

#21-26 wmk: Baptismal font.

21	**500 DINARA**	VG	VF	UNC
	8.10.1991. Lilac on m/c unpt.			
	a. Issued note.	0.50	2.00	9.00
	s. Specimen.	—	—	30.00

22	**1000 DINARA**	VG	VF	UNC
	8.10.1991. Pale blue-violet on m/c unpt.			
	a. Issued note.	0.60	2.50	10.00
	s. Specimen.	—	—	30.00

#23-26 statue of seated Glagolica *Mother Croatia* at ctr. on back.

23	**2000 DINARA**	VG	VF	UNC
	15.1.1992. Deep brown on m/c unpt.			
	a. Issued note.	0.35	1.50	10.00
	s. Specimen.	—	—	30.00

24	**5000 DINARA**	VG	VF	UNC
	15.1.1992. Dark gray on m/c unpt.			
	a. Issued note.	0.40	1.50	10.00
	s. Specimen.	—	—	30.00

25	**10,000 DINARA**	VG	VF	UNC
	15.1.1992. Olive-green on m/c unpt.			
	a. Issued note.	0.20	1.00	10.00
	s. Specimen.	—	—	30.00

26	**50,000 DINARA**	VG	VF	UNC
	30.5.1993. Deep red on m/c unpt.			
	a. Issued note.	0.05	0.15	0.50
	s. Specimen.	—	—	30.00

27	**100,000 DINARA**	VG	VF	UNC
	30.5.1993. Dk. blue-green on m/c unpt.			
	a. Issued note.	0.10	0.25	0.75
	s. Specimen.	—	—	30.00

NARODNA BANKA HRVATSKE

1993 ISSUE

#28-35 shield at upper l. ctr. Printer: G&D.

28	**5 KUNA**	VG	VF	UNC
	31.10.1993 (1994). Dk. green and green on m/c unpt. F. K. Frankopan and P. Zrinski at r. and as wmk. Fortress in Varazdin at l. ctr. on back.			
	a. Issued note.	FV	FV	3.00
	s. Specimen.	—	—	40.00
	x. Error w/o date or sign.	12.00	30.00	60.00

29	**10 KUNA**	VG	VF	UNC
	31.10.1993 (1994). Purple and violet on m/c unpt. J. Dobrila at r. and as wmk. Pula arena at l. ctr. on back.			
	a. Issued note.	FV	FV	7.00
	s. Specimen.	—	—	40.00

30	**20 KUNA**	VG	VF	UNC
	31.10.1993 (1994). Brown, red and violet on m/c unpt. J. Jelacic at r. and as wmk. Pottery dove and castle of Count Eltz in Vukovar at l. ctr. on back.			
	a. Issued note.	FV	FV	10.00
	s. Specimen.	—	—	40.00

31	**50 KUNA**	VG	VF	UNC
	31.10.1993 (1994). Dk. blue and blue-green on m/c unpt. I. Gundulic at r. and as wmk. Aerial view of old Dubrovnik at l. ctr. on back.			
	a. Issued note.	FV	FV	20.00
	s. Specimen.	—	—	40.00

32	**100 KUNA**	VG	VF	UNC
	31.10.1993 (1994). Red-brown and brown-orange on m/c unpt. I. Mazuranic at r. and as wmk. Plan of and church of St. Vitus in Rijeka at l. ctr. on back.			
	a. Issued note.	FV	FV	35.00
	s. Specimen.	—	—	40.00
	x. Error w/o serial #.	12.50	32.50	65.00

36	10 KUNA	VG	VF	UNC
	15.1.1995. Black and brown on green and m/c unpt. Like #29. Printer: G&D.			
	a. Issued note.	FV	FV	4.00
	s. Specimen.	—	—	40.00

HRVATSKA NARODNA BANKA

2001 ISSUE

#37-39 new bank name arrangement. Wmk. as portrait. Perfect registration devices and microprinting on each. Printer: G&D.

37	5 KUNA	VG	VF	UNC
	7.3.2001. M/c. Similar to #28.	FV	FV	2.50

38	10 KUNA	VG	VF	UNC
	7.3.2001. M/c. Similar to #29.	FV	FV	4.00

39	20 KUNA	VG	VF	UNC
	7.3.2001. M/c. Similar to #30.	FV	FV	9.00

33	200 KUNA	VG	VF	UNC
	31.10.1993 (1994). Dk. brown and brown on m/c unpt. S. Radic at r. and as wmk. Town command in Osijek at l. ctr. on back.			
	a. Issued note.	FV	FV	45.00
	s. Specimen.	—	—	40.00

34	500 KUNA	VG	VF	UNC
	31.10.1993 (1994). Dk. brown and olive-brown on m/c unpt. M. Marulic at r. and as wmk. Palace of Diocletian in Spit at l. ctr. on back.			
	a. Issued note.	FV	FV	95.00
	s. Specimen.	—	—	40.00

35	1000 KUNA	VG	VF	UNC
	31.10.1993 (1994). Dk. brown and purple on m/c unpt. A. Starcevic at r. and as wmk. Equestrian statue of Kg. Tomislav at l. ctr., Zagreb Cathedral at ctr. r. on back.			
	a. Issued note.	FV	FV	185.00
	s. Specimen.	—	—	40.00

1995 ISSUE

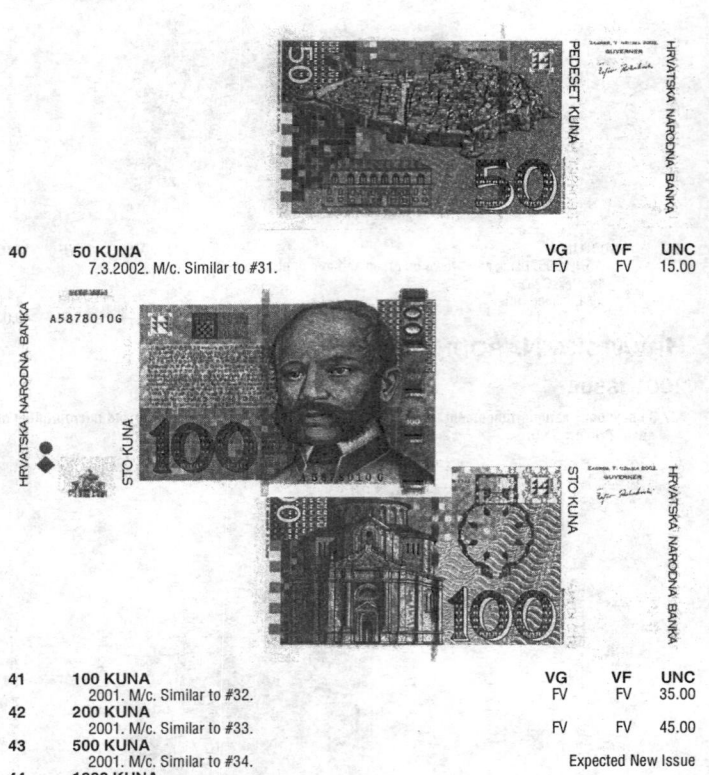

			VG	VF	UNC
40	**50 KUNA**		FV	FV	15.00
	7.3.2002. M/c. Similar to #31.				
41	**100 KUNA**		FV	FV	35.00
	2001. M/c. Similar to #32.				
42	**200 KUNA**		FV	FV	45.00
	2001. M/c. Similar to #33.				
43	**500 KUNA**				Expected New Issue
	2001. M/c. Similar to #34.				
44	**1000 KUNA**				Expected New Issue
	2001. M/c. Similar to #35.				

2004 COMMEMORATIVE ISSUE

#45, 10th Anniversary of the National Bank of Croatia.

			VG	VF	UNC
45	**10 KUNA**		FV	FV	4.00
	2004. Like #38 but large 10 added in wmk. area.				

COLLECTOR SERIES

REPUBLIC OF CROATIA

1998 ISSUE

		Issue Price	Mkt.	Value
CS1	**1991-93 1-100,000 DINARA**	38.50		—
	#16-27 w/matched serial #. (50,000).			
CS2	**1993 5-1000 KUNA**	385.00		—
	#28-36 w/matched serial #. (50,000).			

Note: #CS1 and CS2 are sold by the Croatian National Bank.

REGIONAL

РЕПУБЛИКА СРПСКА КРАЈИНА

REPUBLIKA SRPSKA KRAJINA

1991 ВРИЈЕДНОСНИ БОН ISSUE

#RA1-RA3 Serbian arms at upper l. Uniface.

RA1	**10,000 DINARA**		VG	VF	UNC
	1991.		—	120.00	450.00

RA2	**20,000 DINARA**		VG	VF	UNC
	1991.		—	60.00	350.00

RA3	**50,000 DINARA**		VG	VF	UNC
	1991.		—	80.00	450.00

РЕПУБЛИКА СРПСКА КРАЈИНА

REPUBLIKA SRPSKA KRAJINA

1992 ISSUE

#R1-R6 arms at l., numerals in heartshaped design below guilloche at ctr. r. Curved artistic design at l. ctr., arms at r. on back. Headings in Serbo-Croatian and Cyrillic.

#R1-R3 wmk: Young girl.

Replacement notes: #R1-R34, ZA prefix letters.

Note: For notes identical in color and design to #R1-R19 but differing only in text at top, sign. and place of issue Banja Luka, see Bosnia-Herzegovina #133-147.

R1	**10 DINARA**		VG	VF	UNC
	1992. Deep brown on orange and silver unpt. Back with ochre unpt.				
	a. Issued note.		0.25	1.00	4.00
	b. Specimen.		—	—	12.50

R2	**50 DINARA**		VG	VF	UNC
	1992. Gray on tan and yellow unpt.				
	a. Issued note.		0.30	1.25	5.00
	s. Specimen.		—	—	12.50

NOTICE

Readers with unlisted dates, signature varieties, etc. are invited to submit photocopies of their notes to: Standard Catalog of World Paper Money, 700 East State St. Iola, WI 54990-0001, E-Mail: george.cuhaj@fwpubs.com.

R7	10,000 DINARA	VG	VF	UNC
	1992. Deep gray-green on lt. blue and tan unpt.			
	a. Issued note.	0.50	2.50	20.00
	s. Specimen.	—	—	12.50

R3	100 DINARA	VG	VF	UNC
	1992. Blue-gray on lilac and silver unpt.			
	a. Issued note.	0.25	1.50	6.00
	s. Specimen.	—	—	12.50

R8	50,000 DINARA	VG	VF	UNC
	1992. Brown on pale orange and pale olive-green unpt. Wmk: Young boy.			
	a. Issued note.	0.75	4.00	35.00
	s. Specimen.	—	—	12.50

R4	500 DINARA	VG	VF	UNC
	1992. Blue-gray on pink and m/c unpt. Wmk: Young boy.			
	a. Issued note.	1.00	5.00	20.00
	s. Specimen.	—	—	12.50

R9	100,000 DINARA	VG	VF	UNC
	1993. Dull purple and brown on m/c unpt. Wmk: Young women.			
	a. Issued note.	0.50	2.75	22.50
	s. Specimen.	—	—	12.50

#R10-R12 wmk: Young girl.

R5	1000 DINARA	VG	VF	UNC
	1992. Deep gray on pink and tan unpt.			
	a. Issued note.	1.00	5.00	20.00
	s. Specimen.	—	—	12.50
R6	5000 DINARA			
	1992. Violet on lt. blue, pink and lilac unpt.			
	a. Issued note.	0.75	3.75	15.00
	s. Specimen.	—	—	12.50

НАРОДНА БАНКА РЕПУБЛИКЕ СРПСКЕ КРАЈИНЕ

NARODNA BANKA REPUBLIKE SRPSKE KRAJINE

NATIONAL BANK OF THE SERBIAN REPUBLIC - KRAJINA

1992-93 ISSUE

#R7-R12 replacement notes: Serial # prefix ZA.
#R7-R16 like #R1-R6.

R10	1 MILLION DINARA	VG	VF	UNC
	1993. Deep purple on m/c unpt.			
	a. Issued note.	1.25	4.00	37.50
	s. Specimen.	—	—	12.50

R11 **5 MILLION DINARA**

		VG	VF	UNC
1993. Dk. brown on orange and blue-gray unpt.				
a. Issued note.		0.50	2.00	7.00
s. Specimen.		—	—	12.50

R12 **10 MILLION DINARA**

		VG	VF	UNC
1993. Deep blue on pale olive-green and m/c unpt.				
a. Issued note.		0.25	1.25	5.00
s. Specimen.		—	—	12.50

#R13-R19 wmk: Greek design repeated. Replacement notes: Serial # prefix Z.

R13 **20 MILLION DINARA**

		VG	VF	UNC
1993. Olive-gray on orange and tan unpt.				
a. Issued note.		0.75	3.00	12.00
s. Specimen.		—	—	12.50

R14 **50 MILLION DINARA**

		VG	VF	UNC
1993. Brown-violet on pink and lt. gray unpt.				
a. Issued note.		0.50	2.50	8.00
s. Specimen.		—	—	12.50

R15 **100 MILLION DINARA**

		VG	VF	UNC
1993. Blue-black on lt. blue and gray unpt.				
a. Issued note.		0.25	1.25	5.00
s. Specimen.		—	—	12.50

R16 **500 MILLION DINARA**

		VG	VF	UNC
1993. Orange on lilac and yellow unpt.				
a. Issued note.		0.25	1.25	7.00
s. Specimen.		—	—	12.50

R17 **1 MILLIARD DINARA**

		VG	VF	UNC
1993. Dull brownish orange on pale blue and lt. orange unpt.				
a. Issued note.		0.25	1.25	7.00
s. Specimen.		—	—	12.50

R18 **5 MILLIARD DINARA**

		VG	VF	UNC
1993. Purple on lilac and gray unpt.				
a. Issued note.		0.50	2.50	12.00
s. Specimen.		—	—	12.50

R19 10 MILLIARD DINARA

	VG	VF	UNC
1993. Black on orange and pink unpt.			
a. Issued note.	0.75	3.00	12.50
s. Specimen.			12.50

1993 ISSUE

#R20-R27 Knin fortress on hill at l. ctr. Serbian arms at ctr. r. on back. Wmk: Greek design repeated.
Replacement notes: Serial # prefix Z.

R20 5000 DINARA

	VG	VF	UNC
1993. Red-violet and violet on blue-gray unpt.			
a. Issued note.	0.20	0.75	3.00
s. Specimen.	—	—	12.50

R21 50,000 DINARA

	VG	VF	UNC
1993. Brown, red and red-orange on ochre unpt.			
a. Issued note.	0.15	0.75	3.00
s. Specimen.	—	—	12.50

R22 100,000 DINARA

	VG	VF	UNC
1993. Violet and blue-gray on pink unpt.			
a. Issued note.	0.20	0.75	3.00
s. Specimen.	—	—	12.50

R23 500,000 DINARA

	VG	VF	UNC
1993. Brown and gray-green on pale green unpt.			
a. Issued note.	0.15	0.75	3.00
s. Specimen.	—	—	12.50

R24 5 MILLION DINARA

	VG	VF	UNC
1993. Orange and gray-green on pale orange unpt.			
a. Issued note.	0.15	0.75	3.00
s. Specimen.	—	—	12.50

R25 100 MILLION DINARA

	VG	VF	UNC
1993. Olive-brown and grayish green on lt. blue unpt.			
a. Issued note.	0.15	0.75	3.00
s. Specimen.	—	—	12.50

R26 500 MILLION DINARA

	VG	VF	UNC
1993. Chocolate brown and gray-green on pale olive-green unpt.			
a. Issued note.	0.20	0.75	3.00
s. Specimen.	—	—	12.50

R27 5 MILLIARD DINARA

	VG	VF	UNC
1993. Brown-orange and aqua on gray unpt.			
a. Issued note.	0.25	1.00	5.00
s. Specimen.	—	—	12.50

R28 **10 MILLIARD DINARA**

	VG	VF	UNC
1993. Purple and red on aqua unpt.			
a. Issued note.	0.30	1.25	7.00
s. Specimen.	—	—	12.50

R29 **50 MILLIARD DINARA**

	VG	VF	UNC
1993. Brown and olive-green on reddish brown unpt.			
a. Issued note.	0.25	1.00	5.00
s. Specimen.	—	—	12.50

1994 ISSUE

#R30-R34 like #R2-R29.

Replacement notes: Serial # prefix ZA.

R33 **1 MILLION DINARA**

	VG	VF	UNC
1994. Purple and aqua on lilac unpt.			
a. Issued note.	0.20	0.75	3.00
s. Specimen.	—	—	12.50

R30 **1000 DINARA**

	VG	VF	UNC
1994. Dk. brown and slate-gray on yellow-orange unpt.			
a. Issued note.	0.15	0.50	2.00
s. Specimen.	—	—	12.50

R34 **10 MILLION DINARA**

	VG	VF	UNC
1994. Gray and red-brown on pink unpt.			
a. Issued note.	0.30	1.25	6.50
s. Specimen.	—	—	12.50

R31 **10,000 DINARA**

	VG	VF	UNC
1994. Red-brown and dull purple on ochre unpt.			
a. Issued note.	0.15	0.50	2.00
s. Specimen.	—	—	12.50

R32 **500,000 DINARA**

	VG	VF	UNC
1994. Dk. brown and blue-gray on grayish green unpt.			
a. Issued note.	0.20	0.75	3.00
s. Specimen.	—	—	12.50

CUBA

Gulf of Mexico · U.S.A. · THE BAHAMAS · MEXICO · HAITI · JAMAICA · DOM. REP.

The Republic of Cuba, situated at the northern edge of the Caribbean Sea about 90 miles (145 km.) south of Florida, has an area of 44,218 sq. mi. (114,524 sq. km.) and a population of 11.2 million. Capital: Havana. The Cuban economy is based on the cultivation and refining of sugar, which provides 80 percent of export earnings.

Discovered by Columbus in 1492 and settled by Diego Velasquez in the early 1500s, Cuba remained a Spanish possession until 1898, except for a brief British occupancy in 1762-63. Cuban attempts to gain freedom were crushed, even while Spain was granting independence to its other American possessions. Ten years of warfare, 1868-78, between Spanish troops and Cuban rebels exacted guarantees of right which were never implemented. The final revolt, begun in 1895, evoked American sympathy, and with the aid of U.S. troops independence was proclaimed on May 20, 1902. Fulgencio Batista seized the government in 1952 and established a dictatorship. Opposition to Batista, led by Fidel Castro, drove him into exile on Jan. 1, 1959. A communist-type, 25-member collective leadership headed by Castro was inaugurated in March 1962.

MONETARY SYSTEM:
1 Peso = 100 Centavos
1 Peso Convertible = 1 U.S.A. Dollar, 1995-

REPUBLIC

BANCO NACIONAL DE CUBA

NATIONAL BANK OF CUBA

1961 ISSUE

#94-99 denomination at l. and r. Sign. titles: *PRESIDENTE DEL BANCO* at l., *MINISTRO DE HACIENDA* at r. Printer: STC-P (w/o imprint).

			VG	VF	UNC
94	**1 PESO**				
	1961-65. Olive-green on ochre unpt. Portr. J. Martí at ctr. F. Castro w/rebel soldiers entering Havana in 1959 on back.				
	a. 1961.		1.00	3.00	16.50
	b. 1964.		0.50	2.50	10.00
	c. 1965.		0.40	1.75	7.50
	s. As a. Specimen.		—	—	6.00

			VG	VF	UNC
95	**5 PESOS**				
	1961-65. Dull deep green on pink unpt. Portr. A. Maceo at ctr. Invasion of 1958 on back.				
	a. 1961.		1.00	3.75	18.50
	b. 1964.		0.75	3.00	12.50
	c. 1965.		0.50	2.50	10.00
	s. As a. Specimen.		—	—	6.00

			VG	VF	UNC
96	**10 PESOS**				
	1961-65. Brown on tan and yellow unpt. Portr. M. Gómez at ctr. Castro addressing crowd in 1960 on back.				
	a. 1961.		1.25	5.00	23.00
	b. 1964.		1.00	4.50	17.50
	c. 1965.		1.00	4.00	15.00
	s. As a. Specimen.		—	—	6.00

			VG	VF	UNC
97	**20 PESOS**				
	1961-65. Blue on pink unpt. Portr. C. Cienfuegos at ctr. Soldiers on the beach in 1956 on back.				
	a. 1961.		2.50	12.50	57.50
	b. 1964.		2.00	8.00	32.50
	c. 1965.		1.75	7.50	30.00
	s. As a. Specimen.		—	—	8.00
	x. U.S.A. counterfeit. Series F69; F70, 1961.		3.50	20.00	100.00

Note: Each member of the "Bay of Pigs" invasion force was reportedly issued one hundred each of #97x. They are found w/ or w/o added serial #.

			VG	VF	UNC
98	**50 PESOS**				
	1961. Purple on green unpt. Portr. C. García Iñiguez at ctr. Nationalization of international industries on back.				
	a. Issued note.		10.00	35.00	150.00
	s. Specimen.		—	—	10.00

99 **100 PESOS**
1961. Lt. red on orange unpt. Portr. C. M. de Céspedes at ctr.
Attack on Moncada in 1953 on back.

	VG	VF	UNC
a. Issued note.	25.00	60.00	210.00
s. Specimen.	—	—	10.00

Note: #98 and 99 were recalled shortly after release. A small hoard recently appeared in the marketplace.

1966 ISSUE

#100 and 101 denomination at l. and r. Sign titles: *PRESIDENTE DEL BANCO* at l. and r. Printer: STC-P (w/o imprint).

100 **1 PESO**
1966. Olive-green on ochre unpt. Like #94.

	VG	VF	UNC
a. Issued note.	0.25	1.25	5.00
s. Specimen.	—	—	6.00

101 **10 PESOS**
1966. Brown on tan and yellow unpt. Like #96.

	VG	VF	UNC
a. Issued note.	2.00	7.50	20.00
s. Specimen.	—	—	6.00

1967; 1971 ISSUE

#102-105 denomination at l. Sign. title: *PRESIDENTE DEL BANCO* at lower r. Printer: STC-P (w/o imprint).

102 **1 PESO**
1967-88. Olive-green on ochre unpt. Similar to #94.

	VG	VF	UNC
a. 1967-70; 1972.	0.25	1.00	5.00
b. 1978-85.	0.25	0.50	3.50
c. 1986.	0.25	0.50	3.00
d. 1988.	0.25	0.50	2.50
s. Specimen.	—	—	6.00

103 **5 PESOS**
1967-90. Dull deep green on pink unpt. Similar to #95.

	VG	VF	UNC
a. 1967-68.	0.25	1.00	15.00
b. 1970; 1972.	0.25	0.75	12.50
c. 1984-87.	0.25	0.75	10.00
d. 1988; 1990.	0.25	0.50	4.00
s. Specimen.	—	—	6.00

104 **10 PESOS**
1967-89. Brown on tan and yellow unpt. Similar to #96.

	VG	VF	UNC
a. 1967-71.	0.50	1.00	15.00
b. 1978.	0.50	1.00	15.00
c. 1983-84; 1986-87.	0.50	1.00	10.00
d. 1988-89.	0.50	1.00	10.00
s. Specimen.			

105 **20 PESOS**
1971-90. Blue on pink unpt. Similar to #97.

	VG	VF	UNC
a. 1971.	1.00	3.50	20.00
b. 1978.	1.00	3.50	20.00
c. 1983.	1.00	3.50	15.00
d. 1987-90.	1.00	3.50	10.00
s. Specimen.	—	—	6.00

1975 COMMEMORATIVE ISSUE

#106, 15th Anniversary Nationalization of Banking

106 **1 PESO**
1975. Olive on violet unpt. Portr. J. Martí at l., arms at r. Ship dockside on back.

	VG	VF	UNC
a. Issued note.	0.50	1.25	5.00
s. Specimen.	—	—	5.00

1983 ISSUE

107 **3 PESOS**
1983-89. Red on m/c unpt. Portr. E. "Che" Guevara at ctr. Back red on orange unpt.; "Che" cutting sugar cane at ctr.

	VG	VF	UNC
a. 1983-86.	0.50	1.00	5.00
b. 1988-89.	0.50	1.00	2.00
s. Specimen.	—	—	5.00

1990; 1991 ISSUE

Replacement notes: #108-112: *EX, DX, CX, BX, AX* series #, by denomination.

108   5 PESOS
1991. Deep green and blue on m/c unpt. A. Maceo at r. Conference between A. Maceo and Spanish Gen. A. Martínez Campos at Mangos de Baraguá in 1878 at l. ctr. on back. Wmk: J. Marti.

	VG	VF	UNC
a. Issued note.	0.25	0.50	1.25
s. Specimen.	—	—	5.00

109   10 PESOS
1991. Deep brown and olive-green on m/c unpt. M. Gómez at r. "Guerra de todo el Pueblo" at l. ctr. on back. Wmk: J. Marti.

	VG	VF	UNC
a. Issued note.	FV	FV	2.50
s. Specimen.	—	—	5.00

110   20 PESOS
1991. Blue-black and purple on m/c unpt. C. Cienfuegos at r. Agricultural scenes at l. ctr. on back. Wmk: Celia Sánchez Manduley.

	VG	VF	UNC
a. Issued note.	FV	FV	5.00
s. Specimen.	—	—	5.00

111   50 PESOS
1990. Deep violet and dk. green on m/c unpt. Arms at ctr. C. García Iñiguez at r. Center of Genetic Engineering and Biotechnology at l. ctr. on back. Wmk: Celia Sánchez Manduley.

	VG	VF	UNC
a. Issued note.	FV	FV	6.00
s. Specimen.	—	—	5.00

1995 ISSUE

#112 and 113 arms at upper ctr. r.

112   1 PESO
1995. Dull olive-green and orange on lt. blue and m/c unpt. J. Marti at l., arms at upper ctr. r. F. Castro w/rebel soldiers entering Havana in 1959 on back.

VG	VF	UNC
FV	FV	0.75

113   3 PESOS
1995. Red-brown, purple and green on m/c unpt. E. *Che* Guevara at l. Guevara cutting sugar cane on back.

VG	VF	UNC
FV	FV	1.50

1995 DUAL COMMEMORATIVE ISSUE

#114, 45th anniversary of central banking in Cuba and 100th of death of José Martí

114   1 PESO
1995. Black and olive-green on green and brown unpt. J. Marti at l., arms and commemorative text at ctr. r. Horseback riders at ctr., commemorative text and dates at l. on back. Specimen.

VG	VF	UNC
—	—	200.00

Note: It is reported that only 1300 examples of #114 were printed, only as specimens. The value is speculative.

BANCO CENTRAL DE CUBA

Established in 1997 to replace the Banco Nacional as issuer of coins and paper currency. #115 not assigned.

1997-98 ISSUE

116   5 PESOS
1997; 1998; 2000; 2001. Green on m/c unpt. A. Maceo at r. Back similar to #108.

	VG	VF	UNC
	FV	FV	1.25

117   10 PESOS
1997; 1998; 2001. Brown on m/c unpt. M. Gómez at r. Back similar to #109.

	VG	VF	UNC
	FV	FV	2.50

118   20 PESOS
1998; 2000; 2001. Blue-black and lt. blue on violet and blue unpt. C. Cienfuegos at r. Back similar to #110.

	VG	VF	UNC
	FV	FV	5.00

119   50 PESOS
1998; 1999; 2001. Lt. purple on green unpt. C. Garcia Iñiguez at r. ctr. Back similar to #111.

	VG	VF	UNC
	FV	FV	6.00

2000 COMMEMORATIVE ISSUE

#120, 50th anniversary of central banking in Cuba

120   100 PESOS
2000. Reddish brown on yellow unpt. Carlos Manuel de Cespedes at r., commemorative symbol and text at l. Martí and scene of Havana on back. Wmk: National heroine.

	VG	VF	UNC
	FV	FV	8.00

2001-02 ISSUE

121   1 PESO
2002. Black and olive green. J. Martí at r. Fidel Castro and victory parade scene on back.

	VG	VF	UNC
	FV	FV	1.25

121A   50 PESOS
2002.

	VG	VF	UNC
	FV	FV	7.50

121B   100 PESOS
2001. As #120 but w/o commemorative ovpt.

	VG	VF	UNC
	FV	FV	15.00

2003 FIRST COMMEMORATIVE ISSUE

150th Anniversary birth of Jose Martí.

122   1 PESO
2003. José Martí at r. Martí's birthplace on back.

	VG	VF	UNC
	FV	FV	1.50

2004 COMMEMORATIVE ISSUE

			VG	VF	UNC
123	3 PESOS	2004. Brown on tan unpt. E. "Che" Guevara at r. View of Guevara in sugar cane fields on back.	FV	FV	2.00

FOREIGN EXCHANGE CERTIFICATES

The Banco Nacional de Cuba issued four types of peso certificates in series A, B, C and D. The C and D series was issued in two designs and originally required hand issue date and sign. at redemption. Resembling traveler's checks.

BANCO NACIONAL DE CUBA

SERIES A

#FX1-FX5 red-violet. Arms at l. Various Spanish colonial fortresses on back.

			VG	VF	UNC
FX1	1 PESO	ND (1985). Orange and olive-green unpt. Castillo San Salvador de la Punta on back.	0.25	1.50	3.50

			VG	VF	UNC
FX2	3 PESOS	ND (1985). Orange and pink unpt. Castillo San Pedro de la Roca on back.	0.50	3.50	7.00
FX3	5 PESOS	ND (1985). Orange and blue-green unpt. Castillo de los Tres Reyes del Morro on back.	1.00	5.00	10.00
FX4	10 PESOS	ND (1985). Orange and brown unpt. Castillo Nuestra Señora de Los Angeles de Jagua on back.	2.00	9.00	17.50

			VG	VF	UNC
FX5	20 PESOS	ND (1985). Orange and blue unpt. Castillo de la Real Fuerza on back.	4.00	20.00	40.00

SERIES B

#FX6-FX10 dk. green. Arms at l. Various Spanish colonial fortresses on back.

			VG	VF	UNC
FX6	1 PESO	ND (1985). Lt. green and olive-brown unpt. Back like #FX1.	0.25	1.00	2.50
FX7	5 PESOS	ND (1985). Lt. green and blue-green unpt. Back like #FX3.	1.00	5.00	20.00
FX8	10 PESOS	ND (1985). Lt. green and brown unpt. Back like #FX4.	2.00	10.00	30.00
FX9	20 PESOS	ND (1985). Lt. green and blue unpt. Back like #FX5.	4.00	20.00	40.00

			VG	VF	UNC
FX10	50 PESOS	ND (1985). Lt. green and dull violet unpt. Castillo de la Chorrera on back.	7.50	20.00	70.00

SERIES C FIRST ISSUE

Note: Large quantities were sold into the numismatic market.

#FX11-18 pale blue. Arms at l.

			VG	VF	UNC
FX11	1 PESO	ND. Lt. blue and lt. red-brown unpt.	0.10	0.25	1.50

			VG	VF	UNC
FX12	3 PESOS	ND. Lt. blue and violet unpt.	0.10	0.30	1.75
FX13	5 PESOS	ND. Lt. blue and lt. olive unpt.	0.10	0.50	2.50
FX14	10 PESOS	ND. Lt. blue and lilac unpt.	0.10	0.40	2.25
FX15	20 PESOS	ND. Lt. blue and tan unpt.	0.15	0.50	3.00
FX16	50 PESOS	ND. Lt. blue and rose unpt.	0.20	0.60	3.50
FX17	100 PESOS	ND. Lt. blue and ochre unpt.	0.20	0.75	4.00
FX18	500 PESOS	ND. Lt. blue and tan unpt.	0.20	5.00	20.00

SERIES C SECOND ISSUE

#FX19-FX26 blue-violet. Similar to #FX11-FX18.

			VG	VF	UNC
FX19	1 PESO	ND.	0.15	0.50	1.25
FX20	3 PESOS	ND. Lt. blue and red unpt.	0.15	0.50	1.25
FX21	5 PESOS	ND. Lt. blue and pale olive-green unpt.	0.25	1.00	2.00

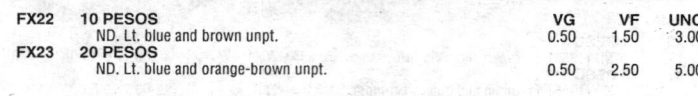

FX22	10 PESOS	VG	VF	UNC
	ND. Lt. blue and brown unpt.	0.50	1.50	3.00
FX23	20 PESOS			
	ND. Lt. blue and orange-brown unpt.	0.50	2.50	5.00

FX24	50 PESOS	VG	VF	UNC
	ND. Lt. blue and violet unpt.	0.50	1.50	5.00
FX25	100 PESOS			
	ND. Lt. blue and gray unpt.	0.50	1.50	5.00
FX26	500 PESOS			
	ND.	2.00	5.00	25.00

SERIES D FIRST ISSUE

#FX27-31 pale red-brown. Arms at l.

FX27	1 PESO	VG	VF	UNC
	ND. Lt. orange and orange-brown unpt.	0.25	1.50	3.50
FX28	3 PESOS			
	ND. Lt. orange and pale blue unpt.	0.50	3.00	7.00

FX29	5 PESOS	VG	VF	UNC
	ND. Lt. orange and lt. green unpt.	1.00	5.00	10.00

FX30	10 PESOS	VG	VF	UNC
	ND. Lt. orange and lilac unpt.	2.00	10.00	17.50

FX31	20 PESOS	VG	VF	UNC
	ND. Lt. orange and ochre unpt.	4.00	20.00	32.50

SERIES D SECOND ISSUE

#FX32-FX36 dk. brown. Similar to #FX19-FX23. W/ or w/o various handstamps *ESPACIO EN BLANCO INUTILIZADO* or *ESPACIO INUTILIZADO* on back.

FX32	1 PESO	VG	VF	UNC
	ND. Tan and pale olive-green unpt.	0.10	0.30	0.60
FX33	3 PESOS			
	ND. Tan and red unpt.	0.15	0.60	1.25
FX34	5 PESOS			
	ND. Tan and green unpt.	0.25	1.00	2.00
FX35	10 PESOS			
	ND. Tan and orange unpt.	0.50	2.00	4.00
FX36	20 PESOS			
	ND. Tan and blue-gray unpt.	1.00	4.00	8.00

1994 PESOS CONVERTIBLES ISSUE

#FX37-FX43 arms at ctr. on back. Wmk: J. Martí.

FX37	1 PESO CONVERTIBLE	VG	VF	UNC
	1994. Orange, brown and olive-green on m/c unpt. J. Martí monument at r. Wmk: J. Marti.	FV	FV	2.50

FX38 3 PESOS CONVERTIBLES
1994. Dull red, deep blue-green and brown on m/c unpt. E. "Che" Guevara monument at r.

VG	VF	UNC
FV	FV	7.00

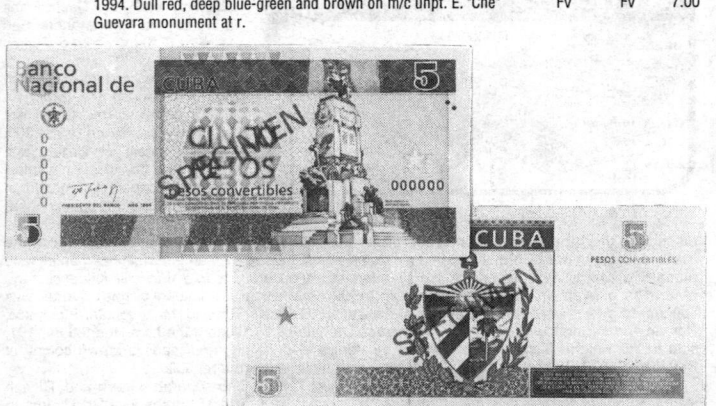

FX39 5 PESOS CONVERTIBLES
1994. Dk. green, orange and blue-black on m/c unpt. A. Maceo monument at r.

VG	VF	UNC
FV	FV	10.00

FX40 10 PESOS CONVERTIBLES
1994. Brown, yellow-green and purple on m/c unpt. M. Gómez monument at r.

VG	VF	UNC
FV	FV	17.50

FX41 20 PESOS CONVERTIBLES
1994. Blue, red and tan on m/c unpt. C. Cienfuegos monument at r.

VG	VF	UNC
FV	FV	35.00

FX42 50 PESOS CONVERTIBLES
1994. Purple, brown and orange on m/c unpt. C. García monument at r.

VG	VF	UNC
FV	FV	70.00

FX43 100 PESOS CONVERTIBLES
1994. Red-violet, brown-orange and purple on m/c unpt. C. Manuel de Céspedes monument at r.

VG	VF	UNC
FV	FV	150.00

BANCO CENTRAL DE CUBA

2004 PESOS CONVERTIBLES ISSUE

FX44 5 PESOS CONVERTIBLES
2004.

VG	VF	UNC
FV	FV	10.00

FX45 10 PESOS CONVERTIBLES
2004.

VG	VF	UNC
FV	FV	17.50

COMPANION CATALOGS
Volume 1 - Specialized Issues
Volume 2 - General Issues, 1368-1960
The Companion Catalogs in the Standard Catalog of World Paper Money series include a volume on Specialized Issues of the World - listed are those banknotes which were issued on a limited circulation basis rather than the central monetary authority note issues detailed in this work. The Specialized volume is currently in its 10th edition, and it is updated periodically. The General Issues volume lists national notes dated and issued, before 1960. The 11th edition is due out in Fall 2006. Inquiries about the availability of both these volumes are invited to contact Book Department, Krause Publications, 700 East State Street, Iola, WI 54990-0001 or you may call 1-800-258-0929 or www.fwpubs.com.

COLLECTOR SERIES

BANCO NACIONAL DE CUBA

1961-1995 ISSUES

The Banco Nacional de Cuba had been selling specimen notes regularly of the 1961-1989 issues. Specimen notes dated 1961-66 have normal block # and serial # while notes from 1967 to date all have normal block # and all zero serial #.

		Issue Price	Mkt.	Value
CS1	1961 1-100 PESOS			
	Ovpt: *SPECIMEN* on #94a-97a, 98, 99.	—		110.00
CS2	1964 1-20 PESOS			
	Ovpt: *SPECIMEN* on #94b-97b.	—		20.00
CS3	1965 1-20 PESOS			
	Ovpt: *SPECIMEN* on #94c-97c.	—		14.00
CS4	1966 1, 10 PESOS			
	Ovpt: *SPECIMEN* on #100, 101.	—		7.00
CS5	1967 1-10 PESOS			
	Ovpt: *SPECIMEN* on #102a-104a.	—		10.00
CS6	1968 1-10 PESOS			
	Ovpt: *SPECIMEN* on #102a-104a.	—		10.00
CS7	1969 1, 10 PESOS			
	Ovpt: *SPECIMEN* on #102a, 104a.	—		7.00
CS8	1970 1-10 PESOS			
	Ovpt: *SPECIMEN* on #102a, 103b, 104a.	—		7.00
CS9	1971 10, 20 PESOS			
	Ovpt: *SPECIMEN* on #104a, 105a.	—		8.00
CS10	1972 1, 5 PESOS			
	Ovpt: *SPECIMEN* on #102a, 103b.	—		7.00
CS11	1975 1 PESO			
	Ovpt: *SPECIMEN* on #106.	—		10.00
CS12	1978 1, 10, 20 PESOS			
	Ovpt: *ESPECIMEN* on #102b, 104b, 105b.	—		11.00
CS13	1979 1 PESO			
	Ovpt: *ESPECIMEN* on #102b.	—		3.00
CS14	1980 1 PESO			
	Ovpt: *ESPECIMEN* on #102b.	—		3.00
CS15	1981 1 PESO			
	Ovpt: *ESPECIMEN* on #102b.	—		3.00
CS16	1982 1 PESO			
	Ovpt: *MUESTRA* on #102b.	—		3.00
CS17	1983 3, 10, 20 PESOS			
	Ovpt: *MUESTRA* on #104c, 105c, 107a.	—		12.00
CS18	1984 3, 5, 10 PESOS			
	Ovpt: *MUESTRA* on #103c, 104c, 107a.	—		12.00
CS19	1985 1, 3, 5 PESOS			
	Ovpt: *MUESTRA* on #102b, 103c, 107a.	—		12.00
CS20	1986 1-10 PESOS			
	Ovpt: *MUESTRA* on #102b, 103c, 104c, 107a.	—		12.50
CS21	1987 5, 10, 20 PESOS			
	Ovpt: *MUESTRA* on #103c-105c.	—		12.00
CS22	1988 1-20 PESOS			
	Ovpt: *MUESTRA* on #102c, 103d-105d, 107b.	—		12.50
CS23	1989 3, 20 PESOS			
	Ovpt: *MUESTRA* on #105d, 107b.	—		7.00
CS24	1990 5, 20, 50 PESOS			
	Ovpt: *SPECIMEN* on #103d, 105d, 111.	—		10.00
CS25	1991 5, 10, 20 PESOS			
	Ovpt: *SPECIMEN* on #108-110.	—		10.00
CS26	1994 1-100 PESO CONVERTIBLES			
	Ovpt: *MUESTRA* on FX37-FX43.	—		60.00
CS27	1995 1, 3 PESOS			
	Ovpt: *MUESTRA* on #112 and 113.	—		5.00

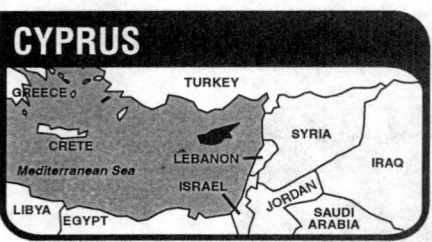

The Republic of Cyprus, a member of the European Commonwealth and Council, lies in the eastern Mediterranean Sea 44 miles (71 km.) south of Turkey and 60 miles (97 km.) west of Syria. It is the third largest island in the Mediterranean Sea, having an area if 3,572 sq. mi. (9,251 sq. km.) and a population of 757,000. Capital: Nicosia. Agriculture and mining are the chief industries. Asbestos, copper, citrus fruit, iron pyrites and potatoes are exported.

The importance of Cyprus dates from the Bronze Age when it was desired as a principal souce of copper (from which the island derived its name) and as a strategic trading center. Its role as an international marketplace made it a prime disseminator of the then prevalent cultures, a role that still influences the civilization of Western man. Because of its fortuitous position and influential role, Cyprus was conquered by a succession of empires; the Assyrian, Egyptian, Persian, Macedonian, Ptolemaic, Roman and Byzantine. It was taken from Isaac Comnenus by Richard the Lion-Hearted in 1191, sold to the Knights Templars, conquered by Venice and Turkey, and made a crown colony of Britain in 1925. Finally on Aug. 16, 1960, it became an independent republic.

In 1964, the ethnic Turks, who favor partition of Cyprus into separate Greek and Turkish states, withdrew from active participation in the government. Turkish forces invaded Cyprus in 1974 and gained control of 40 percent of the island. In 1975, Turkish Cypriots proclaimed their own Federated state in northern Cyprus. The UN held numerous discussions from 1985-92, without any results towards unification.

The president is Chief of State and Head of Government.

MONETARY SYSTEM:
- 1 Shilling = 9 Piastres
- 1 Pound = 20 Shillings to 1963
- 1 Shilling = 50 Mils
- 1 Pound = 1000 Mils, 1963-83
- 1 Pound = 100 Cents, 1983-

DEMOCRATIC REPUBLIC

ΚΥΠΡΙΑΚΗ ΔΗΜΟΚΡΑΤΙΑ

KIBRIS CUMHURIYETI

REPUBLIC OF CYPRUS

1961 ISSUE

#37-40 arms at r., map at lower r. Wmk: Eagle's head. Printer: BWC (w/o imprint).

		VG	VF	UNC
37	**250 MILS**			
	1.12.1961. Blue on m/c unpt. Fruit at l. Mine on back.			
	a. Issued note.	3.00	15.00	85.00
	s. Specimen.	—	—	55.00
38	**500 MILS**			
	1.12.1961. Green on m/c unpt. Mountain road lined w/trees on back.			
	a. Issued note.	5.00	40.00	210.00
	s. Specimen.	—	—	55.00

		VG	VF	UNC
39	**1 POUND**			
	1.12.1961. Brown on m/c unpt. Viaduct and pillars on back.			
	a. Issued note.	10.00	30.00	120.00
	s. Specimen.	—	—	55.00

		VG	VF	UNC
40	**5 POUNDS** 1.12.1961. Dk. green on m/c unpt. Embroidery and floral design on back.			
	a. Issued note.	15.00	55.00	250.00
	s. Specimen.	—	—	55.00

ΚΕΝΤΡΙΚΗ ΤΡΑΠΕΖΑ ΤΗΣ ΚΥΠΡΟΥ

KIBRIS MERKEZ BANKASI

CENTRAL BANK OF CYPRUS

1964-66 ISSUE

#41-44 like #37-40. Various date and sign. varieties.

		VG	VF	UNC
44	**5 POUNDS** 1966-76. Blue on m/c unpt. Like #40.			
	a. 1.8.1966; 1.9.1967; 1.12.1969.	17.50	35.00	175.00
	b. 1.6.1972; 1.11.1972; 1.5.1973.	12.50FV	30.00	110.00
	c. 1.6.1974; 1.7.1975; 1.8.1976.	12.50FV	30.00	105.00

1977-82 ISSUE

#45-48 wmk: Moufflon (ram's) head.

		VG	VF	UNC
41	**250 MILS** 1964-82. Like #37.			
	a. 1.12.1964-1.12.1969; 1.9.1971.	2.00	8.00	55.00
	b. 1.3.1971; 1.6.1972; 1.5.1973; 1.6.1974.	2.00	7.50	42.50
	c. 1.7.1975-1.6.1982.	2.00	6.00	37.50
	ct. Color trial. Brown on m/c unpt.	—	—	200.00
	s. Specimen.	—	—	125.00

		VG	VF	UNC
45	**500 MILS** 1.6.1982. Lt. brown on green and m/c unpt. Woman seated at r., arms at top l. ctr. Yermasoyia Dam on back. Printer: BWC (w/o imprint).			
	a. Issued note.	1.00	7.50	50.00
	s. Specimen.	—	—	115.00

		VG	VF	UNC
42	**500 MILS** 1964-79. Like #38.			
	a. 1.12.1964-1.6.1972.	3.50	10.00	95.00
	b. 1.5.1973; 1.6.1974; 1.7.1975; 1.8.1976.	2.00	7.50	80.00
	c. 1.6.1979; 1.9.1979.	2.00	6.00	60.00
	s. Specimen.	—	—	125.00

		VG	VF	UNC
46	**1 POUND** 1.6.1979. Dk. brown and brown on m/c unpt. Mosaic of nymph Acme at r., arms at top l. ctr. Bellapais Abbey on back. Printer: TDLR (w/o imprint).	2.00	7.50	25.00

		VG	VF	UNC
43	**1 POUND** 1966-78. Like #39.			
	a. 1.8.1966-1.6.1972.	3.50	12.50	90.00
	b. 1.11.1972; 1.5.1973; 1.6.1974; 1.7.1975.	3.50	8.00	75.00
	c. 1.8.1976; 1.5.1978.	3.50	7.50	70.00
	s. Specimen.	—	—	

47 5 POUNDS

	VG	VF	UNC
1.6.1979. Violet on m/c unpt. Limestone head from Hellenistic period at l., arms at upper ctr. r. Ancient Theater at Salamis on back. Printer: TDLR (w/o imprint).	10.00	17.50	67.50

48 10 POUNDS

	VG	VF	UNC
1977-85. Dk. green and blue-black on m/c unpt. Archaic bust at l., arms at r. Two Cyprus warblers on back. Printer: BWC (w/o imprint).			
a. 1.4.1977; 1.5.1978; 1.6.1979.	20.00	35.00	135.00
b. 1.7.1980; 1.10.1981; 1.6.1982; 1.9.1983; 1.6.1985.	20.00	25.00	105.00

1982-87 ISSUE

#49-51 wmk: Moufflon (ram's) head.

49 50 CENTS

	VG	VF	UNC
1.10.1983; 1.12.1984. Brown and m/c. Similar to #45. Printer: BWC (w/o imprint).			
a. Issued note.	1.00	4.00	17.50
s. Specimen.	—	—	115.00

50 1 POUND

	VG	VF	UNC
1.2.1982; 1.11.1982; 1.3.1984; 1.11.1985. Dk. brown and m/c. Like #46 but bank name in outlined (white) letters by dk. unpt. Printer: TDLR (w/o imprint).	1.00	5.00	22.50

51 10 POUNDS

	VG	VF	UNC
1.4.1987; 1.10.1988. Dk. green and blue-black on m/c unpt. Similar to #48 but w/date above at l. of modified arms on r. Printer: TDLR (w/o imprint).	FV	25.00	100.00

1987-92 ISSUE

#53-56 enhanced designs w/micro-printing. Wmk: Moufflon (ram's) head.

52 50 CENTS

	VG	VF	UNC
1.4.1987; 1.10.1988; 1.11.1989. Like #49 but w/bank name in micro-printing alternately in Greek and Turkish just below upper frame. Printer: BABN (w/o imprint).	FV	2.50	11.00

53 1 POUND

	VG	VF	UNC
1987-96. Like #50 but w/bank name in unbroken line of micro-printing with Greek at left and Turkish at right just below upper frame.			
a. W/o lt. beige unpt. color on back. Micro-print line under dark bar at top. Printer: TDLR (w/o imprint). 1.4.1987; 1.10.1988; 1.11.1989.	FV	FV	22.50
b. Lt. beige color added to ctr. unpt. on back for security. Printer: F-CO (w/o imprint). 1.11.1989; 1.2.1992.	FV	FV	12.50
c. Dot added near upper l. corner. 1.3.1993; 1.3.1994.	FV	FV	10.00
d. 1.9.1995.	FV	FV	9.00
e. 1.10.1996.	FV	3.00	17.50

54 **5 POUNDS**
1990; 1995. Violet on m/c unpt. Like #47 but w/line of microprinting added within bank titles. Printer: TDLR (w/o imprint).

	VG	VF	UNC
a. 1.10.1990.	FV	FV	57.50
b. 1.9.1995.	FV	FV	52.50

55 **10 POUNDS**
1989-95. Dk. green and blue-black on m/c unpt. Similar to #51 but
w/enhanced security features. Printer: TDLR (w/o imprint).

	VG	VF	UNC
a. 1.11.1989; 1.10.1990.	FV	FV	95.00
b. 1.2.1992.	FV	FV	90.00
c. 1.6.1994.	FV	FV	85.00
d. 1.9.1995.	FV	FV	70.00

56 **20 POUNDS**
1992; 1993. Deep blue on m/c unpt. Bust of Aphrodite at l., arms
at upper ctr., ancient bird (pottery art) at r. Kyrenia boat at ctr.,
ancient pottery jugs at lower r. on back. Printer: TDLR (w/o
imprint).

	VG	VF	UNC
a. Error: No dot over 'i' in *YIRMI LIRA*. 1.2.1992.	FV	4FV	160.00
b. Corrected: *YiRMi LiRA*. 1.3.1993.	FV	35.00	120.00

1997 FIRST ISSUE

#57-60 arms at upper ctr. Wmk: Bust of Aphrodite. Thin security thread. Printer: F-CO (w/o imprint).

57 **1 POUND**
1.2.1997. Brown on pink and m/c unpt. Cypriot girl at l. Handcrafts
and Kato Drys village scene in background on back.

VG	VF	UNC
FV	FV	9.00

58 **5 POUNDS**
1.2.1997. Purple and violet on m/c unpt. Archaic limestone head of
young man at l. Peristerona church and Turkish mosque on back.

VG	VF	UNC
FV	FV	35.00

59 **10 POUNDS**
1.2.1997. Olive-green and blue-green on m/c unpt. Marble head of
Artemis at l. Ruppell's warbler green turtle, butterfly, moufflon,
tulip and cyclamen plants on back.

VG	VF	UNC
FV	FV	60.00

1997-2001 ISSUE

#60-63 arms at upper ctr. Wmk: Bust of Aphrodite. Wide security foil.

60　1 POUND
1.10.1997; 1.12.1998; 1.2.2001; 1.4.2004. Brown on lt. tan and m/c unpt. Like #57 but w/slightly modified colors. Printer: F-CO (w/o imprint).

		VG	VF	UNC
a.	1.10.1997.	FV	FV	10.00
b.	1.12.1998.	FV	FV	9.00
c.	1.2.2001.	FV	FV	8.00
d.	1.4.2004. Sign. Chr. Christodoulou.	FV	FV	8.00

61　5 POUNDS
1.2.2001; 1.9.2003. Purple and violet on m/c unpt. Like #58.

		VG	VF	UNC
a.	1.2.2001. Printer: F-CO (w/o imprint).	FV	FV	30.00
b.	1.9.2003. Printer: TDLR (w/o imprint). Sign. Chr. Christodoulou.	FV	FV	30.00

62　10 POUNDS
1.10.1997; 1.12.1998; 1.2.2001; 1.9.2003. Olive-green and blue-green on m/c unpt. Like #59.

		VG	VF	UNC
a.	1.10.1997. Printer: F-CO (w/o imprint).	FV	FV	60.00
b.	1.12.1998. Printer: F-CO (w/o imprint).	FV	FV	55.00
c.	1.2.2001. Printer: F-CO (w/o imprint).	FV	FV	52.50
d.	1.9.2003. Printer: TDLR (w/o imprint). Sign. Chr. Christodoulou.	FV	FV	50.00
e.	1.4.2005.	FV	FV	50.00

63　20 POUNDS
1.10.1997; 1.10.2001; 1.4.2004. Deep blue on m/c unpt. Similar to #56b. Printer: TDLR (w/o imprint).

		VG	VF	UNC
a.	1.10.1997.	FV	FV	100.00
b.	1.10.2001.	FV	FV	95.00
c.	1.4.2004. Sign. Chr. Christodoulou.	FV	FV	90.00

CZECHOSLOVAKIA

The Republic of Czechoslovakia, located in central Europe, had an area of 49,365 sq. mi. (127,859 sq. km.). Capital: Prague (Praha). Industrial production in the cities and agriculture and livestock in the rural areas were the chief occupations.

The Czech lands to the west were united with the Slovak to form the Czechoslovak Republic on October 28, 1918 upon the dissolution of the Austrian-Hungarian Empire. Tomas G. Masaryk was the first president. In the 1930s Hitlet provoked Czechoslovakia's German minority in the Sudetenland to agitate for autonomy. The territory was broken up for the benefit of Germany, Poland and Hungary by the Munich agreement signed by the United Kingdom, France, Germany and Italy on September 29, 1938. On March 15, 1939, Germany invaded Czechoslovakia and incorporated the Czech lands into the Third Reich as the "Protectorate of Bohemia and Moravia." eastern Slovakia, was constituted as a republic under Nazi infulence. A government-in-exile was set up in London in 1940. The Soviet and American forces liberated the area by May 1945. After World War II the physical integrity and independence of Czechoslovakia was re-established, while bringing it within the Russian sphere of influence. On February 23-25, 1948, the Communists seized control of the government in a *coup d'etat*, and adopted a constitution making the country a "people's republic." A new constitution adopted June 11, 1960, converted the country into a "socialist republic." Communist infulence increased steadily while pressure for liberalization culminated in the overthrow of the Stalinist leader Antonçin Novotny and his associates in January, 1968. The Communist Party then introduced far reaching reforms which received warnings from Moscow, followed by occupation of Warsaw Pact forces on August 21, 1968 resulting in stationing of Soviet troops. Student demonstrations for reform began in Prague on November 17, 1989. The Federal Assembly abolished the Communist Party's sole right to govern. In December, 1989, communism was overthrown. In January, 1990 the Czech and Slovak Federal Republic (CSFR) was formed. The movement for a democratic Slovakia was apparent in the June 1992 elections with the Slovak National Council adopting a declaration of sovereignty. The CSFR was disolved on December 31, 1992, and both new republics came into being on January 1, 1993.

See the Czech Republic and Slovakia sections for additional listings.

MONETARY SYSTEM:
1 Koruna = 100 Haleru

SPECIMEN NOTES:
Large quantities of specimens were made available to collectors. Notes issued after 1945 are distinguished by a perforation consisting of three small holes or a letter S (for Solvakia). Since the difference in value between issued notes and specimen notes is frequently very great, both types of notes are valued. Earlier issues recalled from circulation were perforated: *SPECIMEN* or *NEPLATNE* or with a letter *S* for collectors. Caution should be exercised while examining notes as examples of perforated notes having the holes filled in are known.

NOTE AVAILABILITY:
The Czech National Bank in 1997 made available to collectors uncirculated examples of #78-98, as a full set or in issue groups. As the notes were demonetized they had no cancellation holes nor were overprinted. They have regular serial #'s.

SOCIALIST REPUBLIC

CESKOSLOVENSKÁ SOCIALISTICKÁ REPUBLIKA

CZECHOSLOVAK SOCIALIST REPUBLI C

1961 ISSUE

#81 and 82 wmk: Star in circle, repeated. Printer: STC-P.

81　3 KORUNY
1961. Blue on blue-green unpt. Large 3 at ctr. and upper corners. Socialist arms at ctr. on back.

		VG	VF	UNC
a.	Issued note. Serial # prefix 2.5mm in height.	0.20	0.50	2.00
b.	Issued note. Serial # prefix 3mm in height.	0.20	0.50	2.00
s.	Perforated w/3 holes or *SPECIMEN*.	—	0.50	2.00

82　5 KORUN
1961. Dull black on pale green unpt. Text in frame. Socialist arms at ctr. on back.

		VG	VF	UNC
a.	Issued note. Serial # prefix 2.5mm in height.	0.20	0.50	2.00
b.	Issued note. Serial # prefix 3mm in height.	0.20	0.50	2.00
s.	Perforated w/3 holes or *SPECIMEN*.	—	0.50	2.00

STÁTNÍ BANKA ČESKOSLOVENSKÁ

CZECHOSLOVAK STATE BANK

1960-64 ISSUE

#88-98 printer: STC-Prague.

#88-91 Printed by wet photogravure or dry photogravure (wet printing has smaller image).

91	100 KORUN	VG	VF	UNC
	1961. Deep green on m/c unpt. Factory at lower l., farm couple at r. Charles Bridge and Hradcany in Prague on back.			
	a. Wmk: Star within linden leaf, repeated. Series prefix: B01-40; C; D (wet printing).	2.50	7.50	20.00
	b. As a. Series prefix: B41-99; P; R; T; Z; X01-24 (dry printing).	1.00	3.00	10.00
	c. Reissue wmk: Multiple stars and linden leaves. Series prefix: X25-96; G; M. (1990-92).	0.50	1.00	7.50

Note: #91b or #91c w/added *C-100* adhesive stamp, see Czech Republic. With *SLOVENSKÁ REPUBLIKA* adhesive stamp, see Slovakia.

1970; 1973 ISSUE

92	20 KORUN	VG	VF	UNC
	1970 (1971). Blue on lt. blue and m/c unpt. Arms at ctr., Jan Zizka at r. Husite soldiers on back. Series prefix: F, H, L, M.	0.25	1.00	2.50

88	10 KORUN	VG	VF	UNC
	1960. Brown on m/c unpt. 2 girls w/flowers at r. Orava Dam on back.			
	a. Series prefix: H; F (wet printing).	2.00	8.00	15.00
	b. Series prefixes: E, J, L, M, S, X (dry printing)	0.10	0.75	3.00
	s. Specimen.	—	—	—

89	25 KORUN	VG	VF	UNC
	1961 (1962). Blue-black on lt. blue unpt. Similar to #87 but different arms.			
	a. Series prefix: E. (wet printing).	5.00	15.00	40.00
	b. Series prefix: Q. (dry printing)	0.75	1.75	7.50
	s. Perforated: *SPECIMEN.*	—	—	2.00

93	500 KORUN	VG	VF	UNC
	1973. Deep brown-violet and m/c. Soldiers at r. Medieval shield at lower ctr., mountain fortress ruins at Devin at r. on back. Series prefix: U, W, Z.	2.00	10.00	30.00

Note: For #93 w/additional "D-500" adhesive stamp, see Czech Republic. *SLOVENSKÁ REPUBLIKA* adhesive stamp, see Slovakia.

1985-89 ISSUE

90	50 KORUN	VG	VF	UNC
	1964 (1965). Red-brown. Arms at l., Russian soldier and partisan at r. Slovnaft refinery in Bratislava on back.			
	a. Series prefix: K. (wet printing).	2.00	5.00	15.00
	b. Series prefix: A; N; G; J (dry printing).	1.00	2.50	7.50

94	10 KORUN	VG	VF	UNC
	1986. Deep brown on blue and m/c unpt. Pavol Orszag-Hviezdoslav at r. Bird at lower l., view of Orava mountains on back. Series prefix: J, P, V.	0.20	0.50	2.00

95   20 KORUN

	VG	VF	UNC
1988. Blue and m/c. Jan Ámos Komensky at r., circular design	0.25	0.75	2.50

w/open book at l. Alphabet at l., Tree of life growing from book at
ctr., young couple at r. on back. Series prefix: E, H.

Note: For #95 w/additional *SLOVENSKÁ REPUBLIKA* adhesive stamp, see Slovakia.

96   50 KORUN

1987. Brown-violet and blue on red and orange unpt. <L/>udovit
Stúr at r., shield and spotted eagle at r. Bratislava castle and town
view on back.

	VG	VF	UNC
a. Series prefix: *F.*	0.50	1.50	3.00
b. Series prefix: *I.*	1.00	2.50	6.00

Note: For #96 w/additional *SLOVENSKÁ REPUBLIKA* adhesive stamp, see Slovakia.

97   100 KORUN

	VG	VF	UNC
1989. Dk. green on green and red unpt. Klement Gottwald at r.	0.75	2.25	10.00

Hradcany in Prague on back. Series prefix: A.

Note: #97 was in circulation only from 1.10.1989 to 31.12.1990.

98   1000 KORUN

	VG	VF	UNC
1985. Blue-black, blue and purple on m/c unpt. Bedrich Smetana at	5.00	20.00	45.00

r. Vysehrad Castle at l. on back. Series prefix: C, U.

Note: For #98 w/additional "M-1000" adhesive stamp or printed, see Czech Republic. With *SLOVENSKÁ REPUBLIKA* adhesive stamp, see Slovakia.

FOREIGN EXCHANGE CERTIFICATES

PODNIKU ZAHRANICNIHO OBCHODU TUZEX

These certificates were issued by the government-owned company *Tuzex*. Foreign visitors could exchange their hard currency for regular Korun or the Tuzex vouchers. These vouchers were accepted at special stores where imported or exported goods could be bought. The common black market rate for Tuzex vouchers was 5-7 regular Korun for 1 Tuzex Koruna.

1961 ISSUE

		VG	VF	UNC
FX25	0.50 KORUNA			
	1961.	5.00	12.50	—
FX26	1 KORUNA			
	1961.	5.00	15.00	—
FX27	5 KORUN			
	1961.	10.00	35.00	—
FX28	10 KORUN			
	1961.	—	Rare	
FX29	20 KORUN			
	1961.	—	Rare	
FX30	50 KORUN			
	1961.	—	Rare	
FX31	71.5 KORUN			
	1961.	—	Rare	
FX32	100 KORUN			
	1962.	—	Rare	

1962-69 ISSUES

Printed date of 1966-69 on FX33-FX39, others w/handstamped date.

		VG	VF	UNC
FX33	0.50 KORUNA			
	1962-69.			
	a. Regular issue.	2.00	5.00	10.00
	b. Z (zahranicni) Foreign issue.	2.00	5.00	10.00

		VG	VF	UNC
FX34	1 KORUNA			
	1962-69.			
	a. Regular issue.	2.00	4.00	10.00
	b. Z (zahranicini) Foreign issue.	2.00	4.00	10.00
FX35	5 KORUN			
	1962-69.	5.00	15.00	50.00
FX36	10 KORUN			
	ND (1962).	10.00	35.00	100.00
FX37	20 KORUN			
	ND (1962).	15.00	50.00	150.00
FX38	50 KORUN			
	ND (1962).	20.00	75.00	200.00
FX39	100 KORUN			
	ND (1962).	25.00	100.00	250.00

1969-73 ISSUES

Printed date on FX40-FX42, all others w/handstamped date.

		VG	VF	UNC
FX40	0.50 KORUNA			
	1969-73.			
	a. Regular issue.	1.25	2.00	5.00
	b. Z (zahranicni) Foreign issue.	3.00	7.50	15.00
FX41	1 KORUNA			
	1969-73.			
	a. Regular issue.	1.25	2.00	5.00
	b. Z (zahranicini) Foreign issue.	3.00	7.50	15.00
FX42	5 KORUN			
	1969-73.			
	a. Regular issue.	2.00	4.00	10.00
	b. Z (zahranicni) Foreign issue.	5.00	12.50	25.00
FX43	10 KORUN			
	1969-73.	5.00	15.00	60.00
FX44	20 KORUN			
	1969-73.	10.00	35.00	100.00

		VG	VF	UNC
FX45	50 KORUN			
	1969-73.	15.00	75.00	150.00
FX46	100 KORUN			
	1969-73.	20.00	100.00	200.00

1973-80 ISSUES

Printed date on FX47-49, all others w/handstamped date.

		VG	VF	UNC
FX47	**0.50 KORUNA** 1973-79.			
	a. Regular issue. 1973-79.	0.20	0.50	1.00
	b. Z (Zahranicni) foreign issue. 1974-78.	0.50	1.50	3.00
FX48	**1 KORUNA** 1973-79.			
	a. Regular issue. 1973-79.	0.20	0.50	1.00
	b. Z (Zahranicni) foreign issue. 1974-78.	0.50	1.50	3.00
FX49	**5 KORUN** 1973-80.			
	a. Regular issue. 1973-80.	0.50	1.50	3.00
	b. Z (Zahranicni) foreign issue. 1974-78.	3.00	7.50	15.00
FX50	**10 KORUN** ND (1973).	4.00	8.00	15.00
FX51	**20 KORUN** ND (1973).	5.00	15.00	30.00
FX52	**50 KORUN** ND (1973).	7.50	25.00	75.00
FX53	**100 KORUN** ND (1974).	15.00	90.00	150.00
FX54	**500 KORUN** ND (1979).	25.00	150.00	350.00

1980-88 ISSUE

#FX55-FX62 white outer edge. *TUZEX* once in text. Date printed for FX55-FX57, others w/handstamped date. Printer: STC-P.

		VG	VF	UNC
FX55	**0.50 KORUNA** 1980-87. Violet and green.	0.25	0.50	1.00

		VG	VF	UNC
FX56	**1 KORUNA** 1980-87. Green on ochre unpt.	0.25	0.50	1.00

		VG	VF	UNC
FX57	**5 KORUN** 1980-87. Violet on blue and ochre unpt.			
	a. 1980.	2.00	4.00	10.00
	b. 1980-87.	0.50	1.50	3.00

		VG	VF	UNC
FX58	**10 KORUN** ND (1980). Dk. green on green unpt.	0.75	2.00	5.00
FX59	**20 KORUN** ND (1980). Brown on orange and green unpt.	2.00	5.00	10.00
FX60	**50 KORUN** ND (1980). Brown on pink and orange unpt.	4.00	10.00	20.00
FX61	**100 KORUN** ND (1980). Violet on green and violet unpt.	5.00	15.00	30.00

		VG	VF	UNC
FX62	**500 KORUN** ND (1980). Gray on brown unpt.	15.00	75.00	150.00

1989-90 ISSUE

#FX63-FX70 lg. globe w/*TUZEX* at l. and r. Colors as previous issue but outer edge w/solid color. Date printed for FX63-65, others w/handstamped date. Printer: STC-P.

		VG	VF	UNC
FX63	**0.50 KORUNA** 1989; 1990. Violet edge.	0.25	0.50	1.00

		VG	VF	UNC
FX64	**1 KORUNA** 1989; 1990. Yellow-brown edge.	0.25	0.50	1.00
FX65	**5 KORUN** 1989; 1990. Blue and ochre edge.	0.50	1.50	3.00

Note: #FX22-FX26 were redeemable 1 year from issue date.

		VG	VF	UNC
FX66	**10 KORUN** ND (1989). Lt. and dk. green edge.	1.25	2.50	5.00
FX67	**20 KORUN** ND (1989). Yellow-brown and green edge.	2.00	5.00	10.00
FX68	**50 KORUN** ND (1989). Pink and orange edge.	4.00	10.00	20.00
FX69	**100 KORUN** ND (1989). Violet and green edge.	5.00	15.00	30.00
FX70	**500 KORUN** ND (1989). Brown edge.	10.00	65.00	100.00

1990-92 ISSUE

#FX71-FX78 globe w/TUZEX. Date printed for FX63-FX65, others w/handstamped date. Printer: VEB Leipzig, Germany.

		VG	VF	UNC
FX71	**0.50 KORUNA** 1990-92.	0.25	0.50	1.00

		VG	VF	UNC
FX72	**1 KORUNA** 1990-92.	0.25	0.50	1.00
FX73	**5 KORUN** 1990-92.	0.50	1.50	3.00
FX74	**10 KORUN** ND (1990).	1.00	2.50	5.00
FX75	**20 KORUN** ND (1990).	2.00	5.00	10.00
FX76	**50 KORUN** ND (1990).	5.00	12.50	20.00
FX77	**100 KORUN** ND (1990).	5.00	15.00	30.00
FX78	**500 KORUN** ND (1990).	10.00	50.00	100.00

The Czech Republic is bordered to the west by Germany, to the north by Poland, to the east by Slovakia and to the south by Austria. It consists of 3 major regions: Bohemia, Moravia and Silesia. It has an area of 30,431 sq. mi. (78,864 sq. km.) and a population of 10.19 million. Capital: Prague (Praha). Industrial production in cities and agriculture and livestock in the rural areas are chief occupations while coal deposits are the main mineral resources.

The Czech Republic was formed on January 1, 1993 upon the peaceful split of the Czech and Slovak Federal Republic. See the Czechslovakia introduction for earlier history.

MONETARY SYSTEM:
1 Czechoslovak Koruna (Kcs) = 100 Haleru Jan. - Feb. 1993
1 Czech Koruna (Kc) = 100 Haleru since Feb. 1993

REPUBLIC

CESKÁ NÁRODNÍ BANKA

CZECH NATIONAL BANK

1993 ND PROVISIONAL ISSUE

#1-3 were released 8.2.1993 having adhesive revalidation stamps affixed (later a printed *1000* was also circulated). Valid until 31.8.1993 but could be exchanged in deposits until 31.5.1994. Old Czechoslovak notes of 100 Korun and higher denominations became obsolete on 7.2.1993. Smaller denominations remained in circulation until 30.11.1993.

Note: In 1997 the CNB made available uncirculated examples of #1-3a and 3b to collectors. The notes are without cancellation marks and have regular serial #.

		VG	VF	UNC
1	**100 KORUN** ND (1993-old date 1961). Dk. green *C-100* adhesive stamp affixed to Czechoslovakia #91a or 91b.			
	a. Stamp on Czechoslovakia #91a.	7.50	12.50	25.00
	b. Stamp on Czechoslovakia #91b.	4.00	7.50	15.00
	c. Stamp on Czechoslovakia #91c.	2.50	5.00	10.00

		VG	VF	UNC
2	**500 KORUN** ND (1993-old date 1973). Dk. green *D-500* adhesive stamp affixed to Czechoslovakia #93. Series prefixes: U, W, Z.	7.50	12.50	30.00

		VG	VF	UNC
3	**1000 KORUN** ND (1993-old date 1985). Deep green *M-1000* revalidation stamp on Czechoslovakia #98.			
	a. Adhesive stamp affixed. Series prefixes: C, U.	7.50	12.50	50.00
	b. Stamp image printed. Series prefix: U.	7.50	12.50	50.00

1993 REGULAR ISSUE

#4-9 arms at ctr. r.; only value in wmk. area on back.

#4-7 replacement notes: Serial # prefix Z.

		VG	VF	UNC
4	**50 KORUN** 1993. Violet and black on pink and gray unpt. St. Agnes of Bohemia at r. and w/crown as wmk. Lg. A within gothic window frame at l. ctr. on back. Printer: TDLR. Serial # prefix A.			
	a. Issued note.	2.00	3.00	8.00
	r. Serial # prefix Z, replacement.	10.00	20.00	50.00

		VG	VF	UNC
5	**100 KORUN** 1993. Blue-green, green and blue-black on lilac and m/c unpt. Kg. Karel IV at r. and as wmk. Lg. seal of Charles University at l. ctr. on back. Printer: TDLR. Serial # prefix A.			
	a. Issued note.	4.00	6.00	12.50
	r. Serial # prefix Z, replacement.	8.00	17.50	35.00

		VG	VF	UNC
6	**200 KORUN** 1993. Deep brown on lt. orange and lt. green unpt. Jan Ámos Komensky at r. and as wmk. Hands outreached at l. ctr. on back. Printer: STC-P. Serial # prefix A.			
	a. Security filament w/*200 KCS*.	FV	FV	25.00
	b. Security filament w/*200 KC*.	FV	FV	15.00
	x. Error. Security filament reads: *REPUBLIQUE DU ZAÏRE*.	100.00	600.00	—

7 500 KORUN
1993. Dk. brown, brown & brown-violet on pink and tan unpt. Rose in unpt. at upper ctr., Bozena Nemcová at r. and as wmk. Laureate young woman's head at l. ctr. on back. Printer: TDLR. Serial # prefix A.

	VG	VF	UNC
a. Issued note.	FV	30.00	60.00
r. Serial # prefix Z, replacement.	20.00	50.00	90.00
s. Specimen.	—	—	—

8 1000 KORUN
1993. Purple and lilac on m/c unpt. Frantisek Palacky and as wmk. Eagle and Kromeriz Castle on back. Printer: STC-P. Serial # prefix A; B.

	VG	VF	UNC
a. Issued ntoe.	FV	FV	100.00
s. Specimen.	—	—	—

9 5000 KORUN
1993. Black, blue-gray and violet on pink and lt. gray unpt. Pres. Tomas Garrigue Masaryk at r. Montage of Prague Gothic and Baroque buildings on back. Printer: STC-P. Serial # prefix A.

	VG	VF	UNC
	FV	FV	350.00

1994-96 ISSUE

#10-16 value and stylized design in wmk. area on back. Printer: STC-P.

10 20 KORUN
1994. Blue-black and gray on lt. blue unpt, Kg. Premysl Otakar 1 at r. and as wmk. Crown with seal above at ctr., stylized crown at lower r. on back.

	VG	VF	UNC
a. Serial # prefix A; B. Security filament at ctr. (74mm from left edge). (1994).	FV	FV	3.00
b. Serial # prefix B. Security filament at l. ctr. (50mm from left edge). (1995).	FV	FV	3.00

11 50 KORUN
1994. Violet and black on m/c unpt. Like #4 but w/o gray in unpt. Stylized heart at lower r. on back. Serial # prefix B.

VG	VF	UNC
FV	FV	4.00

12 100 KORUN
1995. Blue-green, green and blue-black on lilac and m/c unpt. Like #5, but w/stylized K in circle at lower r. on back. Serial # prefix B.

VG	VF	UNC
FV	FV	10.00

13 200 KORUN
1996. Deep brown on pale orange and lt. green unpt. Like #6 but w/stylized open book at lower r. on back. Serial # prefix B.

VG	VF	UNC
FV	FV	15.00

18	**100 KORUN**	VG	VF	UNC
	1997. Dk. green, dk. olive-green and black on m/c unpt. Like #12. Serial # prefix *C, D, E.*	FV	FV	6.00
19	**200 KORUN**			
	1998. Similar to #13, but fibers added in the paper. Serial # prefix *C, D.*	FV	FV	12.00
20	**500 KORUN**			
	1997. Dk. brown, brown and brown-violet on pink and tan unpt. Like #14 but fibers added in the paper. Serial # prefix *C.*	FV	FV	28.00

#21 held in reserve.

14	**500 KORUN**	VG	VF	UNC
	1995. Dk. brown, brown and brown-violet on pink and tan unpt. Like #7 but w/stylized rose at lower r. on back. Serial # prefix *B.*	FV	FV	35.00

15	**1000 KORUN**	VG	VF	UNC
	1996. Purple and lilac on m/c unpt. Like #8 but w/metallic linden leaf at upper ctr. on face, and w/stylized *P* and tree at lower r. on back. Serial # prefix *C, D, E.*	FV	FV	60.00
16	**2000 KORUN**			
	1996. Dk. olive-green, gray and violet on tan unpt. Ema Destinová at r., lyre at at upper l. in spray. Muse of music and lyric poetry Euterpe at l. ctr., violin and cello and a large *D.*, stylized lyre at lower r. on back. Serial # prefix *A*	FV	FV	110.00

22	**2000 KORUN**	VG	VF	UNC
	1999. Similar to #16. 3 Metallic vertical bars in lyre at top ctr. on face. Lyre in wmk. area on back. Fibers added in the paper. Serial # prefix *B.*	FV	FV	100.00

1997-99 ISSUE

#17-23 printer: STC-P. CR used in front-to-back perfect register.

17	**50 KORUN**	VG	VF	UNC
	1997. Violet and purple on m/c unpt. Like #11. Serial # prefix *C, D, E.*	FV	FV	3.00

23	**5000 KORUN**	VG	VF	UNC
	1999. Similar to #9. Metallic hexagon emblem at top ctr. on face. Linden leaf in wmk. area on back. Fibers added in the paper. Serial # prefix *B.*	FV	FV	250.00

DENMARK

The Kingdom of Denmark, a constitutional monarchy located at the mouth of the Baltic Sea, has an area of 16,639 sq. mi. (43,070 sq. km.) and a population of 5.2 million. Capital: Copenhagen. Most of the country is arable. Agriculture, which used to employ the majority of the people, is now conducted by large farms served by cooperatives. The largest industries are food processing, iron and metal, and shipping. Machinery, meats (chiefly bacon), dairy products and chemicals are exported.

Denmark, a great power during the Viking period of the 9th-11th centuries, conducted raids on western Europe and England, and in the 11th century united England, Denmark and Norway under the rule of King Canute. Despite a struggle between the crown and the nobility (13th-14th centuries) which forced the king to grant a written constitution, Queen Margrethe (1353-1412) succeeded in uniting Denmark, Norway, Sweden, Finland and Greenland under the Danish crown, placing all Nordic countries under the rule of Denmark. Sweden and Finland were lost in 1523, and an unwise alliance with Napoleon caused the loss of Norway to Sweden in 1814. In the following years a liberal movement was fostered, which succeeded in making Denmark a constitutional monarchy in 1849.

The present decimal system of currency was introduced in 1874. As a result of a referendum held Sept. 28, 2000, the currency of the European Monetary Union, the Euro, will not be introduced in Denmark in the forseeable future.

RULERS:
Frederik IX, 1947-1972
Margrethe II, 1972-

MONETARY SYSTEM:
1 Krone = 100 Øre

REPLACEMENT NOTES:
#42-45 although dated (19)50, they were issued from 1952 onwards. #42-47, suffix OJ (for whole sheets) or OK (for single notes). Revalued Notes: For early Danish notes with additional printing and signatures on back refer to Danish West Indies, Faeroe Islands and Iceland.

KINGDOM

DANMARKS NATIONALBANK

1944-46 ISSUE

#35-41 first sign. Svendsen for #35, 36, 37a, 38, 39 - 1944-45. Halberg for #35, 37a, 37b, 38, 40, 1945-49. Riim for #35, 37b, 38, 40, 41 - 1948-62.

41	500 KRONER	VG	VF	UNC
	1944-62. Orange. Farmer w/horses at ctr. Arms on back.			
	a. 1944. Prefix D.	120.00	225.00	950.00
	b. 1945. Prefix D.	120.00	225.00	850.00
	c. 1948. Prefix D.	110.00	200.00	650.00
	d. 1951. Prefix D.	110.00	225.00	725.00
	e. 1952. Prefix D.	120.00	225.00	775.00
	f. 1953. Prefix D.	120.00	225.00	725.00
	g. 1954. Prefix D.	110.00	200.00	675.00
	h. 1956. Prefix D.	110.00	200.00	675.00
	i. 1959. Prefix D.	110.00	200.00	675.00
	j. 1961. Prefix D.	110.00	200.00	725.00
	k. 1962. Prefix D.	120.00	200.00	725.00

1950 (1952)-63 ISSUE

Law of 7.4.1936

#42-47 first sign. changes. Usually there are 3 sign. combinations per prefix A0, A1, A2 etc. Second sign. Riim, (19)51-68 for #42, 43, 44a-f, (19)51-68 for #42, 43, 44a-f, 45a-b, 46a-b, 47. Valeur for (19)69 for #44g-h, 45c and 46b. The prefixes mentioned in the listings refer to the first two characters of the left serial #. The middle two digits indicate the date, and the last two characters indicate the sheet position of the note. Replacement Notes: #42-47, Serial # suffix: OJ (for whole sheet replacements) or OK (for single note replacements).

42	5 KRONER	VG	VF	UNC
	(19)50; (19)52; (19)54-60. Blue-green. Portr. Bertil Thorvaldsen at l., 3 Graces at r. Kalundborg city view w/5 spire church at ctr. on back. Wmk: 5 repeated.			
	a. 5 in the wmk. 11mm high. W/o dot after 7 in law date. (19)52. Prefix A0; A1.	9.00	45.00	150.00
	b. As a. (19)52. Prefix A1.	10.00	55.00	155.00
	c. As a., but w/dot after 7 in law date. (19)52. Prefix A2.	7.00	35.00	110.00
	d. As c. (19)52. Prefix A3.	11.00	60.00	160.00
	e. As c. (19)54-55. Prefix A3-A9.	5.00	20.00	70.00
	f. 5 in the wmk. 13mm high. (19)55. Prefix B0.	4.25	16.00	35.00
	g. As f. (19)55. Prefix B1.	6.00	25.00	80.00
	h. As f. (19)56. Prefix B1-B3.	4.00	15.00	32.50
	i. As f. (19)56. Prefix B4.	6.00	25.00	80.00
	j. As f. (19)57. Prefix B4-B6.	3.75	12.50	30.00
	k. As f. (19)58-59. Prefix B7-B9, C0-C1.	3.50	8.00	25.00
	l. As f. (19)59. Prefix C3.	15.00	55.00	175.00
	m. As f. (19)60. Prefix C3-C4.	3.00	7.50	22.50
	r1. As a. Replacement note. (19)50. Suffix OK.	50.00	175.00	300.00
	r2. As e. Replacement note. (19)50. Suffix OJ.	6.50	25.00	85.00
	r3. As e. Replacement note. (19)50. Suffix OK.	35.00	135.00	235.00
	r4. As f, g, j. Replacement note. (19)50. Suffix OJ.	5.00	20.00	45.00
	r5. As k. Replacement note. (19)50. Suffix OJ.	4.50	12.50	35.00
	r6. As m. Replacement note. (19)60. Suffix OJ.	4.00	9.00	27.50
	s. Specimen.	—	—	275.00

43	10 KRONER	VG	VF	UNC
	(19)50-52. Black and olive-brown. Portr. Hans Christian Andersen at l., white storks in nest at r. Green landscape of Egeskov Mølle Fyn at ctr. on back. Wmk: 5 repeated. 125 x 65mm.			
	a. (19)51. Prefix A0; A3; A4.	22.50	55.00	160.00
	b. (19)52. Prefix A1; A2; A5-B0.	17.50	45.00	120.00
	c. (19)52. Prefix B1.	22.50	55.00	160.00

44	10 KRONER	VG	VF	UNC
	(19)50; (19)54-74. Black and brown. Similar to #43, but text line added in upper and lower frame. Portr. Hans Christian Andersen at l. Black landscape at ctr. on back. 125 x 71mm.			
	10. As t or v. Replacement note. (19)71-73. Suffix OK.	6.00	20.00	50.00
	11. As u. Replacement note. (19)71-73. Suffix OK.	12.00	50.00	160.00
	12. As x. Replacement note. (19)74. Suffix OK.	8.00	35.00	100.00
	a. Top and bottom line in frame begins w/10. Wmk: 10 repeated, 11mm high. (19)54. Prefix C0-C1.	9.00	30.00	100.00
	b. Like a but wmk. 13mm high. (19)54-55. Prefix C1-D5.	6.00	17.50	50.00
	c. As b. (19)55. Prefix D6.	9.00	32.50	120.00
	d. As b. (19)56. Prefix D6.	6.00	17.50	50.00
	e. As a. (19)56. Prefix D6-D8.	9.00	30.00	100.00
	f. As b. (19)56-57. Prefix D8-E4.	5.50	15.00	45.00
	g. Top and bottom line in frame begins w/TI. (19)57. Prefix E4.	10.00	40.00	140.00
	h. As g. (19)57. Prefix E5-E6.	5.50	14.00	32.50
	i. As g. (19)57. Prefix E7.	9.00	32.50	120.00
	j. As g. (19)58. Prefix E7-F3.	5.25	12.50	25.00
	k. As g. (19)58-59. Prefix F4.	6.00	15.00	30.00
	l. As g. (19)59-60. Prefix F5-G3.	5.00	12.50	22.50
	m. As g. (19)61. Prefix G4-H6.	4.50	10.00	18.00

	VG	VF	UNC
n. As g. (19)64-67. Prefix H7-K9.	4.00	6.50	12.00
o. As g. (19)68. Prefix A0-A3.	3.75	5.50	10.00
p. As g. (19)68. Second sign. Riim. Prefix A4.	4.50	9.00	17.00
q. As g. (19)69. Second sign. Valeur. Prefix A4.	4.50	9.00	17.00
r1. As c or e. Replacement note. (19)50. Suffix OJ.	10.00	40.00	120.00
r2. As b, d or f. Replacement note. (19)50. Suffix OJ.	7.50	25.00	70.00
r3. As i, k or l.Replacement note. (19)60. Suffix OJ.	6.00	20.00	50.00
r4. As m-r, t. Replacement note. (19)61-74. Suffix OJ.	4.50	10.00	22.50
r5. As u. Replacement note. (19)71. Suffix OJ.	12.00	50.00	160.00
r6. As v or x. Replacement note. (19)72-74. Suffix OJ.	3.00	4.75	7.50
r7. As y. Replacement note. (19)74. Suffix OJ.	3.50	5.00	8.50
r8. As n. Replacement note. (19)64-67. Suffix OK.	12.00	50.00	
r9. As t. Replacement note. (19)70. Suffix OK.	8.00	35.00	100.00
s. Specimen.	—	—	250.00

45 **50 KRONER**

	VG	VF	UNC
(19)50; (19)56-70. Blue on green unpt. Portr. Ole Rømer at l., Round Tower in Copenhagen at r. Back blue; Stone Age burial site Dolmen of Stenvad, Djursland at ctr.			
a. Handmade paper. Wmk: Crowns and *50* (19)56-58.	22.50	65.00	200.00
b. Machine made paper. Wmk: Rhombuses and 50. (19)61/1962; (19)62; (19)63.	15.00	30.00	75.00
c. As b. (19)66, (19)70.	12.00	22.50	55.00
r1. As a. Replacement note. (19)50. Suffix OJ.	17.50	50.00	160.00
r2. As a. 1960. Replacement note. (19)60. Suffix OJ.	16.00	45.00	140.00
r3. As a. Replacement note. (19)50. Suffix OK.	40.00	120.00	300.00
r4. As b. Replacement note. Suffix OJ.	15.00	35.00	80.00
r5. As c. Replacement note. Suffix OJ.	12.00	22.50	55.00
r6. As c. Replacement note. Suffix OK.	30.00	70.00	180.00

46 **100 KRONER**

	VG	VF	UNC
(19)61-70. Red-brown on red-yellow unpt. Portr. Hans Christian Ørsted at l., compass card at r. Back brown; Kronborg castle in Elsinore.			
a. Handmade paper. Wmk: Close wavy lines and compass. (19)61. Prefix A0.	30.00	75.00	275.00
b. Machine made paper. Wmk: *100*. (19)61. Prefix A2, A3; (19)62; (19)65; (19)70.	20.00	30.00	90.00
r1. As a. Replacement note. Suffix OJ.	22.50	40.00	175.00
r2. As a. Replacement note. Suffix OK.	45.00	110.00	325.00
r3. As b. Replacement note. Suffix OJ.	20.00	27.50	70.00
r4. As b. Replacement note. Suffix OK.	35.00	100.00	150.00

47 **500 KRONER**

	VG	VF	UNC
1963-67. Green. Portr. C. D. F. Reventlow at l., farmer plowing at r. Roskilde city view on back.			
a. 1963.	100.00	175.00	500.00
b. 1965.	100.00	200.00	600.00
c. 1967.	90.00	150.00	400.00
r1. As a. Replacement note. Suffix OJ.	100.00	200.00	550.00
r2. As b. Replacement note. Suffix OJ.	120.00	225.00	650.00
r3. As c. Replacement note. Suffix OJ.	75.00	150.00	425.00
s. Specimen.	—	0.00 -	1000.00

1972; 1979 ISSUE

Issued under *L. 1936*. The year of issue is shown by the 2 middle numerals within the series code at lower l. or r. Sign. varieties.

#48-52 portr. at r. on all notes painted by Danish artist Jens Juel (1745-1802).

#48-53 printer: Nationalbanken, Copenhagen (w/o imprint). All w/ *SERIE 1972* at lower r. on back.

48 **10 KRONER**

	VG	VF	UNC
(19)72-78. Black on olive and m/c unpt. Portr. Catherine Sophie Kirchhoff at r. Eider duck at l. on back.			
a. (19)72; (19)75.	FV	3.00	8.00
b. (19)76.	FV	2.50	6.00
c. (19)77-78.	FV	FV	5.00

49 **20 KRONER**

	VG	VF	UNC
(19)79-88. Dk. blue on brown and m/c unpt. Portr. Pauline Tutein at r. Male and female House Sparrow at l. ctr. on back. Wmk: Painter's palette, brushes and *20*.	FV	4.00	12.00

50 **50 KRONER**

	VG	VF	UNC
(19)72-98. Dk. gray on pale blue, dull purple and pale green unpt. Portr. Mrs. Ryberg at r. *Carassius-Carassius* fish at l. on back.			

50		VG	VF	UNC
	a. (19)72.	11.00	17.50	60.00
	b. (19)76; (19)78-79.	FV	12.00	35.00
	c. (19)82; (19)84-85; (19)89-90.	FV	FV	20.00
	d. (19)92-94.	FV	FV	13.50
	e. (19)95.	FV	12.50	25.00
	f. (19)96-98.	FV	FV	15.00
	s. Specimen.	—	—	400.00

51 100 KRONER
(19)72-93. Black and red on m/c unpt. Jens Juel's self-portrait (ca.1773-74) at r. Danish Red Order Ribbon moth at l. on back.

	VG	VF	UNC
a. (19)72.	FV	20.00	75.00
b. (19)75.	FV	FV	55.00
c. (19)76-77.	FV	16.00	60.00
d. (19)78-79; (19)81-85.	FV	FV	40.00
e. (19)85; Prefix H0.	17.50	40.00	100.00
f. (19)86-91.	FV	FV	35.00
g. (19)86; Prefix R1.	17.50	30.00	80.00
h. (19)91; Prefix E2.	FV	15.00	40.00
i. (19)93.	FV	FV	30.00
s. Specimen.	—	—	500.00

52 500 KRONER
(19)72-88. Black on green and m/c unpt. *Unknown Lady* portrait, possibly von Qualen at r. Lizard on back. Wmk: Jens Juel and *500* repeated.

	VG	VF	UNC
a. (19)72.	FV	65.00	200.00
b. (19)76.	FV	FV	170.00
c. (19)80.	FV	FV	140.00
d. (19)88.	FV	FV	130.00

53 1000 KRONER
(19)72-92. Black on gray and m/c unpt. Portr. Thomasine Heiberg at r. European or Red squirrel on back. Wmk: Double portr. Jens Juel and his wife and *1000*.

	VG	VF	UNC
a. (19)72. Prefix A0.	FV	225.00	450.00
b. (19)72. Prefix A1-(19)77.	FV	200.00	375.00
c. (19)80-81.	FV	FV	300.00
d. (19)86.	FV	FV	300.00
e. (19)92.	FV	FV	300.00

1972A ISSUE

54 100 KRONER
(19)94-98. Black and orange on m/c unpt. Like #51 but w/additional security devices. Wmk: Jens Juul. *Series 1972A* at lower r. on back.

	VG	VF	UNC
a. (19)94. Prefix F0.	FV	FV	32.50
b. (19)95. Prefix F1-F2.	FV	FV	32.50
c. (19)95. Prefix F3.	FV	FV	32.50
d. (19)95. Prefix F4-F5.	FV	FV	27.50
e. (19)96. Prefix F6.	FV	FV	30.00
f. (19)97. Prefix F7.	FV	FV	27.50
g. (19)97. Prefix F8.	FV	FV	35.00
h. (19)98. Prefix F9-G0.	FV	FV	27.50

1997-2001 ISSUE

55 50 KRONER
(19)99; (20)00; (20)01; (20)02. Black and dp. purple on m/c unpt. Karen Blixen at r. and as wmk. Centaur stone relief from Landet Church, T<a0>singe at l. ctr. on back. Serial # prefix A.

	VG	VF	UNC
	FV	FV	12.50

59   1000 KRONER
(19)98. Violet, purple and green. Purple iridescent metallic strip. A. and M. Ancher at r. Back purple, turquoise, and orange on m/c unpt. Tournament scene relief from Bislev Church at l. ctr. on back. Serial # prefix A0-A1.

		VG	VF	UNC
		FV	FV	250.00

2002 ISSUE

#60-64 similar to #55-59 but with increased security features. Hologram added at upper left.

60   50 KRONER
(20)05. Black and dp. purple on m/c unpt. Similar to #55.

VG VF UNC
Expected New Issue

56   100 KRONER
(19)99; (20)00; (20)01. Black and red-brown on orange and m/c unpt. Blue latent image at upper l., Carl Nielsen at r. and as wmk. Basilisk stone relief from Tømmerby Church in Thy at l. ctr. on back. Serial # prefix A0-A8.

		VG	VF	UNC
		FV	FV	27.50

61   100 KRONER
(20)02; (20)04. Black and red-brown on orange and m/c unpt. Similar to #56. Serial # prefix B, C.

		VG	VF	UNC
		FV	FV	20.00

62   200 KRONER
(20)03. Black and dk. blue on turquoise green and m/c unpt. Similar to #57. Serial # prefix B.

		VG	VF	UNC
		FV	FV	40.00

57   200 KRONER
(19)97; (20)00. Black and dk. blue on turquoise green and m/c unpt. Pale red-violet latent image at upper l., J. L. Heiberg at r. Stone lion relief from Viborg Cathedral at l. ctr. on back. Serial # prefix A0-A2.

		VG	VF	UNC
		FV	FV	50.00

63   500 KRONER
(20)03. Black on blue, orange and m/c unpt. Similar to #58. Serial # prefix B.

		VG	VF	UNC
		FV	FV	105.00

64   1000 KRONER
(20)04. Violet, purple and green. Similar to #59. Serial # prefix B.

		VG	VF	UNC
		FV	FV	200.00

58   500 KRONER
(19)97; (19)99; (20)00; (20)03. Black on blue, orange and m/c unpt. N. Bohr at r. Knight and dragon relief from Lihme Church at l. ctr. on back. Serial # prefix A0-A2.

		VG	VF	UNC
		FV	FV	125.00

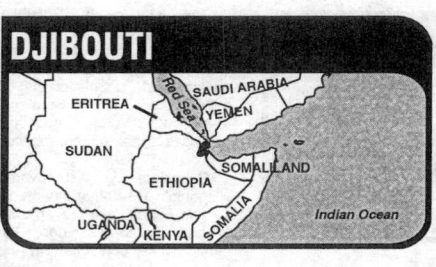

DJIBOUTI

The Republic of Djibouti (formerly French Somaliland or the French Overseas Territory of Afars and Issas), located in northeast Africa at the Bab el Mandeb Strait connecting the Suez ·Canal and the Red Sea with the Gulf of Aden and the Indian Ocean, has an area of 8,494 sq. mi. (22,000 sq. km.) and a population of 687,000. Capital: Djibouti. The tiny nation has less than one sq. mi. of arable land, and few natural resources of salt, sand and camels. The commercial activities of the trans-shipment port of Djibouti and the Addis Ababa-Djibouti railroad are the basis of the economy also French (and now American) military activity. Salt, fish and hides are exported.

French interest in former French Somaliland began in 1839 with concessions obtained by a French naval lieutenant from the provincial sultans. French Somaliland was made a protectorate in 1884 and its boundaries were delimited by the Franco-British and Ethiopian accords of 1887 and 1897. It became a colony in 1896 and a territory within the French Union in 1946. In 1958, it voted to join the new French Community as an overseas territory, and reaffirmed that choice by a referendum in March 1967. Its name was changed from French Somaliland to the French Territory of Afars and Issas on July 5, 1967.

In 1977 Afars and Issas became independent under the name of the Republic of Djibouti.

Note: For earlier issues see French Afars and Issas.

MONETARY SYSTEM:
1 Franc = 100 Centimes

REPUBLIC OF DJIBOUTI

BANQUE NATIONALE DE DJIBOUTI

1979; 1984 ND ISSUE

36	500 FRANCS	VG	VF	UNC
	ND (1979; 1988). M/c. Man at l., rocks in sea, storks at r. Stern of ship at r. on back.			
	a. Blue unpt. W/o sign. (1979).	FV	6.00	16.00
	b. Pale blue unpt. Sign title: *LE GOUVERNEUR* added. (1988).	FV	5.00	13.00

(1979)   (1988)

37	1000 FRANCS
	ND (1979; 1988). Brown and m/c. Woman at l., people by diesel passenger trains at ctr. Trader w/camels at ctr. on back.

37		VG	VF	UNC
	a. Long Arabic text on back. W/o sign. Engraved. (1979).	FV	10.00	30.00
	b. Sign. title: *LE GOUVERNEUR* added above *MILLE*. Short Arabic text at top on back. Lithographed. (1988).	FV	9.00	25.00
	c. Long Arabic text on back. (1991).	FV	9.00	20.00
	d. As c but w/security thread. 2 sign. varieties.	FV	FV	17.50
	e. as d. but bluish microprint frame on both sides.	FV	FV	18.00

38	5000 FRANCS	VG	VF	UNC
	ND (1979). M/c. Man at r., forest scene at ctr. Aerial view at ctr. on back.			
	a. W/o sign.	FV	37.50	85.00
	b. W/sign.	FV	35.00	75.00
	c. As b but w/security thread.	FV	FV	65.00
	d. as c. but fluorescent security stripe.	FV	FV	60.00

39	10,000 FRANCS	VG	VF	UNC
	ND (1984). Brown and red on yellow and green. Woman holding baby at l., goats in tree at r. Fish and harbor scene on back.			
	a. Sign. title: *TRÉSORIER*.	FV	75.00	150.00
	b. Sign. title: *GOUVERNEUR* . W/security thread.	FV	FV	120.00

1997; 1999 ND ISSUE

40	2000 FRANCS	VG	VF	UNC
	ND (1997). Dk. blue, blue-black and black on yellow and m/c unpt. Young girl at r., camel caravan at ctr. Statue w/spear and shield at lower l., government bldg. at ctr. on back.	FV	FV	30.00

Note: #40 reportedly commemorates the 20th anniversary of independence.

41	10,000 FRANCS	VG	VF	UNC
	ND (1999). Blue and m/c. Pres. Hassan Gouled Aptidon at r., undersea life at ctr. bldg. at ctr. on back.	FV	FV	125.00

BANQUE CENTRALE DE DJIBOUTI

2002 ND ISSUE

42	1000 FRANCS	VG	VF	UNC
	(2005) Reddish brown			
	a. Issued note.	FV	FV	16.00
	r. Replacement note. Z prefix.	FV	FV	25.00

43	5000 FRANCS	VG	VF	UNC
	ND (2002). Purple and m/c. Central bank bldg. and M. Harbi. 3 females dancing with swords, rock landscape on back.	FV	FV	55.00

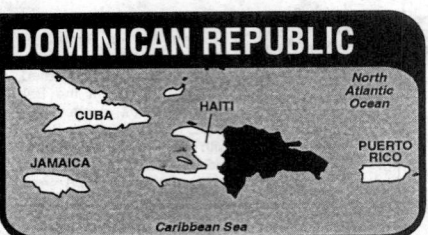

The Dominican Republic, occupying the eastern two-thirds of the island of Hispañola, has an area of 18,816 sq. mi. (48,734 sq. km.) and a population of 8.49 million. Capital: Santo Domingo. The agricultural economy produces sugar, coffee, tobacco and cocoa.

Columbus discovered Hispaniola in 1492, and named it *La Isla Espanola* - "the Spanish Island." Santo Domingo, the oldest white settlement in the Western Hemisphere, was the base from which Spain conducted its exploration of the New World. Later, French buccaneers settled the western third of Hispaniola, which in 1697 was ceded to France by Spain, and in 1804 became the Republic of Haiti - "mountainous country." At this time, the Spanish called their part of Hispaniola Santo Domingo, and the French called their part Saint-Domingue. In 1822, the Haitians conquered the entire island and held it until 1844, when Juan Pablo Duarte, the national hero of the Dominican Republic, drove them out of eastern Hispaniola and established an independent Dominican Republic. The republic returned voluntarily to Spanish dominion - after being rejected by France, Britain and the United States - from 1861 to 1865, when independence was restored.

Dictatorships and democratic rule was intersperced and from 1916 to 1924 it was occupied by the U.S. from 1930 to 1961, Rafael Trujillo was dictator. In the 1994 elections, a reform government gained power.

MONETARY SYSTEM:
1 Peso Oro = 100 Centavos Oro

SPECIMEN NOTES:

In 1998 the Banco Central once again began selling various specimens over the counter to the public. Current market valuations are being reflected, subject to change.

REPLACEMENT NOTES:
#53-61: Z prefix and suffix (TDLR printings).
#117-124: Z prefix and suffix (TDLR printings).

REPUBLIC

BANCO CENTRAL DE LA REPÚBLICA DOMINICANA

1961 ND ISSUES

85	10 CENTAVOS ORO	VG	VF	UNC
	ND (1961). Blue and black. Banco de Reservas in round frame at ctr. Back blue. Printer: ABNC.			
	a. Issued note.	1.00	3.50	15.00
	s. Specimen.	—	—	20.00

86	10 CENTAVOS ORO	VG	VF	UNC
	ND (1961). Black on lt. blue-green safety paper. Banco de Reservas in oval frame at ctr. Back green. Printer: Banco Central.			
	a. Issued note.	2.00	6.00	30.00
	s. Specimen.	—	—	20.00

87	25 CENTAVOS ORO	VG	VF	UNC
	ND (1961). Red and black. Entrance to the Banco Central in rectangular frame at ctr. Back red. Printer: ABNC.			
	a. Issued note.	1.00	4.00	12.50
	s. Specimen.	—	—	20.00

88 25 CENTAVOS ORO

ND (1961). Black. Entrance to the Banco Central in oval frame at ctr. Back green. Printer: Banco Central.

	VG	VF	UNC
a. Pink safety paper.	1.75	5.00	30.00
b. Plain cream paper.	2.50	7.50	35.00
s. Specimen.	—	—	20.00

89 50 CENTAVOS ORO

ND (1961). Purple and black. Palacio Nacional in circular frame at ctr. Back purple. Printer: ABNC.

	VG	VF	UNC
a. Issued note.	1.75	4.00	15.00
s. Specimen.	—	—	20.00

90 50 CENTAVOS ORO

ND (1961). Black on yellow safety paper. Palacio Nacional in oval frame at ctr. Back green. Printer: Banco Central.

	VG	VF	UNC
a. Issued note.	5.50	25.00	80.00
s. Specimen.	—	—	20.00

1962 ND Issue

#91-98 w/text over seal: *SANTO DOMINGO/DISTRITO NACIONAL/REPÚBLICA DOMINICANA.* Medallic portr. Liberty head at l., arms at r. on back. Printer: ABNC.

91 1 PESO ORO

ND (1962-63). Red. Portr. J. P. Duarte at ctr.

	VG	VF	UNC
a. Issued note.	4.00	20.00	65.00
s. Specimen.	—	—	125.00

92 5 PESOS ORO

ND (1962). Red. Portr. J. Sánchez R. at ctr. Back purple.

	VG	VF	UNC
a. Issued note.	6.00	25.00	80.00
s. Specimen.	—	—	150.00

93 10 PESOS ORO

ND (1962). Red. Portr. Mella at ctr. Back brown.

	VG	VF	UNC
a. Issued note.	12.50	50.00	175.00
s. Specimen.	—	—	240.00

94 20 PESOS ORO

ND (1962). Red. *Puerta del Conde* at ctr. Back olive.

	VG	VF	UNC
a. Issued note.	25.00	125.00	350.00
s. Specimen.	—	—	400.00

95 50 PESOS ORO

ND (1962). Red. Tomb of Columbus at ctr. Back blue-gray.

	VG	VF	UNC
a. Issued note.	50.00	200.00	500.00
s. Specimen.	—	—	40.00

96 100 PESOS ORO

ND (1962). Red. Woman w/coffee pot and cup at ctr. Back blue-gray.

	VG	VF	UNC
a. Issued note.	75.00	225.00	550.00
s. Specimen.	—	—	60.00

97	500 PESOS ORO	VG	VF	UNC
	ND (1962). "Obelisco de Ciudad Trujillo" at ctr.			
	a. Issued note.	—	—	—
	s. Specimen.	—	—	100.00

98	1000 PESOS ORO	VG	VF	UNC
	ND (1962). Minor Basilica of Santa Maria at ctr.			
	a. Issued note. Unique.	—	—	—
	s. Specimen.	—	—	150.00

1964 ND Issue

#99-106 orange bank seal at r. Medallic portr. Liberty head at l., arms at r. on back. Sign. varieties. Printer: TDLR.

99	1 PESO ORO	VG	VF	UNC
	ND (1964-73). Black on m/c unpt. Portr. J. P. Duarte at ctr. w/eyes looking l., white bow tie.			
	a. Issued note.	0.50	2.50	12.50
	s. Specimen w/black ovpt: *MUESTRA*.	—	—	15.00

100	5 PESOS ORO	VG	VF	UNC
	ND (1964-74). Brown on m/c unpt. Portr. J. Sánchez R. at ctr.			
	a. Issued note.	3.00	10.00	40.00
	s. Specimen w/black ovpt: *MUESTRA*.	—	—	17.50

101	10 PESOS ORO	VG	VF	UNC
	ND (1964-74). Deep green on m/c unpt. Portr. Mella at ctr.			
	a. Issued note.	5.00	17.50	55.00
	s. Specimen w/black ovpt: *MUESTRA*.	—	—	20.00

102	20 PESOS ORO	VG	VF	UNC
	ND (1964-74). Dk. brown on m/c unpt. *Altar de la Patria* at ctr.			
	a. Issued note.	8.00	30.00	125.00
	s. Specimen w/black ovpt: *MUESTRA*.	—	—	20.00

103	50 PESOS ORO	VG	VF	UNC
	ND (1964-74). Purple on m/c unpt. Ox cart at ctr.			
	a. Issued note.	20.00	75.00	175.00
	s. Specimen w/black ovpt: *MUESTRA*.	—	—	22.50

104	100 PESOS ORO	VG	VF	UNC
	ND (1964-74). Orange-brown on m/c unpt. Banco Central at ctr.			
	a. Issued note.	40.00	125.00	300.00
	s. Specimen.	—	—	40.00

105	500 PESOS ORO	VG	VF	UNC
	ND (1964-74). Dk. blue on m/c unpt. Columbus tomb and cathedral at ctr.			
	a. Issued note.	100.00	400.00	850.00
	s. Specimen w/black ovpt: *MUESTRA*.	—	—	60.00

106   1000 PESOS ORO

	VG	VF	UNC
ND (1964-74). Red and m/c unpt. National Palace at ctr. Medallic portr. Liberty at l. ctr., arms at r. ctr. on back.			
a. Issued note.	200.00	750.00	1750.00
s. Specimen.	—	—	125.00

1973 ND ISSUE

107   1 PESO ORO

	VG	VF	UNC
ND (1973-74). Black on lt. green and pinkish tan unpt. Like #99 but portr. J. P. Duarte w/eyes looking front, black bow tie.	0.50	2.00	10.00
a. Issued note.	0.50	2.00	10.00
s. Specimen.	—	—	12.50

1975 ISSUE

#108-115 dates at ctr. in upper margin on back. Printer: TDLR.

108   1 PESO ORO

	VG	VF	UNC
1975-78. Black on lt. green and pinkish tan unpt. Like #107.			
a. Issued note.	0.25	1.50	7.50
s. Specimen.	—	—	12.50

109   5 PESOS ORO

	VG	VF	UNC
1975-76. Brown on lt. green and lilac unpt. Like #100.			
a. Issued note.	0.50	5.00	20.00
s. Specimen.	—	—	—

110   10 PESOS ORO

	VG	VF	UNC
1975-76. Green on lt. green and lilac unpt. Like #101.			
a. Issued note.	1.50	10.00	35.00
s. Specimen.	—	—	—

111   20 PESOS ORO

	VG	VF	UNC
1975-76. Brown on lt. green and blue unpt. Like #102.			
a. Issued note.	2.50	15.00	55.00
s. Specimen.	—	—	20.00

112   50 PESOS ORO

	VG	VF	UNC
1975-76. Purple on m/c unpt. Like #103.			
a. Issued note.	5.00	35.00	110.00
s. Specimen.	—	—	—

113   100 PESOS ORO

	VG	VF	UNC
1975-76. Orange-brown on m/c unpt. Like #104.			
a. Issued note.	10.00	60.00	190.00
s. Specimen w/black ovpt: *ESPECIMEN*. 1976.	—	—	40.00

114   500 PESOS ORO

	VG	VF	UNC
1975. Dk. blue on m/c unpt. Like #105.			
a. Issued note.	50.00	250.00	750.00
s. Specimen.	—	—	60.00

115   1000 PESOS ORO

	VG	VF	UNC
1975-76. Red on m/c unpt. Like #106.			
a. Issued note.	95.00	500.00	1500.00
s. Specimen w/black ovpt: *ESPECIMEN*. 1975.	—	—	125.00

1977-80 ISSUES

#116-124 dates in upper margin on back. Replacement notes: Serial # prefix and suffix Z.

119	10 PESOS ORO	VG	VF	UNC
	1978-88. Black and green on m/c unpt. Mella at r., medallic Liberty head at ctr. Quarry mining scene on back.			
	a. 1978.	1.25	5.00	20.00
	b. 1980-82.	FV	3.50	15.00
	c. 1985; 1987; 1988.	FV	3.00	10.00
	s1. Specimen w/black ovpt: *ESPECIMEN.* 1978; 1980; 1981.	—	—	17.50
	s2. Specimen w/red ovpt: *MUESTRA SIN VALOR* and TDLR oval seals. 1985; 1987.	—	—	20.00
	s3. Specimen w/black ovpt: *MUESTRA SIN VALOR* and red ovpt: TDLR oval seals. 1988.	—	—	20.00

116	1 PESO ORO	VG	VF	UNC
	1978-79. Black, dk. green and dk. brown on m/c unpt. J. P. Duarte at r., orange seal at l. Sugar refinery on back. Printer: ABNC.			
	a. Issued note.	0.20	1.00	5.00
	s. Specimen w/red ovpt: *MUESTRA - SIN VALOR.* 1978.	—	—	12.50

#117-124 orange bank seal at l. Printer: TDLR.

120	20 PESOS ORO	VG	VF	UNC
	1978-88. Black, dk. brown and olive-brown on m/c unpt. *Altar de la Patria* at ctr. *Puerta del Conde* on back.			
	a. 1978.	2.00	7.00	25.00
	b. 1980-82.	FV	5.50	20.00
	c. 1985; 1987; 1988.	FV	5.00	17.50
	s1. Specimen w/black ovpt: *ESPECIMEN.* 1978; 1980; 1981.	—	—	20.00
	s2. Specimen w/red ovpt: *MUESTRA SIN VALOR* and TDLR oval seals. 1985; 1987.	—	—	22.50
	s3. Specimen w/black ovpt: *MUESTRA SIN VALOR* and red ovpt: TDLR oval seals. 1988.	—	—	22.50

117	1 PESO ORO	VG	VF	UNC
	1980-82. Black, dk. green and dk. brown on m/c unpt. Like #116. Dates very lightly printed.			
	a. Issued note.	0.75	1.00	4.50
	s. Specimen w/black ovpt: *ESPECIMEN.* 1980; 1981.	—	—	12.50

121	50 PESOS ORO	VG	VF	UNC
	1978-87. Black and purple on m/c unpt. Basilica at ctr. First cathedral in America at ctr. r. on back.			
	a. Wmk: Indian head. 1978; 1980; 1981.	5.00	22.50	50.00
	b. Wmk: J. P. Duarte. 1985; 1987.	6.00	25.00	55.00
	s1. As a. Specimen w/black ovpt: *ESPECIMEN.* 1978; 1980; 1981.	—	—	22.50
	s2. As b. Specimen w/perforated *MUESTRA SIN VALOR* and red ovpt: TDLR oval seals. 1985; 1987.	—	—	25.00

118	5 PESOS ORO	VG	VF	UNC
	1978-88. Deep brown, red-brown and red on m/c unpt. J. Sánchez R. at r., arms at ctr. Hydroelectric dam on back.			
	a. 1978.	0.50	2.50	8.50
	b. 1980-82.	FV	2.00	7.00
	c. 1984; 1985; 1987; 1988.	FV	1.50	5.50
	s1. Specimen w/black ovpt: *ESPECIMEN.* 1978; 1980; 1981.	—	—	15.00
	s2. Specimen w/red ovpt: *MUESTRA SIN VALOR* and TDLR oval seals. 1985; 1987.	—	—	15.00
	s3. Specimen w/black ovpt: *MUESTRA SIN VALOR* and red ovpt: TDLR oval seals. 1988.	—	—	15.00

122   100 PESOS ORO

		VG	VF	UNC
1977-87. Violet, brown-orange and yellow-orange on m/c unpt. Entrance to 16th century mint at ctr. Banco Central at ctr. r. on back.				
a. Wmk: Indian head. 1977; 1978; 1980; 1981.		10.00	42.50	125.00
b. Wmk: J.P. Duarte. 1984; 1985; 1987.		FV	50.00	150.00
s1. As a. Specimen w/black ovpt: *ESPECIMEN.* 1978; 1980; 1981.		—	—	30.00
s2. As b. Specimen w/perforated: *MUESTRA SIN VALOR* and red ovpt: TDLR oval seals. 1985; 1987.		—	—	25.00

123   500 PESOS ORO

		VG	VF	UNC
1978-87. Deep blue, blue and brown on m/c unpt. National Theater at ctr. Fort San Felipe at ctr. r. on back.				
a. Wmk: Indian head. 1978; 1980; 1981.		55.00	225.00	450.00
b. Wmk: J. P. Duarte. 1985; 1987.		50.00	200.00	400.00
s1. As a. Specimen w/black ovpt: *ESPECIMEN.* 1978; 1980; 1981.		—	—	40.00
s2. As b. Specimen w/perforated: *MUESTRA SIN VALOR* and red ovpt: TDLR oval seals. 1985; 1987.		—	—	40.00

124   1000 PESOS ORO

		VG	VF	UNC
1978-87. Red, purple and violet on m/c unpt. National Palace at ctr. Columbus' fortress at ctr. r. on back.				
a. Wmk: Indian head. 1978; 1980.		100.00	275.00	550.00
b. Wmk: J. P. Duarte. 1984; 1987.		90.00	225.00	450.00
s1. As a. Specimen w/black ovpt: *ESPECIMEN.* 1978; 1980; 1981.		—	—	50.00
s2. As b. Specimen w/perforated: *MUESTRA SIN VALOR* and red ovpt: TDLR oval seals. 1985; 1987.		—	—	50.00
s3. As b. Specimen w/red ovpt: *MUESTRA SIN VALOR.*		—	—	50.00

1978 COMMEMORATIVE ISSUE

#125, Inauguration of new Banco Central bldg.

125   100 PESOS ORO

		VG	VF	UNC
15.8.1978 (- old date 1977). Special commemorative text ovpt. in black script at l. on back of #122a. Specimen in red folder.		—	—	200.00

1982 COMMEMORATIVE ISSUE

#125A, 35th Anniversary Banco Central, 1947-1982

125A   100 PESOS ORO

		VG	VF	UNC
22.10.1982 (old dates 1978, 1981). Special commemorative text ovpt. in black below bank at r. on back of #122a.				
s1. Old date 1978. Face w/o adhesive stamp or handstamp. Specimen.		—	—	135.00
s2. Old date 1981. Banco Central commemorative adhesive stamp affixed at l., handstamp w/date 22.10.1982 at ctr. l. Specimen.		—	—	150.00

1984 ISSUE

---

126   1 PESO ORO

		VG	VF	UNC
1984; 1987; 1988. Black and brown on m/c unpt. New portr. J. P. Duarte at r., otherwise like #117. Printer: TDLR.				
a. Issued note.		FV	FV	2.00
s1. Specimen w/red ovpt: *MUESTRA SIN VALOR* and TDLR oval seals. 1987.		—	—	10.00
s2. Specimen w/black ovpt: *MUESTRA SIN VALOR* and red ovpt: TDLR oval seals. 1988.		—	—	10.00

1988 ISSUE

#127-130 orange bank seal at l. Wmk: Duarte (profile). Printer: USBNC.

127   50 PESOS ORO

		VG	VF	UNC
1988. Black and purple on m/c unpt. Similar to #121.				
a. Issued note.		FV	FV	17.50
s. Specimen w/red ovpt: *ESPECIMEN MUESTRA SIN VALOR.*		—	—	20.00

128   100 PESOS ORO

		VG	VF	UNC
1988. Violet, brown-orange and brown on m/c unpt. Similar to #122.				
a. Issued note.		FV	FV	25.00
s. Specimen w/red ovpt: *ESPECIMEN MUESTRA SIN VALOR.*		—	—	22.50

129   500 PESOS ORO

		VG	VF	UNC
1988. Deep blue, blue, and brown on m/c unpt. Similar to #123.				
a. Issued note.		FV	FV	75.00
s. Specimen w/red ovpt: *ESPECIMEN MUESTRA SIN VALOR.*		—	—	35.00

130   1000 PESOS ORO

	VG	VF	UNC
1988; 1990. Purple, red-violet and violet on m/c unpt. Similar to #124.			
a. Issued note.	FV	FV	135.00
s. Specimen w/red ovpt: *ESPECIMEN MUESTRA SIN VALOR.* 1988.	—	—	45.00

1990 ISSUE

#131-134 w/silver leaf-like underlays at l. and r. on face. Printer: H&S.

131   5 PESOS ORO

	VG	VF	UNC
1990. Deep brown, red-brown and red on m/c unpt. Similar to #118.	FV	FV	2.50

132   10 PESOS ORO

	VG	VF	UNC
1990. Deep green and black on m/c unpt. Similar to #119.	FV	FV	4.00

133   20 PESOS ORO

	VG	VF	UNC
1990. Deep brown and brown on m/c unpt. Similar to #120.	FV	FV	7.00

134   500 PESOS ORO

	VG	VF	UNC
1990. Deep blue-green, black and brown on m/c unpt. Similar to #123.	FV	FV	70.00

1991 ISSUE

#135-138 orange seal at l. Printer: TDLR.

135   50 PESOS ORO

	VG	VF	UNC
1991; 1994. Black and purple on m/c unpt. Like #127 but wmk: Columbus.			
a. Issued note.	FV	FV	10.00
s. Specimen w/black ovpt: *MUESTRA SIN VALOR* and red ovpt: TDLR oval seals. 1991; 1994.	—	—	20.00

136   100 PESOS ORO

	VG	VF	UNC
1991; 1994. Orange and violet on m/c unpt. Like #128.			
a. Issued note.	FV	FV	20.00
s. Specimen w/black ovpt: *MUESTRA SIN VALOR* and red ovpt: TDLR oval seals. 1994.	FV	FV	35.00

137   500 PESOS ORO

	VG	VF	UNC
1991; 1994. Deep blue, blue and dk. brown on m/c unpt. Like #134.			
a. Issued note.	FV	FV	65.00
s. Specimen w/black ovpt: *MUESTRA SIN VALOR* and red ovpt: TDLR oval seals. 1991; 1994.	—	—	35.00

138   1000 PESOS ORO

	VG	VF	UNC
1991; 1992; 1994. Purple, red-violet and violet on m/c unpt. Like #130.			
a. Issued note.	FV	FV	125.00
s. Specimen w/black ovpt: *MUESTRA SIN VALOR* and red ovpt: TDLR oval seals. 1991; 1994.	—	—	50.00

1992 COMMEMORATIVE ISSUE

#139-142, Quincentennial of First Landfall by Christopher Columbus, 1992

139   20 PESOS ORO

	VG	VF	UNC
1992. Deep brown and brown on m/c unpt. Like #133 but w/brown commemorative text: *1492-1992 V Centenario...* at l. over orange seal. Printer: BABNC.			
a. Issued note.	FV	FV	5.00
s. Specimen w/red ovpt: *ESPECIMEN* and black ovpt: *ESPECIMEN SIN VALOR.*	—	—	20.00

#140-142 wmk: C. Columbus.

140   500 PESOS ORO

	VG	VF	UNC
1992. Brown and blue-black on m/c unpt. Sailing ships at ctr., C. Columbus at ctr. r. Arms at l., Columbus Lighthouse, placement of Cross of Christianity and map outline at ctr. on back. Printer: CBNC.			
a. Issued note.	FV	FV	85.00
s. Specimen w/black ovpt: *MUESTRA SIN VALOR* and red ovpt: TDLR oval seals.	—	—	110.00

141	500 PESOS ORO	VG	VF	UNC
	1992. Deep blue, blue and dk. brown on m/c unpt. Black commemorative text ovpt. at r. on #137. Printer: TDLR.			
	a. Issued note.	FV	FV	85.00
	s. Specimen w/black ovpt: *MUESTRA SIN VALOR* and red ovpt: TDLR oval seals.	—	—	35.00

142	1000 PESOS ORO	VG	VF	UNC
	1992. Purple, red-violet and violet on m/c unpt. Black commemorative text ovpt. at r. on #138. Printer: TDLR.			
	a. Issued note.	FV	FV	125.00
	s. Specimen w/black ovpt: *MUESTRA SIN VALOR* and red ovpt: TDLR oval seals.	—	—	40.00

1993 REGULAR ISSUE

143	5 PESOS ORO	VG	VF	UNC
	1993. Deep brown, red-brown and red on m/c unpt. Similar to #131. Printer: USBNC.	FV	FV	2.00
144	100 PESOS ORO			
	1993. Orange and violet on m/c unpt. Similar to #136. Printer: FNMT.	FV	FV	17.50
145	1000 PESOS ORO			
	1993. Red, purple and violet on m/c unpt. Similar to #138. Printer: FNMT.	FV	FV	120.00

1994 ISSUE

146	5 PESOS ORO	VG	VF	UNC
	1994. Deep brown, red-brown and red on m/c unpt. Similar to #143. Printer: TDLR.	FV	FV	1.75

1995 ISSUE

#147-151 orange bank seal at l. Printer: F-CO.

148	10 PESOS ORO	VG	VF	UNC
	1995. Deep green and black on m/c unpt. Like #132.			
	a. Issued note.	FV	FV	3.00
	s. Specimen w/black ovpt: *ESPECIMEN MUESTRA SIN VALOR.*	—	—	20.00

149	50 PESOS ORO	VG	VF	UNC
	1995. Purple and black on m/c unpt. Like #135.			
	a. Issued note.	FV	FV	7.00
	s. Specimen w/black ovpt: *ESPECIMEN MUESTRA SIN VALOR.*	—	—	20.00

#150 and 151 w/luminescent strip of cross design w/*BCRD* in angles repeated at r. on back.

150	100 PESOS ORO	VG	VF	UNC
	1995. Orange, violet and brown on m/c unpt. Like #136 but w/silver overlays at l. and r., purple design w/*RD* also at r.			
	a. Issued note.	FV	FV	12.50
	s. Specimen w/black ovpt: *ESPECIMEN MUESTRA SIN VALOR.*	—	—	30.00

147	5 PESOS ORO	VG	VF	UNC
	1995. Deep brown, red-brown and red on m/c unpt. Similar to #146 but w/brighter colored arms at ctr.			
	a. Issued note.	FV	FV	1.25
	s. Specimen w/black ovpt: *ESPECIMEN MUESTRA SIN VALOR.*	—	—	15.00

151	500 PESOS ORO	VG	VF	UNC
	1995. Deep blue, blue and brown on m/c unpt. Like #137 but w/silver overlays at l. and r., gold design w/*RD* also at r.			
	a. Issued note.	FV	FV	70.00
	s. Specimen w/black ovpt: *ESPECIMEN MUESTRA SIN VALOR.*	—	—	60.00

1996-97 ISSUE

#152-158 date under bank seal at l. on face. Similar to #147-151 but printer: F-CO.

152	5 PESOS ORO	VG	VF	UNC
	1996; 1997. Deep brown, red-brown and red on m/c unpt. Similar to #147.			
	a. Issued note.	FV	FV	2.00
	s. Specimen.	—	—	7.50

153	10 PESOS ORO	VG	VF	UNC
	1996; 1997; 1998. Deep green and black on m/c unpt. Similar to #148.			
	a. Issued note.	FV	FV	3.00
	s. Specimen w/black ovpt: *ESPECIMEN SIN VALOR.*	—	—	7.50

154	20 PESOS ORO	VG	VF	UNC
	1997; 1998. Deep brown and brown on m/c unpt. Similar to #133.			
	a. Issued note.	FV	FV	5.00
	s. Specimen w/ black ovpt: *ESPECIMEN SIN VALOR.*	—	—	10.00

#155-158 wmk: Duarte.

155	50 PESOS ORO	VG	VF	UNC
	1997; 1998. Purple and black on m/c unpt. Similar to #149.			
	a. Issued note.	FV	FV	10.00
	s. Specimen.	—	—	15.00

156	100 PESOS ORO			
	1997; 1998. Orange and violet on m/c unpt. Similar to #150.			
	a. Issued note.	FV	FV	17.50
	s. Specimen.	—	—	20.00

157	500 PESOS ORO	VG	VF	UNC
	1996; 1997; 1998. Deep blue, blue and brown on m/c unpt. Similar to #151.			
	a. Issued note.	FV	FV	55.00
	s. Specimen.	—	—	25.00

158	1000 PESOS ORO	VG	VF	UNC
	1996; 1997; 1998. Red, purple, violet on m/c unpt. Similar to #145.			
	a. Issued note.	FV	FV	120.00
	s. Specimen.	—	—	40.00

2000 ISSUE

#159-163 printer F-CO.

All Specimen notes w/black ovpt: *ESPECIMEN MUESTRA SIN VALOR* on both sides.

159	10 PESOS ORO	VG	VF	UNC
	2000. Dk. green on m/c unpt. Matías Ramón Mella at r. *Altar de la Patria* on back.			
	a. Issued note.	FV	FV	3.00
	s. Specimen.	—	—	7.50

160	20 PESOS ORO	VG	VF	UNC
	2000. Brown on m/c unpt. Gregorio Luperon at r. *Panteón Nacional* at l. on back.			
	a. Issued note.	FV	FV	4.00
	s. Specimen.	—	—	10.00

#161-163 wmk: Duarte.

161 50 PESOS ORO
2000. Purple and dk. brown on m/c unpt. Santa Maria la Menor
Cathedral at r. Basilica de Nuestra Señora de la Altagracia at l. on
back.

	VG	VF	UNC
a. Issued note.	FV	FV	9.00
s. Specimen.	—	—	12.50

162 500 PESOS ORO
2000. Dk. brown and aqua on m/c unpt. Salome Ureña de
Henriquez and Pedro Henriquez Ureña at r. Banco Central bldg. at
l. on back.

	VG	VF	UNC
a. Issued note.	FV	FV	45.00
s. Specimen.			

163 1000 PESOS ORO
2000. Red and deep lilac on m/c unpt. *Palacio Nacional* at r.
Alcazar de Don Diego Colon at l. on back.

	VG	VF	UNC
a. Issued note.	FV	FV	125.00
s. Specimen.			

164 2000 PESOS ORO
2000. Black and blue on m/c unpt. Emilio Prud-Homme and José
Reyes at r. *Teatro Nacional* on back.

	VG	VF	UNC
a. Issued note.	FV	FV	220.00
s. Specimen.			

Note: #166 has a special rendition of the date and a millennium commemorative text.

2000-01 ISSUE

#166, 167 printer: BABN. Wmk: Duarte.

165 10 PESOS ORO
2000; 2001. Like #159.

	VG	VF	UNC
a. Issued note.	FV	FV	3.00
s. Specimen.	—	—	7.50

166 20 PESOS ORO
2000; 2001. Like #160.

	VG	VF	UNC
a. Issued note.	FV	FV	4.00
s. Specimen.	—	—	10.00

167 100 PESOS ORO
2000; 2001. Dk. brown and orange on m/c unpt. F. R. Sanches, J.
P. Duarte and M. R. Mella at r. *Puerta del Conde at l.* on back.

	VG	VF	UNC
a. Issued note.	FV	FV	20.00
s. Specimen.	—	—	20.00

2001-02 ISSUE

#168-174 like previous issues but for wider border printing at upper ctr. r. on face. Some color shade differences. Printer: (T)DLR.

168 10 PESOS ORO
2002. Dk. green on m/c unpt. Similar to #159.

	VG	VF	UNC
a. Issued note.	FV	FV	2.00
s. Specimen.	—	—	7.50

169 20 PESOS ORO
2001-03. Brown on m/c unpt. Similar to #160.

	VG	VF	UNC
a. Issued note.	FV	FV	3.00
s. Specimen.	—	—	10.00

#170-174 wmk: Duarte.

170	50 PESOS ORO	VG	VF	UNC
	2001-04. Purple and dk. brown on m/c unpt. Similar to #161.			
	a. Issued note.	FV	FV	8.00
	s. Specimen.	—	—	12.50

171	100 PESOS ORO	VG	VF	UNC
	2001-04. Dk. brown and orange on m/c unpt. Similar to #167.			
	a. Issued note.	FV	FV	17.50
	s. Specimen.	—	—	15.00
172	500 PESOS ORO			
	2002-03. Dk. brown and aqua on m/c unpt. Similar to #162.			
	a. Issued note.	FV	FV	40.00
	s. Specimen.	—	—	20.00

173	1000 PESOS ORO	VG	VF	UNC
	2002-03. Red and deep lilac on m/c unpt. Similar to #163.			
	a. Issued note.	FV	FV	105.00
	s. Specimen.	—	—	30.00

174	2000 PESOS ORO	VG	VF	UNC
	2002. Dlack and blue on m/c unpt. Similar to #164.			
	a. Issued note.	FV	FV	200.00
	s. Specimen.	—	—	40.00

2002 COMMEMORATIVE ISSUE

#175, 55th Anniversary of the Central Bank.

175	100 PESOS ORO	VG	VF	UNC
	2002. Dk. Brown and orange on m/c unpt. Commemorative ovpt.	FV	FV	17.50
	on back of #171.			

COLLECTOR SERIES

BANCO CENTRAL DE LA REPÚBLICA DOMINICANA

1974 ISSUES

CS1	1-1000 PESOS ORO	Issue Price	Mkt.	Value
	ND(1974). #99-106. Ovpt: MUESTRA twice on face.	—		450.00
CS2	1-1000 PESOS ORO			
	ND(1974). #99-106. Ovpt: MUESTRA on face and back.	40.00		450.00

1978 ISSUES

CS3	PESOS ORO	Issue Price	Mkt.	Value
	1978. #116, 118-124. Ovpt: MUESTRA/SIN VALOR on face,	40.00		235.00
	ESPECIMEN on back.			

CS4	PESOS ORO	Issue Price	Mkt.	Value
	1978. #116, 118a-120a, 121, 122a, 123, 124a. Ovpt: SPECIMEN	14.00		60.00
	w/serial # prefix Maltese cross. #122a is dated 1977.			

EAST AFRICA

East Africa was an administrative grouping of several neighboring British territories: Kenya, Tanganyika, Uganda and Zanzibar.

The common interest of Kenya, Tanzania and Uganda invited cooperation in economic matters and consideration of political union. The territorial governors, organized as the East Africa High Commission, met periodically to administer such common activities as taxation, industrial development and education. The authority of the Commission did not infringe upon the constitution and internal autonomy of the individual colonies. The common monetary system circulated for the territories by the East African Currency Board and was also used in British Somaliland and the Aden Protectorate subsequent to the independence of India (1947) whose currency had previously circulated in these two territories.

Also see Somaliland Republic, Kenya, Uganda and Tanzania.

RULERS:
British

MONETARY SYSTEM:
1 Shilling = 100 Cents

BRITISH ADMINISTRATION

EAST AFRICAN CURRENCY BOARD, NAIROBI

1961 ND ISSUE

#41-44 portr. Qn. Elizabeth II at upper l. w/3 sign. at l. and 4 at r. Printer: TDLR.

41	5 SHILLINGS	VG	VF	UNC
	ND (1961-63). Brown on lt. red unpt.			
	a. Top l. sign: E. B. David. (1961).	5.00	20.00	250.00
	b. Top l. sign: A. L. Adu. (1962-63).	3.50	15.00	200.00

42	10 SHILLINGS	VG	VF	UNC
	ND (1961-63). Green on m/c unpt.			
	a. Top l. sign: E. B. David. (1961).	9.00	25.00	350.00
	b. Top l. sign: A. L. Adu. (1962-63).	6.00	20.00	300.00
43	20 SHILLINGS			
	ND (1961-63). Blue on lt. pink unpt.			
	a. Top l. sign: E. B. David. (1961).	10.00	50.00	475.00
	b. Top l. sign: A. L. Adu. (1962-63).	7.00	40.00	300.00

44	100 SHILLINGS	VG	VF	UNC
	ND (1961-63). Red on m/c unpt.			
	a. Top l. sign: E. B. David. (1961).	25.00	125.00	950.00
	b. Top l. sign: A. L. Adu. (1962-63).	20.00	90.00	700.00

1964 ND ISSUE

#45-48 wmk: Rhinoceros, wmk. area at l., sailboat at l. ctr. Various plants on back.

45	5 SHILLINGS	VG	VF	UNC
	ND (1964). Brown on m/c unpt.	3.00	12.50	85.00

46	10 SHILLINGS	VG	VF	UNC
	ND (1964). Green on m/c unpt.			
	a. Issued note.	5.00	20.00	120.00
	s. Specimen, punch hole cancelled.	—	—	—

47	20 SHILLINGS	VG	VF	UNC
	ND (1964). Blue on m/c unpt.			
	a. Issued note.	7.50	30.00	300.00
	s. Specimen. Punched hole cancelled.	—	—	—

48	100 SHILLINGS		VG	VF	UNC
	ND (1964). Deep red on m/c unpt.				
	a. Issued note.		9.00	45.00	225.00
	s. Specimen. Punched hole cancelled.		—	—	—

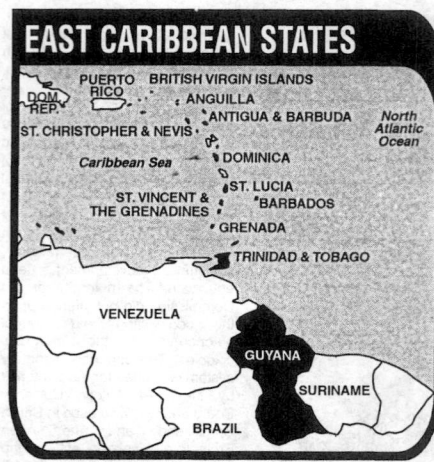

EAST CARIBBEAN STATES

The East Caribbean States, formerly the British Caribbean Territories (Eastern Group), a currency board formed in 1950, comprised the British West Indies territories of Trinidad and Tobago, Barbados, the Leeward Islands of Anguilla, St. Christopher, Nevis and Antigua; the Windward Islands of St. Lucia, Dominica, St. Vincent and Grenada; British Guiana and the British Virgin Islands.

As time progressed, the member countries varied and is reflected on the backs of #13-16. The first issue includes Barbados but not Grenada, while the second issue includes both Barbados and Grenada and the third issue retains Grenada while Barbados is removed. Barbados attained self-government in 1961 and independence on Nov. 30, 1966.

On May 26, 1966 British Guiana became independent as Guyana which later became a cooperative Republic on Feb. 23, 1970.

The British Virgin Islands became a largely self-governing dependent territory of the United Kingdom in 1967. United States currency is the official medium of exchange.

St. Christopher and Nevis became fully independent on Sept. 19, 1983.

Trinidad & Tobago became an independent member state of the Commonwealth on August 31, 1962.

RULERS:
  British

MONETARY SYSTEM:
  1 Dollar = 100 Cents
  The variety letters for numbers 19-46 have changed to match the serial # suffix letter of the respective country of issue.

EAST CARIBBEAN CURRENCY AUTHORITY

SIGNATURE VARIETIES

(signature table, varieties 1–10)

ISLAND PARTICIPATION

Variety I   Variety II   Variety III

VARIETY I: Listing of islands on back includes Barbados but not Grenada.
VARIETY II: Listing includes Barbados and Grenada.
VARIETY III: Listing retains Grenada while Barbados is deleted.

1965 ND Issue

#13-16 map at l., Qn. Elizabeth II at r. and as wmk. Coastline w/rocks and trees at l. ctr. on back. Sign. varieties. Printer: TDLR. Replacement notes: Serial # prefix Z1.

Beginning in 1983, #13-16 were ovpt. with circled letters at l. indicating their particular areas of issue within the Eastern Group. Letters and their respective areas are as follows:

A, Antigua	L, St. Lucia
D, Dominica	M, Montserrat
G, Grenada	U, Anguilla
K, St. Kitts	V, St. Vincent

13 1 DOLLAR

ND (1965). Red on m/c unpt. Fish at ctr.

	VG	VF	UNC
a. Sign. 1; 2. Back variety 1.	1.00	7.50	50.00
b. Sign. 3. Back variety 2.	0.75	4.00	25.00
c. Sign. 4.	1.00	7.50	100.00
d. Sign. 5; 6; 7.	0.50	2.00	25.00
e. Sign. 8. Back variety 3.	0.50	1.50	20.00
f. Sign. 9; 10. Darker red on back as previous varieties, to Series B82.	FV	0.75	15.00
g. Sign. 10. Brighter red on back. Series B83-B91.	FV	0.75	15.00
h. Ovpt: A in circle.	FV	0.50	15.00
i. Ovpt: D in circle.	FV	0.50	17.50
j. Ovpt: G in circle.	FV	0.50	15.00
k. Ovpt: K in circle.	FV	0.50	15.00
l. Ovpt: L in circle.	FV	0.50	17.50
m. Ovpt: M in circle.	FV	0.50	15.00
n. Ovpt: U in circle.	FV	0.50	15.00
o. Ovpt: V in circle.	FV	0.50	15.00
s. As a, j-n. Specimen.	—	—	100.00

14 5 DOLLARS

ND (1965). Green on m/c unpt. Flying fish at ctr.

	VG	VF	UNC
		Reported Not Confirmed	
a. Sign. 1. Back variety 1.	6.00	25.00	150.00
b. Sign. 2.	6.00	25.00	150.00
c. Sign. 3. Back variety 2.			
d. Sign. 4.	4.00	10.00	125.00
e. Sign. 5; 6.	3.50	7.50	70.00
f. Sign. 7.	4.00	10.00	80.00
g. Sign. 8. Back variety 3.	2.00	5.00	40.00
h. Sign. 9; 10.	FV	3.00	25.00
i. Ovpt: A in circle.	FV	2.50	25.00
j. Ovpt: D in circle.	FV	2.50	30.00
k. Ovpt: G in circle.	FV	2.50	25.00
l. Ovpt: K in circle.	FV	2.50	25.00
m. Ovpt: L in circle.	FV	7.50	115.00
n. Ovpt: M in circle.	FV	2.50	27.50
o. Ovpt: U in circle.	FV	2.50	25.00
p. Ovpt: V in circle.	FV	2.50	25.00
s. As a, b. Specimen.	—	—	250.00

15 20 DOLLARS

ND (1965). Purple on m/c unpt. Turtles at ctr.

	VG	VF	UNC
		Reported Not Confirmed	
a. Sign. 1. Back variety 1.	17.50	65.00	500.00
b. Sign. 2.	20.00	75.00	600.00
c. Sign. 3. Back variety 2.			
d. Sign. 4.	12.50	50.00	350.00
e. Sign. 5; 6; 7.	10.00	40.00	250.00
f. Sign. 8. Back variety 3.	10.00	12.50	70.00
g. Sign. 9; 10.	FV	10.00	55.00
h. Ovpt: A in circle.	FV	10.00	50.00
i. Ovpt: D in circle.	FV	10.00	65.00
j. Ovpt: G in circle.	FV	10.00	50.00
k. Ovpt: K in circle.	FV	20.00	115.00
l. Ovpt: L in circle.	FV	10.00	50.00
m. Ovpt: M in circle.	FV	10.00	50.00
n. Ovpt: U in circle.	FV	10.00	50.00
o. Ovpt: V in circle.	FV	10.00	50.00
s. As a. Specimen.	—	—	500.00

16 100 DOLLARS

ND (1965). Black on m/c unpt. Sea horses at ctr.

	VG	VF	UNC
		Reported Not Confirmed	
a. Sign. 1. Back variety 1.	100.00	300.00	1500.00
b. Sign. 2.			
c. Sign. 5. Back variety 2.	110.00	325.00	1600.00
d. Sign. 3; 4; 6; 7.			
e. Sign. 8. Back variety 3.			
f. Sign. 9; 10.	FV	85.00	350.00
g. Ovpt: A in circle.	FV	85.00	350.00
h. Ovpt: D in circle.	60.00	140.00	700.00
i. Ovpt: G in circle.	5FV	120.00	450.00
j. Ovpt: K in circle.	50.00	125.00	650.00
k. Ovpt: L in circle.	FV	85.00	350.00
l. Ovpt: M in circle.	FV	85.00	350.00
m. Ovpt: U in circle.	FV	85.00	350.00
n. Ovpt: V in circle.	FV	85.00	350.00
s. As a. Specimen.	—	—	1000.00

EASTERN CARIBBEAN CENTRAL BANK

SIGNATURE VARIETIES

1	Governor	2	Governor
	[signature]		K. Dwight Venner

1985-87 ND Issue

#17-25 windsurfer at l., Qn. Elizabeth II at ctr. r., map at r. Back similar to #13-16. Wmk: QEII. Printer: TDLR. Replacement notes: Serial # prefix Z1.

Notes w/suffix letter of serial # indicating particular areas of issue (as with ovpt. letters on previous issue).

#17-20 do not have name Anguilla at island near top of map at r. Palm tree, swordfish at ctr. r., shoreline in background on back. No $10 without Anguilla was issued.

1985-88 ND ISSUE

#21-25 with *ANGUILLA* island named near top of map at r.

#21, 22, 24 and 25 harbor at St. Lucia on back.

17	1 DOLLAR	VG	VF	UNC
	ND (1985-88). Red on m/c unpt.			
	a. Suffix letter *A*.	FV	1.00	10.00
	d. Suffix letter *D*.	FV	1.00	10.00
	g. Suffix letter *G*.	FV	1.00	10.00
	k. Suffix letter *K*.	FV	1.00	10.00
	l. Suffix letter *L*.	FV	1.00	10.00
	m. Suffix letter *M*.	FV	1.00	10.00
	u. Ovpt: *U* in circle on suffix letter *V* issue (1988).	FV	1.00	10.00
	v. Suffix letter *V*.	FV	1.00	10.00

21	1 DOLLAR	VG	VF	UNC
	ND (1988-89). Red on m/c unpt. Like #17 but Anguilla named.			
	Sign. 1.			
	d. Suffix letter *D*.	FV	1.00	15.00
	k. Suffix letter *K*.	FV	1.00	15.00
	l. Suffix letter *L*.	FV	1.00	15.00
	m. Suffix letter *M*.	FV	5.00	25.00
	u. Suffix letter *U*.	FV	1.00	15.00

18	5 DOLLARS	VG	VF	UNC
	ND (1986-88). Deep green on m/c unpt.			
	a. Suffix letter *A*.	FV	FV	20.00
	d. Suffix letter *D*.	FV	FV	20.00
	g. Suffix letter *G*.	FV	FV	20.00
	k. Suffix letter *K*.	FV	FV	20.00
	l. Suffix letter *L*.	FV	FV	20.00
	m. Suffix letter *M*.	FV	FV	20.00
	u. Ovpt: *U* in circle on suffix letter *V* issue (1988).	FV	FV	20.00
	ur. Replacement note. Z/1 serial # prefix.	5.00	10.00	45.00
	v. Suffix letter *V*.	FV	FV	20.00

22	5 DOLLARS	VG	VF	UNC
	ND (1988-93). Deep green on m/c unpt. Like #18 but Anguilla			
	named.			
	a1. Suffix letter *A*. Sign. 1.	FV	FV	15.00
	a2. Like a1. Sign. 2.	FV	FV	15.00
	d. Suffix letter *D*. Sign. 1.	FV	FV	15.00
	g. Suffix letter *G*. Sign. 2.	FV	FV	15.00
	k1. Suffix letter *K*. Sign. 1.	FV	FV	15.00
	k2. Like k1. Sign. 2.	FV	FV	15.00
	l1. Suffix letter *L*. Sign. 1.	FV	FV	15.00
	l2. Like l1. Sign. 2.	FV	FV	15.00
	m. Suffix letter *M*. Sign. 1.	FV	FV	15.00
	u. Suffix letter *U*. Sign. 1.	FV	FV	15.00
	v. Suffix letter *V*. Sign. 2.	FV	FV	15.00

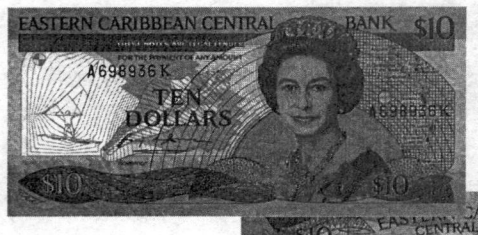

19	20 DOLLARS	VG	VF	UNC
	ND (1987-88). Purple and brown on m/c unpt.			
	a. Suffix letter *A*.	FV	FV	52.50
	d. Suffix letter *D*.	FV	FV	52.50
	g. Suffix letter *G*.	FV	FV	52.50
	k. Suffix letter *K*.	FV	FV	52.50
	l. Suffix letter *L*.	FV	FV	52.50
	m. Suffix letter *M*.	FV	12.50	60.00
	u. Ovpt: *U* in circle.	FV	FV	52.50
	v. Suffix letter *V*.	FV	FV	52.50

23	10 DOLLARS	VG	VF	UNC
	ND (1985-93). Blue on m/c unpt. Harbor at Grenada, sailboats at l.			
	and ctr. on back.			
	a1. Suffix letter *A*. Sign. 1.	FV	FV	30.00
	a2. Like a1. Sign. 2.	FV	FV	30.00
	d1. Suffix letter *D*. Sign. 1.	FV	FV	30.00
	d2. Like d1. Sign. 2.	FV	FV	30.00
	g. Suffix letter *G*. Sign. 1.	FV	FV	30.00
	k1. Suffix letter *K*. Sign. 1.	FV	FV	30.00
	k2. Like k1. Sign. 2.	FV	FV	30.00
	l1. Suffix letter *L*. Sign. 1.	FV	FV	30.00
	l2. Like l1. Sign. 2.	FV	FV	30.00
	m. Suffix letter *M*. Sign. 1.	FV	FV	30.00
	u. Suffix letter *U*. Sign. 1.	FV	FV	30.00
	v1. Suffix letter *V*. Sign. 1.	FV	FV	30.00
	v2. Like v1. Sign. 2.	FV	FV	30.00

20	100 DOLLARS	VG	VF	UNC
	ND (1986-88). Black and orange on m/c unpt.			
	a. Suffix letter *A*.	FV	50.00	225.00
	d. Suffix letter *D*.	FV	50.00	225.00
	g. Suffix letter *G*.	FV	50.00	225.00
	k. Suffix letter *K*.	FV	50.00	225.00
	l. Suffix letter *L*.	FV	50.00	225.00
	m. Suffix letter *M*.	FV	50.00	225.00
	u. Ovpt: *U* in circle on suffix letter *V* issue (1988).	FV	50.00	225.00
	v. Suffix letter *V*.	FV	50.00	225.00

24	20 DOLLARS	VG	VF	UNC
	ND (1988-93). Purple and brown on m/c unpt. Like #19 but Anguilla named.			
	a1. Suffix letter A. Sign. 1.	FV	FV	50.00
	a2. Like a1. Sign. 2.	FV	FV	50.00
	d1. Suffix letter D. Sign. 1.	FV	FV	50.00
	d2. Like d1. Sign. 2.	FV	FV	50.00
	g. Suffix letter G. Sign. 1.	FV	FV	50.00
	k1. Suffix letter K. Sign. 1.	FV	FV	50.00
	k2. Like k1. Sign. 2.	FV	FV	50.00
	l1. Suffix letter L. Sign. 1.	FV	FV	50.00
	l2. Like l1. Sign. 2.	FV	FV	50.00
	m1. Suffix letter M. Sign. 1.	FV	FV	50.00
	m2. Like m1. Sign. 2.	FV	FV	50.00
	u. Suffix letter U. Sign. 1.	FV	FV	50.00
	v. Suffix letter V. Sign. 1.	FV	FV	50.00

26	5 DOLLARS	VG	VF	UNC
	ND (1993). Dk. green, black and violet on m/c unpt. Admiral's House in Antigua and Barbuda at l., Trafalgar Falls in Dominica at r. on back.			
	a. Suffix letter A.	FV	FV	17.50
	d. Suffix letter D.	FV	FV	17.50
	g. Suffix letter G.	FV	FV	17.50
	k. Suffix letter K.	FV	FV	17.50
	l. Suffix letter L.	FV	FV	17.50
	m. Suffix letter M.	FV	FV	25.00
	u. Suffix letter U.	FV	FV	17.50
	v. Suffix letter V.	FV	FV	17.50

25	100 DOLLARS	VG	VF	UNC
	ND (1988-93). Black and orange on m/c unpt. Like #20 but Anguilla named.			
	a1. Suffix letter A. Sign. 1.	FV	FV	200.00
	a2. Like a1. Sign. 2.	FV	FV	200.00
	d1. Suffix letter D. Sign. 1.	FV	FV	200.00
	d2. Like d1. Sign. 2.	FV	FV	200.00
	g. Suffix letter G. Sign. 1.	FV	FV	200.00
	k1. Suffix letter K. Sign. 1.	FV	FV	200.00
	k2. Like k1. Sign. 2.	FV	FV	200.00
	l1. Suffix letter L. Sign. 1.	FV	FV	200.00
	l2. Like l1. Sign. 2.	FV	FV	200.00
	m1. Suffix letter M. Sign. 1.	FV	FV	200.00
	m2. Like m1. Sign. 2.	FV	FV	200.00
	u. Suffix letter U. Sign. 1.	FV	FV	200.00
	v. Suffix letter V. Sign. 1.	FV	FV	200.00

27	10 DOLLARS	VG	VF	UNC
	ND (1993). Dk. blue, black and red on m/c unpt. Admiralty Bay in St. Vincent and Grenadines at l., sailing ship *Warspite* and brown pelican at r. ctr. on back.			
	a. Suffix letter A.	FV	FV	27.50
	d. Suffix letter D.	FV	FV	27.50
	g. Suffix letter G.	FV	FV	27.50
	k. Suffix letter K.	FV	FV	27.50
	l. Suffix letter L.	FV	FV	27.50
	m. Suffix letter M.	FV	FV	35.00
	u. Suffix letter U.	FV	FV	27.50
	v. Suffix letter V.	FV	FV	27.50

1993 ND ISSUE

Antigua (A)	■ ■ ■ ■	St. Lucia (L)	■ ■ ■
Dominica (D)	■ ■ ■	Montserrat (M)	■ ■ ■ ■
Grenada (G)	■ ■	Anguilla (U)	■ ■ ■ ■ ■
St. Kitts (K)	■ ■ ■	St. Vincent (V)	■ ■ ■

#26-30 Qn. Elizabeth II at ctr. r. and as wmk. (profile), turtle at lower ctr., green-throated carib at top l. Island map at ctr. on back. Sign. 2. Printer: TDLR.

28	20 DOLLARS	VG	VF	UNC
	ND (1993). Brown-violet, blue-gray and orange on m/c unpt. Govt. House in Montserrat at l., nutmeg in Grenada at r. on back.			
	a. Suffix letter A.	FV	FV	42.50
	d. Suffix letter D.	FV	FV	42.50
	g. Suffix letter G.	FV	FV	42.50
	k. Suffix letter K.	FV	FV	42.50
	l. Suffix letter L.	FV	FV	42.50
	m. Suffix letter M.	FV	FV	50.00
	u. Suffix letter U.	FV	FV	42.50
	v. Suffix letter V.	FV	FV	42.50

29	**50 DOLLARS**	VG	VF	UNC
	ND (1993). Purple and olive-green on m/c unpt. Brimstone Hill in St. Kitts at l., Les Pitons mountains in St. Lucia and sooty tern at r. on back.			
	a. Suffix letter *A*.	FV	FV	105.00
	d. Suffix letter *D*.	FV	FV	105.00
	g. Suffix letter *G*.	FV	FV	105.00
	k. Suffix letter *K*.	FV	FV	105.00
	l. Suffix letter *L*.	FV	FV	105.00
	m. Suffix letter *M*.	FV	35.00	140.00
	u. Suffix letter *U*.	FV	FV	105.00
	v. Suffix letter *V*.	FV	FV	105.00

32	**10 DOLLARS**	VG	VF	UNC
	ND (1994). Dk. blue, black and red on m/c unpt. Like #27.			
	a. Suffix letter *A*.	FV	FV	25.00
	d. Suffix letter *D*.	FV	FV	25.00
	g. Suffix letter *G*.	FV	FV	25.00
	k. Suffix letter *K*.	FV	FV	25.00
	l. Suffix letter *L*.	FV	FV	25.00
	m. Suffix letter *M*.	FV	7.50FV	35.00
	u. Suffix letter *U*.	FV	FV	25.00
	v. Suffix letter *V*.	FV	FV	25.00

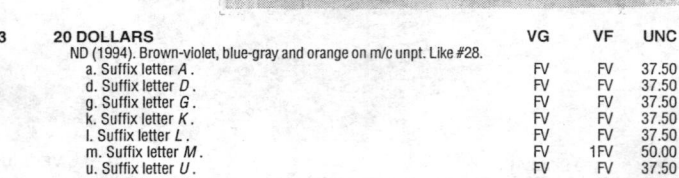

30	**100 DOLLARS**	VG	VF	UNC
	ND (1993). Dk. brown, dk. olive-green and tan on m/c unpt. Sir Arthur Lewis at l., E.C.C.B. Central Bank bldg. and Lesser Antillean Swift at r. on back.			
	a. Suffix letter *A*.	FV	45.00	185.00
	d. Suffix letter *D*.	FV	45.00	185.00
	g. Suffix letter *G*.	FV	45.00	185.00
	k. Suffix letter *K*.	FV	45.00	185.00
	l. Suffix letter *L*.	FV	45.00	185.00
	m. Suffix letter *M*.	FV	55.00	240.00
	u. Suffix letter *U*.	FV	45.00	185.00
	v. Suffix letter *V*.	FV	45.00	185.00

33	**20 DOLLARS**	VG	VF	UNC
	ND (1994). Brown-violet, blue-gray and orange on m/c unpt. Like #28.			
	a. Suffix letter *A*.	FV	FV	37.50
	d. Suffix letter *D*.	FV	FV	37.50
	g. Suffix letter *G*.	FV	FV	37.50
	k. Suffix letter *K*.	FV	FV	37.50
	l. Suffix letter *L*.	FV	FV	37.50
	m. Suffix letter *M*.	FV	1FV	50.00
	u. Suffix letter *U*.	FV	FV	37.50
	v. Suffix letter *V*.	FV	FV	37.50

1994 ND ISSUE

#31-35 like #26-30 but w/clear bold values at upper l. and lower r. Thin security thread. Sign. 2. Replacement notes: Serial # prefix *Z* are scarce and command a premium.

31	**5 DOLLARS**	VG	VF	UNC
	ND (1994). Dk. green, black and violet on m/c unpt. Like #26.			
	a. Suffix letter *A*.	FV	FV	15.00
	d. Suffix letter *D*.	FV	FV	15.00
	g. Suffix letter *G*.	FV	FV	15.00
	k. Suffix letter *K*.	FV	FV	15.00
	l. Suffix letter *L*.	FV	FV	15.00
	m. Suffix letter *M*.	FV	5.00FV	27.50
	u. Suffix letter *U*.	FV	FV	15.00
	v. Suffix letter *V*.	FV	FV	15.00

34	**50 DOLLARS**	VG	VF	UNC
	ND (1994). Tan, red-orange and green on m/c unpt. Like #29.			
	a. Suffix letter *A*.	FV	FV	100.00
	d. Suffix letter *D*.	FV	FV	100.00
	g. Suffix letter *G*.	FV	FV	100.00
	k. Suffix letter *K*.	FV	FV	100.00
	l. Suffix letter *L*.	FV	FV	100.00
	m. Suffix letter *M*.	50.00	95.00	240.00
	u. Suffix letter *U*.	FV	FV	100.00
	v. Suffix letter *V*.	FV	FV	100.00

35	100 DOLLARS		VG	VF	UNC
	ND (1994). Dk. brown and dk. green on m/c unpt. Like #30.				
	a. Suffix letter *A*.		FV	FV	170.00
	d. Suffix letter *D*.		FV	FV	170.00
	g. Suffix letter *G*.		FV	FV	170.00
	k. Suffix letter *K*.		FV	FV	170.00
	l. Suffix letter *L*.		FV	FV	170.00
	m. Suffix letter *M*.		FV	FV	280.00
	u. Suffix letter *U*.		FV	FV	170.00
	v. Suffix letter *V*.		FV	FV	170.00

38	10 DOLLARS	VG	VF	UNC
	ND (2000). Blue and black on m/c unpt. Like #32 but w/ gold foil fish at r.			
	a. Suffix letter *A*.	FV	FV	20.00
	d. Suffix letter *D*.	FV	FV	20.00
	g. Suffix letter *G*.	FV	FV	22.50
	k. Suffix letter *K*.	FV	FV	22.50
	l. Suffix letter *L*.	FV	FV	20.00
	m. Suffix letter *M*.	FV	FV	30.00
	u. Suffix letter *U*.	FV	FV	20.00
	v. Suffix letter *V*.	FV	FV	22.50

1998 ND ISSUE

#36 Building rendering is long, partially covering signature. Printer: (T)DLR.

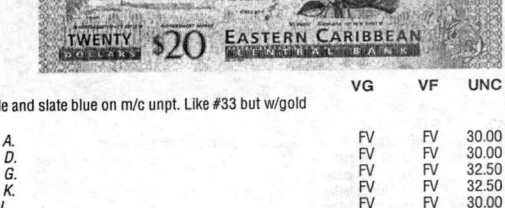

36	100 DOLLARS		VG	VF	UNC
	ND (1998). Dk. brown and dk. green on m/c unpt. Like #35 but w/gold foil flower enhanced colors and segmented foil over security thread.				
	a. Suffix letter *A*.		FV	FV	130.00
	d. Suffix letter *D*.		FV	FV	130.00
	g. Suffix letter *G*.		FV	FV	145.00
	k. Suffix letter *K*.		FV	FV	145.00
	l. Suffix letter *L*.		FV	FV	130.00
	m. Suffix letter *M*.		FV	FV	190.00
	u. Suffix letter *U*.		FV	FV	130.00
	v. Suffix letter *V*.		FV	FV	145.00

39	20 DOLLARS	VG	VF	UNC
	ND (2000). Purple and slate blue on m/c unpt. Like #33 but w/gold foil butterfly at r.			
	a. Suffix letter *A*.	FV	FV	30.00
	d. Suffix letter *D*.	FV	FV	30.00
	g. Suffix letter *G*.	FV	FV	32.50
	k. Suffix letter *K*.	FV	FV	32.50
	l. Suffix letter *L*.	FV	FV	30.00
	m. Suffix letter *M*.	FV	FV	45.00
	u. Suffix letter *U*.	FV	FV	30.00
	v. Suffix letter *V*.	FV	FV	32.50

2000 ND ISSUE

#37-41. Modified security features. Segmented security thread. Gold foil devices in upper r. of face. Shorter building rendering above signature.

37	5 DOLLARS		VG	VF	UNC
	ND (2000). Green, dk. green, slate blue on m/c unpt. Like #31 but w/gold foil fish at r.				
	a. Suffix letter *A*.		FV	FV	10.00
	d. Suffix letter *D*.		FV	FV	10.00
	g. Suffix letter *G*.		FV	FV	13.00
	k. Suffix letter *K*.		FV	FV	13.00
	l. Suffix letter *L*.		FV	FV	10.00
	m. Suffix letter *M*.		FV	FV	27.50
	u. Suffix letter *U*.		FV	FV	10.00
	v. Suffix letter *V*.		FV	FV	13.00

40	50 DOLLARS	VG	VF	UNC
	ND (2000). Bronze and orange on m/c unpt. Like #34 but w/gold foil flower at r.			
	a. Suffix letter *A*.	FV	FV	75.00
	d. Suffix letter *D*.	FV	FV	75.00
	g. Suffix letter *G*.	FV	FV	85.00
	k. Suffix letter *K*.	FV	FV	85.00
	l. Suffix letter *L*.	FV	FV	75.00
	m. Suffix letter *M*.	FV	FV	160.00
	u. Suffix letter *U*.	FV	FV	75.00
	v. Suffix letter *V*.	FV	FV	85.00

41	100 DOLLARS	VG	VF	UNC
	ND (2000). Dk. brown and dk. green on m/c unpt. Like #36.			
a.	Suffix letter A.	FV	FV	115.00
d.	Suffix letter D.	FV	FV	115.00
g.	Suffix letter G.	FV	FV	130.00
k.	Suffix letter K.	FV	FV	130.00
l.	Suffix letter L.	FV	FV	115.00
m.	Suffix letter M.	FV	FV	170.00
u.	Suffix letter U.	FV	FV	115.00
v.	Suffix letter V.	FV	FV	130.00

44	20 DOLLARS	VG	VF	UNC
	ND (2003). Purple and slate blue on m/c unpt.			
a.	Suffix letter A.	FV	FV	25.00
d.	Suffix letter D.	FV	FV	25.00
g.	Suffix letter G.	FV	FV	27.50
k.	Suffix letter K.	FV	FV	27.50
l.	Suffix letter L.	FV	FV	25.00
m.	Suffix letter M.	FV	FV	35.00
u.	Suffix letter U.	FV	FV	25.00
v.	Suffix letter V.	FV	FV	27.50

2003 ND ISSUE

#42-46 like #37-41 but with modified security features which include silver foil devices in the upper r. of the face and a wider security thread. Printer: (T)DLR.

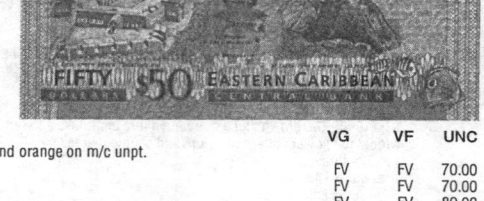

42	5 DOLLARS	VG	VF	UNC
	ND (2003). Green, dk. green, slate blue on m/c unpt.			
a.	Suffix letter A.	FV	FV	8.50
d.	Suffix letter D.	FV	FV	8.50
g.	Suffix letter G.	FV	FV	10.00
k.	Suffix letter K.	FV	FV	10.00
l.	Suffix letter L.	FV	FV	8.50
m.	Suffix letter M.	FV	FV	15.00
u.	Suffix letter U.	FV	FV	8.50
v.	Suffix letter V.	FV	FV	10.00

45	50 DOLLARS	VG	VF	UNC
	ND (2003). Bronze and orange on m/c unpt.			
a.	Suffix letter A.	FV	FV	70.00
d.	Suffix letter D.	FV	FV	70.00
g.	Suffix letter G.	FV	FV	80.00
k.	Suffix letter K.	FV	FV	80.00
l.	Suffix letter L.	FV	FV	70.00
m.	Suffix Letter M.	FV	FV	150.00
u.	Suffix letter U.	FV	FV	70.00
v.	Suffix letter V.	FV	FV	80.00

43	10 DOLLARS	VG	VF	UNC
	ND (2003). Blue and black on m/c unpt.			
a.	Suffix letter A.	FV	FV	17.50
d.	Suffix letter D.	FV	FV	17.50
g.	Suffix letter G.	FV	FV	22.50
k.	Suffix letter K.	FV	FV	22.50
l.	Suffix letter L.	FV	FV	17.50
m.	Suffix letter M.	FV	FV	27.50
u.	Suffix letter U.	FV	FV	17.50
v.	Suffix letter V.	FV	FV	22.50

46	100 DOLLARS	VG	VF	UNC
	ND (2003). Bk. Brown and dk. green on m/c unpt.			
a.	Suffix letter A.	FV	FV	100.00
d.	Suffix letter D.	FV	FV	100.00
g.	Suffix letter G.	FV	FV	115.00
k.	Suffix letter K.	FV	FV	115.00
l.	Suffix letter L.	FV	FV	100.00
m.	Suffix letter M.	FV	FV	150.00
u.	Suffix letter U.	FV	FV	100.00
v.	Suffix letter V.	FV	FV	115.00

COLLECTOR SERIES

GOVERNMENT OF ANTIGUA AND BARBUDA

1983 ND ISSUE

This set is made with thin gold and silver foil bonded to paper.

		Issue Price	Mkt.	Value
CS1	**30 DOLLARS**	—		350.00
	ND (1983). 12 different notes showing various flowers and animals.			

1985 ND ISSUE

		Issue Price	Mkt.	Value
CS2	**30 DOLLARS**	—		350.00
	ND (1984). 12 different notes showing various animals and plants.			
CS3	**30 DOLLARS**	—		250.00
	ND (1985) 10 different notes showing various animals and plants.			

EAST CARIBBEAN CENTRAL BANK

1988 ND ISSUE

This set is made with gold and silver foil bonded to paper.

		Issue Price	Mkt.	Value
CS4	**100 DOLLARS**	1155.00		1100.00
	ND (1988). 30 different notes showing various pirate and treasure sailing ships. (20,000 sets).			

The Republic of Ecuador, located astride the equator on the Pacific coast of South America, has an area of 109,484 sq. mi. (283,561 sq. km.) and a population of 12.65 million. Capital: Quito. Agriculture is the mainstay of the economy but there are appreciable deposits of minerals and petroleum. It is the world's largest exporter of bananas and balsa wood. Coffee, cacao and shrimp are also valuable exports.

Ecuador was first sighted, 1526, by Bartolome Ruiz. Conquest was undertaken by Sebastian de Benalcazar who founded Quito in 1534. Ecuador was part of the province, later Vice-royalty, of Peru until 1739 when it became part of the Vice-royalty of New Granada. After two failed attempts to attain independence in 1810 and 1812, it successfully declared its independence in October 1820, and won final victory over Spanish forces May 24, 1822. Incorporated into the Gran Colombia confederacy, it loosened its ties in 1830 and regained full independence in 1835.

MONETARY SYSTEM:

- 1 Sucre = 10 Decimos = 100 Centavos
- 1 Condor = 25 Sucres
- 1 USA Dollar = 25,000 Sucres (March 2001)

REPUBLIC

BANCO CENTRAL DEL ECUADOR

Multiple signature varieties.

1944-67 ISSUE

#96 and 97 black on m/c unpt. Printer: ABNC.

96	**500 SUCRES**	VG	VF	UNC
	1944-66. Mercury seated at ctr. Back deep orange.			
	a. Sign. title ovpt: *PRESIDENTE* at l. 12.5.1944; 27.6.1944.	175.00	400.00	—
	b. Sign. title ovpt: *GERENTE GENERAL* at l., *VOCAL* at r. 31.7.1944; 7.9.1944.	150.00	375.00	—
	c. Sign. title ovpt: *GERENTE GENERAL* at r. 12.1.1945-12.7.1947.	125.00	300.00	—
	d. As c. 21.4.1961-17.11.1966.	125.00	300.00	—
	s. Specimen. ND.	—	—	400.00

97	**1000 SUCRES**	VG	VF	UNC
	1944-67. Woman reclining ("Telephone Service") at ctr. Back greenish gray.			
	a. Sign. title ovpt: *PRESIDENTE* at l. 12.5.1944; 27.6.1944.	300.00	650.00	—
	b. Sign. title ovpt: *GERENTE GENERAL* at l., *VOCAL* at r. 31.7.1944; 7.9.1944.	275.00	550.00	—
	c. Sign. title ovpt: *PRESIDENTE* at l., *GERENTE GENERAL* at r. 12.1.1945.	250.00	500.00	—
	d. Sign. title ovpt: *GERENTE GENERAL* at r. 16.10.1945; 12.7.1947.	225.00	450.00	—
	e. As d. 21.4.1961; 27.2.1962; 4.3.1964; 23.7.1964; 17.11.1966; 6.4.1967.	150.00	350.00	—
	s. Specimen. ND.	—	—	400.00

Note: The following reduced size notes are listed by printer.

1950 Issue (1950-59)	#98-99 printer: W&S.
1950-71 Issue (1950-74)	#100-107 printer: ABNC.
1975-80 Issue (1975-83)	#108-112 printer: ABNC.
1957-71 Issue (1957-82)	#113-118 printer: TDLR.

1950 ISSUE - REDUCED SIZE NOTES

#98-99 arms at ctr. on back. Printer: W&S.

98	5 SUCRES	VG	VF	UNC
	1950-55. Black on green unpt. Portr. Antonio Jose de Sucre at ctr. Date at l. or r. Back red.			
	a. 11.5.1950-13.7.1953.	2.25	15.00	75.00
	b. Sign. title ovpt: *SUBGERENTE GENERAL* at l. 21.9.1953.	4.50	20.00	85.00
	c. 31.5.1954-28.11.1955.	2.00	12.50	55.00
99	50 SUCRES			
	1950-59. Black on green unpt. National monument at ctr. w/ bldgs. in background. Back green.			
	a. 11.5.1950; 26.7.1950; 13.10.1950; 3.4.1951; 26.9.1951.	7.50	50.00	150.00
	b. Sign. title ovpt: *SUBGERENTE GENERAL* at l. 3.9.1952; 8.10.1954; 24.9.1957.	7.50	50.00	150.00
	c. 10.12.1953; 19.6.1956; 25.11.1957; 25.11.1958; 8.4.1959.	6.00	40.00	125.00
	s1. Specimen. Black ovpt.: *ESPÉCIMEN* on both sides. ND, w/0000 serial #, unsigned.	—	—	175.00
	s2. Specimen. Red ovpt.: *MUESTRA* twice on both sides. ND, w/o serial # or signs. Punched hole cancelled.	—	—	175.00

1950-71 ISSUE

#100-107 black on m/c unpt. Several date varieties, sign. title ovpts. and serial # styles. Arms on back 31mm. wide, w/o flagpole stems below. Printer: ABNC.

100	5 SUCRES	VG	VF	UNC
	1956-73. Portr. Antonio Jose de Sucre at ctr. Back red.			
	a. 19.6.1956; 28.8.1956; 2.4.1957; 19.6.1957; 19.6.1957.	1.00	5.00	40.00
	b. Sign. title ovpt *SUBGERENTE GENERAL*. 24.9.1957; 2.1.1958.	0.75	5.00	40.00
	c. 2.2.1958; 1.1.1966.	0.50	2.50	20.00
	d. 27.2.1970; 3.9.1973. Serial # varieties.	0.25	1.50	3.50
101	10 SUCRES			
	1950-1955. Portr. Sebastian de Benalcazar at ctr. Plain background. Back blue.			
	a. 14.1.1950-28.11.1955.	2.00	8.00	45.00
	b. 21.9.1953; 16.3.1954; 3.10.1955. Ovpt *SUB GERENTE GENERAL*.	2.00	10.00	50.00
	s. Specimen.	—	—	100.00

101A	10 SUCRES	VG	VF	UNC
	1956-74. Like #101 but different guilloches and ornate background.			
	a. 15.6.1956-27.4.1966.	1.00	7.50	35.00
	b. 24.5.1968-2.1.1974.	0.50	3.00	15.00
	s. Specimen.	—	—	100.00

Note: #101A with date of 24.12.1957 has ovpt: *SUB GERENTE GENERAL*.

102	20 SUCRES	VG	VF	UNC
	28.2.1950-28.7.1960. Church facade at ctr. Back brown.	2.50	15.00	50.00

103	20 SUCRES	VG	VF	UNC
	1962-73. Like #102. Church facade at ctr., different guilloches and darker unpt. on face.			
	a. 12.12.1962-4.10.1967.	2.00	5.00	25.00
	b. 24.5.1968-3.9.1973.	1.00	3.00	15.00
	s. Specimen. ND.	—	—	125.00

104	50 SUCRES	VG	VF	UNC
	1968-71. Similar to #99. National monument at ctr. Back green.			
	a. 24.5.1968; 5.11.1969.	2.00	5.00	30.00
	b. 20.5.1971.	1.00	4.00	20.00
	s. Specimen. ND.	—	—	50.00
104A	100 SUCRES			
	1952-57. Portr. Simon Bolivar at ctr. Back purple.			
	a. 3.9.1952-19.6.1957.	15.00	75.00	220.00
	b. Sign. title: *SUBGERENTE*. 3.9.1952; 10.12.1953.	15.00	75.00	220.00
105	100 SUCRES			
	27.4.1966-7.7.1970. Like #104A, but different guilloches. Back purple.	5.00	10.00	50.00
106	500 SUCRES			
	ND (ca.1971). Similar to #96. Mercury seated at ctr. w/different guilloches and other changes. Back red. Archive example.	—	—	1000.00

107	1000 SUCRES	VG	VF	UNC
	30.5.1969-20.9.1973. Banco Central bldg. at ctr. Back olive-gray.			
	a. Issued note.	20.00	85.00	250.00
	s. Specimen. ND.	—	—	75.00

1975-80 ISSUE

#108-112 black on m/c unpt. Face designs like previous issue. New rendition of arms 29mm. wide w/flagpole stems below on back. Printer: ABNC.

108	5 SUCRES	VG	VF	UNC
	1975-83. Like #100. Portr. Antonio Jose de Sucre at ctr. Back red w/new rendition of arms.			
	a. 14.3.1975; 29.4.1977.	0.25	1.50	7.50
	b. 20.8.1982; 20.4.1983.	0.25	1.00	4.00

112	100 SUCRES	VG	VF	UNC
	24.5.1980. Like #105. Portr. S. Bolívar at ctr. Back purple w/new rendition of arms.	0.25	1.50	12.50

1957-71 ISSUE

#113-118 black on m/c unpt. Similar to previous issues. Several sign. title ovpt. varieties. Security thread intermittent through 1969. Printer: TDLR.

109	10 SUCRES	VG	VF	UNC
	14.3.1975; 10.8.1976; 29.4.1977; 24.5.1978. Like #101A. Portr. Sebastian de Benalcazar at ctr. Back blue w/new rendition of arms.	0.25	2.00	10.00

113	5 SUCRES	VG	VF	UNC
	1958-88. Similar to #108. Back red.			
	a. 2.1.1958-7.11.1962.	0.75	4.00	15.00
	b. 23.5.1963-27.2.1970.	0.50	1.00	10.00
	c. 25.7.1979-24.5.1980.	0.25	0.50	5.00
	d. 22.11.1988.	0.10	0.25	2.00
	s. Specimen. ND; 24.5.1968; 24.5.1980.	—	—	50.00

114	10 SUCRES			
	1968-83. Similar to #109. Back blue.			
	a. 24.5.1968; 20.5.1971.	0.50	3.00	20.00
	b. 24.5.1980; 30.9.1982; 20.4.1983.	0.25	1.00	10.00
	s1. Specimen. 24.5.1968.	—	—	75.00
	s2. Specimen. 20.5.1971. Series KY.	—	—	50.00
	s3. Specimen. 30.9.1982. Series LI.	—	—	50.00

110	20 SUCRES	VG	VF	UNC
	10.8.1976. Like #103. Church façade at ctr. Back brown w/new rendition of arms.	0.25	2.50	15.00

115	20 SUCRES	VG	VF	UNC
	1961-83. Similar to #110. Back brown.			
	a. 7.6.1961; 29.8.1961; 27.2.1962; 6.7.1962; 7.11.1962; 12.12.1962.	1.50	5.00	35.00
	b. 1.5.1978; 24.5.1980; 20.4.1983.	1.00	2.50	15.00
	s1. Specimen. ND.	—	—	50.00
	s2. Specimen. Series LE. 24.5.1980.	—	—	50.00

116	50 SUCRES			
	1957-82. Similar to #111.			
	a. 2.4.1957; 7.7.1959.	2.50	15.00	60.00
	b. 7.11.1962; 29.10.1963; 29.1.1965; 6.8.1965.	1.00	8.00	35.00
	c. 1.1.1966; 27.4.1966; 17.11.1966.	1.00	4.00	25.00
	d. 4.10.1967; 30.5.1969; 17.7.1974.	0.75	2.00	15.00
	e. 24.5.1980; 20.8.1982.	0.50	1.25	10.00
	s. Specimen. ND; 1.1.1966.	—	—	20.00

111	50 SUCRES	VG	VF	UNC
	10.8.1976. Like #104. National monument at ctr. Back green w/new rendition of arms.			
	a. Issued note.	1.00	4.00	22.50
	s. Specimen.	—	—	100.00

117   100 SUCRES
29.8.1961-6.8.1965.. Similar to #112 but crude portr. w/lt. clouds behind. Back purple.

	VG	VF	UNC
a. Issued note.	3.50	20.00	50.00
s. Specimen. W/o sign. Series TW.	—	—	75.00

118   100 SUCRES
1971-77. Like #117 but finer portr. w/dk. clouds behind. Back purple.

	VG	VF	UNC
a. 20.5.1971; 17.7.1974.	3.00	8.00	40.00
b. 10.8.1976; 10.8.1977.	2.00	5.00	25.00
s. Specimen. 20.5.1971.	—	—	50.00

1976 ISSUE

#119 and 120 printer: TDLR.

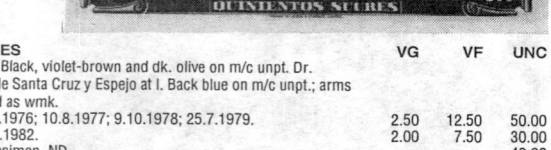

119   500 SUCRES
1976-82. Black, violet-brown and dk. olive on m/c unpt. Dr. Eugenio de Santa Cruz y Espejo at l. Back blue on m/c unpt.; arms at ctr. and as wmk.

	VG	VF	UNC
a. 24.5.1976; 10.8.1977; 9.10.1978; 25.7.1979.	2.50	12.50	50.00
b. 20.7.1982.	2.00	7.50	30.00
s1. Specimen. ND.	—	—	40.00
s2. As b. Specimen.	—	0.00 -	25.00

120   1000 SUCRES
1976-82. Dk. green and red-brown on m/c unpt. Ruminahui at r. Back dk. green on m/c unpt.; arms at ctr. and as wmk.

	VG	VF	UNC
a. 24.5.1976-25.7.1979.	2.50	7.50	50.00
b. 24.5.1980; 20.7.1982.	1.25	5.00	25.00
s1. Specimen. ND.	—	—	50.00
s2. Specimen. Series HP. 24.5.1980.	—	—	25.00

1984-88 ISSUES

#120A-125 w/o text: *SOCIEDAD ANONIMA* below bank title. W/o imprint.

120A   5 SUCRES
22.11.1988. Black on m/c unpt. Portr. A. J. de Sucré at ctr. Arms on back 26mm wide. Back red-violet. Printer: TDLR.

VG	VF	UNC
0.05	0.50	4.00

121   10 SUCRES
29.4.1986; 22.11.1988. Black on m/c unpt. Like #114 Back blue.

VG	VF	UNC
0.10	0.75	3.50

121A   20 SUCRES
1986-88. Black on m/c unpt. Like #115. Back brown.

	VG	VF	UNC
a. 29.4.1986; 22.11.1988.	0.10	0.75	5.00
s. Specimen. 29.4.1986. Series LM.	—	—	20.00

122   50 SUCRES
5.9.1984; 22.11.1988. Black on m/c unpt. Similar to #116. Back green.

	VG	VF	UNC
a. Issued note.	0.25	1.00	7.50
s. Specimen. 5.9.1984.	—	—	40.00

123   100 SUCRES
29.4.1986; 20.4.1990. Black on m/c unpt. Like #118. Back purple. Dark or light blue serial #.

VG	VF	UNC
0.50	2.00	15.00

123A   100 SUCRES
1988-97. Black on m/c unpt. Like #123 but w/plate differences on face and back. Serial # style varieties. Back purple.

	VG	VF	UNC
a. Blue serial #. 8.6.1988; 21.6.1991; 11.10.1991.	0.25	0.50	5.00
b. 9.3.1992; 4.12.1992; 20.8.1993.	0.25	0.50	5.00
c. Black serial #. 21.2.1994.	0.25	0.50	5.00
d. As c. 3.4.1997.	0.25	0.50	5.00
s1. As a. Specimen. 8.6.1988. Punched hole cancelled.	—	—	35.00
s2. As b. Specimen. 21.6.1991; Series WF. 20.8.1993.	—	—	25.00

#124 and 125 wmk: Arms. W/o imprint. Sign. varieties.

124   500 SUCRES
5.9.1984. Black, violet-brown and dk. olive on m/c unpt. Like #119.

	VG	VF	UNC
a. Issued note.	0.50	2.00	15.00
s. Specimen.	—	—	40.00

124A   500 SUCRES
8.6.1988. Black, violet-brown and dk. olive on m/c unpt. Similar to #124 but many minor plate differences.

	VG	VF	UNC
	0.25	1.25	10.00

125   1000 SUCRES
1984-88. Dk. green and red-brown on m/c unpt. Like #120 but w/o *EL* in bank title. Serial # style varieties.

	VG	VF	UNC
a. 5.9.1984; 29.9.1986.	0.25	2.00	15.00
b. 8.6.1988.	0.25	1.50	10.00

Note: Later dates of #123A-#125 were made by different printers (w/o imprint) and vary slightly.

126   5000 SUCRES
1.12.1987. Purple and brown on m/c unpt. Juan Montalvo at l. and as wmk., arms at ctr. Flightless cormoran, Galapagos penguin and Galapagos tortoise on back. Printer: BCdE.

	VG	VF	UNC
a. Issued note.	0.25	2.00	25.00
s. Specimen.	—	—	50.00

Note: #126 designed in Mexico.

127   10,000 SUCRES
1988-98. Dk. brown and reddish brown on m/c unpt. Vicente Rocafuerte at l. and as wmk. Arms upper l. ctr., Independence monument in Quito at ctr. r. on back. Printer: BCdE. Serial # varieties exist.

	VG	VF	UNC
a. Sign. title by itself at l.: *VOCAL.* 30.7.1988; 21.2.1994; 13.10.1994.	0.25	2.00	15.00
b. Sign. title at l.: *PRESIDENTE JUNTA MONETARIA.* 6.2.1995; 8.3.1995; 8.8.1995; 4.1.1996; 23.9.1996.	0.25	2.00	15.00
c. Sign. title at l.: *PRESIDENTE DEL DIRECTORIO.* 14.12.1998.	0.25	0.75	10.00
s1. As a. Specimen. Series AB.	—	—	150.00
s2. As a. Specimen. 13.10.1994 Series AH.	—	0.00 -	150.00
s3. As b. Specimen. 8.3.1995. Series AL.	—	—	125.00

1991-95 ISSUE

128   5000 SUCRES
1991-99. Purple and brown on m/c unpt. Like #126 but w/repositioned sign. and both serial # horizontal. Printer: BCdE.

	VG	VF	UNC
a. Sign. title by itself at l.: *VOCAL.* 21.6.1991; 17.3.1992; 22.6.1992; 20.8.1993.	0.25	1.25	10.00
b. Sign. title at l.: *PRESIDENTE JUNTA MONETARIA.* 31.1.1995; 8.8.1995; 13.1.1996; 31.10.1996.	0.25	1.25	7.50
c. Sign. title at l.: *PRESIDENTE DEL DIRECTORIO.* 6.3.1999.	0.25	1.25	7.50
s1. Specimen. 21.6.1991. Series AG.	—	—	35.00
s2. As a. Specimen. 17.3.1992. Series AJ.	—	—	35.00
s3. As b. Specimen. 31.1.1995.	0.00 -	—	25.00

129   20,000 SUCRES

		VG	VF	UNC
	1995-99. Brown, black and deep blue on m/c unpt. Dr. Gabriel Garcia Moreno at r. and as wmk. Arms at ctr. on back.			
a.	Sign. title at r.: *PRESIDENTE JUNTA MONETARIA.* 31.1.1995; 20.11.1995; 26.3.1999.	0.75	2.00	20.00
b.	Sign. title at r.: *PRESIDENTE JUNTA MONETARIA.* 2.6.1997.	0.75	1.50	15.00
c.	Two security threads. Sign. title at r.: *PRESIDENTE DEL DIRECTORIO.* 10.5.1999.	0.75	1.50	10.00
d.	W/o security thread. Sign. title at r.: *PRESIDENTE DEL DIRECTORIO.* 10.3.1999.	0.75	1.50	7.50
s1.	As a. Specimen, punched hole cancelled. 31.1.1995.	—	—	35.00
s2.	As b. Specimen. 2.6.1997. Series AD.	—	—	25.00
s3.	As c. 10.3.1999.	—	—	25.00

130   50,000 SUCRES

		VG	VF	UNC
	1995-99. Gray and red-brown on m/c unpt. Eloy Alfaro at r. and as wmk. Arms on back. Segmented foil over security thread.			
a.	Two security threads. Sign. title at l.: *PRESIDENTE JUNTA MONETARIA.* 31.1.1995; 2.6.1997; 20.4.1998; 6.3.1999; 26.3.1999.	1.00	2.50	15.00
b.	Decreased security features. W/one security thread. Sign. title at l.: *PRESIDENTE DEL DIRECTORIO.* 10.3.1999.	1.00	2.50	10.00
s.	As a. Specimen. 31.1.1995; 2.6.1997. Series AB.	—	—	25.00

Note: Since September 7, 2000, the U.S. Dollar became legal tender, and the sucre was redeemable until March 30, 2001 at the rate of 25,000 Sucres per U.S. Dollar.

EGYPT

The Arab Republic of Egypt, located on the northeastern corner of Africa, has an area of 386,650 sq. mi. (1,000,000 sq. km.) and a population of 68.12 million. Capital: Cairo. Although Egypt is an almost rainless expanse of desert, its economy is predominantly agricultural. Cotton, rice and petroleum are exported.

Egyptian history dates back to about 4000 B.C. when the empire was established by uniting the upper and lower kingdoms. Following its "Golden Age" (16th to 13th centuries B.C.), Egypt was conquered by Persia (525 B.C.) and Alexander the Great (332 B.C.). The Ptolemies ruled until the suicide of Cleopatra (30 B.C.) when Egypt became a Roman colony. Arab caliphs ruled Egypt from 641 to 1517, when the Turks took it for their Ottoman Empire. Turkish rule, interrupted by the occupation of Napoleon (1798-1801), became increasingly casual, permitting Great Britain to inject its influence by purchasing shares in the Suez Canal. British troops occupied Egypt in 1882, becoming the de facto rulers. On Dec. 14, 1914, Egypt was made a protectorate of Britain. British occupation ended on Feb. 28, 1922, when Egypt became a sovereign, independent kingdom. The monarchy was abolished and a republic proclaimed on June 18, 1952.

On Feb. 1, 1958, Egypt and Syria formed the United Arab Republic. Yemen joined on March 8 in an association known as the United Arab States. Syria withdrew from the United Arab Republic on Sept. 29, 1961, and on Dec. 26 Egypt dissolved its ties with Yemen in the United Arab States. On Sept. 2, 1971, Egypt shed the name United Arab Republic in favor of the Arab Republic of Egypt.

MONETARY SYSTEM:

    1 Pound = 100 Piastres

REPLACEMENT NOTES:

    Starting in 1969, 2 types exist. Earlier system uses a single Arabic letter as series prefix instead of normal number/letter prefix. Known notes: #42. Later system has the equivalent of English "200", "300" or "400" in front of a single Arabic series letter.

SIGNATURE VARIETIES			
11	A. El-Refay, 1961-63	12	A. Zendo, 1962-66
13	A. Nazmy A. A El Hamed, 1967-70	14	A. Zendo, 1972-75
15	M. Ibrahim, 1976-81	16	M. S. A. Shalaby, 1981-84
17	A. Negm, 1985	18	S. Hamed, 1986
19	I. H. Mohamed	20	M. Abou El-Oyoun
21	Farouk Abdel Baky El Okda 1st kind	22	Farouk Abdel Baky El Okda II 2nd kind

REPUBLIC

CENTRAL BANK OF EGYPT

1961-64 ISSUES

#35-41 sign. and date varieties.

35 25 PIASTRES
1.11.1961-18.8.1966. Blue on m/c unpt. U. A. R. arms at r. Sign.
11; 12.

	VG	VF	UNC
a. Issued note.	0.75	2.00	6.00
s. Specimen.	—	—	—

36 50 PIASTRES
1.11.1961-14.8.1966. Blackish green m/c unpt. U. A. R. arms at r.,
also in wmk. Sign. 11; 12.

	VG	VF	UNC
a. Issued note.	0.75	2.00	12.00
s. Specimen.	—	—	—

37 1 POUND
1.11.1961-23.2.1967. Blue-green on lilac and m/c unpt.
Tutankhamen's mask at r. Back green. Wmk: Arms. Sign. 11; 12;
13.

	VG	VF	UNC
a. Issued note.	1.00	2.50	6.00
s. Specimen.	—	—	—

38 5 POUNDS
1.11.1961-12.11.1961. Green and brown on m/c unpt. Circular
guilloche at l., Tutankhamen's mask at r. Wmk: Flower. Sign. 11.

VG	VF	UNC
7.50	25.00	95.00

39 5 POUNDS
13.11.1961-16.6.1964. Green and brown on m/c unpt. Similar to
#38, but circular area at l. is blank. Guilloche at bottom ctr. on face
and back. Wmk: Arms. Sign. 11; 12.

	VG	VF	UNC
a. Issued note.	3.00	7.50	22.50
s. Specimen.	—	—	—

40 5 POUNDS
17.6.1964-13.2.1965. Lilac and brown on m/c unpt. Like #39.
Sign. 12.

VG	VF	UNC
2.00	5.00	20.00

41 10 POUNDS
1.11.1961-13.2.1965. Dk. green and dk. brown on m/c unpt.
Tutankhamen's mask at r. Back brown. Wmk: Arms. Sign. 11; 12.

	VG	VF	UNC
	3.50	7.50	27.50

1967-69 ISSUE

#42-46 wmk: Archaic Egyptian scribe. Replacement notes: Serial # prefix single Arabic letter.

42 25 PIASTRES
6.2.1967-4.1.1975. Blue, green and brown on m/c unpt. Sphinx
w/statue at l. ctr. U.A.R. arms at ctr. on back. Sign. 13; 14.

	VG	VF	UNC
	0.15	0.50	3.00

43 50 PIASTRES
2.12.1967-28.1.1978. Red-brown and brown on m/c unpt. Al Azhar
mosque at r., University of Cairo at l. ctr. Ramses II at ctr. r. on
back. Sign. 13; 14; 15.

	VG	VF	UNC
a. Issued note.	0.25	1.00	3.50
s. Specimen.	—	—	

44 1 POUND
12.5.1967-19.4.1978. Brown and black on m/c unpt. Sultan Quayet
Bey mosque at l. ctr. Archaic statues on back. Sign. 13; 14; 15.

	VG	VF	UNC
a. Issued note.	0.50	1.00	4.00
s. Specimen.	—		

45 5 POUNDS
1.1.1969-78. Black on blue and m/c unpt. Ahmad ibn Tulun
mosque at Cairo at ctr. r. Ruins at l., frieze at ctr. r. on back. Sign.
13; 14; 15.

	VG	VF	UNC
a. Issued note.	2.00	3.50	20.00
s. Specimen.	—		

46 10 POUNDS
1.9.1969-78. Red-brown and brown on m/c unpt. Sultan Hassan
Mosque at Cairo at l. ctr. Pharaoh and pyramids on back. Sign. 13;
14; 15.

	VG	VF	UNC
	3.00	6.00	22.50

1976 ISSUE

#47 and 48 replacement notes: Serial # prefix single Arabic letter.

50 1 POUND

29.5.(19)78-. Brown, purple and deep olive-green on m/c unpt. Sultan Qait Bey mosque at l. ctr. Statues from the Abu Simbel Temple on back.

		VG	VF	UNC
a.	Back deep brown. Solid security thread. 29.5.(19)78-10.4.(19)87. Sign. 15; 16; 17; 18.	FV	FV	1.50
b.	Back pale brown. Solid security thread. 19.11.(19)86-9.8.(19)89. Sign. 18; 19.	FV	FV	1.50
c.	Back pale brown. Segmented security thread with bank name repeated. 10.5.(19)89-(20)01. Sign. 18, 19.	FV	FV	1.50
d.	(20)01-(20)03. Sign. 20.	FV	FV	1.50

47 25 PIASTRES

12.4.1976-28.8.1978. Blue, green and grayish brown on blue and orange unpt. Face and wmk. like #42. A. R. E. arms on back. Sign. 15.

		VG	VF	UNC
a.	Issued note.	0.30	0.75	3.50
s.	Specimen.	—	—	—

51 10 POUNDS

24.6.(19)78-27.9.(20)00. Red-brown and brown-violet on m/c unpt. Al-Rifai mosque at ctr. Pharaoh on back. Sign. 15; 16; 17; 18; 19.

	VG	VF	UNC
	FV	FV	10.00

48 20 POUNDS

5.7.1976; 1978. Green and black on m/c unpt. Mohammed Ali mosque at l., Arabic legends at r. Archaic war chariot at l. ctr., frieze at ctr. r. on back. Wmk: Egyptian scribe. Sign. 15.

VG	VF	UNC
6.00	10.00	35.00

1978-79 ISSUE

#49-62 no longer have conventional dates with Arabic day, month and year. In place of this are six Arabic numerals, the first and last making up the year, the second and third the day, the fourth and fifth the month of issue; YDDMMY; i.e. 825029 will be 25 Feb. 1989. Wmk: Tutankhamen's mask.

Replacement notes: Serial # prefix. Arabic *200* or *300* before single Arabic letter.

52 20 POUNDS

6.9.(19)78-92. Black, gray-violet and deep green on m/c unpt. Muhammed Ali mosque at ctr. Archaic sculptures from Chapel of Sesostris I and archaic war chariot on back.

		VG	VF	UNC
a.	Date below wmk. Solid security thread. 6.9.(19)78-22.4.(19)82. Sign. 15; 16.	FV	FV	30.00
b.	Date at lower r. of wmk. Solid security thread. 9.12.(19)86; 3.3.(19)87; 4.10.(19)87. Sign. 18.	FV	FV	20.00
c.	Segmented security thread w/bank name repeated. (19)88-(19)92. Sign. 19.	FV	FV	17.50

49 25 PIASTRES

2.1.-11.5.(19)79. Black and brown on gray, pale blue and orange unpt. Al-Sayida Aisha mosque at ctr. Stylized A. R. E. arms, cotton, wheat and corn plants at ctr. on back. Sign. 15.

VG	VF	UNC
FV	0.50	2.00

53 100 POUNDS

		VG	VF	UNC
	(19)78; (19)92. Blue and green on m/c unpt. Al-Sayida Zainab mosque at ctr. Pharaoh's mask above frieze at ctr. of vertical format on back.			
a.	Series 1-6.(19)78. Sign. 15.	FV	40.00	120.00
b.	(19)92. Sign. 18.	FV	FV	90.00

1980-81 ISSUE

Replacement notes: Serial # prefix Arabic *200* or *300* before single Arabic series letter.

54 25 PIASTRES

		VG	VF	UNC
	17.1.(19)80-10.1(19)84. Dk. green on lt. green, orange and blue unpt. Like #49. Sign. 15; 16.	FV	0.30	1.50

55 50 PIASTRES

		VG	VF	UNC
	1.1.(19)81-10.6.(19)83. Green and brown on m/c unpt. Al Azhar mosque at ctr. Sculptured wall design at l., Ramses II at ctr., archaic seal at r. on back. Sign. 15; 16.	FV	0.50	2.00

56 5 POUNDS

		VG	VF	UNC
	(19)81; (19)86; (19)87. Olive-black and blue-black on m/c unpt. Ibn Toulon mosque at ctr. Design symbolizing bounty of the Nile River at ctr. on back.			
a.	1.2.(19)81. Sign. 15.	FV	3.00	15.00
b.	(19)86; 6.1.(19)87. Sign. 16; 17; 18.	FV	2.50	10.00

1985 ISSUE

Replacement notes: Serial # prefix Arabic *200* or *300* before single Arabic series letter.

57 25 PIASTRES

		VG	VF	UNC
	(19)85-99. Purple and pale blue on pale lilac and m/c unpt. Face and wmk. like #49 and #54. Standard A.R.E. arms at l. ctr. on back.			
a.	Solid security thread. 12.1.(19)85-30.1.(19)89. Sign. 17; 18.	FV	FV	1.00
b.	Segmented security thread w/bank name repeated. 5.12.(19)90-(19)99. Sign. 18; 19.	FV	FV	0.75
c.	8.1.2001. Sign. 19.	FV	FV	0.75

58 50 PIASTRES

		VG	VF	UNC
	(19)85-94. Black on pale orange, pink and m/c unpt. Al Azhar mosque at ctr. r. Back like #55.			
a.	No text line at lower l. on face. Solid security thead. 2.7.(19)85- . Sign. 17; 18.	FV	0.25	2.00
b.	Text line added at lower l. on face. 1.2.(19)87-17.8.(19)89. Sign. 18; 19.	FV	FV	1.25
c.	Segmented security thread w/bank name repeated. 5.1.(19)90-11.8.(19)94.	FV	FV	1.00

1989-94 ISSUE

Replacement notes: Serial # prefix Arabic *200* or *300* before single Arabic series letter.

62	50 PIASTRES	VG	VF	UNC
	6.7.(19)95-17.7.2002. Dull olive-gray on m/c unpt. Like #58. Sign. 19; 20	FV	FV	0.75

59	5 POUNDS	VG	VF	UNC
	2.4.(19)89- . Black and blue-black on m/c unpt. Like #56 but m/c scrollwork added in unpt. and into wmk. area. Archaic design over wmk. area at r. on back. Sign. 18; 19.	FV	FV	5.00

2000-03 ISSUE

#63-64 w/wide segmented silver security strip and added rosette printed in optical variable ink.

63	5 POUNDS	VG	VF	UNC
	21.2.2002. M/c.	FV	FV	5.00

60	50 POUNDS	VG	VF	UNC
	9.2.(19)93- . Brown, violet and m/c. Abu Hariba Mosque at r. Isis above archaic boat, interior view of Edfu temple at l. ctr. on back. Sign. 18; 19.	FV	FV	30.00

64	10 POUNDS	VG	VF	UNC
	12.8.2003; 31.8.2003. M/c.	FV	FV	8.00

61	100 POUNDS	VG	VF	UNC
	14.9.(19)94; (19)97. Dk. brown and brown-violet on m/c unpt. Sultan Hassan Mosque at lower l. ctr. Sphinx at ctr. on back. Sign. 19.	FV	FV	60.00

1995 ISSUE

65	20 POUNDS	VG	VF	UNC
	3.10.2001-10.12.2003. Black, gray-violet and deep green on m/c unpt. Similar to #52. Sign. 19, 20, 21.	FV	FV	15.00

66	50 POUNDS	VG	VF	UNC
	25.11.2001. M/c.	FV	FV	27.50

67	100 POUNDS	VG	VF	UNC
	2000; 29.12.2003. Dk. brown and brown-violet on m/c unpt. Like #61.	FV	FV	50.00

CURRENCY NOTES

UNITED ARAB REPUBLIC
Law 50 of 1940

Face 4: Main heading unchanged from
Face 3 but *EGYPTIAN REGION* (small line of Arabic text) is deleted.
Back 2: *UNITED ARAB REPUBLIC* in English. Various sign. Imprint: Survey Dept.

1961 ND ISSUE

180	5 PIASTRES	VG	VF	UNC
	L.1940. Lilac. Qn. Nefertiti at r. Wmk: U A R.			
	a. Sign. Baghdady w/titles: *VICE-PRESIDENT AND MINISTER OF TREASURY*. Series 15; 16.	1.25	6.00	25.00
	b. Sign. Kaissouni w/titles: *MINISTER OF TREASURY AND PLANNING*. Series 16-18.	0.25	3.00	10.00
	c. Sign. Daif w/titles: *MINISTER OF TREASURY*. Color lilac to blue. Wmk. 3mm tall. Series 18-22.	0.20	2.00	10.00
	d. Sign. and titles as c. Wmk. 5mm tall. Series 22-26.	0.20	2.00	8.00
	e. Sign. Hegazy w/titles as d. Series 26-33.	0.20	1.00	8.00
180A	5 PIASTRES			
	L.1940. Face like #180. Back w/sign. Kaissouni w/title: MINISTER OF TREASURY (error). Series 16.	15.00	50.00	150.00

181	10 PIASTRES	VG	VF	UNC
	L.1940. Black. Group of militants w/flag having only 2 stars.			
	a. Sign. Baghdady w/titles: *VICE-PRESIDENT AND MINISTER OF TREASURY*. Series 16.	2.00	10.00	30.00
	b. Sign. Kaissouni w/titles: *MINISTER OF TREASURY AND PLANNING*. Series 16-18.	0.50	3.00	10.00
	c. Sign. Kaissouni w/titles: *MINISTER OF TREASURY*. Series 16.	15.00	50.00	175.00
	d. Sign. Daif w/title as c. Series 18-24.	0.25	3.00	10.00
	e. Sign. Hegazy w/title as c. Series 24-29.	0.25	3.00	10.00

ARAB REPUBLIC OF EGYPT
Law 50 of 1940

Face 5: *ARAB REPUBLIC OF EGYPT* in Arabic.
Back 3: *THE ARAB REPUBLIC OF EGYPT* in English. Various sign. Printer: Survey Authority or Postal Printing House.

1971 ND ISSUE

182	5 PIASTRES	VG	VF	UNC
	L.1940. Lilac. Similar to #180. Imprint: Survey of Egypt.			
	a. Sign. Hegazy w/title: *MINISTER OF TREASURY*. Wmk: U A R. Series 33; 34.	1.00	5.00	20.00
	b. Sign. Hegazy w/title: *MINISTER OF TREASURY*. Wmk: A R E. Series 34-36.	0.75	4.00	15.00
	c. Sign. Ibrahim w/title: *MINISTER OF FINANCE*. Wmk: A R E. Series 36; 37.	0.25	1.50	6.00
	d. Sign. El Nashar w/title as c. Series 37.	0.75	2.50	10.00
	e. Sign. Ismail. w/title as c. Series 37-40.	0.20	0.75	3.00
	f. Sign. M. S. Hamed. Series 40-42.	0.25	1.00	4.00
	g. Sign. Loutfy. Series 42-47.	0.20	0.75	3.00
	h. Sign. Meguid. Series 47-50.	0.15	0.60	3.00
	i. Sign. Hamed. Series. 50.	2.00	6.00	25.00
	j. Like c. Printer: Postal Printing House. Sign. Hamed. Series 50-72.	0.10	0.50	2.50
	k. Sign. El Razaz. Series 72.	0.25	1.00	5.00
183	10 PIASTRES			
	L.1940. Black. Simlar to #181. Printer: Survey Authority.			
	a. Sign. Hegazy w/title: *MINISTER OF TREASURY*. Wmk: U A R. Series 29; 30.	2.00	8.00	35.00
	b. Sign. Hegazy w/title: *MINISTER OF TREASURY*. Wmk: A R E. Series 30; 31.	1.00	5.00	20.00
	c. Sign. Ibrahim w/title: *MINISTER OF FINANCE*. Wmk: A R E. Series 31; 32.	0.50	2.00	9.00
	d. Sign. El Nashar w/titles as c. Series 32-33.	1.00	4.00	15.00
	e. Sign. Ismail w/titles as c. Series 33-35.	0.25	1.00	4.00
	f. Sign. M. S. Hamed w/titles as c. Series 35-38.	0.50	1.75	7.00
	g. Sign. Loutfy w/titles as c. Series 38-43.	0.25	1.00	4.00
	h. Sign. Meguid w/titles as c. Series 43-46.	0.20	0.75	3.00
	i. Sign. Hamed w/titles as c. Series 46.	3.00	8.00	30.00

184	10 PIASTRES	VG	VF	UNC
	L.1940. Black. Similar to #183 but new flag w/eagle instead of 2 stars. Sign. title: MINISTER OF FINANCE.			
	a. Sign. Hamed. Series 46-69.	0.15	0.50	2.50
	b. Sign. El Razaz. Series 69-75.	0.20	0.75	3.00

Note: Transitional series numbers from one signature to the next are generally much scarcer and command a premium. As of July, 1991 all Egyptian currency notes had been demonetized and withdrawn from circulation. A new series was released recently because of a coinage shortage.

1997; 1998 ND ISSUE

Law 50 of 1940.

185	5 PIASTRES	VG	VF	UNC
	L.1940. Green and orange. Similar to #182. El-Ghareeb w/title: MINISTER OF FINANCE. Arabic Series 1-2. Printer: Postal Printing House. Wmk: Kg. Tut's mask.	0.10	0.25	1.25
186	5 PIASTRES			
	L.1940. Like #185 but mule issue w/sign. Salah Hamad w/title: MINISTER OF FINANCE on back.	1.00	3.00	12.50

187	10 PIASTRES	VG	VF	UNC
	L.1940. Black and orange. Sphinx, pyramids at r. Mosque of Mohamed Ali at Citadel at l. on back. Sign. El Ghareeb w/title: MINISTER OF FINANCE. Arabic Series 1-2. Wmk: Kg. Tut's mask.	0.10	0.50	1.50

Note: Because of the error note the production of #185-187 ceased.

1998; 1999 ND ISSUE

Law 50 of 1940

#188 and 189 sign. M. Elghareeb w/title: *MINISTER OF FINANCE.*

188	5 PIASTRES	VG	VF	UNC
	L.1940. Blue-gray on blue and lilac unpt. Similar to #185.	0.10	0.25	1.25

189	10 PIASTRES	VG	VF	UNC
	L.1940. Dull purple and blue on m/c unpt. Similar to #187.	0.10	0.25	1.00

EL SALVADOR

GUATEMALA
HONDURAS
NICARAGUA
North Pacific Ocean

The Republic of El Salvador, a Central American country bordered by Guatemala, Honduras and the Pacific Ocean, has an area of 8,260 sq. mi. (21,041 sq. km.) and a population of 6.32 million. Capital: San Salvador. This most intensely cultivated country of Latin America produces coffee (the major crop), sugar and balsam for export. Gold, silver and other metals are largely unexploited.

The first Spanish attempt to subjugate the area was undertaken in 1523 by Pedro de Alvarado, Cortes' lieutenant. He was forced to retreat by superior Indian forces, but returned in 1525 and succeeded in bringing the region under control of the captainy general of Guatemala, where it remained until 1821. In 1821, El Salvador and the other Central American provinces declared their independence from Spain. In 1823, the Federal Republic of Central America was formed by the five Central American States. When this federation was dissolved in 1829, El Salvador became an independent republic.

A twelve-year civil war was ended in 1992 with the signing of a UN sponsored Peace Accord. Free elections, with full participation of all political parties, were held in 1994 and 1997. Armando Calderón-Sol was elected as president in 1994 for a 5-year term.

On January 1, 2001, a monetary reform established the U.S. dollar as the accounting unit for all financial transactions, and fixed the exchange rate as 8.75 colones per dollar. In addition, the Central Reserve Bank has indicated that it will cease issuing coins and notes.

MONETARY SYSTEM:
1 Peso = 100 Centavos to 1919
1 Colón = 100 Centavos 1919-

SUPERINTENDENCIA DE BÁNCOS Y OTRAS INSTITUCIONES FINANCIERAS:

Juan S. Quinteros	1962-1975	Marco T. Guandique	1977-Feb. 1981
Jose A. Mendoza	1968-1975	Rafael T. Carbonell	1981
Jorge A. Dowson	1975-1977	Raul Nolasco	1981-

DATING SYSTEM:
Dates listed for notes are those found on the face, regardless of the ovpt. issue dates on back which were applied practically on a daily basis as notes were needed for circulation.

REPUBLIC

BANCO CENTRAL DE RESERVA DE EL SALVADOR

1962; 1963 ISSUE

#100-146 w/various date and sign. ovpts. on back w/different shields and seals.

#100-130, 132-142, 144 and 145 portr. C. Columbus at ctr. l. on back, and later as wmk.

#100-104 printer: TDLR.

100	1 COLÓN	VG	VF	UNC
	12.3.1963; 25.1.1966; 23.8.1966. Black on m/c unpt. Central Bank at ctr. Back orange.			
	a. Issued note.	1.00	8.50	30.00
	s. Specimen. 12.3.1963.	—	—	—

101 2 COLONES

15.2.1962; 9.6.1964. Black on m/c unpt. Coffee bush at l., workers at l. ctr. Back red-brown.

	VG	VF	UNC
a. Issued note.	3.00	12.50	65.00
s. Specimen. 15.2.1962.	—	—	—

102 5 COLONES

15.2.1962; 12.3.1963. Black on m/c unpt. Woman w/basket of fruit on her head at l. Back green.

	VG	VF	UNC
a. Issued note.	3.00	10.00	50.00
s. Specimen. 15.2.1962.	—	—	—

103 10 COLONES

15.2.1962; 9.6.1964; 27.12.1966. Black on m/c unpt. Portr. Manuel José Arce at ctr., serial # at lower l. and upper r. Back brown.

	VG	VF	UNC
a. Issued note.	3.50	17.50	80.00
s. Specimen. 15.2.1962.	—	—	150.00

104 25 COLONES

1963; 1966. Black on m/c unpt. 5th of November Dam at ctr. Back dk. blue.

	VG	VF	UNC
a. 12.3.1963.	7.50	25.00	125.00
b. 27.12.1966.	750.00	25.00	100.00
s1. As a. Specimen.	—	—	80.00
s2. As b. Specimen.	—	—	75.00

1964; 1965 ISSUE

#105-107 printer: ABNC.

105 1 COLÓN

8.9.1964. Black on pink and green unpt. Farmer plowing at ctr., *SAN SALVADOR* at upper l. Black serial # and series letters. Back orange.

	VG	VF	UNC
a. Issued note.	2.00	7.50	30.00
s. Specimen.	—	—	—

106 5 COLONES

8.9.1964. Black on green and m/c unpt. José Matías Delgado addressing crowd at ctr., *SAN SALVADOR* at upper l. Black serial # at lower l. and upper r. Back deep olive-green.

	VG	VF	UNC
a. Issued note.	2.50	10.00	40.00
s. Specimen.	—	—	—

107 100 COLONES

12.1.1965. Brown and green unpt. Independence monument at ctr. but *SAN SALVADOR* at upper l. Serial # at lower l. and upper r. Back olive-green.

	VG	VF	UNC
a. Issued note.	20.00	75.00	250.00
s. Specimen. Punched hole cancelled.	—	—	150.00

1967 COMMEMORATIVE ISSUE

#108-109 printer: TDLR. These notes are reportedly commemoratives for the Bicentennial of the Birth of José Cañas.

108 1 COLÓN

20.6.1967. Black on m/c unpt. Juan José Cañas at r., *UN COLON* at ctr. *SAN SALVADOR* and date at r. Back orange.

	VG	VF	UNC
a. Issued note.	1.00	4.00	25.00
s. Specimen. Punched hole cancelled.	—	—	40.00

109   5 COLONES

	VG	VF	UNC
20.6.1967. Black on pink and green unpt. Scene of Juan José Cañas freeing the slaves, *31.12.1823* at ctr. Back green.			
a. Issued note.	20.00	125.00	325.00
s. Specimen.	—	—	100.00

1968-70 ISSUE

#110-114 printer: USBNC.

110   1 COLÓN

	VG	VF	UNC
1968; 1970. Black on lt. orange and pale blue unpt. Juan José Cañas at r., *1 COLON* at ctr. Back orange.			
a. Sign. title: *CAJERO* at r. 13.8.1968.	0.75	2.50	17.50
b. Sign. title: *GERENTE* at r. 12.5.1970.	0.75	2.50	17.50
s1. As a. Specimen.	—	—	35.00
s2. As b. Specimen.	—	—	35.00

111   5 COLONES

	VG	VF	UNC
1968-70. Black on green and ochre unpt. José Matías Delgado addressing crowd at ctr., *5 COLONES* at r. Back dk. green.			
a. Sign. title: *CAJERO* at r. 13.8.1968; 4.2.1969.	1.25	5.00	25.00
b. Sign. title: *GERENTE* at r. 12.5.1970.	1.25	5.00	25.00
s1. As a. Specimen. 13.8.1968; 4.2.1969.	—	—	35.00
s2. As b. Specimen.	—	—	35.00

112   10 COLONES

	VG	VF	UNC
13.8.1968. Black on tan and pale blue unpt. Manuel José Arce at r., *10 COLONES* at ctr. Back black.			
a. Issued note.	3.00	12.50	50.00
s. Specimen.	—	—	40.00

113   25 COLONES

	VG	VF	UNC
12.5.1970. Black on lt. orange and pale blue unpt. 5th of November Dam at r. Back dk. blue.			
a. Issued note.	7.00	20.00	80.00
s. Specimen.	—	—	50.00

114   100 COLONES

	VG	VF	UNC
12.5.1970. Black on pink and pale olive-green unpt. Independence monument at ctr. Back olive-green.			
a. Issued note.	20.00	75.00	250.00
s. Specimen.	—	—	200.00

1971; 1972 ISSUE

#115-119 Printer: TDLR.

115   1 COLÓN

	VG	VF	UNC
31.8.1971; 24.10.1972. Black on m/c unpt. *SAN SALVADOR* and date at l., *UN COLON* at ctr., Juan José Cañas at r. Back red.			
a. Issued note.	0.25	1.50	8.00
s. Specimen. 31.8.1971; 24.10.1972.	—	—	30.00

119	25 COLONES	VG	VF	UNC
	31.8.1971. Black on m/c unpt. 5th of November Dam at ctr. Back blue.			
	a. Issued note.	7.50	15.00	55.00
	s. Specimen.	—	—	32.50

1974 ISSUE

#120-122 black on m/c unpt. Printer: TDLR.

116	2 COLONES	VG	VF	UNC
	1972; 1974. Black on m/c unpt. Colonial church of Panchimalco at ctr., *DOS COLONES* at r. Back red-brown.			
	a. 24.10.1972.	0.25	2.00	10.00
	b. 15.10.1974.	0.25	1.75	10.00
	s. As a, b. Specimen.	—	—	30.00

Note: #116 w/o wmk. is reported, not confirmed.

120	1 COLÓN	VG	VF	UNC
	15.10.1974. Cerron Grande Dam at ctr., w/o *UN COLON=* at l. Back red; like #115.	0.25	1.50	7.50

117	5 COLONES	VG	VF	UNC
	31.8.1971-24.6.1976. Black on pale blue and m/c unpt. Face like #111 w/o *5 COLONES* at l., José Matías Delgado addressing crowd at ctr. Back green.			
	a. Issued note.	FV	2.50	17.50
	s. Specimen. 31.8.1971; 24.10.1972; 15.10.1974.	—	—	30.00

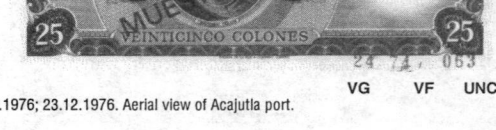

121	25 COLONES	VG	VF	UNC
	15.10.1974; 24.6.1976; 23.12.1976. Aerial view of Acajutla port. Back blue.			
	a. Issued note.	5.00	12.50	45.00
	s. Specimen. 15.10.1974.	—	—	

118	10 COLONES	VG	VF	UNC
	31.8.1971-23.12.1976. Black on m/c unpt. *DIEZ COLONES* at ctr., Manuel José Arce at r. Back dull black.			
	a. Issued note.	2.50	6.00	30.00
	s. Specimen. 31.8.1971; 24.10.1972; 15.10.1974.	—	—	35.00

122	100 COLONES	VG	VF	UNC
	1974-79. Indian pyramid at Tazumal at ctr., arms at lower r. Back olive-green on m/c unpt.			
	a. Regular serial #. 15.10.1974-11.5.1978.	15.00	20.00	95.00
	b. Electronic sorting serial #. 3.5.1979.	15.00	17.50	75.00
	s. As a. Specimen. 15.10.1974.	—	—	60.00

1976 ISSUE

#123 and 124 black on m/c unpt. Printer: TDLR.

123	1 COLÓN	VG	VF	UNC
	28.10.1976. Similar to #120 but *UN COLON* at l. Back like #125. W/o wmk.			
	a. Issued note.	0.25	1.00	7.50
	s. Specimen.	—	—	30.00

124	2 COLONES	VG	VF	UNC
	24.6.1976. Black on m/c unpt. Like #116 but w/*DOS COLONES* at l. and r. Denomination added to face at l. Back brown-violet; w/o wmk.			
	a. Issued note.	0.25	1.75	10.00
	s. Specimen.	—	—	30.00

1977-79 ISSUES

#125-126, 129-130 black on m/c unpt. w/unpt. in margins on face.

125	1 COLÓN	VG	VF	UNC
	1977-80. Like #123. Printer: TDLR.			
	a. Regular style serial #. 7.7.1977; 11.5.1978.	FV	1.50	7.50
	b. Electronic sorting serial #. 3.5.1979; 19.6.1980.	FV	1.00	6.50
	s. As b. Specimen.	—	—	—

126	5 COLONES	VG	VF	UNC
	6.10.1977. Like #117, but *5 COLONES* at l. and r. W/o wmk. Printer: TDLR.			
	a. Issued note.	FV	2.00	10.00
	s. Specimen.	—	—	30.00

Note: For similar 5 Colones dated 19.6.1980, see #132A.

127	10 COLONES			
	7.7.1977. Black on m/c unpt. *DIEZ COLONES* at ctr., Manuel José Arce at ctr. r. Back black. Printer: ABNC.	FV	4.00	15.00

128	10 COLONES	VG	VF	UNC
	13.10.1977. Like #127 but blue arms added to face and back. W/o wmk. Printer: ABNC.	FV	4.00	15.00

129	10 COLONES	VG	VF	UNC
	1978-80. Manuel José Arce at r. Back black. Printer: TDLR.			
	a. Regular serial #. 11.5.1978.	FV	2.25	10.00
	b. Electronic sorting serial #. 3.5.1979; 21.7.1980.	FV	1.50	8.00
	s. As b. Specimen. 3.5.1979.	—	—	30.00

130	25 COLONES	VG	VF	UNC
	1978-80. Like #121. Printer: TDLR.			
	a. Regular serial #. 11.5.1978.	FV	5.00	30.00
	b. Electronic sorting serial #. 3.5.1979; 19.6.1980.	FV	3.00	15.00
	s. As b. Specimen. 19.6.1980.	—	—	30.00

131	50 COLONES	VG	VF	UNC
	1979; 1980. Purple on m/c unpt. Lg. bldg. and statue at l., Capt. Gen. Gerardo Barrios at r. Ships at l., Christopher Columbus at ctr. on back. Printer: TDLR.			
	a. 3.5.1979.	FV	8.00	42.50
	b. 19.6.1980.	FV	5.00	20.00
	s. As a. Specimen.	—	—	30.00

132	100 COLONES	VG	VF	UNC
	7.7.1977. Deep olive-green on m/c unpt. Independence monument at r. Printer: ABNC.	FV	20.00	75.00

1980 ISSUE

132A	5 COLONES	VG	VF	UNC
	19.6.1980 (1992). Like #134. Printer: ABNC.	FV	FV	5.00

133	100 COLONES	VG	VF	UNC
	17.7.1980. Black on m/c unpt. Like #122 but w/flag below date at upper l. Printer: TDLR.	FV	17.50	42.50

1982; 1983 ISSUE

#133A-137 w/o sign. title *GERENTE* at r.

#133A-136 black on m/c unpt. W/o unpt. in margins.

133A	1 COLÓN	VG	VF	UNC
	3.6.1982. Black on m/c unpt. Like #125. Back red. Printer: TDLR.			
	a. Issued note.	FV	FV	6.00
	s. Specimen.	—	—	30.00

#134-137 printer: ABNC.

134	5 COLONES	VG	VF	UNC
	1983; 1988. Black on m/c unpt. Back green. Like #132A.			
	a. 25.8.1983.	FV	FV	5.00
	b. 17.3.1988.	FV	FV	4.00
	s1. As a. Specimen.	—	—	55.00
	s2. As b. Specimen.	—	—	30.00

135	10 COLONES	VG	VF	UNC
	1983; 1988. Black on m/c unpt. Like #127.			
	a. 25.8.1983.	FV	FV	7.50
	b. 17.3.1988.	FV	FV	7.00
	s1. As a. Specimen.	—	—	55.00
	s2. As b. Specimen.	—	—	30.00

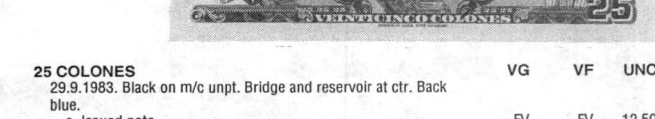

136	25 COLONES	VG	VF	UNC
	29.9.1983. Black on m/c unpt. Bridge and reservoir at ctr. Back blue.			
	a. Issued note.	FV	FV	12.50
	s. Specimen.	—	—	30.00

137	100 COLONES	VG	VF	UNC
	1983; 1988. Deep olive-green on m/c unpt. Like #132.			
	a. 29.9.1983.	FV	FV	37.50
	b. 17.3.1988.	FV	FV	30.00
	s1. As a. Specimen.	—	—	30.00
	s2. As b. Specimen.	—	—	27.50

1990-93 ISSUES

#138 and 140 unpt. in margins on face.

138	5 COLONES	VG	VF	UNC
	16.5.1990. Black on m/c unpt. Like #126 but w/o sign., title: *GERENTE* at r., w/electronic sorting serial #. Back olive-green and dk. gray. Printer: TDLR.			
	a. Issued note.	FV	FV	3.00
	s. Specimen.	—	—	25.00

#139 *Deleted. See #132A.*

140	100 COLONES	VG	VF	UNC
	12.3.1993; 22.12.1994; 26.5.1995. Black, blue-green and violet on pink, blue and pale green unpt. Like #133 but w/arms at upper l., flag at lower r. Printer: TDLR.			
	a. Issued note.	FV	FV	30.00
	s. Specimen.	FV	FV	40.00

1995 ISSUE

#141-143 w/ascending size serial # at upper r. Wmk: Columbus wearing cap. Printer: TDLR.

141	10 COLONES	VG	VF	UNC
	26.5.1995. Like #129.			
	a. Issued note.	FV	FV	6.00
	s. Specimen.	—	—	40.00

142	25 COLONES	VG	VF	UNC
	26.5.1995; 9.2.1996. Similar to #130 but w/o sign., title: *GERENTE* at r.			
	a. Issued note.	FV	FV	12.50
	s. Specimen.	—	—	40.00
143	50 COLONES			
	26.5.1995. Purple on m/c unpt. Like #131 but w/o sign., title: *GERENTE* at r.			
	a. Issued note.	FV	FV	17.50
	s. Specimen.	—	—	40.00

1996 ISSUE

#144-146 wmk: C. Columbus wearing cap. Printer: CBNC.

144	10 COLONES	VG	VF	UNC
	9.2.1996. Black on m/c unpt. Similar to #141.			
	a. Issued note.	FV	FV	5.00
	s. Specimen.	—	—	40.00

#145 and 146 w/segmented foil over security thread.

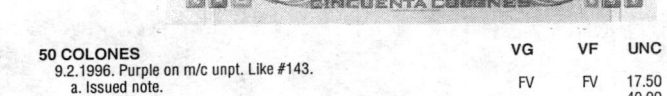

145	50 COLONES	VG	VF	UNC
	9.2.1996. Purple on m/c unpt. Like #143.			
	a. Issued note.	FV	FV	17.50
	s. Specimen.	—	—	40.00

146	100 COLONES	VG	VF	UNC
	9.2.1996. Black, blue-green and violet on pink, blue and pale green unpt. Like #140.			
	a. Issued note.	FV	FV	25.00
	s. Specimen.	—	—	50.00

1997 ISSUE

#147-152 w/special marks for poor of sight above arms at l. ctr. C. Columbus wearing hat at l. on back and as wmk., continents over his 3 ships at ctr. Sign. titles *PRESIDENTE* and *DIRECTOR*.

147	5 COLONES	VG	VF	UNC
	18.4.1997; 2.3.1998. Black, dk. green and brown on m/c unpt. National Palace at ctr. r.			
	a. Issued note. Series D, E, K.	FV	FV	3.00
	s. Specimen. Series A.	—	—	22.50

148   10 COLONES

	VG	VF	UNC
18.4.1997; 2.3.1998. Dk. blue-violet, brown and deep blue-green m/c unpt. Izalco volcano at ctr. r.			
Issued note. Series A; C.	FV	FV	5.00
Specimen. Series A.	—	—	22.50

149   25 COLONES

	VG	VF	UNC
1997; 1998. Black, brown and blue-black on m/c unpt. San Andres pyramid at ctr. r.			
a. Issued note. Series A-D. 18.4.1997.	FV	FV	10.00
b. Issued note. Series F. 2.3.1998.	FV	FV	9.00
s. Specimen. Series A.	—	—	22.50

150   50 COLONES

	VG	VF	UNC
18.4.1997. Purple, brown and blue-black on m/c unpt. Lake Coatepeque at ctr. r.			
a. Issued note. Series A.	FV	FV	17.50
s. Specimen. Series A.	—	—	50.00

151   100 COLONES

	VG	VF	UNC
18.4.1997; 4.5.1998. Deep olive-green and dk. brown on m/c unpt. Tazumal pyramid at ctr. r.			
a. Issued note. Series A.	FV	FV	22.50
s. Specimen. Series A.	—	—	27.50

152   200 COLONES

	VG	VF	UNC
1997-98. Brown, red-violet and purple on m/c unpt. *EL SALVADOR DEL MUNDO* monument at ctr. r.			
a. 1997; 1998. Series B.	FV	FV	40.00
s. Specimen. Series A.	—	—	35.00

1999 ISSUE

#153-158 like #147-152 except for added security features.

153   5 COLONES

	VG	VF	UNC
19.4.1999. Green and olive on m/c unpt. National Palace. Like #147.	FV	FV	2.50

NOTICE

Readers with unlisted dates, signature varieties, etc. are invited to submit photocopies of their notes to: Standard Catalog of World Paper Money, 700 East State St. Iola, WI 54990-0001, E-Mail: george.cuhaj@fwpubs.com.

154   10 COLONES
19.4.1999. Purple and green on m/c unpt. Izalco Volcano. Like #148.

	VG	VF	UNC
	FV	FV	5.00

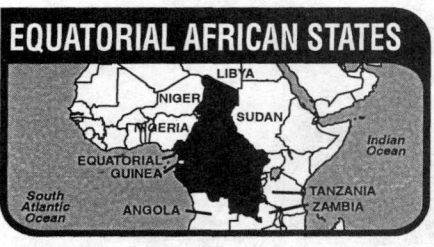

Equatorial African States (Central African States), a monetary union comprising the former French possessions and now independent states of the Republic of Congo (Brazzaville), Gabon, Central African Republic, Chad and Cameroon, issues a common currency for the member states from a common central bank. The monetary unit, the African Financial Community Franc, is tied to and supported by the French franc.

In 1960, an abortive attempt was made to form a union of the newly independent republics of Chad, Congo, Central Africa and Gabon. The proposal was discarded when Chad refused to become a constituent member. The four countries then linked into an Equatorial Customs Unit, to which Cameroon became an associate member in 1961. A more extensive cooperation of the five republics, identified as the Central African Customs and Economic Union, was entered into force at the beginning of 1966.

In 1974 the Central Bank of the Equatorial African States, which had issued coins and paper currency in its own name and with the names of the constituent member nations, changed its name to the Bank of the Central African States.

MONETARY SYSTEM:
1 Franc (C.F.A.) = 100 Centimes

CONTROL LETTER or SYMBOL CODE

Country	1961-72
Cameroun	*
Central African Republic	B
Chad	A
Congo	C
Equatorial Guinea	
Gabon	D

155   25 COLONES
19.4.1999. Brown and green on m/c. San Andres Pyramid. Like #149.

	VG	VF	UNC
	FV	FV	9.50

EQUATORIAL AFRICAN STATES

BANQUE CENTRALE DES ÉTATS DE L'AFRIQUE

ÉQUATORIALE ET DU CAMEROUN

1961 ND ISSUES

		VG	VF	UNC
1	**100 FRANCS** ND (1961-62). Blue and m/c. Portr. Gov. Felix Eboue at ctr., woman w/jug at l., people in canoe at r. Cargo ships at ctr., man at r. on back.			
	a. Code letter *A*.	20.00	125.00	450.00
	b. Code letter *B*.	20.00	150.00	500.00
	c. Code letter *C*.	20.00	125.00	450.00
	d. Code letter *D*.	20.00	125.00	450.00
	e. * for Cameroun.	50.00	200.00	750.00
	f. W/o code letter.	15.00	40.00	300.00
	s. Specimen. Prefix letter O, serial #0s	—	—	500.00
2	**100 FRANCS** ND (1961-62). M/c. Like #1 but denomination also in English. W/* for Cameroun.	50.00	150.00	500.00

Note: For similar 100 Francs w/FRANÇAISE in the title see French Equatorial Africa #32. (Vol. II).

156   50 COLONES
19.4.1999. Violet and orange on m/c unpt. Coatepeque Lake. Like #150.

	VG	VF	UNC
	FV	FV	20.00

BANQUE CENTRALE

ÉTATS DE L'AFRIQUE ÉQUATORIALE

1963 ND ISSUE

157   100 COLONES
19.4.1999. Dk. green and lt. green on m/c unpt. Tazumal Pyramid. Like #151.

	VG	VF	UNC
	FV	FV	30.00

158   200 COLONES
19.4.1999. Brown, red and m/c. Like #152.

	VG	VF	UNC
	FV	FV	50.00

Note: U.S. Dollars have replaced Salvadorian Colones.

		VG	VF	UNC
3	**100 FRANCS** ND (1963). Brown and m/c. Musical instrument at l., hut at l. ctr., man at r. Elephant at l., tools at r. on back.			
	a. Code letter *A*.	10.00	40.00	125.00
	b. Code letter *B*.	15.00	50.00	150.00
	c. Code letter *C*.	10.00	40.00	125.00
	d. Code letter *D*.	10.00	40.00	125.00

6 **5000 FRANCS**

ND (1963). M/c. Girl at l., village scene at ctr. Carving at l., airplane, train crossing bridge and tractor hauling logs at ctr., man smoking a pipe at r. on back.

	VG	VF	UNC
a. Code letter *A*.	150.00	375.00	1150.00
b. Code letter *B*.	150.00	375.00	1150.00
c. Code letter *C*.	150.00	375.00	1150.00
d. Code letter *D*.	150.00	375.00	1150.00

7 **10,000 FRANCS**

	VG	VF	UNC
ND (1968). M/c. Pres. Bokassa at r., Rock Hotel, Bangui, C.A.R. in background, arms of Central African Republic at lower l.	275.00	650.00	2150.00

4 **500 FRANCS**

ND (1963). Green and m/c. Girl wearing bandana at r., track mounted crane w/ore bucket in background. Radar unit at l., man on camel at r. on back.

	VG	VF	UNC
a. Engraved. Code letter *A*. Block #1-4.	15.00	70.00	260.00
b. As a. Code letter *B*.	20.00	125.00	400.00
c. As a. Code letter *C*.	17.50	70.00	260.00
d. As a. Code letter *D*.	15.00	70.00	260.00
e. Lithographed. Code letter *A*. Block #5-.	10.00	55.00	240.00
f. As e. Code letter *B*.	10.00	65.00	260.00
g. As e. Code letter *C*.	12.00	55.00	240.00
h. As e. Code letter *D*.	10.00	55.00	240.00

5 **1000 FRANCS**

ND (1963). M/c. People gathering cotton. Young men logging on back.

	VG	VF	UNC
a. Engraved. Code letter *A*. Block #1-5.	15.00	125.00	400.00
b. As a. Code letter *B*.	20.00	150.00	450.00
c. As a. Code letter *C*.	15.00	125.00	400.00
d. As a. Code letter *D*.	15.00	125.00	400.00
e. Lithographed. Code letter *A*. Block #7-.	10.00	100.00	350.00
f. As e. Code letter *B*.	15.00	125.00	400.00
g. As e. Code letter *C*.	10.00	100.00	350.00
h. As e. Code letter *D*.	10.00	100.00	350.00

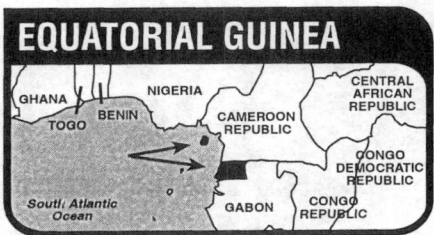

EQUATORIAL GUINEA

The Republic of Equatorial Guinea (formerly Spanish Guinea) consists of Rio Muni, located on the coast of west-central Africa between Cameroon and Gabon, and the offshore islands of Fernando Po, Annobon, Corisco, Elobey Grande and Elobey Chico. The equatorial country has an area of 10,831 sq. mi. (28,051 sq. km.) and a population of 452,000. Capital: Malabo. The economy is based on agriculture and forestry. Cacao, wood and coffee are exported.

Fernando Po was discovered between 1474 and 1496 by Portuguese navigators charting a route to the spice islands of the Far East. Portugal retained control of it and the adjacent islands until 1778 when they, together with trading rights to the African coast between the Ogooue and Niger rivers, were ceded to Spain. Fernando Po was administered, with Spanish consent, by the British from 1827 to 1844 when it was reclaimed by Spain. Mainland Rio Muni was granted to Spain by the Berlin Conference of 1885. The name of the colony was changed from Spanish Guinea to Equatorial Guinea in Dec. of 1963. Independence was attained on Oct. 12, 1968.

Additional listings can be found under Central African States.

MONETARY SYSTEM:

1 Peseta Guineana = 100 Centimos to 1975
1 Ekuele = 100 Centimos, 1975-80
1 Epkwele (pl. Bipkwele) = 100 Centimos, 1980-85
1 Franc (C.F.A.) = 100 Centimes, 1985-
1 Franco (C.F.A.) = 4 Bipkwele

REPUBLIC

BANCO CENTRAL

1969 ISSUE

#1-3 printer: FNMT.

		VG	VF	UNC
1	**100 PESETAS GUINEANAS** 12.10.1969. Red-brown on lt. tan unpt. Banana tree at l. Shoreline and man w/boat on back. Wmk: Woman's head.	1.00	4.00	15.00

		VG	VF	UNC
2	**500 PESETAS GUINEANAS** 12.10.1969. Green on m/c unpt. Derrick loading logs at l., shoreline at ctr. Woman w/bundle on head at r. on back. Wmk: Man's head.	2.00	6.00	22.50

		VG	VF	UNC
3	**1000 PESETAS GUINEANAS** 12.10.1969. Blue on m/c unpt. Pres. M. Nguema Biyogo at ctr. Tree at l., arms at ctr. on back. Wmk: King and queen.	2.75	8.50	35.00

BANCO POPULAR

1975 FIRST DATED ISSUE

#4-8 w/portr. Pres. M. N. Biyogo at r. and as wmk. Name under portrait: *MACIAS NGUEMA BIYOGO.*
Printer: TDLR. Replacement notes: Serial # prefix *Z1.*

		VG	VF	UNC
4	**25 EKUELE** 7.7.1975. Purple on lt. orange and green unpt. Trees at ctr. Arms at l., bridge at ctr. on back. Name underneath: *PUENTE MACIAS NGUEMA BIYOGO.*	0.50	1.50	5.00

		VG	VF	UNC
5	**50 EKUELE** 7.7.1975. Brown on green and pink unpt. Plants at ctr. Arms at l., logging at ctr. on back.	0.50	1.75	5.00

#6-8 arms at ctr.

6	100 EKUELE			
	7.7.1975. Green on pink and m/c unpt. Bridge and boats on back.	0.75	2.00	5.00

7	500 EKUELE	VG	VF	UNC
	7.7.1975. Blue on m/c unpt. National Palace on back.	1.25	4.00	12.50

8	1000 EKUELE	VG	VF	UNC
	7.7.1975. Red on m/c unpt. Bank on back.	2.00	4.00	15.00

1975 SECOND DATED ISSUE

#9-13 like #4-8 but name under portrait: *MASIE NGUEMA BIYOGO NEGUE NDONG.* Different sign. at l. Replacement notes: Serial # prefix *Z1.*

9	25 EKUELE	VG	VF	UNC
	7.7.1975. Like #4 except for name change on both sides.	1.00	2.00	7.50

10	50 EKUELE	VG	VF	UNC
	7.7.1975. Like #5 except for name change.	1.00	2.00	7.50

11	100 EKUELE	VG	VF	UNC
	7.7.1975. Like #6 except for name change on both sides.	1.00	2.50	7.50

12	500 EKUELE	VG	VF	UNC
	7.7.1975. Like #7 except for name change.	1.50	4.00	10.00
13	1000 EKUELE			
	7.7.1975. Like #8 except for name change.	1.50	4.00	10.00

BANCO DE GUINEA ECUATORIAL

1979 ISSUE

#14-17 wmk: T.E. Nkogo. Printer: FNMT.

14	100 BIPKWELE	VG	VF	UNC
	3.8.1979. Dk. olive-green and m/c. Arms at ctr., T. E. Nkogo at r. Boats along pier of Puerto de Bata on back.	1.75	4.00	10.00

15	500 BIPKWELE	VG	VF	UNC
	3.8.1979. Black on green and pink unpt. Arms at ctr., R. Uganda at r. Back brown and black; sailboat, shoreline and trees at l. ctr.	4.00	15.00	45.00

16	1000 BIPKWELE	VG	VF	UNC
	3.8.1979. Brown, black and m/c. Arms at ctr., R. Bioko at r. Back maroon and brown; men cutting food plants at l. ctr.	5.00	12.50	35.00

17	5000 BIPKWELE	VG	VF	UNC
	3.8.1979. Blue-gray on m/c unpt. Arms at ctr., E. N. Okenve at r. Back blue-gray and blue; logging scene at ctr.	3.00	7.50	30.00

1980 PROVISIONAL ISSUE

18	1000 BIPKWELE ON 100 PESETAS	VG	VF	UNC
	21.10.1980 (-old date 12.10.1969). Black ovpt. of new denomination and date on #1. (Not issued).	—	3.50	15.00

19	5000 BIPKWELE ON 500 PESETAS	VG	VF	UNC
	21.10.1980 (-old date 12.10.1969). Similar red ovpt. on #2. (Not issued).	—	6.00	20.00

Note: #18 and 19 were prepared for issue but not released to circulation. Shortly afterwards, Equatorial Guinea began the use of CFA franc currency. #3 was not ovpt. because it carries the portrait of former Pres. Biyogo.

BANQUE DES ÉTATS DE L'AFRIQUE CENTRALE

1985 ISSUE

#20-22 wmk: Carving (as printed on notes). Sign. 9. For sign. see Central African States listings.

20	500 FRANCOS	VG	VF	UNC
	1.1.1985. Brown on m/c unpt. Carving and jug at ctr. Man carving mask at l. ctr. on back.	1.00	2.50	7.50

21	1000 FRANCOS	VG	VF	UNC
	1.1.1985. Dk. blue on m/c unpt. Animal carving at lower l., map at ctr., starburst at lower r. Incomplete map of Chad at upper ctr. Elephant at l., statue at r. on back.	2.00	6.00	12.00

22	5000 FRANCOS	VG	VF	UNC
	1.1.1985; 1.1.1986. Brown, yellow and m/c. Carved mask at l., woman carrying bundle at r. Farmer plowing w/tractor at l., ore lift at r. on back.			
	a. 1.1.1985.	10.00	20.00	75.00
	b. 1.1.1986.	10.00	17.50	65.00

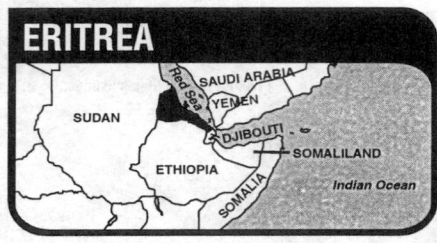

ERITREA

The State of Eritrea, a former Ethiopian province fronting on the Red Sea, has an area of 45,300 sq. mi. (117,600 sq. km.) and a population of 3.53 million. It was an Italian colony from 1889 until its incorporation into Italian East Africa in 1936. It was under the British Military Administration from 1941 to 1952, when the United Nations designated it an autonomous unit within the federation of Ethiopia and Eritrea. On Nov. 14, 1962, it was annexed with

Ethiopia. In 1991 the Eritrean Peoples Liberation Front extended its control over the entire territory of Eritrea. Following 2 years of provisional government, Eritrea held a referendum on independence in May 1993. Overwhelming popular approval led to the proclamation of an independent Republic of Eritrea on May 24.

MONETARY SYSTEM:
1 Nakfa = 100 Cents

BANK OF ERITREA

1997 ISSUE

#1-6 flag raising at I. Wmk: Camel's head.

Design by Clarence Holbert of the USBEP. Printer: G&D (w/o imprint).

			VG	VF	UNC
1	**1 NAKFA**				
	24.5.1997. Dk. brown and black on m/c unpt. 3 girls at ctr. Back dk. green; children in bush school at ctr. r.		FV	FV	1.00

#2-6 Kinnegram vertical foil strip at I. w/camels repeated.

			VG	VF	UNC
2	**5 NAKFA**				
	24.5.1997. Dk. brown and black on m/c unpt. Young boy, young and old man at ctr. Back dk. green; cattle grazing under huge Jacaranda tree at ctr. r.		FV	FV	3.50

			VG	VF	UNC
3	**10 NAKFA**				
	24.5.1997. Dk. brown and black on m/c unpt. 3 young women at ctr. Back dk. green; truck on rails hauling box cars across viaduct over the Dogali River at ctr. r.		FV	FV	7.50

			VG	VF	UNC
4	**20 NAKFA**				
	24.5.1997. Dk. brown and black on m/c unpt. 3 young girls at ctr. Back dk. green; farmer plowing w/camel, woman harvesting, woman on farm tractor at ctr. r.		FV	FV	12.50

			VG	VF	UNC
5	**50 NAKFA**				
	24.5.1997. Dk. brown and black on m/c unpt. 3 young women at ctr. Back dk. green; ships in Port of Masawa at ctr. r.		FV	FV	20.00

			VG	VF	UNC
6	**100 NAKFA**				
	24.5.1997. Dk. brown and black on m/c unpt. 3 young girls at ctr. Back dk. green; farmers plowing w/oxen at ctr. r.		FV	FV	37.50

ESTONIA

The Republic of Estonia (formerly the Estonian Soviet Socialist Republic of the U.S.S.R.) is the northernmost of the three Baltic states in eastern Europe. It has an area of 17,413 sq. mi. (45,100 sq. km.) and a population of 1.42 million. Capital: Tallinn. Agriculture and dairy farming are the principal industries. Butter, eggs, bacon, timber are exported.

This small and ancient Baltic state has enjoyed but two decades of independence since the 13th century. After having been conquered by the Danes, the Livonian Knights, the Teutonic Knights of Germany, the Swedes, the Poles and the Russians, Estonia declared itself an independent republic on Nov. 15, 1917, The peace treaty was signed Feb. 2, 1920. Shortly after the start of World War II, it was again occupied by Russia and incorporated as the 16th state of the U.S.S.R. Germany occupied Estonia from 1941 to 1944, after which it was retaken by Russia.

On August 20, 1991, the Parliament of the Estonian S.S.R. voted to reassert the republic's independence.

MONETARY SYSTEM
1 Kroon = 100 Senti

EESTI PANK
BANK OF ESTONIA

1991-92 ISSUE

#69-71 replacement notes: Serial # prefix *.

#69 and 70 wmk: Fortress.

		VG	VF	UNC
69	**1 KROON**			
	1992. Brownish black on yellow-orange and dull violet-brown unpt. K. Raud at l. Toampea castle w/Tall Hermann (national landmarks) on back.			
	a. Issued note.	FV	FV	1.50
	s. Specimen.	—	—	45.00

		VG	VF	UNC
70	**2 KROONI**			
	1992. Black on lt. blue-violet and grayish green unpt. K. E. von Baer at l. Tartu University bldg. at ctr. on back.			
	a. Issued note.	FV	FV	1.50
	s. Specimen.	—	—	45.00

#71-75 wmk: Arms (3 lions).

		VG	VF	UNC
71	**5 KROONI**			
	1991 (92); 1992 (94). Black and tan on m/c unpt. P. Keres at ctr., chessboard and arms at upper r. Teutonic fortress along Narva River, church on back.			
	a. 1991.	FV	FV	2.00
	b. 1992.	FV	FV	2.00
	s. Specimen.	—	—	60.00

		VG	VF	UNC
72	**10 KROONI**			
	1991 (92); 1992 (94). Purple and red on m/c unpt. J. Hurt at l. ctr. Tamme-lauri oak tree at Urvaste at r. on back.			
	a. 1991.	FV	FV	4.00
	b. 1992.	FV	FV	2.50
	s. Specimen.	—	—	60.00

		VG	VF	UNC
73	**25 KROONI**			
	1991 (92); 1992 (94). Deep olive-green on m/c unpt. A. Hansen-Tammsaare at l. ctr., wilderness in background at r. Early rural log construction farm; view of Vargamäe on back.			
	a. 1991.	FV	FV	10.00
	b. 1992.	FV	FV	4.50
	s. Specimen.	—	—	70.00

		VG	VF	UNC
74	**100 KROONI**			
	1991 (92); 1992 (94). Black and deep blue on lt. blue and m/c unpt. L. Koidula at l. ctr., cuckoo bird at lower r. Waves breaking against rocky cliffs of north coast at ctr. to r. on back.			
	a. 1991.	FV	FV	15.00
	b. 1992.	FV	FV	15.00
	s. Specimen.	—	—	85.00

75   500 KROONI

		VG	VF	UNC
1991 (92). Blue-black and purple on m/c unpt. C. R. Jakobson at l. ctr., harvest between 2 farmers with Sakala above at r. Barn swallow in flight over rural pond at r., value at upper r. on back.				
a. Issued note.		FV	FV	75.00
s. Specimen.		—	—	200.00

1994 ISSUE

#76-80 ascending size serial # at r.

76   5 KROONI

		VG	VF	UNC
1994 (97). Black and tan on m/c unpt. Like #71 but w/modified design at lower r. on face and lower l. on back.				
a. Issued note.		FV	FV	1.00
s. Specimen.		—	—	60.00

77   10 KROONI

		VG	VF	UNC
1994 (97). Purple and red on m/c unpt. Like #72 but w/modified design at lower r. on face and lower l. on back.				
a. Issued note.		FV	FV	1.50
s. Specimen.		—	—	60.00

78   50 KROONI

		VG	VF	UNC
1994. Green and black on m/c unpt. R. Tobias at l. ctr., gates at lower ctr. r. Opera house in Tallinn at ctr. r. on back.				
a. Issued note.		FV	FV	10.00
s. Specimen.		—	—	60.00

79   100 KROONI

		VG	VF	UNC
1994. Black and dk. blue on m/c unpt. Like #74 but w/gray seal at upper r. on face. Different rosette at lower l. on back.				
a. Issued note.		FV	FV	17.50
s. Specimen.		—	—	75.00

80   500 KROONI

		VG	VF	UNC
1994 (95). Blue-black and purple on m/c unpt. Like #75 but w/dk. gray bank seal at upper r. Different rosette at lower l. on back.				
a. Issued note.		FV	FV	80.00
s. Specimen.		—	—	200.00

1996 ISSUE

81   500 KROONI

		VG	VF	UNC
1996 (97). Blue, black and purple on m/c unpt. Like #80 but w/hologram at upper l. Value at lower r. on back.				
a. Issued note.		FV	FV	75.00
s. Specimen.		—	—	200.00

1999-2000 ISSUE

82	100 KROONI	VG	VF	UNC
	1999. Blue on lt. blue and m/c unpt. Holographic strip at l. Similar to #79, but many differences. L. Koidula at l. ctr.; cuckoo bird at lower ctr. Back blue on lt. red unpt. Waves breaking against rocky cliffs of north coast at ctr. to r.			
	a. Issued note.	FV	FV	15.00
	s. Specimen w/ovpt: *PROOV.*	—	—	35.00

83	500 KROONI	VG	VF	UNC
	2000. Dk. blue and blue on m/c unpt. Similar to #81, but w/some differences. C. R. Jakobson at l. and as wmk. Barn swallow on back.	FV	FV	75.00

2002 ISSUE

84	25 KROONI	VG	VF	UNC
	2002. Green, black and lilac on m/c unpt. Anton Hansen-Tammsaare at l., arms at upper r. Estonian farm view Vargamae on back. Wide holographic band at l.	FV	FV	8.00

COLLECTOR SERIES

EESTI PANK

BANK OF ESTONIA

1999 COLLECTOR'S SET

80th Anniversary of Bank

CS1	100 KROONI	Issue Price	Mkt.	Value
	1999. Set includes: 100 Krooni specimen note (#82), 5 Krooni coin, and 4 stamps. 3,000 pcs.	20.00		35.00

The Federal Republic of Ethiopia (formerly the Peoples Democratic Republic and the Empire of Ethiopia) is located in east-central Africa. The country has an area of 424,214 sq. mi. (1.099,900 sq. km.) and a population of 66.18 million people who are divided among 40 tribes that speak some 270 languages and dialects. Capital: Addis Ababa. The economy is predominantly agricultural and pastoral. Gold and platinum are mined and petroleum fields are being developed. Coffee, oilseeds, hides and cereals are exported.

Legend claims that Menelik I, the son born to Solomon, King of Israel, by the Queen of Sheba, settled in Axum in northern Ethiopia to establish the dynasty which then reigned - with only brief interruptions - until 1974. Modern Ethiopian history began with the reign of Emperor Menelik II (1889-1913) under whose guidance the country emerged from medieval isolation. Ethiopia was invaded by fascist Italy in 1935, and together with Italian Somaliland and Eritrea became part of Italian East Africa until liberated by British and Ethiopian troops in 1941. Haile Selassie I, 225th consecutive Solomonic ruler, was deposed by a military committee on Sept. 12, 1974. In July 1976, Ethiopia's military provisional government referred to the country as Socialist Ethiopia. After establishing a new regime in 1991, Ethiopia became a federated state.

Eritrea, a former Ethiopian province fronting on the Red Sea, was an Italian colony from 1890 until its incorporation into Italian East Africa in 1936. It was under British military administration from 1941 to Sept. 15, 1952, when the United Nations designated it an autonomous unit within the federation of Ethiopia and Eritrea. On Nov. 14, 1962, it was fully integrated with Ethiopia. On May 24, 1993, Eritrea became an independent nation.

RULERS:
Haile Selassie I, 1930-1936, 1941-1974

MONETARY SYSTEM:
1 Birr (Dollar) = 100 Santeems (Cents), since 1944

EMPIRE

STATE BANK OF ETHIOPIA

1961 ND ISSUE

Dollar System

#18-24 Emperor Haile Selassie at r. Arms at ctr. on back. Printer: BWC.

18	1 DOLLAR	VG	VF	UNC
	ND (1961). Green on lilac and lt. orange unpt. Coffee bushes at l.			
	a. Issued note.	4.00	15.00	50.00
	s. Specimen. Punched hole cancelled.	—	—	25.00

19	5 DOLLARS	VG	VF	UNC
	ND (1961). Orange on green and m/c unpt. Addis Ababa University (old palace) at l.			
	a. Issued note.	4.00	25.00	80.00
	s. Specimen. Punched hole cancelled.	—	—	50.00

20	10 DOLLARS	VG	VF	UNC
	ND (1961). Red on m/c unpt. Harbor at Massawa at l.			
	a. Issued note.	10.00	40.00	125.00
	s. Specimen. Punched hole cancelled.	—	—	110.00

21 20 DOLLARS
ND (1961). Brown on m/c unpt. Ancient stone monument (Axum) at l.

	VG	VF	UNC
a. Issued note.	25.00	80.00	250.00
s. Specimen. Punched hole cancelled.	—	—	125.00

22 50 DOLLARS
ND (1961). Blue on m/c unpt. Bridge over Blue Nile at l.

	VG	VF	UNC
a. Issued note.	50.00	100.00	300.00
s. Specimen. Punched hole cancelled.	—	—	175.00

23 100 DOLLARS
ND (1961). Purple on m/c unpt. Trinity Church at Addis Ababa at l.

	VG	VF	UNC
a. Sign. title: *GOVERNOR.*	80.00	150.00	400.00
b. Sign. title: *ACTING GOVERNOR.*	65.00	125.00	350.00
s. Specimen.	—	—	200.00

24 500 DOLLARS
ND (1961). Dk. green on m/c unpt. Fasilides castle at Gondar at l.

	VG	VF	UNC
a. Issued note.	250.00	600.00	1500.00
s. Specimen. Punched hole cancelled.	—	—	300.00

NATIONAL BANK OF ETHIOPIA

1966 ND ISSUE

#25-29 Emperor Haile Selassie at r. Arms at ctr. on back. Printer: TDLR.

25 1 DOLLAR
ND (1966). Dk. green on m/c unpt. Aerial view of Massawa harbor, city at l.

	VG	VF	UNC
a. Issued note.	1.50	6.00	20.00
s. Specimen.	—	—	30.00

26 5 DOLLARS
ND (1966). Brown on m/c unpt. Bole Airport, Addis Ababa at l. Back orange.

	VG	VF	UNC
a. Issued note.	3.00	17.50	80.00
r. Replacement note. Serial # prefix *X.*	6.00	30.00	140.00
s. Specimen.	—	—	35.00

27 10 DOLLARS
ND (1966). Dk. red on m/c unpt. National Bank at Addis Ababa at l.

	VG	VF	UNC
a. Issued note.	4.00	20.00	75.00
s. Specimen.	—	—	50.00

28 50 DOLLARS
ND (1966). Blue on m/c unpt. Koka High Dam on the Awash River on back.

	VG	VF	UNC
a. Issued note.	15.00	75.00	190.00
s. Specimen.	—	—	165.00

29 100 DOLLARS
ND (1966). Purple on green and m/c unpt. Rock church "Bet Giorgis" in Lalibela at l.

	VG	VF	UNC
a. Issued note.	5.00	20.00	125.00
s. Specimen.	—	—	125.00

PEOPLES DEMOCRATIC REPUBLIC

ARMS VARIETIES			
Type A 1975-1987	Type B 1987	Type C	Type D

SIGNATURE VARIETIES			
1	Teferra Deguefe, 1974-76 CHAIRMAN OF THE BOARD	2	Tadesse G. Kidan, 1978-87 ADMINISTRATOR
3	Bekele Tamirat, 1987-91 ADMINISTRATOR	4	Leikun Berhanu, 1991-97 GOVERNOR
5	Thbale Tala, 1997-98 GOVERNOR	6	Teklewold Atnafu, 1998- GOVERNOR

NATIONAL BANK OF ETHIOPIA

1976 ND ISSUE

Birr System

law EE Masharam 1969 (Sept. 1976 AD) #30-34 have map at l., lion's head in unpt. at l. ctr. Arms Type A at r. on back. Replacement notes: Serial # prefix *ZZ*.

			VG	VF	UNC
30	**1 BIRR** L.EE1969 (1976). Black and dk. green on lt. brown and green unpt. Young man at ctr. r., longhorns at r. Back black on m/c unpt.; whited-throated bee-eaters and Tisisat waterfalls of Blue Nile on back.				
	a. Sign. 1.		0.25	2.00	5.00
	b. Sign. 2.		0.25	1.50	2.50

			VG	VF	UNC
31	**5 BIRR** L.EE1969 (1976). Black and brown-orange on m/c unpt. Man picking coffee beans at ctr. r., plant at r. Kudu, caracal and Semien Mountains on back.				
	a. Sign. 1.		0.75	3.25	9.00
	b. Sign. 2.		0.75	2.75	7.00
32	**10 BIRR** L.EE1969 (1976). Brown-violet and red on m/c unpt. Woman weaving basket at ctr. r., wicker work dining table w/lid at r. Plowing w/tractor on back.				
	a. Sign. 1.		2.00	6.00	15.00
	b. Sign. 2.		2.00	4.00	12.00

NOTICE
Readers with unlisted dates, signature varieties, etc. are invited to submit photocopies of their notes to: Standard Catalog of World Paper Money, 700 East State St. Iola, WI 54990-0001, E-Mail: george.cuhaj@fwpubs.com.

			VG	VF	UNC
33	**50 BIRR** L.EE1969 (1976). Blue-black and dk. brown on lilac and m/c unpt. Science students at ctr. r., musical instrument at r. Fasilides Castle at Gondar on back.				
	a. Sign. 1.		10.00	25.00	60.00
	b. Sign. 2.		10.00	20.00	50.00

			VG	VF	UNC
34	**100 BIRR** L.EE1969 (1976). Purple, violet and dk. brown on m/c unpt. Warrior standing at ctr. r., flowers at r. Young man w/microscope on back.				
	a. Sign. 1.		20.00	40.00	100.00
	b. Sign. 2.		20.00	32.50	85.00

1987 ND ISSUE

Law EE Masharam 1969 (Sept. 1976 AD).

#36-40 similar to #30-34 but w/ornate tan design at l. and r. edges on back. Sign. 3. Arms Type A at r. on back. Replacement notes: Serial # prefix *ZZ*.

			VG	VF	UNC
36	**1 BIRR** L.EE1969 (1987). Black and green on lt. brown and green unpt. Like #30.		0.25	1.00	2.50
37	**5 BIRR** L.EE1969 (1987). Black and brown-orange on m/c unpt. Like #31.		0.75	2.50	6.00
38	**10 BIRR** L.EE1969 (1987). Brown-violet and red on m/c unpt. Like #32.		1.00	3.50	10.00
39	**50 BIRR** L.EE1969 (1987). Blue-black and dk. brown on lilac and m/c unpt. Like #33.		7.50	17.50	40.00
40	**100 BIRR** L.EE1969 (1976). Purple, violet and dk. brown on m/c unpt. Like #34 but w/flowers and dark silvered shield at r.		15.00	35.00	70.00

FEDERAL DEMOCRATIC REPUBLIC
NATIONAL BANK OF ETHIOPIA

1991 ND ISSUE

Law EE Masharam 1969 (Sept. 1976 AD).

#41-45 like #36-40 but w/new arms Type B, C or D at r. on back.

			VG	VF	UNC
41	**1 BIRR** L.EE1969 (1991). Dk. green on lt. brown and green unpt. Like #36. Arms Type D.				
	a. Sign. 3 w/title in Amharic script. Serial # prefix larger sans-serif letters.		0.25	0.75	1.50
	b. Sign. 4 w/title: *GOVERNOR* and also in Amharic script.		0.20	0.75	1.50
	c. As b. but w/serial # prefix smaller serif letters.		0.25	0.75	2.00

45	100 BIRR	VG	VF	UNC
	L.EE1969 (1991). Purple, violet and dk. brown on m/c unpt. Like #40. Arms Type D.			
	a. Sign. 3 w/title in Amharic script.	8.00	25.00	50.00
	b. Sign. 4 w/title: *GOVERNOR* and also in Amharic script.	7.00	22.50	45.00

1997/EE1989 ISSUE

#46-48 similar to #41-43 but w/latent image (map of Ethiopia) w/value at l. W/o arms on back. Sign. 5; 6.

42	5 BIRR	VG	VF	UNC
	L.EE1969 (1991). Black and brown-orange on m/c unpt. Like #37.	Reported Not Confirmed		
	a. Sign 3 w/title in Amharic script. Arms Type B.	0.50	2.00	4.50
	b. Sign. 4 w/title *GOVERNOR* and also in Amharic script. Arms Type C.	0.50	2.00	4.00
	c. As b. Arms Type D.			

46	1 BIRR	VG	VF	UNC
	1997/EE1989; 2000/EE1992. Black on m/c unpt. Similar to #41.			
	a. 1997/EE 1989. Sign. 5.	FV	FV	0.75
	b. 2000/EE 1992. Sign. 6.	FV	FV	0.75
	c. 2003/EE 1995. Sign. 6.	FV	FV	0.75

#47-50 w/segmented foil over security thread.

43	10 BIRR	VG	VF	UNC
	L.EE1969 (1991). Brown-violet and red on m/c unpt. Like #38. Arms Type D.			
	a. Sign. 3 w/title in Amharic script.	0.75	3.75	7.50
	b. Sign. 4 w/title: *GOVERNOR* and also in Amharic script.	0.75	3.00	6.00

47	5 BIRR	VG	VF	UNC
	1997/EE1989; 2000/EE1992. Dk. blue on m/c unpt. Similar to #42.			
	a. 1997/EE1989. Sign. 5.	FV	FV	3.00
	b. 2000/EE1992. Sign. 6.	FV	FV	2.50
	c. 2003/EE 1995. Sign. 6.	FV	FV	2.50

44	50 BIRR	VG	VF	UNC
	L.EE1969 (1991). Blue-black and dk. brown on lilac and m/c unpt. Like #39.			
	a. Sign. 3 w/title in Amharic script. Arms Type B.	5.00	20.00	40.00
	b. Sign. 4 w/title: *GOVERNOR* and also in Amharic script. Arms Type C.	5.00	17.50	35.00
	c. As b. Arms Type D.	4.00	15.00	30.00

48	10 BIRR	VG	VF	UNC
	1997/EE1989; 2000/EE1992. Deep brown, red and green on m/c unpt. Similar to #43.			
	a. 1997/EE1989. Sign.5.	FV	FV	4.00
	b. 2000/EE1992. Sign. 6.	FV	FV	3.00
	c. 2003/EE 1995. Sign. 6.	FV	FV	3.00

49   50 BIRR

1997/EE1989; 2000/EE1992. Tan and orange-brown on m/c unpt.
Farmer plowing w/oxen at ctr. Back similar to #33.

	VG	VF	UNC
a. 1997/EE1989. Sign. 5.	FV	FV	15.00
b. 2000/EE1992. Sign. 6.	FV	FV	12.50
c. 2003/EE1995. Sign. 6.	FV	FV	10.00

50   100 BIRR

1997/EE1989; 2000/EE1992. Deep blue-green, olive-green and dk.
green on m/c unpt. Face like #49. Back similar to #34.

	VG	VF	UNC
a. 1997/EE1989. Sign. 5.	FV	FV	30.00
b. 2000/EE1992. Sign. 6.	FV	FV	27.50

2003/EE1997; 2004/EE1999 ISSUE

#51-52 increased security features.

51   50 BIRR

	VG	VF	UNC
2004/EE 1997. Tan and orange-brown on m/c unpt. Farmer plowing w/oxen at ctr.	FV	FV	10.00

52   100 BIRR

	VG	VF	UNC
2003/EE1995; 2004/EE1997. Deep blue-green, olive-green and dk. green on m/c unpt.	FV	FV	22.50

EUROPEAN UNION

The Treaty of Rome (1958) declared a common European market as a European objective with the aim of increasing economic prosperity and contributing to an ever closer union among the peoples of Europe.

The Single European Act (1986) and the Treaty on European Union (1992) have built on this, introducing the Economic and Monetary Union and laying the foundations for the single currency.

In January 1999 the exchange rate was irrevocably set for the original participating countries. These were: Austria, Belgium, Finland, France, Germany, Ireland, Italy, Luxembourg, Netherlands, Portugal and Spain. Greece became a participating member in January 2001.

Denmark, Sweden and the United Kingdom, although members of the European Union, decided not to participate in the single currency at its inception. The currency was introduced on January 1, 2002.

The French overseas departments: French Guiana, Guadeloupe, Martinique; these dependencies: Saint Martin, Saint Barthélemy; and territories: Saint Pierre et Miquelon and Mayotte all use the Euro Currency, and are depicted on the map section on the notes along with Réunion and the Canary Islands.

MONETARY SYSTEM:

1 Euro = 100 Cent

Central Bank	Serial # Prefix	Printer Code Letters (on face)	Printer
Sweden	K (reserved)	A	Bank of England Printing Works
Finland	L	C	AB Tumba Bruk, Sweden
Portugal	M	D	Setec Oy, Finland
Austria	N	E	F.C. Oberthur, France
Netherlands	P	F	Oesterreichische Nationalbank
Luxembourg	R (reserved)	G	John. Enschede Security Printing
Italy	S	H	Thomas De La Rue, Great Britian
Ireland	T	J	Banca d'Italia
France	U	K	Central Bank of Ireland
Spain	V	L	Banque de France
Denmark	W (reserved)	M	Fabrica Nacional de Moneda y Timbre
Germany	X	N	Bank of Greece
Greece	Y	P	Giesecke & Devrient, Germany
Belgium	Z	R	Bundesdruckerei, Germany
		S	Danmarks Nationalbank
		T	Banque Nationale de Belgique

EUROPEAN UNION

EUROPEAN CENTRAL BANK

2002 ISSUE

#1-7 various windows, arches and gateways on face. Bridges, map of Europe and European Union flag on back. The theme of the issue is "the ages and styles of Europe," and a differnt architectural era is portraied on each note. 2 Sign. var.

1	5 EURO		VG	VF	UNC
	2002. Gray and m/c. Classical architecture.				
	l. Serial # prefix *L*.		FV	FV	14.00
	m. Serial # prefix *M*.		FV	FV	11.00
	n. Serial # prefix *N*.		FV	FV	10.00
	p. Serial # prefix *P*.		FV	FV	10.00
	s. Serial # prefix *S*.		FV	FV	10.00
	t. Serial # prefix *T*.		FV	FV	11.00
	u. Serial # prefix *U*.		FV	FV	10.00
	v. Serial # prefix *V*.		FV	FV	11.00
	x. Serial # prefix *X*.		FV	FV	10.00
	y. Serial # prefix *Y*.		FV	FV	10.00
	z. Serial # prefix *Z*.		FV	FV	11.00

2	10 EURO		VG	VF	UNC
	2002. Red and m/c. Romanesque architecture.				
	l. Serial # prefix *L*.		FV	FV	25.00
	m. Serial # prefix *M*.		FV	FV	22.50
	n. Serial # prefix *N*.		FV	FV	20.00
	p. Serial # prefix *P*.		FV	FV	21.50
	s. Serial # prefix *S*.		FV	FV	20.00
	t. Serial # prefix *T*.		FV	FV	20.00
	u. Serial # prefix *U*.		FV	FV	20.00
	v. Serial # prefix *V*.		FV	FV	21.50
	x. Serial # prefix *X*.		FV	FV	20.00
	y. Serial # prefix *Y*.		FV	FV	20.00
	z. Serial # prefix *Z*.		FV	FV	20.00

3	20 EURO		VG	VF	UNC
	2002. Blue and m/c. Gothic architecture.				
	l. Serial # prefix *L*.		FV	FV	45.00
	m. Serial # prefix *M*.		FV	FV	42.50
	n. Serial # prefix *N*.		FV	FV	37.50
	p. Serial # prefix *P*.		FV	FV	37.50
	s. Serial # prefix *S*.		FV	FV	37.50
	t. Serial # prefix *T*.		FV	FV	37.50
	u. Serial # prefix *U*.		FV	FV	42.50
	v. Serial # prefix *V*.		FV	FV	37.50
	x. Serial # prefix *X*.		FV	FV	37.50
	y. Serial # prefix *Y*.		FV	FV	37.50
	z. Serial # prefix *Z*.		FV	FV	37.50

4	50 EURO		VG	VF	UNC
	2002. Orange and m/c. Renaissance architecture.				
	l. Serial # prefix *L*.		FV	FV	100.00
	m. Serial # prefix *M*.		FV	FV	95.00
	n. Serial # prefix *N*.		FV	FV	90.00
	p. Serial # prefix *P*.		FV	FV	90.00
	s. Serial # prefix *S*.		FV	FV	90.00
	t. Serial # prefix *T*.		FV	FV	90.00
	u. Serial # prefix *U*.		FV	FV	90.00
	v. Serial # prefix *V*.		FV	FV	100.00
	x. Serial # prefix *X*.		FV	FV	90.00
	y. Serial # prefix *Y*.		FV	FV	90.00
	z. Serial # prefix *Z*.		FV	FV	90.00

5	100 EURO		VG	VF	UNC
	2002. Green and m/c. Baroque and Rococo architecture.				
	l. Serial # prefix *L*.		FV	FV	185.00
	m. Serial # prefix *M*.		FV	FV	180.00
	n. Serial # prefix *N*.		FV	FV	175.00
	p. Serial # prefix *P*.		FV	FV	175.00
	s. Serial # prefix *S*.		FV	FV	175.00
	t. Serial # prefix *T*.		FV	FV	175.00
	u. Serial # prefix *U*.		FV	FV	175.00
	v. Serial # prefix *V*.		FV	FV	180.00
	x. Serial # prefix *X*.		FV	FV	175.00
	y. Serial # prefix *Y*.		FV	FV	175.00
	z. Serial # prefix *Z*.		FV	FV	175.00

6	200 EURO		VG	VF	UNC
	2002. Yellow-brown and m/c. Iron and glass architecture.				
	l. Serial # prefix *L*.		FV	FV	360.00
	n. Serial # prefix *N*.		FV	FV	350.00
	p. Serial # prefix *P*.		FV	FV	335.00
	s. Serial # prefix *S*.		FV	FV	335.00
	t. Serial # prefix *T*.		FV	FV	335.00
	u. Serial # prefix *U*.		FV	FV	335.00
	v. Serial # prefix *V*.		FV	FV	350.00
	x. Serial # prefix *X*.		FV	FV	335.00
	y. Serial # prefix *Y*.		FV	FV	335.00
	z. Serial # prefix *Z*.		FV	FV	335.00

7	500 EURO	VG	VF	UNC
	2002. Purple and m/c. Modern 20th century architecture.			
	l. Serial # prefix *L*.	FV	FV	900.00
	n. Serial # prefix *N*.	FV	FV	875.00
	p. Serial # prefix *P*.	FV	FV	850.00
	s. Serial # prefix *S*.	FV	FV	850.00
	t. Serial # prefix *T*.	FV	FV	850.00
	u. Serial # prefix *U*.	FV	FV	850.00
	v. Serial # prefix *V*.	FV	FV	875.00
	x. Serial # prefix *X*.	FV	FV	850.00
	y. Serial # prefix *Y*.	FV	FV	850.00
	z. Serial # prefix *Z*.	FV	FV	850.00

FAEROE ISLANDS

The Faroes, a self-governing community within the kingdom of Denmark, are situated in the North Atlantic between Iceland and the Shetland Islands. The 17 inhabited islets and reefs have an area of 540 sq. mi. (1,399 sq. km.) and a population of 43,678. Capital: Thorshavn. The principal industries are fishing and grazing. Fish and fish products are exported.

While it is thought that Irish hermits lived on the islands in the 7th and 8th centuries, the present inhabitants are descended from the 6th century Norse settlers. The Faroes became a Norwegian fief in 1035 and became Danish in 1380 when Norway and Denmark were united. They have ever since remained in Danish possession and were granted self-government (except for an appointed governor-general) with their own legislature, executive and flag in 1948.

The islands were occupied by British troops during World War II, while the Germans occupied Denmark.

RULERS:
Danish

MONETARY SYSTEM:
1 Króne = 100 Øre

DANISH ADMINISTRATION

FØROYAR

1964-74 ISSUE

#16-18 have coded year dates in the l. series # (the 2 middle digits). Wmk: Anchor chain. Replacement notes: Serial # suffix *OJ; OK*.

16	10 KRÓNUR	VG	VF	UNC
	L.1949 (19)74. Green. Shield w/ram at l. Rural scene at ctr. on back. Sign. L. Groth and A. P. Dam.			
	a. Issued note.	FV	FV	8.00
	s. Specimen.	—	—	—

17	50 KRÓNUR	VG	VF	UNC
	L.1949 (19)67. Black on lt. blue and blue-green unpt. Portr. Nólsoyar Páll at l. Back blue on green unpt. Drawing of homes and church across ctr. Sign. M. Wahl and P. M. Dam.	12.50	25.00	65.00

18	100 KRÓNUR	VG	VF	UNC
	L.1949 (19)64; 69; 72; 75. Black on pink and gold unpt. Portr. V. U. Hammershaimb at l. Back blue on tan unpt. Drawing of house and mountains on back.			
	a. (19)75. Sign. L. Groth and A.P. Dam.	20.00	30.00	80.00
	r1. (19)64. Sign. M. Wahl and H. Djurhuus. Suffix OJ.	27.50	75.00	150.00
	r2. (19)64. As r1 but suffix OK.	50.00	175.00	—
	r3. (19)69. Sign. M. Wahl and H. Djurhuus. Suffix OJ.	25.00	50.00	130.00
	r4. (19)72. Sign. as r3. Suffix OJ.	22.50	45.00	125.00
	r5. (19)75. Sign. L. Groth and A.P. Dam. Suffix OJ.	20.00	30.00	80.00
	s. Specimen. As d.	—	—	—

1978-86 ISSUE

#19-23 have coded year dates in the l. series # (the 2 middle digits). Wmk: Anchor chain. Replacement notes: Serial # suffix *OJ; OK.*

19	20 KRÓNUR	VG	VF	UNC
	L.1949 (19)86; 88. Deep purple on pink and aqua unpt. Man w/ice tool at r. Back red and black; drawing of animals at ctr.			
	a. Sign. N. Bentsen and A. P. Dam. (19)86.	FV	FV	14.00
	b. Sign. B. Klinte and A. P. Dam. (19)88.	FV	FV	10.00

20	50 KRÓNUR	VG	VF	UNC
	L.1949 (19)78-94. Black on lt. blue and gray unpt. Similar to #17 but reduced size. 140 x 72mm. Back black on gray unpt. Wmk: Chain links.			
	a. Sign. L. Groth and A. P. Dam. (19)78.	FV	FV	40.00
	b. Sign. as a. (19)87.	FV	25.00	90.00
	c. Sign. N. Bentsen and A. P. Dam. (19)87.	FV	FV	25.00
	d. Sign. B. Klinte and E. Joensen (19)94.	FV	FV	20.00
	s. Specimen. As a.	—	—	—

21	100 KRÓNUR	VG	VF	UNC
	L.1949 (19)78-94. Black on tan unpt. Similar to #18 but reduced size. Back black and green on ochre unpt. Wmk: Chain links.			
	a. Sign. L. Groth and A. P. Dam. (19)78.	FV	FV	80.00
	b. Sign. N. Bentsen and P. Ellefsen. (19)83.	FV	FV	75.00
	c. Sign. N. Bentsen and A. P. Dam. (19)87.	FV	FV	70.00
	d. Sign. B. Klinte and A. P. Dam. (19)88.	FV	FV	65.00
	e. Sign. B. Klinte and J. Sun Stein. (19)90.	FV	FV	50.00
	f. Sign. B. Klinte and E. Joensen. (19)94.	FV	FV	40.00
	s. Specimen. As a.	—	—	—

22	500 KRÓNUR	VG	VF	UNC
	L.1949 (19)78; (19)94. Black on green and dull purple unpt. Sketch of fisherman at r. Sketch of fishermen in boat at sea on back.			
	a. Sign. L. Groth and A. P. Dam. (19)78.	FV	FV	175.00
	b. Sign. B. Klinte and E. Joensen. (19)94.	FV	FV	165.00

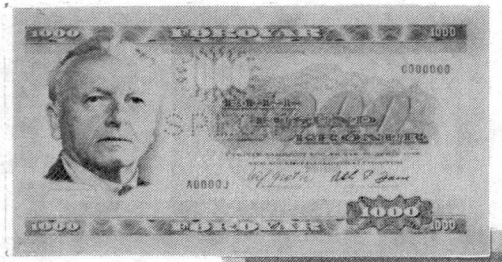

23	1000 KRÓNUR	VG	VF	UNC
	L.1949 (19)78; 83; 87; 89; 94. Blue-green, black and green. J. H. O. Djurhuus at l. Street scene sketch on back.			
	a. Sign. L. Groth and A. P. Dam. (19)78.	FV	FV	400.00
	b. Sign. N. Bentsen and P. Ellefsen. (19)83.	FV	FV	350.00
	c. Sign. N. Bentsen and A. P. Dam. (19)87.	FV	FV	350.00
	d. Sign. B. Klinte and A. P. Dam. (19)89.	FV	FV	325.00
	e. Sign. B. Klinte and M. Petersen. (19)94.	FV	FV	300.00

2001 ISSUE

24	50 KRÓNUR		VG	VF	UNC
	(20)01. Black on gray unpt. Ram's horn at r. Hillside in Sumba on back. Lilac segmented security strip at r.		FV	FV	14.00

25	100 KRÓNUR		VG	VF	UNC
	(20)02. Dull yellow. Fish tail at r. View from Klaksvík at back.		FV	FV	20.00

26	200 KRÓNUR		VG	VF	UNC
	(20)03. Dull purple. Moth at r. View from Vágum on back.		FV	FV	60.00
27	500 KRÓNUR				
	(20)04. Dull green. Crab's claw at r. View from Hvannasundi on back.		FV	FV	125.00
28	1000 KRÓNUR				
	(20)05. Dull red. Bird's wing at r. View from Sandoy on back.		FV	FV	225.00

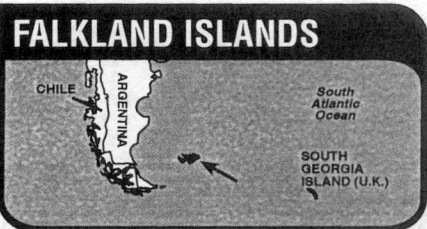

FALKLAND ISLANDS

The Colony of the Falkland Islands and Dependencies, a British colony located in the South Atlantic about 500 miles northeast of Cape Horn, has an area of 4,700 sq. mi. (12,173 sq. km.) and a population of 2,564. East Falkland, West Falkland, South Georgia, and South Sandwich are the largest of the 200 islands. Capital: Port Stanley. Fishing and sheep are the industry. Wool, whale oil, and seal oil are exported.

The Falklands were discovered by British navigator John Davis (Davys) in 1592, and named by Capt. John Strong - for Viscount Falkland, treasurer of the British navy - in 1690. French navigator Louis De Bougainville established the first settlement, at Port Louis, in 1764. The following year Capt. John Byron claimed the islands for Britain and left a small party at Saunders Island. Spain later forced the French and British to abandon their settlements but did not implement its claim to the islands. In 1829 the Republic of Buenos Aires, which claimed to have inherited the Spanish rights, sent Louis Vernet to develop a colony on the islands. In 1831 he seized three American sailing vessels, whereupon the men of the corvette *U.S.S. Lexington*, destroyed his settlement and proclaimed the Falklands to be "free of all governance." Britain, which had never renounced its claim, re-established its settlement in 1833.

The Islands were important in the days of sail and steam shipping as a location to re-stock fresh food and fuel, and make repairs after trips around Cape Horn. Argentine forces In 1990 the Argentine congrees declared the Falklands and other islands in the region part of the province of Tierra del Fuego. occupied the islands in April 1982, and after a short military campaign Britain regained control in June.

RULERS:
  British

MONETARY SYSTEM:
  1 Shilling = 12 Pence
  1 Pound = 20 Shillings to 1966
  1 Pound = 100 Pence, 1966-

GOVERNMENT

1960-67 ISSUE

#7-9 portr. Qn. Elizabeth II at r. Printer: TDLR.

7	10 SHILLINGS	VG	VF	UNC
	10.4.1960. Brown on gray unpt.			
	a. Issued note.	15.00	65.00	450.00
	s. Specimen.	—	—	—

8	1 POUND	VG	VF	UNC
	1967-82. Blue on gray-green and lilac unpt.			
	a. 2.1.1967.	5.00	20.00	80.00
	b. 20.2.1974.	4.00	10.00	65.00
	c. 1.12.1977.	6.00	25.00	100.00
	d. 1.1.1982.	4.00	10.00	70.00
	e. 15.6.1982.	4.00	8.50	70.00
	s. Specimen. As a-e.	—	—	—

9	5 POUNDS	VG	VF	UNC
	1960; 1975. Red on green unpt.			
	a. Sign: L. Gleadell: 10.4.1960.	20.00	60.00	300.00
	b. Sign: H. T. Rowlands: 30.1.1975.	17.50	50.00	250.00
	s. Specimen. As a-b.	—	—	—

1969; 1975 ISSUE

#10 and 11 portr. Qn. Elizabeth II at r. Printer: TDLR.

10	50 PENCE	VG	VF	UNC
	1969; 1974. Brown on gray unpt. Like #7.			
	a. Sign: L. Gleadell. 25.9.1969.	2.50	6.00	35.00
	b. Sign: H. T. Rowlands. 20.2.1974.	2.50	6.00	30.00
	s. Specimen. As a-b.			

11	10 POUNDS	VG	VF	UNC
	1975-82. Green on lt. orange and yellow-green unpt. Sign. H. T. Rowlands.			
	a. 5.6.1975.	25.00	75.00	325.00
	b. 1.1.1982.	27.50	85.00	425.00
	c. 15.6.1982.	25.00	75.00	300.00
	s. Specimen. As a.	—	—	—

1983 COMMEMORATIVE ISSUE

#12, 150th Anniversary of English rule, 1833-1983

12	5 POUNDS	VG	VF	UNC
	14.6.1983. Red on m/c unpt. Like #13. Commemorative legend at lower ctr.			
	a. Issued note.	FV	FV	37.50
	s. Specimen.			

1984-90 REGULAR ISSUE

#13-16 Qn. Elizabeth II at r. King penguins and shield at l., seals at r. Governor's home and church on back.

13	1 POUND	VG	VF	UNC
	1.10.1984. Blue on brown and yellow unpt. Like #12.	FV	7.50	35.00

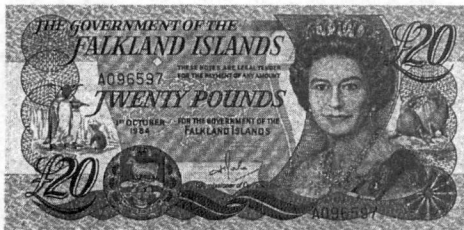

14	10 POUNDS	VG	VF	UNC
	1.9.1986. Green on blue and m/c unpt. Like #12.			
	a. Issued note.	FV	FV	55.00
	s. Specimen.	—	—	—

15	20 POUNDS	VG	VF	UNC
	1.10.1984. Brown on m/c unpt. Like #12.			
	a. Issued note.	FV	55.00	100.00
	s. Specimen.	—	—	—

16	50 POUNDS	VG	VF	UNC
	1.7.1990. Blue on m/c unpt. Like #12.			
	a. Issued note.	FV	FV	195.00
	s. Specimen.	—	—	—

FIJI ISLANDS

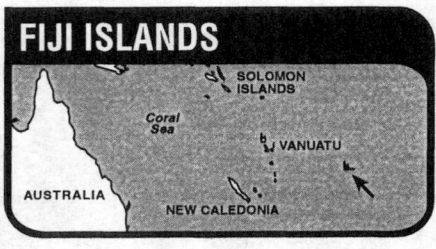

The republic of Fiji is an independent member of the British Commonwealth. It consists of about 320 islands located in the southwestern Pacific 1,100 miles (1,770 km.) north of New Zealand. The islands have a combined area of 7,056 sq. mi. (18,274 sq. km.) and a population of 848,000. Capital: Suva, on the island of Viti Levu. Fiji's economy is based on agriculture and mining. Sugar, coconut products, manganese and gold are exported.

The first European to sign Fiji was the Dutch navigator Abel Tasman in 1643. The island was visited by British naval captain James Cook in 1774. The first complete survey of the island was conducted by the United States in 1840. Settlement by missionaries from Tonga and traders attracted by the sandalwood trade began in 1835. Following a lengthy period of intertribal warfare, the islands were unconditionally and voluntarily ceded to Great Britain in 1874 by King Cakobau. The trading center was Levuka on the island of Ovalau which was also the capital under the British from 1874-82. Fiji became an independent nation on Oct 10, 1970, the 96th anniversary of the cession of the islands to Queen Victoria.

RULERS:
British, 1874-

MONETARY SYSTEM:
1 Shilling = 12 Pence
1 Pound = 20 Shillings to 1969
1 Dollar = 100 Cents, 1969-

REPLACEMENT NOTES:
#37-72: Z/1 prefix.

BRITISH ADMINISTRATION

GOVERNMENT

1954-57 ISSUE

#51-57 arms at upper ctr., portr. Qn. Elizabeth II at r. Wmk: Fijian youth's bust. Printer: BWC.

51	5 SHILLINGS	VG	VF	UNC
	1957-65. Green and blue on lilac and green unpt.			
	a. 1.6.1957. Sign. Davidson, Griffiths, Marais.	10.00	75.00	350.00
	b. 28.4.1961. Sign. Bevington, Griffiths, Cruickshank.	10.00	75.00	350.00
	c. 1.12.1962. Sign. Ritchie, Griffiths, Cruickshank.	8.00	60.00	325.00
	cs. Commercial (false color) specimen.			350.00
	d. 1.9.1964. Sign. Ritchie, Griffiths, Cruickshank.	7.50	50.00	275.00
	e. 1.10.1965. Sign. Ritchie, Griffiths, Cruickshank.	7.50	40.00	225.00
	s. Specimen. Various dates.	—	—	450.00

52	10 SHILLINGS	VG	VF	UNC
	1957-65. Brown on lilac and green unpt.			
	a. 1.6.1957. Sign. Davidson, Griffiths, Marais.	17.50	100.00	500.00
	b. 28.4.1961. Sign. Bevington, Griffiths, Cruickshank.	17.50	120.00	550.00
	c. 1.12.1962. Sign. Ritchie, Griffiths, Cruickshank.	10.00	80.00	450.00
	cs. Commercial (false color) specimen.			500.00
	d. 1.9.1964. Sign. Ritchie, Griffiths, Cruickshank.	12.50	125.00	600.00
	e. 1.10.1965. Sign. Ritchie, Griffiths, Cruickshank.	10.00	95.00	600.00
	s. Specimen. Various dates.	—	—	650.00

53	1 POUND	VG	VF	UNC
	1954-67. Green on yellow and blue unpt.			
	a. 1.7.1954. Sign. Davidson, Donovan, Davis.	20.00	130.00	625.00
	b. 1.6.1957. Sign. Davidson, Griffiths, Marais.	25.00	145.00	725.00
	c. 1.9.1959. Sign. Ritchie, Griffiths, Cruickshank.	20.00	130.00	625.00
	cs. Commercial (false color) specimen.			700.00
	d. 1.12.1961. Sign. ritchie, Griffiths, Cruickshank.	27.50	145.00	725.00
	e. 1.12.1962. Sign. Ritchie, Griffiths, Cruickshank.	25.00	145.00	700.00
	f. 20.1.1964. Sign. Ritchie, Griffiths, Cruickshank.	22.50	140.00	625.00
	g. 1.5.1965. Sign. Ritchie, Griffiths, Cruickshank.	20.00	130.00	600.00
	h. 1.12.1965. Sign. Ritchie, Griffiths, Cruickshank.	25.00	135.00	575.00
	i. 1.1.1967. Sign. Ritchie, Griffiths, Cruickshank.	17.50	125.00	575.00
	s. Specimen. Various dates.	—	—	850.00

54	5 POUNDS	VG	VF	UNC
	1954-67. Purple on lt. orange and green unpt.			
	a. 1.7.1954. Sign. Davidson, Donovan, Davis.	125.00	750.00	1500.00
	b. 1.9.1959. Sign. Bevington, Griffiths, Marais.	125.00	750.00	1500.00
	c. 1.10.1960. Sign. Bevington, Griffiths, Cruickshank.	95.00	750.00	1500.00
	cs. Commercial (false color) specimen.	—	—	850.00
	d. 1.12.1962. Sign. Ritchie, Griffiths, Cruickshank.	85.00	725.00	1250.00
	e. 20.1.1964. Sign. Ritchie, Griffiths, Cruickshank.	85.00	700.00	1100.00
	f. 1.1.1967. Sign. Ritchie, Griffiths, Cruickshank.	80.00	700.00	1100.00
	s. Specimen. Various dates.	—	—	1000.00

55	10 POUNDS	VG	VF	UNC
	1954-64. Blue on blue, orange and green unpt.			
	a. 1.7.1954. Sign. Davidson, Donovan, Davis.	250.00	1250.00	2000.00
	b. 1.9.1959. Sign. Bevington, Griffiths, Marais.	250.00	1250.00	2000.00
	c. 1.10.1960. Sign. Bevington, Griffiths, Cruickshank.	180.00	1100.00	2000.00
	cs. Commercial (false color) specimen.	—	—	950.00
	d. 20.1.1964. Sign. Ritchie, Griffiths, Cruickshank.	170.00	1000.00	1850.00
	e. 11.6.1964. Sign. Ritchie, Griffiths, Cruickshank.	160.00	900.00	1750.00
	f. 1.5.1965. Not released. Sign. Ritchie, Griffiths, Cruickshank.	—	—	—
	s. Specimen. Various dates.	—	—	1100.00

56	20 POUNDS	VG	VF	UNC
	1.1.1953. Black and purple on purple unpt.			
	a. 1.1.1953. Sign. Davidson, Donovan, Smith.	950.00	1250.00	4000.00
	cs. Commercial (false color) specimen.	—	—	1200.00
	s. Specimen.	—	—	3500.00

318 FIJI

57	20 POUNDS	VG	VF	UNC
	1.7.1954; 1.11.1958. Red on red and green unpt.			
	a. 1.7.1954. Sign. Davidson, Donovan, Davis.	750.00	1250.00	3000.00
	b. 1.11.1958. Sign. Bevington, Griffiths, Marais.	600.00	1000.00	2500.00
	cs. Commercial (false color) specimen.	—	—	1000.00
	s. Specimen.	—	—	2000.00

1969 CURRENCY BOARD ISSUE

#58-63 Qn. Elizabeth at r. Arms and heading: *GOVERNMENT OF FIJI* at upper ctr. Sign. Ritchie and Barnes. Wmk: Profile Fijian head. Printer: TDLR.

58	50 CENTS	VG	VF	UNC
	ND (1968). Blue-green on m/c unpt. Thatched bure (house) and coconut palms on back.			
	a. Issued note.	1.00	5.00	30.00
	s. Specimen.	—	—	200.00

59	1 DOLLAR	VG	VF	UNC
	ND (1968). Brown on brown, green and pink unpt. Yanuca beach scene in Yasewas on back.			
	a. Issued note.	2.00	10.00	85.00
	s. Specimen.	—	—	250.00

#52-55 w/o pictorial scenes on back.

60	2 DOLLARS			
	ND (1968). Green on brown and and lt. blue unpt. Geometric lathe pattern on back.			
	a. Issued note.	4.00	25.00	150.00
	s. Specimen.	—	—	300.00
61	5 DOLLARS			
	ND (1968). Orange on purple and gray unpt. Geometric lathe pattern on back.			
	a. Issued note.	7.00	40.00	350.00
	s. Specimen.	—	—	400.00
62	10 DOLLARS			
	ND (1968). Purple on orange and purple unpt. Geometric lathe pattern on back.			
	a. Issued note.	12.50	75.00	650.00
	s. Specimen.	—	—	700.00

63	20 DOLLARS			
	ND (1968). Blue on lt. green, orange and blue unpt. Geometric lathe pattern on back.			
	a. Issued note.	25.00	100.00	950.00
	s. Specimen.	—	—	1000.00

1971-73 AD-INTERIM CURRENCY

#64-69 like #68-63 but w/only 1 sign. Wmk: Profile Fijian head. Printer: TDLR.

64	50 CENTS	VG	VF	UNC
	ND (1971). Green on m/c unpt. Like #58.			
	a. Sign. Wesley Barrett.	1.00	5.00	35.00
	ar. As a. Replacement *Z/1* prefix.	5.00	15.00	75.00
	b. Sign. C. A. Stinson.	1.00	3.00	30.00
	br. As b. Replacement *Z/I* prefix.	7.50	12.50	65.00
	s. Specimen.	—	—	150.00
65	1 DOLLAR			
	ND (1971). Brown on lilac and lt. green unpt. Like #59.			
	a. Sign. Wesley Barrett.	1.50	20.00	100.00
	ar. As a. Replacement. *Z/I* prefix.	25.00	150.00	550.00
	b. Sign. C. A. Stinson.	2.00	25.00	125.00
	br. As b. Replacement. *Z/I* prefix.	10.00	50.00	250.00
	s. Specimen.	—	—	200.00
66	2 DOLLARS			
	ND (1971). Green on yellow and lt. blue unpt. Like #60.			
	a. Sign. Wesley Barrett.	4.00	15.00	185.00
	ar. As a. Replacement. *Z/I* prefix.	15.00	125.00	400.00
	b. Sign. C. A. Stinson. Not issued.	—	—	—
	br. As b. Replacement. *Z/I* prefix. Not issued.	—	—	—
	s. Specimen.	—	—	350.00

67	5 DOLLARS	VG	VF	UNC
	ND (1971). Like #61.			
	a. Sign. Wesley Barrett.	6.00	40.00	400.00
	ar. As a. Replacement. *Z/I* prefix.	20.00	200.00	850.00
	b. Sign. C. A. Stinson.	7.00	50.00	500.00
	br. As b. Replacement. *Z/I* prefix.	40.00	350.00	1000.00
	s. Specimen.	—	—	500.00
68	10 DOLLARS			
	ND (1971). Like #62.			
	a. Sign. Wesley Barrett.	10.00	150.00	550.00
	ar. As a. Replacement. *Z/I* prefix.	60.00	325.00	1000.00
	b. Sign. C. A. Stinson.	12.50	200.00	750.00
	br. As b. Replacement. *Z/I* prefix.	85.00	400.00	1250.00
	s. Specimen.	—	—	700.00
69	20 DOLLARS			
	ND (1971). Like #63.			
	b. Sign. C. A. Stinson.	30.00	125.00	925.00
	s. Specimen.	25.00	85.00	700.00

CENTRAL MONETARY AUTHORITY
1974 ND ISSUE

#70-75 like #58-63 but w/heading: *FIJI* at top ctr., and issuing authority name across lower ctr. 2 sign. Wmk: Profile Fijian head. Printer: TDLR.

70	50 CENTS	VG	VF	UNC
	ND (1974). Like #58. Sign. D. J. Barnes and R. J. A. Earland. (Not issued.)	—	—	—
	s. Specimen.	—	—	—

71	1 DOLLAR	VG	VF	UNC
	ND (1974). Like #59.			
	a. Sign. D. J. Barnes and R. J. Earland.	1.00	5.00	17.50
	ar. As a. Replacement. *Z/I* prefix.	2.50	9.00	30.00
	b. Sign. D. J. Barnes and H. J. Tomkins.	1.00	4.00	17.50
	br. As b. Replacement. *Z/I* prefix.	2.00	7.50	25.00
	s. As a, b. Specimen.	—	—	100.00

72 2 DOLLARS

ND (1974). Like #60.

	VG	VF	UNC
a. Sign. D. J. Barnes and I. A. Craik.	12.50	85.00	275.00
ar. As a. Replacement. Z/I prefix.	35.00	200.00	550.00
b. Sign. D. J. Barnes and R. J. Earland.	2.00	8.50	40.00
br. As b. Replacement. Z/I prefix.	3.00	25.00	135.00
c. Sign. D. J. Barnes and H. J. Tomkins.	2.00	10.00	60.00
cr. As c. Replacement. Z/I prefix.	2.50	15.00	95.00
s. Specimen.	—	—	175.00

73 5 DOLLARS

ND (1974). Like #61.

	VG	VF	UNC
a. Sign. D. J. Barnes and I. A. Craik.	20.00	100.00	550.00
ar. As a. Replacement. Z/I prefix.	85.00	350.00	1000.00
b. Sign. D. J. Barnes and R. J. Earland.	5.00	45.00	190.00
br. As b. Replacement. Z/I prefix.	12.50	225.00	750.00
c. Sign. D. J. Barnes and H. J. Tomkins.	6.00	85.00	250.00
cr. As c. Replacement. Z/I prefix.	15.00	95.00	350.00
s. Specimen.	—	—	500.00

74 10 DOLLARS

ND (1974). Like #62.

	VG	VF	UNC
a. Sign. D. J. Barnes and I. A. Craik.	20.00	75.00	700.00
b. Sign. D. J. Barnes and R. J. Earland.	8.50	20.00	250.00
c. Sign. D. J. Barnes and H. J. Tomkins.	7.50	17.50	185.00
s. As a. Specimen.	—	—	—

75 20 DOLLARS

ND (1974). Like #63.

	VG	VF	UNC
a. Sign. D. J. Barnes and I. A. Craik.	125.00	425.00	1850.00
ar. As a. Replacement. Z/I prefix.	375.00	850.00	2500.00
b. Sign. D. J. Barnes and R. J. Earland.	20.00	65.00	450.00
br. As b. Replacement. Z/I prefix.	65.00	225.00	900.00
c. Sign. D. J. Barnes and H. J. Tomkins.	20.00	85.00	500.00
cr. As c. Replacement. Z/I prefix.	95.00	325.00	1000.00
s. Specimen.	—	—	650.00

1980 ND ISSUE

#76-80 Qn. Elizabeth II at r. ctr., arms at ctr., artifact at r. Denomination figures 8mm high. Wmk: Profile Fijian head. Sign. D. J. Barnes and H. J. Tomkins. Printer: TDLR.

76 1 DOLLAR

ND (1980). Brown on m/c unpt. Open air Suva markets at ctr. on back.

	VG	VF	UNC
a. Issued note.	FV	4.00	15.00
r. As a. Replacement. Z/I prefix.	6.00	12.50	60.00
s. Specimen.	—	—	350.00

77 2 DOLLARS

ND (1980). Green on m/c unpt. Back khaki, sugar cane harvest at ctr. on back.

	VG	VF	UNC
a. Issued note.	FV	8.00	20.00
r. As a. Replacement. Z/I prefix.	7.50	18.50	90.00
s. Specimen.	—	—	400.00

78 5 DOLLARS

ND (1980). Orange on m/c unpt. Circle of fishermen w/net at ctr. on back.

	VG	VF	UNC
a. Issued note.	FV	12.50	30.00
r. As a. Replacement. Z/I prefix.	10.00	35.00	150.00
s. Specimen.	—	—	450.00

79	10 DOLLARS	VG	VF	UNC
	ND (1980). Purple on m/c unpt. Ceremonial tribal dance scene at ctr. on back.			
	a. Issued note.	FV	15.00	40.00
	r. As a. Replacement. *Z/I* prefix.	12.50	75.00	225.00
	s. Specimen.	—	—	550.00

80	20 DOLLARS	VG	VF	UNC
	ND (1980). Blue on m/c unpt. Fijian bure (house) at ctr. on back.			
	a. Issued note.	FV	20.00	60.00
	r. As a. Replacement. *Z/I* prefix.	15.00	95.00	375.00
	s. Specimen.	—	—	650.00

1983-86 ND ISSUE

#81-85 like #76-80. Backs retouched and lithographed. Denomination figures 9.5mm high. Wmk: Profile Fijian head. Sign. D. J. Barnes and S. Siwatibau. Printer: TDLR.

81	1 DOLLAR	VG	VF	UNC
	ND (1983). Dk. gray on m/c unpt. Like #76.			
	a. Issued note.	FV	3.00	9.00
	r. As a. Replacement. *Z/I* prefix.	4.00	10.00	45.00
	s1. Specimen. Signatures punched out.	—	—	225.00
	s2. Specimen. Corners punched out.	—	—	150.00

82	2 DOLLARS	VG	VF	UNC
	ND (1983). Green on m/c unpt. Like #77 but back green.			
	a. Issued note.	FV	7.00	15.00
	r. As a. Replacement. *Z/I* prefix.	5.00	18.50	85.00
	s1. Specimen. Signatures punched out.	—	—	275.00
	s2. Specimen. Corners punched out.	—	—	175.00

83	5 DOLLARS	VG	VF	UNC
	ND (1986). Brown-orange and purple on m/c unpt. Like #78.			
	a. Issued note.	FV	8.50	22.50
	r. As a. Replacement. *Z/I* prefix.	8.50	30.00	125.00
	s1. Specimen. Signatures punched out.	—	—	325.00
	s2. Specimen. Corners punched out.	—	—	225.00

84	10 DOLLARS	VG	VF	UNC
	ND (1986). Purple and brown on m/c unpt. Like #79.			
	a. Issued note.	FV	12.50	35.00
	r. As a. Replacement. *Z/I* prefix.	12.50	50.00	185.00
	s1. Specimen. Signatures punched out.	—	—	400.00
	s2. Specimen. Corners punched out.	—	—	285.00

85	20 DOLLARS	VG	VF	UNC
	ND (1986). Blue on m/c unpt. Like #80.			
	a. Issued note.	FV	17.50	50.00
	r. As a. Replacement. *Z/I* prefix.	17.50	85.00	225.00
	s1. Specimen. Signatures punched out.	—	—	450.00
	s2. Specimen. Corners punched out.	—	—	350.00

RESERVE BANK OF FIJI

1987-88 ND ISSUE

#86-88 modified portr. of Qn. Elizabeth II at r., and new banking authority. Similar to #81-2, 85. Sign. S. Siwatibau. Wmk: Profile Fijian head. No replacement notes. Printer: BWC.

86	1 DOLLAR	VG	VF	UNC
	ND (1987). Dk. gray on m/c unpt. Similar to #73.			
	a. Issued note.	FV	FV	4.50
	s. Specimen.	—	—	25.00

87 2 DOLLARS

	VG	VF	UNC
ND (1988). Green on m/c unpt. Similar to #74.			
a. Issued note.	FV	FV	7.00
s. Specimen.	—		35.00

88 20 DOLLARS

	VG	VF	UNC
ND (1988). Dk. blue, blue-green and black on m/c unpt. Similar to #77.			
a. Issued note.	FV	35.00	60.00
s. Specimen.	—		95.00

1991 ND Issue

#89-92 modified portr. Qn. Elizabeth II at r. Like #81-84. Wmk: Profile Fijian head. Sign. J. Kuabuabola. Printer: TDLR. No replacement notes.

89 1 DOLLAR

	VG	VF	UNC
ND (1993). Dk. gray on m/c unpt. Similar to #78. W/o segmented security thread.			
a. Issued note.	FV	FV	3.00
s. Specimen.	—		25.00

90 2 DOLLARS

	VG	VF	UNC
ND (1995). Deep green on m/c unpt. Similar to #79.			
a. Issued note.	FV	FV	6.00
s. Specimen.	—		35.00

91 5 DOLLARS

	VG	VF	UNC
ND (ca.1991). Brown-orange and purple on m/c unpt. Similar to #75.			
a. Issued note.	FV	17.50	30.00
s. Specimen.	—		55.00

92 10 DOLLARS

	VG	VF	UNC
ND (1989). Purple and brown on m/c unpt. Similar to #76.			
a. Issued note.	FV	27.50	45.00
s. Specimen.	—		75.00

1992 ND Issue

#93-95 like #86-92 but vertical and horizontal serial #. single letter serial # prefix, segmented security thread. Wmk: Profile Fijian head. Sign. J. Kubuabola. Printer: TDLR.

93 5 DOLLARS

	VG	VF	UNC
ND (1992). Brown-orange and purple on m/c unpt. Similar to #80.			
a. Issued note.	FV	8.00	15.00
s. Specimen.	—		50.00

94 10 DOLLARS

	VG	VF	UNC
ND (1992). Purple and brown on m/c unpt. Similar to #81.			
a. Issued note.	FV	12.50	27.50
s. Specimen.	—		75.00

95 20 DOLLARS

	VG	VF	UNC
ND (1992). Dk. blue, blue-green and black on m/c unpt. Similar to #82.			
a. Issued note.	FV	25.00	45.00
s. Specimen.	—		100.00

1992-95 ND Issue

#96-100 mature bust of Qn. Elizabeth II at r., arms at upper r. Segmented foil security thread. Wmk: Profile Fijian head. Printer: TDLR. Replacement notes: Serial # prefix Z.

96	2 DOLLARS	VG	VF	UNC
	ND (1996). Dk. green, blue and olive-brown on m/c unpt. Kaka bird (Masked Shining Parrot) at lower l. Fijian family of 5 at l. ctr. on back.			
	a. Single letter prefix.	FV	FV	7.50
	b. Double letter prefix. Amended security thread.	FV	FV	5.00
	r. Replacement. Z prefix.	FV	5.00	10.00
	s. Specimen.	—	—	30.00

100	50 DOLLARS	VG	VF	UNC
	ND (1996). Black, red, orange and violet on m/c unpt. Kaka bird at lower l. Ascending size vertical serial # at l. Flag raising ceremony at l., signing of Deed of Cession over Cession Stone at ctr. on back.			
	a. Singla letter prefix. Novel numbering on l. serial only.	FV	FV	65.00
	r. Replacement. Z prefix.	FV	60.00	90.00
	s. Specimen.	—	—	150.00

1998 ND ISSUE

101	5 DOLLARS	VG	VF	UNC
	ND (1998). Brown and orange on m/c unpt. Like #89.			
	a. Sign. Kubuabola.	FV	FV	10.00
	ar. As a. Replacement. Z prefix.	FV	10.00	20.00
	b. Sign. Narube.	FV	FV	12.50
	br. As b. Replacement. Z prefix.	FV	10.00	20.00
	s1. As a. Specimen.	—	—	50.00
	s2. As b. Specimen.	—	—	65.00

2000 COMMEMORATIVE ISSUE

#102-103 arms at upper r. *Y2K* at ctr. Segmented foil security thread. Wmk: Profile Fijian head.

97	5 DOLLARS	VG	VF	UNC
	ND (1995). Brown-orange on violet and m/c unpt. Bunedamu bird (White-throated Pigeon) at lower l. Aerial view Nadi International Airport at l. ctr., ferry boat at lower ctr. r. on back.			
	a. Issued note.	FV	FV	12.50
	r. Replacement. Z prefix.	5.00	12.50	25.00
	s. Specimen.	—	—	50.00

98	10 DOLLARS	VG	VF	UNC
	ND (1996). Purple, violet and brown on m/c unpt. Kikau bird at lower l. Children swimming at l. in background, family in boat constructed of reeds with thatched roof shelter at l. ctr. on back.			
	a. Single letter prefix.	FV	FV	25.00
	b. Double letter prefix.	FV	FV	18.50
	r. Replacement. Z prefix.	10.00	25.00	40.00
	s. Specimen.	—	—	75.00

102	2 DOLLARS	VG	VF	UNC
	2000. Green and blue on m/c unpt. Kaka bird at l., Sir Penaia Ganilau at r. Group portrait of islanders and turtle on back.			
	a. Issued note.	FV	FV	4.00
	b. Uncut pair.	FV	FV	7.50
	c. Uncut sheet of 20.	FV	FV	75.00
	s. Specimen.	—	—	20.00

99	20 DOLLARS	VG	VF	UNC
	ND (1996) Blue, purple and dk. blue on m/c unpt. Manusa bird at lower l. Parliament House at l., Reserve Bank bldg. at ctr. r. on back.			
	a. Single letter prefix. Novel numbering on l. serial # only.	FV	FV	65.00
	b. Double letter prefix.	FV	FV	35.00
	r. Replacement. Z prefix.	FV	60.00	90.00
	s. Specimen.	—	—	150.00

103	2000 DOLLARS	VG	VF	UNC
	2000. M/c. Sir Kamisese Mara at r. Earth, rising sun; island map on back.			
	a. Isused note.	FV	FV	1500.00
	s. Specimen, individually numbered.	—	—	450.00

2002 ND ISSUE

#104-108 similar to #104-106 but with additional security features. Ascending size serial #. Sign. Savenaca Narube.

104	2 DOLLARS	VG	VF	UNC
	ND (2002). Dk. green, blue and olive-brown on m/c unpt. Similar to #88.			
	a. Double letter prefix.	FV	FV	3.00
	r. Replacement. Z prefix.	3.00	6.00	10.00
	s. Specimen.	—	—	20.00

105	5 DOLLARS	VG	VF	UNC
	ND (2002). Brown-orange on violet and m/c unpt. Similar to #89.			
	a. Single letter prefix.	FV	FV	8.00
	b. Double letter prefix.	FV	FV	8.00
	r. Replacement. Z prefix.	FV	7.00	15.00
	s. Specimen.	—	—	45.00

106	10 DOLLARS	VG	VF	UNC
	ND (2002). Purple, violet and brown on m/c unpt. Similar to #90.			
	a. Double letter prefix.	FV	FV	13.00
	r. Replacement. Z prefix.	FV	10.00	20.00
	s. Specimen.	—	—	65.00

107	20 DOLLARS	VG	VF	UNC
	ND (2002). Blue, purple and dk. blue on m/c unpt. Similar to #91.			
	a. Double letter prefix.	FV	FV	25.00
	r. Replacement. Z prefix.	FV	15.00	30.00
	s. Specimen.	—	—	85.00

108	50 DOLLARS	VG	VF	UNC
	ND (2002). Black, red, orange and violet on m/c unpt. Similar to #92.			
	a. Single letter prefix.	FV	FV	55.00
	r. Replacement. Z prefix.	FV	30.00	70.00
	s. Specimen.	—	—	120.00

FINLAND

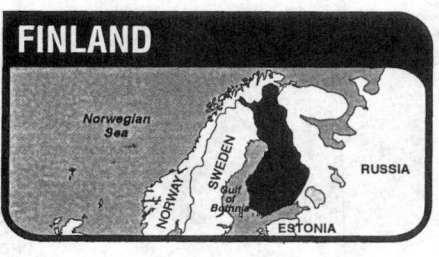

The Republic of Finland, the second most northerly state of the European continent, has an area of 130,120 sq. mi. (337,009 sq. km.) and a population of 5.21 million. Capital: Helsinki. Electrical/optical equipment, shipbuilding, metal and woodworking are the leading industries. Paper, wood pulp, plywood and telecommunication equipment are exported.

The Finns, who probably originated in the Volga region of Russia, took Finland from the Lapps late in the 7th century. They were conquered in the 12th century by Eric IX of Sweden, and brought into contact with Western Christendom. In 1809, Sweden was invaded by Alexander I of Russia, and the peace terms gave Finland to Russia. It became a grand duchy within the Russian Empire until Dec. 6, 1917, when, shortly after the Bolshevik revolution, it declared its independence. After a brief but bitter civil war between the Russian sympathizers and Finnish nationalists in which the Whites (nationalists) were victorious, a new constitution was adopted, and on Dec. 6, 1917 Finland was established as a republic. In 1939 Soviet troops invaded Finland over disputed territorial concessions which were later granted in the peace treaty of 1940. When the Germans invaded Russia, Finland also became involved and in the Armistice of 1944 lost the Petsamo area also to the USSR.

MONETARY SYSTEM:
  1 Markka = 100 Penniä, 1963-2001
  1 Euro = 100 Cents, 2002

REPUBLIC

SUOMEN PANKKI - FINLANDS BANK

1963 DATED ISSUE

#98-102 arms at ctr. or ctr. r. on back. W/o Litt. designation.

98	1 MARKKA	VG	VF	UNC
	1963. Lilac-brown on olive unpt. Wheat ears.			
	a. Issued note.	0.30	0.50	1.50
	r. Replacement note. Serial # suffix *.	1.00	7.00	15.00
	s. Specimen.	—	—	100.00

99	5 MARKKAA	VG	VF	UNC
	1963. Blue and blue-green. Conifer branch.			
	a. Issued note.	1.00	3.00	8.00
	r. Replacement note. Serial # suffix *.	1.00	20.00	
	s. Specimen.	—	—	125.00

324 FINLAND

100	10 MARKKAA	VG	VF	UNC
	1963. Dk. green and blue. Juho Kusti Paasikivi at l. (Wmk. direction varies.)			
	a. Issued note.	3.00	10.00	25.00
	r. Replacement note. Serial # suffix *.	50.00	125.00	250.00
	s. Specimen.	—	—	150.00

104	10 MARKKAA	VG	VF	UNC
	1963. Dk. green and blue. Like #100. (Wmk. position varies.)			
	a. Issued note.	2.00	3.00	8.00
	r. Replacement note. Serial # suffix *.	2.00	5.00	10.00

105	50 MARKKAA	VG	VF	UNC
	1963. Brown. Like #101.			
	a. Issued note.	10.00	20.00	35.00
	r. Replacement note. Serial # suffix *.	75.00	150.00	200.00

101	50 MARKKAA	VG	VF	UNC
	1963. Brown. Kaarlo Juho St<a0>hlberg at l.			
	a. Issued note.	10.00	20.00	40.00
	r. Replacement note. Serial # suffix *.	200.00	400.00	
	s. Specimen.	—	—	175.00

106	100 MARKKAA	VG	VF	UNC
	1963. Violet. Like #102.			
	a. Issued note.	20.00	25.00	40.00
	r. Replacement note. Serial # suffix *.	20.00	30.00	50.00

1963 DATED ISSUE, LITT. B

106A	5 MARKKAA	VG	VF	UNC
	1963. Blue and blue-green. Like #99.			
	a. Issued note.	1.00	1.50	2.50
	r. Replacement note. Serial # suffix *.	1.00	2.00	3.00

107	50 MARKKAA	VG	VF	UNC
	1963. Brown. Like #101 and #105. (Wmk. direction varies.)			
	a. Issued note.	10.00	15.00	35.00
	r. Replacement note. Serial # suffix *.	10.00	25.00	40.00

102	100 MARKKAA	VG	VF	UNC
	1963. Violet. Juhana Vilhelm Snellman at l.			
	a. Issued note.	20.00	25.00	50.00
	r. Replacement note. Serial # suffix *.	100.00	250.00	500.00
	s. Specimen.	—	—	200.00

1963 DATED ISSUE, LITT. A

1975-77 ISSUE

103	5 MARKKAA	VG	VF	UNC
	1963. Blue and blue-green. Similar to #99 but border and date designs are more detailed.			
	a. Issued note.	1.00	2.50	5.00
	r. Replacement note. Serial # suffix *.	1.00	4.00	8.00

108	50 MARKKAA	VG	VF	UNC
	1977. Brown and m/c. Kaarlo Juho St<a0>hlberg at l. and as wmk. (Wmk. position and direction varies.)			
	a. Issued note.	10.00	12.50	20.00
	r. Replacement note. Serial # suffix *.	10.00	15.00	25.00
	s. Specimen.	—	—	200.00

109 100 MARKKAA

	VG	VF	UNC
1976. Violet. Juhana Vilhelm Snellman at l. and as wmk. (Wmk. position and direction varies.)			
a. Issued note.	20.00	25.00	40.00
r. Replacement note. Serial # suffix *.	20.00	25.00	40.00

110 500 MARKKAA

	VG	VF	UNC
1975. Blue and violet. Urho Kaleva Kekkonen at l. and as wmk. Arms and 9 small shields on back. (Wmk. position varies.)			
a. Thin metallic security thread.	100.00	150.00	200.00
b. Broad yellow plastic security thread.	100.00	100.00	150.00
r1. As a. Replacement note. Serial # suffix *.	150.00	250.00	500.00
r2. As b. Replacement note. Serial # suffix *.	125.00	175.00	250.00
s. Specimen.	—	—	350.00

1980 ISSUE

111 10 MARKKAA

	VG	VF	UNC
1980. Green and brown on orange and m/c unpt. Like #100 except for color and addition of 4 raised discs at r. ctr. for denomination identification by the blind. Back green and purple. Wmk: Paasikivi.			
a. Issued note.	2.00	3.00	6.00
r. Replacement note. Serial # suffix *.	2.50	5.00	10.00

1980 ISSUE; LITT. A

112 10 MARKKAA

	VG	VF	UNC
1980. Similar to #111 but date under portr., and 5 small circles at bottom. Litt. A.			
a. Issued note.	2.00	3.00	6.00
r. Replacement note. 99 as 2nd and 3rd numerial in serial #.	2.50	5.00	10.00

1986 ISSUE

#113-117 portr. as wmk. Circles above lower r. serial #.

#113-115, and 117 replacement notes: w/99 as 2nd and 3rd digits in serial # and command a premium.

113 10 MARKKAA

	VG	VF	UNC
1986. Deep blue on blue and green unpt. Paavo Nurmi at l. and as wmk. Helsinki Olympic Stadium on back.			
a. Issued note.	2.00	2.50	6.00
r. Replacement note.	2.25	4.00	9.00

114 50 MARKKAA

	VG	VF	UNC
1986. Black on red-brown and m/c unpt. Alvar Aalto at l. and as wmk. 4 raised circles at lower r. for the blind. Finlandia Hall on back.			
a. Issued note.	12.50	15.00	30.00
r. Replacement note.	15.00	30.00	50.00

115 100 MARKKAA

	VG	VF	UNC
1986. Black on green and m/c unpt. Jean Sibelius at l. and as wmk. 3 raised circles at lower r. for the blind. Whooper Swans on back.			
a. Issued note.	20.00	30.00	55.00
r. Replacement note.	25.00	40.00	60.00

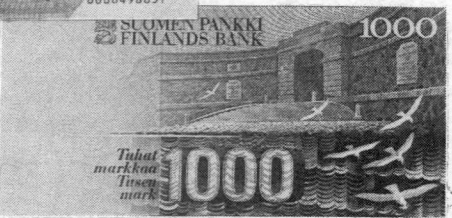

116   500 MARKKAA
1986. Black on red, brown and yellow unpt. Elias Lönnrot at l. and as wmk. Punkaharju on back.

	VG	VF	UNC
a. Issued note.	100.00	125.00	175.00
r. Replacement note.	125.00	150.00	200.00

117   1000 MARKKAA
1986. Blue and purple on m/c unpt. Anders Chydenius at l. and as wmk. King's gate, sea fortress of Suomenlinna in Helsinki harbor, seagulls on back.

	VG	VF	UNC
a. Issued note.	FV	200.00	300.00
r. Replacement note.	200.00	250.00	325.00

1986 DATED (1991) ISSUE, LITT. A

#118-122 like #114-117 with w/*Litt. A* above denomination added to lower l. and optical variable device (OVD) added at upper r. to higher denominations. Circles above bank name. Portr. as wmk.

		VG	VF	UNC
118	**50 MARKKAA** 1986 (1991). Similar to #114. Latent image at upper r.	FV	10.00	22.50
119	**100 MARKKAA** 1986 (1991). Similar to #115. Latent image at upper r.	FV	17.50	35.00

		VG	VF	UNC
120	**500 MARKKAA** 1986 (1991). Similar to #116.	FV	100.00	150.00

		VG	VF	UNC
121	**1000 MARKKAA** 1986 (1991). Similar to #117.	FV	200.00	250.00

1993 ISSUE

		VG	VF	UNC
122	**20 MARKKAA** 1993. Black on blue and gold unpt. Väinö Linna at l. and as wmk. Latent image at upper r. Tampere street scene on back.	4.00	7.50	12.50

1993 DATED (1997) ISSUE; LITT. A.

		VG	VF	UNC
123	**20 MARKKAA** 1993 (1997). Black on blue and green unpt. Like #122 but w/optical variable device at upper r. *Litt. A.* at lower l.	4.00	5.00	7.50

Note: For later issues made for use in Finland see European Union listings.

FRANCE

The French Republic, largest of the West European nations, has an area of 220,668 sq. mi. (547,026 sq. km.) and a population of 60 million. Capital: Paris. Agriculture, manufacturing and tourism are the most important elements of France's diversified economy. Textiles and clothing, iron and steel products, machinery and transportation equipment, agricultural products and wine are exported.

France, the Gaul of ancient times, emerged from the Renaissance as a modern centralized national state which reached its zenith during the reign of Louis XIV (1643-1715) when it became an absolute monarchy and the foremost power in Europe. Although his reign marks the golden age of French culture, the domestic abuses and extravagance of Louis XIV plunged France into a series of costly wars. This, along with a system of special privileges granted the nobility and other favored groups, weakened the monarchy, brought France to bankruptcy - and laid the way for the French Revolution of 1789-94 that shook Europe and affected the whole world.

The monarchy was abolished and the First Republic formed in 1793. The new government fell in 1799 to a coup led by Napoleon Bonaparte who, after declaring himself First Consul for life, had himself proclaimed emperor of France and king of Italy. Napoleon's military victories made him master of much of Europe, but his disastrous Russian campaign of 1812 initiated a series of defeats that led to his abdication in 1814 and exile to the island of Elba. The monarchy was briefly restored under Louis XVIII. Napoleon returned to France in March 1815, but his efforts to regain power were totally crushed at the Battle of Waterloo. He was exiled to the island of St. Helena where he died in 1821.

The monarchy under Louis XVIII was again restored in 1815, but the ultrareactionary regime of Charles X (1824-30) was overthrown by a liberal revolution and Louis Philippe of Orleans replaced him as monarch. The monarchy was ousted by the Revolution of 1848 and the Second Republic proclaimed. Louis Napoleon Bonaparte (nephew of Napoleon I) was elected president of the Second Republic. He was proclaimed emperor in 1852. As Napoleon III, he gave France two decades of prosperity under a stable, autocratic regime, but led it to defeat in the Franco-Prussian War of 1870, after which the Third Republic was established.

The Third Republic endured until 1940 and ended with the capitulation of France to the swiftly maneuvering German forces. Marshal Henri Petain formed a puppet government that sued for peace and ruled unoccupied France from Vichy. Meanwhile, General Charles de Gaulle escaped to London where he formed a wartime government in exile and the Free French army. Charles de Gaulle's provisional exile government was officially recognized by the Allies after the liberation of Paris in 1944, and de Gaulle, who had been serving as head of the provisional government, was formally elected to that position. In October 1945, the people overwhelmingly rejected a return to the prewar government, thus paving the way for the formation of the Fourth Republic.

Charles de Gaulle was unanimously elected president of the Fourth Republic, but resigned in January 1946 when leftists withdrew their support. In actual operation, the Fourth Republic was remarkably like the Third, with the National Assembly the focus of power. The later years of the Fourth Republic were marked by a burst of industrial expansion unmatched in modern French history. The growth rate, however, was marred by a nagging inflationary trend that weakened the franc and undermined the competitive posture of France's export trade. This and the Algerian conflict led to the recall of de Gaulle to power, the adoption of a new constitution vesting strong powers in the executive, and establishment in 1958 of the current Fifth Republic.

MONETARY SYSTEM:

1 Nouveau Franc = 100 "old" Francs, 1960-1962
1 Franc = 100 Centimes, 1962-2002
1 Euro = 100 Cents, 2002-

REPUBLIC

BANQUE DE FRANCE

1959 ISSUE

#141-145 denomination: *NOUVEAUX FRANCS* (NF).

		VG	VF	UNC
142	**10 NOUVEAUX FRANCS**			
	5.3.1959-4.1.1963. M/c. Like #134. Palais Cardinal across, Armand du Plessis, Cardinal Richelieu at r. Town gate (of Richelieu, in Indre et Loire) at r. on back.	5.00	15.00	125.00
143	**50 NOUVEAUX FRANCS**			
	5.3.1959-6.7.1961. M/c. Like #135. Henry IV at ctr., Paris' Point Neuf bridge in background. Henry IV at ctr., Château de Pau at l. on back.	30.00	100.00	1000.00
144	**100 NOUVEAUX FRANCS**			
	5.3.1959-2.4.1964. M/c. Like #136. Arc de Triomphe at l., Napoléon Bonaparte at r. Church of the Invalides in Paris at r., Bonaparte at l. on back.	20.00	40.00	700.00

		VG	VF	UNC
145	**500 NOUVEAUX FRANCS**			
	1959-66. M/c. Like #136A. Jean Baptiste Poquelin called Molière at ctr. Paris' Palais Royal in background. Theater in Versailles on back.			
	a. Sign. G. Gouin D'Ambrières, R. Tondu and P. Gargam. 2.7.1959-8.1.1965.	FV	200.00	1000.00
	b. Sign. H. Morant, R. Tondu and P. Gargam. 6.1.1966; 1.9.1966.	FV	200.00	1000.00
	s. Specimen. As b.	—	—	—

Note: #145b dated 1.9.1966 was not released for circulation, but examples with pin-hole cancelations are known.

1962-66 ISSUE

		VG	VF	UNC
146	**5 FRANCS**			
	1966-70. Brown, purple and m/c. Louis Pasteur at l., Pasteur Institute in Paris at r. Laboratory implements, man fighting a rabid dog, Pasteur at r. on back.			
	a. Sign. R. Tondu, P. Gargam and H. Morant. 5.5.1966-4.11.1966.	5.00	10.00	100.00
	b. Sign. R. Tondu, H. Morant and G. Bouchet. 5.5.1967-8.1.1970.	5.00	10.00	100.00

		VG	VF	UNC
141	**5 NOUVEAUX FRANCS**			
	5.3.1959-5.11.1965. Blue, orange and m/c. Like #133. Panthéon in Paris at l., Victor Hugo at r. Village at r., Victor Hugo at l. on back.			
	a. Issued note.	5.00	20.00	200.00
	s. Specimen.	—	—	—

147   10 FRANCS

1963-73. Red and m/c. Paris' Palais des Tuileries at ctr., François Voltaire at r. and as wmk. Château de Cirey at r., Voltaire at l. on back.

	VG	VF	UNC
a. Sign. G. Gouin D'Ambrières, P. Gargam and R. Tondu. 4.1.1963-2.12.1965.	FV	10.00	100.00
b. Sign. H. Morant, P. Gargam and R. Tondu. 6.1.1966-6.4.1967.	FV	8.00	60.00
c. Sign. G. Bouchet, H. Morant and R. Tondu. 6.7.1967-4.2.1971.	FV	6.00	40.00
d. Sign. G. Bouchet, H. Morant and P. Vergnes. 3.6.1971-6.12.1973.	FV	7.50	15.00
s. Specimen. As a-c. Ovpt. and perforated SPECIMEN.	—	—	500.00

148   50 FRANCS

1962-76. M/c. Port Royal des Champs Abbey at ctr., Jean Racine at r. Jean Racine at l., View of La Ferté-Milon on back.

	VG	VF	UNC
a. Sign. G. Gouin d'Ambrieres, R. Tondu and P. Gargam. 7.6.1962-4.3.1965.	6.00	20.00	120.00
b. Sign. H. Morant, R. Tondu and P. Gargam. 2.2.1967.	10.00	20.00	125.00
c. Sign. H. Morant, R. Tondu and G. Bouchet. 7.12.1967-5.11.1970.	6.00	15.00	100.00
d. Sign. G. Bouchet, P. Vergnes and H. Morant. 3.6.1971-3.10.1974.	6.00	15.00	80.00
e. Sign. G. Bouchet, J. J. Tronche and H. Morant. 6.3.1975-2.10.1975.	6.00	15.00	80.00
f. Sign. P. A. Strohl, G. Bouchet and J. J. Tronche. 2.1.1976-3.6.1976.	6.00	15.00	100.00
s. Specimen. Ovpt. and perforated SPECIMEN.	—	—	500.00

149   100 FRANCS

1964-79. M/c. Pierre Corneille at ctr., Theater in Versailles around. His bust in cartouche at ctr., View of Rouen on back.

	VG	VF	UNC

	VG	VF	UNC
a. Sign. R. Tondu. G. Gouin D'Ambrières and P. Gargam. 2.4.1964-2.12.1965.	10.00	35.00	150.00
b. Sign. R. Tondu, H. Morant and P. Gargam. 3.2.1966-6.4.1967.	10.00	25.00	120.00
c. Sign. R. Tondu, G. Bouchet and H. Morant. 5.10.1967-1.4.1971.	10.00	25.00	100.00
d. Sign. P. Vergnes, G. Bouchet and H. Morant. 1.7.1971-3.10.1974.	10.00	25.00	100.00
e. Sign. J. J. Tronche, G. Bouchet and H. Morant. 6.2.1975-6.11.1975.	10.00	25.00	100.00
f. Sign. P. A. Strohl, G. Bouchet and J. J. Tronche. 2.1.1976-1.2.1979.	10.00	25.00	70.00
s. Specimen. Ovpt. and perforated SPECIMEN.	—	—	600.00

1968-81 ISSUE

150   10 FRANCS

1972-78. Red, brown and olive. Hector Berlioz at r. conducting in the Chapelle des Invalides, Berlioz at l., musical instrument at r. and Rome's Villa Medici on back.

	VG	VF	UNC
a. Sign. H. Morant, G. Bouchet and P. Vergnes. 23.11.1972-3.10.1974.	FV	6.00	45.00
b. Sign. H. Morant, G. Bouchet and J. J. Tronche. 6.2.1975-4.12.1975.	FV	5.00	20.00
c. Sign. P. A. Strohl, G. Bouchet and J. J. Tronche. 2.1.1976-6.7.1978.	FV	4.00	15.00
s. Specimen. As b. Ovpt. and perforated SPECIMEN.	—	—	500.00

151   20 FRANCS

1980-97. Dull violet, brown and m/c. Claude Debussy at r. and as wmk., sea scene in background (La Mer). Back similar but w/lake scene.

	VG	VF	UNC
a. Sign. P. A. Strohl, J. J. Tronche and B. Dentaud. 1980-86.	FV	5.00	40.00
b. Sign. P. A. Strohl, D. Ferman and B. Dentaud. 1987.	FV	4.00	30.00
c. W/o security thread. Sign. D. Ferman, B. Dentaud and A. Charriau. 1988; 1989.	FV	3.00	25.00
d. W/security thread. Sign. as c. 1990.	FV	FV	20.00
e. Sign. D. Bruneel, B. Dentaud and A. Charriau. 1991.	FV	FV	15.00
f. Sign. D. Bruneel, J. Bonnardin and A. Charriau. 1992; 1993.	FV	FV	15.00
g. Sign. D. Bruneel, J. Bonnardin and C. Vigier. 1993.	FV	FV	15.00
h. Sign. as g. New Ley (law) on back. 1995.	FV	FV	10.00
i. Sign. D. Bruneel, J. Bonnardin and Y. Barroux. 1997.	FV	FV	10.00

152 50 FRANCS

1976-92. Deep blue-black on m/c unpt. Maurice Quentin de la Tour at ctr. r. and as wmk., and Palace of Versailles at l. ctr. in background. Q. de la Tour and St. Quentin City Hall at ctr. r. in background on back.

	VG	VF	UNC
a. Sign. P. A. Strohl, G. Bouchet and J. J. Tronche. 1976-79.	FV	FV	45.00
b. Sign. P. A. Strohl, J. J. Tronche and B. Dentaud. 1979-86.	FV	FV	40.00
c. Sign. P. A. Strohl, D. Ferman and B. Dentaud. 1987.	FV	FV	35.00
d. Sign. D. Ferman, B. Dentaud and A. Charriau. 1988; 1989.	FV	FV	30.00
e. Sign. D. Bruneel, B. Dentaud and A. Charriau. 1990; 1991.	FV	FV	20.00
f. Sign. D. Bruneel, J. Bonnardin and A. Charriau. 1992.	FV	FV	20.00

153 100 FRANCS

	VG	VF	UNC
1978. Brown. Eugène Delacroix at l. ctr. and as wmk., Marianne holding tricolor, part of Delacroix's painting *La Liberté Guidant le Peuple* at r. Sign. P. A. Strohl, G. Bouchet and J. J. Tronche.	FV	50.00	150.00

154 100 FRANCS

1978-95. Brown. Like #153 but *100 CENT FRANCS* retouched w/heavier diagonal lines at upper l.

	VG	VF	UNC
a. Sign. P. A. Strohl, G. Bouchet and J. J. Tronche. 1978-79.	FV	30.00	100.00
b. Sign. P. A. Strohl, J. J. Tronche and B. Dentaud. 1979-86.	FV	FV	60.00
c. Sign. P. A. Strohl, D. Ferman and B. Dentaud. 1987.	FV	FV	50.00
d. Sign. D. Ferman, B. Dentaud and A. Charriau. 1988-90.	FV	FV	50.00
e. Sign. D. Bruneel, B. Dentaud and A. Charriau. 1990-91.	FV	FV	40.00
f. Sign. D. Bruneel, J. Bonnardin and A. Charriau. 1991.	FV	FV	40.00
g. Sign. D. Bruneel, J. Bonnardin and C. Vigier. 1993.	FV	FV	35.00
h. Sign. as g. New Ley (law) on back. 1994; 1995.	FV	FV	30.00

155 200 FRANCS

1981-94. Blue-green, yellow and m/c. Figure w/staff at at l., Charles Baron de Montesquieu at r. and as wmk. Similar but w/Castle of Labrède on back (Montesquieu's birthplace).

	VG	VF	UNC
a. Sign. P. A. Strohl, J. J. Tronche and B. Dentaud. 1981-86.	FV	FV	120.00
b. Sign. P. A. Strohl, D. Ferman and B. Dentaud. 1987.	FV	FV	120.00
c. Sign. D. Ferman, B. Dentaud and A. Charriau. 1988; 1989.	FV	FV	95.00
d. Sign. D. Bruneel, B. Dentaud and A. Charriau. 1990; 1991.	FV	FV	90.00
e. Sign. D. Bruneel, J. Bonnardin and A. Charriau. 1992.	FV	FV	70.00
f. Sign. D. Bruneel, J. Bonnardin and C. Vigier. New Ley (law) on back. 1994.	FV	FV	100.00

156 500 FRANCS

1968-93. Yellow-brown and dk. brown. Tower of St. Jacques Church in Paris at l., Blaise Pascal at ctr. Blaise Pascal at l., abbey of Port Royal on back.

	VG	VF	UNC
a. Sign. G. Bouchet, R. Tondu and H. Morant. 4.1.1968-8.1.1970.	FV	115.00	250.00
b. Sign. G. Bouchet, P. Vergnes and H. Morant. 5.8.1971-5.9.1974.	FV	120.00	300.00
c. Sign. G. Bouchet, J. J. Tronche and H. Morant. 5.12.1974-6.11.1975.	FV	80.00	250.00
d. Sign. P. A. Strohl, G. Bouchet and J. J. Tronche. 1.4.1976-7.6.1979.	FV	70.00	150.00
e. Sign. P. A. Strohl, J. J. Tronche and B. Dentaud. 7.6.1979-6.2.1986.	FV	FV	130.00
f. Sign. P. A. Strohl, D. Ferman and B. Dentaud. 8.1.1987; 22.1.1987; 5.11.1987.	FV	FV	125.00
g. Sign. of D. Ferman, B. Dentaud and A. Charriau. 3.3.1988-1.2.1990.	FV	FV	125.00
h. Sign. D. Bruneel, B. Dentaud and A. Charriau. 5.7.1990-2.5.1991.	FV	FV	125.00

156   500 FRANCS

	VG	VF	UNC
i. Sign. D. Bruneel, J. Bonnardin and A. Charriau. 3.10.1991-7.1.1993.	FV	FV	125.00
j. Sign. D. Bruneel, J. Bonnardin and C. Vigier. 2.9.1993.	FV	FV	200.00
s. Specimen. Ovpt. and perforated *SPECIMEN*.	—	—	600.00

1993-97 ISSUE

#157-160 Many technical anti-counterfeiting devices added

157   50 FRANCS

1992-93. Purple and dk. blue on blue, green and m/c unpt. Drawing of *le Petit Prince* at l. Old airplane at top l., topographical map of Africa at ctr., Antoine de Saint-Exupéry at r. and as wmk. Breguet XIV biplane on back. Name as Éxupéry, ol

	VG	VF	UNC
a. Sign. D. Bruneel, J. Bonnardin and A. Charriau. 1992.	FV	FV	30.00
b. Sign. D. Bruneel, J. Bonnardin and C. Vigier. 1993.	FV	FV	25.00

157A   50 FRANCS

1994-99. As 157 but corrected to Exupéry, new law clause on back.

	VG	VF	UNC
a. Sign. D. Bruneel, J. Bonnardin and C. Vigier. 1994. 8 cardinal points in compass solid. Underline *al.* in sign. titles.	FV	FV	12.50
b. Sign. D. Bruneel, J. Bonnardin and C. Vigier. 1994. 8 cardinal points in compass striped. W/o underlined *al.* in sign. title.	FV	FV	12.50
c. Sign. D. Bruneel, J. Bonnardin and Y. Barroux. 1996.	FV	FV	25.00
d. Sign. as c. 1997, 1998.	FV	FV	10.00

158   100 FRANCS

1997; 1998. Deep brown on orange, pink and lt. green unpt. Paul Cézanne at r. and as wmk. Painting of fruit at l. on back. Sign. as #157Ab.

	VG	VF	UNC
	FV	FV	25.00

159   200 FRANCS

1995-99. Brown and pink on m/c unpt. Gustave Eiffel at r. and as wmk., observatory at upper l. ctr., Eiffel tower truss at ctr. View through tower base across exhibition grounds at l. ctr. on back.

	VG	VF	UNC
a. Sign. D. Bruneel, J. Bonnardin and C. Vigier. 1995; 1996.	FV	FV	50.00
b. Sign. D. Bruneel, J. Bonnardin and Y. Barroux. 1996; 1997.	FV	FV	45.00
c. Sign. D. Bruneel, J. Bonnardin and Y. Barroux. 1999.	FV	FV	40.00

160   500 FRANCS

1994-2000. Dk. green and black on m/c unpt. Marie and Pierre Curie at ctr. r. Segmented foil strip at l. Laboratory utensils at l. ctr. on back. Wmk: M. Curie.

	VG	VF	UNC
a. 1994-95. Sign. as #159a.	FV	FV	130.00
b. 1996. Sign. as #159a.	FV	120.00	200.00
c. 1998. Sign. as #157b.	FV	FV	120.00
d. 2000. Sign. Y. Barroux, J. Bonnardin, A. Vienney.	FV	FV	140.00

Note: For later issues made for use in France see European Union listings.

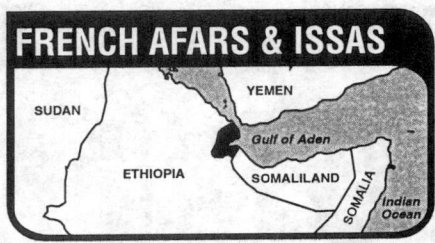

FRENCH AFARS & ISSAS

The French Overseas Territory of Afars and Iassas (formerly French Somaliland, later to be independent as Djibouti) is located in northeast Africa at the Bab el Mandeb Strait connecting the Suez Canal and the Red Sea with the Gulf of Aden and the Indian Ocean, has an area of 8,494 sq. mi. (22,000 sq. km.) and a population of 542,000. Capital: Djibouti. The tiny nation has less than one sq. mi. of arable land, and no natural resources except salt, sand and camels. The commercial activities of the trans-shipment port of Djibouti and the Addis Ababa-Djibouti railroad are the basis of the economy. Salt, fish and hides are exported.

French interest in former French Somaliland began in 1839 with concessions obtained by a French naval lieutenant from the provincial sultans. French Somaliland was made a protectorate in 1884 and its boundaries were delimited by the Franco-British and Ethiopian accords of 1887 and 1897. It became a colony in 1896 and a territory within the French Union in 1946. In 1958, it voted to join the new French Community as an overseas territory, and reaffirmed that choice by a referendum in March 1967. Its name was changed from French Somaliland to the French Territory of Afars and Issas on July 5, 1967.

The French Tricolor, which had flown over the strategically important territory for 115 years, was lowered for the last time on June 27, 1977, when French Afars and Issas became Djibouti.

Note: For later issues see Djibouti.

RULERS:
    French to 1977

MONETARY SYSTEM:
    1 Franc = 100 Centimes

FRENCH ADMINISTRATION

TRÉSOR PUBLIC, TERRITOIRE FRANÇAIS DES AFARS ET DES ISSAS

1969 ND ISSUE

30	5000 FRANCS	VG	VF	UNC
	ND (1969). M/c. Aerial view of Djibouti harbor at ctr. Ruins at ctr. on back.	75.00	275.00	750.00

1973; 1974 ND ISSUE

31	500 FRANCS	VG	VF	UNC
	ND (1973). M/c. Ships at l. ctr. Rearing antelope at ctr. on back.	12.00	50.00	185.00

32	1000 FRANCS	VG	VF	UNC
	ND (1974). M/c. Woman holding jug at l. ctr. on face. Reversed image as face on back.	20.00	80.00	325.00

1975 ND ISSUE

33	500 FRANCS	VG	VF	UNC
	ND (1975). M/c. Man at l., rocks in sea, storks at r. Stern of ship at r. on back.	7.00	20.00	80.00

34	1000 FRANCS	VG	VF	UNC
	ND (1975). M/c. Woman at l., people by diesel passenger trains at ctr. Trader w/camels on back.	10.00	35.00	150.00

35	5000 FRANCS	VG	VF	UNC
	ND (1975). M/c. Man at r., forest scene at ctr. Aeriel view at ctr. on back.	45.00	85.00	350.00

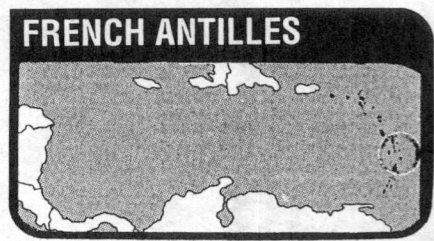

FRENCH ANTILLES

Three French overseas departments, Guiana, Guadeloupe and Martinique which issued a common currency from 1961-1975. Since 1975 Bank of France notes have circulated.

RULERS:
French

MONETARY SYSTEM:
1 Nouveau Franc = 100 "old" Francs
1 Franc = 100 Centimes

SIGNATURE VARIETIES

	Le Directeur Général	Le Président du Conseil de Surveillance
1	André POSTEL-VINAY	Pierre CALVET 1059-1965
2	André POSTEL-VINAY	Bernard CLAPPIER 1966-1972

FRENCH ADMINISTRATION

INSTITUT D'EMISSION DES DÉPARTEMENTS D'OUTRE-MER

1961 ND PROVISIONAL ISSUE

Nouveau Franc System

#1-3 ovpt: *GUADELOUPE, GUYANE, MARTINIQUE.* Sign. 1.

			VG	VF	UNC
1	1 NOUVEAU FRANC ON 100 FRANCS	ND (1961). M/c. La Bourdonnais at l. Woman at r. on back.	15.00	75.00	425.00

			VG	VF	UNC
2	10 NOUVEAUX FRANCS ON 1000 FRANCS	ND (1961). M/c. Fishermen from the Antilles.	75.00	500.00	2000.00
3	50 NOUVEAUX FRANCS ON 5000 FRANCS	ND (1961). M/c. Woman w/fruit bowl at ctr. r.	150.00	750.00	2500.00

SECOND 1961 ND PROVISIONAL ISSUE

#4, ovpt: *DÉPARTEMENT DE LA GUADELOUPE - DÉPARTEMENT DE LA GUYANE - DÉPARTEMENT DE LA MARTINIQUE.* Sign. 1.

			VG	VF	UNC
4	5 NOUVEAUX FRANCS ON 500 FRANCS	ND (1961). Brown on m/c unpt. Sailboat at l., 2 women at r. Men w/carts containing plants and wood on back.	75.00	350.00	1500.00

INSTITUT D'EMISSION DES DÉPARTEMENTS D'OUTRE-MER RÉPUBLIQUE FRANCAISE

1963 ND ISSUE

#5-10 ovpt: *DÉPARTEMENT DE LA GUADELOUPE - DÉPARTEMENT DE LA GUYANE - DÉPARTEMENT DE LA MARTINIQUE.* Sign. 1.

			VG	VF	UNC
5	10 NOUVEAUX FRANCS	ND (1963). Brown and green on m/c unpt. Girl at r., coastal scenery in background. People cutting sugar cane on back.			
		a. Issued note.	5.00	40.00	250.00
		s. Specimen.	—	—	125.00

6	50 NOUVEAUX FRANCS	VG	VF	UNC
	ND (1963). Green on m/c unpt. Banana harvest. Shoreline w/houses at l., man and woman at r. on back.			
	a. Issued note.	15.00	75.00	400.00
	s. Specimen.	—	—	185.00

1964 ND ISSUE

7	5 FRANCS	VG	VF	UNC
	ND (1964). Like #4, but smaller size.			
	a. Sign. 1.	15.00	60.00	500.00
	b. Sign. 2.	7.50	50.00	400.00
	s. As b. Specimen.	—	—	—

10	100 FRANCS	VG	VF	UNC
	ND (1964). Brown and m/c. Gen. Schoelcher at ctr. r. Schoelcher at l. ctr., various arms and galleon around on back.			
	a. Sign. 1.	75.00	250.00	900.00
	b. Sign. 2.	50.00	150.00	850.00

8	10 FRANCS	VG	VF	UNC
	ND (1964). Like #5.			
	a. Sign. 1.	7.00	25.00	175.00
	b. Sign. 2.	5.00	20.00	150.00

9	50 FRANCS	VG	VF	UNC
	ND (1964). Like #6.			
	a. Sign. 1.	15.00	100.00	400.00
	b. Sign. 2.	10.00	40.00	350.00

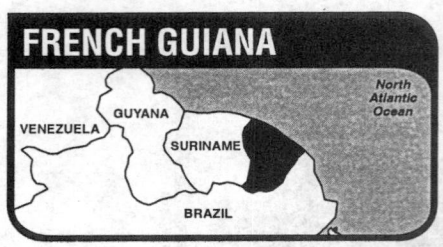

FRENCH GUIANA

The French Overseas Department of French Guiana, located on the northeast coast of South America, bordered by Surinam and Brazil, has an area of 32,252 sq. mi. (91,000 sq. km.) and a population of 173,000. Capital: Cayenne. Placer gold mining and shrimp processing are the chief industries. Shrimp, lumber, gold, cocoa and bananas are exported.

The coast of Guiana was sighted by Columbus in 1498 and explored by Amerigo Vespucci in 1499. The French established the first successful trading stations and settlements, and placed the area under direct control of the French Crown in 1674. Portuguese and British forces occupied French Guiana for five years during the Napoleonic Wars. Devil's Island, the notorious penal colony in French Guiana where Capt. Alfred Dreyfus was imprisoned, was established in 1852 - and finally closed in 1947. When France adopted a new constitution in 1946, French Guiana voted to remain within the French Union as an overseas department.

RULERS:
French

MONETARY SYSTEM:
1 Nouveau (new) Franc = 100 "old" Francs, 1961-

FRENCH ADMINISTRATION

CAISSE CENTRALE DE LA FRANCE D'OUTRE-MER
1961 ND PROVISIONAL ISSUE

#29-33 ovpt: *GUYANE* and nouveau franc denominations on earlier issue. (Vol. 2.)

		VG	VF	UNC
29	**1 NOUVEAU FRANC ON 100 FRANCS** ND (1961). M/c. Ovpt. on #23. B. d'Esnambuc at l., sailing ship at r.	15.00	45.00	325.00

		VG	VF	UNC
30	**5 NOUVEAUX FRANCS ON 500 FRANCS** ND (1961). M/c. Ovpt. on #24. Sailboat at l., 2 women at r.	50.00	165.00	675.00
31	**10 NOUVEAUX FRANCS ON 1000 FRANCS** ND (1961). M/c. Ovpt. on #27. Fishermen.	125.00	500.00	1300.00

		VG	VF	UNC
32	**10 NOUVEAUX FRANCS ON 1000 FRANCS** ND. M/c. Ovpt. on #25. Woman at r.	110.00	350.00	900.00
33	**50 NOUVEAUX FRANCS ON 5000 FRANCS** ND. Ovpt. on #28. Woman w/fruit bowl.	375.00	800.00	1800.00

Note: For later issues see French Antilles.

FRENCH PACIFIC TERRITORIES

The French Pacific Territories include French Polynesia, New Caledonia and formerly the New Hebrides Condominium. For earlier issues also refer to French Oceania and Tahiti.

FRENCH ADMINISTRATION

INSTITUT D'EMISSION D'OUTRE-MER
1985-96 ND ISSUE

Notes w/o *NOUMEA* or *PAPEETE*.

		VG	VF	UNC
1	**500 FRANCS** ND (1992). M/c. Sailboat at ctr., fisherman at r., Man at l., objects at r. on back.			
	a. 2 sign. W/o security thread. Sign. 2.	FV	FV	25.00
	b. 3 sign. W/security thread. Sign. 3.	FV	FV	20.00

		VG	VF	UNC
2	**1000 FRANCS** ND (1996). M/c. Hut in palm trees at l., girl at r.			
	a. Sign. 3.	FV	FV	32.50
	b. Sign. 4.	FV	FV	30.00

3   5000 FRANCS
　ND (1996). M/c. Bougainville at l., sailing ships at ctr. Sign. 3.

	VG	VF	UNC
	FV	FV	140.00

4   10,000 FRANCS
　ND (1985). M/c. Tahitian girl w/floral headdress at upper l.
　to?puristic bungalows at ctr. Fish at ctr., Melanesian girl wearing
　flower at r. on back. Wmk: 2 ethnic heads.

	VG	VF	UNC
a. 2 sign. W/o security thread. Sign. 1.	FV	FV	250.00
b. 3 sign. W/security thread. (New Ley on back.) Sign. 5.	FV	FV	225.00

fNote: Above notes in CFP francs (change franc Pacifique). Common currency of French Polynesia, New Caledonia, and Wallis & Futuna Islands. Design types of #1-3 like issues for New Caledonia and New Hebrides but w/o *NOUMEA* or *PAPEETE*. Sign. varieties correspond to those used for New Caledonia and New Hebrides issues.

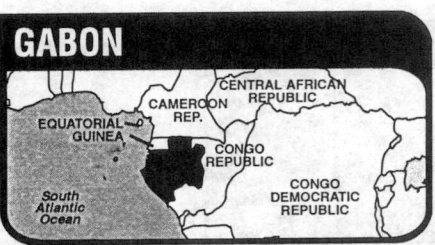

The Gabonese Republic, a member of the French Community, straddles the equator on the west coast of Africa. The hot and humid rain forest country has an area of 103,347 sq. mi. (267,667 sq. km.) and a population of 1.23 million, almost all of Bantu origin. Capital: Libreville. Extravagantly rich in resources, Gabon exports crude oil, manganese ore, gold and timbers.

　Gabon was first visited by Portuguese navigator Diego Cam in the 15th century. Dutch, French and British traders, lured by the rich stands of hard woods and oil palms, quickly followed. The French founded their first settlement on the left bank of the Gabon River in 1839 and established their presence by signing treaties with the tribal chiefs. After gradually extending their influence into the interior during the last half of the 19th century, France occupied Gabon in 1885 and, in 1910, organized it as one of the four territories of French Equatorial Africa. It became an autonomous republic within the French Union in 1946, and on Aug. 17, 1960, became a completely independent republic within the new French Community.

　Note: For related currency, see the Equatorial African States.

MONETARY SYSTEM:
　1 Franc = 100 Centimes

SIGNATURE VARIETIES:
　Refer to introduction to Central African States.

RÉPUBLIQUE GABONAISE

BANQUE CENTRALE

1971 ND ISSUE

1   10,000 FRANCS
　ND (1971). M/c. Pres. O. Bongo at r., mask at l., mine elevator at
　ctr. Statue at l. and r., tractor plowing at ctr. on back. Sign. 1.

	VG	VF	UNC
	40.00	125.00	375.00

BANQUE DES ÉTATS DE L'AFRIQUE CENTRALE

1974 ND ISSUE

2   500 FRANCS
　ND (1974); 1978. Lilac-brown on m/c unpt. Woman wearing
　kerchief at l., logging at ctr. Mask at l., students and chemical
　testing at ctr., statue at r. on back.

	VG	VF	UNC
a. Engraved. Sign. 6. ND (1974).	1.75	4.50	22.50
b. Lithographed. Sign. 9. 1.4.1978.	1.00	3.00	15.00

5   **10,000 FRANCS**
ND (1974; 1978). M/c. Like #1 except for new bank name on back.

	VG	VF	UNC
a. Sign. 6 w/titles: *LE DIRECTEUR GÉNÉRAL* and *UN CENSEUR*. ND (1974).	27.50	75.00	200.00
b. Sign. 9 w/titles: *LE GOUVERNEUR* and *UN CENSEUR*. ND (1978).	20.00	50.00	175.00

1983; 1984 ND ISSUE

3   **1000 FRANCS**
ND (1974; 1978); 1978-84. Red and blue on m/c unpt. Ship and oil refinery at ctr., Pres. O. Bongo at r. Mask at l., trains, planes and bridge at ctr., statue at r. on back.

	VG	VF	UNC
a. Sign. 4 w/titles: *LE DIRECTEUR GÉNÉRAL* and *UN CENSEUR*. Engraved. Wmk: Antelope head in half profile. ND (1974).	45.00	150.00	350.00
b. Like a. Sign. 6.	4.00	15.00	55.00
c. Sign. 6 w/titles: *LE DIRECTEUR GÉNÉRAL* and *UN CENSEUR*. Lithographed. Wmk. Antelope head in profile. ND (1978).	3.50	10.00	40.00
d. Sign. 9 w/titles: *LE GOUVERNEUR* and *UN CENSEUR*. Lithographed. Wmk. like b. 1.4.1978; 1.1.1983; 1.6.1984.	3.25	8.00	20.00

6   **5000 FRANCS**
ND (1984-91). Brown on m/c unpt. Mask at l., woman w/fronds at r. Plowing and mine ore conveyor on back. Sign. 9; 14.

	VG	VF	UNC
a. Sign. 9. (1984).	5.00	15.00	50.00
b. Sign. 14. (1991).	5.00	12.50	40.00

4   **5000 FRANCS**
ND (1974; 1978). Brown. Oil refinery at l., open pit mining and Pres. O. Bongo at r. Mask at l., bldgs. at ctr., statue at r. on back.

	VG	VF	UNC
a. Sign. 4 w/titles: *LE DIRECTEUR GENERAL* and *UN CENSEUR*. ND (1974).	35.00	100.00	400.00
b. Like a. Sign. 6.	17.50	50.00	200.00
c. Sign. 9 w/titles: *LE GOUVERNEUR* and *UN CENSEUR*. ND (1978).	10.00	25.00	150.00
x1. Error. As a. W/o sign.	25.00	60.00	180.00
x2. Error. As c. W/o sign.	20.00	50.00	155.00

7   **10,000 FRANCS**
ND (1983-91). Brown and green on m/c unpt. Stylized antelope heads at l., woman at r. Loading fruit onto truck at l. on back. Sign. 9; 14.

	VG	VF	UNC
a. Sign. 9. (1984).	7.50	27.50	90.00
b. Sign. 14. (1991).	7.50	25.00	75.00

1985 ISSUE

#8-10 wmk: Carving (same as printed on notes).

8   **500 FRANCS**
1.1.1985. Brown on orange and m/c unpt. Carving and jug at ctr.
Man carving mask at l. ctr. on back. Sign. 9.

VG	VF	UNC
1.25	2.25	7.00

9   **1000 FRANCS**
1.1.1985. Deep blue on m/c unpt. Carving at l., map at ctr., Pres. O.
Bongo at r. Incomplete outline map of Chad at top ctr. Elephant at
l., animals at ctr., man carving at r. on back. Sign. 9.

VG	VF	UNC
FV	9.50	20.00

1986 ISSUE

10   **1000 FRANCS**
1986-91. Deep blue on m/c unpt. Like #9 but w/outline map of
Chad at top completed.

	VG	VF	UNC
a. Sign. 9. 1.1.1986; 1.1.1987; 1.1.1990.	FV	7.50	20.00
b. Sign. 14. 1.1.1991.	FV	7.00	15.00

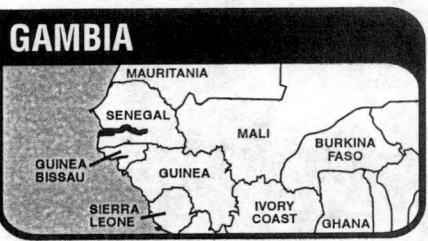

The Republic of The Gambia, an independent member of the British Commonwealth, occupies a strip of land 7 miles (11 km.) to 20 miles (32 km.) wide and 200 miles (322 km.) long encompassing both sides of West Africa's Gambia River, and completely surrounded by Senegal. The republic, one of Africa's smallest countries, has an area of 4,361 sq. mi. (11,295 sq. km.) and a population of 1.24 million. Capital: Banjul. Agriculture and tourism are the principal industries. Peanuts constitute 95 per cent of export earnings.

The Gambia was once part of the great empires of Ghana and Songhay. When Portuguese gold seekers and slave traders visited The Gambia in the 15th century, it was part of the Kingdom of Mali. In 1588 the territory became, through purchase, the first British colony in Africa. English slavers established Fort James, the first settlement, on a small island a dozen miles up the Gambia River in 1664. After alternate periods of union with Sierra Leone and existence as a separate colony, The Gambia became a British colony in 1888. On Feb. 18, 1965, The Gambia achieved independence as a constitutional monarchy within the Commonwealth of Nations, with Elizabeth II as Head of State as Queen of The Gambia. It became a republic on April 24, 1970, remaining a member of the Commonwealth, but with the president as Chief of State and Head of Government.

RULERS:
British to 1970

MONETARY SYSTEM:
1 Shilling = 12 Pence
1 Pound = 20 Shillings to 1970
1 Dalasi = 100 Bututs 1970-

SIGNATURE VARIETIES			
1	CHAIRMAN DIRECTOR	**8**	
2	GENERAL MANAGER GOVERNOR	**9**	GENERAL MANAGER GOVERNOR
3	S. S. Sisay	**10**	GENERAL MANAGER GOVERNOR
4	S. S. Sisay	**11**	
5	S. S. Sisay	**12**	
6	S. S. Sisay	**13**	
7		**14**	

BRITISH ADMINISTRATION
THE GAMBIA CURRENCY BOARD

1965 ND ISSUE

Pound System

#1-3 sailboat at l. Wmk. Crocodile's head. Sign. 1.

1   10 SHILLINGS
ND (1965-70). Green and brown on m/c unpt. Workers in field on back.

	VG	VF	UNC
a. Issued note.	5.00	15.00	45.00
ct. Color trial. Blue and green on m/c unpt.	—	—	250.00
s. Specimen.	—	—	175.00

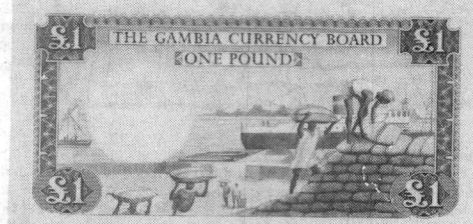

2   1 POUND
ND (1965-70). Red and brown on m/c unpt. Loading sacks at dockside on back.

	VG	VF	UNC
a. Issued note.	6.00	22.50	70.00
ct. Color trial. Brown and gray on m/c unpt.	—	—	250.00
s. Specimen.	—	—	175.00

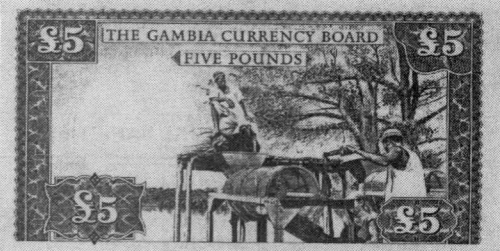

3   5 POUNDS
ND (1965-70). Blue and green on m/c unpt. Back blue; man and woman operating agricultural machine at ctr. r.

	VG	VF	UNC
a. Issued note.	15.00	40.00	125.00
ct. Color trial. Gray-brown and green on m/c unpt.	—	—	250.00
s. Specimen.	—	—	175.00

REPUBLIC

CENTRAL BANK OF THE GAMBIA

1971; 1972 ND ISSUE

Dalasi System

#4-8 sailboat at l., Pres. D. Kairaba Jawara at r. Sign. varieties. Wmk: Crocodile's head.

4   1 DALASI
ND (1971-87). Purple on m/c unpt. Back similar to #1.

	VG	VF	UNC
a. Sign. 2.	4.00	15.00	50.00
b. Sign. 3.	4.50	15.00	65.00
c. Sign. 4.	2.50	9.00	20.00
d. Sign. 5.	1.50	5.00	10.00
e. Sign. 6.	0.75	2.50	5.00
f. Sign. 7.	0.50	2.00	4.00
g. Sign. 8.	1.00	4.00	7.00
p. Proof.	—	—	250.00
s. Specimen.	—	—	65.00

5   5 DALASIS
ND (1972-86). Red on m/c unpt. Back similar to #2.

	VG	VF	UNC
a. Sign. 2.	17.50	35.00	140.00
b. Sign. 4.	3.00	7.00	25.00
c. Sign. 6.	2.00	5.00	15.00
d. Sign. 7.		3.00	8.00
s. Specimen.	—	—	100.00

6   10 DALASIS
ND (1972-86). Green on m/c unpt. Fishermen in boat w/net on back.

	VG	VF	UNC
		Reported Not Confirmed	
a. Sign. 3.	5.00	15.00	40.00
b. Sign. 4.			
c. Sign. 6.	3.25	6.00	14.00
ct. Color trial. Purple-brown on m/c unpt.	—	—	200.00
d. Sign. 7.	1.50	4.00	10.00
s. Specimen.	—	—	100.00

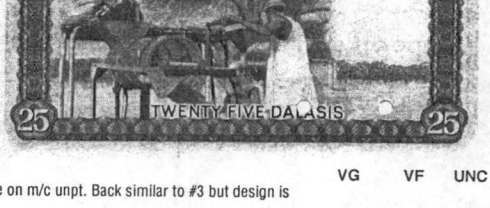

7   25 DALASIS
ND (1972-83). Blue on m/c unpt. Back similar to #3 but design is at l. ctr.

	VG	VF	UNC
a. Sign. 2.	30.00	65.00	240.00
b. Sign. 6.	9.00	17.50	40.00
ct. Color trial. Slate on m/c unpt.	—	—	400.00
s. As a, b. Specimen.	—	—	100.00

1978 ND COMMEMORATIVE ISSUE

#8, Opening of Central Bank on 18.2.1978

8   1 DALASI
ND (1978). Purple on m/c unpt. Central bank bldg. on back; commemorative legend beneath. Sign. 5.

	VG	VF	UNC
	6.00	12.50	55.00

1987 ND Issue

#9-11 w/line of microprinting under text: *PROMISE TO PAY....* Wmk: Crocodile's head.

9   5 DALASIS
ND (1987-90). Red and orange on m/c unpt. Like #5.

	VG	VF	UNC
a. Sign. 8.	1.00	2.25	9.00
b. Sign. 10.	1.00	2.00	8.00

10   10 DALASIS
ND (1987-90). Green on m/c unpt. Like #6 but back green and lt. olive.

	VG	VF	UNC
a. Sign. 8 w/title: *GOVERNOR* at r.	1.50	3.75	12.00
b. Sign. 9 w/title: *ACTING GOVERNOR* at r.	1.50	4.00	12.00

11   25 DALASIS
ND (1987-90). Blue on m/c unpt. Like #7 but back blue, black and aqua.

	VG	VF	UNC
a. Sign. 8 w/title: *GOVERNOR* at r.	5.00	12.00	45.00
b. Sign. 9 w/title: *ACTING GOVERNOR* at r.	4.00	9.00	35.00
c. Sign. 10.	3.75	7.50	32.50
s. Specimen.	—	—	100.00

18	25 DALASIS	VG	VF	UNC
	ND (1996). Deep blue-violet, black and blue on m/c unpt. Carmine Bee Eater at ctr., man at r. Back like #14.			
	a. Issued note.	FV	6.00	10.00
	s. Specimen.	—	—	40.00

15	50 DALASIS	VG	VF	UNC
	ND (1989-95). Purple and violet on m/c unpt. Hoopoe birds at ctr. Stone circles at Wassu on back. Sign. 10.			
	a. Issued note.	FV	FV	20.00
	s. Specimen.	—	—	40.00

1996 ND ISSUE

#16-19 backs similar to #12-15. Wmk: Crocodile's head. W/o imprint. Sign. 12. Replacement notes: Serial # prefix Z.

19	50 DALASIS	VG	VF	UNC
	ND (1996). Purple and violet on m/c unpt. Hoopoe birds at ctr., woman at r. Back like #15.			
	a. Issued note.	FV	FV	15.00
	s. Specimen.	—	—	40.00

2001 ND ISSUE

#20-24 like #16-19 except that vertical serial # is in ascending size.

16	5 DALASIS	VG	VF	UNC
	ND (1996). Red, orange and dk. brown on m/c unpt. Giant Kingfisher at ctr., young girl at r. Back like #12.			
	a. Issued note.	FV	FV	2.50
	s. Specimen.	—	—	35.00

20	5 DALASIS	VG	VF	UNC
	ND (2001). M/c. Like #16 but w/ascending size vertical serial #.			

17	10 DALASIS	VG	VF	UNC
	ND (1996). Dk. green, bright green and olive-green on m/c unpt. Sacred Ibis at ctr., young boy at r. Back like #13.			
	a. Issued note.	FV	FV	4.00
	s. Specimen.	—	—	35.00

21	10 DALASIS	VG	VF	UNC
	ND (2001). M/c. Like #17 but w/ascending size vertical serial #.			

22	25 DALASIS	VG	VF	UNC
	ND (2001). M/c. Like #18 but w/ascending size vertical serial #. Sign. 13; 14.			
	a. Sign. 13.	FV	FV	6.00
	b. Sign. 14.	FV	FV	4.00

23	50 DALASIS	VG	VF	UNC
	ND (2001). M/c. Like #19 but w/ascending size vertical serial #.			

24	100 DALASIS	VG	VF	UNC
	ND (2001). M/c. Senegal Parrot at ctr., male bust facing at r. Sign. 13; 14.			
	a. Sign. 13.	FV	FV	20.00
	b. Sign. 14.	FV	FV	20.00

Georgia is bounded by the Black Sea to the west and by Turkey, Armenia and Azerbaijan. It occupies the western part of Transcaucasia covering an area of 26,900 sq. mi. (69,700 sq. km.), and a population of 5.42 million. Capital: Tbilisi. Hydro-electricity, minerals, forestry and agriculture are the chief industries.

The Georgian dynasty first emerged after the Macedonian victory over the Achaemenid Persian empire in the 4th century B.C. Roman "friendship" was imposed in 65 B.C. after Pompey's victory over Mithradates. The Georgians embraced Christianity in the 4th century A.D. During the next three centuries Georgia was involved in the ongoing conflicts between the Byzantine and Persian empires. The latter developed control until Georgia regained its independence in 450-503 A.D. but then it reverted to a Persian province in 533 A.D., then restored as a kingdom by the Byzantines in 562 A.D. It was established as an Arab emirate in the 8th century. Over the following centuries Turkish and Persian rivalries along with civil strife, divided the area under the two influences.

Russian interests increased and a treaty of alliance was signed on July 24, 1773 whereby Russia guaranteed Georgian independence while it acknowledged Russian suzerainty. Persia invaded again in 1795. Russia slowly took over annexing piece by piece and soon developed total domination. After the Russian Revolution, the Georgians, Armenians and Azerbaijanis formed the short- lived Transcaucasian Federal Republic on Sept. 20, 1917, which broke up into three independent republics on May 26, 1918. A Germano-Georgian treaty was signed on May 28, 1918, followed by a Turko-Georgian peace treaty on June 4. The end of WW I and the collapse of the central powers allowed free elections.

On May 20, 1920, Soviet Russia concluded a peace treaty recognizing its independence, but later invaded on Feb. 11, 1921 and a soviet republic was proclaimed. On March 12, 1922 Stalin included Georgia in a newly formed Transcaucasian Soviet Federated Socialist Republic. On Dec. 5, 1936, the T.S.F.S.R. was dissolved and Georgia became a direct member of the U.S.S.R. The collapse of the U.S.S.R. allowed full transition to independence and on April 9, 1991, the republic, as an independent state, based on its original treaty of independence of May 1918 was declared.

MONETARY SYSTEM:
1 Lari = 1,000,000 'old' Laris, 1995-
1 Lari = 100 Thetri to 1995

REPUBLIC OF GEORGIA

GEORGIAN NATIONAL BANK

FIRST 1993 *KUPONI* ND ISSUE

#25-32, view of Tbilisi at ctr. r. w/equestrian statue of Kg. V. Gorgosal in foreground, Mt. Tatzminda in background. Cave dwellings at l. ctr. on back. Fractional serial # prefix w/1 as denominator. Wmk: Hexagonal design repeated.

#25-28 w/o ornate triangular design at l. and r. of lg. value in box at l. ctr. on face, or at sides of value at r. on back.

#23 and 24 not used.

25	5 (LARIS)	VG	VF	UNC
	ND (1993). Dull brown on lilac unpt. W/rosettes at sides of value on face and back.	0.05	0.25	2.50

26	10 (LARIS)	VG	VF	UNC
	ND (1993). Yellow-brown on lilac unpt.	0.05	0.30	3.00

27	50 (LARIS)		VG	VF	UNC
	ND (1993). Lt. blue on lilac unpt.		0.10	0.50	4.00
28	100 (LARIS)				
	ND (1993). Greenish gray and lt. brown on lilac unpt.		0.15	0.75	5.00

29	500 (LARIS)		VG	VF	UNC
	ND (1993). Purple on lilac unpt.		0.20	0.75	5.00

30	1000 (LARIS)		VG	VF	UNC
	ND (1993). Blue-gray and brown on lilac unpt.		0.30	1.50	10.00

31	5000 (LARIS)		VG	VF	UNC
	ND (1993). Green and brown on lilac unpt. Back green on pale brown-orange.		0.20	1.00	5.00
32	10,000 (LARIS)				
	ND (1993). Violet on lilac and brown unpt.		0.50	3.00	15.00

SECOND 1993 *KUPONI* ND ISSUE

#33-38 like #25-28 but w/ornate triangular design at l. and r. of lg. value in box at l. ctr. on face, and at sides of value at r. on back. Fractional serial # prefix w/2 as denominator. Wmk: Hexagonal design repeated.

33	1 (LARIS)		VG	VF	UNC
	ND (1993). Red-orange and lt. brown on lilac unpt. Similar to #25.		0.05	0.15	0.75

34	3 (LARIS)		VG	VF	UNC
	ND (1993). Purple and lt. brown on lilac unpt. Similar to #25.		0.05	0.15	0.75

35	5 (LARIS)		VG	VF	UNC
	ND (1993). Like #25.		0.05	0.15	0.75

36	10 (LARIS)		VG	VF	UNC
	ND (1993). Like #26.		0.05	0.15	0.75

37	50 (LARIS)		VG	VF	UNC
	ND (1993). Like #27.		0.05	0.20	1.25

38	100 (LARIS)		VG	VF	UNC
	ND (1993). Like #28.		0.10	0.50	2.50

THIRD 1993 DATED ISSUE

#39-42 similar to first 1993 issue but fractional serial # prefix w/3 as denominator.

39	10,000 (LARIS)		VG	VF	UNC
	1993. Violet on lilac and brown unpt.		0.15	0.50	3.25

40	25,000 (LARIS)		VG	VF	UNC
	1993. Orange and dull brown on lilac unpt.		0.20	1.00	4.50

41	50,000 (LARIS)		VG	VF	UNC
	1993. Pale red-brown and tan on lilac unpt. Back dull red-brown on pale brown-orange unpt.		0.20	1.00	3.00

42	100,000 (LARIS)		VG	VF	UNC
	1993. Olive-green and brown on lilac unpt. Back pale olive-green on dull brown-orange unpt.		0.20	1.00	5.00

FOURTH 1993 DATED ISSUE

#43-46 griffin at l. and r. of ornate round design at ctr. on face. 2 bunches of grapes w/vine above and below value on vertical format back. Wmk: Isometric rectangular design.

48	50,000 (LARIS)	VG	VF	UNC
	1994. Dk. olive-green and dull black on pale olive-green and tan unpt.	0.15	1.00	5.00

43	250 (LARIS)	VG	VF	UNC
	1993. Dk. blue on green, lilac and lt. blue unpt.			
	a. W/security thread.	0.05	0.15	1.25
	b. W/o security thread.	—	—	—

48A	100,000 (LARIS)	VG	VF	UNC
	1994. Dk. gray on lt. blue and lt. gray unpt.			
	a. W/security thread. Lg. wmk.	0.20	0.75	5.00
	b. W/o security thread. Sm. wmk.	0.20	0.75	5.00

44	2000 (LARIS)	VG	VF	UNC
	1993. Green and blue on gold and green unpt.	0.10	0.50	2.00

45	3000 (LARIS)	VG	VF	UNC
	1993. Brown and yellow on lt. brown unpt.	0.10	0.50	2.00

49	150,000 (LARIS)	VG	VF	UNC
	1994. Dk. blue-green on pale blue, lt. gray and lilac unpt.	0.20	1.00	6.00

46	20,000 (LARIS)	VG	VF	UNC
	1993; 1994. Purple on lt. red and blue unpt.			
	a. Lg. wmk. 1993.	0.10	0.50	3.00
	b. W/security foil printing at l. edge of design. Sm. wmk. 1994.	0.10	0.50	2.50

50	250,000 (LARIS)	VG	VF	UNC
	1994. Brown-orange on pale orange and lt. green unpt.	0.20	0.75	4.50

1994 ISSUE

#47-52 similar to #43-46 but w/security foil printing at l. edge of design. Wmk: Isometric rectangular design repeated.

51	500,000 (LARIS)	VG	VF	UNC
	1994. Deep violet on pale purple and pink unpt.	0.20	0.75	3.00

47	30,000 (LARIS)	VG	VF	UNC
	1994. Dull red-brown on pale orange and lt. gray unpt.	0.10	1.00	5.00

52	1 MILLION (LARIS)	VG	VF	UNC
	1994. Red on pink and pale yellow-brown unpt.	0.25	1.00	7.00

1994 PRIVATIZATION CHECK VOUCHER ISSUE

52A	VARIOUS DENOMINATIONS	VG	VF	UNC
	1994. Orange, black and m/c.	3.50	7.50	25.00

1995 ISSUE

#57-59 wmk: Griffin.

#53-59 arms at l. to ctr.

53	1 LARI	VG	VF	UNC
	1995. Dull purple on m/c unpt. N. Pirosmani between branches at ctr. View of Tbilisi, painting of deer at ctr. r. on back.	0.50	1.25	3.00

54	2 LARI	VG	VF	UNC
	1995. Deep olive-green on m/c unpt. Bars of music at l., Z. Paliashvili at ctr. r. Opera House in Tbilisi at ctr. r. on back.	0.75	1.50	6.00

55	5 LARI	VG	VF	UNC
	1995. Brown on m/c unpt. I. Javakhishvili at ctr. Map above ornate lion statue at l. ctr., Tbilisi State University above open book at r.	0.75	1.50	10.00

56	10 LARI	VG	VF	UNC
	1995. Blue-black on m/c unpt. Flowers at l., A. Tsereteli and barn swallow at ctr. r. Woman seated on stump while spinning yarn with a crop spindle between ornamental branches at ctr. r. on back. Wmk: Arms repeated vertically.	0.75	5.00	12.50

57	20 LARI	VG	VF	UNC
	1995. Dk. brown on m/c unpt. Open book and newspaper at upper l., I. Chavchavadze at ctr. Statue of Kg. V. Gorgosal between views of Tbilisi at ctr. r. on back.	5.00	10.00	35.00

58	50 LARI	VG	VF	UNC
	1995. Dk. brown and deep blue-green on m/c unpt. Griffin at l., Princess Tamara at ctr. r. Mythical figure at ctr. r. on back.	5.00	25.00	50.00

59	100 LARI	VG	VF	UNC
	1995. Dk. brown, purple and black on m/c unpt. Carved bust of S. Rustaveli at ctr. r. Frieze at upper ctr. r. on back.	5.00	45.00	75.00
60	500 LARI			
	1995. Deep purple on m/c unpt. Kg. David "The Builder" w/bldg. at ctr. Early Georgian inscriptions, cross on back. (Not issued).	—	—	500.00

1999 ISSUE

#61-67 similar to #53-59 but for country name change in English to *GEORGIA*.

61	1 LARI	VG	VF	UNC
	1999. Deep purple on m/c unpt. Similar to #53.	0.50	0.75	1.50
62	2 LARI			
	1999. Deep olive-green on m/c unpt. Similar to #54.	0.50	0.75	3.00
63	5 LARI			
	1999. Brown on m/c unpt. Similar to #55.	0.50	2.00	4.50
64	10 LARI			
	1999. Blue-black on m/c unpt. Similar to #56.	5.00	7.50	17.50
65	20 LARI			
	1999. Dk. brown on m/c unpt. Similar to #57.	8.00	10.00	20.00

		VG	VF	UNC
66	**50 LARI**			
	1999. Dk. brown and deep blue-green on m/c unpt. Similar to #58.	15.00	20.00	30.00

		VG	VF	UNC
67	**100 LARI**			
	1999. Dk. brown, purple and black on m/c unpt. Similar to #59.	25.00	30.00	55.00

2002 ISSUE

		VG	VF	UNC
68	**1 LARI**			
	2002. Deep purple on m/c unpt.	0.50	0.75	1.50

		VG	VF	UNC
69	**2 LARI**			
	2002. Deep olive-green on m/c unpt.	0.75	1.00	3.50

		VG	VF	UNC
70	**5 LARI**			
	2002. Brown on m/c unpt.	1.25	1.50	4.50

		VG	VF	UNC
71	**10 LARI**			
	2002. Blue-black on m/c unpt.	2.50	3.00	17.50

		VG	VF	UNC
72	**20 LARI**			
	2002. Dk. brwn on m/c unpt.	5.00	6.00	20.00

		VG	VF	UNC
73	**50 LARI**			
	2004.	20.00	25.00	50.00

		VG	VF	UNC
74	**100 LARI**			
	2004.	40.00	50.00	100.00
75	**200 LARI**			
	2004.	75.00	110.00	200.00

Note: The 1991-1992 ND Provisional Issues, R1-R6, and the 1993 Georgia Military Issues, M1-M8 have been determined to be spurious in nature and have been eliminated from the listings.

346 GERMAN FEDERAL REPUBLIC

GERMANY-FEDERAL REP.

The Federal Republic of Germany (formerly West Germany), located in north-central Europe, since 1990 with the unification of East Germany, has an area of 137,782 sq. mi. (356,854 sq. km.) and a population of 82.69 million. Capital: Berlin. The economy centers about one of the world's foremost industrial establishments. Machinery, motor vehicles, iron, steel, chemicals, yarns and fabrics are exported.

During the post-Normandy phase of World War II, Allied troops occupied the western German provinces of Schleswig-Holstein, Hamburg, Lower Saxony, Bremen, North Rhine-Westphalia, Hesse, Rhineland-Palatinate, Baden-Wurttemberg, Bavaria and Saarland. The conquered provinces were divided into American, British and French occupation zones.

Five eastern German provinces were occupied and administered by the forces of the Soviet Union.

The western occupation forces restored the civil status of their zones on Sept. 21, 1949, and resumed diplomatic relations with the provinces on July 2, 1951. On May 5, 1955, nine of the ten western provinces, organized as the Federal Republic of Germany, became fully independent. The tenth province, Saarland, was restored to the republic on Jan. 1, 1957.

The post-WW II division of Germany ended on Oct. 3, 1990, when the German Democratic Republic (East Germany) ceased to exist and its five constituent provinces were formally admitted to the Federal Republic of Germany. An election Dec. 2, 1990, chose representatives to the united federal parliament (Bundestag), which then conducted its opening session in Berlin in the old Reichstag building.

MONETARY SYSTEM:
1 Deutsche Mark (DM) = 100 Pfennig, 1948-2001
1 Euro = 100 Cents, 2002-

FEDERAL REPUBLIC

DEUTSCHE BUNDESBANK

1960 ISSUE

#18-24 portr. as wmk. Replacement notes: Serial # prefix Y, Z.
#18-22 w/ or w/o ultraviolet sensitive features.

18	5 DEUTSCHE MARK	VG	VF	UNC
	2.1.1960. Green on m/c unpt. Young Venetian woman by Albrecht Dürer (1505) at r. Oak sprig at l. ctr. on back.			
	a. Issued note.	FV	FV	14.00
	s. Specimen.	—	—	100.00

19	10 DEUTSCHE MARK	VG	VF	UNC
	2.1.1960. Blue on m/c unpt. Young man by Albrecht Dürer at r. Sail training ship Gorch Fock on back.			
	a. Issued note.	FV	12.00	50.00
	s. Specimen.	—	—	100.00

20	20 DEUTSCHE MARK	VG	VF	UNC
	2.1.1960. Black and green on m/c unpt. Elsbeth Tucher by Albrecht Dürer (1499) at r. Violin, bow and clarinet on back.			
	a. Issued note.	FV	20.00	65.00
	s. Specimen.	—	—	100.00

21	50 DEUTSCHE MARK	VG	VF	UNC
	2.1.1960. Brown and olive-green on m/c unpt. Portrait of Hand Urmiller by Barthel Beham (about 1525) at r. Holsten-Tor gate in Lübeck on back.			
	a. Issued note.	FV	20.00	80.00
	s. Specimen.	—	—	100.00

22	100 DEUTSCHE MARK	VG	VF	UNC
	2.1.1960. Blue on m/c unpt. Master Sebastian Münster by Christoph Amberger (1552) at r. Eagle on back.			
	a. Issued note.	FV	75.00	190.00
	s. Specimen.	—	—	150.00

	2 DEUTSCHE MARK	VG	VF	UNC
29	ND. Purple and tan on m/c unpt. (Not issued).	—	—	20.00
29A	5 DEUTSCHE MARK			
	1.7.1963. Brown. Young Venetian woman by Albrecht Dürer. Like #18.	—	—	—

DEUTSCHE BUNDESBANK

1970-80 ISSUE

#30-36 portr. as wmk. Replacement notes: Serial # prefix Y, Z, YA-, ZA-. Values are significantly higher.

	5 DEUTSCHE MARK	VG	VF	UNC
30	1970; 1980. Green on m/c unpt. Like #18.			
	a. 2.1.1970.	FV	25.00	60.00
	b. W/ © DEUTSCHE BUNDESBANK 1963 on back. 2.1.1980.	FV	6.00	9.00
	s. Specimen. As a.	—	—	100.00

#31a-34a letters of serial # either 2.8 or 3.3mm in height.

	10 DEUTSCHE MARK	VG	VF	UNC
31	1970-80. Blue on m/c unpt. Like #19.			
	a. 2.1.1970.	FV	10.00	32.50
	b. 1.6.1977.	FV	10.00	25.00
	c. W/o © notice. 2.1.1980.	FV	10.00	25.00
	d. W/ © DEUTSCHE BUNDESBANK 1963 on back. 2.1.1980.	FV	7.50	12.50
	s. Specimen.	—	—	100.00

	20 DEUTSCHE MARK	VG	VF	UNC
32	1970-80. Black and green on m/c unpt. Like #20.			
	a. 2.1.1970.	FV	20.00	60.00
	b. 1.6.1977.	FV	20.00	60.00
	c. W/o © notice. 2.1.1980.	FV	20.00	60.00
	d. W/ © DEUTSCHE BUNDESBANK 1961 on back. 2.1.1980.	FV	7.50	35.00
	s. Specimen.	—	—	100.00

	500 DEUTSCHE MARK	VG	VF	UNC
23	2.1.1960. Brown-lilac on m/c unpt. Male portrait by Hans Maler zu Schwaz. Eltz Castle on back.			
	a. Issued note.	FV	375.00	750.00
	s. Specimen.	—	—	400.00

	1000 DEUTSCHE MARK	VG	VF	UNC
24	2.1.1960. Dk. brown on m/c unpt. Astronomer Johann Schöner by Lucas Cranach the Elder at r. Cathedral of Limburg on the Lahn on back.			
	a. Issued note.	FV	700.00	1100.00
	s. Specimen.	—	—	600.00

BUNDESKASSENSCHEIN

1967 ND ISSUE

#25-29A small change notes. Printed for use in a coin shortage which never developed. Not issued. Replacement notes: Serial # prefix 4 petals (+). Printer: BDDK (w/o imprint).

	5 PFENNIG	VG	VF	UNC
25	ND. Black and dk. green on lilac unpt. (Not issued).	—	—	0.00

	10 PFENNIG	VG	VF	UNC
26	ND. Dk. brown on tan unpt. (Not issued).	—	—	15.00
27	50 PFENNIG			
	ND. (Not issued).	—	—	—

	1 DEUTSCHE MARK	VG	VF	UNC
28	ND. Brown and blue on m/c unpt. (Not issued).	—	—	75.00

33   50 DEUTSCHE MARK

		VG	VF	UNC
1970-80. Brown and olive-green on m/c unpt. Like #21.				
a. 2.1.1970.		FV	35.00	85.00
b. 1.6.1977.		FV	30.00	75.00
c. W/o © notice. 2.1.1980.		FV	30.00	75.00
d. W/ © *DEUTSCHE BUNDESBANK 1962* on back. 2.1.1980.		FV	30.00	70.00
s. Specimen.		—	—	100.00

34   100 DEUTSCHE MARK

		VG	VF	UNC
1970-80. Blue on m/c unpt. Like #22.				
a. 2.1.1970.		FV	70.00	140.00
b. 1.6.1977.		FV	70.00	140.00
c. W/o © notice. 2.1.1980.		FV	70.00	140.00
d. W/ © *DEUTSCHE BUNDESBANK 1962* on back. 2.1.1980.		FV	65.00	125.00
s. Specimen.		—	—	100.00

35   500 DEUTSCHE MARK

		VG	VF	UNC
1970-80. Brown-lilac on m/c unpt. Like #23.				
a. 2.1.1970.		FV	335.00	625.00
b. 1.6.1977.		FV	300.00	500.00
c. 2.1.1980.		FV	300.00	550.00
s. Specimen.		—	—	400.00

36   1000 DEUTSCHE MARK

		VG	VF	UNC
1977-80. Dk. brown on m/c unpt. Astronomer Johannes Schöner by Lucas Cranach "the elder" at r. and as wmk. Cathedral of Limburg on the Lahn on back.				
a. 1.6.1977.		FV	675.00	1100.00
b. 2.1.1980.		FV	625.00	950.00
s. Specimen.		—	—	600.00

1989-91 ISSUE

#37-44 replacement notes: Serial # prefix *ZA; YA.*

37   5 DEUTSCHE MARK

		VG	VF	UNC
1.8.1991. Green and olive-green on m/c unpt. Bettina von Arnim (1785-1859) at r. Bank seal and Brandenburg Gate in Berlin at l. ctr., script on open envelope at lower r. in wmk. area on back. Sign. Schlesinger-Tietmeyer.		FV	FV	7.50

38   10 DEUTSCHE MARK

		VG	VF	UNC
1989-99. Purple, violet and blue on m/c unpt. Carl Friedrich Gauss (1777-1855) at r. Sextant at l. ctr., mapping at lower r. in wmk. area on back.				
a. Sign. Pöhl-Schlesinger. 2.1.1989.		FV	FV	20.00
b. Sign. Schlesinger-Tietmeyer. 1.8.1991.		FV	FV	15.00
c. Sign. Tietmeyer-Gaddum. 1.10.1993.		FV	FV	10.00
d. Sign. Welteke-Stark. 1.9.1999.		FV	FV	12.50
e. Uncut sheet of 54 notes, sign. as c or d.		—	—	400.00

39   20 DEUTSCHE MARK

		VG	VF	UNC
1991; 1993. Green and red-violet on m/c unpt. Annette von Droste-Hülshoff (1797-1848) at r. Quill pen and beech-tree at l. ctr., open book at lower r. in wmk. area on back.				
a. Sign. Schlesinger-Tietmeyer. 1.8.1991.		FV	FV	30.00
b. Sign. Tietmeyer-Gaddum. 1.10.1993.		FV	FV	30.00

40 50 DEUTSCHE MARK

	VG	VF	UNC
1989-93. Dk. brown and red-brown on m/c unpt. Balthasar Neuman (1687-1753) at r. Architectural drawing of Bishop's residence in Würzburg at l. ctr., bldg. blueprint at lower r. in wmk. area on back.			
a. Sign. Pöhl-Schlesinger. 2.1.1989.	FV	FV	75.00
b. Sign. Schlesinger-Tietmeyer. 1.8.1991.	FV	FV	70.00
c. Sign. Tietmeyer-Gaddum. 1.10.1993.	FV	FV	70.00

41 100 DEUTSCHE MARK

	VG	VF	UNC
1989-93. Deep blue and violet on m/c unpt. Clara Schumann (1819-1896) at ctr. r. Bldg. at l. in background, grand piano at ctr., multiple tuning forks at lower r. in wmk. area on back.			
a. Sign. Pöhl-Schlesinger. 2.1.1989.	FV	FV	140.00
b. Sign. Schlesinger-Tietmeyer. 1.8.1991.	FV	FV	130.00
c. Sign. Tietmeyer-Gaddum. 1.10.1993.	FV	FV	135.00

42 200 DEUTSCHE MARK

	VG	VF	UNC
2.1.1989. Red-orange and blue on m/c unpt. Paul Ehrlich (1854-1915) at r. Microscope at l. ctr., medical science symbol at lower r. in wmk. area on back. Sign. Pöhl-Schlesinger.	FV	FV	225.00

43 500 DEUTSCHE MARK

	VG	VF	UNC
1991; 1993. Red-violet and blue on m/c unpt. Maria Sibylla Merian (1647-1717) at r. Dandelion w/butterfly and caterpillar at ctr., flower at lower r. in wmk. area on back.			
a. Sign. Schlesinger-Tietmeyer. 1.8.1991.	FV	FV	425.00
b. Sign. Tietmeyer-Gaddum. 1.10.1993.	FV	FV	400.00

44 1000 DEUTSCHE MARK

	VG	VF	UNC
1.8.1991; 1.10.1993. Deep brown-violet and blue-green on m/c unpt. City drawing at ctr., Wilhelm and Jakob Grimm (1786-1859 and 1785-1863) at ctr. r. Bank seal at l., book frontispiece of *Deutches Wörterbuch* over entry for freedom at l. ctr.,			
a. Sign. Schlesinger-Tietmeyer. 1.8.1991.	FV	FV	775.00
b. Sign. Tietmeyer-Gaddum. 1.10.1993.	FV	FV	800.00

1996 ISSUE

#45-47 like #40-42 but w/Kinegram foil added at l. ctr. Sign. Tietmeyer-Gaddum.

45 50 DEUTSCHE MARK

	VG	VF	UNC
2.1.1996. Dk. brown and violet on m/c unpt. Square-shaped Kinegram foil.	FV	FV	65.00

46   **100 DEUTSCHE MARK**   VG   VF   UNC
        2.1.1996. Deep blue and violet on m/c unpt. Lyre-shaped Kinegram   FV   FV   130.00
        foil.

47   **200 DEUTSCHE MARK**   VG   VF   UNC
        2.1.1996. Red-orange and blue on m/c unpt. Double hexagon-   FV   FV   225.00
        shaped Kinegram foil.

Note: For later issues made for use in Germany see European Union listings.

GERMANY-DEMOCRATIC REP.

The German Democratic Republic (East Germany), located on the great north European plain, ceased to exist in 1990. During the closing days of World War II in Europe, Soviet troops advancing into Germany from the east occupied the German provinces of Mecklenburg, Brandenburg, Saxony-Anhalt, Saxony and Thuringia. These five provinces comprised the occupation zone administered by the Soviet Union after the cessation of hostilities. The other three zones were administered by the United States, Great Britain and France. Under the Potsdam agreement, questions affecting Germany as a whole were to be settled by the commanders in chief of the occupation zones acting jointly and by unanimous decision. When Soviet intransigence rendered the quadripartite commission inoperable, the three western zones were united to form the Federal Republic of Germany, May 23, 1949. Thereupon the Soviet Union dissolved its occupation zone and established it as the Democratic Republic of Germany, Oct. 7, 1949. East and West Germany became reunited as one country on Oct. 3, 1990.

MONETARY SYSTEM:
    1 Mark = 100 Pfennig

DEMOCRATIC REPUBLIC

DEUTSCHE NOTENBANK

1964 ISSUE

#22-26 replacement notes: Serial # prefix *YA-YZ; ZA-ZZ.*

#22 and 25 arms at l. on back.

#23, 24 and 26 arms at upper ctr. r. on back.

22   **5 MARK**   VG   VF   UNC
        1964. Brown on m/c unpt. Alexander von Humboldt at r. Humboldt
        University in Berlin at l. ctr. on back. Wmk: Hammer and compass.
           a. Issued note.   1.25   3.00   8.00
           s. Specimen.   —   —   25.00

23   **10 MARK**   VG   VF   UNC
        1964. Green on m/c unpt. Friedrich von Schiller at r. Zeiss factory
        in Jena at l. ctr. on back. Wmk: Hammer and compass.
           a. Issued note.   3.00   6.00   12.50
           s. Specimen.   —   —   25.00

24   20 MARK

1964. Red-brown on m/c unpt. Johann Wolfgang von Goethe at r. and as wmk. National Theater in Weimar at l. ctr. on back.

		VG	VF	UNC
a.	Issued note.	2.00	7.50	15.00
s.	Specimen.	—	—	25.00

25   50 MARK

1964. Deep green on m/c unpt. Friedrich Engels at r. and as wmk. Wheat threshing at l. ctr. on back.

		VG	VF	UNC
a.	Issued note.	5.00	10.00	30.00
r.	Replacement note. Serial # prefix ZA-ZE.	5.00	12.50	35.00
s.	Specimen.	—	—	25.00

26   100 MARK

1964. Blue on m/c unpt. Karl Marx at r. and as wmk. Brandenburg Gate in Berlin at l. ctr. on back.

		VG	VF	UNC
a.	Issued note.	4.00	12.50	45.00
r.	Replacement note. Serial # prefix ZA, ZB.	4.00	15.00	50.00
s.	Specimen.	—	—	25.00

STAATSBANK DER DDR

1971-85 ISSUE

#27-31 arms at upper l. on face. Arms at l. on back. Portr. as wmk. Replacement notes: Serial # prefix *YA-YI, YZ, ZA-ZQ*.

27   5 MARK

1975. Purple on m/c unpt. Thomas Müntzer at r. Harvesting on back.

		VG	VF	UNC
a.	6 digit wide serial #.	0.40	1.00	2.50
b.	6 digit narrow serial #. (1987).	0.50	1.25	3.00
s.	As b. Specimen.	—	—	25.00

Note: A large quanity of #27 are known with mis-matched serial numbers. Value $100.00 in EF.

28   10 MARK

1971. Brown on m/c unpt. Clara Zetkin at r. Woman at radio station on back.

		VG	VF	UNC
a.	6 digit wide serial #.	0.75	1.75	4.50
b.	7 digit narrow serial #. (1985).	0.40	1.00	3.50
s.	As a. Specimen.	—	—	25.00

29   20 MARK

1975. Green on m/c unpt. Johann Wolfgang von Goethe at r. Children leaving school on back.

		VG	VF	UNC
a.	6 digit wide serial #.	0.75	2.00	5.00
b.	7 digit narrow serial #. (1986).	1.25	3.00	7.50
s.	As b. Specimen.	—	—	25.00

30   50 MARK

1971. Dk. red on m/c unpt. Friedrich Engels at r. Oil refinery on back.

		VG	VF	UNC
a.	7 digit wide serial #.	1.35	4.50	15.00
b.	7 digit narrow serial #. (1986).	1.25	3.50	10.00
s.	Specimen.	—	—	25.00

31   100 MARK

1975. Blue on m/c unpt. Karl Marx at r. Street scene in East Berlin on back.

		VG	VF	UNC
a.	7 digit wide serial #.	1.75	4.50	20.00
b.	7 digit narrow serial #. (1986).	1.75	4.50	12.00
s.	Specimen.	—	—	25.00

AC 4037556

32   200 MARK

	VG	VF	UNC
	—	—	40.00

1985. Dk. olive-green and dk. brown on m/c unpt. Family at r.
Teacher dancing w/children in front of modern school bldg. at ctr.
on back. Wmk: Dove. (Not issued.)

AB 9293471

33   500 MARK

	VG	VF	UNC
	—	—	40.00

1985. Dk. brown on m/c unpt. Arms at r. and as wmk. Govt. bldg.
Staatsrat (in Berlin) at ctr. on back. (Not issued.)

COLLECTOR SERIES

STAATSBANK DER DDR

1989 COMMEMORATIVE ISSUE

#CS1, Opening of Brandenburg Gate, 1989. Not legal tender.

GB 0385361

CS1   20 MARK 22.12.1989

	Issue Price	Mkt.	Value
	—		300.00

Black and purple on m/c unpt. Brandenburg Gate in Berlin at ctr.
Note: As stated on this item, #CS1 was never intended to be legal tender.

NOTICE

Readers with unlisted dates, signature varieties, etc.
are invited to submit photocopies of their notes to:
Standard Catalog of World Paper Money,
700 East State St. Iola, WI 54990-0001,
E-Mail: george.cuhaj@fwpubs.com.

FOREIGN EXCHANGE CERTIFICATES

FORUM-AUSSENHANDELSGESELLSCHAFT M.B.H.

1979 ISSUE

Certificates issued by state-owned export-import company. These were in the form of checks for specified
amounts for purchase of special (mostly imported) goods.

1 Mark = 1 DM (West German Mark)

#FX1-FX7 replacement notes: Serial # prefix ZA, ZB.

FX1   50 PFENNIG

	VG	VF	UNC
	0.25	0.75	2.00

1979. Violet on m/c unpt. Back violet and orange.

FX2   1 MARK

	VG	VF	UNC
	0.25	0.75	3.00

1979. Brown and rose.

FX3   5 MARK

	VG	VF	UNC
	0.50	1.50	5.00

1979. Green and peach.

FX4   10 MARK

	VG	VF	UNC
	0.50	1.50	5.00

1979. Blue and lt. green.

FX5   50 MARK

	VG	VF	UNC
	0.50	1.50	5.00

1979. Lt. red and orange.

FX6   100 MARK

	VG	VF	UNC
1979. Olive and green. Back olive and yellow.	1.00	3.00	7.50

FX7   500 MARK

	VG	VF	UNC
1979. Gray-brown and purple. Back gray-brown and blue.	2.50	5.00	10.00

A set of specimens of FX1-FX7 are available in two varieties: w/ovpt: *MUSTER* and w/o serial #s, or perforation *SPECIMEN* and serial # AA000000. Value at $700.

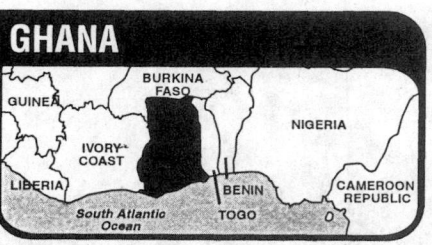

The Republic of Ghana, a member of the British Commonwealth situated on the West Coast of Africa between the Ivory Coast and Togo, has an area of 92,098 sq. mi. (238,537 sq. km.) and a population of 19.93 million, almost entirely African. Capital: Accra. Traditional exports include cocoa, coffee, timber, gold, industrial diamonds, maganese and bauxite. Additional exports include pineapples, bananas, yams, tuna, cola and salt.

Ghana was first visited by Portuguese traders in 1470, and through the 17th century was used by various European powers - England, Denmark, Holland, Germany - as a center for their slave trade. Britain achieved control of the Gold Coast in 1821, and established the colony of Gold Coast in 1874. In 1901, Britain annexed the neighboring Ashanti Kingdom; the same year a northern region known as the Northern Territories became a British protectorate. Part of the former German colony of Togoland was mandated to Britain by the League of Nations and administered as part of the Gold Coast. The state of Ghana, comprising the Gold Coast and British Togoland, obtained independence on March 6, 1957, becoming the first black African colony to do so. On July 1, 1960, Ghana adopted a republican constitution, changing from a ministerial to a presidential form of government. The government was overthrown, the constitution suspended and the National Assembly dissolved by the Ghanaian Army and police on Feb. 24, 1966. The government was returned to civilian authority in Oct. 1969, but was again seized by military officers in a bloodless coup on Jan. 13, 1972. The country was again returned to civilian rule on Sept. 24, 1979. The junior military officers once again seized power on Dec. 31, 1981 and ruled the country until Jan. 7, 1993 when power was handed over to a civilian government. Ghana remains a member of the Commonwealth of Nations, with executive authority vested in the Supreme Military Council.

Ghana's monetary denomination of "cedi" is derived from the word "sedie" meaning cowrie, a shell money commonly employed by coastal tribes.

MONETARY SYSTEM:
1 Shilling = 12 Pence
1 Pound = 20 Shillings to 1965
1 Cedi = 100 Pesewas, 1965-

REPUBLIC

BANK OF GHANA
1958-63 ISSUE

#1-3 wmk: *GHANA* in star.

1   10 SHILLINGS

	VG	VF	UNC
1958-63. Green and brown on m/c unpt. Bank of Ghana bldg. in Accra at ctr. r. Star on back.			
a. 2 sign. Printer: TDLR. 1.7.1958.	4.00	20.00	55.00
b. W/o imprint. 1.7.1961.	2.50	12.50	35.00
c. W/o imprint. 1.7.1962.	4.25	20.00	57.50
d. 1 sign. 1.7.1963.	1.25	7.00	27.50
s. As a. Specimen.	—	—	75.00

2   1 POUND

	VG	VF	UNC
1958-62. Red-brown and blue on m/c unpt. Bank of Ghana bldg. in Accra at ctr. Cocoa pods in 2 heaps on back.			
a. Printer: TDLR. 1.7.1958; 1.4.1959.	3.25	10.00	30.00
b. W/o imprint. 1.7.1961; 1.7.1962.	3.00	9.00	25.00
s. As a. Specimen.	—	—	75.00

		VG	VF	UNC
3	**5 POUNDS** 1.7.1958-1.7.1962. Purple and orange on m/c unpt. Bank of Ghana bldg. in Accra at ctr. Cargo ships, logs in water on back.			
	a. Issued note.	10.00	25.00	80.00
	s1. Specimen. 1.7.1958.	—	—	100.00
	s2. Specimen. Perforated: *CANCELLED*.	—	—	200.00

		VG	VF	UNC
4	**1000 POUNDS** 1.7.1958. Blackish brown. Bank of Ghana bldg. in Accra at lower r. Ornate design on back.	10.00	100.00	300.00

Note: #4 was used in interbank transactions.

1965 ISSUE

#5-9 wmk: Kwame Nkrumah.

		VG	VF	UNC
5	**1 CEDI** ND (1965). Blue on m/c unpt. Portr. K. Nkrumah at upper r. Bank on back.			
	a. Issued note.	2.50	5.50	10.00
	ct. Color trial. Red m/c unpt.	—	—	200.00
	s. Specimen, punch hole cancelled.	—	—	35.00

		VG	VF	UNC
6	**5 CEDIS** ND (1965). Dk. brown on m/c unpt. Portr. K. Nkrumah at upper r. Parliament House at l. ctr. on back.			
	a. Issued note.	2.50	6.00	14.00
	ct. Color trial. Green m/c unpt.	—	—	200.00
	s. Specimen, punch hole cancelled.	—	—	35.00

		VG	VF	UNC
7	**10 CEDIS** ND (1965). Green on m/c unpt. Portr. K. Nkrumah at upper l. Independence Square at ctr. on back.			
	a. Issued note.	4.00	9.00	25.00
	ct. Color trial. Dk. blue m/c unpt.	—	—	200.00
	s. Specimen, punch hole cancelled.	—	—	35.00

		VG	VF	UNC
8	**50 CEDIS** ND (1965). Red on m/c unpt. Portr. K. Nkrumah at upper l. Island and coconut trees on back.			
	a. Issued note.	8.00	25.00	60.00
	ct. Color trial. Lt. blue on m/c unpt.	—	—	250.00
	s. Specimen, punch hole cancelled.	—	—	35.00

9	100 CEDIS	VG	VF	UNC
	ND (1965). Purple on m/c unpt. Portr. K. Nkrumah at upper r. Hospital on back.			
	a. Issued note.	15.00	35.00	80.00
	ct. Color trial. Brown m/c unpt.	—	—	300.00
	s. Specimen.	—	—	55.00

11	5 CEDIS	VG	VF	UNC
	23.2.1967; 8.1.1969. Dk. brown on m/c unpt. Wood carving of a bird at r. Animal carvings on back.			
	a. 23.2.1967.	3.00	9.00	35.00
	b. 8.1.1969.	3.00	8.50	32.50
	s. Specimen.	—	—	45.00

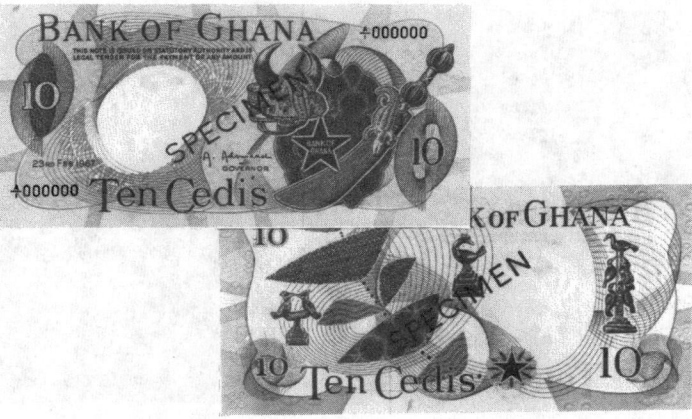

9A	1000 CEDIS	VG	VF	UNC
	ND(1965). Black. Lg. star at upper l. Bank of Ghana bldg. in Accra at r. on back.			
	a. Issued note.	—	175.00	450.00
	ct. Color trial. Purple.	—	—	700.00
	s. Specimen.	—	—	—

12	10 CEDIS	VG	VF	UNC
	23.2.1967; 8.1.1969; 1.10.1970. Red on m/c unpt. Art products at r. Small statuettes on back.			
	a. 23.2.1967.	2.50	7.00	30.00
	b. 8.1.1969.	2.50	8.00	35.00
	c. 1.10.1970.	2.50	6.50	27.50
	s. Specimen.	—	—	45.00

1967 ISSUE

Various date and sign. varieties.

#10-16 wmk: Arms - Eagle's head above star. Replacement notes: Serial # prefix *Z/99*.

1972-73 ISSUE

#13-16 wmk: Arms - Eagle's head above star.

10	1 CEDI	VG	VF	UNC
	23.2.1967; 8.1.1969; 1.10.1970; 1.10.1971. Blue on m/c unpt. Cacao tree with pods at r. Shield and ceremonial sword on back.			
	a. 23.2.1967.	1.50	4.00	7.00
	b. 8.1.1969.	2.00	5.00	10.00
	c. 1.10.1970.	1.25	4.00	7.00
	d. 1.10.1971.	1.00	3.50	6.50
	s. Specimen.	—	—	45.00

13	1 CEDI	VG	VF	UNC
	1973-76. Dk. blue, deep green, and purple on m/c unpt. Young boy w/slingshot at r. Man cutting Cacao pods from tree at l. ctr. on back.			
	a. 2.1.1973.	1.25	3.00	7.50
	b. 2.1.1975.	0.50	2.50	6.00
	c. 2.1.1976.	0.50	2.00	5.00
	d. 2.1.1978.	0.30	0.75	4.00
	s. As a. Specimen.	—	—	45.00

Note: Date 2.1.1976 has two minor varieties in length of *"2nd"* as part of date.

14   2 CEDIS

		VG	VF	UNC
1972-78. Green on m/c unpt. Young man w/hoe at r. Workers in field at l. ctr. on back.				
	a. 21.6.1972. Sign. 1. J. J. Ansah.	2.00	4.00	13.00
	b. 21.6.1972. Sign. 2. G. Nikoi.	2.00	3.50	9.00
	c. 2.1.1977; 2.1.1978.	0.50	1.25	4.00
	s. As a. Specimen.	—	—	45.00

15   5 CEDIS

		VG	VF	UNC
1973-78. Brown on m/c unpt. Woman wearing lg. hat at r. Huts on back.				
	a. 2.1.1973; 2.1.1975.	0.75	1.50	6.00
	b. 2.1.1977; 4.7.1977; 2.1.1978.	0.50	1.00	3.50
	s. As a. Specimen.	—	—	45.00

16   10 CEDIS

		VG	VF	UNC
1973-78. Red, violet and dk. brown on m/c unpt. Elderly man smoking a pipe at r. Dam on back.				
	a. 2.1.1973. Sign. 1. Serial # prefix *A/1*.	2.00	5.00	8.00
	b. 2.1.1973. Sign. 2. Serial # prefix *B/1-*.	1.50	5.00	8.00
	c. 2.1.1975.	2.00	6.00	10.00
	d. 2.1.1976.	0.75	2.00	3.75
	e. 2.1.1977.	0.75	2.00	3.50
	f. 2.1.1978.	0.50	1.50	3.25
	s. As a. Specimen.	—	—	45.00

1979 ISSUE

#17-22 wmk: Arms - Eagle's head above star. Replacement notes: Serial # prefix *XX; ZZ*.

#17-21, 2 serial # varieties.

17   1 CEDI

		VG	VF	UNC
7.2.1979; 6.3.1982. Green and m/c. Young man at r. Man weaving at ctr. r. on back.				
	a. 7.2.1979.	1.00	1.75	5.00
	b. 6.3.1982.	0.50	1.00	3.25
	s. Specimen.	—	—	50.00

18   2 CEDIS

		VG	VF	UNC
7.2.1979; 2.1.1980; 2.7.1980; 6.3.1982. Blue and m/c. School girl at r. Workers tending plants in field at ctr. r. on back.				
	a. 7.2.1979.	0.75	1.25	4.00
	b. 2.1.1980.	1.00	1.50	5.50
	c. 2.7.1980.	0.50	0.75	3.00
	d. 6.3.1982.	0.75	1.25	3.75
	s. Specimen.	—	—	50.00

19   5 CEDIS

		VG	VF	UNC
7.2.1979; 2.1.1980; 6.3.1982. Red and m/c. Elderly man at r. Men cutting log at l. ctr. on back.				
	a. 7.2.1979.	0.50	1.75	5.00
	b. 2.1.1980.	0.50	1.75	5.00
	c. 6.3.1982.	0.50	1.50	4.50
	s. Specimen.	—	—	60.00

20 10 CEDIS
7.2.1979; 2.1.1980; 2.7.1980; 6.3.1982. Purple, green and m/c.
Young woman at r. Fishermen w/long net at l. ctr. on back.

	VG	VF	UNC
a. 7.2.1979.	1.25	6.00	18.00
b. 2.1.1980.	1.25	5.00	11.00
c. 2.7.1980.	1.25	5.00	13.00
d. 6.3.1982.	1.25	5.75	16.00
s. Specimen.	—	—	75.00

21 20 CEDIS
7.2.1979; 2.7.1980; 6.3.1982. Green and m/c. Miner at r. Man
weaving at ctr. r. on back.

	VG	VF	UNC
a. 7.2.1979.	1.50	5.50	22.00
b. 2.7.1980.	1.25	5.00	18.00
c. 6.3.1982.	1.25	5.00	17.00
s. Specimen.	—	—	75.00

22 50 CEDIS
7.2.1979; 2.7.1980. Brown and m/c. Old man at r. Men splitting
cacao pods on back.

	VG	VF	UNC
a. 7.2.1979.	0.75	3.00	10.00
b. 2.7.1980.	0.75	2.50	7.50
s. Specimen.	—	—	90.00

1983-91 ISSUE

#23-31 Replacement notes: Serial # prefix Z/1.

#23-27 arms at top ctr. r.

23 10 CEDIS
15.5.1984. Purple and m/c. W. Larbi, F. Otoo, E. Nukpor at l. People
going to rural bank at ctr. on back. W/o security thread.

	VG	VF	UNC
a. Issued note.	0.50	1.25	4.00
s. Specimen.	—	—	—

#24-28 wmk: Arms - Eagle's head above star.

24 20 CEDIS
15.5.1984; 15.7.1986. Shades of green and aqua. Qn. Mother Yaa
Asantewa at l. Workers and flag procession on back.
VG 0.75 VF 1.25 UNC 6.00

25 50 CEDIS
1.4.1983; 15.5.1984; 15.7.1986. Brown, violet and m/c. Boy w/hat
at l. ctr. Drying grain at ctr. on back.
VG 0.75 VF 1.25 UNC 6.00

26 100 CEDIS
1983-91. Purple, blue and m/c. Woman at l. ctr. Loading produce
onto truck at ctr. on back.

	VG	VF	UNC
a. Sign. J. S. Addo. 1.4.1983; 15.5.1984; 15.7.1986.	0.75	1.50	7.00
b. Sign. G. K. Agama. 19.7.1990; 19.9.1991.	0.75	1.50	6.00

27	200 CEDIS	VG	VF	UNC
	1983-93. Lt. brown, orange and m/c. Old man at l. ctr. Children in classroom at ctr. on back.			
	a. Sign. J. S. Addo. 1.4.1983; 15.5.1984; 15.7.1986.	0.50	1.75	6.00
	b. Sign. G. K. Agama. 20.4.1989; 19.7.1990; 19.9.1991; 14.10.1992; 10.8.1993.	0.40	1.50	5.00
	s. Specimen. 1.4.1983.	—	—	75.00

31	5000 CEDIS	VG	VF	UNC
	29.6.1994; 6.1.1995; 23.2.1996. Green and red-orange on m/c unpt. Lg. stars in unpt. at ctr., supported shield of arms at upper r. Map at l. ctr., freighter in harbor at ctr., log flow in foreground on back.			
	a. 26.6.1994.	FV	7.00	35.00
	b. 6.1.1995.	FV	6.00	28.00
	c. 23.2.1996.	FV	6.00	25.00

28	500 CEDIS	VG	VF	UNC
	1986-94. Purple and blue-green on m/c unpt. Arms at r. Cacao trees w/cacao pods and miner at ctr. on back.			
	a. Sign. J. S. Addo. 31.12.1986.	FV	2.00	15.00
	b. Sign. G. K. Agama. 20.4.1989; 19.7.1990.	FV	FV	7.00
	c. Sign. as a. 19.9.1991; 14.10.1992; 10.8.1993; 10.6.1994.	FV	FV	5.50
	s. Specimen.	—	—	75.00

#29-31 arms at lower l. and as wmk. Sign. G. K. Agama.

1996 ISSUE

#32-34 like #29-31 but reduced size.

29	1000 CEDIS	VG	VF	UNC
	1991-96. Dk. brown, dk. blue and dk. green on m/c unpt. Jewels at r. Harvesting, splitting cacao pods at l. ctr. on back.			
	a. 22.2.1991.	FV	1.00	9.00
	b. Segmented foil security thread. 22.7.1993; 6.1.1995; 23.2.1996.	FV	1.00	6.00

32	1000 CEDIS	VG	VF	UNC
	1996-2003. Dk. brown, dk. blue and dk. green on m/c unpt. Like #29.			
	a. 5.12.1996.	FV	FV	5.50
	b. 2.12.1997; 2.5.1998; 1.7.1999; 1.7.2000.	FV	FV	4.00
	c. 3.9.2001.	FV	FV	10.00
	d. 22.10.2001; 2.9.2002; 4.8.2003.	FV	FV	3.00
	s. Specimen. 1.7.2000.	—	—	35.00

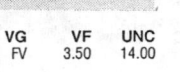

33	2000 CEDIS	VG	VF	UNC
	5.12.1996; 1.12.1997; 2.5.1998; 1.7.1999; 1.7.2000; 22.10.2001; 2.9.2002; 4.8.2003. Red-brown, green and m/c. Like #30.			
	a. Issued note.	FV	FV	5.00
	s. Specimen. 2.5.1998.	—	—	35.00

30	2000 CEDIS	VG	VF	UNC
	15.6.1994; 6.1.1995. 23.2.1996. Red-brown, green and m/c. Suspension bridge at r. Fisherman loading nets into boat at l. ctr. on back.	FV	3.50	14.00

34   **5000 CEDIS**

5.12.1996; 1.12.1997; 2.5.1998; 1.7.1999; 1.7.2000; 22.10.2001; 2.9.2002; 4.8.2003. Green and red-orange on m/c unpt. Like #31.

	VG	VF	UNC
	FV	FV	8.00

2002 ISSUE

35   **10,000 CEDIS**

2.9.2002; 4.8.2003. Purple and red-yellow on m/c unpt. Kwame Nkrumah and five other leaders at r.

	VG	VF	UNC
a. 2.9.2002.	FV	FV	13.00
b. 4.8.2003.	FV	FV	10.00

36   **20,000 CEDIS**

2.9.2002; 4.8.2003. Red-orange and pink-yellow on m/c unpt. Ephraim Amu, musician, at r.

	VG	VF	UNC
a. 2.9.2002.	FV	FV	20.00
b. 4.8.2003.	FV	FV	17.50

COLLECTOR SERIES

BANK OF GHANA

1977 ISSUE

			Issue Price	Mkt.	Value
CS1	**1977 1-10 CEDIS**				
	#13b, 14c, 15b, 16d. w/ovpt: *SPECIMEN* and Maltese cross prefix serial #.		14.00		40.00

GIBRALTAR

The British Colony of Gibraltar, located at the southernmost point of the Iberian Peninsula, has an area of 2.25 sq. mi. (5.8 sq. km.) and a population of 29,000. Capital (and only town): Gibraltar. Aside from its strategic importance as guardian of the western entrance to the Mediterranean Sea, Gibraltar is also a free port and a British naval base.

Gibraltar, rooted in Greek mythology as one of the Pillars of Hercules, has long been a coveted stronghold. Moslems took it from Spain and fortified it in 711. Spain retook it in 1309, lost it again to the Moors in 1333, and retook it in 1462. After Barbarossa sacked Gibraltar in 1540, Spain strengthened its defenses and held it until the War of the Spanish Succession when it was captured by a combined British and Dutch force, 1704. Britain held it against the Franco-Spanish attacks of 1704-05 and through the historic "Great Siege" of 1779-83. Recently Spain has attempted to discourage British occupancy by harassment and economic devices. In 1967, Gibraltar's inhabitants voted to remain under British rule.

RULERS:

British

MONETARY SYSTEM:

1 Shilling = 12 Pence
1 Pound = 20 Shillings to 1971
1 Pound = 100 New Pence, 1971-

BRITISH ADMINISTRATION

GOVERNMENT OF GIBRALTAR

1934 ORDINANCE; 1958 ISSUE

#17-19 arms at ctr. on back. Printer: TDLR.

17   **10 SHILLINGS**

3.10.1958; 1.5.1965. Blue on yellow-brown unpt. Like #11. Rock of Gilbraltar at l.

	VG	VF	UNC
	10.00	60.00	250.00

18   **1 POUND**

1958-75. Green on yellow-brown unpt. Like #12. Rock of Gibraltar at bottom ctr.

	VG	VF	UNC
a. Sign. title: *FINANCIAL SECRETARY*. 3.10.1958; 1.5.1965.	4.00	15.00	90.00
b. Sign. title: *FINANCIAL AND DEVELOPMENT SECRETARY*. 20.11.1971.	3.00	10.00	50.00
c. 20.11.1975.	7.50	30.00	175.00
s. Specimen. As a-c.	—	—	—

19   **5 POUNDS**

1958-75. Brown. Like #13. Rock of Gibraltar at bottom ctr.

	VG	VF	UNC
a. Sign. title: *FINANCIAL SECRETARY*. 3.10.1958; 1.5.1965.	25.00	100.00	575.00
b. Sign. title: *FINANCIAL AND DEVELOPMENT SECRETARY*. 1.5.1965; 20.11.1971; 20.11.1975.	17.50	80.00	400.00
s. Specimen. As a-b.	—	—	—

ORDINANCE CAP 39; 1975; 1986 ISSUE

#20-24 Qn. Elizabeth II at ctr. r. and as wmk. Sign. varieties. Printer: TDLR.

20	1 POUND	VG	VF	UNC
	1975-88. Brown and red on m/c unpt. The Covenant of Gibraltar at l. ctr. on back. 3 sign. varieties.			
	a. 20.11.1975 (1978).	FV	5.00	45.00
	b. 15.9.1979.	FV	4.00	42.50
	c. 10.11.1983.	FV	4.00	40.00
	d. 21.10.1986.	FV	2.50	35.00
	e. 4.8.1988.	FV	FV	12.50
	s. Specimen. As a; b; d.	—	—	—

23	20 POUNDS	VG	VF	UNC
	1975-86. Lt. brown on m/c unpt. Back similar to #22.			
	a. 20.11.1975 (1978).	FV	60.00	325.00
	b. 15.9.1979.	FV	60.00	375.00
	c. 1.7.1986.	FV	60.00	150.00

21	5 POUNDS	VG	VF	UNC
	1975; 1988. Green on m/c unpt. Back like #20.			
	a. 20.11.1975.	FV	17.50	80.00
	b. 4.8.1988.	FV	FV	32.50

24	50 POUNDS	VG	VF	UNC
	27.11.1986. Purple on m/c unpt. Rock of Gibraltar on back.	FV	FV	210.00

1995 ISSUE

#25-28 mature image of Qn. Elizabeth at r. and as wmk., shield of arms at l.

22	10 POUNDS	VG	VF	UNC
	1975; 1986. Deep violet, dk. brown and deep blue-green on m/c unpt. Governor's house on back.			
	a. 20.11.1975 (1977).	FV	25.00	95.00
	b. 21.10.1986.	FV	FV	60.00

25	5 POUNDS	VG	VF	UNC
	1.7.1995. Green and purple on m/c unpt. Urn above gateway at l. ctr. Tavik ibn Zeyad w/sword at r., Moorish castle at upper l. on back.			
	a. Issued note.	FV	FV	30.00
	s. Specimen.	—	—	—

26 10 POUNDS
1.7.1995. Orange-brown and violet on m/c unpt. Lighthouse above cannon at l. ctr. Portr. Gen. Eliott at r., scene of "The Great Siege, 1779-85" at upper l. ctr. on back.

	VG	VF	UNC
a. Issued note.	FV	FV	55.00
s. Specimen.	—	—	—

27 20 POUNDS
1.7.1995. Purple and violet on m/c unpt. Bird above cannon at l. ctr. Portr. Admiral Nelson at r., H.M.S. Victory at upper l. ctr. on back.

	VG	VF	UNC
a. Issued note.	FV	FV	100.00
s. Specimen.	—	—	—

28 50 POUNDS
1.7.1995. Red and violet on m/c unpt. Gibraltar monkey above horse and carriage at l. ctr. Portr. W. Churchill at upper r., Spitfire airplanes at the North Front, 1942 at upper l. ctr. on back.

	VG	VF	UNC
a. Issued note.	FV	FV	180.00
s. Specimen.	—	—	—

Note: #28 also honored the 30th anniversary of the death of Churchill.

2000 ISSUE
#29, Millennium Commemorative

29 5 POUNDS
2000. Green on m/c unpt. Face similar to #25, but with enhanced security devices. Gibraltar monkey at l., city & harbor view at ctr., gondola on r. on back.

VG	VF	UNC
FV	FV	30.00

30 10 POUNDS
10.9.2002. Orange-brown and violet on m/c unpt. Large square with butterflies and grouse within on back.

VG	VF	UNC
FV	FV	50.00

2004 COMMEMORATIVE ISSUE

31 20 POUNDS
4.8.2004. Mauve, tan and black on m/c unpt. Back blue, tan and brown; John Mackintosh Square at ctr., 19th century townfolk at r. edge.

	VG	VF	UNC
a. Issued note.	FV	FV	100.00
s. Specimen.	—	—	—

COLLECTOR SERIES

GOVERNMENT OF GIBRALTAR

1975 ISSUE

		Issue Price	Mkt. Value
CS1	1975 1-20 POUNDS		
	#20a, 21a, 22, 23a. w/ovpt: *SPECIMEN* and serial # prefix: Maltese cross.	14.00	110.00

GREAT BRITAIN

The United Kingdon of Great Britain and Northern Ireland, (including England, Scotland, Wales and Norhtern Ireland) is located off the northwest coast of the European continent, has an area of 94,227 sq. mi. (244,046 sq. km.), and a population of 59.45 million. Capital: London.

The economy is based on industrial activity, trading and financial services. Machinery, motor vehicles, chemicals and textile yarns and fabrics are exported.

After the departure of the Romans, who brought Britain into an active relationship with Europe, Britain fell prey to invaders from Scandinavia and the Low Countries who drove the original Britons into Scotland and Wales, and established a profusion of kingdoms that finally united in the 11th century under the Danish King Canute. Norman rule, following the conquest of 1066, stimulated the development of those institutions which have since distinguished British life. Henry VIII (1509-47) turned Britain from continental adventuring and faced it to the sea - a decision that made Britain a world power during the reign of Elizabeth I (1558-1603). Strengthened by the Industrial Revolution and the defeat of Napoleon, 19th century Britain turned to the remote parts of the world and established a colonial empire of such extent and prosperity that the world has never seen its like. World Wars I and II sealed the fate of the Empire and relegated Britain to a lesser role in world affairs by draining her resources and inaugurating a worldwide movement toward national self-determination in her former colonies.

By the mid-20th century, most of the former British Empire had gained independence and had evolved into the Commonwealth of Nations. This association of equal and and autonomous states, set out to agree views and special relationships with one another (appointing High Commissioners rather than Ambassadors) for mutual benefit, trade interests, etc. The Commonwealth is presently (1999) composed of 54 member nations, including the United Kingdom. All recognize the monarch as Head of the Commonwealth; 16 continue to recognize Queen Elizabeth II as Head of State. In addition to the United Kingdom, they are: Antigua & Barbuda, Australia, The Bahamas, Barbados Belize, Canada, Grenada, Paupa New Guinea, St. Christopher & Nevis, St. Lucia, St. Vincent & the Grenadines, Solomon Islands.

RULERS:
Elizabeth II, 1952-

MONETARY SYSTEM:
1 Shilling = 12 Pence
1 Pound = 20 Shillings to 1971
1 Pound = 100 (New) Pence, 1971-

KINGDOM

BANK OF ENGLAND

1957-61 ND ISSUE

			VG	VF	UNC
371	5 POUNDS				
	ND (1957-67). Blue and m/c. Helmeted Britannia hd. at l., St. George and dragon at lower ctr., denomination £5 in blue print on back. Sign. L. K. O'Brien.		15.00	50.00	120.00
372	5 POUNDS				
	ND (1961-63). Blue and m/c. Like #371 but denomination £5 recessed in white on back.		15.00	50.00	120.00

1960-64 ND ISSUE

#373-376 portr. Qn. Elizabeth II at r.

#373-375 wmk: Laureate heads in continuous vertical row at l.

373	10 SHILLINGS	VG	VF	UNC
	ND (1960-70). Brown on m/c unpt. Britannia seated w/shield in circle at ctr. r. on back.			
	a. Sign. L. K. O'Brien. (1960-61).	1.50	4.00	15.00
	b. Sign. J. Q. Hollom. (1962-66).	1.00	3.00	12.50
	c. Sign. J. S. Fforde. (1966-70).	1.00	2.50	10.00
	s. Specimen. As a; c.			

374	1 POUND	VG	VF	UNC
	ND (1960-77). Deep green on m/c unpt. Back similar to #373.			
	a. Sign. L. K. O'Brien. (1960-61).	2.00	4.00	12.00
	b. Sign. as a. Small letter *R* (for Research) at lower l. ctr. on back. (Notes printed on reel-fed web press.) Serial # prefixes A01N; A05N; A06N.	125.00	350.00	1000.00
	c. Sign. J. Q. Hollom. (1962-66).	FV	4.00	10.00
	d. Sign. as c. Letter *G* at lower l. ctr. on back. (Printed on experimental German Goebel Press.)	4.00	12.50	25.00
	e. Sign. J. S. Fforde. (1966-70).	FV	4.00	9.00
	f. Sign. as e. Letter *G* at lower ctr. on back.	4.00	12.50	30.00
	g. Sign. J. B. Page. (1970-77).	FV	4.00	9.00
	s. Specimen. As a-c.	—	—	—

375	5 POUNDS	VG	VF	UNC
	ND (1963-71). Deep blue on m/c unpt. Britannia seated w/shield in 8-petalled pattern at ctr. on back.			
	a. Sign. J. Q. Hollom. (1963-66).	FV	20.00	65.00
	b. Sign. J. S. Fforde. (1966-70).	FV	20.00	65.00
	c. Sign. J. B. Page. (1970-71).	FV	22.50	70.00
	s. Specimen. As a.	—	—	—

376	10 POUNDS	VG	VF	UNC
	ND (1964-75). Deep brown on m/c unpt. Lion facing l. at ctr. on back. Wmk: Qn. Elizabeth II.			
	a. Sign. J. Q. Hollom. (1964-66).	FV	35.00	80.00
	b. Sign. J. S. Fforde. (1966-70).	FV	35.00	80.00
	c. Sign. J. B. Page. (1970-75).	FV	35.00	80.00
	r. As c. Replacement note. Serial # prefix *M*.	20.00	45.00	95.00
	s. Specimen. As a.	—		

1971-82 ND Issue

#377-381 Qn. Elizabeth II in court robes at r.

377	1 POUND	VG	VF	UNC
	ND (1978-84). Deep green on m/c unpt. Back guilloches gray at lower l. and r. corners. Sir I. Newton at ctr. r. on back and in wmk.			
	a. Green sign. J. B. Page. (1978-80).	FV	4.00	9.00
	b. Back guilloches lt. green at lower l. and r. Black sign. D. H. F. Somerset. (1981-84).	FV	4.00	9.00
	s. Specimen. As a-b.	—	—	—

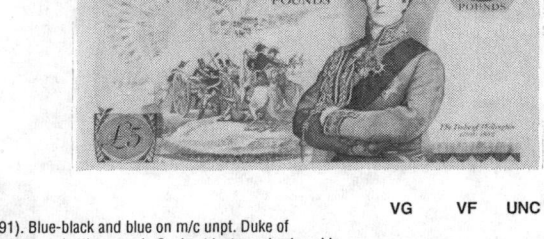

378	5 POUNDS	VG	VF	UNC
	ND (1971-91). Blue-black and blue on m/c unpt. Duke of Wellington at ctr. r., battle scene in Spain at l. ctr. on back and in wmk.			
	a. Blue-gray sign. J. B. Page. (1971-72).	FV	17.50	50.00
	b. Black sign. J. B. Page. Litho back w/small *L* at lower l. (1973-80).	FV	15.00	45.00
	c. Black sign. D. H. F. Somerset. (1980-87). Thin security thread.	FV	12.00	32.50
	d. As c. W/o sign.	50.00	110.00	250.00
	e. Sign. D. H. F. Somerset. Thick security thread. (1987-88).	FV	18.00	55.00
	f. Sign. G. M. Gill (1988-91).	FV	12.50	37.50
	s. Specimen. As a.	—	—	—

379 10 POUNDS
ND (1978-92). Deep brown on m/c unpt. Florence Nightingale at
ctr. r., hospital scene w/Florence Nightingale as the "Lady w/lamp"
at l. ctr. on back and as wmk.

	VG	VF	UNC
a. J. B. Page. (1975-80).	FV	30.00	75.00
b. D. H. F. Somerset (1980-84).	FV	40.00	95.00
c. Sign. D. H. F. Somerset. Litho printing w/L on back. (1984-86).	FV	20.00	65.00
d. D. H. F. Somerset. W/segmented security thread. (1987-88).	FV	20.00	65.00
e. Sign. G. M. Gill (1988-91).	FV	20.00	65.00
f. Sign. G. E. A. Kentfield (1991-92).	FV	30.00	75.00

380 20 POUNDS
ND (1970-91). Purple on m/c unpt. Shakespeare statue at ctr. r.
on back.

	VG	VF	UNC
a. Wmk: Qn. Elizabeth II. Sign. J. S. Fforde. (1970).	60.00	175.00	450.00
b. Wmk. as a. Sign. J. B. Page. (1970-80).	FV	55.00	150.00
c. Wmk. as a. Sign. D. H. F. Somerset. (1981-84).	FV	55.00	150.00
d. Wmk: Shakespeare. Modified background colors. Segmented security thread. D. H. F. Somerset. (1984-88).	FV	55.00	150.00
e. Sign. G. M. Gill (1988-91).	FV	45.00	125.00
s. Specimen. As c.	—	—	—

381 50 POUNDS
ND (1981-93). Olive-green and brown on m/c unpt. Wmk: Qn.
Elizabeth II at l., w/o imprint. View and plan of St. Paul's Cathedral
at l., Sir C. Wren at ctr. r. on back.

	VG	VF	UNC
a. Black sign. D. H .F. Somerset (1981-88).	FV	100.00	240.00
b. Modified background and guilloche colors. Segmented foil on security thread on surface. Sign. G. M. Gill (1988-91).	FV	110.00	265.00
c. Sign. G. E. A. Kentfield (1991-93).	FV	100.00	250.00

1990-92 ISSUE

#382-384 Qn. Elizabeth II at r. and as wmk. Crown at upper r. corner on face.

382 5 POUNDS
©1990 (1990-92). Dk. brown and deep blue-green on m/c unpt.
Britannia seated at upper l. Rocket locomotive at l., G. Stephenson
at r. on back.

	VG	VF	UNC
a. Sign. G. M. Gill (1990-91).	FV	FV	27.50
b. Sign. G. E. A. Kentfield (1991-92).	FV	FV	25.00

383 10 POUNDS
©1992 (1992-93). Black, brown and red on m/c unpt. Britannia at
l. Cricket match at l., Charles Dickens at r. on back. Sign. G. E. A.
Kentfield (1992).

	VG	VF	UNC
	FV	FV	47.50

384 20 POUNDS
©1991 (1991-93). Black, teal-violet and purple on m/c unpt.
Britannia at l. Broken vertical foil strip and purple optical device at
l. ctr. M. Faraday w/students at l., portr. at r. on back. Serial # olive-
green to maroon at upper l. and dk. blue at

	VG	VF	UNC
a. Sign. G. M. Gill (1990-91).	FV	FV	90.00
b. Sign. G. E. A. Kentfield (1991-93).	FV	FV	90.00

1993 MODIFIED ISSUE

#385-388 Qn. Elizabeth II at r. and as wmk. Value at upper r. corner on face.

		VG	VF	UNC
385	**5 POUNDS**			
	©1990 (1993-2002). Like #382 but w/dk. value symbol at upper l. corner, also darker shading on back.			
	a. Sign. G. E. A. Kentfield (1993-98).	FV	FV	22.50
	b. Sign. M. Lowther (1999-2002).	FV	FV	22.50

Note: For #385 with HK serial # prefix, see CS4.

		VG	VF	UNC
386	**10 POUNDS**			
	©1993 (1993-2000). Like #383 but w/enhanced symbols for value and substitution of value £10 for crown at upper r. on face. Additional value symbol at top r. on back.			
	a. Sign. G. E. A. Kentfield (1993-98).	FV	FV	40.00
	b. Sign. M. Lowther (1999-2000).	FV	FV	40.00

		VG	VF	UNC
387	**20 POUNDS**			
	©1993 (1993-99). Like #384 but w/dk. value symbol at upper l. corner and substitution of value symbol for crown at upper r. corner on face. Additional value symbol at top r. on back.			
	a. Sign. G. E. A. Kentfield (1993-98).	FV	FV	80.00
	b. Sign. M. Lowther (1999).	FV	FV	90.00

		VG	VF	UNC
388	**50 POUNDS**			
	©1994 (1993-). Brownish-black, red and violet on m/c unpt. Allegory in oval in unpt. at l. Bank gatekeeper at lower l., his house at l. and Sir J. Houblon at r. on back.			
	a. Sign. G. E. A. Kentfield (1993-98).	FV	FV	175.00
	b. Sign. M. Lowther (1999-).	FV	FV	160.00

Note: #388 also honors the 300th anniversary of the Bank of England.

1999-2000 ISSUE

		VG	VF	UNC
389	**10 POUNDS**			
	2000. Brown, orange and m/c. Brown and m/c. Charles Darwin at r. on back. Hummingbird magnifying glass and flora to l.			
	a. Copyright notice reads: *THE GOVERNOR AND THE COMPANY...* Sign. M. Lowther (2000).	FV	FV	35.00
	b. Copyright notice reads: *THE GOVERNOR AND COMPANY...* Sign. M. Lowther (2000-2003).	FV	FV	32.50
	c. Sign. A. Bailey (2004-).	FV	FV	30.00

		VG	VF	UNC
390	**20 POUNDS**			
	© 1999. Brown and purple on red and green unpt. 20 and Britannia in OVD, modified top l. and r. value numerals. Worchester Cathedral at l., Sir Edward Elgar at r. on back.			
	a. Sign. M. Lowther (1999-2003).	FV	FV	65.00
	b. Sign. A. Bailey (2004-).	FV	FV	60.00

2002 ISSUE

		VG	VF	UNC
391	**5 POUNDS**			
	2002. Brown and green on m/c unpt. Back lt. blue and m/c.; Elizabeth Fry at r., scene of women and children in workhouse at l.			
	a. Serial # on varnished paper, easily rubbed off. Withdrawn. From serial # prefix: HA 01. Sign. M. Lowther (2002).	FV	FV	25.00
	b. Serial # prefix on paper, varnished. From serial # prefix: HC 01. Sign. M. Lowther (2002-03).	FV	FV	17.50
	c. Sign. A. Bailey (2004).	FV	FV	16.00

COLLECTOR SERIES

BANK OF ENGLAND

1995 ISSUE

#CS1 and CS2, 200th Anniversary of the First 5 Pound Note

			Issue Price	Mkt.	Value
CS1	5 POUNDS	Uncut sheet of 3 notes #385 in folder. Serial #AB16-AB18. Last sheet printing.	68.00		100.00
CS2	5 POUNDS	Uncut sheet of 3 notes #385 in folder. Serial #AC01-AC03. First web printing.	68.00		100.00
CS3	10 POUNDS	As #386 w/serial #HM70. 70th Birthday of Queen Elizabeth II. Issued in a case w/£5 Proof coin. 2,000 sets.	—		—
CS4	20 POUNDS	Uncut pair of #384b. Kentfield first issue. 1000 pair in folder.	—		—

1996 ISSUE

			Issue Price	Mkt.	Value
CS5	5 POUNDS	As #386 w/serial # prefix HM70 for the 70th Birthday of Queen Elizabeth II. Limited to 5000.	—		—
CS6	5 POUNDS	Uncut sheet of 8 of #383c. Limited to 5000 sheets.	—		—

1997 ISSUE

			Issue Price	Mkt.	Value
CS7	5 POUNDS	As #385a w/serial # prefix HK issued commemorating the Return of Hong Kong to the People's Republic of China.			
		a. Single note in a special card.			25.00
		b. Uncut sheet of 12.	—		—
		c. Uncut sheet of 35.	—		—
CS8	5, 10, 20 POUNDS	As #385b, 386b, 387b w/serial # prefix BE98 with matching numbers. Limited to 1888.			100.00

1999 ISSUE

			Issue Price	Mkt.	Value
CS9	5, 10, 20, 50 POUNDS	New Lowther issue. In folder: #385b, 386b, 387b and 388b.	—		—

2000 ISSUE

			Issue Price	Mkt.	Value
CS10	5 POUNDS	As 385b but w/serial # prefix YR20. Millenium. Limited to 1500.	—		—
CS11	10 POUNDS	As #386b w/serial # prefix YR20. Millenium. Limited to 1500.	—		—
CS12	5 POUNDS	As #385b w/serial # prefix QM10. Queen Mother's 100th birthday. Limited to 10,000.	—		—
CS13	5 POUNDS	As #CS12 w/CN crown in folder. Limited to 1000.	—		—

MILITARY

BRITISH ARMED FORCES, SPECIAL VOUCHERS

Note: The Ministry of Defense sold large quantities of remainders including #M32 and M35 w/2-hole punch cancelled w/normal serial # some years ago. Original Specimens of #M35 have one punched hole and special serial # 123456 and 789012.

1962 ND FOURTH SERIES

#M30-M36 w/o imprint. (Not issued).

			VG	VF	UNC
M30	3 PENCE	ND (1962). Slate on violet and lt. green unpt. Specimen.	—	Rare	—

			VG	VF	UNC
M31	6 PENCE	ND (1962). Blue on violet and lt. green unpt. Specimen.	—	Rare	—
M32	1 SHILLING	ND. Dk. brown on olive and orange unpt.			
		a. Normal serial #, but w/o punch cancellations.	6.00	25.00	100.00
		b. Cancelled remainder w/2 punched holes.	—	—	3.50
		c. Specimen w/1 punched hole.	—	Rare	—
M33	2 SHILLINGS - 6 PENCE	ND (1962). Red-orange on violet and lt. green unpt. Specimen.	—	Rare	—

			VG	VF	UNC
M34	5 SHILLINGS	ND. Green on lt. brown unpt. Specimen only.	—	Rare	—

			VG	VF	UNC
M35	10 SHILLINGS	ND. Violet on blue and green unpt.			
		a. Normal serial # but w/o punch cancellations.	5.00	25.00	125.00
		b. Cancelled remainder w/normal serial # and 2 punched holes.	—	—	5.00
		c. Specimen w/special serial # and 1 punched hole.	—	Rare	—

			VG	VF	UNC
M36	1 POUND	ND. Violet on pale green and lilac unpt.			
		a. Normal serial #, w/o punch cancellations.	—	—	1.00
		b. Specimen w/special serial # and 1 punched hole.	—	Rare	—

1960s FIFTH SERIES

#M37-M43 known in specimen form and a few as proofs.

			VG	VF	UNC
M37	3 PENCE	ND. Red-brown, purple and green. Specimen.	—	Rare	—
M38	6 PENCE	ND. Green, turquoise and lt. brown. Specimen.	—	Rare	—
M39	1 SHILLING	ND. Lilac and green. Specimen.	—	Rare	—
M40	2 SHILLINGS - 6 PENCE	ND. Purple, turquoise and lt. brown. Specimen.	—	Rare	—
M41	5 SHILLINGS	ND. Blue, red and turquoise. Specimen.	—	Rare	—
M42	10 SHILLINGS	ND. Orange, green and slate. Specimen.	—	Rare	—
M43	1 POUND	ND. Olive and red-brown. Specimen.	—	Rare	—

1972 SIXTH SERIES

#M44-M46 printer: TDLR.

			VG	VF	UNC
M44	5 NEW PENCE	ND (1972). Orange-brown and green.			
		a. Issued note.	—	—	2.00
		s. Specimen.	—	—	5.00

M45	10 NEW PENCE	VG	VF	UNC
	ND (1972). Violet, green and olive.			
	a. Issued note.	—	—	3.00
	s. Specimen.	—	—	5.00

M46	50 NEW PENCE	VG	VF	UNC
	ND (1972). Green on pink unpt.			
	a. Issued note.	—	—	4.00
	s. Specimen.	—	—	5.00

1972 SIXTH SERIES SECOND ISSUE

#M47-M49 printer: BWC.

M47	5 NEW PENCE	VG	VF	UNC
	ND (1972). Like #M44.	—	—	0.50
M48	10 NEW PENCE			
	ND (1972). Like #M45.	—	—	0.50
M49	50 NEW PENCE			
	ND (1972). Like #M46.	—	—	0.75

GREECE

The Hellenic Republic of Greece is situated in southeastern Europe on the southern tip of the Balkan Peninsula. The republic includes many islands, the most important of which are Crete and the Ionian Islands. Greece (including islands) has an area of 50,949 sq. mi. (131,957 sq. km.) and a population of 10.6 million. Capital: Athens. Greece is still largely agricultural. Tobacco, cotton, fruit and wool are exported.

Greece, the Mother of Western civilization, attained the peak of its culture in the 5th century BC, when it contributed more to government, drama, art and architecture than any other people to this time. Greece fell under Roman domination in the 2nd and 1st centuries BC, becoming part of the Byzantine Empire until Constantinople fell to the Crusaders in 1202. With the fall of Constantinople to the Turks in 1453, Greece became part of the Ottoman Empire. Independence from Turkey was won with the revolution of 1821-27. In 1833, Greece was established as a monarchy, with sovereignty guaranteed by Britain, France and Russia. After a lengthy power struggle between the monarchist forces and democratic factions, Greece was proclaimed a republic in 1925. The monarchy was restored in 1935 and reconfirmed by a plebiscite in 1946. The Italians invaded Greece via Albania on Oct. 28, 1940 but were driven back well within the Albanian border. Germany began its invasion on April 6, 1941 and quickly overran the entire country, driving off a British Expeditionary force by the end of April. King George II and his new government went into exile. The German - Italian occupation of Greece lasted until Oct. 1944. On April 21, 1967, a military junta took control of the government and suspended the constitution. King Constantine II made an unsuccessful attempt against the junta in the fall of 1968 and consequently fled to Italy. The monarchy was formally abolished by plebiscite, Dec. 8, 1974, and Greece established as the "Hellenic Republic," the third republic in Greek history.

The island of Crete (Kreti), located 60 miles southeast of the Peloponnesus, was the center of a brilliant civilization that flourished before the advent of Greek culture. After being conquered by the Romans, Byzantines, Moslems and Venetians, Crete became part of the Turkish Empire in 1669. As a consequence of the Greek Revolution of the 1820s, it was ceded to Egypt. Egypt returned the island to the Turks in 1840, and they ceded it to Greece in 1913, after the Second Balkan War.

The Ionian Islands, situated in the Ionian Sea to the west of Greece, is the collective name for the islands of Corfu, Cephalonia, Zante, Santa Maura, Ithaca, Cthera and Paxo, with their minor dependencies. Before Britain acquired the islands, 1809-1814, they were at various times subject to the authority of Venice, France, Russia and Turkey. They remained under British control until their cession to Greece on March 29, 1864.

RULERS:
Paul I, 1947-1964
Constantine II, 1964-1973

MONETARY SYSTEM:
1 Drachma = 100 Lepta, 1841-2001
1 Euro = 100 Cents, 2002-

GREEK ALPHABET

Α	α	Alpha	(ä)	Ι	ι	Iota	(ē)	Ρ	ρ	Rho	(r)
Β	β	Beta	(b)	Κ	κ	Kappa	(k)	Σ	σ	Sigma	(s)6
Γ	γ	Gamma	(g)	Λ	λ	Lambda	(l)	Τ	τ	Tau	(t)
Δ	δ	Delta	(d)	Μ	μ	Mu	(m)	Υ	υ	Upsilon	(oo)
Ε	ε	Epsilon	(e)	Ν	ν	Nu	(n)	Φ	φ	Phi	(f)
Ζ	ζ	Zeta	(z)	Ξ	ξ	Xi	(ks)	Χ	χ	Chi	(H)
Η	η	Eta	(ā)	Ο	ο	Omicron	(o)	Ψ	ψ	Psi	(ps)
Θ	θ	Theta	(th)	Π	π	Pi	(p)	Ω	ω	Omega	(ō)

KINGDOM - POST WWII

ΤΡΑΠΕΖΑ ΤΗΣ ΕΛΛΑΔΟΣ

BANK OF GREECE

1964-70 ISSUE

#195-197 wmk: Head of Ephebus.

195 **50 DRACHMAI**
1.10.1964. Blue on m/c unpt. Arethusa at l., galley at bottom r. Shipyard on back.

	VG	VF	UNC
a. Issued note.	0.50	1.00	2.50
s. Specimen.	—	—	45.00

196 **100 DRACHMAI**
1966-67. Red-brown on m/c unpt. Demokritos at l., bldg. and atomic symbol at r. University at ctr. on back.

	VG	VF	UNC
a. Sign. Zolotas as Bank President. 1.7.1966.	8.00	15.00	45.00
b. Sign. Galanis as Bank President. 1.10.1967.	0.75	1.00	3.00
s. Specimen. As b.	—	—	100.00

197 **500 DRACHMAI**
1.11.1968. Olive on m/c unpt. Relief of Elusis at ctr. Relief of animals at bottom l., fruit at bottom ctr. on back.

	VG	VF	UNC
a. Issued note.	2.50	6.00	25.00
s. Specimen.	—	—	150.00

198 **1000 DRACHMAI**
1.11.1970. Brown on m/c unpt. Zeus at l., stadium at bottom ctr. Back brown and green; woman at l. and view of city Hydra on the Isle of Hydra.

	VG	VF	UNC
a. Wmk: Head of Aphrodite of Knidus (hair in knot at top of head) profile (1970).	20.00	40.00	120.00
b. Wmk: Head of Ephebus of Anticythera in 3/4 profile (1972).	3.00	10.00	30.00
s. As b. Specimen.	—	—	150.00

REPUBLIC

ΤΡΑΠΕΖΑ ΤΗΣ ΕΛΛΑΔΟΣ

BANK OF GREECE

1978 ISSUE

#199 and 200 wmk: Head of Charioteer Polyzalos of Delphi.

199 **50 DRACHMAI**
8.12.1978. Blue on m/c unpt. Poseidon at l. Sailing ship at l. ctr., man and woman at r. on back.

	VG	VF	UNC
a. Issued note.	FV	FV	2.50
r. Replacement note. Series 00A.	FV	FV	45.00
s. Specimen.	—	—	50.00

200 **100 DRACHMAI**
8.12.1978. Brown and violet on m/c unpt. Athena Peiraios at l. Back maroon, green and orange; A. Koraes at l., Church of Arkadi Monastery in Crete at bottom r.

	VG	VF	UNC
a. Original issue. W/o "L" at lower left on back.	FV	FV	2.50
b. Second issue. W/ "L" at lower left on back.	FV	FV	2.00
r. As b. Replacement note. Series 00A.	FV	FV	35.00

1983-87 ISSUE

#201-203 wmk: Head of Charioteer Polyzalos of Delphi.

201 **500 DRACHMAES**
1.2.1983. Deep green on m/c unpt. I. Capodistrias at l. ctr., his birthplace at lower r. Fortress overlooking Corfu on back.

	VG	VF	UNC
a. Issued note.	FV	FV	4.50
r. Replacement note. Series 00A.	FV	FV	100.00
s. Specimen.	—	—	50.00

202 1000 DRACHMAES
1.7.1987. Brown on m/c unpt. Apollo at ctr. r., ancient coin at bottom l. ctr. Discus thrower and Hera Temple ruins at Olympia on back.

	VG	VF	UNC
a. Issued note.	FV	FV	4.50
r. Replacement note. Series OOA.	FV	FV	100.00
s. Specimen.	—	—	50.00

203 5000 DRACHMAES
23.3.1984. Deep blue on m/c unpt. T. Kolokotronis at l., Church of the Holy Apostles at Calamata at bottom ctr. r. Landscape and view of town of Karytaina at ctr. r. on back.

	VG	VF	UNC
a. Issued note.	FV	FV	35.00
r. Replacement note. Series OOA.	FV	FV	100.00
s. Specimen.	—	—	150.00

1995-98 ISSUE

#204 and 205 wmk: Bust of Philip of Macedonia.

204 200 DRACHMAES
2.9.1996. Deep orange on m/c unpt. R. Velestinlis-Feraios at l. Velestinlis-Feraios singing his patriotic song at lower, r. Secret school run by Greek priests (during the Ottoman occupation) at ctr. r. on back.

	VG	VF	UNC
a. Issued note.	FV	FV	3.75
s. Specimen.	—	—	100.00

205 5000 DRACHMAES
1.6.1997. Purple and yellow-green on m/c unpt. Similar to #203 but reduced size.

a. Issued note.	FV	FV	30.00
r. Replacement note. Series OOA.	FV	FV	150.00
s. Specimen.	—	—	150.00

206 10,000 DRACHMAES
16.1.1995. Deep purple on m/c unpt. Dr. Georgios Papanikolaou at l. ctr., microscope at lower ctr. r. Medical care frieze at bottom ctr., statue of Asklepios at ctr. r. on back.

	VG	VF	UNC
a. Issued note.	FV	FV	55.00
r. Replacement note. Series OOA.	FV	FV	200.00
s. Specimen.	—	—	200.00

Note: For later issues made for use in Greece see European Union listings.

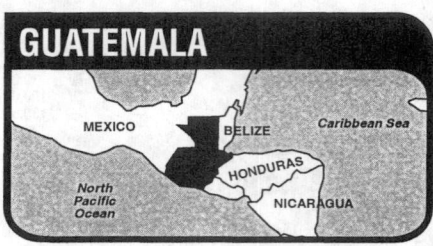

GUATEMALA

MEXICO   BELIZE   *Caribbean Sea*

North Pacific Ocean   HONDURAS

NICARAGUA

The Republic of Guatemala, the northernmost of the five Central American republics, has an area of 42,042 sq. mi. (108,889 sq. km.) and a population of 12.22 million. Capital: Guatemala City. The economy of Guatemala is heavily dependent on resources which are being developed. Coffee, cotton and bananas are exported.

Guatemala, once the site of the ancient Mayan civilization, was conquered by Pedro de Alvarado, the lieutenant of Cortes who undertook the conquest from Mexico. Skilled in strategy and cruelty, he progressed rapidly along the Pacific coastal lowlands to the highland plain of Quezaltenango where the decisive battle for Guatemala was fought. After routing the Mayan forces, he established the first capital of Guatemala in 1524.

Guatemala of the colonial period included all of Central America but Panama. Guatemala declared its independence of Spain in 1821 and was absorbed into the short-lived Mexican empire of Augustin Iturbide, 1822-23. From 1823 to 1839 Guatemala was a constituent state of the Central American Republic. Upon dissolution of the federation, Guatemala became an independent republic.

MONETARY SYSTEM:
1 Peso = 100 Centavos to 1924
1 Quetzal = 100 Centavos, 1924-

REPUBLIC

BANCO DE GUATEMALA

1957-63 ISSUE

#35-50 sign. title: *JEFE DE...* at r.

#35-39 Printer: ABNC.

		VG	VF	UNC
35	**1/2 QUETZAL** 22.1.1958. Brown on m/c unpt. Like #23. Hermitage of Cerro del Carmen at l. Two Guatemalans on back.	3.00	15.00	75.00
36	**1 QUETZAL** 16.1.1957; 22.1.1958. Green on m/c unpt. Like #24. Palace of the Captains General at l. Lake Atitlan on back.	3.00	10.00	50.00

		VG	VF	UNC
37	**5 QUETZALES** 22.1.1958. Purple. Like #25. Vase *Vasija de Uaxactum* at l. Mayan-Spanish battle scene on back.	8.00	35.00	125.00
38	**10 QUETZALES** 22.1.1958; 12.1.1962; 9.1.1963; 8.1.1964. Red. Like #26. Round stone carving *Ara de Tikal* at l. Founding of old Guatemala on back.	12.50	65.00	200.00

		VG	VF	UNC
39	**20 QUETZALES** 9.1.1963; 8.1.1964; 15.1.1965. Blue. Like #27. R. Landivar at l. Meeting of Independence on back.	20.00	75.00	250.00

1959-60 ISSUES

#40-50 sign. varieties. Printer: W&S.

		VG	VF	UNC
40	**1/2 QUETZAL** 18.2.1959. Like #29. Lighter brown shadings around value guilloche at l. Printed area 2mm smaller than #41. 6-digit serial #.	2.00	10.00	60.00

		VG	VF	UNC
41	**1/2 QUETZAL** 18.2.1959; 13.1.1960; 18.1.1961. Similar to #40 but darker brown shadings around value guilloche at l. 7-digit serial #.			
	a. Issued note.	2.00	7.50	40.00
	s. Specimen.	—	—	30.00
42	**1 QUETZAL** 18.2.1959. Green palace. Like #30. Dull green back. 6-digit serial #.			
	a. Issued note.	2.00	10.00	60.00
	s. Specimen.	—	—	—

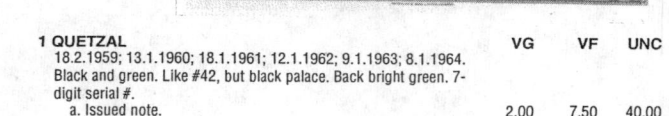

		VG	VF	UNC
43	**1 QUETZAL** 18.2.1959; 13.1.1960; 18.1.1961; 12.1.1962; 9.1.1963; 8.1.1964. Black and green. Like #42, but black palace. Back bright green. 7-digit serial #.			
	a. Issued note.	2.00	7.50	40.00
	s. Specimen.	—	—	—

		VG	VF	UNC
44	**5 QUETZALES** 18.2.1959. Like #31. Value at l. ctr. Vase in purple.	8.00	30.00	110.00

		VG	VF	UNC
45	**5 QUETZALES** 18.2.1959-8.1.1964. Similar to #44 but redesigned guilloche. Value at ctr and vase in brown.			
	a. Issued note.	5.00	25.00	100.00
	s. Specimen.	—	—	—
46	**10 QUETZALES** 18.2.1959. Like #32. Stone in red.	15.00	50.00	200.00

47	**10 QUETZALES**	VG	VF	UNC
	18.2.1959; 13.1.1960; 18.1.1961. Similar to #46 but redesigned guilloche. Stone in brown.			
	a. Issued note.	15.00	35.00	150.00
	s. Specimen.	—	—	—

48	**20 QUETZALES**	VG	VF	UNC
	13.1.1960-15.1.1965. Blue. Similar to #33, but portr. R. Landivar at r.			
	a. Issued note.	20.00	65.00	200.00
	s. Specimen.	—	—	—
49	**100 QUETZALES**			
	18.2.1959. Dk. blue. Like #34, w/*Indio de Nahuala* in blue at ctr.	115.00	250.00	550.00

50	**100 QUETZALES**	VG	VF	UNC
	13.1.1960-15.1.1965. Dk. blue. Portr. *Indio de Nahuala* in brown at r.			
	a. Issued note.	115.00	250.00	500.00
	s. Specimen.	—	—	—

1964-67 ISSUE

#51-57 sign. varieties. Printer: TDLR.

51	**1/2 QUETZAL**	VG	VF	UNC
	8.1.1964-5.1.1972. Brown on m/c unpt. Like #41. Hermitage of Cerro del Carmen at l. Two Guatemalans at ctr. on back.	1.50	5.00	30.00

52	**1 QUETZAL**	VG	VF	UNC
	8.1.1964; 15.1.1965; 21.1.1966; 13.1.1967; 3.1.1968; 3.1.1969; 7.1.1970; 6.1.1971; 5.1.1972. Black and green on m/c unpt. Like #43. Palace of the Captains General at ctr. r. Lake Atitlan on back.	1.50	5.00	30.00

#53-57 two wmk. varieties.

53	**5 QUETZALES**	VG	VF	UNC
	8.1.1964; 15.1.1965; 21.1.1966; 13.1.1967; 3.1.1968; 3.1.1969; 7.1.1970; 6.1.1971. Purple on m/c unpt. Like #45. Vase *Vasija de Uaxactum* at r.	3.00	7.50	50.00
54	**10 QUETZALES**			
	15.1.1965-7.1.1970. Red on m/c unpt. Similar to #47. Round carved stone *Arade Tikal* at r. Mayan-Spanish battle scene on back.	8.00	25.00	100.00
55	**20 QUETZALES**			
	15.1.1965-6.1.1971. Blue on m/c unpt. Like #48. R. Landivar at r. Founding of Guatemala on back.	17.50	45.00	200.00

56	**50 QUETZALES**	VG	VF	UNC
	13.1.1967-5.1.1973. Orange and blue on m/c unpt. Gen. J. M. Orellana at r. Back orange; bank at ctr.	50.00	175.00	450.00

57	**100 QUETZALES**	VG	VF	UNC
	21.1.1966; 13.1.1967; 3.1.1968; 3.1.1969; 7.1.1970. Blue-black and brown on pale green and m/c unpt. Face like #50. *Indio de Nahuala* at r. City and mountain in valley Antihua on back.	60.00	150.00	400.00

1969-75 ISSUE

#58-64 Quetzal bird at upper ctr. Various date and sign. varieties. Printer: TDLR.

#60-64 wmk: Tecun Uman.

58	**1/2 QUETZAL**	VG	VF	UNC
	1972-83. Brown on m/c unpt. Tecun Uman (national hero) at r. Tikal temple on back.			
	a. W/o security (flourescent) imprint. 5.1.1972; 5.1.1973.	0.25	1.75	10.00
	b. Security (flourescent) imprint on back. 2.1.1974; 3.1.1975; 7.1.1976; 20.4.1977.	0.25	1.25	8.00
	c. 4.1.1978; 3.1.1979; 2.1.1980; 7.1.1981; 6.1.1982; 6.1.1983.	0.25	1.50	9.00
	s. Specimen. As c.	—	—	10.00

62	20 QUETZALES	VG	VF	UNC
	1972-83; 1988. Blue on m/c unpt. Dr. M. Galvez at r. Granting of Independence to Central America on back.			
	a. 5.1.1972; 5.1.1973.	4.00	10.00	65.00
	b. 2.1.1974; 3.1.1975; 7.1.1976; 5.1.1977; 20.4.1977.	3.75	8.50	45.00
	c. 4.1.1978; 2.1.1979; 2.1.1980; 7.1.1981; 6.1.1982; 6.1.1983.	3.50	8.50	35.00
	d. 6.1.1988.	FV	6.00	30.00

59	1 QUETZAL	VG	VF	UNC
	1972-83. Green on m/c unpt. Gen. J. M. Orellana at r. Banco de Guatemala bldg. on back.			
	a. Security (flourescent) imprint on face. Date at lower r. 5.1.1972; 5.1.1973.	0.50	2.50	14.00
	b. Security imprint as a. on face and back. 2.1.1974; 3.1.1975; 7.1.1976.	0.40	2.00	10.00
	c. Date at ctr. r. 5.1.1977; 20.4.1977; 4.1.1978; 3.1.1979; 2.1.1980; 7.1.1981; 6.1.1982; 6.1.1983; 30.12.1983.	0.25	1.00	7.50
	s. Specimen. As c.	—	—	10.00

60	5 QUETZALES	VG	VF	UNC
	1969-83. Purple on m/c unpt. Gen. (later Pres.) J. R. Barrios at r. Classroom scene on back.			
	a. 3.1.1969; 6.1.1971; 5.1.1972; 5.1.1973.	1.25	5.00	27.50
	b. 2.1.1974; 3.1.1975; 7.1.1976; 5.1.1977; 20.4.1977.	1.00	4.00	22.50
	c. 4.1.1978; 3.1.1979; 2.1.1980; 7.1.1981; 6.1.1982; 6.1.1983.	1.00	3.00	17.50
	s. Specimen. As c. ND.	—	—	10.00

63	50 QUETZALES	VG	VF	UNC
	1974; 1981-83. Orange on m/c unpt. C. O. Zachrisson at r. Crop workers on back.			
	a. 2.1.1974.	10.00	40.00	150.00
	b. 7.1.1981; 6.1.1982; 6.1.1983.	10.00	30.00	100.00

64	100 QUETZALES	VG	VF	UNC
	1972-83. Brown on m/c unpt. F. Marroquin at r. University of San Carlos de Borromeo on back.			
	a. 5.1.1972.	22.50	70.00	200.00
	b. 3.1.1975; 7.1.1976; 3.1.1979.	20.00	50.00	150.00
	c. 6.1.1982; 6.1.1983.	17.50	40.00	125.00

1983 ISSUE

#65-71 similar to #58-64. Wmk: Tecun Uman. Printer: G&D.

61	10 QUETZALES	VG	VF	UNC
	1971-83. Red on m/c unpt. Gen. M. G. Granados at r. National Assembly session of 1872 on back.			
	a. 6.1.1971; 5.1.1972; 3.1.1973.	2.50	10.00	45.00
	b. 2.1.1974; 3.1.1975; 7.1.1976; 5.1.1977; 20.4.1977.	2.25	7.50	35.00
	c. 4.1.1978; 3.1.1979; 2.1.1980; 7.1.1981; 6.1.1982; 6.1.1983.	2.00	5.00	22.50
	s. Specimen. As c. ND.	—	—	10.00

65	1/2 QUETZAL	VG	VF	UNC
	6.1.1983-4.1.1989. Brown on m/c unpt. Tecun Uman at r. Tikal temple on back. Similar to #58.	FV	FV	5.00

66	1 QUETZAL		VG	VF	UNC

66 1 QUETZAL
30.12.1983-4.1.1989. Blue-green and green on m/c unpt. Gen. J.
Orellana at r. Banco de Guatemala bldg. on back. Similar to #59.
VG FV   VF FV   UNC 5.00

67 5 QUETZALES
6.1.1983-6.1.1988. Purple on m/c unpt. J. R. Barrios at r.
Classroom scene on back. Similar to #60.
VF 2.50   UNC 12.50

68 10 QUETZALES
30.12.1983-6.1.1988. Red and red-brown on m/c unpt. Gen. M. G.
Granados at r. National Assembly session of 1872 on back. Similar
to #61.
VG FV   VF 5.00   UNC 20.00

69 20 QUETZALES
6.1.1983-7.1.1987. Blue on m/c unpt. Dr. M. Galvez at r. Similar to
#62.
VF 5.00   UNC 35.00

70 50 QUETZALES
30.12.1983-7.1.1987. Orange and yellow-orange on m/c unpt. C.
O. Zachrisson at r. Crop workers on back. Similar to #63.
VG FV   VF 17.50   UNC 45.00

71 100 QUETZALES
30.12.1983-7.1.1987. Brown on m/c unpt. F. Marroquin at r.
Similar to #64.
VF 25.00   UNC 70.00

1989; 1990 ISSUE

#72-74 printer: CBN. Sign. varieties.

72 1/2 QUETZAL
4.1.1989; 14.2.1992. Brown on m/c unpt. Similar to #65. W/o
wmk.
VG FV   VF FV   UNC 5.00

73 1 QUETZAL
3.1.1990; 6.3.1991; 22.1.1992; 14.2.1992. Blue-green on m/c
unpt. Similar to #66. W/o wmk.
VG FV   VF FV   UNC 4.00

74 5 QUETZALES
3.1.1990; 6.3.1991; 22.1.1992. Purple on m/c unpt. Similar to #67.
VG FV   VF FV   UNC 7.50

#75-78 similar to #68-71. Vertical serial # at l. Wmk: Tecun Uman. Printer: TDLR. Sign. varieties.

75 10 QUETZALES
4.1.1989; 3.1.1990; 22.1.1992. Brown-violet and red on m/c unpt.
Similar to #68.
VG FV   VF FV   UNC 12.50

76	20 QUETZALES	VG	VF	UNC
	4.1.1989; 3.1.1990; 22.1.1992. Blue-black, purple and blue on m/c unpt. Similar to #69.	FV	FV	17.50

77	50 QUETZALES	VG	VF	UNC
	4.1.1989; 3.1.1990. Orange and green on m/c unpt. Similar to #70.	FV	FV	30.00

78	100 QUETZALES	VG	VF	UNC
	4.1.1989; 3.1.1990; 22.1.1992. Brown and red-brown on m/c unpt. Similar to #71. Back lilac and m/c.	FV	20.00	50.00

1992 ISSUE

#79-82 similar to #65-68 but more colorful backs. Printer: F-CO.

79	1/2 QUETZAL	VG	VF	UNC
	16.7.1992. Brown on m/c unpt. Similar to #65.	FV	FV	2.50
80	1 QUETZAL			
	16.7.1992. Blue-green on m/c unpt. Similar to #66.	FV	FV	3.50

81	5 QUETZALES	VG	VF	UNC
	16.7.1992. Purple on m/c unpt. Similar to #67.	FV	FV	7.00

#82-85 wmk: Tecun Uman.

82	10 QUETZALES			
	16.7.1992. Brown-violet and red on m/c unpt. Similar to #68.	FV	FV	10.00

#83-85 similar to #69-71 but more colorful backs. Printer: BABN.

83	20 QUETZALES			
	12.8.1992. Blue-black, purple and blue on m/c unpt. Similar to #69.	FV	FV	15.00
84	50 QUETZALES			
	12.8.1992. Orange and green on m/c unpt. Similar to #70.	FV	FV	30.00

85	100 QUETZALES	VG	VF	UNC
	27.5.1992. Brown on m/c unpt. Date at lower l., gold colored device at r. Back lt. brown and m/c. Similar to #71.	FV	FV	40.00

1993; 1995 ISSUE

#86-89 printer: CBNC.

86	1/2 QUETZAL	VG	VF	UNC
	27.10.1993; 27.9.1994; 6.9.1995. Brown on m/c unpt. Similar to #79 but w/colorful back.	FV	FV	2.00

87	1 QUETZAL	VG	VF	UNC
	27.10.1993; 6.9.1994; 6.9.1995. Dk. green on green and m/c unpt. Similar to #80 but w/colorful back.	FV	FV	3.00

88	5 QUETZALES	VG	VF	UNC
	1993; 1995. Purple on m/c unpt. Similar to #81 but w/colorful back.			
	a. 27.10.1993; 16.6.1995.	FV	FV	5.50
	b. W/o imprint. 16.6.1995.	FV	FV	4.50

		VG	VF	UNC
89	**10 QUETZALES** 16.6.1995. Brown-violet and red on m/c unpt. Similar to #82 but w/colorful back. Large and small, printer imprint on back.	FV	FV	7.50

1994 ISSUE

#90 and 91 printer: F-CO.

		VG	VF	UNC
90	**1 QUETZAL** 27.9.1994. Dk. green on green and m/c unpt. Similar to #73 but w/colorful back.	FV	FV	1.50
91	**10 QUETZALES** 29.6.1994. Brown-violet and red on m/c unpt. Similar to #75 but w/colorful back.	FV	FV	7.50

Note: Formerly listed #90A has been determined to be #92.

1994; 1995 ISSUE

#92-94 Printer: TDLR.

		VG	VF	UNC
92	**5 QUETZALES** 29.6.1994. Purple on m/c unpt. Similar to #74 but w/colorful back.	FV	FV	3.50

		VG	VF	UNC
93	**50 QUETZALES** 16.6.1995. Orange and green on m/c unpt. Similar to #77 but w/colorful back.	FV	FV	20.00

		VG	VF	UNC
94	**100 QUETZALES** 29.6.1994; 16.6.1995. Brown on m/c unpt. Similar to #78 but w/colorful back.	FV	FV	35.00

1995 ISSUE

		VG	VF	UNC
95	**20 QUETZALES** 16.6.1995. Blue-black, purple and blue on m/c unpt. Similar to #69 but w/colorful back. Printer: G&D.	FV	FV	10.00

1996 ISSUE

#96 and 97 printer: H&S.

		VG	VF	UNC
96	**1/2 QUETZAL** 28.8.1996. Brown on m/c unpt. Similar to #86.	FV	FV	1.00
97	**1 QUETZAL** 28.8.1996. Dk. green on green and m/c unpt. Similar to #87.	FV	FV	1.50

1998 ISSUE

#98 and 99 printer: (T)DLR.

		VG	VF	UNC
98	**1/2 QUETZAL** 9.1.1998. Brown on m/c unpt. Similar to #96.	FV	FV	0.75
99	**1 QUETZAL** 9.1.1998. Dk. green and green on m/c unpt. Similar to #90.	FV	FV	1.00

		VG	VF	UNC
100	**5 QUETZALES** 29.7.1998. Purple on m/c unpt. Similar to #92.	FV	FV	2.50

1998-99 ISSUE

#100-103 printer: BABN.

		VG	VF	UNC
101	**10 QUETZALES** 29.7.1998. Brown-violet and red on m/c unpt. Similar to #91.	FV	FV	5.00

		VG	VF	UNC
102	**20 QUETZALES** 17.6.1999. Similar to #83.	FV	FV	10.00

2001 ISSUE

103   100 QUETZALES
       29.7.1998. M/c.

	VG	VF	UNC
	FV	FV	35.00

104   100 QUETZALES
       2001. M/c. Printer: G&D.

	VG	VF	UNC
	FV	FV	30.00

108   20 QUETZALES
       12.2.2003. Blue-black, purple and blue on m/c unpt. Printer: G&D.

	VG	VF	UNC
	FV	FV	8.00

2001 SECOND ISSUE

105   50 QUETZALES
       9.4.2001. Orange and green on m/c unpt. Printer: G&D.

	VG	VF	UNC
	FV	FV	20.00

2003 ISSUE

106   5 QUETZALES
       12.2.2003. Purple on m/c unpt. Printer: F-CO.

	VG	VF	UNC
	FV	FV	3.50

107   10 QUETZALES
       12.2.2003. Brown-violet and red on m/c unpt. Printer: F-CO.

	VG	VF	UNC
	FV	FV	5.00

GUERNSEY

The Bailiwick of Guernsey, a British crown dependency located in the English Channel 30 miles (48 km.) west of Normandy, France, has an area of 30 sq. mi. (78 sq. km.), including the Isles of Alderney, Jethou, Herm, Brechou and Sark, and a population of 58,681. Capital: St. Peter Port. Agriculture and cattle breeding are the main occupations.

Militant monks from the Duchy of Normandy established the first permanent settlements on Guernsey prior to the Norman invasion of England, but the prevalence of prehistoric monuments suggests an earlier occupancy. The island, the only part of the Duchy of Normandy belonging to the British crown, has been a possession of Britain since the Norman Conquest of 1066. During the Anglo-French Wars, the harbors of Guernsey were employed in the building and outfitting of ships for the English privateers preying on French shipping. Guernsey is administered by its own laws and customs. Acts passed by the British Parliament are not applicable to Guernsey unless the island is specifically mentioned. During World War II, German troops occupied the island from 1940 to 1944.

United Kingdom bank notes and coinage circulate concurrently with Guernsey money as legal tender.

RULERS:
British to 1940, 1944-

MONETARY SYSTEM:
1 Penny = 8 Doubles
1 Shilling = 12 Pence
1 Pound = 20 Shillings to 1971
1 Pound = 100 New Pence 1971-

BRITISH ADMINISTRATION
STATES OF GUERNSEY
1945; 1956 ISSUE
#42-44 printer: PBC.

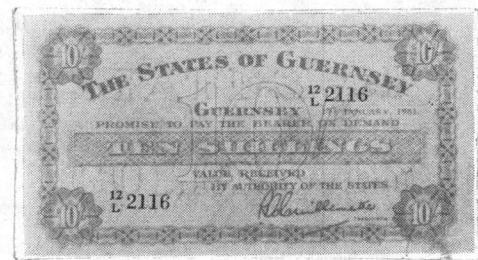

		VG	VF	UNC
42	**10 SHILLINGS**			
	1945-66. Lilac on lt. green unpt. Back purple.			
	a. 1.8.1945-1.9.1957.	20.00	75.00	400.00
	b. 1.7.1958-1.3.1965.	10.00	60.00	150.00
	c. 1.7.1966.	5.00	35.00	85.00
	s. As c. Specimen.	—	—	—

		VG	VF	UNC
43	**1 POUND**			
	1945-66. Purple on green unpt. Harbor entrance across ctr. Back green.			
	a. 1.8.1945-1.3.1957.	10.00	75.00	500.00
	b. 1.9.1957-1.3.1962; 1.6.1963; 1.3.1965.	8.00	50.00	250.00
	c. 1.7.1966.	6.00	30.00	125.00
	s. As c. Specimen.	—	—	—

		VG	VF	UNC
44	**5 POUNDS**			
	1.12.1956; 1.3.1965; 1.7.1966. Green and blue. Flowers at l.	60.00	325.00	850.00

1969; 1975 ND ISSUE
#45-47 printer: BWC. Replacement notes: Serial # prefix Z.

		VG	VF	UNC
45	**1 POUND**			
	ND (1969-75). Olive on pink and yellow unpt. Arms at ctr. Castle Cornet on back.			
	a. Sign. Guillemette.	2.00	6.00	45.00
	b. Sign. Hodder.	FV	5.00	25.00
	c. Sign. Bull.	FV	4.50	20.00

		VG	VF	UNC
46	**5 POUNDS**			
	ND (1969-75). Purple on lt. brown unpt. Arms at r. City view and harbor wall on back.			
	a. Sign. Guillemette.	15.00	50.00	225.00
	b. Sign. Hodder.	FV	30.00	120.00
	c. Sign. Bull.	FV	25.00	100.00
	s. Specimen.	—	—	—

		VG	VF	UNC
47	**10 POUNDS**			
	ND (1975-80). Blue, green and m/c. Britannia w/lion and shield at l. Sir I. Brock and Battle of Queenston Hgts. on blue back. Sign. Hodder.	20.00	65.00	300.00

1980 ND ISSUE
#48-51 Guernsey States seal at lower l. on face and as wmk. Printer: TDLR. Replacement notes: Serial # prefix Z.

48	1 POUND	VG	VF	UNC
	ND (1980-89). Dk. green and black on m/c unpt. Market square scene of 1822 at lower ctr. in unpt. D. De Lisle Brock and Royal Court of St. Peter Port on back. 135 x 67mm.			
	a. Sign. W. C. Bull.	FV	FV	10.00
	b. Black sign. M. J. Brown.	FV	FV	8.00

49	5 POUNDS	VG	VF	UNC
	ND (1980-89). Purple, dk. brown and olive-brown on m/c unpt. Fort Grey at lower ctr. in unpt. T. De La Rue and Fountain St. at ctr., workers at envelope making machine at lower r. on back. Sign. W. C. Bull. 146 x 78mm.	FV	12.00	40.00

50	10 POUNDS	VG	VF	UNC
	ND (1980-89). Purple, blue and blue-black on m/c unpt. Castle Cornet at lower ctr. Maj. Sir Isaac Brock and battle of Queenston Hgts. on back. 151 x 85mm.			
	a. Sign. W. C. Bull.	FV	20.00	70.00
	b. Black sign. M. J. Brown.	FV	20.00	70.00

51	20 POUNDS	VG	VF	UNC
	ND (1980-89). Red, red-violet, brown and orange on m/c unpt. 1815 scene of Saumarez Park at lower ctr. in unpt. Adm. Lord de Saumarez and ships on back. 161 x 90mm.			
	a. Sign. W. C. Bull.	FV	40.00	140.00
	b. Black sign. M. J. Brown.	FV	40.00	140.00

1990; 1991 ND ISSUE

#52-55 similar to #48-51 but reduced size. Wmk: Guernsey States seal. Printer: (T)DLR. Replacement notes: Serial # prefix Z.

52	1 POUND	VG	VF	UNC
	ND (ca.1991-). Dk. green and black on m/c unpt. Similar to #48. 128 x 65mm.			
	a. Green sign. M. J. Brown.	FV	FV	7.00
	b. Sign. D. P. Trestain.	FV	FV	6.00
	c. Sign. D. M. Clark.	FV	FV	5.50

53	5 POUNDS	VG	VF	UNC
	ND (1990-95). Purple, dk. brown and olive-brown on m/c unpt. Similar to #49. 136 x 70mm.			
	a. Brown sign. M. J. Brown.	FV	10.00	30.00
	b. Sign. D. P. Trestain.	FV	10.00	27.50
54	10 POUNDS			
	ND (ca.1991-95). Purple, blue and blue-black on m/c unpt. Similar to #50. 142 x 75mm.			
	a. Blue sign. M. J. Brown.	FV	FV	40.00
	b. Sign. D. P. Trestain.	FV	FV	40.00

55	20 POUNDS	VG	VF	UNC
	ND (ca.1991-95). Red, red-violet, brown and orange on m/c unpt. Similar to #51. 149 x 80mm.			
	a. Red-orange sign. M. J. Brown.	FV	FV	80.00
	b. Sign. D. P. Trestain.	FV	FV	75.00

1994-96 ND ISSUE

#56-59 Qn. Elizabeth II at r. and as wmk., Guernsey States seal at bottom ctr. r. Printer: TDLR.

56	5 POUNDS	VG	VF	UNC
	ND (1996). Dk. brown and purple on m/c unpt. St. Peter Port Town Church at lower l., brown seal at lower ctr. Fort Grey at upper l. ctr., Hanois Lighthouse at ctr. r. on back.			
	a. Sign. D. P. Trestain.	FV	FV	25.00
	b. Sign. D. M. Clark.	FV	FV	22.50

59	50 POUNDS	VG	VF	UNC
	ND (1994). Dk. brown, dk. green and blue-black on m/c unpt. Royal Court House at lower l. Stone carving, letter of Marque at lower l., St. Andrew's Church at ctr. r. on back.	FV	FV	150.00

2000 ISSUE

#60, Millennium Commemorative

57	10 POUNDS	VG	VF	UNC
	ND (1995). Violet, blue and dk. blue on m/c unpt. Elizabeth College at lower l. Saumarez Park above Le Niaux Watermill and Le Trepid Dolmen at l. ctr. on back.			
	a. Sign. D. P. Trestain.	FV	FV	35.00
	b. Sign. D. M. Clark.	FV	FV	35.00

60	5 POUNDS	VG	VF	UNC
	2000. Dk. brown and purple on m/c unpt. Similar to #56 but with added commemorative text at l. on face. Blue seal at lower ctr. Printer: (T)DLR.	FV	FV	17.50

58	20 POUNDS	VG	VF	UNC
	ND (1996). Pink, dk. brown and orange on m/c unpt. St. James Concert Hall at lower l. Flowers at lower l., St. Sampson's Church at l. ctr., sailboats below Vale Castle at ctr. r., ship at upper r. on back.			
	a. Sign. D. P. Trestain.	FV	FV	60.00
	b. Sign. D. M. Clark.	FV	FV	60.00

The Republic of Guinea (formerly French Guinea), situated on the Atlantic coast of Africa between Sierra Leone and Guinea-Bissau, has an area of 94,964 sq. mi. (245,957 sq. km.) and a population of 7.86 million. Capital: Conakry. Although Guinea contains one-third of the world's reserves of bauxite and significant deposits of iron ore, gold and diamonds, the economy is still dependent on agriculture. Aluminum, bananas, copra and coffee are exported.

The coast of Guinea was known to Portuguese navigators of the 15th century but was seldom visited by European traders of the 16th-18th centuries because of its dangerous coastal waters. French penetration of the area began in the mid-19th century with the entering into of protectorate treaties with several of the coastal chiefs. After a long struggle with Guinea's native leader Samory Toure, France secured the area and until 1890 administered it as a part of Senegal. In 1895 the colony (Guinee Francaise) became an autonomous part of the federation of French West Africa. The inhabitants were extended French citizenship in 1946 when the colony became an overseas territory of the French Union. Guinea became an independent republic on Oct. 2, 1958, when it declined to enter the new French Community.

MONETARY SYSTEM:
1 Franc = 100 Centimes to 1971
1 Syli = 10 Francs, 1971-1980
Franc System, 1985-

REPUBLIC

BANQUE CENTRALE DE LA RÉPUBLIQUE DE GUINÉE

1960 ISSUE

#12-15A Pres. Sekou Toure at l. Wmk: Dove.

12	50 FRANCS	VG	VF	UNC
	1.3.1960. Brown on m/c unpt. Heavy machinery on back.			
	a. Issued note.	1.00	4.00	20.00
	s. Specimen.	—	—	25.00

13	100 FRANCS	VG	VF	UNC
	1.3.1960. Dk. brown on pale olive-green, pale orange, pink and lilac unpt. Back dk. brown on orange and pink unpt., pineapple field workers.			
	a. Issued note.	2.00	6.00	35.00
	s. As a. Specimen.	—	—	25.00
	x. (Error). Dk. brown and pale olive-green, lt. blue and pale yellow-orange unpt. Back dk. brown on yellow unpt.	—	—	—

14	500 FRANCS	VG	VF	UNC
	1.3.1960. Blue on m/c unpt. Men pulling long boats ashore on back.			
	a. Issued note.	3.00	20.00	150.00
	s. Specimen.	—	—	35.00

15	1000 FRANCS	VG	VF	UNC
	1.3.1960. Green on m/c unpt. Banana harvesting on back.			
	a. Issued note.	3.00	15.00	75.00
	s. Specimen.	—	—	35.00

15A	5000 FRANCS	VG	VF	UNC
	1.3.1960. Purple on green and m/c unpt. Pres. Sekou Toure at l. Woman in headdress at l. huts at r. on back. (Not issued). Specimen.	—	—	400.00

1971 ISSUE

#16-19 issued under Law of 1960.

19	100 SYLIS		VG	VF	UNC
	1971. Purple on m/c unpt. A. S. Toure at l. Steam shovel and two dump trucks on back.		0.50	2.00	9.00

16	10 SYLIS		VG	VF	UNC
	1971. Brown on m/c unpt. Patrice Lumumba at r. People w/bananas on back.		0.20	0.50	1.75

1980; 1981 ISSUE

#20-27 issued under Law of 1960.

20	1 SYLI		VG	VF	UNC
	1981. Olive on green unpt. Mafori Bangoura at r.				
	a. Issued note.		0.05	0.15	0.50
	s. Specimen.		—	—	6.00

21	2 SYLIS		VG	VF	UNC
	1981. Black and brown on orange unpt. Green guilloche at ctr. Kg. Mohammed V of Morocco at l.				
	a. Issued note.		0.05	0.25	0.75
	s. Specimen.		—	—	7.00

17	25 SYLIS		VG	VF	UNC
	1971. Dk. brown on m/c unpt. Man smoking a pipe at r. Man and cows on back.		0.25	0.75	3.00

22	5 SYLIS		VG	VF	UNC
	1980. Blue on pink unpt. Kwame Nkrumah at r. Back like #16.				
	a. Issued note.		0.20	0.50	2.00
	s. Specimen.		—	—	8.00

23	10 SYLIS		VG	VF	UNC
	1980. Red and red-orange on m/c unpt. Like #16.				
	a. Issued note.		0.25	0.50	2.50
	s. Specimen.		—	—	9.00

18	50 SYLIS		VG	VF	UNC
	1971. Green on m/c unpt. Bearded man at l. Landscape w/large dame and reservoir on back.		0.50	2.00	10.00

27	**500 SYLIS**	VG	VF	UNC
	1980. Dk. brown on m/c unpt. J. Broz Tito at l. Modern bldg. on back.			
	a. Issued note.	0.50	2.00	12.50
	s. Specimen.	—	—	20.00

Note: #27 is purported to commemorate Marshal Tito's visit to Guinea.

1985 ISSUE

#28-33 arms at ctr. on face. Issued under Law of 1960.

24	**25 SYLIS**	VG	VF	UNC
	1980. Dk. green on m/c unpt. Like #17.			
	a. Issued note.	0.25	0.50	4.00
	s. Specimen.	—	—	10.00

28	**25 FRANCS**	VG	VF	UNC
	1985. Blue on m/c unpt. Young boy at l. Girl by huts at ctr. r. on back.			
	a. Issued note.	0.05	0.20	1.25
	s. Specimen.	—	—	3.00

25	**50 SYLIS**	VG	VF	UNC
	1980. Dk. red and brown on m/c unpt. Like #18.			
	a. Issued note.	0.50	1.50	7.00
	s. Specimen.	—	—	10.00

29	**50 FRANCS**	VG	VF	UNC
	1985. Red-violet on m/c unpt. Bearded man at l. Plowing w/water buffalo at ctr. on back.			
	a. Issued note.	0.10	0.25	1.50
	s. Specimen.	—	—	50.00

26	**100 SYLIS**	VG	VF	UNC
	1980. Blue on m/c unpt. Like #19.			
	a. Issued note.	1.00	4.00	17.50
	s. Specimen.	—	—	15.00

30	**100 FRANCS**	VG	VF	UNC
	1985. Purple on m/c unpt. Young woman at l. Harvesting bananas at ctr. on back.			
	a. Issued note.	0.10	0.25	1.75
	s. Specimen.	—	—	50.00

31   500 FRANCS
      1985. Green on m/c unpt. Woman at l. Minehead at ctr. on back.

	VG	VF	UNC
a. Issued note.	0.25	1.00	4.50
s. Specimen.	—	—	65.00

36   500 FRANCS
      1998. M/c. Woman at l. Minehead at ctr. on back. Similar to #31.

VG	VF	UNC
FV	FV	3.50

32   1000 FRANCS
      1985. Brown and blue on m/c unpt. Girl at l. Shovel loading ore into
      open end dump trucks at ctr., mask at r. on back.

	VG	VF	UNC
a. Issued note.	FV	1.50	6.50
s. Specimen.	—	—	65.00

37   1000 FRANCS
      1998. Brown and red-brown on m/c unpt. Female head at l. Mining
      scene on back. Similar to #32.

VG	VF	UNC
FV	FV	5.00

33   5000 FRANCS
      1985. Blue and brown on m/c unpt. Woman at l. Dam at ctr., mask
      at r. on back.

	VG	VF	UNC
a. Issued note.	FV	4.50	20.00
s. Specimen.	—	—	100.00

#34 not assigned.

1998 ISSUE

38   5000 FRANCS
      1998. M/c. Woman at l. Dam at ctr., mask at r. on back. Similar to
      #33 but w/thick security thread.

VG	VF	UNC
FV	FV	17.50

35   100 FRANCS
      1998. M/c. Young woman at l. Harvesting bananas at ctr. on back.
      Similar to #30.

VG	VF	UNC
FV	FV	1.50

GUINEA-BISSAU

The Republic of Guinea-Bissau, a former Portuguese overseas province on the west coast of Africa between Senegal and Guinea, has an area of 13,948 sq. mi. (36,125 sq. km.) and a population of 1.18 million. Capital: Bissau. The country has undeveloped deposits of oil and bauxite. Peanuts, oil-palm kernels and hides are exported.

The African Party for the Independence of Guinea-Bissau was founded in 1956, and several years later began a guerrilla warfare that grew in effectiveness until 1974, when the rebels controlled most of the colony. Portugal's costly overseas wars in her African territories resulted in a military coup in Portugal in April 1974, that appreciably brightened the prospects for freedom for Guinea-Bissau. In August 1974, the Lisbon government signed an agreement granting independence to Portuguese Guinea effective Sept. 10, 1974. The new republic took the name of Guinea-Bissau.

On Jan. 1, 1997, Guinea-Bissau became a member of the West African States, and has issued CFA currency notes with the code letter `S'. Refer to West African States listings.

RULERS:
Portuguese until 1974

MONETARY SYSTEM:
1 Peso = 100 Centavos, 1975-1997
1 Franc = 65 Pesos, 1997-

REPUBLIC

BANCO NACIONAL DA GUINÉ-BISSAU

1975 ISSUE

#1-3 wmk: A. Cabral. Printed in Algeria.

		VG	VF	UNC
1	**50 PESOS**			
	24.9.1975. Blue and brown on m/c unpt. P. Nalsna at I., group at ctr. Field workers at ctr., woman at r. on back.	2.00	5.00	30.00

		VG	VF	UNC
2	**100 PESOS**			
	24.9.1975. Brown (shades) on m/c unpt. D. Ramos at I., group in open hut at lower I. ctr. Objects and woman on back.	1.50	5.00	27.50

		VG	VF	UNC
3	**500 PESOS**			
	24.9.1975. Green, black and brown on m/c unpt. Pres. A. Cabral at I., arms at ctr., soldier at r. Carving and two youths on back.	8.00	30.00	120.00

#4 *Deleted*. See #8.

1978-84 ISSUE

#5-9 arms at lower r. on face. Wmk: A. Cabral. Replacement notes: Serial # prefix Z.

		VG	VF	UNC
5	**50 PESOS**			
	28.2.1983. Orange on blue and m/c unpt. Artifact at I. ctr., P. Nalsna at r. Local scene on back. Printer: BWC.	0.50	2.50	9.00

		VG	VF	UNC
6	**100 PESOS**			
	28.2.1983. Red on m/c unpt. Carving at I., D. Ramos at r. Bldg. at I. ctr. on back. W/o imprint.	0.25	1.25	4.50

		VG	VF	UNC
7	**500 PESOS**			
	28.2.1983. Deep blue on m/c unpt. Carving at I., F. Mendes at r. Slave trade scene on back. W/o imprint.	0.50	2.00	6.00

15	**10,000 PESOS**	VG	VF	UNC
	1990; 1993. Green, olive-brown and blue on m/c unpt. Statue at lower l. ctr., outline map at ctr., A. Cabral at r. Local people fishing w/nets in river at ctr. on back.			
	a. Sign titles: *MINISTRO-GOVERNADOR* and *VICE-GOVERNADOR*. 1.3.1990.	0.30	2.00	12.50
	b. Sign. titles: *GOVERNADOR* and *VICE-GOVERNADOR*. 1.3.1993.	0.30	1.00	10.00

The Cooperative Republic of Guyana, (formerly British Guiana) an independent member of the British Commonwealth situated on the northeast coast of South America, has an area of 83,000 sq. mi. (214,969 sq. km.) and a population of 874,000. Capital: Georgetown. The economy is basically agrarian. Sugar, rice and bauxite are exported.

The original area of Guyana, which included present-day Surinam, French Guiana, and parts of Brazil and Venezuela, was sighted by Columbus in 1498. The first European settlement was made late in the 16th century by the Dutch. For the next 150 years, possession alternated between the Dutch and the British, with a short interval of French control. The British exercised de facto control after 1796, although the area, which included the Dutch colonies of Essequebo, Demerary and Berbice, wasn't ceded to them by the Dutch until 1814. From 1803 to 1831, Essequebo and Demerary were administered separately from Berbice. The three colonies were united in the British Crown Colony of British Guiana in 1831. British Guiana won internal self-government in 1952 and full independence, under the traditional name of Guyana, on May 26, 1966.

Notes of the British Caribbean Currency Board circulated from 1950-1965.

RULERS:
British to 1966

MONETARY SYSTEM:
1 Dollar = 4 Shillings 2 Pence, 1837-1965
1 Dollar = 100 Cents, 1966-

SIGNATURE VARIETIES

1	GOVERNOR MINISTER OF FINANCE	2	GOVERNOR MINISTER OF FINANCE
3	GOVERNOR MINISTER OF FINANCE	4	GOVERNOR MINISTER OF FINANCE
4A	GOVERNOR MINISTER OF FINANCE	5	GOVERNOR MINISTER OF FINANCE
6	GOVERNOR VICE PRESIDENT ECONOMIC MINISTER OF FINANCE	7	GOVERNOR MINISTER OF FINANCE
8	GOVERNOR MINISTER OF FINANCE	9	GOVERNOR MINISTER OF FINANCE
10	GOVERNOR MINISTER OF FINANCE	11	GOVERNOR MINISTER OF FINANCE
12	GOVERNOR MINISTER OF FINANCE		

REPUBLIC

BANK OF GUYANA

1966 ND ISSUE

#21-29 wmk: Macaw's (parrot) head. Printer: TDLR.

#21-27 arms at ctr., Kaieteur Falls at r. Color shading variations.

21 1 DOLLAR
ND (1966-92). Red on m/c unpt. Black bush polder at l., rice harvesting at r. on back.

	VG	VF	UNC
a. Sign. 1; 2.	0.75	3.00	15.00
b. Sign. 3; 4.	1.25	6.00	30.00
c. Sign. 4A.	0.05	0.25	1.50
d. Sign. 5.	0.20	1.00	4.00
e. Sign. 6 (1983).	0.05	0.25	1.50
f. Serial # prefix *B/1* or higher. Sign. 7 (1989).	FV	FV	1.00
g. Sign. 8 (1992); 9. Back darker red.	FV	FV	0.75
s. As a. Specimen.	—	—	25.00

22 5 DOLLARS
ND (1966-92). Dk. green on m/c unpt. Cane sugar harvesting at l., conveyor at r. on back.

	VG	VF	UNC
a. Sign. 1; 2.	1.50	8.00	40.00
b. Sign. 3.	2.00	10.00	50.00
c. Sign. 5.	0.20	1.00	5.00
d. Sign. 6 (1983).	0.15	0.50	3.00
e. Serial # prefix *A/27* or higher. Sign. 7 (1989).	FV	FV	1.00
f. Sign. 8 (1992); 9.	FV	FV	0.75
s. As a. Specimen.	—	—	25.00

23 10 DOLLARS
ND (1966-92). Dk. brown on m/c unpt. Bauxite mining at l., aluminum plant at r. on back.

	VG	VF	UNC
a. Sign. 1; 2; 3.	2.00	10.00	50.00
b. Sign. 4; 5.	0.50	2.50	12.50
c. Sign. 6 (1983).	0.25	1.25	6.00
d. Serial # prefix *A/16* or higher. Sign. 7 (1989).	FV	FV	1.00
e. Sign. 8 (1992).	FV	FV	1.50
f. Sign. 9.	FV	FV	1.00
s. As a. Specimen.	—	—	25.00

24 20 DOLLARS
ND (1966-89). Brown and purple on m/c unpt. Shipbuilding at l., ferry *Malali* at r. on back.

	VG	VF	UNC
a. Sign. 1; 2; 4; 4A.	2.00	10.00	50.00
b. Sign. 5.	FV	3.00	15.00
c. Sign. 6 (1983).	FV	2.50	12.50
d. Serial # prefix *A/42* or higher. Sign. 7 (1989).	FV	FV	1.50
s. As a. Specimen.	—	—	25.00

#25 and 26 not used.

1989; 1992 ND Issue
#27-29 printer: TDLR.

27 20 DOLLARS
ND (1989). Brown and purple on m/c unpt. Similar to #24, but design element in colored border at l. and r. Sign. 7; 9.

	VG	VF	UNC
	FV	FV	2.50

#28 and 29 map of Guyana at r., bank arms at ctr.

28 100 DOLLARS
ND (1989). Blue on m/c unpt. Cathedral at ctr. on back. Sign. 7; 8.

	VG	VF	UNC
	FV	FV	6.00

29 500 DOLLARS
ND (ca. 1992). Lilac-brown and purple on m/c unpt. Public bldgs. in Georgetown on back.

	VG	VF	UNC
a. Sign. 8.	FV	FV	35.00
b. Sign. 9.	FV	FV	10.00
c. Sign. 10.	FV	FV	10.00

1996; 1999 ND ISSUE

#30-33 map of Guyana at r., bank arms at ctr. Ascending size serial # at upper r. Wmk: Macaw's (parrot) head.

30	**20 DOLLARS**	VG	VF	UNC
	ND (1996). Brown and purple on m/c unpt. Like #27. Sign. 10; 11; 12.	FV	FV	1.00

31	**100 DOLLARS**	VG	VF	UNC
	ND (1999). Like #28. Sign. 10; 11; 12.	FV	FV	4.00

32	**500 DOLLARS**	VG	VF	UNC
	ND (1996). Lilac-brown and purple on m/c unpt. Silver OVD map at r. Segmented foil over security thread. Like #29. Sign. 10; 11.	FV	FV	8.50

33	**1000 DOLLARS**	VG	VF	UNC
	ND (1996). Dk. green, deep red and brown on m/c unpt. Gold OVD map at r. Segmented foil over security thread. Bank bldg. at ctr. on back. Sign. 10.	FV	FV	15.00

2000 ND ISSUE

34	**500 DOLLARS**	VG	VF	UNC
	ND (2002). Lilac-brown and purple on m/c unpt. OVD in wmk. area at r. Similar to #32.	FV	FV	8.50

35	**1000 DOLLARS**	VG	VF	UNC
	ND (2000). Similar to #33 but w/gold OVD shield at r. Various small design and color adjustments also.	FV	FV	15.00

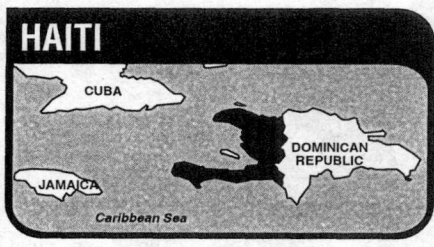

HAITI

The Republic of Haiti, occupying the western one third of the island of Hispañola in the Caribbean Sea between Puerto Rico and Cuba, has an area of 10,714 sq. mi. (27,750 sq. km.) and a population of 7.82 million. Capital: Port-au-Prince. The economy is based on agriculture, light manufacturing and tourism which is becoming increasingly important. Coffee, bauxite, sugar, essential oils and handicrafts are exported.

Columbus discovered Hispañola in 1492. Spain colonized the island, making Santo Domingo the base for exploration of the Western Hemisphere. Later French buccaneers settled the western third of Hispañola which was ceded to France by Spain in 1697. Slaves brought over from Africa to work the coffee and sugar cane plantations made it one of the richest colonies of the French Empire. The Republic of Haiti was established in 1804 after the slave revolts of the 1790's.

As a republic from 1915-1934 it was occupied by the U.S. Francois Duvalier was president 1957-1981, and his son 1981-1986, when a quick succession of governments continued with U.N. and U.S. intervention through the 1990's.

MONETARY SYSTEM:
1 Gourde = 100 Centimes
5 Gourdes = 1 U.S. Dollar, 1919-89

REPUBLIC

BANQUE NATIONALE DE LA RÉPUBLIQUE D'HAITI

CONVENTION DU 12 AVRIL 1919

SIXTH ISSUE (CA.1951-64)

#178-184 arms at ctr. on back. First sign. title: *Le President*. Printer: ABNC.

		VG	VF	UNC
178	**1 GOURDE** L.1919. Dk. brown on lt. blue and m/c unpt. Closeup view of Citadel Rampart at ctr. Prefix letters AS-BM. 5 sign. varieties.			
	a. Issued note.	0.75	2.00	17.50
	s. Specimen.	—	—	35.00

		VG	VF	UNC
179	**2 GOURDES** L.1919. Blue and m/c. Lt. green in unpt. Citadel rampart at ctr. Prefix letters Y-AF. 6 sign. varieties.			
	a. Issued note.	1.00	4.00	25.00
	s. Specimen.	—	—	60.00
180	**5 GOURDES** L.1919. Orange and m/c. Green in unpt. Woman harvesting coffee at I. Prefix letters G-M. 3 sign. varieties.			
	a. Issued note.	1.25	6.00	35.00
	s. Specimen, punch hole cancelled.	—	—	50.00

		VG	VF	UNC
181	**10 GOURDES** L.1919. Green on m/c unpt. Coffee plant at ctr. Prefix letters B-D. 2 sign. varieties.			
	a. Issued note.	3.00	12.50	55.00
	s. Specimen, punch hole cancelled.	—	—	70.00

#182 not assigned.

		VG	VF	UNC
183	**50 GOURDES** L.1919. Olive-green on m/c unpt. Cotton bolls at ctr. Specimen.			225.00

		VG	VF	UNC
184	**100 GOURDES** L.1919. Purple on m/c unpt. Field workers at I. Prefix letter A.			
	a. Issued note.	30.00	125.00	350.00
	s. Specimen, punched hole cancelled.	—	—	175.00

Note: For similar notes but w/new guilloche patterns w/o green unpt., printer: ABNC, see Vol. 3.

Note: For similar notes but printed by TDLR, see Vol. 3.

CONVENTION DU 12 AVRIL 1919

SEVENTH ISSUE (CA.1964)

#185-189 like #178-180 but new guilloche patterns, w/o green in unpt. Arms at ctr. on back. Printer: ABNC.

		VG	VF	UNC
185	**1 GOURDE** L.1919. Dk. brown on lt. blue and m/c unpt. Citadel rampart at ctr. Like #178. Prefix letters BK-BT.			
	a. Issued note.	0.50	1.50	7.50
	s. Specimen.	—	—	25.00
186	**2 GOURDES** L.1919. Blue on lt. blue and m/c unpt. Citadel rampart at ctr. Like #179. Prefix letters AE-AJ.			
	a. Issued note.	0.50	1.50	7.50
	s. Specimen.	—	—	25.00

		VG	VF	UNC
187	**5 GOURDES** L.1919. Orange on lt. blue and m/c unpt. Woman harvesting coffee beans at I. Like #180. Prefix letter N.			
	a. Issued note.	0.50	1.00	7.00
	s. Specimen.	—	—	25.00

Note: It is reported that the entire shipment of #187 was stolen and never officially released.

		VG	VF	UNC
188	**50 GOURDES** L.1919. Olive-green on blue and magenta unpt. Like #183. Cotton bolls at ctr. (Not issued.) Archive example.	—	—	—
189	**100 GOURDES** L.1919. Purple on m/c unpt. Like #184. Field workers at I. (Not issued.) Archive example.	—	—	—

CONVENTION DU 12 AVRIL 1919

EIGHTH ISSUE (CA.1967)

#190-195 arms at ctr. on back. Printer: TDLR.

#190-193, 195 second sign. title: *LE DIRECTEUR*.

		VG	VF	UNC
190	**1 GOURDE** L.1919. Brown on m/c unpt. Similar to #185. Prefix letters DA-DL.			
	a. Issued note.	0.25	1.00	7.50
	s. Specimen.	—	—	27.50

191	2 GOURDES	VG	VF	UNC
	L.1919. Grayish blue on m/c unpt. Similar to #186. Prefix letters DA-DF.			
	a. Issued note.	0.50	1.50	10.00
	s. Specimen.	—	—	27.50

192	5 GOURDES	VG	VF	UNC
	L.1919. Orange on lt. blue and m/c unpt. Similar to #187. Prefix letters DA-DK.			
	a. Issued note.	1.00	4.00	12.50
	s. Specimen.	—	—	27.50

193	10 GOURDES	VG	VF	UNC
	L.1919. Green on m/c unpt. Coffee plant at ctr. Similar to #181. Prefix letters DA.			
	a. Issued note.	3.00	8.00	30.00
	s. Specimen.	—	—	35.00

194	50 GOURDES	VG	VF	UNC
	L.1919. Olive-green on m/c unpt. Cotton bolls at ctr. Similar to #188. Prefix letters DA. Second sign. title: UN DIRECTEUR.			
	a. Issued note.	10.00	17.50	80.00
	s. Specimen.	—	—	170.00

195	100 GOURDES	VG	VF	UNC
	L.1919. Purple on m/c unpt. Field workers at l. Similar to #189. Prefix letters DA.			
	a. Issued note.	20.00	35.00	150.00
	s. Specimen.			

CONVENTION DU 12 AVRIL 1919

NINTH ISSUE

#196-198 Pres. Dr. François Duvalier at ctr. or l. Arms at ctr. on back. Printer: TDLR.

196	1 GOURDE	VG	VF	UNC
	L.1919. Dk. brown on m/c unpt. Prefix letters DK-DT.			
	a. Issued note.	0.25	0.75	3.50
	s. Specimen.	—	—	20.00

197	2 GOURDES	VG	VF	UNC
	L.1919. Grayish blue on m/c unpt. Like #196. Prefix letters DG-DK.			
	a. Issued note.	0.50	1.25	4.50
	s. Specimen.	—	—	25.00

198	5 GOURDES	VG	VF	UNC
	L.1919. Orange on m/c unpt. Portr. Pres. Duvalier at l. Prefix letters DG-DK.			
	a. Issued note.	1.00	2.50	7.50
	s. Specimen.	—	—	25.00

CONVENTION DU 12 AVRIL 1919

TENTH ISSUE

#200-203 arms at ctr. on back. Printer: ABNC.

200	1 GOURDE	VG	VF	UNC
	L.1919. Dk. brown on m/c unpt. Portr. Pres. Dr. F. Duvalier at ctr. Prefix letters A-Z; AA-CR. 3 sign. varieties.			
	a. Issued note.	0.25	0.75	3.00
	s. Specimen.	—	—	20.00

#201-207 w/4 lines of text on back (like previous issues).

			VG	VF	UNC
201	**2 GOURDES**				
	L.1919. Blue on m/c unpt. Like #200. First issued w/o prefix, then letters A-Q.		0.50	1.25	3.50

			VG	VF	UNC
202	**5 GOURDES**				
	L.1919. Orange on m/c unpt. Portr. Pres. Dr. F. Duvalier at l. First issued w/o prefix, then letters A-Z; AA-AP. 3 sign. varieties.				
	a. Issued note.		1.00	2.00	6.50
	s. Specimen.		—	—	25.00
203	**10 GOURDES**				
	L.1919. Dk. green on m/c unpt. Portr. Pres. Dr. F. Duvalier at ctr. First issued w/o prefix, then letter A.				
	a. Issued note.		2.50	5.00	12.50
	s. Specimen.		—	—	30.00

			VG	VF	UNC
204	**50 GOURDES**				
	L.1919. Dk. gray on m/c unpt. Portr. Pres. Lysius Félicité Salomon Jeune at ctr. First issued w/o prefix, then letters A-C. 2 sign. varieties.				
	a. Issued note.		10.00	17.50	30.00
	s. Specimen.		—	—	27.50

			VG	VF	UNC
205	**100 GOURDES**				
	L.1919. Purple on m/c unpt. Portr. Henri Christophe (Pres., later Kg.) at l. W/o prefix letter. 2 sign. varieties.		20.00	40.00	75.00

			VG	VF	UNC
206	**250 GOURDES**				
	L.1919. Dk. yellow-green on m/c unpt. Jean-Jacques Dessalines at r. W/o prefix letter.				
	a. Issued note.		55.00	110.00	225.00
	s. Specimen.		—	—	225.00

			VG	VF	UNC
207	**500 GOURDES**				
	L.1919. Red on m/c unpt. Similar to #203. W/o prefix letter.				
	a. Issued note.		80.00	165.00	350.00
	s. Specimen.		—	—	350.00

#208 and 209 not assigned.

ELEVENTH ISSUE (CA.1973)

Lois des 21 Mai 1935 et 15 Mai 1953 et au Décret du 22 Novembre 1973 (issued 1979)

#210-214 arms at ctr. on back. Printer: ABNC.

			VG	VF	UNC
210	**1 GOURDE**				
	L.1973, etc. Dk. brown on m/c unpt. Like #200. Prefix letters A-Z; AA-AC.		0.30	0.60	3.00

#211-214 w/3 lines of text on back.

			VG	VF	UNC
211	**2 GOURDES**				
	L.1973, etc. Blue on m/c unpt. Like #201. Prefix letters A-J.		0.60	1.25	4.50

			VG	VF	UNC
212	**5 GOURDES**				
	L.1973, etc. Orange on m/c unpt. Like #202. Prefix letters A-AA.		1.00	2.00	7.50

			VG	VF	UNC
213	**50 GOURDES**				
	L.1973, etc. Dk. gray on m/c unpt. Like #204. Prefix letter A.		10.00	17.50	35.00
214	**100 GOURDES**				
	L.1973, etc. Purple on m/c unpt. Like #205. W/o prefix letter. Two serial # varieties.		20.00	35.00	70.00

#215-217 not assigned.

TWELFTH ISSUE

Lois des 21 Mai 1935 et 15 Mai 1953 et au Décret du 22 Novembre 1973

			VG	VF	UNC
218	**25 GOURDES**				
	L.1973, etc. Dk. blue and brown-violet on m/c unpt. Pres. Jean-Claude Duvalier at l., antenna at r. Prefix letters DA-DD. National Palace on back. Printer: TDLR.				
	a. Issued note.		3.00	7.50	17.50
	s. Specimen.		—	—	30.00

#219-229 not assigned.

BANQUE DE LA RÉPUBLIQUE D'HAITI

LOI DU 17 AOUT 1979 (1980-82)

#230-232, 235-238 sign. titles: *LE GOUVERNEUR, LE GOUVERNEUR ADJOINT* and *LE DIRECTEUR.* Arms at ctr. on back. Printer: ABNC.

			VG	VF	UNC
230	**1 GOURDE**				
	L.1979. Dr. brown on m/c unpt. Like #210. W/ or w/o prefix letter. Printed on paper w/planchettes. Small size numerals in serial #.		FV	0.50	1.75
230A	**1 GOURDE**				
	L.1979. Like #230. Printed on Tyvek. Larger size numerals in serial #.				
	a. Issued note.		FV	0.50	3.00
	s. Specimen.		—	—	25.00

			VG	VF	UNC
231	**2 GOURDES**				
	L.1979. Blue on m/c unpt. Like #230. W/o or w/prefix letter. Printed on paper w/planchettes. Smaller size numerals in serial #.		FV	0.50	3.00
231A	**2 GOURDES**				
	L.1979. Like #231. Printed on Tyvek. Larger size numerals in serial #.		FV	1.00	5.00
232	**5 GOURDES**				
	L.1979. Orange on m/c unpt. Like #212. Prefix letters A-T, AA-.		FV	1.25	7.50
#233 and 234 held in reserve.					
235	**50 GOURDES**				
	L.1979. Dk. brown on green and m/c unpt. Like #213. Printed on dull white paper w/planchettes. W/o prefix letter or w/A, B, G.				
	a. Issued note.		FV	12.50	30.00
	s. Specimen.		—	—	35.00
235A	**50 GOURDES**				
	L.1979. Like #235. Printed on Tyvek.				
	a. Prefix letter C. Wmk: American bald eagle symbol of ABNC.		FV	12.50	35.00
	b. W/o wmk. Prefix letter D, F.		FV	12.50	32.50
	s. Specimen.		—	—	40.00

			VG	VF	UNC
236	**100 GOURDES**				
	L.1979. Purple on m/c unpt. Like #205. Printed on paper w/planchettes. Prefix letters A; B.				
	a. Issued note.		FV	20.00	55.00
	s. Specimen.		—	—	35.00
236A	**100 GOURDES**				
	L.1979. Like #236. Printed on Tyvek. Prefix letter C, D, E.		FV	20.00	55.00
237	**250 GOURDES**				
	L.1979. Dk. yellow-green on m/c unpt. Similar to #206. Printed on Tyvek.				
	a. Issued note.		FV	45.00	125.00
	s. Specimen.		—	—	100.00
238	**500 GOURDES**				
	L.1979. Red on m/c unpt. Similar to #207. Printed on Tyvek.				
	a. Issued note.		FV	90.00	250.00
	s. Specimen.		—	—	300.00

1984; 1985 ND ISSUE

#239-240 arms at ctr. on back. Printer: TDLR. Replacement notes: Serial # prefix ZZ.

			VG	VF	UNC
239	**1 GOURDE**				
	L.1979 (1984). Dk. brown on m/c unpt. Like #196. Double prefix letters. Sign. titles like #230.		FV	0.25	1.50
240	**2 GOURDES**				
	L.1979 (1985). Grayish blue on m/c unpt. Similar to #191.		FV	0.50	2.50

#241-243 sign. title at r: *LE DIRECTEUR GENERAL.* Arms at ctr. on back.

			VG	VF	UNC
241	**5 GOURDES**				
	L.1979 (1985). Orange on m/c unpt. Portr. Pres. Jean-Claude Duvalier at l. and as wmk. Printer: G&D.				
	a. Issued note.		FV	1.00	4.00
	s. Specimen.		—	—	35.00

242	**10 GOURDES**	VG	VF	UNC
	L.1979 (1984). Green on m/c unpt. Similar to #203, but portr. Jean-Claude Duvalier at ctr. Printer: ABNC.			
	a. Issued note.	FV	2.00	7.50
	s. Specimen.	—	—	27.50

243	**25 GOURDES**	VG	VF	UNC
	L.1979 (1985). Blue on pink and m/c unpt. Like #241. Printer: G&D.			
	a. Issued note.	FV	4.50	15.00
	s. Specimen.	—	—	30.00

#244 *Deleted.* See #240.

1986-88 Issue

#245-252 sign. title at r: *LE DIRECTEUR GENERAL.* Arms at ctr. on back.

245	**1 GOURDE**	VG	VF	UNC
	1987. Dk. brown and brown-black on m/c unpt. Toussaint L'Ouverture w/long hair at ctr. Printer: G&D.			
	a. Issued note.	FV	FV	1.00
	s. Specimen.	—	—	22.50

245A	**2 GOURDES**	VG	VF	UNC
	L.1979. Grayish blue on m/c unpt. Like #240.	FV	0.25	2.00

246	**5 GOURDES**	VG	VF	UNC
	1987. Orange and brown on m/c unpt. Statue of Combat de Vertiéres at upper ctr. Wmk: Palm tree. Printer: G&D.			
	a. Issued note.	FV	FV	4.00
	s. Specimen.	—	—	25.00

247	**10 GOURDES**	VG	VF	UNC
	1988. Green, red and blue on m/c unpt. Catherine Flon Arcahaie seated sewing the first flag of the Republic at r. Back green. Printer: ABNC.			
	a. Issued note.	FV	FV	6.00
	s. Specimen.	—	—	27.50

248	**25 GOURDES**	VG	VF	UNC
	1988. Dk. blue and purple on m/c unpt. Palace of Justice at ctr. Wmk: Palm tree. Printer: G&D.			
	a. Issued note.	FV	FV	12.50
	s. Specimen.	—	—	28.50

249	**50 GOURDES**	VG	VF	UNC
	1986. Dk. brown on green and m/c unpt. Design and sign. titles like #235. Printer: ABNC.			
	a. Issued note.	FV	FV	30.00
	s. Specimen.	—	—	25.00
250	**100 GOURDES**			
	1986. Purple on m/c unpt. Similar to #236 (but more colorful). Printer: TDLR.			
	a. Issued note.	FV	FV	45.00
	s. Specimen.	—	—	35.00
251	**250 GOURDES**			
	1988. Tan on m/c unpt. Similar to #237. Printer: ABNC.			
	a. Issued note.	FV	FV	80.00
	s. Specimen.	—	—	70.00
252	**500 GOURDES**			
	1988. Red on m/c unpt. Pres. Alexandre Pétion at r. Printer: ABNC.			
	a. Issued note.	FV	FV	150.00
	s. Specimen.	—	—	85.00

1989-91 ISSUE

#253-255 arms at ctr. on back. Printer: USBC.

253	1 GOURDE	VG	VF	UNC
	1989. Dk. brown and brown-black on m/c unpt. Toussaint L'Ouverture w/short hair at ctr. Legal clause includes reference to the United States.			
	a. Issued note.	FV	FV	1.00
	s. Specimen.	—	—	22.50

254	2 GOURDES	VG	VF	UNC
	1990. Blue-black on m/c unpt. Citadel rampart at ctr. Legal clause w/o reference to the United States.			
	a. Issued note.	FV	0.50	3.00
	s. Specimen.	—	—	25.00

255	5 GOURDES	VG	VF	UNC
	1989. Orange and brown on m/c unpt. Like #246. Legal clause includes reference to the United States.			
	a. Issued note.	FV	FV	2.00
	s. Specimen.	—	—	25.00

#256-258 legal clause on face and back w/o reference to the United States. Arms at ctr. on back. Wmk: Palm tree. Printer: G&D.

256	10 GOURDES	VG	VF	UNC
	1991; 1998; 1999. Dk. green, red and blue on m/c unpt. Similar to #247, but w/C. F. Arcahaie at ctr.			
	a. Issued note.	FV	FV	4.00
	s. Specimen.	—	—	25.00

257	50 GOURDES	VG	VF	UNC
	1991; 1999. Dk. olive-green on m/c unpt. Portr. Pres. L. F. Salomon Jeune at ctr.			
	a. Issued note.	FV	FV	10.00
	s. Specimen.	—	—	50.00

258	100 GOURDES	VG	VF	UNC
	1991. Purple on m/c unpt. Portr. H. Christophe at l.			
	a. Issued note.	FV	FV	20.00
	s. Specimen.	—	—	25.00

1992-94 ISSUE

#259-264 w/o laws. Shortened clause on face and back: *CE BILLET EST EMIS CONFORMEMENT...* Arms at ctr. on back.

#259-261 printer: TDLR. Replacement notes: Serial # prefix *ZZ*.

259	1 GOURDE	VG	VF	UNC
	1992; 1993. Dk. brown and brown-black on m/c unpt. Like #245.			
	a. Issued note.	FV	FV	0.75
	s. Specimen.	FV	FV	25.00

260	2 GOURDES	VG	VF	UNC
	1992. Blue-black on m/c unpt. Like #254.			
	a. Issued note.	FV	FV	1.25
	s. Specimen.	—	—	25.00

261	5 GOURDES	VG	VF	UNC
	1992. Orange and brown on m/c unpt. Like #246.			
	a. Issued note.	FV	FV	2.00
	s. Specimen.	—	—	22.50

262	25 GOURDES	VG	VF	UNC
	1993. Dk. blue and purple on m/c unpt. Like #248. Printer: G&D.			
	a. Issued note.	FV	FV	4.50
	s. Specimen.	—	—	25.00

263	250 GOURDES	VG	VF	UNC
	1994. Olive-brown and dk. brown on m/c unpt. Portr. J. J. Dessalines at l. Printer: G&D.			
	a. Issued note.	FV	FV	35.00
	s. Specimen.	—	—	100.00

264	500 GOURDES	VG	VF	UNC
	1993. Red-violet on m/c unpt. Portr. Pres. A. Pétion at l. Printer: G&D.			
	a. Issued note.	FV	FV	60.00
	s. Specimen.	—	—	200.00

NOTICE

Readers with unlisted dates, signature varieties, etc. are invited to submit photocopies of their notes to: Standard Catalog of World Paper Money, 700 East State St. Iola, WI 54990-0001, E-Mail: george.cuhaj@fwpubs.com.

2000 ISSUE

#265-270 more colorful, especially on borders. Ascending size serial #. Letters BRH at r. in various color combinations on face.

#265, 267, 269 and 270 printer: (T)DLR. #266 and 268 printer: G&D.

265	10 GOURDES	VG	VF	UNC
	2000-2005. Dk. green and m/c. Similar to #256.	FV	FV	2.50

266	25 GOURDES	VG	VF	UNC
	2000; 2005. Dk. blue and black on m/c unpt. Similar to #262.	FV	FV	3.00

267	50 GOURDES	VG	VF	UNC
	2000; 2003. Dk. olive-green and black on m/c unpt. Similar to #257.	FV	FV	8.00

268	100 GOURDES	VG	VF	UNC
	2000. Purple on m/c unpt. Similar to #258.	FV	FV	18.00

269 250 GOURDES
2000; 2003. Olive-brown and dk. brown on m/c unpt. Similar to #263.

	VG	VF	UNC
	FV	FV	30.00

270 500 GOURDES
2000; 2003. Red and violet on m/c unpt. Similar to #264.

	VG	VF	UNC
	FV	FV	45.00

2001 COMMEMORATIVE ISSUE

Bicentennial of the Constitution, 1801-2001

271 20 GOURDES
2001. Brown, orange and yellow. Bust at l. Foil impressions flank center wreath. Open Constitution book on back.

	VG	VF	UNC
	FV	FV	4.00

2004 COMMEMORATIVE ISSUE

#272-277 Bicentennial of Haiti. Signature titles in Frence French and Haitian Creole.

272 10 GOURDES
2004. Blue. Sanite Belair. Fort Cap-Rouge (Jacmel) on back.

	VG	VF	UNC
	FV	FV	2.50

273 20 GOURDES
2004. Purple on tan and green unpt. Nicolas Gieffrard. Fortress des Plantons (Dussio) on back.

	VG	VF	UNC
	FV	FV	3.00

274 50 GOURDES
2004. Purple. Francois Cappiox. Fort Jalousiere (Marmelade) on back.

	VG	VF	UNC
	FV	FV	8.00

275 100 GOURDES
2004. Blue and gray. Henry Christophé. Citadelle Henry (Milot) on back.

	VG	VF	UNC
	FV	FV	18.00

276 250 GOURDES
2004. Blue on tan and brown unpt. Jean-Jacques Dessalines. Fort Decidé (Marchand) on back.

	VG	VF	UNC
	FV	FV	30.00

277	500 GOURDES	VG	VF	UNC
	2004. Purple on tan unpt. Alexandre Petion. Fort Jacques (Fermathe) on back.	FV	FV	45.00

2000 DATED 2004 ISSUE

278	1000 GOURDES	VG	VF	UNC
	1999 (2006). Purple.			
	a. Issued note.	—	—	—
	s. Specimen.	—	—	—

CERTIFICAT DE LIBERATION ECONOMIQUE

The C.L.E. was an internal loan made by the Haitian government. A certain percentage of an employee's wage was paid in C.L.E. notes.

LOI DU 17 SEPTEMBRE 1962

501	1 GOURDE	VG	VF	UNC
	1.10.1962. Green w/black text.	5.00	25.00	65.00
502	5 GOURDES			
	1.10.1962. Red w/black text.			
	a. Series A.	5.00	25.00	65.00
	b. Series B.	5.00	25.00	65.00
	c. Series C.	5.00	25.00	65.00
503	25 GOURDES			
	1.10.1962. Yellow-orange w/black text.	10.00	30.00	80.00

504	100 GOURDES	VG	VF	UNC
	1.10.1962. Blue w/black text.	30.00	100.00	250.00

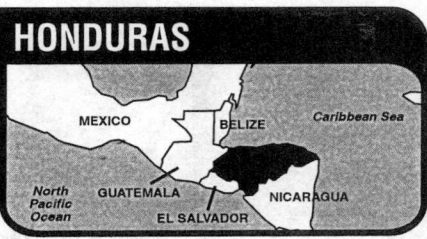

The Republic of Honduras, situated in Central America between El Salvador, Nicaragua and Guatemala, has an area of 43,277 sq. mi. (112,088 sq. km.) and a population of 6.48 million. Capital: Tegucigalpa. Tourism, agriculture, mining (gold and silver), and logging are the chief industries. Bananas, timber and coffee are exported.

Honduras, a site of the ancient Mayan Empire, was claimed for Spain by Columbus in 1502, during his last voyage to the Americas. The first settlement was made by Cristobal de Olid under orders of Hernan Cortes, then in Mexico. The area, regarded as one of the most promising sources of gold and silver in the New World, was a part of the Captaincy General of Guatemala throughout the colonial period. After declaring its independence from Spain in 1821, Honduras fell briefly to the Mexican Empire of Agustin de Iturbide, and then joined the Central American Federation (1823-39). Upon dissolution of the federation, Honduras became an independent republic.

MONETARY SYSTEM:
I Peso = 100 Centavos, 1871-1926
1 Lempira = 100 Centavos, 1926-

REPÚBLICA DE HONDURAS

BANCO CENTRAL DE HONDURAS

Established July 1, 1950 by merger of Banco Atlantida and Banco de Honduras. Various date and sign. varieties.

1950-51 ISSUE

49	100 LEMPIRAS	VG	VF	UNC
	1951-73. Yellow on m/c unpt. Valle at l., arms at r. Village and bridge on back.		Reported Not Confirmed	
	a. W/o security thread, lilac-pink unpt. Printer: W&S. 16.3.1951; 8.3.1957.	70.00	300.00	1000.00
	b. W/o security thread, w/fibers at r. ctr., lt. green and lt. orange unpt. Printer: W&S. 5.2.1964; 5.11.1965; 22.3.1968; 10.12.1969.	100.00	300.00	1250.00
	c. W/security thread, yellow unpt. 13.10.1972.			
	d. As c. but w/o security thread. 13.10.1972; 23.3.1973.	45.00	175.00	375.00
	s. Specimen, punched hole cancelled.	—		250.00

#50 not assigned.

1953-56 ISSUE

51	5 LEMPIRAS	VG	VF	UNC
	1953-68. Gray on m/c unpt. Morazán at l., arms at r. Serial # at upper l. and upper r. Battle of Trinidad on back. Printer: ABNC.			
	a. Date horizontal. 17.3.1953; 19.3.1954; 7.5.1954.	6.00	35.00	175.00
	b. As a. 22.11.1957-7.1.1966.	4.00	25.00	125.00
	c. Date vertical. 15.4.1966; 29.9.1967; 22.3.1968.	3.50	17.50	70.00

52	10 LEMPIRAS	VG	VF	UNC
	1954-69. Brown on m/c unpt. Cabañas at l., arms at r. Old bank on back. Date and sign. style varieties. Printer: TDLR.			
	a. R. sign. title: MINISTRO DE HACIENDA... 19.11.1954.	15.00	75.00	300.00
	b. R. sign. title: MINISTRO DE ECONOMIA... 19.2.1960-10.1.1969.	10.00	35.00	250.00

53	20 LEMPIRAS	VG	VF	UNC
	1954-72. Green. D. de Herrera at l., arms at r. Waterfalls on back. Printer: TDLR.			
	a. 4.6.1954; 26.11.1954; 5.4.1957; 6.3.1959; 8.5.1959.	22.50	75.00	325.00
	b. 19.2.1960; 27.4.1962; 19.4.1963; 6.3.1964.	17.50	50.00	275.00
	c. 7.1.1966-18.2.1972.	15.00	45.00	250.00

1961 ISSUE

54A	1 LEMPIRA	VG	VF	UNC
	10.2.1961; 30.7.1965. Red on m/c unpt. Lempira at l., modified design of #45 w/black serial #. Dios del Maiz/Idolo Maya and Mayan artifacts on back. 2 sign. varieties. Printer: TDLR.			
	a. Issued note.	0.75	4.00	25.00
	s. Specimen. Punched hole cancelled. 10.2.1961.	—	—	50.00

1968; 1970 ISSUE

55	1 LEMPIRA	VG	VF	UNC
	1968; 1972. Red-orange on green and pink unpt. Lempira at l., design different from #45 and 54A. *Ruinas de Copan Juego de Pelota* on back. Printer: TDLR.			
	a. R. sign. title: *MINISTRO DE ECONOMIA*... 25.10.1968.	0.50	3.00	17.50
	b. R. sign. title: *MINISTRO DE HACIENDA*... 21.1.1972.	0.25	1.00	12.50

56	5 LEMPIRAS	VG	VF	UNC
	1968-74. Black on m/c unpt. Morazan at l., arms at r. Similar to #51. Serial # at lower l. and upper r. Battle scene of Trinidad at ctr. on back. Printer: ABNC.			
	a. Date horizontal. 29.11.1968; 11.4.1969; 10.3.1970.	3.00	30.00	65.00
	b. Date vertical. 20.11.1970-24.8.1974.	2.00	10.00	60.00

57	10 LEMPIRAS	VG	VF	UNC
	27.8.1970-13.11.1975. Brown on m/c unpt. Cabañas at l., arms at r. Ruins and new bank on back. Printer: ABNC.	3.50	15.00	65.00

1973; 1974 ISSUE

58	1 LEMPIRA	VG	VF	UNC
	11.3.1974. Red on green and lilac unpt. Lempira w/o feather at l., arms at r. Different view of Ruinas de Copan on back. Printer: TDLR.	0.25	1.00	8.00

59	5 LEMPIRAS	VG	VF	UNC
	1974-78. Black on m/c unpt. Morazán at l., arms at r. Battle of Trinidad at l. on back. Printer: ABNC.			
	a. Date vertical. 24.10.1974.	2.50	8.00	40.00
	b. Date horizontal. 12.12.1975; 26.2.1976; 16.9.1976; 9.12.1976; 13.1.1977; 3.6.1977; 25.11.1977; 13.2.1978.	2.00	4.00	25.00

60 20 LEMPIRAS

	VG	VF	UNC
2.3.1973; 13.8.1973; 30.11.1973; 1.3.1974; 22.4.1974; 5.6.1975;	12.50	40.00	150.00

15.1.1976; 18.3.1976; 13.1.1977; 3.6.1977. Green on m/c unpt. D. de Herrera at l., arms at r. Presidential residence on back. Date placement varieties. Printer: (T)DLR.

1976 COMMEMORATIVE ISSUE

#61, Centennial of the Marco Aurelio Soto Government

61 2 LEMPIRAS

	VG	VF	UNC
23.9.1976. Purple on m/c unpt. Arms at l., M. A. Soto at r. Island	FV	0.75	5.00

and Port of Amapala on back. Printer: TDLR.

1975-78 REGULAR ISSUE

#62-63 printer: TDLR.

62 1 LEMPIRA

	VG	VF	UNC
30.6.1978. Red. Like #58 but Indian symbols added below bank name on back.	FV	0.75	5.00

63 5 LEMPIRAS

1978-94. Black, dk. blue, and deep olive-green on m/c unpt. Arms at l., Morazán at r. Battle of Trinidad Nov. 11, 1827 on back.

	VG	VF	UNC
a. 4.10.1978; 8.5.1980.	FV	2.00	10.00
b. 8.12.1985; 30.3.1989.	FV	1.50	7.50
c. Red serial # at upper l. in ascending size. 14.1.1993; 25.2.1993.	FV	FV	4.00
d. Brown serial # as c. 12.5.1994.	FV	FV	4.00
s. As d. Specimen. *MUESTRA SIN VALOR.*	—	—	—

#64-66 printer: ABNC.

64 10 LEMPIRAS

1976-89. Brown on m/c unpt. Cabañas at l. Scene of City University on back.

	VG	VF	UNC
a. 18.3.1976-10.5.1979.	FV	5.00	25.00
b. 23.6.1982-5.10.1989.	FV	3.00	17.50

65 20 LEMPIRAS

1978-93. Green on m/c unpt. D. de Herrera at r. and as wmk. Port of Puerto Cortes on back. Date placement varieties.

	VG	VF	UNC
a. 2.11.1978; 10.9.1979.	FV	8.00	30.00
b. Vertical date at r. 8.1.1981-10.2.1989.	FV	4.00	20.00
c. Horizontal date at upper l. 22.6.1989-2.10.1992.	FV	3.50	12.50
d. 10.12.1992; 18.3.1993; 1.7.1993.	FV	FV	7.50

66 50 LEMPIRAS

1976-93. Deep blue on m/c unpt. J. M. Galvez D. at l. National Agricultural Development bank on back. Wmk: tree.

	VG	VF	UNC
a. Vertical date at r. 29.1.1976-10.9.1979.	FV	15.00	55.00
b. 5.1.1984; 3.7.1986; 24.9.1987; 10.2.1989.	FV	8.00	35.00
c. Horizontal date at upper l. 1.3.1990; 13.12.1990; 29.8.1991.	FV	7.00	25.00
d. 18.3.1993; 1.7.1993.	FV	FV	17.50

67 100 LEMPIRAS

	VG	VF	UNC
16.1.1975; 29.1.1976; 18.3.1976; 13.1.1977; 12.1.1978;	FV	25.00	150.00

10.9.1979. Brown-orange on m/c unpt. Valle at l. Signatepeque school of forestry on back. Printer: TDLR.

1980-81 ISSUE

#68-69 printer: TDLR.

68 1 LEMPIRA

1980; 1984; 1989. Red on m/c unpt. Arms at l., Lempira at r. Ruins of Copan on back.

	VG	VF	UNC
a. W/o security thread. 29.5.1980; 18.10.1984.	FV	0.50	4.00
b. W/security thread. 30.3.1989.	FV	FV	3.00

		VG	VF	UNC
69	**100 LEMPIRAS**			
	1981-94. Brown-orange, dk. olive-green, and deep purple on m/c unpt. J. C. del Valle at r. and as wmk. Different view of forestry school on back.			
	a. Regular serial #. 8.1.1981; 23.6.1982; 8.9.1983.	FV	15.00	75.00
	b. 5.1.1984-13.12.1989.	FV	12.50	50.00
	c. 21.12.1989-1.7.1993.	FV	FV	35.00

1989 ISSUE

		VG	VF	UNC
70	**10 LEMPIRAS**			
	21.9.1989. Dk. brown and red on m/c unpt. (of vertical stripes). Arms at l., Cabañas at r. City University on back. Printer: TDLR.			
	a. Issued note.	FV	2.50	10.00
	s. Specimen. *MUESTRA SIN VALOR.*	—	—	—

1992-93 ISSUE

		VG	VF	UNC
71	**1 LEMPIRA**			
	10.9.1992. Dk. red on m/c unpt. Similar to #68 but back in paler colors. Printer: CBNC.	FV	FV	2.00

#72-75 printer: TDLR. 1993 dates have red serial #. 1994 and later dates have brown serial #.

		VG	VF	UNC
72	**2 LEMPIRAS**			
	14.1.1993; 25.2.1993; 12.5.1994. Purple on m/c unpt. Like #61 but w/lt. blue unpt. at l. Ascending size serial # at upper l.			
	a. Issued note.	FV	FV	3.00
	s. Specimen. *MUESTRA SIN VALOR.*	—	—	—

		VG	VF	UNC
73	**20 LEMPIRAS**			
	14.1.1993; 25.2.1993; 12.5.1994; 12.12.1996; 18.9.1997. Deep green and dk. brown on m/c unpt. D. de Herrera at r. and as wmk. Back vertical; Presidential House at ctr.			
	a. Issued note.	FV	FV	6.00
	s. Specimen. *MUESTRA SIN VALOR.* 12.5.1994.			
73A	**20 LEMPIRAS**			
	3.9.1998. As #73 but Printer: FC-O.	FV	FV	6.00

		VG	VF	UNC
74	**50 LEMPIRAS**			
	14.1.1993; 25.2.1993; 12.5.1994; 12.12.1996; 18.9.1997; 3.9.1998. Blue-black and dk. brown on m/c unpt. J. M. Galvez D. at r. and as wmk. Back vertical; Central Bank Annex at ctr.			
	a. Issued note.	FV	FV	14.00
	s. Specimen. *MUESTRA SIN VALOR.* 12.5.1994.	—	—	—

		VG	VF	UNC
75	**100 LEMPIRAS**			
	14.1.1993; 25.2.1993; 12.5.1994. Brown-orange, dk. olive-green and dk. brown on m/c unpt. Like #69 but w/engraved date. Serial # at upper l. in ascending size. Enhanced unpt. in wmk. area on back. Black sign. Red serial #. Printer: DLR.			
	a. Issued note.	FV	FV	27.50
	s. Specimen. *MUESTRA SIN VALOR.* 12.5.1994.	—	—	—

1994; 1995 ISSUE

				VG	VF	UNC
76	1 LEMPIRA					
	12.5.1994. Red on m/c unpt. Similar to #71 but w/brown ascending size serial # at upper l. Printer: TDLR.					
	a. Issued note.			FV	FV	1.50
	s. Specimen. *MUESTRA SIN VALOR.*			—	—	

				VG	VF	UNC
77	100 LEMPIRAS					
	1994-2003. Brown-orange, black and olive-green on m/c unpt. J. C. del Valle at ctr. r. and as wmk., bridge over the Choluteca River at r. Valle's house at l. on back. Brown serial #. Printer: TDLR (w/o imprint).					
	a. Sign. titles: *MINISTRO DE HACIENDA Y CREDITO PÚBLICO.* 12.5.1994.			FV	FV	25.00
	b. Sign. titles: *SECRETARIO DE FINANZAS.* 18.9.1997; 3.9.1998; 14.12.2000; 30.8.2001; 23.1.2003; 26.8.2004.			FV	FV	25.00
78	500 LEMPIRAS					
	1995-2003. Violet and purple on m/c unpt. Dr. R. Rosa at r. and as wmk., National Gallery of Art in background. View of Rosario de San Juancito at l. ctr. on back.					
	a. Sign. titles: *MINISTRO DE HACIENDA Y CREDITO PUBLICO.* 16.11.1995.			FV	FV	90.00
	b. Sign. titles: *SECRETARIO DE FINANZAS.* 3.9.1998; 14.12.2000; 30.8.2001; 23.1.2003.			FV	FV	90.00

1996-98 ISSUE

#79-81 brown serial # w/ascending size serial # at upper l.

				VG	VF	UNC
79	1 LEMPIRA					
	12.12.1996; 3.9.1998. Dk. red on m/c unpt. Like #71. Printer: F-CO.			FV	FV	1.00

				VG	VF	UNC
79A	1 LEMPIRA					
	18.9.1997. Dk. red on m/c unpt. Like #79 but printer: TDLR (w/o imprint).			FV	FV	1.00
80	2 LEMPIRAS					
	18.9.1997 Purple on m/c unpt. Similar to #72. Printer: TDLR.			FV	FV	1.50
80A	2 LEMPIRAS					
	3.9.1998; 14.12.2000; 30.8.2001; 23.1.2003. Purple on m/c unpt. Like #80 but printer: F-CO.			FV	FV	1.50

				VG	VF	UNC
81	5 LEMPIRAS					
	12.12.1996; 18.9.1997; 3.9.1998. Black, dk. blue and deep olive-green on m/c unpt. Like #63. Printer: DLR.			FV	FV	2.00

				VG	VF	UNC
82	10 LEMPIRAS					
	12.12.1996; 18.9.1997; 3.9.1998; 14.12.2000. Dk. brown and red on m/c unpt. Like #70. Printer: TDLR.			FV	FV	3.50

2000 COMMEMORATIVE ISSUE

#83, 50th Anniversary of the Central Bank and Year 2000

				VG	VF	UNC
83	20 LEMPIRAS					
	30.3.2000. Dk. green and brown on m/c unpt. D. Herrera and Government House at r. Work, effort and unity sculpture on back.			FV	FV	4.50

2000 ISSUE

84   **1 LEMPIRA**

	VG	VF	UNC
14.12.2000; 30.8.2001; 23.1.2003. Dk. red on m/c unpt. Similar to #79. Printer: CBNC.	FV	FV	0.75

88   **50 LEMPIRAS**

	VG	VF	UNC
30.8.2001; 23.1.2003. M/c. Similar to #74, but vertical serial # at l. Printer: TDLR.	FV	FV	6.50

85   **5 LEMPIRAS**

	VG	VF	UNC
14.12.2000; 30.8.2001; 23.1.2003. M/c. Similar to #81. Printer: CBNC.	FV	FV	1.25

86   **10 LEMPIRAS**

	VG	VF	UNC
30.8.2001; 23.1.2003. M/c. Similar to #82. Printer: FC-O.	FV	FV	2.50

87   **20 LEMPIRAS**

	VG	VF	UNC
30.8.2001; 23.1.2003. M/c. Printer: G&D.	FV	FV	4.00

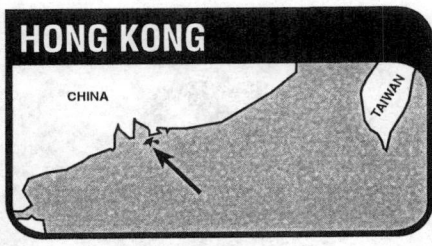

HONG KONG

CHINA

TAIWAN

Hong Kong S.A.R., a former British Colony, is situated at the mouth of the Canton or Pearl River 90 miles (145 km.) southeast of Canton, has an area of 409 sq. mi. (1,091 sq. km.) and an estimated population of nearly 7 million. Capital: Central (formerly Victoria). The port of Hong Kong had developed as the commercial center of the Far East, a transshipment point for goods destined for China and the countries of the Pacific rim. Light manufacturing and tourism are important components of the economy.

Long a haven for fishermen-pirates and opium smugglers, the island of Hong Kong was ceded to Britain at the conclusion of the first Opium War (1839-1842). At the time, the acquisition of "a barren rock" was ridiculed by both London and English merchants operating in the Far East. The Kowloon Peninsula and Stonecutter's Island were ceded in 1860 and the so-called New Territories, comprising most of the mainland of the colony, were leased to Britain for 99 years in 1898.

Hong Kong was returned to the Peoples Republic of China on July 1, 1997 and was made a Special Administrative Region, enjoying a high degree of autonomy and vested with executive, legislative and independent judicial power.

RULERS:
British (1842-1997)

MONETARY SYSTEM:
1 Dollar = 100 Cents

COMMERCIAL BANKS:
Chartered Bank - #68-81
Hong Kong & Shanghai Banking Corporation - #184-205
Mercantile Bank Limited - #244-245
Standard Chartered Bank - #278-289
Government of Hong Kong - #325-327
Bank of China - #329-333

CHARTERED BANK

行銀打渣[1]

Cha Ta Yin Hang

Prior to December 1956, it was in business as The Chartered Bank of India, Australia & China. In the 1980s it became the Standard Bank, then later became the Standard Chartered Bank.

1961; 1967 ND ISSUES

#68-72 wmk: Helmeted warrior's head. Printer: TDLR.

		VG	VF	UNC
68	**5 DOLLARS** 1961-62; ND. Black and green on m/c unpt. Arms at lower l. Chinese junk and sampan at ctr. on back.			
	a. 1.7.1961.	20.00	65.00	180.00
	b. 3.3.1962.	22.50	75.00	275.00
	c. ND (1962-70).	10.00	32.50	90.00
	s. Specimen. As a.	—	—	—

		VG	VF	UNC
69	**5 DOLLARS** ND (1967). Black and yellow-brown on m/c unpt. Like #68.	6.00	25.00	80.00

		VG	VF	UNC
70	**10 DOLLARS** 1961-62; ND. Black and red-violet on red unpt. Arms at l. Chartered Bank bldg. at ctr. on back.			
	a. 1.7.1961.	25.00	85.00	200.00
	b. 3.3.1962.	15.00	50.00	110.00
	c. ND (1962-70).	7.50	22.50	50.00
	s. Specimen. As c.	—	—	—

		VG	VF	UNC
71	**100 DOLLARS** 1961; ND. Dk. green and brown on m/c unpt. Arms at ctr. Harbor view on back.			
	a. 1.7.1961.	150.00	550.00	900.00
	b. ND (1961-70).	100.00	300.00	500.00

		VG	VF	UNC
72	**500 DOLLARS** 1961-77. Black and dk. brown on m/c unpt. Male portr. at l. Ship, harbor view at ctr. on back.			
	a. Sign. titles: *ACCOUNTANT* and *MANAGER.* 1.7.1961.	350.00	1000.00	1750.00
	b. Sign. titles as a. ND (1962-?).	150.00	400.00	100.00
	c. Sign. titles: *ACCOUNTANT* and *CHIEF MANAGER IN HONG KONG.* ND (?-1975).	150.00	400.00	900.00
	d. Sign. titles as c. 1.1.1977.	100.00	275.00	450.00
	s. Specimen. As d.	—	—	375.00

1970 ND; 1975-77 ISSUE

#73-76 bank bldg. at l., bank crest at ctr. Wmk: Helmeted warrior's head. Printer: TDLR.

		VG	VF	UNC
73	**5 DOLLARS** ND (1970-75); 1975. Dk. brown on m/c unpt. City Hall at ctr. r. on back.			
	a. Sign. titles: *ACCOUNTANT* and *MANAGER.* ND (1970-75).	0.75	3.00	12.50
	b. Sign. titles: *ACCOUNTANT* and *CHIEF MANAGER IN HONG KONG* at r. ND; 1.6.1975.	1.50	6.50	27.50
	s. Specimen. As b.	—	—	—

77	10 DOLLARS	VG	VF	UNC
	1.1.1980; 1.1.1981. Green on m/c unpt. Stylistic carp at r.	FV	4.00	8.00

74	10 DOLLARS	VG	VF	UNC
	ND; 1975; 1977. Dk. green on m/c unpt. Ocean terminal at ctr. r.			
	a. Sign. titles: *ACCOUNTANT* and *MANAGER.* ND (1970-75).	3.00	10.00	45.00
	b. Sign. titles: *ACCOUNTANT* and *CHIEF MANAGER IN HONG KONG.* ND; 1.6.1975.	3.00	12.00	40.00
	c. Sign. titles as b. 1.1.1977.	1.50	6.00	22.50
	s. Specimen. As b.	—	—	125.00

78	50 DOLLARS	VG	VF	UNC
	1979-82. Blue on m/c unpt. Chinze at r.			
	a. 1.1.1979.	FV	20.00	75.00
	b. 1.1.1981; 1.1.1982.	FV	FV	50.00
	s. Specimen.	—	—	160.00

75	50 DOLLARS	VG	VF	UNC
	ND (1970-75). Blue on m/c unpt. City Hall at ctr. r. on back.			
	a. Issued note.	50.00	150.00	400.00
	s. Specimen.	—	—	175.00

79	100 DOLLARS	VG	VF	UNC
	1979-82. Red on m/c unpt. Mythical horse *Qilin* at r.			
	a. 1.1.1979.	FV	20.00	90.00
	b. 1.1.1980.	FV	17.50	65.00
	c. 1.1.1982.	FV	15.00	50.00
	s. Specimen.	—	—	175.00

76	100 DOLLARS	VG	VF	UNC
	ND; 1977. Red on m/c unpt.			
	a. ND (1970-75).	40.00	125.00	325.00
	b. 1.1.1977.	30.00	60.00	125.00
	s. Specimen. As a.	—	—	160.00

1979; 1980 ISSUE

#77-81 bank bldg. at l., arms at ctr. on back. Wmk: Helmeted warrior's head. Printer: TDLR (w/o imprint).

80	500 DOLLARS	VG	VF	UNC
	1979; 1982. Brown on m/c unpt. Mythical phoenix at r.			
	a. 1.1.1979.	FV	FV	200.00
	b. 1.1.1982.	FV	FV	170.00
	s. Specimen.	—	—	225.00

81	1000 DOLLARS	VG	VF	UNC
	1979; 1982. Yellow-orange on m/c unpt. Dragon at r.			
	a. 1.1.1979.	FV	FV	350.00
	b. 1.1.1982.	FV	FV	275.00
	s. Specimen.	—	—	350.00

HONG KONG & SHANGHAI BANKING CORPORATION

行銀理滙海上港香   *Hsiang K'ang Shang Hai Hui Li Yin Hang*

HONG KONG

1932-35 ISSUE

179	500 DOLLARS	VG	VF	UNC
	1935-69. Brown and blue. Arms at top ctr., Sir T. Jackson at r. Back blue; allegorical female head at l., bank bldg. at ctr.			
	a. Handsigned. 1.6.1935-1.7.1937.	225.00	1250.00	3000.00
	b. Printed sign. 1.4.1941-1.8.1952.	175.00	450.00	1250.00
	c. 11.7.1960-1.8.1966.	150.00	250.00	900.00
	d. 31.7.1967.	150.00	200.00	400.00
	e. 11.2.1968.	FV	100.00	250.00
	f. 27.3.1969.	FV	100.00	300.00

1959 ISSUE

#181-183 wmk: Helmeted warrior's head. Printer: BWC.

181	5 DOLLARS	VG	VF	UNC
	1959-75. Brown on m/c unpt. Woman seated at r. New bank bldg. at ctr. on back.			
	a. Sign. titles: CHIEF ACCOUNTANT and CHIEF MANAGER. 2.5.1959-29.6.1960.	3.00	15.00	45.00
	b. 1.5.1963.	50.00	175.00	550.00
	c. 1.5.1964-27.3.1969.	1.50	4.00	15.00
	d. Sign. titles: CHIEF ACCOUNTANT and GENERAL MANAGER. 1.4.1970-18.3.1971.	1.00	3.50	12.50
	e. 13.3.1972; 31.10.1972.	0.75	2.00	8.00
	f. Sm. serial #. 31.10.1973; 31.3.1975.	0.75FV	1.25	6.00
	s. Specimen.	—	—	—

182	10 DOLLARS	VG	VF	UNC
	1959-83. Dk. green on m/c unpt. Portr. woman w/sheaf of grain at upper l., arms below. Back similar to #184.			
	a. Sign. titles: CHIEF ACCOUNTANT and CHIEF MANAGER. 21.5.1959-1.9.1962.	5.00	15.00	45.00
	b. 1.5.1963; 1.9.1963.	6.00	20.00	60.00
	c. 1.5.1964; 1.9.1964.	5.00	15.00	55.00
	d. 1.10.1964.	40.00	165.00	575.00
	e. 1.2.1965; 1.8.1966; 31.7.1967.	2.00	6.00	20.00
	f. 20.3.1968; 23.11.1968; 27.3.1969.	2.00	6.00	18.00
	g. Sign. titles: CHIEF ACCOUNTANT and GENERAL MANAGER. 1.4.1970-31.3.1976.	1.50	3.75	10.00
	h. Sign. titles: CHIEF ACCOUNTANT and EXECUTIVE DIRECTOR. 31.3.1977; 31.3.1978; 31.3.1979.	1.50	3.00	12.00
	i. Sign. titles: CHIEF ACCOUNTANT and GENERAL MANAGER. 31.3.1980; 31.3.1981.	1.50	2.00	9.00
	j. Sign. titles: MANAGER and GENERAL MANAGER. 31.3.1982; 31.3.1983.	1.50	2.00	9.00
	s. Specimen.	—	—	—

183	100 DOLLARS	VG	VF	UNC
	1959-72. Red on m/c unpt. Woman seated at l. w/open book, arms at upper ctr. Wmk: Helmeted warrior's head and denomination.			
	a. Sign. titles: CHIEF ACCOUNTANT and CHIEF MANAGER. 12.8.1959-1.10.1964.	20.00	50.00	175.00
	b. 1.2.1965-27.3.1969.	20.00	35.00	125.00
	c. Sign. titles: CHIEF ACCOUNTANT and GENERAL MANAGER. 1.4.1970; 18.3.1971; 13.3.1972.	15.00	30.00	90.00

NOTICE
Readers with unlisted dates, signature varieties, etc. are invited to submit photocopies of their notes to: Standard Catalog of World Paper Money, 700 East State St. Iola, WI 54990-0001, E-Mail: george.cuhaj@fwpubs.com.

1968-73 ISSUE

#184-186 printer: BWC.

184	50 DOLLARS	VG	VF	UNC
	1968-83. Dk. blue on lt. blue and m/c unpt. Arms at r. New bank bldg. at l. ctr. on back. Wmk: Helmeted warrior's head and denomination.			
	a. Sign. titles: *CHIEF ACCOUNTANT* and *CHIEF MANAGER.* 31.5.1968; 27.3.1969.	8.50	30.00	80.00
	b. Sign. titles: *CHIEF ACCOUNTANT* and *GENERAL MANAGER.* 31.10.1973; 31.3.1975; 31.3.1978.	8.00	25.00	60.00
	c. Sign. titles as b. 31.3.1977.	8.00	25.00	60.00
	d. Sign. titles: *CHIEF ACCOUNTANT* and *EXECUTIVE DIRECTOR.* 31.3.1977.	8.00	25.00	60.00
	e. 31.3.1979.	30.00	100.00	225.00
	f. Sign. titles: *CHIEF ACCOUNTANT* and *GENERAL MANAGER.* 31.3.1980.	FV	12.50	45.00
	g. 31.3.1981.	FV	12.00	40.00
	h. Sign. titles: *MANAGER* and *GENERAL MANAGER.* 31.3.1982; 31.3.1983.	FV	9.00	37.50
	s. Specimen.	—	—	—

185	100 DOLLARS	VG	VF	UNC
	1972-76. Red on m/c unpt. Arms at l. Facing lions at lower l. and r., bank bldg. at ctr., dragon in medallion at r. on back.			
	a. W/4 lg. serial # on back. 13.3.1972; 31.10.1972.	15.00	30.00	80.00
	b. Smaller electronic sorting serial # on face. W/o serial # on back. 31.10.1972.	20.00	50.00	140.00
	c. 31.10.1973.	15.00	30.00	75.00
	d. 31.3.1975; 31.3.1976.	15.00	25.00	50.00

186	500 DOLLARS	VG	VF	UNC
	1973-76. Brown on m/c unpt. Arms at l. Bank bldg. at l., lion's head at r. on back.			
	a. 31.10.1973.	FV	130.00	250.00
	b. 31.3.1975.	FV	150.00	300.00
	c. 31.3.1976.	FV	125.00	250.00

1977; 1978 ISSUE

#187, 189 and 190 wmk: Lion's head. Printer: BWC.

187	100 DOLLARS	VG	VF	UNC
	1977-83. Red on lighter m/c unpt. Similar to #185.			
	a. Sign. titles: *CHIEF ACCOUNTANT* and *EXECUTIVE DIRECTOR.* 31.3.1977; 31.3.1978.	FV	25.00	65.00
	b. Sign. titles as a. 31.3.1979.	12.50	25.00	125.00
	c. 31.3.1980; 31.3.1981.	FV	FV	45.00
	d. Sign. titles: *MANAGER* and *GENERAL MANAGER.* 31.3.1982; 31.3.1983.	FV	FV	35.00

#188 *Deleted.* See #186.

189	500 DOLLARS	VG	VF	UNC
	1978-83. Brown and black on m/c unpt. Similar to #186 but w/modified frame designs.			
	a. 31.3.1978; 31.3.1980; 31.3.198 1981.	FV	FV	215.00
	b. 31.3.1983.	FV	FV	165.00

190 1000 DOLLARS

		VG	VF	UNC
1977-83. Gold and black on m/c unpt. Arms at r. Lion at l., bank bldg. at ctr. r. on back.				
a. 31.3.1977.		FV	FV	350.00
b. 31.3.1979; 31.3.1980; 31.3.1981; 31.3.1983.		FV	FV	300.00

1985-87 ISSUE

#191-196 arms at l. Facing lions at lower l. and r. w/new bank bldg. at ctr. on back. Sign. varieties. Wmk: Lion's head. Printer: TDLR. Replacement notes: Serial # prefix *ZZ*.

191 10 DOLLARS

		VG	VF	UNC
1985-92. Deep green on m/c unpt. Sampan and ship at r. on back.				
a. Sign. title: *GENERAL MANAGER.* 1.1.1985; 1.1.1986; 1.1.1987.		FV	FV	4.50
b. Sign. title: *EXECUTIVE DIRECTOR.* 1.1.1988.		FV	FV	4.00
c. Sign. title: *GENERAL MANAGER.* 1.1.1989; 1.1.1990; 1.1.1991; 1.1.1992.		FV	FV	3.50
s. Specimen. As a.		—	—	100.00

192 20 DOLLARS

		VG	VF	UNC
1986-89. Deep gray-green and brown on purple and m/c unpt. Clock tower, ferry in harbor view at r. on back.				
a. Sign. title: *GENERAL MANAGER.* 1.1.1986; 1.1.1987.		FV	FV	10.00
b. Sign. title: *EXECUTIVE DIRECTOR.* 1.1.1988.		FV	FV	7.50
c. Sign. title: *GENERAL MANAGER.* 1.1.1989.		FV	FV	6.50
s. Specimen. As a.		—	—	100.00

193 50 DOLLARS

		VG	VF	UNC
1985-92. Purple on m/c unpt. Men in boats at r. on back.				
a. Sign. title: *GENERAL MANAGER.* 1.1.1985; 1.1.1986; 1.1.1987.		FV	FV	25.00
b. Sign. title: *EXECUTIVE DIRECTOR.* 1.1.1988.		FV	FV	20.00
c. Sign. title: *GENERAL MANAGER.* 1.1.1989; 1.1.1990; 1.1.1991; 1.1.1992.		FV	FV	15.00
s. Specimen.		—	—	100.00

194 100 DOLLARS

		VG	VF	UNC
1985-88. Red on m/c unpt. Tiger Balm Garden pagoda at r.				
a. Sign. title: *GENERAL MANAGER.* 1.1.1985; 1.1.1986; 1.1.1987.		FV	FV	27.50
b. Sign. title: *EXECUTIVE DIRECTOR.* 1.1.1988.		FV	FV	25.00
s. Specimen.		—	—	100.00

195 500 DOLLARS

		VG	VF	UNC
1987-92. Brown on m/c unpt. Old tower at r. on back.				
a. Sign. title: *GENERAL MANAGER.* 1.1.1987.		FV	FV	120.00
b. Sign. title: *EXECUTIVE DIRECTOR.* 1.1.1988.		FV	FV	110.00
c. Sign. title: *GENERAL MANAGER.* 1.1.1989; 1.1.1990; 1.1.1991; 1.1.1992.		FV	FV	110.00

196 1000 DOLLARS

		VG	VF	UNC
1.1.1985; 1.1.1986; 1.1.1987. Red, brown and orange on m/c unpt. Old Supreme Court bldg. at r. on back.		FV	FV	180.00

1988-90 ISSUE

#197-199 printer: TDLR. Replacement notes: Serial # prefix *ZZ*.

197   20 DOLLARS

	VG	VF	UNC
1.1.1990; 1.1.1991; 1.1.1992. Like #192 but gray and black on orange, pink and m/c unpt. Sign. title: *GENERAL MANAGER*.	FV	FV	6.00

198   100 DOLLARS

	VG	VF	UNC
1.1.1989; 1.1.1990; 1.1.1991; 1.1.1992. Similar to #194. Sign. title: *GENERAL MANAGER*. Back red and black on m/c unpt.	FV	FV	22.50

199   1000 DOLLARS

	VG	VF	UNC
1988-91. Similar to #196. Back orange, brown and olive-brown on m/c unpt.			
a. Sign. title: *EXECUTIVE DIRECTOR*. 1.1.1988.	FV	FV	210.00
b. Sign title: *GENERAL MANAGER*. 1.1.1989; 1.1.1990; 1.1.1991.	FV	FV	190.00

HONG KONG & SHANGHAI BANKING CORPORATION LIMITED

1993; 1995 ISSUE

#201-205 lion's head at l. and as wmk., city view in unpt. at ctr. Latent image of value in box at lower r. New bank bldg. at ctr. between facing lions on back. Printer: TDLR. Notes dated 1.1.1996 and after w/o imprint. Replacement notes: Serial # prefix ZZ.

#200 not assigned.

201   20 DOLLARS

	VG	VF	UNC
1993-99. Gray and brown on m/c unpt.			
a. Sign. title: *EXECUTIVE DIRECTOR*. 1.1.1993; 1.1.1994.	FV	FV	10.00
b. Sign. titles as a. Copyright clause on both sides. 1.1.1995; 1.1.1996.	FV	FV	7.50
c. Sign. title: *GENERAL MANAGER*. 1.1.1997; 1.7.1997.	FV	FV	6.00
d. Sign. title as c. 1.1.1998; 1.1.1999; 1.1.2000; 1.1.2001; 1.1.2002.	FV	FV	6.00

202   50 DOLLARS

	VG	VF	UNC
1993-99. Purple, violet and black on m/c unpt.			
a. Sign. title: *EXECUTIVE DIRECTOR*. 1.1.1993; 1.1.1994.	FV	FV	17.50
b. Sign. title as a. Copyright clause on both sides. 1.1.1995; 1.1.1996.	FV	FV	15.00
c. Sign. title: *GENERAL MANAGER*. 1.1.1997; 1.7.1997.	FV	FV	10.00
d. Sign. title as a. 1.1.1998; 1.1.2000; 1.1.2001.	FV	FV	10.00
e. Sign. title as c. 1.1.2002.	FV	FV	10.00

203   100 DOLLARS

	VG	VF	UNC
1993-99. Red, orange and black on m/c unpt. Ten Thousand Buddha Pagoda at Shatin at r. on back.			
a. Sign. title: *EXECUTIVE DIRECTOR*. 1.1.1993; 1.1.1994; 1.1.1996.	FV	FV	30.00
b. Sign. title: *GENERAL MANAGER*. 1.1.1997; 1.7.1997; 1.1.1998.	FV	FV	25.00
c. Sign. title as a. 1.1.1999; 1.1.2000.	FV	FV	20.00
d. Sign. title as b. 1.1.2001.	FV	FV	20.00
e. Sign. titles as a.	FV	FV	20.00

204 500 DOLLARS

		VG	VF	UNC
1993-99. Brown and red-orange on m/c unpt. Government house at upper r. on back.				
a. Sign. title: *EXECUTIVE DIRECTOR*. 1.1.1993; 1.1.1994.		FV	FV	105.00
b. Sign. title as a. Copyright clause on both sides. 1.1.1995; 1.1.1996.		FV	FV	100.00
c. Sign. title: *GENERAL MANAGER*. 1.1.1997; 1.7.1997.		FV	FV	95.00
d. Sign. title as a. 1.1.1998; 1.1.1999.		FV	FV	95.00
e. Sign. title as c. 1.1.2002.		FV	FV	90.00

205 1000 DOLLARS

		VG	VF	UNC
1993-99. Orange, red-brown and olive-green on pink and m/c unpt. Legislative Council bldg. at r. on back.				
a. Sign. title: *EXECUTIVE DIRECTOR*. 1.1.1993; 1.1.1994.		FV	FV	200.00
b. Sign. title: *GENERAL MANAGER*. 1.1.1997; 1.7.1997.		FV	FV	185.00
c. Sign. titles as a. 1.1.1998; 1.1.1999.		FV	FV	185.00

2000 ISSUE

Wide security thread added.

206 1000 DOLLARS

	VG	VF	UNC
1.9.2000; 1.1.2002. Orange, red-brown and olive-green on pink and m/c unpt. Sign. title: *GENERAL MANAGER*.	FV	FV	185.00

2003 ISSUE

207 20 DOLLARS

	VG	VF	UNC
1.7.2003. Dk. blue on lt. blue and m/c unpt. The Peak Tram on back. Sign. title: *GENERAL MANAGER*.	FV	FV	5.00

208 50 DOLLARS

	VG	VF	UNC
1.7.2003. Green on m/c unpt. Po Lin Temple on back.	FV	FV	15.00

209 100 DOLLARS

	VG	VF	UNC
1.7.2003. Red on m/c unpt. Tsing-Ma Bridge on back.	FV	FV	20.00

210 500 DOLLARS

	VG	VF	UNC
Brown on m/c unpt. 1.7.2003. Hong Kong Airport on back.	FV	FV	90.00

211	1000 DOLLARS	VG	VF	UNC
	1.7.2003. Orange, red-brown and olive-green on m/c unpt. Hong Kong Convention and Exhibition Center on back.	FV	FV	175.00

MERCANTILE BANK LIMITED

行銀利有港香

Hsiang K'ang Yu Li Yin Hang

Formerly The Mercantile Bank of India Limited. In 1959 this bank was absorbed by the Hong Kong & Shanghai Banking Corporation. In July 1984 it was sold to Citibank N.A. which resold the Mercantile's Hong Kong banking license to the Mitsubishi Bank in January 1987.

1964 ISSUE

244	100 DOLLARS	VG	VF	UNC
	1964-73. Red-brown on m/c unpt. Aerial view of coastline. Woman standing w/pennant and shield at ctr. on back. Wmk: Dragon. Printer: TDLR.			
	a. 28.7.1964.	250.00	800.00	2200.00
	b. 5.10.1965.	150.00	450.00	1250.00
	c. 27.7.1968.	160.00	550.00	1500.00
	d. 16.4.1970.	80.00	325.00	1000.00
	e. 1.11.1973.	75.00	300.00	900.00

1974 ISSUE

245	100 DOLLARS	VG	VF	UNC
	4.11.1974. Red, purple and brown on m/c unpt. Woman standing w/pennant and shield at l. Back red on m/c unpt., city view at ctr. Wmk: Dragon. Printer: TDLR.	17.00	50.00	200.00

NOTICE

Readers with unlisted dates, signature varieties, etc. are invited to submit photocopies of their notes to: Standard Catalog of World Paper Money, 700 East State St. Iola, WI 54990-0001, E-Mail: george.cuhaj@fwpubs.com.

STANDARD CHARTERED BANK

Hong Kong Cha Ta Yin Hang

1985-89 ISSUES

#278 -283 bank bldg. at l., bank arms at ctr. on back. Wmk: Helmeted warrior's head.

278	10 DOLLARS	VG	VF	UNC
	1985-91. Dk. green on yellow-green and m/c unpt. Mythological carp at r.			
	a. Sign. titles: *FINANCIAL CONTROLLER* and *AREA GENERAL MANAGER*. 1.1.1985.	FV	FV	10.00
	b. Sign. titles: *AREA FINANCIAL CONTROLLER* and *AREA GENERAL MANAGER*. 1.1.1986; 1.1.1987; 1.1.1988; 1.1.1989.	FV	FV	7.00
	c. Sign. titles: *AREA FINANCIAL CONTROLLER* and *GENERAL MANAGER*. 1.1.1990.	FV	FV	6.00
	d. Sign. titles: *CHIEF FINANCIAL OFFICER* and *GENERAL MANAGER*. 1.1.1991.	FV	FV	6.00

279	20 DOLLARS	VG	VF	UNC
	1985; 1992. Dk. gray, orange and brown on m/c unpt. Mythological tortoise at r.			
	a. Sign. titles: *FINANCIAL CONTROLLER* and *AREA GENERAL MANAGER*. 1.1.1985.	FV	FV	10.00
	b. Sign. titles: *CHIEF FINANCIAL OFFICER* and *AREA GENERAL MANAGER*. 1.1.1992.	FV	FV	7.00

280	50 DOLLARS	VG	VF	UNC
	1985-91. Purple, violet and dk. gray on m/c unpt. Mythological lion at r.			
	a. Sign. titles: *FINANCIAL CONTROLLER* and *AREA GENERAL MANAGER*. 1.1.1985.	FV	FV	35.00
	b. Sign. titles: *AREA FINANCIAL CONTROLLER* and *AREA GENERAL MANAGER*. 1.1.1987; 1.1.1988.	FV	FV	30.00
	c. Sign. titles: *AREA FINANCIAL CONTROLLER* and *GENERAL MANAGER*. 1.1.1990.	FV	FV	25.00
	d. Sign. titles: *CHIEF FINANCIAL OFFICER* and *GENERAL MANAGER*. 1.1.1991.	FV	FV	25.00

285 20 DOLLARS
1993-2002. Dk. gray, orange and brown on m/c unpt. Face like #279.

	VG	VF	UNC
a. Sign. titles: *CHIEF FINANCIAL OFFICER* and *AREA GENERAL MANAGER*. 1.1.1993.	FV	FV	10.00
b. Sign. titles: *HEAD OF FINANCE* and *GENERAL MANAGER*. 1.1.1994; 1.1.1995; 1.1.1996; 1.1.1997; 1.7.1997.	FV	FV	7.50
c. Sign. titles: *HEAD OF FINANCE* and *CHIEF EXECUTIVE*. 1.1.1998; 1.1.1999; 1.1.2000; 1.1.2001.	FV	FV	6.00
d. Sign. titles: *CHIEF FINANCIAL OFFICER* and CHIEF EXECUTIVE & GENERAL MANAGER. 1.1.2002.	FV	FV	5.00

286 50 DOLLARS
1993-2002. Purple, violet and dk. gray on m/c unpt. Face like #280.

	VG	VF	UNC
a. Sign. titles: *CHIEF FINANCIAL OFFICER* and *AREA GENERAL MANAGER*. 1.1.1993.	FV	FV	17.50
b. Sign. titles: *HEAD OF FINANCE* and *GENERAL MANAGER*. 1.1.1994; 1.1.1995; 1.1.1997; 1.7.1997.	FV	FV	15.00
c. Sign. titles: *HEAD OF FINANCE* and *CHIEF EXECUTIVE*. 1.1.1998; 1.1.1999; 1.1.2000; 1.1.2001; 1.1.2002.	FV	FV	15.00

281 100 DOLLARS
1985-92. Red on m/c unpt. Mythological horse (unicorn) at r.

	VG	VF	UNC
a. Sign. titles: *FINANCIAL CONTROLLER* and *AREA GENERAL MANAGER*. 1.1.1985.	FV	FV	45.00
b. Sign. titles: *FINANCIAL CONTROLLER* and *AREA GENERAL MANAGER*. 1.1.1986-1.1.1989.	FV	FV	35.00
c. Sign. titles: *FINANCIAL CONTROLLER* and *AREA GENERAL MANAGER*. 1.1.1990.	FV	FV	30.00
d. Sign. titles: *FINANCIAL CONTROLLER* and *AREA GENERAL MANAGER*. 1.1.1991; 1.1.1992.	FV	FV	27.50

282 500 DOLLARS
1988-92. Maroon, gray and green on m/c unpt. Mythological phoenix at r.

	VG	VF	UNC
a. Sign. titles: *FINANCIAL CONTROLLER* and *AREA GENERAL MANAGER*. 1.1.1988; 1.1.1989; 1.10.1989.	FV	FV	125.00
b. Sign. titles: *FINANCIAL CONTROLLER* and *AREA GENERAL MANAGER*. 1.1.1990.	FV	FV	120.00
c. Sign. titles: *FINANCIAL CONTROLLER* and *AREA GENERAL MANAGER*. 1.1.1991; 1.1.1992.	FV	FV	110.00

283 1000 DOLLARS
1985-92. Yellow-orange on m/c unpt. Mythological dragon at r.

	VG	VF	UNC
a. Sign. titles: *FINANCIAL CONTROLLER* and *AREA GENERAL MANAGER*. 1.1.1985.	FV	FV	225.00
b. Sign. titles: *AREA FINANCIAL CONTROLLER* and *AREA GENERAL MANAGER*. 1.1.1987.	FV	FV	285.00
c. Sign. titles as b. 1.1.1988.	FV	FV	220.00
d. Sign. titles: *FINANCIAL CONTROLLER* and *AREA GENERAL MANAGER*. 1.1.1992.	FV	FV	200.00

287 100 DOLLARS
1993-2002. Red and purple on m/c unpt. Face like #281.

	VG	VF	UNC
a. Sign. titles: *CHIEF FINANCIAL OFFICER* and *AREA GENERAL MANAGER*. 1.1.1993.	FV	FV	30.00
b. Sign. titles: *HEAD OF FINANCE* and *GENERAL MANAGER*. 1.1.1994; 1.1.1995; 1.1.1996; 1.1.1997; 1.7.1997.	FV	FV	25.00
c. Sign. titles: *HEAD OF FINANCE* and *CHIEF EXECUTIVE*. 1.1.1998; 1.1.1999; 1.1.2000; 1.1.2001.	FV	FV	22.50
d. Sign. titles: *CHIEF FINANCIAL OFFICER* and *CHIEF EXECUTIVE & GENERAL MANAGER*. 1.1.2001; 1.1.2002.	FV	FV	20.00

1993 ISSUE

#284-289 Bauhinia flower blossom replaces bank arms at ctr. on back. Wmk: *SCB* above helmeted warrior's head.

284 10 DOLLARS
1993-95. Dk. green on yellow-green unpt. Face like #278.

	VG	VF	UNC
a. Sign. titles: *CHIEF FINANCIAL OFFICER* and *AREA GENERAL MANAGER*. 1.1.1993.	FV	FV	6.00
b. Sign. titles: *HEAD OF FINANCE* and *GENERAL MANAGER*. 1.1.1994; 1.1.1995.	FV	FV	5.00

288 500 DOLLARS
1993-2002. Brown and blue-green on m/c unpt. Face like #282.

	VG	VF	UNC
a. Sign. titles: *CHIEF FINANCIAL OFFICER* and *AREA GENERAL MANAGER*. 1.1.1993.	FV	FV	105.00
b. Sign. titles: *HEAD OF FINANCE* and *GENERAL MANAGER*. 1.1.1994; 1.1.1995; 1.1.1996; 1.1.1997; 1.7.1997; 1.1.1998; 1.1.1999; 1.1.2000.	FV	FV	95.00
c. Sign. titles: *CHIEF FINANCIAL OFFICER* and CHIEF EXECUTIVE & GENERAL MANAGER. 1.1.2001; 1.1.2002.	FV	FV	90.00

289 1000 DOLLARS
1993-2002. Yellow-orange on m/c unpt. Face like #283.

	VG	VF	UNC
a. Sign. titles: *CHIEF FINANCIAL OFFICER* and *AREA GENERAL MANAGER*. 1.1.1993.	FV	FV	200.00
b. Sign. titles: *HEAD OF FINANCE* and *GENERAL MANAGER*. 1.1.1994; 1.1.1995; 1.1.1997; 1.7.1997; 1.1.1998.	FV	FV	185.00

289	1000 DOLLARS		VG	VF	UNC
	c. Sign. titles: *HEAD OF FINANCE* and *CHIEF EXECUTIVE*. 1.1.1999; 1.1.2000.		FV	FV	175.00
	d. Sign. titles: *CHIEF FINANCIAL OFFICER* and *CHIEF EXECUTIVE & GENERAL MANAGER.* 1.1.2001; 1.1.2002.		FV	FV	175.00

2002 ISSUE

290	1000 DOLLARS	VG	VF	UNC
	1.1.2002. Yellow-orange and blue-green on m/c unpt. Like #289 but with enhanced security features. Sign. title: *CHIEF FINANCIAL OFFICER* and CHIEF EXECUTIVE & GENERAL MANAGER.	FV	FV	185.00

2003 ISSUE

291	20 DOLLARS	VG	VF	UNC
	1.7.2003. Dk. Blue on m/c unpt. Victoria Harview view ca. 1850 on back. Sign. titles: *CHIEF FINANCIAL OFFICER* and *DIRECTOR.*	FV	FV	6.00

292	50 DOLLARS	VG	VF	UNC
	1.7.2003. Dk. green and brown on m/c unpt. Victoria Harbor view ca. 1890 on back.	FV	FV	15.00

293	100 DOLLARS	VG	VF	UNC
	1.7.2003. Red and brown on m/c unpt. Victoria Harbor view ca. 1930 on back.	FV	FV	22.50

294	500 DOLLARS	VG	VF	UNC
	1.7.2003. Dk. brown and dk. blue on m/c unpt. Victoria Harbor view ca. 1970 on back.	FV	FV	95.00

295	1000 DOLLARS	VG	VF	UNC
	1.7.2003. Red-brown, orange and olive on m/c unpt. Victoria Harbor view ca. 2003 on back.	FV	FV	185.00

GOVERNMENT OF HONG KONG

香港政府

Hsiang K'ang Cheng Fu

SIGNATURE VARIETIES			
1	J.J. Cowperthwaite, 1961-71	4	Sir Piers Jacobs, 1986-92
2	C.P. Haddon-Cave, 1971-81	5	Sir Hamish Macleod, 1992-95
3	Sir J.H. Bremridge, 1981-86		

1961 ND ISSUE

#325-327 portr. Qn. Elizabeth II at r. Uniface.

325	1 CENT	VG	VF	UNC
	ND (1961-95). Brown on lt. blue unpt.			
	a. Sign. 1. (1961-71).	0.05	0.10	0.25
	b. Sign. 2. (1971-81).	0.05	0.25	0.50
	c. Sign. 3. (1981-86).	0.05	0.75	2.00
	d. Sign. 4. (1986-92).	0.05	0.10	0.25
	e. Sign. 5. (1992-95).	0.05	0.25	0.50

326 5 CENTS
ND (1961-65). Green on lilac unpt.

VG	VF	UNC
0.25	1.75	8.00

327 10 CENTS
ND (1961-65). Red on grayish unpt.

VG	VF	UNC
0.25	1.00	5.00

HONG KONG SPECIAL ADMINISTRATION REGION

BANK OF CHINA (HONG KONG) LIMITED 中國銀行

Chung Kuo Yin Hang

1994 ISSUE

#329-#333 Bank of China Tower at l. Wmk: Chinze. Printer: TDLR (HK) Ltd. (W/o imprint).

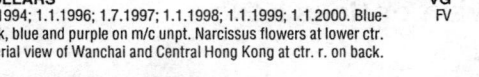

329 20 DOLLARS
1.5.1994; 1.1.1996; 1.7.1997; 1.1.1998; 1.1.1999; 1.1.2000. Blue-black, blue and purple on m/c unpt. Narcissus flowers at lower ctr. r. Aerial view of Wanchai and Central Hong Kong at ctr. r. on back.

VG	VF	UNC
FV	FV	6.00

330 50 DOLLARS
1.5.1994; 1.1.1996; 1.7.1997; 1.1.1998; 1.1.1999; 1.1.2000. Purple and blue on violet and m/c unpt. Chrysanthemum flowers at lower ctr. r. Aerial view of cross-harbor tunnel at ctr. r. on back.

VG	VF	UNC
FV	FV	12.50

331 100 DOLLARS
1.5.1994; 1.1.1996; 1.7.1997; 1.1.1998; 1.1.1999; 1.1.2000. Red-violet, orange and red on m/c unpt. Lotus flowers at lower ctr. r. Aerial view of Tsimshatsui, Kowloon Peninsula at ctr. r. on back.

VG	VF	UNC
FV	FV	22.50

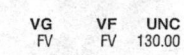

332 500 DOLLARS
1.5.1994; 1.1.1995; 1.1.1996; 1.7.1997; 1.1.1998; 1.1.1999; 1.1.2000. Dk. brown and blue on m/c unpt. Peony flowers at lower ctr. r. Hong Kong Container Terminal in Kwai Chung at ctr. r. on back.

VG	VF	UNC
FV	FV	130.00

333 1000 DOLLARS
1.5.1994; 1.1.1995; 1.1.1996; 1.7.1997; 1.1.1998; 1.1.1999; 1.1.2000. Reddish brown, orange and pale olive-green on m/c unpt. Bauhinia flowers at lower ctr. r. Aerial view overlooking the Central district at ctr. r. on back.

VG	VF	UNC
FV	FV	215.00

NOTICE
Readers with unlisted dates, signature varieties, etc. are invited to submit photocopies of their notes to: Standard Catalog of World Paper Money, 700 East State St. Iola, WI 54990-0001, E-Mail: george.cuhaj@fwpubs.com.

2001 ISSUE

334   1000 DOLLARS

    1.1.2001. Reddish brown, orange and pale olive-green on m/c unpt. Like #333 but enhanced security features.

	VG	VF	UNC
	FV	FV	200.00

2003 ISSUE

335   20 DOLLARS

    1.7.2003. Dk. blue on m/c unpt. The Peak on back. Sign. title: *CHIEF EXECUTIVE*.

	VG	VF	UNC
	FV	FV	6.00

336   50 DOLLARS

    1.7.2003. Dk. green on m/c unpt. Aerial view of Tsimshatsui, Kowloon Peninsula on back.

	VG	VF	UNC
	FV	FV	12.50

337   100 DOLLARS

    1.7.2003. Red on pink and m/c unpt. Tsing-Ma Bridge on back.

	VG	VF	UNC
	FV	FV	22.50

338   500 DOLLARS

    1.7.2003. Dk. brown on m/c unpt. Hong Kong Airport on back.

	VG	VF	UNC
	FV	FV	95.00

339   1000 DOLLARS

    1.7.2003. Reddish-brown, orange and olive-green on m/c unpt. Hong Kong Convention and Exhibition Center on back.

	VG	VF	UNC
	FV	FV	185.00

GOVERNMENT OF HONG KONG

2002 ISSUE

400   10 DOLLARS

    1.7.2002; 1.1.2003. Purple, blue and m/c. Geometric patterns.

	VG	VF	UNC
	FV	FV	3.00

HUNGARY

The Hungarian Republic, located in central Europe, has an area of 35,919 sq. mi. (93,030 sq. km.) and a population of 9.81 million. Capital: Budapest. The economy is based on agriculture and a rapidly expanding industrial sector. Machinery, chemicals, iron and steel, and fruits and vegetables are exported.

The ancient kingdom of Hungary, founded by the Magyars in the 9th century, expanded its greatest power and authority in the mid-14th century. After suffering repeated Turkish invasions, Hungary accepted Habsburg rule to escape Turkish occupation, regaining independence in 1867 with the Emperor of Austria as king of a dual Austro-Hungarian Empire.

Sharing the defeat of the Central Powers in World War I, Hungary lost the greater part of its territory and population and underwent a period of drastic political revision. The short-lived republic of 1918 was followed by a chaotic interval of communist rule during 1919, and the restoration of the kingdom in 1920 with Admiral Horthy as regent of a kingdom without a king. Although a German ally in World War II, Hungary was occupied by German troops who imposed a pro-Nazi dictatorship in 1944. Soviet armies drove out the Germans in 1945 and assisted the communist minority in seizing power. A revised constitution published on Aug. 20, 1949, had established Hungary as a "People's Republic" of the Soviet type, but it is once again a republic as of Oct. 23, 1989. Entered the European Union in 2004.

MONETARY SYSTEM:
1 Forint = 100 Fillér 1946-

PEOPLES REPUBLIC

MAGYAR NEMZETI BANK

HUNGARIAN NATIONAL BANK

1957-83 ISSUE

#168-171 The variety in the serial # occurs in 1975 when the letter and numbers are narrower and larger.
#170, 172 and 173 arms of 3-bar shield w/star in grain spray.

168	10 FORINT	VG	VF	UNC
	1957-75. Green and slate black on orange and lilac unpt. Like #164 but new arms and sign. Value at l., port. Sándar Petöfi at r. Trees and river, *Birth of the Song* by János Jankó at ctr. on back.			
	a. 23.5.1957.	0.30	2.00	10.00
	b. 24.8.1960.	0.25	0.50	9.50
	c. 12.10.1962.	0.10	0.50	5.00
	d. 30.6.1969. Blue-green ctr. on back.	0.10	0.40	5.00
	e. Serial # varieties. 28.10.1975.	0.10	0.25	7.50
	s1. As a, b, c. Specimen w/red ovpt. and perforated: *MINTA*.	—	—	45.00
	s2. As d, e. Specimen.	—	—	27.50

169	20 FORINT	VG	VF	UNC
	1957-80. Blue and green on lt. green and pink unpt. Like #165 but new arms and sign. Value at l., portr. György Dózsa at r. Penthathlete Csaba Hegedüs with hammer and wheat at ctr. on back.			
	a. 23.5.1957.	0.25	3.00	12.50
	b. 24.8.1960.	2.00	7.50	45.00
	c. 12.10.1962.	0.20	1.50	12.50
	d. 3.9.1965.	0.20	1.00	12.50
	e. 30.6.1969.	0.20	0.75	9.00
	f. Serial # varieties. 28.10.1975.	0.15	0.50	12.50
	g. 30.9.1980.	0.15	0.40	12.50
	s1. As a; c; d. Specimen w/red ovpt. and perforated: *MINTA*.	—	—	27.50
	s2. As b. Specimen.	—	—	35.00
	s3. As e; f; g. Specimen.	—	—	25.00

170	50 FORINT	VG	VF	UNC
	1965-89. Brown on blue and orange unpt. Value at l., Like #167 but new arms and sign. portr. Prince Ferencz Rákóczi II at r. Battle of the Hungarian insurrectionists (Kuruc) against pro-Austrian soldiers (Labanc) scene at ctr. on back.			
	a. 3.9.1965.	0.25	1.50	25.00
	b. 30.6.1969.	0.25	1.50	20.00
	c. Serial # varieties. 28.10.1975.	1.00	2.00	12.50
	d. Serial # prefix D. 30.9.1980.	0.20	0.75	12.50
	e. Serial # prefix H. 30.9.1980.	1.00	2.50	15.00
	f. 10.11.1983.	0.10	0.50	9.00
	g. 4.11.1986.	0.10	0.50	27.50
	h. 10.1.1989.	0.10	0.50	17.50
	s1. As a. Specimen. Ovpt *MINTA*.	—	—	50.00
	s2. As b-h. Specimen.	—	—	25.00

171	100 FORINT	VG	VF	UNC
	1957-89. Red-violet on blue and orange unpt. Like #166 but new arms and sign. Value at l., portr. Lajos Kossuth at r. Horse-drawn wagon from *Took Refuge from the Storm* by Károly Lotz at ctr. on back.			
	a. 23.5.1957.	1.00	3.00	15.00
	b. 24.8.1960.	2.00	4.00	15.00
	c. 12.10.1962.	1.00	3.00	12.50
	d. 24.10.1968.		2.00	12.50
	e. 28.10.1975. Serial # varieties.	FV	2.00	10.00
	f. 30.9.1980.	FV	FV	10.00
	g. 30.10.1984.	FV	FV	10.00
	h. 10.1.1989.	FV	FV	9.00
	s1. As a. Specimen w/red ovpt. and perforted: *MINTA*.	—	—	65.00
	s2. As b; c. Specimen.	—	—	
	s3. As d; e. Specimen.	—	—	35.00
	s4. As f; g. Specimen.	—	—	30.00
	s5. As h. Specimen.	—	—	30.00

		VG	VF	UNC
172	**500 FORINT**			
	1969-80. Purple on m/c unpt. Portr. Endre Ady at r. Aerial view of			
	Budapest and Danube river on back.			
	a. 30.6.1969.	FV	FV	12.50
	b. Serial # varieties. 28.10.1975.	FV	FV	12.50
	c. 30.9.1980.	FV	FV	10.00
	s. As a-c. Specimen.	—	—	30.00

		VG	VF	UNC
173	**1000 FORINT**			
	1983. Deep green and olive-green on m/c unpt. Béla Bartók at r.			
	Back green on m/c unpt.; *Anya* sculpture, mother nursing child by			
	F. Medgyessy at ctr.			
	a. Serial # prefix: *A; B.* 25.3.1983.	FV	FV	17.50
	b. Serial # prefix: *B; C; D;.* 10.11.1983.	FV	FV	17.50
	s. As a, b. Specimen w/red ovpt. and perforated: *MINTA.*	—	—	45.00

REPUBLIC

MAGYAR NEMZETI BANK

HUNGARIAN NATIONAL BANK

1990; 1992 ISSUE

#174-177 St. Stephan's Crown over Hungarian Arms replaces 3-bar shield.

#174-177 numerous photocopy counterfeits began appearing in mid-1999.

		VG	VF	UNC
174	**100 FORINT**			
	1992-95. Red-violet on m/c unpt. Like #171 but w/new arms.			
	a. 15.1.1992.	FV	FV	3.00
	b. 16.12.1993.	FV	FV	3.00
	c. 20.12.1995.	FV	FV	12.50
	s1. As a, b. Specimen w/red. ovpt. and perforated *MINTA.*	—	—	25.00
	s2. As c. Specimen.	—	—	65.00

		VG	VF	UNC
175	**500 FORINT**			
	31.7.1990. Purple on m/c unpt. Like #172 but w/new arms.			
	a. Issued note.	FV	FV	10.00
	s. Specimen.	—	—	30.00
176	**1000 FORINT**			
	1992-96. Deep green and olive-green on m/c unpt. Like #173 but			
	w/new arms.			
	a. Serial # prefix: *D.* 30.10.1992.	FV	FV	17.50
	b. Serial # prefix: *D; E.* 16.12.1993.	FV	FV	17.50
	c. Serial # prefix: *E; F.* 15.1.1996.	FV	FV	17.50
	s. Specimen. Serial # prefix: *A-F.*	—	—	30.00

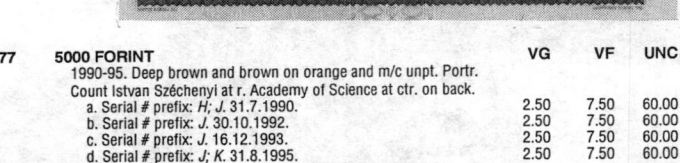

		VG	VF	UNC
177	**5000 FORINT**			
	1990-95. Deep brown and brown on orange and m/c unpt. Portr.			
	Count Istvan Széchenyi at r. Academy of Science at ctr. on back.			
	a. Serial # prefix: *H; J.* 31.7.1990.	2.50	7.50	60.00
	b. Serial # prefix: *J.* 30.10.1992.	2.50	7.50	60.00
	c. Serial # prefix: *J.* 16.12.1993.	2.50	7.50	60.00
	d. Serial # prefix: *J; K.* 31.8.1995.	2.50	7.50	60.00
	s. As a-d. Specimen w/red ovpt. and perforated: *MINTA.*	—	—	50.00

1997-99 ISSUE

#178-183 crowned arms at l. ctr. Latent image in cartouche at upper l.

		VG	VF	UNC
178	**200 FORINT**			
	1998. Dk. green and grayish purple on m/c unpt. Kg. Robert Károly			
	at r. and as wmk. Diósgyóri castle ruins at l. on back. Serial # prefix:			
	FA-FH.			
	a. Issued note.	FV	FV	5.00
	s. Specimen.	—	—	25.00

	182	**5000 FORINT**	**VG**	**VF**	**UNC**
		1999. Dp. violet and purple on m/c unpt. István Széchenyi at r. and as wmk. Széchenyi's home at Nagycenk on back. Serial # prefixes: *BA-BJ*.			
		a. Issued note.	FV	FV	60.00
		s. Specimen.	—	—	75.00

	179	**500 FORINT**	**VG**	**VF**	**UNC**
		1998. Brown-violet and brown on m/c unpt. Ferenc Rákóczi II at r. and as wmk. Sárospatak Castle on back. Serial # prefix *EA-EF*.			
		a. Issued note.	FV	FV	10.00
		s. Specimen.	—	—	30.00

	180	**1000 FORINT**	**VG**	**VF**	**UNC**
		1998; 1999. Blue and blue-green on m/c unpt. Kg. Mátyás at r. and as wmk. Fountain in the palace at Visegrád on back.			
		a. 1998. Serial # prefix: *DA-DJ*.	FV	FV	17.50
		b. 1999. Serial # prefix: *DA-DD*.	FV	FV	17.50
		s. As a, b. Specimen.	—	—	30.00

#181-183 w/hologram.

	183	**10,000 FORINT**	**VG**	**VF**	**UNC**
		1997-1999. Violet, dull purple and blue-black on m/c unpt. unpt. Kg. St. Stephan at r. and as wmk. View of Esztergom at l. ctr. on back.			
		a. Serial # prefixes: *AA-AK*. 1997.	FV	FV	120.00
		b. Serial # prefixes: *AA-AC* w/additional security devices. 1998.	FV	FV	120.00
		c. 1999. Serial # prefix: *AA-AE*.	FV	FV	120.00
		s. As a-c. Specimen.	—	—	120.00

	181	**2000 FORINT**	**VG**	**VF**	**UNC**
		1998. Dk. brown and brown on m/c unpt. Prince Gabor Bethlen at r. and as wmk. Prince G. Bethlen amongst scientists at l. ctr. on back. Serial # prefix: *CA-CG*.			
		a. Issued note.	FV	FV	30.00
		s. Specimen.	—	—	50.00

	184	**20,000 FORINT**	**VG**	**VF**	**UNC**
		1999. Slate gray on red and m/c unpt. Ferenc Deák at r. and as wmk. Plaza on back. Serial # prefix: *GA-GE*.			
		a. Issued note.	FV	FV	200.00
		s. Specimen.	—	—	225.00

2000 COMMEMORATIVE ISSUES

#185, Millennium Celebration

185 1000 FORINT
2000. Blue, light yellow brown on m/c unpt. Similar to #180 but with MNB in seal at upper l. and *MILLENNIUM* at lower l. Serial # prefix: *DA-DE*.

	VG	VF	UNC
a. Issued note.	FV	FV	17.50
s. Specimen.	—	—	30.00

#186, 1000 Years of the Hungarian State

186 2000 FORINT
20.8.2000. Brown on tan and m/c unpt. Crown of St. Stephan at r. St. Stephan as bishop baptizing on back. Serial # prefix: *MM*.

	VG	VF	UNC
a. Issued note.	FV	FV	45.00
s. Specimen.	—	—	50.00

2001-02 ISSUE

#187-192 enhanced security features added.

187 200 FORINT
2001-04. Green and m/c. Like #178.

	VG	VF	UNC
a. 2001. Serial # prefix: *FA-FE*.	FV	FV	5.00
b. 2002. Serial # prefix: *FA-FC*.	FV	FV	5.00
c. 2003. Serial # prefix: *FA-FC*.	FV	FV	9.00
d. 2004. Serial # prefix: *FA-FC*.	FV	FV	9.00
e. 2005. Serial # prefix: *FA-FC*.	FV	FV	9.00
s. Specimen.	—	—	25.00

188 500 FORINT
2001-03. Brown-violet and brown on and m/c unpt. Like #179.

	VG	VF	UNC
a. 2001. Serial # prefix: *EA-EC*.	FV	FV	10.00
b. 2002. Serial # prefix: *EA-EB*.	FV	FV	10.00
c. 2003. Serial # prefix: *EA-EC*.	FV	FV	10.00
d. 2005. Serial # prefix: *EA-EC*.	FV	FV	10.00
s. Specimen.	—	—	30.00

189 1000 FORINT
2002-04. Blue and light yellow brown on m/c unpt. Like #180.

	VG	VF	UNC
a. 2002. Serial # prefix: *DA, DB*.	FV	FV	17.50
b. 2003. Serial # prefix: *DA-DC*.	FV	FV	17.50
c. 2004. Serial # prefix: *DA-DC*.	FV	FV	15.00
s. Specimen.	—	—	30.00

190 2000 FORINT
2002-04. Dk. brown and brown on m/c unpt. Like #181.

	VG	VF	UNC
a. 2002. Serial # prefix: *CA, CB*.	FV	FV	25.00
b. 2003. Serial # prefix: *CA*.	FV	FV	25.00
c. 2004. Serial # prefix: *CA-CC*.	FV	FV	25.00
s. Specimen.	—	—	50.00

191 5000 FORINT
2005.

	VG	VF	UNC
a. 2005. Serial # prefix: *BA-BC*.	FV	FV	60.00
s. Specimen.	—	—	75.00

192 10,000 FORINT
2001, 2003.

	VG	VF	UNC
a. 2001. Serial # prefix: *AA-AC*.	FV	FV	120.00
b. 2003. Serial # prefix: *AA-AC*.	FV	FV	120.00
c. 2005. Serial # prefix: *AA-AC*.	FV	FV	120.00
s. Specimen.	—	—	120.00

193 20,000 FORINT
2004; 2005.

	VG	VF	UNC
a. 2004. Serial # prefix: *GA-GB*.	FV	FV	200.00
b. 2005. Serial # prefix: *GA-GC*.	FV	FV	200.00
s. Specimen.	—	—	225.00

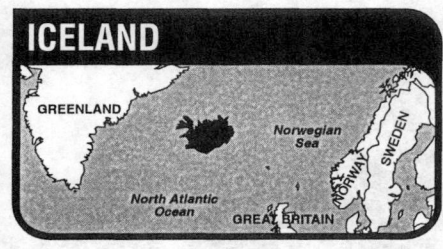

ICELAND

The Republic of Iceland, an island of recent volcanic origin in the North Atlantic east of Greenland and immediately south of the Arctic Circle, has an area of 39,768 sq. mi. (103,000 sq. km.) and a population of 283,000. Capital: Reykjavík. Fishing is the chief industry and accounts for more than 60 percent of the exports.

Iceland was settled by Norwegians in the 9th century and established as an independent republic in 930. The Icelandic assembly called the "Althing," also established in 930, is the oldest parliament in the world. Iceland came under Norwegian sovereignty in 1262, and passed to Denmark when Norway and Denmark were united under the Danish crown in 1384. In 1918, it was established as a virtually independent kingdom in union with Denmark. On June 17, 1944, while Denmark was still under occupation by troops of the Third Reich, Iceland was established by plebiscite as an independent republic.

MONETARY SYSTEM:
1 Krona = 100 Aurar, 1874-

SIGNATURE VARIETIES			
31	V. Thor - J.G. Mariasson, 1961-64	32	J. Nordal - V. Thor, 1961-64
33	J.G. Mariasson - J. Nordal, 1961-67	34	J. Nordal - J.G. Mariasson, 1961-67
35	S. Klemenzson - J.G. Mariasson, 1966-67	36	J. Nordal - S. Klemenzson, 1966-67
37	J. Nordal - D. Olafsson, 1967-86	38	D. Olafsson - J. Nordal, 1967-86
39	S. Klemenzson - D. Olafsson, 1967-71	40	S. Frimannsson - D. Olafsson, 1971-73
41	J. Nordal - S. Frimannsson, 1971-73	42	G. Hjartarson - D. Olafsson, 1974-84
43	J. Nordal - G. Hjartarson, 1974-84	44	G. Hjartarson - T. Arnason, 1984
45	T. Arnason - J. Nordal, 1984-93	46	T. Arnason - D. Olafsson, 1984-93
47	J. Nordal - T. Arnason, 1984-93	48	G. Hallgrimsson - T. Arnason, 1986-90
49	J. Nordal - G. Hallgrimsson, 1986-90	50	B. I. Gunnarsson - T. Arnason, 1991-93
51	J. Nordal - B. I. Gunnarsson, 1991-93	52	J. Sigurthsson - B. I. Gunnarsson, 1994
53	B. I. Gunnarsson - J. Sigurthsson, 1994	54	E. Guthnason - S. Hermannsson, 1994
55	S. Hermannsson - E. Guthnason, 1994	56	E. Guthnason - S. Hermannsson, 1994

REPUBLIC

SEDLABANKI ÍSLANDS
CENTRAL BANK OF ICELAND

LAW OF 29.3.1961

#42-47 printer: BWC (w/o imprint).
#43-47 wmk: S. Bjornsson.

	10 KRÓNUR		VG	VF	UNC
42	L.1961. Brown-violet on green and orange unpt. Jón Eriksson at l., ships in Port of Reykjavík at lower ctr. Back green; ships moored at pier. Sign. 33; 34.		1.50	3.00	6.00

	25 KRÓNUR		VG	VF	UNC
43	L.1961. Purple on m/c unpt. Magnús Stephensen at l. Fjord at ctr. Fishing boats near Westmen Islands on back. Sign. 34.		1.00	2.00	5.00

	100 KRÓNUR		VG	VF	UNC
44	L.1961. Dk. blue-green on m/c unpt. Tryggvi Gunnarsson at l. Sheepherders on horseback, sheep in foreground, Mt. Mekla in background on back. Sign. 31-33; 35; 36; 38-43.				
	a. Issued note.		0.50	1.50	3.25
	s. Specimen.		—	—	—

			VG	VF	UNC
45	**500 KRÓNUR**				
	L.1961. Green on lilac and m/c unpt. Hannes Hafstein at l. Sailors on back. Sign. 36; 38-43.				
	a. Issued note.		1.00	2.50	7.00
	s. Specimen.				

			VG	VF	UNC
49	**50 KRÓNUR**				
	L.1961 (1981). Brown on m/c unpt. Bishop Guthbranthur Thorláksson at l. 2 printers on back. Sign. 37; 38; 42; 43.				
	a. Issued note.		FV	FV	2.00
	s. Specimen.		—		50.00

			VG	VF	UNC
46	**1000 KRÓNUR**				
	L.1961. Blue on m/c unpt. Jón Sigurthsson at r., bldg. at lower ctr. Rock formations on back. Sign. 31-34; 36; 38-43.				
	a. Issued note.		2.50	6.00	15.00
	s. Specimen.				

			VG	VF	UNC
50	**100 KRÓNUR**				
	L.1961 (1981). Dk. green on m/c unpt. Prof. Arni Magnússon at r. Monk w/illuminated manuscript on back. Sign. 37; 38; 42; 43; 45-53.				
	a. Issued note.		FV	FV	4.00
	s. Specimen.		—		60.00

			VG	VF	UNC
47	**5000 KRÓNUR**				
	L.1961. Brown on m/c unpt. Similar to #41. Einer Benediktsson at l., dam at lower ctr. Man overlooking waterfalls on back. Sign. 36; 38-43.				
	a. Issued note.		5.00	15.00	35.50
	s. Specimen.		—	—	

LAW 29 MARCH 1961 (1981-86) ISSUE

#48-52 Printer: BWC (w/o imprint), then later by TDLR (w/o imprint). These made after takeover of BWC by TDLR.

#48-53 wmk: J. Sigurthsson.

			VG	VF	UNC
51	**500 KRÓNUR**				
	L.1961 (1981). Red on m/c unpt. Jón Sigurthsson at l. ctr. Sigurthsson working at his desk on back. Sign. 37; 38; 42; 43; 45; 48-53.				
	a. Issued note.		FV	FV	16.50
	s. Specimen. .		—		65.00

			VG	VF	UNC
48	**10 KRÓNUR**				
	L.1961 (1981). Blue on m/c unpt. Arngrimúr Jónsson at r. Old Icelandic household scene on back. Sign. 37; 38; 42; 43.				
	a. Issued note.		FV	FV	1.00
	s. Specimen.		—		50.00

		VG	VF	UNC
52	**1000 KRÓNUR** L.1961 (1984-91). Purple on m/c unpt. Bishop Byrnijólfur Sveinsson w/book at r. Church at ctr. on back. Sign. 38; 42; 43; 45; 48-51.			
	a. Issued note.	FV	FV	27.50
	s. Specimen.	—	—	70.00

		VG	VF	UNC
56	**1000 KRÓNUR** L.1986 (1994). Sign. 45; 50; 51; 54-56.	FV	FV	20.00

		VG	VF	UNC
53	**5000 KRÓNUR** L.1961 (1986-95). Blue on m/c unpt. Ragnheithur Jónsdóttir at ctr. Bishop G. Thorláksson w/two previous wives at r. Jónsdóttir teaching two girls embroidery on back.			
	a. Sign. 38; 46; 47.	FV	FV	160.00
	b. Sign. 54-56. (1995).	FV	FV	110.00

		VG	VF	UNC
57	**2000 KRÓNUR** L.1986 (1995). Brown and blue-violet on m/c unpt. Painting Inside, Outside at ctr., Johannes S. Kjarval at r. Painting Yearning for Flight (Leda and the Swan) and Woman with Flower on back. Sign. 54-56.	FV	FV	40.00
58	**5000 KRÓNUR** 22.5.2001. Blue on m/c unpt. Similar to #53, enhanced security decives.	FV	FV	85.00

LAW 5 MAI 1986 (1994-) ISSUE

#54-56 like #50-52 but w/new sign. and law date.

LAW 5 MAI 1986 (2001) ISSUE

Design extended to end of paper.

		VG	VF	UNC
59	**500 KRÓNUR** 22.5.2001. M/c.	FV	FV	12.50
60	**1000 KRÓNUR** 22.5.2001. M/c.	FV	FV	20.00

		VG	VF	UNC
54	**100 KRÓNUR** L.1986 (1994). Sign 52; 53.	FV	FV	3.00

		VG	VF	UNC
55	**500 KRÓNUR** L.1986 (1994). Sign. 45; 50-53.	FV	FV	12.50

INDIA

The Republic of India, a subcontinent jutting southward from the mainland of Asia, has an area of 1,266,595 sq. mi. (3,287,590 sq. km.) and a population of 1,006.8 million, second only to that of the Peoples Republic of China. Capital: New Delhi. India's economy is based on agriculture and industrial activity. Engineering goods, cotton apparel and fabrics, handicrafts, tea, iron and steel are exported.

The people of India have had a continuous civilization since about 2500 BC, when an urban culture based on commerce and trade, and to a lesser extent, agriculture, was developed by the inhabitants of the Indus River Valley. The origins of this civilization are uncertain, but it declined about 1500 B.C., when the region was conquered by the Aryans. Over the following 2,000 years, the Aryans developed a Brahmanic civilization and introduced the caste system.

Several successive empires flourished in India over the following centuries, notably those of the Mauryans, Guptas and Mughals. In the 7th and 8th centuries AD, the Arabs expanded into western India, bringing with them the Islamic faith. A Muslim dynasty (the Mughal Empire) controlled virtually the entire subcontinent during the period preceding the arrival of the Europeans; an Indo-Islamic style of art and architecture evolved, of which the Taj Mahal is a splendid example.

The Portuguese were the first to arrive, off Calicut in May 1498. It was not until 1612, after Portuguese and Spanish power began to wane, that the English East India Company established its initial settlement at Surat. By the end of the century, English traders were firmly established in Bombay, Madras and Calcutta, as well as in some parts of the interior, and Britain was implementing a policy to create the civil and military institutions that would insure British dominion over the country. By 1757, following the successful conclusion of a war of colonial rivalry with France, the British were firmly established in India not only as traders, but as conquerors. During the next 60 years, the English East India Company acquired dominion over most of India by bribery and force, and ruled directly or through puppet princelings.

The Indian Mutiny (also called Sepoy Mutiny) of 1857-59, begun by Indian troops in the service of the British East India Company, revealed the intensity of the growing resentment against British domination. The widespread rebellion against British rule was unsuccessful, but resulted in the transfer of government from the company to the British crown.

Following World War I, in which India sent six million troops to fight at the side of the Allies, Indian nationalism intensified under the banner of the Indian National Congress and the leadership of Mohandas Gandhi, who called the non-violent revolt against British authority. The Government of India Act of 1935 proposed a federal status linking the British India provinces with the many princely states; in addition, provincial legislatures were to be created. The federal status was never implemented, but the legislatures were created after the election of 1937, with the National Congress winning majorities in most of the provinces.

When Britain declared war on Germany in Sept., 1939, the viceroy declared India also to be at war with a common enemy. The Congress, however, demanded independence as a condition for cooperation. Britain refused. But as the Japanese advanced into Asia, Britain offered to transfer to Indians power over all but military affairs during the war, and set forth a plan for postwar independence. Congress was willing to accept the wartime transfer of power, but both Congress and the Muslim League rejected Britain's plan for independence; Congress because it did not sufficiently safeguard Indian unity, the Muslims (who wanted a separate Muslim state) because of fears of what would happen to Muslims within a united India.

Early in 1947, Prime Minister Clement Attlee announced that Britain would leave India "by a date not later than June 1948," even though the Hindus and Muslims could not agree among themselves on a plan for self-government. The National Congress, aware that the Muslim League would revolt rather than accept an all-India government, reluctantly agreed to the formation of a separate Muslim state. The Muslim-populated provinces of the northwest frontier, Sindh and West Punjab in the west, and East Bengal in the east were separated from India to form the Muslim state of Pakistan, which became independent on August 14, 1947. India became independent on the following day. Initially, Pakistan consisted of East and West Pakistan, two areas separated by 1,000 miles of Indian territory. East Pakistan seceded from Pakistan on March 26, 1971, and with the support of India established itself as the independent Peoples Republic of Bangladesh.

The Republic of India is a member of the Commonwealth of Nations. The president is the Chief of State. The prime minister is the Head of Government.

MONETARY SYSTEM:
1 Rupee = 100 Naye Paise, 1957-1964
1 Rupee = 100 Paise, 1964-

Note: Staple holes and condition:

Perfect uncirculated notes are rarely encountered without having at least two tiny holes made by staples, stick pins or stitching having been done during age old accounting practices before and after a note is released to circulation. Staples were officially discontinued in 1998.

COLONIAL OFFICES

	Allahabad	**K**	Karachi
B	Bombay	**L**	Lahore
C	Calcutta	**M**	Madras
	Calicut	**R**	Rangoon, refer to Myanmar listings
A	Cawnpore		

DENOMINATION LANGUAGE PANELS

Bengali	Marathi
Burmese	Tamil
Gujarati	Telugu
Gujarati (var.)	Persian (Farsi)
Hindi	Urdu
Kannada	

SIGNATURE VARIETIES
GOVERNORS OF THE RESERVE BANK OF INDIA

No.	Governor	No.	Governor
71	Sir C.D. Deshmukh February 1943-June 1949	72	Sir B. Rama Rue July 1949-1957
73	K. G. Ambegoankar January 1957-February 1957	74	H. V. R. Iengar March 1957-February 1962
75	P. C. Bhattacharyya March 1962-June 1967	76	L. K. Jha MJuly 1967-May 1970
77	B. N. Adarkar May 1970-June1970	78	B. N. Adarkar May 1970-June1970
79	N. C. Sengupta May 1975-August 1975	80	K. R. Puri August 1975-May 1975
81	M. Narasimham May 1977-November 1977	82	I. G. Patel December 1977-September 1982
83	Manmohan Singh September 198 January 1984-February 1985	84	Abhitam Ghosh January 1985-February 1985
85	R. N. Malhotra February 1985-December 1990	86	S. Venkitaramanan November 1997-
87	C. Rangarajan December 1992-97 November 1987-88	88	Bimal Jalan November 1997-

REPUBLIC OF INDIA

RESERVE BANK OF INDIA

FIRST SERIES

#27-47 Asoka column at r. Lg. letters in unpt. beneath serial #. Wmk: Asoka column.

Error singular Hindi = *RUPAYA*   Corrected plural Hindi = *RUPAYE*

VARIETIES: #27-28, 33, 38, 42, 46, 48 and 50 have large headings in Hindi expressing value incorrectly in the singular form Rupaya.

Note: For similar notes but in different colors, please see Haj Pilgrim and Persian Gulf listings at the end of this country listing.

		VG	VF	UNC
27	**2 RUPEES** ND. Red-brown on violet and green unpt. Tiger head at l. on back. Value in English and error Hindi on face and back. Hindi numeral *2* at upper r. 8 value text lines on back. Sign. 72.	1.50	6.00	20.00
28	**2 RUPEES** ND. Similar to #27 but English *2* at upper l. and r. Redesigned panels on face. 7 value text lines on back; third line 18mm long. Sign 72.	0.50	2.00	5.00

		VG	VF	UNC
29	**2 RUPEES** ND. Red-brown on violet and green unpt. Like #28 but value in English and corrected Hindi on both sides. Tiger head at l. looking to l., third value text line on back 24mm long.			
	a. Sign. 72.	1.00	6.00	10.00
	b. Sign. 74.	0.75	2.00	5.00

		VG	VF	UNC
30	**2 RUPEES** ND. Red-brown on green unpt. Face like #29. Tiger head at l. looking to r., w/13 value text lines at ctr. on back. Sign. 75.	0.75	4.00	10.00

		VG	VF	UNC
31	**2 RUPEES** ND. Olive on tan unpt. Like #30. Sign. 75.	0.50	2.50	12.50

		VG	VF	UNC
32	**5 RUPEES** ND. Green on brown unpt. English value only on face, serial # at ctr. *Rs. 5* and antelope on back. Sign. 72 .	1.00	8.00	40.00
33	**5 RUPEES** ND. Like #32 but value in English and error Hindi on face, serial # at r. 8 value lines on back, fourth line 21mm long. Sign. 72.	0.50	2.00	5.00

		VG	VF	UNC
34	**5 RUPEES** ND. Like #33 but Hindi corrected. Fourth value text line on back 26mm long. Sign. 72.	1.00	8.00	50.00
35	**5 RUPEES** ND. Green on brown unpt. Like #34 but redesigned panels at l. and r.			
	a. W/o letter. Sign. 74.	0.75	4.00	15.00
	b. Letter A. Sign. 74.	0.50	3.50	10.00
	c. Letter A. Sign. 75.	0.75	5.00	15.00
	d. Letter B. Sign. 75.	0.75	5.00	15.00

Note: For similar note but in orange, see #R2 (Persian Gulf listings).

		VG	VF	UNC
36	**5 RUPEES** ND (1962-67). Green on brown unpt. Like #35 but sign. title: *GOVERNOR* centered. 13 value text lines on back.			
	a. Letter A. Sign. 75.	0.50	2.00	10.00
	b. Letter B. Sign. 75.	0.50	3.00	15.00

		VG	VF	UNC
37	**10 RUPEES** ND. Purple on m/c unpt. English value only on face. *Rs. 10* at lower ctr., 1 serial #. English in both lower corners, dhow at ctr. on back.			
	a. Sign. 71.	4.00	17.50	100.00
	b. Sign. 72.	3.00	10.00	25.00

		VG	VF	UNC
38	**10 RUPEES** ND. Like #37 but value in English and error Hindi on face and back. 2 serial #. Third value text line on back 24mm long. Sign. 72.	0.75	2.00	5.00
39	**10 RUPEES** ND. Purple on m/c unpt. Like #38 but Hindi corrected. Third value text line on back 29mm long.			
	a. W/o letter. Sign. 72.	1.00	5.00	15.00
	b. W/o letter. Sign. 74.	1.00	5.00	15.00
	c. Letter A. Sign. 74.	0.75	2.00	5.00

Note: For similar note but in red, see #R3 (Persian Gulf listings); in blue, see #R5 (Haj Pilgrim listings).

		VG	VF	UNC
40	**10 RUPEES** ND. Like #39 but title: *GOVERNOR* centered. Green on brown unpt. 13 value text lines on back.			
	a. Letter A. Sign. 75.	0.75	3.00	12.50
	b. Letter B. Sign. 75.	0.75	3.00	5.00

		VG	VF	UNC
41	**100 RUPEES** ND. Blue on m/c unpt. English value only on face. Two elephants at ctr. 8 value text lines below and bank emblem at l. on back.			
	a. Dk. blue. Sign. 72.	25.00	60.00	140.00
	b. Lt. blue. Sign. 72.	25.00	60.00	140.00
42	**100 RUPEES** ND. Purplish-blue on m/c unpt. Like #41 but value in English and error Hindi on face and back. 7 value text lines on back; third 27mm long.			
	a. Black serial #. Sign. 72.	15.00	45.00	120.00
	b. Red serial #. Sign. 72.	15.00	45.00	120.00

		VG	VF	UNC
43	**100 RUPEES** ND. Purplish blue on m/c unpt. Like #42 but Hindi corrected. Third value text line 40mm long.			
	a. W/o letter, thin paper. Sign. 72.	15.00	45.00	120.00
	b. W/o letter, thin paper. Sign. 74.	12.50	40.00	100.00

Note: For similar note but in green, see #R4 (Persian Gulf listings); in red, see #R6 (Haj Pilgrim listings).

		VG	VF	UNC
44	**100 RUPEES** ND. Purple and m/c. Heading in rectangle at top, serial # at upper l. and lower r. Title: *GOVERNOR* at ctr. r. Dam at ctr. w/13 value text lines at l. on back. Sign. 74.	12.50	30.00	60.00
45	**100 RUPEES** ND. Violet and m/c. Like #44 but sign. title: *GOVERNOR* centered. Sign. 75.	12.50	30.00	60.00

46 1000 RUPEES
ND. Brown on green and blue unpt. Value in English and error Hindi on face and back. Tanjore Temple at ctr. w/7 value text lines at l. on back.

	VG	VF	UNC
a. *BOMBAY*. Sign. 72.	100.00	200.00	—
b. *CALCUTTA*. Sign. 72.	100.00	200.00	—
c. *DELHI*. Sign. 72.	300.00	500.00	—
d. *KANPUR*. Sign. 72.	200.00	400.00	—
e. *MADRAS*. Sign. 72.	200.00	400.00	—
s. Like a. Specimen.	—	—	1400.00

47 1000 RUPEES
ND. Brown on green and blue unpt. Like #46 but Hindi corrected. Tanjore Temple at ctr. 13 value text lines on back.

	VG	VF	UNC
a. *BOMBAY*. Sign. 72.	200.00	400.00	—
b. *CALCUTTA*. Sign. 72.	200.00	400.00	—
c. *BOMBAY*. Sign. 74.	400.00	800.00	—
d. *BOMBAY*. Sign. 75.	100.00	200.00	

48 5000 RUPEES
ND. Green, violet and brown. Asoka column at l. Value in English and error Hindi on face and back. Gateway of India on back.

	Good	Fine	XF
a. *BOMBAY*. Sign. 72.			Rare
b. *CALCUTTA*. Sign. 72.			Rare
c. *DELHI*. Sign. 72.			Rare

49 5000 RUPEES
ND. Green, violet and brown. Like #48 but Hindi corrected.

a. *BOMBAY*. Sign. 74.	200.00	375.00	800.00
b. *MADRAS*. Sign. 74.	200.00	375.00	800.00

50 10,000 RUPEES
ND. Blue, violet and brown. Asoka column at ctr. Value in English and error Hindi on face and back.

	VF	XF	UNC
a. *BOMBAY*. Sign. 72.	300.00	700.00	1500.00
b. *CALCUTTA*. Sign. 72.	300.00	700.00	1500.00
s. As B. Specimen. Sign. 72.			3700.00

50A 10,000 RUPEES
ND. Like #50 but Hindi corrected.

a. *BOMBAY*. Sign. 74.	300.00	700.00	1500.00
b. *MADRAS*. Sign. 74.	400.00	800.00	1750.00
c. *NEW DELHI*. Sign. 74.	400.00	800.00	1750.00
d. *BOMBAY*. Sign. 76.	400.00	800.00	1750.00

SECOND SERIES

Most notes of reduced size. Large letters found in unpt. beneath serial #.

#51-65 Asoka column at r.

Urdu Incorrect

Corrected Urdu (actually Farsi)

51 2 RUPEES
ND. Brown and m/c. Numeral *2* at ctr. 7mm high. Incorrect Urdu inscription at bottom l., tiger at ctr. on back.

	VG	VF	UNC
a. Sign. 75 w/title: *GOVERNOR* centered at bottom.	0.25	1.00	5.00
b. Sign. 76 w/title: *GOVERNOR* at ctr. r.	0.25	1.00	5.00

52 2 RUPEES
ND. Deep pink and m/c. Numeral *2* at ctr. 15mm high. Back like #51, tiger at ctr. Sign. 78.

	VG	VF	UNC
	0.20	1.00	4.00

53 2 RUPEES
ND. Deep pink and m/c. English text at l. on face. Like #52 but corrected Urdu at bottom l. on back.

a. W/o letter. Sign. 78.	0.20	1.00	3.00
b. W/o letter. Sign. 80.	0.25	1.00	4.00
c. Letter A. Sign. 80.	0.20	1.00	3.00
d. Letter A. Sign. 82.	0.20	0.75	2.50
e. Letter B. Sign. 82.	0.20	0.75	2.50
f. Letter C. Sign. 82.	0.20	0.75	2.50
g. Letter C. Sign. 83.	0.15	0.75	2.50

53A 2 RUPEES
ND. Deep pink and m/c. English text at r. on face. Otherwise like #53. Smaller size serial #.

	VG	VF	UNC
a. W/o letter. Sign. 83.	0.15	0.50	2.00
b. W/o letter. Sign. 84.	0.75	2.00	6.00
c. Letter A. Sign. 85.	0.15	0.50	2.00
d. Letter B. Sign. 85.	0.15	0.50	2.00
e. Letter B. Sign. 86.	0.15	0.50	2.00

54 5 RUPEES
ND. Green and m/c. Numeral *5* at ctr. 11mm high. Incorrect Urdu inscription at bottom l. antelope at ctr. on back.

	VG	VF	UNC
a. Sign. 75 w/title: *GOVERNOR* centered at bottom.	0.25	2.00	7.00
b. Sign. 76 w/title: *GOVERNOR* at ctr. r.	0.25	2.00	7.00

55 5 RUPEES
ND. Dk. green on m/c unpt. Numeral *5* at ctr. 17mm high. Back like #54, antelope at ctr. Sign. 78.

	VG	VF	UNC
	0.50	2.00	6.00

56 5 RUPEES
ND. Dk. green on m/c unpt. Like #55 but antelope at ctr., corrected Urdu at bottom l. on back.

a. W/o letter. Sign. 78.	0.50	2.00	6.00
b. Letter A. Sign. 78.	0.50	2.00	6.00

#57-58 incorrect Urdu at bottom l. on back.

57	10 RUPEES	VG	VF	UNC
	ND. Purple and m/c. Numeral *10* at ctr. 30mm broad. Dhow at ctr. on back.			
	a. Sign. 75 w/title: *GOVERNOR* centered at bottom.	1.00	2.50	10.00
	b. Sign. 76 w/title: *GOVERNOR* at ctr. r.	1.00	2.50	10.00
58	10 RUPEES			
	ND. Black on brown and pale green unpt. Numeral *10* at ctr. 18mm broad. Heading in English and Hindi on back. Sign. 76.	2.00	6.00	17.50

61	20 RUPEES	VG	VF	UNC
	ND. Orange and m/c. Parliament House at ctr. on back. Sign. 78.			
	a. Dk. colors under sign., error in Kashmiri in fifth line on back.	2.00	6.00	20.00
	b. Lt. colors under sign., error in Kashmiri in fifth line on back.	1.50	4.00	10.00
61A	20 RUPEES			
	ND. Orange and m/c. Like #61b but corrected Kashmiri in fifth line on back.	1.50	4.00	10.00

59	10 RUPEES	VG	VF	UNC
	ND. Dk. brown on m/c unpt. Like #58. Heading only in Hindi on back.			
	a. W/o letter. Sign. 78.	0.75	1.50	4.00
	b. Letter A. Sign. 78.	0.75	1.50	4.00
60	10 RUPEES			
	ND. Dk. brown on m/c unpt. Like #59 but corrected Urdu at bottom l. on back.			
	a. Letter A. Sign. 78.	1.00	2.50	9.00
	b. Letter B. Sign. 78.	1.00	7.50	40.00
	c. Letter B. Sign. 80.	1.00	2.50	9.00
	d. Letter B. Sign. 81.	1.00	10.00	50.00
	e. Letter C. Sign. 81.	0.75	1.50	4.00
	f. Letter C. Sign. 82.	0.75	1.50	4.00
	g. Letter D. Sign. 82.	0.75	1.50	4.00
	h. Letter D. Sign. 83.	0.75	1.50	4.00
	i. Letter E. Sign. 83.	0.75	1.50	4.00
	j. Letter E. Sign. 84.	0.75	1.50	4.00
	k. Letter F. Sign. 85.	0.75	1.50	4.00
	l. Letter G. Sign. 85.	0.75	1.50	4.00

62	100 RUPEES	VG	VF	UNC
	ND. Blue and m/c. Numeral *100* at ctr. 43mm broad. Dam at ctr. w/only English heading on back.			
	a. Sign. 75.	6.00	15.00	50.00
	b. Sign. 76.	6.00	15.00	50.00
63	100 RUPEES			
	ND. Blue and m/c. Numeral *100* at ctr. 28mm broad. Dam at ctr. w/only Hindi heading on back. Sign. 78.	5.00	12.50	35.00

64	100 RUPEES	VG	VF	UNC
	ND. Like #63 but corrected Urdu value line on back.			
	a. W/o letter. Sign. 78.	5.00	12.50	35.00
	b. W/o letter. Sign. 80.	5.00	12.50	35.00
	c. W/o letter. Sign. 81.	5.00	12.50	35.00
	d. Letter A. Sign. 82.	5.00	12.50	35.00

60A	10 RUPEES	VG	VF	UNC
	ND. Dk. brown on m/c unpt. but w/Hindi title above *RESERVE BANK OF INDIA* and Hindi text at l. of *10* and *I PROMISE...* at r. Sanskrit title added under Asoka column at r.			
	a. Sign. 85.	0.50	1.50	4.00
	b. Sign. 86. Lg. serial #.	0.75	1.50	4.00
	c. Sign. 86. Sm. serial #.	0.50	1.50	4.00

Incorrect Kashmiri   Corrected Kashmiri (actually Farsi)

NOTICE
Readers with unlisted dates, signature varieties, etc. are invited to submit photocopies of their notes to: Standard Catalog of World Paper Money, 700 East State St. Iola, WI 54990-0001, E-Mail: george.cuhaj@fwpubs.com.

		VG	VF	UNC
65	1000 RUPEES ND. Brown on m/c unpt. Text in English and Hindi on face. Temple at ctr. on back. *BOMBAY*.			
	a. Sign. 79.	40.00	100.00	200.00
	b. Sign. 80.	40.00	100.00	200.00

GOVERNMENT OF INDIA -
1969 ND COMMEMORATIVE ISSUE

#66, Centennial - Birth of M. K. Gandhi

		VG	VF	UNC
66	1 RUPEE ND (1969-70). Violet and m/c. Coin w/Gandhi and *1869-1948* at r. Reverse of Gandhi coin on back at l. Sign. 82.	0.75	2.00	6.00

RESERVE BANK OF INDIA -
1969 ND COMMEMORATIVE ISSUE

#67-70, Centennial - Birth of M. K. Gandhi

		VG	VF	UNC
67	2 RUPEES ND (1969-70). Red-violet and m/c. Face like #52. Gandhi seated at ctr. on back.			
	a. Sign. 76.	0.50	3.00	8.50
	b. Sign. 77.	0.50	3.00	8.50

		VG	VF	UNC
68	5 RUPEES ND (1969-70). Dk. green on m/c unpt. Face like #55. Back like #67.			
	a. Sign. 76.	0.50	3.00	9.00
	b. Sign. 77.	0.50	4.00	12.50

		VG	VF	UNC
69	10 RUPEES ND (1969-70). Brown and m/c. Face like #59. Back like #68.			
	a. Sign. 76.	0.50	3.50	10.00
	b. Sign. 77.	1.00	4.00	12.50
	s. Specimen.	—	—	—

		VG	VF	UNC
70	100 RUPEES ND (1969-70). Blue and m/c. Face like #63. Back like #68.			
	a. Sign. 76.	5.00	30.00	80.00
	b. Sign. 77.	5.00	30.00	80.00
	s. Specimen.	—	—	—

GOVERNMENT OF INDIA

SIGNATURE VARIETIES	
SECRETARIES, MINISTRY OF FINANCE (1 Rupee notes only)	
K. R. K. Menon, 1944	A. K. Roy, 1957
K. G. Ambegaonkar, 1949-1951	L. K. Jha, 1957-1963
H. M. Patel, 1951-1957	

Note: The sign. H.M. Patel is often misread as "Mehta". There was never any such individual serving as Secretary. Also, do not confuse H.M. Patel with I.G. Patel who served later.

1957; 1963 ISSUE

		VG	VF	UNC
75	1 RUPEE 1957. Violet on m/c unpt. Redesigned coin w/Asoka column at r. Coin dated 1957 and *100 Naye Paise* in Hindi, 7 value text lines on back. Wmk: Asoka column.			
	a. Letter A. Sign. H. M. Patel w/sign. title: *SECRETARY...* (1957).	0.50	3.00	10.00
	b. Letter A. Sign. H. M. Patel w/sign. title: *PRINCIPAL* *SECRETARY...* 1957.	0.25	2.00	8.00
	c. Letter B. Sign. A. K. Roy. 1957.	0.50	4.00	12.50
	d. Letter B. Sign. L. K. Jha. 1957.	0.75	6.00	40.00
	e. Letter C. Sign. L. K. Jha. 1957.	0.25	1.25	5.00
	f. Letter D. Sign. L. K. Jha. 1957.	0.25	1.25	5.00

Note: For similar note but in red, see #R1 (Persian Gulf listings).

76	1 RUPEE	VG	VF	UNC
	1963-65. Violet on m/c unpt. Redesigned note. Coin w/various dates and *1 Rupee* in Hindi, 13 value text lines on back.			
	a. Letter A. Sign. 35. 1963.	0.25	1.25	5.00
	b. Letter B. Sign. 36. 1964.	1.50	10.00	60.00
	c. Letter B. Sign. 36. 1965.	0.25	1.25	5.00

77	1 RUPEE	VG	VF	UNC
	1966-80. Violet on m/c unpt. Redesigned note, serial # at l. Coin w/various dates on back.			
	a. W/o letter. Sign. 36. 1966.	0.20	0.75	3.00
	b. Letter A. Sign. 37. 1967.	0.25	1.25	5.00
	c. Letter A. Sign. 37. 1968.	0.25	1.00	4.00
	d. Letter B. Sign. 38 w/sign. title: *SPECIAL SECRETARY...* 1968.	0.20	0.75	3.00
	e. Letter B. Sign. 38 w/sign. title: *SPECIAL SECRETARY...* 1969.	0.20	0.75	3.00
	f. Letter C. Sign. 38 w/title: *SPECIAL SECRETARY...* 1969.	0.20	0.75	3.00
	g. Letter C. Sign. 38. 1970.	0.20	0.75	3.00
	h. Letter C. Sign. 38. 1971.	0.20	0.75	3.00
	i. Letter D. Sign. 38. 1971.	0.20	0.75	3.00
	j. Letter D. Sign. 38. 1972.	0.20	0.75	3.00
	k. Letter E. Sign. 38. 1972.	0.20	0.75	3.00
	l. Letter E. Sign. 39. 1973.	0.20	0.75	3.00
	m. Letter F. Sign. 39. 1973.	0.20	0.75	3.00
	n. Letter F. Sign. 39. 1974.	0.20	0.75	3.00
	o. Letter G. Sign. 39. 1974.	0.20	0.75	3.00
	p. Letter G. Sign. 39. 1975.	0.20	0.75	3.00
	q. Letter H. Sign. 39. 1975.	0.25	1.00	4.00
	r. Letter H. Sign. 39. 1976.	0.20	0.75	3.00
	s. Letter I. Sign. 39. 1976.	0.25	1.25	5.00
	t. W/o letter. Sm. serial #. Sign. 40. 1976.	0.20	0.75	3.00
	u. Sm. serial #. Sign. 40. 1977.	0.20	0.75	3.00
	v. Letter A. Sign. 40. 1978.	0.20	0.75	3.00
	w. Letter A. Sign. 40. 1979.	0.20	0.75	3.00
	x. Letter A. Sign. 40. 1980.	0.20	0.75	3.00
	y. Letter A. Sign. 41. 1980.	0.20	0.75	3.00
	z. Letter B. Sign. 41. 1980.	0.20	0.75	3.00

78	1 RUPEE	VG	VF	UNC
	1981. Purple and violet on lt. blue, brown and m/c unpt. Coin w/Asoka column at upper r. Offshore oil drilling platform and reverse of coin w/date on back.			
	a. Sign. 41. 1981.	0.10	0.25	1.00
	b. Sign. 42. 1981.	0.10	0.50	2.00

78A	1 RUPEE	VG	VF	UNC
	1983-1994. Similar to #78 but w/new coin design.			
	a. Sign. 43 w/title: *SECRETARY...* 1983-85.	0.10	0.20	1.00
	b. Sign. 44 w/title: *FINANCE SECRETARY...* 1985.	0.10	0.20	1.00
	c. Letter A. Sign. 44. 1986-89.	0.10	0.20	1.00
	d. Letter B. Sign. 45. 1989.	0.10	0.50	2.00
	e. Letter B. Sign. 46. 1990.	0.10	0.50	2.00
	f. Letter B. Sign. 47. 1991.	0.10	0.75	2.50
	g. Letter B. Sign. 48 w/title: *SECRETARY...* 1991.	0.10	0.75	2.50
	h. Letter B. Sign. 48. 1992.	0.10	0.75	2.50
	i. Letter B. Sign. 48 w/title: *FINANCE SECRETARY...* 1993.	0.10	0.75	2.50
	j. Letter B. Sign. 48. 1994.	0.20	1.00	3.00

RESERVE BANK OF INDIA

THIRD SERIES

Lg. letters in unpt. beneath serial #.
#79-88 Asoka column at r. and as wmk.

79	2 RUPEES	VG	VF	UNC
	ND(1976). Orange on m/c unpt. Space craft at ctr. on back.			
	a. Sign. 80.	0.20	0.75	2.00
	b. Sign. 81.	0.20	0.75	2.00
	c. W/o letter. W/o wmk. Sign. 82.	0.25	0.75	2.00
	d. W/o letter. W/wmk: 6 wheels surrounding Asoka column. Sign. 82.	0.15	0.60	2.00
	e. Letter A. Sign. 82.	0.15	0.60	2.00
	f. Letter A. Sign. 83.	0.20	0.75	2.00
	g. Letter A. Sign. 84.	0.20	0.75	2.00
	h. Letter A. Sign. 85.	0.15	0.60	2.00
	i. Letter B. Sign. 85.	0.15	0.60	2.00
	j. W/o letter. Sign. 85 with *Satyameva Jayate* added below the Ashoka Pillar.	0.15	0.60	2.00
	k. Letter A. Sign. 85 with *Satyameva Jayate* added below the Ashoka Pillar.	0.15	0.60	2.00
	l. Letter B. Sign. 86.	0.10	0.50	2.00
	m. Letter B. Sign. 87.	0.10	0.50	2.00

80	5 RUPEES	VG	VF	UNC
	ND(1975). Grayish green on lt. blue and orange unpt. Farmer plowing w/tractor at ctr. on back.			
	a. W/o letter. Sign. 78.	0.50	1.00	2.00
	b. W/o letter. Sign. 80.	0.50	1.00	2.00
	c. Letter A. Sign. 80.	0.50	1.00	2.00
	d. Letter A. Sign. 81.	0.50	1.00	2.00
	e. Letter A. Sign. 82.	0.50	1.00	2.00
	f. Letter B. Sign. 82.	0.50	1.00	2.00
	g. Letter C. Sign. 82.	0.50	1.00	2.00
	h. Letter C. Sign. 83.	0.25	0.75	2.00
	i. Letter D. Sign. 83.	0.25	0.75	2.00
	j. Letter D. Sign. 84.	0.50	1.00	2.00
	k. Letter D. Sign. 85.	0.25	0.75	2.00
	l. Letter E. Sign. 85.	0.25	0.75	2.00
	m. Letter F. Sign. 85.	0.25	0.75	2.00
	n. Letter G. Sign. 85.	0.25	0.75	2.00
	o. W/o letter. New Seal in Hindi & English. Sign. 85.	0.25	0.75	2.00
	p. Letter A. New Seal - do - Sign. 85.	0.25	0.75	2.00
	q. Letter B. Sign. 86.	0.15	0.50	2.00
	r. Letter B. Sign. 87.	0.15	0.50	2.00
	s. W/o letter. Sign. 88.	0.15	0.50	2.00

81	10 RUPEES	VG	VF	UNC
	ND. Brown on m/c unpt. Tree w/peacocks at ctr. on back.			
	a. W/o letter. Sign. 78.	0.50	2.00	7.00
	b. W/o letter. Sign. 80.	0.50	2.00	7.00
	c. W/o letter. Sign. 81.	0.50	2.50	10.00
	d. Letter A. Sign. 82.	0.50	1.50	3.00
	e. W/o letter. Sign. 82.	0.50	1.50	3.00
	f. Letter A. Sign. 83.	0.50	1.50	3.00
	g. Letter B. Sign. 85.	0.50	1.50	3.00
	h. Letter C. Sign. 85.	0.50	1.50	3.00

82	20 RUPEES	VG	VF	UNC
	ND. Red and purple on m/c unpt. Back orange on m/c unpt.; Hindu Wheel of Time at lower ctr.			
	a. Sign. 78.	0.50	3.50	12.50
	b. Sign. 80.	0.50	2.50	5.00
	c. Sign. 81.	0.50	7.50	25.00
	d. W/o letter. Sign. 82.	0.50	3.00	9.00
	e. Letter A. Sign. 82.	0.50	2.50	5.00
	f. Letter A. Sign. 83.	0.50	2.00	6.00
	g. Letter A. Sign. 85.	0.50	2.00	6.00
	h. Letter B. Sign. 85.	0.50	2.00	6.00
	i. Letter B. Sign. 87.	0.50	1.50	4.00
	j. Letter C. Sign. 87.	0.50	1.50	4.00
	k. Letter C. Sign. 88.	0.50	1.50	4.00
	l. Letter C. Sign. 89.	0.50	1.50	4.00

85	100 RUPEES	VG	VF	UNC
	ND(1975). Black and blue-violet on brown and m/c unpt. (tan at ctr.). Dam, agricultural work at ctr. on back. Denomination above bar at lower r. Black sign.			
	a. Sign. 78.	3.00	15.00	100.00
	b. Sign. 80.	2.00	6.00	20.00
	c. Sign. 81.	3.00	12.50	35.00
	d. Sign. 82.	2.00	6.00	15.00

83	50 RUPEES	VG	VF	UNC
	ND(1975). Black and purple on lilac and m/c unpt. Parliament House at ctr. w/o flag at top of flagpole on back.			
	a. Sign. 78.	0.75	5.00	15.00
	b. Sign. 80.	0.75	4.00	12.50
	c. Sign. 81.	0.75	7.50	30.00
	d. Sign. 82.	0.75	3.50	10.00

85A	100 RUPEES	VG	VF	UNC
	ND. Like #85 but w/o bar under denomination at lower r. Sign. 85.	2.00	6.00	15.00

84	50 RUPEES	VG	VF	UNC
	ND(1978). Black and purple on orange, lilac and m/c unpt. Similar to #83 but w/flag at top of flagpole on back.	Reported Not Confirmed		
	a. Sign. 82.	0.75	3.00	9.00
	b. Sign. 83.	0.75	3.00	9.00
	c. Sign. 85.	0.75	2.50	9.00
	d. Letter A. Sign. 85.	0.75	3.00	9.00
	e. Letter B. Sign. 85.	0.75	3.00	9.00
	f. Letter A. Sign. 86.	0.75	2.50	7.00
	g. Letter B. Sign. 86.	0.75	2.50	7.00
	h. Letter A. Sign. 87.	0.75	2.00	5.00
	i. Letter B. Sign. 87.	0.75	2.00	5.00
	j. Letter C. Sign. 87.	0.75	2.00	5.00
	k. W/o letter. Sign. 87.			
	l. Letter B. Sign. 88.	1.00	2.00	5.00

86	100 RUPEES	VG	VF	UNC
	ND(1979). Black, deep red and purple on m/c unpt. (pink at ctr.). Like #85A. Deep red sign.			
	a. Sign. 82.	1.50	5.00	15.00
	b. Sign. 83.	1.50	5.00	15.00
	c. Sign. 85.	1.50	4.00	12.50
	d. Sign. 86.	1.50	4.00	8.50
	e. Letter A. Sign. 86.	1.50	4.00	8.50
	f. W/o letter. Sign. 87.	1.50	4.00	8.50
	g. Letter A. Sign. 87.	1.50	4.00	8.50
	h. Letter B. Sign. 87.	1.50	4.00	8.50

87	500 RUPEES	VG	VF	UNC
	ND (1987). Brown, deep blue-green and deep blue on m/c unpt. M. K. Gandhi at ctr. r. Electronic sorting marks at lower l. Gandhi leading followers across back.			
	a. Sign. 85.	FV	20.00	40.00
	b. Sign. 86.	FV	FV	37.50
	c. Sign. 87.	FV	FV	35.00

1992 ISSUE

88	10 RUPEES	VG	VF	UNC
	ND (1992). Dull brown-violet on orange, green and m/c unpt. Back red-violet; rural temple at l. ctr.			
	a. Sign. 86.	0.50	1.25	3.00
	b. Letter A. Sign. 86.	0.50	1.25	3.00
	c. Letter A. Sign. 87.	0.50	1.25	3.00
	d. Letter B. Sign. 87.	0.50	1.25	3.00
	e. Letter C. Sign. 87.	0.50	1.25	3.00
	f. Letter D. Sign. 87.	0.25	1.25	2.50
	g. Letter E. Sign. 87.	0.25	1.25	2.50

1996-2002 ND ISSUE

#89-93 M. K. Gandhi at r. and as wmk. Reserve Bank seal at lower r. In 1999 the name was spelled out as Mahatma Gandhi.

88A	5 RUPEES	VG	VF	UNC
	ND(2002). Green-orange on m/c unpt. Mahatma Gandhi at r. & as wmk. Farmer plowing w/tractor at ctr. on back.			
	a. W/o letter. Sign. 88.	FV	FV	1.00
	b. Letter L; R. Sign. 88.	FV	FV	1.00
	c. W/o letter. Sign. 89.	FV	FV	1.00
	d. Letter L, R. Sign. 89.	FV	FV	1.00

89	10 RUPEES	VG	VF	UNC
	ND (1996). Pale brown-violet on m/c unpt. Ornamented rhinoceros and elephant heads behind tiger at l. ctr. on back.			
	a. W/o letter. Sign. 87.	FV	FV	1.00
	b. Letter L; M; R. Sign. 87.	FV	FV	1.00
	c. Letter R; N; A; P; Q; S; T; L; B; M. Sign. 88.	FV	FV	1.00
	d. W/o letter. Sign. 89.	FV	FV	1.00
	e. Letter A, R. Sign. 89.	FV	FV	1.00

89A	20 RUPEES	VG	VF	UNC
	ND(2002). Red-orange on m/c unpt. Mahatma Gandhi at r. & as wmk. Coconut trees on back.			
	a. W/o letter. Sign. 88.	FV	FV	2.00
	b. Letter A; R. Sign. 88.	FV	FV	2.00
	c. W/o letter. Sign. 89.	FV	FV	2.00
	d. Letter A; R. Sign. 89.	FV	FV	2.00

90	50 RUPEES	VG	VF	UNC
	ND (1997). Black and purple on m/c unpt. Parliament house at l. ctr. on back.			
	a. W/o letter. Sign. 87.	FV	FV	4.00
	b. W/o letter. Sign. 88.	FV	FV	3.50
	c. Letter A. Sign. 88.	FV	FV	3.50
	d. Letter R. Sign. 88.	FV	FV	3.50
	e. Letter E. Sign. 88.	FV	FV	3.50
	f. Letter E. Sign. 88.	FV	FV	3.50
	g. Letter L. Sign. 88.	FV	FV	3.50
	h. W/o letter. Sign. 89.	FV	FV	3.50
	i. Letter A. Sign. 89.	FV	FV	3.50
	j. Letter E. Sign. 89.	FV	FV	3.50
	k. Lertter R. Sign. 89.	FV	FV	3.50

91	100 RUPEES	VG	VF	UNC
	ND (1996). Black, purple and dk. olive-green on pale blue-green and m/c unpt. Himalaya mountains at l. ctr. on back. Segmented foil over security thread.			
	a. W/o letter. Sign. 87.	FV	2.50	9.00
	b. Letter E. Sign. 87.	FV	2.50	9.00
	c. Letter L. Sign. 87.	FV	2.50	9.00
	d. Letter A. Sign. 87.	FV	FV	7.00
	e. Letter L. Sign. 88.	FV	FV	7.00
	f. Letter E. Sign. 88.	FV	FV	7.00
	g. W/o letter. Sign. 88.	FV	FV	7.00
	h. Letter R. Sign. 88.	FV	FV	7.00
	i. Letter F. Sign. 88.	FV	FV	7.00
	j. Letter B. Sign. 88.	FV	FV	7.00
	k. W/o letter. Sign. 89.	FV	FV	7.00
	l. Letter L. Sign. 89.	FV	FV	7.00
	m. Letter R. Sign. 89.	FV	FV	

92	500 RUPEES	VG	VF	UNC
	ND (1997). Dk. brown, olive-green and purple on m/c unpt. Similar to #87. Segmented foil over security thread.			
	a. W/o letter. Sign. 87.	FV	FV	40.00
	b. W/o letter. Sign. 88.	FV	FV	40.00
	c. Letter A. Sign. 88.	FV	FV	40.00
	d. Letter C. Sign. 88.	FV	FV	40.00

2000-02 ND ISSUE

93	500 RUPEES	VG	VF	UNC
	ND (2000-02). Pale yellow, mauve and brown. Like #92 but different colors. Value at ctr. in optical variable ink.			
	a. W/o letter. Sign. 88.	FV	FV	37.50
	b. Letter A. Sign. 88.	FV	FV	37.50
	c. Letter B. Sign. 88.	FV	FV	37.50
	d. Letter C. Sign. 88.	FV	FV	37.50
	e. W/o letter. Sign. 89.	FV	FV	33.50
	f. Letter A. Sign. 89.	FV	FV	33.50
	g. Letter B. Sign. 89.	FV	FV	33.50
	h. Letter C. Sign. 89.	FV	FV	33.50

94	1000 RUPEES	VG	VF	UNC
	ND (2000). Pink and gray. M. K. Gandhi at r. Back brown, red and black; allegory of Indian economy.			
	a. W/o letter. Sign. 88.	FV	FV	65.00
	b. Letter A. Sign. 88.	FV	FV	65.00
	c. W/o letter. Sign. 89.	FV	FV	65.00
	d. Letter A. Sign. 89.	FV	FV	65.00

PERSIAN GULF

Intended for circulation in areas of Oman, Bahrain, Qatar and Trucial States during 1950's and early 1960's.

"Z" prefix in serial # Known as "Gulf Rupees".

GOVERNMENT OF INDIA

ND ISSUE

R1	1 RUPEE	VG	VF	UNC
	ND. Red. Like #75c. Sign. A. K. Roy; L. K. Jha or H. V. R. Iengar.	25.00	50.00	200.00

RESERVE BANK OF INDIA

ND ISSUE

R2	5 RUPEES	VG	VF	UNC
	ND. Orange. Like #35a. Sign. H. V. R. Iengar.	100.00	200.00	500.00

R3 10 RUPEES
ND. Red. Like #39c. Letter A. Sign. H. V. R. Iengar.

	VG	VF	UNC
	25.00	125.00	350.00

R4 100 RUPEES
ND. Green. Like #43b. Sign. H. V. R. Iengar.

	VG	VF	UNC
	65.00	350.00	1350.00

HAJ PILGRIM
Intended for use by Moslem pilgrims in Mecca, Saudi Arabia.

RESERVE BANK OF INDIA

(ND) ISSUE
#R5 and R6 Asoka column at r. Letters *HA* near serial #, and *HAJ* at l. and r. of bank title at top.

R5 10 RUPEES
ND. Blue. Like #39c. Sign. H. V. R. Iengar.

R6 100 RUPEES
ND. Red. Like #43b. Sign. H. V. R. Iengar.

	VG	VF	UNC
R5	250.00	500.00	1000.00
R6	500.00	1000.00	—

INDONESIA

The Republic of Indonesia, the world's largest archipelago, extends for more than 3,000 miles (4,827 km.) along the equator from the mainland of southeast Asia to Australia. The 13,667 islands comprising the archipelago have a combined area of 735,268 sq. mi. (2,042,005 sq. km.) and a population of 202 million, including East Timor. Capital: Jakarta. Petroleum, timber, rubber and coffee are exported.

Had Columbus succeeded in reaching the fabled Spice Islands, he would have found advanced civilizations a millennium old, and temples still ranked among the finest examples of ancient art. During the opening centuries of the Christian era, the islands were influenced by Hindu priests and traders who spread their culture and religion. Moslem invasions began in the 13th century, fragmenting the island kingdoms into small states which were unable to resist Western colonial infiltration. Portuguese traders established posts in the 16th century, but they were soon outnumbered by the Dutch who arrived in 1602 and gradually asserted control over the islands comprising present-day Indonesia. Dutch dominance, interrupted by British incursions during the Napoleonic Wars, established the Netherlands East Indies as one of the richest colonial possessions in the world.

The Indonesian independence movement, which began between the two world wars, was encouraged by the Japanese during their 3-year occupation during World War II. Indonesia proclaimed its independence on Aug. 17, 1945, three days after the surrender of Japan, and was established on Dec. 28, 1949, after four years of Dutch military efforts to reassert control. West Irian, formerly Netherlands New Guinea, came under the administration of Indonesia on May 1, 1963.

MONETARY SYSTEM:
1 Rupiah = 100 Sen, 1945-

REPUBLIC

REPUBLIK INDONESIA

1961 ISSUE

78 1 RUPIAH
1961. Dk. green on orange unpt. Like #76.

	VG	VF	UNC
	0.10	0.25	0.75

79 2 1/2 RUPIAH
1961. Black, dk. blue and brown on blue-green unpt. Like #77.

	VG	VF	UNC
	0.10	0.25	0.75

1961 BORNEO ISSUE
#79A and 79B portr. Pres. Sukarno at l. Javanese dancer at r. on back.

79A 1 RUPIAH
1961. Green on orange unpt.

	VG	VF	UNC
	1.00	4.00	10.00

79B 2 1/2 RUPIAH
1961. Blue on gray-brown unpt.

	VG	VF	UNC
	1.00	4.00	10.00

1964 ISSUE (1960 DATED)

#80 and 81 portr. Pres. Sukarno at l. Wmk: Arms at ctr.

		VG	VF	UNC
80	**1 RUPIAH**			
	1964. Black, red and brown.			
	a. Imprint: *Pertjetakan Kebajoran* at bottom ctr. on face.	0.25	1.00	3.00
	b. W/o imprint.	0.50	2.00	6.00

		VG	VF	UNC
86	**100 RUPIAH**	Reported Not Confirmed		
	1960. Red-brown. Man and woman dancer on back.			
	a. Printer: Pertjetakan. Wmk: Sukarno.	2.50	10.00	22.50
	b. Wmk: Water buffalo.			

		VG	VF	UNC
81	**2 1/2 RUPIAH**			
	1964. Black, blue and brown.			
	a. Imprint like #80a.	0.75	2.50	7.50
	b. W/o imprint.	0.85	3.00	8.00

#82-88 Pres. Sukarno at l. Javanese dancers on most backs.

		VG	VF	UNC
82	**5 RUPIAH**			
	1960. Lilac. Female dancer at r. on back.			
	a. Wmk: Sukarno.	0.25	1.50	5.00
	b. Wmk: Water buffalo.	0.30	0.60	6.00

BANK INDONESIA

1960 DATED (1964) ISSUE

#82-88 Pres. Sukarno at l. Dancers on back.

		VG	VF	UNC
83	**10 RUPIAH**			
	1960. Green. 2 female dancers. Wmk: Sukarno.	0.50	2.00	6.00

		VG	VF	UNC
87	**500 RUPIAH**			
	1960. Black. Two dancers on back.			
	a. Printer: TDLR. Wmk: Sukarno.	7.50	15.00	75.00
	b. Printer: Pertjetakan. Wmk: Sukarno.	7.50	15.00	75.00
	c. Printer like b. Wmk: Water buffalo.	7.50	15.00	75.00
	d. Printer like b. Wmk: Arms.	10.00	20.00	80.00

		VG	VF	UNC
84	**25 RUPIAH**			
	1960. Green on yellow. Female dancer on back.			
	a. Printer: TDLR. Wmk: Sukarno.	1.00	4.00	10.00
	b. Printer: Pertjetakan. Wmk: Water buffalo.	1.00	4.00	10.00

		VG	VF	UNC
88	**1000 RUPIAH**			
	1960. Dk. green. 2 dancers on back.			
	a. Printer: TDLR. Wmk: Sukarno.	25.00	60.00	150.00
	b. Printer: Pertjetakan. Wmk: Water buffalo.	15.00	40.00	110.00

1963 ISSUE

		VG	VF	UNC
85	**50 RUPIAH**			
	1960. Dk. blue. Female dancer and 2 men on back.			
	a. Printer: TDLR. Wmk: Sukarno.	2.00	8.00	20.00
	b. Printer: Pertjetakan. Wmk: Water buffalo.	1.50	4.50	12.50

89 **10 RUPIAH**
1963. Pale blue and brown on m/c unpt. A Balinese wood carver at l. Balinese houses at ctr., mythical figure at r. on back. Wmk: Water buffalo.

VG	VF	UNC
0.15	0.50	1.50

1964 ISSUE

90 **1 SEN**
1964. Green-blue and brown. Peasant w/straw hat at r.

	VG	VF	UNC
a. Issued note.	—	0.05	0.10
s. Specimen.			15.00

91 **5 SEN**
1964. Lilac-brown. Female volunteer in uniform at r.

	VG	VF	UNC
a. Issued note.	—	0.05	0.10
s. Specimen.		—	15.00

92 **10 SEN**
1964. Dk. blue on yellow-green unpt. Like #91.

	VG	VF	UNC
a. Issued note.	—	0.05	0.10
s. Specimen.		—	15.00

93 **25 SEN**
1964. Red on yellow-green unpt. A volunteer in uniform at r.

	VG	VF	UNC
a. Issued note.	—	0.05	0.15
s. Specimen.		—	15.00

94 **50 SEN**
1964. Purple and red. Like #93.

	VG	VF	UNC
a. Issued note.		0.10	0.25
s. Specimen.		—	15.00

95 **25 RUPIAH**
1964. Green on lt. brown unpt. Batak woman weaver at l., printed arms in brown at r. Batak house at ctr. on back.

VG	VF	UNC
0.20	0.50	2.00

96 **50 RUPIAH**
1964. Black and green on aqua unpt. Timor woman spinner at l., printed arms in pale green at r. Rice barns at ctr. on back.

VG	VF	UNC
0.15	0.50	1.50

97 **100 RUPIAH**
1964. Brown and red on lt. tan unpt. Rubber tapper at l. Kalimantan house at ctr. on back. Wmk: Water buffalo.

	VG	VF	UNC
a. Printer's name: *P. T. Pertjetakan Kebajoran Imp.* 16mm. long at r. on back.	0.50	2.00	6.00
b. Printer's name: *PN Pertjetakan Kebajoran Imp.* 22mm. long at r. on back.	0.25	1.25	4.00

98 **100 RUPIAH**
1964. Blue on lt. tan unpt. Like #97b. Printed arms in brown at l.

VG	VF	UNC
0.50	1.50	5.00

99 **10,000 RUPIAH**
1964. Red and dk. brown on m/c unpt. Two fishermen at l. Floating houses at ctr. on back. Wmk: Water buffalo.

VG	VF	UNC
1.50	4.00	20.00

100 **10,000 RUPIAH**
1964. Green. Like #99.

VG	VF	UNC
0.75	2.00	6.00

105	10 RUPIAH	VG	VF	UNC
	1968. Brown on green and m/c unpt. Oil refinery on back.			
	a. Issued note.	0.25	1.00	3.00
	s. Specimen.	—	—	15.00

101	10,000 RUPIAH	VG	VF	UNC
	1964. Green. Like #100, but wmk. w/printed arms in pale green at r.			
	a. Wmk. in paper at ctr.	1.25	5.00	22.50
	b. Wmk. in paper at l. and r.	1.25	5.00	22.50

1968 ISSUE

#102-112 Gen. Sudirman at l.

#102 and 103 wmk: Arms at ctr.

106	25 RUPIAH	VG	VF	UNC
	1968. Green on lt. brown and m/c unpt. Back brown; Ampera lift bridge over Musi River at ctr. r.			
	a. Issued note.	0.50	1.50	4.50
	s. Specimen.	—	—	15.00

102	1 RUPIAH	VG	VF	UNC
	1968. Lt. red on lt. blue and purple unpt. Arms at r. Woman collecting copra at l. on back.			
	a. Issued note.	0.25	0.75	2.25
	s. Specimen.	—	—	15.00

103	2 1/2 RUPIAH	VG	VF	UNC
	1968. Dk. blue on red and blue unpt. Arms at r. Woman gathering paddy rice stalks at l. on back.			
	a. Issued note.	0.25	0.75	2.25
	s. Specimen.	—	—	15.00

#104-110 wmk: Arms at r. upper ctr.

107	50 RUPIAH	VG	VF	UNC
	1968. Purple and dk. blue on m/c unpt. Airplanes in repair hangar at ctr. r. on back.			
	a. Issued note.	0.75	2.50	7.50
	s. Specimen.	—	—	15.00

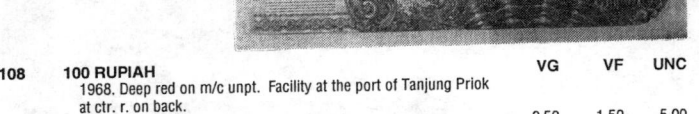

104	5 RUPIAH	VG	VF	UNC
	1968. Pale purple on m/c unpt. Jatiluhur Dam construction on back.			
	a. Issued note.	0.50	1.50	4.50
	s. Specimen.	—	—	15.00

108	100 RUPIAH	VG	VF	UNC
	1968. Deep red on m/c unpt. Facility at the port of Tanjung Priok at ctr. r. on back.			
	a. Issued note.	0.50	1.50	5.00
	s. Specimen.	—	—	15.00

109 **500 RUPIAH**
1968. Black and dk. green on m/c unpt. Yarn spinning in cotton mill on back.

	VG	VF	UNC
a. Issued note.	0.75	2.50	7.50
s. Specimen.	—	—	15.00

110 **1000 RUPIAH**
1968. Orange and black on m/c unpt. P.T. Pusri fertilizer plant at ctr. r. on back.

	VG	VF	UNC
a. Issued note.	1.00	3.00	12.00
s. Specimen.	—	—	15.00

Note: Deceptive forgeries of #110 exist.

#111 and 112 wmk: Prince Diponegoro. Two serial # varieties.

111 **5000 RUPIAH**
1968. Blue-green on m/c unpt. Tonasa cememt plant at ctr. r. on back.

	VG	VF	UNC
a. Issued note.	5.00	22.50	70.00
s. Specimen.	—	—	15.00

112 **10,000 RUPIAH**
1968. Red-brown and dk. brown on m/c unpt. Back purple; tin mininig facility in Bangla at ctr. r.

	VG	VF	UNC
a. Issued note.	5.00	20.00	60.00
s. Specimen.	—	—	15.00

1975; ND ISSUE

#112 A, B, C, 113A, 114A wmk: Prince Diponegoro.

112A **100 RUPIAH**
ND. Red on m/c unpt. Prince Diponegoro at l. Mountain scenery at l. ctr. on back. (Not issued.)

	VG	VF	UNC
a. Normal serial #.	—	—	—
s. Specimen.			

112B **500 RUPIAH**
ND. Green on m/c unpt. Prince Diponegoro at l. Terraced rice fields in Sianok Gorge on back. (Not issued.)

	VG	VF	UNC
a. Normal serial #.	—	—	—
s. Specimen.			

113 **1000 RUPIAH**
ND; 1975. Blue-green and blue on m/c unpt. Prince Diponegoro at l. Farmer plowing in terraced rice fields on back.

	VG	VF	UNC
a. 1975. Wmk: Majapahit statue.	0.50	2.00	7.50
s. ND. Specimen. (Not issued.)	—	—	—

| 115 | **10,000 RUPIAH**
1975. Brown, red and m/c. Stone relief at Borobudur Temple. Large
mask from Bali at l. on back. Wmk: Surkano. | **VG**
7.50 | **VF**
25.00 | **UNC**
75.00 |

1977 ISSUE

| 116 | **100 RUPIAH**
1977. Red on m/c unpt. Java Rhinoceros at l. Java Rhinoceros in
jungle scene at ctr. on back. Wmk: Arms. | **VG**
0.25 | **VF**
0.50 | **UNC**
2.00 |

| 113A | **5000 RUPIAH**
ND. Brown on m/c unpt. Prince Diponegoro at r. Three sailing ships
on back. (Not issued.)
 a. Normal serial #.
 s. Specimen. | **VG**
—
— | **VF**
—
— | **UNC**
—
— |

| 114 | **5000 RUPIAH**
1975. Brown and red-brown on m/c unpt. Fisherman w/net at r.
Back like #113A. Wmk: Tjut Njak Din. | **VG**
2.50 | **VF**
7.50 | **UNC**
25.00 |

| 117 | **500 RUPIAH**
1977. Green on pink and m/c unpt. Woman w/orchids at l. Bank of
Indonesia at ctr. on back and as wmk. | **VG**
0.25 | **VF**
1.00 | **UNC**
4.00 |

1979 ISSUE

| 114A | **10,000 RUPIAH**
ND. Green and red on m/c unpt. Face like #113A. Peasants at ctr.
on back. (Not issued.)
 a. Normal serial #.
 s. Specimen. | **VG**
—
— | **VF**
—
— | **UNC**
—
— |

| 118 | **10,000 RUPIAH**
1979. Purple on m/c unpt. Javanese Gamelan Orchestra at ctr.
Prambanan Temple on back. Wmk: Dr. Soetomo. | **VG**
3.00 | **VF**
9.00 | **UNC**
25.00 |

1980 ISSUE

119	1000 RUPIAH	VG	VF	UNC
	1980. Blue on m/c unpt. Dr. Soetomo at ctr. r. Mountain scene in Sianok Valley on back. Wmk: Sultan Hasanudin.	0.25	1.00	3.50

123	500 RUPIAH	VG	VF	UNC
	1988. Brown and dk. green on m/c unpt. Rusa Deer at l. Bank of Indonesia Cirebon branch at r. on back. Wmk: Gen. A. Yani.			
	a. Issued note.	0.20	0.50	1.50
	s. Specimen.	—	—	15.00

120	5000 RUPIAH	VG	VF	UNC
	1980. Brown on m/c unpt. Diamond cutter at ctr. Back brown, green and m/c. 3 Torajan houses from Celebes at ctr.			
	a. Wmk: D. Sartika.	2.00	6.00	20.00
	p. Proof. Wmk: Prince Diponegoro.			

1982 ISSUE

121	500 RUPIAH	VG	VF	UNC
	1982. Dk. green on m/c unpt. Man standing by Amorphophallus Titanum giant flower at l. Bank of Indonesia on back. Wmk: Gen. A. Yani.	0.25	0.75	2.50

1984-88 ISSUE

122	100 RUPIAH	VG	VF	UNC
	1984. Red on m/c unpt. Victoria crowned pigeon at l. Asahan Dam on back. Wmk: Arms.			
	a. Engraved.	0.10	0.30	1.25
	b. Litho.	0.05	0.25	0.75
	s. As a. Specimen.	—	—	15.00

124	1000 RUPIAH	VG	VF	UNC
	1987. Blue-black on m/c unpt. Raja Sisingamangaraja XII at ctr., arms at l. Yogyakarta Court at ctr. on back. Wmk: Sultan Hasanudin.			
	a. Issued note.	0.25	1.00	2.00
	s. Specimen.	—	—	15.00

125	5000 RUPIAH	VG	VF	UNC
	1986. Dk. brown on m/c unpt. Teuku Umar at ctr. Minaret of Kudus mosque at r. on back. Wmk: C. Martha Tijahahu.			
	a. Issued note.	1.50	3.50	10.00
	s. Specimen.	—	—	15.00

NOTICE

Readers with unlisted dates, signature varieties, etc. are invited to submit photocopies of their notes to: Standard Catalog of World Paper Money, 700 East State St. Iola, WI 54990-0001, E-Mail: george.cuhaj@fwpubs.com.

126	**10,000 RUPIAH**	VG	VF	UNC
	1985. Purple on m/c unpt. R. A. Kartini at l. Prambanan Temple at ctr. Female graduate at ctr. r. on back. Wmk: Dr. T. Mangoenkoesoemo.			
	a. Issued note.	2.00	6.00	15.00
	s. Specimen.	—	—	15.00

1992 ISSUE

#127-132 arms at upper r. area. Printer: Perum Percetakan Uang.

#127-129 second date appears after imprint.

127	**100 RUPIAH**	VG	VF	UNC
	1992-2000. Pale red on orange and m/c unpt. Sailboat *Pinisi* at l. Volcano *Anak Krakatau* at r. on back. Wmk: Ki Hajar Dewantara.			
	a. 1992.	FV	FV	0.75
	b. 1992/1993.	FV	FV	0.50
	c. 1992/1994.	FV	FV	0.50
	d. 1992/1995.	FV	FV	0.45
	e. 1992/1996.	FV	FV	0.25
	f. 1992/1997.	FV	FV	0.25
	g. 1992/1999.	FV	FV	0.25
	h. 1992/2000.	FV	FV	0.20

128	**500 RUPIAH**	VG	VF	UNC
	1992-99. Brown and green on m/c unpt. Orangutan resting on limb at l. Native huts at E. Kalimantan at r. on back. Wmk: H. O. S. Cokroaminoto.			
	a. 1992.	FV	FV	1.25
	b. 1992/1993.	FV	FV	1.00
	c. 1992/1994.	FV	FV	1.00
	d. 1992/1995.	FV	FV	1.00
	e. 1992/1996.	FV	FV	0.50
	f. 1992/1997.	FV	FV	0.40
	g. 1992/1998.	FV	FV	0.30
	h. 1992/1999.	FV	FV	0.20

129	**1000 RUPIAH**	VG	VF	UNC
	1992-2000. Deep blue on lt. blue and m/c unpt. Aerial view of Lake Toba at l. ctr. Stone jumping attraction on Nias Island at ctr. on back. Wmk: Cut Nyak Meutia.			

129	**1000 RUPIAH**	VG	VF	UNC
	a. 1992.	FV	FV	2.00
	b. 1992/1993.	FV	FV	1.75
	c. 1992/1994.	FV	FV	1.75
	d. 1992/1995.	FV	FV	1.50
	e. 1992/1996.	FV	FV	1.00
	f. 1992/1997.	FV	FV	0.75
	g. 1992/1998.	FV	FV	0.75
	h. 1992/1999.	FV	FV	0.50
	i. 1992/2000.	FV	FV	0.50

130	**5000 RUPIAH**	VG	VF	UNC
	1992-2001. Black, brown and dk. brown on m/c unpt. Sasando musical instrument and Rote Island tapestry at ctr. Volcano w/3-color Lake Kelimutu at ctr. on back. Wmk: Tjut Njak Din.			
	a. 1992.	FV	FV	7.50
	b. 1992/1993.	FV	FV	7.00
	c. 1992/1994.	FV	FV	7.00
	d. 1992/1995.	FV	FV	6.50
	e. 1992/1996.	FV	FV	3.50
	f. 1992/1997.	FV	FV	2.50
	g. 1992/1998.	FV	FV	1.50
	h. 1992/1999.	FV	FV	1.25
	i. 1992/2000.	FV	FV	1.25
	j. 1999/2001.	FV	FV	1.25
	s. Specimen.	—	—	—

131	**10,000 RUPIAH**	VG	VF	UNC
	1992-98. Purple and red on m/c unpt. Sri Sultan Hamengku Buwono IX at l., girl scouts at ctr. r. Borobudur Temple on hillside on back. Wmk: W. R. Soepratman.			
	a. 1992.	2.00	6.00	12.50
	b. 1992/1993.	2.00	6.00	12.00
	c. 1992/1994.	2.00	5.00	12.00
	d. 1992/1995.	2.00	5.00	10.00
	e. 1992/1996.	1.50	3.00	6.00
	f. 1992/1997.	1.00	2.00	4.00
	g. 1992/1998 & letter prefix.	2.00	7.50	15.00
	s. Specimen.	—	—	—

132 20,000 RUPIAH
1992-95. Black, dk. grayish green and red on m/c unpt. Red bird of paradise at ctr. Cloves flower at ctr., map of Indonesian Archipelago at r. on back. Wmk: K. H. Dewantara.

	VG	VF	UNC
a. 1992.	3.00	10.00	22.50
b. 1992/1993.	3.00	10.00	20.00
c. 1992/1994.	—	8.00	17.50
d. 1992/1995.	4.00	12.50	25.00
s. Specimen.			

1993 COMMEMORATIVE ISSUES

#133 and 134, 25 Years of Development

133 50,000 RUPIAH
1993-94. Greenish blue, tan and gray on m/c unpt. Pres. Soeharto at l. ctr., surrounded by various scenes of development activities. Anti-counterfeiting design at r. Jet plane over Soekarno-Hatta International Airport at ctr. on back. Wmk: W. R. Soep

	VG	VF	UNC
a. 1993.	8.00	20.00	40.00
b. 1993/1994.	8.00	17.50	35.00

134 50,000 RUPIAH
1993. Design like #133, but pale gray. Plastic. Pres. Soeharto in OVD at r.

	VG	VF	UNC
a. Note alone.	8.00	20.00	40.00
b. Included in souvenir folder.	—	—	50.00

1995 ISSUE

135 20,000 RUPIAH
1995-98. Black, dark grayish green and red on m/c unpt. Like #132 but w/new engraved date, new sign. and segmented foil over security thread.

	VG	VF	UNC
a. 1995.	FV	5.00	15.00
b. 1995/1996.	FV	4.00	9.00
c. 1995/1997.	FV	3.00	5.00
d. 1995/1998.	FV	3.00	5.00

136 50,000 RUPIAH
1995-98. Greenish blue, tan tan and gray on m/c unpt. Like #133 but w/new engraved date, new sign. and segmented foil over security thread.

	VG	VF	UNC
a. 1995.	FV	7.00	42.50
b. 1995/1996.	FV	5.00	25.00
c. 1995/1997.	FV	5.00	15.00
d. 1995/1998.	FV	5.00	15.00

1998-99 ISSUE

#137 and 138 printer: Perum Peruri.

137 10,000 RUPIAH
1998-. Deep brownish purple and black on m/c unpt. Tjut Njak Dhien at r., arms at upper r., bank monogram at lower r. Segara Anak Volcanic Lake at ctr. r. on back. Wmk.: W. R. Soepratman.

	VG	VF	UNC
a. 1998.	FV	FV	3.25
b. 1998/1999.	FV	FV	3.25
c. 1998/2000.	FV	FV	3.25
d. 1998/2001.	FV	FV	3.25
e. 1998/2002.	FV	FV	3.25
f. 1998/2003.	FV	FV	3.25
g. 1998/2004.	FV	FV	3.25

138 20,000 RUPIAH
1998-. Deep green and dk. brown on m/c unpt. Ki Hadjar Dewantara at ctr. and as wmk., arms at upper l., Ganesha at l., bank monogram at r. Classroom at ctr. r. on back.

	VG	VF	UNC
a. 1998.	FV	FV	6.00
b. 1998/1999.	FV	FV	5.00
c. 1998/2000.	FV	FV	5.00
d. 1998/2001.	FV	FV	5.00
e. 1998/2002.	FV	FV	5.00
f. 1998/2003.	FV	FV	5.00
g. 1998/2004.	FV	FV	5.00

139 50,000 RUPIAH
1999-. Grayish brown on m/c unpt. W. R. Soepratman at ctr. Military personnel hoisting flag on Independence Day on back.

	VG	VF	UNC
a. 1999.	FV	FV	22.50
b. 1999/2000.	FV	FV	20.00
c. 1999/2001.	FV	FV	20.00
d. 1999/2002.	FV	FV	20.00
e. 1999/2003.	FV	FV	20.00
f. 1999/2004.	FV	FV	20.00

140   100,000 RUPIAH

	VG	VF	UNC
1999. Lilac brown, green and orange. Soekarno and Hatta at ctr. Parliament bldg. on back. Polymer plastic.	FV	FV	30.00

2000 ISSUE

141   1000 RUPIAH

	VG	VF	UNC
2000-. Purple on red, blue and m/c unpt. Kapitan Pattimura at ctr. Fishing boat and volcano on back.			
a. 2000.	FV	FV	0.50
b. 2000/2001.	FV	FV	0.50
c. 2000/2002.	FV	FV	0.50
d. 2000/2003.	FV	FV	0.50
e. 2000/2004.	FV	FV	0.50

2001 ISSUE

142   5000 RUPIAH

	VG	VF	UNC
2001-. Brown and green on m/c unpt. Tuanku Imam Bondjol at ctr. Purple and green on m/c unpt.; female at hand loom at ctr.			
a. 2001.	FV	FV	2.50
b. 2001/2002.	FV	FV	2.50
c. 2001/2003.	FV	FV	2.50
d. 2001/2004.	FV	FV	2.50

143   20,000 RUPIAH

	Good	Fine	XF
2004. Blue on m/c unpt. Otto Iskandar Dinata at ctr.			Expected New Issue

144   100,000 RUPIAH

	VG	VF	UNC
2004. Red-brown on m/c unpt. Similar to #140 but paper.	FV	FV	30.00

REGIONAL - IRIAN BARAT

REPUBLIK INDONESIA

1963 ND PROVISIONAL ISSUE

#R1 and R2 Pres. Sukarno at l. w/ovpt: *IRIAN BARAT* at lower r. on Republik Indonesia issue.

R1   1 RUPIAH

	VG	VF	UNC
ND (1963 - old date 1961). Orange.	4.00	10.00	30.00

R2   2 1/2 RUPIAH

	VG	VF	UNC
ND (1963 - old date 1961). Violet.	5.00	12.00	35.00

BANK INDONESIA

1963 ND PROVISIONAL ISSUE

#R3-R5 Pres. Sukarno at l. w/ovpt: *IRIAN BARAT* on Bank Indonesia issue.

R3   5 RUPIAH

	VG	VF	UNC
ND (1963 - old date 1960). Gray-olive.	7.50	20.00	60.00

R4   10 RUPIAH
ND (1963 - old date 1960). Red.

	VG	VF	UNC
	6.00	17.50	50.00

R5   100 RUPIAH
ND (1963 - old date 1960). Green.

	VG	VF	UNC
	20.00	45.00	110.00

REGIONAL - RIAU

REPUBLIK INDONESIA

1963 ND PROVISIONAL ISSUE

#R6 and R7 Pres. Sukarno at l. w/ovpt: *RIAU* at lower r. on Republik Indonesia issue.

R6   1 RUPIAH
ND (1963 - old date 1961). Orange.

	VG	VF	UNC
	7.50	20.00	50.00

R7   2 1/2 RUPIAH
ND (1963 - old date 1961). Blue.
Note: Contemporary counterfeits on fragile paper w/artificial blue fibers exist.

	VG	VF	UNC
	7.50	20.00	60.00

BANK INDONESIA

1963 ND PROVISIONAL ISSUE

#R8-R10 Pres. Sukarno at l. w/ovpt: *RIAU* on Bank Indonesia issue.

R8   5 RUPIAH
ND (1963 - old date 1960). Violet. Ovpt. on #82b, w/prefix *X* in serial #.
Note: Modern counterfeits on #82a but w/o prefix X on serial # exist.

	VG	VF	UNC
	7.50	22.50	55.00

R9   10 RUPIAH
ND (1963 - old date 1960). Red.

	VG	VF	UNC
	6.00	17.50	45.00

R10   100 RUPIAH
ND (1963 - old date 1960). Green.

	VG	VF	UNC
	25.00	100.00	400.00

IRAN

The Islamic Republic of Iran, located between the Caspian Sea and the Persian Gulf in southwestern Asia, has an area of 636,296 sq. mi. (1,648,000 sq. km.) and a population of 76.43 million. Capital: Tehran. Although predominantly an agricultural state, Iran depends heavily on oil for foreign exchange. Crude oil, carpets and agricultural products are exported.

Iran (historically known as Persia) is one of the world's most ancient and resilient nations. Strategically astride the lower land gate to Asia, it has been conqueror and conquered, sovereign nation and vassal state, ever emerging from its periods of glory or travail with its culture and political individuality intact. Iran (Persia) was a powerful empire under Cyrus the Great (600-529 B.C.), its borders extending from the Indus to the Nile. It has also been conquered by the predatory empires of antique and recent times - Assyrian, Medean, Macedonian, Seljuq, Turk, Mongol - and more recently been coveted by Russia, Germany and Great Britain. Revolts against the absolute power of the Shahs resulted in the establishment of a constitutional monarchy in 1906. In 1931 the Kingdom of Persia became known as the Kingdom of Iran. In 1979, the Pahlavi monarchy was toppled and an Islamic Republic proclaimed.

RULERS:
Mohammad Reza Pahlavi, SH1320-58/1941-79AD

PRESIDENTS:
Islamic Republic of Iran
Abolhassan Bani Sadr, SH1358-60 (AD1979-Jun 81)
Mohammad Ali Rajai, SH1360 (AD-1981 Jun-Oct)
Hojjatoleslam Ali Khamene'i, SH1360-(AD1981-)

MONETARY SYSTEM:
1 Rial 100 Dinars = 20 Shahis
1 Toman = 10 Rials SH1310- (1932-)

SIGNATURE AND TITLE VARIETIES		
Kingdom: Mohammad Reza Pahlavi		
	GENERAL DIRECTOR	MINISTER OF FINANCE
7	Ebrahim Kashani	Abholbagi Shoaii
8	Dr. Ali Asghar Pouhomayoun	Abdul Hossein Behnia
9	Mehdi Samii	Abdul Hossein Behnia
10	Mehdi Samii	Amir Abbas Hoveyda
11	Mehdi Samii	Dr. Jamshid Amouzegar
12	Khodadad Famanfarmaian	Dr. Jamshid Amouzegar
13	Abdul Ali Jahanshahi	Dr. Jamshid Amouzegar
14	Mohammad Yeganeh	Dr. Jamshid Amouzegar
	GENERAL DIRECTOR	MINISTER OF ECONOMIC AND FINANCIAL AFFAIR
15	Mohammad Yeganeh	Hushang Ansary

SIGNATURE AND TITLE VARIETIES		
Kingdom: Mohammad Reza Pahlavi		
	GENERAL DIRECTOR	MINISTER OF FINANCE
16	Hassan Ali Mehran	Hushang Ansary
17	Hassan Ali Mehran	Mohammad Yeganeh

Note: Some signers used more than one signature (Jamshid Amouzegar), some held more than one term of office (Mehdi Samii) and others held the office of both General Director and Minister of Finance (Mohammad Yeganeh) at different times.

Shah Mohammad Reza Pahlavi, SH1323-58/1944-79 AD

Type V. Imperial Iranian Army (IIA) uniform. Full face. SH1337-40.

Type VI. Imperial Iranian Air Force (IIAF) uniform. Three quarter face. SH1341-44.

Type VII. Imperial Iranian Army (IIA) uniform. Full face. SH1347-48.

Type VIII. Commander in Chief of Iran's Armed Forces. Three quarter face. Large portrait. MS2535 to SH1358.

Type IX. Shah Pahlavi in CinC uniform and his father Shah Reza in Imperial Iranian Army (IIA) uniform. MS2535.

KINGDOM OF IRAN

BANK MARKAZI IRAN

1961; 1962 ISSUE

#71 and 72 Type V portr. of Shah Pahlavi in army uniform at r. Wmk: Young Shah Pahlavi. Yellow security security thread runs vertically. Sign. 7. Printer: Harrison (w/o imprint).

#73-75 Type VI portr. of Shah Pahlavi in air force uniform. Wmk: Young Shah Pahlavi. Yellow security thread runs vertically. Sign. 8. Printer: Harrison (w/o imprint).

		VG	VF	UNC
71	10 RIALS	2.00	4.00	10.00
	SH1340 (1961). Blue on green and orange unpt. Geometric design at ctr. Amir Kabir Dam near Karaj on back.			

72	20 RIALS	VG	VF	UNC

SH1340 (1961). Dk. brown on green and pink unpt. Geometric
design at ctr. Statue of Shah and Ramsar Hotel on back.   2.00   6.00   14.00

73	50 RIALS	VG	VF	UNC

SH1341 (1962). Green on orange and blue unpt. Shah Pahlavi at r.
Koohrang Dam and tunnel on back.
   a. Sm. date 2.5mm high.   2.00   6.00   14.00
   b. Lg. date 4.0mm high.   3.00   8.00   16.00

74	500 RIALS	VG	VF	UNC

SH1341 (1962). Black on pink and m/c unpt. Shah Pahlavi at ctr.   40.00   100.00   250.00
Winged horses on back.

75	1000 RIALS	VG	VF	UNC

SH1341 (1962). Brown on red and blue unpt. Shah Pahlavi at ctr.   40.00   125.00   350.00
Tomb of Hafez in Shiraz on back.

1963; 1964 ISSUE

#76 and 77 Type VI portr. of Shah Pahlavi in armed forces uniform at r. Wmk: Young Shah Pahlavi. Yellow
security thread. Printer: Harrison (w/o imprint).

76	50 RIALS	VG	VF	UNC

SH1343 (1964). Dk. green on orange and blue unpt. Like #73.   3.00   10.00   20.00
Ornate design at ctr. Koohrang Dam and tunnel on back. Sign. 9.

77	100 RIALS	VG	VF	UNC

SH1342 (1963). Maroon on lt. green and m/c unpt. Ornate design   3.00   10.00   20.00
at ctr. Oil refinery at Abadan on back. Sign. 9.

1965 ND ISSUE

#78-83 Type VI portr. of Shah Pahlavi in armed forces uniform at r. Wmk: Young Shah Pahlavi. Yellow
security thread. Printer: Harrison (w/o imprint).

78	20 RIALS	VG	VF	UNC

ND (1965). Dk. brown on pink and green unpt. Ornate design at ctr.
Oriental hunters on horseback on back.
   a. Sign. 9.   1.00   3.00   7.00
   b. Sign. 10.   1.00   3.00   7.00

79   50 RIALS
ND (1965). Dk. green on orange and blue unpt. Like #73. Ornate design at ctr. Koohrang Dam and tunnel on back.

	VG	VF	UNC
a. Sign. 9.	3.00	8.00	20.00
b. Sign. 10.	3.00	8.00	20.00

80   100 RIALS
ND (1965). Maroon on olive-green and m/c unpt. Like #77. Ornate design at ctr. Oil refinery at Abadan on back. Sign. 10.

VG	VF	UNC
3.00	8.00	20.00

81   200 RIALS
ND (1965). Dk. blue on orange and lavender unpt. M/c ornate design at ctr. Railroad bridge on back. Sign. 9.

VG	VF	UNC
6.00	20.00	50.00

82   500 RIALS
ND (1965). Black on pink and purple unpt. Like #74. Shah at ctr. Winged horses on back. Sign. 9.

VG	VF	UNC
40.00	100.00	250.00

83   1000 RIALS
ND (1965). Brown on red and blue unpt. Like #75. Shah at ctr. Tomb of Hafez at Shiraz on back. Sign. 9.

VG	VF	UNC
50.00	125.00	350.00

1969 ND ISSUE

#84-87 Type VII portr. of Shah Pahlavi in army uniform at r. Wmk: Young Shah Pahlavi. Yellow security thread runs vertically. Sign. 11 or 12. Printer: Harrison (w/o imprint).

#84-89A are called *Dark Panel* notes. The bank name is located on a contrasting dk. ornamental panel at the top ctr.

84   20 RIALS
ND (1969). Dk. brown on pink and green unpt. Ornate design at ctr. Oriental hunters on horseback on back. Sign. 11.

VG	VF	UNC
2.00	4.00	10.00

85   50 RIALS
ND (1969-71). Green on orange and blue unpt. Ornate design at ctr. Koohrang Dam and tunnel on back.

	VG	VF	UNC
a. Sign. 11.	2.00	5.00	10.00
b. Sign. 12.	2.00	5.00	10.00

86   100 RIALS
ND (1969-71). Maroon on lt. green and m/c unpt. Ornate design at ctr. Oil refinery at Abadan on back.

	VG	VF	UNC
a. Sign. 11.	2.00	6.00	12.00
b. Sign. 12.	2.00	6.00	12.00

87   200 RIALS
ND (1969-71). Dk. blue on orange and purple unpt. M/c ornate design. Railroad bridge on back.

	VG	VF	UNC
a. Sign. 11.	5.00	15.00	35.00
b. Sign. 12.	7.00	20.00	50.00

#88-89A Type VII portr. of Shah Pahlavi in army uniform at ctr. Sign. 11.

88	**500 RIALS**	VG	VF	UNC
	ND (1969). Black on pink and purple unpt. Ornate frame at ctr. Winged horses on back.	6.00	25.00	80.00

89	**1000 RIALS**	VG	VF	UNC
	ND (1969). Brown on red and blue unpt. Ornate frame at ctr. Tomb of Hafez at Shiraz on back.	10.00	40.00	150.00
89A	**5000 RIALS**			
	ND (1969). Purple on red and m/c unpt. Ornate frame at ctr. Golestan Palace in Tehran on back. Printed in Pakistan.	350.00	1000.00	2000.00

1971 ND Issue

#90-96 are called *Light Panel* notes. The bank name is located on a contrasting lt. ornamental background panel at the top ctr.

#90-92 Type VII portr. of Shah Pahlavi in army uniform at r. Wmk: Young Shah Pahlavi. Yellow security thread runs vertically. Printer: Harrison (w/o imprint).

90	**50 RIALS**	VG	VF	UNC
	ND (1971). Dk. green on orange and blue unpt. Like #85 but w/light panel. Sign. 13.	2.00	4.00	10.00

91	**100 RIALS**	VG	VF	UNC
	ND (1971-73). Maroon on olive-green and m/c unpt. Like #86 but w/light panel.			
	a. Sign. 11.	2.00	5.00	15.00
	b. Sign. 12.	2.00	8.00	18.00
	c. Sign. 13.	2.00	5.00	15.00

92	**200 RIALS**	VG	VF	UNC
	ND (1971-73). Dk. blue on orange and lavender unpt. Like #87 but w/light panel.			
	a. Sign. 11.	4.00	16.00	50.00
	b. Sign. 12.	6.00	20.00	60.00
	c. Sign. 13.	3.00	8.00	20.00

#93-96 Type VII portr. of Shah Pahlavi in army uniform at ctr. Wmk: Young Shah Pahlavi.

93	**500 RIALS**	VG	VF	UNC
	ND (1971-73). Black on orange, green and m/c unpt. Like #88 but w/light panel.			
	a. Sign. 11.	8.00	20.00	50.00
	b. Sign. 12.	15.00	40.00	150.00
	c. Sign. 13.	12.00	30.00	100.00

94	**1000 RIALS**	VG	VF	UNC
	ND (1971-73). Brown on red, blue and m/c unpt. Like #89 but w/light panel.			
	a. Sign. 11.	20.00	60.00	200.00
	b. Sign. 12.	15.00	50.00	150.00
	c. Sign. 13.	12.00	40.00	125.00

95	**5000 RIALS**	VG	VF	UNC
	ND (1971-72). Purple on red and m/c unpt. Ornate frame at ctr. Golestan Palace in Tehran on back.			
	a. Sign. 12.	100.00	300.00	900.00
	b. Sign. 13.	70.00	200.00	600.00

96   10,000 RIALS

	VG	VF	UNC
ND (1972-73). Dk. green and brown. Ornate frame at ctr. National Council of Ministries in Tehran on back.			
a. Sign. 11.	300.00	600.00	2000.00
b. Sign. 13.	200.00	400.00	1250.00

1971 ND COMMEMORATIVE ISSUE

#97 and 98, 2,500th Anniversary of the Persian Empire

#97 and 98 Type VIII portr. of Shah Pahlavi in the "Commander in Chief" of Iranian armed forces uniform at r. Wmk: Young Shah Pahlavi. Yellow security thread runs vertically. Printer: TDLR.

97   50 RIALS

	VG	VF	UNC
SH1350 (1971). Green on blue, brown and m/c unpt. Floral design at ctr. Shah Pahlavi giving land deeds to villager on back.			
a. Sign. 11.	2.00	6.00	12.00
b. Sign. 13.	2.50	8.00	16.00

98   100 RIALS

	VG	VF	UNC
SH1350 (1971). Maroon on orange and m/c unpt. M/c geometric and floral design. 3 vignettes labeled: *HEALTH, AGRICULTURE* and *EDUCATION* on back. Sign. 11.	3.00	8.00	20.00

#99 *Deleted.* See #101a.

1974 ND ISSUE

#100-107 Type VIII portr. of Shah Pahlavi at r. Wmk: Young Shah Pahlavi. Yellow security thread runs vertically. Printer: TDLR. Replacement notes: For sign. 14, 15, 16 where the prefix for regular notes is a whole number such as 1, 2, 3 or 4, the replacemnt is 01, 02, 03 or 04. For sign. 17 and 18 where the prefix for regular notes is a fraction, the replacemnt is 99/9, 98/9 or 97/9.

100   20 RIALS

	VG	VF	UNC
ND (1974-79). Brown on orange, lilac and m/c unpt. Persian carpet design, shepherd and ram. Amir Kabir Dam near Karaj on back.			
a1. Sign. 16. Farsi denomination short.	1.00	2.00	6.00
a2. Sign. 16. Farsi denomination long.	1.00	2.00	6.00
b. Sign. 17.	2.00	4.00	8.00
c. Sign. 18.	2.50	5.00	10.00

101   50 RIALS

	VG	VF	UNC
ND (1974-79). Green on brown, blue and m/c unpt. Persian carpet design. Tomb of Cyrus the Great at Pasargarde at l. ctr. on back.			
a. Yellow security thread. Sign. 14.	2.50	5.00	10.00
b. Yellow security thread. Sign. 15.	2.00	4.00	8.00
c. Yellow security thread. Sign. 16.	2.00	4.00	8.00
d. Black security thread. Sign: 17.	2.00	4.00	8.00
e. Black security thread. Sign. 18.	2.50	5.00	10.00

102   100 RIALS

	VG	VF	UNC
ND (1974-79). Maroon on orange, green and m/c unpt. Persian carpet design. Pahlavi Museum at l. ctr. on back.			
a. Yellow security thread. Sign. 15.	2.50	5.00	12.50
b. Yellow security thread. Sign. 16.	3.00	6.00	15.00
c. Black security thread. Sign. 17.	3.00	7.00	18.00
d. Black security thread. Sign. 18.	3.00	6.00	15.00

103 **200 RIALS**

		VG	VF	UNC
ND (1974-79). Blue on green and m/c unpt. Persian carpet design. Shahyad Square in Tehran on back.				
a. 6 point star in design on back. Yellow security thread. Monument name as Maidane Shahyad at lower l. on back. Sign. 15.		6.00	20.00	50.00
b. 12 point star in design on back. Yellow security thread. Monument name as Maidane Shahyad. Sign. 16.		3.00	10.00	30.00
c. 12 point star in design on back. Yellow security thread. Monument name changed to Shahyad Aryamer. Sign. 16.		2.00	8.00	25.00
d. 12 point star in design on back. Black security thread and Shahyad Aryamer monument. Sign. 17.		2.00	8.00	25.00
e. 12 point star in design on back. Black security thread and Shahyad Aryamer monument. Sign. 18.		2.00	8.00	25.00

106 **5000 RIALS**

		VG	VF	UNC
ND (1974-79). Purple on pink, green and m/c unpt. Persian carpet design. Golestan Palace in Tehran on back.				
a. Yellow security thread. Sign. 15.		50.00	100.00	300.00
b. Yellow security thread. Sign. 16.		3.00	10.00	50.00
c. Black security thread. Sign. 17.		25.00	75.00	200.00
d. Black security thread. Sign. 18.		50.00	100.00	250.00

104 **500 RIALS**

		VG	VF	UNC
ND (1974-79). Black, dk. brown and green on orange and m/c unpt. Persian carpet design. Winged horses on back.				
a. 6 point star in design below Shah Pahlavi. Yellow security thread. Sign. 15.		5.00	15.00	40.00
b. 6 point star in design below Shah Pahlavi. Yellow security thread. Sign. 16.		4.00	10.00	25.00
c. Diamond design below Shah Pahlavi. Black security thread. Sign. 17.		5.00	15.00	35.00
d. Diamond design below Shah Pahlavi. Black security thread. Sign. 18.		4.00	10.00	25.00

107 **10,000 RIALS**

		VG	VF	UNC
ND (1974-79). Dk. brown and green on m/c unpt. Persian carpet design. National Council of Ministries in Tehran on back.				
a. Yellow security thread. Sign. 15.		75.00	200.00	550.00
b. Yellow security thread. Sign. 16.		10.00	30.00	100.00
c. Black security thread. Sign. 17.		25.00	100.00	300.00
d. Black security thread. Sign. 18.		35.00	125.00	350.00

1976 ND COMMEMORATIVE ISSUE

#108, 50th Anniversary of the Founding of the Pahlavi Dynasty

#108 Type IX portr. of Shah Pahlavi w/Shah Reza at r. Wmk: Young Shah Pahlavi. Yellow security thread runs vertically. Sign. 16. Printer: TDLR.

105 **1000 RIALS**

		VG	VF	UNC
ND (1974-79). Brown on green, red, yellow and m/c unpt. Persian carpet design. Tomb of Hafez in Shiraz on back.				
a. Yellow security thread. Sign. 15.		10.00	30.00	100.00
b. Yellow security thread. Sign. 16.		5.00	10.00	30.00
c. Black security thread. Sign. 17.		5.00	10.00	30.00
d. Black security thread. Sign. 18.		5.00	10.00	30.00

108 **100 RIALS**

		VG	VF	UNC
ND (1976). Maroon on orange, green and m/c unpt. Persian carpet design w/old Bank Melli at bottom ctr. 50th anniversary design in purple and lavender consisting of 50 suns surrounding Pahlavi Crown on back.		4.00	10.00	25.00

ISLAMIC REPUBLIC

REVOLUTIONARY OVERPRINTS

After the Islamic Revolution of 1978-79, the Iranian government used numerous overprints on existing stocks of unissued paper money to obliterate Shah Pahlavi's portrait. There were many unauthorized and illegal crude stampings such as a large "X" and hand obliterations used by zealous citizens which circulated freely, but only three major types types of official overprints were used by the government.

PROVISIONAL ISSUES

All provisional government ovpt. were placed on existing notes of Shah Pahlavi already printed. Overprinting was an interim action meant to discredit and disgrace the deposed Shah as well as to publicize and give credence to the new Islamic Republic. The overprints themselves gave way to more appropriate seals and emblems, changes of watermarks and finally to a complete redesigning of all denominations of notes.

In all cases the Shah's portr. was covered by an arabesque design. Eight different styles and varieties of this ovpt. were used. Watermark ovpt., when used, are either the former Iranian national emblem of Lion and Sun or the calligraphic Persian text of *JUMHURI-YE-ISLAMI-YE-IRAN* (Islamic Republic of Iran) taken from the obverse of the country's new emblem. All ovpt. colors are very dark and require careful scrutiny to distinguish colors other than black.

PORTRAIT OVERPRINT

Overprint A · Overprint B · Overprint C · Overprint D · Overprint E · Overprint F · Overprint G · Overprint H

Obverse 1

Obverse 2

Reverse 1 / Obverse 3

GOVERNMENT

TYPE 1 ND PROVISIONAL ISSUE

#110-116 Type I ovpt: Arabesque design over Shah at r. Wmk. area at l. w/o ovpt. Replacement notes: Refer to #100-107.

110	20 RIALS	VG	VF	UNC
	ND.			
	a. Black type A ovpt. on #100a1 (short Farsi).	2.00	8.00	15.00
	b. Black type A ovpt. on #100a2 (long Farsi).	3.00	8.00	30.00
	c. Black type C ovpt. on #100a2.	250.00	400.00	800.00
	d. Black type C ovpt. on 100b.	300.00	500.00	1000.00
	e. Black type C. ovpt. on #100c.	600.00	1000.00	2000.00

111	50 RIALS	VG	VF	UNC
	ND. Ovpt. on #101b.			
	a. Black type B ovpt.	2.00	5.00	12.00
	b. Green type B ovpt.	3.00	6.00	20.00

112	100 RIALS	VG	VF	UNC
	ND. Ovpt. on #102c.			
	a. Black type C ovpt.	2.50	10.00	25.00
	b. Maroon type C ovpt.	2.50	10.00	25.00
	c. Black type G. ovpt.	75.00	150.00	300.00

113   200 RIALS
ND. Ovpt. on #103.

	VG	VF	UNC
a. Black type E ovpt. on #103a.	200.00	400.00	1200.00
b. Black type E ovpt. on #103b.	250.00	500.00	1400.00
c. Black type E ovpt. on #103d.	3.00	12.00	30.00
d. Black type G ovpt. on #103d.	75.00	150.00	300.00

114   500 RIALS
ND. Ovpt. on #104.

	VG	VF	UNC
a. Black type F ovpt. on #104b.	5.00	15.00	50.00
b. Black type F ovpt. on #104c.	200.00	400.00	900.00
c. Black type F ovpt. on #104d.	5.00	16.00	60.00

115   1000 RIALS
ND. Ovpt. on #105.

	VG	VF	UNC
a. Black type G ovpt. on #105b.	5.00	15.00	50.00
b. Black type G ovpt. on #105d.	7.00	20.00	65.00
c. Brown type G ovpt. on #105d.	7.00	20.00	100.00

116   5000 RIALS
ND. Black type H ovpt. on #106d.

VG	VF	UNC
500.00	1000.00	2000.00

TYPE 2 ND PROVISIONAL ISSUE

#117-122 Type II ovpt: Arabesque design over Shah at r. and lion and sun national emblem over wmk. area at l.

117   50 RIALS
ND. Ovpt. on #101.

	VG	VF	UNC
a. Black type B ovpt. on #101c.	5.00	12.00	30.00
b. Black type B ovpt. on #101d.	200.00	400.00	1000.00
c. Black type B ovpt. on #101e.	100.00	200.00	600.00

118   100 RIALS
ND. Ovpt. on #102.

	VG	VF	UNC
a. Black type C ovpt. on #102c.	70.00	150.00	400.00
b. Black type D ovpt. on #102d.	2.00	4.00	10.00

119   200 RIALS
ND. Ovpt. on #103.

	VG	VF	UNC
a. Black Type E ovpt. on #103d.	8.00	25.00	60.00

120   500 RIALS
ND. Ovpt. on #104.

	VG	VF	UNC
a. Black type F ovpt. on #104b.	350.00	700.00	2000.00
b. Black type F ovpt. on #104d.	10.00	30.00	80.00

121   1000 RIALS
ND. Ovpt. on #105.

	VG	VF	UNC
a. Black type G ovpt. on #105b.	400.00	800.00	3000.00
b. Brown type G ovpt. on #105b.	8.00	20.00	75.00
c. Black type G ovpt. on #105d.	8.00	20.00	75.00

122   5000 RIALS
ND. Ovpt. on #106.

	VG	VF	UNC
a. Black type H ovpt. on #106b.	500.00	1000.00	2750.00
b. Black type H ovpt. on #106c.	700.00	1500.00	3000.00
c. Black type H ovpt. on #106d.	350.00	800.00	1750.00

TYPE 3 ND PROVISIONAL ISSUE

#123-126 Type III ovpt: Arabesque design over Shah at r. and calligraphic Persian text *JUMHURI-YE ISL-AMI-YE-IRAN* (Islamic Republic of Iran) over wmk. area at l.

			VG	VF	UNC
123	**50 RIALS**				
	ND. Ovpt. on #101.				
	a. Black type B ovpt., dk. green script on #101c.		2.00	6.00	20.00
	b. Black type D ovpt., black script on #101e.		1.50	4.00	10.00

			VG	VF	UNC
124	**500 RIALS**				
	ND. Ovpt. on #104.				
	a. Black type F ovpt., black script on #104b.		5.00	15.00	50.00
	b. Black type D ovpt., black script on #104d.		3.00	10.00	30.00

			VG	VF	UNC
125	**1000 RIALS**				
	ND. Ovpt. on #105.				
	a. Black type G ovpt., black script on #105b.		5.00	15.00	50.00
	b. Black type G ovpt., black script on #105d.		5.00	15.00	50.00
	c. Brown type G ovpt., violet script on #105b.		7.50	20.00	75.00
	d. Brown type G ovpt., brown script on #105b.		7.50	20.00	75.00

			VG	VF	UNC
126	**5000 RIALS**				
	ND. Ovpt. on #106.				
	a. Purple type H ovpt., purple script on #106b.		500.00	1000.00	2500.00
	b. Black type H ovpt., purple script on #106d.		75.00	150.00	350.00

Note: Some notes w/Shah portr. are found w/unofficial ovpts., i.e. large purple or black stamped *X* on portr. and wmk. area.

1980 EMERGENCY CIRCULATING CHECK ISSUE

The emergency checks were issed by Bank Melli, the National Bank and not Bank Markazi, the Central Bank, which is only authorized to issue currency. The checks were valid in the country only, not abroad. No English text on the checks.

			VG	VF	UNC
126A	**10,000 RIALS**				
	ND (1980). Dk. blue w/black text on green unpt. Bank Melli bldg. at l. and ctr. 2 Wmk varieties: Bank name repeated. Uniface.		100.00	250.00	6000.00

Note: These Emergency Checks were issued by Bank Melli the National Bank, and not Bank Markazi, the Central Bank which is only authorized to issue currency. The checks were valid in Iran and not abroad. No English text on the check.

BANK MARKAZI IRAN

Notes of the Islamic Republic of Iran		
18	Yousef Khoshkish (on ovpt.)	Mohammad Yeganeh (on ovpt.)
19	Mohammad Ali Mowlavi	Ali Ardalan
20	Ali Reza Nobari	Abol Hassan Bani-Sadr
21	Dr. Mohsen Nourbakhsh	Hossein Nemazi
22	Dr. Mohsen Nourbakhsh	Iravani
23	Ghasemi	Iravani
24	Ghasemi	Dr. Mohsen Nourbakhsh
25	Mohammad Hosein Adeli	Dr. Mohsen Nourbakhsh
26	Mohammad Hosein Adeli	Mohammad Khan
27	Dr. Mohsen Nourbakhsh	Mohammad Khan
28	Dr. Mohsen Nourbakhsh	Hossein Nemazi

1981 ND FIRST ISSUE

#127-131 calligraphic Persian (Farsi) text from circular republic seal at l., Imam Reza mosque at r. W/o wmk. Yellow security thread w/*BANK MARKAZI IRAN* in black runs through vertically. Back has circular shield w/stars and points at r. Sign. 19. Printer: TDLR (w/o imprint).

#127 and #130 have calligraphic seal printed in the same color as the note (blue and lavender, respectively) and with no variation. #128, 129 and 131 had the calligraphic seal applied locally after notes were printed. Numerous color varieties, misplacement or total omission can be seen on face or back, or both.

			VG	VF	UNC
127	**200 RIALS**				
	ND (1981). Blue and green on m/c unpt. Tomb of Ibn-E-Sina in Hamadan at l. on back. Ovpt. dark blue calligraphic seal at r.				
	a. Ovpt. on wmk: Shah profile.		0.75	2.00	6.00
	b. Ovpt. on wmk: Lion & Sun.		1.50	4.00	10.00

130   5000 RIALS   VG   VF   UNC
ND (1981). Lavender on green and m/c unpt. Oil refinery at Tehran
on back.
a. Security thread.   10.00   30.00   80.00
b. W/o security thread.   15.00   50.00   100.00

127A   200 RIALS   VG   VF   UNC
ND (1981). Blue, blue-violet and deep green on m/c unpt. Face like   2500.00   5000.00 12000.0
#127 w/ovpt. lion and sun. Victory Monument renamed *Banaye*   0
Azadi at l. on back. Sign. 19.

131   10,000 RIALS   VG   VF   UNC
ND (1981). Deep green, olive-brown and dk. brown on m/c unpt.
National Council of Ministries in Tehran on back.
a. Dk. brown circular seal at l. Dk. brown circular shield seal at r.   20.00   50.00   200.00
on back.

**Note: #131 first ovpt. w/circular gray-yellow lion and sun on both sides, then additional ovpt. regular black
calligraphic seal on top of first ovpt. Notes w/o black seal, or misplaced seal, are errors.**

128   500 RIALS   VG   VF   UNC
ND (1981). Dk. brown on orange, green and m/c unpt. Winged   2.00   5.00   12.00
horses on back.

1981 ND SECOND ISSUE

#132-134 Islamic motifs. White security thread w/*BANK MARKAZI IRAN* in black Persian script runs verti-
cally. Sign. 20 unless otherwise noted. Printer: TDLR (w/o imprint). Replacement notes: Serial # prefix *99/99; 98/99; 97/99;* etc.

129   1000 RIALS   VG   VF   UNC
ND (1981). Rust and brown on green and m/c unpt. Tomb of Hafez   2.50   8.00   22.50
in Shiraz on back.

132   100 RIALS   VG   VF   UNC
ND (1981). Maroon and lt. brown on m/c unpt. Imam Reza shrine   1.00   2.00   5.00
at Mashad at r. Madressa Chahr-Bagh in Isfahan on back. Wmk:
Republic seal. Sign. 20; 21.

133   5000 RIALS
ND (1981). Violet, red-orange and brown on m/c unpt. Mullahs leading marchers carrying posters of Ayatollah Khomeini at ctr. Hazrat Masoumeh shrine at l. ctr. on back. Wmk: Arms.

VG	VF	UNC
7.00	25.00	80.00

134   10,000 RIALS
ND (1981). Dk. blue and green on yellow and m/c unpt. Face like #133. Imam Reza shrine in Mashad at ctr. on back.

	VG	VF	UNC
a. Sign. 20. Wmk: Republic seal.	10.00	30.00	125.00
b. Sign. 21. Wmk: Arms.	10.00	30.00	125.00
c. Sign. 22. Wmk: Arms.	10.00	30.00	125.00

1982; 1983 ND Issue

#135-139 Islamic motifs. White security thread w/black *BANK MARKAZI IRAN* in Persian letters repeatedly runs vertically. Printer: TDLR (w/o imprint).

135   100 RIALS
ND (1982). Maroon on lt. brown and m/c unpt. Like #132 except for wmk. Sign. 21.

VG	VF	UNC
1.00	2.00	4.00

136   200 RIALS
ND (1982-). Aqua and blue-black on m/c unpt. Mosque at ctr. Farmers and farm tractor at l. ctr. on back.

	VG	VF	UNC

136   200 RIALS
a. Sign. 21. Wmk: Arms.
b. Sign. 23.
c. Sign. 28. Wmk: Khomeini.
d. Sign. 31. Wmk: Khomeini.

VG	VF	UNC
1.00	3.00	6.00
FV	FV	4.00
FV	FV	3.00
FV	FV	3.00

137   500 RIALS
ND (1982-2002). Gray and olive. Feyzieh Madressa Seminary at lower l., lg. prayer gathering at ctr. Tehran University on back.

	VG	VF	UNC
a. Sign. 21. Wmk: Arms.	FV	FV	12.00
b. Sign. 22.	5.00	15.00	40.00
c. Sign. 23.	FV	FV	10.00
d. Sign. 23. Wmk: Mohd. H. Fahmideh (youth).	FV	FV	8.00
e. Sign. 24.	FV	FV	6.00
f. Sign. 25.	FV	FV	4.00
g. Sign. 26.	FV	FV	4.00
h. Sign. 27. Wmk: Arms.	FV	FV	3.00
i. Sign. 27. Wmk: Mohd. H. Fahmideh (youth).	FV	FV	3.00
j. Sign. 28. Wmk: Khomeini.	FV	FV	3.00
k. Sign. 28. Wmk: Mohd. H. Fahmideh (youth).	FV	FV	3.00
l. Sign. 28. Wmk: Arms.	FV	FV	3.00

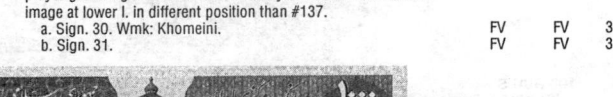

137A   500 RIALS
ND (2003-). Gray and olive. Feyzieh Madressa Seminary at lower l. prayer gathering at ctr. Tehran University on back. Architectural image at lower l. in different position than #137.

	VG	VF	UNC
a. Sign. 30. Wmk: Khomeini.	FV	FV	3.00
b. Sign. 31.	FV	FV	3.00

138   1000 RIALS
ND (1982-2002). Dk. olive-green, red-brown and brown on m/c unpt. Feyzieh Madressa Seminary at ctr. Mosque of Omar (Dome of the Rock) in Jerusalem on back.

	VG	VF	UNC
a. Sign. 21. Additional short line of text under mosque on back. Wmk: Arms.	FV	FV	20.00
b. Sign. like a. No line of text under bldg. on back.	FV	FV	50.00
c. Sign. 22.	FV	FV	25.00
d. Sign. 23.	FV	FV	15.00

138	1000 RIALS	VG	VF	UNC
	e. Sign. 23. Wmk: Mohd. H. Fahmideh (youth).	FV	FV	7.00
	f. Sign. 25.	FV	FV	4.00
	g. Sign. 26.	FV	FV	4.00
	h. Sign. 27.	FV	FV	4.00
	i. Sign. 28. Wmk: Mohd. H. Fahmideh (youth).	FV	FV	4.00
	j. Sign. 28. Wmk: Arms.	FV	FV	4.00
138A	1000 RIALS			

ND (2003-). Dk. olive-green, red-brown and brown on m/c unpt. Feyzieh Madressa Seminary at ctr. Mosque of Omar (Dome of the rock) in Jerusalem on back. Architectural element at lower l. in different position than on #138.

	a. Sign. 30.	FV	FV	4.00

139	5000 RIALS	VG	VF	UNC

ND (1983-). Violet, red-orange and brown on m/c unpt. Similar to #133; reduced crowd. Radiant sun removed from upper l. on face. 2 small placards of Khomeini added to crowd. Wmk: Arms.

	a. Sign. 21.	FV	FV	75.00
	b. Sign. 22.	FV	FV	75.00

Note: #139 exists w/2diff. sign. 21 style of Nemazi.

CENTRAL BANK OF THE ISLAMIC REPUBLIC OF IRAN

1985; 1986 ND ISSUE

140	100 RIALS	VG	VF	UNC

ND (1985-). Purple on m/c unpt. Ayatollah Moddaress at r. Parliament at l. on back. Printer: TDLR (w/o imprint).

	a. Sign. 21. Wmk. Arms.	FV	FV	3.00
	b. Sign. 22.	FV	FV	2.50
	c. Sign. 23.	FV	FV	1.50
	d. Sign. 25.	FV	FV	1.25
	e. Sign. 26.	FV	FV	1.25
	f. Sign. 28. Wmk: Khomeini.	FV	FV	1.25
	g. Sign. 31.	FV	FV	1.25

141	2000 RIALS	VG	VF	UNC

ND(1986-). Purple, olive-green and dk. brown on m/c unpt. Revolutionists before mosque at ctr. r. Kaabain Mecca on back.

	a. Sign. 21. Wmk: Arms.	FV	FV	10.00
	b. Sign. 22.	FV	FV	10.00
	c. Sign. 23.	FV	FV	10.00
	d. Sign.23. Wmk: Mohd. H. Fahmideh (youth).	FV	FV	6.00
	e. Sign.24.	FV	FV	4.00
	f. Sign. 25.	FV	FV	4.00
	g. Sign. 25. Wmk: Arms.	10.00	25.00	125.00
	h. Sign. 26.	FV	FV	3.00
	i. Sign. 27. Wmk: Arms.	FV	FV	3.00
	j. Sign. 27. Wmk: Mohd. H. Fahmideh (youth).	FV	FV	3.00
	k. Sign. 28. Wmk: Khomeini.	FV	FV	3.00
	l. Sign. 28. Wmk: Mohd. H. Fahmideh (youth).	FV	FV	3.00

1992; 1993 ND ISSUE

#142 not assigned.

#143-146 Khomeini at r. Sign. 25.

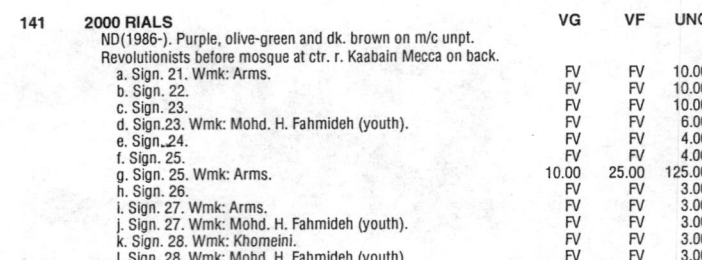

143	1000 RIALS	VG	VF	UNC

ND (1992-). Brown and dk. green on m/c unpt. Mosque of Omar (Dome of the Rock) in Jerusalem at ctr. on back.

	a. Sign. 25. Wmk: Mohd. H. Fahmideh (youth).	FV	FV	12.50
	b. Sign. 27.	FV	FV	5.00
	c. Sign. 28. Wmk: Khomeini.	FV	FV	3.00
	d. Sign. 31. Wmk: Khomeini.	FV	FV	3.00
144	2000 RIALS			
	ND (2005).	FV	FV	4.50

#145 and 146 wmk: Khomeini.

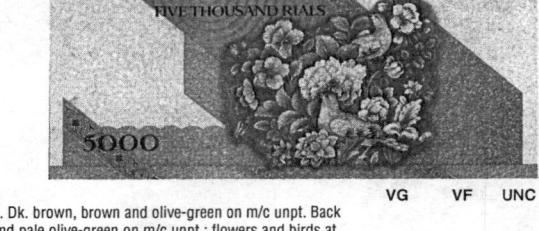

145	5000 RIALS	VG	VF	UNC

ND (1993-). Dk. brown, brown and olive-green on m/c unpt. Back red-violet and pale olive-green on m/c unpt.; flowers and birds at ctr. r.

	a. Sign. 25.	FV	FV	10.00
	b. Sign. 27.	FV	FV	9.00
	c. Sign. 28 (same as 21).	FV	FV	6.00
	d. Sign. 29.	FV	FV	6.00
	e. Sign. 30.	FV	FV	6.00

146 **10,000 RIALS**
ND (1992-). Deep blue-green, blue and olive-green on m/c unpt.
Mount Damavand at ctr. r. on back.

		VG	VF	UNC
a. Sign. 25.		FV	FV	20.00
b. Sign. 26.		FV	FV	20.00
c. Sign. 27.		FV	FV	12.50
d. Sign. 28 (same as 21).		FV	FV	12.50
e. Sign. 29.		FV	FV	9.00
f. Sign. 30.		FV.	FV	9.00
g. Sign. 31.		FV	FV	8.00

Note: Dr. Nourbaksh & Nemazi (sign. 21) were re-appointed to the positions they held several years ago and therefore sign. 28 is the same as sign. 21.

147 **20,000 RIALS**
ND (2004-5). Blue and green on m/c unpt. Large Imam Khomeini
at r. Khomeini square in Isfahan on back.

		VG	VF	UNC
a. Sign. 30.		FV	FV	18.00
b. Sign. 31 (Small variety).		FV	FV	18.00

148 **20,000 RIALS**   **VG**   **VF**   **UNC**
2005. Blue and green on m/c unpt. Smaller Iman Khomeini at r.   FV   FV   15.00
Khomeini square in Isfahan on back. Large sign. 31.

The Republic of Iraq, historically known as Mesopotamia, is located in the Near East and is bordered by Kuwait, Iran, Turkey, Syria, Jordan and Saudi Arabia. It has an area of 167,925 sq. mi. (434,924 sq. km.) and a population of 23.11 million. Capital: Baghdad. The economy of Iraq is based on agriculture and petroleum. Crude oil accounts for 94 percent of the exports before the war with Iran began in 1980.

Iraq was the site of a number of flourishing civilizations of antiquity - Sumerian, Assyrian, Babylonian, Parthian, Persian - and of the Biblical cities of Ur, Nineveh and Babylon. Desired because of its favored location which embraced the fertile alluvial plains of the Tigris and Euphrates Rivers, Mesopotamia - "land between the rivers" - was conquered by Cyrus the Great of Persia, Alexander of Macedonia and by Arabs who made the legendary city of Baghdad the capital of the ruling caliphate. Suleiman the Great conquered Mesopotamia for Turkey in 1534, and it formed part of the Ottoman Empire until 1623, and from 1638 to 1917. Great Britain, given a League of Nations mandate over the territory in 1920, recognized Iraq as a kingdom in 1922. Iraq became an independent constitutional monarchy presided over by the Hashemite family, direct descendants of the prophet Mohammed, in 1932. In 1958, the army-led revolution of July 14 overthrew the monarchy and proclaimed a republic. After several military coups, Saddam Hussein became president in 1979. In 2003 he was overthrown by a coalition of foreign forces lead by the United States.

MONETARY SYSTEM:
  1 Dinar = 1000 Fils

REPUBLIC

CENTRAL BANK OF IRAQ

1959 ISSUE

#51-55 new Republic arms w/1958 at r. and as wmk. Sign. 10, 11, 12.

51 **1/4 DINAR**
ND (1959). Green on m/c unpt. Palm trees at ctr. on back.

	VG	VF	UNC
a. W/o security thread. 1 sign. varieties.	1.00	5.00	15.00
b. W/security thread. 2 sign. varieties.	1.00	5.00	5.00
s. Specimen. Punched hole cancelled.	—		30.00

52 **1/2 DINAR**   **VG**   **VF**   **UNC**
ND (1959). Brown on m/c unpt. Ruins of the mosque and spiral
minaret at Samarra on back.

	VG	VF	UNC
a. W/o security thread. 1 sign. variety.	2.00	7.50	30.00
b. W/security thread. 2 sign. varieties.	2.00	7.50	30.00
s. Specimen. Punched hole cancelled.	—		30.00

#56-60 wmk: Falcon's head. Sign. #13, 14.

		VG	VF	UNC
53	**1 DINAR**			
	ND (1959). Blue on m/c unpt. The *Harp of Ur* at ctr. on back.			
	a. W/o security thread. 1 sign. variety.	1.50	5.00	20.00
	b. W/security thread. Blue lines over wmk. area. 2 sign. varieties.	1.50	5.00	20.00
	s. Specimen. Punched hole cancelled.	—	—	30.00

		VG	VF	UNC
54	**5 DINARS**			
	ND (1959). Lt. purple on m/c unpt. Ancient carving of Hammurabi receiving the laws on back.			
	a. W/o security thread. 1 sign. variety.	2.50	12.50	35.00
	b. W/security thread.	2.50	12.50	35.00
	s. Specimen. Punched hole cancelled.	—	—	30.00

		VG	VF	UNC
55	**10 DINARS**			
	ND (1959). Purple on m/c unpt. Carvings of a winged Assyrian ox and an Assyrian priest on back.			
	a. W/o security thread. 1 sign. variety.	3.00	10.00	50.00
	b. W/security thread. 2 sign. varieties.	3.00	10.00	50.00
	s. Specimen. Punched hole cancelled.	—	—	30.00

Note: Various hoards of #51-55 have appeared on the market during the past several years. Values shown are speculative for all these pieces.

		VG	VF	UNC
56	**1/4 DINAR**			
	ND (1971). Green and brown on m/c unpt. Harbor at ctr. *1/4 Dinar* at l., palm trees at ctr. on back.	1.00	3.00	9.00

		VG	VF	UNC
57	**1/2 DINAR**			
	ND (1971). Brown and blue on m/c unpt. Cement factory at ctr. *1/2 Dinar* at l., spiral minaret and runins of mosque at Samarra at ctr. on back.	2.50	7.50	25.00

		VG	VF	UNC
58	**1 DINAR**			
	ND (1971). Blue and brown on m/c unpt. Oil refinery at ctr. Entry to the al-Mustansiriyah School at ctr., *1 Dinar* at l. on back. 2 sign. varieties.	2.00	6.00	17.50

59 5 DINARS

ND (1971). Lilac on brown and m/c unpt. Parliament bldg. across face. Hammurabi (l.) in conversation with sun god Shamash at ctr. *5 Dinars* at l. on back. 2 sign. varieties.

VG	VF	UNC
5.00	15.00	45.00

60 10 DINARS

ND (1971). Purple, blue and brown on m/c unpt. Dockdan dam at ctr. Winged statues from the palace complex of Sargon II at Khorsabad at ctr. on back. *10 Dinars* at l. on back.

VG	VF	UNC
5.00	15.00	45.00

1973 ND; 1978 ISSUE

#61-66 wmk: Falcon's head. Sign. #14, 15.

61 1/4 DINAR

ND (1973). Green and black on m/c unpt. Similar to #56. *Quarter Dinar* at bottom r. on back. 2 sign. varieties.

VG	VF	UNC
0.50	1.50	5.00

62 1/2 DINAR

ND (1973). Brown on m/c unpt. Face design similar to #57. *Half Dinar* below Minaret of the Great Mosque at Samarra at ctr. on back. 2 sign. varieties.

VG	VF	UNC
1.25	4.00	12.50

63 1 DINAR

ND (1973). Dk. blue and aqua on m/c unpt. Similar to #58. *One Dinar* at bottom r. on back.

	VG	VF	UNC
a. 1 line of Arabic caption (factory name) below.	1.00	4.50	32.50
b. W/o Arabic caption below factory.	1.00	3.00	10.00

64 5 DINARS

ND (1973). Deep lilac on m/c unpt. Similar to #59. *Five Dinars* at bottom on back. 2 sign. varieties.

VG	VF	UNC
0.75	2.50	7.50

65 10 DINARS

ND (1973). Purple and red-brown on blue and m/c unpt. Dockdan dam at r. Back similar to #60, but *Ten Dinars* at bottom. 2 sign. varieties.

VG	VF	UNC
1.50	4.50	12.50

66   25 DINARS
1978; 1980. Green and brown on m/c unpt. 3 Arabian horses at ctr., date below sign. at lower r. Abbasid Palace on back. 182 x 88mm. 2 sign. varieties.

	VG	VF	UNC
a. 1978/AH1398.	5.00	10.00	30.00
b. 1980/AH1400.	2.50	7.50	22.50
s. Specimen.	—	—	—

1979-86 ISSUE

#67-72 wmk: Arabian horse's head. Sign. varieties.

67   1/4 DINAR
1979/AH1399. Green and m/c. Palm trees at ctr. Bldg. on back.

	VG	VF	UNC
a. Issued note.	0.15	0.30	1.00
s. Specimen.	—	—	—

68   1/2 DINAR
1980/AH1400; 1985/AH1405. Brown and m/c. Astrolabe at r. Minaret of Samarra on back. 2 sign. varieties.

	VG	VF	UNC
a. Issued note.	0.10	0.20	0.75
s. Specimen.	—	—	—

69   1 DINAR
1979/AH1399; 1980/AH1400; 1984/AH1405. Olive-green and deep blue on m/c unpt. Coin design at ctr. Mustansiriyah School in Baghdad on back. 3 sign. varieties.

	VG	VF	UNC
a. Issued note.	0.10	0.20	0.75
s. Specimen.			

70   5 DINARS
1980/AH1400; 1981/AH1401; 1982/AH1402. Brown-violet and deep blue on m/c unpt. Gali-Ali Beg waterfall at ctr. Al-Ukhether castle at ctr. on back.

	VG	VF	UNC
a. Issued note.	0.25	1.00	3.00
s. Specimen.	—	—	—

71   10 DINARS
1980/AH1400; 1981/AH1401; 1982/AH1402. Purple on blue, violet and m/c unpt. Al-Hassan ibn al-Haitham (scientist) at r. Hadba minaret in Mosul on back.

	VG	VF	UNC
	0.25	1.00	3.00

72 **25 DINARS**
1981/AH1401; 1982/AH1402. Green and brown. Similar to #66 but date below horses. Reduced size, 175 x 80mm.

VG	VF	UNC
0.25	0.75	1.25

73 **25 DINARS**
1986. Brown, green and black on blue and m/c unpt. Charging horsemen at ctr., Saddam Hussein at r. and as wmk. City gate at l., Martyr's monument at ctr. on back.

VG	VF	UNC
0.25	0.75	2.50

Note: In a sudden economic move during summer of 1993, it was announced that all previous 25 Dinar notes issued before #74 had become worthless.

1990 EMERGENCY GULF WAR ISSUE

#74-76 Iraq printing. Many color shade varieties exist because of poor printing quality.

74 **25 DINARS**
1990/AH1411. Similar to #72 but green and gray. Lithograph, w/o wmk.

	VG	VF	UNC
a. Green unpt. w/ pink highlights and brown ink.	—	0.10	0.50
b. Green unpt. w/o pink highlights and black ink.	—	0.10	0.50
c. Green and pink unpt. with pink highlights and brown ink.	—	0.10	0.50

75 **50 DINARS**
1991/AH1411. Brown and blue-green on peach and m/c unpt. Saddam Hussein at r. Minaret of the Great Mosque at Samarra at ctr. r. on back. Lithograph.

VG	VF	UNC
—	—	0.75

76 **100 DINARS**
1991/AH1411. Dk. blue-green on lilac and m/c unpt. Saddam Hussein at at r. Victory Arch Monument of crossed swords at ctr. on back.

VG	VF	UNC
5.00	15.00	40.00

1992-93 EMERGENCY ISSUE

#77-79 dull lithograph printing. W/faint indelible ink wmk. Printed in China.

77 **1/4 DINAR**
1993/AH1413. Green on m/c unpt. Like #67.

VG	VF	UNC
—	—	0.40

78 **1/2 DINAR**
1993/AH1413. Brown on m/c unpt. Like #68.

	VG	VF	UNC
a. Dk. brown unpt.	—	—	0.40
b. Lt. lilac unpt.	—	—	0.40

79 **1 DINAR**
1992/AH1412. Green and blue-black on m/c unpt. Like #69.

VG	VF	UNC
—	—	0.40

#80 and 81 Saddam Hussein at r. Printed in China.

			VG	VF	UNC
80	**5 DINARS**				
	1992/AH1412. Dull red-brown on pale orange, lilac and m/c unpt. Temple at ctr. Hammurabi in conversation with the sun god Shamash at l. Tomb of the unknown soldier in ctr. on back. Shade varieties.				
	a. W/border around embossed text at ctr.		—	—	3.00
	b. W/o border around embossed text at ctr.		—	—	3.00
	c. As b. W/o embossed text at ctr.		—	—	0.60

			VG	VF	UNC
81	**10 DINARS**				
	1992/AH1412. Purplish black, blue-green and m/c. Statue of winged beast from the palace complex of Sargon II at Khorsabad at l. on back.		—	—	1.50

#82 held in reserve.

1994-95 ISSUE

#83-85 Saddam Hussein at r.

			VG	VF	UNC
83	**50 DINARS**				
	1994/AH1414. Brown and pale green on m/c unpt. Ancient statuette, monument at l. ctr. "Aljahad Project" double deck Saddam bridge at ctr. on back.		—	—	1.50

			VG	VF	UNC
84	**100 DINARS**				
	1994/AH1414. Dk. blue on lt. blue and pale ochre unpt. Al-Ukhether castle at ctr. Baghdad clock at ctr. on back. Printed wmk: Falcon's head.				
	a1. First diacritical mark in the text of the denomination is above the first letter (from the right). Printed on white paper which fluoresces.		—	—	1.00
	a2. As a. but printed on dark paper which does not fluoresce under UV light.		—	—	1.00
	b. First diacritical mark in the text of the denomination is below the second letter (from the right).		—	—	1.00

Note: Shade varieties exist.

			VG	VF	UNC
85	**250 DINARS**				
	1995/AH1415. Lavender on blue and m/c unpt. Hydroelectric dam at l. ctr. Friese from the Liberty Monument across back.				
	a1. First word of the text for the denomination has its second letters as a long 'a.' Printed on white paper which fluoresces.		—	—	1.25
	a2. As a. but printed on dark paper which does not fluoresce under UV light.		—	—	1.25
	b. First word of the text for the denomination has its second last letters as a long 'i', also w/different diacritical marks.		—	—	1.25

2001-02 ISSUE

#86-88 Saddam Hussein at r.

86 25 DINARS
2001/AH1422. Brown on lt. green unpt.

	VG	VF	UNC
	—	—	0.75

87 100 DINARS
2002/AH1422. Blue on blue and yellow unpt. Shenashils of old Baghdad on back.

	VG	VF	UNC
	—	—	1.50

88 250 DINARS
2002/AH1422. Purple on rose and blue unpt. Dome Rock on back.

	VG	VF	UNC
	—	—	1.50

89 10,000 DINARS
2002/AH1423. Tomb of unknown soldier in ctr. Saddam Hussein at r. Al-Mustansiriyah University in Baghdad and Arabic astrolabe on back.

	VG	VF	UNC
	—	—	7.00

DEMOCRATIC REPUBLIC

CENTRAL BANK OF IRAQ

2003-04 ISSUE

#90-96 printer: TDLR.

90 50 DINARS
2003/AH1424. Purple on m/c unpt. Grain silo at Basrah. Date palms on back.

	VG	VF	UNC
	FV	FV	0.50

91 250 DINARS
2003/AH1424. Lt. and dk. blue on m/c unpt. Astrolobe. Spiral Minaret in Samarra on back.

	VG	VF	UNC
	FV	FV	1.00

92 500 DINARS
2004/AH1425. Green and blue on m/c unpt. Ducan Dam at ctr. Winged bull statue on back.

	VG	VF	UNC
	FV	FV	1.75

93 1000 DINARS
2003/AH1424. Lt. and dk. brown. Medieval dinar coin. Al-Mustansiriyah University in Baghdad on back.

	VG	VF	UNC
	FV	FV	2.50

94 5000 DINARS
2003/AH1424. Dk. blue on m/c unpt. Gali Ali Beg and waterfall. Al-Ukhether fortress on back.

	VG	VF	UNC
	FV	FV	10.00

95 10,000 DINARS
2003/AH1424; 2004/AH1425. Green on m/c unpt. Abu Ali Hasan Ibn al-Haitham (known as Alhazen), physicist and mathematician. Hadba Minaret at the Great Nurid Mosque in Mosul on back. on back. 2 sign. varieties.

	VG	VF	UNC
	FV	FV	15.00

96 25,000 DINARS
2003/AH1424; 2004;AH1425. Red, purple and tan on m/c unpt. Kurdish farmer holding sheaf of wheat, tractor in background. Ancient Babylonian Kg. Hammurabi on back. 2 sign. varieties.

	VG	VF	UNC
	FV	FV	27.50

IRELAND REPUBLIC

The Republic of Ireland, occupying five-sixths of the island of Ireland located in the Atlantic Ocean west of Great Britain, has an area of 27,136 sq. mi. (70,283 sq. km.) and a population of 3.71 million. Capital: Dublin.

Agriculture and dairy farming are the principal industries. Meat, livestock, dairy products and textiles are exported.

The Irish Free State was established as a dominion on Dec. 6, 1921. Ireland withdrew from the Commonwealth and proclaimed itself a republic on April 18, 1949.

RULERS:
British to 1921

MONETARY SYSTEM:
1 Shilling = 12 Pence
1 Pound = 20 Shillings to 1971
1 Pound = 100 Pence, 1971-2001
1 Euro = 100 Cent, 2002-

REPUBLIC

BANC CEANNAIS NA HÉIREANN

CENTRAL BANK OF IRELAND
1961-63 ISSUE

#63-69 representation of river gods at ctr. on back. Replacement notes: From 1974-1976 single letter prefix plus 6-digit serial number for £1-£20. For £1 and £5 dated 1975 a "OO" was used in front of a prefix letter.

#63-65 portr. Lady Hazel Lavery at l., denomination at bottom ctr.

63 10 SHILLINGS
3.1.1962-6.6.1968. Orange on lt. green and lilac unpt. Sign. M. O'Muimhneacháin and T. K. Whitaker.

	VG	VF	UNC
a. Issued note.	3.00	10.00	45.00
s. Specimen.	—	—	—

64 1 POUND
1962-76. Green on pale gold unpt.

	VG	VF	UNC
a. Sign. M. O'Muimhneacháin and T. K. Whitaker. 16.3.1962-8.10.1968.	FV	12.00	60.00
b. Sign. T. K. Whitaker and C. H. Murray. 1.3.1969-17.9.1970.	FV	10.00	40.00
c. Sign. like b, but metallic security thread at l. of ctr. 8.7.1971-21.4.1975.	FV	6.00	27.50
d. Sign. C. H. Murray and M. O'Murchu. 30.9.1976.	FV	5.00	25.00
s. Specimen.	—	—	—

Note: Replacement notes: Serial # prefix S or OOA.

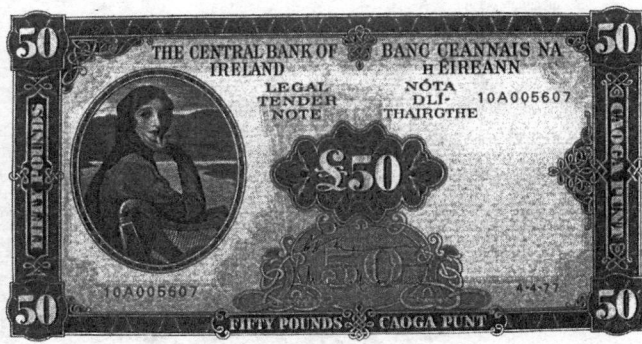

67	**20 POUNDS**	**VG**	**VF**	**UNC**
	1961-76. Red on m/c unpt.			
	a. Sign. M. O'Muimhneachain and T. K. Whitaker. 1.6.1961-15.6.1965.	FV	110.00	375.00
	b. Sign. T. K. Whitaker and C. H. Murray. 3.3.1969-6.1.1975.	FV	80.00	275.00
	c. Sign. C. H. Murray and M. O'Murchu. 24.3.1976.	FV	65.00	200.00

Note: Replacement notes: Serial # prefix V.

65	**5 POUNDS**	**VG**	**VF**	**UNC**
	1961-75. Dk. brown on lt. gold and orange unpt.			
	a. Sign. M. O'Muimhneachain and T. K. Whitaker. 15.8.1961-12.8.1968.	FV	35.00	175.00
	b. Sign. T. K. Whitaker and C. H. Murray. 12.5.1969; 27.2.1970.	FV	27.50	140.00
	c. Sign. like b., but metallic security thread at l. of ctr. 18.1.1971-5.9.1975.	FV	25.00	125.00

Note: Replacement notes: Serial # prefix R or OOK.

#66-69 Lady Hazel Lavery in Irish national costume w/chin resting on her hand and leaning on an Irish harp.

68	**50 POUNDS**	**VG**	**VF**	**UNC**
	1962-77. Purple on m/c unpt.			
	a. Sign. M. O'Muimhneachain and T. K. Whitaker. 1.2.1962-6.9.1968.	FV	175.00	525.00
	b. Sign. T. K. Whitaker and C. H. Murray. 4.11.1970-16.4.1975.	FV	160.00	475.00
	c. Sign. C. H. Murray and M. O'Murchu. 4.4.1977.	FV	150.00	450.00

66	**10 POUNDS**	**VG**	**VF**	**UNC**
	1962-76. Blue on m/c unpt.			
	a. Sign. M. O'Muimhneachain and T. K. Whitaker. 2.5.1962-16.7.1968.	FV	60.00	190.00
	b. Sign. T. K. Whitaker and C. H. Murray. 5.5.1969; 9.3.1970.	FV	50.00	170.00
	c. Sign. like b, but metallic security thread at l. of ctr. 19.5.1971-10.2.1975.	FV	45.00	150.00
	d. Sign. C. H. Murray and M. O'Murchu. 2.12.1976.	FV	40.00	140.00

Note: Replacement notes: Serial # prefix T.

69	**100 POUNDS**	**VG**	**VF**	**UNC**
	1963-77. Green on m/c unpt.			
	a. Sign. M. O'Muimhneachain and T. K. Whitaker. 16.1.1963-9.9.1968.	FV	350.00	850.00
	b. Sign. T. K. Whitaker and C. H. Murray. 26.10.1970; 3.3.1972; 26.2.1973; 10.4.1975.	FV	300.00	750.00
	c. Sign. C. H. Murray and M. O'Murchu. 4.4.1977.	FV	275.00	725.00

1976-82 ISSUE

#70-74 replacement notes: Serial # prefixes AAA; BBB; etc.

70 1 POUND
1977-89. Dk. olive-green and green on m/c unpt. Qn. Medb at r. Old
writing on back. Wmk: Lady Lavery.

	VG	VF	UNC
a. Sign. C. H. Murray and M. O'Murchu. 10.6.1977-29.11.1977.	2.00	5.00	15.00
b. Sign. C. H. Murray and T. F. O'Cofaigh. 30.8.1978-30.10.1981.	FV	5.00	14.00
c. Sign. T. F. O'Cofaigh and M. F. Doyle. 30.6.1982-24.4.1987.	FV	5.00	14.00
d. Sign. M. F. Doyle and S. P. Cromien. 23.3.1988-17.7.1989.	FV	4.00	12.50
s. Specimen. As a, c.	—		

71 5 POUNDS
1976-93. Brown and red-violet on m/c unpt. John Scotus Eriugena
at r. Old writing on back.

	VG	VF	UNC
a. Sign. T. K. Whitaker and C. H. Murray. 26.2.1976.	FV	30.00	60.00
b. Sign. C. H. Murray and M. O'Murchu. 18.5.1976-17.10.1977.	FV	25.00	55.00
c. Sign. C. H. Murray and T. F. O'Cofaigh. 25.4.1979-29.10.1981.	FV	17.50	40.00
d. Sign. T. F. O'Cofaigh and M. F. Doyle. 1982; 17.10.1983-22.4.1987.	FV	17.50	40.00
e. Sign. M. F. Doyle and S. P. Cromien. 12.8.1988-7.5.1993.	FV	15.00	35.00
s. Specimen. As b, d.	—	—	—

72 10 POUNDS
1978-92. Violet and purple on m/c unpt. Jonathan Swift at r. Old
street map and canal on back.

	VG	VF	UNC
a. Sign. C. H. Murray and T. F. O'Cofaigh. 1.6.1978-28.10.1981.	FV	35.00	85.00
b. Sign. T. F. O'Cofaigh and M. F. Doyle. 1982; 25.2.1983-9.2.1987.	FV	30.00	70.00
c. Sign. M. F. Doyle and S. P. Cromien. 22.12.1987-15.4.1992.	FV	27.50	65.00
s. Specimen. As a, b.	—	—	—

73 20 POUNDS
1980-92. Blue on m/c unpt. William Butler Yeats at r., Abbey
Theatre symbol at ctr. Map on back.

	VG	VF	UNC
a. Sign. C. H. Murray and T. F. O'Cofaigh. 7.1.1980-28.10.1981.	FV	55.00	140.00
b. Sign. T. F. O'Cofaigh and M. F. Doyle. 11.7.1983-28.8.1986.	FV	50.00	125.00
c. Sign. M. F. Doyle and S. P. Cromien. 12.8.1987-14.2.1992.	FV	45.00	100.00
s. Specimen. As b.			

74 50 POUNDS
1982; 1991. Red and brown on m/c unpt. Turlough O'Carolan
playing harp in front of group. Musical instruments on back.

	VG	VF	UNC
a. Sign. T. F. O'Cofaigh and M. F. Doyle. 1.11.1982.	FV	120.00	325.00
b. Sign. M. F. Doyle and S. P. Cromien. 5.11.1991.	FV	100.00	275.00

1992-96 I**SSUE**

#75-78 wmk: Lady Lavery and value. Replacement notes: Serial # prefixes *BBB; CCC,* etc.

75 5 POUNDS
1994-99. Dk. brown, reddish brown, and grayish purple on m/c
unpt. Mater Misericordiae Hospital at bottom l. ctr., Sister
Catherine McAuley at r. School children at ctr. on back.

	VG	VF	UNC
a. Sign. M. F. Doyle and S. P. Cromien. 15.3.1994-28.4.1994.	FV	FV	27.50
b. Sign. M. O'Conaill and P. H. Mullarkey. 21.12.1994-15.10.1999.	FV	FV	20.00

76 10 POUNDS
1993-99. Dk. green and brown on m/c unpt. Aerial view of Dublin
at ctr., James Joyce at r. Sculpted head representing Liffey River at
l., map in unpt. on back.

	VG	VF	UNC
a. Sign. M. F. Doyle and S. P. Cromien. 14.7.1993-27.4.1994.	FV	FV	37.50
b. Sign. M. O'Conaill and P. H. Mullarkey. 13.3.1995-2.7.1999.	FV	FV	30.00

IRELAND - NORTHERN

From 1800 to 1921 Ireland was an integral part of the United Kingdom. The Anglo-Irish treaty of 1921 established the Irish Free State of 26 counties within the Commonwealth of Nations and recognized the partition of Ireland. The six predominantly Protestant counties of northeast Ulster chose to remain a part of the United Kingdom with a limited self-government.

Up to 1928 banknotes issued by six of the nine joint stock commercial banks were circulating in the whole of Ireland. After the establishment of the Irish Free State, the commercial notes were issued for circulation only in Northern Ireland, with the Consolidated Banknotes being issued by the eight commercial banks operating in the Irish Free State.

RULERS:
British

MONETARY SYSTEM:
1 Shilling = 12 Pence
1 Pound = 20 Shillings to 1971
1 Pound = 100 New Pence, 1971-

BRITISH ADMINISTRATION

ALLIED IRISH BANKS LTD.
Formerly Provincial Bank of Ireland Ltd., later became First Trust Bank.

1982 ISSUE
#1-5 designs similar to Provincial Bank of Ireland Ltd. (#247-251) except for bank title and sign. Printer: TDLR.

		VG	VF	UNC
1	**1 POUND**			
	1.1.1982; 1.7.1983; 1.12.1984. Green on m/c unpt. Young girl at r. Sailing ship *Girona* at ctr. on back.	3.00	12.00	40.00

		VG	VF	UNC
77	**20 POUNDS**			
	1992-99. Violet, brown and dk. grayish blue on m/c unpt. Derryname Abbey at l. ctr., Daniel O'Connell at r. Writings and Four Courts bldg., Dublin, on back.			
	a. Sign. M. F. Doyle and S. P. Cromien. 10.9.1992-29.4.1994.	FV	FV	70.00
	b. Sign. M. O'Conaill and P. H. Mullarkey. 14.6.1995-9.12.1999.	FV	FV	65.00

		VG	VF	UNC
78	**50 POUNDS**			
	1995-2001. Dk. blue and violet on m/c unpt. Douglas Hyde at r., Áras an Uachtaráin bldg. in background at ctr. Back dk. gray and deep olive-green on m/c unpt.; Uilinn Piper at l., crest of Conradh na Gaeilge at upper ctr. r.			
	a. Sign. M. O'Conaill and P. H. Mullarkey. 6.10.1995; 14.2.1996; 19.3.1999.	FV	FV	180.00
	b. Sign. M. O'Conaill and J. A. Hurley. 8.3.2001.	FV	FV	180.00

		VG	VF	UNC
2	**5 POUNDS**			
	1.1.1982; 1.7.1983. Blue and purple on m/c unpt. Young woman at r. Dunluce Castle at ctr. on back.	12.50	27.50	65.00

		VG	VF	UNC
79	**100 POUNDS**			
	22.8.1996. Lilac brown, lt. orange-brown and slate. Charles Stewart Parnell at r., Avondale House and gardens in Rathdrum at lower l. ctr., Irish Wolfhound at lower l. Parts of the Parnell monument in Dublin on back. Sign. M. O'Conaill and P. H. Mull	FV	FV	325.00

Note: For later issues made for use in the Republic of Ireland, see European Union listings.

3	10 POUNDS	VG	VF	UNC
	1.1.1982; 1.12.1984. Brown and gray-green on m/c unpt. Young man at r. Wreck of the *Girona* at ctr. on back.	22.50	35.00	125.00

4	20 POUNDS	VG	VF	UNC
	1.1.1982; 1.7.1983; 1.12.1984. Purple and green. Elderly woman at r. Chimney at Lacada Pt. at ctr. on back.	40.00	60.00	250.00
5	100 POUNDS			
	1.1.1982. Black, olive and green. Elderly man at r. The *Armada* at ctr. on back.	200.00	375.00	750.00

ALLIED IRISH BANKS PUBLIC LIMITED COMPANY

Formerly Allied Irish Banks Ltd., later became First Trust Bank.

1987-88 ISSUE

#6-9 like #2-5 except for bank title and sign. Printer: TDLR.

6	5 POUNDS	VG	VF	UNC
	1.1.1987; 1.1.1990. Similar to #2.	12.50	25.00	55.00

7	10 POUNDS	VG	VF	UNC
	1.6.1988; 1.1.1990; 18.5.1993. Similar to #3.	22.50	37.50	80.00

8	20 POUNDS	VG	VF	UNC
	1.4.1987; 1.1.1990. Similar to #4.	40.00	65.00	170.00

9	100 POUNDS	VG	VF	UNC
	1.12.1988. Similar to #5.	200.00	350.00	700.00

BANK OF IRELAND

BELFAST

1967 ND ISSUE

#56-64 Mercury at l., woman w/harp at r. Airplane, bank bldg. and boat on back. Sign. title as Agent.

56	1 POUND	VG	VF	UNC
	ND (1967). Black on green and lilac unpt. 151 x 72mm. Sign. W. E. Guthrie.	2.75	9.00	40.00
57	5 POUNDS			
	ND (1967-68). Brown-violet.			
	a. Sign. W. E. Guthrie. (1967).	15.00	50.00	175.00
	b. Sign. H. H. M. Chestnutt. (1968).	12.50	45.00	120.00
58	10 POUNDS			
	ND (1967). Brown and yellow. Sign. W. E. Guthrie.	35.00	175.00	450.00

#59 and 60 *Deleted*.

1971-74 ND ISSUES

W/o word *Sterling* after Pound.

#61-63 replacement notes: Serial # prefix *Z*.

61	1 POUND	VG	VF	UNC
	ND (1972-77). Black on lt. green and lilac unpt. Like #56 but smaller size. 134 x 66mm.			
	a. Sign. H. H. M. Chestnutt. (1972).	3.00	13.00	50.00
	b. Sign. A. S. J. O'Neill. (1977).	2.50	12.00	42.50
62	5 POUNDS			
	ND (1971-77). Blue on lt. green and lilac unpt. 146 x 78mm.			
	a. Sign. H. H. M. Chestnutt. (1971).	17.50	52.50	150.00
	b. Sign. A. S. J. O'Neill. (1977).	14.00	47.50	120.00
63	10 POUNDS			
	ND (1971-77). Brown on lt. green and pale orange unpt.			
	a. Sign. H. H. M. Chestnutt. (1971).	25.00	120.00	450.00
	b. Sign. A. S. J. O'Neill. (1977).	22.50	90.00	300.00
64	100 POUNDS			
	ND (1974-78). Red on m/c unpt.			
	a. Sign. H. H. M. Chestnutt. (1974).	275.00	850.00	1200.00
	b. Sign. A. S. J. O'Neill. (1978).	250.00	575.00	900.00

1980s ND Issue

Word *Sterling* added after Pound.

65	1 POUND	VG	VF	UNC
	ND. Black on lt. green and lilac unpt. Like #61 but w/*STERLING* added below value. Wmk: Bank name repeated. Sign. A. S. J. O'Neill.	2.50	6.00	15.00
66	5 POUNDS			
	ND. Blue on lt. green and lilac unpt. Like #62 but w/£ signs added in corners.			
	a. Sign. A. S. J. O'Neill.	15.00	60.00	100.00
	b. Sign. D. F. Harrison.	12.50	40.00	70.00

67	10 POUNDS	VG	VF	UNC
	ND (1984). Dk. brown on lt. green and pale orange unpt. Like #63.			
	a. Sign. A. S. J. O'Neill.	22.50	90.00	140.00
	b. Sign. D. F. Harrison.	20.00	80.00	110.00
67A	20 POUNDS			
	ND. Dk. olive-green on m/c unpt.			
	a. Sign. A. S. J. O'Neill.	50.00	160.00	225.00
	b. Sign. D. F. Harrison.	50.00	150.00	200.00
68	100 POUNDS			
	ND. Red on m/c unpt. Similar to #64 but w/£ sign at upper r. and lower l. corners on face and back. *Sterling* added at lower ctr. on face.			
	a. Sign. A. S. J. O'Neill.	250.00	525.00	700.00
	b. Sign. D. F. Harrison.	225.00	400.00	600.00

1983 Commemorative Issue

#69, Bank of Ireland Bicentenary, 1783-1983

69	20 POUNDS	VG	VF	UNC
	1983. Dk. olive-green on m/c on unpt. Like #67A but commemorative text below bank title. Sign. A. S. J. O'Neill.	125.00	400.00	900.00

1990-95 Issue

#70-74 bank seal (Hibernia seated) at l., six county shields at upper ctr. Queen's University in Belfast on back. Sign. D. F. Harrison. Wmk: Medusa head.

70	5 POUNDS	VG	VF	UNC
	28.8.1990; 16.1.1992. Blue and purple on m/c unpt.			
	a. Issued note.	10.00	22.50	37.50
	s. Specimen.	—	—	27.50

71	10 POUNDS	VG	VF	UNC
	14.5.1991. Purple and maroon on m/c unpt.			
	a. Issued note.	18.00	27.50	50.00
	s. Specimen.	—	—	45.00

72	20 POUNDS	VG	VF	UNC
	9.5.1991. Green and brown on m/c unpt.			
	a. Issued note.	37.50	55.00	110.00
	s. Specimen.	—	—	100.00
73	100 POUNDS			
	28.8.1992. Red on m/c unpt.			
	a. Issued note.	210.00	250.00	375.00
	s. Specimen.	—	—	300.00

Note: Specimens and 3-subject sheets were sold to collectors. Low numbers were also available to special folders.

1995; 1998 ISSUE

#74-76, 78 like #70-73 except for somewhat different color arrangements.

#74-78 w/ascending size serial # at lower r.

			VG	VF	UNC
74	5 POUNDS		FV	12.50	25.00
	4.8.1998; 5.9.2000. Blue and purple on m/c unpt. Like #74.				

			VG	VF	UNC
75	10 POUNDS		FV	22.50	37.50
	1.7.1995; 1.7.1998; 5.9.2000. Purple and maroon on m/c unpt. Like #75.				

			VG	VF	UNC
76	20 POUNDS		FV	52.50	72.50
	1995; 1.1.1999. Green and brown on m/c unpt. Like #76.				
77	50 POUNDS		FV	125.00	180.00
	1.7.1995; 1.9.1999. Brown, olive and m/c. Seated woman at l. The Queen's University in Belfast on back.				

			VG	VF	UNC
78	100 POUNDS		FV	200.00	325.00
	1.7.1995. Red on m/c unpt. Like #73.				

2003 ISSUE

			VG	VF	UNC
79	5 POUNDS		FV	FV	12.50
	1.3.2003. Blue and violet on m/c unpt. Queen's University, Belfast on back.				

BELFAST BANKING COMPANY LIMITED

BELFAST

1922-23 ISSUE

#126-131 arms at top or upper ctr. w/payable text: *. . . at our Head Office, Belfast.*

#127-131 arms at top or upper ctr. w/payable text: *. . . at our Head Office, Belfast.*

			VG	VF	UNC
127	5 POUNDS				
	1923-66. Black on red unpt.				
	a. Black serial #. 3.1.1923; 3.5.1923; 7.9.1927.		30.00	42.50	375.00
	b. Red serial #. 8.3.1928-2.10.1942.		22.50	75.00	240.00
	c. Red serial #. 6.1.1966.		18.00	45.00	130.00

			VG	VF	UNC
128	10 POUNDS				
	1923-65. Black on green unpt.				
	a. Black serial #. 3.1.1923.		90.00	160.00	650.00
	b. Green serial #. 9.1.1929-1.1.1943.		50.00	100.00	300.00
	c. Green serial #. 3.12.1963; 5.6.1965.		35.00	80.00	190.00
129	20 POUNDS				
	1923-65. Black on purple unpt.				
	a. Black serial #. 3.1.1923.		90.00	275.00	850.00
	b. Mauve serial #. 9.11.1939; 10.8.1940.		65.00	180.00	425.00
	c. Black serial #. 3.2.1943.		55.00	130.00	350.00
	d. Black serial #. 5.6.1965.		50.00	110.00	275.00

130	50 POUNDS	VG	VF	UNC
	1923-63. Black on orange unpt.			
	a. Black serial #. 3.1.1923; 3.5.1923.	250.00	475.00	1100.00
	b. Yellow serial #. 9.11.1939; 10.8.1940.	190.00	325.00	700.00
	c. Black serial #. 3.2.1943.	150.00	300.00	650.00
	d. Black serial #. 3.12.1963.	130.00	275.00	500.00

131	100 POUNDS	VG	VF	UNC
	1923-68. Black on red unpt.			
	a. 3.1.1923; 3.5.1923.	325.00	800.00	1400.00
	b. 9.11.1939; 3.2.1943.	300.00	650.00	1100.00
	c. 3.12.1963.	275.00	500.00	750.00
	d. 8.5.1968.	275.00	500.00	700.00

FIRST TRUST BANK

Formerly Allied Irish Banks PLC, which acquired the Trustee Savings Bank. Member AIB Group Northern Ireland PLC.

1994 ISSUE

#132-135 five shields at bottom ctr. Printer: TDLR. Sign. title: *GROUP MANAGING DIRECTOR*. Wmk: Young woman.

132	10 POUNDS	VG	VF	UNC
	10.1.1994; 1.3.1996. Dk. brown and purple. Face similar to #3. Sailing ship Girona at ctr. on back.	FV	32.50	60.00

133	20 POUNDS	VG	VF	UNC
	10.1.1994. Violet, dk. brown and red-brown on m/c unpt. Face similar to #4. Chimney at Lacada Pt. at ctr. on back.	FV	55.00	100.00

134	50 POUNDS	VG	VF	UNC
	10.1.1994. Black, dk. olive-green and blue on m/c unpt. Face similar to #5. Cherubs holding Armada medallion at ctr. on back.	100.00	140.00	200.00

135	100 POUNDS	VG	VF	UNC
	10.1.1994; 1.3.1996. Black and olive-brown on m/c unpt. Elderly couple at r. The Armada at ctr. on back.	FV	240.00	375.00

1998 ISSUE

#136-139 like #132-135 but w/added security features.

136	10 POUNDS	VG	VF	UNC
	1998. Dk. brown and purple. Like #132 but w/scalloped gold seal over value at upper r.	FV	FV	35.00
137	20 POUNDS			
	1998. Violet, dk. brown and red-brown on m/c unpt. Like #133 but w/windowed security thread and gold seal at upper r.	FV	FV	60.00
138	50 POUNDS			
	1998. Black, dk. olive-green and blue on m/c unpt. Like #134 but w/windowed security thread and silver seal at upper r.	FV	FV	125.00
139	100 POUNDS			
	1998. Black and olive-brown on m/c unpt. Like #135 but w/windowed security thread and gold seal at upper r.	FV	FV	275.00

NORTHERN BANK LIMITED

1929 REGULAR ISSUE

#178; 181 sailing ship, plow and man at grindstone at upper ctr.

178	1 POUND	VG	VF	UNC
	1929-68. Black. Blue guilloche.			
	a. Red serial #. 6.5.1929; 1.7.1929; 1.8.1929.	22.50	65.00	160.00
	b. Black prefix letters and serial #. 1.1.1940.	12.00	40.00	100.00
	c. 1.10.1968.	10.00	30.00	70.00

181	10 POUNDS	VG	VF	UNC
	1930-68. Black on red unpt.			
	a. Red serial #. 1.1.1930-1.1.1940.	100.00	225.00	450.00
	b. Black serial #. 1.8.1940; 1.9.1940.	70.00	150.00	350.00
	c. Red serial #. 1.1.1942-1.11.1943.	65.00	140.00	300.00
	d. Imprint on back below central design. 1.10.1968.		35.00	180.00

1968 ISSUE

184	5 POUNDS	VG	VF	UNC
	1.10.1968. Black on green unpt.	25.00	55.00	110.00
185	50 POUNDS			
	1.10.1968. Black on dk. blue unpt. *NBLD* monogram on back.	200.00	400.00	725.00
186	100 POUNDS			
	1.10.1968. Black on dk. blue unpt. *NBLD* monogram on back.	300.00	600.00	950.00

1970 ISSUE

#187-192 cows at l., shipyard at bottom ctr., loom at r. Stylized arms at ctr. on back. Sign. varieties.

187	1 POUND	VG	VF	UNC
	1970-82. Green on pink unpt. Printer: BWC.			
	a. 1.7.1970; 1.10.1971; 1.1.1976.	5.00	20.00	40.00
	b. 1.8.1978; 1.7.1979; 1.4.1982.	4.00	17.50	30.00
188	5 POUNDS			
	1.7.1970-1.4.1982. Lt. blue.	20.00	40.00	75.00
189	10 POUNDS			
	1970-88. Brown.			
	a. 1.7.1970; 1.10.1971.	45.00	100.00	200.00
	b. 1.1.1976; 1.4.1982; 15.6.1988.	40.00	90.00	175.00
190	20 POUNDS			
	1.7.1970; 1.3.1981; 2.3.1987; 15.6.1988. Purple.	70.00	130.00	225.00

191	50 POUNDS	VG	VF	UNC
	1.7.1970; 1.3.1981. Orange.	125.00	275.00	400.00
192	100 POUNDS			
	1.7.1970; 1.10.1971; 1.1.1975; 1.7.1976; 1.1.1980. Red.	240.00	375.00	750.00

1988-90 ISSUE

#193-197 dish antenna at l., stylized *N* at ctr. and computer on back. Printer: TDLR.

193	5 POUNDS	VG	VF	UNC
	24.8.1988; 24.8.1989; 24.8.1990. Blue and m/c. Station above trolley car at ctr., W. A. Traill at r.			
	a. 24.8.1988; 24.8.1989.	FV	22.50	50.00
	b. 24.8.1990.	FV	20.00	40.00

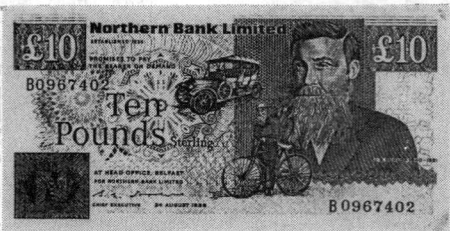

194	10 POUNDS	VG	VF	UNC
	24.8.1988; 14.5.1991; 24.8.1993. Red and brown on m/c unpt. Early automobile above bicyclist at ctr., J. B. Dunlop at r.			
	a. 24.8.1988; 24.8.1990.	40.00	90.00	160.00
	b. 14.5.1991; 24.8.1993.	FV	75.00	130.00

195	20 POUNDS	VG	VF	UNC
	24.8.1988; 24.8.1989; 24.8.1990; 9.5.1991; 30.3.1992; 8.24.1993. Purple-brown, red and m/c. Airplane at ctr., H. G. Ferguson at r., tractor at bottom r.	50.00	110.00	175.00

196	50 POUNDS	VG	VF	UNC
	1.11.1990. Bluish green, black and m/c. Tea dryer, centrifugal machine at ctr, Sir S. Davidson at r.	100.00	160.00	225.00

197	100 POUNDS	VG	VF	UNC
	1.11.1990. Lilac, black, blue and m/c. Airplanes and ejection seat at ctr., Sir J. Martin at r.	250.00	375.00	500.00

1997; 1999 ISSUE

#198-201 city hall in Belfast at ctr., bldgs. and architectural drawings in unpt. on back.

198	10 POUNDS	VG	VF	UNC
	24.2.1997. Dk. brown and violet on m/c unpt. J. B. Dunlop at r. and as wmk., bicycle at lower l.	FV	25.00	37.50
199	20 POUNDS			
	24.2.1997; 1.9.1999. Purple and dk. brown on m/c unpt. H. Ferguson at r. and as wmk., farm tractor at lower l.	FV	50.00	60.00
200	50 POUNDS			
	8.10.1999. Olive brown on m/c unpt. Sir Samuel Davidson at r.	FV	110.00	175.00
201	100 POUNDS			
	8.10.1999. Brown olive on m/c unpt. Sir James Martin at r. Martin Baker ejection seat at l.	FV	FV	275.00

1999 COMMEMORATIVE ISSUE

#202, 175 Years of Banking, 1824-1999

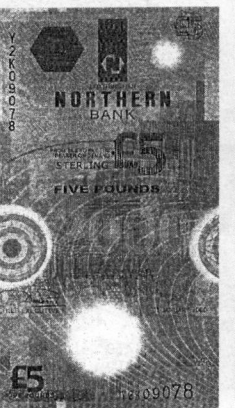

202	20 POUNDS	VG	VF	UNC
	1.9.1999 Purple and dk. brown on m/c unpt. Like #199 but w/commemorative text and gold rectangle at upper l. ctr. on face.	FV	55.00	85.00

2000 COMMEMORATIVE ISSUE

#203, Millennium and Y2K Commemoratives

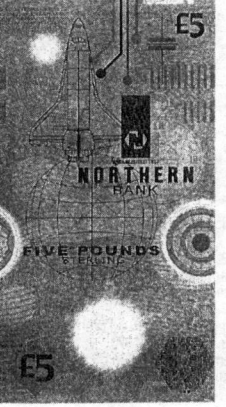

203	5 POUNDS	VG	VF	UNC
	1999; 2000. Blue, red and m/c. Ovals, globe pattern. Space shuttle, electronics on back. Polymer plastic.			
	a. 8.10.1999. Serial # prefix MM.	FV	FV	15.00
	b. 1.1.2000. Serial # prefix Y2K.	FV	FV	25.00

PROVINCIAL BANK OF IRELAND LIMITED

See also Ireland-Republic and Northern - Allied Irish Banks Ltd.

BELFAST

1948; 1951 ISSUE

240	10 POUNDS	VG	VF	UNC
	10.1.1948. Green on red unpt. and green and pink mesh.			
	a. Sign. H. Robertson.	25.00	60.00	125.00
	b. Sign. F. S. Forde.	22.00	55.00	110.00
	c. Sign. G. A. Kennedy.	20.00	50.00	100.00

1954 ISSUE

241	1 POUND	VG	VF	UNC
	1.10.1954. Green. 148 x 84mm.	20.00	70.00	140.00
242	5 POUNDS			
	5.10.1954-5.7.1961. Brown.	30.00	90.00	200.00

1965 ISSUE

#243 and 244 cameo portr. archaic woman at upper ctr. Bank bldg. at ctr. on back.

#243-246 printer: TDLR.

243	1 POUND	VG	VF	UNC
	1.12.1965. Green.	17.50	70.00	150.00
244	5 POUNDS			
	6.12.1965. Brown.	25.00	80.00	180.00

1968 ISSUE

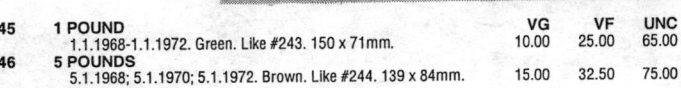

245	1 POUND	VG	VF	UNC
	1.1.1968-1.1.1972. Green. Like #243. 150 x 71mm.	10.00	25.00	65.00
246	5 POUNDS			
	5.1.1968; 5.1.1970; 5.1.1972. Brown. Like #244. 139 x 84mm.	15.00	32.50	75.00

1977; 1981 ISSUE

247	1 POUND	VG	VF	UNC
	1977; 1979. Green on m/c unpt. Like #1. Young girl at r. Sailing ship *Girona* at ctr. on back.			
	a. Sign. J. G. McClay. 1.1.1977.	4.00	20.00	35.00
	b. Sign. F. H. Hollway. 1.1.1979.	4.00	20.00	30.00

		VG	VF	UNC
248	**5 POUNDS** 1977; 1979. Blue and purple on m/c unpt. Like #2. Young woman at r. Dunluce Castle at ctr. on back.			
	a. Sign. J. G. McClay. 1.1.1977.	20.00	45.00	125.00
	b. Sign. F. H. Hollway. 1.1.1979.	15.00	35.00	90.00
249	**10 POUNDS** 1977; 1979. Brown and gray-green on m/c unpt. Like #3. Young man at r. Wreck of the *Girona* at ctr. on back.			
	a. Sign. J. G. McClay. 1.1.1977.	32.50	90.00	160.00
	b. Sign. F. H. Hollway. 1.1.1979.	32.50	90.00	150.00
250	**20 POUNDS** 1.3.1981. Purple and green. Like #4. Elderly woman at r. Chimney at Lacada Pt. at ctr. on back.	60.00	130.00	275.00
251	**100 POUNDS** 1.3.1981. Black, olive and green. Like #5. Elderly man at r. The *Armada* at ctr. on back.	250.00	400.00	900.00

ULSTER BANK LIMITED

BELFAST

1966-70 ISSUE

#321-324 rural and urban views of Belfast at lower l. and r., port w/bridge at lower ctr. below sign., date to r. Arms at ctr. on back. Sign. Jno. J. A. Leitch. Printer: BWC.

		VG	VF	UNC
321	**1 POUND** 4.10.1966. Blue-black on m/c unpt. 151 x 72mm.			
	a. Issued note.	10.00	25.00	60.00
	s. Specimen.	—	—	70.00

		VG	VF	UNC
322	**5 POUNDS** 4.10.1966. Brown on m/c unpt. 140 x 85mm.			
	a. Issued note.	20.00	50.00	160.00
	s. Specimen, punch hole cancelled.	—	—	120.00

		VG	VF	UNC
323	**10 POUNDS** 4.10.1966. Green on m/c unpt. 151 x 93mm.			
	a. Issued note.	40.00	80.00	275.00
	s. Specimen, punch hole cancelled.	—	—	150.00

		VG	VF	UNC
324	**20 POUNDS** 1.7.1970. Lilac on m/c unpt. 161 x 90mm. Specimen, punch hole cancelled.	—	—	225.00

1971-82 ISSUE

#325-330 printer: BWC.

#325-328 similar to #321-324 but date at l., sign. at ctr. r.

		VG	VF	UNC
325	**1 POUND** 1971-76. Blue-black on m/c unpt. Wmk: Bank name repeated. 135 x 67mm.			
	a. Sign. H. E. O'B. Traill. 15.2.1971.	7.00	20.00	50.00
	b. Sign. R. W. Hamilton. 1.3.1973; 1.3.1976.	5.00	10.00	27.50
	s. As a. Specimen.	—	—	70.00
326	**5 POUNDS** 1971-86. Brown on m/c unpt. 146 x 78mm.			
	a. Sign. H. E. O'B. Traill. 15.2.1971.	17.50	50.00	160.00
	b. Sign R. W. Hamilton. 1.3.1973; 1.3.1976.	15.00	30.00	120.00
	c. Sign. V. Chambers. 1.10.1982; 1.10.1983; 1.9.1986.	12.00	22.50	47.50

327	10 POUNDS	VG	VF	UNC
	1971-89. Green on m/c unpt. 151 x 86mm.			
	a. Sign. H. E. O'B. Traill. 15.2.1971.	30.00	80.00	190.00
	b. Sign. R. W. Hamilton. 1.3.1973; 1.3.1976; 2.6.1980.	25.00	50.00	110.00
	c. Sign. V. Chambers. 1.10.1982; 1.10.1983; 1.2.1988.	25.00	45.00	100.00
	d. Sign. J. Wead. 1.12.1989.	25.00	45.00	90.00
328	20 POUNDS			
	1976-83. Violet on m/c unpt.			
	a. Sign. R. W. Hamilton. 1.3.1976.	60.00	120.00	190.00
	b. Sign. V. Chambers. 1.10.1982; 1.10.1983.; 1.2.1988	60.00	120.00	180.00
329	50 POUNDS			
	1.10.1982. Brown on m/c unpt. Sign. V. Chambers.	130.00	250.00	400.00
330	100 POUNDS			
	1.3.1973. Red on m/c unpt. Sign. R. W. Hamilton.			
	a. Issued note.	200.00	400.00	600.00
	s. Specimen.	—	—	350.00

1989-90 ISSUE

#331-334 similar to previous issue but smaller size notes. Sign. J. Wead. Printer: TDLR.

Note: The Bank of Ireland sold to collectors matched serial # sets of £5-10-20 notes as well as 100 sets of replacement serial # prefix Z.

331	5 POUNDS	VG	VF	UNC
	1.12.1989; 1.1.1992; 4.1.1993. Brown on m/c unpt. Similar to #326.	FV	17.50	35.00

332	10 POUNDS	VG	VF	UNC
	1.12.1990. Green on m/c unpt. Similar to #327.	FV	25.00	60.00
333	20 POUNDS			
	1.11.1990. Violet on m/c unpt. Similar to #328.	FV	50.00	130.00
334	100 POUNDS			
	1.12.1990. Red on m/c unpt. Similar to #330.	FV	250.00	350.00

1996; 1998 ISSUE

#335-338 similar to #329, 331-333 but w/ascending size serial # at l. and r.

335	5 POUNDS	VG	VF	UNC
	2.1.1998; 1.7.1998; 1.1.2001. Similar to #331.	FV	FV	15.00

336	10 POUNDS	VG	VF	UNC
	1.1.1997. Blue and green on m/c unpt. Similar to #332.	FV	FV	30.00

337	20 POUNDS	VG	VF	UNC
	1.1.1996; 1.7.1999. Purple and violet on m/c unpt. Similar to #333 but w/hologram at upper ctr. r.	FV	FV	55.00

338	50 POUNDS	VG	VF	UNC
	1.1.1997. Brown on m/c unpt. Similar to #329 but w/hologram at upper ctr. r.	FV	FV	140.00

COLLECTOR SERIES

BANK OF IRELAND

Note: The Bank of Ireland sold to collectors matched serial # sets of £5-10-20 notes as well as 100 sets of replacement serial # prefix Z.

1978 ND ISSUE

		Issue Price	Mkt.	Value
CS1	ND (1978). 1, 5, 10, 100 POUNDS			
	#61b-64b ovpt: *SPECIMEN* and Maltese cross prefix serial #.	7.00		85.00

PROVINCIAL BANK OF IRELAND LIMITED

1978 ISSUE

		Issue Price	Mkt.	Value
CS2	1978 1, 5, 10 POUNDS			
	#247a-249a dated 1.1.1977. Ovpt: *SPECIMEN* and Maltese cross prefix serial #.	7.00		60.00

BANK OF IRELAND

Note: The Bank of Ireland sold to collectors matched serial # sets of £5-10-20 notes as well as 100 sets of replacement serial # prefix *Z*.

1995 ND ISSUE

		Issue Price	Mkt.	Value
CS3	ND (1995). 5, 10, 100 POUNDS			
	#62b-64b ovpt: *SPECIMEN*.	—		400.00

ISLE OF MAN

The Isle of Man, a dependency of the British Crown located in the Irish Sea equidistant from Ireland, Scotland and England, has an area of 227 sq. mi. (588 sq. km.) and a population of 71,714. Capital: Douglas. Agriculture, dairy farming, fishing and tourism are the chief industries.

The prevalence of prehistoric artifacts and monuments on the island gives evidence that its mild, almost sub-tropical climate was enjoyed by mankind before the dawn of history. Vikings came to the Isle of Man during the 9th century and remained until ejected by Scotland in 1266. The island came under the protection of the English Crown in 1288, and in 1406 was granted, in perpetuity, to the Earls of Derby. In 1736 it was inherited by the Duke of Atholl. Rights and title were purchased from the Duke of Atholl in 1765 by the British Crown; the remaining privileges of the Atholl family were transferred to the crown in 1829. The Sovereign of the United Kingdom (currently Queen Elizabeth II) holds the title Lord of Man. The Isle of Man is ruled by its own legislative council and the House of Keys, one of the oldest legislative assemblies in the world. Acts of Parliament passed in London do not affect the island unless it is specifically mentioned.

United Kingdom bank notes and coinage circulate concurrently with Isle of Man money as legal tender.

RULERS:
British

MONETARY SYSTEM:
1 Pound = 20 Shillings to 1971
1 Pound = 100 New Pence, 1971-

BRITISH ADMINISTRATION

LLOYDS BANK LIMITED

1955 ISSUE

		Good	Fine	XF
13	1 POUND			
	21.1.1955-14.3.1961. Black on green unpt. Bank arms at upper ctr. Like #12 but bank title enlarged on back.			
	a. Issued note.	90.00	180.00	400.00
	r. Unsigned remainder. ND.	—	—	120.00

WESTMINSTER BANK LIMITED

Formerly the London County Westminster and Parr's Bank Limited.

1955 ISSUE

#23A, various date and sign. varieties.

		Good	Fine	XF
23A	1 POUND			
	1955-61. Black on lt. yellow unpt. Like #23 but w/text: *INCORPORATED IN ENGLAND* added below bank name. Printer: W&S.			
	a. 23.11.1955.	100.00	200.00	500.00
	b. 4.4.1956-10.3.1961.	40.00	100.00	225.00

NOTICE

Readers with unlisted dates, signature varieties, etc. are invited to submit photocopies of their notes to: Standard Catalog of World Paper Money, 700 East State St. Iola, WI 54990-0001, E-Mail: george.cuhaj@fwpubs.com.

GOVERNMENT

1961 ND ISSUE

#24-27 Triskele arms at lower ctr. and as wmk., young portr. Qn. Elizabeth II at r. Printer: BWC.

	SIGNATURE VARIETIES		
1	Garvey	2	Stallard
3	Paul (26mm)	4	Paul (20mm)
5	Dawaon	6	Cashen

24	10 SHILLINGS	VG	VF	UNC
	ND (1961). Red on m/c unpt. Old sailing boat on back.			
	a. Sign. 1.	5.00	25.00	75.00
	b. Sign. 2.	5.00	20.00	60.00
	s1. Sign. 1. Specimen. 00000 serial #. (150 issued).	—	—	180.00
	s2. Sign. 2. Specimen.			

25	1 POUND	VG	VF	UNC
	ND (1961). Purple on m/c unpt. Tynwald Hill on back.			
	a. Sign. 1.	6.00	30.00	110.00
	b. Sign. 2.	5.00	25.00	100.00
	s1. Sign. 1. Specimen. 00000 serial #. (150 issued).	—	—	200.00
	s2. Sign. 2. Specimen.	—	—	200.00

26	5 POUNDS	VG	VF	UNC
	ND (1961). Green and blue on m/c unpt. Castle Rushen on back.			
	a. Sign. 1.	40.00	200.00	1100.00
	b. Sign. 2.	35.00	150.00	950.00
	s1. Specimen w/normal serial #.	—	—	500.00
	s2. Sign. 1. Specimen w/normal serial # blocked out, punch hole cancelled. (50 issued).	—	—	350.00
	s3. Sign. 1. Specimen. 000000 serial #. (150 issued).	—	—	200.00

1969 ND ISSUE

27	50 NEW PENCE	VG	VF	UNC
	ND (1969). Blue on m/c unpt. Back like #24. 139 x 66mm. Sign. 2.	2.00	8.50	30.00

1972 ND ISSUE

#28-31 Triskele arms at ctr. and as wmk., older portr. Qn. Elizabeth II at r. Sign. title: *LIEUTENANT GOVERNOR*. Printer: BWC.

28	50 NEW PENCE	VG	VF	UNC
	ND (1972). Blue on m/c unpt. Back like #24. 126 x 62mm.			
	a. Sign. 2.	3.00	15.00	55.00
	b. Sign. 3.	2.00	10.00	30.00
	c. Sign. 4.	2.00	10.00	25.00
	s1. As a. Specimen. Punched hole cancelled.	—	—	200.00
	s2. As b, c. Specimen.	—	—	200.00

29	1 POUND	VG	VF	UNC
	ND (1972). Purple on m/c unpt. Back similar to #25.			
	a. Sign. 2.	5.00	25.00	110.00
	b. Sign. 3.	5.00	32.50	120.00
	c. Sign. 4.	2.50	7.50	25.00
	s1. As a. Specimen. Punched hole cancelled.	—	—	200.00
	s2. As b, c. Specimen.	—	—	200.00

		VG	VF	UNC
30	**5 POUNDS** ND (1972). Blue-black and violet on m/c unpt. Back gray-green; similar to #26.			
	a. Sign. 2.	20.00	60.00	400.00
	b. Sign. 3.	15.00	35.00	200.00
	s. As a, b. Specimen. Punched hole cancelled.	—	—	325.00

		VG	VF	UNC
31	**10 POUNDS** ND (1972). Brown and dk. green on m/c unpt. Back brown and orange; Peel Castle ca.1830 at ctr.			
	a. Sign. 2.	150.00	350.00	1200.00
	b. Sign. 3.	60.00	150.00	600.00
	s. As a, b. Specimen, punched hole cancelled.	—	—	600.00

1979 COMMEMORATIVE ISSUE

#32, Millennium Year 1979

		VG	VF	UNC
32	**20 POUNDS** 1979. Red-orange, orange and dk. brown on m/c unpt. Triskele at ctr. Qn. Elizabeth II at r. Island outline at upper r. Commemorative text at lower r. of triskele. Laxey wheel ca. 1854, crowd of people w/ hills in background on back. Printer: BWC.	40.00	100.00	325.00

1979 ND ISSUE

#33-37 Qn. Elizabeth II at r., arms at ctr. Sign. title: *TREASURER OF THE ISLE OF MAN*. Wmk: Triskele arms. Printer: BWC.

#33s-38s were mounted on a board for bank display.

		VG	VF	UNC
33	**50 NEW PENCE** ND. Blue on m/c unpt. Like #28. Sign. 5.			
	a. Issued note.	FV	FV	7.00
	s. Specimen. Normal serial #, punched hole cancelled.	—	—	175.00

		VG	VF	UNC
34	**1 POUND** ND. Purple on m/c unpt. Like #29. Sign. 5.			
	a. Issued note.	FV	FV	12.00
	s. Specimen. Normal serial #, punched hole cancelled.	—	—	175.00

		VG	VF	UNC
35	**5 POUNDS** ND. Blue-black and violet on m/c unpt. Like #30.			
	a. Sign. 5. Series A-C.	12.50	45.00	150.00
	b. Sign. 5. Series D. Lg. 'D' with serifs.	20.00	60.00	200.00
35A	**5 POUNDS** ND. Blue-black and violet on m/c unpt. Like #35 but w/modified guilloche. Series D. Narrow 'D' w/o serifs.			
	a. Issued note.	12.50	45.00	150.00
	s. Specimen. Normal serial #, punched hole cancelled.	—	—	275.00

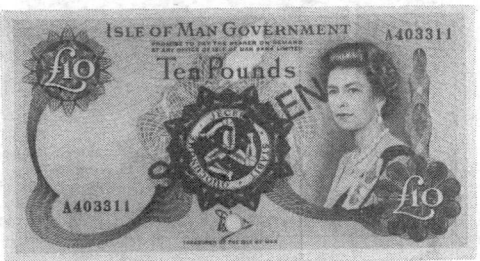

		VG	VF	UNC
36	**10 POUNDS** ND. Brown and dk. green on m/c unpt. Like #31. Sign. 5.			
	a. W/o prefix.	25.00	90.00	350.00
	b. Prefix A.	25.00	90.00	350.00
	c. Prefix B. (10,000 printed).	250.00	500.00	1250.00
	s. Specimen. Prefix A, normal serial #, punched hole cancelled.	—	—	40—

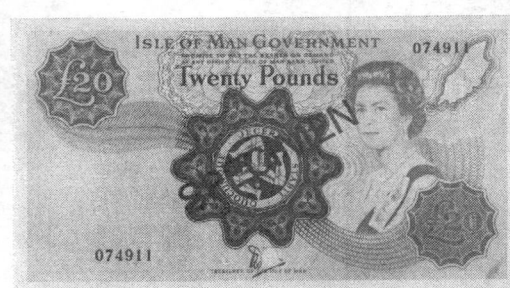

		VG	VF	UNC
37	**20 POUNDS** ND (1979). Red-orange, orange and dk. brown on m/c unpt. Like #32 but w/o commemorative text.			
	a. Issued note.	40.00	100.00	375.00
	s. Specimen. Normal serial #, punched hole cancelled.	—	—	350.00

1983 ND ISSUE

38	1 POUND		VG	VF	UNC
	ND (1983). Green on m/c unpt. Like #25 but printed on Bradvek, a special plastic.		2.00	5.00	22.50

42	10 POUNDS		VG	VF	UNC
	ND. Brown and green on m/c unpt. Like #31. Back brown, orange and m/c.				
	b. Sign. 6.		FV	FV	40.00

39	50 POUNDS		VG	VF	UNC
	ND (1983). Blue gray, deep green and olive-green on m/c unpt. Douglas Bay on back.				
	a. Issued note.		FV	100.00	175.00
	s. Specimen. Normal serial #, punched hole cancelled.		—	—	500.00

1983 ND REDUCED SIZE ISSUE

#40-44 smaller format. Qn. Elizabeth II at r., arms at ctr. Wmk: Triskele. Printer: TDLR. Replacement notes: Serial # prefix Z.

43	20 POUNDS		VG	VF	UNC
	ND. Brown and red-orange on m/c unpt. Back like #32.				
	a. Sign. 5.		40.00	75.00	325.00
	b. Sign. 6.		FV	FV	80.00

1998; 2000 ND ISSUE

#44-45 like #42-43 but w/LIMITED deleted from payment clause.

40	1 POUND		VG	VF	UNC	44	10 POUNDS		VG	VF	UNC
	ND. Purple on m/c unpt. Back like #25.						ND (1998). Brown and green on m/c unpt. Like #42.		FV	FV	37.50
	a. Sign. 5.		FV	4.00	12.00	45	20 POUNDS				
	b. Sign. 6.		FV	FV	5.00		ND (2000). Brown and red-orange on m/c unpt. Like #43b.		FV	FV	70.00

41	5 POUNDS		VG	VF	UNC
	ND. Greenish blue and lilac-brown on m/c unpt. Back like #30.				
	a. Sign. 5.		FV	15.00	35.00
	b. Sign. 6.		FV	10.00	20.00

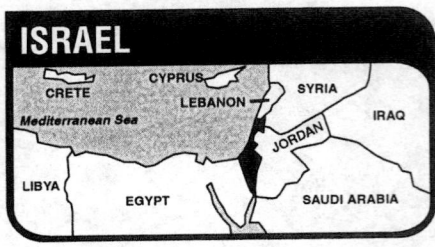

The State of Israel, at the eastern end of the Mediterranean Sea, bounded by Lebanon on the north, Syria on the northeast, Jordan on the east, and Egypt on the southwest, has an area of 7,847 sq. mi. (23,309 sq. km.) and a population of 6.08 million. Capital: Jerusalem. Diamonds, chemicals, citrus, textiles, and minerals are exported, local tourism to religious sites.

Palestine, which corresponds to Canaan of the Bible, was settled by the Philistines about the 12th century B.C. and shortly thereafter was invaded by the Jews who established the kingdoms of Israel and Judah. Because of its position as part of the land bridge connecting Asia and Africa, Palestine was invaded and conquered by nearly all of the historic empires of ancient Europe and Asia. In the 16th century it became a Turkish satrap. After falling to the British in World War I, it, together with Transjordan, was mandated to Great Britain by the League of Nations in 1922.

For more than half a century prior to the termination of the British mandate over Palestine in 1948, Zionist leaders had sought to create a Jewish homeland for Jews dispersed throughout the world. Israel was the logical location choice as it had long been the Jewish religious and cultural homeland. Also, for almost as long, Jews fleeing persecution had immigrated to Palestine. The Nazi persecutions of the 1930s and 1940s increased the Jewish relocation to Palestine and generated international support for the creation of a Jewish state, first promulgated by the Balfour Declaration of 1917 which asserted British support for the endeavor. The dream of a Jewish homeland was realized on May 14, 1948 when Palestine was proclaimed the State of Israel.

MONETARY SYSTEM:
1 Lira = 100 Agorot, 1958-1980
1 Sheqel = 10 "old" Lirot, 1980-85
1 Sheqel = 100 New Agorot, 1980-1985
1 New Sheqel = 1000 "old" Sheqalim, 1985-
1 New Sheqel = 100 New Agorot, 1985-

BANK OF ISRAEL

1958-60 / 5718-20 ISSUE

Lira system
#29-33 wmk. as portrait.
#29, 30 and 33 printer: JEZ (w/o imprint).

29	1/2 LIRA	VG	VF	UNC
	1958/5718. Green on green and peach unpt. Woman soldier w/basket full of oranges at l. Tombs of the Sanhedrin at r. on back.			
	a. Issued note.	0.50	1.50	5.00
	s. Specimen.	—	—	295.00

30	1 LIRA	VG	VF	UNC
	1958/5718. Blue on lt. blue and peach unpt. Fisherman w/net and anchor at l. Synagogue mosaic at r. on back.			
	a. Paper w/security thread at l. Black serial #.	0.50	1.25	4.00
	b. Red serial #.	0.50	1.25	4.00
	c. Paper w/security thread and morse tape, brown serial #.	0.50	1.00	3.00
	s. Specimen.	—	—	295.00

#31 and 32 printer: TDLR (w/o imprint).

31	5 LIROT	VG	VF	UNC
	1958/5718. Brown on m/c unpt. Worker w/hammer in front of factory at l. Seal of Shema at r. on back.			
	a. Issued note.	0.50	2.00	5.00
	s. Specimen.	—	—	295.00

32	10 LIROT	VG	VF	UNC
	1958/5718. Lilac and purple on m/c unpt. Scientist w/microscope and test tube at l. Dead Sea scroll and vases at r. on back.			
	a. Paper w/security thread. Black serial #.	0.50	2.00	10.00
	b. Paper w/security thread and morse tape. Red serial #.	0.50	2.00	18.00
	c. Paper w/security thread and morse tape. Blue serial #.	0.50	2.00	18.00
	d. Paper w/security thread and morse tape. Brown serial #.	0.50	1.50	7.50
	s. Specimen.	—	—	295.00

33	50 LIROT	VG	VF	UNC
	1960/5720. Brown and m/c. Boy and girl at l. Mosaic of menorah at r. on back.			
	a. Paper w/security thread. Black serial #.	2.00	10.00	45.00
	b. Paper w/security thread. Red serial #.	2.00	10.00	45.00
	c. Paper w/security thread and morse tape. Blue serial #.	1.50	6.00	45.00
	d. Paper w/security thread and morse tape. Green serial #.	1.50	6.00	30.00
	e. Paper w/security thread and morse tape. Brown serial #.	1.50	5.00	30.00
	s. Specimen.	—	—	400.00

1968 / 5728 ISSUE

#34-37 printer: JEZ (w/o imprint).

34	5 LIROT	VG	VF	UNC
	1968/5728. Gray-green and blue on m/c unpt. Albert Einstein at r. and as wmk. Atomic reactor at Nahal Sorek on back.			
	a. Black serial #.	0.75	3.00	10.00
	b. Red serial #.	0.75	3.00	10.00

37	100 LIROT	VG	VF	UNC
	1968/5728. Blue and lt. green on m/c unpt. Dr. Theodor Herzl at r. and as wmk. Menorah and symbols of the 12 tribes of Israel at l. ctr. on back.			
	a. Wmk: Profile. Black serial #. 3.5mm.	1.50	10.00	35.00
	b. Wmk: 3/4 profile r. Red serial #.	1.50	10.00	35.00
	c. Wmk: Profile. Black serial #. 2.8mm. W/o series letter.	1.50	7.50	30.00
	d. Wmk: Profile. Brown serial #.	1.50	5.00	30.00

1973-75 / 5733-35 ISSUE

#38-51 printer: JEZ (w/o imprint).

All the following notes except #41 and 45 have marks for the blind on the face. #38-46 have barely discernible bar code strips at lower l. and upper r. on back. All have portr. as wmk. Various gates in Jerusalem on backs.

35	10 LIROT	VG	VF	UNC
	1968/5728. Brown, purple and m/c. Chaim Nahman Bialik at r. and as wmk. Bialik's house in Tel Aviv on back.			
	a. Black serial #.	0.25	1.00	5.00
	b. Green serial #.	0.25	1.00	5.00
	c. Blue serial #.	0.25	1.00	5.00

38	5 LIROT	VG	VF	UNC
	1973/5733. Lt. and dk. brown. Henrietta Szold at r. Lion's Gate on back.	0.15	0.50	1.50

36	50 LIROT	VG	VF	UNC
	1968/5728. Lt. and dk. brown and green on m/c unpt. Pres. Chaim Weizmann at r. and as wmk. Knesset bldg. in Jerusalem on back.			
	a. Black serial #.	0.50	2.00	7.50
	b. Blue serial #.	0.50	2.00	7.50

39	10 LIROT	VG	VF	UNC
	1973/5733. Purple on lilac unpt. Sir Moses Montefiore at r. Jaffa Gate on back.			
	a. Issued note.	0.15	0.50	1.50
	s. Specimen.	—	—	—

		VG	VF	UNC
40	**50 LIROT**	0.25	1.00	6.00
	1973/5733. Green on olive-green unpt. Chaim Weizmann at r. Sichem Gate on back.			

		VG	VF	UNC
44	**5 SHEQALIM**	0.25	0.75	3.00
	1978/5738 (1980). Green on olive-green unpt. Like #40.			

		VG	VF	UNC
41	**100 LIROT**	0.50	1.50	5.00
	1973/5733. Blue on blue and brown unpt. Dr. Theodor Herzl at r. Zion Gate on back.			

		VG	VF	UNC
45	**10 SHEQALIM**	0.50	1.50	5.00
	1978/5738 (1980). Blue on blue and brown unpt. Like #41.			

		VG	VF	UNC
42	**500 LIROT**	2.50	10.00	45.00
	1975/5735. Black on tan and brown unpt. David Ben-Gurion at r. Golden Gate on back.			

1978-84 / 5738-44 ISSUE

Sheqel system

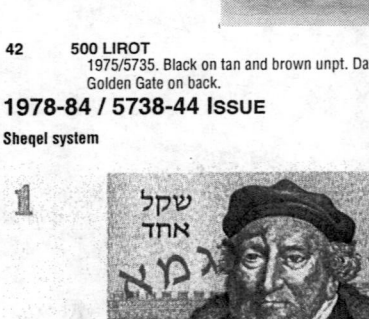

		VG	VF	UNC
46	**50 SHEQALIM**			
	1978/5738 (1980). Black on tan and brown unpt. Like #42.			
	a. W/o small bars below serial # or barely discernible bar code strips on back.	0.15	0.50	2.00
	b. W/o small bars below serial #, but w/bar code strips on back.	1.00	4.00	25.00
	c. 2 green bars below serial # on back.	20.00	45.00	225.00
	d. 4 black bars below serial # on back.	15.00	35.00	175.00
	e. As a. 12-subject sheet.	—	—	25.00

Note: Colored bars were used to identify various surface-coated papers, used experimentally.

		VG	VF	UNC
43	**1 SHEQEL**			
	1978/5738 (1980). Purple on lilac unpt. Like #39.			
	a. Issued note.	0.15	0.50	2.00
	s. Specimen.	—	—	—

47	100 SHEQALIM	VG	VF	UNC
	1979/5739. Red-brown on lt. tan unpt. Ze'ev Jabotinsky at r. Herod's Gate on back.			
	a. W/o bars below serial # on back.	0.50	1.50	8.00
	b. 2 bars below serial # on back.	6.00	30.00	100.00

51	10,000 SHEQALIM	VG	VF	UNC
	1984/5744. Brown, black, orange and dk. green on m/c unpt. Stylized tree at ctr., Golda Meir at r. and as wmk. Gathering in front of Moscow synagogue on back.			
	a. Issued note.	2.00	10.00	35.00
	b. Uncut sheet of 3 (2,720 sheets).	—	—	75.00

1985-92 / 5745-52 ISSUE

#51A-56 portr. as wmk. Printer: JEZ (w/o imprint). All with marks for the blind.

SIGNATURE VARIETIES			
5	Mandelbaum, 1986	6	Shapira and Mandelbaum, 1985
7	Lorincz and Bruno, 1987-91	8	Lorincz and Frankel, 1992
9	Lorincz and ...		

48	500 SHEQALIM	VG	VF	UNC
	1982/5742. Red on m/c unpt. Farm workers at ctr., Baron Edmond de Rothschild at r. Vine leaves on back.	0.50	1.50	9.00

49	1000 SHEQALIM	VG	VF	UNC
	1983/5743. Green on m/c unpt. Rabbi Moses Maimonides at r. View of Tiberias at l. on back.			
	a. Error in first letter he of second word at r. in vertical text (right to left), partly completed letter resembling 7.	1.50	7.50	30.00
	b. Corrected letter resembling 17.	0.75	4.00	22.50
	c. As a. Uncut sheet of 3 (3,610 sheets).	—	—	45.00
	d. As b. Uncut sheet of 3 (3,365 sheets).	—	—	35.00

51A	1 NEW SHEQEL	VG	VF	UNC
	1986/5746. Like #49 except for denomination. Sign. 5.			
	a. Issued note.	0.25	0.50	2.00
	b. Uncut sheet of 3 (2,017 sheets).	—	—	7.00
	c. Uncut sheet of 12 (1,416 sheets).	—	—	35.00
	d. Uncut sheet of 18 (1.503 sheets).	—	—	50.00

50	5000 SHEQALIM	VG	VF	UNC
	1984/5744. Blue on m/c unpt. City view at ctr., Levi Eshkol at r. Water pipe and modern design on back.			
	a. Issued note.	1.50	7.50	45.00
	b. Uncut sheet of 3 (2,755 sheets).	—	—	45.00

52	5 NEW SHEQALIM	VG	VF	UNC
	1985/5745; 1987/5747. Like #50 except for denomination.			
	a. Sign. 6. 1985/5745.	0.75	4.00	25.00
	b. Sign. 7. 1987/5747.	0.50	2.50	20.00
	c. As a. Uncut sheet of 3 (1,630 sheets).	—	—	50.00

	100 NEW SHEQALIM	VG	VF	UNC
56	1986/5746; 1989/5749; 1995/5755. Brown on m/c unpt. Itzhak Ben-Zvi at r. and as wmk. Stylized village of Peki'in and carob tree on back.			
	a. Sign. 5. Plain security thread and plain white paper. 1986/5746.	FV	FV	100.00
	b. Sign. 6. W/security thread inscribed: *Bank Israel,* paper w/colored threads. 1989/5749.	FV	FV	100.00
	c. Sign. 8. 1995/5755.	FV	FV	85.00

	10 NEW SHEQALIM	VG	VF	UNC
53	1985/5745; 1987/5747; 1992/5752. Like #51 except for denomination.			
	a. Sign. 6. 1985/5745.	1.00	6.00	32.50
	b. Sign. 7. 1987/5747.	0.75	4.00	20.00
	c. Sign. 8. 1992/5752.	0.50	2.00	12.50
	d. As a. Uncut sheet of 3 (1,571 sheets).	—	—	50.00

	20 NEW SHEQALIM	VG	VF	UNC
54	1987/5747; 1993/5753. Dk. gray on m/c unpt. Moshe Sharett standing holding flag at ctr., his bust at r. and as wmk. Herzlya High School at ctr. on back.			
	a. W/o sm. double circle w/dot in wmk. area face and back. Sign. 7. 1987/5747.	FV	FV	40.00
	b. W/sm. double circle w/dot in wmk. area face and back. Sign. 7. 1987/5747.	FV	FV	40.00
	c. Sign. 8. 1993/5753.	FV	FV	20.00

	200 NEW SHEQALIM	VG	VF	UNC
57	1991/5751; 1994/5754. Deep red, purple and blue-green on m/c unpt. Zalman Shazar at r. and as wmk. School girl writing at ctr. on back.			
	a. Sign. 7. 1991/5751.	FV	FV	135.00
	b. Sign. 8. 1994/5754.	FV	FV	120.00

1998 COMMEMORATIVE ISSUE

#58, 50th Anniversary - State of Israel

	50 NEW SHEQALIM	VG	VF	UNC
58	1998/5758. Purple on m/c unpt. Like #55 but w/OVI *50* at upper l., 5-digit serial # below. Sign. 8.	FV	FV	45.00

Note: #58 was issued in sheets of three in a special folder (10,001) sets. Value $100.

	50 NEW SHEQALIM	VG	VF	UNC
55	1985/5745-1992/5752. Purple on m/c unpt. Shmuel Yosef Agnon at r. r. and as wmk. Various bldgs. and book titles on back.			
	a. Sign. 6. 1985/5745.	FV	FV	100.00
	b. Sign. 7. Slight color variations. 1988/5748.	FV	FV	90.00
	c. Sign. 8. 1992/5752.	FV	FV	50.00

1998 DATED 1999 ISSUE

#59-62 vertical format.

59	20 NEW SHEQALIM	VG	VF	UNC
	1998; 2001. Dk. green on m/c unpt. Moshe Sharett at bottom, flags in background. Scenes of his life and work on back.			
	a. 1998 (1999).	FV	FV	20.00
	b. 2001 (2003).	FV	FV	18.00

60	50 NEW SHEQALIM	VG	VF	UNC
	1998; 2001. Purple on m/c unpt. Shmuel Yosef Agnon at bottom, library shelves in background. Scenes of his life and work on back.			
	a. 1998.	FV	FV	40.00
	b. 2001 (2003).	FV	FV	30.00

61	100 NEW SHEQALIM	VG	VF	UNC
	1998; 2002. Dk. brown on m/c unpt. Itzhak Ben-Zvi at bottom. Scenes of his life and work on back.			
	a. 1998.	FV	FV	50.00
	b. 2002 (2003).	FV	FV	50.00

62	200 NEW SHEQALIM	VG	VF	UNC
	1999, 2002. Red and red-orange on m/c unpt. Zalman Shazar at bottom, classroom in background. Scenes of his life and work on back.			
	a. 1999.	FV	FV	100.00
	b. 2002 (2003).	FV	FV	100.00

COLLECTOR SERIES

BANK OF ISRAEL

1990 ISSUE

CS1	(1990). 1-50 NEW SHEQALIM	Issue Price	Mkt.	Value
	1985-87. #51Aa-55a w/matching serial #. Issued in special packaging. (2,000).	75.00		95.00

1991 ISSUE

CS2	(1991). 100, 200 NEW SHEQALIM	Issue Price	Mkt.	Value
	1985-86. #56a and 57a w/matching serial # issued in special packaging. (2,000).	149.00		150.00

ITALY

The Italian Republic, a 700-mile-long peninsula extending into the heart of the Mediterranean Sea, has an area of 116,304 sq. mi. (301,308 sq. km.) and a population of 57.46 million. Captal: Rome. The economy centers about agriculture, manufacturing, forestry and fishing. Machinery, textiles, clothing and motor vehicles are exported.

From the fall of Rome until modern times, "Italy" was little more than a geographical expression. Although nominally included in the Empire of Charlemagne and the Holy Roman Empire, it was in reality divided into a number of independent states and kingdoms presided over by wealthy families, soldiers of fortune or hereditary rulers. The 19th century unification movement fostered by Mazzini, Garibaldi and Cavor attained fruition in 1860-1870 with the creation of the Kingdom of Italy and the installation of Victor Emanuele, King of Italy. Benito Mussolini came to power during the post-World War I period of economic and political unrest, installed a Fascist dictatorship with a figurehead king as titular Head of State.

Mussolini entered Italy into the German-Japanese anti-Comintern pact (Tri-Partite Pact) and withdrew from the League of Nations. The war did not go well for Italy and Germany was forced to assist Italy in its failed invasion of Greece. The Allied invasion of Sicily on July 10, 1943 and bombing Rome brought the Fascist council to a no vote of confidence on July 24, 1943. Mussolini was arrested but soon escaped and set up a government in Saló. Rome fell to the Allied forces in June 1944 and the country was allowed the status of co-belligerent against Germany. The Germans held northern Italy for another year. Mussolini was eventually captured and executed by partisans. Following the defeat of the Axis powers the Italian monarchy was dissolved by plebiscite, and the Italian Republic proclaimed on June 10, 1946.

MONETARY SYSTEM:
1 Lira = 100 Centesimi, to 2001
1 Euro = 100 Cents, 2001-

DECREES:
There are many different dates found on the following notes of the Banca d'Italia. These include ART. DELLA LEGGE (law date) and the more important DECRETO MINISTERIALE (D. M. date). The earliest D.M. date is usually found on the back of the note while later D.M. dates are found grouped together. The actual latest date (of issue) is referred to in the following listings.

FACE SEAL VARIETIES:

Type B
Facing head of Medusa

Type C
Winged lion of St. Mark of Venice above 3 shields of Genoa, Pisa and Amalfi

REPUBLIC

REPUBBLICA ITALIANA - BIGLIETTO DI STATO

1966 ISSUE

			VG	VF	UNC
93	**500 LIRE**				
	1966-75. Dk. gray on blue and m/c unpt. Eagle w/snake at l., Arethusa at r. 3 sign. varieties.				
	a. 20.6.1966; 20.10.1967; 23.2.1970.		1.00	2.00	20.00
	b. 23.4.1975.		18.00	70.00	400.00

DECRETO MINISTERIALE 14.2.1974

			VG	VF	UNC
94	**500 LIRE**		0.50	1.00	2.00
	14.2.1974; 2.4.1979. Grayish purple on blue and m/c unpt. Mercury at r. Wmk: star in wreath. 3 sign. varieties.				

DECRETO MINISTERIALE 5.6.1976

			VG	VF	UNC
95	**500 LIRE**		0.50	1.50	3.50
	20.12.1976. Like #94.				

BANCA D'ITALIA

BANK OF ITALY

1962 ISSUE

Decreto Ministeriale 12.4. 1962; Decreto Ministeriale 28.6.1962.

			VG	VF	UNC
96	**1000 LIRE**				
	1962-68. Blue on red and lt. brown unpt. G. Verdi at r. Wmk: Laureate head. Seal: Type B.				
	a. Sign. Carli and Ripa. 14.7.1962; 14.1.1964.		FV	8.00	80.00
	b. Sign. Carli and Ripa. 5.7.1963; 25.7.1964.		FV	9.00	120.00
	c. Sign. Carli and Febbraio. 10.8.1965; 20.5.1966.		FV	9.00	80.00
	d. Sign. Carli and Pacini. 4.1.1968.		FV	9.00	300.00

			VG	VF	UNC
97	**10,000 LIRE**				
	1962-73. Brown, purple, orange and red-brown w/dk. brown text on m/c unpt. Michaelangelo at r. Piazza del Campidoglio in Rome. Wmk: Roman head. Seal: Type B.				
	a. Sign. Carli and Ripa. 3.7.1962; 14.1.1964; 27.7.1964.		FV	10.00	60.00
	b. Sign. Carli and Febbraio. 20.5.1966.		FV	10.00	60.00
	c. Sign. Carli and Pacini. 4.1.1968.		FV	10.00	90.00
	d. Sign. Carli and Lombardo. 8.6.1970.		FV	10.00	60.00
	e. Sign. Carli and Barbarito. 15.2.1973; 27.11.1973.		FV	FV	60.00

1964 ISSUE

Decreto Ministeriale 20.8.1964.

98	5000 LIRE	VG	VF	UNC
	1964-70. Green on pink unpt. Columbus at r. Ship at l. ctr. on back. Seal: Type B.			
	a. Sign. Carli and Ripa. 3.9.1964.	10.00	40.00	220.00
	b. Sign. Carli and Pacini. 4.1.1968.	10.00	40.00	220.00
	c. Sign. Carli and Lombardo. 20.1.1970.	10.00	40.00	220.00

1967 ISSUE

Decreto Ministeriale 27.6.1967.

99	50,000 LIRE	VG	VF	UNC
	1967-74. Brownish black, dk. brown and reddish brown w/black text on m/c unpt. Leonardo da Vinci at r. City view at ctr. on back. Wmk: bust of Madonna. Seal: Type B.			
	a. Sign. Carli and Febbraio. 4.12.1967.	FV	150.00	800.00
	b. Sign. Carli and Lombardo. 19.7.1970.	FV	100.00	600.00
	c. Sign. Carli and Barbarito. 16.5.1972; 4.2.1974.	FV	100.00	600.00

100	100,000 LIRE	VG	VF	UNC
	1967-74. Brownish black, brown and deep olive-green on m/c unpt. A. Manzoni at r. Mountain lake scene at ctr. on back. Wmk: Archaic female bust. Seal: Type B.			
	a. Sign. Carli and Febbraio. 3.7.1967.	80.00	160.00	1300.00
	b. Sign. Carli and Lombardo. 19.7.1970.	80.00	150.00	650.00
	c. Sign. Carli and Barbarito. 6.2.1974.	80.00	150.00	720.00

1969; 1971 ISSUE

Decreto Ministeriale 26.2.1969; Decreto Ministeriale 15.5.1971.

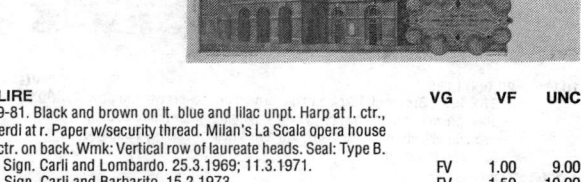

101	1000 LIRE	VG	VF	UNC
	1969-81. Black and brown on lt. blue and lilac unpt. Harp at l. ctr., G. Verdi at r. Paper w/security thread. Milan's La Scala opera house at l. ctr. on back. Wmk: Vertical row of laureate heads. Seal: Type B.			
	a. Sign. Carli and Lombardo. 25.3.1969; 11.3.1971.	FV	1.00	9.00
	b. Sign. Carli and Barbarito. 15.2.1973.	FV	1.50	10.00
	c. Sign. Carli and Barbarito. 5.8.1975.	FV	1.00	8.00
	d. Sign. Baffi and Stevani. 10.1.1977; 10.5.1979.	FV	2.00	15.00
	e. Sign. Ciampi and Stevani. 20.2.1980; 6.9.1980; 30.5.1981.	FV	1.00	8.00

102	5000 LIRE	VG	VF	UNC
	1971-77. Olive, blue and brown on lt. olive unpt. Mythical seahorse at ctr., Columbus at r. 3 sailing ships of Columbus' at l. ctr. on back. Seal: Type C.			
	a. Sign. Carli and Lombardo. 20.5.1971.	FV	14.00	85.00
	b. Sign. Carli and Barbarito. 11.4.1973.	FV	14.00	80.00
	c. Sign. Baffi and Stevani. 10.11.1977.	FV	14.00	80.00

1973; 1974 ISSUE

Decreto Ministeriale 10.9.1973; Decreto Ministeriale 20.12.1974.

103	2000 LIRE	VG	VF	UNC
	1973; 1976; 1983. Brown and green on lt. tan and olive unpt. Galileo at ctr., ornate arms at l., bldgs. and leaning tower of Pisa at r. Signs of the Zodiac on back. Wmk: Man's head. Seal: Type C.			
	a. Sign. Carli and Barbarito. 8.10.1973.	FV	3.00	30.00
	b. Sign. Baffi and Stevani. 20.10.1976.	FV	2.00	15.00
	c. Sign. Ciampi and Stevani. 24.10.1983.	FV	FV	5.00

104   20,000 LIRE
21.2.1975. Brownish black and dk. brown on red-brown and pale olive-green unpt. Titian at ctr. Titian's painting *Amor Sacro e Amor Profano* at l. ctr. on back. Wmk: Woman's head. Seal: Type C. Sign. Carli and Barbarito.

	VG	VF	UNC
	30.00	60.00	340.00

1976-79 ISSUE

Decreto Ministeriale 2.3.1979; Decreto Ministeriale 25.8.1976; Decreto Ministeriale 20.6.1977; Decreto Ministeriale 16.6.1978.

105   5000 LIRE
1979-83. Brown and green. Man at l. Bldg. and statuary at ctr. r. on back. Wmk: Man w/cap. Seal: Type C.

	VG	VF	UNC
a. Sign. Baffi and Stevani. 9.3.1979.	FV	5.00	20.00
b. Sign. Ciampi and Stevani. 1.7.1980; 3.11.1982; 19.10.1983.	FV	5.00	20.00

106   10,000 LIRE
1976-84. Black and m/c. Man at l. and as wmk. Column at r. on back. Seal: Type C.

	VG	VF	UNC
a. Sign. Baffi and Stevani. 30.10.1976; 29.12.1978.	FV	10.00	30.00
b. Sign. Ciampi and Stevani. 6.9.1980; 3.11.1982; 8.3.1984.	FV	7.50	30.00

107   50,000 LIRE
1977-82. Blue, red and green. Young women and lion of St. Mark at l. Modern design of arches on back. Seal: Type C.

	VG	VF	UNC
a. Sign. Baffi and Stevani. 20.6.1977; 12.6.1978; 23.10.1978.	FV	40.00	100.00
b. Sign. Ciampi and Stevani. 11.4.1980.	FV	40.00	100.00
c. Sign. Ciampi and Stevani. 2.11.1982.	FV	50.00	250.00

108   100,000 LIRE
D.1978. Red-violet and black on m/c unpt. Woman's bust at l. and as wmk. Modern bldg. design at r. on back. Seal: Type C.

	VG	VF	UNC
a. Sign. Baffi and Stevani. 20.6.1978.	FV	65.00	180.00
b. Sign. Ciampi and Stevani. 1.7.1980-10.5.1982.	FV	65.00	220.00

1982; 1983 ISSUE

Decreto Ministeriale 6.1.1982; Decreto Ministeriale 1.9.1983.

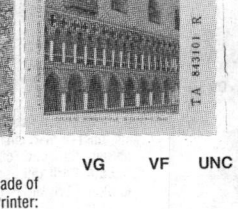

109   1000 LIRE
D.1982. Dk. green and tan. Marco Polo at r. and as wmk. Facade of Doge Palace in Venice at bottom of vertical format on back. Printer: ODBI. Seal: Type C.

	VG	VF	UNC
a. Sign. Ciampi and Stevani. 6.1.1982.	FV	FV	3.00
b. Sign. Ciampi and Speziali. 6.1.1982.	FV	FV	3.00

110   100,000 LIRE
D.1983. Dk. brown and brown on green and olive-green unpt. Couple at ctr., Caravaggio at r. and as wmk. Fruit basket at l., castle at upper ctr. on back. Seal: Type C.

	VG	VF	UNC
a. Sign. Ciampi and Stevani. 1.9.1983.	FV	FV	150.00
b. Sign. Ciampi and Speziali. 1.9.1983.	FV	FV	120.00

1984; 1985 ISSUE

Decreto Ministeriale 4.1.1985; Decreto Ministeriale 3.9.1984; Decreto Ministeriale 6.2.1984.

			VG	VF	UNC
111	**5000 LIRE**				
	D.1985. Olive-green and blue on m/c unpt. Coliseum at ctr., V. Bellini at r. and as wmk. Scene from opera Norma at l. ctr. on back. Seal: Type C.				
	a. Sign. Ciampi and Stevani. 4.1.1985.		FV	FV	30.00
	b. Sign. Ciampi and Speziali. 4.1.1985.		FV	FV	10.00
	c. Sign. Fazio and Amici.		FV	FV	7.50

			VG	VF	UNC
112	**10,000 LIRE**				
	D.1984. Dk. blue on m/c unpt. Lab instrument at ctr., A. Volta at r. and as wmk. Mausoleum at l. ctr. on back. Seal: Type C.				
	a. Sign. Ciampi and Stevani. 3.9.1984.		FV	FV	30.00
	b. Sign. Ciampi and Speziali. 3.9.1984.		FV	FV	14.00
	c. Sign. Fazio and Speziali. 3.9.1984.		FV	FV	12.50
	d. Sign. Fazio and Amici. 3.9.1984.		FV	FV	12.50

			VG	VF	UNC
113	**50,000 LIRE**				
	D.1984. Red-violet and m/c. Figurine at ctr., G.L. Bernini at r. and as wmk. Equestrian statue at l. ctr. on back. Seal: Type C.				
	a. Sign. Ciampi and Stevani. 6.2.1984; 5.12.1984; 28.10.1985; 1.12.1986.		FV	FV	80.00
	b. Sign. Ciampi and Speziali. 25.1.1990.		FV	FV	60.00
	c. Sign. Fazio and Speziali.		FV	FV	55.00

1990-94 ISSUE

Decreto Ministeriale 3.10.1990; Decreto Ministeriale 27.5.1992; Decreto Ministeriale 6.5.1994.

			VG	VF	UNC
114	**1000 LIRE**				
	D.1990. Red-violet and m/c. M. Montessori at r. and as wmk. Teacher and student at l. ctr. on back. Seal: Type C.				
	a. Sign. Ciampi and Speziali.		FV	FV	3.00
	b. Sign. Fazio and Speziali.		FV	FV	3.00
	c. Sign. Fazio and Amici.		FV	FV	3.00

			VG	VF	UNC
115	**2000 LIRE**				
	D.1990. Dk. brown on m/c unpt. Arms at l. ctr., G. Marconi at r. and as wmk. Marconi's yacht Elettra at upper l. ctr., radio towers at l., early radio set at ctr. on back. Seal: Type C. Sign. Ciampi and Speziali.		FV	FV	4.50

			VG	VF	UNC
116	**50,000 LIRE**				
	D.1992. Violet and dull green on m/c unpt. Similar to #113. Seal: Type C.				
	a. Sign. Ciampi and Speziali.		FV	FV	70.00
	b. Sign. Fazio and Amici.		FV	FV	60.00

117	100,000 LIRE	VG	VF	UNC
	D.1994. Dk. brown, reddish brown and pale green on m/c unpt. Similar to #110. Seal: Type C.			
	a. Sign. Fazio and Speziali. 6.5.1994.	FV	FV	125.00
	b. Sign. Fazio and Amici.	FV	FV	120.00

1997 ISSUE

Decreto Ministeriale 6.5.1997.

118	500,000 LIRE	VG	VF	UNC
	D.1997. Deep purple, dk. blue and bright green on m/c unpt. Raphaël at r., painting of Triumph of Galatée at ctr. The School of Athens at l. ctr. on back. Seal: Type C. Sign. Fazio and Amici.	FV	FV	400.00

Note: For later issues made for use in Italy, see European Union listings.

JAMAICA

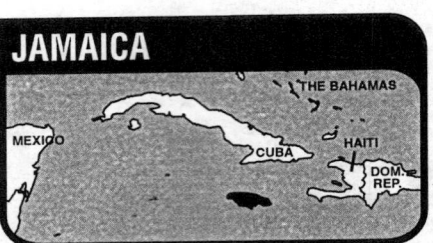

Jamaica, a member of the British Commonwealth situated in the Caribbean Sea 90 miles south of Cuba, has an area of 4,232 sq. mi. (10,991 sq. km.) and a population of 2.59 million. Capital: Kingston. The economy is founded chiefly on mining, tourism and agriculture. Alumina, bauxite, sugar, rum and molasses are exported.

Jamaica was discovered by Columbus on May 3, 1494, and settled by Spain in 1509. The island was captured in 1655 by a British naval force under the command of Admiral William Penn, and ceded to Britain by the Treaty of Madrid in 1670. For more than 150 years, the Jamaican economy of sugar, slaves and piracy was one of the most prosperous in the New World. Dissension between the property-oriented island legislature and the home government prompted Parliament to establish a crown colony government for Jamaica in 1866. From 1958 to 1961 Jamaica was a member of the West Indies Federation, withdrawing when Jamaican voters rejected the association. The colony attained independence on Aug. 6, 1962.

Jamaica is a member of the Commonwealth of Nations. Elizabeth II is the Head of State, as Queen of Jamaica.

A decimal standard currency system was adopted on Sept. 8, 1969.

RULERS:
British

MONETARY SYSTEM:
1 Shilling = 12 Pence
1 Pound = 20 Shillings to 1969
1 Dollar = 100 Cents, 1969-

BRITISH ADMINISTRATION

BANK OF JAMAICA

SIGNATURE VARIETIES			
1	Stanley W. Payton, 1960-64	2	Richard T. P. Hall Acting Governor, 1964-66
3	Richard T. P. Hall Governor, 1966-67	4	G. Arthur Brown, 1967-77
5	Herbert Samuel Walker, 1977-81	6	Dr. Owen C. Jefferson, Acting Governor, 1981-83
7	Horace G. Barber, 1983-86	8	Headley A. Brown, 1986-89
9	Dr. Owen C. Jefferson Acting Governor, 1989-90	10	G. A. Brown, 1990-93
11	R. Rainsford, 1993	12	J. Bussieres, 1994-
13			

LAW 1960

1961 ND ISSUE

Pound System

#49-51 Qn. Elizabeth II at l. Latin motto below arms. Sign. 1. Printer: TDLR.

49	5 SHILLINGS	VG	VF	UNC
	L.1960. (1961). Red on m/c unpt. River rapids on back.	5.00	20.00	100.00
50	10 SHILLINGS			
	L.1960. (1961). Purple on m/c unpt. Men w/bananas on back.	7.50	45.00	300.00

51	1 POUND	VG	VF	UNC
	L.1960. (1961). Green on m/c unpt. Harvesting on back.	7.50	40.00	285.00

1964 ND ISSUE

#51A-51C like #49-51, but English motto below arms. Printer: TDLR.

51A	5 SHILLINGS	VG	VF	UNC
	L.1960. (1964). Red on m/c unpt. Like #49.			
	a. Sign. 1. Gothic serial #.	3.00	15.00	85.00
	b. Sign. 1. Roman numeral serial #.	3.50	25.00	120.00
	c. Sign. 2.	2.50	15.00	100.00
	d. Sign. 4.	2.00	7.50	75.00
	e. Specimen. As b.	—	—	—

51B	10 SHILLINGS	VG	VF	UNC
	L.1960. (1964). Purple on m/c unpt. Like #50.			
	a. Sign. 1. Gothic serial #.	3.50	10.00	160.00
	b. Sign. 1. Roman numeral serial #.	3.50	15.00	170.00
	c. Sign. 2.	3.50	12.50	185.00
	d. Sign. 3.	5.00	17.50	225.00
	e. Sign. 4.	3.00	8.50	140.00

51C	1 POUND	VG	VF	UNC
	L.1960. (1964). Green on m/c unpt. Like #51.			
	a. Sign. 1. Gothic serial #.	5.00	20.00	285.00
	b. Sign. 1. Roman numeral serial #.	7.50	35.00	325.00
	c. Sign. 2.	5.00	20.00	250.00
	d. Sign. 3.	7.50	35.00	300.00
	e. Sign. 4.	4.00	25.00	250.00
	s. Specimen. As c.	—	—	—

52	5 POUNDS	VG	VF	UNC
	L.1960. Blue on m/c unpt. Storage plant at ctr., woman w/fruit basket at r. on back.			
	a. Sign. 1. Gothic serial #.	35.00	300.00	1500.00
	b. Sign. 1. Roman numeral serial #.	40.00	350.00	1750.00
	c. Sign. 3.	30.00	325.00	1550.00
	d. Sign. 4.	30.00	275.00	1400.00

LAW 1960

1970 ND ISSUE

Dollar System

#53-58 wmk: Pineapple. Sign. 4. Printer: TDLR. Replacement notes: Serial # prefix ZZ.

53	50 CENTS	VG	VF	UNC
	L.1960 (1970). Red on m/c unpt. Marcus Garvey at l., arms in unpt. at ctr. National shrine at r. on back.			
	a. Issued note.	0.50	2.00	8.00
	s. Specimen.	—	—	—

54	1 DOLLAR	VG	VF	UNC
	L.1960 (1970). Purple on m/c unpt. Sir Alexander Bustamante at l., arms at bottom ctr. r. Tropical harbor at r. on back.	0.50	2.00	8.00

55	2 DOLLARS	VG	VF	UNC
	L.1960 (1970). Dk. green and red-brown on m/c unpt. Paul Bogle, arms at l., Red-billed streamer trail at ctr. Group of people on back.			
	a. Issued note.	1.00	4.00	12.50
	s. Specimen.	—	—	—

Note: For #54 and 55 w/red serial # see #CS1-CS3.

56	**5 DOLLARS**	VG	VF	UNC
	L.1960 (1970). Dk. brown, green and blue-gray on m/c unpt. Norman Manley at l., arms at bottom ctr. Old Parliament at ctr. r. on back.	2.50	10.00	55.00

57	**10 DOLLARS**	VG	VF	UNC
	L.1960 (1970). Blue-black, brown and black on m/c unpt. George William Gordon at l., arms in unpt. at ctr. Bauxite mining scene at ctr. r. on back.	5.00	30.00	175.00

1973 FAO COMMEMORATIVE ISSUE

#58, 25th Anniversary Declaration of Human Rights 1948-73

58	**2 DOLLARS**	VG	VF	UNC
	1973. Like #55 but *Universal Declaration of Human Rights/1948 - 10 December - 1973. Toward Food Education Employment for All/Articles 23-26* added on back. Serial # double prefix FA-O. Sign. 4.	1.00	3.00	15.00

1976; 1977 ND ISSUE

#59-63 new guilloches in corners and some larger denomination numerals on face and back. Wmk: Pineapple. Printer: TDLR. Replacement notes: Serial # prefix *ZY* or *ZZ*.

59	**1 DOLLAR**	VG	VF	UNC
	L.1960 (1976). Purple on m/c unpt. Like #54 but w/corner design modifications.			
	a. Sign. 4.	0.25	1.50	6.00
	b. Sign. 5.	0.25	1.00	5.00
60	**2 DOLLARS**			
	L.1960 (1976). Dk. green on m/c unpt. Like #55 but w/corner design modifications.			
	a. Sign. 4.	0.50	2.00	12.50
	b. Sign. 5.	0.50	1.50	10.00

61	**5 DOLLARS**	VG	VF	UNC
	L.1960 (1976). Dk. brown, green and blue-green on m/c unpt. Like #56 but w/corner design modifications.			
	a. Sign. 4.	1.00	5.00	32.50
	b. Sign. 5.	0.75	3.50	20.00
62	**10 DOLLARS**			
	L.1960 (1976). Blue-black and black on m/c unpt. Like #57 but w/corner design modifications. Sign. 4.	3.00	20.00	175.00

63	**20 DOLLARS**	VG	VF	UNC
	L.1960 (1977). Maroon on m/c unpt. Noel Nethersole at l., flag in unpt. at ctr., arms below. Bank of Jamaica bldg. on back. Sign. 4.	5.00	35.00	200.00

1978-84 ISSUE

Bank of Jamaica Act

#64-68 wmk: Pineapple. Printer: TDLR. Replacement notes: Serial # prefix *ZY* or *ZZ*.

64	**1 DOLLAR**	VG	VF	UNC
	ND (1982-86). Purple on m/c unpt. Like #59.			
	a. Sign. 6.	0.15	0.50	2.50
	b. Sign. 7.	0.10	0.25	1.50
65	**2 DOLLARS**			
	ND (1982-86). Dk. green and red-brown on m/c unpt. Like #60.			
	a. Sign. 6.	0.25	1.50	7.50
	b. Sign. 7.	0.20	1.00	6.00
66	**5 DOLLARS**			
	ND (1984). Dk. brown, green and blue-gray on m/c unpt. Similar to #61. Sign. 7.	0.15	2.00	10.00

69 | **2 DOLLARS** | | **VG** | **VF** | **UNC**

1985-93. Dk. green and red-brown on m/c unpt. Similar to #65 but corner numerals modified. Horizontal sorting bar at r.

		VG	VF	UNC
a. Sign. 7. 1.1.1985.		FV	FV	3.00
b. Sign. 8. 1.3.1986; 1.2.1987; 1.9.1987.		FV	FV	2.25
c. Sign. 9. 1.7.1989.		FV	FV	2.00
d. Sign. 10. 1.1.1990; 29.5.1992.		FV	FV	1.25
e. Sign. 11. 1.2.1993.		FV	FV	1.25

#70-72 arms at bottom ctr.

67	**10 DOLLARS**	**VG**	**VF**	**UNC**
	1978-81. Bluish purple on m/c unpt. Like #62.			
	a. Sign. 5. 1.10.1978; 1.10.1979.	0.50	2.50	25.00
	b. Sign. 9. 1.12.1981.	0.25	1.00	7.50

68	**20 DOLLARS**	**VG**	**VF**	**UNC**
	1978-83. Red and purple on m/c unpt. Like #63.			
	a. Sign. 5. 1.10.1978; 1.10.1979; 1.10.1981.	1.00	5.00	40.00
	b. Sign. 6. 1.12.1981.	0.75	3.00	30.00
	c. Sign. 7. 1.12.1983.	0.75	2.50	25.00

70 | **5 DOLLARS** | **VG** | **VF** | **UNC**

1985-92. Dk. brown, green and blue-gray on m/c unpt. Similar to #66 but w/2 horizontal blue-green sorting bars at l. and r.

		VG	VF	UNC
a. Sign. 7. 1.1.1985.		FV	FV	5.00
b. Sign. 8. 1.9.1987.		FV	FV	3.50
c. Sign. 9. 1.5.1989.		FV	FV	3.00
d. Sign. 10. 1.7.1991; 1.8.1992.		FV	FV	1.75

1985 REDUCED SIZE ISSUE

#68A-72 note size: 144 x 68mm. Wmk: Pineapple. Printer: TDLR. Replacement notes: Serial # prefix ZY or ZZ.

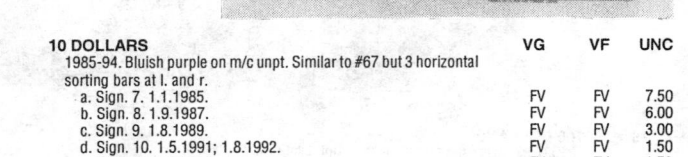

71	**10 DOLLARS**	**VG**	**VF**	**UNC**
	1985-94. Bluish purple on m/c unpt. Similar to #67 but 3 horizontal sorting bars at l. and r.			
	a. Sign. 7. 1.1.1985.	FV	FV	7.50
	b. Sign. 8. 1.9.1987.	FV	FV	6.00
	c. Sign. 9. 1.8.1989.	FV	FV	3.00
	d. Sign. 10. 1.5.1991; 1.8.1992.	FV	FV	1.50
	e. Sign. 12. 1.3.1994.	FV	FV	1.50

68A	**1 DOLLAR**	**VG**	**VF**	**UNC**
	1985-90. Purple on m/c unpt. Similar to #64; lower corner guilloches modified.			
	a. Sign. 7. 1.1.1985.	FV	FV	4.00
	b. Sign. 8. 1.3.1986; 1.2.1987; 1.9.1987.	FV	FV	2.25
	c. Sign. 9. 1.7.1989.	FV	FV	2.00
	d. Sign. 10. 1.1.1990.	FV	FV	1.00

72	**20 DOLLARS**	**VG**	**VF**	**UNC**
	1985-99. Red-orange, purple and black on m/c unpt. Similar to #68 but circular electronic sorting mark at l.			
	a. Sign. 7. 1.1.1985.	FV	FV	10.00
	b. Sign. 8. 1.3.1986; 1.2.1987; 1.9.1987.	FV	FV	8.00
	c. Sign. 9. 1.9.1989.	FV	FV	7.00
	d. Sign. 10. 1.10.1991.	FV	FV	4.50
	e. Sign. 12. 1.2.1995.	FV	FV	3.50
	f. Sign. 13. 24.5.1996; 12.1.1998; 15.2.1999.	FV	FV	3.00

1986-91 ISSUE

#73-75 wmk: Pineapple. Printer: TDLR. Replacement notes: Serial # prefix *ZZ; ZY.*

			VG	VF	UNC
73	**50 DOLLARS**				
	1988-. Brown, purple and red-violet on m/c unpt. Sam Sharpe at l. Doctor's Cave Beach, Mointego Bay, on back.				
	a. Sign. 8. 1.8.1988.		FV	FV	12.00
	b. Sign. 11. 1.2.1993.		FV	FV	7.50
	c. Sign. 12. 1.2.1995.		FV	FV	5.00
	d. Sign. 13. 24.5.1996; 12.1.1998.		FV	FV	4.50

			VG	VF	UNC
74	**100 DOLLARS**				
	1.12.1986; 1.9.1987. Black and purple on m/c unpt. Sir Donald Sangster at l. Dunn's River Falls, St. Ann, at r. on back. Sign. 8.		FV	7.00	35.00

			VG	VF	UNC
75	**100 DOLLARS**				
	1991-93. Black and purple on lilac unpt. Like #74. 2 circles at r., each w/vertical orange bar. More silver waves added to both *$100* and across bottom on back.				
	a. Sign. 10. 1.7.1991.		FV	FV	12.50
	b. 1.6.1992.		FV	FV	10.00
	c. Sign. 11. 1.2.1993.		FV	FV	10.00

1994 ISSUE

#76-78 printer: TDLR. Replacement notes: Serial # prefix *ZY* or *ZZ.*

			VG	VF	UNC
76	**100 DOLLARS**				
	1994-2002. Black and purple on lilac unpt. Like #75 but w/ascending size serial # and segmented foil over security thread.				
	a. Sign. 12. 1.3.1994.		FV	FV	8.50
	b. Sign. 13. 24.5.1996; 12.1.1998; 15.2.1999.		FV	FV	7.50
	c. 15.3.2000. Wmk: swallow-tailed hummingbird. Improved security thread.		FV	FV	7.00

			VG	VF	UNC
77	**500 DOLLARS**				
	1994-99. Purple, violet and brown on m/c unpt. Nanny of the Maroons at l. Historical map of the islands above Port Royal architecture at ctr. r. on back. Wmk: Pineapple.				
	a. Sign. 12. 1.5.1994.		FV	FV	25.00
	b. Sign. 13. 24.5.1996; 12.2.1998; 15.2.1999.		FV	FV	25.00

2000 ISSUE

			VG	VF	UNC
78	**1000 DOLLARS**				
	15.2.2000; 15.10.2000; 15.1.2001. Dk. blue, green and purple on m/c unpt. Michael Manley at l. Jamaica House on back. Sign. 13. Printer: TDLR. (w/o imprint).		FV	FV	45.00

2001; 2002 ISSUE

			VG	VF	UNC
79	**50 DOLLARS**				
	15.3.2000; 15.1.2001; 15.1.2002; 15.1.2003; 15.1.2004. M/c. Like #73. Wmk: Swallow-tailed Hummingbird. Sign. 13.		FV	FV	4.00
80	**100 DOLLARS**				
	15.1.2001; 15.1.2002; 15.1.2004. Black and purple on lilac unpt.		FV	FV	7.00
81	**500 DOLLARS**				
	15.1.2002; 15.1.2003; 15.1.2004. Like #77. Wmk: Swallow-Tailed Hummingbird.		FV	FV	22.50
82	**1000 DOLLARS**				
	15.1.2002; 15.1.2003; 15.1.2004. Like #78. Sign. 13. Printer: (T)DLR.		FV	FV	40.00

NOTICE

Readers with unlisted dates, signature varieties, etc. are invited to submit photocopies of their notes to: Standard Catalog of World Paper Money, 700 East State St. Iola, WI 54990-0001, E-Mail: george.cuhaj@fwpubs.com.

COLLECTOR SERIES

BANK OF JAMAICA

1976 ISSUE

CS1	1976 1-10 DOLLARS		Issue Price	Mkt.	Value
	#54-57 w/matching red star prefix serial # and *SERIES 1976*. (5000 sets issued).		30.00		20.00

1977 ISSUE

CS2	1977 1-10 DOLLARS		Issue Price	Mkt.	Value
	#59-61a, 62 w/matching red star prefix serial # and *SERIES 1977*. (7500 sets issued).		29.50		15.00

1978 ISSUE

CS3	1978 1-10 DOLLARS		Issue Price	Mkt.	Value
	#54-57 in double set. One is like #CS1-2 w/ *SERIES 1978* and the other w/additional ovpt: *Twenty-fifth Anniversary of the Coronation June 2, 1953* and *SERIES 1978* at r. All w/matching red star prefix serial #. (6250 sets issued).		61.00		30.00

JAPAN

Japan, a constitutional monarchy situated off the east coast of Asia, has an area of 145,856 sq. mi. (377,819 sq. km.) and a population of 127.13 million. Capital: Tokyo. Japan, one of the three major industrial nations of the free world, exports machinery, motor vehicles, textiles and chemicals.

Founded (so legend holds) in 660 BC by a direct descendant of the Sun Goddess, the country was first brought into contact with the west by a storm-blown Portuguese ship in 1542. European traders and missionaries proceeded to enlarge the contact until the Shogunate, sensing a military threat in the foreign presence, expelled all foreigners and severed relations with the outside world in the 17th century. (Except for one Dutch outpost in Nagasaki.) After contact was reestablished by Commodore Perry of the U.S. Navy in 1854, Japan rapidly industrialized, abolished the Shogunate and established a parliamentary form of government, and by the end of the 19th century achieved the status of a modern economic and military power. A series of wars with China and Russia, and participation with the Allies in World War I, enlarged Japan territorially but brought its interests into conflict with the Far Eastern interests of the United States and Britain, causing it to align with the Axis powers for the pursuit of World War II. After its defeat in World War II, Japan renounced military aggression as a political instrument, established democratic self-government, and quickly reasserted its position as an economic world power.

RULERS:
Yoshihito (Taisho), 1912-1926
Hirohito (Showa), 1926-1989
Akihito (Heisei), 1989-

MONETARY SYSTEM:
1 Sen = 10 Rin
1 Yen = 100 Sen

CONSTITUTIONAL MONARCHY

BANK OF JAPAN

日 本 銀 行 券
Nip-pon Gin-ko Ken

1963-69 ND ISSUE

		VG	VF	UNC
95	**500 YEN** ND (1969). Blue on m/c unpt. Tomomi Iwakura at r. Back steel blue; Mt. Fuji at l. ctr. Wmk: 5-petaled flowers.			
	a. Single letter serial # prefix.	FV	10.00	25.00
	b. Double letter serial # prefix.	FV	6.00	10.00
	s. As b. Specimen.	—	—	—

96	**1000 YEN**	VG	VF	UNC
	ND (1963). Dk. green and brown on m/c unpt. Hirobumi Ito at r. and as wmk. Back brown; Bank of Japan at ctr.			
	a. Single letter serial # prefix. Black serial #.	FV	20.00	60.00
	b. As a., but w/double letter serial # prefix.	FV	10.00	20.00
	c. Single letter serial # prefix. Blue serial #.	FV	10.00	35.00
	d. As c., but w/double letter serial # prefix.	FV	FV	16.00
	s. As b. Specimen.	—	—	—

1984 ND ISSUE

#97-99 wmk. same as portr.

#97s-99s were released in a special booklet by Printing Bureau, Ministry of Finance.

97	**1000 YEN**	VG	VF	UNC
	ND (1984-93). Blue on m/c unpt. Soseki Natsume at r. and as wmk. Two Manchurian cranes on back.			
	a. Single letter serial # prefix. Black serial #	FV	10.00	20.00
	b. As a., but w/double letter serial # prefix.	FV	FV	15.00
	c. Single letter serial # prefix. Blue serial #.	FV	10.00	20.00
	d. As c., but w/double letter serial # prefix.	FV	FV	15.00
	s. As b. Specimen. Perforated *mihon*.	—	—	1500.00

98	**5000 YEN**	VG	VF	UNC
	ND (1984-93). Purple on m/c unpt. Inazo Nitobe at r. and as wmk. Lake and Mt. Fuji at ctr. on back.			
	a. Single letter serial # prefix. Black serial #.	FV	55.00	75.00
	b. As a., but w/double letter serial # prefix.	FV	FV	65.00
	s. As b. Specimen. Perforated *mihon*.	—	—	1500.00

99	**10,000 YEN**	VG	VF	UNC
	ND (1984-93). Lt. brown on m/c unpt. Yukichi Fukuzawa at r. and as wmk. Pheasant at l. and r. on back.			
	a. Single letter serial # prefix.	FV	110.00	150.00
	b. As a., but w/double letter serial # prefix.	FV	FV	120.00
	s. As b. Specimen. Perforated *mihon*.	—	—	1500.00

1993 ND ISSUE

#100-102 microprinting added to upper or lower r. corner.

Due to a government reorganization, the Okurasho (Finance Ministry) was renamed Zaimusho (Ministry of Finance). The imprint on the notes (made at the Finance Ministry Pinting Bureau) was changed accordingly in 2001. In 2003 the imprint was changed again, to National Printing Bureau.

Printer a. 8 characters starting *O*.

Printer b. 8 characters starting *Zai*.

Printer c. 7 characters.

100	**1000 YEN**	VG	VF	UNC
	ND (1993-). Blue on m/c unpt. Soseki Natsume at r. Like #97.			
	a. Single letter serial # prefix. Brown serial #. Printer a. (1993).	FV	10.00	18.00
	b. As a. Double letter serial # prefix.	FV	FV	12.50
	c. Single letter serial # prefix. Green serial #.	FV	FV	18.00
	d. As c. Double letter serial # prefix. Printer b. (2001).	FV	FV	12.50
	e. As d, printer c. (2003).	FV	FV	13.00
101	**5000 YEN**			
	ND (1993-). Violet on m/c unpt. Inazo Nitobe at r. Like #98.			
	a. Single letter serial # prefix. Brown serial # Printer a. (1993).	FV	70.00	80.00
	b. As a., but w/double letter serial # prefix.	FV	FV	70.00
	c. As b. Printer b. (2001).	FV	FV	70.00
	d. As c. Printer c. (2003).	FV	FV	65.00
102	**10,000 YEN**			
	ND (1993-). Lt. brown on m/c unpt. Yukichi Fukuzawa at r. Like #99.			
	a. Single letter serial # prefix. Brown serial # (1993).	FV	110.00	150.00
	b. As a., but w/double letter serial # prefix.	FV	FV	125.00
	c. As b. printer b. (2001).	FV	FV	125.00
	d. As b. Printer c. (2003).	FV	FV	125.00

2000 COMMEMORATIVE ISSUE

#103, G-8 Economic Summit in Okinawa

103	**2000 YEN**	VG	VF	UNC
	ND (2000). Slate, green and brown on m/c unpt. Shureimon Gate in Naha, Okinawa at r. and as wmk. Scene from *Genji Monogatari* (Tale of Genji) on back.	FV	FV	25.00

2004 ND ISSUE

#104-106 include enhanced security features and bar wmk. (in addition to portr. wmk.) Iridescent ink feature is observed by holding the note at a shallow angle to incident light. The iridescent ink glistens like mother of pearl from the surface of the note; it is otherwise virtually invisible and impossible to copy using available copying technologies.

104	**1000 YEN**	VG	VF	UNC
	ND (2004). Blue on m/c unpt. Hideo Noguchi (bacteriologist) at r. and as wmk. Mt. Fuji on back.	FV	FV	13.00
105	**5000 YEN**			
	ND (2004). Violet on m/c unpt. Ichiyo Higuchi (novelist) at r. and as wmk. Irises (painting by Korin Ogata) on back.	FV	FV	65.00
106	**10,000 YEN**			
	ND (2004). Brown on m/c unpt. Yukichi Fukuzawa (educator, futurist) at r. and as wmk. Phoenix from Boydo-in Temple on back.	FV	FV	125.00

JERSEY

The Bailiwick of Jersey, a British Crown dependency located in the English Channel 12 miles (19 km.) west of Normandy, France, has an area of 45 sq. mi. (117 sq. km.) and a population of 90,000. Capital: St. Helier. The economy is based on agriculture and cattle breeding - the importation of cattle is prohibited to protect the purity of the island's world-famous strain of milk cows.

Jersey was occupied by Neanderthal man 100,000 years B.C., and by Iberians of 2000 B.C. who left their chamber tombs in the island's granite cliffs. Roman legions almost certainly visited the island although they left no evidence of settlement. The country folk of Jersey still speak an archaic form of Norman-French, lingering evidence of the Norman annexation of the island in 933 B.C. Jersey was annexed to England in 1206, 140 years after the Norman Conquest. The dependency is administered by its own laws and customs; laws enacted by the British Parliament do not apply to Jersey unless it is specifically mentioned. During World War II, German troops occupied the island from 1940 until 1944.

United Kingdom bank notes and coinage circulate concurrently with Jersey money as legal tender.

RULERS:
British

MONETARY SYSTEM:
1 Shilling = 12 Pence
1 Pound = 20 Shillings to 1971
1 Pound = 100 New Pence, 1971-

	SIGNATURE VARIETIES		
1	F. N. Padgham, 1963-72	2	J. Clennett, 1972-83
3	Leslie May, 1983-93	4	George Baird Baird, 1993

BRITISH ADMINISTRATION

STATES OF JERSEY, TREASURY

1963 ND ISSUE

#7-10 Qn. Elizabeth II at r. looking l., wearing cape. Wmk: Jersey cow's head. Sign. 3. Printer: TDLR. Replacement notes: Serial # prefix Z.

10 SHILLINGS

	VG	VF	UNC
ND (1963). Brown on m/c unpt. St. Ouen's Manor on back.			
a. Issued note.	3.00	10.00	35.00
s. Specimen.	—	—	200.00

8 **1 POUND**

	VG	VF	UNC
ND (1963). Green on m/c unpt. Mont Orgueil Castle on back. 2 sign. varieties.			
a. Sign. 1.	7.50	35.00	90.00
b. Sign. 2.	5.00	20.00	50.00
c. W/o sign.	30.00	85.00	300.00
s. As a. Specimen. Black or red ovpt. Serial # prefix A-G.	—	—	75.00

9 **5 POUNDS**

	VG	VF	UNC
ND (1963). Dk. red on m/c unpt. St. Aubin's Fort on back.			
a. Sign. 1.	40.00	100.00	400.00
b. Sign. 2.	10.00	30.00	90.00
s1. As a. Specimen. Black or red ovpt.	—	—	100.00
s2. As b. Specimen. Red overprint.	—	—	100.00

10 **10 POUNDS**

	VG	VF	UNC
ND (1972). Purple on m/c unpt. Back similar to #7.			
a. Sign. 2.	20.00	40.00	100.00
s. Specimen. Red overprint.	—	—	135.00

1976 ND ISSUE

#11-14 Qn. Elizabeth at ctr. r. looking l., wearing a tiara. Wmk: Jersey cow's head. Printer: TDLR. Replacement notes: Serial # prefixes ZB; ZC.

11 **1 POUND**
ND (1976-88). Blue on m/c unpt. Battle of Jersey scene on back.

	VG	VF	UNC
a. Sign. 2.	FV	5.00	12.00
b. Sign. 3.	FV	4.00	9.00
s. As a. Specimen.	—		17.50

12 **5 POUNDS**
ND (1976-88). Brown on m/c unpt. Elizabeth Castle, sailing ships in foreground on back.

	VG	VF	UNC
a. Sign. 2.	FV	20.00	50.00
b. Sign. 3.	FV	20.00	45.00
s. Specimen.	—		27.50

13 **10 POUNDS**
ND (1976-88). Green on m/c unpt. Victoria College on back.

	VG	VF	UNC
a. Sign. 2.	FV	35.00	85.00
b. Sign. 3.	FV	30.00	75.00
s. Specimen.	—		45.00

14 **20 POUNDS**
ND (1976-88). Red-brown on m/c unpt. Sailing ship, Gorey Castle on back.

	VG	VF	UNC
a. Sign. 2.	FV	60.00	140.00
b. Sign. 3.	FV	60.00	150.00
s. Specimen.	—		80.00

1989 ND ISSUE

#15-19 Birds at l. corner, arms at ctr., older Qn. Elizabeth II at r. facing, wearing cape. Wmk: Jersey cow's head. Sign. 3. Replacement notes: Serial # prefix *CZ*.

15 **1 POUND**
ND (1989). Dk. green and violet on m/c unpt. Treecreepers at lower l. Church at l. ctr. on back.

	VG	VF	UNC
a. Issued note.	FV	FV	8.00
s. Specimen.	—		6.00

16 **5 POUNDS**
ND (1989). Rose on m/c unpt. Whitethroat at lower l. La Corbiere lighthouse on back.

	VG	VF	UNC
a. Issued note.	FV	FV	25.00
s. Specimen.	—		17.50

17 **10 POUNDS**
ND (1989). Orange-brown on m/c unpt. Oystercatchers at lower l. Battle of Jersey on back.

	VG	VF	UNC
a. Issued note.	FV	FV	45.00
s. Specimen.	—		25.00

18 **20 POUNDS**
ND (1989). Blue on m/c unpt. Brent goose at lower l. St. Ouen's Manor on back.

	VG	VF	UNC
a. Issued note.	FV	FV	85.00
s. Specimen.	—		35.00

19 50 POUNDS

	VG	VF	UNC
ND (1989). Dk. gray on m/c unpt. Fulmers at lower l. Government House on back			
a. Issued note.	FV	FV	165.00
s. Specimen.	—	—	75.00

1993 ND ISSUE

#20-24 like #15-19 but w/solid color denomination at upper r. Wmk: Jersey cow's head.

20	1 POUND	VG	VF	UNC
	ND (1993). Dk. green on m/c unpt. Like #15.			
	a. Sign. 4.	FV	FV	6.00
	s. Specimen.	—	—	6.00

21	5 POUNDS	VG	VF	UNC
	ND (1993). Rose on m/c unpt. Like #16.			
	a. Sign. 4.	FV	FV	20.00
	s. Specimen.	—	—	15.00
22	10 POUNDS			
	ND (1993). Orange-brown on m/c unpt. Like #17.			
	a. Sign. 4.	FV	FV	40.00
	s. Specimen.	—	—	22.50

23	20 POUNDS	VG	VF	UNC
	ND (1993). Blue on m/c unpt. Like #18.			
	a. Sign. 4.	FV	FV	70.00
	s. Specimen.	—	—	30.00
24	50 POUNDS			
	ND (1993). Dk. gray on m/c unpt. Like #19.			
	a. Sign. 4	FV	FV	150.00
	s. Specimen.	—	—	85.00

1995 COMMEMORATIVE ISSUE

#25, 50th Anniversary Liberation of Jersey

25	1 POUND	VG	VF	UNC
	9.5.1995. Dk. green and purple on m/c unpt. Face like #20 w/island outline at upper r., w/text: *50th Anniversary*... at l. in wmk. area. Serial # prefix: *LJ*. Face and back of German occupation 1 Pound #6 on back. Wmk: Cow's head. Sign. 4			
	a. Issued note.	FV	FV	8.00
	s. Specimen.	—	—	25.00

Note: #25 also issued in a special wallet w/commemorative £2 coin. (6000 pcs.). Current market value: $20.00.

2000 ND ISSUE

#26-30 like #20-24 but sign. Ian Black.

26	1 POUND	VG	VF	UNC
	ND (2000). Dk. green on m/c unpt. Like #20.	FV	FV	5.00
27	5 POUNDS			
	ND (2000). Rose on m/c unpt. Like #21.	FV	FV	17.50

28	10 POUNDS	VG	VF	UNC
	ND (2000). Orange-brown on m/c unpt. Like #17.	FV	FV	35.00
29	20 POUNDS			
	ND (2000). Blue on m/c unpt. Like #23.	FV	FV	65.00
30	50 POUNDS			
	ND (2000). Dk. gray on m/c unpt. Like #24.	FV	FV	140.00

2004 COMMEMORATIVE ISSUE

800th Anniversary of the special relationship between Jersey and the British Crown.

31	1 POUND	VG	VF	UNC
	2004. Dk. green and purple on m/c unpt. Mount Orgueil Castle on back.			
	a. Issued note.	FV	FV	7.50
	s. Specimen.	—	—	12.50

COLLECTOR SERIES

STATES OF JERSEY, TREASURY

1978 ISSUE

CS1	ND (1978) 1-20 POUNDS		Issue Price	Mkt.	Value
	#11a-14a w/ovpt: *SPECIMEN* and Maltese cross prefix serial #.		14.00		75.00

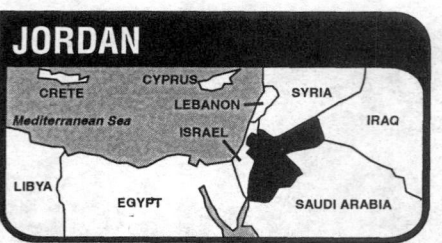

The Hashemite Kingdom of Jordan, a constitutional monarchy in southwest Asia, has an area of 37,738 sq. mi. (97,740 sq. km.) and a population of 5.46 million. Capital: Amman. Agriculture and tourism comprise Jordan's economic base. Chief exports are phosphates, tomatoes and oranges.

Jordan is the Edom and Moab of the time of Moses. It became part of the Roman province of Arabia in 106 AD, was conquered by the Arabs in 633-36, and was part of the Ottoman Empire from the 16th century until World War I. At that time, the regions presently known as Jordan and Israel were mandated to Great Britain by the League of Nations as Transjordan and Palestine. In 1922 Transjordan was established as the semi-autonomous Emirate of Transjordan, ruled by the Hashemite Prince Abdullah but still nominally a part of the British mandate. The mandate over Transjordan was terminated in 1946, the country becoming the independent Hashemite Kingdom of Transjordan. The kingdom was renamed The Hashemite Kingdom of The Jordan in 1950.

RULERS:

Hussein I, 1952-1999
Abdullah II, 1999-

MONETARY SYSTEM:

1 Dinar = 10 Dirhams
1 Dirham = 10 Piastres = 10 Qirsh
1 Piastre = 1 Qirsh = 10 Fils

REPLACEMENT NOTES:

#9-27, jj prefix (YY).

KINGDOM

CENTRAL BANK OF JORDAN

SIGNATURE VARIETIES					
9			10		
11			12A		
12			13		
14			15		
16			17		
18			19		
20			21		
22			23		
24			25		

FIRST ISSUE - LAW 1959

#9-12 Kg. Hussein at I. w/law date 1959 (in Arabic *1909*).

9 500 FILS
L.1959. Brown on m/c unpt. Jerash Forum on back. FIVE
HUNDRED FILS at bottom margin on back. Sign. 10.

	VG	VF	UNC
a. Issued note.	10.00	50.00	100.00
s. Specimen.	—	—	100.00

10 1 DINAR
L.1959. Green on m/c unpt. Al-Aqsa Mosque "Dome of the Rock" at
ctr. w/columns at r. on back. Sign. 10.

	VG	VF	UNC
a. Issued note.	4.00	20.00	65.00
s. Specimen.	—	—	100.00

11 5 DINARS
L.1959. Red-brown on m/c unpt. Al-Hazne, Treasury of Pharaoh at
Petra at ctr. r. on back.

	VG	VF	UNC
a. Sign. 10; 11; 12.	10.00	35.00	125.00
s. Specimen. Sign. 10.	—	—	125.00

12 10 DINARS
L.1959. Blue-gray on m/c unpt. Baptismal site on River Jordan on
back.

	VG	VF	UNC
a. Sign. 10; 11, 12.	25.00	65.00	235.00
s. Specimen. Sign. 10.	—	—	125.00

SECOND ISSUE - LAW 1959

#13-16 like #9-12. Kg. Hussein I at l., but w/o law date *1959* (in Arabic *1909*). Wmk: Kg. Hussein wearing turban.

13 1/2 DINAR
ND. Like #9, but *HALF DINAR* at bottom margin on back.

	VG	VF	UNC
a. Sign. 12.	2.00	8.00	30.00
b. Sign. 12A.	2.00	8.00	30.00
c. Sign. 14.	1.00	3.00	12.00

14 1 DINAR
ND. Like #10.

	VG	VF	UNC
a. Sign. 13.	FV	10.00	40.00
b. Sign. 14.	FV	6.00	25.00

15 5 DINARS
ND. Like #11.

	VG	VF	UNC
a. Sign. 12.	FV	15.00	60.00
b. Sign. 15.	FV	12.00	35.00
s. Specimen. Sign. 10.	—	—	100.00

19	5 DINARS	VG	VF	UNC
	ND (1975-92). Red on m/c unpt. Al-Hazne, Treasury of the Pharaoh at r. on back.			
	a. Sign. 15.	FV	FV	30.00
	b. Sign. 16.	FV	FV	27.50
	c. Sign. 18.	FV	FV	22.50
	d. Sign. 19.	FV	FV	27.50
	s. Specimen. As a.	—	—	250.00

16	10 DINARS	VG	VF	UNC
	ND. Like #12.			
	a. Sign. 12; 12A.	FV	45.00	150.00
	b. Sign. 13; 14.	FV	55.00	175.00
	c. Sign. 15.	FV	FV	85.00

THIRD ISSUE

#17-21 Kg. Hussein at l. Wmk: Kg. Hussein wearing turban.

17	1/2 DINAR	VG	VF	UNC
	ND (1975-92). Brown on m/c unpt. Jerash at r. on back.			
	a. Sign. 15. Serial # prefix starts with 'I.'	FV	2.00	5.00
	b. Sign. 15. Serial # prefix starts with an 'u.'	3.00	5.00	10.00
	c. Sign. 16, 18.	FV	1.00	3.25
	d. Sign. 17.	FV	2.00	5.00
	s. Specimen. Sign. 15.	—	—	85.00

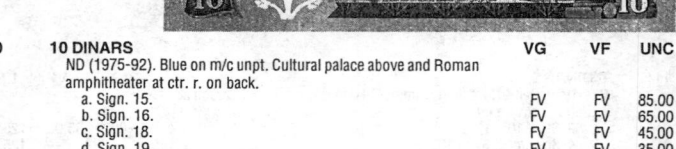

20	10 DINARS	VG	VF	UNC
	ND (1975-92). Blue on m/c unpt. Cultural palace above and Roman amphitheater at ctr. r. on back.			
	a. Sign. 15.	FV	FV	85.00
	b. Sign. 16.	FV	FV	65.00
	c. Sign. 18.	FV	FV	45.00
	d. Sign. 19.	FV	FV	35.00
	s. Specimen. As a.	—	—	—

18	1 DINAR	VG	VF	UNC
	ND (1975-92). Dk. green on m/c unpt. Al-Aqsa Mosque "Dome of the Rock" behind columns at r. on back.			
	a. Text above doorway on back. Sign. 15.	FV	FV	15.00
	b. W/o text above doorway on back. Sign. 15.	FV	FV	12.50
	c. Text above doorway on back. Sign. 16.	FV	FV	10.00
	d. Sign. 17.	FV	FV	8.00
	e. Sign. 18.	FV	FV	8.00
	f. Sign. 19.	FV	FV	5.00
	s. Specimen. As b. Sign. 15.	—	—	200.00

21	20 DINARS	VG	VF	UNC
	1977-1988. Deep brown on m/c unpt. Electric power station of Zerga on back. Sign. 16-18.			
	a. Sign. 16. 1977; 1981.	FV	FV	80.00
	b. Sign. 17. 1985.	FV	FV	75.00
	c. Sign. 18. 1987; 1988.	FV	FV	70.00
	s. Specimen. Sign. 15. 1977.	FV	FV	300.00

22 20 DINARS

	VG	VF	UNC
1977-85. Blue on m/c unpt. Like #21.			
a. Sign. 16. 1977 (1991).	FV	45.00	100.00
b. Sign. 15. 1982 (1991).	FV	45.00	95.00
c. Sign. 17. 1985 (1992).	FV	45.00	85.00

FOURTH ISSUE (1992-93)

#23-27 Kg. Hussein wearing headdress at ctr. r. and as wmk. Sign. 19.

23 1/2 DINAR

	VG	VF	UNC
AH1412/1992-AH1413/1993. Lilac-brown and dk. brown on m/c unpt. Qusayr Amra fortress at r. on back.			
a. AH1412/1992.	FV	FV	4.00
b. AH1413/1993.	FV	FV	3.50
s1. As a. Specimen.	—	—	40.00
s2. As b. Specimen.	—	—	25.00

24 1 DINAR

	VG	VF	UNC
AH1412/1992-AH1413/1993. Green on olive and m/c unpt. Ruins of Jerash at ctr. r. on back.			
a. AH1412/1992.	FV	FV	6.50
b. AH1413/1993.	FV	FV	5.00
s1. As a. Specimen.	—	—	45.00
s2. As b. Specimen.	—	—	30.00

25 5 DINARS

	VG	VF	UNC
AH1412/1992-AH1413/1993. Red and violet-brown on m/c unpt. Treasury of Petra on back.			
a. AH1412/1992.	FV	FV	30.00
b. AH1413/1993.	FV	FV	25.00
s1. As a. Specimen.	—	—	60.00
s2. As b. Specimen.	—	—	35.00

26 10 DINARS

	VG	VF	UNC
AH1412/1992. Blue, gray-violet and green on m/c unpt. al-Rabadh Castle ruins on back.			
a. Issued note.	FV	FV	45.00
s. Specimen.	—	—	75.00

27 20 DINARS

	VG	VF	UNC
AH1412/1992. Dk. brown, green and red-brown on m/c unpt. Al-Aqsa Mosque "Dome of the Rock" at l. ctr. on back.			
a. Issued note.	FV	FV	95.00
s. Specimen.	—	—	105.00

Note: Kg. Hussein financed the restoration of the Al-Aqsa Mosque, as well as the gold-leaf treatment on the dome.

FIFTH ISSUE (1995-2002)

#28-32 w/title: *THE HASHEMITE KINGDOM OF JORDAN* added on back.

28	1/2 DINAR	VG	VF	UNC
	AH1415/1995-. Lilac-brown and dk. brown on m/c unpt. Like #23.			
	a. AH1415/1995. Sign. 19.	FV	FV	3.50
	b. AH1417/1997. Sign. 21.	FV	FV	3.00
	s. Specimen.	—	—	25.00

31	10 DINARS	VG	VF	UNC
	AH1416/1996; AH1422/2001. Purple, dk. blue and black on m/c unpt. Like #26 but castle ruins renamed *AJLOUN CASTLE*.			
	a. AH1416/1996. Sign. 20.	FV	FV	35.00
	b. AH1422/2001. Sign. 24.	FV	FV	27.50
	s. As a. Specimen.	—	—	85.00

29	1 DINAR	VG	VF	UNC
	AH1415/1995-. Green and olive on m/c unpt. Like #24.			
	a. AH1415/1995. Sign. 19.	FV	FV	6.00
	b. AH1416/1996. Sign. 21.	FV	FV	5.00
	c. AH1417/1997. Sign. 21.	FV	FV	5.00
	d. AH1422/2001. Sign. 24.	FV	FV	4.00
	e. AH1423/2001. Sign. 24.	FV	FV	3.50
	s. As a, b. Specimen.	—	—	35.00

32	20 DINARS	VG	VF	UNC
	AH1415/1995; AH1422/2001. Dk. brown, green and red-brown on m/c unpt. Like #27.			
	a. AH1415/1995. Sign. 19.	FV	FV	65.00
	b. AH1422/2001. Sign. 24.	FV	FV	45.00
	s. Specimen.	—	—	100.00

30	5 DINARS	VG	VF	UNC
	AH1415/1995-. Red-violet, purple and orange on m/c unpt. Similar to #25.			
	a. AH1415/1995. Sign. 19.	FV	FV	17.50
	b. AH1417/1997. Sign. 22.	FV	FV	15.00
	c. AH1423/2001. Sign. 24.	FV	FV	17.50
	s. As a, b. Specimen.	—	—	50.00

33	50 DINARS	VG	VF	UNC
	AH1420/1999. Lt. green, blue, red and brown on m/c unpt. Kg. Abdullah II at r. wearing business suit. Raghadan Palace at r. ctr. Coat of Arms at l. on back. Sign. 23.	FV	FV	125.00

SIXTH ISSUE (2002-)
Wmk: same as the portr. Printer: (T)DLR.

34	1 DINAR	VG	VF	UNC
	AH1423/2002. Green, gold and brown on m/c unpt. Sherif Hussein ibn Ali at r. Silver coins, Great Arab Revolt scene on back. Sign. 24.	FV	FV	3.00

35	5 DINARS	VG	VF	UNC
	AH1423/2002. Orange, brown and gold on m/c unpt. Kg. Abdullah I at r., calvary at ctr. Ma'an Palace on back. Sign. 24.			
	a. Issued note.	FV	FV	12.50
	s. Specimen.	—	—	—

36	10 DINARS	VG	VF	UNC
	AH1423/2002. Blue, green and red on m/c unpt. Kg. Talal ibn Abdullah at r. First Parliament at ctr. Camels at Petra on back.			
	a. Sign. 24. Foil on vertical serial #.	FV	FV	30.00
	b. Sign. 25. Foil to left of vertical serial #.	FV	FV	25.00
	s. Specimen.	—	—	—

37	20 DINARS	VG	VF	UNC
	AH1423/2002. Blue-green and grey on m/c unpt. Kg. Hussein at r. Al-Aqsa Mosque "Dome of the Rock" on back. Sign. 24.	FV	FV	50.00

38	50 DINARS	VG	VF	UNC
	AH1423/2002; AH1425/2004. Lt. green, blue, red and brown on m/c unpt. Kg. Abdullah II at r. Raghadan Palace on back. Sign. 24; 25.	FV	FV	110.00

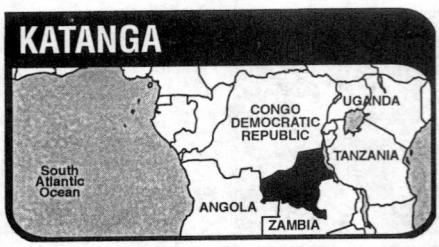

Katanga, the southern province of the former Zaïre extends northeast to Lake Tanganyika, east and south to Zambia, and west to Angola. It was inhabited by Luba and Bantu peoples, and was one of Africa's richest mining areas.

In 1960, Katanga, under the leadership of provincial president Moise Tshombe and supported by foreign mining interests, seceded from newly independent Republic of the Congo. A period of political confusion and bloody fighting involving Congolese, Belgian and United Nations forces ensued. At the end of the rebellion in 1962, Katanga was reintegrated into the republic, and is known as the Shaba region.

For additional history, see Zaïre.

MONETARY SYSTEM:
1 Franc = 100 Centimes

GOVERNMENT

1961 ND PROVISIONAL ISSUE

#1-4 w/red ovpt: *GOUVERNEMENT KATANGA* on face and back of Banque D'Emission du Rwanda et du Burundi notes.

		Good	Fine	XF
1	**5 FRANCS** ND (1961 - old date 15.5.1961). Ovpt. on Rwanda & Burundi #1.	—	—	—
2	**10 FRANCS** ND (1961 - old date 15.9.1960; 5.10.1960). Ovpt. on Rwanda & Burundi #2.		Rare	

		Good	Fine	XF
3	**20 FRANCS** ND (1961 - old date/15.9.1960; 5.10.1960). Ovpt. on Rwanda & Burundi #3.		Rare	

		Good	Fine	XF
4	**50 FRANCS** ND (1961 - old date 1.10.1960). Ovpt. on Rwanda & Burundi #4.		Rare	

BANQUE NATIONALE DU KATANGA

1960 ISSUE

#5-10 Moise Tshombe at r. Bldg. at l. on back. Sign. 1.

#5A and 6A Moise Tshombe at l., flag at r. Printer: W&S. (Not issued).

		VG	VF	UNC
5	**10 FRANCS** 1.12.1960; 15.12.1960. Lilac and yellow.			
	a. Issued note.	20.00	60.00	125.00
	r. Remainder, w/o serial #.	—	—	80.00
	s. Specimen.	—	75.00	100.00

		VG	VF	UNC
5A	**10 FRANCS** 1.12.1960. Green, brown and red. Reservoir at ctr. Foundry at ctr. on back.			
	r. Remainder w/o date or serial #.	—	—	500.00
	s. Specimen.	—	—	150.00

		VG	VF	UNC
6	**20 FRANCS** 1960. Blue-green and brown.			
	a. 21.11.1960.	30.00	75.00	150.00
	b. 1.12.1960.	50.00	120.00	250.00
	r. Remainder, w/o serial #.	—	—	125.00
	s. Specimen.	—	80.00	150.00

10	1000 FRANCS	VG	VF	UNC
	31.10.1960. Blue and brown.			
	a. Issued note.	150.00	450.00	900.00
	r. Remainder, w/o serial #.	—	—	450.00
	s. Specimen.	—	275.00	325.00

#11 Not assigned.

1962 ISSUE

#12-14 wheel of masks and spears on back. Wmk: Elephant. Sign. 2, 3.

6A	20 FRANCS	Good	Fine	XF
	1.12.1960. M/c. Aerial view at ctr. Miners at ctr. on back.			
	Specimen.		Rare	

12	100 FRANCS	VG	VF	UNC
	18.5.1962; 15.8.1962; 15.9.1962. Dk. green and brown on m/c			
	unpt. Woman carrying ears of corn at r.			
	a. Issued note.	30.00	75.00	180.00
	b. 15.1.1963.	50.00	125.00	250.00
	s. Specimen.	—	—	125.00

7	50 FRANCS	VG	VF	UNC
	10.11.1960. Red-brown and blue.			
	a. Issued note.	40.00	90.00	200.00
	r. Remainder, w/o serial #.	—	—	125.00
	s. Specimen.	—	100.00	150.00

13	500 FRANCS	VG	VF	UNC
	17.4.1962. Purple and m/c. Man w/fire at r.			
	a. Issued note.	125.00	350.00	600.00
	s. Specimen.	—	—	450.00

8	100 FRANCS	VG	VF	UNC
	31.10.1960. Brown, green and yellow.			
	a. Issued note.	40.00	100.00	250.00
	r. Remainder, w/o serial #.	—	—	175.00
	s. Specimen.	—	150.00	200.00

9	500 FRANCS	VG	VF	UNC
	31.10.1960. Green, violet and olive.			
	a. Issued note.	150.00	400.00	750.00
	r. Remainder, w/o serial #.	—	—	450.00
	s. Specimen.	—	200.00	300.00

14	1000 FRANCS	VG	VF	UNC
	26.2.1962. Dk. blue, red and brown on m/c unpt. Woman carrying			
	child on back while picking cotton at r. Ornate wheel at l.			
	a. Issued note.	75.00	180.00	350.00
	s. Specimen.	—	—	300.00

KAZAKHSTAN

The Republic of Kazakhstan is bordered to the west by the Caspian Sea and Russia, to the north by Russia, in the east by the Peoples Republic of China and in the south by Uzbekistan and Kyrgyzstan. It has an area of 1,049,155 sq. mi. (2,717,300 sq. km.) and a population of 16.93 million. Capital: Astana. The country is rich in mineral resources including coal, tungsten, copper, lead, zinc and manganese with huge oil and natural gas reserves. Agriculture is important also non-ferrous metallurgy, heavy engineering and chemical industries are leaders in its economy.

The Kazakhs are a branch of the Turkic peoples which led the nomadic life of herdsman until WW I. In the 13th century they come under Genghis Khan's eldest son Juji and later became a part of the Golden Horde, a western Mongol empire. Around the beginning of the 16th century they were divided into 3 confederacies, known as zhuz or hordes, in the steppes of Turkistan. At the end of the 17th century an incursion by the Kalmucks, a remnant of the Oirat Mongol confederacy, facilitated Russian penetration. Resistance to Russian settlements varied throughout the 1800's, but by 1900 over 100 million acres was declared Czarist state property and used for a planned peasant colonization. In 1916 the Czarist government ordered mobilization of all males, between 19 and 43 for auxiliary service. The Kazakhs rose in defiance which led the governor general of Turkestan to send troops against the rebels. Shortly after the Russian revolution, Kazakh nationalists asked for full autonomy. The Communist coup d'état of Nov. 1917 led to civil war. In 1919-20 the Red army defeated the "White" Russian forces and occupied Kazakhstan and fought against the Nationalist government formed by Ali Khan Bukey Khan. The Kazakh Autonomous Soviet Socialist Republic was proclaimed on Aug. 26, 1920 within the R.S.F.S.R. Russian and Ukrainian colonization continued. On Dec. 5, 1936, Kazakhstan qualified for full status as an S.S.R. and held its first congress in 1937. Independence was declared on Dec. 16, 1991 and the new Republic joined the C.I.S.

MONETARY SYSTEM:
1 Tengé = 100 Tyin = 500 Rubles (Russian), 1993 -

ҚАЗАҚСТАН ҰЛТТЫҚ БАНКІ

KAZAKHSTAN NATIONAL BANK

1993-98 ISSUE

#1-6 ornate denomination in circle at r. Circular arms at l. on back. Serial # at l. or lower l. Wmk. paper.

		VG	VF	UNC
1	**1 TYIN**			
	1993. Red, blue and purple on yellow and m/c unpt. 2 wmk. varieties.			
	a. Wmk: large diamond lattice pattern.	0.10	0.15	0.50
	b. Wmk: small snowflake pattern.	0.10	0.15	0.50

		VG	VF	UNC
2	**2 TYIN**			
	1993. Blue-violet on lt. blue and m/c unpt.			
	a. Wmk: large diamond pattern.	0.10	0.15	0.50
	b. Wmk: small snowflake pattern.	0.10	0.15	0.50
	c. W/o wmk.	0.10	0.15	0.45

		VG	VF	UNC
3	**5 TYIN**			
	1993. Violet on lt. blue and m/c unpt.	0.10	0.15	0.60

		VG	VF	UNC
4	**10 TYIN**			
	1993. Deep red on pink and m/c unpt.	0.10	0.15	0.75

		VG	VF	UNC
5	**20 TYIN**			
	1993. Black and blue-gray on yellow and m/c unpt.	0.10	0.15	0.75

		VG	VF	UNC
6	**50 TYIN**			
	1993. Dk. brown and black on m/c unpt.	0.10	0.15	1.50

#7-15 arms at upper ctr. r. on back.

#7-9 wmk: symmetrical design repeated.

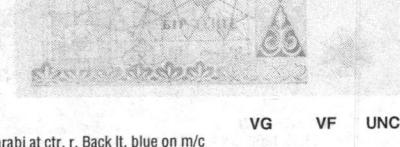

		VG	VF	UNC
7	**1 TENGÉ**			
	1993. Dk. blue on m/c unpt. Al-Farabi at ctr. r. Back lt. blue on m/c unpt; architectural drawings of mosque at l. ctr., arms at upper r.			
	a. Issued note.	0.10	0.15	1.50
	s. Specimen.	—	—	100.00

		VG	VF	UNC
8	**3 TENGÉ**			
	1993. Dk. green on m/c unpt. Suinbai at ctr. r. Mountains, forest, and river at l. ctr. on back.			
	a. Issued note.	0.10	0.15	2.50
	s. Specimen.	—	—	100.00

12   50 TENGÉ
1993. Red-brown and deep violet on m/c unpt. Abilkhair Khan at
ctr. r. and as wmk. Native artwork at l. ctr. on back.

	VG	VF	UNC
a. Issued note.	0.30	1.25	7.00
s. Specimen.	—	—	125.00

13   100 TENGÉ
1993. Purple and dk. blue on m/c unpt. Abylai Khan at ctr. r. and as
wmk. Domed bldg. at l. ctr. on back.

	VG	VF	UNC
a. Issued note.	0.60	1.20	7.50
s. Specimen.	—	—	125.00

#14-17 al-Farabi at r. and as wmk.

14   200 TENGÉ
1993. Red and brown on m/c unpt. Back blue and m/c; domes of
bldg. at l. on back.

	VG	VF	UNC
a. Issued note.	FV	FV	12.00
s. Specimen.	—	—	135.00

15   500 TENGÉ
1994. Blue-black and violet on m/c unpt. Ancient bldg. on back.

	VG	VF	UNC
a. Issued note.	FV	FV	17.50
s. Specimen.	—	—	150.00

16   1000 TENGÉ
1994. Deep green, red and orange on m/c unpt. Ancient bldg. on
back.

	VG	VF	UNC
a. Issued note.	FV	FV	32.50
s. Specimen.	—	—	150.00

9   5 TENGÉ
1993. Dk. brown-violet on m/c unpt. Kurmangazy at ctr. r.
Cemetery at l. ctr. on back.

	VG	VF	UNC
a. Issued note.	0.25	0.45	2.50
s. Specimen.	—	—	100.00

10   10 TENGÉ
1993. Dk. green on m/c unpt. Shoqan Valikhanov at ctr. r. and as
wmk. Mountains, forest, and lake at l. ctr. on back.

	VG	VF	UNC
a. Issued note.	0.25	0.50	3.00
s. Specimen.	—	—	100.00

11   20 TENGÉ
1993. Brown on m/c unpt. Abai Kunanbrev at ctr. r. and as wmk.
Equestrian hunter at l. ctr. on back.

	VG	VF	UNC
a. Issued note.	0.25	0.50	5.00
s. Specimen.	—	—	100.00

17 **2000 TENGÉ**
1996. Dk. brown and green on m/c unpt. Gate on back.

	VG	VF	UNC
	12.50	25.00	60.00

18 **5000 TENGÉ**
1998. Lt. brown on m/c unpt. Al Farabi at ctr. Mausoleum on back.

	VG	VF	UNC
	30.00	35.00	75.00

19 *Deleted.*

1999-2001 ISSUE

20 **200 TENGÉ**
1999. Brown and tan on m/c unpt. Similar to #14.

	VG	VF	UNC
	1.00	2.00	5.00

21 **500 TENGÉ**
1999. Dk. blue and violet on m/c unpt. Similar to #15.

	VG	VF	UNC
	3.00	5.00	7.50

22 **1000 TENGÉ**
2000. Dk. green, red and slate blue on m/c unpt. Similar to #16.

	VG	VF	UNC
	6.00	12.50	27.50

23 **2000 TENGÉ**
2000. Green, brown and purple on m/c unpt. Similar to #17.
Mausoleum of Khodka Akhemd Yassavi on back.

	VG	VF	UNC
	FV	FV	35.00

24 **5000 TENGÉ**
2001. Lt. brown and red on m/c unpt. Similar to #18.

	VG	VF	UNC
	FV	FV	65.00

25 **10,000 TENGÉ**
2003. Blue and dark brown on m/c unpt. Snow leopard with
mountains in background on back.

	VG	VF	UNC
	FV	FV	125.00

2001 COMMEMORATIVE ISSUE

26 **5000 TENGÉ**
2001. Lt. brown and red on m/c unpt. Blue ovpt. at top of wmk.
area on face of #18.

	VG	VF	UNC
	FV	FV	65.00

2004 ISSUE

27 **500 TENGÉ**
1999 (2004). Dk. blue and blue on violet and m/c unpt. Al-Farabi at
r. Mausoleum of Khodka Akhmed Yassavi on back. Like #21 but
additional security features at r.

	VG	VF	UNC
	FV	FV	7.50

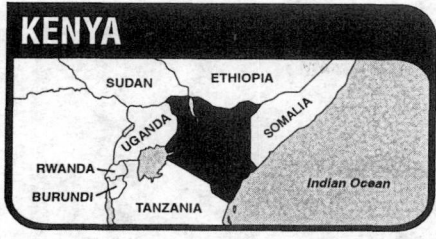

KENYA

The Republic of Kenya, located on the east coast of Central Africa, has an area of 224,961 sq. mi. (582,646 sq. km.) and a population of 30.34 million. Capital: Nairobi. The predominantly agricultural country exports coffee, tea and petroleum products.

The Arabs came to the coast of Kenya in the 8th century and established posts to conduct an ivory and slave trade. The Portuguese, the inveterate wanderers of the Age of Exploration, followed in the 16th century. After a lengthy and bitter struggle with the sultans of Zanzibar who controlled much of the southeastern coast of Africa, the Portuguese were driven away (late 17th century) and for many years Kenya was simply a port of call on the route to India. German and British interests in the 19th century produced agreements defining their respective spheres of influence. The British sphere was administered by the Imperial East Africa Co. until 1895, when the British government purchased the company's rights in the East Africa Protectorate which in 1920 was designated as Kenya Colony and protectorate - the latter being a 10-mile wide coastal strip together with Mombasa, Lamu and other small islands nominally retained by the Sultan of Zanzibar. Kenya achieved self-government in June of 1963 as a consequence of the 1952-60 Mau Mau terrorist campaign to secure land reforms and political rights for Africans. Independence was attained on Dec. 12, 1963. Kenya became a republic in 1964. It is a member of the Commonwealth of Nations. The president is Chief of State and Head of Government.

Notes of the East African Currency Board were in use during the first years.

RULERS:
British to 1964

MONETARY SYSTEM:
1 Shilling (Shilingi) = 100 Cents

REPUBLIC

CENTRAL BANK OF KENYA

1966 ISSUE

#1-5 Mzee Jomo Kenyatta at l., arms at ctr. in unpt. Values also in Arabic numerals and letters. Wmk: Lion's head.

1	5 SHILLINGS	VG	VF	UNC
	1966-68. Brown on m/c unpt. Woman picking coffee beans at r. on back.			
	a. 1.7.1966.	4.00	20.00	95.00
	b. 1.7.1967.	3.00	17.50	90.00
	c. 1.7.1968.	3.50	17.50	85.00
	s. As a. Specimen, punched hole cancelled.	—	—	—

2	10 SHILLINGS	VG	VF	UNC
	1966-68. Green on m/c unpt. Tea pickers in field on back.			
	a. 1.7.1966.	5.00	25.00	95.00
	b. 1.7.1967.	5.00	27.50	140.00
	c. 1.7.1968.	4.00	20.00	120.00
	s. As a. Specimen, punched hole cancelled.	—	—	—

3	20 SHILLINGS	VG	VF	UNC
	1966-68. Blue on m/c unpt. Plants and train w/sisal on back.			
	a. 1.7.1966.	10.00	60.00	250.00
	b. 1.7.1967.	10.00	60.00	250.00
	c. 1.7.1968.	10.00	60.00	250.00
	s. As a. Specimen, punched hole cancelled.	—	—	—

4	50 SHILLINGS	VG	VF	UNC
	1966-68. Dk. brown on m/c unpt. Cotton picking below Mt. Kenya on back.			
	a. 1.7.1966.	55.00	300.00	850.00
	b. 1.7.1967.	65.00	350.00	1300.00
	c. 1.7.1968.	50.00	325.00	1250.00
	s. As a. Specimen, punched hole cancelled.	—	—	—

5	100 SHILLINGS	VG	VF	UNC
	1966; 1968. Purple on m/c unpt. Workers at pineapple plantation on back.			
	a. 1.7.1966.	12.50	55.00	475.00
	b. 1.7.1968.	15.00	60.00	500.00
	s. As a. Specimen, punched hole cancelled.	—	—	—

1969 ISSUE

#6-10 Mzee Jomo Kenyatta at l., values w/o Arabic numerals and letters. Different text at lower ctr. Wmk: Lion's head.

		VG	VF	UNC
6	**5 SHILLINGS**			
	1969-73. Brown on m/c unpt. Similar to #1.			
	a. Sign. 2. 1.7.1969.	1.00	5.00	25.00
	b. Sign. 3. 1.7.1971.	1.50	6.00	30.00
	c. Sign. 3. 1.7.1972.	0.75	2.00	22.50
	d. Sign. 3. 1.7.1973.	0.75	4.00	20.00

		VG	VF	UNC
7	**10 SHILLINGS**			
	1969-74. Green on m/c unpt. Similar to #2.			
	a. Sign. 2. 1.7.1969.	2.50	8.00	60.00
	b. Sign. 3. 1.7.1971.	2.00	6.00	50.00
	c. Sign. 3. 1.7.1972.	1.50	7.00	55.00
	d. Sign. 3. 1.7.1973.	1.50	7.00	55.00
	e. Sign. 3. 1.7.1974.	1.50	7.00	52.50

		VG	VF	UNC
8	**20 SHILLINGS**			
	1969-73. Blue on m/c unpt. Similar to #3.			
	a. Sign. 2. 1.7.1969.	3.00	20.00	160.00
	b. Sign. 3. 1.7.1971.	7.00	40.00	275.00
	c. Sign. 3. 1.7.1972.	4.00	25.00	180.00
	d. Sign. 3. 1.7.1973.	5.00	30.00	200.00
9	**50 SHILLINGS**			
	1969; 1971. Dk. brown on m/c unpt. Similar to #4.			
	a. Sign. 2. 1.7.1969.	50.00	175.00	600.00
	b. Sign. 3. 1.7.1971.	15.00	65.00	200.00

		VG	VF	UNC
10	**100 SHILLINGS**			
	1969-73. Purple on m/c unpt. Similar to #5.			
	a. Sign. 2. 1.7.1969.	25.00	125.00	500.00
	b. Sign. 3. 1.7.1971.	10.00	40.00	275.00
	c. Sign. 3. 1.7.1972.	10.00	40.00	275.00
	d. Sign. 3. 1.7.1973.	20.00	100.00	350.00

1974 ISSUE

#11-14 Mzee Jomo Kenyatta at l., values in latent images at bottom l. Wmk: Lion's head.

		VG	VF	UNC
11	**5 SHILLINGS**			
	1974-77. Brown-orange on m/c unpt. Woman picking coffee beans at r. on back.			
	a. Sign. 3. 12.12.1974.	0.50	2.00	15.00
	b. Sign. 4. 1.1.1975.	1.00	4.00	30.00
	c. Sign. 4. 1.7.1976.	0.25	1.50	10.00
	d. Sign. 5. 1.7.1977.	0.50	2.00	15.00

		VG	VF	UNC
12	**10 SHILLINGS**			
	1.1.1975; 1.7.1976; 1.7.1977. Dk. green and dk. brown on m/c unpt. Back green; cattle at ctr. r. on back.			
	a. Sign. 4. 1.1.1975.	1.00	3.00	15.00
	b. Sign. 4. 1.7.1976.	1.50	6.00	25.00
	c. Sign. 5. 1.7.1977.	1.25	4.00	17.50

13	20 SHILLINGS	VG	VF	UNC
	1974-77. Dk. blue on m/c unpt. Lions on back.			
	a. Sign. 3. 12.12.1974.	3.00	15.00	60.00
	b. Sign. 4. 1.1.1975.	2.00	7.50	35.00
	c. Sign. 4. 1.7.1976.	4.00	12.50	65.00
	d. Sign. 5. 1.7.1977.	3.00	9.00	45.00

14	100 SHILLINGS	VG	VF	UNC
	1974-77. Purple on lt. green and m/c unpt. Kenyatta statue and tower on back. 153 x 79mm.			
	a. Sign. 3. 12.12.1974.	10.00	35.00	150.00
	b. Sign. 4. 1.1.1975.	5.00	17.50	125.00
	c. Sign. 4. 1.7.1976.	7.50	25.00	140.00
	d. Sign. 5. 1.7.1977.	7.50	30.00	220.00

1978 ISSUE

#15-18 Mzee Jomo Kenyatta at l., w/English value only in 3rd line on face. Wmk: Lion's head.

Note: #15-18 were withdrawn soon after Kenyatta's death. A shortage of currency resulted in a limited reissue during Dec. 1993 - Jan. 1994 of mostly circulated notes.

15	5 SHILLINGS	VG	VF	UNC
	1.7.1978. Brown-orange on m/c unpt. Similar to #11. W/English value only in third line on face. Sign. 5.	0.50	1.50	4.00

16	10 SHILLINGS	VG	VF	UNC
	1.7.1978. Dk. green and dk. brown on m/c unpt. Similar to #12. Sign. 5.	0.50	1.00	4.00

17	20 SHILLINGS	VG	VF	UNC
	1.7.1978. Blue-black and blue on m/c unpt. Similar to #13. Sign. 5.	1.25	2.75	10.00

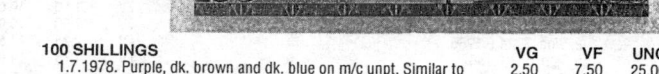

18	100 SHILLINGS	VG	VF	UNC
	1.7.1978. Purple, dk. brown and dk. blue on m/c unpt. Similar to #14 but w/different colors in guilloches. 157 x 81mm. Sign. 5.	2.50	7.50	25.00

1980-81 ISSUE

#19-23 arms at ctr., Pres. Daniel Toroitich Arap Moi at r. Wmk: Lion's head.

19	5 SHILLINGS	VG	VF	UNC
	1981-84. Orange-brown on m/c unpt. 3 rams w/giraffes and mountain in background on back.			
	a. Sign. 6. 1.1.1981.	FV	0.50	4.00
	b. Sign. 6. 1.1.1982.	FV	4.00	3.00
	c. Sign. 7. 1.7.1984.	FV	6.00	5.00

20 **10 SHILLINGS**

1981-88. Green, blue and brown on m/c unpt. 2 cows at l., 2 school children drinking milk at ctr. on back.

	VG	VF	UNC
a. Sign. 6. 1.1.1981.	FV	1.50	8.00
b. Sign. 6. 1.1.1982.	FV	1.25	7.00
c. Sign. 7. 1.7.1984.	FV	1.75	9.00
d. Sign. 7. 1.7.1985.	FV	2.00	10.00
e. Sign. 7. 14.9.1986.	FV	1.50	8.00
f. Sign. 8. 1.7.1987.	FV	1.25	8.00
g. Sign. 9a. 1.7.1988.	FV	1.25	7.00

21 **20 SHILLINGS**

1981-87. Blue on m/c unpt. 4 women reading newspaper at ctr. on back.

	VG	VF	UNC
a. Sign. 6. 1.1.1981.	FV	1.75	14.00
b. Sign. 6. 1.1.1982.	FV	1.50	10.00
c. Sign. 7. 1.7.1984.	FV	1.50	10.00
d. Sign. 7. 1.7.1985.	FV	2.00	16.00
e. Sign. 7. 14.9.1986.	FV	2.25	17.50
f. Sign. 8. 1.7.1987.	FV	1.75	14.00

22 **50 SHILLINGS**

1980-88. Dk. red and m/c. Back olive; jet aircraft flying over Jomo Kenyatta airport.

	VG	VF	UNC
a. Sign. 4. 1.6.1980.	FV	3.00	16.00
b. Sign. 7. 1.7.1985.	FV	4.00	20.00
c. Sign. 7. 14.9.1986.	FV	3.50	18.00
d. Sign. 8. 1.7.1987.	FV	5.00	22.00
e. Sign. 9a. 1.7.1988.	FV	7.00	30.00

23 **100 SHILLINGS**

1980-88. Purple and m/c. Kenyatta statue, tower and mountains on back.

	VG	VF	UNC
a. Sign. 4. 1.6.1980.	FV	5.00	25.00
b. Sign. 6. 1.6.1981.	FV	6.00	35.00
c. Sign. 7. 1.7.1984.	FV	5.00	30.00
d. Sign. 7. 14.9.1986.	FV	6.50	40.00
e. Sign. 8. 1.7.1987.	FV	7.00	50.00
f. Sign. 9a. 1.7.1988.	FV	4.00	22.00

23A **200 SHILLINGS**

1986-88. Dk. brown on m/c unpt. Triangle in lower l. border. No silvering on value at upper r. Fountain at ctr. on back.

	VG	VF	UNC
a. Sign. 7. 14.9.1986.	FV	7.50	50.00
b. Sign. 8. 1.7.1987.	FV	25.00	200.00
c. Sign. 9a. 1.7.1988.	FV	35.00	225.00

1986-90 ISSUE

#24-30 Pres. Daniel Toroitich Arap Moi at r. ctr., arms at l. ctr. Vertical serial # at l. Wmk: Lion's head. Replacement notes: Serial # prefix ZZ.

Note: H&S printed the small date of 2.1.1992.

24 **10 SHILLINGS**

1989-94. Dk. green, dk. blue and brown on m/c unpt. University at l. ctr. on back.

	VG	VF	UNC
a. Sign. 9a. 14.10.1989	FV	FV	3.00
b. Sign. 9a. 1.7.1990.	FV	FV	2.50
c. Sign. 9a. 1.7.1991.	FV	FV	1.75
d. Sign. 10a. 2.1.1992. Small date font.	FV	1.00	4.50
e. Sign. 10a. 1.7.1993. Large date font.	FV	1.00	4.50
f. Sign. 11. 1.1.1994.	FV	1.50	6.00

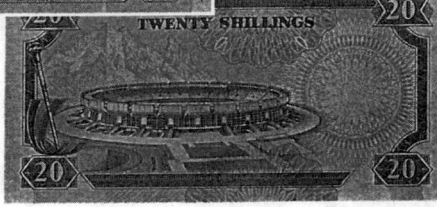

25 20 SHILLINGS

		VG	VF	UNC
1988-92. Dk. blue and m/c. Moi International Sports Complex on back.				
a. Sign. 9b. 12.12.1988.		1.25	4.00	15.00
b. Sign. 9b. 1.7.1989.		FV	1.00	5.00
c. Sign. 9b. 1.7.1990.		FV	FV	3.50
d. Sign. 9b. 1.7.1991.		FV	2.00	6.00
e. Sign. 10a. 2.1.1992. Large date font.		FV	2.00	6.00

Note: #25 dated 12.12.1988 is believed to be a commemorative for the 25th Anniversary of Independence.

26 50 SHILLINGS

		VG	VF	UNC
1990; 1992. Red-brown on m/c unpt. Back green; modern bldgs. at l., flag at r.				
a. Sign. 9b. 10.10.1990.		FV	4.00	16.00
b. Sign. 10b. 1.7.1992.		FV	3.00	14.00

27 100 SHILLINGS

		VG	VF	UNC
1989-95. Purple, dk. green and red on m/c unpt. Monument to 25th Anniversary of Independence w/Mt. Kenya on back.				
a. Sign. 9a. 14.10.1989.		FV	3.00	12.50
b. Sign. 9a. 1.7.1990.		FV	2.00	10.00
c. Sign. 9a. 1.7.1991.		FV	2.00	10.00
d. Sign. 10a. 2.1.1992. Small date font.		FV	2.00	10.00
e. Sign. 10a. 1.7.1992. Large date font.		FV	4.00	17.50
f. Sign. 11. 1.1.1994.		FV	3.00	15.00
g. Sign. 12. 1.1.1995.		FV	4.00	17.50

#28 Deleted. See #23A.

29 200 SHILLINGS

		VG	VF	UNC
1989-94. Similar to #23A but rose replaces colored triangle to r. of *200* at lower l. Additional silver diamond design under 200 at upper r. Vertical serial # at l.				
a. Sign. 9a. 14.10.1989.		FV	4.50	27.50
b. Sign. 9a. 1.7.1990.		FV	4.50	25.00
c. Sign. 10a. 2.1.1992. Small date font.		FV	5.00	35.00
d. Sign. 10a. 1.7.1992. Large date font.		FV	4.00	22.50
e. Sign. 11. 14.9.1993.		FV	3.50	20.00
f. Sign. 11. 1.1.1994.		FV	4.00	25.00

30 500 SHILLINGS

		VG	VF	UNC
1988-95. Black, deep green and red on m/c unpt. Roses at l. Parliament bldg., Mt. Kenya on back.				
a. Sign. 9b. 14.10.1988.		10.00	50.00	250.00
b. Sign. 9b. 1.7.1989.		FV	25.00	100.00
c. Sign. 9b. 1.7.1990.		FV	15.00	55.00
d. Sign. 10a. 2.1.1992. Small date font.		FV	20.00	75.00
e. Sign. 10a. 1.7.1992. Large date font.		FV	15.00	55.00
f. Sign. 11. 14.9.1993.		FV	17.50	60.00
g. Sign. 12. 1.1.1995.		FV	17.50	65.00

1993 ISSUE

#31 Pres. Daniel Toroitich Arap Moi at ctr. r.

31 20 SHILLINGS

		VG	VF	UNC
1993-94. Similar to #25 but w/roses added to l. border, vertical red serial #. Male runner and other artistic enhancements added on back.				
a. Sign. 11. 14.9.1993.		FV	2.00	5.00
b. Sign. 11. 1.1.1994.		FV	2.00	6.00

1994-95 ISSUE

#32-34 Pres. Daniel Toroitich Arap Moi at l. ctr., arms at upper ctr. r. Ascending size serial #. W/o segmented foil over security thread. Wmk: Lion head facing.

32 20 SHILLINGS

		VG	VF	UNC
1.7.1995. Dk. blue, brown and blue-green on m/c unpt. Baton at l., Moi Int'l Sports Complex at l. ctr., runner at ctr. r. on back. Sign. 13.		FV	FV	2.50

33 500 SHILLINGS

		VG	VF	UNC
1.1.1995. Black, green and red on m/c unpt. Parliament bldg. at l. ctr. on back.		FV	FV	22.50

34 1000 SHILLINGS

		VG	VF	UNC
12.12.1994; 1.7.1995. Brown on m/c unpt. Water buffalo, elephants and egret on back.		FV	FV	50.00

1996-97 ISSUE

#35-40 like previous issue but w/segmented foil over security thread.

35 20 SHILLINGS

1996-2001. Dk. blue on m/c unpt. Like #32. W/security thread.

	VG	VF	UNC
a. 1.1.1996.	FV	FV	3.00
b. 1.7.1997.	FV	FV	5.00
c. 1.7.1998.	FV	FV	7.00

36 50 SHILLINGS

1996-2002 Brown-violet and blue-black on m/c unpt. Dromedary caravan on back.

	VG	VF	UNC
a. 1.1.1996. Reddish-brown or black sign.	FV	FV	5.00
b. 1.7.1997.	FV	FV	7.00
c. 1.7.1998.	FV	FV	4.00
d. 1.7.1999.	FV	FV	4.00
e. 1.7.2000.	FV	FV	3.00
f. 1.7.2001.	FV	FV	15.00
g. 1.7.2002.	FV	FV	2.50

37 100 SHILLINGS

1996-2002. Purple, red and deep green on m/c unpt. People by Monument to 25th Anniversary of Independence at ctr., branch of fruit at l. on back.

	VG	VF	UNC
a. 1.7.1996.	FV	FV	6.00
b. 1.7.1997.	FV	FV	12.00
c. 1.7.1998.	FV	FV	5.00
d. 1.7.1999.	FV	FV	5.00
e. 1.7.2000.	FV	FV	4.00
f. 1.7.2001.	FV	FV	8.00
g. 1.7.2002.	FV	FV	4.00
h. 1.9.2002.	FV	FV	5.00

38 200 SHILLINGS

1996-2002. Dk. brown, blue-gray and dk. green on m/c unpt. Unity monument at ctr., women harvesting at l. on back.

	VG	VF	UNC
a. 1.7.1996.	FV	FV	16.00
b. 1.7.1997.	FV	FV	12.50
c. 1.7.1998.	FV	FV	16.00
d. 1.7.1999.	FV	FV	16.00
e. 1.7.2000.	FV	FV	16.00
f. 1.7.2001.	FV	FV	8.00
g. 1.9.2002.	FV	FV	7.00

39 500 SHILLINGS

1997-2002. Black, green and red on m/c unpt. Like #33

	VG	VF	UNC
a. 1.7.1997.	FV	7.50	28.00
b. 1.7.1999.	FV	FV	26.00
c. 1.7.2000.	FV	FV	24.00
d. 1.7.2001.	FV	FV	18.00

2003-04 ISSUE

#41-45 like previous issue but w/enhanced security features. 2003 dates ahve thin security thread, 2004 onwards have a thick thread.

40	1000 SHILLINGS	VG	VF	UNC
	1997-2002. Brown-violet and olive-green on m/c unpt. Like #34.			
	a. 1.7.1997.	FV	FV	60.00
	b. 1.7.1999.	FV	FV	45.00
	c. 1.7.2000.	FV	FV	35.00
	d. 1.7.2001.	FV	FV	40.00
	e. 1.7.2002.	FV	FV	35.00

2003-04 ISSUE

#41-45 like previous issue but w/enhanced security features. 2003 dates ahve thin security thread, 2004 onwards have a thick thread.

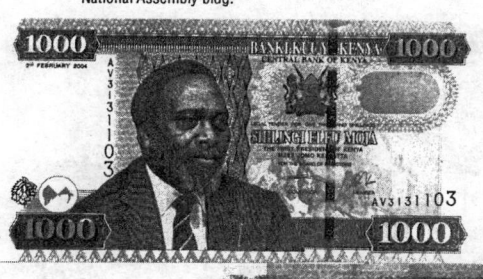

44	500 SHILLINGS	VG	VF	UNC
	1.4.2003; 2.2.2004; 2.8.2004. Black and green on m/c unpt. National Assembly bldg.	FV	FV	16.00

41	50 SHILLINGS	VG	VF	UNC
	1.4.2003; 2.2.2004; 2.8.2004; 1.6.2005. Brown-violet and blue-black on m/c unpt. Dromedary caravan on back.			
	a. Issued note.	FV	FV	2.50
	s. Specimen.	—		

45	1000 SHILLINGS	VG	VF	UNC
	1.4.2003; 2.2.2004; 2.8.2004; 1.6.2005. Brown, lilac and light olive on m/c unpt. Elephants and other animals on back.	FV	FV	32.50

2003 COMMEMORATIVE ISSUE

40th Anniversary of Independence.

42	100 SHILLINGS	VG	VF	UNC
	2.2.2004; 2.8.2004; 1.6.2005. Purple, orange and green on m/c unpt. Nyayo monument on back.	FV	FV	3.50

2003 COMMEMORATIVE ISSUE

40th Anniversary of Independence.

43	200 SHILLINGS	VG	VF	UNC
	2.2.2004; 2.8.2004; 1.6.2005. Brown, blue and light green on m/c unpt. Jomo Kenyatta at l. ctr. Cotton pickers on back. Like #45 but w/o commemorative text.	FV	FV	6.50

46	200 SHILLINGS	VG	VF	UNC
	12.12.2003. Brown, blue and light green on m/c unpt. Jomo Kenyatta at l. ctr., commemorative text in wmk. area at l. Cotton pickers on back.	FV	FV	6.50

KOREA-NORTH

The Democratic Peoples Republic of Korea, situated in in northeastern Asia on the northern half of the Korean peninsula between the Peoples Republic of China and the Republic of Korea, has an area of 46,540 sq. mi. (120,538 sq. km.) and a population of 23.26 million. Capital: Pyongyang. The economy is based on heavy based on heavy industry and agriculture. Metals, minerals and farm produce are exported.

Japan replaced China as the predominant foreign influence in Korea in 1895 and annexed the peninsular country in 1910. Defeat in World War II brought an end to Japanese rule. U.S. troops entered Korea from the south and Soviet forces entered from the north. The Cairo conference (1943) had established that Korea should be "free and independent." The Potsdam conference (1945) set the 38th parallel as the line dividing the occupation forces of the United States and Russia. When Russia refused to permit a U.N. commission designated to supervise reunification elections to enter North Korea, an election was held in South Korea which established the Republic of Korea on Aug. 15, 1948. North Korea held an unsupervised election on Aug. 25, 1948, and on the following day proclaimed the establishment of the Democratic Peoples Republic of Korea.

MONETARY SYSTEM:
1 Won = 100 Chon

KOREAN CENTRAL BANK

1959 ISSUE

#12-17 arms at l. or upper l. Wmk. paper.

			VG	VF	UNC
12	50 CHON		0.15	0.50	2.00
	1959. Blue on m/c unpt. Arms at upper l.				

			VG	VF	UNC
13	1 WON		0.15	0.50	2.00
	1959. Red-brown on m/c unpt. Fishing boat at ctr.				

			VG	VF	UNC
14	5 WON		0.15	0.50	2.00
	1959. Green on m/c unpt. Lg. bldg. at ctr.				

			VG	VF	UNC
15	10 WON		0.20	0.50	2.00
	1959. Red on m/c unpt. Fortress gateway at ctr. r. Woman picking fruit on back.				

			VG	VF	UNC
16	50 WON		0.20	0.50	2.50
	1959. Purple on m/c unpt. Bridge and city at ctr. Woman w/wheat on back.				

			VG	VF	UNC
17	100 WON		0.25	0.75	3.00
	1959. Green on m/c unpt. Steam freight train in factory area at ctr. River w/cliffs on back.				

1978 ISSUE

#18-22 arms at upper l.

Note: Circulation of varieties #18-21:

a. For general circulation.

b. For Socialist visitors.

c. For non-Socialist visitors.

d. Replaced a for general circulation.

e. Use not known.

18	1 WON	VG	VF	UNC
	1978. Olive-green on m/c unpt. 2 adults and 2 children at ctr. Back purple and m/c; soldier at l., woman w/flowers at ctr., woman at r.			
	a. Red and black serial #. No seal on back.	0.20	0.50	3.00
	b. Black serial #. Green seal at l. on back.	0.20	0.50	2.50
	c. Red serial #. Red seal at l. on back.	0.20	0.50	2.50
	d. Red serial #. Lg. numeral 1 in red guilloche on back.	0.20	0.50	2.50
	e. Black serial #. Lg. numeral 1 in blue guilloche on back.	0.20	0.50	2.50
	s. Specimen.	—	—	—

21	50 WON	VG	VF	UNC
	1978. Olive-green on m/c unpt. Soldier w/man holding torch, woman w/wheat, man w/book at ctr. Lake scene on back.			
	a. Red and black serial #. No seal on back.	0.35	1.25	6.00
	b. Black serial #. Green seal at lower r. on back.	0.35	1.25	4.50
	c. Red serial #. Red seal at lower r. on back.	0.35	1.25	4.50
	d. Red serial #. Lg. numeral 50 in red guilloche on back.	0.50	1.25	4.50
	e. Black serial #. Lg. numeral 50 in blue guilloche on back.	0.35	1.25	4.50
	s. Specimen.	—	—	—

19	5 WON	VG	VF	UNC
	1978. Blue-gray on m/c unpt. Worker w/book and gear, and woman w/wheat at ctr. Mt. Gumgang on back.			
	a. Red and black serial #. No seal on back.	0.25	0.75	3.00
	b. Black serial #. Green seal at l. on back.	0.25	0.75	3.50
	c. Red serial #. Red seal at l. on back.	0.25	0.75	3.50
	d. Red serial #. Lg. numeral 5 in red guilloche on back.	0.25	0.75	3.50
	e. Black serial #. Lg. numeral 5 in blue guilloche on back.	0.25	0.75	3.50
	s. Specimen.	—	—	—

22	100 WON	VG	VF	UNC
	1978. Brown on lilac and m/c unpt. Kim Il Sung at ctr. r. House w/trees on back. Red and black serial #. No seal on back.			
	a. Issued note.	0.75	2.50	10.00
	s. Specimen. Ovpt. in red on face.	—	—	200.00

1988 "CAPITALIST VISITOR" ISSUE

#23-26 arms at upper l. on face; red serial #. "Value" backs.

 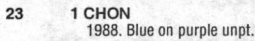

23	1 CHON	VG	VF	UNC
	1988. Blue on purple unpt.	0.10	0.20	0.40

24	5 CHON	VG	VF	UNC
	1988. Blue on pink unpt.	0.15	0.25	0.50

20	10 WON	VG	VF	UNC
	1978. Brown on m/c unpt. Winged equestrian statue "Chonllima" at ctr. Waterfront factory on back.			
	a. Red and black serial #. No seal on back.	0.30	1.00	7.50
	b. Black serial #. Green seal at upper r. on back.	0.30	1.00	4.00
	c. Red serial #. Red seal at upper r. on back.	0.30	1.00	4.00
	d. Red serial #. Lg. numeral 10 in red guilloche on back.	0.30	1.00	4.00
	e. Black serial #. Lg. numeral 10 in blue guilloche on back.	0.30	1.00	4.00
	s. Specimen.	—	—	—

25	10 CHON	VG	VF	UNC
	1988. Blue and black on green-yellow unpt.	0.20	0.40	0.75

26 50 CHON
1988. Blue on yellow unpt.

	VG	VF	UNC
	0.25	0.50	1.00

#27-30 dk. green on blue and pink unpt. w/winged equestrian statue "Chonllima" at ctr., arms at upper r. Red serial #.

27 1 WON
1988.

	VG	VF	UNC
	0.25	0.75	2.50

28 5 WON
1988.

	VG	VF	UNC
	0.25	1.50	7.50

29 10 WON
1988.

	VG	VF	UNC
	0.75	3.00	12.50

30 50 WON
1988.

	VG	VF	UNC
	1.50	8.00	40.00

1988 "SOCIALIST VISITOR" ISSUE

#31-38 arms at upper r. Denomination on back. Black serial #.

31 1 CHON
1988. Red-brown on pink and blue unpt.

	VG	VF	UNC
	FV	FV	1.25

32 5 CHON
1988. Purple on pink and blue unpt.

	VG	VF	UNC
	FV	FV	1.75

33 10 CHON
1988. Olive-green on pink and blue unpt.

	VG	VF	UNC
	FV	FV	2.50

34 50 CHON
1988. Brown-violet on pink and blue unpt.

	VG	VF	UNC
	FV	FV	3.00

#35-38 red on blue and ochre unpt. Temple at ctr., olive sprig on globe at r. Olive sprig on globe on back.

35 1 WON
1988.

	VG	VF	UNC
	FV	FV	3.50

36 5 WON
1988.

	VG	VF	UNC
	FV	FV	12.50

37 10 WON
1988.

	VG	VF	UNC
	FV	FV	25.00

		VG	VF	UNC
38	**50 WON** 1988.	FV	FV	100.00

1992; 1998 ISSUE

#39-42 arms at upper l. Wmk: Winged equestrian statue "Chonllima".

		VG	VF	UNC
42	**50 WON** 1992; 1998. Deep brown and deep olive-brown on m/c unpt. Monument to 5 year plan at l. and as wmk., young professionals at ctr. r., arms at upper r. Landscape of pine trees and mountains on back.	FV	FV	10.00

		VG	VF	UNC
39	**1 WON** 1992; 1998. Grayish olive-green and olive-brown on m/c unpt. Young woman w/flower basket at ctr. r. Mt. Gumgang on back.	FV	FV	1.50

		VG	VF	UNC
43	**100 WON** 1992; 1998. Deep brown and brown-violet on m/c unpt. Arms at lower l. ctr., Kim Il Sung at r. Rural home at ctr. on back. Wmk: Arched gateway.	FV	FV	7.50

		VG	VF	UNC
40	**5 WON** 1992; 1998. Blue-black and deep purple on m/c unpt. Students at ctr. r. w/modern bldg. and factory in background. Palace on back.	FV	FV	4.00

		VG	VF	UNC
44	**500 WON** 1998. Slate gray on lt. blue and purple unpt. Assembly Hall. Back red and black. Suspension bridge.	FV	FV	25.00

2002 ISSUE

		VG	VF	UNC
41	**10 WON** 1992; 1998. Deep brown and red-brown on m/c unpt. Factory worker, winged equestrian statue "Chonllima" at ctr., factories in background at r. Flood gates on back.	FV	FV	6.00

		VG	VF	UNC
45	**1000 WON** 2002. Dk. green on m/c unpt. Back slate blue on m/c unpt. Rural home at ctr. Like #43.	FV	FV	75.00

		VG	VF	UNC
46	**5000 WON** 2002. Purple on m/c unpt. Rural home at ctr. on back. Like #43.	FV	FV	150.00

COLLECTOR SERIES

KOREAN CENTRAL BANK

1978 ISSUE

		Issue Price	Mkt.	Value
CS1	**1978 1-100 WON.** Red ovpt. Korean characters for specimen on #18a-21a, 22 (w/all zero serial #).	—		30.00

1992 ISSUE

		Issue Price	Mkt.	Value
CS2	**1992 1-100 WON.** Red, rectangular ovpt. Korean characters for specimen on #39-43. (39, 42 and 43 w/all zero serial #, 40-41 w/normal serial #).	—		20.00

2000 ISSUE

#CS3-CS8 ovpt. in Korean or English: *The 55th Anniversary of Foundation of the Workers' Party of Korea 10th.10.Juche 89 (2000).*

		Issue Price	Mkt.	Value
CS3	**1 WON** Black ovpt. in English on face of #18e.	—		3.00
CS4	**5 WON** Red ovpt. in Korean on face of #19d.	—		3.00
CS5	**10 WON** Black ovpt. in English on face of #20e.	—		3.00
CS6	**50 WON** Red ovpt. in Korean on face of #21b.	—		3.00
CS7	**50 WON** Red ovpt. in English on face of #21b.	—		3.00
CS8	**50 WON** Black ovpt. in English on face of #21b.	—		3.00

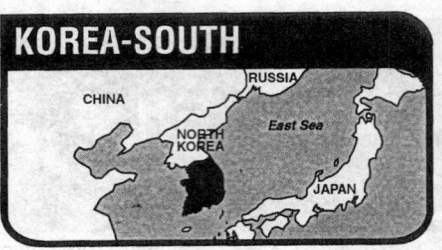

The Republic of Korea, situated in northeastern Asia on the southern half of the Korean peninsula between North Korea and the Korean Strait, has an area of 38,025 sq. mi. (98,484 sq. km.) and a population of 44.61 million. Capital: Seoul. The economy is based on agriculture and textiles. Clothing, plywood and textile products are exported. Japan replaced China as the predominant foreign influence in Korea in 1895 and annexed the peninsular country in 1910.

Defeat in World War II brought an end to Japanese rule. U.S. troops entered Korea from the south and Soviet entered from the north. The Cairo Conference (1943) had established that Korea should be "free and independent." The Potsdam Conference (1945) set the 38th parallel as the line dividing the occupation forces of the United States and Russia. When Russia refused to permit a U.N. commission designated to supervise reunification elections to enter North Korea, an election was held in South Korea on May 10, 1948. By its determination, the Republic of Korea was inaugurated on Aug. 15, 1948.

MONETARY SYSTEM:
1 Won (Hwan) = 100 Chon
1 new Won = 10 old Hwan, 1962-

REPLACEMENT NOTES:
#30-32, 34, 36-37, sm. crosslet design in front of serial #. #35, 38, 38A, 39, 43-49: notes w/first digit 9 in serial number.

DATING:
The modern notes of Korea are dated according to the founding of the first Korean dynasty, that of the house of Tangun, in 2333 BC.

REPUBLIC

BANK OF KOREA

1958-60 ISSUE

		VG	VF	UNC
23	**50 HWAN** 4291 (1958). Green-blue on olive-green unpt. Archway at l. Back green; statue at ctr., medieval tortoise warship at r.	20.00	60.00	350.00

		VG	VF	UNC
24	**500 HWAN** 4291 (1958); 4292 (1959). Dk. green. Portr. Syngman Rhee at r. Back brownish purple.	7.50	40.00	350.00

		VG	VF	UNC
25	**1000 HWAN** 4293 (1960); 4294 (1961); 1962. Black on olive unpt. Kg. Sejong the Great at r. Back blue-green and lt. brown; flaming torch at ctr.			
	a. 4293 (1960).	2.50	10.00	100.00
	b. 4294 (1961).	1.50	6.00	60.00
	c. 1962.	1.75	7.00	65.00

1961-62 ISSUE

Hwan System.

			VG	VF	UNC
26	**100 HWAN**				
	1962. Green on orange and m/c unpt. Woman reading to child at r. Archway at l., date at bottom r. margin on back.		15.00	60.00	325.00

			VG	VF	UNC
27	**500 HWAN**				
	4294 (1961). Blue-green on m/c unpt. Kg. Sejong the Great at r. Back green; bldg. at r. 8-character imprint.		17.50	80.00	475.00

1962 ND ISSUES

Won System

			VG	VF	UNC
28	**10 JEON**				
	1962. Deep blue on pale blue and pink unpt.		0.05	0.10	0.40

			VG	VF	UNC
29	**50 JEON**				
	1962. Black on pale green and ochre unpt. Back brown.		0.05	0.10	0.50

			VG	VF	UNC
30	**1 WON**				
	ND (1962). Violet on brown unpt.				
	a. Issued note.		0.05	0.10	1.00
	s. Specimen.		—	—	—

			VG	VF	UNC
31	**5 WON**				
	ND (1962). Black on gray-green unpt.				
	a. Issued note.		0.10	0.25	2.00
	s. Specimen.		—	—	—

			VG	VF	UNC
32	**10 WON**				
	ND (1962). Brown on green unpt.				
	a. Issued note.		0.50	2.00	10.00
	s. Specimen.		—	—	—

			VG	VF	UNC
33	**10 WON**				
	1962-65; ND. Brown on lilac and green unpt. Tower at l. Medieval tortoise warship at ctrr., date at lower l. on back.				
	a. 1962.		2.50	8.00	50.00
	b. 1963.		2.75	8.50	52.50
	c. 1964.		1.50	4.50	27.50
	d. 1965.		1.00	3.00	20.00
	e. ND.		0.15	0.50	3.00

			VG	VF	UNC
34	**50 WON**				
	ND (1962). Red-brown on blue and lilac unpt. Rock in the sea at l. Torch at ctr. on back.				
	a. Issued note.		4.00	15.00	95.00
	s. Specimen.		—	—	—

			VG	VF	UNC
35	**100 WON**				
	1962-69. Green on olive unpt. Archway at l. Unpt: 100 Won at ctr. Pagoda and date on back.				
	a. 1962.		5.00	17.50	110.00
	b. 1963.		4.00	12.50	80.00
	c. 1964.		4.00	12.50	75.00
	d. 1965.		4.00	12.50	75.00
	e. 1969.		5.00	15.00	90.00

36	100 WON	VG	VF	UNC
	ND (1962). Green on blue and gold unpt. Archway similar to #35 at l. 5-petaled blossom at ctr. in unpt. Back similar to #34.			
	a. Issued note.	2.00	12.50	80.00
	s. Specimen.	—	—	—

37	500 WON	VG	VF	UNC
	ND (1962). Blue on lilac and green unpt. Pagoda portal at l. Back similar to #34.			
	a. Issued note.	5.00	22.50	135.00
	s. Specimen.	—	—	—

1965; 1966 ND Issue

38	100 WON	VG	VF	UNC
	ND (1965). Dk. green and blue on m/c unpt. Bank name and denomination in red. Kg. Sejong the Great at r. Bldg. on back.			
	a. Issued note.	0.75	1.75	5.50
	s. Specimen.	—	—	—

38A	100 WON	VG	VF	UNC
	ND (1965). Dk. blue-green. Bank name and denomination in brown. Like #38.	0.75	2.25	10.00

39	500 WON	VG	VF	UNC
	ND (1966). Black on m/c unpt. City gate at l. Medieval turtle warships on back.			
	a. Issued note.	0.75	1.50	9.00
	s. Specimen.	—	—	—

1969-73 ND Issue

40	50 WON	VG	VF	UNC
	ND (1969). Black on green and brown unpt. Pavilion at l. Back blue; torch at ctr.			
	a. Issued note.	0.25	1.00	4.00
	s. Specimen.	—	—	—

41	5000 WON	VG	VF	UNC
	ND (1972). Brown on green and m/c unpt. Yi l at r. and as wmk. Lg. bldg. on back.	7.50	12.50	40.00

42	10,000 WON	VG	VF	UNC
	ND (1973). Dk. brown on m/c unpt. Kg. Sejong the Great at l. ctr. Bldgs. and pavilion on back. Wmk: Woman w/headdress.	15.00	25.00	60.00

1973-79 ND Issue

	VG	VF	UNC
43 **500 WON**	FV	1.00	3.50

ND (1973). Blue and green on m/c unpt. Adm. Yi Sun-shin at l., medieval turtle warship at ctr. Bldg. w/steps on back.

	VG	VF	UNC
44 **1000 WON**	FV	2.00	5.00

ND (1975). Purple on m/c unpt. Yi Hwang at r. Do-San Academy in black on back. Wmk: Flowers.

	VG	VF	UNC
45 **5000 WON**	FV	8.50	20.00

ND (1977). Brown on m/c unpt. Yi I at r. and as wmk. Sm. bldg. w/steps on back.

	VG	VF	UNC
46 **10,000 WON**	FV	20.00	40.00

ND (1979). Black and dk. green on m/c unpt. Water clock at l., Kg. Sejong at r. and as wmk. Pavilion at ctr. on back.

1983 ND Issue

	VG	VF	UNC
47 **1000 WON**	FV	FV	4.00

ND (1983). Purple on m/c unpt. Yi Hwang at r. and as wmk. One raised colored dot for blind at lower l. Bldgs. of Tosansowon Academy on back.

	VG	VF	UNC
48 **5000 WON**	FV	FV	12.00

ND (1983). Brown on m/c unpt. Yi I at r. and as wmk. Two raised colored dots for blind at lower l. Ojukon, birthplace of Yi I on back.

	VG	VF	UNC
49 **10,000 WON**	FV	FV	22.50

ND (1983). Dk. green on m/c unpt. Water clock at l., Kg. Sejong at r. and as wmk in clear area. Three raised colored dots in green for visually impaired at lower l. Kyonghoeru Pavilion at ctr. on back.

	VG	VF	UNC
50 **10,000 WON**	FV	FV	20.00

ND (1994). Dk. green on m/c unpt. Like #49, but w/circular dk. green lines over wmk. area at l., microprinting added under water tower, segmented silver security thread at l. ctr.

2000-2002 Issue

			VG	VF	UNC
51	**5000 WON**		FV	FV	9.00
	2002. Brown and orange on m/c unpt. Scholar Yi l. Ojukon on back.				

			VG	VF	UNC
52	**10,000 WON**		FV	FV	20.00
	2000. Dk. green on m/c unpt. Like #50, but wmk. area clear. Three raised colored dots in variable ink (brown to green). Copyright 2000 notice in Korean at lower l. on face, in English at lower r. on back.				

2004 BANK CHECK ISSUE

			VG	VF	UNC
53	**1,000,000 WON**		FV	FV	1250.00
	6.2004.				

AUXILIARY MILITARY PAYMENT CERTIFICATE COUPONS

Issued to Korean troops in Vietnam to facilitate their use of United States MPC. These coupons could not be used as currency by themselves.

SERIES I

#M1-M8 were issued on Dec. 29, 1969, and were valid only until June or Oct. 7, 1970. Anchor on glove crest. Validation stamp on back. Uniface.

			VG	VF	UNC
M1	**5 CENTS**		—	—	—
	ND (1969). Maroon, red-brown and yellow ctr. Flowering branch at l., lg. *5* at r.				
M2	**10 CENTS**		—	—	—
	ND (1969). Dk. blue w/lt. blue-green ctr. Flowers at l., lg. *10* at r.				
M3	**25 CENTS**		—	—	—
	ND (1969). Brown and yellow ctr. Flower at l., lg. *25* at r.				
M4	**50 CENTS**		—	—	—
	ND (1969). Green and yellow ctr. Flower at l., lg. *50* at r.				
M5	**1 DOLLAR**		—	—	—
	ND (1969). Brown and yellow ctr. Korean flag at l., lg. *1* at r.				
M6	**5 DOLLARS**		—	—	—
	ND (1969). Blue and turquoise ctr. Flowers at l., lg. *5* at r.				
M7	**10 DOLLARS**		—	—	—
	ND (1969). Brown and yellow ctr. Flowers at l.				
M8	**20 DOLLARS**		—	—	—
	ND (1969). Green and yellow ctr. Flowers at l.				

SERIES II

#M9-M16 were issued June (or Oct.) 1970. Anchor symbol ctr., 702 at l., lg. denomination numerals r. Face and back similar.

			VG	VF	UNC
M9	**5 CENTS**		20.00	65.00	200.00
	ND (1970). Maroon and violet on ochre unpt. Space capsule at l.				

			VG	VF	UNC
M10	**10 CENTS**		30.00	90.00	275.00
	ND (1970). Red and yellow on green paper. Flowers at l. Back red.				

			VG	VF	UNC
M11	**25 CENTS**		90.00	225.00	—
	ND (1970). Green and blue. Crown at l.				

			VG	VF	UNC
M12	**50 CENTS**		90.00	225.00	—
	ND (1970). Blue and green. Pottery w/legs at l.				
M13	**1 DOLLAR**		—	—	—
	ND (1970). Maroon and red on lt. green paper. Torch at l.				
M14	**5 DOLLARS**		—	—	—
	ND (1970). Red, ochre and yellow on lt. blue paper. Holed coin at l.				
M15	**10 DOLLARS**		—	—	—
	ND (1970). Blue on yellow paper. Pagoda at l.				
M16	**20 DOLLARS**		—	—	—
	ND (1970). Green on pink paper. Vignette at l.				

SERIES III

#M17-M24, military symbol in circle at ctr. on face.

			VG	VF	UNC
M17	**5 CENTS**		20.00	65.00	200.00
	ND. Brown and maroon on yellow paper. "5" at l., clam shell and pearl at ctr. Kettle on back.				
M18	**10 CENTS**		30.00	75.00	275.00
	ND. Blue w/green tint. "10" at l., snail at ctr. Candle holder on back.				

			VG	VF	UNC
M19	**25 CENTS**		90.00	225.00	—
	ND. Red, lilac and ochre. "25" at l., crest seal on turtle at r. Back pink; archway at ctr.				
M20	**50 CENTS**		90.00		—
	ND. Green and blue. "50" at l., tiger at ctr. Balancing rock on back.				

			VG	VF	UNC
M21	**1 DOLLAR**		—	—	—
	ND. Brown and maroon. Flowers at l. Shrine on back.				

M22	**5 DOLLARS**	VG	VF	UNC
	ND. Blue and lt. blue on yellow paper. Bush at l., crest seal on rayed cloud at r. Tower at ctr. on back.	—	—	—
M23	**10 DOLLARS**			
	ND. Yellow and maroon. Pagoda on face. Turtle boat on back.	—	—	—
M24	**20 DOLLARS**			
	ND. 2 dragons at ctr. Korean house on back.	—	—	—

SERIES IV

#M25-M32, Korean warrior at ctr. on face.

M25	**5 CENTS**	VG	VF	UNC
	ND. Pink, deep green and lt. blue. Beams and steel mill at ctr. on back.	20.00	40.00	185.00

M26	**10 CENTS**	VG	VF	UNC
	ND. Deep green on yellow-green. Modern city complex on back. Thick or thin paper.	20.00	40.00	185.00
M27	**25 CENTS**			
	ND. Yellow and maroon. 2 bridges on back.	60.00	200.00	—
M28	**50 CENTS**			
	ND. Blue-green and maroon. Back blue-green and red; dam.	90.00	225.00	—

M29	**1 DOLLAR**	VG	VF	UNC
	ND. Green on lt. green unpt. Oil refinery on back.	35.00	100.00	250.00

M31	**10 DOLLARS**	VG	VF	UNC
	ND. Pink and green. Back pink and blue; loading area at docks.	60.00	200.00	—
M32	**20 DOLLARS**			
	ND. Blue and purple. Back green; 4-lane superhighway.	—	—	—

M30	**5 DOLLARS**	VG	VF	UNC
	ND. Brown on gold unpt. Back red-orange; natural gas tank.	350.00	700.00	—

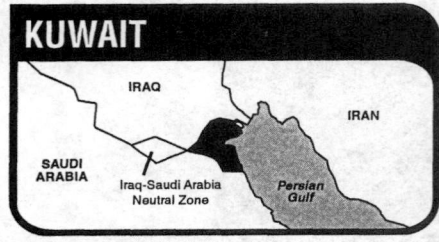

The State of Kuwait, a constitutional monarchy located on the Arabian Peninsula at the northwestern corner of the Persian Gulf, has an area of 6,880 sq. mi. (17,818 sq. km.) and a population of 1.97 million. Capital: Kuwait. Petroleum, the basis of the economy, provides 95 per cent of the exports.

The modern history of Kuwait began with the founding of the men who wandered northward from the region of the Qatar Peninsula of eastern Arabia.

Fearing that the Turks would take over the sheikhdom, Shaikh Mubarak entered into an agreement with Great Britain, 1899, placing Kuwait under the protection of Britain and empowering Britain to conduct its foreign affairs. Britain terminated the protectorate on June 19, 1961, giving Kuwait its independence (by a simple exchange of notes) but agreeing to furnish military aid on request.

The Kuwait dinar, one of the world's strongest currencies, is backed 100 percent by gold and foreign exchange holdings.

On Aug. 2, 1990 Iraqi forces invaded and rapidly overran Kuwaiti forces. Annexation by Iraq was declared on Aug. 8. The Kuwaiti government established itself in exile in Saudi Arabia. The United Nations forces attacked on Feb. 24, 1991 and Kuwait City was liberated on Feb. 26. Iraq quickly withdrew remaining forces.

RULERS:
British to 1961
Abdullah, 1961-1965
Sabah Ibn Salim Al Sabah, 1965-1977
Jabir Ibn Ahmad Al Sabah, 1977-

MONETARY SYSTEM:
1 Dinar = 1000 Fils

SIGNATURE VARIETIES

1	Amir Sheikh Jaber al-Ahmed			
	BANK GOVERNOR	**FINANCE MINISTER**	**BANK GOVERNOR**	**FINANCE MINISTER**
2	Hamza Abbas	A. R. al-Atiquel	3 Hamza Abbas	A. L. al-Hamad
4	A. al-Tammar	A. K. al-Sabah	5 A. al-Tammar	J. M. al-Kharafi
6	S. A. al-Sabah	N. A. al-Rodhan	7 S. A. al-Sabah	A. K. al-Sabah
8	S. A. al-Sabah	N. A. al-Rodhan	9 S. A. al-Sabah	A. S. al-Sabah
10	S. A. al-Sabah	A. A. al-Sabah	11 S. A. al-Sabah	Y. H. Al-Ibrahim

KUWAIT CURRENCY BOARD

LAW OF 1960, 1961 ND ISSUE

#1-5 Amir Shaikh Abdullah at r. and as wmk. Sign. 1.

1	1/4 DINAR	VG	VF	UNC
	L.1960 (1961). Brown on m/c unpt. Aerial view, Port of Kuwait at ctr. on back.	4.00	15.00	45.00

2	1/2 DINAR	VG	VF	UNC
	L.1960 (1961). Purple on m/c unpt. School at ctr. on back.	5.00	25.00	90.00

3	1 DINAR	VG	VF	UNC
	L.1960 (1961). Red-brown on m/c unpt. Cement plant at ctr. on back.	7.50	40.00	125.00

4	5 DINARS	VG	VF	UNC
	L.1960 (1961). Blue on m/c unpt. Street scene on back.	30.00	150.00	500.00

5	10 DINARS	VG	VF	UNC
	L.1960 (1961). Green on m/c unpt. Dhow on back.	30.00	150.00	475.00

CENTRAL BANK OF KUWAIT

LAW #32 OF 1968, FIRST ND ISSUE

#6-10 Amir Shaikh Sabah at r. and as wmk. Sign. #2.

6   1/4 DINAR
L.1968. Brown on m/c unpt. Back similar to #1.

	VG	VF	UNC
a. Black sign.	1.25	6.00	22.50
b. Brown sign.	1.25	6.00	22.50
s. As a. Specimen.	—	—	250.00

7   1/2 DINAR
L.1968. Purple on m/c unpt. Back similar to #2.

	VG	VF	UNC
a. Black sign.	2.00	7.50	30.00
b. Purple sign.	2.00	7.50	30.00
s. As a. Specimen.	—	—	250.00

8   1 DINAR
L.1968. Red-brown and blue on m/c unpt. Oil refinery on back.

	VG	VF	UNC
a. Issued note.	4.00	8.00	40.00
s. Specimen.	—	—	350.00

9   5 DINARS
L.1968. Blue and aqua on m/c unpt. View of Kuwait on back.

	VG	VF	UNC
a. Issued note.	15.00	45.00	100.00
s. Specimen.	—	—	350.00

10   10 DINARS
L.1968. Green and brown on m/c unpt. Back similar to #5.

	VG	VF	UNC
a. Issued note.	22.50	60.00	140.00
s. Specimen.	—	—	475.00

LAW #32 OF 1968, SECOND ND ISSUE

#11-16 arms at r. Black serial #. #11-15 wmk.: Dhow.

11   1/4 DINAR
L.1968 (1980-91). Brown and purple on m/c unpt. Oil rig at l. Oil refinery on back.

	VG	VF	UNC
a. Overall ornate unpt. Sign. 2-4.	1.00	3.00	8.00
b. Clear margins at top and bottom. Sign. 6.	0.75	1.50	6.00

Note: Contraband stolen by invading Iraqi forces included prefix denominators #54-68.

12   1/2 DINAR
L.1968 (1980). Purple on m/c unpt. Kuwait Towers at l. Harbor scene on back.

	VG	VF	UNC
a. Overall ornate unpt. Sign. 2-4.	1.25	4.00	10.00
b. Clear margins at top and at bottom. Sign. 6.	1.00	3.00	7.00

Note: Contraband stolen by invading Iraqi forces include prefix denominators #30-37.

16   **20 DINARS**

		VG	VF	UNC
	L.1968 (1986-91). Brown and olive-green on m/c unpt. Façade of Kuwait Stock Exchange at l. The Justice Center of Kuwait at l. ctr. on back. Wmk: Eagle's head.			
a.	Sign. 5.	20.00	60.00	150.00
b.	Sign. 6.	3.00	8.00	32.50

Note: Contraband stolen by invading Iraqi forces include prefix denominators #9-13.

LAW #32 OF 1968, 1992 ND POST LIBERATION ISSUE

Note: After the 1991 Gulf War, Kuwait declared all previous note issues worthless.

#17-22 like previous issue. Red serial # at top r. Wmk: Dhow. Sign. 7.

13   **1 DINAR**

		VG	VF	UNC
	L.1968 (1980-91). Red-violet and purple on on m/c unpt. Telecommunications Center in Kuwait City at l. Old fortress on back.			
a.	Overall ornate unpt. Sign. 2.	2.00	7.00	20.00
b.	As a. Sign. 3.	1.50	4.00	10.00
c.	As a. Sign. 4.	1.50	3.50	8.00
d.	Plain colored unpt. at top and bottom. Sign. 6.	1.00	3.00	7.00
s.	As a. Specimen.	—	—	100.00

Note: Contraband stolen by invading Iraqi forces include prefix denominators #47-53.

17   **1/4 DINAR**

	VG	VF	UNC
L.1968 (1992). Violet and black on silver and m/c unpt. Back brown on m/c unpt. Like #11.	FV	FV	4.00

14   **5 DINARS**

		VG	VF	UNC
	L.1968 (1980-91). Deep blue and black on m/c unpt. Minaret at l. The Seif Palace (the Amir's Administration HQ) on back.			
a.	Overall ornate unpt. Sign. 2, 4.	5.00	10.00	40.00
b.	Clear margins at top and at bottom. Sign. 6.	3.00	7.50	22.50
s.	Specimen.	—	—	—

Note: Contraband stolen by invading Iraqi forces include prefix denominators #18-20.

18   **1/2 DINAR**

	VG	VF	UNC
L.1968 (1992). Deep blue, blue-green and deep violet on silver and m/c unpt. Like #12.	FV	FV	7.00

15   **10 DINARS**

		VG	VF	UNC
	L.1968 (1980-91). Green on m/c unpt. Falcon at l. Sailing boat on back.			
a.	Overall ornate unpt. Sign. 2-4.	6.00	12.50	50.00
b.	Clear margins at top and at bottom. Sign. 6.	3.00	7.50	32.50

Note: Contraband stolen by invading Iraqi forces include prefix denominators #70-87.

19   **1 DINAR**

	VG	VF	UNC
L.1968 (1992). Deep olive-green, green and deep blue on silver and m/c unpt. Like #13.	FV	FV	9.00

20 **5 DINARS**
L.1968 (1992). Olive-brown, green and pink on m/c unpt. Like #14.

VG	VF	UNC
FV	FV	45.00

21 **10 DINARS**
L.1968 (1992). Orange-red, olive-brown on m/c unpt. Like #15.
Sign. 7, 8.

VG	VF	UNC
FV	FV	75.00

22 **20 DINARS**
L.1968 (1992). Violet-brown on m/c unpt. Like #16. Sign. 7, 8.

VG	VF	UNC
FV	FV	125.00

LAW #32 OF 1968, 1994 ND ISSUE

#23-28 arms at l., segmented silver vertical thread at ctr. r. Wmk: Falcon's head. Sign. 8-12.

23 **1/4 DINAR**
L.1968 (1994). Brown, grayish purple and deep orange on m/c
unpt. Ship at bottom ctr. r. Outline of falcon's head at lower r. near
value. Girls playing game on back. Sign. 8, 10, 11, 12.

VG	VF	UNC
FV	FV	3.00

#24-28 outline of falcon's head at upper l. near value.

24 **1/2 DINAR**
L.1968 (1994). Brown and dk. grayish green on m/c unpt. Souk
shops at lower r. Boys playing game on back. Sign. 8, 10, 11, 12.

VG	VF	UNC
FV	FV	6.00

25 **1 DINAR**
L.1968 (1994). Deep brown, purple and dk. gray on blue and m/c
unpt. Pinnacles at ctr. r. Aerial view of harbor docks on back. Sign.
8, 10, 11, 12.

VG	VF	UNC
FV	FV	10.00

#26-28 silver foiling of falcon's head at l. ctr.

26 **5 DINARS**
L.1968 (1994). Dk. red and grayish green on m/c unpt. Pinnacle at
r. Oil refinery at ctr. on back. Sign. 8, 9, 11, 12.

VG	VF	UNC
FV	FV	40.00

27 **10 DINARS**
L.1968 (1994). Purple, dk. blue and dk. brown on m/c unpt. Mosque at lower r. Pearl fisherman at l. ctr., dhow at r. on back. Sign. 8, 12.

	VG	VF	UNC
	FV	FV	75.00

Note: #23-27 were withdrawn in early 1995 because the word *Allah* being present.

28 **20 DINARS**
L.1968 (1994). Dk. olive-green, orange and olive-brown on m/c unpt. Fortress at lower r. Central bank at bottom l. ctr., old fortress gate, pinnacle at r. on back. Sign. 8, 9, 10, 11, 12.

	VG	VF	UNC
	FV	FV	110.00

COLLECTOR SERIES

CENTRAL BANK OF KUWAIT

1993 ISSUE

#CS1 Issued in a special folder for "Second Anniversary of Liberation of Kuwait."

CS1 **1 DINAR**
26.2.1993. Orange-red, violet-blue and blue. Polymer w/silver on window. Text on back includes: *THIS IS NOT LEGAL TENDER.*

	Issue Price	Mkt.	Value
	—		20.00

Note: Replacement notes for #CS1 have serial # CK000091 and a market value of $175.

2001 ISSUE

#CS2 issued in a special folder for "10th Anniversary of the Liberation of the State of Kuwait."

CS2 **1 DINAR**
26.2.2001. Lt. blue and lilac. Arms at r. Military man holding flag, town view on back. Polymer plastic w/silver foil window. Text on back includes: *NOT A LEGAL TENDER*... at lower l.

	Issue Price	Mkt.	Value
	—		17.50

KYRGYZSTAN

The Republic of Kyrgyzstan, an independent state since Aug. 31, 1991, is a member of the UN and of the C.I.S. It was the last state of the Union Republics to declare its sovereignty. Capital: Bishkek (formerly Frunze). Population of 4.54 million.

Originally part of the Autonomous Turkestan S.S.R. founded on May 1, 1918, the Kyrgyz ethnic area was established on October 14, 1924 as the Kara-Kirghiz Autonomous Region within the R.S.F.S.R. Then on May 25, 1925 the name Kara (black) was dropped. It became an A.S.S.R. on Feb. 1, 1926 and a Union Republic of the U.S.S.R. in 1936. On Dec. 12, 1990, the name was then changed to the Republic of Kyrgyzstan.

MONETARY SYSTEM:
1 COM = 100 ТЫЙЫН
1 SOM = 100 Tyiyn

REPUBLIC

КЫРГЫЗ РЕСПУБЛИКАСЫ

KYRGYZ REPUBLIC

1993 ND ISSUE

#1-3 bald eagle at ctr. Ornate design at ctr. on back. Wmk: Eagle in repeating pattern.

1 **1 TYIYN**
ND (1993). Dk. brown on pink and brown-orange unpt.

	VG	VF	UNC
	0.05	0.10	0.50

2 **10 TYIYN**
ND (1993). Brown on pale green and brown-orange unpt.

	VG	VF	UNC
	0.10	0.25	0.75

3 **50 TYIYN**
ND (1993). Gray on blue and brown-orange unpt.

	VG	VF	UNC
	0.15	0.35	1.00

КЫРГЫЗСТАН БАНКЫ

KYRGYZSTAN BANK

1993; 1994 ND ISSUE

#4-6 Equestrian statue of Manas the Noble at ctr. r. Manas Mausoleum at l. ctr. on back. Wmk: Eagle in repeating pattern.

4   1 SOM
ND (1993). Red on m/c unpt.

	VG	VF	UNC
	0.20	0.35	1.75

5   5 SOM
ND (1993). Deep grayish green on m/c unpt.

	VG	VF	UNC
	0.10	1.50	5.00

6   20 SOM
ND (1993). Purple on m/c unpt.

	VG	VF	UNC
	0.25	3.00	20.00

КЫРГЫЗ БАНКЫ

KYRGYZ BANK

1994 ND ISSUE

Replacement notes: Serial # prefix *ZZ*.

7   1 SOM
ND (1994). Brown on yellow and m/c unpt. A. Maldybayev at r. and as wmk. String musical instruments, Bishkek's Philharmonic Society and Manas Architectural Ensemble at l. ctr. on back.

	VG	VF	UNC
	0.10	0.50	2.00

8   5 SOM
ND (1994). Dk. blue on yellow and m/c unpt. B. Beishenaliyeva at r. and as wmk. National Opera Theatre at l. ctr. on back.

	VG	VF	UNC
	0.25	1.00	4.50

9   10 SOM
ND (1994). Green and brown on m/c unpt. Kassim at r. and as wmk. Mountains on back.

	VG	VF	UNC
	0.50	1.50	6.00

10   20 SOM
ND (1994). Red-orange on m/c unpt. T. Moldo at r. and as wmk. Manas Mausoleum on back.

	VG	VF	UNC
	1.00	1.50	6.00

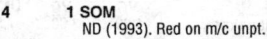

11   50 SOM
ND (1994). Reddish brown on m/c unpt. Czarina Kurmanjan Datka at r. and as wmk., Uzgen Architectural Ensemble, mausoleum and minaret on back.

	VG	VF	UNC
	1.00	1.50	12.50

		VG	VF	UNC
12	**100 SOM**	2.00	5.00	25.00

ND (1994). Dk. brown on m/c unpt. Toktogul at r. and as wmk. Hydroelectric dam at l. ctr. on back.

1997 ISSUE

Replacement notes: Serial # prefix *BZ*.

		VG	VF	UNC
13	**5 SOM**	0.15	0.75	2.00

1997. Dk. blue and violet on m/c unpt. Similar to #8.

		VG	VF	UNC
14	**10 SOM**	0.15	0.75	3.25

1997. Dk. green, purple and red on m/c unpt. Similar to #9.

2000 ND ISSUE

		VG	VF	UNC
15	**1 SOM**	0.05	0.25	1.25

1999. Brown and tan on m/c unpt. Abdilas Maldibayeff at l. Musical instruments on back.

		VG	VF	UNC
16	**200 SOM**	1.00	3.00	7.50

2000. Brown and tan on m/c unpt. Alikul Osmonov at r. Poetry verse and lake scene on back.

		VG	VF	UNC
17	**500 SOM**	1.00	3.50	15.00

2000. Rose, brown and olive on m/c unpt. Sayakbai Karalaiev at r. Karalaiev seated, in background horseman chasing an eagle on back.

		VG	VF	UNC
18	**1000 SOM**	1.00	4.00	25.00

2000. Olive, slate, brown and m/c. Jusul Balasagbin at r. Gate, tree and mountains on back.

2002 ND ISSUE

#19-20 wmk. as portr.

		VG	VF	UNC
19	**20 SOM**	0.25	1.00	5.00

ND (2002). Dark brown and orange on m/c unpt. Togolok Moldo at r. Manas Mausoleum on back.

20	50 SOM		VG	VF	UNC

ND (2002). Brown and blue on m/c unpt. Czarina Krumanjan-Datka at r. Uzgen Architectural ensemble: mausoleum and minaret on back. — 0.50 | 1.00 | 7.50

21	100 SOM		VG	VF	UNC

ND (2002). Green, pink and blue on m/c unpt. Toktogul at r. Khan Tenyiri Mountains at l. ctr. on back. — 0.50 | 1.00 | 12.50

22	200 SOM		VG	VF	UNC

ND (2004). Brown and tan on m/c unpt. Alikul Osmonov at r. Poetry verse and lake scene on back. — 0.50 | 1.00 | 7.50

The Lao People's Democratic Republic, located on the Indo-Chinese Peninsula between the Socialist Republic of Vietnam and the Kingdom of Thailand, has an area of 91,429 sq. mi. (236,800 sq. km.) and a population of 5.69 million. Captial: Vientiane. Agriculture employs 95 percent of the people. Tin, lumber and coffee are exported.

The first United Kingdom of Laos was established in the mid-14th century by King Fa Ngum who ruled an area including present Laos, northeastern Thailand, and the southern part of China's Yunnan province from his capital at Luang Prabang. Thailand and Vietnam obtained control over much of the present Lao territory in the 18th century and remained dominant until France established a protectorate over the area in 1893 and incorporated it into the Union of Indo-China. The Independence of Laos was proclaimed in March of 1945, during the last days of the Japanese occupation of World War II. France reoccupied Laos in 1946, and established it as a constitutional monarchy within the French Union in 1949. In 1953, war erupted between the government and the Pathet Lao, a Communist movement supported by the Vietnamese Communist forces. Peace was declared in 1954 with Laos becoming fully independent in 1955 and the Pathet Lao being permitted to occupy two northern provinces. Civil war broke out again in 1960 with the United States supporting the government of the Kingdom of Laos and the North Vietnamese helping the Communist Pathet Lao, and continued, with intervals of truce and political compromise, until the formation of the Lao People's Democratic Republic on Dec. 2, 1975.

RULERS:
Sisavang Vong, 1949-1959
Savang Vatthana, 1959-1975

MONETARY SYSTEM:
1 Kip = 100 At, 1955-1978
1 new Kip = 100 old Kip, 1979-

BANQUE NATIONALE DU LAOS

	SIGNATURE VARIETIES	
	LE GOUVERNEUR	UN CENSEUR
1	*Phoy Panya*	*Lt Crundos*
2	*Phoy Panya*	*Reinly*
3	*Oudong Panya*	*Leva*
4	*mony Mannary*	*Leva*
5	*mony Mannary*	
6	*mony Mannary*	

1962-63 ISSUE

8	1 KIP		VG	VF	UNC

ND (1962). Brown on pink and bue unpt. Stylized figure at l. Tricephalic elephant arms at ctr. on back.

a. Sign. 3; 4. — 0.10 | 0.20 | 0.50
s. Sign. 3. Specimen. — — | — | 40.00

12   50 KIP
ND (1963). Purple on brown and blue unpt. Pagoda at ctr. Back purple; bldg. at r.

	VG	VF	UNC
a. Sign. 5; 6.	0.10	0.25	2.00
s1. Sign. 5. Specimen. Ovpt: *SAN VALEUR*.	—	—	40.00
s2. Sign. 5. Specimen. Ovpt: TDLR oval.	—	—	40.00

9   5 KIP
ND (1962). Green on m/c unpt. S. Vong at r. Temple at l., man on elephant at ctr. on back. Wmk: Tricephalic elephant arms.

	VG	VF	UNC
a. Sign. 2.	4.50	17.50	50.00
b. Sign. 5.	0.15	0.50	1.25
s. As a. Specimen.	—	—	50.00

13   200 KIP
ND (1963). Blue on green and gold unpt. Temple of That Luang at ctr. Waterfalls on back.

	VG	VF	UNC
a. Sign. 4.	0.20	1.00	6.00
b. Sign. 6.	0.20	0.50	3.00
s1. As a. Specimen. Ovpt: *SAN VALEUR*.	—	—	50.00
s2. As a. Specimen. Ovpt: TDLR oval.	—	—	60.00

10   10 KIP
ND (1962). Blue on yellow and green unpt. Woman at l. (like back of Fr. Indochina #102). Stylized sunburst on back (like face of #102). Wmk: Elephant's head.

	VG	VF	UNC
a. Sign. 1.	7.50	22.50	50.00
b. Sign. 5.	0.15	0.50	1.75
s1. As a. Specimen.	—	—	100.00
s2. As b. Specimen.	—	—	100.00

#11-14, Kf. Savang Vatthana at l. Wmk: Tricephalic elephant arms. Replacement notes: Serial # prefix *S9* (=Z9 in English).

14   1000 KIP
ND (1963). Brown on blue and gold unpt. Temple at ctr. 3 long canoes on back.

	VG	VF	UNC
a. Sign. 5.	0.25	1.00	6.00
b. Sign. 6.	0.25	0.75	4.00
s1. As a. Specimen. Ovpt: *SAN VALEUR*.	—	—	60.00
s2. As a. Specimen. Ovpt: TDLR oval.	—	—	60.00

11   20 KIP
ND (1963). Brown on tan and blue unpt. Temple or pagoda at ctr. Pagoda at ctr. r. on back.

	VG	VF	UNC
a. Sign 5.	0.10	0.40	2.00
b. Sign 6.	0.10	0.30	1.50
s1. As a. Specimen. Ovpt: *SAN VALEUR*.	—	—	40.00
s2. As a. Specimen. Ovpt: TDLR oval.	—	—	40.00

1974; 1975 ND Issue

039

15   10 KIP
ND (1974). Blue on m/c unpt. Kg. Savang Vatthana at ctr. r. Back
blue and brown; ox cart. Sign. 6.

	VG	VF	UNC
a. Normal serial #. (Not issued).	—	—	10.00
s. Specimen. Ovpt: *SAN VALEUR*.	—	—	350.00

#16-19 Kg. Savang Vatthana at l. Wml: Tricephalic elephant arms. Sign. 6.

16   100 KIP
ND (1974). Brown on blue, green and pink unpt. Pagoda at ctr. Ox
cart on back.

	VG	VF	UNC
a. Issued note.	0.15	0.50	3.00
s. Specimen. Ovpt: *SAN VALEUR*.	—	—	50.00

17   500 KIP
ND (1974). Red on m/c unpt. Pagoda at ctr. Hydroelectric dam
on back.

	VG	VF	UNC
a. Issued note.	0.20	0.75	4.00
s. Specimen. Ovpt: *SAN VALEUR*.	—	—	75.00

18   1000 KIP
ND. Black on m/c unpt. Elephant on back.

	VG	VF	UNC
a. Normal serial #. (Not issued.)	—	—	15.00
s. Specimen. Ovpt: *SAN VALEUR*.	—	—	500.00

19   5000 KIP
ND (1975). Blue-gray on m/c unpt. Pagoda at ctr. Musicians
w/instruments on back.

	VG	VF	UNC
a. Issued note.	0.75	2.25	9.00
s. Specimen. Ovpt: *SAN VALEUR*.	—	—	75.00

STATE OF LAO

PATHET LAO GOVERNMENT

ND ISSUE

#19A-24 printed in Peoples Republic of China and circulated in areas under control of Pathet Lao insurgents. Later these same notes became the accepted legal tender for the entire country.

19A   1 KIP
ND. Green and blue on yellow and pink unpt. Threshing grain at ctr.
Medical clinic scene on back.

	VG	VF	UNC
a. Issued note.	—	—	10.00
s. Specimen.	—	—	150.00

20   10 KIP
ND. Red on lt. blue and gold unpt. Medical examination scene.
Fighters in the brush on back.

	VG	VF	UNC
a. Wmk: Temples.	0.05	0.15	2.00
b. Wmk: 5-pointed stars.	0.05	0.15	1.00
s. As b. Specimen. Ovpt. in Lao.	—	—	50.00

21   20 KIP

		VG	VF	UNC
ND. Brown on lt. pink and olive-brown unpt. Rice distribution. Forge workers on back.				
a. Wmk: Temples.		0.10	0.20	3.00
b. Wmk: 5-pointed stars.		0.10	0.20	2.00
s. As b. Specimen. Ovpt. in Lao.		—	—	50.00

22   50 KIP

		VG	VF	UNC
ND. Purple on m/c unpt. Factory workers. Plowing ox on back.				
a. Wmk: Temples.		0.10	0.25	3.00
b. Wmk: 5-pointed stars.		0.10	0.25	2.00
s. As b. Specimen. Ovpt. in Lao.		—	—	50.00

23   100 KIP

		VG	VF	UNC
ND. Blue on m/c unpt. Long boats on lake. Scene in textile store on back. Wmk: Temples.				
a. Issued note.		1.00	3.00	6.00
s. Specimen. Ovpt. in Lao.		—	—	50.00

23A   200 KIP

		VG	VF	UNC
ND. Green on m/c unpt. Road and trail convoys. Factory scene on back. Wmk: Temples.				
a. Issued note.		2.00	4.00	12.00
s. Specimen. Ovpt. in Lao.		—	—	50.00
x. Lithograph counterfeit (1974) on plain paper, w/o serial #. Ho Chi Minh at r. on back.		100.00	200.00	400.00

24   500 KIP

		VG	VF	UNC
ND. Brown on m/c unpt. Armed field workers in farm scene. Soldiers shooting down planes on back. Wmk: Temples.				
a. Issued note.		2.00	5.00	15.00
s. Specimen. Ovpt. in Lao.		—	—	50.00

LAO PEOPLES DEMOCRATIC REPUBLIC

GOVERNMENT

1979 PROVISIONAL ISSUE

24A   50 KIP ON 500 KIP

		VG	VF	UNC
ND. New legends and denomination ovpt. on #24. (Not issued).		25.00	165.00	500.00

BANK OF THE LAO PDR

1979 ND; 1988 ISSUE

#25-32 wmk: Stars, hammer and sickles.

#25-29 replacement notes: Serial # prefixes ZA; ZB; ZC.

25   1 KIP

		VG	VF	UNC
ND (1979). Blue-gray on m/c unpt. Militia unit at l., arms at upper r. Schoolroom scene at l. on back.				
a. Issued note.		0.05	0.15	1.00
s. Specimen. Ovpt. in Lao.		—	—	15.00

26   5 KIP
ND (1979). Green on m/c unpt. Shoppers at a store, arms at upper
r. Logging elephants at l. on back.

	VG	VF	UNC
a. Issued note.	0.05	0.15	1.00
s. Specimen. Ovpt. in Lao.	—	—	15.00

27   10 KIP
ND (1979). Dk. brown on m/c unpt. Lumber mill at l., arms at upper
r. Medical scenes at l. on back.

	VG	VF	UNC
a. Issued note.	0.05	0.15	1.00
s. Specimen. Ovpt. in Lao.	—	—	15.00

28   20 KIP
ND (1979). Brown and red-brown on unpt. Arms at l., tank w/troop
column at ctr. Back brown and maroon; textile mill at ctr.

	VG	VF	UNC
a. Issued note.	0.10	0.20	1.00
s. Specimen. Ovpt. in Lao.	—	—	15.00

29   50 KIP
ND (1979). Violet on m/c unpt. Rice planting at l. ctr., arms at
upper r. Back red and brown; hydroelectric dam at ctr.

	VG	VF	UNC
a. Issued note.	0.10	0.20	1.00
s. Specimen. Ovpt. in Lao.	—	—	15.00

#30-32 replacement notes: Serial # prefixes *AM; ZL; ZK.*

30   100 KIP
ND (1979). Deep blue-green and deep blue on m/c unpt. Grain
harvesting at l., arms at upper r. Bridge, storage tanks, and soldier
on back.

	VG	VF	UNC
a. Issued note.	FV	FV	2.00
s. Specimen. Ovpt. in Lao.	—	—	17.50

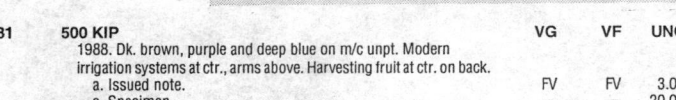

31   500 KIP
1988. Dk. brown, purple and deep blue on m/c unpt. Modern
irrigation systems at ctr., arms above. Harvesting fruit at ctr. on back.

	VG	VF	UNC
a. Issued note.	FV	FV	3.00
s. Specimen.	—	—	20.00

1998-2003 ISSUE

32   1000 KIP
1992-2003. Dk. green, deep purple and green on m/c unpt. 3
women at l., temple at ctr. r., arms at upper r. Cattle at ctr. on back.
Wmk: star.

	VG	VF	UNC
a. W/o security thread. 1992. Red serial #.	FV	FV	6.00
b. W/security thread. 1994.	FV	FV	3.50
c. As b. 1995.	FV	FV	3.50
d. As b. 1996.	FV	FV	3.50
e. Red and green serial #. 1998.	FV	FV	3.00
f. 2003.	FV	FV	3.00
s. As a; e. Specimen.	—	—	20.00

#33 and 34 Kaysone Phomvihane at l., arms at upper r.

33   2000 KIP
1997; 2003. Blue-black and purple on m/c unpt. Temple in unpt. at
ctr. r. Hydroelectric complex at ctr. on back.

	VG	VF	UNC
a. Issued note.	FV	FV	2.00
s. Specimen. Ovpt: *SPECIMEN* on both sides.	—	—	20.00

34 **5000 KIP**
Dark brown 1997; 2003. and purple on m/c unpt. Temple in unpt.
at ctr. r. Cememt factory at at ctr. on back. Wmk.: Temple.
  a. Issued note.
  s. Specimen. Ovpt: *SPECIMEN* on both sides.

	VG	VF	UNC
a.	FV	FV	3.00
s.	—	—	20.00

35 **10,000 KIP**
2002-03. Slate blue and brown on m/c unpt. Kaysone Phomuihane
at l., temple at ctr. Bridge over Mekong river at ctr. on back. Brown
and green serial #. Blue and green, road at ctr. on back.

VG	VF	UNC
FV	FV	5.00

36 **20,000 KIP**
2002-03. Red-brown on m/c unpt. Brown and green serial #.
Hydroelectric complex at ctr. on back.

VG	VF	UNC
FV	FV	9.00

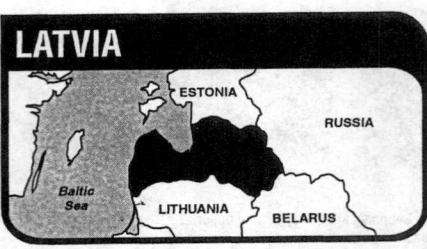

LATVIA

The Republic of Latvia, the central Baltic state in east Europe, has an area of 24,595 sq. mi. (43,601 sq. km.) and a population of 2.4 million. Capital: Riga. Livestock raising and manufacturing are the chief industries. Butter, bacon, fertilizers and telephone equipment are exported.

The Latvians, of Aryan descent, were nomadic tribesmen who settled along the Baltic prior to the 13th century. Lacking a central government, they were easily conquered by the German Teutonic knights, Russia, Sweden and Poland. Following the third partition of Poland by Austria, Prussia and Russia in 1795, Latvia came under Russian domination and did not experience autonomy until the Russian Revolution of 1917 provided an opportunity for freedom. The Latvian republic was established on Nov. 18, 1918. It was occupied by Soviet troops in 1939 and annexed to the Soviet Union in 1940. Following the German occupation of 1941-44, it was retaken by Russia and reestablished as a member S.S. Republic of the Soviet Union. Western countries, including the United States, did not recognize Latvia's incorporation into the Soviet Union. Latvia declared its independence from the former U.S.S.R. on Aug. 22, 1991.

MONETARY SYSTEM:
  1 Lats = 100 Santimu, 1923-40; 1992
  1 Lats = 200 Rublu, 1993
  1 Rublis = 1 Russian Ruble, 1992

REPUBLIC

GOVERNMENT

1992 ISSUE

#35-40 wmk: Symmetrical design.

35 **1 RUBLIS**
1992. Violet on yellow and ochre unpt. Back violet-brown on lt.
green and yellow unpt.

VG	VF	UNC
—	0.10	0.30

36 **2 RUBLI**
1992. Purple on brown-orange and yellow unpt.

VG	VF	UNC
—	0.10	0.50

37 **5 RUBLI**
1992. Deep blue on lt. blue and lt. yellow-orange unpt. Back blue-
black on blue and lt. blue unpt.

VG	VF	UNC
0.20	0.75	2.75

38	**10 RUBLU**		**VG**	**VF**	**UNC**
	1992. Purple on red-orange and pale orange unpt.		0.10	0.25	2.00

39	**20 RUBLU**		**VG**	**VF**	**UNC**
	1992. Violet on lilac and pink unpt.		0.15	0.50	3.00

40	**50 RUBLU**		**VG**	**VF**	**UNC**
	1992. Gray-green on lt. blue and pink unpt.		0.20	0.75	4.00

41	**200 RUBLU**		**VG**	**VF**	**UNC**
	1992. Greenish black on yellow and blue-green unpt. Back greenish black on lt. blue and pink unpt.		1.00	3.50	10.00

42	**500 RUBLU**		**VG**	**VF**	**UNC**
	1992. Violet-brown on gray and dull orange unpt.		1.50	5.00	18.00

LATVIJAS BANKAS NAUDAS ZIME

1992 DATED 1993-1998 ISSUE

43	**5 LATI**		**VG**	**VF**	**UNC**
	1992 (1993); 1996; 2001. Varied shades of green on tan and pale green unpt. Oak tree at ctr. r. Local art at ctr. on back.				
	a. Small foil strip. 1992.		FV	FV	15.00
	b. Broad foil strip. 1996.		FV	FV	10.00

44	**10 LATU**		**VG**	**VF**	**UNC**
	1992 (1993). Violet and purple on m/c unpt. Panoramic view of Daugava River at ctr. Traditional bow broach at ctr. on back.		FV	FV	30.00

45	**20 LATU**		**VG**	**VF**	**UNC**
	1992 (1993). Brown and dk. brown on m/c unpt. Rural homestead at r. Traditional ornamented woven linen at l. ctr. on back.		FV	FV	60.00

46	**50 LATU**		**VG**	**VF**	**UNC**
	1992 (1994). Deep blue on m/c unpt. Sailing ship at r. Two crossed keys and a cross on back (Historical seal of Riga) superimposed on medieval fortifications of Riga.		FV	FV	120.00

47 100 LATU

		VG	VF	UNC
1992 (1994). Red and dk. brown on m/c unpt. Krisjanis Barons at r. Lielvarde belt ornaments on back.		FV	FV	150.00

48 500 LATU

		VG	VF	UNC
1992 (1998). Purple on m/c unpt. Young woman in national costume at r. Small ornamental brass crowns on back.		FV	FV	625.00

2000-01 ISSUE

		VG	VF	UNC
49 5 LATI				
2001. Similar to #43.		FV	FV	10.00
50 10 LATU				
2000. Violet and purple on m/c unpt. Similar to # 44 but for some engraving and color modifications.		FV	FV	17.50
51 20 LATU				
2004.		FV	FV	32.50

LEBANON

The Republic of Lebanon, situated on the eastern shore of the Mediterranean Sea between Syria and Israel, has an area of 4,015 sq. mi. (10,400 sq. km.) and a population of 3.29 million. Capital: Beirut. The economy is based on agriculture, trade and tourism. Fruit, other foodstuffs and textiles are exported.

Almost at the beginning of recorded history, Lebanon appeared as the well-wooded hinterland of the Phoenicians who exploited its famous forests of cedar. The mountains were a Christian refuge and a Crusader stronghold. Lebanon, the history of which is essentially the same as that of Syria, came under control of the Ottoman Turks early in the 16th century. Following the collapse of the Ottoman Empire after World War I, Lebanon, along with Syria, became a French mandate. The French drew a border around the predominantly Christian Lebanon Sanjak or administrative subdivision and on Sept. 1, 1920 proclaimed the area the State of Grand Lebanon (Etat du Grand Liban), a republic under French control. France announced the independence of Lebanon during WWII after Vichy control was deposed on Nov. 26, 1941. It became fully independent on Jan. 1, 1944, but the last British and French troops did not leave until the end of Aug. 1946.

Since the late 1950's the independent Palestinian movement caused government friction. By 1976 large-scale fighting broke out, which continued thru 1990. In April 1996, Israel staged a 17 day bombardment of the southern areas.

MONETARY SYSTEM
1 Livre (Pound) = 100 Piastres

RÉPUBLIQUE LIBANAISE

BANQUE DE SYRIE ET DU LIBAN

1952; 1956 ISSUE

#55-60 all dated 1st of January. Sign. varieties. Printer: TDLR.

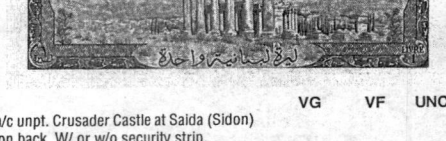

55 1 LIVRE

		VG	VF	UNC
1.1.1952-64. Brown on m/c unpt. Crusader Castle at Saida (Sidon) at l. Columns of Baalbek on back. W/ or w/o security strip.				
a. Issued note.		1.00	8.00	40.00
s. Specimen. Oval TDLR stamp, punch hole cancelled.		—	—	30.00

56 5 LIVRES

		VG	VF	UNC
1.1.1952-64. Blue on m/c unpt. Courtyard of the Palais de Beit-ed-Din. Snowy mountains w/trees on back. W/ or w/o security strip.				
a. Issued note.		3.00	35.00	140.00
s. Specimen. Oval TDLR stamp, punch hole cancelled.		—	—	40.00

60 100 LIVRES

	VG	VF	UNC
1.1.1952; 1.1.1953; 1.1.1958; 1.1.1963. Blue on m/c unpt. View of Beirut and harbor. Cedar tree at ctr. on back and as wmk.			
a. Issued note.	12.50	35.00	150.00
s. Specimen. Oval TDLR stamp, punch hole cancelled.	—	—	120.00

REPUBLIC

BANQUE DU LIBAN

1964; 1978 ISSUE

#61-67 printer: TDLR.

57 10 LIVRES

	VG	VF	UNC
1.1.1956; 1.1.1961; 1.1.1963. Green on m/c unpt. Ruins of Temple of Bacchus temple at Baalbek. Shoreline w/city in hills on back.			
a. Issued note.	6.00	45.00	200.00
s. Specimen. Oval TDLR stamp, punch hole cancelled.	—	—	—

61 1 LIVRE

	VG	VF	UNC
1964-80. Brown on lt. blue unpt. Columns of Baalbek. Jeita Cavern on back. Wmk: 2 eagles.			
a. 1964; 1968.	1.00	3.00	15.00
b. 1971; 1972; 1973; 1974.	1.00	2.00	10.00
c. 1978; 1980.	0.50	1.50	3.50

58 25 LIVRES

	VG	VF	UNC
1.1.1952; 1.1.1953. Blue-gray on m/c unpt. Harbor town. Stone arch bridge at ctr. r. on back. Wmk: Lion's head.			
a. Issued note.	50.00	175.00	750.00
s. Specimen. Oval TDLR stamp, punch hole cancelled.	—	—	120.00

62 5 LIVRES

	VG	VF	UNC
1964-86. Green on blue and lt. yellow unpt. Bldgs. Bridge over Kalb at ctr. r. on back. Wmk: Ancient galley.			
a. 1964.	1.50	5.00	15.00
b. 1967; 1968.	1.00	3.00	12.50
c. 1972; 1974; 1.2.1978; 1.4.1978.	0.50	1.25	4.00
d. 1986.	0.20	0.40	1.25

59 50 LIVRES

	VG	VF	UNC
1.1.1952; 1.1.1953; 1.1.1964. Deep brown on m/c unpt. Coast landscape. Lg. rock formations in water on back. Wmk: Lion's head.			
a. Issued note.	45.00	165.00	725.00
s. Specimen. Oval TDLR stamp, punch hole cancelled.	—	—	125.00

63 10 LIVRES

1964-86. Purple on m/c unpt. Ruins of Anjar. Lg. rocks in water near Beirut on back. Wmk: Man's head.

	VG	VF	UNC
a. 1964.	2.00	7.50	20.00
b. 1967; 1968.	1.50	5.00	15.00
c. 1971; 1972; 1973; 1974.	1.00	2.75	10.00
d. 1.2.1978.	2.00	7.50	20.00
e. 1.4.1978.	1.00	2.75	10.00
f. 1986.	0.20	0.40	1.25

64 25 LIVRES

1964-83. Brown on gold unpt. Crusader Castle at Saida (Sidon). Ruin on rocks on back. Wmk: Lion's head.

	VG	VF	UNC
a. 1964; 1967; 1968.	4.00	12.50	35.00
b. 1972; 1973; 1974; 1978.	2.50	8.50	27.50
c. 1983.	0.50	0.75	2.00

65 50 LIVRES

1964-88. Dk. gray, purple and dk. olive-green on m/c unpt. Ruins of Temple of Bacchus at Baalbek. Bldg. on back. Wmk: Cedar tree.

	VG	VF	UNC
a. 1964; 1967; 1968.	4.50	15.00	45.00
b. 1972; 1973; 1974; 1978.	3.50	10.00	30.00
c. Guilloche added above temple ruins w/10-petaled rosette at l. in unpt. Clear wmk. area on back. 1983; 1985.	0.50	0.75	2.00
d. W/o control # above ruins on face. 1988.	FV	FV	2.00

66 100 LIVRES

1964-88. Blue on lt. pink and lt. blue unpt. Palais Beit-ed-din w/inner courtyard. Snowy cedars on Lebanon mountains on back. Wmk: bearded male elder.

	VG	VF	UNC
a. 1964; 1967; 1968.	5.00	12.50	40.00
b. 1972; 1973; 1974; 1977; 1978; 1980.	4.00	8.50	25.00
c. Guilloche added under bank name on face and back. Clearer wmk. area on back. 1983; 1985.	0.25	1.00	3.00
d. W/o control # at upper ctr. 1988.	0.25	0.50	1.75

67 250 LIVRES

1978-88. Deep gray-green and blue-black on m/c unpt. Ruins at Tyras on face and back. Wmk: Ancient circular sculpture w/head at ctr. from the Grand Temple Podium.

	VG	VF	UNC
a. 1978.	3.00	17.50	50.00
b. 1983. Control # at top ctr.	1.25	5.00	15.00
c. 1985.	0.20	1.00	5.00
d. 1986.	0.15	1.00	4.50
e. W/o control # above sign. at archway on face. 1986; 1987; 1988.	FV	0.50	4.00

1988; 1993 ISSUE

Law of 1988
#68 and 69 printer: TDLR.

68 500 LIVRES

1988. Brown and olive-green on m/c unpt. Beirut city view at ctr. Back brown on m/c unpt.; ruins at l. ctr. Wmk: Lion's head.

	VG	VF	UNC
	1.00	1.50	3.50

69 1000 LIVRES

1988; 1990-92. Dk. blue, blue-black and green on m/c unpt. Map at r. Ruins at ctr., modern bldg. at ctr. back. Wmk: Cedar tree.

	VG	VF	UNC
a. 1988.	0.75	1.50	3.00
b. 1990; 1991.	0.75	1.00	2.50
c. 1992.	FV	FV	2.00

70   **10,000 LIVRES**
       1993 Purple and olive-brown on m/c unpt. Ancient ruins at Tyros
       at ctr. City ruins w/5 archaic statues on back. Wmk: Ancient circular
       sculpture w/head at ctr. from the Grand Temple Podium.

	VG	VF	UNC
	FV	FV	15.00

1994 ISSUE

#71-74 ornate block designs as unpt. Arabic serial # and matching bar code, #. Wmk: Cedar tree. Printer: BABN.

71   **5000 LIVRES**
       1994; 1995. Dk. purple and red on pink and m/c unpt. Geometric
       designs on back.

		VG	VF	UNC
a. 1994.		FV	7.00	12.00
b. 1995.		FV	6.00	12.00

72   **20,000 LIVRES**
       1994; 1995. Red-brown and orange on yellow and m/c unpt.
       Geometric designs w/lg. *LIBAN* l. ctr. on back.

	VG	VF	UNC
	FV	17.50	35.00

73   **50,000 LIVRES**
       1994; 1995. Blue-black and brown-violet on m/c unpt. Cedar tree
       at upper l., artistic boats at lower l. ctr. Lg. diamond w/BDL at l. ctr.,
       cedar tree at lower l. on back.

	VG	VF	UNC
	FV	40.00	80.00

74   **100,000 LIVRES**
       1994; 1995. Dk. blue-green and dk. green on m/c unpt. Cedar tree
       at lower r. Artistic bunch of grapes and grain stalks at l. ctr. on
       back.

	VG	VF	UNC
	FV	FV	110.00

1998-99 ISSUE

75   **5000 LIVRES**
       1999. Dk. purple and red on m/c unpt. Like #71 but smaller size and
       new sign.

	VG	VF	UNC
	FV	FV	8.00

76	10,000 LIVRES	VG	VF	UNC
	1998. Orange and green on yellow and m/c unpt. Patriotic Monument, stylized landscape on back. Embedded iridescent planchets in paper.	FV	FV	17.50

Note: #76 issued on Martyr's Day 1998.

77	50,000 LIVRES	VG	VF	UNC
	1999. Blue-black and brown-violet on m/c unpt. Similar to #73 but w/enhanced security features and holographic foil strip at l.	FV	FV	70.00

81	20,000 LIVRES	VG	VF	UNC
	2001. Red-brown and orange on m/c unpt.	FV	FV	35.00

78	100,000 LIVRES	VG	VF	UNC
	1999. Dk. blue-green and dk. green on m/c unpt. Similar to #74 but w/enhanced security features.	FV	FV	100.00

82	50,000 LIVRES	VG	VF	UNC
	2001.	FV	FV	70.00

2001 ISSUE

#79-82 wide security thread. Printer: BABN.

79	5000 LIVRES	VG	VF	UNC
	2001. Dk. purple and red on m/c unpt.	FV	FV	6.00
80	10,000 LIVRES			
	2001.		Expected New Issue	

83	100,000 LIVRES	VG	VF	UNC
	2001. Dk. blue-green and dk. green on m/c unpt.	FV	FV	100.00

LESOTHO

The Kingdom of Lesotho, a constitutional monarchy located within the east-central part of the Republic of South Africa, has an area of 11,716 sq. mi. (30,355 sq. km.) and a population of 2.29 million. Capital: Maseru. The economy is based on subsistence agriculture and livestock raising. Wool, mohair, water through Katse Dam, and cattle are exported. Lesotho (formerly Basutoland) was sparsely populated until the end of the 16th century. Between the 16th and 19th centuries an influx of refugees from tribal wars led to the development of a distinct Basotho group. During the reign of tribal chief Moshoeshoe I (1823-70), a series of wars with the Orange Free State resulted in the loss of large areas of territory to South Africa. Moshoeshoe II appealed to the British for help, and Basutoland was constituted a native state under British protection. In 1871 it was annexed to Cape Colony, but was restored to direct control by the Crown in 1884. From 1884 to 1959 legislative and executive authority was vested in a British High Commissioner. The constitution of 1959 recognized the expressed wish of the people for independence, which was attained on Oct. 4, 1966, when Lesotho became a monarchy under King Moshoeshoe II. Following his death in an automobile accident in Jan. 1996 his eldest son Prince Bereng Seeiso became King Letsie III on Oct. 17, 1997. Lesotho is a member of the Commonwealth of Nations. The king of Lesotho is Chief of State.

RULERS:
King Motlotlehi Moshoeshoe II, 1966-1996
King Letsi III, 1997-

MONETARY SYSTEM:
1 Loti = 100 Lisente

KINGDOM

LESOTHO MONETARY AUTHORITY

1979 ISSUE

#1-3A arms at ctr., military bust of Kg. Moshoeshoe II at r. Wmk: Basotho hat. Sign. 1.

Dating: Partial date given in the 2 numbers of the serial # prefix for #1-8.

		VG	VF	UNC
1	2 MALOTI			
	(19)79. Dk. brown on m/c unpt. Bldg. and Lesotho flag at l. on back.			
	a. Blue and brown unpt. at r. of Kg.	2.00	4.50	24.00
	s. Specimen. Serial # prefix R/79.	—	—	135.00

		VG	VF	UNC
2	5 MALOTI			
	(19)79. Deep blue on m/c unpt. Craftsmen weaving at l. ctr. on back.			
	a. Issued note.	4.00	12.50	37.00
	s. Specimen. Serial # prefix J/79.	—	—	135.00

		VG	VF	UNC
3	10 MALOTI			
	(19)79. Red and purple on m/c unpt. Basotho horseman in maize field at ctr. on back.			
	a. Issued note.	8.00	30.00	145.00
	s. Specimen. Serial # prefix C/79.	—	—	135.00

		VG	VF	UNC
3A	20 MALOTI			
	(19)79. Herdsmen w/cattle at l. ctr. on back. Specimen (Not issued.)	—	—	—

CENTRAL BANK OF LESOTHO

SIGNATURE VARIETIES		
	MINISTER OF FINANCE	GOVERNOR
1	E. R. Sekhonyana	E. K. Molemohi
2A	K. Rakhetla	S. Schoenbeg 08.11.1982-08.11.1985
2B	K. Rakhetla	S. Schoenbeg 08.11.1982-08.11.1985
2C	K. Rakhetla	S. Schoenbeg 08.11.1982-08.11.1985
1985-1988	K. Rakhetla	Mr. E. L. Karlsson 09.11.1985-30.6.1988
3	E. R. Sekhonyana	Dr. A. M. Maruping 01.07.1988-15.05.1998
4	E. L. Thoahlane	Dr. A. M. Maruping 01.07.1988-15.05.1998
5	Dr. L. V. Ketso	Dr. A. M. Maruping 01.07.1988-15.05.1998
6	Dr. L. V. Ketso	S. M. Swaray 9.9.1998

1981; 1984 ISSUE

#4-8 arms at ctr., military bust of Kg. Moshoeshoe II at r. Partial year date given as the denominator of the serial # prefix. Wmk: Basotho hat.

4	2 MALOTI	VG	VF	UNC
	(19)81; 84. Like #1.			
	a. Sign. 1 (19)81.	1.50	4.00	15.00
	b. Sign. 2 (19)84.	1.00	3.00	12.50
	s1. Specimen. Serial # prefix A/81.	—	—	135.00
	s2. Specimen. Serial # prefix D/84.	—	—	135.00

5	5 MALOTI	VG	VF	UNC
	(19)81. Face like #2. Waterfalls at ctr. on back. Sign 1.			
	a. Issued note.	1.50	5.00	22.00
	s. Specimen. Serial # prefix A/81.	—	—	135.00

6	10 MALOTI	VG	VF	UNC
	(19)81. Like #3.			
	a. Sign. 1 (19)81.	5.00	15.00	55.00
	b. Sign. 2 (19)81 (issued 1984).	1.50	5.00	22.50
	s1. Specimen. Serial # prefix A/81.	—	—	135.00
	s2. Specimen. Serial # prefix C/81.	—	—	135.00

7	20 MALOTI	VG	VF	UNC
	(19)81; 84. Dk. green and olive-green on m/c unpt. Mosotho herdsboy w/cattle at l. ctr. on back.			
	a. Sign. 1 (19)81.	10.00	30.00	110.00
	b. Sign. 2 (19)84.	7.50	12.50	50.00
	s1. Specimen. Serial # prefix A/81.	—	—	135.00
	s2. Specimen. Serial # prefix A/84.	—	—	135.00

8	50 MALOTI	VG	VF	UNC
	(19)81. Purple and deep blue on m/c unpt. "Qiloane" mountain at l. on back. Sign. 1.			
	a. Issued note.	20.00	80.00	375.00
	s. Specimen. Serial # prefix A/81.	—	—	175.00

1989 ISSUE

#9-13 arms at ctr., civilian bust of Kg. Moshoeshoe II in new portr. at r. Designs similar to #4-8 but w/Kg. also as wmk. Sign. 3.

9	2 MALOTI	VG	VF	UNC
	1989. Similar to #4.			
	a. Issued note.	FV	1.25	2.75
	s. Specimen. Serial # prefix G.	—	—	115.00

10	5 MALOTI	VG	VF	UNC
	1989. Similar to #5.			
	a. Issued note.	FV	2.00	7.50
	s. Specimen. Serial # prefix C.	—	—	115.00

11	10 MALOTI	VG	VF	UNC
	1990. Similar to #6.			
	a. Issued note.	FV	3.50	12.50
	s. Specimen. Serial # prefix R.	—	—	115.00

12	20 MALOTI	VG	VF	UNC
	1990. Dk. green and blue-black on m/c unpt. Similar to #7.			
	a. 1990.	FV	10.00	40.00
	b. 1993.	20.00	100.00	400.00
	s1. As a. Specimen. Serial # prefix F.	—	—	115.00
	s2. As b. Specimen. Serial # prefix J.	—	—	160.00
13	50 MALOTI			
	1989. Purple and deep blue on m/c unpt. Similar to #18.			
	a. Issued note.	12.00	30.00	135.00
	s. Specimen. Serial # prefix A.	—	—	115.00

16	20 MALOTI	VG	VF	UNC
	1994; 1999; 2001. Deep olive-green and blue-black on m/c unpt. Mosotho herdsboy w/cattle near huts at ctr. r. on back. Printer: TDLR.			
	a. Sign. 5. 1994.	FV	6.00	20.00
	b. Sign. 6. 1999.	FV	FV	9.00
	c. Sign. 6. 2001.	FV	FV	6.50
	s1. As a. Specimen. Serial # prefix A.	—	—	100.00
	s2. As b. Specimen. Serial # prefix F.	—	—	100.00

1992 ISSUE

14	50 MALOTI	VG	VF	UNC
	1992. Purple, dk. olive-green and dk. blue on m/c unpt. Seated Kg. Moshoeshoe I at r. "Qiloane" mountain at l. ctr. on back. Sign. 4.			
	a. Issued note.	10.00	20.00	90.00
	s1. As a. 1992. Specimen. Serial # prefix A.	—	—	110.00
	s2. As b. 1993. Specimen. Serial # prefix B.	—	—	160.00

1994-2000 ISSUE

#15-20 seated Kg. Moshoeshoe I at l., arms at ctr. and as wmk.

15	10 MALOTI	VG	VF	UNC
	2000; 2003. Red and purple on m/c unpt. Traditionally dressed Masotho on horseback, maize crops and mountain on back. Printer: TDLR.			
	a. Sign. 6. 2000.	FV	FV	4.50
	b. Sign. 7. 2003.	FV	FV	3.50
	s. Specimen. Serial # prefix A.	—	—	100.00

17	50 MALOTI	VG	VF	UNC
	1994; 1997; 1999; 2001. Purple, olive-green and dk. blue on m/c unpt. Herdsman on horseback w/pack mule at ctr., *Qiloane* mountain at r. on back. Printer: TDLR.			
	a. Sign. 5. 1994.	FV	12.50	50.00
	b. Sign. 5. 1997.	FV		30.00
	c. Sign. 6. 1999.	FV	FV	20.00
	d. Sign. 6. 2001.	FV	FV	17.00
	s1. As a. Specimen. Serial # prefix A.	—	—	100.00
	s2. As b. Specimen. Serial # prefix C.	—	—	100.00
	s3. As c. Specimen. Serial # prefix F.	—	—	100.00
18	100 MALOTI			
	1994. Dk. olive-green, orange and brown on m/c unpt. Sheep by shed and home at ctr. r. on back. Printer: BABN.			
	a. Sign. 5.	FV	20.00	65.00
	s. Specimen. Serial # prefix AA.	—	—	100.00

19	100 MALOTI	VG	VF	UNC
	1999; 2001. Similar to #18. Printer: TDLR.			
	a. Sign 6.	FV	15.00	55.00
	b. Sign. 6. 2001.	FV	FV	45.00
	s. As a. Specimen. Serial # prefix A.	—	—	100.00

			VG	VF	UNC
20	**200 MALOTI**				
	1994; 2001. Dk. brown, brown and orange on m/c unpt. Herdsman w/sheep on back. Kinogram strip vertically at r. Printer: TDLR.				
	a. Sign. 5. 1994.		FV	FV	80.00
	b. Sign. 6. 2001.		FV	FV	100.00
	s. As a. Specimen. Serial # prefix A.		—	—	100.00

LIBERIA

The Republic of Liberia, located on the southern side of the west African bulge between Sierra Leone and the Ivory Coast, has an area of 38,250 sq. mi. (111,369 sq. km.) and a population of 3.26 million. Capital: Monrovia. The major industries are agriculture, mining and lumbering. Iron ore, diamonds, rubber, coffee and cocoa are exported.

The Liberian coast was explored and chartered by Portuguese navigator Pedro de Cintra in 1461. For the following three centuries Portuguese traders visited the area regularly to trade for gold, slaves and pepper. The modern country of Liberia, Africa's first republic, was settled in 1822 by the American Colonization Society as a homeland for American freed slaves, with the U.S. government furnishing funds and assisting in negotiations for procurement of land from the indigenous chiefs. The various settlements united in 1839 to form the Commonwealth of Liberia, and in 1847 established the country as a republic with a constitution modeled after that of the United States.

Notes were issued from 1857 through 1880; thereafter the introduction of dollar notes of the United States took place. U.S. money was declared legal tender in Liberia in 1943, replacing British West African currencies. Not until 1989 was a distinctive Liberian currency again issued.

MONETARY SYSTEM:
1 Dollar = 100 Cents

REPLACEMENT NOTES:
#19, 20: ZZ prefix.

NATIONAL BANK OF LIBERIA

1989 ISSUE

#19 replacement note: Serial # prefix *ZZ.*

		VG	VF	UNC
19	**5 DOLLARS**	1.00	2.50	7.00
	12.4.1989. Black and deep green on m/c unpt. Latent image star at l., portr. J. J. Roberts at ctr., tapping trees at r. Back deep green on m/c unpt.; National Bank bldg. at ctr. Printer: TDLR.			

1991 ISSUE

#20 replacement note: Serial # prefix *ZZ.*

		VG	VF	UNC
20	**5 DOLLARS**	1.00	2.00	6.00
	6.4.1991. Similar to #19 but w/arms at ctr. Printer: TDLR.			

CENTRAL BANK OF LIBERIA

1999 ISSUE

#21-23 arms at l.

21 5 DOLLARS
1999. Red and brown on yellow unpt. Edward J. Roye at ctr. Female farmer harvesting rice on back. Date for establishment of Central Bank shown as 1974.

	VG	VF	UNC
	FV	FV	2.50

22 10 DOLLARS
1999. Purple and black on m/c unpt. Joseph Jenkins Roberts at ctr. Worker tapping rubber on back.

	VG	VF	UNC
	FV	FV	3.50

23 20 DOLLARS
1999. Brown, black and olive on m/c unpt. William V. S. Tubman, Sr. at ctr. Market on back.

	VG	VF	UNC
	FV	FV	5.00

#24-25 wmk: Arms.

24 50 DOLLARS
1999. Purple; red and blue on m/c unpt. Samuel Kayon Doe at ctr. Palm nut harvesting on back.

	VG	VF	UNC
	FV	FV	7.50

25 100 DOLLARS
1999. Green, brown and black on m/c unpt. William R. Tolbert, Jr. at ctr. Market woman and child on back.

	VG	VF	UNC
	FV	FV	15.00

2003 Issue

#26-30, Bank name replaces country name at top of back.

26 5 DOLLARS
2003. Red and brown on yellow unpt.

	VG	VF	UNC
	FV	FV	2.50

27 10 DOLLARS
2003. Purple and black on m/c unpt.

	VG	VF	UNC
	FV	FV	3.50

28 20 DOLLARS
2003. Brown, black and olive on m/c unpt.

	VG	VF	UNC
	FV	FV	5.00

30 100 DOLLARS
2003. Green, brown and black on m/c unpt.

	VG	VF	UNC
	FV	FV	15.00

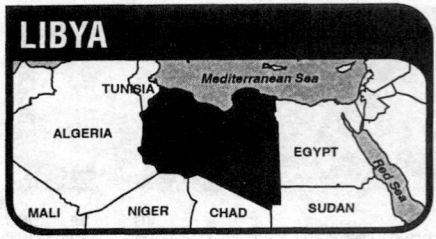

The Socialist People's Libyan Arab Jamahiriya, located on the north central coast of Africa between Tunisia and Egypt, has an area of 679,359 sq. mi. (1,759,540 sq. km.) and a population of 6.39 million. Capital: Tripoli. Crude oil, which accounts for 90 percent of the export earnings, is the mainstay of the economy.

Libya has been subjected to foreign rule throughout most of its history, various parts of it having been ruled by the Phoenicians. Carthaginians, Vandals, Byzantines, Greeks, Romans, Egyptians, and in the following centuries the Arab's language, culture and religion were adopted by the indigenous population. Libya was conquered by the Ottoman Turks in 1553, and remained under Turkish domination, becoming a Turkish vilayet in 1835, until it was conquered by Italy and made into a colony in 1911. The name "Libya", the ancient Greek name for North Africa exclusive of Egypt, was given to the colony by Italy in 1934. Libya came under Allied administration after the fall of Tripoli on Jan. 23, 1943 and was divided into zones of British and French control. On Dec. 24, 1951, in accordance with a United Nations resolution, Libya proclaimed its independence as a constitutional monarchy, thereby becoming the first country to achieve independence through the United Nations. The monarchy was overthrown by a coup d'etat on Sept. 1, 1969, and Libya was established as a republic.

RULERS:
Idris I, 1951-1969

MONETARY SYSTEM:
1 Piastre = 10 Milliemes
1 Pound = 100 Piastres = 1000 Milliemes, 1951-1971
1 Dinar = 1000 Dirhams, 1971-

CONSTITUTIONAL MONARCHY

BANK OF LIBYA

LAW OF 5.2.1963 - FIRST ISSUE

Pound System
#23-27 crowned arms at l. Wmk: Arms.

23	1/4 POUND	VG	VF	UNC
	L.1963/AH1382. Red on m/c unpt.			
	a. Issued note.	3.50	15.00	125.00
	s. Specimen.	—	—	—
24	1/2 POUND			
	L.1963/AH1382. Purple on m/c unpt.	5.00	30.00	185.00
25	1 POUND			
	L.1963/AH1382. Blue on m/c unpt.	8.00	45.00	350.00

26	5 POUNDS	VG	VF	UNC
	L.1963/AH1382. Green on m/c unpt.	17.50	120.00	—

NOTICE
Readers with unlisted dates, signature varieties, etc. are invited to submit photocopies of their notes to: Standard Catalog of World Paper Money, 700 East State St. Iola, WI 54990-0001, E-Mail: george.cuhaj@fwpubs.com.

27	10 POUNDS	VG	VF	UNC
	L.1963/AH1382. Brown on m/c unpt.	22.50	185.00	—

LAW OF 5.2.1963 - SECOND ISSUE

#28-32 crowned arms at l. Reduced size notes. Wmk: Arms.

28	1/4 POUND	VG	VF	UNC
	L.1963/AH1382. Red on m/c unpt.	4.00	17.50	150.00
29	1/2 POUND			
	L.1963/AH1832. Purple on m/c unpt.	5.00	27.50	250.00
30	1 POUND			
	L.1963/AH1382. Blue on m/c unpt.	7.00	35.00	350.00

31	5 POUNDS	VG	VF	UNC
	L.1963/AH1382. Green on m/c unpt.	15.00	95.00	650.00
32	10 POUNDS			
	L.1963/AH1382. Brown on m/c unpt.	25.00	150.00	1200.00

SOCIALIST PEOPLES REPUBLIC

CENTRAL BANK OF LIBYA

SIGNATURE VARIETIES			
1		3	
2		4	
5		6	

1971 ISSUE - SERIES 1

Dinar System

#33-37 w/ or w/o Arabic inscription at bottom of wmk. area at lower r. on face. Wmk: Arms (Heraldic eagle).

33	1/4 DINAR	VG	VF	UNC
	ND. Orange-brown on m/c unpt. Arms at l. Doorway on back.			
	a. W/o inscription (1971).	5.00	20.00	150.00
	b. W/ inscription (1972).	1.00	3.50	25.00

34	1/2 DINAR	VG	VF	UNC
	ND. Purple on m/c unpt. Arms at l. Oil refinery on back.			
	a. W/o inscription (1971).	7.50	35.00	225.00
	b. W/inscription (1972).	2.00	5.00	35.00

35	1 DINAR	VG	VF	UNC
	ND. Blue on m/c unpt. Gate and minaret at l. Hilltop fortress on back.			
	a. W/o inscription (1971).	10.00	45.00	425.00
	b. W/ inscription (1972).	3.00	7.50	50.00

36	5 DINARS	VG	VF	UNC
	ND. Olive on m/c unpt. Arms at l. Fortress at ctr. on back.			
	a. W/o inscription (1971).	20.00	75.00	500.00
	b. W/ inscription (1972).	5.00	15.00	125.00

37	10 DINARS	VG	VF	UNC
	ND. Blue-gray on m/c unpt. Omar El Mukhtar at l. 3 horsemen at ctr. on back.			
	a. W/o inscription (1971).	35.00	100.00	650.00
	b. W/ inscription (1972).	4.00	12.50	55.00

#38-42 *Deleted.* See #33b-37b.

1980-81 ISSUE - SERIES 2

#42A-46 wmk: Heraldic falcon.

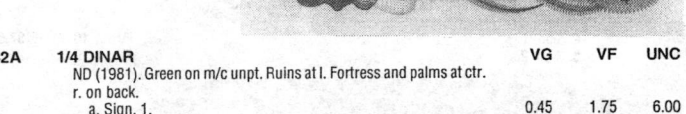

42A	1/4 DINAR	VG	VF	UNC
	ND (1981). Green on m/c unpt. Ruins at l. Fortress and palms at ctr. r. on back.			
	a. Sign. 1.	0.45	1.75	6.00
	b. Sign. 2.	0.40	1.50	4.50

43	1/2 DINAR	VG	VF	UNC
	ND (1981). Green on m/c unpt. Petroleum refinery at l. Irrigation system above wheat field on back.			
	a. Sign. 1.	0.75	3.00	7.50
	b. Sign. 2.	0.50	2.25	6.00

44   1 DINAR

	VG	VF	UNC
ND (1981). Green on m/c unpt. Mosque at l. Interior of mosque at ctr. r. on back.			
a. Sign. 1.	2.00	4.00	11.50
b. Sign. 2.	1.65	3.00	10.00

45   5 DINARS

	VG	VF	UNC
ND (1980). Green on m/c unpt. Camels at l. Crowd around monument at ctr. r. on back.			
a. Sign. 1.	FV	10.00	37.50
b. Sign. 2.	FV	9.00	20.00

46   10 DINARS

	VG	VF	UNC
ND (1980). Green on m/c unpt. Omar El Mukhtar at l. Lg. crowd below hilltop fortress at ctr. on back.			
a. Sign. 1.	FV	22.00	85.00
b. Sign. 2.	FV	20.00	45.00

1984 Issue - Series 3

#47-51 designs generally similar to previous issue. Sign. 2.

47   1/4 DINAR

	VG	VF	UNC
ND (1984). Green and brown on m/c unpt. Similar to #42A.	FV	1.50	4.00

48   1/2 DINAR

	VG	VF	UNC
ND (1984). Green and purple on m/c unpt. Similar to #43.	FV	2.00	4.00

49   1 DINAR

	VG	VF	UNC
ND (1984). Green and dk. blue on m/c unpt. Similar to #44.	FV	4.00	12.50

50	**5 DINARS**	VG	VF	UNC
	ND (1984). Dk. olive-green and lt. green on m/c unpt. Similar to #45.	FV	8.50	27.50

51	**10 DINARS**	VG	VF	UNC
	ND (1984). Dk. green and blue-green on m/c unpt. Similar to #46.	FV	15.00	40.00

54	**1 DINAR**	VG	VF	UNC
	ND (1988). Blue and green on m/c unpt. M. Kadaffy at l. ctr. Temple at lower ctr. r. on back.	FV	2.00	7.50
55	**5 DINARS**			
	ND (ca.1991). Brown and violet on m/c unpt. Camel at ctr. Crowd and monument on back. English text at top.	FV	7.50	25.00
56	**10 DINARS**			
	ND (1989). Green on m/c unpt. Omar el-Mukhtar at l. Arabic text; lg. crowd before hilltop fortress at ctr. Octagonal frame w/o unpt. at upper r. on back.	FV	14.00	40.00

1988-90 ISSUE - SERIES 4

#52-58 wmk: Heraldic falcon. Sign. 3.

1991-93 ISSUE - SERIES 4

52	**1/4 DINAR**	VG	VF	UNC
	ND (ca.1990). Green, blue and black on m/c unpt. Ruins at ctr. Back brown; English text at top, fortress w/palm trees at l. ctr. Design features similar to #47.	FV	1.00	2.00

57	**1/4 DINAR**	VG	VF	UNC
	ND (ca.1991). Green, blue and black on m/c unpt. Like #52, but w/all Arabic text on back. More pink in unpt. on face.			
	a. Sign. 3.	FV	FV	4.00
	b. Sign. 4.	FV	FV	3.00
	c. Sign. 5.	FV	FV	2.50

53	**1/2 DINAR**	VG	VF	UNC
	ND (ca.1990). Deep purple and aqua on m/c unpt. Oil refinery at l ctr. Back purple; English text at top, irrigation system at l. ctr. Similar to #48.	FV	1.75	3.00

58	**1/2 DINAR**	VG	VF	UNC
	ND (ca. 1991). Deep purple and blue on m/c unpt. Like #53, but w/all Arabic text on back. More color in unpt. at upper corners.			
	a. Sign. 3.	FV	FV	4.00
	b. Sign. 4.	FV	FV	4.00
	c. Sign. 5.	FV	FV	4.00

		VG	VF	UNC
59	**1 DINAR** ND (1993). Blue and green on m/c unpt. Like #54, but w/modified green and pink unpt.			
	a. Sign. 4.	FV	FV	6.00
	b. Sign. 5.	FV	FV	5.00

62   **1/4 DINAR**
ND (2002). Ochre on m/c unpt. Ruins at ctr. Walled compound on back. Sign. 4.

	VG	VF	UNC
	FV	FV	2.00

		VG	VF	UNC
60	**5 DINARS** ND (ca. 1991). Brown and violet on m/c unpt. Like #55, but w/all Arabic text on back.			
	a. Sign. 3.	FV	FV	15.00
	b. Sign. 4.	FV	FV	14.00
	c. Sign. 5.	FV	FV	12.50

63   **1/2 DINAR**
ND (2002). Dk. blue on blue and m/c unpt. Oil refinery at ctr. Irrigation system on back. Sign. 4.

	VG	VF	UNC
	FV	FV	3.00

64   **1 DINAR**
ND (2002). Blue and green on m/c unpt. Muammar Qadhafy at ctr. Mosque on back. Sign. 4; 5.

	VG	VF	UNC
	FV	FV	6.00

		VG	VF	UNC
61	**10 DINARS** ND (1991). Green on m/c unpt. Like #56, but w/unpt. in octagonal frame at upper r. on back. Sign. 4; 5.	FV	FV	37.50

65   **5 DINARS**
ND (2002). Green and yellow on m/c unpt. Camels at ctr. Monument and crowd on back. Sign. 4; 5.

	VG	VF	UNC
	FV	FV	12.50

66   **10 DINARS**
ND (2002). Green and dk. green on m/c unpt. Omar el-Mukhtar at ctr. l. Fortress and crowd on back. Sign. 4.

	VG	VF	UNC
	FV	FV	22.50

67   **20 DINARS**
9.9.1999 (2002). Green, blue and brown on m/c unpt. Map w/water tunnels at ctr. Mohmar Kadaffy w/OAU members at ctr, map of Africa at r. on back. Sign. 6. Series 1.

	VG	VF	UNC
	FV	FV	40.00

2004 ISSUE - SERIES 6

#68-70 like #64-66 but reduced in size.

			VG	VF	UNC
68	**1 DINAR**	ND (2004). M/c. Muammar Qadhafy at ctr. Mosque on back.	FV	FV	7.50
69	**5 DINARS**	ND (2004). M/c. Camels at ctr. Monument and crowd on back.	FV	FV	12.50
70	**10 DINARS**	ND (2004). M/c. Omar el-Mukhtar at ctr. Fortress and crowd on back.	FV	FV	22.50

The Republic of Lithuania southernmost of the Baltic states in east Europe, has an area of 26,173 sq. mi. (65,301 sq. km.) and a population of 3.69 million. Capital: Vilnius. The economy is based on livestock raising and manufacturing. Hogs, cattle, hides and electric motors are exported.

Lithuania emerged as a grand duchy joined to Poland through the Lublin Union in 1569. In the 15th century it was a major power of central Europe, stretching from the Baltic to the Black Sea. Following the 1795 partition of Poland by Austria, Prussia and Russia, Lithuania came under Russian domination and did not regain its independence until shortly before the end of World War I when it declared itself a sovereign republic. The republic was occupied by Soviet troops in June of 1940 and annexed to the U.S.S.R. Following the German occupation of 1941-44, it was retaken by Russia and reestablished as a member republic of the Soviet Union. Western countries, including the United States, did not recognize Lithuania's incorporation into the Soviet Union.

Lithuania declared its independence March 11, 1990. Lithuania was seated in the UN General Assembly on Sept. 17, 1991; and joined the European Union on May 1, 2004.

MONETARY SYSTEM:
1 Litas = 100 Centu

REPUBLIC

LIETUVOS BANKAS

BANK OF LITHUANIA

1991 ISSUE

Talonas System

#29-31 plants on face, arms at ctr. in gray on back. W/ and w/o counterfeiting clause at bottom. Wmk. paper.

29   **0.10 TALONAS**
1991. Brown on green and gold unpt.

	VG	VF	UNC
a. W/o 3 lines of black text at ctr.	0.05	0.15	1.00
b. W/3 lines of black text at ctr.	0.05	0.10	0.25
x. Error. As b. but w/ text: *PAGAL ISTATYMA* repeated.	0.50	0.75	3.00

30   **0.20 TALONAS**
1991. Lilac on green and gold unpt. W/3 lines of black text at ctr.

	VG	VF	UNC
	0.05	0.10	0.50

31   **0.50 TALONAS**
1991. Blue-green on green and gold unpt.

	VG	VF	UNC
a. W/o 3 lines of black text at ctr.	0.05	0.15	2.00
b. W/3 lines of black text at ctr.	0.05	0.15	0.50
x1. As b. but first word of text: *VALSTYBINIS.* (error).	0.50	0.75	3.00
x2. As x1 but w/inverted text. (contemporary counterfeit).	—	—	—

#32-38 value w/plants at ctr., arms in gray at r. Animals or birds on back. Wmk: Lg. squarish diamond w/symbol of the republic throughout paper. W/ and w/o counterfeiting clause at bottom of face.

32 1 (TALONAS)

1991. Brown on yellow-gold unpt. Numeral w/cranberry branch at ctr. 2 lizards on back.

	VG	VF	UNC
a. W/o text.	0.10	0.25	2.00
b. W/ text.	0.10	0.25	2.00

33 3 (TALONAS)

1991. Dk. green and gray on blue-green, ochre and brown unpt. Numeral w/juniper branch at ctr. 2 Grey Herons on back.

	VG	VF	UNC
a. W/o text.	0.10	0.25	3.00
b. W/ text.	0.10	0.25	3.00

34 5 (TALONAS)

1991. Dk. purple and gray on blue and gray unpt. Numeral w/oak tree branch at ctr. Osprey at ctr. on back.

	VG	VF	UNC
a. W/o text.	0.75	1.00	4.00
b. W/ text.	0.50	0.75	3.00

35 10 (TALONAS)

1991. Brown on pinkish unpt. Numerals w/walnut tree branch at ctr. 2 martens on back.

	VG	VF	UNC
a. W/o text.	0.50	1.50	10.00
b. W/ text.	0.50	1.00	4.00

36 25 (TALONAS)

1991. Purplish gray on blue and orange unpt. Numerals w/pine tree branch at ctr. Lynx on back.

	VG	VF	UNC
a. W/o text.	1.00	2.50	15.00
b. W/ text.	0.50	1.00	5.00

37 50 (TALONAS)

1991. Green and orange on orange unpt. Numerals w/seashore plant at ctr. Moose on back.

	VG	VF	UNC
a. W/o text.	1.00	2.00	10.00
b. W/ text.	0.50	1.00	4.00

38 100 (TALONAS)

1991. Green and brown on brown unpt. Numerals and dandelions at ctr. European bison on back.

	VG	VF	UNC
a. W/o text.	1.50	3.00	15.00
b. W/ text.	0.50	2.00	5.00

1992 ISSUE

#39-44 value on plant at ctr., shield of arms at r. on face. Wmk. as #32-38. Smaller size than #32-38.

39 1 (TALONAS)

1992. Brown on orange and ochre unpt., dk. brown shield. Two Eurasian lapwings on back.

	VG	VF	UNC
	0.05	0.15	1.00

40 10 (TALONAS)

1992. Brown on tan and ochre unpt., gray shield. Nest of mistle thrush on back.

	VG	VF	UNC
	0.10	1.00	10.00

41 50 (TALONAS)

1992. Dk. grayish green on lt. green and gray unpt., dk. gray-green shield. Two black grouse on back.

	VG	VF	UNC
	1.00	4.00	20.00

42	100 (TALONAS)	VG	VF	UNC
	1992. Grayish purple on blue and red-orange unpt., gray shield. Two otters on back.	0.25	0.75	6.00

43	200 (TALONAS)	VG	VF	UNC
	1992. Dk. brown on red and brown unpt., gray shield. 2 Red Deer on back.			
	a. Issued note.	0.40	1.50	6.00
	x. Error. W/o gray shield at r.	—	—	

44	500 (TALONAS)	VG	VF	UNC
	1992. Brown-violet on blue unpt., brown shield. Brown Bear on back.	1.00	2.25	5.00

1993 ISSUE

#45 and 46 arms in brown at l., value w/branches at ctr. Animals on back. Wmk: Pattern repeated, circle w/design inside.

45	200 TALONU	VG	VF	UNC
	1993. Brown and red on blue unpt. 2 Red Deer on back.	0.50	1.25	3.00

46	500 TALONU	VG	VF	UNC
	1993. Brown on blue and brown unpt. 2 wolves on back.	0.20	0.75	2.50

Note: #46 was withdrawn after 6 weeks.

1991 Dated Issue (1993)

Litu System

#47-49 arms "Vytis" at upper r. on back and as wmk. Printer: USBNC (w/o imprint).

47	10 LITU	VG	VF	UNC
	1991 (1993). Brownish black and brown on tan unpt. Aviators Steponas Darius and Stasys Girénas at ctr. Monoplane "Lituanica" at upper ctr. on back.			
	a. GIRENAS name w/o accent dot on E (error).	FV	4.00	15.00
	b. GIRÉNAS name w/accent dot on E.	FV	5.00	20.00
	x. Quadrupled engraved face printing. Error.	—	—	250.00

48	20 LITU	VG	VF	UNC
	1991 (1993). Dk. brown and green on violet and tan unpt. Jonas Maironis at r. Liberty at l., Museum of History in Kaunas at ctr. on back.	FV	7.00	30.00

49	50 LITU	VG	VF	UNC
	1991 (1993). Yellowish black and brown on ochre and tan unpt. Jonas Basanavicius at r. Cathedral at Vilnius at l. on back.			
	a. VALDYBOS w/regular L.	5.00	20.00	45.00
	b. VALDYBOS w/heel on L (error).	—	30.00	50.00

50	100 LITU	VG	VF	UNC
	1991 (1993); 1994. Deep green, blue and brown on m/c unpt. Arms "Vytis" at ctr., Simonas Daukantas at r. Back brown and green; aerial view of University of Vilnius at l. ctr.			
	a. 1991. One sign.	FV	40.00	120.00
	b. 1994. Two sign. (Not issued.)	—	—	—
51	500 LITU			
	1991. Arms "Vytis" at ctr., Vincas Kudirka at r. Liberty bell on back. (Not issued.)	—	—	—
52	1000 LITU			
	1991. Arms "Vytis" at ctr., Mykolas Ciurlionis at r. 2 kings on back. (Not issued.)	—	—	—

1993; 1994 ISSUE

#53-58 wmk: Arms "Vytis." Shield w/"Vytis" at ctr. r. on back. Printer: TDLR (w/o imprint).

53	**1 LITAS**		**VG**	**VF**	**UNC**
	1994. Black and dk. brown on orange and m/c unpt. Julija Zemaite at r. Old church at l. on back.				
	a. Issued note.		0.25	0.50	3.00
	b. Uncut sheet of 40.		—	—	120.00
	r. Replacement note, ZZ serial # prefix.		0.75	1.00	7.50

57	**20 LITU**		**VG**	**VF**	**UNC**
	1993. Dk. brown, purple and deep blue-green on m/c unpt. Similar to #48.				
	a. Issued note.		FV	FV	20.00
	r. Replacement note, * serial # prefix.		4.00	8.00	17.50

54	**2 LITAI**		**VG**	**VF**	**UNC**
	1993. Black and dk. green on pale green and m/c unpt. Samogitian Bishop Motiejus Valancius at ctr. r. Trakai castle at l. on back.				
	a. Issued note.		0.25	0.75	5.00
	b. Uncut sheet of 40.		—	—	200.00
	r. Replacement note, ZZ serial # prefix.		1.00	2.00	7.50

58	**50 LITU**		**VG**	**VF**	**UNC**
	1993. Dk. brown, red-brown and blue-black on m/c unpt. Similar to #49.				
	a. Issued note.		FV	FV	40.00
	r. Replacement note, * serial # prefix.		12.50	16.00	50.00

1997-2000 ISSUE

#59-61 printer: G&D (w/o imprint).

55	**5 LITAI**		**VG**	**VF**	**UNC**
	1993. Purple, violet and dk. blue-green on m/c unpt. Jonas Jablonskis at ctr. r. Mother and daughter at spinning wheel at l. ctr. on back.				
	a. Issued note.		0.25	1.50	7.50
	b. Uncut sheet of 40.		—	—	350.00
	r. Replacement note, ZZ serial # prefix.		1.00	4.00	12.50

59	**10 LITU**		**VG**	**VF**	**UNC**
	1997. Dk. blue, dk. green and brown-violet on m/c unpt. Like #56 but w/1 sign. Wmk: Arms "Vytis".		FV	FV	15.00

56	**10 LITU**		**VG**	**VF**	**UNC**
	1993. Dk. blue, dk. green, and brown-violet on m/c unpt. Similar to #47 but pilots at r.				
	a. Issued note.		FV	FV	15.00
	r. Replacement note, * serial # prefix.		3.00	7.50	20.00

60	**20 LITU**		**VG**	**VF**	**UNC**
	1997. Dk. brown, purple and deep green on m/c unpt. Like #57 but w/1 sign. Wmk: Jonas Maironis.		FV	FV	20.00

2001-03 ISSUE

#65-67 printer: OFZ. Replacement notes *AZ* serial # prefix.

			VG	VF	UNC
65	**10 LITU**		FV	FV	9.00

2001. Violet and blue on m/c unpt. Like #59 but w/additional security features and airplane hologram at lower l. Wmk: "Vytis."

			VG	VF	UNC
66	**20 LITU**		FV	FV	12.50

2001. Dk. brown on m/c unpt. Similar to #60 but w/additional security features. Book and quill hologram at lower l. Wmk: Jonas Maironis.

			VG	VF	UNC
67	**50 LITU**		FV	FV	30.00

2003. Brown and green on ochre and m/c unpt. Jonas Basanavicius at r. and as wmk. Vilnius Cathedral, belfry and Gediminas hill on back. Like #61 but w/addtional security features.

			VG	VF	UNC
61	**50 LITU**		FV	FV	40.00

1998. Brown and green on ochre and m/c unpt. Jonas Basanavicius at r. Vilnius Cathedral, belfry and Gediminas hill on back.

			VG	VF	UNC
62	**100 LITU**		FV	FV	80.00

2000. Dk. green and green on m/c unpt. Simonas Daukantas at r. View of Vilnius's Old Town section on back. Printer: OFZ.

			VG	VF	UNC
63	**200 LITU**		FV	FV	100.00

1997. Dk. blue on blue and m/c unpt. Vilius Vydūnas at r., "Vytis" at lower l. ctr. Klaipeda Lighthouse at l. on back. Printer: G&D.

			VG	VF	UNC
64	**500 LITU**		FV	FV	200.00

2000. Brown and rose on m/c unpt. Vincas Kudirka at r. Bell of Freedom of Lithuania against landscape view on back. Printer: G&D.

The Grand Duchy of Luxembourg is located in western Europe between Belgium, Germany and France. It has an area of 998 sq. mi. (2,586 sq. km.) and a population of 430,000. Capital: Luxembourg. The economy is based on steel - Luxembourg's per capita production of 16 tons is the highest in the world.

Founded about 963, Luxembourg was a prominent country of the Holy Roman Empire; one of its sovereigns became Holy Roman Emperor as Henry VII, 1308. After being made a duchy by Emperor Charles IV, 1534, Luxembourg passed under the domination of Burgundy, Spain, Austria and France in 1443-1815. It regained autonomy under the Treaty of Vienna, 1815, as a grand duchy in union with the Netherlands, though ostensibly a member of the German Confederation. When Belgium seceded from the Kingdom of the Netherlands, in 1830, Luxembourg was forced to cede its greater western section to Belgium. The tiny duchy left the German Confederation in 1867 when the Treaty of London recognized it as an independent state and guaranteed its perpetual neutrality. Luxembourg was occupied by Germany and liberated by American forces in both world wars.

RULERS:
Charlotte, 1919-64
Jean, 1964-

MONETARY SYSTEM:
1 Franc = 100 Centimes, to 2001
1 Euro = 100 Cents, 2001-

BANQUE INTERNATIONALE A LUXEMBOURG

INTERNATIONAL BANK IN LUXEMBOURG

1968 ISSUE

		VG	VF	UNC
14	**100 FRANCS**			
	1.5.1968. Green-blue and blue on m/c unpt. Tower at l., portr. Grand Duke Jean at r. Steelworks and dam on back. Wmk: *BIL*. Printer: F-CO.			
	a. Issued note.	1.25	4.00	15.00
	s. Specimen.	—	—	65.00

1981 ISSUE

		VG	VF	UNC
14A	**100 FRANCS**			
	8.3.1981. Brown and tan on m/c unpt. Bridge to Luxembourg City at l., Grand Duke Jean at r., Prince Henry of the Netherlands in the background. Back purple on m/c unpt; 2 stylized female figures swirling around wmk. area. Wmk: *BIL*.	1.00	3.50	12.50

GRAND DUCHÉ DE LUXEMBOURG

1961; 1963 ISSUE

#51-52B Portr. Grand Duchess Charlotte at r. and as wmk.

		VG	VF	UNC
51	**50 FRANCS**			
	6.2.1961. Brown on m/c unpt. Landscape w/combine harvester on back.			
	a. Issued note.	2.00	4.00	10.00
	s. Specimen, punched hole cancelled.	—	—	45.00
52	**100 FRANCS**			
	18.9.1963. Dk. red on m/c unpt. Hydroelectric dam on back.			
	a. Issued note.	5.00	10.00	30.00
	s. Specimen, punched hole cancelled.	—	—	65.00

		VG	VF	UNC
52A	**500 FRANCS**			
	ND. Ducal Palace on back. Specimen only.	—	—	2400.00

		VG	VF	UNC
52B	**1000 FRANCS**			
	ND. Crowned and mantled arms at ctr. on back. Specimen only.	—	—	3000.00

1966-72 ISSUE

#53-56 Grand Duke Jean at l. ctr.

53	10 FRANCS	VG	VF	UNC
	20.3.1967. Green on m/c unpt. Grand Duchess Charlotte Bridge in city on back.			
	a. Issued note.	0.75	2.25	5.00
	s. Specimen, punched hole cancelled.	—	—	75.00

54	20 FRANCS	VG	VF	UNC
	7.3.1966. Blue on m/c unpt. Moselle River w/dam and lock on back.			
	a. Issued note.	1.00	2.25	5.00
	s. Specimen, punched hole cancelled.	—	—	250.00

55	50 FRANCS	VG	VF	UNC
	25.8.1972. Dk. brown on m/c unpt. Guilloche unpt at l. Factory on back.			
	a. Sign. title: *LE MINISTRE DES FINANCES.*	2.00	4.00	8.50
	b. Sign. title: *LE MINISTRE D'ÉTAT.*	2.00	3.50	7.00
	s. As a. Specimen, punched hole cancelled.	—	—	175.00

56	100 FRANCS	VG	VF	UNC
	15.7.1970. Red on m/c unpt. View of Adolphe Bridge on back.			
	a. Issued note.	FV	4.00	12.50
	s. Specimen, punched hole cancelled.	—	—	50.00

1980 ISSUE

57	100 FRANCS	VG	VF	UNC
	14.8.1980. Brownish red on m/c unpt. Grand Duke Jean at ctr. r., bldg. at l. Back gold and red; city of Luxembourg scene. Sign. varieties.			
	a. Issued note.	FV	4.50	7.50
	s. Specimen.	—	—	140.00

INSTITUT MONETAIRE LUXEMBOURGEOIS

SIGNATURE VARIETIES			
MINISTRE DU TRESOR			
1	J. Poos	2	J. Santer

1985-93 ND ISSUE

#58-60 Grand Duke Jean at ctr. r. and as wmk.

58	100 FRANCS	VG	VF	UNC
	ND (1986). Red on m/c unpt. Like #57, but w/new issuer's name.			
	a. W/o © symbol. Sign. 1. Series A-K.	FV	FV	6.50
	b. W/© symbol. Sign. 2. Series L-.	FV	FV	4.50

59 1000 FRANCS

ND (1985). Brown on m/c unpt. Castle of Vianden at l., Grand Duke Jean at ctr. Bldg. sketches at ctr. r. on back.

	VG	VF	UNC
a. Issued note.	FV	FV	45.00
s. Specimen.	—	—	275.00

60 5000 FRANCS

ND(1993); 1996. Green, orange and olive-green on brown and m/c unpt. Chateau de Clevaux at l. 17th century map, European Center at Luxembourg-Kirchberg at ctr. r. on back. 2 sign. varieties.

	VG	VF	UNC
a. Serial # prefix A. ND.	FV	200.00	300.00
b. Serial # Prefix B. 10.1996.	FV	FV	225.00

Note: For later issues used in Luxembourg see European Union listings.

The Macau R.A.E.M., a former Portuguese overseas province located in the South China Sea 35 miles (56 km.) southwest of Hong Kong, consists of the peninsula and the islands of Taipa and Coloane. It has an area of 14 sq. mi. (21.45 sq. km.) and a population of 415,850. Capital: Macau. The economy is based on tourism, gambling, commerce and gold trading - Macau is one of the few entirely free markets for gold in the world. Cement, textiles, vegetable oils and metal products are exported.

Established by the Portuguese in 1557, Macau is the oldest European settlement in the Far East. The Chinese, while agreeing to Portuguese settlement, did not recognize Portuguese sovereign rights and the Portuguese remained largely under control of the Chinese until 1849, when the Portuguese abolished the Chinese custom house and declared the independence of the port. The Manchu government formally recognized the Portuguese right to *perpetual occupation* of Macau in 1887. In March 1940 the Japanese army demanded recognition of the nearby "puppet" government at Changshan. In Sept. 1943 they demanded installation of their "advisors" in lieu of a military occupation.

Macao became a special administrative area known as Macau R.A.E.M under The Peoples Republic of China on December 20, 1999.

RULERS:
Portuguese from 1849-1999

MONETARY SYSTEM:
1 Pataca = 100 Avos

PORTUGUESE ADMINISTRATION

BANCO NACIONAL ULTRAMARINO

大西洋國海外滙理銀行

Ta Hsi Yang Kuo Hai Wai Hui Li Yin Hang

1963-68 ISSUE

#49, 50, and 52 portr. Bishop D. Belchior Carneiro at lower r. and as wmk. Bank seal w/sailing ship at l. Woman and sailing ships at ctr. on back. Printer: BWC.

49 5 PATACAS

21.3.1968. Brown on m/c unpt. Sign. varieties.

	VG	VF	UNC
a. Issued note.	10.00	40.00	90.00
s. Specimen.	—	—	110.00

50 10 PATACAS

8.4.1963. Deep blue-violet on m/c unpt. Sign. varieties.

	VG	VF	UNC
a. Issued note.	7.50	20.00	65.00
s. Specimen.	—	—	150.00

54	5 PATACAS	VG	VF	UNC
	18.11.1976. Brown on m/c unpt. Like #49. Sign. varieties.			
	a. Issued note.	2.50	10.00	65.00
	s. Specimen.	—	—	150.00

51	100 PATACAS	VG	VF	UNC
	1.8.1966. Brown on m/c unpt. Portr. M. de Arriaga Brum da Silveira at r. Arms at l., flag atop archway at ctr. on back. Printer: TDLR.			
	a. Issued note.	100.00	300.00	900.00
	s. Specimen.	—	—	650.00

55	10 PATACAS	VG	VF	UNC
	7.12.1977. Deep blue-violet on m/c unpt. Like #50.			
	a. Issued note.	5.00	15.00	75.00
	s. Specimen.	—	—	160.00

52	500 PATACAS	VG	VF	UNC
	8.4.1963. Green on m/c unpt.			
	a. Issued note.	200.00	400.00	1000.00
	s. Specimen.	—	—	700.00

1973 ISSUE

53	100 PATACAS	VG	VF	UNC
	13.12.1973. Deep blue-violet on m/c unpt. Ruins of S. Paulo Cathedral at r. and as wmk. Junk at l., bank seal w/sailing ship at ctr. on back. Sign. titles: *GOVERNADOR* and *ADMINISTRADOR* above signs.			
	a. Issued note.	100.00	225.00	600.00
	s. Specimen.	—	—	450.00

1976-79 ISSUE

#54-57 w/text: *CONSELHO DE GESTAO* at ctr.

56	50 PATACAS	VG	VF	UNC
	1.9.1976. Greenish-gray on m/c unpt. Portr. L. de Camoes at r. Bank seal w/sailing ship at l., woman and sailing ships at ctr. on back.			
	a. Issued note.	50.00	175.00	500.00
	s. Specimen.	—	—	250.00

57	100 PATACAS	VG	VF	UNC
	8.6.1979. Blue on m/c unpt. Like #53. Sign. title: *PRESIDENTE* at l. sign.			
	a. Issued note.	75.00	175.00	450.00
	s. Specimen.	—	—	375.00

001 — 100

57A 500 PATACAS
24.4.1979. Green on m/c unpt. Like #52.

	VG	VF	UNC
a. Issued note.	125.00	300.00	800.00
s. Specimen. 2 different sign. varieties r.h. side.	—	—	550.00

1981; 1988 ISSUE

#58-62 bank seal w/sailing ship at l., 19th century harbor scene on back.

58 5 PATACAS
8.8.1981. Green on m/c unpt. Temple at r.

	VG	VF	UNC
a. W/sign. title: *PRESIDENTE* at l.	4.00	10.00	30.00
b. W/sign. title: *VICE-PRESIDENTE* at l.	4.00	10.00	30.00
c. W/o sign. title: *PRESIDENTE* at l.	4.00	10.00	30.00
s. As b. Specimen.	—	—	120.00

59 10 PATACAS
1981; 1984. Brown on m/c unpt. Lighthouse w/flag at r.

	VG	VF	UNC
a. W/sign. title: *PRESIDENTE* at l. 2 decrees at upper l. 8.8.1981.	3.00	10.00	40.00
b. As a. w/o sign. title at l. 8.8.1981.	2.00	6.00	40.00
c. Sign. title as a. 3 decrees at upper l. 12.5.1984.	2.00	6.00	30.00
d. W/Sign. title: *VICE-PRESIDENTE* at l. 12.5.1984.	1.50	5.00	30.00
e. W/o sign. title under sign. at l. 3 sign. varieties. 12.5.1984.	1.25	4.00	30.00
s1. As a. Specimen.	—	—	100.00
s2. As d. Specimen.	—	—	100.00

60 50 PATACAS
8.8.1981. Purple on m/c unpt. Portr. L. de Camoes at r. and as wmk.

	VG	VF	UNC
a. W/sign. title: *PRESIDENTE* at l.	10.00	17.50	80.00
b. W/o sign. title: *PRESIDENTE* at l.	10.00	17.50	80.00
s1. As a. Specimen.	—	—	150.00
s2. As b. Specimen.	—	—	150.00

61 100 PATACAS
1981; 1984. Blue and purple on m/c unpt. Portr. C. Pessanha at r. Wmk: Man's head.

	VG	VF	UNC
a. W/sign. title: *PRESIDENTE* at l. 8.8.1981; 12.5.1984.	12.50	20.00	100.00
b. W/o sign. title: *PRESIDENTE* at l. 8.8.1981; 12.5.1984.	12.50	20.00	90.00
s1. As a. Specimen. 8.8.1981; 12.5.1984.	—	—	180.00
s2. As b. Specimen. 2 sign. varieties. 8.8.1981.	—	—	180.00

62 500 PATACAS
1981; 1984. Olive-green on m/c unpt. Portr. V. de Morais at r. Peninsula on back.

	VG	VF	UNC
a. 8.8.1981; 12.5.1984. Sign. title: *PRESIDENTE* at l.	65.00	90.00	350.00
b. 8.8.1981; 12.5.1984. Sign. title: *ADMINISTRADOR* at l.	65.00	90.00	325.00
s1. As a. Specimen.	—	—	350.00
s2. As b. Specimen.	—	—	350.00
s3. Specimen. 12.5.1984. Sign. title: *VICE-PRESIDENTE* at l.	—	—	700.00

63   1000 PATACAS

	VG	VF	UNC
1988. Brown and yellow-orange on m/c unpt. Stylized dragon at r. Modern view of bridge to Macao on back.			
a. Issued note.	130.00	175.00	450.00
b. Specimen.	—	—	600.00

1988 COMMEMORATIVE ISSUE

#64, 35th Anniversary Grand Prix

64   10 PATACAS

	VG	VF	UNC
11.26-27.1988 (- old date 1984). Black ovpt. at l. on face, at ctr. on back of #59a. Issued in a small folder.	3.00	10.00	40.00

1990-96 ISSUE

#65-70 bank seal w/sailing ship at l., bridge and city view on back. Wmk: Junk.

65   10 PATACAS

	VG	VF	UNC
8.7.1991. Brown and olive-green on m/c unpt. Bldg. at r.			
a. Issued note.	3.00	6.00	15.00
s. Specimen.	—	—	150.00

66   20 PATACAS

	VG	VF	UNC
1.9.1996. Lilac and purple on lt. green and m/c unpt. B.N.U. bldg. at r., facing dragons in border at l. and r.			
a. Issued note.	4.00	10.00	25.00
s. As a. Specimen.	—	—	250.00

67   50 PATACAS

	VG	VF	UNC
13.7.1992. Olive-brown on m/c unpt. Holiday marcher w/dragon costume at ctr. r., man at r.			
a. Issued note.	12.00	20.00	40.00
s. As a. Specimen.	—	—	300.00

68   100 PATACAS

	VG	VF	UNC
13.7.1992. Black on m/c unpt. Early painting of Settlement at ctr., junk at r.			
a. Issued note.	25.00	30.00	75.00
s. As a. Specimen.	—	—	400.00

69   500 PATACAS

	VG	VF	UNC
3.9.1990. Olive-green on m/c unpt. Bldg. at r. 2 sign. varieties.			
a. Issued note.	75.00	125.00	300.00
s1. Specimen. Sign. as a. Serial # AA00000.	—	—	600.00
s2. Specimen. Sign. different. Serial # AW00000.	—	—	565.00

70 1000 PATACAS

	VG	VF	UNC
8.7.1991. Brown and yellow-orange on m/c unpt. Like #63. 2 sign. varieties.			
a. 8.7.1991. Sign. title at l.: *ADMINISTRATOR*. Serial # prefix AP.	175.00	200.00	450.00
b. 8.7.1991. Sign. title at l.: *PRESIDENTE*. Serial # prefix AQ.	175.00	200.00	425.00
s. As b. Specimen but different sign. Serial # AF00000.	—	—	600.00

1999 ISSUE

All notes issued since 20 December 1999 are issued under Macao as a Special Administrative Region in China.

71 20 PATACAS

	VG	VF	UNC
20.12.1999. Similar to #66.			
a. Issued note.	FV	FV	12.50
b. Uncut sheet of 12. Serial # prefix *JJ* or *KK*.	—	—	200.00
s. As a. Specimen.	—	—	100.00

72 50 PATACAS

	VG	VF	UNC
20.12.1999. Similar to #67.			
a. Issued note.	FV	FV	27.50
b. Uncut sheet of 12. Serial # prefix: *CC*.	—	—	375.00
s. As a. Specimen.	—	—	125.00

73 100 PATACAS

	VG	VF	UNC
20.12.1999. Similar to #68.			
a. Issued note.	FV	FV	45.00
s. Specimen.	—	—	150.00

74 500 PATACAS

	VG	VF	UNC
20.12.1999. Similar to #69.			
a. Issued note.	FV	FV	195.00
s. Specimen.	—	—	300.00

75 1000 PATACAS

	VG	VF	UNC
20.12.1999. Similar to #70.			
a. Sign. title: *PRESIDENTE*.	FV	FV	375.00
b. Sign. title: *ADMINISTRADOR*.	FV	FV	325.00
s. Specimen. As a.	FV	FV	400.00

2001 ISSUE

76 10 PATACAS

	VG	VF	UNC
8.1.2001. Dark red and orange with m/c unpt. Like #65.			
a. Sign. title: *PRESIDENTE*.	FV	FV	9.50
b. Sign. title: *ADMINISTRATOR*	FV	FV	8.50
c. Uncut sheet of 4. Archive use only.	—	—	—
d. Uncut sheet of 40.	—	—	285.00
s. As a. Specimen.	—	—	125.00

2003 ISSUE

		VG	VF	UNC
77	**10 PATACAS**	FV	FV	8.50
	8.6.2003. Dark red and orange on m/c unpt. Like #76.			

		VG	VF	UNC
78	**100 PATACAS**	FV	FV	40.00
	8.6.2003. Black on m/c unpt. Similar to #68.			
79	**500 PATACAS**	FV	FV	185.00
	8.6.2003. Olive-green on m/c unpt. Similar to #74.			

2005 ISSUE

Begining with the 2005 Issue, the 50 Pataca note was no longer issued.

		VG	VF	UNC
80	**10 PATACAS**	FV	FV	7.50
	8.8.2005 (2006).			

		VG	VF	UNC
81	**20 PATACAS**	FV	FV	12.50
	8.8.2005 (2006).			

		VG	VF	UNC
82	**100 PATACAS**	FV	FV	40.00
	8.8.2005 (2006).			

		VG	VF	UNC
83	**500 PATACAS**	FV	FV	165.00
	8.8.2005 (2006).			

		VG	VF	UNC
84	**1000 PATACAS**	FV	FV	300.00
	8.8.2005 (2006).			

BANCO DA CHINA

Chung Kuo Yin Hang

1995; 1996 ISSUE

#90-95 Bank of China - Macau bldg. at l., lotus blossom at lower ctr. on back. Wmk: Lotus blossom(s).

		VG	VF	UNC
90	**10 PATACAS**	FV	FV	15.00
	16.10.1995. Dk. brown and deep green on m/c unpt. Farel de Guia lighthouse at r.			

91 20 PATACAS
1.9.1996. Purple and violet on m/c unpt. Ama Temple at r.

VG	VF	UNC
FV	FV	25.00

92 50 PATACAS
1995; 1997. Black, dk. brown and brown on m/c unpt. University of
Macao at r.

	VG	VF	UNC
a. 16.10.1995.	FV	FV	50.00
b. 1.11.1997.	FV	FV	40.00

93 100 PATACAS
16.10.1995. Black, brown and purple on m/c unpt. New terminal of
Port Exterior at r.

VG	VF	UNC
FV	FV	75.00

94 500 PATACAS
16.10.1995. Dk. green and dk. blue on m/c unpt. Ponte de Amizade
bridge at r.

VG	VF	UNC
FV	FV	300.00

95 1000 PATACAS
16.10.1995. Brown, orange and red on m/c unpt. Aerial view of
Praia Oeste at r.

VG	VF	UNC
FV	FV	600.00

1999 ISSUE

All notes issued since 20 December 1999 are issued under Macau as a Special Administrative Region in
China.

96 20 PATACAS
20.12.1999. Purple and violet on m/c unpt. Similar to #91.

VG	VF	UNC
FV	FV	12.50

97 50 PATACAS
20.12.1999. Black, dk. brown and brown on m/c unpt. Similar to #92.

VG	VF	UNC
FV	FV	27.50

98 100 PATACAS
1999; 2002. Black, brown and purple on m/c unpt. Similar to #93.

	VG	VF	UNC
a. 20.12.1999.	FV	FV	42.50
b. 2.2.2002.	FV	FV	40.00

99	500 PATACAS	VG	VF	UNC
	1999; 2002. Dk. green and dk. blue on m/c unpt. Similar to #94.			
	a. 20.12.1999.	FV	FV	200.00
	b. 2.2.2002.	FV	FV	185.00

100	1000 PATACAS	VG	VF	UNC
	20.12.1999. Brown, orange and red on m/c unpt. Similar to #95.	FV	FV	325.00

2001 ISSUE

101	10 PATACAS	VG	VF	UNC
	2001; 2002. Red and orange on m/c unpt. Like #90.			
	a. 8.1.2001.	FV	FV	8.50
	b. 2.2.2002.	FV	FV	8.00
	c. Uncut sheet of 30. 8.1.2001.	—	—	235.00

2003 ISSUE

#102-106 similar to previous issue but include increased security features, two metallic threads, champagne bubbles in the design and graduated serial #s.

Begining with the 2003 issue the 50 Pataca note was no longer issued.

102	10 PATACAS	VG	VF	UNC
	8.12.2003 (2004). Red and orange on m/c unpt.	FV	FV	7.50
103	20 PATACAS			
	8.12.2003 (2005).	FV	FV	13.50
104	100 PATACAS			
	8.12.2003 (2005).	FV	FV	42.50
105	500 PATACAS			
	8.12.2003 (2005).	FV	FV	185.00
106	1000 PATACAS			
	8.12.2003 (2005).	FV	FV	325.00

COLLECTOR SERIES

BANCO NACIONAL ULTRAMARINO

1999 ISSUE

CS1	20-1000 PATACAS	Issue Price	Mkt.	Value
	One each of #71-74 in a special folder. Matching serial #.	—		675.00

BANCO DA CHINA AND BANCO NACIONAL

ULTRAMARINO

2001 ISSUE

CS2	10 PATACA SHEETLETS OF 4	Issue Price	Mkt.	Value
	One mini-sheet from each bank in a special folder.	—		150.00

MACEDONIA

The Republic of Macedonia is land-locked, and is bordered in the north by Yugoslavia, to the east by Bulgaria, in the south by Greece and to the west by Albania. It has an area of 9,923 sq. mi. (25,713 sq. km.) and its population at the 1991 census was 2.23 million. of which the predominating ethnic groups were Macedonians. The capital is Skopje.

The Slavs, settled in Macedonia since the 6th century, who had been Christianized by Byzantium, were conquered by the non-Slav Bulgars in the 7th century and in the 9th century formed a Macedo-Bulgarian empire, the western part of which survived until Byzantine conquest in 1014. In the 14th century it fell to Serbia, and in 1355 to the Ottomans. After the Balkan Wars of 1912-13 Turkey was ousted, and Serbia received the greater part of the territory, the balance going to Bulgaria and Greece. In 1918, Yugoslav Macedonia was incorporated into Serbia as "South Serbia," becoming a republic in the S.F.R. of Yugoslavia. Claims to the historical Macedonian territory have long been a source of contention between Bulgaria and Greece.

On Nov. 20, 1991 parliament promulgated a new constitution, and declared its independence on Nov. 20, 1992 and was admitted to the UN on April 8, 1993.

MONETARY SYSTEM:
1 ДЕНАР (Denar) = 100 ДЕНИ (Deni)

REPUBLIC

НАРОДНА БАНКА НА МАКЕДОНИЈА

NATIONAL BANK OF MACEDONIA

1992 ISSUE

#1-8 wmk. paper.
#1-6 farmers harvesting at l. Ilenden monument in Krushevo at l. on back.

		VG	VF	UNC
1	**10 (DENAR)**			
	1992. Pale blue on lilac unpt.			
	a. Issued note.	0.10	0.20	0.75
	s. Specimen. Red ovpt. PRIMHROK.	—	—	—

		VG	VF	UNC
2	**25 (DENAR)**			
	1992. Red on lilac unpt.			
	a. Issued note.	0.10	0.20	1.00
	s. Specimen.	—	—	—

		VG	VF	UNC
3	**50 (DENAR)**			
	1992. Brown on ochre unpt.			
	a. Issued note.	0.10	0.20	1.00
	s. Specimen.	—	—	—

		VG	VF	UNC
4	**100 (DENAR)**			
	1992. Blue-gray on lt. blue unpt.			
	a. Issued note.	—	0.20	1.00
	s. Specimen.	—	—	—

		VG	VF	UNC
5	**500 (DENAR)**			
	1992. Bright green on ochre unpt.			
	a. Issued note.	0.15	0.20	1.25
	s. Specimen.	—	—	—

		VG	VF	UNC
6	**1000 (DENAR)**			
	1992. Dull blue-violet on pink unpt.			
	a. Issued note.	0.25	0.75	1.75
	s. Specimen.	—	—	—

7   5000 (DENAR)

1992. Deep brown and dull red on m/c unpt. Woman at desk top computer at ctr. Ilenden monument at l. on back.

	VG	VF	UNC
a. Issued note.	0.25	1.50	6.00
s. Specimen.	—	—	—

10   20 DENARI

1993. Wine-red on m/c unpt. 16th century clock Tower in Skopje in vertical format on face. Turkish bath in Skopje at l. ctr. on back.

	VG	VF	UNC
a. Issued note.	FV	FV	2.50
s. Specimen.	—	—	15.00

8   10,000 (DENAR)

1992. Blue-black on pink and gray unpt. Bldgs. at ctr. r. Musicians at l. of Ilenden monument at ctr. r. on back.

	VG	VF	UNC
a. Issued note.	0.50	2.50	8.50
s. Specimen.	—	—	—

11   50 DENARI

1993. Lt. red on m/c unpt. National Bank bldg. in Skopje at r. 12th century Orthodox Church of St. Pantileimon at l. on back.

	VG	VF	UNC
a. Issued note.	FV	FV	4.00
s. Specimen.	—	—	15.00

НАРОДНА БАНКА НА РЕПУБЛИКА МАКЕДОНИЈА

NATIONAL BANK OF THE REPUBLIC OF MACEDONIA

1993 ISSUE

Currency Reform

1 "New" Denar = 100 "Old" Denars

#9-12 wmk: Ilenden monument in Krushevo.

12   100 DENARI

1993. Brown on m/c unpt. Bovev Palace, National Museum in Ohrid at r. 11th century Monestery of St. Sophia in Ohrid at l. on back.

	VG	VF	UNC
a. Issued note.	FV	FV	8.00
s. Specimen.	—	—	15.00

9   10 DENARI

1993. Lt. blue on m/c unpt. Houses on mountainside in Krushevo at ctr. r. Ilenden monument at l. ctr. on back.

	VG	VF	UNC
a. Issued note.	FV	FV	1.50
s. Specimen.	—	—	15.00

13   500 DENARI
1993. Greenish gray on m/c unpt. Ohrid castle ruins at at. upper ctr.
12th century Orthodox church of St. John in Ohrid at l. and as wmk.
on back.

	VG	VF	UNC
a. Issued note.	FV	FV	35.00
s. Specimen.			15.00

1996 ISSUE

14   10 DENARI
8.9.1996; 8.1997; 1.2001; 1.2003. Deep olive-green w/black text
on m/c unpt. Statue torso of Goddess Isida at ctr. r. and as wmk.
Back blue-green, deep olive-green w/black text on m/c unpt.
Mosaic of branch over peacock and duck.

	VG	VF	UNC
a. Issued note.	FV	FV	1.50
s. Specimen.	—	—	20.00

15   50 DENARI
8.9.1996; 8.1997; 1.2001. Brown w/black text on m/c unpt.
Byzantine copper follis of Anastasia at ctr. r. and as wmk.
Archangel Gabriel at l. ctr. on back.

	VG	VF	UNC
a. Issued note.	FV	FV	3.00
s. Specimen.	—	—	20.00

16   100 DENARI
8.9.1996; 8.1997; 1.2000; 1.2002; 5.2004. Brown w/purple text on
m/c unpt. Lg. baroque wooden ceiling rosette in Debar town house
at ctr. r. and as wmk. J. Harevin's engraving of Skopje "seen"
through town house window frame at l. ctr.

	VG	VF	UNC
a. Issued note.	FV	FV	5.00
s. Specimen.	—	—	25.00

17   500 DENARI
8.9.1996. Black and violet on m/c unpt. 6th century golden death
mask, Trebenista, Ohrid at r. and as wmk. Violet poppy flower and
plant at l. ctr. on back.

	VG	VF	UNC
a. Issued note.	FV	FV	22.50
s. Specimen.	—	—	25.00

18   1000 DENARI
8.9.1996. Brown and orange on m/c unpt. 14th century icon of
Madonna Episkepsis and Christ Child, church of St. Vrach-Mali,
Ohrid at ctr. r. Partial view of the St. Sophia church in Ohrid at l. ctr.
Wmk: Madonna.

	VG	VF	UNC
a. Issued note.	FV	FV	40.00
s. Specimen.	—	—	30.00

19   5000 DENARI
8.9.1996. Black and violet on olive-green and m/c unpt. 6th century
bronze figurine of Tetovo Maenad VI (horizontally) at ctr. r. and as
wmk. 6th century mosaic of Cerberus the Dog tied to a fig tree,
representing the watcher of Heaven (horizontally)

	VG	VF	UNC
a. Issued note.	FV	FV	175.00
s. Specimen.	—	—	60.00

2000 COMMEMORATIVE ISSUE

20 100 DENARI
1.2000. Brown w/purple text on m/c unpt. As #16 but with *2000* added at l.

	VG	VF	UNC
	—	35.00	80.00

2003 ISSUE

21 500 DENARI
1.2003. Black and violet on m/c unpt. gold foil at ctr. Similar to #17.

	VG	VF	UNC
a. Issued note.	FV	FV	22.50
s. Specimen.	FV	FV	25.00

22 1000 DENARI
1.2003. Brown and orange on m/c unpt. As #18 but with hologram added on ctr. top.

	VG	VF	UNC
a. Issued note.	FV	FV	40.00
s. Specimen.	—	—	25.00

The Democratic Republic of Madagascar, an independent member of the French Community located in the Indian Ocean 250 miles (402 km.) off the southeast coast of Africa, has an area of 226,658 sq. mi. (587,041 sq. km.) and a population of 17.39 million. Capital: Antananarivo. The economy is primarily agricultural; large bauxite deposits are presently being developed. Coffee, vanilla, graphite and rice are exported.

Diago Diaz, a Portuguese navigator, sighted the island of Madagascar on Aug. 10, 1500, when his ship became separated from an India-bound fleet. Attempts at settlement by the British during the reign of Charles I and by the French during the 17th and 18th centuries were of no avail, and the island became a refuge and supply base for Indian Ocean pirates. Despite considerable influence on the island, the British accepted the imposition of a French protectorate in 1886 in return for French recognition of Britain's sphere of influence in Zanzibar. Madagascar was made a French colony in 1896 after absolute control had been established by military force. Britain occupied the island after the fall of France in 1942, to prevent its seizure by the Japanese, and gave it to the Free French in 1943. On Oct. 14, 1958, following a decade of intermittent but bitter warfare, Madagascar, as the Malagasy Republic, became an autonomous state within the French Community. On June 27, 1960, it became a sovereign independent nation, though remaining nominally within the French Community. The Malagasy Republic was renamed the Democratic Republic of Madagascar in 1976.

MONETARY SYSTEM:
1 CFA Franc = 0.02 French Franc, 1959-1961
5 Malagasy Francs (F.M.G.) = 1 Ariary, 1961-2003
1 Ariary = 5 Francs, 2003-

MALAGASY

INSTITUT D'EMISSION MALGACHE

1961 ND PROVISIONAL ISSUE

#51-55 new bank name and new Ariary denominations ovpt. on previous issue of Banque de Madagascar et des Comores. Wmk: Woman's head.

51 50 FRANCS = 10 ARIARY
ND (1961). M/c. Woman w/hat at ctr. r. Man at ctr. on back. Ovpt. on #45.

	VG	VF	UNC
a. Sign. title: LE CONTROLEUR GENERAL.	2.00	17.50	70.00
b. Sign. title: LE DIRECTEUR GENERAL ADJOINT.	2.50	20.00	75.00

52 100 FRANCS = 20 ARIARY
ND (1961). M/c. Woman at ctr. r., palace of the Qn. of Tananariva in background. Woman, boats and animals on back. Ovpt. on #46b.

	VG	VF	UNC
	3.00	30.00	110.00

53 500 FRANCS = 100 ARIARY
ND (1961 - old date 9.10.1952). M/c. Man w/fruit at ctr. Ovpt. on #47.

	VG	VF	UNC
	15.00	90.00	400.00

54	1000 FRANCS = 200 ARIARY	VG	VF	UNC
	ND (1961 - old date 9.10.1952). M/c. Man and woman at l. ctr. Ox cart at ctr. r. on back. Ovpt. on #48.	20.00	175.00	500.00
55	5000 FRANCS = 1000 ARIARY			
	ND (1961). M/c. Gallieni at upper l., woman at r. Woman and baby on back. Ovpt. on #49.	50.00	325.00	800.00

Note: #53-55 some notes also have old dates of intended or original issue (1952-55).

1963 ND REGULAR ISSUE

56	1000 FRANCS = 200 ARIARY	VG	VF	UNC
	ND (1963). M/c. Portr. Pres. P. Tsiranana, people in canoes at l. Ox cart at ctr. r. on back. Wmk: Woman's head.			
	a. W/o sign. and title.	50.00	375.00	800.00
	b. W/sign. and title.	40.00	250.00	700.00

1966 ND ISSUE

#57-60 wmk: Woman's head.

57	100 FRANCS = 20 ARIARY	VG	VF	UNC
	ND (1966). M/c. 3 women spinning. Trees on back. 2 sign. varieties.			
	a. Issued note.	2.50	10.00	30.00
	s. Specimen.	—	—	25.00

58	500 FRANCS = 100 ARIARY	VG	VF	UNC
	ND (1966). M/c. Woman at l., landscape in background. River scene on back. 2 sign. varieties.			
	a. Issued note.	5.00	45.00	185.00
	s. Specimen.	—	—	35.00

59	1000 FRANCS = 200 ARIARY	VG	VF	UNC
	ND (1966). M/c. Woman and man at l. Similar to #48 and #54 but size 150 x 80mm.			
	a. Issued note.	7.50	65.00	250.00
	s. Specimen.	—	—	35.00

60	5000 FRANCS = 1000 ARIARY	VG	VF	UNC
	ND (1966). M/c. Portr. Pres. P. Tsiranana at l., workers in rice field at r. Woman and boy on back.			
	a. Issued note.	10.00	45.00	200.00
	s. Specimen.	—	—	45.00

1969 ND ISSUE

61	50 FRANCS = 10 ARIARY	VG	VF	UNC
	ND (1969). M/c. Like #51. Different sign. title.	2.25	7.50	25.00

MADAGASCAR DEMOCRATIC REPUBLIC
BANKY FOIBEN'NY REPOBLIKA MALAGASY
BANQUE CENTRALE DE LA RÉPUBLIQUE MALGACHE
1974 ND ISSUE

#62-66 replacement notes: Serial # prefix Z/.
#64-66 wmk: Zebu's head.

65	1000 FRANCS = 200 ARIARY	VG	VF	UNC
	ND. Blue on m/c unpt. Ring-tailed Lemurs at l., man in straw hat at r. Trees and designs on back.			
	a. Issued note.	2.00	8.00	45.00
	s. Specimen.	—	—	25.00

62	50 FRANCS = 10 ARIARY	VG	VF	UNC
	ND (1974-75). Purple on m/c unpt. Young man at ctr. r. Fruit stand under umbrella at l. ctr. on back.			
	a. Issued note.	0.50	4.00	12.50
	s. Specimen.	—	—	25.00

66	5000 FRANCS = 1000 ARIARY	VG	VF	UNC
	ND. Red and violet on m/c unpt. Oxen at l., young woman at ctr. r. Back violet and orange; tropical plants and African carving at ctr.			
	a. Issued note.	7.00	30.00	80.00
	s. Specimen.	—	—	25.00

63	100 FRANCS = 20 ARIARY	VG	VF	UNC
	ND. Brown on m/c unpt. Old man at r. Rice planting on back.			
	a. Issued note.	0.50	3.00	10.00
	s. Specimen.	—	—	25.00

BANKY FOIBEN'I MADAGASIKARA
1983 ND ISSUE

#67-70 wmk: Zebu's head. Sign. varieties. Replacement notes: Serial # prefix Z/.

67	500 FRANCS = 100 ARIARY	VG	VF	UNC
	ND (1983-87). Brown and red on m/c unpt. Boy w/fish in net at ctr. Aerial view of port at r. on back.	0.25	1.50	5.00

64	500 FRANCS = 100 ARIARY	VG	VF	UNC
	ND. Green on m/c unpt. Butterfly at l., young woman at ctr. r. holding ornate bag on head. Dancers at ctr. on back.			
	a. Issued note.	1.00	6.00	30.00
	s. Specimen.	—	—	25.00

		VG	VF	UNC
68	**1000 FRANCS = 200 ARIARY**	0.25	2.00	7.50
	ND (1983-87). Violet and brown on m/c unpt. Man w/hat playing flute at ctr. Fruits and vegetables at r. on back.			

		VG	VF	UNC
72	**1000 FRANCS = 200 ARIARY**	0.25	2.00	7.50
	ND (1988-93). Similar to #68, but modified unpt.			

		VG	VF	UNC
69	**5000 FRANCS = 1000 ARIARY**	1.50	10.00	35.00
	ND (1983-87). Blue on m/c unpt. Woman and child at ctr. Book at upper ctr., school at ctr. r., monument at lower r. on back.			

		VG	VF	UNC
72A	**2500 FRANCS = 500 ARIARY**	0.20	0.75	2.50
	ND (1993). Red, green, blue and black on m/c unpt. Older woman at ctr. Grey heron, tortoise, Verreaux's Sifaka and butterfly in foliage on vertical format back.			

		VG	VF	UNC
70	**10,000 FRANCS = 2000 ARIARY**	2.50	20.00	65.00
	ND (1983-87). Green on m/c unpt. Young girl w/sheaf at ctr. Harvesting rice at ctr. r. on back.			

1988 ND ISSUE

#71-74 vertical serial # at r. Sign. varieties. Wmk: Zebu's head. Replacement notes: Serial # prefix ZZ.

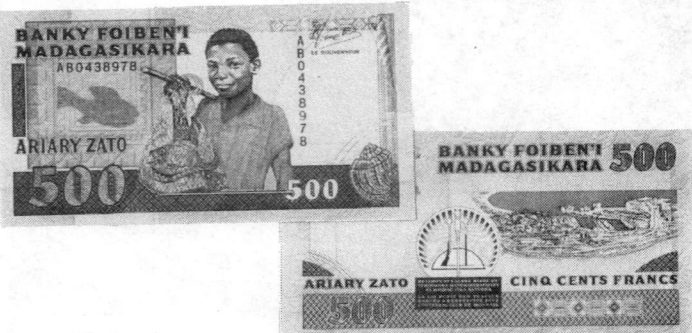

		VG	VF	UNC
73	**5000 FRANCS = 1000 ARIARY**	1.25	4.00	15.00
	ND (1988-94). Similar to #69, but modified unpt.			

		VG	VF	UNC
71	**500 FRANCS = 100 ARIARY**	0.25	1.50	5.00
	ND (1988-93). Similar to #67, but modified unpt.			

		VG	VF	UNC
74	**10,000 FRANCS = 2000 ARIARY**	2.00	10.00	30.00
	ND (1988-94). Similar to #70, but modified unpt.			

74A 25,000 FRANCS = 5000 ARIARY

	VG	VF	UNC
	1.00	5.00	17.50

ND (1993) Olive-green and green on m/c unpt. Old man at ctr., island outline at l. Scene of traditional bullfighting at r. on back.

1994-95 ND Issue

#75-80 wmk: Zebu's head.

75 500 FRANCS = 100 ARIARY

	VG	VF	UNC
	0.10	0.50	1.75

ND (1994). Dk. brown and dk. green on m/c unpt. Girl at ctr. r., village in unpt. at upper ctr. Herdsmen w/Zebus, village in upper background at l. ctr. on back.

76 1000 FRANCS = 200 ARIARY

	VG	VF	UNC
	0.20	0.50	1.50

ND (1994). Dk. brown and dk. blue on m/c unpt. Young man at ctr. r., boats in background. Young woman w/basket of shellfish at ctr., fisherman w/net at l. ctr. on back.

#77 renumbered to 72A.

78 5000 FRANCS = 1000 ARIARY

	VG	VF	UNC
	0.75	1.25	6.00

ND (1995). Dk. brown and purple on lilac and m/c unpt. Young male head at r., ox cart, cane cutters at ctr. Ringtailed Lemur, Diademed Sifaka, Red-ruffed Lemur and birds - Madagascar pigmy kingfisher, Madagascar fody and helmet vanga, plus seashells

79 10,000 FRANCS = 2000 ARIARY

	VG	VF	UNC
	1.00	2.50	10.00

ND (1995). Dk. brown on tan and m/c unpt. Old man at r., statuette, local artifacts at ctr. Artisans at work on back.

#80 renumbered to #74A.

1998 ND Issue

81 2500 FRANCS = 500 ARIARY

	VG	VF	UNC
	0.25	0.75	3.50

ND (1998). M/c. Woman at r., village in background. Woman weaving at l. ctr. on back.

82 25,000 FRANCS = 5000 ARIARY

	VG	VF	UNC
	1.00	3.00	25.00

ND (1998). M/c. Mother w/child at ctr. r., fruit trees in background. Woman harvesting at ctr. on back.

2003 Issue

83	2000 ARIARY	VG	VF	UNC
	ND (2003). M/c.	FV	FV	10.00

84	5000 ARIARY	VG	VF	UNC
	ND (2003). M/c.	FV	FV	20.00

85	10,000 ARIARY	VG	VF	UNC
	ND (2003). M/c.	FV	FV	35.00

2004 ISSUE

86	100 ARIARY	VG	VF	UNC
	2004. Blue and tan on m/c unpt.	FV	FV	0.75

87	200 ARIARY	VG	VF	UNC
	2004. Green and tan on m/c unpt.	FV	FV	1.00

88	500 ARIARY	VG	VF	UNC
	2004. Tan on blue unpt.	FV	FV	2.50

89	1000 ARIARY	VG	VF	UNC
	2004. Purple on m/c unpt.	FV	FV	3.50

MALAWI

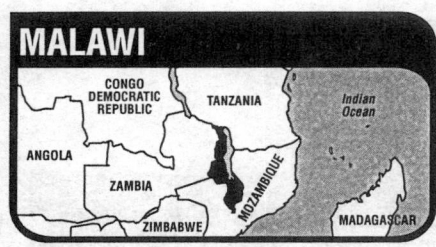

The Republic of Malawi (formerly Nyasaland), located in southeastern Africa to the west of Lake Malawi (Nyasa), has an area of 45,747 sq. mi. (118,484 sq. km.) and a population of 10.98 million. Capital: Lilongwe. The economy is predominantly agricultural. Tobacco, tea, peanuts and cotton are exported. Although the Portuguese, heirs to the restless spirit of Prince Henry, were the first Europeans to reach the Malawi area, the first meaningful contact was made by missionary-explorer Dr. David Livingstone who arrived at Lake Malawi on Sept. 16, 1859, and remained to make extensive explorations in the 1860s. Subsequent clashes between settlements of Scottish missionaries and Arab slave traders, and the procurement of development rights by Cecil Rhodes, 1884, stimulated British interest and brought about the establishment of the Nyasaland protectorate in 1891. In 1953, Nyasaland reluctantly joined the Federation of Rhodesia and Nyasaland and, after prolonged protest, was granted self-government within the federation. Nyasaland became the independent nation of Malawi on July 6, 1964, and became a republic two years later. As a one party dictatorship lasting 30 years until 1994 when elections returned Malawi to a multi-party democracy. Malawi is a member of the Commonwealth of Nations. The president is the Chief of State and Head of Government.

Also see Rhodesia, Rhodesia and Nyasaland.

RULERS:
    British to 1964

MONETARY SYSTEM:
    1 Pound = 20 Shillings to 1971
    1 Kwacha = 100 Tambala 1971-

REPLACEMENT NOTES:
    #13-17, ZZ prefix. #18-22, V/1, W/1, X/1, Y/1, Z/1 prefix by denomination. #23-27, ZZ prefix.

REPUBLIC

RESERVE BANK OF MALAWI

1964 RESERVE BANK ACT; FIRST ISSUE

Pound System

#1-4 portr. Dr. Hastings Kamuzu Banda at l., fishermen in boat on Lake Malawi at ctr. Sign. title: GOVERNOR only. Wmk: Rooster.

		VG	VF	UNC
1	**5 SHILLINGS** L.1964. Blue-gray on m/c unpt. Arms w/bird on back.	5.00	17.50	95.00

		VG	VF	UNC
2	**10 SHILLINGS** L.1964. Brown on m/c unpt. Workers in tobacco field on back.	7.50	75.00	250.00
3	**1 POUND** L.1964. Green on m/c unpt. Workers picking cotton at ctr. r. on back.	10.00	85.00	350.00

		VG	VF	UNC
4	**5 POUNDS** L.1964. Blue and brown on m/c unpt. Tea pickers below Mt. Mulanje on back.	40.00	300.00	1200.00

1964 RESERVE BANK ACT; SECOND ISSUE

#1A-3A portr. Dr. Hastings Kamusu Banda at l., fishermen at ctr. Sign. titles: GOVERNOR and GENERAL MANAGER.

		VG	VF	UNC
1A	**5 SHILLINGS** L.1964. Blue-gray on m/c unpt. Like #1. a. Issued note. s. Specimen.	3.50 —	10.00 —	70.00 —

		VG	VF	UNC
2A	**10 SHILLINGS** L.1964. Brown on m/c unpt. Like #2. a. Issued note. s. Specimen.	5.00 —	17.50 —	100.00 —

		VG	VF	UNC
3A	**1 POUND** L.1964. Green on m/c unpt. Like #3. a. Issued note. s. Specimen.	5.00 —	40.00 —	200.00 —

1964 RESERVE BANK ACT; 1971 ISSUE

Kwacha System

		VG	VF	UNC
5	**50 TAMBALA** L.1964 (1971). Blue-gray on m/c unpt. Face like #1A. Independence Arch in Blantyre at r. on back. a. Issued note. s. Specimen.	10.00 —	50.00 —	325.00 —

6	**1 KWACHA**	VG	VF	UNC
	L.1964 (1971). Brown on m/c unpt. Like #2A.			
	a. Issued note.	12.50	50.00	325.00
	s. Specimen.	—	—	—

7	**2 KWACHA**	VG	VF	UNC
	L.1964 (1971). Green on m/c unpt. Like #3A.			
	a. Issued note.	15.00	50.00	300.00
	s. Specimen.	—	—	—

10	**1 KWACHA**	VG	VF	UNC
	L.1964 (ND); 1974-75. Red-brown on m/c unpt. Plantation worker, hill in background on back.			
	a. ND (1973).	5.00	20.00	135.00
	b. 30.6.1974.	4.00	15.00	85.00
	c. 31.1.1975.	3.00	7.00	75.00
	ct. Color trial. Orange on m/c unpt.	—	—	250.00

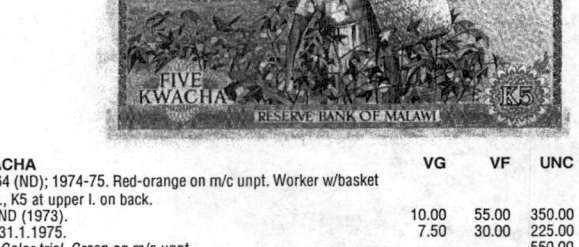

11	**5 KWACHA**	VG	VF	UNC
	L.1964 (ND); 1974-75. Red-orange on m/c unpt. Worker w/basket at ctr., K5 at upper l. on back.			
	a. ND (1973).	10.00	55.00	350.00
	b. 31.1.1975.	7.50	30.00	225.00
	ct. Color trial. Green on m/c unpt.	—	—	550.00

12	**10 KWACHA**			
	L.1964 (ND); 1974-75. Blue and brown on m/c unpt. Plantation workers w/mountains in background on back.			
	a. ND (1973).	15.00	65.00	400.00
	b. 30.6.1974.	12.50	75.00	450.00
	c. 31.1.1975.	9.00	45.00	325.00

8	**10 KWACHA**	VG	VF	UNC
	L.1964 (1971). Blue and brown on m/c unpt. Like #4 but 2 signs.			
	a. Issued note.	30.00	175.00	900.00
	s. Specimen.	—	—	—

1973-74 ISSUE

#9-12 portr. Dr. Hastings Kamuzu Banda as Prime Minister at r., fishermen in boat on Lake Malawi and palm tree at ctr. W/ or w/o dates. Wmk: Rooster.

1976; 1983 ISSUE

#13-17 portr. Dr. Hastings Kamuzu Banda as President at r. Wmk: Rooster. Sign. varieties.

9	**50 TAMBALA**	VG	VF	UNC
	L.1964 (ND); 1974-75. Blue-gray on m/c unpt. Sugar cane harvesting on back.			
	a. ND (1973).	5.00	30.00	200.00
	b. 30.6.1974.	3.00	15.00	100.00
	c. 31.1.1975.	2.00	5.00	40.00
	ct. Color trial. Purple on m/c unpt.	—	—	275.00
	s. As a. Specimen.	—	—	—

13	**50 TAMBALA**	VG	VF	UNC
	1976-84. Blue-gray on m/c unpt. Cotton harvest on back.			
	a. 31.1.1976.	0.50	3.00	25.00
	b. 1.7.1978.	0.50	4.50	30.00
	c. 1.1.1981.	0.50	5.00	40.00
	d. 1.5.1982.	0.50	2.50	12.50
	e. 1.1.1983.	0.50	5.00	35.00
	f. 1.11.1984.	1.00	7.50	60.00
	s. As a. Specimen.	—	—	35.00

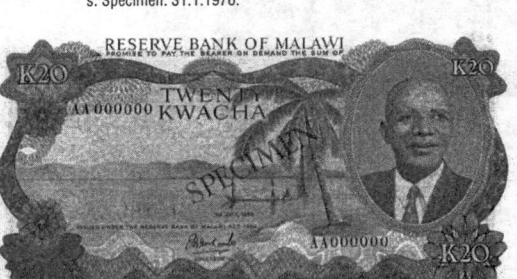

16	10 KWACHA	VG	VF	UNC
	a. 31.1.1976.	7.50	30.00	400.00
	b. 1.7.1978.	7.50	25.00	385.00
	c. 30.6.1979.	8.50	40.00	500.00
	d. 1.1.1981.	7.50	25.00	350.00
	e. 1.1.1983.	7.50	22.50	300.00
	f. 1.11.1984.	8.00	27.50	400.00
	g. 1.8.1985.	7.50	27.50	375.00
	s. Specimen. 31.1.1976.	—		45.00

17	20 KWACHA	VG	VF	UNC
	1983; 1984. Green, brown-violet on m/c unpt. Back green; Reserve Bank at in Lilongwe at ctr.			
	a. 1.7.1983.	4.50	15.00	125.00
	b. 1.11.1984.	10.00	35.00	300.00
	s. Specimen.	—	—	240.00

1986 ISSUE

#18-22 portr. Pres. Dr. Hastings Kamuzu Banda at r. Wmk; Rooster.

18	50 TAMBALA	VG	VF	UNC
	1.3.1986. Black and dk. brown on m/c unpt. Picking corn on back.	0.25	1.00	9.00

19	1 KWACHA	VG	VF	UNC
	1986; 1988. Red-brown on m/c unpt. Cultivating tobacco on back.			
	a. 1.3.1986.	0.50	1.75	10.00
	b. 1.4.1988.	0.25	0.75	6.50

14	1 KWACHA	VG	VF	UNC
	1976-84. Red-brown on m/c unpt. Workers harvesting, mountains in background on back.			
	a. 31.1.1976.	0.50	3.00	22.50
	b. 1.7.1978.	0.50	3.00	25.00
	c. 30.6.1979.	2.00	15.00	100.00
	d. 1.1.1981.	0.50	2.00	20.00
	e. 1.5.1982.	0.25	1.50	12.50
	f. 1.1.1983.	0.50	3.00	25.00
	g. 1.4.1984.	0.25	1.50	12.50
	h. 1.11.1984.	0.50	2.00	15.00
	s. Specimen. 31.1.1976.	—		40.00

15	5 KWACHA	VG	VF	UNC
	1976-84. Red on m/c unpt. Field workers, K5 at upper r. on back.			
	a. 31.1.1976.	2.00	20.00	175.00
	b. 1.7.1978.	2.00	20.00	175.00
	c. 30.6.1979.	3.00	30.00	275.00
	d. 1.1.1981.	1.50	7.50	60.00
	e. 1.1.1983.	1.00	5.00	50.00
	f. 1.11.1984.	2.00	15.00	175.00
	s. Specimen. 31.1.1976.	—	—	50.00

16	10 KWACHA
	1976-85. Deep blue and brown on m/c unpt. Capital bldg. at Lilongwe on back.

1989 ACT; 1990; 1993 ISSUE
#23-28 palm tree, man in dugout canoe, and rayed silver circle at ctr., portr. Dr. Hastings Kamuzu Banda as President at r. Ascending size vertical serial # at l. and lower r. Wmk: Rooster.

		VG	VF	UNC
20	**5 KWACHA**			
	1986; 1988. Red-orange on m/c unpt. University of Malawi at Zomba on back.			
	a. 1.3.1986.	1.75	7.00	40.00
	b. 1.4.1988.	1.00	5.00	30.00

		VG	VF	UNC
23	**1 KWACHA**			
	1990; 1992. Red-brown on m/c unpt. Back similar to #19.			
	a. 1.12.1990.	FV	FV	5.00
	b. 1.5.1992.	FV	FV	2.00

		VG	VF	UNC
21	**10 KWACHA**			
	1986; 1988. Deep blue and brown on m/c unpt. Lilongwe, capital city, on back.			
	a. 1.3.1986.	3.00	12.50	80.00
	b. 1.4.1988.	2.00	8.50	45.00

		VG	VF	UNC
24	**5 KWACHA**			
	1990; 1994. Red-orange and olive-green on m/c unpt. University of Malawi at l. ctr. on back.			
	a. 1.12.1990.	FV	FV	6.50
	b. 1.1.1994.	FV	FV	4.50

		VG	VF	UNC
22	**20 KWACHA**			
	1986; 1988. Deep green on m/c unpt. Kamuzu International Airport on back.			
	a. 1.3.1986.	6.00	25.00	250.00
	b. 1.4.1988.	3.00	15.00	135.00

		VG	VF	UNC
25	**10 KWACHA**			
	1990-94. Blue-gray, blue-violet and dk. brown on m/c unpt. Lilongwe City municipal bldg. at l. ctr. on back.			
	a. 1.12.1990.	FV	FV	12.50
	b. 1.9.1992.	FV	FV	6.00
	c. Smaller sign. as b. 1.1.1994.	FV	FV	4.00
	s. As b. Specimen.	—	—	135.00
26	**20 KWACHA**			
	1.9.1990. Green, orange and blue on m/c unpt. Kamuzu International Airport at l. ctr. on back.	FV	FV	50.00

27 20 KWACHA
  1.7.1993. Like #26 but w/larger airplane on back.

	VG	VF	UNC
	FV	FV	10.00

28 50 KWACHA
  1990; 1994. Pale purple, violet and blue on m/c unpt.
  Independence Arch at Blantyre at ctr. on back.

	VG	VF	UNC
a. 1.6.1990.	FV	12.50	55.00
b. 1.1.1994.	FV	FV	30.00

29 100 KWACHA
  1993; 1994. Blue, green and dk. brown on m/c unpt. Trucks hauling
  maize to storage facility at ctr. on back.

	VG	VF	UNC
a. 1.4.1993.	FV	30.00	65.00
b. 1.1.1994.	FV	FV	40.00

1995 ISSUE

#30-35 Pres. Muluzi at r., bird at upper l., sunrise above fisherman in boat on Lake Malawi at ctr., bird over silver segmented sunburst at l. Wmk: Fish.

30 5 KWACHA
  1.6.1995. Red and orange-brown on m/c unpt. Spoonbill at top l.
  Zebras at l. on back.

	VG	VF	UNC
	FV	FV	1.75

31 10 KWACHA
  1.6.1995. Black, dk. blue and dk. brown on m/c unpt. Crowned
  crane at top l. Capital Hill, Lilongwe at l. ctr. on back.

	VG	VF	UNC
	FV	FV	4.00

32 20 KWACHA
  1.6.1995. Deep green and dk. brown on m/c unpt. Lesser striped
  swallow at top l. Harvesting tea leaves at l. ctr. on back.

	VG	VF	UNC
	FV	FV	7.50

33 50 KWACHA
  1.6.1995. Purple and violet on m/c unpt. Pink-backed pelican at top
  l. Independence Arch in Blantyre at l. ctr. on back.

	VG	VF	UNC
	FV	FV	12.00

34 100 KWACHA
1.6.1995. Purple and deep ultramarine on m/c unpt. Sacred ibis at top l. Trucks hauling maize to storage facility at l. ctr. on back.

	VG	VF	UNC
	FV	FV	25.00

35 200 KWACHA
1.6.1995. Brown-violet and blue-green and silver on m/c unpt. African fish eagle at top l. Elephants on back.

	VG	VF	UNC
	FV	FV	40.00

1989 Act; 1997 Issue

#36-41 J. Chilembwe at r. and as wmk., sunrise, fishermen at ctr., bank stylized logo at lower l.

#36-39 bank seal at top ctr. r. on back.

36 5 KWACHA
1.7.1997. Deep olive-green, green and olive-brown on m/c unpt. Villagers mashing grain at l. on back.

	VG	VF	UNC
	FV	FV	1.25

37 10 KWACHA
1.7.1997. Dk. brown and brown-violet on m/c unpt. Children in "bush" school at l. ctr. on back.

	VG	VF	UNC
	FV	FV	1.50

38 20 KWACHA
1.7.1997. Blackish purple, purple and violet on m/c unpt. Workers harvesting tea leaves, mountains in background at l. on back.

	VG	VF	UNC
a. Even height serial #s.	FV	FV	3.50
b. Ascending size serial #.	FV	FV	3.25

39 50 KWACHA
1.7.1997. Dk. green, deep blue and aqua on m/c unpt. Independence arch in Blantyre at l. ctr. on back.

	VG	VF	UNC
	FV	FV	5.00

40 100 KWACHA
1.7.1997. Purple, red and violet on m/c unpt. Circular kinegram bank seal at r. Capital Hill Lilongwe at l. ctr. on back.

	VG	VF	UNC
	FV	FV	12.50

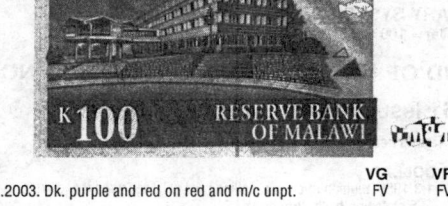

41	200 KWACHA	VG	VF	UNC
	1.7.1997. Dk. gray, dull blue and deep blue-green on m/c unpt.	FV	FV	17.50
	Oval kinegram bank seal at r. Reserve Bank bldg. in Lilongwe at l.			
	ctr. on back.			

#42 has been merged into #48.

2001-03 Issue

#43-48 with ascending size serial #.

46	100 KWACHA	VG	VF	UNC
	1.10.2001; 1.1.2003. Dk. purple and red on red and m/c unpt.	FV	FV	10.00
47	200 KWACHA			
	1.7.2001; 1.6.2003. M/c. As #41 but w/holographic band at r.	FV	FV	15.00
48	500 KWACHA			
	1.12.2001; 1.6.2003. M/c.			
	a. 1.12.2001. Holographic square at l.	FV	FV	30.00
	b. 1.6.2003. Holographic strip at r.	FV	FV	25.00

2004 Commemorative Issue

#49, 40th Anniversary of Independence.

43	10 KWACHA	VG	VF	UNC
	1.1.2003; 1.10.2003. Dk. brown and brown-violet on m/c unpt.	FV	FV	1.50
	Children in "bush" school at l. ctr. on back.			

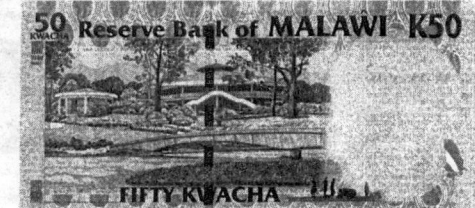

49	50 KWACHA	VG	VF	UNC
	6.7.2004. Blue on yellow-orange unpt. Modern buildings on back.	FV	FV	4.00

2004 Regular Issue

Denomination added to wmk.

50	20 KWACHA	VG	VF	UNC
	1.6.2004. M/c. Similar to # 44.	FV	FV	2.50
51	200 KWACHA			
	1.6.2004. M/c. 1.6.2004.	FV	FV	15.00

44	20 KWACHA	VG	VF	UNC
	1.10.2001; 1.1.2003; 1.4.2004. Black and purple on m/c unpt.	FV	FV	2.50

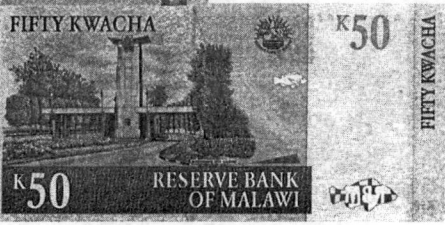

45	50 KWACHA	VG	VF	UNC
	1.10.2001; 1.1.2003. Dk. green, deep blue and aqua on m/c unpt.	FV	FV	4.00

MALAYA & BRITISH BORNEO

Malaya and British Borneo, a Currency Commission named the Board of Commissioners of Currency, Malaya and British North Borneo, was initiated on Jan. 1, 1952, for the purpose of providing a common currency for use in Johore, Kelantan, Kedah, Perlis, Trengganu, Negri Sembilan, Pahang, Perak, Salangor, Penang, Malacca, Singapore, North Borneo, Sarawak and Brunei.

For later issues see Brunei, Malaysia and Singapore.

RULERS:
British

MONETARY SYSTEM:
1 Dollar = 100 Cents

BOARD OF COMMISSIONERS OF CURRENCY

1959-61 ISSUE

#8-9 wmk: Tiger's head.

		VG	VF	UNC
8	**1 DOLLAR** 1.3.1959. Blue on m/c unpt. Sailing boat at l. Men w/boat and arms of 5 states on back. Printer: W&S.			
	a. Issued note.	6.00	20.00	120.00
	s. Specimen.	—	—	—
8A	**1 DOLLAR** 1.3.1959. Blue on m/c unpt. Like #8. Printer: TDLR.	4.00	12.50	60.00

		VG	VF	UNC
9	**10 DOLLARS** 1.3.1961. Red and dk. brown on m/c unpt. Farmer plowing w/ox at r. Printer: TDLR.			
	a. Sm. serial #. Series A.	35.00	100.00	400.00
	b. Lg. serial #. Series A.	100.00	180.00	500.00
	c. Lg. serial #. Series B.	100.00	225.00	700.00
	s. As a. Specimen.	—	—	—

MALAYSIA

Malaysia, an independent federation of southeast Asia consisting of 11 states of West Malaysia on the Malay Peninsula and two states of East Malaysia on the island of Borneo, has an area of 127,316 sq. mi. (329,747 sq. km.) and a population of 22.3 million. Capital: Kuala Lumpur. The federation came into being on Sept. 16, 1963. Rubber, timber, tin, iron ore and bauxite are exported.

The constituent states of Malaysia are Johore, Kedah, Kelantan, Malacca, Negri Sembilan, Pahang, Penang, Perak, Perlis, Selangor and Trengganu of West Malaysia; and Sabah and Sarawak of East Malaysia. Singapore joined the federation in 1963, but broke away on Aug. 9, 1965, to become an independent republic. Malaysia is a member of the Commonwealth of Nations. The "Paramount Ruler" is Chief of State. The prime minister is Head of Government.

MONETARY SYSTEM:
1 Ringgit (Dollar) = 100 Sen

DEMONETIZED NOTES:
All 500 and 1000 Ringgitt notes ceased to be legal tender on July 1, 1999.

BANK NEGARA MALAYSIA

All notes w/Yang Di-Pertuan Agong, Tunku Abdul Rahman, first Head of State of Malaysia (died 1960).

1967 ND ISSUE

#1-6 old spelling of *DI-PERLAKUKAN*. Arms on back. Wmk: Tiger's head. Sign. of Ismail Md. Ali w/title: *GABENOR*.

#1, 2, and 6 printer: BWC.

		VG	VF	UNC
1	**1 RINGGIT** ND (1967-72). Blue on m/c unpt.			
	a. Solid security thread.	FV	3.00	10.00
	b. Broken security thread.	FV	5.00	12.00

		VG	VF	UNC
2	**5 RINGGIT** ND (1967-72). Green on m/c unpt.			
	a. Solid security thread.	FV	8.00	42.50
	b. Broken security thread.	FV	8.00	47.50

#3-5 printer: TDLR. Replacement notes: Serial # prefix *Z/.*

		VG	VF	UNC
3	**10 RINGGIT** ND (1967-72). Red-orange on m/c unpt. *(SA-PULOH).*			
	a. Solid security thread.	FV	15.00	55.00
	b. Broken security thread.	FV	15.00	60.00
4	**50 RINGGIT** ND (1967-72). Blue and greenish gray on m/c unpt. *(LIMA PULOH).*			
	a. Solid security thread.	FV	60.00	220.00
	b. Broken security thread.	FV	50.00	180.00

		VG	VF	UNC
5	**100 RINGGIT** ND (1967-72). Purple and brown on m/c unpt. unpt. *(SA-RATUS).*			
	a. Solid security thread.	FV	200.00	500.00
	b. Broken security thread.	FV	175.00	500.00

6   1000 RINGGIT
ND (1967-72). Brown-violet on m/c unpt. *(SA-RIBU)*. Printer: BWC.

	VG	VF	UNC
	450.00	1250.00	2250.00

1972; 1976 ND Issue

#7-12 new spelling *DIPERLAKUKAN*. Arms on back. Wmk: Tiger's head. Sign. of Ismail Md. Ali w/title: *GABENUR*.

#7, 8, 11 and 12 printer: BWC.

7   1 RINGGIT
ND (1972-76). Blue on m/c unpt. Like #1.

	VG	VF	UNC
	FV	2.00	6.00

8   5 RINGGIT
ND (1976). Green on m/c unpt. Like #2.

	VG	VF	UNC
a. Issued note.	FV	6.00	20.00
s. Specimen.	—	—	—

#9 and 10 printer: TDLR.

9   10 RINGGIT
ND (1972-76). Red-orange and brown on m/c unpt. *(SEPULUH)*. Like #3.

	VG	VF	UNC
a. Solid security thread.	FV	6.00	40.00
b. Broken security thread.	FV	6.00	40.00
s. Specimen.	—	—	—

10   50 RINGGIT
ND (1972-76). Blue and greenish gray on m/c unpt. *(LIMA PULUH)*. Like #4.

	VG	VF	UNC
a. Solid security thread.	FV	80.00	200.00
b. Broken security thread.	FV	80.00	210.00

11   100 RINGGIT
ND (1972-76). Purple and brown on m/c unpt. *(SERATUS)*. Like #5.

	VG	VF	UNC
	FV	140.00	350.00

12   1000 RINGGIT
ND (1972-76). Brown-violet on m/c unpt. *(SERIBU)*. Like #6.

	VG	VF	UNC
	500.00	800.00	2250.00

1976; 1981 ND Issues

#13-18 arms on back. Wmk: Tiger's head.

#13-16 different guilloche w/latent image numeral at lower l.

#13-15 printer: BWC.

13   1 RINGGIT
ND (1976-81). Blue on m/c unpt. Like #7.

	VG	VF	UNC
a. Sign. Ismail Md. Ali. (1976).	FV	1.00	5.00
b. Sign. Abdul Aziz Taha. (1981).	FV	1.00	6.00
s. Specimen.	—	—	—

14   5 RINGGIT
ND (1976-81). Green on m/c unpt. Like #8.

	VG	VF	UNC
a. Sign. Ismail Md. Ali. (1976).	FV	5.00	20.00
b. Sign. Abdul Aziz Taha. (1981).	FV	5.00	18.00
s. Specimen.	—	—	—

15   10 RINGGIT
ND (1976-81). Red-orange and brown on m/c unpt. Like #9. Sign. Ismail Md. Ali. (1976).

	VG	VF	UNC
	FV	15.00	30.00

#15A, 16A and 17b replacement notes: Serial # prefix *X/*.

15A   10 RINGGIT
ND (1976-81). Like #15 but printer: TDLR. Sign. Abdul Aziz Taha.

	VG	VF	UNC
a. Issued note.	FV	15.00	30.00
s. Specimen.			

16   50 RINGGIT
ND (1976-81). Blue and greenish gray on m/c unpt. Like #10. Sign. Ismail Md. Ali. (1976). Printer: BWC.

	VG	VF	UNC
	FV	70.00	145.00

16A   50 RINGGIT
ND (1981-83). Blue and greenish gray on m/c unpt. Like #16 but printer: TDLR. Sign. Abdul Aziz Taha (1981).

	VG	VF	UNC
	FV	70.00	160.00

17   100 RINGGIT
ND (1976-81). Purple and brown on m/c unpt. Like #11. Printer: TDLR.

	VG	VF	UNC
a. Sign. Ismail Md. Ali. (1976).	FV	80.00	210.00
b. Sign. Abdul Aziz Taha. (1981).	FV	250.00	550.00

18	1000 RINGGIT	VG	VF	UNC
	ND (1976-81). Purple and green on m/c unpt. Face like #12. Parliament bldg. in Kuala Lumpur on back. Sign. Ismail Md. Ali. Printer: BWC.	—	600.00	1500.00

1981-83 ND ISSUES

#19-26 new design w/marks for the blind. Sign. of Abdul Aziz Taha. T. A. Rahman at r. and as wmk.
Replacement notes: Serial # prefixes BA; WA; UZ; ZZ.

19	1 RINGGIT	VG	VF	UNC
	ND (1982-84). Dk. blue and brown on pink and m/c unpt. National Monument Kuala Lumpurate at ctr. on back. Printer: BWC.	FV	2.00	5.00
19A	1 RINGGIT			
	ND (1981-83). Like #19 except for printer: TDLR.	FV	2.00	5.00
20	5 RINGGIT	VG	VF	UNC
	ND (1983-84). Dk. green and blue on m/c unpt. King's Palace at Kuala Lumpur on back. Printer: TDLR.	FV	8.00	20.00

21	10 RINGGIT	VG	VF	UNC
	ND (1983-84). Red and brown on m/c unpt. Railway station at Kuala Lumpur on back. Printer: TDLR.	FV	15.00	30.00

22	20 RINGGIT	VG	VF	UNC
	ND (1982-84). Deep brown and dk. blue on m/c unpt. Bank Negara Malaysia bldg. in Kuala Lumpur on back. Printer: BWC.	FV	15.00	30.00

23	50 RINGGIT	VG	VF	UNC
	ND (1983-84). Black and blue-gray on m/c unpt. National Museum at Kuala Lumpur on back. Printer: TDLR.	FV	60.00	100.00

24	100 RINGGIT	VG	VF	UNC
	ND (1983-84). Red-brown and violet on m/c unpt. National Mosque in Kuala Lumpur on back. Printer: TDLR.	FV	80.00	150.00

25	500 RINGGIT	VG	VF	UNC
	ND (1982-84). Dk. red and purple on m/c unpt. High Court bldg. in Kuala Lumpur on back. Printer: BWC.	FV	300.00	425.00

26	1000 RINGGIT	VG	VF	UNC
	ND (1983-84). Gray-green on m/c unpt. Parliament bldg. in Kuala Lumpur on back. Printer: TDLR.	450.00	675.00	1000.00

1986-95 ND ISSUES

#27-34 similar to #19-26 but no mark for the blind, white space for wmk. (both sides), and vertical serial #. Sign. Datuk Jaafar Hussein. Wmk: T. A. Rahman.

#27-31, 32, 33 and 34 printer: TDLR. Replacement notes: Serial # prefixes BA; WA; UZ or ZZ.

27	1 RINGGIT	VG	VF	UNC
	ND (1986; 1989). Dk. blue and purple on m/c unpt. Similar to #19.			
	a. Usual security thread (1986).	FV	FV	2.50
	b. Segmented foil over security thread (1989).	FV	FV	2.50

31	50 RINGGIT	VG	VF	UNC
	ND (1987). Blue and black on m/c unpt. Segmented foil over security thread. Sign. Jafar Hussein. Similar to #23.	FV	FV	40.00
31A	50 RINGGIT			
	ND (1991-92). Like #31, but printer: BABN. Sign. Jafar Hussein.	FV	FV	50.00
31B	50 RINGGIT			
	ND (1995). Like #31, but printer: F-CO. Sign. Ahmad M. Don.	FV	FV	40.00
31C	50 RINGGIT			
	ND (1995). Like #31, but printer: TDLR. Sign. Ahmad M. Don.	FV	FV	40.00
31D	50 RINGGIT			
	ND (1997). Like #31 but printer: BABN. Sign. Ahmad M. Don.	FV	FV	40.00

28	5 RINGGIT	VG	VF	UNC
	ND (1986-91). Dk. green and green on m/c unpt. Similar to #20.			
	a. Usual security thread (1986).	FV	FV	9.00
	b. Segmented foil over security thread (1989).	FV	FV	7.00
	c. Flagpole w/o crossbar at top of back (1991).	FV	FV	5.00

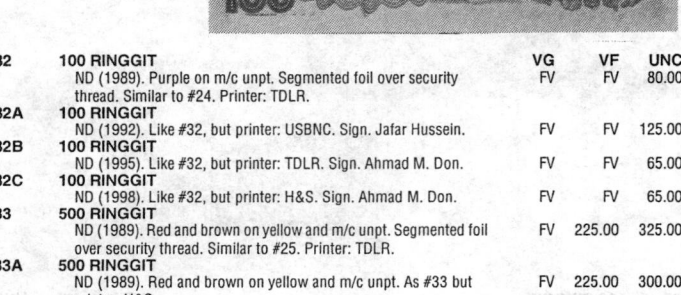

29	10 RINGGIT	VG	VF	UNC
	ND (1989). Red-orange and brown on m/c unpt. Segmented foil over security thread. Similar to #21.	FV	FV	12.50
29A	10 RINGGIT			
	ND (1989). Brown, red-orange and violet on m/c unpt. Like #29 but printer: BABN.	FV	FV	10.00

32	100 RINGGIT	VG	VF	UNC
	ND (1989). Purple on m/c unpt. Segmented foil over security thread. Similar to #24. Printer: TDLR.	FV	FV	80.00
32A	100 RINGGIT			
	ND (1992). Like #32, but printer: USBNC. Sign. Jafar Hussein.	FV	FV	125.00
32B	100 RINGGIT			
	ND (1995). Like #32, but printer: TDLR. Sign. Ahmad M. Don.	FV	FV	65.00
32C	100 RINGGIT			
	ND (1998). Like #32, but printer: H&S. Sign. Ahmad M. Don.	FV	FV	65.00
33	500 RINGGIT			
	ND (1989). Red and brown on yellow and m/c unpt. Segmented foil over security thread. Similar to #25. Printer: TDLR.	FV	225.00	325.00
33A	500 RINGGIT			
	ND (1989). Red and brown on yellow and m/c unpt. As #33 but printer: H&S.	FV	225.00	300.00

30	20 RINGGIT	VG	VF	UNC
	ND (1989). Deep brown and olive on m/c unpt. Similar to #22.	FV	FV	15.00

34	1000 RINGGIT	VG	VF	UNC
	ND (1987). Blue, green and purple on m/c unpt. Segmented foil over security thread. Printer: TDLR. Similar to #26. Sign. Jafar Hussein.	FV	500.00	650.00
34A	1000 RINGGIT			
	ND (1995). Blue, green and purple on m/c unpt. As #34 but printer: G&D. Sign. Ahmad M. Don.	FV	425.00	550.00

1995 ND ISSUES

#35-38 sign. Ahmed Mohd. Don. Wmk: T.A. Rahman.

		VG	VF	UNC
35	**5 RINGGIT** ND (1995). Dk. blue on m/c unpt. Like #28. Printer: TDLR.	FV	FV	3.50
35A	**5 RINGGIT** ND (1998). Dk. green. Like #35. Segmented security thread. Printer: CBN.	FV	FV	3.50

		VG	VF	UNC
36	**10 RINGGIT** ND (1995). Dk. brown, red-orange and violet on m/c unpt. Like #29. Printer: F-CO.	FV	FV	6.50

		VG	VF	UNC
37	**10 RINGGIT** ND (1995). Dk. brown, red-orange and violet on m/c unpt. Like #29. Printer: BABN.	FV	FV	10.00

		VG	VF	UNC
38	**10 RINGGIT** ND (1995). Dk. brown, red-orange and violet on m/c unpt. Like #29. Printer: G&D.	FV	FV	6.50

1996-2000 ND ISSUE

#39-44 T. A. Rahman at r. and as wmk. Ascending size serial #. 3 sign. varieties.

		VG	VF	UNC
39	**1 RINGGIT** ND (2000). Blue and m/c. Flora and mountain landscape w/lake on back.	FV	FV	0.75

		VG	VF	UNC
40	**2 RINGGIT** ND (1996-99). Purple and red-violet on m/c unpt. Modern tower at l., communications satellite at upper ctr. on back. Printer: NBM (w/o imprint). a. Sign. Ahmad M. Don vertical at l. b. Sign. Ali Abu Hassan vertical at left. c. Sign. Ali Abu Hassan horizontal at lower ctr.	 FV FV FV	 FV FV FV	 1.50 1.50 1.50

		VG	VF	UNC
41	**5 RINGGIT** ND (1999; 2001). Green on m/c unpt. Modern bldgs. on back. Printer: CBNC. a. ND (1999). Sign. Ali Abu Hassan. b. ND (2001). Sign. Zeti Akhtar Aziz.	 FV FV	 FV FV	 2.00 2.00

42	10 RINGGIT	VG	VF	UNC
	ND (1997-). Red on m/c unpt. Modern passenger train at l., passenger jet airplane, freighter ship at ctr. on back.			
	a. ND (1997). Sign. Ahmad M. Don vertical at l.	FV	FV	5.00
	b. ND (1999). Sign. Ali Abu Hassan vertical at l.	FV	FV	5.00
	c. ND (1999). Sign. Ali Abu Hassan at ctr.	FV	FV	5.00
	d. ND (2001). Sign. Zeti Akhtar Aziz.	FV	FV	5.00

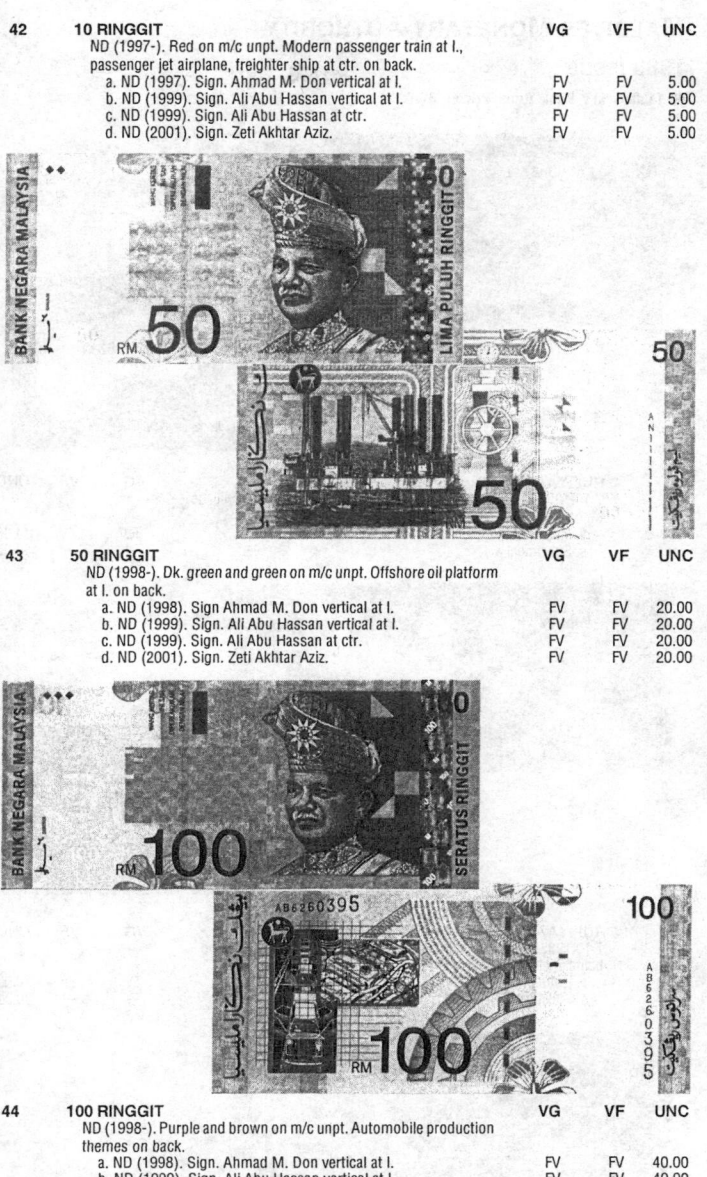

43	50 RINGGIT	VG	VF	UNC
	ND (1998-). Dk. green and green on m/c unpt. Offshore oil platform at l. on back.			
	a. ND (1998). Sign Ahmad M. Don vertical at l.	FV	FV	20.00
	b. ND (1999). Sign. Ali Abu Hassan vertical at l.	FV	FV	20.00
	c. ND (1999). Sign. Ali Abu Hassan at ctr.	FV	FV	20.00
	d. ND (2001). Sign. Zeti Akhtar Aziz.	FV	FV	20.00

44	100 RINGGIT	VG	VF	UNC
	ND (1998-). Purple and brown on m/c unpt. Automobile production themes on back.			
	a. ND (1998). Sign. Ahmad M. Don vertical at l.	FV	FV	40.00
	b. ND (1999). Sign. Ali Abu Hassan vertical at l.	FV	FV	40.00
	c. ND (1999). Sign. Ali Abu Hassasn at ctr.	FV	FV	40.00
	d. ND (2001). Sign. Zeti Akhtar Aziz.	FV	FV	40.00

1998 COMMEMORATIVE ISSUE

#45, XVI Commonwealth Games, Kuala Lumpur, 1998. Polymer plastic.

45	50 RINGGIT	VG	VF	UNC
	(19)98. Black and purple on m/c unpt. T. A. Rahman at r., Petronas Towers at ctr., multimedia corridor in unpt. at r. Utama Bukit Jalil Stadium at ctr., games logo at l. on back. Serial # prefix: KL/98.	FV	FV	40.00

2004 ND FIRST ISSUE

46	10 RINGGIT	VG	VF	UNC
	ND (2004). Red and orange on m/c unpt. Wide holographic strip at r.	FV	FV	20.00

2004 ND POLYMER ISSUE

47	5 RINGGIT	VG	VF	UNC
	ND (2004). Green. Polymer plastic.	FV	FV	2.00
48	10 RINGGIT			
	ND (2004).	FV	FV	20.00

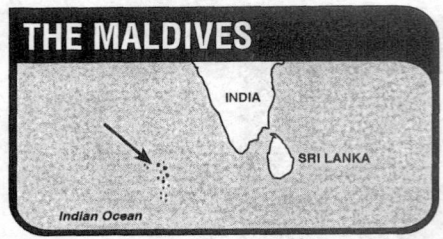

THE MALDIVES

The Republic of Maldives, an archipelago of about 2,000 coral islets in the northern Indian Ocean 417 miles (671 km.) southwest of Ceylon, has an area of 115 sq. mi. (298 sq. km.) and a population of 302,000. Capital: Malé. Fishing employs 95 percent of the work force. Dried fish, copra and coir yarn are exported.

The Maldive Islands were visited by Arab traders and converted to Islam in 1153. After being harassed in the 16th and 17th centuries by Mopla pirates of the Malabar coast and Portuguese raiders, the Maldivians voluntarily placed themselves under the suzerainty of Ceylon. In 1887, the islands became an internally self-governing British protectorate and a nominal dependency of Ceylon. Traditionally a sultanate, the Maldives became a republic in 1953 but restored the sultanate in 1954. The Sultanate of the Maldive Islands attained complete internal and external autonomy within the Commonwealth on July 26, 1965, and on Nov. 11, 1968 again became a republic.

RULERS:
British to 1965

MONETARY SYSTEM:
1 Rufiyaa (Rupee) = 100 Lari

MALDIVIAN STATE, GOVERNMENT TREASURER

1951; 1960; 1980 ISSUE

6	50 RUPEES	VG	VF	UNC
	1951-80. Blue on m/c unpt. Royal Embarkation Gate at Male at ctr. on back			
	a. 1951/AH1371.	35.00	150.00	400.00
	b. 4.6.1960/AH1379.	4.00	20.00	60.00
	c. Litho. 1.8.1980/AH17.7.1400.	5.00	25.00	85.00
	s. As c. Specimen.	—	—	175.00

7	100 RUPEES	VG	VF	UNC
	1951; 1960. Green on m/c unpt. Back brown, violet and m/c; park and bldg. complex at ctr.			
	a. 1951/AH1371.	45.00	175.00	500.00
	b. 4.6.1960/AH1379.	7.50	30.00	100.00

#8 not assigned.

MALDIVES MONETARY AUTHORITY

1983 ISSUE

#9-14 dhow at r. Wmk: Arms. Printer: BWC.

9	2 RUFIYAA	VG	VF	UNC
	7.10.1983/AH1404. Dk. olive-green on m/c unpt. Shoreline village on back.			
	a. Issued note.	FV	FV	4.00
	s. Specimen.	—	—	30.00

10	5 RUFIYAA	VG	VF	UNC
	7.10.1983/AH1404. Deep purple on green and m/c unpt. Fishing boats at ctr. on back.			
	a. Issued note.	FV	FV	4.00
	s. Specimen.	—	—	30.00

11	10 RUFIYAA	VG	VF	UNC
	7.10.1983/AH1404. Brown on green and m/c unpt. Villagers working at ctr. on back.			
	a. Issued note.	FV	FV	4.00
	s. Specimen.	—	—	30.00

12	20 RUFIYAA	VG	VF	UNC
	1983; 1987. Red-violet on m/c unpt. Fishing boats at dockside in Malé Harbour on back.			
	a. 7.10.1983/AH1404. Imprint at bottom ctr. on back.	FV	FV	7.00
	b. 25.8.1987/AH1408. W/o imprint at bottom ctr. on back.	FV	FV	5.50
	s. Specimen. As a.	—	—	30.00

13	50 RUFIYAA	VG	VF	UNC
	1983; 1987. Blue-violet on m/c unpt. Village market in Malé at ctr. on back.			
	a. 7.10.1983/AH1404. Imprint at bottom ctr. on back.	FV	FV	25.00
	b. 25.8.1987/AH1408. W/o imprint at bottom ctr. on back.	FV	FV	17.50
	s. Specimen.	—	—	30.00

14	100 RUFIYAA	VG	VF	UNC
	1983; 1987. Dk. green and brown on m/c unpt. Tomb of Medhuziyaaraiy at ctr. on back.			
	a. 7.10.1983/AH1404. Imprint at bottom ctr. on back.	FV	FV	35.00
	b. 25.8.1987/AH1408. W/o imprint at bottom ctr. on back.	FV	FV	27.50
	s. Specimen.	—	—	30.00

1990 ISSUE

#15-17 wmk: Arms. Printer: TDLR.

15	2 RUFIYAA	VG	VF	UNC
	26.7.1990/AH1411. Dk. olive-green on m/c unpt. Like #9, but darker dhow and trees, also slightly different unpt. colors and less clouds.	FV	FV	2.50

16	5 RUFIYAA	VG	VF	UNC
	26.7.1990/AH1411. Deep purple on m/c unpt. Like #10, but brown unpt. at ctr., also darker boats on back.	FV	FV	3.00

17	500 RUFIYAA	VG	VF	UNC
	26.7.1990/AH1411. Orange and green on m/c unpt. Grand Friday Mosque and Islamic Center on back.	FV	FV	120.00

1995-98 ISSUE

#18-21 w/design into borders. Ascending size serial # at l. and lower r. Wmk: Arms. Printer: TDLR.

18	5 RUFIYAA	VG	VF	UNC
	27.4.1998/AH1419; 2000/AH1421. Deep purple, dk. blue and violet on m/c unpt. Like #16.	FV	FV	2.00

19	10 RUFIYAA	VG	VF	UNC
	25.10.1998/AH1419. Dk. brown, green and orange on m/c unpt. Like #11.	FV	FV	3.00

20	20 RUFIYAA	VG	VF	UNC
	2000/AH1421. Red-violet and green on m/c unpt. Like #12.	FV	FV	5.50

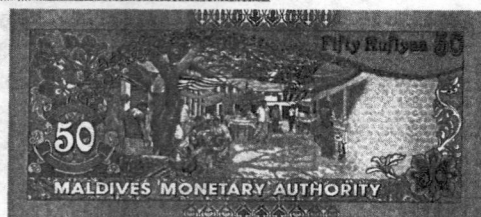

			VG	VF	UNC
21	**50 RUFIYAA**		VG	VF	UNC
	2000/AH1421. Blue-violet and lt. green on m/c unpt. Like #13.		FV	FV	12.50
22	**100 RUFIYAA**		VG	VF	UNC
	29.7.1995/AH1416; 2000/AH1421. Dk. green and brown on m/c unpt. Like #14 but lt. blue unpt. at l.		FV	FV	22.50

			VG	VF	UNC
23	**500 RUFIYAA**		VG	VF	UNC
	1.5.1996/AH1416. Orange and green on m/c unpt. Like #17 but ship and other design elements in dark color.		FV	FV	90.00

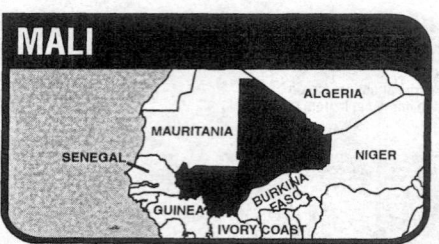

MALI

The Republic of Mali, a landlocked country in the interior of West Africa southwest of Algeria, has an area of 478,764 sq. mi. (1,240,000 sq. km.) and a population of 12.56 million. Capital: Bamako. Livestock, fish, cotton and peanuts are exported.

Malians are descendants of the ancient Malinke Kingdom of Mali that controlled the middle Niger from the 11th to the 17th centuries. The French penetrated the Sudan (now Mali) about 1880, and established their rule in 1898 after subduing fierce native resistance. In 1904 the area became the colony of Upper Senegal-Niger (changed to French Sudan in 1920), and became part of the French Union in 1946. In 1958 French Sudan became the Sudanese Republic with complete internal autonomy. Senegal joined with the Sudanese Republic in 1959 to form the Mali Federation which, in 1960, became a fully independent member of the French Community. Upon Senegal's subsequent withdrawal from the Federation, the Sudanese, on Sept. 22, 1960, proclaimed their nation the fully independent Republic of Mali and severed all ties with France.

Mali seceded from the African Financial Community in 1962, then rejoined in 1984. Issues specially marked with letter *D* for Mali were made by the Banque des Etats de l'Afrique de l'Ouest. See also French West Africa, and West African States.

MONETARY SYSTEM:
  1 Franc = 100 Centimes

	SIGNATURE VARIETIES	
1	*Ministre Des Finances*	*Gouverneur de La Banque*
2	*Ministre d'Etat* *Ministre Des Finances*	*Gouverneur de La Banque*
3	*Le Président du Council d' Administration*	*Le Directeur Général*
4	*Le Président du Council d' Administration*	*Le Directeur Général*
5	*Le Président du Council d' Administration*	*Le Directeur Général*
6	*Le Président du Council d' Administration*	*Le Directeur Général*
7	*Le Président du Council d' Administration*	*Le Directeur Général*
8	*Le Président du Council d' Administration*	*Le Directeur Général*
9	*Le Président du Council d' Administration*	*Le Directeur Général*

BANQUE DE LA RÉPUBLIQUE DU MALI
FIRST 1960 (1962) ISSUE
Note: Post-dated on Day of Independence.
#1-5 Pres. Modibo Keita at l. Sign. 1.

1	50 FRANCS	VG	VF	UNC
	22.9.1960. Purple on m/c unpt. Village on back.	10.00	35.00	125.00

6	50 FRANCS	VG	VF	UNC
	22.9.1960 (1967). Purple on blue and lt. green unpt. Dam at lower l. Back purple; woman and village.	17.50	50.00	220.00

2	100 FRANCS	VG	VF	UNC
	22.9.1960. Brown on yellow unpt. Cattle on back.	10.00	50.00	165.00
3	500 FRANCS			
	22.9.1960. Red on lt. blue and orange unpt. Woman and tent on back.	60.00	400.00	1000.00

7	100 FRANCS	VG	VF	UNC
	22.9.1960 (1967). Brown on green and lilac unpt. Tractors at lower l. Back brown; old man at r., canoes at ctr., city view behind.	15.00	50.00	215.00

4	1000 FRANCS	VG	VF	UNC
	22.9.1960. Blue on lt. green and orange unpt. Farmers w/oxen at lower r. Back blue; man and huts.	25.00	100.00	500.00
5	5000 FRANCS			
	22.9.1960. Green on m/c unpt. 2 farmers plowing w/oxen at r. Market scene and bldg. on back.	85.00	285.00	—

Second 1960 (1967) Issue

Note: Post-dated on Day of Independence.

#6-10 Modibo Keita at r. Sign 2. Printer: TDLR.

8	500 FRANCS	VG	VF	UNC
	22.9.1960 (1967). Green on yellow, blue and red unpt. Bldg. at lower l. Longhorn cattle on back.	30.00	125.00	450.00

9	1000 FRANCS	VG	VF	UNC
	22.9.1960 (1967). Blue on lilac and brown unpt. Bank at lower l. Back blue; people and Djenne mosque.	60.00	300.00	950.00

10	5000 FRANCS	VG	VF	UNC
	22.9.1960 (1967). Dk. red on green unpt. Farmers at ctr. Market scene and bldgs. on back.	65.00	225.00	700.00

BANQUE CENTRALE DU MALI
1970-73 ND ISSUES

#12-15 wmk: Man's head. Sign. varieties.

11	100 FRANCS	VG	VF	UNC
	ND (1972-73). Brown and m/c. Woman at l., hotel at r. Woman at l., boats docking at ctr. on back. Sign. 4.	6.00	25.00	100.00

12	500 FRANCS	VG	VF	UNC
	ND (1973-84). Brown and m/c. Soldier at l., tractors at r. Men and camels on back.			

12	500 FRANCS	VG	VF	UNC
	a. Sign. 4.	4.00	12.50	60.00
	b. Sign. 5.	2.50	8.00	30.00
	c. Sign. 6.	2.50	8.00	30.00
	d. Sign. 7.	2.50	8.00	30.00
	e. Sign. 8.	2.50	8.00	30.00
	f. Sign. 9.	7.50	30.00	75.00

13	1000 FRANCS	VG	VF	UNC
	ND (1970-84). Brownish black, purple and m/c. Bldg. at l., older man at r. Carvings at l., mountain village at ctr. on back.			
	a. Sign. 4.	3.50	12.50	35.00
	b. Sign. 5.	3.50	12.50	35.00
	c. Sign. 6.	3.50	10.00	30.00
	d. Sign. 7.	3.50	10.00	30.00
	e. Sign. 8.	3.50	10.00	30.00

14	5000 FRANCS	VG	VF	UNC
	ND (1972-84). Blue, brown and m/c. Cattle at lower l., man w/turban at r. Woman and flowers at l. ctr., woman at textile machinery at r. on back.			
	a. Sign. 4.	12.50	35.00	225.00
	b. Sign. 5.	12.50	30.00	200.00
	c. Sign. 6.	12.50	30.00	200.00
	d. Sign. 7.	12.50	30.00	200.00
	e. Sign. 8.	12.50	30.00	175.00

15	10,000 FRANCS	VG	VF	UNC
	ND (1970-84). M/c. Man w/fez at l., factory at lower r. Weaver at l., young woman w/coin headband at r. on back.			
	a. Sign. 3.	20.00	65.00	300.00
	b. Sign. 4.	20.00	60.00	225.00
	c. Sign. 5.	20.00	60.00	275.00
	d. Sign. 6.	25.00	75.00	225.00
	e. Sign. 7.	20.00	60.00	225.00
	f. Sign. 8.	20.00	60.00	225.00
	g. Sign. 9.	20.00	65.00	275.00

MALTA

The Republic of Malta, an independent parliamentary democracy within the British Commonwealth, is situated in the Mediterranean Sea between Sicily and North Africa. With the islands of Gozo and Comino, Malta has an area of 122 sq. mi. (316 sq. km.) and a population of 379,000. Capital: Valletta. With the islands of Gozo (Ghawdex), Comino, Cominetto and Filfla, Malta has no proven mineral resources, an agriculture insufficient to its needs and a small but expanding, manufacturing facility. Clothing, textile yarns and fabrics, and knitted wear are exported.

For more than 3,500 years Malta was ruled, in succession, by Phoenicians, Carthaginians, Romans, Arabs, Normans, the Knights of Malta, France and Britain. Napoleon seized Malta by treachery in 1798. The French were ousted by a Maltese insurrection assisted by Britain, and in 1814, Malta, of its own free will, became part of the British Empire. The island was awarded the George Cross for conspicuous corrage during World War II. Malta obtained full independence in September 1964, electing to remain within the Commonwealth with Elizabeth II as Head of State as Queen of Malta.

RULERS:
British to 1974

REPUBLIC

GOVERNMENT

1949 ORDINANCE; 1963 ND ISSUE

#25-27 Qn. Elizabeth II at r. Printer: BWC.

25	10 SHILLINGS	VG	VF	UNC
	L.1949 (1963). Green and blue on m/c unpt. Cross at ctr. Mgarr Harbor, Gozo on back.			
	a. Issued note.	9.00	50.00	225.00
	s. Specimen.	—	—	—

26	1 POUND	VG	VF	UNC
	L.1949 (1963). Brown and violet on m/c unpt. Cross at ctr. Industrial Estate, Marsa on back.			
	a. Issued note.	10.00	50.00	225.00
	s. Specimen.	—	—	—

27	5 POUNDS	VG	VF	UNC
	L.1949 (1961). Blue on m/c unpt. Cross at ctr. Grand Harbor on back.			
	a. Sign. D. A. Shepherd (1961).	35.00	200.00	1100.00
	b. Sign. R. Soler (1963).	40.00	225.00	1250.00
	s. As a. Specimen, punch hole cancelled.	—	—	450.00

CENTRAL BANK OF MALTA

1967 CENTRAL BANK ACT; 1968-69 ND ISSUE

#28-30 designs similar to #25-27. Printer: BWC.

28	10 SHILLINGS	VG	VF	UNC
	L.1967 (1968). Red on m/c unpt. Similar to #25.			
	a. Issued note.	4.00	15.00	80.00
	ct. Color trial. Dark olive on m/c unpt.	—	—	250.00

29	1 POUND	VG	VF	UNC
	L.1967 (1969). Olive-green on m/c unpt. Similar to #26.			
	a. Issued note.	7.50	25.00	125.00
	ct. Color trial. Blue on m/c unpt.	—	—	275.00
	s. Specimen.	—	—	100.00

30	5 POUNDS	VG	VF	UNC
	L.1967 (1968). Brown and violet on m/c unpt. Similar to #27.	20.00	50.00	200.00

BANK CENTRALI TA' MALTA

1967 CENTRAL BANK ACT; 1973 ND ISSUE

#31-33 arms at r., map at ctr. Wmk: Allegorical head of Malta. Printer: TDLR. Replacement notes: Serial # prefix X/1, Y/1 or Z/1 (by denomination).

			VG	VF	UNC
31	**1 LIRA**				
	L.1967 (1973). Green on m/c unpt. War Memorial at I. Prehistoric Temple in Tarxien at l., old capital city of Medina at ctr. on back.				
	a. Sign. J. Sammut and A. Camilleri.		1.00	7.50	35.00
	b. Sign. H. de Gabriele and J. Laspina.		1.00	7.50	35.00
	c. Sign. H. de Gabriele and A. Camilleri.		1.00	7.50	35.00
	d. Sign. J. Laspina and J. Sammut.		1.00	7.50	35.00
	e. Sign. A. Camilleri and J. Laspina.		1.00	7.50	35.00
	f. Sign. J. Sammut and H. de Gabriele.		1.00	7.50	35.00

			VG	VF	UNC
32	**5 LIRI**				
	L.1967 (1973). Blue on m/c unpt. Neptune at I. Marina at l., boats at ctr. r. on back.				
	a. Sign. H. de Gabriele and J. Laspina.		3.00	15.00	80.00
	b. Sign. H. de Gabriele and A. Camilleri.		3.00	15.00	80.00
	c. Sign. J. Laspina and J. Sammut.		3.00	15.00	80.00
	d. Sign. A. Camilleri and J. Laspina.		3.00	10.00	70.00
	e. Sign. J. Sammut and H. de Gabriele.		3.00	10.00	70.00
	f. Sign. J. Sammut and A. Camilleri.		3.00	10.00	70.00

			VG	VF	UNC
33	**10 LIRI**				
	L.1967 (1973). Brown on m/c unpt. Like #32. View of Grand Harbour and boats on back.				
	a. Sign. H. de Gabriele and A. Camilleri.		4.50	35.00	180.00
	b. Sign. J. Laspina and J. Sammut.		4.50	35.00	220.00
	c. Sign. A. Camilleri and J. Laspina.		4.50	35.00	220.00
	d. Sign. J. Sammut and H. de Gabriele.		4.50	35.00	220.00
	e. Sign. L. Spiteri w/title: DEPUTAT GOVERNATUR.		4.50	35.00	150.00

1979 ND ISSUE

Central Bank Act, 1967

#34-36 map at upper l., arms at upper r. Wmk: Allegorical head of Malta. Printer: TDLR. Replacement notes: Serial prefix X/2, Y/2 or Z/2 (by denomination).

			VG	VF	UNC
34	**1 LIRA**				
	L.1967 (1979). Brown on m/c unpt. Watch tower "Gardjola" at ctr. New University at l. ctr. on back.				
	a. W/o dot.		FV	5.00	14.00
	b. W/1 dot added for blind at upper r.		FV	5.00	12.50

			VG	VF	UNC
35	**5 LIRI**				
	L.1967 (1979). Purple and violet on m/c unpt. Statue of "Culture" at ctr. Aerial view of Marsa Industrial Estate at l. ctr. on back.				
	a. W/o 2 dots.		FV	20.00	50.00
	b. W/2 dots added for blind at upper r.		FV	17.50	42.50

			VG	VF	UNC
36	**10 LIRI**				
	L.1967 (1979). Gray and pink on m/c unpt. Statue of "Justice" at ctr. Aerial view of Malta drydocks at l. ctr. on back.				
	a. W/o 3 dots.		FV	35.00	80.00
	b. W/3 dots added for blind at upper r.		FV	35.00	90.00

1986 ND Issue

#37-40 sailing craft and map of Malta at ctr., A. Barbara at r. Wmk: Allegorical head of Malta. Printer: TDLR. Replacement notes: Serial # prefix W/2, X/2, Y/2 or Z/2 (by denomination).

		VG	VF	UNC
37	2 LIRI	FV	FV	25.00
	L.1967 (1986). Red-orange on m/c unpt. Dockside crane at l., aerial harbor view at r. on back.			

		VG	VF	UNC
38	5 LIRI	FV	FV	50.00
	L.1967 (1986). Gray-green and blue on m/c unpt. w/2 black horizontal accounting bars at lower r. Sailboats in harbor and repairing of fishing nets on back.			

		VG	VF	UNC
39	10 LIRI	FV	FV	85.00
	L.1967 (1986). Olive and dk. green on m/c unpt. w/3 dk. green horizontal accounting bars at lower r. Shipbuilding on back.			

		VG	VF	UNC
40	20 LIRA	FV	FV	165.00
	L.1967 (1986). Brown and red-brown on m/c unpt. w/4 brown horizontal accounting bars at lower r. Statue and govt. bldg. at ctr. on back.			

1989 ND Issue

#41-44 doves at l., Malta standing w/rudder at ctr. r. Wmk: Turreted head of Malta. Printer: TDLR. Replacement notes: Serial # prefix W/2, X/2, Y/2 or Z/2 (by denomination).

		VG	VF	UNC
41	2 LIRI	FV	FV	22.50
	L.1967 (1989). Purple on m/c unpt. Bldgs. in Malta and Gozo on back.			
42	5 LIRI	FV	FV	40.00
	L.1967 (1989). Blue on m/c unpt. Historical tower on back.			
43	10 LIRI	FV	FV	70.00
	L.1967 (1989). Green on m/c unpt. Wounded people being brought into National Assembly on back.			
44	20 LIRA	FV	FV	140.00
	L.1967 (1989). Brown on m/c unpt. Prime Minister Dr. G. B. Olivier on back.			

1994 ND Issue

#45-48 like #41-44 but w/enhanced colors, segmented foil over security threads and ascending size serial # at upper l.

		VG	VF	UNC
45	2 LIRI			
	L.1967 (1994). Purple on m/c unpt. Like #41.			
	a. Sign. Anthony P. Galdes.	FV	FV	15.00
	b. Sign. Francis J. Vasallo.	FV	FV	14.00
	c. Sign. Emanuel Ellul.	FV	FV	12.50
46	5 LIRI			
	L.1967 (1994). Blue on m/c unpt. Like #42.			
	a. Sign. Anthony P. Galdes.	FV	FV	35.00
	b. Sign. Francis J. Vassallo.	FV	FV	32.50
	c. Sign. Emanuel Ellul.	FV	FV	30.00

		VG	VF	UNC
47	10 LIRI			
	L.1967 (1994). Green on m/c unpt. Like #43.			
	a. Sign. Anthony P. Galdes.	FV	FV	65.00
	b. Sign. Emanuel Ellul.	FV	FV	60.00
	c. Sign. Michael P. Bonello.	FV	FV	60.00

		VG	VF	UNC
48	20 LIRA	FV	FV	120.00
	L.1967 (1994). Brown on m/c unpt. Sign. Anthony P. Galdes. Like #44.			

2000 ISSUE

#49-51 Millennium Commemorative issue.

#49-51 like #45-47 but w/map and clock hologram on wmk. area.

			VG	VF	UNC
49	2 LIRI		FV	FV	
	2000. (L. 1967.) Purple on m/c unpt. Like #45.				15.00

			VG	VF	UNC
50	5 LIRI		FV	FV	
	2000. (L.1967.) Blue on m/c unpt. Like #46.				30.00

			VG	VF	UNC
51	10 LIRI		FV	FV	
	2000. (L. 1967.) Green on m/c unpt. Like #47.				50.00

COLLECTOR SERIES

BANK CENTRALI TA' MALTA

1979 ISSUE

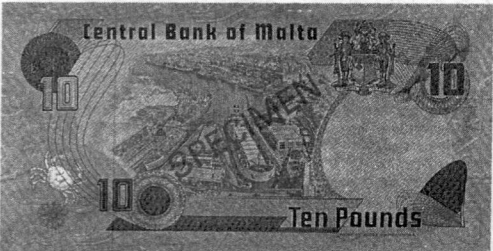

		Issue Price	Mkt.	Value
CS1	ND (1979) 1-10 LIRI	14.00		50.00
	#34a-36a w/ovpt: SPECIMEN and Maltese cross prefix serial #.			

2000 ISSUE

		Issue Price	Mkt.	Value
CS2	ND (2000) 2-5-10 LIRI	—		100.00
	#49-51 in individual folders titled: Special Millennium Issue. Hologram on wmk. area: 1999 Towards a New Millennium 2000. 25,000 sets issued.			

MAURITANIA

The Islamic Republic of Mauritania, located in northwest Africa bounded by Spanish Sahara, Mali, Algeria, Senegal and the Atlantic Ocean, has an area of 397,955 sq. mi. (1,030,700 sq. km.) and a population of 2.58 million. Capital: Nouakchott. The economy centers on herding, agriculture, fishing and mining. Iron ore, copper concentrates and fish products are exported.

The indigenous Negroid inhabitants were driven out of Mauritania by Berber invaders of the Islamic faith in the 11th century. The Berbers in turn were conquered by Arab invaders, the Beni Hassan, in the 16th century. Arab traders carried on a gainful trade in gum arabic, gold and slaves with Portuguese, Dutch, English and French traders until late in the 19th century when France took control of the area, and in 1920 made it a part of French West Africa. Mauritania became a part of the French Union in 1946 and was made an autonomous republic within the new French Community in 1958, when the Islamic Republic of Mauritania was proclaimed. The republic became independent on November 28, 1960, and withdrew from the French Community in 1966.

On June 28, 1973, in a move designed to emphasize its non-alignment with France, Mauritania converted its currency from the old French-supported CFA franc unit to a new unit called the Ouguiya.

MONETARY SYSTEM:
1 Ouguiya = 5 Khoum
100 Ouguiya = 500 CFA Francs, 1973-

Note: Issues specially marked with letter *E* for Mauritania were issued by the Banque Centrale des Etats de l'Afrique de l'Ouest. These issues were used before Mauritania seceded from the French Community of the West African States in 1973. For those listings see West African States.

REPUBLIC

BANQUE CENTRALE DE MAURITANIE

1973 ISSUE

#1-3 printed in Algeria.

			VG	VF	UNC
1	100 OUGUIYA				
	20.6.1973. Blue on m/c unpt. Mauritanian girl at ctr. Men loading boat on back.				
	a. Issued note.		10.00	20.00	65.00
	s. Specimen.		—		25.00

			VG	VF	UNC
2	200 OUGUIYA				
	20.6.1973. Brown on m/c unpt. Bedouin woman at l., tents in background. Camels and huts on back.				
	a. Issued note.		12.50	25.00	75.00
	s. Specimen.		—	—	27.50

3   **1000 OUGUIYA**

	VG	VF	UNC
20.6.1973. Green and m/c. Woman weaving on loom at l., metal worker at r. ctr. Local musicians and scenes on back.			
a. Issued note.	15.00	35.00	140.00
s. Specimen.	—	—	50.00

1974; 1979 ISSUE

#4-7 wmk: Old man w/beard. Sign. varieties. Printer: G&D (w/o imprint).

4   **100 OUGUIYA**

	VG	VF	UNC
1974-. Purple, violet and brown on m/c unpt. Musical instruments at l., cow and tower at r. on back.			
a. 28.11.1974. Narrow black security thread.	3.00	10.00	25.00
b. 28.11.1983.	6.00	15.00	35.00
c. 28.11.1985.	2.00	7.50	15.00
d. 28.11.1989. Wide green security thread.	1.50	5.00	12.50
e. 28.11.1992.	FV	4.00	10.00
f. 28.11.1993.	FV	3.00	9.00
g. 28.11.1995.	FV	2.50	6.00
h. 28.11.1996.	FV	2.00	5.00
i. 28.11.1999.	FV	2.00	5.00
j. 28.11.2001.	FV	2.00	5.00
k. 28.11.2002.	FV	2.00	5.00
s. As a. Specimen.	—	—	20.00

5   **200 OUGUIYA**

	VG	VF	UNC
1974-. Brown, dk. olive-green and brown-orange on m/c unpt. Bowl and rod at l., dugout canoe and palm tree at r. on back.			
a. 28.11.1974. Thin security thread.	6.00	15.00	30.00
b. 28.11.1985.	4.00	10.00	25.00
c. 28.11.1989. Thick security thread.	3.00	6.00	22.50
d. 28.11.1992.	FV	5.00	20.00
e. 28.11.1993.	FV	5.00	15.00
f. 28.11.1995.	FV	5.00	10.00
g. 28.11.1996.	FV	5.00	9.00
h. 28.11.1999.	FV	5.00	8.50
i. 28.11.2001.	FV	5.00	8.00
j. 28.11.2002.	FV	FV	8.00
s. As a. Specimen.	—	—	30.00

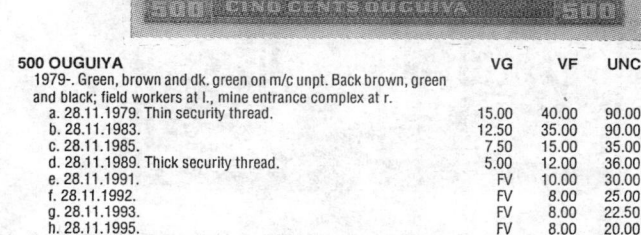

6   **500 OUGUIYA**

	VG	VF	UNC
1979-. Green, brown and dk. green on m/c unpt. Back brown, green and black; field workers at l., mine entrance complex at r.			
a. 28.11.1979. Thin security thread.	15.00	40.00	90.00
b. 28.11.1983.	12.50	35.00	90.00
c. 28.11.1985.	7.50	15.00	35.00
d. 28.11.1989. Thick security thread.	5.00	12.00	36.00
e. 28.11.1991.	FV	10.00	30.00
f. 28.11.1992.	FV	8.00	25.00
g. 28.11.1993.	FV	8.00	22.50
h. 28.11.1995.	FV	8.00	20.00
i. 28.11.1996.	FV	8.00	20.00
s. As a. Specimen.	—	—	40.00

7   **1000 OUGUIYA**

	VG	VF	UNC
1974-. Blue, violet and blue-black on m/c unpt. Bowl of fish at l., camel, hut and tower at r. back.			
a. 28.11.1974. Thin security thread.	17.50	40.00	85.00
b. 28.11.1985.	10.00	30.00	55.00
c. 28.11.1989. Thick security thread.	8.00	25.00	45.00
d. 28.10.1991.	FV	20.00	40.00
e. 28.11.1992.	FV	15.00	40.00
f. 28.11.1993.	FV	15.00	35.00
g. 28.11.1995.	FV	15.00	27.50
h. 28.11.1996.	FV	12.50	25.00
s. As a. Specimen.	—	—	60.00

1999 ISSUE

			VG	VF	UNC
11	**200 OUGUIYA** 28.11.2004. M/c.		FV	FV	5.00

			VG	VF	UNC
8	**500 OUGUIYA** 28.11.1999; 28.11.2001; 28.11.2002. Green, brown and dk. green on m/c unpt. Similar to #6 but hologram image added to r. ctr.		FV	FV	17.50

			VG	VF	UNC
12	**500 OUGUIYA** 28.11.2004. M/c.		FV	FV	10.00

			VG	VF	UNC
9	**1000 OUGUIYA** 28.11.1999; 28.11.2001; 28.11.2002. Blue on tan unpt. Similar to #7 but w/hologram value added at r. ctr.		FV	FV	22.50

2004 ISSUE

#10-14 Printer: G&D (w/o imprint)

			VG	VF	UNC
10	**100 OUGUIYA** 28.11.2004. M/c.		FV	FV	3.00

			VG	VF	UNC
13	**1000 OUGUIYA** 28.11.2004. M/c.		FV	FV	15.00
14	**2000 OUGUIYA** 28.11.2004. M/c.		FV	FV	25.00

MAURITIUS

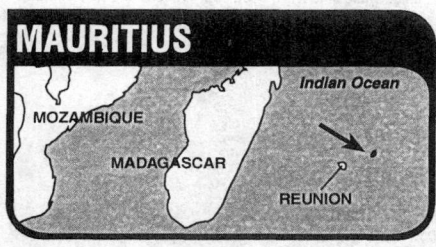

The island of Mauritius, a member of the British Commonwealth located in the Indian Ocean 500 miles (805 km.) east of Madagascar, has an area of 790 sq. mi. (2,045 sq. km.) and a population of 1.18 million. Capital: Port Louis. Sugar provides 90 percent of the export revenue.

Cartographic evidence indicates that Arabs and Malays arrived at Mauritius during the Middle Ages. Domingo Fernandez, a Portuguese navigator, visited the island in the early 16th century, but Portugal made no attempt at settlement. The Dutch took possession, and named the island, in 1598. Their colony failed to prosper and was abandoned in 1710. France claimed Mauritius in 1715 and developed a strong and prosperous colony that endured until the island was captured by the British in 1810, during the Napoleonic Wars. British possession was confirmed by the Treaty of Paris, 1814. Mauritius became independent on March 12, 1968, with Elizabeth II as Head of State as Queen of Mauritius. Mauritius became a Republic on March 12, 1992, with a President as Head of State.

RULERS:
 British

MONETARY SYSTEM:
 1 Rupee = 100 Cents, 1848-

BRITISH ADMINISTRATION

BANK OF MAURITIUS

SIGNATURE VARIETIES		
	GOVERNOR	MANAGING DIRECTOR
1	Mr. A. Beejadhur 1.7.1967-31.12.1972	Mr. D. G. H. Cook 1.7.1967-27.7.1968
2	Mr. A. Beejadhur 1.7.1967-31.12.1972	Mr. D. C. Keys 28.7.1968-27.21920
3	Mr. A. Beejadhur 1.7.1967-31.12.1972	Mr. G. Bunwaree 28.2.1970-31.12.1972
4	Mr. G. Bunwaree 1.1.1973-9.6.1982	Sir I. Ramphul 1.1.1973-9.6.1982
5	Sir I. Ramphul 10.6.1982-31.3.1996	Mr. R. Tacouri 10.6.1982-28.2.1997
6	Mr. D. Maraye 1.4.1996-30.11.1998	Mr. B. Gujadhur 1.3.1997-1.12.1998
7	Mr. R. Basant Roi 1.12.1998-	Mr. B. R. Gujadhur 17.12.1998-

NOTICE

Readers with unlisted dates, signature varieties, etc. are invited to submit photocopies of their notes to: Standard Catalog of World Paper Money, 700 East State St. Iola, WI 54990-0001, E-Mail: george.cuhaj@fwpubs.com.

1967 ND ISSUE

#30-33 Qn. Elizabeth II at r. Wmk: Dodo bird. Printer: TDLR. Replacement notes: Serial # prefix Z/#.

30	5 RUPEES	VG	VF	UNC
	ND (1967). Blue on m/c unpt. Sailboat on back.			
	a. Sign. 1.	1.00	5.00	35.00
	b. Sign. 3.	1.50	7.50	50.00
	c. Sign. 4.	0.75	2.50	10.00
	s. As a. Specimen.			

31	10 RUPEES	VG	VF	UNC
	ND (1967). Red on m/c unpt. Government bldg. on back.			
	a. Sign. 1.	1.50	7.50	50.00
	b. Sign. 2.	2.50	10.00	75.00
	c. Sign. 4.	0.75	3.00	12.50

32	25 RUPEES	VG	VF	UNC
	ND (1967). Green on m/c unpt. Ox cart on back.			
	a. Sign. 1.	2.50	10.00	75.00
	b. Sign. 4.	2.25	8.50	60.00

33	50 RUPEES ND (1967). Purple on m/c unpt. Ships docked at Port Louis harbor on back.	VG	VF	UNC
	a. Sign. 1.	12.50	40.00	185.00
	b. Sign. 2.	12.50	50.00	225.00
	c. Sign. 4.	5.00	20.00	85.00

1985-91 ND ISSUE

#34-41 replacement notes: Serial # prefix *Z/#*.

#34-36 outline of Mauritius map on back. Wmk: Dodo bird. Printer: TDLR. Sign. 5.

34	5 RUPEES ND (1985). Dk. brown. Arms at lower l. ctr., bldg. w/flag at r. Bank on back.	VG FV	VF FV	UNC 3.00

35	10 RUPEES ND (1985). Green on m/c unpt. Arms at lower l. ctr., bldg. w/flag at ctr. r. Bridge on back.	VG	VF	UNC
	a. Orange UV latent printing. Dk. green printing.	FV	0.75	4.00
	b. Dk. green printing. Green UV latent printing.	FV	FV	3.00

Note: the light green variety formerly listed is the result of fading.

36	20 RUPEES ND. Bluish purple, blue-green, blue and orange on m/c unpt. Lady Jugnauth at l., arms at ctr., bldg. w/flag at lower r. Satellite dishes at ctr. on back.	VG FV	VF FV	UNC 7.00

#37 and 38 arms at lower l. to lower ctr., bldg. w/flag at r. Wmk: Dodo bird. Printer: BWC (w/o imprint).

37	50 RUPEES ND (1986). Dk. blue on m/c unpt. 2 deer, butterfly and Mauritius Kestrel on back.	VG	VF	UNC
	a. Printer's name on back.	FV	2.50	15.00
	b. W/o printer's name on back.	FV	FV	10.00

38	100 RUPEES ND (1986). Red on m/c unpt. Landscape on back.	VG FV	VF FV	UNC 20.00

39	200 RUPEES ND (1985). Blue on m/c unpt. Sir Seewoodsagur Ramgoolam at l. Lg. home (Le Réduit) on back. Printer: TDLR.	VG	VF	UNC
	a. Orange UV latent printing.	FV	7.50	45.00
	b. Green UV latent printing.	FV	FV	35.00

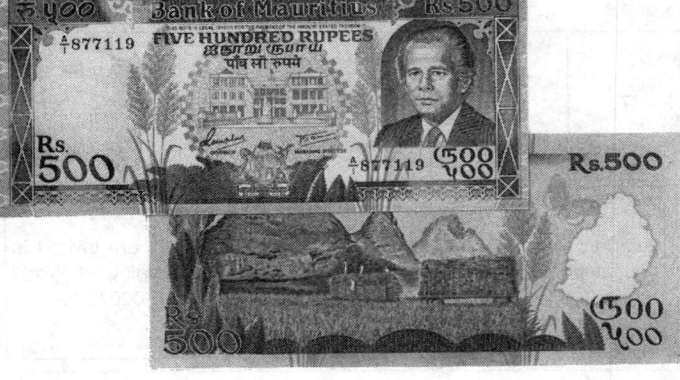

40 500 RUPEES
ND (1988). Brown and orange on m/c unpt. Bldg. w/flag at ctr., arms below, Sir A. Jugnaurh (Prime Minister) at r. Sugar cane field workers loading wagon w/mountains in background on back. Wmk: Dodo bird. Printer: TDLR (w/o imprint).

	VG	VF	UNC
a. Orange UV latent printing.	FV	20.00	100.00
b. Green UV latent printing.	FV	FV	90.00

41 1000 RUPEES
ND (1991). Blue and red on m/c unpt. Sir V. Ringadoo at l., palm trees and bldg. w/flag at ctr. Port Louis harbor on back. Wmk: Dodo bird. Printer: TDLR.

VG	VF	UNC
FV	FV	160.00

1998 ISSUE

#42-48 arms at lower l., bldg. facades at ctr., standing Justice w/scales at lower r. in unpt. Wmk: Dodo bird's head. Ascending size serial #.

#42-48 raised much public controversy being printed w/the values in English/ Sanskrit/ Tamil instead of the normal order of English/ Tamil/ Sanskrit. They have been withdrawn and replaced with #49-55.

42 25 RUPEES
1998. Black, violet and brown on m/c unpt. Sir M. J. Ah-chuen at l. Bldg. facade at ctr., worker at r. on back.

VG	VF	UNC
FV	FV	6.00

43 50 RUPEES
1998. Black, purple and deep blue on m/c unpt. J. M. Paturau at l. Bldg. complex at ctr. r. on back.

VG	VF	UNC
FV	FV	10.00

44 100 RUPEES
1998. Black, blue and deep blue-green on m/c unpt. R. Seeneevassen at l. Bldg. at l. on back.

VG	VF	UNC
FV	FV	17.50

45 200 RUPEES
1998. Black, deep green and violet on m/c unpt. Sir A. R. Mohamed at l. Market street scene at r. on back.

VG	VF	UNC
FV	FV	30.00

46 500 RUPEES
1998. Black, brown and orange on m/c unpt. S. Bissoondoyal at l. University of Mauritius at ctr. r. on back.

VG	VF	UNC
FV	FV	60.00

47 1000 RUPEES
1998. Black and blue on m/c unpt. Sir Charles G. Duval aat l. Women dancing at ctr. r. on back.

VG	VF	UNC
FV	FV	135.00

48 **2000 RUPEES**
1998. Rose, orange, black, yellow-brown on m/c unpt.
Seewoosagur Ramgoolam at I. Ox cart on back.

	VG	VF	UNC
	FV	FV	220.00

1999 ISSUE

#49-55 as 42-48 but language text correctly ordered as: English/Tamil/Sanskrit. Sign. 7.

49 **25 RUPEES**
1999; 2003. Similar to #42.

	VG	VF	UNC
	FV	FV	3.50

50 **50 RUPEES**
1999; 2001; 2003. Similar to #43.

	VG	VF	UNC
a. 1999.	FV	FV	7.50
b. 2001.	FV	FV	6.50

51 **100 RUPEES**
1999; 2001. Similar to #44.

	VG	VF	UNC
a. 1999.	FV	FV	15.00
b. 2001.	FV	FV	13.50

52 **200 RUPEES**
1999; 2001. Similar to #45.

	VG	VF	UNC
a. 1999.	FV	FV	25.00
b. 2001.	FV	FV	22.50

53 **500 RUPEES**
1999. Similar to #46.

	VG	VF	UNC
a. 1999.	FV	FV	55.00

54 **1000 RUPEES**
1999. Slate black, lt. blue and red unpt. Sir Charles Duval at I. Back
lt. blue and red. Bldg. at ctr.

	VG	VF	UNC
a. 1999.	FV	FV	100.00

55	2000 RUPEES	VG	VF	UNC
	1999. Similar to #48.	FV	FV	195.00

2001 ISSUE

56	100 RUPEES	VG	VF	UNC
	2001. Similar to #51 but iridescent strip added.	FV	FV	22.50
57	200 RUPEES			
	2001. Similar to #52 but iridescent strip added.	FV	FV	22.50
58	500 DOLLARS			
	2003.	FV	FV	45.00

59	1000 DOLLARS	VG	VF	UNC
	2003.	FV	FV	75.00
60	2000 RUPEES			
	2003.	FV	FV	195.00

COLLECTOR SERIES

BANK OF MAURITIUS

1978 ND ISSUE

CS1	ND (1978) 5-50 RUPEES	Issue Price	Mkt.	Value
	#30c, 31c, 32b, 33c w/ovpt.: *SPECIMEN* and Maltese cross prefix serial #.	14.00		80.00

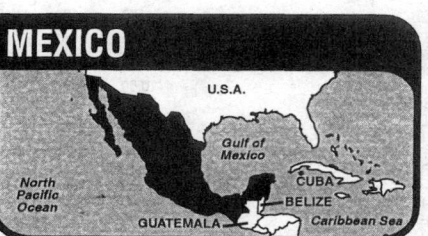

The United States of Mexico, located immediately south of the United States, has an area of 1,222,612 sq. mi. (1,967,183 sq. km.) and a population of 98.88 million. Capital: Mexico City. The economy is based on agriculture, manufacturing and mining. Cotton, sugar, coffee and shrimp are exported.

Mexico was the site of highly advanced Indian civilizations 1,500 years before conquistador Hernando Cortes conquered the wealthy Aztec empire of Montezuma, 1519-1521, and founded a Spanish colony which lasted for nearly 300 years. During the Spanish period, Mexico, then called New Spain, stretched from Guatemala to the present states of Wyoming and California, its present northern boundary having been established by the secession of Texas (1836) and the war of 1846-1848 with the United States.

Independence from Spain was declared by Father Miguel Hidalgo on Sept. 16, 1810, Mexican Independence Day, and was achieved by General Agustin de Iturbide in 1821. Iturbide became emperor in 1822 but was deposed when a republic was established a year later. For more than half a century following the birth of the republic, the political scene of Mexico was characterized by turmoil which saw two emperors (including the unfortunate Maximilian), several dictators and an average of one new government every nine months passing swiftly from obscurity to oblivion. The land, social, economic and labor reforms promulgated by the Reform Constitution of Feb. 5, 1917 established the basis for a sustained economic development and participative democracy that have made Mexico one of the most politically stable countries of modern Latin America.

MONETARY SYSTEM:
1 Peso = 100 Centavos, 1863-
1 Nuevo Peso = 1000 "old" Pesos, 1992-1996
1 Peso = 1 Nuevo Peso, 1996-

ESTADOS UNIDOS MÉXICANOS

UNITED STATES OF MEXICO

BANCO DE MÉXICO

1945-51 ISSUE

#49-53 sign. varieties. Printer: ABNC.

49	50 PESOS	VG	VF	UNC
	1948-72. Blue on m/c unpt.Like #41 but middle sign. title: *INTERVENTOR DE LA COM. NAC. BANCARIA.* Engraved dates. Back blue; Independence Monument at ctr.			
	a. 22.12.1948. Black series letters. Series: BA-BD.	3.00	6.00	15.00
	b. 23.11.1949. Series: BU-BX.	3.00	6.00	15.00
	c. 26.7.1950. Series: BY-CF.	3.00	5.00	15.00
	d. 27.12.1950. Series: CS-DH.	3.00	5.00	15.00
	e. 19.1.1953. Series: DK-DV.	2.00	4.00	15.00
	f. 10.2.1954. Series: DW-EE.	2.00	4.00	15.00
	g. 8.9.1954. Series: EF-FF.	2.00	4.00	15.00
	h. 11.1.1956. Series: FK-FV.	2.00	4.00	15.00
	i. 19.6.1957. Series: FW-GP.	2.00	4.00	15.00
	j. 20.8.1958. Series: HC-HR.	2.00	4.00	15.00
	k. 18.3.1959. 2 red series letters. Series: HS-IP.	2.00	4.00	15.00
	l. 20.5.1959. Series: IQ-JN.	2.00	4.00	15.00
	m. 25.1.1961. Series: JO-LB.	1.00	3.00	8.00
	n. 8.11.1961. Series: LC-AID.	1.00	3.00	8.00
	o. 24.4.1963. Series: AIE-BAP.	1.00	3.00	6.00
	p. 17.2.1965. Series: BAQ-BCD.	1.00	2.50	6.00
	q. 10.5.1967. Series: BCY-BEN.	1.00	2.50	6.00
	r. 19.11.1969. Series: BGK-BIC.	1.00	2.50	4.00
	s. 22.7.1970. Series: BIG-BKN.	1.00	2.50	4.00
	t. 27.6.1972. Series: BLI-BMG.	1.00	2.50	3.00
	u. 29.12.1972. Series: BMO-BRB.	1.00	2.00	3.00
	v. Specimen, punched hole cancelled.	—	—	135.00

50	100 PESOS	VG	VF	UNC
	17.1.1945. Brown on m/c unpt. Portr. M. Hidalgo at l., series letters above serial #. Middle sign. title: *INTERVENTOR DEL GOBIERNO.* Printed date. Back olive-green. Coin w/national coat-of-arms at ctr. Series: S-Z.			
	a. Issued note.	5.00	15.00	70.00
	s. Specimen, punched hole cancelled.	—	—	200.00

51 **500 PESOS**
1948-78. Black on m/c unpt. Like #43 but w/o *No.* above serial #.
Middle sign. title: *INTERVENTOR DE LA COM. NAC. BANCARIA.*
Back green; Palace of Mining at ctr.

	VG	VF	UNC
a. 22.12.1948. Series: BA.	10.00	40.00	125.00
b. 27.12.1950. Series: CS; CT.	4.00	12.00	30.00
c. 3.12.1951. Series: DI; DJ.	4.00	12.00	30.00
d. 19.1.1953. Series: DK-DN.	4.00	12.00	30.00
e. 31.8.1955. Series: FG-FJ.	4.00	12.00	30.00
f. 11.1.1956. Series: FK-FL.	4.00	12.00	30.00
g. 19.6.1957. Series: FW-GB.	4.00	12.00	30.00
h. 20.8.1958. Series: HC-HH.	4.00	12.00	30.00
i. 18.3.1959. Series: HS-HX.	4.00	12.00	30.00
j. 20.5.1959. Series: IQ-IV.	4.00	12.00	30.00
k. 25.1.1961. Series: JO-JT.	3.00	8.00	25.00
l. 8.11.1961. Series: LC-MP.	2.00	7.00	20.00
m. 17.2.1965. Series: BAQ-BCN.	4.00	12.00	25.00
n. 24.3.1971. Series: BKO-BKT.	2.50	5.00	12.50
o. 27.6.1972. Series: BLI-BLT.	2.50	5.00	12.50
p. 29.12.1972. Series: BNG-BNP.	2.50	5.00	12.50
q. 18.7.1973. Series: BUY-BWB.	1.50	5.00	10.00
r. 2.8.1974. Series: BXV-BZI.	1.50	3.50	10.00
s. 18.2.1977. Series: BZJ-CCK.	1.00	3.50	10.00
t. 18.1.1978. Series: CCL-CDY.	1.00	3.50	8.50

52 **1000 PESOS**
1948-77. Black on m/c unpt. Like #44 but middle sign. title: *IN-TERVENTOR DE LA COM. NAC. BANCARIA.* Back brown; Chichen Itza pyramid at ctr.

	VG	VF	UNC
a. 22.12.1948. Series: BA.	5.00	15.00	60.00
b. 23.11.1949. Series: BU.	5.00	15.00	60.00
c. 27.12.1950. Series: CS.	5.00	15.00	60.00
d. 3.12.1951. Series: DI; DJ.	5.00	15.00	60.00
e. 19.1.1953. Series: DK; DL.	5.00	15.00	60.00
f. 31.8.1955. Series: FG; FH.	5.00	15.00	60.00
g. 11.1.1956. Series: FK; FL.	5.00	15.00	60.00
h. 19.6.1957. Series: FW-FZ.	5.00	15.00	60.00
i. 20.8.1958. Series: HC-HE.	5.00	15.00	60.00
j. 18.3.1959. Series: HS-HU.	5.00	15.00	60.00
k. 20.5.1959. Series: IQ-IS.	5.00	15.00	60.00
l. 25.1.1961. Series: JO-JQ.	5.00	15.00	60.00
m. 8.11.1961. Series: LC-LV.	3.00	10.00	20.00
n. 17.2.1965. Series: BAQ-BCN.	2.00	8.00	15.00
o. 24.3.1971. Series: BKO-BKT.	2.00	6.00	10.00
p. 27.6.1972. Series: BLI-BLM.	2.00	6.00	10.00
q. 29.12.1972. Series: BNG-BNK.	1.00	3.00	5.00
r. 18.7.1973. Series: BUY-BWB.	2.00	6.00	10.00
s. 2.8.1974. Series: BXV-BYY.	1.00	5.00	8.00
t. 18.2.1977. Series: BZJ-CBQ.	1.00	5.00	8.00
x. Error: *EERIE HD* rather than SERIE at left.	25.00	45.00	85.00

1950; 1951 ISSUE

#53-55 sign. varieties. Printer: ABNC.

53 **10 PESOS**
1951; 1953. Black on m/c unpt. Like #47 but w/o *No.* above serial #.

	VG	VF	UNC
a. 3.12.1951. Series: DI, DJ.	0.25	2.00	5.00
b. 19.1.1953. Series: DK-DL.	0.25	2.00	5.00

1950 ISSUE

#54 and 55 sign. varieties. Printer: ABNC.

54 **20 PESOS**
1950-70. Black on m/c unpt. Like #48 but w/o *No.* above serial #.
Back olive-green; Federal Palace courtyard at ctr.

	VG	VF	UNC
a. 27.12.1950. Black series letters. Series: CS; CT.	1.00	3.00	15.00
b. 19.1.1953. Series: DK.	1.00	3.00	15.00
c. 10.2.1954. Red series letters. Series: DW.	1.00	2.00	10.00
d. 11.1.1956. Series: FK.	1.00	2.00	10.00
e. 10.6.1957. Series: FW.	1.00	2.00	10.00
f. 20.8.1958. Series: HC, HD.	1.00	2.00	10.00

54 **20 PESOS**

	VG	VF	UNC
g. 18.3.1959. Series: HS, HT.	1.00	2.00	10.00
h. 20.5.1959. Series: IQ, IR.	1.00	2.00	10.00
i. 25.1.1961. Series: JO, JP.	0.50	1.50	10.00
j. 8.11.1961. Series: LC-LG.	0.50	1.50	10.00
k. 24.4.1963. Series: AIE-AIH.	0.50	1.50	5.00
l. 17.2.1965. Series: BAQ-BAV.	0.50	1.50	5.00
m. 10.5.1967. Series: BCY-BDB.	0.50	1.50	5.00
n. 27.8.1969. Series: BGA; BGB.	0.50	1.50	5.00
o. 18.3.1970. Series: BID-BIF.	0.50	1.50	5.00
p. 22.7.1970. Series: BIG-BIK.	0.50	1.50	5.00
s. Specimen, punched hole cancelled.	—	—	135.00

55 **100 PESOS**
1950-61. Brown on m/c unpt. Like #50 but middle sign. title:
INTERVENTOR DE LA COM. NAC. BANCARIA. Engraved dates.
Back olive-green; coin w/national seal at ctr.

	VG	VF	UNC
a. 27.12.1950. Black series letters. Series: CS-CZ.	4.00	8.00	30.00
b. 19.1.1953. Series: DK-DP.	2.00	7.00	25.00
c. 10.2.1954. Series: DW-DZ.	2.00	7.00	25.00
d. 8.9.1954. Series: EI-ET.	2.00	7.00	25.00
e. 11.1.1956. Series: FK-FV.	2.00	7.00	25.00
f. 19.6.1957. Series: FW-GH.	2.00	7.00	25.00
g. 20.8.1958. Series: HC-HR.	2.00	7.00	25.00
h. 18.3.1959. Series: HS-IH.	2.00	7.00	25.00
i. 20.5.1959. Series: IQ-JF.	2.00	7.00	25.00
j. 25.1.1961. Series: JO-KL.	2.00	7.00	25.00

1954 ISSUE

58 **10 PESOS**
1954-67. Black on m/c unpt. Portr. E. Ruiz de Velazquez at r. Like
#53 but w/text: *MEXICO D.F.* above series letters. Back brown; road
to Guanajuato at ctr. Printer: ABNC.

	VG	VF	UNC
a. 10.2.1954. Series: DW, DX.	0.50	1.50	5.00
b. 8.9.1954. Series: EI-EN.	0.50	1.50	5.00
c. 19.6.1957. Series: FW, FX.	0.50	1.50	5.00
d. 24.7.1957. Series: GQ.	0.50	1.50	5.00
e. 20.8.1958. Series: HC-HF.	0.25	1.50	6.00
f. 18.3.1959. Series: HS-HU.	0.25	1.00	5.00
g. 20.5.1959. Series: IQ-IS.	0.25	1.00	4.00
h. 25.1.1961. Series: JO-JT.	0.25	1.00	4.00
i. 8.11.1961. Series: LC-LV.	0.25	1.00	4.00
j. 24.4.1963. Series: AIE-AIT.	0.25	1.00	3.00
k. 17.2.1965. Series: BAQ-BAX.	0.25	1.00	3.00
l. 10.5.1967. Series: BCY-BDA.	0.25	1.00	3.00
s. Specimen, punched hole cancelled.	—	—	150.00

1957; 1961 ISSUE

#59-61 printer: ABNC.

59 **1 PESO**
1957-70. Black on m/c unpt. Aztec calendar stone at ctr. Like #56
but w/text: *MEXICO D.F.* added above date at lower l. Back red,
Independence monument at ctr.

	VG	VF	UNC
a. 19.6.1957. Series: FW-GF.	0.10	1.00	4.50
b. Deleted.	—	—	—
c. 4.12.1957. Series: GS-HB.	0.10	1.00	4.50
d. 20.8.1958. Series: HC-HL.	0.10	0.75	2.50
e. 18.3.1959. Series: HS-IB.	0.10	0.50	2.50
f. 20.5.1959. Series: IQ-IZ.	0.10	0.50	2.50
g. 25.1.1961. Series: JO-KC.	0.10	0.25	2.00
h. 8.11.1961. Series: LC; LD.	0.10	0.50	2.00
i. 9.6.1965. Series: BCO-BCX.	0.10	0.25	2.00
j. 10.5.1967. Series: BCY-BEB.	0.10	0.25	1.00
k. 27.8.1969. Series: BGA-BGJ.	0.10	0.25	1.00
l. 22.7.1970. Series: BIG-BIP.	0.10	0.20	1.00
s. Specimen.	—	—	—

60 **5 PESOS**

1957-70. Black on m/c unpt. Portr. gypsy at ctr. Like #57 but w/Text: *MEXICO D.F.* before date. Back gray; Independence Monument at ctr.

	VG	VF	UNC
a. 19.6.1957. Series: FW, FX.	0.25	2.00	7.00
b. 24.7.1957. Series: GQ, GR.	0.25	2.00	7.00
c. 20.8.1958. Series: HC-HJ.	0.25	1.50	6.00
d. 18.3.1959. Series: HS-HV.	0.25	1.50	6.00
e. 20.5.1959. Series: IQ-IT.	0.25	1.50	6.00
f. 25.1.1961. Series: JO-JV.	0.15	0.50	4.00
g. 8.11.1961. Series: LC-MP.	0.15	0.50	3.00
h. 24.4.1963. Series: AIE-AJJ.	0.15	0.50	2.50
i. 27.8.1969. Series BGJ.	0.15	0.50	2.50
j. 19.11.1969. Series: BGK-BGT.	0.15	0.50	2.50
k. 22.7.1970. Series: BIG-BII.	0.15	0.50	2.50

61 **100 PESOS**

1961-73. Brown on m/c unpt. Like #55 but series letters below serial #.

	VG	VF	UNC
a. 8.11.1961. Red series letters. Series: LE-ZZ; AAA-AEG.	2.00	5.00	12.50
b. 24.4.1963. Series: AIK-AUG.	2.00	5.00	12.50
c. 17.2.1965. Series: BAQ-BCD.	1.00	3.00	8.00
d. 10.5.1967. Series: BCY-BFZ.	1.00	3.00	8.00
e. 22.7.1970. Series: BIO-BJK.	1.00	3.00	8.00
f. 24.3.1971. Series: BKP-BLH.	1.00	3.00	8.00
g. 27.6.1972. Series: BLI-BNF.	1.00	3.00	8.00
h. 29.12.1972. Series: BNG-BUX.	0.50	1.50	5.00
i. 18.7.1973. Series: BUY-BXU.	0.50	1.50	5.00

1969-74 ISSUE

#62-66 bank title w/*S.A.* 3 sign. and sign. varieties. Printer: BdM.

62 **5 PESOS**

1969-72. Black on m/c unpt. J. Ortiz de Dominguez at r. Yucca plant, aqueduct, village of Queretaro and national arms on back.

	VG	VF	UNC
a. 3.12.1969.	0.15	0.50	3.00
b. 27.10.1971.	0.15	0.25	2.00
c. 27.6.1972.	0.15	0.25	1.50

63 **10 PESOS**

1969-77. Dk. green on m/c unpt. Bell at l., M. Hidalgo y Castilla at r. National arms and Dolores Cathedral on back.

	VG	VF	UNC
a. 16.9.1969.	0.25	0.50	5.00
b. 3.12.1969.	0.15	0.25	1.50
c. 22.7.1970.	0.15	0.25	1.50
d. 3.2.1971.	0.15	0.25	1.25
e. 29.12.1972.	0.15	0.25	1.25

63 **10 PESOS**

	VG	VF	UNC
f. 18.7.1973.	0.10	0.20	1.25
g. 16.10.1974.	0.10	0.20	1.00
h. 15.5.1975.	0.10	0.20	0.75
i. 18.2.1977.	0.10	0.20	0.75
s. Specimen.	—	—	—

Note: #63a bears the date of Mexican Independence Day.

64 **20 PESOS**

1972-77. Red and black on m/c unpt. J. Morelos y Pavon at r. w/bldg. in background. Pyramid of Quetzalcoatl on back.

	VG	VF	UNC
a. 29.12.1972.	0.25	0.50	3.00
b. 18.7.1973.	0.10	0.30	2.25
c. 8.7.1976.	0.10	0.20	2.00
d. 8.7.1977.	0.10	0.20	1.50

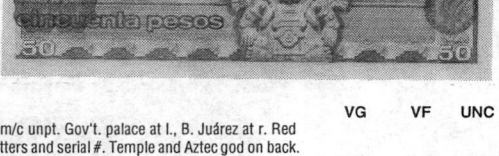

65 **50 PESOS**

1973-78. Blue on m/c unpt. Gov't. palace at l., B. Juárez at r. Red and black series letters and serial #. Temple and Aztec god on back.

	VG	VF	UNC
a. 18.7.1973.	0.30	1.00	4.00
b. 8.7.1976.	0.20	0.50	3.00
c. 5.7.1978.	0.20	0.50	3.00

66 **100 PESOS**

1974; 1978. Purple on m/c unpt. V. Carranza at l., "La Trinchera" painting at ctr. Red and black series letters and serial #. Stone figure on back.

	VG	VF	UNC
a. 30.5.1974.	0.30	1.00	3.00
b. 5.7.1978.	0.30	1.00	3.00
s. Specimen.	—	—	—

1978-80 ISSUE

#67-71 bank title w/*S.A.* W/3 sign. Printer: BdM.

	50 PESOS	VG	VF	UNC
67	1978; 1979. Blue on m/c unpt. Like #65 but only red series letters and a black serial #.			
	a. 5.7.1978.	0.30	0.75	2.00
	b. 17.5.1979.	0.20	0.40	1.50
68	100 PESOS			
	1978-79. Purple on m/c unpt. Like #66 but only red series letters and a black serial #.			
	a. 5.7.1978.	0.20	0.40	1.50
	b. 17.5.1979. Engraved. Litho back. Series before LL.	0.20	0.40	1.00
	c. 17.5.1979. Litho back. Series LS and later.	0.20	0.40	1.00

	500 PESOS	VG	VF	UNC
69	29.6.1979. Black on dk. olive-green on m/c unpt. F. I. Madero at l. and as wmk. Aztec calendar stone on back. Pink paper.	1.00	3.00	11.00

	1000 PESOS	VG	VF	UNC
70	1978-79. Dk. brown and brown on m/c unpt. J. de Asbaje at r. and as wmk. Santo Domingo plaza at l. ctr. on back. Lt. tan paper.			
	a. 5.7.1978.	2.00	4.50	20.00
	b. 17.5.1979.	1.00	4.00	12.50
	c. 29.6.1979.	1.00	3.00	10.00

	5000 PESOS	VG	VF	UNC
71	25.3.1980. Red on m/c unpt. Cadets at l. ctr., one of them as wmk. Chapultepec castle on back. Lt. blue paper.	5.00	15.00	45.00

	10,000 PESOS	VG	VF	UNC
72	18.1.1978. Purple on m/c unpt. Portr. M. Romero at l. Back green; National Palace at ctr. Printer: ABNC. Series CCL-CES.	5.00	20.00	75.00

1981 ISSUE

#73-78 bank title w/*S.A.* W/4 sign. and sign. varieties. Printer: BdM.

	50 PESOS	VG	VF	UNC
73	27.1.1981. Blue on m/c unpt. Like #67 but 4 sign.	0.10	0.25	1.00

	100 PESOS	VG	VF	UNC
74	1981-82. Purple on m/c unpt. Like #68 but 4 sign.			
	a. 27.1.1981.	0.10	0.30	1.50
	b. 3.9.1981.	0.10	0.30	1.50
	c. 25.3.1982.	0.10	0.20	0.75

	500 PESOS	VG	VF	UNC
75	1981-82. Green on m/c unpt. Like #69 but 4 sign. and narrow serial # style.			
	a. 27.1.1981.	0.25	1.25	4.50
	b. 25.3.1982.	0.25	1.25	4.50

	1000 PESOS	VG	VF	UNC
76	1981-82. Dk. brown and brown on m/c unpt. Like #70 but 4 sign. and narrow serial # style.			

76	1000 PESOS	VG	VF	UNC
	a. Engraved bldgs. on back. 27.1.1981. Black or red serial #.	0.50	2.00	10.00
	b. Litho. bldgs. on back. 27.1.1981.	0.50	2.00	10.00
	c. 3.9.1981.	0.50	2.00	9.00
	d. 25.3.1982.	0.50	1.50	7.00
77	5000 PESOS			
	1981; 1982. Red and black on m/c unpt., lt. blue paper. Like #71 but 4 sign. and narrower serial #.			
	a. 27.1.1981.	1.00	6.00	30.00
	b. 25.3.1982.	1.00	6.00	30.00

78	10,000 PESOS	VG	VF	UNC
	1981-82. Blue-black, brown and deep blue-green on m/c unpt. Power plant at ctr., Gen. Lazaro Cardenas at r. and as wmk. Back dk. green, red and blue; Coyolxauhqui stone carving at ctr. Lt. green paper.			
	a. 8.12.1981.	10.00	25.00	55.00
	b. 25.3.1982.	2.00	15.00	50.00
	c. Red and blue serial #. 30.9.1982.	2.00	15.00	50.00
	d. Green and red serial #. 30.9.1982.	2.00	15.00	50.00

1983-84 ISSUES

#79-84 *S.A.* removed from bank title. W/4 sign. Printer: BdM.

79	500 PESOS	VG	VF	UNC
	1983; 1984. Green on m/c unpt. Similar to #75 but w/silk threads and w/o wmk. Design continued over wmk. area on both sides. White paper.			
	a. 14.3.1983.	0.25	1.00	4.00
	b. 7.8.1984.	0.20	0.75	2.50

80	1000 PESOS	VG	VF	UNC
	1983; 1984. Dk. brown and brown on m/c unpt. Like #76 but *S.A.* removed from title.			
	a. 13.5.1983.	0.50	2.00	5.00
	b. 7.8.1984.	0.50	2.00	5.00
81	1000 PESOS			
	30.10.1984. Dk. brown and brown on m/c unpt. Similar to #80 but rayed quill pen printed over wmk. area at l.	0.25	0.75	3.00

82	2000 PESOS	VG	VF	UNC
	1983-84. Black, dk. green and brown on m/c unpt. J. Sierra at l. ctr., University bldg. at r. 19th century courtyard on back.			
	a. 26.7.1983.	1.00	3.00	10.00
	b. 7.8.1984.	0.75	1.25	5.00
	c. 30.10.1984.	0.75	1.25	5.00

83	5000 PESOS	VG	VF	UNC
	1983. Red and black on m/c unpt. Like #77 but *S.A.* removed from title.			
	a. 13.5.1983.	1.25	3.50	12.50
	b. 26.7.1983.	1.00	3.00	9.00
	c. 5.12.1983.	1.00	3.00	9.50
84	10,000 PESOS			
	1983. Blue-black, brown and deep blue-green on m/c unpt. Similar to #78 but *S.A.* removed from bank title.			
	a. 13.5.1983.	2.00	4.50	15.00
	b. Red and dk. blue serial #. 26.7.1983.	2.00	4.50	15.00
	c. Green and blue serial #. 26.7.1983.	2.00	4.50	15.00
	d. Purple and blue serial #. 26.7.1983.	2.00	4.50	17.50
	e. 5.12.1983.	2.00	5.00	20.00

1985 ISSUES

#85-94 w/3 sign. *S.A.* removed from bank title. Printer: BdM.

85	1000 PESOS	VG	VF	UNC
	19.7.1985. Dk. brown and brown on m/c unpt. Like #81 but only 3 sign.	0.35	0.75	2.50

86   2000 PESOS

	VG	VF	UNC
1985-89. Black, dk. green and brown on m/c unpt. Like #82 but only 3 sign.			
a. W/*SANTANA* at lower l. 2 date positions. 19.7.1985.	0.60	1.25	4.00
b. As a. 24.2.1987.	0.60	1.25	3.00
c. W/o *SANTANA*. 28.3.1989.	0.60	1.00	2.25

87   5000 PESOS

	VG	VF	UNC
19.7.1985. Red on m/c unpt. Blue tint paper. Like #83 but only 3 sign.	1.75	2.25	7.50

88   5000 PESOS

	VG	VF	UNC
1985-89. Purple and brown-orange on m/c unpt. Similar to #87 but design continued over wmk. area. W/o wmk. Lt. tan paper.			
a. W/*SANTANA* vertically at lower l. 19.7.1985.	0.60	2.00	6.00
b. As a. 24.2.1987.	0.60	1.75	5.00
c. W/o *SANTANA*. 28.3.1989.	0.50	1.50	3.00

89   10,000 PESOS

	VG	VF	UNC
1985; 1987. Blue-black, brown and deep blue-green on m/c unpt. Like #84 but only 3 sign.			
a. Purple and blue serial #. 19.7.1985.	2.00	5.00	12.50
b. Green and blue serial #. 19.7.1985.	2.00	5.00	12.50
c. Red and blue serial #. 24.2.1987.	2.00	5.00	12.50
d. Green and blue serial #. 24.7.1987.	2.00	5.00	12.50

90   10,000 PESOS

	VG	VF	UNC
1987-91. Deep blue-black on brown and blue-green unpt. Similar to #89 but wmk. area filled in. Lt. tan paper.			
a. W/*SANTANA*. at lower l. under refinery design. 24.2.1987.	1.50	3.00	10.00
b. W/o *SANTANA*. 1.2.1988.	1.50	2.50	7.00
c. 28.3.1989.	1.50	2.50	6.00
d. 16.5.1991.	1.25	2.00	6.00

91   20,000 PESOS

	VG	VF	UNC
1985-87. Deep blue on blue and m/c unpt. Fortress above coastal cliffs at ctr. Don A. Quintana Roo at r. and as wmk. Artwork on back.			
a. 19.7.1985.	4.00	7.00	22.50
b. 24.2.1987.	3.50	6.50	17.50
c. 27.8.1987.	3.50	6.50	17.50

92   20,000 PESOS

	VG	VF	UNC
1988; 1989. Blue-black on blue and pink unpt. Similar to #91 but design continued over wmk. area.			
a. 1.2.1988.	3.50	5.00	15.00
b. 28.3.1989.	3.50	5.00	12.50

93   50,000 PESOS

	VG	VF	UNC
1986-90. Purple on m/c unpt. Aztec symbols at ctr., Cuauhtémoc at r. and as wmk. Aztec and Spaniard fighting at l. ctr. on back. Pink paper.			
a. 12.5.1986; 24.2.1987; 27.8.1987; 1.2.1988.	7.50	17.50	60.00
b. 28.3.1989; 10.1.1990; 20.12.1990.	6.50	15.00	45.00

94 **100,000 PESOS**
1988; 1991. Blue-black and maroon on m/c unpt. P. E. Calles at l. and as wmk, Banco de Mexico at ctr. Desert Mule Deer, cactus, lake and mountain at ctr. r. on back.

	VG	VF	UNC
a. 4.1.1988.	12.50	27.50	85.00
b. 2.9.1991.	12.50	27.50	85.00

1992 FIRST ISSUE

Nuevos Pesos System

1000 "old" Pesos = 1 Nuevo Peso

#95-98 similar to #90-94. 3 sign. and sign. varieties. Printer: BdM.

95 **10 NUEVOS PESOS** — VG FV · VF FV · UNC 7.50
31.7.1992. Blue-black, brown and deep blue-green on m/c unpt. Similar to #90. Series A-Y.

96 **20 NUEVOS PESOS** — VG FV · VF FV · UNC 12.50
31.7.1992. Deep blue on blue and m/c unpt. Similar to #92. Series A-Q.

97 **50 NUEVOS PESOS** — VG FV · VF FV · UNC 27.50
31.7.1992. Purple on m/c unpt. Similar to #93. Series A-P.

98 **100 NUEVOS PESOS** — VG FV · VF FV · UNC 40.00
31.7.1992. Blue-black and maroon on m/c unpt. Similar to #94. Series A-Q.

1992 (1994) SECOND ISSUE

#99-104 printer: BdM.

99 **10 NUEVOS PESOS** — VG FV · VF FV · UNC 4.00
10.12.1992 (1994). Deep blue-green and gold on m/c unpt. E. Zapata at r., hands holding corn at ctr. Machinery at lower l., statue of Zapata on horseback near peasant at ctr. r., bldg. in background. Series A-T.

100 **20 NUEVOS PESOS** — VG FV · VF FV · UNC 6.50
10.12.1992 (1994). Purple and dk. blue on m/c unpt. B. Juárez at r., eagle on cactus w/snake (arms) at ctr. Monument, statues "Hemiciclo a Juárez" on back. Series A-T.

101 **50 NUEVOS PESOS** — VG FV · VF FV · UNC 15.00
10.12.1992 (1994). Red-violet and black on m/c unpt. J. M. Morelos at r., crossed cannons on outlined bow and arrow below his flag at l. ctr. Butterflies at l., boat fishermen at ctr. on back. Series A-AF.

102	100 NUEVOS PESOS	VG	VF	UNC
	10.12.1992 (1994). Red and brown on m/c unpt. Nezahualcóyotl at r. and as wmk., Aztec figure at ctr. Xochipilli statue on back. Series A-V.	FV	FV	25.00

103	200 NUEVOS PESOS	VG	VF	UNC
	10.12.1992 (1994). Dk. olive-green, dk. brown and olive-brown on m/c unpt. J. de Asbaje at r. and as wmk., open book and quill pen at ctr. Temple de San Jerónimo on back. Series A-E.	FV	FV	45.00

104	500 NUEVOS PESOS	VG	VF	UNC
	10.12.1992 (1994). Red-brown, deep purple and dk. brown-violet on m/c unpt. I. Zaragoza at ctr. r. and as wmk., Battle of Puebla at l. ctr. Cathedral at Puebla at ctr. on back. Series A-C.	FV	FV	110.00

1994; 1995 (1996) ISSUE

#105-116 similar to #99-104 but *EL* omitted from bank title, *NUEVOS* and *PAGARÁ A LA VISTA AL PORTA-DOR* are omitted. 2 sign. Printer: BdM.

105	10 PESOS	VG	VF	UNC
	1994 (1996); 1996. Deep blue-green and gold on m/c unpt. Similar to #99. Series A-.			
	a. 6.5.1994.	FV	FV	3.00
	b. 10.5.1996.	FV	FV	3.00

106	20 PESOS	VG	VF	UNC
	1994 (1996); 1996. Purple and dk. blue on m/c unpt. Similar to #100. Series A-.			
	a. 6.5.1994.	FV	FV	6.00
	b. 10.5.1996.	FV	FV	5.50
	c. 3.17.1998.	FV	FV	5.50
	d. 23.4.1999.	FV	FV	5.50

107	50 PESOS	VG	VF	UNC
	1994-98 (1996). Red-violet and black on m/c unpt. Similar to #101. Series A-.			
	a. 6.5.1994.	FV	FV	15.00
	b. 10.5.1996.	FV	FV	10.00
	c. 17.3.1998.	FV	FV	10.00
	d. 23.4.1999.	FV	FV	10.00

108	100 PESOS	VG	VF	UNC
	1994 (1996); 1996. Red and brown-orange on m/c unpt. Similar to #102. Series A-.			
	a. 6.5.1994.	FV	FV	22.50
	b. 10.5.1996.	FV	FV	22.50
	c. 23.4.1999.	FV	FV	22.50

		VG	VF	UNC
109	**200 PESOS**			
	1995-98 (1996). Dk. olive-green, dk. brown and olive-brown on m/c unpt. Similar to #103. Series A-.	FV	FV	45.00
	a. 7.2.1995.	FV	FV	37.50
	b. 10.5.1996.	FV	FV	37.50
	c. 17.3.1998.	FV	FV	37.50
	d. 23.4.1999.	FV	FV	37.50

		VG	VF	UNC
110	**500 PESOS**			
	1995 (1996); 1996. Red-brown, deep purple and dk. brown-violet on m/c unpt. Similar to #104. Series A-.			
	a. 7.2.1995.	FV	FV	95.00
	b. 10.5.1996.	FV	FV	95.00
	c. 17.3.1998.	FV	FV	95.00
	d. 23.4.1999.	FV	FV	95.00

2000 COMMEMORATIVE ISSUE

#111-115, 75th Anniversary Banco de Mexico. Commemorative text immediately below bank name.

		VG	VF	UNC
111	**20 PESOS**			
	25.8.2000. Purple and dk. blue on m/c unpt. Like #106.	FV	3.50	9.50

		VG	VF	UNC
112	**50 PESOS**			
	25.8.2000. Red-violet and black on m/c unpt. Like #107.	FV	9.00	17.50

		VG	VF	UNC
113	**100 PESOS**			
	25.8.2000. Red and brown-orange on m/c unpt. Like #108.	FV	15.00	35.00

		VG	VF	UNC
114	**200 PESOS**			
	25.8.2000. Dk. olive-green, dk. brown and olive-brown on m/c unpt. Like #109.	FV	30.00	70.00

		VG	VF	UNC
115	**500 PESOS**			
	25.8.2000. Red-brown, deep purple and dk. brown-violet on m/c unpt. Like #110.	FV	65.00	150.00

2000-01 ISSUE

		VG	VF	UNC
116	**20 PESOS**			
	2001; 2002; 2003. Blue and m/c unpt. Similar to #106. Polymer plastic. Printer: NPA and BdM.			
	a. 17.5.2001. Series A-F. Two electronic sorting bars at upper l.	FV	FV	5.50
	b. 17.5.2001. Series G-T. Three electronic sorting bars at upper l.	FV	FV	4.50

#117-120 w/vertical iridescent strip at l. Additional enhanced security features.

		VG	VF	UNC
117	**50 PESOS**			
	18.10.2000 (2001); 26.3.2002; 23.5.2003. Similar to #107.	FV	FV	10.00

		VG	VF	UNC
118	**100 PESOS** 18.10.2000 (2001); 26.3.2002; 23.5.2003; 21.11.2003. Similar to #108.	FV	FV	18.00
119	**200 PESOS** 18.10.2000 (2001); 23.3.2002. Similar to #109.	FV	FV	32.50
120	**500 PESOS** 18.10.2000 (2001). Similar to #110.	FV	FV	80.00

		VG	VF	UNC
121	**1000 PESOS** 26.3.2002. M/c. Similar to #111.	FV	FV	150.00

The area of Moldova is bordered in the north, east, and south by the Ukraine and on the west by Romania.

The historical Romanian principality of Moldova was established in the 14th century. It fell under Turkish suzerainty in the 16th century. From 1812 to 1918, Russians occupied the eastern portion of Moldova which they named Bessarabia. In March 1918, the Bessarabian legislature voted in favor of reunification with Romania.

At the Paris Peace Conference of 1920, the union was officially recognized by several nations, but the new Soviet government did not accept the union. In 1924, to pressure Romania, a Moldovan Autonomous Soviet Socialist Republic (A.S.S.R.) was established within the USSR on the border, consisting of a strip extending east of the Dniester River. Today it is Transnistria (see country listing).

Soviet forces reoccupied the region in June 1940, and the Moldovan S.S.R. was proclaimed. Transniestria was transferred to the new republic. Ukrainian S.S.R. obtained possession of the southern part of Bessarabia. The region was liberated by the Romanian army in 1941. The Soviets reconquered the territory in 1944. A declaration of independence was adopted in June 1990 and the area was renamed Moldova. It became an independent republic in August 1991. In December 1991, Moldova became a member of the Commonwealth of Independent States.

MONETARY SYSTEM:
100 Rubles = 1000 Cupon, 1992
1 Leu = 1000 Cupon, 1993-

REPUBLIC

MINISTER OF FINANCE
RUBLE CONTROL COUPONS

A11	**VARIOUS AMOUNTS** 1992. a. Full sheet. b. Coupon.	VG — —	VF 0.50 —	UNC 1.00 0.10

BANCA NATIONALA A MOLDOVEI
1992; 1993 "CUPON" ISSUE
#1-4 arms at l. Castle at r. on back. Wmk. paper (varies).

1	50 CUPON	VG	VF	UNC
	1992. Gray-green on gray unpt.	0.10	0.40	2.25

2	200 CUPON	VG	VF	UNC
	1992. Purple on gray unpt. Back purple on lilac unpt.	0.10	0.40	2.25

3	1000 CUPON	VG	VF	UNC
	1993. Brown on pale blue-green and ochre unpt. Bank monogram at upper l.	0.15	0.75	3.00

4	5000 CUPON	VG	VF	UNC
	1993. Pale brown-violet on orange and pale olive-green unpt. Bank monogram at upper l. Back pale brown-violet on pale brown-orange unpt.	0.50	1.50	5.00

1992 (1993) Issue

#5-7 Kg. Stefan at l., arms at upper ctr. r. Soroca Fortress at ctr. r. on back. Sign. L. Talmaci. Printed in Romania on watermarked paper.

5	1 LEU	VG	VF	UNC
	1992 (1993). Brown and dk. olive-green on ochre unpt.	0.10	0.50	2.00

6	5 LEI	VG	VF	UNC
	1992 (1993). Purple on lt. blue and ochre unpt.	0.25	1.00	5.00

7	10 LEI	VG	VF	UNC
	1992 (1993). Red brown and olive-green on pale orange unpt.	0.50	1.50	7.50

1992; 1994 Issue

#8-16 Kg. Stefan at l. and as wmk., arms at upper ctr. r.

#8-14 bank monogram at upper r. corner.

8	1 LEU	VG	VF	UNC
	1994; 1995; 1997; 1998; 1999; 2002; 2005. Brown on ochre, pale yellow-green and m/c unpt. Monastery at Capriana at ctr. r. on back.	0.10	0.50	1.50

9	5 LEI	VG	VF	UNC
	1994; 1995; 1999. Blue-green on lilac and pale aqua unpt. Basilica of St. Dumitru in Orhei at ctr. r. on back.	0.25	1.00	2.75

10	10 LEI	VG	VF	UNC
	1994; 1995; 1998; 2005. Red-brown on pale blue and gold unpt. Monastery at Hîrjauca at ctr. r. on back.	0.75	1.25	4.00

#11 and 12 held in reserve.

1992 (1999) ISSUE

17	500 LEI	VG	VF	UNC
	1992 (1999). Slate black, orange and green on m/c unpt. Chisinau Cathedral on back.	35.00	60.00	100.00

13	20 LEI	VG	VF	UNC
	1992 (1994); 1995; 1997; 1999; 2002; 2005. Blue-green on lt. green, aqua and ochre unpt. Soroca Fortress at ctr. r. on back.	1.50	3.00	8.00

18	1000 LEI	VG	VF	UNC
	1992 (2003). Blue and purple on m/c unpt. Kg. Stefan at l.	FV	100.00	150.00

14	50 LEI	VG	VF	UNC
	1992 (1994); 2002; 2005. Red-violet on lilac and m/c unpt. Monastery at Hîrbovet at ctr. r. on back.	2.00	5.00	15.00

1992 (1995) ISSUE

15	100 LEI	VG	VF	UNC
	1992 (1995). Brown on m/c unpt. Thighina Fortress on back.	5.00	7.50	25.00

16	200 LEI	VG	VF	UNC
	1992 (1995). Purple on m/c unpt. Chisinau City Hall on back.	12.50	17.50	45.00

MONGOLIA

RUSSIA

KAZAKHSTAN

CHINA

Yellow Sea

The State of Mongolia, a landlocked country in central Asia between Russia and the Peoples Republic of China, has an area of 604,247 sq. mi. (1,565,000 sq. km.) and a population of 2.74 million. Capital: Ulan Bator. Animal herds and flocks are the chief economic asset. Wool, cattle, butter, meat and hides are exported.

Mongolia (often referred to as Outer Mongolia), one of the world's oldest countries, attained its greatest power in the 13th century when Genghis Khan and his successors conquered all of China and extended their influence westward as far as Hungary and Poland. The empire dissolved in later centuries and in 1691 was brought under suzerainty of the Manchus, who had conquered China in 1644. Mongolia, with the support of Russia, proclaimed its independence from China on March 13, 1921, when the Provisional Peoples Government was established. Later, on November 26, 1924, the government proclaimed the Mongolian Peoples Republic. Opposition to the communist party developed in late 1989 and on March 12, 1990 and the new State of Mongolia was organized.

RULERS:
Chinese to 1921

MONETARY SYSTEM:
1 Tugrik (Tukhrik) = 100 Mongo

REPLACEMENT NOTES:
#28-41, 3A, 3B, or ЯA prefix.
#42-48, ЯA, ЯB prefix.

STATE

УЛСЫН БАНК

STATE BANK

1966 ISSUE

#35-41 Socialist arms at upper l. Backs are m/c. Wmk: Circles forming a 6-petaled flower-like pattern.
#36-41 portr. Sukhe-Bataar at r.

		VG	VF	UNC
35	**1 TUGRIK** 1966. Brown on pale green and yellow unpt.			
	a. Issued note.	0.20	0.40	0.75
	s. Specimen.	—	—	15.00
36	**3 TUGRIK** 1966. Dk. green on lt. green and pink unpt.			
	a. Issued note.	0.25	0.50	1.00
	s. Specimen.	—	—	15.00
37	**5 TUGRIK** 1966. Dk. blue on lt. blue and pale green unpt.			
	a. Issued note.	0.25	0.50	1.00
	s. Specimen.	—	—	15.00
38	**10 TUGRIK** 1966. Red on pale red and blue unpt.			
	a. Issued note.	0.25	0.75	1.25
	s. Specimen.	—	—	15.00
39	**25 TUGRIK** 1966. Brown-violet on pale green unpt.			
	a. Issued note.	0.50	1.00	1.50
	s. Specimen.	—	—	15.00
40	**50 TUGRIK** 1966. Dk. green on lt. green and gold unpt. Govt. bldg. at Ulan-Bator on back.			
	a. Issued note.	1.00	2.50	3.00
	s. Specimen.	—	—	15.00

		VG	VF	UNC
41	**100 TUGRIK** 1966. Dk. brown on ochre and blue-green unpt. Back like #40.			
	a. Issued note.	2.00	4.00	7.50
	s. Specimen.	—	—	15.00

1981-83 ISSUE

#42-45 and 47-48 like #36-41. Replacement notes: Serial # prefix WA.

		VG	VF	UNC
42	**1 TUGRIK** 1983. Brown on pale green and yellow unpt. Like #35.	0.05	0.25	1.00

		VG	VF	UNC
43	**3 TUGRIK** 1983. Dk. green on lt. green and pink unpt. Like #36.	0.10	0.25	1.25

		VG	VF	UNC
44	**5 TUGRIK** 1981. Blue on lt. blue and pale green unpt. Like #37.	0.10	0.25	1.75

		VG	VF	UNC
45	**10 TUGRIK** 1981. Red on pale red and blue unpt. Like #38.	0.10	0.25	2.00

		VG	VF	UNC
46	**20 TUGRIK** 1981. Yellow-green on lt. green and brown unpt. Sukhe-Bataar at ctr., arms at l. Power station at Ulan-Bator at ctr. r. on back.	0.10	0.35	2.25

47	50 TUGRIK	VG	VF	UNC
	1981. Dk. green on lt. green and gold unpt. Like #40.	0.10	1.00	5.00

48	100 TUGRIK	VF	XF	UNC
	1981. Dk. brown on ochre and blue-green unpt. Like #41.	2.50		9.00

МОНГОЛ БАНК

MONGOL BANK

1993 ND; 1994-95 ISSUE

#49-51 "Soemba" arms at upper ctr. Replacement notes: Serial # prefix ZZ.

#49   #50   #51

49	10 MONGO	VG	VF	UNC
	ND (1993). Red-violet on pale red-orange unpt. 2 archers at lower ctr. on face and back.	—	0.10	0.75
50	20 MONGO			
	ND (1993). Brown on ochre and yellow-brown unpt. 2 athletes at lower ctr. on face and back.	—	0.15	0.75
51	50 MONGO			
	ND (1993). Greenish-black on blue and pale green unpt. 2 horsemen at lower ctr. on face and back.	—	0.50	0.75

#52-60 wmk: Genghis Khan.

52	1 TUGRIK	VG	VF	UNC
	ND (1993). Dull olive-green and brown-orange on ochre unpt. Chinze at l. "Soemba" arms at ctr. r. on back.	0.05	0.15	1.00

#53-57 youthful portr. Sukhe-Bataar at l., "Soemba" arms at ctr. Horses grazing in mountainous landscape at ctr. r. on back.

53	5 TUGRIK	VG	VF	UNC
	ND (1993). Deep orange, ochre and brown on m/c unpt.	0.05	0.25	1.25

54	10 TUGRIK	VG	VF	UNC
	ND (1993). Green, blue and lt. green on m/c unpt.	0.05	0.25	1.25

55	20 TUGRIK	VG	VF	UNC
	ND (1993). Violet, orange and red on m/c unpt.	0.05	0.25	1.25

56	50 TUGRIK	VG	VF	UNC
	ND (1993). Dk. brown on m/c unpt.	0.05	0.25	1.50

57	100 TUGRIK	VG	VF	UNC
	ND (1993); 1994. Purple, brown and dk. blue on m/c unpt.	0.05	0.50	2.00

#58-61 Genghis Khan at l. and as wmk., "Soemba" arms at ctr. Ox drawn yurte, village at ctr. r. on back.

	63	**20 TUGRIK**	VG	VF	UNC
		2000; 2002. M/c.	FV	FV	0.75

58	**500 TUGRIK**		VG	VF	UNC
	ND (1993; 1997). Dk. green, brown and yellow-green on m/c unpt.		0.25	1.00	5.00

64	**50 TUGRIK**	VG	VF	UNC
	2000. Brown-gold. Sukhe-Bataar at l. Segmented security thread. Microprinting, UV ink and embossed *50* below arms.	FV	FV	1.25

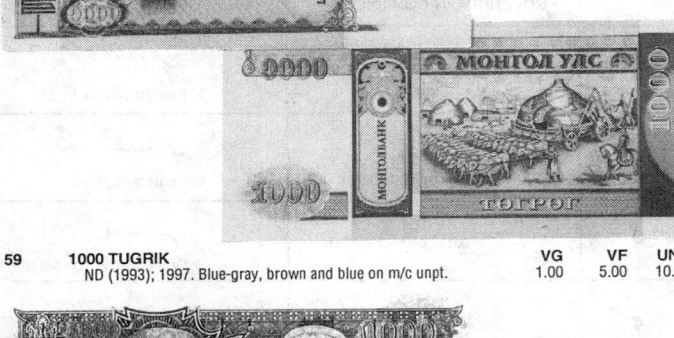

59	**1000 TUGRIK**	VG	VF	UNC
	ND (1993); 1997. Blue-gray, brown and blue on m/c unpt.	1.00	5.00	10.00

65	**100 TUGRIK**	VG	VF	UNC
	2000. M/c.	FV	FV	2.00
65A	**500 TUGRIK**			
	2000. M/c.	FV	FV	5.00

60	**5000 TUGRIK**	VG	VF	UNC
	1994. Purple, violet and red on m/c unpt. Bldg. complex, tree, people on back.	4.00	7.50	17.50
61	**10,000 TUGRIK**			
	1995. Black, dk. olive-green and orange on m/c unpt. Bldg. complex, tree, people on back.	8.50	16.00	35.00

2000; 2003 ISSUE

62	**10 TUGRIK**	VG	VF	UNC
	2000; 2002; 2005. Dark green and m/c.	FV	FV	0.50

66	**500 TUGRIK**	VG	VF	UNC
	2003. Blue and brown on m/c unpt. Wide security thread added to #65A.	FV	FV	5.00

67	1000 TUGRIK	VG	VF	UNC
	2003. Blue and brown on m/c unpt.	FV	FV	10.00

68	5000 TUGRIK	VG	VF	UNC
	2003. Purple and orange on m/c unpt.	FV	FV	17.50

69	10,000 TUGRIK	VG	VF	UNC
	2003. Dk. green and orange on m/c unpt.	FV	FV	35.00

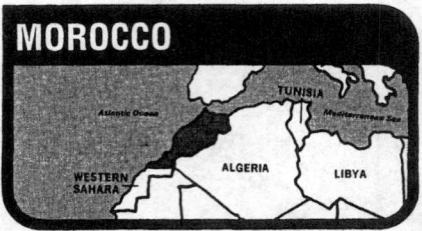

MOROCCO

The Kingdom of Morocco, situated on the northwest corner of Africa south of Spain, has an area of 172,413 sq. mi. (712,550 sq. km.) and a population of 28.98 million. Capital: Rabat. The economy is essentially agricultural. Phosphates, fresh and preserved vegetables, canned fish and raw material are exported.

Morocco's strategic position at the gateway to western Europe has been the principal determinant of its violent, frequently unfortunate history. Time and again the fertile plain between the rugged Atlas Mountains and the sea has echoed the battle's trumpet as Phoenicians, Romans, Vandals, Visigoths, Byzantine Greeks and Islamic Arabs successively conquered and occupied the land. Modern Morocco is a remnant of an early empire formed by the Arabs at the close of the 7th century which encompassed all of northwest Africa and most of the Iberian Peninsula. During the 17th and 18th centuries, while under the control of native dynasties, it was the headquarters of the famous Sale pirates. Morocco's strategic position involved it in the competition of 19th century European powers for political influence in Africa, and resulted in the division of Morocco into French and Spanish spheres of interest which were established as protectorates in 1912. Morocco became independent on March 2, 1956, after France agreed to end its protectorate. Spain signed similar agreements on April 7 of the same year.

RULERS:
Muhammad V, AH1346-1380/1927-1961AD
Hassan II, AH1380-1420 /1961-1999AD
Muhammad VI, AH1420- /1999- AD

MONETARY SYSTEM:
1 Dirham = 100 Francs, 1921-1974
1 Dirham = 100 Centimes = 100 Santimat, 1974-

SIGNATURE VARIETIES		
	GOVERNMENT COMISSONER	GOVERNOR
1	Mohamed Tahiri, 1960	M'hamed Zeghari
2	Ahmed Ben Nani, 1963-65	M'Hamed Zeghari
3	Ahmed Ben Nani	Driss Slaovi
4	Mohamed Lemniai, 1966	Driss Slaovi
5	Abdelaziz El Alami, 1967	Driss Slaovi
6	Abdelkrim Lazrek, 1968	M'hamed Zeghari
7	Abdelkrim Lazrek, 1969	Prince Moulay Hassan Ben Mehdi El Alaovi
8	Mohamed El Mdaghri, 1970	Prince Moulay Hassan Ben Mehdi El Alaovi
9	Hassan Lukash, 1985-89	Ahmed Ben Nani
10	Hassan Lukash	Mohamed Es Sakat
11	Abdul el Fatah ben Mansour	Mohamed Es Sakat
12	Noureddin Omary	Mohamed Es Sakat

KINGDOM

BANQUE DU MAROC
Established June 30, 1959

1960 (ND); 1965 ISSUE
#53-55 wmk: Lion's head. French printing.

53 5 DIRHAMS
ND (1960); 1965-69. Brown and m/c. Kg. Muhammad V wearing a fez at r. Harvesting at l., man holding sheaf at r. on back.

	VG	VF	UNC
a. Sign. 1. ND (1960).	2.00	8.50	40.00
b. Sign. 2. ND (1963).	1.75	7.50	35.00
c. Sign. 3. 1965/AH1384.	1.50	6.00	35.00
d. Sign. 4. 1966/AH1386.	1.25	5.00	35.00
e. Sign. 6. 1968/AH1387.	1.25	5.00	35.00
f. Sign. 7. 1969/AH1389.	1.25	5.00	35.00

54 10 DIRHAMS
ND (1960); 1965-69. Brown and m/c. Kg. Muhammad V wearing fez at l., Hassan Tower in Rabat at ctr. Orange picking on back.

	VG	VF	UNC
a. Sign. 1. ND (1960).	2.75	12.50	50.00
b. Sign. 2. ND (1963).	2.50	10.00	45.00
c. Sign. 3. 1965/AH1384.	2.00	8.00	40.00
d. Sign. 6. 1968/AH1387.	2.00	8.00	40.00
e. Sign. 7. 1969/AH1389.	2.00	8.00	40.00

55 50 DIRHAMS
1965-69. Brown and m/c. Kg. Hassan II at r. Miners at work on back.

	VG	VF	UNC
a. Sign. 3. 1965/AH1385.	15.00	60.00	375.00
b. Sign. 5. 1966/AH1386.	12.50	55.00	350.00
c. Sign. 6. 1968/AH1387.	10.00	45.00	300.00
d. Sign. 7. 1969/AH1389.	10.00	42.50	285.00

1970 ISSUE
#56-59 Kg. Hassan II at l. and as wmk. Printer: TDLR.

56 5 DIRHAMS
1970/AH1390. Purple on lt. blue and m/c unpt. Castle at ctr. Industrial processing on back. Sign. 8. Replacement notes: Serial # prefix Z.

	VG	VF	UNC
a. Issued note.	0.50	1.50	4.50
s. Specimen.	—	—	32.50

57 10 DIRHAMS
1970; 1985. Brown on lt. green and m/c unpt. Villa at ctr. Processing oranges on back. Replacement notes: Serial # prefix Y.

	VG	VF	UNC
a. Sign. 8. 1970/AH1390.	0.75	2.00	6.50
b. Sign. 9. 1985/AH1405.	0.75	1.50	5.50
s. As a. Specimen.	—	—	35.00

58 50 DIRHAMS
1970; 1985. Green and brown on m/c unpt. City at ctr. Dam on back. Replacement notes: Serial # prefix X.

	VG	VF	UNC
a. Sign. 8. 1970/AH1390.	3.00	10.00	22.50
b. Sign. 9. 1985/AH1405.	3.00	8.00	20.00
s. As b. Specimen.	—	—	50.00

59   **100 DIRHAMS**

1970; 1985. Brown and blue on lt. green and m/c unpt. Bldg. at ctr. Oil refinery on back. Replacement notes: Serial # prefix *W*.

	VG	VF	UNC
a. Sign. 8. 1970/AH1390.	5.00	15.00	37.50
b. Sign. 9. 1985/AH1405.	5.00	12.50	35.00
s. As b. Specimen.	—	—	70.00

BANK AL-MAGHRIB

1987 ISSUE

#60-62 Kg. Hassan II facing at r. and as wmk. 2 sign. varieties.

60   **10 DIRHAMS**

1987/AH1407. Red-brown and red on m/c unpt. Musical instrument and pillar at l. ctr. on back.

	VG	VF	UNC
a. Sign. 9.	FV	3.00	10.00
b. Sign. 10.	FV	2.50	8.00

61   **50 DIRHAMS**

1987/AH1407. Green on m/c unpt. Mounted militia charging, flowers at ctr. on back.

	VG	VF	UNC
a. Sign. 9.	FV	FV	25.00
b. Sign. 10.	FV	FV	20.00

62   **100 DIRHAMS**

1987/AH1407. Brown on m/c unpt. Demonstration on back.

	VG	VF	UNC
a. Sign. 9.	FV	FV	30.00
b. Sign. 10.	FV	FV	30.00

1987 (1991) ISSUE

#63-66 older bust of Kg. Hassan II at r. facing half l. Wmk: Kg. facing.

63   **10 DIRHAMS**

1987/AH407 (ca.1991). Brown-violet and purple on m/c unpt. Back like #60, but diff. colors of unpt.

	VG	VF	UNC
a. Sign. 10.	FV	FV	6.00
b. Sign. 11.	FV	FV	3.50

64   **50 DIRHAMS**

1987/AH1407 (ca.1991). Green on m/c unpt. Back like #61.

	VG	VF	UNC
a. Sign. 10.	FV	FV	20.00
b. Sign. 11.	FV	FV	15.00
c. Sign. 12.	FV	FV	12.50
d. Sign. 13.	FV	FV	12.50

65   **100 DIRHAMS**

1987/AH1407 (ca.1991). Brown and blue on m/c unpt. Back like #62.

	VG	VF	UNC
a. Sign. 10.	FV	FV	30.00
b. Sign. 11.	FV	FV	25.00
c. Sign. 12.	FV	FV	20.00
d. Sign. 13.	FV	FV	20.00

66   **200 DIRHAMS**

1987/AH1407 (ca.1991). Blue-violet and blue on m/c unpt. Mausoleum of Kg. Muhammad V at ctr. Sailboat, shell and coral on back.

	VG	VF	UNC
a. Sign. 10.	FV	FV	50.00
b. Sign. 11.	FV	FV	47.50
c. Sign. 12.	FV	FV	45.00
d. Sign. 13.	FV	FV	40.00
e. Sign. 16.	FV	FV	37.50

1996 ISSUE

67	20 DIRHAMS	VG	VF	UNC
	1996. M/c. Kg. Hassan II at l., Great Mosque of Casablanca at ctr. Fountain on back.			
	a. Sign. 12.	FV	FV	5.00
	b. Sign. 13.	FV	FV	4.50
	c. Sign. 14.	FV	FV	4.50
	d. Sign. 15.	FV	FV	4.50
	e. Sign. 16.	FV	FV	4.50

2002 (2004-) ISSUE

68	20 DIRHAMS	Good	Fine	XF
	2004. Mohammed VI.		Expected New Issue	
69	50 DIRHAMS			
	2002/AH1423. Mohammed VI.	FV	FV	12.50

70	100 DIRHAMS	VG	VF	UNC
	2002/AH1423. Brown on m/c unpt. Mohammed VI, Hassan II and Mohammed V at r. People with flags marching on back.	FV	FV	20.00

71	200 DIRHAMS	VG	VF	UNC
	2002/AH1423. Mohammed VI and Hassan II.	FV	FV	35.00

The People's Republic of Mozambique, a former overseas province of Portugal stretching for 1,430 miles (2,301 km.) along the southeast coast of Africa, has an area of 309,494 sq. mi. (783,030 sq. km.) and a population of 19.56 million. Capital: Maputo. Agriculture is the chief industry. Cashew nuts, cotton, sugar, copra and tea are exported.

Vasco da Gama explored all the coast of Mozambique in 1498 and found Arab trading posts already along the coast. Portuguese settlement dates from the establishment of the trading post of Mozambique in 1505. Within five years Portugal absorbed all the former Arab sultanates along the east African coast. The area was organized as a colony in 1907 and became an overseas province in 1952. In Sept. of 1974, after more than a decade of guerrilla warfare with the forces of the Mozambique Liberation Front, Portugal agreed to the independence of Mozambique, effective June 25, 1975. Mozambique became a member of the Commonwealth of Nations in November 1995. The President is Head of State; the Prime Minister is Head of Government.

RULERS:
Portuguese to 1975

MONETARY SYSTEM:
1 Escudo = 100 Centavos, 1911-1975
1 Escudo = 1 Metica = 100 Centimos, 1975-

REPLACEMENT NOTES:
#116, 117, 119: Z prefix.
#125-133, ZA, ZB, ZC prefix.
#134-137, AW, BW, CY, DZ prefix by denomination.

BANCO NACIONAL ULTRAMARINO

MOÇAMBIQUE BRANCH

1961; 1967 ISSUE

#109 and 110 printer: BWC.

109	100 ESCUDOS	VG	VF	UNC
	27.3.1961. Green on m/c unpt. Portr. A. de Ornelas at r., arms at upper ctr. Bank steamship seal at l. on back. W/o printer imprint.			
	a. Wmk: Arms.	1.50	4.00	17.50
	b. W/o wmk.	1.00	3.00	10.00
	s. As a. Specimen.	—	—	140.00

110	500 ESCUDOS	VG	VF	UNC
	22.3.1967. Purple on m/c unpt. Portr. C. Xavier at r., arms at upper ctr.			
	a. Issued note.	4.00	20.00	75.00
	s. Specimen.	—	—	150.00

1970 ISSUE

Sign. varieties.

111	50 ESCUDOS		VG	VF	UNC
	27.10.1970. Black on m/c unpt. J. de Azevedo Coutinho at l. ctr., arms at upper ctr. r. Back green; bank steamship seal at l. Wmk: Arms.		1.00	3.00	15.00

FIRST 1972 ISSUE

112	1000 ESCUDOS		VG	VF	UNC
	16.5.1972. Black-blue on m/c unpt. Kg. Afonso V at r. and as wmk., arms at upper ctr. Allegorical woman w/ships at l. on back, bank steamship seal at upper ctr. 3 sign. varieties.		10.00	22.50	125.00

Note: #112 has 2 1/2mm. serial # w/o prefix or 3mm. serial # and 3-letter prefix.

SECOND 1972 ISSUE

113	100 ESCUDOS		VG	VF	UNC
	23.5.1972. Blue on m/c unpt. G. Coutinho and S. Cabral at l. ctr. Surveyor at ctr. on back. Wmk: Coutinho.		2.00	7.50	50.00

114	500 ESCUDOS		VG	VF	UNC
	23.5.1972. Purple on m/c unpt. G. Coutinho at l. ctr. and as wmk. Cabral and airplane on back.		4.00	15.00	85.00

115	1000 ESCUDOS		VG	VF	UNC
	23.5.1972. Green on m/c unpt. Face similar to #114. 2 men in cockpit of airplane at l. ctr. on back.		5.00	25.00	120.00

PEOPLES REPUBLIC

BANCO DE MOÇAMBIQUE

1976 ND PROVISIONAL ISSUE

#116-119 black ovpt. of new bank name.

116	50 ESCUDOS		VG	VF	UNC
	ND (1976 - old date 27.10.1970). Black on m/c unpt. Ovpt. on #111.		0.10	0.25	1.00

117	100 ESCUDOS		VG	VF	UNC
	ND (1976 - old date 27.3.1961). Green on m/c unpt. Ovpt. on #109.				
	a. Issued note.		0.10	0.25	1.50
	s. Specimen.		—	—	100.00

118	**500 ESCUDOS**	VG	VF	UNC
	ND (1976 - old date 22.3.1967). Purple on m/c unpt. Ovpt. on #110.			
	a. Issued note.	0.25	0.50	2.50
	s. Specimen.	—	—	115.00

119	**1000 ESCUDOS**	VG	VF	UNC
	ND (1976 - old date 23.5.1972). Green on m/c unpt. Ovpt. on #115.	0.25	0.75	3.00

1976 ISSUE

#120-124 Pres. S. Machel at l. ctr. Printer: TDLR. These appear to be unadopted designs.

120	**5 METICAS**	VG	VF	UNC
	25.6.1976. Brown and m/c. Kudu on back. Specimen, punched hole cancelled.	—	—	—
121	**10 METICAS**			
	25.6.1976. Blue on m/c. Lions on back. Specimen, punched hole cancelled.	—	—	—
122	**20 METICAS**			
	25.6.1976. Red and m/c. Giraffes on back. Specimen, punched hole cancelled.	—	—	—
123	**50 METICAS**			
	25.6.1976. Purple and m/c. Cape buffalo on back. Specimen, punched hole cancelled.	—	—	—

124	**100 METICAS**	VG	VF	UNC
	25.6.1976. Green and m/c. Elephants on back. Specimen, punched hole cancelled.	—	—	—

REPÚBLICA POPULAR DE MOÇAMBIQUE

1980 ISSUE

#125-128 arms at ctr. Large size serial #.

125	**50 METICAIS**	VG	VF	UNC
	16.6.1980. Dk. brown and brown on m/c unpt. Soldiers at l., flag ceremony at r. Soldiers in training on back.	0.15	0.50	2.00

126	**100 METICAIS**	VG	VF	UNC
	16.6.1980; 16.6.1983. Green on m/c unpt. Soldiers at flagpole at l., E. Mondlane at r. Public ceremony on back.	0.20	0.75	3.00

127	**500 METICAIS**	VG	VF	UNC
	16.6.1980. Deep blue-violet and dk. blue-green on m/c unpt. Government assembly at l., chanting crowd at r. Chemists and school scene on back.	0.25	0.50	4.50

128 1000 METICAIS

16.6.1980. Deep red on m/c unpt. Pres. S. Machel w/3 young boys at r., revolutionary monument at l. Mining and harvesting scenes on back.

	VG	VF	UNC
	0.75	1.75	8.50

1983-88 ISSUE

#129-132 modified arms at ctr. Smaller size serial #.

132 1000 METICAIS

16.6.1983; 16.6.1986; 16.6.1989. Similar to #128 except for arms.

	VG	VF	UNC
	0.50	1.50	3.00
a. 16.6.1983.	0.50	1.50	6.00
b. 16.6.1986.	0.50	2.00	7.50
c. 16.6.1989.	0.50	0.50	3.00

129 50 METICAIS

16.6.1983; 16.6.1986. Similar to #125 except for arms.

	VG	VF	UNC
	0.10	0.25	1.50

133 5000 METICAIS

3.2.1988; 3.2.1989. Purple, brown and violet on m/c unpt. Carved statues at l., painting at r. Dancers and musicians on back.

	VG	VF	UNC
	0.75	1.75	5.00

1991-93 ISSUE

#134-137 arms at upper ctr. r. printed on silver or gold underlay. Bank seal at lower l. on back. Wmk: J. Chissano. Printer: TDLR.

130 100 METICAIS

16.6.1983; 16.6.1986; 16.6.1989. Similar to #126 except for arms.

	VG	VF	UNC
	0.15	0.50	2.00

134 500 METICAIS

16.6.1991. Brown and blue on m/c unpt. Native carving of couple in grief at l. ctr., native art at r. Dancing warriors at ctr. on back.

	VG	VF	UNC
	FV	FV	1.00

131 500 METICAIS

16.6.1983; 16.6.1986; 16.6.1989. Similar to #127 except for arms.

	VG	VF	UNC
	0.25	0.50	2.50

135 1000 METICAIS

16.6.1991. Brown and red on m/c unpt. E. Mondlane at l. ctr., military flag raising ceremony at r. Monument at l. ctr. on back.

	VG	VF	UNC
	FV	FV	2.00

136 5000 METICAIS
16.6.1991. Purple, violet and orange-brown on m/c unpt. S.
Machel at l. ctr., monument to the Socialist vanguard at r. Foundry
workers at ctr. on back.

VG	VF	UNC
FV	FV	1.50

137 10,000 METICAIS
16.6.1991. Blue-green, brown and orange on m/c unpt. J. Chissano
at l. ctr., high tension electrical towers at r. w/farm tractor in field
and high-rise city view in background at r. Plowing with oxen at ctr.
on back.

VG	VF	UNC
FV	FV	1.50

**#138 and 139 Bank of Mozambique bldg. at l. ctr., arms at upper r. Cabora Bassa hydroelectric dam on
back. Wmk: Bank monogram.**

138 50,000 METICAIS
16.6.1993 (1994). Dk. brown, red-brown on m/c unpt.

VG	VF	UNC
FV	FV	6.50

139 100,000 METICAIS
16.6.1993 (1994). Red, brown-orange and olive-brown on m/c unpt.

VG	VF	UNC
FV	FV	12.50

1999 ISSUE

140 20,000 METICAIS
16.6.1999. Green on m/c unpt. Young woman seated writing at ctr.
Maputo city hall on back.

VG	VF	UNC
FV	FV	2.50

2004 ISSUE

141 200,000 METICAIS
16.6.2003 (2004). Dk. blue and aqua on m/c unpt. Dancing
warriors on back.

VG	VF	UNC
FV	FV	25.00

142 500,000 METICAIS
16.6.2003 (2004). Purple, tan and m/c. Holographic seal at right.
Serial #s in green and black.

VG	VF	UNC
FV	FV	55.00

MYANMAR (Burma)

The Socialist Republic of the Union of Myanmar (formally called Burma), a country of Southeast Asia fronting on the Bay of Bengal and the Andaman Sea, has an area of 261,789 sq. mi. (676,552 sq. km.) and a population of 49.34 million. Capital: Rangoon. Myanmar is an agricultural country heavily dependent on its leading product (rice) which embodies two-thirds of the cultivated area and accounts for 40 percent of the value of exports. Petroleum, lead, tin, silver, zinc, nickel, cobalt and precious stones are exported.

The first European to reach Burma, about 1435, was Nicolo Di Conti, a merchant of Venice. During the beginning of the reign of Bodawpaya (1782-1819AD) the kingdom comprised most of the same area as it does today including Arakan which was taken over in 1784-85. The British East India Company, while unsuccessful in its 1612 effort to establish posts along the Bay of Bengal, was enabled by the Anglo-Burmese Wars of 1824-86 to expand to the whole of Burma and to secure its annexation to British India. In 1937, Burma was separated from India, becoming a separate British colony with limited self-government. The Japanese occupied Burma in 1942, and on Aug. 1, 1943 Burma became an "independent and sovereign state" under Dr. Ba Maw who was appointed the Adipadi (head of state) which collpased with the surrender of Japanese forces. Burma became an independent nation outside the British Commonwealth on Jan. 4, 1948, the constitution of 1948 providing for a parliamentary democracy and the nationalization of certain industries. However, political and economic problems persisted, and on March 2, 1962, Gen. Ne Win took over the government, suspended the constitution, installed himself as chief of state, and pursued a socialist program with nationalization of nearly all industry and trade. On Jan. 4, 1974, a new constitution adopted by referendum established Burma as a "socialist republic" under one-party rule. The country name in English was changed to Union of Myanmar in 1989.

MONETARY SYSTEM:
1 Kyat = 100 Pyas, 1943-1945, 1952-

REPUBLIC

CENTRAL BANK OF MYANMAR

1990 ND ISSUE

		VG	VF	UNC
67	**1 KYAT**	FV	FV	0.30
	ND (1990). Pale brown and orange on m/c unpt. Gen. Aung San at l. and as wmk. Dragon carving at l. on back.			

1991-98 ND ISSUE

		VG	VF	UNC
68	**50 PYAS**	FV	FV	0.30
	ND (1994). Dull purple and dull brown on gray and tan unpt. Musical string instrument at ctr. Wmk: B/CM.			

		VG	VF	UNC
69	**1 KYAT**	FV	FV	0.30
	ND (1996). Gray, blue and purple on m/c unpt. Chinze at r. Wmk: B/CM.			

		VG	VF	UNC
70	**5 KYATS**			
	ND (1996). Dk. brown and blue-green on m/c unpt. Chinze at l. ctr. Ball game scene on back.			
	a. Wmk: Chinze. (1996).	FV	FV	0.75
	b. Wmk: Chinze bust over value. (1997).	FV	FV	0.50

		VG	VF	UNC
71	**10 KYATS**			
	ND (1996). Deep purple and violet on m/c unpt. Chinze at r. ctr. Elaborate barge on back.			
	a. Wmk: Chinze. (1996).	FV	FV	1.00
	b. Wmk: Chinze bust over value. (1997).	FV	FV	0.50

		VG	VF	UNC
72	**20 KYATS**	FV	FV	1.00
	ND (1994). Deep olive-green, brown and blue-green on m/c unpt. Chinze at l. Fountain of elephants in park at ctr. r. on back. Wmk: Chinze bust over value.			

		VG	VF	UNC
73	**50 KYATS**			
	ND (1994-). Red-brown, tan and dk. brown on m/c unpt. Chinze at r. and as wmk. Coppersmith at l. ctr. on back.			
	a. Wmk: Chinze. (1994).	FV	FV	3.00
	b. Wmk: Chinze bust over value. (1997).	FV	FV	2.00

77 1000 KYATS

	VG	VF	UNC
ND (1998). Deep green and purple on m/c unpt. Chinze at r. Central Bank bldg. at l. ctr. on back.			
a. Security thread in negative script. Wmk: Chinze.	FV	FV	15.00
b. Security thread in positive script. Wmk: Chinze above value.	FV	FV	15.00

2004 ND REDUCED SIZE ISSUE

		VG	VF	UNC
78 200 KYATS	ND (2004).	FV	FV	6.00
79 500 KYATS	ND (2004).	FV	FV	10.00

74 100 KYATS

	VG	VF	UNC
ND (1994). Blue-violet, blue-green and dk. brown on m/c unpt. Chinze at l. Workers restoring temple and grounds at ctr. r. on back.			
a. Security thread in negative script. Wmk: Chinze.	FV	FV	4.00
b. Security thread in positive script. Wmk: Chinze above value.	FV	FV	3.00

75 200 KYATS

	VG	VF	UNC
ND (ca.1991; 1998). Dk. blue and green on m/c unpt. Chinze at r., his head as wmk. Elephant pulling log at ctr. r. on back.			
a. Security thread in negative script. Wmk: Chinze.	FV	FV	8.00
b. Security thread in positive script. Wmk: Chinze above value.	FV	FV	6.00

80 1000 KYATS

	VG	VF	UNC
ND (2004).	FV	FV	15.00

FOREIGN EXCHANGE CERTIFICATES

CENTRAL BANK

1993 ND ISSUE

76 500 KYATS

	VG	VF	UNC
ND (1994). Brown, purple and brown-orange on m/c unpt. Chinze at l. Workers restoring medieval statue, craftsman and water hauler at ctr. r. on back.			
a. Security thread in negative script. Wmk: Chinze.	FV	FV	14.00
b. Security thread in positive script. Wmk: Chinze above value.	FV	FV	10.00

FX1 1 DOLLAR (USA)

	VG	VF	UNC
ND (1993). Blue, brown, yellow and green.	—	—	4.00

FX2   **5 DOLLARS (USA)**   **VG**   **VF**   **UNC**
ND (1993). Maroon, yellow and blue.   —   —   12.50

FX3   **10 DOLLARS (USA)**   **VG**   **VF**   **UNC**
ND (1993). Blue, green and gray.   —   —   27.50
FX4   **20 DOLLARS (USA)**
ND (1997). Maroon, yellow and brown.   —   —   35.00

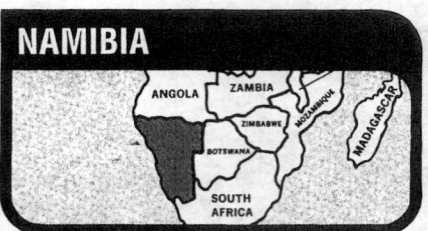

NAMIBIA

The Republic of Namibia, once the German colonial territory of German South West Africa, is situated on the Atlantic coast of southern Africa, bounded on the north by Angola, on the east by Botswana, and on the south by South Africa. It has an area of 318,261 sq. mi. (824,290 sq. km.) and a population of 1.73 million. Capital: Windhoek. Diamonds, copper, lead, zinc and cattle are exported.

South Africa undertook the administration of South West Africa under the terms of a League of Nations mandate on Dec. 17, 1920. When the League of Nations was dissolved in 1946, its supervisory authority for South West Africa was inherited by the United Nations. In 1946 the UN denied South Africa's request to annex South West Africa. South Africa responded by refusing to place the territory under a UN trusteeship. In 1950 the International Court of Justice ruled that South Africa could not unilaterally modify the international status of South West Africa. A 1966 UN resolution declaring the mandate terminated was rejected by South Africa, and the status of the area remained in dispute. In June 1968 the UN General Assembly voted to rename the territory Namibia. In 1971 the International Court of Justice ruled that South Africa's presence in Namibia was illegal. In Dec. 1973 the UN appointed a UN Commissioner, and a multi-racial Advisory Council was also appointed. An interim government was formed in 1977 and independence was to be declared by Dec. 31, 1978. This resolution was rejected by major UN powers. In April 1978 South Africa accepted a plan for UN-supervised elections which led to political abstention by the South West Africa People's Organization (SWAPO) party. The result was the dissolution of the Minister's Council and National Assembly in Jan. 1983. A Multi-Party Conference (MPC) was formed in May 1984 which held talks with SWAPO. The MPC petitioned South Africa for Namibian self-government and on June 17, 1984 the Transitional Government of National Unity was installed. Negotiations were held in 1988 between Angola, Cuba and South Africa reaching a peaceful settlement on Aug. 5, 1988. By April 1, 1989, Cuban troops were to withdraw from Angola and South African troops from Namibia. The Transitional Government resigned on Feb. 28, 1988 for the upcoming elections of the constituent assembly in Nov. 1989. Independence was finally achieved on March 21, 1990, within the Commonwealth of Nations. The President is Head of State; the Prime Minister is Head of Government.

MONETARY SYSTEM:
   1 Namibia Dollar = 100 Cents

Note: For notes of the 3 commercial banks circulating until 1963, see Southwest Africa listings in Vol. II.

SIGNATURE VARIETIES	
	Dr. W. L. Benard 16 July 1990-31 August 1991
1	*Erik L. Karlsson* Mr. Erik L. Karlsson Acting: 1 Semtember 1991-24 November 1992 25 November 1992-31 December 1993
2	*Jaafar B Ahmad* Dr. Jaafar B. Ahmad 1 January 1994-31 December 1996
3	*Kalweendo* Mr. Tom K. Alweendo 1 January 1997-

REPUBLIC

NAMIBIA RESERVE BANK

1990 ISSUE

#A1-E1 printer: BWC. Unadopted designs.

A1   **2 KALAHAR**   **VG**   **VF**   **UNC**
ND. Red on m/c unpt. Zebra head at l. Plant at ctr., rock formation   —   —   —
at r. Unissued specimen.

B1 5 KALAHAR | VG | VF | UNC
ND. Red and purple on m/c unpt. Oryx head at l. Back blue; road graders at ctr. Unissued specimen. | — | — | —

C1 10 KALAHAR | VG | VF | UNC
ND. Red and purple on m/c unpt. Oryx head at l. Commercial fishing boat at ctr. on back. Unissued specimen. | — | — | —

D1 20 KALAHAR | VG | VF | UNC
ND. Purple on m/c unpt. Lion head in round frame at l., watermark circle at r. Sheep herd on back, herdsman on horseback. Unissued specimen. | — | — | —

E1 20 KALAHAR | VG | VF | UNC
ND. Purple on m/c unpt. Lion head at l., flag at ctr. Sheep herd on back, walking herdsman. Unissued specimen. | — | — | —

BANK OF NAMIBIA
1993 ND ISSUE

#1-3 Capt. H. Wittbooi at l. ctr. and as wmk. Printer: Tumba Bruk A.B. (Sweden - w/o imprint). Sign. 1.
Replacement notes: Serial # prefix *X; Y; Z* for #1, 2 and 3 respectively.

1	**10 NAMIBIA DOLLARS**	VG	VF	UNC
	ND (1993). Blue-black on m/c unpt. Arms at upper l. Springbok at r. on back.			
	a. Sign. 1.	FV	2.00	8.25
	s. Specimen. Serial # prefix *S*.	—	—	150.00

2	**50 NAMIBIA DOLLARS**	VG	VF	UNC
	ND (1993). Blue-green and dk. brown on m/c unpt. Arms at upper ctr. Kudu at r. on back.			
	a. Sign. 1.	FV	11.00	38.50
	s. Specimen. Serial # prefix *S*.	—	—	150.00

3	**100 NAMIBIA DOLLARS**	VG	VF	UNC
	ND (1993). Red, brown and red-brown on m/c unpt. Arms at upper ctr. r. Oryx at r. on back.			
	a. Sign. 1.	FV	20.00	70.00
	s. Specimen. Serial # prefix *S*.	—	—	150.00

#4 not assigned.

1996-2001 ND ISSUE

#4-8 Capt. H. Wittbooi at l. ctr. and as wmk. Segmented foil over security thread and ascending size serial #. Replacement notes: Serial # prefix *X; V; Y; Z; W* respectively for #4-8.

4	10 NAMIBIA DOLLARS	VG	VF	UNC
	ND (2001). Blue on m/c unpt. Arms at upper l. Springbok on back. Sign 3. Like #1. Printer: F-CO.			
	a. Issue note.	FV	FV	3.75
	s. Specimen. Serial # prefix A.	—	—	120.00

5	20 NAMIBIA DOLLARS	VG	VF	UNC
	ND (1996). Orange and violet on m/c unpt. Arms at upper l. Red hartebeest at ctr. r. on back. Printer: TDLR. 7-digit serial #.			
	a. Sign. 2.	FV	FV	15.00
	s. Specimen. Serial # prefix H.	—	—	140.00
6	20 NAMIBIA DOLLARS	VG	VF	UNC
	ND (2002). Similar to #5. Printer: SABN.			
	a. Sign. 3. 8-digit serial #.	FV	FV	6.75
	s. Specimen. Serial # prefix J.	—	—	120.00

7	50 NAMIBIA DOLLARS	VG	VF	UNC
	ND (1999). Blue-green and dk. brown on m/c unpt. Arms at upper ctr. Kudu at r. on back. Like #2. Printer: TDLR.			
	a. Sign. 3. 7-digit serial #.	FV	FV	23.00
	s. Specimen. Serial # prefix P.	—	—	130.00
8	50 NAMIBIA DOLLARS			
	ND (1999). Similar to #7. Printer: SABN.			
	a. Sign. 3. 8-digit serial #.	FV	FV	17.00
	s. Specimen. Serial # prefix N.	—	—	120.00

9	100 NAMIBIA DOLLARS	VG	VF	UNC
	ND (1999). Red, brown and red-brown on m/c unpt. Arms at ctr. r. Oryx at r. on back. Like #3. Printer: TDLR.			
	a. Sign. 3. Seven digit serial #.	FV	FV	47.50
	b. Sign. 3. Eight digit serial #.	FV	FV	35.00
	c. Sign. 3. 7-digit serial #. Prefix TT.	FV	30.00	100.00
	s. Specimen. Serial # prefix T.	—	—	130.00

10	200 NAMIBIA DOLLARS	VG	VF	UNC
	ND (1996). Purple and violet on m/c unpt. Arms at upper ctr. Roan antelope at ctr. r. on back. Printer: TDLR.			
	a. Sign. 2.	FV	FV	80.00
	s. Specimen. Serial # prefix U.	—	—	130.00

2003 ISSUE

#11-12 8-digit serial #: Printer:SABN.

11	50 NAMIBIA DOLLARS	VG	VF	UNC
	ND (2003). Blue-green and dk. brown on m/c unpt.	FV	FV	22.50
12	100 NAMIBIA DOLLARS			
	ND (2003). Red, brown and red-brown on m/c unpt.	FV	FV	30.00

COLLECTOR SERIES

BANK OF NAMIBIA

1993 ND ISSUE

CS1	10, 50, 100 DOLLARS	Issue Price	Mkt.	Value
	ND (1993). #1-3 w/matched serial # mounted in a special plexiglass frame.	150.00		225.00

1996; 1999 ND ISSUE

CS2	20, 50, 100, 200 DOLLARS	Issue Price	Mkt.	Value
	ND (1996; 1999). #5, 7, 9, 10 w/matched serial #.	—		330.00

Note: Issued only to current owners of #CS1 to complete matched serial sets.

NEPAL

The Kingdom of Nepal, the world's only Hindu kingdom, is a landlocked country located in central Asia along the southern slopes of the Himalayan Mountains. It has an area of 56,136 sq. mi. (140,797 sq. km.) and a population of 24.35 million. Capital: Káthmandu. Nepal has substantial deposits of coal, copper, iron and cobalt but they are largely unexploited. Agriculture is the principal economic activity. Livestock, rice, timber and jute are exported.

Prithvi Narayan Shah, ruler of the principality of Gurkha, formed Nepal from a number of independent mountain states in the latter half of the 18th century. After his death a period of political instability ensued which lasted until the 1840's when the Rana family reduced the monarch to a figurehead and established itself as hereditary Prime Ministers. A popular revolution (1950-51) toppled the Rana family and reconstituted the power in the throne. In 1959 King Mahendra declared Nepal a constitutional monarchy. A new constitution promulgated in 1962 instituted a system of panchayat (village council) democracy from the village to the national levels. In 1990, following political unrest, the king's powers were reduced, and the country adopted a system of parliamentary democracy.

RULERS:
Mahendra Vira Vikrama Shahi Deva, 1955-1972
Birendra Bir Bikram Shahi Deva, 1972-2001
Ginendra, 2001-

MONETARY SYSTEM:
1 Rupee = 100 Paisa, 1961-

SIGNATURE VARIETIES			
1	जनक राज Janak Raj	2	भरत राज Bharat Raj
3	नरेन्द्र राज Narendra Raj	4	Himalaya Shamsher (J.B. Rama)
5	Lekshmi Nath Gautam	6	Pradhumna Lai (Rajbhandari)
7	Bekh Bahadur Thapa	8	Yadav Prasad Pant
9	Kul Shekhar Sharma	10	Kalyan Dikram Adhikary
11	Ganesh Bahadur Thapa	12	Harishankar Trfipathi
13	Satyendra Pyara Shrestha	14	Dipendra Purush Dhakal
15	Dr. Tilak Rawal	16	

KINGDOM

CENTRAL BANK OF NEPAL

1961; 1965 ND ISSUE

#12-15 denominations in Nepalese language changed from "Mohru" on previous issue to "Rupees" on both face and back. Wmk: Plumed crown.

		VG	VF	UNC
12	**1 RUPEE** ND (1965). Lilac and olive-green. Like #8. Coin at l., temple at ctr. Back lilac and green; arms at ctr., coin at r. Sign. 8.	0.25	0.75	3.50

#13-15 portr. Kg. Mahendra Vira Vikrama at upper l.

		VG	VF	UNC
13	**5 RUPEES** ND (1961). Purple and aqua. Like #9. Stupa at ctr. Himalayas on back. Sign. 5; 7; 8.	0.50	1.50	4.00

		VG	VF	UNC
14	**10 RUPEES** ND (1961). Dk. brown and red. Like # 10. Temple at ctr. Arms at ctr. on back. Sign. 5; 6; 7; 8.	1.00	3.00	8.00

		VG	VF	UNC
15	**100 RUPEES** ND (1961). Green and brown. Like #11. Temple at Lalitpor at ctr. Indian rhinoceros at ctr. on back. Sign. 5; 6; 7; 8.	3.00	10.00	35.00

1972 ND ISSUE

#16-21 Kg. Mahendra Vira Vikrama wearing military uniform w/white cap at l. Wmk: Plumed crown. Sign. 8.

		VG	VF	UNC
16	**1 RUPEE** ND (1972). Lt. brown on blue unpt. Back brown and purple; 4-chair rotary swing at ctr. r., arms at upper r. on back.	0.20	0.75	1.75

17 **5 RUPEES**
ND (1972). Lt. green on lilac unpt. Back green and blue; terraced hillside w/Himalayas in background.

	VG	VF	UNC
	0.25	1.00	2.50

18 **10 RUPEES**
ND (1972). Lt. brown on dull olive-green and lt. blue unpt. Back green and brown; Singha Dunbar at Kathmandu at ctr.

	VG	VF	UNC
	0.25	1.00	2.50

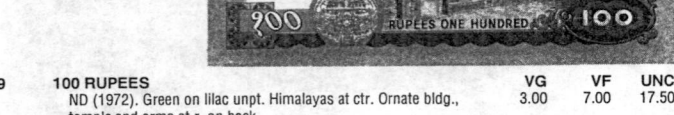

19 **100 RUPEES**
ND (1972). Green on lilac unpt. Himalayas at ctr. Ornate bldg., temple and arms at r. on back.

	VG	VF	UNC
	3.00	7.00	17.50

20 **500 RUPEES**
ND (1972). Brown and violet. 2 tigers on back.

	VG	VF	UNC
	25.00	75.00	200.00

21 **1000 RUPEES**
ND (1972). Blue and m/c. Great Stupa at Bodhnath. House and mountains on back.

	VG	VF	UNC
	25.00	75.00	200.00

NOTICE
Readers with unlisted dates, signature varieties, etc. are invited to submit photocopies of their notes to: Standard Catalog of World Paper Money, 700 East State St. Iola, WI 54990-0001, E-Mail: george.cuhaj@fwpubs.com.

1974 ND ISSUE
#22-28 Kg. Birendra Bir Bikram in military uniform w/dk. cap at l. Wmk: Plumed crown.

22 **1 RUPEE**
ND (1974). Blue on purple and gold unpt. Temple at ctr. Back blue and brown; 2 musk deer at ctr., arms at upper r. Sign. 9; 10; 11; 12.

	VG	VF	UNC
	0.05	0.25	1.00

23 **5 RUPEES**
ND (1974). Red, brown and green. Temple at ctr. Back red and brown; 2 yaks at ctr. r. Sign. 9; 10; 11.

	VG	VF	UNC
a. Issued note.	0.15	0.50	3.25
ct. Color trial. Green and purple face, back blue.	—	—	165.00
s. Specimen.	—	—	100.00

24 **10 RUPEES**
ND (1974). Dk. and lt. brown on m/c unpt. Vishnu on Garnda at ctr. Back brown and green; 2 Black Buck Antelope at ctr., arms at r. Sign. 9; 10; 11.

	VG	VF	UNC
a. Issued note.	0.25	0.75	3.25
ct. Color trial. Green and purple on m/c unpt.	—	—	165.00
s. Specimen.	—	—	100.00

25 **50 RUPEES**
ND (1974). Purple on green and m/c unpt. Bldg. at ctr. Back blue and brown; Himalayan Tahr standing facing r. at ctr., arms at r. Sign. 9.

	VG	VF	UNC
a. Issued note.	1.50	3.50	10.00
s. Specimen.	—	—	135.00

	30	5 RUPEES	VG	VF	UNC
		ND (1987-). Brown on red and m/c unpt. Temple at ctr. Back similar to #23.			
		a. Serial # 24mm long. Sign. 11; 12; 13.	FV	FV	1.25
		b. Serial # 20mm long. Sign. 12.	FV	FV	1.25

	26	100 RUPEES	VG	VF	UNC
		ND (1974). Green and purple on m/c unpt. Mountains at ctr., temple at r. Back green; Indian Rhinoceros walking l., "eye" at upper l. corner, arms at upper r. Sign. 9.	3.00	7.00	20.00

	31	10 RUPEES	VG	VF	UNC
		ND (1985-87). Dk. brown and orange on lilac and m/c unpt. Vishnu on Garnda at ctr. Antelopes at ctr., arms at r. on back.			
		a. Serial # 24mm long. Sign. 11; 12.	FV	FV	2.00
		b. Segmented foil over security thread. Sign. 13.	FV	FV	1.75

	27	500 RUPEES	VG	VF	UNC
		ND (1974). Brown on m/c unpt. Monastery at ctr. Back brown and gold; 2 tigers at ctr. r., arms at upper r. Sign. 9; 10.	25.00	75.00	200.00

	32	20 RUPEES	VG	VF	UNC
		ND (1982-87). Orange on m/c unpt. Janakpur Temple at ctr. Back orange and m/c; Sambar Deer at ctr. r., arms at r. Serial # 24mm long. Sign. 10; 11.			
		a. Issued note.	FV	FV	5.00
		s. Specimen.	—	—	135.00

	28	1000 RUPEES	VG	VF	UNC
		ND (1974). Blue on m/c unpt. Temple and Great Stupa at ctr. Elephant at ctr., arms at upper r. on back. Sign. 9.			
		a. Issued note.	25.00	80.00	225.00
		s. Specimen.	—	—	—

1981-87 ND ISSUE

#29-36 Kg. Birendra Bir Bikram wearing plumed crown at l. Wmk: Plumed crown.

	29	2 RUPEES	VG	VF	UNC
		ND (1981-). Green on lt. blue and lilac unpt. Temple at ctr. Back m/c; leopard at ctr.			
		a. Line from king's lower lip extending downward. Serial # 24mm long. Sign. 10.	FV	FV	2.00
		b. No line from king's lower lip. Sign. 10; 11; 13.	FV	FV	0.50
		c. As b. Serial # 20mm long. Sign. 12.	FV	FV	0.75

	33	50 RUPEES	VG	VF	UNC
		ND (1983-). Blue on m/c unpt. Palace at ctr. Himalayan Tahr at ctr., arms at r. on back.			
		a. W/title at r. Serial # 24mm long. Sign. 10. (1983).	FV	FV	5.50
		b. W/title at ctr. Serial # 20mm long. Sign. 11; 12.	FV	FV	3.50
		c. Segmented foil over security thread. Sign. 13.	—	—	3.00

34   100 RUPEES

		VG	VF	UNC
ND (1981-). Green on pale lilac and m/c unpt. Temple at r. Rhinoceros walking l., arms at upper r. on back. Similar to #26, but w/o "eye" at upper l.				
a. Line from king's lower lip extending downward. W/security thread. Serial # 24mm long. Sign. 10.		FV	FV	6.50
b. No line from king's lower lip. Serial # at lower l. Sign. 10.		FV	FV	6.00
c. Serial # 20mm long. Sign. 11.		FV	FV	5.50
d. As b. Segmented foil over security thread. Sign. 12.		FV	FV	5.00
e. Serial # 20mm long. Sign. 13.		FV	FV	4.50
f. Serial # 24mm long. Sign. 13.		FV	FV	4.50

38   20 RUPEES

		VG	VF	UNC
ND (1988-). Orange on m/c unpt. Like #32, but m/c border on face and back.				
a. Serial # 24mm long. Sign. 11; 12.		FV	FV	2.25
b. Segmented foil over security thread. Serial # 20mm long. Sign. 13.		FV	FV	2.00
s. As a. Specimen.		—	—	115.00

Note: #39 and 40 have been renumbered 35d and 36d respectively.

1997 ND COMMEMORATIVE ISSUE

#41 and 42, Silver Jubilee of Accession, 1972-1997

#41 and 42 portr. Kg. Birenda Bir Bikram wearing plumed crown at l. Wmk: Plumed crown.

35   500 RUPEES

		VG	VF	UNC
ND (1981-). Brown and blue-violet on m/c unpt. Temple at ctr. Back brown and gold on blue unpt.; 2 tigers at ctr. r., arms at upper r.				
a. Line from King's lip extending downwards. Serial # 24mm long. Sign. 10.		FV	FV	45.00
b. Serial # 20mm long. Sign. 11.		FV	FV	20.00
c. Segmented foil over security thread. Sign. 12.		FV	FV	17.50
d. Sign. 13. (1996).		FV	FV	17.50

41   25 RUPEES

		VG	VF	UNC
ND (1997). Black and dk. brown on m/c unpt. Royal palace at ctr. r. Back dull green and orange; pillars w/chinze at l., steer at ctr., arms at r.		FV	FV	2.25

36   1000 RUPEES

		VG	VF	UNC
ND (1981-). Red-brown and gray on m/c unpt. Stupa and temple on face. Elephant at ctr., arms at upper r. on back.				
a. Line from King's lip extending downwards. Serial # 24mm long. Sign. 10.		FV	FV	85.00
b. Serial # 20mm long. Sign. 11.		FV	FV	37.50
c. Segmented foil over security thread. Sign. 12.		FV	FV	37.50
d. Sign. 13. (1996).		FV	FV	35.00

1988-96 ND ISSUE

#37 and 38 Kg. Birendra Bir Bikram wearing plumed crown at l. Wmk: Crown.

37   1 RUPEE

		VG	VF	UNC
ND (1991-) Purple and dull blue on m/c unpt. Back like #22. Sign. 12; 13.		FV	FV	0.40

42   250 RUPEES

		VG	VF	UNC
ND (1997). Dk. gray and blue-gray on m/c unpt. House of Representatives in unpt. at ctr., royal palace at ctr. r. Back blue and orange on green unpt.; pillars w/chinze at l., steer at ctr., arms at r.		FV	FV	17.50

#42 was also issued in a special folder.

2000 ND ISSUE

		VG	VF	UNC
43	**500 RUPEES** ND (2000). Brown, blue-violet and silver on m/c unpt. Similar to #39 but larger portrait.	FV	FV	17.50
44	**1000 RUPEES** ND (2000). Blue, brown and silver on m/c unpt. Similar to #40 but larger portrait.	FV	FV	35.00

2002 ND COMMEMORATIVE ISSUE

Accession to the throne of Kg. Gyanendra Bir Bikram

		VG	VF	UNC
45	**10 RUPEES** ND (30.9.2002). M/c. Commemorative text in horse-shoe shaped window: *This is issued on the occasion of King Gyanendra Bir Bikram Shah Dev's accession to the throne in BS 2058.* Printer: NPA.	FV	FV	1.50

2002 ND ISSUE

#46-51 portr. Kg. Gyanendra Bir Bikram at r. Sign. Tilak Rawal.

		VG	VF	UNC
46	**5 RUPEES** ND (2002). a. Darkly engraved portr. (Withdrawn). b. Lightly engraved portr.	 FV FV	 FV FV	 2.50 0.50

		VG	VF	UNC
47	**20 RUPEES** ND (2002). Deer at ctr.	FV	FV	2.25

		VG	VF	UNC
48	**50 RUPEES** ND (2002). Black and blue on m/c unpt. Bldg. at ctr. Himalayan Tahr at ctr. on back.	FV	FV	4.00

		VG	VF	UNC
49	**100 RUPEES** ND (2002). Rhinocerous walking l. at ctr. on back.	FV	FV	6.00

		VG	VF	UNC
50	**500 RUPEES** ND (2002). Black and orange on m/c unpt. Bldg. at ctr. 2 tigers at ctr. on back.	FV	FV	17.50

		VG	VF	UNC
51	**1000 RUPEES** ND (2002). Black and red on m/c unpt. Temple at ctr. Elephant at ctr. on back.	FV	FV	35.00

NETHERLANDS

The Kingdom of the Netherlands, a country of western Europe fronting on the North Sea and bordered by Belgium and Germany, has an area of 15,770 sq. mi. (40,844 sq. km.) and a population of 15.87 million. Capital: Amsterdam, but the seat of government is at The Hague. The economy is based on dairy farming and a variety of industrial activities. Chemicals, yarns and fabrics, and meat products are exported.

After being a part of Charlemagne's empire in the 8th and 9th centuries, the Netherlands came under the control of Burgundy and the Austrian Hapsburgs, and finally were subjected to Spanish domination in the 16th century. Led by William of Orange, the Dutch revolted against Spain in 1568. The seven northern provinces formed the Union of Utrecht and declared their independence in 1581, becoming the Republic of the United Netherlands. In the following century, the "Golden Age" of Dutch history, the Netherlands became a great sea and colonial power, a patron of the arts and a refuge for the persecuted. In 1814, all the provinces of Holland and Belgium were merged into the Kingdom of the United Netherlands under William I. The Belgians withdrew in 1830 to form their own kingdom, the last substantial change in the configuration of European Netherlands. German forces invaded in 1940 and the royal family fled to England where a government in exile was formed. German High Commissioner Arthur Seyss-Inquart was placed in command until 1945 when the arrival of Allied military forces ended the occupation. Reigning since 1948, Queen Juliana abdicated in 1981. Her daughter, Beatrix, is now Queen.

RULERS:
Juliana, 1948-1981
Beatrix, 1981-

MONETARY SYSTEM:
1 Gulden = 100 Cents, to 2001
1 Euro = 100 Cents, 2002-

KONINKRIJK - KINGDOM

DE NEDERLANDSCHE BANK

NETHERLANDS BANK

1966-72 ISSUE

		VG	VF	UNC
90	**5 GULDEN**			
	26.4.1966. Green on m/c unpt. Joost van den Vondel at r. Modern design of Amsterdam Play-house on back. Wmk: Inkwell, quill pen and scroll.			
	a. Serial # at upper l. and lower r. Gray paper w/clear wmk.	FV	FV	10.00
	b. Serial # at upper l. and lower r. White paper w/vague wmk. Series XA/XM.	FV	FV	12.50
	c. Serial # at upper l. and ctr. r. in smaller type. (Experimental issue; circulated initally in the province of Utrecht.) Series 6AA.	50.00	125.00	625.00

		VG	VF	UNC
91	**10 GULDEN**			
	25.4.1968. Dk. blue on violet and m/c unpt. Stylized self-portrait of Frans Hals at r. Modern design on back. Wmk: Cornucopia.			
	a. *O* in "bullseye" at upper l. on back.	FV	6.00	12.00
	b. Plain "bullseye" at upper l. on back.	FV	FV	10.00

		VG	VF	UNC
92	**25 GULDEN**			
	10.2.1971. Red on orange and pink unpt. Jan Pietersz. Sweelinck at r. Modern design on back. Wmk: Rectangular wave design.			
	a. Issued note.	FV	FV	35.00
	s. Specimen.	—	—	950.00

		VG	VF	UNC
93	**100 GULDEN**			
	14.5.1970. Dk. brown on m/c unpt. Michiel Adriaensz. de Ruyter at r. Compass-card or rhumbcard design at ctr. on back.			
	a. Issued note.	FV	FV	165.00
	s. Specimen.	—	—	1100.00

		VG	VF	UNC
94	**1000 GULDEN**			
	30.3.1972. Black and dk. green on m/c unpt. Baruch d' Espinoza at r. Wmk: Pyramid in bowl on slab.			
	a. Issued note.	FV	FV	750.00
	s. Specimen.	—	—	1400.00

1973 ISSUE

95 5 GULDEN
28.3.1973. Dk. green on green and m/c unpt. Joost van den Vondel
at r. Wmk. like #90.
  a. Issued note.
  s. Specimen.

VG	VF	UNC
FV	FV	7.50
—	—	1300.00

1977-85 ISSUE

96 50 GULDEN
4.1.1982. Orange and yellow on m/c unpt. Sunflower w/bee at
lower ctr. Vertical format. Map and flowers on back. Wmk: Bee.

VG	VF	UNC
FV	FV	35.00

97 100 GULDEN
28.7.1977 (1981). Dk. brown on m/c unpt. Snipe at r. Head of great
snipe on back and as wmk.
  a. Issued note.
  s. Specimen.

VG	VF	UNC
FV	FV	140.00
—	—	1200.00

NOTICE
Readers with unlisted dates, signature varieties, etc. are invited to
submit photocopies of their notes to: Standard Catalog of World
Paper Money, 700 East State St. Iola, WI 54990-0001, E-Mail:
george.cuhaj@fwpubs.com.

98 250 GULDEN
25.7.1985 (1986). Violet on m/c unpt. Lighthouse. Vertical format.
Lighthouse and map on back. Wmk: Rabbit and *VHP*.
  a. Issued note.
  s. Specimen.

VG	VF	UNC
FV	FV	150.00
—	—	1700.00

1989-97 ISSUE

99 10 GULDEN
1.7.1997. Purple and blue-violet on m/c unpt. Value and geometric
designs on face and back. Wmk: Bird.

VG	VF	UNC
FV	FV	7.50

100 25 GULDEN
5.4.1989. Red on m/c unpt. Value and geometric designs on face
and back. Wmk: Robin.

VG	VF	UNC
FV	FV	17.50

		VG	**VF**	**UNC**
101	**100 GULDEN** 9.1.1992 (7.9.1993). Dk. and lt. brown, gray and gold on m/c unpt. Value and geometric designs on face and back. Wmk: Little owl.	FV	FV	75.00

		VG	**VF**	**UNC**
102	**1000 GULDEN** 2.6.1994 (1996). Dk. gray and green. Geometric designs on face and back. Wmk: Lapwing's head.	FV	FV	600.00

Note: For later issues used in the Netherlands see European Union listings.

The Netherlands Antilles, part of the Netherlands realm, comprise two groups of islands in the West Indies: Bonaire and Curacao near the Venezuelan coast; and St. Eustatius, and the southern part of St. Martin (St. Maarten) southeast of Puerto Rico. The island group has an area of 385 sq. mi. (961 sq. km.) and a population of 210,000. Capital: Willemstad. Chief industries are the refining of crude oil, and tourism. Petroleum products and phosphates are exported.

On Dec. 15, 1954, the Netherlands Antilles were given complete domestic autonomy and granted equality within the Kingdom with Surinam and the Netherlands. The island of Aruba gained independence in 1986.

RULERS:
  Dutch

MONETARY SYSTEM:
  1 Gulden = 100 Cents

DUTCH ADMINISTRATION

NEDERLANDSE ANTILLEN

1955 MUNTBILJET NOTE ISSUE

		VG	**VF**	**UNC**
A1	**2 1/2 GULDEN** 1955; 1964. Blue. Ship in dry dock at ctr. Crowned supported arms at ctr. on back. Printer: ABNC.			
	a. 1955.	7.50	35.00	200.00
	b. 1964.	5.00	25.00	175.00
	s. As a or b. Specimen.	—	—	240.00

1962 ISSUE

#1-7 woman seated w/scroll and flag in oval at l. Crowned arms at ctr. r. on back. Wmk: *NA* monogram.
  Printer: JEZ.

		VG	**VF**	**UNC**
1	**5 GULDEN** 2.1.1962. Blue on m/c unpt. View of Curaçao at ctr.			
	a. Issued note.	4.00	15.00	75.00
	s. Specimen.	—	—	35.00

2	**10 GULDEN**	VG	VF	UNC
	2.1.1962. Green on m/c unpt. High-rise bldg. (Aruba) at ctr.			
	a. Issued note.	7.50	25.00	110.00
	s. Specimen.	—	—	45.00

3	**25 GULDEN**	VG	VF	UNC
	2.1.1962. Black-gray on m/c unpt. View of Bonaire at ctr.			
	a. Issued note.	FV	25.00	145.00
	s. Specimen.	—	—	60.00

4	**50 GULDEN**	VG	VF	UNC
	2.1.1962. Brown on m/c unpt. City by the seaside (St. Maarten) at ctr.			
	a. Issued note.	35.00	100.00	300.00
	s. Specimen.	—	—	75.00

5	**100 GULDEN**	VG	VF	UNC
	2.1.1962. Violet on m/c unpt. Monument (St. Eustatius) at ctr.			
	a. Issued note.	60.00	175.00	450.00
	s. Specimen.	—	—	100.00

6	**250 GULDEN**	VG	VF	UNC
	2.1.1962. Olive-green on m/c unpt. Boats on the beach (Saba) at ctr.			
	a. Issued note.	125.00	375.00	—
	s. Specimen.	—	—	135.00

7	**500 GULDEN**	VG	VF	UNC
	2.1.1962. Red on m/c unpt. Oil refinery (Curaçao) at ctr.			
	a. Issued note.	250.00	450.00	—
	s. Specimen.	—	—	185.00

1967 ISSUE

#8-13 monument *Steunend op eigen Kracht...* at l. Crowned arms at ctr. on back. Wmk: *NA* monogram. Printer: JEZ.

8	**5 GULDEN**	VG	VF	UNC
	1967; 1972. Dk. blue and green on m/c unpt. View of Curaçao at ctr.			
	a. 28.8.1967.	3.50	7.50	45.00
	b. 1.6.1972.	3.50	5.00	35.00
	s. As a. Specimen.	—	—	30.00

9	**10 GULDEN**	VG	VF	UNC
	1967; 1972. Green on m/c unpt. View of Aruba at ctr.			
	a. 28.8.1967.	FV	10.00	55.00
	b. 1.6.1972.	FV	7.50	47.50
	s. As a. Specimen.	—	—	—

10	**25 GULDEN**	VG	VF	UNC
	1967; 1972. Black-gray on m/c unpt. View of Bonaire at ctr.			
	a. 28.8.1967.	FV	27.50	125.00
	b. 1.6.1972.	FV	20.00	95.00
	s. As a. Specimen.	—	—	—

16	**10 GULDEN**	VG	VF	UNC
	1979; 1984. Green and blue-green on m/c unpt. Like #9.			
	a. 14.7.1979.	FV	10.00	50.00
	b. 1.6.1984.	FV	7.50	45.00
17	**25 GULDEN**			
	14.7.1979. Blue and blue-green on m/c unpt. Like #10.	FV	50.00	200.00
18	**50 GULDEN**			
	23.12.1980. Red on m/c unpt. Like #11.	FV	65.00	325.00
19	**100 GULDEN**			
	14.7.1979. Red-brown and violet on m/c unpt. Like #12.			
	a. 14.7.1979.	FV	90.00	450.00
	b. 9.12.1981.	FV	100.00	500.00

1970 MUNTBILJET ISSUE

#20 and 21 crowned arms at r. on back. Printer: JEZ.

11	**50 GULDEN**	VG	VF	UNC
	1967; 1972. Brown on m/c unpt. Beach (St. Maarten) at ctr.			
	a. 28.8.1967.	FV	65.00	225.00
	b. 1.6.1972.	FV	45.00	175.00
	s. As a. Specimen.	—	—	—

20	**1 GULDEN**	VG	VF	UNC
	8.9.1970. Red on orange unpt. Aerial view of harbor at l. ctr.			
	a. Issued note.	FV	2.00	8.50
	s. Specimen.	—	—	90.00

12	**100 GULDEN**	VG	VF	UNC
	1967; 1972. Violet on m/c unpt. Boats and fishermen on the beach (St. Eustatius) at ctr.			
	a. 28.8.1967.	FV	125.00	365.00
	b. 1.6.1972.	FV	85.00	275.00
	s. As a. Specimen.	—	—	150.00

21	**2 1/2 GULDEN**	VG	VF	UNC
	8.9.1970. Blue on lt. blue unpt. Jetliner at l. ctr.			
	a. Issued note.	FV	3.00	17.50
	s. Specimen.	—	—	90.00

1986 BANK ISSUE

#22-27 back and wmk: Shield-like bank logo. Sign. and sign. title varieties. Printer: JEZ.

13	**250 GULDEN**	VG	VF	UNC
	28.8.1967. Olive-green on m/c unpt. Mountains (Saba) at ctr.			
	a. Issued note.	125.00	250.00	525.00
	s. Specimen.	—	—	350.00

#14 *Deleted.* See #A1.

1979; 1980 ISSUE

#15-19 like #8-13. Printer: JEZ.

15	**5 GULDEN**	VG	VF	UNC
	1980; 1984. Purplish blue on m/c unpt. Like #8.			
	a. 23.12.1980.	FV	7.50	35.00
	b. 1.6.1984.	FV	6.00	32.50

22	5 GULDEN	VG	VF	UNC
	1986; 1990; 1994. Dk. blue on m/c unpt. Troupial at ctr.			
	a. Sign. titles: *SEKRETARIS; PRESIDENT.* 31.3.1986.	FV	FV	30.00
	b. Sign. titles: *DIRECTEUR SEKRETARIS; PRESIDENT.*	FV	FV	27.50
	1.1.1990.			
	c. 1.5.1994.	FV	FV	27.50
	s. As a. Specimen.	—	—	—

23	10 GULDEN	VG	VF	UNC
	1986; 1990; 1994. Dk. green on m/c unpt. Purple-throated carib at			
	l. ctr.			
	a. 31.3.1986. Sign. titles as 22a.	FV	FV	42.50
	b. 1.1.1990. Sign. titles as 22b.	FV	FV	37.50
	c. 1.5.1994.	FV	FV	32.50
	s. As a. Specimen.	—	—	—

24	25 GULDEN	VG	VF	UNC
	1986; 1990; 1994. Red on m/c unpt. Flamingo at l. ctr.			
	a. 31.3.1986. Sign. titles as 22a.	FV	FV	90.00
	b. 1.1.1990. Sign. titles as 22b.	FV	FV	85.00
	c. 1.5.1994.	FV	FV	80.00
	s. As a. Specimen.	—	—	—

25	50 GULDEN	VG	VF	UNC
	1986; 1990; 1994. Brown and orange on m/c unpt. Rufous-collared			
	sparrow at l. ctr.			
	a. 31.3.1986. Sign. titles as 22a.	FV	FV	145.00
	b. 1.1.1990. Sign. titles as 22b.	FV	FV	135.00
	c. 1.5.1994.	FV	FV	125.00
	s. As a. Specimen.	—	—	—

26	100 GULDEN	VG	VF	UNC
	1986; 1990; 1994. Brown on m/c unpt. Bananaquit at l. ctr.			
	a. 31.3.1986.	FV	FV	245.00
	b. 1.1.1990.	FV	FV	230.00
	c. 1.5.1994.	FV	FV	205.00
	s. As a. Specimen.	—	—	—

27	250 GULDEN	VG	VF	UNC
	31.3.1986. Purple and red-violet on m/c unpt. Caribbean			
	mockingbird at l. ctr.			
	a. Issued note.	FV	FV	475.00
	s. Specimen.	—	—	—

1998; 2001; 2003 ISSUE

#28-31 similar to #23-26 but w/gold foil at lower r. Additional enhanced security devices include surface overlays on face and small sparkling dots at top and bottom on back. 2 sign. varieties.

28	10 GULDEN	VG	VF	UNC
	1998; 2001; 2003. Dk. and lt. green on m/c unpt. Similar to #23.			
	a. 1.1.1998.	FV	FV	30.00
	b. 1.12.2001.	FV	FV	27.50
	c. 1.12.2003.	FV	FV	20.00

29	25 GULDEN	VG	VF	UNC
	1998; 2001; 2003. Red on m/c unpt. Similar to #24.			
	a. 1.1.1998.	FV	FV	70.00
	b. 1.12.2001.	FV	FV	50.00
	c. 1.12.2003.	FV	FV	40.00

30	50 GULDEN	VG	VF	UNC
	1998; 2001; 2003. Brown-orange on m/c unpt. Similar to #25.			
	a. 1.1.1998.	FV	FV	105.00
	b. 1.12.2001.	FV	FV	90.00
	c. 1.12.2003.	FV	FV	75.00

31	100 GULDEN	VG	VF	UNC
	1998; 2001; 2003. Brown on m/c unpt. Similar to #26.			
	a. 1.1.1998.	FV	FV	185.00
	b. 1.12.2001.	FV	FV	160.00
	c. 1.12.2003.	FV	FV	140.00

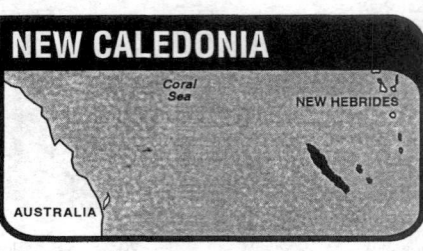

NEW CALEDONIA

The French Overseas Territory of New Caledonia, a group of about 25 islands in the South Pacific, is situated about 750 miles (1,207 km.) east of Australia. The territory, which includes the dependencies of Ile des Pins, Loyalty Islands, Ile Huon, Islés Belep, Isles Chesterfield, and Ile Walpole, has a total land area of 6,530 sq. mi. (19,058 sq. km.) and a population of 152,000. Capital: Noumea. The islands are rich in minerals; New Caledonia has the world's largest known deposit of nickel. Nickel, nickel castings, coffee and copra are exported.

British navigator Capt. James Cook discovered New Caledonia in 1774. The French took possession in 1853, and established a penal colony on the island in 1854. The European population of the colony remained disproportionately convict until 1894. New Caledonia became an overseas territory within the French Community in 1946, and in 1958 and 1972 chose to remain affiliated with France.

RULERS:
French

MONETARY SYSTEM:
1 Franc = 100 Centimes

	SIGNATURE VARIETIES	
	DIRECTEUR GÉNÉRAL	PRÉSIDENT DU CONSEIL DE SURVEILLANCE
1	André Postel-Vinay, 1967-1972	Bernard Clappier, 1966-1972
2	Claude Panouillot, 1972-1973	André De Lattre, 1973
3	Claude Panouillot, 1974-1978	Marcel Theron, 1974-1979
4	Yves Roland-Billecart, 1979-1984	Gabriel Lefort, 1980-1984
5	Yves Roland-Billecart, 1985-1973	Jacques Waitzenegger, 1985-

INSTITUT D'EMISSION D'OUTRE-MER

NOUMÉA

1969 ND ISSUE

59	100 FRANCS	VG	VF	UNC
	ND (1969). Brown on m/c unpt. Girl wearing wreath and playing guitar at r. W/o ovpt: *REPUBLIQUE FRANÇAISE* at lower ctr. Girl at l., harbor scene at ctr. on back. Intaglio. Sign. 1.	5.00	22.50	75.00

60	**500 FRANCS** ND (1969-92). Blue, brown and m/c. Dugout canoe w/sail at ctr., fisherman at r. Man at l., rock formation at l. ctr., native art at r. on back.	**VG**	**VF**	**UNC**
	a. Sign. 1.	7.00	12.00	35.00
	b. Sign. 2.	7.00	12.00	32.50
	c. Sign. 3.	6.50	10.00	30.00
	d. Sign. 4.	6.50	10.00	30.00
61	**1000 FRANCS** ND (1969). Orange, brown and m/c. Hut under palm tree at l., girl at r. W/o ovpt: *RÉPUBLIQUE FRANÇAISE* at lower l. Bldg., kagu bird at l., deer near hut at r. on back. Sign. 1.	12.50	25.00	125.00

#62 *Deleted*. See #65.

1971 ND ISSUE

63	**100 FRANCS** ND (1971; 1973). Brown on m/c unpt. Like #59 but w/ovpt: *RÉPUBLIQUE FRANÇAISE* at lower ctr.	**VG**	**VF**	**UNC**
	a. Intaglio. Sign. 1 (1971).	2.00	5.00	35.00
	b. Lithographed. Series beginning #H2, from #51,000. Sign. 1 (1973).	1.75	4.00	25.00
	c. As. b. Sign. 2 (1975).	1.50	3.50	20.00
	d. As b. Sign. 3 (1977).	1.50	3.00	17.50
	s. As a. Specimen.	—	—	—
64	**1000 FRANCS** ND (1971; 1983). Orange, brown and m/c. Like #61 but w/ovpt: *RÉPUBLIQUE FRANÇAISE* ovpt. at lower l.			
	a. Sign. 1 (1971).	12.50	20.00	35.00
	b. Sign. 4 (1983).	10.00	17.50	32.50

65	**5000 FRANCS** ND (1971-84). M/c. Bougainville at l., sailing ships at ctr. Ovpt: *RÉPUBLIQUE FRANÇAISE*. Admiral Febvrier-Despointes at r., sailboat at ctr. r. on back.	**VG**	**VF**	**UNC**
	a. Sign. 1 (1971).	60.00	100.00	200.00
	b. Sign. 2 (1975).	55.00	95.00	190.00
	c. Sign. 4 (1982-84).	55.00	90.00	175.00
	s. As a. Specimen.	—	—	150.00

Note: For current 500 and 10,000 Francs see French Pacific Territories.

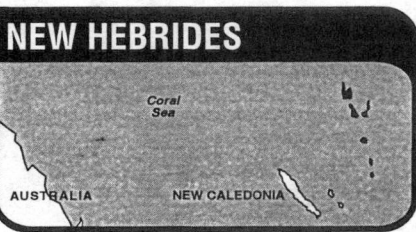

NEW HEBRIDES

New Hebrides Condominium, a group of islands located in the South Pacific 500 miles (800 km.) west of Fiji, were under the joint sovereignty of Great Britain and France. The islands have an area of 5,700 sq. mi. (14,763 sq. km.) and a population of mainly Melanesians of mixed blood. Capital: Port-Vila. The volcanic and coral islands, while malarial and subject to frequent earthquakes, are extremely fertile, and produce copra, coffee, tropical fruits and timber for export.

The New Hebrides were discovered by Portuguese navigator Pedro de Quiros in 1606, visited by French explorer Bougainville in 1768, and named by British navigator Capt. James Cook in 1774. Ships of all nations converged on the islands to trade for sandalwood, prompting France and Britain to relinquish their individual claims and declare the islands a neutral zone in 1878. The New Hebrides were placed under the control of a mixed Anglo-French commission of naval officers during the native uprisings of 1887, and established as a condominium under the joint sovereignty of France and Great Britain in 1906.

RULERS:
British and French to 1980

MONETARY SYSTEM:
1 Franc = 100 Centimes

SIGNATURE VARIETIES		
	DIRECTEUR GÉNÉRAL	**PRÉSIDENT DU CONSEIL DE SURVEILLANCE**
1	André Postel-Vinay, 1967-1972	Bernard Clappier, 1966-1972
2	Claude Panouillot, 1972-1973	André De Lattre, 1973
3	Claude Panouillot, 1974-1978	Marcel Theron, 1974-1979
4	Yves Roland-Billecart, 1979-1984	Gabriel Lefort, 1980-1984
5	Yves Roland-Billecart, 1985-1973	Jacques Waitzenegger, 1985-

INSTITUT D'EMISSION D'OUTRE-MER, NOUVELLES HEBRIDES

1965; 1967 ND ISSUE

16	**100 FRANCS** ND (1965-71). Brown and m/c. Girl w/guitar at r. Girl at l., harbor scene at ctr. w/ovpt: *NOUVELLES-HÉBRIDES* in capital letters on back. Sign. 1.	**VG**	**VF**	**UNC**
		7.50	40.00	175.00

17	**1000 FRANCS**		**VG**	**VF**	**UNC**

17 **1000 FRANCS**
ND (1967-71). Red. Hut under palm tree at l., girl at r. Bldg., Kagu
bird at l., deer near hut at r. w/ovpt: *NOUVELLES HÉBRIDES* in
capital letters at upper ctr. on back. Sign. 1.

		VG	**VF**	**UNC**
		17.50	80.00	275.00

1970 ND ISSUE

18 **100 FRANCS**
M/c. Like #16, but red and blue unpt. *Nouvelles Hébrides*. ND
(1970; 1972; 1977). in script on face and back.

	VG	**VF**	**UNC**
a. Intaglio plates. Sign. 1. (1970).	2.00	5.00	27.50
b. Lithographed series beginning E1, from no. 51,000. Sign. 1. (1972).	1.50	4.00	25.00
c. As b. Sign. 2. (1975).	1.50	3.50	20.00
d. As b. Sign. 3. (1977).	1.50	3.00	17.50

19 **500 FRANCS**
ND (1970-80). Blue, brown and m/c. Dugout canoe w/sail at ctr.,
fisherman at. r. Man at l., rock formation at l. ctr., native art at r on
back.

	VG	**VF**	**UNC**
a. Sign. 1. (1970).	7.50	12.50	45.00
b. Sign. 3. (1979).	7.00	12.00	42.50
c. Sign. 4. (1980).	6.00	10.00	40.00

20 **1000 FRANCS**
ND (1970-80). Orange, brown and m/c. Like #17. *Nouvelles
Hébrides* in script on face and back.

	VG	**VF**	**UNC**
a. Sign. 1. (1970).	15.00	25.00	75.00
b. Sign. 2. (1975).	12.50	22.50	65.00
c. Sign. 3. (1980).	12.50	20.00	55.00

Note: For later issues see Vanuatu.

NEW ZEALAND

New Zealand, a parliamentary state located in the southwestern Pacific 1,250 miles (2,011 km.) east of Australia, has an area of 103,736 sq. mi. (269,056 sq. km.) and a population of 3.8 million. Capital: Wellington. Wool, meat, dairy products and some manufactured items are exported.

New Zealand was discovered and named by Dutch navigator Abel Tasman in 1642, and explored by British navigator Capt. James Cook who surveyed it in 1769 and annexed the land to Great Britain. The British government disavowed the annexation and for the next 70 years the only white settlers to arrive were adventurers attracted by the prospects of lumbering, sealing and whaling. Great Britain annexed the land in 1840 by treaty with the native chiefs and made it a dependency of New South Wales. The colony was granted self-government in 1852, a ministerial form of government in 1856, and full dominion status on Sept. 26, 1907. Full internal and external autonomy, which New Zealand had in effect possessed for many years, was formally extended in 1947. New Zealand is a member of the Commonwealth of Nations. Elizabeth II is Head of State as Queen of New Zealand.

RULERS:
British

MONETARY SYSTEM:
1 Shilling = 12 Pence
1 Pound = 20 Shillings to 1967
1 Pound = 20 Shillings (also 2 Dollars) to 1967
1 Dollar = 100 Cents, 1967-

RESERVE BANK OF NEW ZEALAND

1940 ND ISSUE

#158-162 portr. Capt. J. Cook at lower r. Sign. title: *CHIEF CASHIER*. Wmk: Maori chief. Printer: TDLR.

158 **10 SHILLINGS**
ND (1940-67). Brown on m/c unpt. Arms at upper ctr. Kiwi at l.,
Waitangi Treaty signing scene at ctr. on back.

	VG	**VF**	**UNC**
a. Sign. T. P. Hanna. (1940-55).	10.00	45.00	225.00
b. Sign. G. Wilson. (1955-56).	12.50	55.00	325.00
c. Sign. R. N. Fleming. W/o security thread. (1956-67).	10.00	50.00	300.00
d. As c. W/security thread. (1967).	5.00	12.50	55.00

159 **1 POUND**
ND (1940-67). Purple on m/c unpt. Arms at upper ctr. Sailing ship
on sea at l. on back.

	VG	**VF**	**UNC**
a. Sign. T. P. Hanna. (1940-55).	8.00	30.00	200.00
b. Sign. G. Wilson. (1955-56).	10.00	40.00	275.00
c. Sign. R. N. Fleming. W/o security thread. (1956-67).	8.00	30.00	215.00
d. As c. W/security thread. (1967).	4.00	13.50	65.00

160	5 POUNDS	VG	VF	UNC
	ND (1940-67). Blue on m/c unpt. Crowned arms at upper ctr. Lake Pukaki and Mt. Cook on back.			
	a. Sign. T. P. Hanna. (1940-55).	12.50	60.00	225.00
	b. Sign. G. Wilson. (1955-56).	12.50	65.00	275.00
	c. Sign. R. N. Fleming. W/o security thread. (1956-67).	12.50	40.00	275.00
	d. As c. W/security thread. (1967).	12.50	30.00	120.00

161	10 POUNDS	VG	VF	UNC
	ND (1940-67). Green on m/c unpt. Crowned arms, sailing ship at l. Flock of sheep at l. ctr. on back.			
	a. Sign. T. P. Hanna. (1940-55).	55.00	130.00	875.00
	b. Sign. G. Wilson. (1955-56).	70.00	225.00	1000.00
	c. Sign. R. N. Fleming. (1956-67).	50.00	100.00	425.00
	d. As c. W/security thread. (1967).	40.00	90.00	275.00

162	50 POUNDS	VG	VF	UNC
	ND (1940-67). Red on m/c unpt. Crowned arms, sailing ship at l. Dairy farm and Mt. Egmont on back.			
	a. Sign. T. P. Hanna. (1940-55).	450.00	1100.00	5000.00
	b. Sign. G. Wilson. (1955-56).	500.00	1150.00	5500.00
	c. Sign. R. N. Fleming. (1956-67).	225.00	750.00	2500.00

1967 ND ISSUE

#163-168 Qn. Elizabeth II at r. on face. Birds and plants on back. Wmk: Capt. J. Cook. Printer: TDLR.

#163b-168b replacement notes: Special serial # prefix and * suffix.

163	1 DOLLAR	VG	VF	UNC
	ND (1967-81). Brown on m/c unpt. Pied fantail at ctr. on back.			
	a. Sign. R. N. Fleming. (1967-68).	6.00	20.00	55.00
	b. Sign. D. L. Wilks. (1968-75).	3.50	10.00	25.00
	c. Sign. R. L. Knight. (1975-77).	2.00	7.50	17.50
	d. Sign. H. R. Hardie. (1977-81).	2.00	7.50	17.50
	s. Specimen.	—	—	—

164	2 DOLLARS	VG	VF	UNC
	ND (1967-81). Purple on m/c unpt. Rifleman at ctr. on back.			
	a. Sign. R. N. Fleming. (1967-68).	5.00	17.50	60.00
	b. Sign. D. L. Wilks. (1968-75).	5.00	15.00	40.00
	c. Sign. R. L. Knight. (1975-77).	4.00	12.50	30.00
	d. Sign. H. R. Hardie. (1977-81).	3.50	10.00	25.00
	s. Specimen.	—	—	—

165	5 DOLLARS	VG	VF	UNC
	ND (1967-81). Orange on m/c unpt. Tui at ctr. on back.			
	a. Sign. R. N. Fleming. (1967-68).	7.50	25.00	80.00
	b. Sign. D. L. Wilks. (1968-75).	12.50	50.00	250.00
	c. Sign. R. L. Knight. (1975-77).	6.00	20.00	60.00
	d. Sign. H. R. Hardie. (1977-81).	5.00	15.00	55.00
	s. Specimen.			

170	2 DOLLARS	VG	VF	UNC
	ND (1981-92). Purple on m/c unpt. Back similar to #164.			
	a. Sign. H. R. Hardie w/title: *CHIEF CASHIER.* (1981-85).	FV	4.50	9.00
	b. Sign. S.T. Russell w/title: *GOVERNOR.* (1985-89).	FV	4.00	9.00
	c. Sign. D. T. Brash. (1989-92).	FV	3.50	7.00

166	10 DOLLARS	VG	VF	UNC
	ND (1967-81). Blue on m/c unpt. Kea at ctr. on back.			
	a. Sign. R. N. Fleming. (1967-68).	15.00	35.00	140.00
	b. Sign. D. L. Wilks. (1968-75.)	15.00	45.00	225.00
	c. Sign. R. L. Knight. (1975-77).	15.00	35.00	200.00
	d. Sign. H. R. Hardie. (1977-81).	12.00	25.00	120.00
	s. Specimen.	—	—	—

167	20 DOLLARS	VG	VF	UNC
	ND (1967-81). Green on m/c unpt. New Zealand pigeon at ctr. on back.			
	a. Sign. R. N. Fleming. (1967-68).	25.00	50.00	180.00
	b. Sign. D. L. Wilks. (1968-75).	35.00	75.00	400.00
	c. Sign. R. L. Knight. (1975-77).	30.00	65.00	300.00
	d. Sign. H. R. Hardie. (1977-81).	20.00	40.00	125.00
	s. Specimen.	—	—	—

171	5 DOLLARS	VG	VF	UNC
	ND (1981-92). Orange on m/c unpt. Back similar to #165.			
	a. Sign. H. R. Hardie w/title: *CHIEF CASHIER.* (1981-85).	FV	12.00	25.00
	b. Sign. S.T. Russell w/title: *GOVERNOR.* (1985-89).	FV	10.00	20.00
	c. Sign. D. T. Brash. (1989-92).	FV	10.00	20.00

168	100 DOLLARS	VG	VF	UNC
	ND (1967-77). Red on m/c unpt. Takahe at ctr. on back.			
	a. Sign. R. N. Fleming. (1967-68).	120.00	300.00	1400.00
	b. Sign. R. L. Knight. (1975-77).	100.00	250.00	900.00
	s. Specimen.	—	—	—

1981-83 ND ISSUE

#169-175 new portr. of Qn. Elizabeth II on face. Birds and plants on back. Wmk: Capt. J. Cook. Printer: BWC.

#169a, 170a, 171a, 171b, 172a, 172b and 173a replacement note: Special serial # prefix and * suffix.

172	10 DOLLARS	VG	VF	UNC
	ND (1981-92). Blue on m/c unpt. Back similar to #166.			
	a. Sign. H. R. Hardie w/title: *CHIEF CASHIER.* (1981-85).	FV	22.50	47.50
	b. Sign. S.T. Russell w/title: *GOVERNOR.* (1985-89).	FV	15.00	32.50
	c. Sign. D. T. Brash. (1989-92).	FV	9.00	35.00

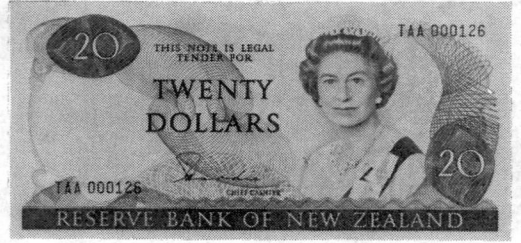

169	1 DOLLAR	VG	VF	UNC
	ND (1981-92). Dk. brown on m/c unpt. Back similar to #163.			
	a. Sign. H. R. Hardie w/title: *CHIEF CASHIER.* (1981-85).	FV	3.50	6.50
	b. Sign. S. T. Russell w/title: *GOVERNOR.* (1985-89).	FV	3.00	6.00
	c. Sign. D. T. Brash. (1989-92).	FV	2.50	5.00

173	20 DOLLARS	VG	VF	UNC
	ND (1981-92). Green on m/c unpt. Back similar to #167.			
	a. Sign. H. R. Hardie w/title: *CHIEF CASHIER.* (1981-85).	FV	40.00	100.00
	b. Sign. S.T. Russell w/title: *GOVERNOR.* (1985-89).	FV	35.00	65.00
	c. Sign. D. T. Brash. (1989-92).	FV	30.00	55.00

174	50 DOLLARS	VG	VF	UNC
	ND (1981-92). Yellow-orange on m/c unpt. Morepork Owl at ctr. on back.			
	a. Sign. H. R. Hardie, w/title: Chief Cashier. (1981-85).	FV	70.00	200.00
	b. Sign. D. T. Brash, w/title: Governor. (1989-92).	FV	65.00	130.00

175	100 DOLLARS	VG	VF	UNC
	ND (1981-89). Red on m/c unpt. Back similar to #168.			
	a. Sign. H. R. Hardie w/title: *CHIEF CASHIER.* (1981-85).	FV	150.00	350.00
	b. Sign. S.T. Russell w/title: *GOVERNOR.* (1985-89).	FV	135.00	275.00

1990 COMMEMORATIVE ISSUE

#176, 150th Anniversary - Treaty of Waitangi, 1840-1990

176	10 DOLLARS	VG	VF	UNC
	1990. Blue-violet and pale blue on m/c unpt. Face design like #172, w/addition of 1990 Commission logo, the White Heron (in red and white w/date 1990) at r. of Qn. Special inscription and scene of treaty signing on back. Wmk: Capt. J. Cook. Serial #	FV	FV	25.00

Note: #176 w/prefix letters *AAA* was issued in 2, 4, 8, 16 and 32 subject panes. Market value is 10% over face value.

Note: #176 w/serial # prefix *BBB* was also issued in a special folder.

1992 ND ISSUE

#177-181 wmk: Qn. Elizabeth II. Sign. D.T. Brash. Replacement notes: Serial # prefix *ZZ*. Printer: TDLR.

177	5 DOLLARS	VG	VF	UNC
	ND (1992-). Brown and brown-orange on m/c unpt. Mt. Everest at l., Sir Edmund Hillary at ctr. Back brown and blue; flora w/Yellow-eyed penguin at ctr. r..			
	a. Issued note.	FV	6.00	15.00
	b. Uncut block of 4 in special folder.	—	—	50.00
	c. Uncut block of 8 in special folder.	—	—	140.00

178	10 DOLLARS	VG	VF	UNC
	ND (1992). Blue and purple on m/c unpt. Camellia flowers at l., K. Sheppard at ctr. r. Pair of blue ducks at ctr. r. on back.			
	a. Issued note.	FV	14.00	35.00
	b. Uncut pair in special folder.	—	—	35.00
	c. Uncut block of 4 in special folder.	—	—	65.00

179 20 DOLLARS
ND (1992). Green on m/c unpt. Qn. Elizabeth II at r., gov't. bldg. at l. in unpt. Back pale green and blue; New Zealand falcons at ctr.

	VG	VF	UNC
a. Issued note.	FV	25.00	50.00
b. Uncut block of 4 in special folder.	—	—	125.00

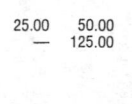

1999 ISSUE

#185-189 printer: NPA (w/o imprint).

Note: See Collector Series for special sets.

180 50 DOLLARS
ND (1992). Purple, violet and deep blue on m/c unpt. Sir A. Ngata at r., Maori meeting house at l. in unpt. Kokako at r. on back.

	VG	VF	UNC
a. Issued note.	FV	50.00	70.00
b. Uncut block of 4 in special folder.	—	—	285.00

185 5 DOLLARS
ND (1999). Similar to #177 but polymer plastic.

VG	VF	UNC
FV	FV	8.50

186 10 DOLLARS
ND (1999). Blue and m/c. Similar to #178 but polymer plastic.

VG	VF	UNC
FV	FV	14.00

181 100 DOLLARS
ND (1992). Violet-brown and red on m/c unpt. Lord Rutherford of Nelson at ctr., Nobel prize medal in unpt. at l. Yellowhead on tree trunk at ctr. r., moth at lower l. on back.

	VG	VF	UNC
a. Issued note.	FV	90.00	140.00
b. Uncut block of 4 in special folder.	—	—	550.00
s. Specimen.	—	—	—

1994 ND ISSUE

#182 and 183 replacement notes: Serial # prefix ZZ.

182 10 DOLLARS
ND (1994). Like #178 but bright blue at ctr. behind Whio ducks on back.

VG	VF	UNC
FV	FV	22.50

183 20 DOLLARS
ND (1994). Like #179 but bright green at ctr. behind Karearea falcon on back.

VG	VF	UNC
FV	FV	40.00

187 20 DOLLARS
ND (1999). Gray and m/c. Similar to #179 but polymer plastic.

VG	VF	UNC
FV	FV	27.50

1996 COMMEMORATIVE ISSUE

#184, 70th Birthday - Qn. Elizabeth II

184 20 DOLLARS
ND (1996). Green on m/c unpt. Commemorative ovpt. on #183. Serial # prefix ER.

VG	VF	UNC
FV	FV	200.00

Note: Issued in a special folder w/a $5 Commemorative coin (3000).

188 50 DOLLARS
ND (1999). Purple and m/c. Similar to #180 but polymer plastic.

VG	VF	UNC
FV	FV	50.00

189 100 DOLLARS
ND (1999). Brownish red and m/c. Similar to #181 but polymer plastic.

	VG	VF	UNC
	FV	FV	95.00

2000 COMMEMORATIVE ISSUE

#190, Millennium Commemorative
#190 printer: NPA (w/o imprint).

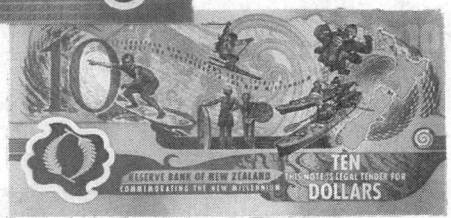

190 10 DOLLARS
2000. Blue, orange and m/c. Earth, map of New Zealand at l., ceremonial boat at ctr. Five sport activities on back. Polymer plastic.

	VG	VF	UNC
a. Black serial #. Serial # prefix *AA; AB*.	FV	FV	17.50
b. Red serial #. Serial # prefix *NZ*.	FV	FV	17.50

COLLECTOR SERIES

RESERVE BANK OF NEW ZEALAND

1990 ND COMMEMORATIVE ISSUE

CS176 10 DOLLARS
1990. W/special serial # prefix.

	Issue Price	Mkt.	Value
a. Serial # prefix *CWB* (for Country Wide Bank).	—		9.00
b. Serial # prefix *FTC* (for Farmers Trading Co.).	—		9.00
c. Serial # prefix *MBL* (for Mobil Oil Co.).	—		9.00
d. Serial # prefix *RNZ* (for Radio New Zealand).	—		9.00
e. Serial # prefix *RXX* (for Rank Xerox Co.).	—		9.00
f. Serial # prefix *TNZ* (for Toyota New Zealand).	—		9.00

1992 ISSUE

CS180 50 DOLLARS
ND (1993). Red serial #.

	Issue Price	Mkt.	Value
	—		65.00

Note: Issued w/$50 phone card.

1993 ND ISSUE

CS183 20 DOLLARS
As #183.

	Issue Price	Mkt.	Value
a. Uncut pair. W/serial # prefix: *TRBNZA* on back in folder.	—		—
b. In folder w/$20 phone card. 2500 sets.	—		40.00

1999 ISSUE

CS185 5 DOLLARS
As #185. Serial # prefix: *AA*.

	Issue Price	Mkt.	Value
a. Uncut pair.	12.50		20.00
b. Uncut sheet of 40 notes. 150 sheets.	130.00		150.00

CS186 10 DOLLARS
As #186. Serial # prefix: *AA*.

	Issue Price	Mkt.	Value
a. Uncut pair. 2,000 pairs.	19.00		25.00
b. Uncut sheet of 40 notes. 150 sheets.	255.00		300.00

CS187 20 DOLLARS
As #187. Serial # prefix: *AA*.

	Issue Price	Mkt.	Value
a. Uncut pair. 4,000 pairs.	38.00		50.00
b. Uncut sheet of 40. 150 sheets.	500.00		600.00

CS188 50 DOLLARS

			Expected New Issue

CS189 100 DOLLARS
As #189. Serial # prefix: *AA*.

	Issue Price	Mkt.	Value
a. Uncut pair. 1,000 pairs.	130.00		150.00
b. Uncut sheet of 28. 100 sheets.	1720.00		1800.00

1999 COMMEMORATIVE ISSUE

#CS190, Millennium Commemorative

CS190 10 DOLLARS
As #190 but w/bank ovpt. in red under 10 on face. Red serial #.

	Issue Price	Mkt.	Value
a. Single note in folder w/serial # prefix: *NZ*.	18.00		12.50
b. Uncut pair in folder w/serial # prefix: *NZ*.	19.00		25.00
c. Uncut sheet of 20 w/serial # prefix: *NZ*.	175.00		225.00

The Republic of Nicaragua, situated in Central America between Honduras and Costa Rica, has an area of 50,193 sq. mi (130,000 sq. km.) and a population of 4.69 million. Capital: Managua. Agriculture, mining (gold and silver) and hardwood logging are the principal industries. Cotton, meat, coffee, tobacco and sugar are exported.

Columbus sighted the coast of Nicaragua in 1502 during the course of his last voyage of discovery. It was first visited in 1522 by conquistadors from Panama, under command of Gonzalez Davila. After the first settlements were established in 1524 at Granada and Leon, Nicaragua was incorporated, for administrative purpose, in the Captaincy General of Guatemala, which included every Central American state but Panama. The Captaincy General declared its independence from Spain on Sept. 15, 1821. The next year Nicaragua united with the Mexican Empire of Agustin de Iturbide, then in 1823 with the Central American Republic. When the federation was dissolved, Nicaragua declared itself an independent republic in 1838.

MONETARY SYSTEM:
1 Peso = 100 Centavos to 1912
1 Córdoba = 100 Centavos, 1912-1987
1 New Córdoba = 1000 Old Córdobas, 1988-90
1 Córdoba Oro = 100 Centavos, 1990-

REPLACEMENT NOTES:
1985-dated issues printed by TDLR, ZA; ZB prefix.

REPUBLIC

BANCO CENTRAL DE NICARAGUA

DECRETO 26.4.1962

Series A

#107-114 portr. F. Hernandez Córdoba at ctr. on back. Printer: ABNC.

		VG	VF	UNC
107	**1 CÓRDOBA**			
	D.1962. Blue on m/c unpt. Banco Central at upper ctr.	0.15	1.00	7.50

		VG	VF	UNC
108	**5 CÓRDOBAS**			
	D.1962. Green on m/c unpt. C. Nicarao at upper ctr. Similar to #100.	0.75	3.00	15.00

		VG	VF	UNC
109	**10 CÓRDOBAS**			
	D.1962. Red on m/c unpt. Portr. M. de Larreynaga at upper ctr.	1.50	5.00	22.50

		VG	VF	UNC
110	**20 CÓRDOBAS**			
	D.1962. Orange-brown on m/c unpt. Portr. T. Martinez at upper ctr.	3.00	10.00	45.00

		VG	VF	UNC
111	**50 CÓRDOBAS**			
	D.1962. Purple on m/c unpt. Portr. M. Jerez at upper ctr.	6.00	25.00	85.00

		VG	VF	UNC
112	**100 CÓRDOBAS**			
	D.1962. Red-brown on m/c unpt. Portr. J. D. Estrada at upper ctr.	4.00	12.50	60.00
113	**500 CÓRDOBAS**			
	D.1962. Black on m/c unpt. Portr. R. Dario at upper ctr.			
	a. Issued note.	50.00	175.00	425.00
	s. Specimen.	—	—	500.00
114	**1000 CÓRDOBAS**			
	D.1962. Brown on m/c unpt. Portr. A. Somoza at upper ctr.			
	a. Issued note.	60.00	200.00	550.00
	s. Specimen.	—	—	500.00

DECRETO 25.5.1968

Series B

#115-120 portr. F. Hernandez Córdoba on back. Printer: TDLR.

115   1 CÓRDOBA
D.1968. Blue on m/c unpt. Like #107.
a. W/3 sign.
b. Pres. A. Somoza hand sign. at l.

	VG	VF	UNC
a.	0.10	0.50	2.00
b.	—	—	—

116   5 CÓRDOBAS
D.1968. Green on m/c unpt. Like #108.

VG	VF	UNC
0.50	1.50	5.00

117   10 CÓRDOBAS
D.1968. Red on m/c unpt. Like #109.

VG	VF	UNC
0.75	2.00	7.50

Note: Some of #118-120 were apparently released w/o r.h. sign. after the Managua earthquake of 1972 damaged the Central Bank building.

118   20 CÓRDOBAS
D.1968. Orange-brown on m/c unpt. Like #110.
a. W/3 sign.
b. W/o r.h. sign.

	VG	VF	UNC
a.	1.00	3.00	12.50
b.	—	—	—

119   50 CÓRDOBAS
D.1968. Purple on m/c unpt. Like #111.
a. W/3 sign.
b. W/o r.h. sign.

	VG	VF	UNC
a.	4.00	8.00	30.00
b.	—	—	—

120   100 CÓRDOBAS
D.1968. Red-brown on m/c unpt. Like #112.
a. W/3 sign.
b. W/o r.h. sign.

	VG	VF	UNC
a.	3.00	8.00	30.00
b.	—	—	—

DECRETO 27.4.1972

Series C
#121-128 printer: TDLR.

121   2 CÓRDOBAS
D.1972. Olive-green on m/c unpt. Banco Central at r. Furrows at l. on back.
a. W/3 sign.
b. W/o l.h. sign.
s. As a. Specimen.

	VG	VF	UNC
a.	0.10	0.25	3.00
b.	—	—	400.00
s.	—	—	35.00

122   5 CÓRDOBAS
D.1972. Dk. green on m/c unpt. C. Nicarao standing at r. w/bow. Fruitseller at l. on back.

VG	VF	UNC
0.25	0.75	4.00

123   10 CÓRDOBAS
D.1972. Red on m/c unpt. A. Castro standing at r. atop rocks. Hacienda at l. on back.

VG	VF	UNC
0.25	1.00	6.00

124   20 CÓRDOBAS
D.1972. Orange-brown on m/c unpt. R. Herrera igniting cannon at r. Signing ceremony of abrogation of Chamorro-Bryan Treaty of 1912, Somoza at ctr. on back.

VG	VF	UNC
0.50	2.00	10.00

Note: #124 was issued on the 60th anniversary of the Chamorro-Bryan Treaty of 1912.

125	50 CÓRDOBAS	VG	VF	UNC
	D.1972. Purple on m/c unpt. M. Jerez at r. Cows at l. on back.	10.00	30.00	85.00

129	20 CÓRDOBAS	VG	VF	UNC
	D.1978. Like #124.	0.25	1.50	7.50

126	100 CÓRDOBAS	VG	VF	UNC
	D.1972. Violet on m/c unpt. J. Dolores Estrada at r. National flower at l. on back.	0.50	2.50	10.00

130	50 CÓRDOBAS	VG	VF	UNC
	D.1978. Like #125.	0.25	2.50	9.00

DECRETO 16.8.1979

Series E, first issue

#131-133 w/square outer frame. Engraved. Printer: TDLR.

127	500 CÓRDOBAS	VG	VF	UNC
	D.1972. Black on m/c unpt. R. Darío at r. National Theater at l. on back.	10.00	25.00	100.00

131	50 CÓRDOBAS	VG	VF	UNC
	D.1979. Purple on m/c unpt. Comdt. C. F. Amador at r. Liberation of 19.7.1979 on back.	0.50	1.50	5.00

128	1000 CÓRDOBAS	VG	VF	UNC
	D.1972. Brown on m/c unpt. A. Somoza G. at r. View of Managua at l. on back.			
	a. 3 sign.	12.00	30.00	125.00
	b. 2 sign. (w/o r.h. sign.).	—	—	80.00

132	100 CÓRDOBAS	VG	VF	UNC
	D.1979. Dk. brown on m/c unpt. Like #126.	0.50	1.50	5.00

DECRETO 20.2.1978

Series D

#129-130 printer: TDLR.

		VG	VF	UNC
133	500 CÓRDOBAS	0.50	2.50	7.00
	D.1979. Deep blue on m/c unpt. Like #127.			

1979 ND Second Issue

Series E, second issue

#134-139 underprint to edge. Wmk: Sandino. Printer: TDLR.

#134-137 lithographed.

		VG	VF	UNC
134	10 CÓRDOBAS	0.25	0.75	3.00
	D.1979. Red on m/c unpt. A. Castro standing atop rocks at r. Miners on back.			

		VG	VF	UNC
135	20 CÓRDOBAS	0.25	0.75	3.50
	D.1979. Orange-brown on m/c unpt. Comdt. G. P. Ordoñez at r. Marching troops on back.			

		VG	VF	UNC
136	50 CÓRDOBAS	0.25	1.00	4.00
	D.1979. Purple on m/c unpt. Comdt. C. F. Amador at r. Liberation of 19.7.1979 on back.			

		VG	VF	UNC
137	100 CÓRDOBAS	0.50	1.00	4.00
	D.1979. Brown on m/c unpt. J. D. Estrada at r. Flower on back. Sign. varieties.			

		VG	VF	UNC
138	500 CÓRDOBAS	0.50	1.75	6.00
	D.1979. Deep olive-green on m/c unpt. Engraved. R. Darío at r. Teatro Popular at l. on back. Sign. varieties.			

		VG	VF	UNC
139	1000 CÓRDOBAS	2.50	15.00	45.00
	D.1979. Blue-gray on m/c unpt. Engraved. Gen. A. C. Sandino at r. Hut (Sandino's birthplace) on back. Sign. varieties.			

RESOLUTION OF 6.8.1984

Series F

#140-143 wmk: Sandino. Printer: TDLR.

		VG	VF	UNC
140	50 CÓRDOBAS	0.20	0.50	2.00
	L.1984 (1985). Purple on m/c unpt. Like #136.			

141	100 CÓRDOBAS	VG	VF	UNC
	L.1984 (1985). Brown on m/c unpt. Like #137.	0.25	1.00	3.00
142	500 CÓRDOBAS			
	L.1984 (1985). Deep olive-green on m/c unpt. Like #138.	0.20	1.00	5.00
143	1000 CÓRDOBAS			
	L.1984 (1985). Blue-gray on m/c unpt. Like #139.	0.50	2.00	9.00

RESOLUTION OF 11.6.1985

Series G

#144-146 wmk: Sandino. Replacement notes: Serial # prefix ZA; ZB. Printer: TDLR.

144	500 CÓRDOBAS	VG	VF	UNC
	L.1985 (1987). Deep olive-green on m/c unpt. Like #142. Lithographed.	0.20	0.75	4.00

145	1000 CÓRDOBAS	VG	VF	UNC
	L.1985 (1987). Dk. gray on m/c unpt. Like #143.			
	a. Engraved.	0.25	1.00	3.00
	b. Lithographed.	0.15	0.50	2.00

146	5000 CÓRDOBAS	VG	VF	UNC
	L.1985 (1987). Brown, orange and black on m/c unpt. Map at upper ctr., Gen. B. Zeledon at r. National Assembly bldg. on back.	0.15	0.50	2.50

A.P.E. DEL 26 OCT.

1987 ND PROVISIONAL ISSUE

#147-150 black ovpt. new denomination on face and back of old Series F and G notes printed by TDLR.

147	20,000 CÓRDOBAS ON 20 CÓRDOBAS	VG	VF	UNC
	D.1987 (1987). Ovpt. on unissued 20 Cordobas Series F. Colors and design like #135.	0.20	0.75	2.50

148	50,000 CÓRDOBAS ON 50 CÓRDOBAS	VG	VF	UNC
	D.1987 (1987). Ovpt. on #140.	0.25	0.75	3.00

149	100,000 CÓRDOBAS ON 500 CÓRDOBAS	VG	VF	UNC
	D.1987 (1987). Ovpt. on #144.	0.25	0.75	4.00

150	500,000 CÓRDOBAS ON 1000 CÓRDOBAS	VG	VF	UNC
	D.1987 (1987). Ovpt. on #145b. (Not issued).	0.50	2.00	5.50

1985 (1988) ISSUE

#151-156 wmk: Sandino. Replacement notes: Serial # prefix *ZA; ZB.*

151	10 CÓRDOBAS	VG	VF	UNC
	1985 (1988). Green and olive on m/c unpt. Comdt. C. F. Amador at r. Troop formation marching at l. on back.	0.10	0.50	2.00

152	20 CÓRDOBAS	VG	VF	UNC
	1985 (1988). Blue-black and blue on m/c unpt. Comdt. G. P. Ordoñez at r. Demonstration for agrarian reform at l. on back.	0.10	0.50	2.50

153	50 CÓRDOBAS	VG	VF	UNC
	1985 (1988). Brown and dk. red on m/c unpt. Gen. J. D. Estrada at r. Medical clinic scene at l. on back.	0.10	0.50	3.50

154	100 CÓRDOBAS	VG	VF	UNC
	1985 (1988). Deep blue, blue and gray on m/c unpt. R. Lopez Perez at r. State council bldg. at l. on back.	0.20	0.50	4.00

155	500 CÓRDOBAS	VG	VF	UNC
	1985 (1988). Purple, blue and brown on m/c unpt. R. Dario at r. Classroom w/students at l. on back.	0.25	0.75	4.00

156	1000 CÓRDOBAS	VG	VF	UNC
	1985 (1988). Brown on m/c unpt. Gen. A. C. Sandino at r. Liberation of 19.7.1979 on back.			
	a. Engraved w/wmk. at l. Serial # prefix FA.	0.25	0.75	5.00
	b. Lithographed w/o wmk. at l. Serial # prefix FC.	0.25	0.50	2.00

1988-89 ND PROVISIONAL ISSUE

157	5000 CÓRDOBAS	VG	VF	UNC
	ND (1988). Ovpt. elements in black on face and back of #146. Face ovpt.: sign. and title: *PRIMER VICE PRESIDENTE BANCO CENTRAL DE NICARAGUA* at l., 2 lines of text at lower ctr. blocked out, guilloche added at r. Ovpt: guilloche at l. and r., s	0.25	0.50	2.50

#158 and 159 black ovpt. of new denominations on face and back of earlier notes. Ovpt. errors exist and are rather common.

		VG	VF	UNC
158	10,000 CÓRDOBAS ON 10 CÓRDOBAS ND (1989). Ovpt. on #151.	0.25	0.75	3.00

		VG	VF	UNC
159	100,000 CÓRDOBAS ON 100 CÓRDOBAS ND (1989). Ovpt. on #154.	0.25	1.00	5.00

1989 ND EMERGENCY ISSUE

#160 and 161 grid map of Nicaragua at ctr. on face and back. Wmk: Sandino.

		VG	VF	UNC
160	20,000 CÓRDOBAS ND (1989). Black on blue, yellow and m/c unpt. Comdt. Cleto Ordoñez at r. Church of San Francisco Granada at l., map at ctr. on back.	0.25	1.00	4.50

		VG	VF	UNC
161	50,000 CÓRDOBAS ND (1989). Brown on purple, orange and m/c unpt. Gen. J. D. Estrada at r. Hacienda San Jacinto at l., map at ctr. on back.	0.25	0.75	3.50

NOTICE

Readers with unlisted dates, signature varieties, etc. are invited to submit photocopies of their notes to: Standard Catalog of World Paper Money, 700 East State St. Iola, WI 54990-0001, E-Mail: george.cuhaj@fwpubs.com.

1990 ND PROVISIONAL ISSUE

#162-164, black ovpt. new denomination on face and back of earlier notes.

Note: Ovpt. errors exist and are rather common.

		VG	VF	UNC
162	200,000 CÓRDOBAS ON 1000 CÓRDOBAS ND (1990). Ovpt on #156b.	0.15	0.40	1.75

		VG	VF	UNC
163	500,000 CÓRDOBAS ON 20 CÓRDOBAS ND (1990). Ovpt. on #152.	0.25	1.00	3.50

		VG	VF	UNC
164	1 MILLION CÓRDOBAS ON 1000 CÓRDOBAS ND (1990). Ovpt. on #156b.	0.25	1.00	3.50

1990 ND EMERGENCY ISSUE

#165 and 166 wmk: Sandino head, repeated.

		VG	VF	UNC
165	5 MILLION CÓRDOBAS ND (1990). Purple and orange on red and m/c unpt. Like #160.	0.20	0.50	2.00

		VG	VF	UNC
170	**25 CENTAVOS** ND (1991). Blue on pale green and m/c unpt. 2 sign. varieties.			
	a. Issued note.	FV	0.15	0.25
	s. Specimen.	—	—	100.00

#171 and 172 printer: CBNC.

		VG	VF	UNC
171	**1/2 CÓRDOBA** ND (1991). Brown and green on m/c unpt. F. H. de Córdoba at l., plant at r. Arms at ctr. on green back.	FV	FV	0.50

		VG	VF	UNC
172	**1/2 CÓRDOBA** ND (1992). Face like #171. Arms at l., national flower at r. on green back.	FV	FV	0.50

#173-177, 2 sign. varieties.

		VG	VF	UNC
173	**1 CÓRDOBA** 1990. Blue on purple and m/c unpt. Sunrise over field of maize at l., F. H. Córdoba at r. Back green and m/c; arms at ctr. Printer: TDLR. 2 sign. varieties.	FV	FV	1.00

		VG	VF	UNC
166	**10 MILLION CÓRDOBAS** ND (1990). Purple and lilac on blue and m/c unpt. Like #161.	0.25	0.75	2.50

1990; 1991-92 ND ISSUES

#173-177, 2 sign. varieties.

#167-170, F. H. Córdoba at r. Arms at l., flower at r. on back. Printer: Harrison.

		VG	VF	UNC
167	**1 CENTAVO** ND (1991). Purple on pale green and m/c unpt.	FV	0.05	0.15

		VG	VF	UNC
168	**5 CENTAVOS** ND (1991). Red-violet on pale green and m/c unpt. 2 sign. varieties.			
	a. Issued note.	FV	0.05	0.20
	s. Specimen.	—	—	100.00

		VG	VF	UNC
169	**10 CENTAVOS** ND (1991). Olive-green on lt. green and m/c unpt. 2 sign. varieties.			
	a. Issued note.	FV	0.10	0.25
	b. Specimen.	—	—	100.00

174 **5 CÓRDOBAS**
ND (1991). Red-violet and deep olive-green on m/c unpt. Indian Chief Diriangén at l., sorghum plants at r. R. Herrera firing cannon at British warship on green back. Printer: CBNC. 2 sign. varieties.

	VG	VF	UNC
	FV	FV	2.00

175 **10 CÓRDOBAS**
1990. Green on blue and m/c unpt. Sunrise over rice field at l., M. de Larreynaga at r. Back dk. green and m/c; arms at ctr. Printer: TDLR. 2 sign. varieties.

	VG	VF	UNC
	FV	FV	3.50

176 **20 CÓRDOBAS**
ND (1990). Pale red-orange and dk. brown on m/c unpt. Sandino at l., coffee plant at r. E. Mongalo at l., fire in the Mesón de Rivas (1854) at ctr. on green back. 2 sign. varieties. Printer: CBNC.

	VG	VF	UNC
	FV	FV	6.00

177 **50 CÓRDOBAS**
ND (1991). Purple and violet on m/c unpt. Dr. P. J. Chamorro at l., banana plants at r. Toppling of Somoza's statue and scene at polling place on green back. Series A: three sign.; Series B: two sign. Printer: CBNC.

	VG	VF	UNC
	FV	FV	12.50

178 **100 CÓRDOBAS**
1990. Blue and red on m/c unpt. Sunrise over cotton field at l., R. Darío at r. Back green and m/c; arms at ctr. Printer: TDLR. 3 sign. Series A.

	VG	VF	UNC
	FV	FV	25.00

178A **500 CÓRDOBAS**
ND (1991). Brown and red on m/c unpt. Estrada at r., cattle and sunrise at l. Arms at ctr. on back. Printer: H&S.
  a. Issued note.
  s. Specimen.

	VG	VF	UNC
a.	FV	FV	50.00
s.	—	—	175.00

178B **1000 CÓRDOBAS**
ND (1991). Purple and brown on m/c unpt. Coffee plants at l., peace demonstration at r. Printer: H&S.
  a. Issued note.
  s. Specimen.

	VG	VF	UNC
a.	FV	FV	90.00
s.	—	—	200.00

1992-96 ISSUE

179 **1 CÓRDOBA**
1995. Blue on purple and m/c unpt. Similar to #173. Printer: BABN. Series B.

	VG	VF	UNC
	FV	FV	1.00

180 **5 CÓRDOBAS**
1995. Red, deep olive-green and brown on m/c unpt. Similar to #174. Printer: F-CO.

	VG	VF	UNC
	FV	FV	1.75

181 **10 CÓRDOBAS**
1996. Green on blue and m/c unpt. Similar to #175. Printer: G&D.

	VG	VF	UNC
	FV	FV	3.00

182 **20 CÓRDOBAS**
1995. Pale red-orange and dk. brown on m/c unpt. Similar to #176. Printer: F-CO.

	VG	VF	UNC
	FV	FV	5.00

183 **50 CÓRDOBAS**
1995. Purple and brown on m/c unpt. Face similar to #177 but w/2 sign. Arms at ctr. on back. Printer: F-CO.

	VG	VF	UNC
	FV	FV	10.00

184 **100 CÓRDOBAS**
1992. Blue and red on m/c unpt. Like #178 but w/2 sign. Series B.

	VG	VF	UNC
	FV	FV	22.50

1997 ISSUE

#185-187 printer: TDLR.

185 **20 CÓRDOBAS**
1997. Orange-brown, green and m/c. J. Santos Zelaya at r. Arms at ctr. on back. Series C.

	VG	VF	UNC
	FV	FV	6.00

#186 Not assigned.

187 **100 CÓRDOBAS**
1997. Blue and red on m/c unpt. Like #184. Series C.

	VG	VF	UNC
	FV	FV	17.50

1999 ISSUE

188 **10 CÓRDOBAS**
1999. M/c. Series D. Printer: F-CO.

	VG	VF	UNC
	FV	FV	2.50

189	20 CÓRDOBAS	VG	VF	UNC
	1999. Similar to #182. Printer F-CO.	FV	FV	5.00
189A	50 CÓRDOBAS			
	2001, Printer: G&D.	FV	FV	7.50
190	100 CÓRDOBAS			
	1999. Blue and red on m/c unpt. Like #187 but with windowed security thread.	FV	FV	15.00

2002 ISSUE

191	10 CÓRDOBAS	VG	VF	UNC
	2002. Green on blue and m/c unpt.	FV	FV	3.00

195	500 CÓRDOBAS	VG	VF	UNC
	2002. Brown and red on m/c unpt.	FV	FV	50.00

192	20 CÓRDOBAS	VG	VF	UNC
	2002. Pale red-orange and dk. brown on m/c unpt.	FV	FV	5.00

193	50 CÓRDOBAS	VG	VF	UNC
	2002. Purple and brown on m/c unpt.	FV	FV	10.00

194	100 CÓRDOBAS	VG	VF	UNC
	2002. Blue and red on m/c unpt.	FV	FV	15.00

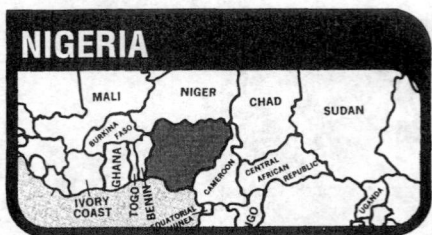

The Federal Republic of Nigeria, situated on the Atlantic coast of Africa between Benin and Cameroon, has an area of 356,667 sq. mi. (923,768 sq. km.) and a population of 128.79 million. Capital: Abuja. The economy is based on petroleum and agriculture. Crude oil, cocoa, tobacco and tin are exported.

Following the Napoleonic Wars, the British expanded their trade with the interior of Nigeria. British claims to a sphere of influence in that area were recognized by the Berlin Conference of 1885, and in the following year the Royal Niger Company was chartered. Direct British control of the territory was initiated in 1900, and in 1914 the amalgamation of northern and southern Nigeria into the Colony and Protectorate of Nigeria was effected. In 1960, following a number of territorial and constitutional changes, Nigeria was granted independence within the British Commonwealth as a federation of the northern, western and eastern regions. Nigeria altered its political relationship with Great Britain on Oct. 1, 1963, by proclaiming itself a republic. It did, however, elect to remain a member of the Commonwealth. The Supreme Commander of Armed Forces is the Head of the Federal Military Government.

On May 30, 1967, the Eastern Region of the republic - an area occupied principally by the proud and resourceful Ibo tribe - seceded from Nigeria and proclaimed itself the independent Republic of Biafra. Civil war erupted and raged for 31 months. Casualties, including civilian, were about two million, the majority succumbing to malnutrition and disease. Biafra surrendered to the federal government on January 15, 1970. After military coups in 1983 and 1985 the government was assumed by an Armed Forces Ruling Council. A transitional civilian council was formed in 1993. Nigeria was suspended from the Commonwealth in November 1995, but was re-admitted on May 29, 1999.

RULERS:
British to 1963

MONETARY SYSTEM:
1 Shilling = 12 Pence
1 Pound = 20 Shillings to 1973
1 Naira (10 Shillings) = 100 Kobo, 1973-

SIGNATURE VARIETIES

	GOVERNOR	CHIEF OF BANKING OPERATIONS		GOVERNOR	CHIEF OF BANKING OPERATIONS
1			2		
3			4		DIRECTOR OF DOMESTIC OPERATIONS
5			6		
	GOVERNOR	DIRECTOR OF CURRENCY OPERATIONS			DIRECTOR OF CURRENCY OPERATIONS
7			8		
9			10		
11			12		
13					

FEDERAL REPUBLIC OF NIGERIA

CENTRAL BANK OF NIGERIA

1967 ND ISSUE

Pound System

#6-13 bank bldg. at l. Wmk: Lion's head.

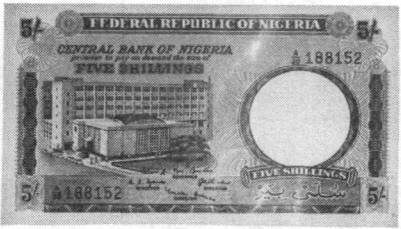

6	5 SHILLINGS	VG	VF	UNC
	ND (1967). Lilac and blue. Back lilac; log cutting.	2.00	20.00	140.00
7	10 SHILLINGS			
	ND (1967). Green and brown. Back green; stacking grain sacks.	4.00	35.00	200.00

8	1 POUND	VG	VF	UNC
	ND (1967). Red and dk. brown. Back red; man beating cluster from date palm at r.	0.75	2.00	8.00
9	5 POUNDS			
	ND (1967). Blue-gray and blue-green on m/c unpt. Back blue-gray; food preparation.	1.00	30.00	350.00

1968 ND ISSUE

#10-13 designs similar to previous issue. Wmk: Lion's head.

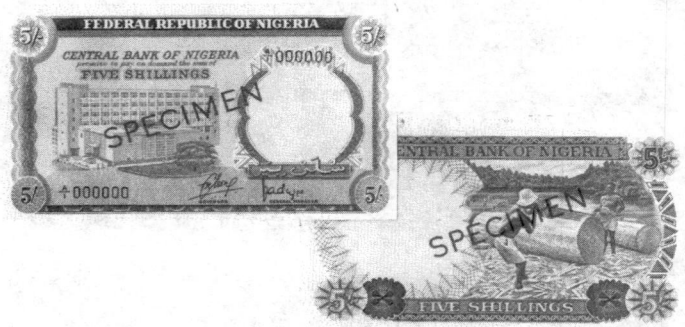

10	5 SHILLINGS	VG	VF	UNC
	ND (1968). Green and orange on m/c unpt. Back green. Similar to #6.			
	a. R. sign. title: *GENERAL MANAGER*.	2.00	15.00	150.00
	b. R. sign. title: *CHIEF OF BANKING OPERATIONS*.	3.00	25.00	200.00
	s. As a. Specimen.	—	—	25.00

11	10 SHILLINGS	VG	VF	UNC
	ND (1968). Blue and black on m/c unpt. Back blue; similar to #7.			
	a. R. sign. title: *GENERAL MANAGER*.	4.50	25.00	200.00
	b. R. sign. title: *CHIEF OF BANKING OPERATIONS*.	7.50	35.00	325.00
	s. As a. Specimen.	—	—	25.00

12 1 POUND
ND (1968). Olive-brown and purple on m/c unpt. Back olive-brown.
Similar to #8.

	VG	VF	UNC
a. R. sign. title: *GENERAL MANAGER*.	4.50	25.00	200.00
b. R. sign. title: *CHIEF OF BANKING OPERATIONS*.	7.50	35.00	325.00
s. As a. Specimen.	—	—	25.00

13 5 POUNDS
ND (1968). Red-brown and blue on m/c unpt. Back red-brown.
Similar to #9.

	VG	VF	UNC
a. R. sign. title: *GENERAL MANAGER*.	20.00	75.00	500.00
b. R. sign. title: *CHIEF OF BANKING OPERATIONS*.	25.00	100.00	550.00
s. As a. Specimen.	—	—	60.00

1973; 1977 ND ISSUE

Naira System

#14-17 bank bldg. at l. ctr. Wmk: Heraldic eagle. Replacement notes: Serial # prefix *DZ/*.

14 50 KOBO
ND (1973-78). Blue and purple on m/c unpt. Back brown; logging
at r.

	VG	VF	UNC
a. Sign. 1.	0.50	4.00	8.00
b. Sign. 2.	0.50	5.00	35.00
c. Sign. 3.	0.50	2.00	15.00
d. Sign. 4.	0.50	2.00	15.00
e. Sign. 5.	0.50	2.00	15.00
f. Sign. 6.	0.25	1.75	10.00
g. Sign. 7; 8; 9.	FV	FV	1.50

15 1 NAIRA
ND (1973-78). Red and brown on m/c unpt. Back red; stacking
grain sacks.

	VG	VF	UNC
a. Sign. 1.	0.75	5.00	12.50
b. Sign. 2.	0.75	4.00	12.50
c. Sign. 3.	0.75	4.00	12.50
d. Sign. 4.	2.00	17.50	50.00

16 5 NAIRA
ND (1973-78). Blue-gray and olive-green on m/c unpt. Back blue-
gray; man beating cluster from date palm at r.

	VG	VF	UNC
a. Sign. 1.	5.00	15.00	70.00
b. Sign. 2.	3.00	10.00	50.00
c. Sign. 3.	15.00	60.00	275.00
d. Sign. 4.	20.00	75.00	325.00

17 10 NAIRA
ND (1973-78). Carmine and dk. blue on m/c unpt. Back carmine;
dam at ctr.

	VG	VF	UNC
a. Sign. 1.	15.00	35.00	110.00
b. Sign. 2.	7.00	22.50	85.00
c. Sign. 3.	35.00	125.00	400.00
d. Sign. 4.	40.00	150.00	475.00

18 20 NAIRA
ND (1977-84). Yellow-green and black on red and m/c unpt. Gen
M. Muhammed at l. Arms at ctr. r. on back.

	VG	VF	UNC
a. Sign. 2.	30.00	100.00	325.00
b. Sign. 3.	20.00	60.00	200.00
c. Sign. 4.	8.00	20.00	65.00
d. Sign. 5.	6.00	15.00	45.00
e. Sign. 6.	4.00	10.00	35.00

1979 ND ISSUE

#19-22 sign. titles: *GOVERNOR* and *DIRECTOR OF DOMESTIC OPERATIONS*. Wmk: Heraldic eagle.

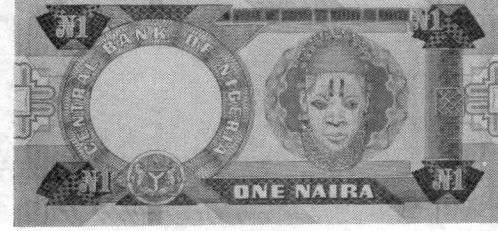

19 1 NAIRA
ND (1979-84). Red on orange and m/c unpt. H. Macaulay at l. Mask
at ctr. r. on back.

	VG	VF	UNC
a. Sign. 4.	0.25	2.00	7.50
b. Sign. 5.	0.25	1.00	5.00
c. Sign. 6.	0.25	0.75	3.00

20	5 NAIRA	VG	VF	UNC
	ND (1979-84). Green on m/c unpt. Alhaji Sir Abubakar Tafawa Balewa at l. Dancers at ctr. r. on back.			
	a. Sign. 4.	1.00	5.00	15.00
	b. Sign. 5.	1.00	4.00	12.50
	c. Sign. 6.	0.50	3.00	10.00

21	10 NAIRA	VG	VF	UNC
	ND (1979-84). Brown, purple and violet on m/c unpt. A. Ikoku at l. 2 women w/bowls on heads at ctr. r. on back.			
	a. Sign. 4.	2.50	12.00	30.00
	b. Sign. 5.	1.50	8.00	25.00
	c. Sign. 6.	5.00	20.00	—

1984; 1991 ND ISSUE

#23-27 new colors and sign. Like #18-21 but reduced size. Wmk: Heraldic eagle.

23	1 NAIRA	VG	VF	UNC
	ND (1984-). Red, violet and green. Like #19. Back olive and lt. violet.			
	a. Sign. title at r.: *DIRECTOR OF DOMESTIC OPERATIONS*. Sign. 6.	FV	1.00	3.00
	b. Sign. title at r.: *DIRECTOR OF CURRENCY OPERATIONS*. Sign. 7.	FV	FV	2.50
	c. Titles as b. Sign. 8.	FV	FV	2.50
	d. Titles as b. Sign. 9.	FV	FV	2.50

24	5 NAIRA	VG	VF	UNC
	ND (1984-). Purple and brown-violet on m/c unpt. Like #20.			
	a. Sign. title at r.: *DIRECTOR OF DOMESTIC OPERATIONS*. Sign. 6.	FV	2.00	6.50
	b. Sign. title at r.: *DIRECTOR OF CURRENCY OPERATIONS*. Sign. 7.	FV	1.00	4.00
	c. Titles as b. Sign. 8.	FV	FV	2.00
	d. Titles as b. Sign. 9.	FV	FV	2.00
	e. Titles as b. Sign. 10.	FV	FV	1.75
	f. Sign. 11. 2001.	FV	FV	1.75
	g. 2002.	FV	FV	1.75

25	10 NAIRA	VG	VF	UNC
	ND (1984-). Red-violet and orange on m/c unpt. Back red. Like #21.			
	a. Sign. title at r.: *DIRECTOR OF DOMESTIC OPERATIONS*. Sign. 6.	FV	2.50	9.00
	b. Sign. title at r.: *DIRECTOR OF CURRENCY OPERATIONS*. Sign. 7.	FV	2.50	6.00
	c. Titles as b. Sign. 8.	FV	FV	3.25
	d. Titles as b. Sign. 9.	FV	FV	3.00
	e. Titles as b. Sign. 10.	FV	FV	3.00
	f. Titles as b. Sign. 11. 2001.	FV	FV	3.00
	g. 2003.	FV	FV	3.00

26	20 NAIRA	VG	VF	UNC
	ND (1984-). Dk. blue-green, dk. green and green on m/c unpt. Like #18.			
	a. Sign. title at r.: *DIRECTOR OF DOMESTIC OPERATIONS*. Sign. 6.	FV	5.00	20.00
	b. Sign. title at r.: *DIRECTOR OF CURRENCY OPERATIONS*. Sign. 7.	FV	FV	6.00
	c. Titles as b. Sign. 8.	FV	FV	4.00
	d. Titles as b. Sign. 9.	FV	FV	4.00
	e. Titles as b. Sign. 10.	FV	FV	3.00
	f. 2001.	FV	FV	3.00
	g. 2003.	FV	FV	3.00

27	50 NAIRA	VG	VF	UNC
	ND (1991-). Dk. blue, black and gray on m/c unpt. Four busts reflecting varied citizenry at l. ctr. Three farmers in field at ctr. r., arms at lower r. on back.			
	a. Sign. 8.	FV	3.50	12.50
	b. Sign. 9.	FV	FV	7.50
	c. Sign. 10.	FV	FV	6.50
	d. Sign. 11. 2001.	FV	FV	6.50

1999-2001 ND Issue

#28-30 sign. 11.

28	100 NAIRA	VG	VF	UNC
	ND (1999-). Brown and red on m/c unpt. Chief Obafemi Awolowo at l. Zuma rock on back.			
	a. Back w/*Abuja Province* identification by rock. (1999).	FV	FV	10.00
	b. Back modified w/o identification. (2000).	FV	FV	8.00
	c. 2001.	FV	FV	8.00
	d. 2003.	FV	FV	8.00

29	200 NAIRA	VG	VF	UNC
	2000; 2003. Brown, dk. blue and green on m/c unpt. Sir Ahmadu Bello at l. and as wmk. Two cows and agricultural products on back.	FV	FV	10.00

30	500 NAIRA	VG	VF	UNC
	2001; 2002. Purple and olive-green on rose and m/c unpt. Dr. Nnamdi Azikiwe at l. and as wmk. Wide segmented security thread at l. ctr. Oil platform at ctr. r. on back.	FV	FV	18.00

NORWAY

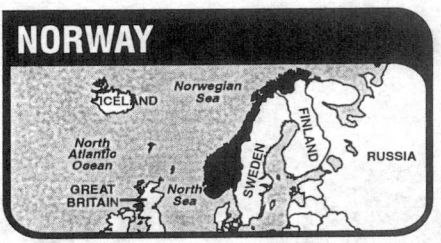

The Kingdom of Norway, a constitutional monarchy located in northwestern Europe, has an area of 150,000 sq. mi. (388,500 sq. km.) including the island territories of Spitzbergen (Svalbard) and Jan Mayen, and a population of 4.46 million. Capital: Oslo. The diversified economic base of Norway includes shipping, fishing, forestry, agriculture and manufacturing. Nonferrous metals, paper and paperboard, paper pulp, iron, steel and oil are exported.

A United Norwegian kingdom was established in the 9th century, the era of the indomitable Norse Vikings who ranged far and wide, visiting the coasts of northwestern Europe, the Mediterranean, Greenland and North America. In the 13th century, the Norse kingdom was united briefly with Sweden, then passed, through the Union of Kalmar, 1397, to the rule of Denmark which was maintained until 1814. In 1814, Norway fell again under the rule of Sweden. The union lasted until 1905 when the Norwegian Parliament arranged a peaceful separation and invited a Danish prince (King Haakon VII) to occupy the throne of an independent Kingdom of Norway.

RULERS:
Olav V, 1957-1991
Harald V, 1991-

MONETARY SYSTEM:
1 Krone = 100 Øre, 1873-

KINGDOM

NORGES BANK

1948-55 Issue

#30-33 Replacement notes: Serial # prefix Z. Wmk: value repeated.

30	5 KRONER	VG	VF	UNC
	1955-63. Blue on gray and m/c unpt. Portr. Fridtjof Nansen at l. Fishing scene on back.			
	a. Sign. Brofoss - Thorp. 1955-57. Prefix A-F.	10.00	20.00	75.00
	b. Sign. Brofoss - Ottesen. 1959-63. Prefix F-L.	7.50	17.50	65.00
	s. As a. Specimen.	—	150.00	300.00

31	10 KRONER	VG	VF	UNC
	1954-73. Yellow-brown on gray unpt. Portr. Christian Michelsen at l. Mercury w/ships on back.			
	a. Sign. Jahn - Thorp. 1954. Prefix A-D.	2.50	7.50	40.00
	b1. Sign. Brofoss - Thorp. 1954-55. Prefix D-G.	2.00	7.00	35.00
	b2. Sign. Brofoss - Thorp. 1955. Prefix H.	180.00	350.00	800.00
	b3. Sign. Brofoss - Thorp. 1956. Prefix H-I.	2.00	7.00	35.00
	b4. Sign. Brofoss - Thorp. 1957. Prefix I.	12.50	40.00	100.00
	b5. Sign. Brofoss - Thorp. 1957-58. Prefix J-M.	2.00	7.00	35.00
	b6. Sign. Brofoss - Thorp. 1958. Prefix N.	7.00	30.00	85.00
	c. Sign. Brofoss - Ottesen. 1959-65. Prefix N-E.	2.00	4.00	20.00
	d. Sign. Brofoss - Petersen. 1965-69. Prefix F-V.	FV	3.00	12.50
	e. Sign. Brofoss - Odegaard. 1970. Prefix W-Ø.	FV	2.00	10.00
	f. Sign. Wold - Odegaard. 1971-73. Prefix Å-R.	FV	1.75	7.50
	s. As a, d, f. Specimen.	—	150.00	300.00

#31 replacement notes: Serial # prefix X (1966-72) Z (1954-73).

32   50 KRONER
1950-65. Dk. green. Portr. Bjørnstjerne Björnson at upper l. and as wmk., crowned arms at upper ctr. Harvesting on back.

	VG	VF	UNC
a1. Sign. Jahn - Thorp. 1950-52. Prefix A.	15.00	55.00	200.00
a2. Sign. Jahn - Thorp. 1952. Prefix B.	60.00	120.00	550.00
a3. Sign. Jan - Thorp. 1953-54. Prefix B.	15.00	55.00	200.00
b1. Sign. Brofoss - Thorp. 1954. Prefix B.	70.00	150.00	650.00
b2. Sign. Brofoss - Thorp. 1955-58. Prefix B; C.	17.50	50.00	170.00
b3. Sign. Brofoss - Thorp. 1958. Prefix D.	24.00	95.00	350.00
c. Sign. Brofoss - Ottesen. 1959-65. Prefix D-F.	12.50	35.00	130.00
s. As a. 1951. Specimen.	—	—	—

33   100 KRONER
1949-62. Red. Portr. Henrik Wergeland at upper l. and as wmk., crowned arms at upper ctr. Logging on back.

	VG	VF	UNC
a1. Sign. Jahn - Thorp. 1949-52. Prefix A.	22.50	50.00	175.00
a2. Sign. Jahn - Thorp. 1952. Prefix C.	800.00	1250.00	—
a3. Sign. Jahn - Thorp. 1953-54. Prefix C.	22.50	50.00	175.00
b. Sign. Brofoss - Thorp. 1954-58. Prefix D-G.	20.00	50.00	175.00
c. Sign. Brofoss - Ottesen. 1959-62. Prefix G-I.	20.00	40.00	140.00

34   500 KRONER
1948-76. Dk. green. Portr. Niels Henrik Abel at upper l. and as wmk., crowned supported arms at upper ctr. Factory workers on back. Prefix A.

	VG	VF	UNC
a. Sign. Jahn - Thorp. 1948; 1951.	175.00	350.00	1000.00
b1. Sign. Brofoss - Thorp. 1954; 1956.	175.00	350.00	1000.00
b2. Sign. Brofoss - Thorp. 1958.	100.00	200.00	675.00
c. Sign. Brofoss - Ottesen. 1960-64.	90.00	160.00	550.00
d. Sign. Brofoss - Petersen. 1966-69.	85.00	140.00	400.00
e. Sign. Brofoss - Odegaard. 1970.	80.00	130.00	325.00
f. Sign. Wold - Odegaard. 1971-76.	75.00	120.00	275.00
s. As a. Specimen.	—	600.00	850.00

35   1000 KRONER
1949-74. Red-brown. Portr. H. Ibsen at l. and as wmk., crowned supported arms at upper ctr. Old man and child on back. Prefix A.

	VG	VF	UNC
a. Sign. Jahn - Thorp. 1949; 1951; 1953.	175.00	425.00	800.00
b. Sign. Brofoss - Thorp. 1955; 1958.	160.00	290.00	600.00
c. Sign. Brofoss - Ottesen. 1961; 1962.	150.00	225.00	500.00
d. Sign. Brofoss - Petersen. 1965-70.	140.00	210.00	400.00
e. Sign. Brofoss - Odegaard. 1971-74.	130.00	200.00	325.00
s. As a. Specimen.	—	600.00	850.00

#34 and 35 replacement notes: Serial # prefix *G*.

1962-78 ISSUE

#36-40 arms at ctr.

#36 and 41 replacement notes: Serial # prefix *H* or *Q*.

36	10 KRONER	VG	VF	UNC
	1972-84. Dk. blue on m/c unpt. Fridtjof Nansen at l. Fisherman and cargo ship at r. on back. Wmk: Value *10* repeated.			
	a. 1972. Replacement Prefix *Q*.	30.00	50.00	100.00
	b. Sign. Wold and Odegaard. 1973-76.	FV	4.00	11.00
	c. Sign. Wold and Sag<a0>rd. 1977-79; 1981-84.	FV	2.00	6.50
	s. As a. Specimen.	—	500.00	900.00

#37-40 replacement notes: Serial # prefix *X* or *Z*.

37	50 KRONER	VG	VF	UNC
	1966-83. Green on m/c unpt. Bjørnstjerne Björnson at l. and as wmk. Old church at r. on back.			
	a. Sign. Brofoss and Petersen. 1966-67; 1969. Prefix A-C.	12.00	25.00	80.00
	b. Sign. Wold and Odegaard. 1971-73. Prefix C-E.	12.00	17.50	60.00
	c. As b. W/security thread. 1974-75. Prefix F-G.	12.00	15.00	40.00
	d. Sign. Wold and Sag<a0>rd. 1976-83. Prefix H-R.	FV	12.50	35.00
	s. As a. Specimen.	—	450.00	750.00

38	100 KRONER	VG	VF	UNC
	1962-77. Red-violet on m/c unpt. H. Wergeland at l. and as wmk. Establishment of Constitution in 1814 at r. on back.			
	a. Sign. Brofoss and Ottesen. 1962-65. Prefix A-D.	FV	20.00	80.00
	b. Sign. Brofoss and Petersen. 1965-69. Prefix D-H.	FV	17.50	80.00
	c. Sign. Brofoss and Odegaard. 1970. Prefix M-P.	FV	17.50	55.00
	d. Sign. Wold and Odegaard. 1971-76. Prefix P-C.	FV	17.50	50.00
	e. Sign. Wold and Sag<a0>rd. 1977. Prefix D-K.	FV	FV	40.00
	s. As a. Specimen.	—	450.00	800.00

39	500 KRONER	VG	VF	UNC
	1978-85. Green on brown unpt. Niels Henrik Abel at l. and as wmk. University of Oslo at r. on back.			
	a. Sign. Wold and Sag<a0>rd. 1978; 1982.	FV	100.00	200.00
	b. Sign. Sk<a0>nland and Sag<a0>rd. 1985.	FV	100.00	200.00
	s. As a. Specimen.	—	1000.00	1900.00

40	1000 KRONER	VG	VF	UNC
	1975-87. Brown and violet on m/c unpt. Henrik Ibsen at l. and as wmk. Scenery on back.			
	a. Sign. Wold and Odegaard. 1975. Prefix A.	FV	200.00	275.00
	b. Sign. Wold and Sag<a0>rd. 1978; 1980; 1982-85. Prefix A-C.	FV	160.00	250.00
	c. Sign. Sk<a0>nland and Sag<a0>rd. 1985-87. Prefix C-E.	FV	140.00	225.00
	s. As a. Specimen.	—	800.00	1400.00

1977 ISSUE

41	100 KRONER	VG	VF	UNC
	1977-82. Purple on pink and m/c unpt. Cahilla Collett at l. and as wmk. Date at top l. ctr. Filigree design on back. Sign. Wold and Sag<a0>rd.			
	a. Brown serial #. 1977.	FV	17.50	55.00
	b. Black serial #. 1979; 1980.	FV	17.50	45.00
	c. 1981; 1982.	FV	17.50	45.00
	s. As a. Specimen.	—	800.00	1400.00

1983-91 ISSUE

42 50 KRONER

	VG	VF	UNC
1984-95. Green on m/c unpt. Aasmund Olavsson Vinje at l. Stone carving w/soldier slaying dragon on back. Wmk: 50 repeated within diagonal bars.			
a. Sign. Wold and Sag<a0>rd. 1984.	FV	15.00	30.00
b. Sign. Sk<a0>nland and Sag<a0>rd. 1985-87.	FV	9.00	22.50
c. Sign. Sk<a0>nland and Johansen. 1989-90; 1993.	FV	9.00	17.50
d. Sign. Moland and Johansen. 1995.	FV	FV	15.00
s. As a. Specimen.	—	800.00	1400.00

Note: #42d was also issued in a special "Last Edition" folder w/50 Øre coin dated 1996. (8400 pieces), Value $50.00.

43 100 KRONER

	VG	VF	UNC
1983-94. Red-violet on pink and m/c unpt. Similar to #41 but smaller printing size, and date at lower r.			
a. Sign. Wold and Sag<a0>rd. 1983.	FV	17.50	40.00
b. As a. but lg. date. 1984.	FV	17.50	40.00
c. Sign. Sk<a0>nland and Sag<a0>rd. 1985-87.	FV	17.50	35.00
d. Sign. Sk<a0>nland and Johansen. 1988-93.	FV	15.00	27.50
e. Sign. Moland and Johansen. 1994.	FV	FV	27.50

Note: #43e was also issued in a special "Last Edition" folder w/1 Krone coin dated 1996. (6000 issued). Value $50.

44 500 KRONER

	VG	VF	UNC
1991; 1994; 1996; 1997. Blue-violet on m/c unpt. Edvard Grieg at l. Floral mosaic at ctr. on back. Wmk: Multiple portr. of Grieg vertically.			
a. Sign. Sk<a0>nland and Johansen. 1991.	FV	FV	125.00
b. Sign. Moland and Johansen. 1994.	FV	FV	100.00
c. Sign. Storvik and Johansen. 1996; 1997.	FV	FV	100.00

45 1000 KRONER

	VG	VF	UNC
1989; 1990. Purple and dk. blue on m/c unpt. C. M. Falsen at l. 1668 royal seal on back. Sign. Sk<a0>nland and Johansen.			
a. Sign. Sk<a0>nland and Johansen. 1989; 1990.	FV	FV	200.00
b. Sign. Storvik and Johansen. 1998.	FV	FV	190.00

1994-96 ISSUE

#46 and 47 sign. K. Storvik and S. Johansen.

46 50 KRONER

	VG	VF	UNC
1996; 1998. Dark green on pale green and m/c unpt. P. C. Asbjörnsen at r. and as repeated vertical wmk. Water lilies and dragonfly on back.			
a. Sign. Storvik and Johansen. 1996; 1998.	FV	FV	12.50
b. Sign. Gjedrem and Johansen. 1999; 2000.	FV	FV	10.00

47 100 KRONER

	VG	VF	UNC
1995; 1997-99. Deep brown-violet and red-violet on m/c unpt. Kirsten Flagstad at r. and as repeated vertical wmk. Theatre layout on back.			
a. Sign. Storvik and Johansen. 1995; 1997; 1998. 10-digit serial # upper l. and lower r. on face. Date on back.	FV	FV	25.00
b. Sign. Gjedrem and Johansen. 1999. 10-digit serial # upper l., 8-digit # lower r. on face, where last four digits are the date.	FV	FV	20.00

Note: #47 was issued on the 100th birthday of famed singer Kirsten Flagstad in 1895.

48   200 KRONER

	VG	VF	UNC
1994; 1998; 1999. Blue-black and dk. blue on m/c unpt. Kristian Birkeland at r. and as repeated vertical wmk. Map of the North Pole; North America and Northern Europe at l. ctr. on back.			
a. Sign. Moland and Johansen. 1994.	FV	FV	40.00
b. Sign. Storvik and Johansen. 1998.	FV	FV	37.50
c. Sign. Gjedrem and Johansen. 1999; 2000.	FV	FV	35.00

1999-2002 ISSUE

49   100 KRONER

	VG	VF	UNC
2003. Similar to #49 but w/wide holographic strip at r. Sign. Gjdren and Eklund.	FV	FV	20.00

50   200 KRONER

	VG	VF	UNC
2002-03. Similar to #48 but w/wide holographic strip at r.	FV	FV	30.00
a. 2002. Sign. Gjedrem and Johansen.	FV	FV	40.00
b. 2003. Sign. Gjdrem and Eklund.	FV	FV	35.00

51   500 KRONER

	VG	VF	UNC
1999; 2000; 2002. Brown on tan and m/c unpt. Sigrid Undste and wide holographic strip at r. Wreath of wheat and roses on back. Sign. Gjedrem and Johansen.	FV	FV	90.00

52   1000 KRONER

	VG	VF	UNC
2001. Lilac, blue, yellow and m/c. Edvard Munch at r., wide holographic strip at r. edge., part of his painting *Melancholy* at l. ctr. Munch's great work *The Sun* on back. Sign. Gjedrem and Johansen.	FV	FV	180.00

Listings for

Nouméa, see New Caledonia

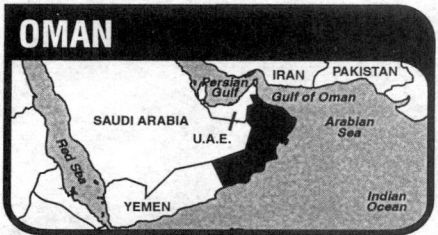

The Sultanate of Oman (formerly Muscat and Oman), an independent monarchy located in the southeastern part of the Arabian Peninsula, has an area of 82,030 sq. mi. (212,457 sq. km.) and a population of 2.72 million. Capital: Muscat. The economy is based on agriculture, herding and petroleum. Petroleum products, dates, fish and hides are exported.

The first European contact with Muscat and Oman was made by the Portuguese who captured Muscat, the capital and chief port, in 1508. They occupied the city, utilizing it as a naval base and factory and holding it against land and sea attacks by Arabs and Persians until finally ejected by local Arabs in 1650. It was next occupied by the Persians who maintained control until 1741, when it was taken by Ahmed ibn Sa'id of the present ruling family. Muscat and Oman was the most powerful state in Arabia during the first half of the 19th century, until weakened by the persistent attack of interior nomadic tribes. British influence, initiated by the signing of a treaty of friendship with the Sultanate in 1798, remains a dominant fact of the civil and military phases of the government, although Britain recognizes the Sultanate as a sovereign state and there is no colonial relationship between them.

Sultan Sa'id bin Taimur was overthrown by his son, Qaboos bin Sa'id, on July 23, 1970. He changed the nation's name to the Sultanate of Oman.

RULERS:

Sa'id bin Taimur, AH1351-1390/1932-1970 AD
Qaboos bin Sa'id, AH1390-1419/1970-1999AD

MONETARY SYSTEM:

1 Rial Omani = 1000 Baiza (Baisa)
1 Rial Saidi = 1000 Baiza (Baisa)

SULTANATE OF MUSCAT AND OMAN

1970 ND ISSUE

#1-6 arms at r. and as wmk.

1   100 BAIZA

	VG	VF	UNC
ND (1970). Brown on blue-green and m/c unpt.			
a. Issued note.	1.00	2.00	5.00
s. Specimen.	—	—	40.00

2   1/4 RIAL SAIDI

	VG	VF	UNC
ND (1970). Blue and brown on m/c unpt. Jalali Fortress on back.			
a. Issued note.	1.25	3.00	6.00
s. Specimen.	—	—	45.00

3   1/2 RIAL SAIDI

	VG	VF	UNC
ND (1970). Green and purple on m/c unpt. Sumail Fortress on back.			
a. Issued note.	2.00	4.00	10.00
s. Specimen.	—	—	60.00

4   1 RIAL SAIDI
ND (1970). Red and olive-green on m/c unpt. Sohar Fort on back.

	VG	VF	UNC
a. Issued note.	4.00	9.00	22.50
s. Specimen.	—	—	90.00

5   5 RIALS SAIDI
ND (1970). Purple and blue on m/c unpt. Nizwa Fort on back.

	VG	VF	UNC
a. Issued note.	20.00	40.00	80.00
s. Specimen.	—	—	120.00

6   10 RIALS SAIDI
ND (1970). Dk. brown and blue on m/c unpt. Mirani Fort on back.

	VG	VF	UNC
a. Issued note.	30.00	70.00	160.00
s. Specimen.	—	—	175.00

OMAN

OMAN CURRENCY BOARD

1973 ND ISSUE

#7-12 arms at r. and as wmk. Like #1-6.
#8-12 different fortresses on back.

7   100 BAIZA
ND (1973). Brown on blue-green and m/c unpt. Like #1.

	VG	VF	UNC
a. Issued note.	1.00	2.25	4.25
ct. Color trial. Brown on m/c unpt.	—	—	65.00
s. Specimen.	—	—	35.00

8   1/4 RIAL OMANI
ND (1973). Blue and brown on m/c unpt. Like #2.

	VG	VF	UNC
a. Issued note.	1.25	2.50	6.00
ct. Color trial. Green on m/c unpt.	—	—	75.00
s. Specimen.	—	—	35.00

9   1/2 RIAL OMANI
ND (1973). Green and purple on m/c unpt. Like #3.

	VG	VF	UNC
a. Issued note.	2.00	3.00	9.00
ct. Color trial. Black and purple on m/c unpt.	—	—	80.00
s. Specimen.	—	—	35.00

10   1 RIAL OMANI
ND (1973). Red and olive-green on m/c unpt. Like #4.

	VG	VF	UNC
a. Issued note.	3.00	9.00	17.50
ct. Color trial. Blue on m/c unpt.	—	—	125.00
s. Specimen.	—	—	50.00

14 200 BAISA
ND (1985). Purple on m/c unpt. Rustaq Fortress on back.

	VG	VF	UNC
	FV	2.00	3.50

11 5 RIALS OMANI
ND (1973). Purple and blue on m/c unpt. Like #5.

	VG	VF	UNC
a. Issued note.	17.50	30.00	70.00
ct. Color trial. Red and blue on m/c unpt.	—	—	240.00
s. Specimen.	—	—	100.00

15 1/4 RIAL
ND (1977). Blue and brown on m/c unpt. Back similar to #2.

	VG	VF	UNC
a. Issued note.	FV	2.50	5.00
s. Specimen.	—	—	135.00

12 10 RIALS OMANI
ND (1973). Dk. brown and blue on m/c unpt. Like #6.

	VG	VF	UNC
a. Issued note.	32.50	60.00	125.00
s. Specimen.	—	—	140.00

16 1/2 RIAL
ND (1977). Green and purple on m/c unpt. Back similar to #3.

	VG	VF	UNC
a. Issued note.	FV	4.00	8.00
s. Specimen.	—	—	135.00

CENTRAL BANK OF OMAN

1977; 1985 ND ISSUE

#13-19 arms at r. and as wmk.

17 1 RIAL
ND (1977). Red and brown on m/c unpt. Back similar to #14.

	VG	VF	UNC
a. Issued note.	FV	8.00	16.00
s. Specimen.	—	—	135.00

13 100 BAISA
ND (1977). Lt. brown on m/c unpt. Port of Qaboos on back.

	VG	VF	UNC
a. Issued note.	FV	2.00	3.00
s. Specimen.	—	—	100.00

	50 RIALS	VG	VF	UNC
21	ND. Olive-brown, blue and dk. brown on m/c unpt. Sultan at r. Jabreen Fort at l. ctr. on back.			
	a. Issued note.	150.00	250.00	375.00
	s. Specimen.	—	—	350.00

1985-90 ISSUE

#22-30 Sultan Qaboos bin Sa'id at r. and as wmk.

	5 RIALS	VG	VF	UNC
18	ND (1977). Lilac and blue on m/c unpt. Back similar to #15.			
	a. Issued note.	FV	25.00	40.00
	s. Specimen.	—	—	35.00

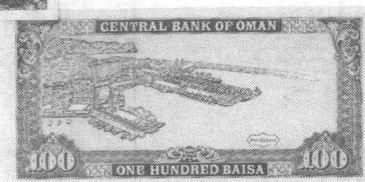

	100 BAISA	VG	VF	UNC
22	AH1408-1414/1987-1994AD. Lt. brown on m/c unpt. Port of Qaboos on back.			
	a. 1987/AH1408.	1.25	2.00	3.50
	b. 1989/AH1409.	1.00	1.50	2.25
	c. 1992/AH1413.	2.00	4.00	18.00
	d. 1994/AH1414.	0.75	1.50	2.00

	10 RIALS	VG	VF	UNC
19	ND (1977). Brown and blue on m/c unpt. Back similar to #16.			
	a. Issued note.	FV	42.50	100.00
	s. Specimen.	—	—	35.00

	200 BAISA	VG	VF	UNC
23	AH1407-1414/1987-1994AD. Purple on m/c unpt. Rustaq Fort on back.			
	a. 1987/AH1407.	1.25	2.25	4.00
	b. 1993/AH1413.	1.25	2.00	3.50
	c. 1994/AH1414.	1.00	2.00	2.75

	20 RIALS	VG	VF	UNC
20	ND (1977). Gray-blue and orange on m/c unpt. Sultan Qaboos bin Sa'id at r. Central Bank at l. ctr. on back. Wmk: Arms.			
	a. Issued note.	FV	75.00	150.00
	s. Specimen.	—	—	60.00

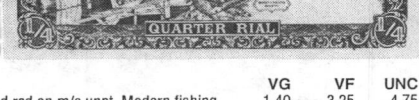

	1/4 RIAL	VG	VF	UNC
24	1989/AH1409. Blue, brown and red on m/c unpt. Modern fishing industry on back.	1.40	3.25	4.75

25	1/2 RIAL	VG	VF	UNC
	1987/AH1408. Green on m/c unpt. Aerial view of Sultan Qaboos University on back.	2.25	5.25	7.00

26	1 RIAL	VG	VF	UNC
	AH1407-1414/1987-1994AD. Red, black and olive-brown on m/c unpt. Sohar Fort at l. on back.			
	a. 1987/AH1407.	5.00	10.00	15.00
	b. 1989/AH1409.	5.00	10.00	12.50
	c. 1994/AH1414.	FV	FV	8.00

27	5 RIALS	VG	VF	UNC
	1990/AH1411. Dk. rose, brown-violet and m/c unpt. Fort Nizwa on back.	FV	27.50	45.00

28	10 RIALS	VG	VF	UNC
	AH1408/1987AD; AH1413/1993AD. Dk. brown, red-brown and blue on m/c unpt. Fort Mirani at l. ctr. on back.			
	a. 1987/AH1408.	FV	55.00	80.00
	b. 1993/AH1413.	FV	50.00	70.00

29	20 RIALS	VG	VF	UNC
	AH1407/1987AD; AH1414/1994AD. Brown, dk. olive-brown and blue-gray on m/c unpt. Similar to #20.			
	a. 1987/AH1408.	FV	110.00	140.00
	b. 1994/AH1414.	FV	100.00	130.00

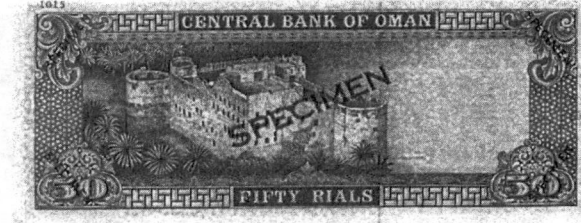

30	50 RIALS	VG	VF	UNC
	AH1405/1985AD; AH1413/1992AD. Olive-brown, blue and dk. brown on m/c unpt. Like #21 but w/*Jabreen Fort* added at lower r. on back.			
	a. 1985/AH1405.	FV	220.00	325.00
	b. 1992/AH1413.	FV	210.00	300.00
	s. As a. Specimen.	—	—	375.00

Note: For note with similar design but w/o date, see #21.

1995 ISSUE

#31-38 Sultan Qaboos at r. and as wmk.

#31-36, 38 arms at upper l.

31	100 BAISA	VG	VF	UNC
	1995/AH1416. Deep olive-green, dk. green-blue and purple on m/c unpt. Faslajs irrigation system at ctr. Verreaux's eagle and white oryx at ctr. on back.	FV	FV	0.50

35 5 RIALS
1995/AH1416. Red on pale blue and m/c unpt. Sultan Qaboos University bldg. w/clock tower at ctr. Nizwa city view at l. ctr. on back.

		VG	VF	UNC
a.	W/o reflective pattern of Khanjars (State Emblem) on back.	FV	FV	45.00
b.	W/reflective pattern of Khanjars on back.	FV	FV	32.50

32 200 BAISA
1995/AH1416. Black, deep blue and green on m/c unpt. Seeb & Salalah Airports at l. ctr. Raysut Port and Marine Science & Fisheries Center at lower l., aerial view of Sultan Qaboos port ctr. on back.

	VG	VF	UNC
	FV	FV	1.00

36 10 RIALS
1995/AH1416. Dk. brown on pale blue and m/c unpt. al-Nahdha in Salalah Tower, Jabreen coconut palm and frankincense tree at ctr. Mutrah Fort and Corniche at l. ctr. on back.

	VG	VF	UNC
	FV	FV	60.00

33 1/2 RIAL
1995/AH1416. Dk. brown and gray on m/c unpt. Bahla Castle at ctr. Nakhl Fort and Al-Hazm castle at lower l., Nakhl Fort at ctr. on back.

	VG	VF	UNC
	FV	FV	3.50

37 20 RIALS
1995/AH1416. Dk. blue-green and olive-green on m/c unpt. Central Bank of Oman bldg. at ctr., minaret at r. Muscat Security Market at l., aerial view of Rysayl Industrial Area at ctr., Oman Chamber of Commerce bldg. at upper r. on back.

	VG	VF	UNC
	FV	FV	120.00

34 1 RIAL
1995/AH1416. Deep purple, purple and blue-green on m/c unpt. Sultan Qaboos Sports Complex, Burj al-Sahwa, road overpass at ctr. Omani Khanjar, traditional silver bracelets and ornaments w/shipbuilding in background unpt. on back.

	VG	VF	UNC
	FV	FV	6.00

38 50 RIALS
1995/AH1416. Purple and violet on m/c unpt. Ministry of Finance and Economy bldg. at ctr., Mirani Fort at r. Cabinet Bldg. at l., Ministry of Commerce and Industry bldg. at ctr. r. on back.

	VG	VF	UNC
	FV	FV	300.00

NOTICE
Readers with unlisted dates, signature varieties, etc. are invited to submit photocopies of their notes to: Standard Catalog of World Paper Money, 700 East State St. Iola, WI 54990-0001, E-Mail: george.cuhaj@fwpubs.com.

2000 ISSUE

#39-42 like #35-38 but w/holographic strip added at r.

39	5 RIALS	VG	VF	UNC
	2000/AH1420. Red on m/c unpt. Like #5.	FV	FV	27.50

40	10 RIALS	VG	VF	UNC
	2000/1420AH. Brown on m/c unpt. Like #36.	FV	FV	45.00

41	20 RIALS	VG	VF	UNC
	2000/1420AH. Green on m/c unpt. Like #37.	FV	FV	95.00

42	50 RIALS	VG	VF	UNC
	2000/1420AH. Purple on m/c unpt. Like #38.	FV	FV	225.00

PAKISTAN

The Islamic Republic of Pakistan, located on the Indian subcontinent between India and Afghanistan, has an area of 310,404 sq. mi. (803,943 sq. m.) and a population of 156 million. Capital: Islamabad. Pakistan is mainly an agricultural land. Yarn, cotton, rice and leather are exported.

Afghan and Turkish intrusions into northern India between the 11th and 18th centuries resulted in large numbers of Indians being converted to Islam. The idea of a separate Moslem state independent of Hindu India developed in the 1930's and was agreed to by Britain in 1946. The Islamic majority areas of India, consisting of the separate geographic entities known as East and West Pakistan, achieved self-government as Pakistan, with dominion status in the British Commonwealth, when the British withdrew from India on Aug. 14, 1947. Pakistan became a republic in 1956. When a basic constitutional crisis initiated by the election of Dec. 1, 1970 - the first direct general election in Pakistani history - could not be resolved by the leaders of East and West Pakistan, the East Pakistanis seceded from the Islamic Republic of Pakistan (March 26, 1971) and formed the independent People's Republic of Bangladesh.

Pakistan was expelled from the Commonwealth on January 20, 1972 and re-admitted again on October 1, 1989.

MONETARY SYSTEM:
1 Rupee = 16 Annas to 1961
1 Rupee = 100 Paisa (Pice), 1961-

REPLACEMENT NOTES:
#24, 24A, 24B, 1/X or 2/X prefix. #25-33, X as first of double prefix letters.

GOVERNMENT OF PAKISTAN

1951-73 ND ISSUES

8	1 RUPEE	VG	VF	UNC
	ND (1951). Blue on m/c unpt. Back violet. Archway at l. ctr. Like #4. 2 sign. varieties.	15.00	60.00	100.00

9	1 RUPEE	VG	VF	UNC
	ND (1953-63). Blue on m/c unpt. Like #8 but larger size serial #. Back blue. 6 sign. varieties.	3.00	5.00	10.00

Note: The scarce sign. is Abdul Qadir, valued at $50. in Unc.

9A	1 RUPEE	VG	VF	UNC
	ND (1964). Blue on m/c unpt. Back violet. Like #8 but differnt font for serial #. 3 sign. varieties.	1.00	2.50	4.50

10	1 RUPEE	VG	VF	UNC
	ND (1973). Brown on m/c unpt. Like #9.			
	a. Sign. 1. *Attab Qazi.*	0.50	1.50	3.50
	b. Sign. 2. *Abdul Rauf.*	0.50	1.50	3.00

STATE BANK OF PAKISTAN

CITY OVERPRINT VARIETIES

চাকা ঢাকা করাচী کراچی লাহোর لاہور

| Dacca | Karachi | Lahore |

Some notes exist w/Urdu and some w/Bengali ovpt. denoting city of issue, Dacca, Karachi or Lahore. These are much scarcer than the regular issues. Sign. varieties.

1957-66 ND ISSUE

#15-19 Portr. Mohammed Ali Jinnah and as wmk.

15	5 RUPEES	VG	VF	UNC
	ND (1966). Purple on lt. blue and maroon unpt. Mohammed Ali Jinnah at ctr. Terraces on back. 3 sign. varieties	2.00	3.50	6.00

16	10 RUPEES	VG	VF	UNC
	ND (1970). Brown on m/c unpt. Portr. Mohammed Ali Jinnah at l. Shalimar Gardens on back. 2 sign. varieties.			
	a. Latin sign.	2.50	7.50	15.00
	b. Urdu & Bengali sign.	2.00	6.00	12.50

17	50 RUPEES	VG	VF	UNC
	ND (1964). Blue-green on peach unpt. Portr. Mohammed Ali Jinnah at ctr. Back green; sailing ships. 3 sign. varieties.			
	a. Latin sign. 2 sign. varieties.	2.50	6.00	10.00
	b. 1 Urdu and 1 Bengali sign. of the same signatory.	2.50	6.00	10.00

18	100 RUPEES	VG	VF	UNC
	ND (1957). Green on violet and peach unpt. Mohammed Ali Jinnah at ctr. back. Badshahi Mosque in Lahore on			
	a. W/o overprint. 2 sign. varieties.	3.00	6.00	10.00
	b. Ovpt. *Dhaka*. 2 sign. varieties.	3.00	6.00	10.00
	c. Ovpt. *Karachi*. 2 sign. varieties.	3.00	6.00	10.00
	d. Ovpt. *Lahore*. 2 sign. varieties.	3.00	6.00	10.00

19	500 RUPEES	VG	VF	UNC
	ND (1964). Red on gold and lt. green unpt. Mohammed Ali Jinnah at ctr. State Bank of Pakistan bldg. on back.			
	a. Ovpt. *Dhaka*.	15.00	25.00	50.00
	b. Ovpt. *Karachi*. 2 sign. varieties.	10.00	20.00	35.00
	c. Ovpt. *Lahore*.	10.00	20.00	35.00

1973 ND ISSUE

#20-23 Mohammed Ali Jinnah at ctr. or l. and as wmk.

20	5 RUPEES	VG	VF	UNC
	ND (1972-78). Orange-brown on pale blue and dull green unpt. Mohammed Ali Jinnah at ctr. Terraces on back. 3 sign. varieties.			
	a. Serial # prefix of single or double letters.	2.00	5.00	8.00
	b. Serial # prefix fractional w/double letters over numerals.	2.00	5.00	8.00

21	10 RUPEES	VG	VF	UNC
	ND (1972-75). Green on m/c unpt. Mohammed Ali Jinnah at l. Shalimar Gardens, Lahore on back. 2 sign. varieties.			
	a. Sans-serif font for serial #.	2.50	5.00	10.00
	b. Serif font for serial #. Printer :TDLR w/o imprint.	5.00	10.00	20.00
	c. Serial # prefix with two **.	15.00	40.00	100.00

22 50 RUPEES
ND (1972-78). Blue on m/c unpt. Mohammed Ali Jinnah at ctr.
Sailing ships on back. 3 sign. varieties.

	VG	VF	UNC
	5.00	12.50	25.00

23 100 RUPEES
ND (1973-78). Dk. blue on m/c unpt. Mohammed Ali Jinnah at l.
Badshahi Mosque, Lahore, on back. 2 sign. varieties.

	VG	VF	UNC
	7.50	20.00	55.00

Note: The signature variety of Osman Ali is valued at $150. in Unc.

GOVERNMENT OF PAKISTAN (RESUMED)

	SIGNATURE VARIETIES		
1	Abdur Rauf Shaikh	2	Aftab Ahmad Khan
3	Habibullah Baig	4	Izharul-Haq
5	Saeed Ahmad Qureshi	6	R. A. Akhund
7	Qazi Alimullah	8	Khalid Javed
9	Javed Talat	10	Mian Tayeb Hasan
11	Moeen Afzal	12	Mohammad Younus Khan

1975 ND ISSUE

24 1 RUPEE
ND (1974). Blue on lt. green and lilac unpt. Arms at r. and as wmk.
Minar-i-Pakistan monument at l on back. Lower border on face is
14mm high and includes text in 4 languages. Sign. 1.

	VG	VF	UNC
	5.00	10.00	35.00

24A 1 RUPEE
ND (1975-81). Blue on lt. green and lilac unpt. Like #24, but new
broader panel is 22mm high and w/o 4-language text along bottom
face. Arms at r. and as wmk. Minar-i-Pakistan monument at l. on
back. Sign 1-3.

	VG	VF	UNC
	1.00	2.00	3.50

1981-83 ND ISSUE

URDU TEXT LINE A   URDU TEXT LINE B

25 1 RUPEE
ND (1981-82). Dull brown on m/c unpt. Arms at r. and as wmk.
Tomb of Allama Mohammed Iqbal on back. No Urdu text line at
bottom on back. Serial # at upper ctr. Sign. 3.

	VG	VF	UNC
	1.00	2.00	3.50

26 1 RUPEE
ND (1982). Dull brown on m/c unpt. Like #25 but w/Urdu text line
A at bottom on back.

	VG	VF	UNC
a. Serial # at upper ctr. Sign. 3.	1.00	2.00	3.00
b. Serial # at lower r. Sign. 3.	1.00	2.00	3.00

27 1 RUPEE
ND (1983-). Like #26 but w/Urdu text line B at bottom on back.

	VG	VF	UNC
a. Serial # at upper ctr. Sign. 3.	0.50	1.00	2.00
b. Serial # at lower r. Sign. 3.	0.25	0.50	1.00
c. As a. Sign. 4.	0.50	1.00	2.00
d. As b. Sign. 4.	0.25	0.50	1.00
e. As a. Sign. 5.	0.50	1.00	2.00
f. As b. Sign. 5.	0.25	0.50	1.00
g. As a. Sign. 6.	0.50	1.00	2.00
h. As b. Sign. 6.	0.25	0.50	1.00
i. As a. Sign. 7.	0.50	1.00	2.00
j. As b. Sign. 7.	0.25	0.50	1.00
k. As b. Sign. 8.	0.25	0.50	1.00
l. As b. Sign. 9.	0.25	0.50	1.00
m. As b. Sign. 10.	0.25	0.50	1.00
n. As b. Sign. 11.	0.25	0.50	1.00
o. As b. Sign. 13.	0.25	0.50	1.00

STATE BANK OF PAKISTAN
1976-77 ND ISSUE
#28-31 Mohammed Ali Jinnah at r. and as wmk. Serial # and sign. varieties.

28   5 RUPEES
ND (1976-84). Dk. brown on tan and pink unpt. Khajak railroad
tunnel on back. No Urdu text line beneath upper title on back. 2
sign. varieties.

VG	VF	UNC
1.00	2.50	4.00

35   50 RUPEES
ND (1981-82). Purple on m/c unpt. Like #30 but w/Urdu text line A
beneath upper title on back.

VG	VF	UNC
3.00	7.50	12.50

29   10 RUPEES
ND (1976-84). Pale olive-green on m/c unpt. View of Moenjodaro
on back. No Urdu text line beneath upper title on back. 2 sign.
varieties.

VG	VF	UNC
1.00	2.50	4.00

30   50 RUPEES
ND (1977-84). Purple on m/c unpt. Main gate of Lahore fort on
back. No Urdu text line beneath upper title on back. 2 sign.
varieties.

VG	VF	UNC
2.50	5.00	12.50

36   100 RUPEES
ND (1981-82). Red and orange on m/c unpt. Like #31 but w/Urdu
text line A beneath upper title on back.

VG	VF	UNC
5.00	12.50	25.00

1983-88 ND ISSUE

37   2 RUPEES
ND (1985-99). Pale purple on m/c unpt. Arms at r. and as wmk.
Badshahi mosque on back. Urdu text line B beneath upper title on
back. 5 sign. varieties.

VG	VF	UNC
1.00	2.00	4.00

Note: #37 shade varieties exist.

#38-43 Mohammed Ali Jinnah at r. and as wmk.

31   100 RUPEES
ND (1976-84). Red and orange on m/c unpt. Islamic College,
Peshawar, on back. No Urdu text line beneath upper title on back.
2 sign. varieties.

VG	VF	UNC
5.00	12.50	25.00

1981-82 ND ISSUE

#33-36 Mohammed Ali Jinnah at r. and as wmk.

#32 *Deleted.*

33   5 RUPEES
ND (1981-82). Dk. brown on tan and pink unpt. Like #28 but
w/Urdu text line A beneath upper title on back.

VG	VF	UNC
1.00	2.50	5.00

34   10 RUPEES
ND (1981-82). Pale olive-green on m/c unpt. Like #29 but w/Urdu
text line A beneath upper title on back.

VG	VF	UNC
1.00	2.50	5.00

38   5 RUPEES
ND (1983-84). Dk. brown on tan and pink unpt. Like #28 but
w/Urdu text line B beneath upper title on back. 6 sign. varieties.

VG	VF	UNC
FV	FV	1.00

39 10 RUPEES
ND (1983-84). Pale olive-green on m/c unpt. Like #29 but w/Urdu
text line B beneath upper title on back. 6 sign. varieties.

VG	VF	UNC
FV	FV	1.50

44 5 RUPEES
1997. Dull violet on lt. green and pale orange-brown unpt. Starburst w/text and dates at l., Mohammed Ali Jinnah at r. and as wmk.
Tomb of Shah Ruke-e-Alam at l. ctr., bank seal at upper r. on back.

VG	VF	UNC
2.00	3.50	5.00

REGIONAL
STATE BANK OF PAKISTAN
1950 ND HAJ PILGRIM ISSUE

R3 10 RUPEES
ND. Green on m/c unpt. Like #16 but w/ovpt. 2 sign. varieties.

VG	VF	UNC
15.00	40.00	75.00

40 50 RUPEES
ND (1986-). Purple on m/c unpt. Like #30 but w/Urdu text line B
beneath upper title on back. 6 sign. varieties.

VG	VF	UNC
FV	FV	6.00

41 100 RUPEES
ND (1986-). Red and orange on m/c unpt. Like #31 but w/Urdu text
line B beneath upper title on back. 6 sign. varieties.

	VF	UNC
FV	FV	7.50

R4 10 RUPEES
ND. Purple on m/c unpt. Like #16 and #21 but w/ovpt.

VG	VF	UNC
5.00	7.00	10.00

42 500 RUPEES
ND (1986-). Deep blue-green and olive-green on m/c unpt. State
Bank of Pakistan bldg. at ctr. on back. 6 sign. varieties.

VG	VF	UNC
FV	FV	30.00

R5 100 RUPEES
ND. Brown on m/c unpt. Like #23; black ovpt.

VG	VF	UNC
50.00	100.00	225.00

1970 ND HAJ PILGRIM ISSUE
Haj Pilgrim notes were discontinued in 1994 and notes on hand were destroyed.

43 1000 RUPEES
ND (1988-). Deep purple and blue-black on m/c unpt. Tomb of
Jahangir on back. 4 sign. varieties.

VG	VF	UNC
FV	FV	50.00

1997 COMMEMORATIVE ISSUE

#44, Golden Jubilee of Independence, 1947-1997

R6 10 RUPEES
ND (1978). Blue-black on m/c unpt. Like #34; black ovpt.

VG	VF	UNC
4.00	7.00	10.00

R7 100 RUPEES
ND (1975-78). Gold on m/c unpt. Like #31; dk. brown ovpt. 2 sign.
varieties.

VG	VF	UNC
5.00	10.00	20.00

Papua New Guinea, an independent member of the British Commonwealth, occupies the eastern half of the island of New Guinea. It lies north of Australia near the equator and borders on West Irian. The country, which includes nearby Bismarck Archipelago, Buka and Bougainville, has an area of 176,280 sq. mi. (461,691 sq. km.) and a population of 4.81 million who are divided into more than 1,000 separate tribes speaking more than 700 mutually unintelligible languages. Capital: Port Moresby. The economy is agricultural, and exports include copra, rubber, cocoa, coffee, tea, gold and copper.

New Guinea, the world's largest island after Greenland, was discovered by Spanish navigator Jorge de Menezes, who landed on the northwest shore in 1527. European interests, attracted by exaggerated estimates of the resources of the area, resulted in the island being claimed in whole or part by Spain, the Netherlands, Great Britain and Germany.

Papua (formerly British New Guinea), situated in the southeastern part of the island of New Guinea, has an area of 90,540 sq. mi. (234,499 sq. km.) and a population of 740,000. It was temporarily annexed by Queensland in 1883 and by the British Crown in 1888. Papua came under control of the Australian Commonwealth in 1901 and became the Territory of Papua in 1906. Japan invaded New Guinea and Papua early in 1942, but Australian control was restored before the end of the year in Papua and in 1945 in New Guinea.

In 1884 Germany annexed the area known as German New Guinea (also Neu-Guinea or Kaiser Wilhelmsland) comprising the northern section of eastern New Guinea, and granted its administration and development to the New-Guinea Compagnie. Administration reverted to Germany in 1889 following the failure of the company to exercise adequate administration. While a German protectorate, German New Guinea had an area of 92,159 sq. mi. (238,692 sq. km.) and a population of about 250,000. Capital: Herbertshohe, later named Rabaul. Copra was the chief crop. Australian troops occupied German New Guinea in Aug. 1914, shortly after Great Britain declared war on Germany. It was mandated to Australia by the League of Nations in 1920 and known as the Territory of New Guinea. The territory was invaded and occupied by Japan in 1942. Following the Japanese surrender, it came under U.N. trusteeship, Dec. 13, 1946, with Australia as the administering power.

The Papua and New Guinea Act, 1949, provided for the government of Papua and New Guinea as one administrative unit. On Dec. 1, 1973, Papua New Guinea became self-governing with Australia retaining responsibility for defense and foreign affairs. Full independence was achieved on Sept. 16, 1975 and Papua New Guinea is now a member of the Commonwealth of Nations. The Queen of England is Chief of State.

RULERS:
British

MONETARY SYSTEM:
1 Kina = 100 Toea, 1975-

BRITISH ADMINISTRATION

BANK OF PAPUA NEW GUINEA

SIGNATURE VARIETIES		
1		
2		
3		
4		
5		
6		
7		
8		
9		
10		

1975 ISSUE

#1-4 stylized Bird of Paradise at l. ctr. and as wmk.

1	2 KINA	VG	VF	UNC
	ND (1975). Black on lt green and m/c unpt. Artifacts on back. Sign. 1.			
	a. Issued note.	1.50	6.00	17.50
	s. Specimen.	—	—	35.00

2	5 KINA	VG	VF	UNC
	ND (1975). Violet and purple on m/c unpt. Mask at ctr. r. on back. Sign. 1.	3.00	8.50	27.50

3	10 KINA	VG	VF	UNC
	ND (1975). Dk. blue-green and purple on m/c unpt. Bowl, ring and other artifacts on back. Sign. 1.	7.50	20.00	60.00

4	20 KINA	VG	VF	UNC
	ND (1977). Dk. brown and deep red on m/c unpt. Boar's head at r. on back. Sign. 1.	10.00	25.00	80.00

1981-85 ISSUES

		VG	VF	UNC
5	**2 KINA** ND (1981). Black and dk. green on lt. green and m/c unpt. Like #1. White strip 16mm wide at r.			
	a. Sign. 1.	FV	FV	10.00
	b. Sign. 2.	FV	7.50	30.00
	c. Sign. 3.	FV	FV	7.50
6	**5 KINA** ND (1981). Violet and purple on m/c unpt. Like #2. White strip 22mm wide at r.			
	a. Sign. 1.	FV	6.50	30.00
	b. Sign. 2.	FV	7.00	32.50
7	**10 KINA** ND (1985). Dk. blue, purple and green on m/c unpt. Like #3. White strip 18mm wide at r. Sign. 1.	FV	10.00	50.00

#8 Held in Reserve.

		VG	VF	UNC
9	**10 KINA** ND (1988). Dk. blue, dk. green and brown-violet on m/c unpt. Similar to #7 but different design elements in unpt. representing a modern bldg. Ornate corner designs omitted on face and back.			
	a. Sign. 2.	FV	15.00	85.00
	b. Sign. 3.	FV	FV	25.00
	c. Sign. 5.	FV	FV	22.50
	d. Sign. 7.	FV	FV	22.50
	e. Sign. 8.	FV	FV	22.50

		VG	VF	UNC
10	**20 KINA** ND. Dk. brown and deep red on m/c unpt. Similar to #4 but different design elements in unpt.			
	a. Sign. 3.	FV	FV	50.00
	b. Sign. 6.	FV	FV	40.00
	c. Sign. 8.	FV	FV	30.00
	d. Sign. 10.	FV	FV	35.00

		VG	VF	UNC
11	**50 KINA** ND (1989). Brown, red, blue and m/c unpt. National Parliament bldg. at ctr. Foreign Affairs Minister M. Somare at l. ctr., ceremonial masks at r. on back. Wmk: Central Bank logo. Sign. 3. Paper.	FV	FV	75.00

1991 COMMEMORATIVE ISSUE

#12, 9th South Pacific Games 1991

		VG	VF	UNC
12	**2 KINA** 1991. Black and dk. green on lt. green and m/c unpt. Similar to #5 but w/stylized Bird of Paradise in clear circle at lower r. Polymer plastic. Sign. 3. Printer: NPA (w/o imprint).	FV	FV	6.50

1992; 1993 ND REGULAR ISSUES

#12A, 13 and 14: stylized Bird of Paradise at l. ctr. and as wmk.

		VG	VF	UNC
12A	**2 KINA** ND (1992). Black and dk. green on lt. green and m/c unpt. Like #5 but most design elements much lighter. Serial # darker and heavier type face. Sign. 3. Paper.	FV	FV	6.00

13   5 KINA
ND (1992). Violet and purple on m/c unpt. Like #6 but most design
elements much lighter. Serial # darker, heavier type face. Paper.

	VG	VF	UNC
a. Sign. 3.	FV	FV	15.00
b. Sign. 7.	FV	FV	15.00
c. Sign. 9.	FV	FV	7.50
d. Sign. 10.	FV	FV	5.00

14   5 KINA
ND (1993). Violet and purple on m/c unpt. Like #13 but
w/segmented security thread and new sign. title: *Secretary for
Finance and Planning*. Paper.

	VG	VF	UNC
a. Sign. 4.	FV	FV	12.50
b. Sign. 5.	FV	FV	12.50

1995 ND COMMEMORATIVE ISSUE

#15, 20th Anniversary of Independence

15   2 KINA   VG   VF   UNC
ND (1995). Black and dk. green on lt. green and m/c unpt. Similar   FV   FV   7.50
to #12 but w/ornate *20 ANNIVERSARY* logo at l., *PNG 20* at lower
l. Sign 5. Polymer plastic. Printer: NPA (w/o imprint).

1996 ND REGULAR ISSUE

16   2 KINA
ND (1996). Black and dk. green on lt. green and m/c unpt. Similar
to #12A and 15. Polymer plastic.

	VG	VF	UNC
a. Sign. 6.	FV	FV	5.50
b. Sign. 7.	FV	FV	5.50
c. Sign. 10.	FV	FV	5.00

1998 COMMEMORATIVE ISSUE

#17, Bank's 25th Anniversary

17   10 KINA   VG   VF   UNC
1998. Dk. blue, dk. green and brown-violet on m/c unpt. Like #9,   FV   FV   20.00
but sign. 8. Silver Jubilee foil w/arms and commemorative dates
1973-1998 at l., and *SJ XXV* at lower l. ctr. Paper.

1999 ISSUE

18   50 KINA
1999. Black and red on orange, yellow and m/c unpt. Similar to #11
but w/ornate window design. Polymer plastic. Printer: NPA (w/o
imprint).

	VG	VF	UNC
a. Sign. 9.	FV	FV	70.00
b. Sign. 10.	FV	FV	65.00

2000 COMMEMORATIVE ISSUE

19   5 KINA   VG   VF   UNC
2000. Violet and purple on m/c unpt. Similar to #14 but w/*YEAR*   FV   FV   11.00
2000 at lower l. ctr. in dull gold and serial # prefix: *PNG20*. Sign.
9. Paper.

2000 SECOND COMMEMORATIVE ISSUE

#20 Currency Silver Jubilee

20	5 KINA	VG	VF	UNC
	2000. Similar to #19 but w/silver imprint at lower ctr. r. and red inscription ovpt. at lower ctr.: *PNG1942000 (19 4 2000 date)*. Paper. Sign. 10.	FV	FV	10.00

2000 THIRD COMMEMORATIVE ISSUE

#21-25, Silver Jubilee of PNG. Sign. 10.

21	2 KINA	VG	VF	UNC
	(20)00. Black and dk. green on lt. green and m/c unpt. Similar to #16 but w/25th Anniversary logo at l. Polymer plastic.	FV	FV	5.00

22	5 KINA	VG	VF	UNC
	ND (2000). Similar to # 13 but w/25th Anniversary logo at lower r. Paper. Sign. 10.	FV	FV	10.00

23	10 KINA	VG	VF	UNC
	(20)00. Similar to #17 but w/25th Anniversary logo at l. Polymer plastic.	FV	FV	18.50

24	20 KINA	VG	VF	UNC
	(20)00. Similat to #10 but w/25th Anniversary logo at l. Paper.	FV	FV	35.00

25	50 KINA	VG	VF	UNC
	(20)00. Similar to #11 but w/25th Anniversary logo at upper l. ctr. Polymer plasic. Sign. 10.	FV	FV	65.00

2000 ISSUE

26	10 KINA	VG	VF	UNC
	July, 2000. Similar to #9. Polymer plastic. Sign. 10.	FV	FV	20.00

2004 ISSUE

#27, 30th Anniversary of the Bank.

27	20 KINA	VG	VF	UNC
	2004. Polymer plastic.	FV	FV	35.00

The Republic of Paraguay, a landlocked country in the heart of South America surrounded by Argentina, Bolivia and Brazil, has an area of 157,042 sq. mi. (406,752 sq. km.) and a population of 5.5 million, 95 percent of whom are of mixed Spanish and Indian descent. Capital: Asunción. The country is predominantly agrarian, with no important mineral deposits or oil reserves. Meat, timber, oilseeds, tobacco and cotton account for 70 percent of Paraguay's export revenue.

Paraguay was first visited by Alejo Garcia, a shipwrecked Spaniard, in 1520. The interior was explored by Sebastian Cabot in 1526 and 1529, when he sailed up the Paraná and Paraguay Rivers. Asunción, which would become the center of a province embracing much of southern South America, was established by the Spanish explorer Juan de Salazar on Aug. 15, 1537. For a century and a half the history of Paraguay was largely the history of the agricultural colonies established by the Jesuits in the south and east to Christianize the Indians. In 1811, following the outbreak of the South American wars of independence, Paraguayan patriots overthrew the local Spanish authorities and proclaimed their country's independence.

MONETARY SYSTEM:
1 Guaraní = 100 Céntimos, 1944-

REPUBLIC

BANCO CENTRAL DEL PARAGUAY

DECRETO LEY DE NO. 18 DEL 25 DE MARZO DE 1952

(FROM AUG.1963)

#192-201 arms at l. Sign. size and name varieties. Replacement notes: Serial # prefix Z. Printer: TDLR.

	192	1 GUARANÍ	VG	VF	UNC
		L.1952. Green on m/c unpt. Soldier at r. Black serial # at lower l. and lower r. Banco Central on back. 1 sign. variety.	0.25	1.00	4.00

193	1 GUARANÍ	VG	VF	UNC
	L.1952. Green on m/c unpt. Soldier at r. Palacio Legislativo on back. 2 sign. varieties.			
	a. Black serial # at lower l. and lower r.	0.10	0.25	1.75
	b. Black serial # at upper l. and lower r.	0.10	0.25	1.25
	s. As a. Specimen.	—	—	25.00
194	5 GUARANÍES			
	L.1952. Blue on m/c unpt. Girl holding jug at r., black serial # at lower l. and lower r. Hotel Guarani on back. 1 sign. variety.	0.25	1.50	6.00

195	5 GUARANÍES	VG	VF	UNC
	L.1952. Black on m/c unpt. Like #194. 2 sign. varieties.			
	a. Red serial # at lower l. and lower r.	0.10	0.25	1.50
	b. Red serial # at upper l. and lower r.	0.10	0.25	1.25
	s. As a. Specimen.	—	—	25.00

196	10 GUARANÍES	VG	VF	UNC
	L.1952. Deep red on m/c unpt. General Eugenio A. Garay at r. International bridge on back. 2 sign. varieties.			
	a. Black serial # at lower l. and lower r.	0.15	0.40	2.25
	b. Black serial # at upper l. and lower r.	0.15	0.40	2.00
	s. As a. Specimen.	—	—	25.00

197	50 GUARANÍES	VG	VF	UNC
	L.1952. Brown on m/c unpt. Mariscal José F. Estigarribia at r. Country road on back. 2 sign. varieties.			
	a. Black serial # at lower l. and lower r.	0.50	1.75	7.00
	b. Black serial # at upper l. and lower r.	0.20	0.75	4.00
	s. As a. Specimen.	—	—	25.00

198	100 GUARANÍES	VG	VF	UNC
	L.1952. Green on m/c unpt. General José E. Diaz at r. Black serial # at lower l. and lower r. Ruins of Humaita on back. 1 sign. variety (large sign.)			
	a. Issued note.	0.50	3.00	15.00
	s. Specimen.	—	—	25.00

Note: Do not confuse green #198 w/later issue #205 also in green. #198 w/value: *CIEN GUARANIES* at bottom on back.

199 100 GUARANÍES

	VG	VF	UNC
L.1952. Orange on m/c unpt. Like #198. 2 sign. varieties (small size).			
a. Black serial # at lower l. and lower r.	0.50	2.50	7.00
b. Black serial # at upper l. and lower r.	0.50	1.00	3.00

200 500 GUARANÍES

	VG	VF	UNC
L.1952. Blue-gray on m/c unpt. General Bernardino Caballero at r. Federal merchant ship on back. 2 sign. varieties.			
a. Black serial # at lower l. and lower r.	0.75	4.00	10.00
b. Black serial # at upper l. and lower r.	0.50	2.00	6.00
s. As a. Specimen.	—	—	25.00

201 1000 GUARANÍES

	VG	VF	UNC
L.1952. Purple on m/c unpt. Mariscal Francisco Solano Lopez r. National shrine on back. 2 sign. varieties.			
a. Black serial # at lower l. and lower r.	2.00	7.50	20.00
b. Black serial # at upper l. and lower r.	1.00	6.00	15.00
s. As a. Specimen.	—	—	25.00

#202-204 printer: TDLR.

202 5000 GUARANÍES

	VG	VF	UNC
L.1952. Red-orange on m/c unpt. Arms at ctr., Don Carlos Antonio López at r. López Palace on back. 2 sign. varieties.			
a. Black serial # at lower l. and lower r.	7.50	25.00	60.00
b. Black serial # at upper l. and lower r.	5.00	75.00	45.00
s. As a. Specimen.	—	—	25.00

203 10,000 GUARANÍES

	VG	VF	UNC
L.1952. Dk. brown on m/c unpt. Arms at ctr., Dr. José Caspar Rodriguez De Francia at r., black serial # at lower l. and lower r. Historical scene from 14.5.1811 on back. 1 sign. variety.			
a. Issued note.	10.00	40.00	100.00
s. Specimen.	—	—	25.00

204 10,000 GUARANÍES

	VG	VF	UNC
L.1952. Dk. brown on m/c unpt. Like #203 but CASPAR changed to GASPAR below Francia. 2 sign. varieties.			
a. Black serial # at lower l. and lower r.	10.00	40.00	100.00
b. Black serial # at upper l. and lower r.		30.00	75.00

1982; 1990 ND ISSUE

#205-210 replacement notes: Serial # prefix Z.

#205-209 like #199-203 except expression of values changed on back from Spanish to native Guaraní.
    Printer: TDLR.

205 100 GUARANÍES

	VG	VF	UNC
L.1952 (1982). Green on m/c unpt. Like #199 but value on back stated: SA GUARANI. 4 sign. varieties.	0.10	0.25	1.25

206 **500 GUARANÍES**
L.1952 (1982). Blue-gray on m/c unpt. Like #200 but value on back
stated: PO SA GUARANI. 6 sign. varieties.

	VG	VF	UNC
	FV	FV	1.75

207 **1000 GUARANÍES**
L.1952 (1982). Purple on m/c unpt. Like #201 but value on back
stated: SU GUARANI. 6 sign. varieties.

	VG	VF	UNC
	FV	FV	2.00

208 **5000 GUARANÍES**
L.1952 (1982). Red-orange on m/c unpt. Like #202 but value on
back stated: PO SU GUARANI. 6 sign. varieties.

	VG	VF	UNC
	FV	FV	7.50

209 **10,000 GUARANÍES**
L.1952 (1982). Dk. brown on m/c unpt. Like #203 but value on
back stated: PA SU GUARANI. 5 sign. varieties.

	VG	VF	UNC
	FV	FV	10.00

210 **50,000 GUARANÍES**
L.1952 (1990). Deep purple and lt. blue on m/c unpt. Soldier at r.,
outline map of Paraguay at ctr. Back purple and olive-green on m/c
unpt. House of Independence at ctr. Wmk: Bust of soldier. Plain
security thread. 3 sign. varieties. Printer:

	VG	VF	UNC
	FV	FV	45.00

1994 ND ISSUE

211 **50,000 GUARANÍES**
L.1952 (1994). Purple and lt. blue on m/c unpt. Like #210 but
w/segmented foil over security thread. 3 sign. varieties. Series A.

	VG	VF	UNC
	FV	FV	40.00

1995 ND ISSUE

#212 and 213 printer: F-GO.

212 **500 GUARANÍES**
L.1952 (1995). Blue-gray on m/c unpt. Like #206. 2 sign. varieties.

	VG	VF	UNC
	FV	FV	1.25

213 **1000 GUARANÍES**
L.1952 (1995). Purple on m/c unpt. Like #207.

	VG	VF	UNC
	FV	FV	2.00

LEY 489 DEL 29 DE JUNIO DE 1995; 1997-98 ISSUE

214 **1000 GUARANÍES**
1998; 2001; 2003. Purple on m/c unpt. Like #213. Series B. Printer:
Ciccone Calcogra, S.A.

	VG	VF	UNC
	FV	FV	1.75

		VG	VF	UNC
215	**5000 GUARANÍES** 1997; 1998. Red-orange on m/c unpt. Like #208. Silver foil over security thread. Printer: TDLR. 2 sign. varieties. Series B.	FV	FV	5.00
216	**10,000 GUARANÍES** 1998; 2003. Brown. Like #209. Series B. Printer Ciccone Calcogra, S.A.	FV	FV	7.50

		VG	VF	UNC
217	**50,000 GUARANÍES** 1997. Purple and lt. blue on m/c unpt. Like #211. Printer: TDLR. Series B.	FV	FV	27.50
218	**50,000 GUARANÍES** 1998. Like #217 but w/staircase metallic impression at lower l. corner on face. Series B. Imprint: *De La Rue.*	FV	FV	27.50
219	**100,000 GUARANÍES** 1998. Green, yellow-brown and m/c. San Rogue González de Santa Cruz at r. *Represa de Itaipu,* Itaipu Hydroelectric Dam on back. Printer: TDLR.	FV	FV	50.00

2000 ISSUE

		VG	VF	UNC
220	**5000 GUARANÍES** 2000; 2003. Similar to #215. Series C. Printer: CC.	FV	FV	5.00

2002 COMMEMORATIVE ISSUE
50th Anniversary of the Banco Cenral del Paraguay

		VG	VF	UNC
221	**1000 GUARANÍES** 2002. Purple on m/c unpt. Like #214 but w/anniversary text below date. Printer: FC-O.	FV	FV	1.75

2004 ISSUE

		VG	VF	UNC
222	**1000 GUARANÍES** 2004. Like #221 but w/o anniversary text. Printer: F-CO.	FV	FV	1.75
223	**5000 GUARANÍES** 2004. Brown.		FV	5.00
224	**10,000 GUARANÍES** 2004. Green. Printer: CCSA.		FV	10.00
225	**20,000 GUARANÍES** 2004.		FV	20.00

COLLECTOR SERIES
BANCO CENTRAL DEL PARAGUAY
1979 ISSUE

		Issue Price	Mkt. Value
CS1	**100-10,000 GUARANÍES** L.1972 (1979). 199b-202b, 204b ovpt: SPECIMEN and w/serial # prefix Maltese cross.	14.00	25.00

The Republic of Perú, located on the Pacific coast of South America, has an area of 496,222 sq. mi. (1,285,216 sq. km.) and a population of 25.66 million. Capital: Lima. The diversified economy includes mining, fishing and agriculture. Fish meal, copper, sugar, zinc and iron ore are exported.

Once part of a great Inca Empire that reached from northern Ecuador to central Chile, Perú was conquered in 1531-33 by Francisco Pizarro. Desirable as the richest of the Spanish viceroyalties, it was torn by warfare between avaricious Spaniards until the arrival in 1569 of Francisco de Toledo, who initiated 2 1/2 centuries of efficient colonial rule which made Lima the most aristocratic colonial capital and the stronghold of Spain's South American possessions. José de San Martín of Argentina proclaimed Perú's independence on July 28, 1821; Simón Bolívar of Venezuela secured it in Dec. of 1824 when he defeated the last Spanish army in South America. After several futile attempts to re-establish its South-American empire, Spain recognized Perú's independence in 1879.

MONETARY SYSTEM:
1 Sol = 1 Sol de Oro = 100 Centavos, 1879-1985
1 Libra = 10 Soles
1 Inti = 1000 Soles de Oro, 1986-1991
1 Nuevo Sol = 100 Centimes = 1 Million Intis, 1991-

REPÚBLICA DEL PERÚ
BANCO CENTRAL DE RESERVA DEL PERU
LEY 10535, 1956 ISSUE
#76-80 seated Liberty holding shield and staff at ctr. Arms at ctr. on back. Sign. varieties.

		VG	VF	UNC
76	**5 SOLES** 22.3.1956; 18.3.1960. Green on patterned lt. blue unpt. Like #70. Printer: TDLR.	0.50	1.50	5.00

		VG	VF	UNC
77	**10 SOLES** 9.7.1956. Orange on m/c unpt. Similar to #71. Printer: G&D.	2.00	6.00	20.00

#78-80 printer: TDLR.

		VG	VF	UNC
78	**50 SOLES** 22.3.1956; 24.10.1957; 13.5.1959. Dk. blue on lilac unpt. Like #72. Serial # at upper l. and r.			
	a. Issued note.	1.50	4.50	17.50
	s. Specimen.	—	—	—
79	**100 SOLES** 1956-61. Black on lt. blue unpt. Like #73 but different guilloche. Back black.			
	a. *LIMA* at lower l. 22.3.1956; 24.10.1957.	4.00	12.00	30.00
	b. *LIMA* at lower r. w/date. 13.5.1959.	4.00	12.00	30.00
	c. As b. Series and serial # at lower l. and upper r. 1.2.1961.	4.00	12.00	30.00
	s. As a. Specimen.	—	—	—

80	500 SOLES	VG	VF	UNC
	1956-61. Brown on lt. brown and lilac unpt. Similar to #74. Back brown.			
	a. Series and serial # at upper corners. 22.3.1956; 24.10.1957.	8.00	25.00	75.00
	b. Series and serial # at lower l. and upper r. 10.12.1959; 16.6.1961.	8.00	25.00	75.00
	s. As b. Specimen.	—	—	—

1958 ISSUE

#81-82 printer: W&S.

81	5 SOLES	VG	VF	UNC
	21.8.1958. Green. Like #70 but different guilloche on back.	1.00	4.00	7.50

82	10 SOLES	VG	VF	UNC
	21.8.1958. Orange on m/c unpt. Similar to #71.	1.00	4.00	15.00

1960 ISSUE

82A	10 SOLES	VG	VF	UNC
	8.7.1960; 1.2.1961. Orange on m/c unpt. Liberty seated holding shield and staff at ctr. Serial # and series at lower l. and upper r. Printer: TDLR.	0.75	1.50	6.00

LEY 13958, 1962; 1964 ISSUE

#83-87 Liberty seated holding shield and staff at ctr. Arms at ctr. on back. Printer: TDLR.

83	5 SOLES DE ORO	VG	VF	UNC
	9.2.1962; 20.9.1963; 18.6.1965; 18.11.1966; 23.2.1968. Green on m/c unpt. Serial # at lower l. and upper r. Series J.			
	a. Issued note.	0.25	1.00	4.00
	s. Specimen.	—	—	25.00

84	10 SOLES DE ORO	VG	VF	UNC
	8.6.1962; 20.9.1963; 20.5.1966; 25.5.1967; 23.2.1968. Orange on m/c unpt. Series I.			
	a. Issued note.	0.25	1.50	4.00
	s. Specimen.	—	—	25.00

85	50 SOLES DE ORO	VG	VF	UNC
	9.2.1962; 20.9.1963; 23.2.1968. Blue on m/c unpt. Serial # at lower l. and upper r. Series H.			
	a. Issued note.	0.75	3.50	12.50
	s. Specimen.	—	—	25.00
86	100 SOLES DE ORO			
	13.3.1964; 23.2.1968. Black on lt. blue and m/c unpt. Series G.			
	a. Issued note.	2.00	6.00	20.00
	s. Specimen.	—	—	25.00

87	500 SOLES DE ORO	VG	VF	UNC
	9.2.1962; 20.9.1963; 20.5.1966; 23.2.1968. Brown on lt. brown and m/c unpt. Series L.			
	a. Issued note.	3.00	10.00	40.00
	s. Specimen.	—	—	25.00

1962; 1965 ISSUE

#88-91 like #84-87. *Pagará al Portador* added under bank name at top ctr. Printer: ABNC.

88	10 SOLES DE ORO	VG	VF	UNC
	26.2.1965. Red-orange on lt. green and m/c unpt. Series C.	0.50	2.00	7.50

91	500 SOLES DE ORO	VG	VF	UNC
	26.2.1965. Brown on m/c unpt. Series P.	7.50	25.00	70.00

LEY 13 958 1968 ISSUE

#92-98 arms at ctr. 3 sign. Printer: TDLR.

Replacement notes: Serial # *Z999 . . .*

89	50 SOLES DE ORO	VG	VF	UNC
	20.8.1965. Blue on m/c unpt. Series B.			
	a. Issued note.	1.00	5.00	20.00
	s. Specimen.	—	—	100.00

92	5 SOLES DE ORO	VG	VF	UNC
	23.2.1968. Green on m/c unpt. Artifacts at l., Inca Pachacútec at r. Fortaleza de Sacsahuaman on back. Series J.			
	a. Issued note.	0.25	0.75	3.00
	s. Specimen.	—	—	25.00

90	100 SOLES DE ORO	VG	VF	UNC
	12.9.1962; 20.8.1965. Black on lt. blue and m/c unpt. Series A.			
	a. Issued note.	2.00	6.50	22.50
	s. Specimen.	—	—	100.00

93	10 SOLES DE ORO	VG	VF	UNC
	23.2.1968. Red-orange on m/c unpt. Bldg. at l., Garcilaso Inca de la Vega at r. Lake Titicaca, boats on back. Series I.			
	a. Issued note.	0.20	0.50	2.00
	s. Specimen.	—	—	25.00

94	50 SOLES DE ORO	VG	VF	UNC
	23.2.1968. Blue-gray on m/c unpt. Workers at l., Tupac Amaru II at r. Scene of historic town of Tinta on back. Series H.			
	a. Issued note.	0.25	1.00	5.00
	s. Specimen.	—	—	25.00

95	100 SOLES DE ORO	VG	VF	UNC
	23.2.1968. Black on m/c unpt. Dock workers at l., Hipolito Unanue at r. Church, site of first National Congress on back. Series G.			
	a. Issued note.	0.50	1.50	6.50
	s. Specimen.	—	—	25.00

96	200 SOLES DE ORO	VG	VF	UNC
	23.2.1968. Purple on m/c unpt. Fishermen at l., Ramon Castilla at r. Frigate *Amazonas* at ctr. on back. Series Q.			
	a. Issued note.	1.00	3.50	12.50
	s. Specimen.	—	—	25.00

97	500 SOLES DE ORO	VG	VF	UNC
	23.2.1968. Brown on m/c unpt., tan near ctr. Builders at l., Nicolas de Pierola at r. National mint on back. Series L.			
	a. Issued note.	2.00	3.00	20.00
	s. Specimen.	—	—	25.00
98	1000 SOLES DE ORO	VG	VF	UNC
	23.2.1968. Violet on m/c unpt. Miguel Grau at l., Francisco Bolognesi (misspelled BOLOGÑESI) at r. Scene of Machu Picchu on back. Series R.			
	a. Issued note.	4.00	12.50	30.00
	s. Specimen.	—	—	25.00

1969 ISSUE

#99-105 like #92-98 but text changed to: *De Acuerdo Con Su Ley Organica.* 2 sign. Printer: TDLR.

Replacement notes: Serial # *Z999 . . .*

99	5 SOLES DE ORO	VG	VF	UNC
	1969-74. Like #92. Series J.			
	a. 20.6.1969.	0.10	0.25	2.50
	b. 16.10.1970; 9.9.1971; 4.5.1972.	0.10	0.25	2.00
	c. 24.5.1973; 16.5.1974; 15.8.1974.	0.10	0.25	1.25

100	10 SOLES DE ORO	VG	VF	UNC
	1969-74. Like #93. Series I.			
	a. 20.6.1969.	0.10	0.25	2.00
	b. 16.10.1970; 9.9.1971.	0.10	0.25	1.50
	c. 4.5.1972; 24.5.1973; 16.5.1974.	0.10	0.25	1.50
101	50 SOLES DE ORO			
	1969-74. Like #94. Series H.			
	a. 20.6.1969.	0.20	0.50	5.00
	b. 16.10.1970; 9.9.1971; 4.5.1972.	0.20	0.50	4.00
	c. 24.5.1973; 16.5.1974; 15.8.1974.	0.20	0.50	2.50

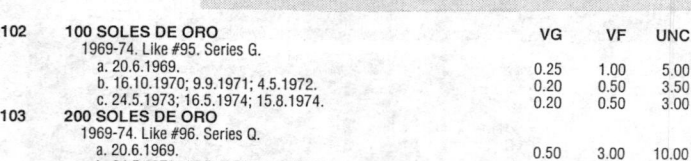

102	100 SOLES DE ORO	VG	VF	UNC
	1969-74. Like #95. Series G.			
	a. 20.6.1969.	0.25	1.00	5.00
	b. 16.10.1970; 9.9.1971; 4.5.1972.	0.20	0.50	3.50
	c. 24.5.1973; 16.5.1974; 15.8.1974.	0.20	0.50	3.00
103	200 SOLES DE ORO			
	1969-74. Like #96. Series Q.			
	a. 20.6.1969.	0.50	3.00	10.00
	b. 24.5.1973; 16.5.1974; 15.8.1974.	0.50	2.00	9.00

104	500 SOLES DE ORO	VG	VF	UNC
	1969-74. Like #97. Series L.			
	a. 20.6.1969.	1.00	5.00	20.00
	b. 16.10.1970; 9.9.1971; 4.5.1972; 24.5.1973.	1.00	4.00	15.00
	c. 16.5.1974; 15.8.1974.	0.50	2.50	10.00

105	1000 SOLES DE ORO	VG	VF	UNC
	1969-73. Like #98 but *BOLOGNESI* correctly spelled at r. Series R.			
	a. 20.6.1969; 16.10.1970.	1.50	7.50	30.00
	b. 9.9.1971; 4.5.1972; 24.5.1973.	1.50	5.00	25.00

1975 ISSUE

#106-111 3 sign. Printer: TDLR.

Replacement notes: Serial # *Z999 . . .*

106	10 SOLES DE ORO	VG	VF	UNC
	2.10.1975. Like #93. Series I.	0.10	0.25	1.50

107	50 SOLES DE ORO	VG	VF	UNC
	2.10.1975. Like #94. Series H.	0.10	0.25	1.50
108	100 SOLES DE ORO			
	2.10.1975. Like #95. Series G.	0.20	0.50	2.50

#109 Not assigned.

110	500 SOLES DE ORO	VG	VF	UNC
	2.10.1975. Like #97. Pale green unpt. near ctr. Series L.	1.00	3.00	15.00

111	1000 SOLES DE ORO	VG	VF	UNC
	2.10.1975. Like #98. Name correctly spelled. Series R.	2.00	5.00	27.50

1976-77 ISSUES

#112 and 113 w/o *Pagará al Portador* at top. W/o security thread. 3 sign. Printer: TDLR. Replacement notes: Serial # *Z999....*

112	10 SOLES DE ORO	VG	VF	UNC
	17.11.1976. Like #106. Series I. Printer: TDLR.	0.10	0.25	1.50

113	50 SOLES DE ORO	VG	VF	UNC
	15.12.1977. Like #107. Series H. Printer: TDLR.	0.10	0.25	1.25

#114-115 printer: IPS-Roma.

114	100 SOLES DE ORO	VG	VF	UNC
	22.7.1976. Green, brown and m/c. Arms at l., Tupac Amaru II at r. Machu Picchu on back.	0.10	0.25	1.25

115 500 SOLES DE ORO

	VG	VF	UNC
22.7.1976. Green, blue and yellow. Arms at ctr., Jose Quiñones at r. Logging scene on back.	0.05	0.25	1.50

#116 and 117 printer: BDDK. Replacement notes: Serial # prefix *Y*, and suffix letter *A*.

116 1000 SOLES DE ORO

	VG	VF	UNC
22.7.1976. Black, green, brown and m/c. Arms at ctr., Miguel Grau at r. Fishermen on back.	0.50	2.00	7.50

117 5000 SOLES DE ORO

	VG	VF	UNC
1976-85. Brown and maroon on m/c unpt. Arms at ctr., Col. Bolognesi at r. and as wmk. 2 miners in mine at l. on back.			
a. 22.7.1976.	1.00	2.50	10.00
b. 5.11.1981.	0.15	0.50	2.50
c. 21.6.1985.	0.05	0.25	1.50

1979 ISSUE

#117A *Deleted*. See #125A.

#118-120 denominations below coat-of-arms. Printer: TDLR. Replacement notes: Serial # prefix *Y* and suffix letter *A*.

118 1000 SOLES DE ORO

	VG	VF	UNC
1.2.1979; 3.5.1979. Black, green and m/c. Adm. Grau at r. and as wmk., arms at ctr. Fishermen and boats at l. on back.	0.50	1.00	3.00

119 5000 SOLES DE ORO

	VG	VF	UNC
1.2.1979. Brown-violet and m/c. Similar to #117 but *CINCO MIL* added at bottom on face. Miners on back.	0.50	1.50	7.50

120 10,000 SOLES DE ORO

	VG	VF	UNC
1.2.1979; 5.11.1981. Black, blue-violet and purple on m/c unpt. Inca Garcilaso Inca de la Vega at r. and as wmk. Indian digging at l., woman w/flowers at ctr. on back.	0.50	3.00	15.00

1981 ISSUE

#121 *Deleted*. See #125B.

#122-125 portr. as wmk. Printer: ABNC. Replacement notes: Serial # prefix *Y*, suffix *A*.

122	1000 SOLES DE ORO	VG	VF	UNC
	5.11.1981. Black, green and m/c. Similar to #118 but slightly modified guilloche in unpt. at ctr.			
	a. Issued note.	0.10	0.30	1.50
	s. Specimen.	—	—	100.00

123	5000 SOLES DE ORO	VG	VF	UNC
	5.11.1981. Black and red-brown on m/c unpt. Similar to #119 but denomination is above signs. at ctr.	0.25	1.00	5.00

124	10,000 SOLES DE ORO	VG	VF	UNC
	5.11.1981. Black, blue-violet and purple on m/c unpt. Similar to #120 but slight variations on borders.	0.50	2.00	7.00

125	50,000 SOLES DE ORO	VG	VF	UNC
	5.11.1981; 2.11.1984. Black and orange on m/c unpt. Arms at ctr., Nicolas de Pierola at r. Drilling rig at l. on back, helicopter approaching.			
	a. Issued note.	1.00	3.00	12.50
	s. Specimen.	—	—	150.00

1982; 1985 ISSUE

Replacement notes: Serial # prefix *Y*, suffix *A* and *ZZ* respectively.

125A	500 SOLES DE ORO	VG	VF	UNC
	18.3.1982. Like #115 but printer: (T)DLR.	0.25	0.50	3.00
125B	50,000 SOLES DE ORO			
	23.8.1985. Black, orange and m/c. Like #125. Printer: TDLR.	0.75	2.25	6.50

1985 PROVISIONAL ISSUE

126	100,000 SOLES DE ORO	VG	VF	UNC
	23.8.1985. Ovpt. bank name and new denomination in red on face and back of #122.	50.00	150.00	375.00
127	500,000 SOLES DE ORO			
	23.8.1985. Ovpt. bank name and new denomination in red on face and back of #123.	—	—	—

1985-91 ISSUES

During the period from around 1984 and extending beyond 1990, Perú suffered from a hyperinflation that saw the Sol depreciate in value dramatically and drastically. A sudden need for new Inti banknotes caused the government to approach a number of different security printers in order to satisfy the demand for new notes.

#128-150 involve 7 different printers: BdM, BDDK, CdM-B, FNMT, G&D, IPS-Roma and TDLR. Listings proceed by denomination and in chronological order. All portr. appear also as wmk., and all notes have arms at ctr. on face.

Replacement notes:

BdM - Serial # prefix *Y; Z.* BDDK - Serial # prefix *Y.* FNMT - Serial # prefix *Y. IPS-Roma - Serial # prefix Y; Z. TDLR - Serial # prefix Y; Z.*

128	10 INTIS	VG	VF	UNC
	3.4.1985; 17.1.1986. Black, dk. blue and purple on m/c unpt. Ricardo Palma at r. Back aqua and purple; Indian farmer digging at l. and another picking cotton at ctr. Printer: TDLR.	0.05	0.20	0.50

129	10 INTIS	VG	VF	UNC
	26.6.1987. Black, dk. blue and purple on m/c unpt. Like #128. Printer: IPS-Roma.	0.05	0.10	0.35

		VG	VF	UNC
130	**50 INTIS**			
	3.4.1985. Black, orange and green on m/c unpt. Nicolas de Pierola at r. Drilling rig at l. on back, helicopter approaching. Printer: TDLR.	0.15	0.50	2.00
131	**50 INTIS**			
	1986; 1987. Black, orange and green on m/c unpt. Like #130. Printer: CdM-Brazil.			
	a. 6.3.1986.	0.05	0.20	0.75
	b. 26.6.1987.	0.05	0.20	0.50

		VG	VF	UNC
134	**500 INTIS**			
	1985; 1987. Deep brown-violet and olive-brown on m/c unpt. Jose Cabriel Condorcanqui Tupac Amaru II at r. Mountains and climber at ctr. on back. Printer: BDDK.			
	a. 1.3.1985.	0.15	0.30	3.00
	b. 26.6.1987. Ornate red-orange vertical strip at l. end of design w/added security thread underneath.	0.05	0.20	0.50

		VG	VF	UNC
132	**100 INTIS**			
	1985-86. Black and dk. brown on m/c unpt. Ramon Castilla at r. Women workers by cotton spinning frame at l. ctr. on back. Printer: CdM-Brazil.			
	a. 1.2.1985; 1.3.1985.	0.50	2.00	12.00
	b. 6.3.1986. W/add'l pink and lt. green vertical unpt. at r.	0.15	0.50	2.00

		VG	VF	UNC
135	**500 INTIS**			
	6.3.1986. Deep brown-violet and olive-brown on m/c unpt. Similar to #134b. Printer: FNMT.	1.00	3.50	12.50

		VG	VF	UNC
133	**100 INTIS**			
	26.6.1987. Black and dk. brown on m/c unpt. Like #132b. Printer: BDDK.	0.05	0.10	0.35

		VG	VF	UNC
136	**1000 INTIS**			
	1986-88. Deep green, olive-brown and red on m/c unpt. Mariscal Andres Avelino Caceres at r. Ruins off Chan Chan on back. Printer: TDLR.			
	a. 6.3.1986.	0.10	0.50	2.00
	b. 26.6.1987; 28.6.1988.	0.05	0.25	1.50

		VG	VF	UNC
142	**50,000 INTIS** 28.6.1988. Red, violet and dk. blue on m/c unpt. Victor Raul Haya de la Torre at r. Chamber of National Congress on back. Printer: IPS-Roma.	0.25	0.75	3.50
143	**50,000 INTIS** 28.6.1988. Red, violet and dk. blue on m/c unpt. Like #142 but w/segmented foil security thread. Printer: TDLR.	0.50	1.50	5.00

#144-150 arms at ctr. Various printers.

		VG	VF	UNC
137	**5000 INTIS** 28.6.1988. Purple, deep brown and red-orange on m/c unpt. Admiral Miguel Grau at r. Fishermen repairing nets on back. Printer: G&D.	0.05	0.15	0.50
138	**5000 INTIS** 28.6.1988. Purple, deep brown and red-orange on m/c unpt. Like #137. Printer: IPS-Roma.	0.25	1.00	3.50
139	**5000 INTIS** 9.9.1988. Purple, deep brown and red-orange on m/c unpt. Like #137. W/o wmk. Printer: TDLR.	0.25	1.00	4.50

		VG	VF	UNC
144	**100,000 INTIS** 21.11.1988. Brown and black on m/c unpt. Francisco Bolognesi at r. Local boats in Lake Titicaca on back. Bolognesi's printed image on wmk. area at l. Printer: TDLR.	0.25	0.75	2.25

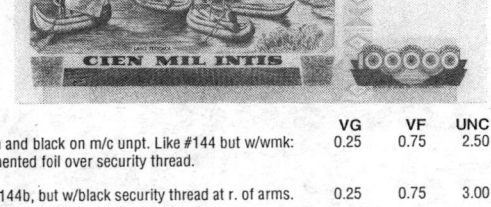

		VG	VF	UNC
140	**10,000 INTIS** 28.6.1988. Aqua, blue and orange on lt. green and m/c unpt. Cesar Vallejo at r. Black and red increasing size serial # (anti-counterfeiting device). Santiago de Chuco street scene on back. Printer IPS-Roma.	0.05	0.25	0.75

		VG	VF	UNC
144A	**100,000 INTIS** 21.12.1988. Brown and black on m/c unpt. Like #144 but w/wmk: *F. Bolognesi.* Segmented foil over security thread.	0.25	0.75	2.50
145	**100,000 INTIS** 21.12.1989. Like #144b, but w/black security thread at r. of arms. Printer: BdeM.	0.25	0.75	3.00
146	**500,000 INTIS** 21.11.1988. Blue and blue-violet on m/c unpt. Face like #128. Church of *La Caridád* (charity), site of first National Congress, on back. Ricardo Palma's printed image on wmk. area at l. Printer: TDLR.	0.25	1.00	6.50

		VG	VF	UNC
141	**10,000 INTIS** 28.6.1988. Dk. blue and orange on lt. green and m/c unpt. Like #140 but w/broken silver security thread. Printer: TDLR.	0.25	0.75	3.00

		VG	VF	UNC
146A	**500,000 INTIS** 21.12.1988. Blue and blue-violet on m/c unpt. Like #146 but w/wmk: *R. Palma.* Segmented foil over security thread.	0.25	1.75	7.50

147	500,000 INTIS	VG	VF	UNC
	21.12.1989. Blue and blue-violet on m/c unpt. Like #146A, but w/black security thread at r. Printer: BdeM.	0.25	1.25	5.50

148	1,000,000 INTIS	VG	VF	UNC
	5.1.1990. Red-brown, green and m/c. Hipolito Unanue at r. and as wmk. Medical college at San Fernando at l. ctr. on back. Printer: TDLR.	0.25	1.00	5.00

149	5,000,000 INTIS	VG	VF	UNC
	5.1.1990. Brown, red and m/c. Antonio Raimondi at r. and as wmk. Indian comforting Raimundi on back. Printer: BdeM.	2.25	7.50	20.00

150	5,000,000 INTIS	VG	VF	UNC
	16.1.1991. Similar to #149 but plants printed on wmk. area at l. on face. Old bldg. at r. on back. Printer: IPS-Roma.	0.50	2.00	7.50

1991; 1992 ISSUES

MONETARY REFORM: 1 Nuevo Sol = 1 Million Intis

#151-155 arms at upper r.

151	10 NUEVOS SOLES	VG	VF	UNC
	1.2.1991. Dk. green and blue-green on m/c unpt. WW II era fighter plane as monument at upper ctr., José Abelardo Quiñones at r. and as wmk. Biplane inverted (signifying pilot's death) at l. ctr. on back. Printer: TDLR.	FV	FV	9.50
151A	10 NUEVOS SOLES	FV	FV	9.50
	10.9.1992. Dk. green and blue-green on m/c unpt. Like #151 but printer: IPS-Roma.			

152	20 NUEVOS SOLES	VG	VF	UNC
	1.2.1991. Black, brown and orange on m/c unpt. Patio of San Marcos University at ctr., Raul Porras B. at r. and as wmk. Palace of Torre Tagle at l. ctr. on back. Printer: TDLR.	FV	FV	22.50

#153-155 printer: IPS-Roma.

153	20 NUEVOS SOLES			
	25.6.1992. Black, brown and orange on m/c unpt. Like #152.	FV	FV	17.50

154	50 NUEVOS SOLES	VG	VF	UNC
	1.2.1991; 25.6.1992. Red-brown, blue-violet and black on m/c unpt. Bldg. at ctr., Abraham Valdelomar at r. and as wmk. Laguna de Huacachina at l. ctr. on back.	FV	FV	40.00

155	100 NUEVOS SOLES	VG	VF	UNC
	1.2.1991; 25.6.1992; 10.9.1992. Black, blue-black, red-violet and deep green on m/c unpt. Arch monument at ctr., Jorge Basadre (Grohmann) at r. and as wmk. National Library at l. ctr. on back.			
	a. W/Jorge Basadre. 1.2.1991.	FV	FV	75.00
	b. W/Jorge Basadre Grohmann. 10.9.1992.	FV	FV	70.00

1994; 1995 ISSUE

#156-161 similar to #151-155 but w/clear wmk. area.

156	10 NUEVOS SOLES	VG	VF	UNC
	16.6.1994. Dk. green and blue-green on m/c unpt. Like #151. Printer: TDLR.	FV	FV	7.50

157	10 NUEVOS SOLES	VG	VF	UNC
	20.4.1995. Dk. green and blue-green on m/c unpt. Like #156. Printer: G&D.	FV	FV	7.00

158	20 NUEVOS SOLES	VG	VF	UNC
	16.6.1994. Black, brown and orange on m/c unpt. Like #152. Printer: TDLR.	FV	FV	15.00
159	20 NUEVOS SOLES			
	20.4.1995. Similar to #158.	FV	FV	14.00

#160-162 printer: IPS-Roma.

160	50 NUEVOS SOLES	VG	VF	UNC
	16.6.1994; 20.4.1995. Brown, deep blue and black on m/c unpt. Like #154.	FV	FV	37.50

161	100 NUEVOS SOLES	VG	VF	UNC
	20.4.1995. Black, blue-black, red-violet and deep green on m/c unpt. Like #155b.	FV	FV	65.00

162	200 NUEVOS SOLES	VG	VF	UNC
	20.4.1995. Red, brown-violet and dk. blue on m/c unpt. Isabel Flores de Oliva, St. Rose of Lima at r. and as wmk., well in unpt. at ctr. Convent of Santo Domingo at l. on back.	FV	FV	120.00

1996 ISSUE

#163-165 printer: IPS-Roma.

163	10 NUEVOS SOLES	VG	VF	UNC
	25.4.1996. Like #156.	FV	FV	10.00

164	20 NUEVOS SOLES	VG	VF	UNC
	25.4.1996; 11.6.1997. Like #158.	FV	FV	15.00
165	100 NUEVOS SOLES			
	25.4.1996. Like #161.	FV	FV	65.00

1997 ISSUE

#166-167 printer: BABN.

166	10 NUEVOS SOLES	VG	VF	UNC
	11.6.1997; 6.8.1998; 20.5.1999. Dk. green and blue-green on m/c unpt. Like #157.	FV	FV	9.00
167	20 NUEVOS SOLES	VG	VF	UNC
	11.6.1997. Like #158.	FV	FV	15.00

		VG	VF	UNC
168	**50 NUEVOS SOLES**			
	11.6.1997; 6.8.1998. Like #154. Printer: IPS-Roma.	FV	FV	37.50

1999 ISSUE

		VG	VF	UNC
169	**20 NUEVOS SOLES**			
	20.5.1999. Like #167. Printer: FNMT.	FV	FV	15.00

		VG	VF	UNC
169A	**50 NUEVOS SOLES**			
	20.5.1999. Like #168. Printer: De La Rue.	FV	FV	37.50
170	**100 NUEVOS SOLES**			
	20.5.1999. Like #161. Printer: BABN.	FV	FV	65.00

BANCO DE CREDITO DEL PERÚ /BANCO CENTRAL DE RESERVA DEL PERÚ

1985 EMERGENCY CHECK ISSUE

		VG	VF	UNC
R2	**100,000 SOLES**			
	2.9.1985. Black text on lt. blue text unpt. 2 sign. varieties.	35.00	150.00	—

BANCO DE LA NACIÓN/ BANCO CENTRAL DE RESERVA DEL PERÚ

1985 CHEQUES CIRCULARES DE GERENCIA ISSUE
#R6-R8 bank monogram at upper l.

		VG	VF	UNC
R6	**50,000 SOLES**			
	9.9.1985; 16.9.1985. Black text on tan unpt. Bank at ctr.	35.00	125.00	—
R7	**100,000 SOLES**			
	2.9.1985. Black text on lt. blue unpt. Like #R6.	35.00	125.00	—
R8	**200,000 SOLES**			
	2.9.1985. Black text on pink unpt. Like #R6.	35.00	125.00	—

PHILIPPINES

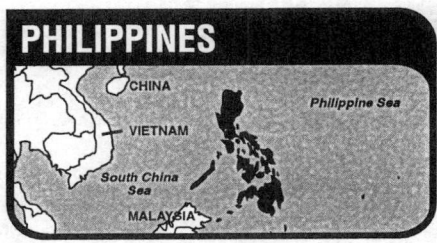

The Republic of the Philippines, an archipelago in the western Pacific 500 miles (805 km.) from the southeast coast of Asia, has an area of 115,830 sq. mi. (300,000 sq. km.) and a population of 75.04 million. Capital: Manila. The economy of the 7,000-island group is based on agriculture, forestry and fishing. Timber, coconut products, sugar and hemp are exported.

Migration to the Philippines began about 30,000 years ago when land bridges connected the islands with Borneo and Sumatra. Ferdinand Magellan claimed the islands for Spain in 1521. The first permanent settlement was established by Miguel de Legazpi at Cebu in April of 1565; Manila was established in 1572. A British expedition captured Manila and occupied the Spanish colony in Oct. of 1762, but it was returned to Spain by the treaty of Paris, 1763. Spain held the Philippines amid a growing movement of Filipino nationalism until 1898 when they were ceded to the United States at the end of the Spanish-American War. The Filipinos then fought unsuccessfully against the United States to maintain their independent Republic proclaimed by Emilio Aguinaldo. The country became a self-governing Commonwealth of the United States in 1935, and attained independence as the Republic of the Philippines on July 4, 1946. During World War II the Japanese had set up a puppet republic, but this quasi-government failed to achieve worldwide recognition. The occupation lasted from late 1941 to 1945. Ferdinand Marcos lost to Corazón Aquino in elections of 1986. Marcos then fled the country. In 1992 Fidel Ramos was elected president. He was succeeded in 1998 by Joseph E. Estrada, who was deposed in January 2001 and replaced by his vice-president Gloria Macapagal Arroyo.

MONETARY SYSTEM:
1 Peso = 100 Centavos to 1967
1 Piso = 100 Sentimos, 1967-

Type1 Type 2 Type 3 Type 4 Type 5

SIGNATURE VARIETIES

1	E. Quirino	L. Cuaderno
2	R. Magsaysay	M. Cuaderno
3	C. Garcia	M. Cuaderno
4	C. Garcia	A. Castillo
5	D. Macapagal	A. Castillo
6	F. Marcos	A. Castillo
7	F. Marcos	A. Calalang
8	F. Marcos	G. Licaros
9	F. Marcos	J. Laya

SIGNATURE VARIETIES

10	F. Marcos	J. Fernandez
11	C. Aquino	J. Fernandez
12	C. Aquino	J. Cuisia
13	M. Ramos	J. Cuisia
14	M. Ramos	G.C. Singson
15	J. E. Estrada	G. C. Singson
16	J.E. Estrada	R. B. Buenaventura
17	G. Macapagal-Arroyo	R. B. Buenaventura

REPUBLIC

CENTRAL BANK OF THE PHILIPPINES

1949 ND "ENGLISH" ISSUES

#125, 127, and 129 sign. 1. Central Bank Seal at l., Type 1. Printer: SBNC.

125	5 CENTAVOS	VG	VF	UNC
	ND (1949). Red on tan unpt. Back red.	0.15	0.50	1.75

126	5 CENTAVOS	VG	VF	UNC
	ND. Like #125. Sign. 2. Printer: W&S.			
	a. Issued note.	0.10	0.25	1.50
	p. Proof.	—	—	250.00
127	10 CENTAVOS			
	ND. Brownish purple on tan unpt. Back brownish purple.			
	a. Issued note.	0.25	0.50	2.50
	r. Remainder w/o serial #.	—	100.00	250.00

128	10 CENTAVOS	VG	VF	UNC
	ND. Like #127. Sign. 2. Printer: W&S.	0.25	0.50	1.25
129	20 CENTAVOS			
	ND. Green on lt. green unpt. Back green.			
	a. Issued note.	0.25	0.75	2.50
	r. Remainder w/o serial #.	—	100.00	250.00

#130-141 printer: TDLR.

130	20 CENTAVOS	VG	VF	UNC
	ND. Green on lt. green unpt. Back green.			
	a. Sign. 2.	0.20	0.50	2.00
	b. Sign. 3.	0.20	0.50	2.00

131	50 CENTAVOS	VG	VF	UNC
	ND. Blue on lt. blue unpt. Back blue. Sign. 2.			
	a. Issued note.	0.20	0.50	2.00
	p. Proof.	—	—	250.00

#132-141 large Central Bank Seal Type 1 bank seal at lower r.

132	1/2 PESO	VG	VF	UNC
	ND. Green on yellow and blue unpt. Ox-cart w/Mt. Mayon in background at ctr. Back green. Sign. 2.	0.25	1.00	3.50

134	2 PESOS	VG	VF	UNC
	ND. Black on blue and gold unpt. Portr. J. Rizal at l. Back blue; landing of Magellan in the Philippines.			
	a. Sign. 1.	1.50	7.50	15.00
	b. Sign. 2.	0.75	2.00	5.00
	c. Sign. 4.	1.00	2.50	10.00
	d. Sign. 5.	0.15	0.50	2.00
	p. Sign. as b. Proof.	—	—	125.00
	s1. Sign. as a. Specimen. (De La Rue) Cancelled.	—	—	250.00
	s2. Sign. as b. Specimen.	—	—	60.00
	s3. Sign. as b. Specimen. (De La Rue).	—	—	250.00
	s5. Sign. as d. Specimen.	—	—	60.00

135	5 PESOS	VG	VF	UNC
	ND. Black on yellow and gold unpt. Portr. M. H. del Pilar at l., Lopez Jaena at r. Back gold; newspaper "La Solidaridad".			
	a. Sign. 1.	1.50	7.50	40.00
	b. Sign. 2.	0.75	3.50	12.50
	c. Sign. 3.	0.75	5.00	17.50
	d. Sign. 4.	0.75	3.00	10.00
	e. Sign. 5.	0.20	0.50	3.00
	f. Sign. 8.	0.20	0.50	2.00
	p. Proof.	—	—	150.00
	s1. Sign. as a. Specimen. (De La Rue).	—	—	250.00
	s2. Sign. as b. Specimen. (De La Rue).	—	—	250.00
	s3. Sign. as d. Specimen. (De La Rue).	—	—	250.00
	s4. Sign. as e. Specimen.	—	—	65.00
	s5. Sign. as e. Specimen. (De La Rue).	—	—	200.00
	s6. Sign. as f. Specimen.	—	—	65.00

136	10 PESOS	VG	VF	UNC
	ND. Black on tan and lt. red unpt. Fathers Burgos, Gomez and Zamora at l. Back brown; monument.			
	a. Sign. 1.	75.00	200.00	500.00
	b. Sign. 2.	2.50	5.00	25.00
	c. Sign. 3.	2.50	5.00	25.00
	d. Sign. 4.	2.50	5.00	30.00
	e. Sign. 5.	0.25	0.50	2.00
	f. Sign. 8.	1.00	2.00	5.00
	s1. Sign. as b. Specimen.	—	—	70.00
	s2. Sign. as c. Specimen.	—	—	70.00
	s3. Sign. as c. Specimen. (De La Rue).	—	—	250.00
	s4. Sign. as d. Specimen	—	—	75.00
	s5. Sign. as d. Specimen. (De La Rue).	—	—	250.00
	s6. Sign. as e. Specimen. (De La Rue).	—	—	200.00
	s7. Sign. as f. Specimen.	—	—	70.00

133	1 PESO	VG	VF	UNC
	ND. Black on lt. gold and blue unpt. Portr. A. Mabini at l. Back black; Barasoain Church at ctr.			
	10. Sign. as h. Specimen.	—	—	30.00
	11. Sign. as h. Specimen. (De La Rue).	—	—	250.00
	a. Sign. 1. *GENUINE* in very lt. tan letters just beneath top heading on face.	7.50	25.00	110.00
	b. Sign. 1. W/o *GENUINE* on face.	0.50	2.00	10.00
	c. Sign. 2.	0.75	2.50	15.00
	d. Sign. 3.	0.25	2.00	12.50
	e. Sign. 4.	0.50	1.25	8.00
	f. Sign. 5.	0.25	1.00	5.00
	g. Sign. 6.	0.10	0.50	2.50
	h. Sign. 7.	0.10	1.00	3.00
	s1. Sign. as a. Specimen.	—	—	200.00
	s2. Sign. as b. Specimen. (De La Rue).	—	—	200.00
	s3. Sign. as c. Specimen. (De La Rue).	—	—	200.00
	s4. Sign. as d. Specimen. (De La Rue).	—	—	200.00
	s5. Sign. as e. Specimen. (De La Rue).	—	—	200.00
	s6. Sign. as f. Specimen.	—	—	45.00
	s7. Sign. as f. Specimen. (De La Rue).	—	—	250.00
	s8. Sign. as g. Specimen.	—	—	50.00
	s9. Sign. as g. Specimen. (De La Rue).	—	—	250.00

137	20 PESOS	VG	VF	UNC
	ND. Black on yellow unpt. Portr. A. Bonifacio at l., E. Jacinto at r. Back brownish orange; flag and monument.			
	a. Sign. 1.	10.00	75.00	200.00
	b. Sign. 2.	3.00	20.00	50.00
	c. Sign. 4.	3.00	10.00	20.00
	d. Sign. 5.	0.50	1.50	2.25
	e. Sign. 8.	0.25	1.00	2.50

137	20 PESOS	VG	VF	UNC
	p. Sign. as d. Proof.	—	—	150.00
	s1. Sign. as a. Specimen.	—	—	175.00
	s2. Sign. as c. Specimen. (De La Rue).	—	—	200.00
	s3. Sign. as d. Specimen.	—	—	125.00
	s4. Sign. as d. Specimen (De La Rue).	—	—	175.00
	s5. Sign. as e. Specimen.	—	—	70.00

138	50 PESOS	VG	VF	UNC
	ND. Black on pink and lt. tan unpt. Portr. A. Luna at l. Back red; scene of blood compact of Sikatuna and Legaspi.			
	a. Sign. 1.	125.00	500.00	—
	b. Sign. 2.	15.00	50.00	125.00
	c. Sign. 3.	5.00	15.00	40.00
	d. Sign. 5.	0.25	1.00	2.50
	p. Sign. as d. Proof.	—	—	175.00
	s1. Sign. as a. Specimen. (De La Rue).	—	—	500.00
	s2. Sign. as b. Specimen. (De La Rue).	—	—	300.00
	s3. Sign. as d. Specimen.	—	—	75.00
	s4. Sign. as d. Specimen. (De La Rue).	—	—	500.00

139	100 PESOS	VG	VF	UNC
	ND. Black on gold unpt. Portr. T. Sora at l. Back yellow; regimental flags. Sign. 1.			
	a. Issued note.	2.00	6.00	15.00
	s. Specimen.	—	—	85.00

140	200 PESOS	VG	VF	UNC
	ND. Green on pink and lt. blue unpt. Portr. Pres. Manuel Quezon at l. Back green; Legislative bldg. Sign. 1.			
	a. Issued note.	3.00	7.50	20.00
	s. Specimen (De La Rue).	—	—	350.00

141	500 PESOS	VG	VF	UNC
	ND. Black on purple and lt. tan unpt. Portr. Pres. Manuel Roxas at l. Back purple; Central Bank. Sign. 1.			
	a. Issued note.	10.00	25.00	70.00
	s. Specimen. (De La Rue).	—	—	300.00

BANGKO SENTRAL NG PILIPINAS

1969 ND "PILIPINO" ISSUE

#142-147 heading at top in double outline. Replacement notes: Serial # prefix "+".

142	1 PISO	VG	VF	UNC
	ND (1969). Blue and black on m/c unpt. J. Rizal at l. and as wmk. Central Bank Seal Type 2. Scene of Aguinaldo's Independence Declaration of June 12, 1898 on back.			
	a. Sign. 7.	0.20	0.50	1.75
	b. Sign. 8.	0.15	0.50	1.00
	s1. Sign. as a. Specimen. (De La Rue).	—	—	100.00
	s2. Sign. as b. Specimen.	—	—	40.00

#143-145 printer: G&D (w/o imprint).
Central Bank Seal Type 3.

143	5 PISO	VG	VF	UNC
	ND (1969). Green and brown on m/c unpt. A. Bonifacio at l. in brown and as wmk. Scene of the Katipunan organization on back.			
	a. Sign. 7.	0.25	1.50	3.25
	b. Sign. 8.	0.25	1.00	3.00
	s1. Sign. as a. Specimen.	—	—	125.00
	s2. Sign. as b. Specimen.	—	—	25.00

144	10 PISO	VG	VF	UNC
	ND (1969). Brown on m/c unpt. A. Mabini at l. and as wmk. Barasoain Church on back.			
	a. Sign. 7.	0.25	1.50	5.00
	b. Sign. 8.	0.25	1.50	4.00
	s1. Sign. as a. Specimen.	—	—	100.00
	s2. Sign. as b. Specimen.	—	—	20.00

145 20 PISO
ND (1969). Orange and brown on m/c unpt. M. L. Quezon at l. in brown and as wmk. Malakanyang Palace on back.

	VG	VF	UNC
a. Sign. 7.	0.50	2.00	10.00
b. Sign. 8.	0.50	2.00	6.00
s1. Sign. as a. Specimen.	—	—	100.00
s2. Sign. as b. Specimen.	—	—	325.00

146 50 PISO
ND (1969). Red on m/c unpt. S. Osmeña at l. and as wmk. Central Bank Seal Type 2. Legislative bldg. on back.

	VG	VF	UNC
a. Sign. 7.	2.00	5.00	18.00
b. Sign. 8.	1.75	3.00	13.00
s1. Sign. as a. Specimen. (De La Rue).	—	—	275.00
s2. Sign. as b. Specimen.	—	—	30.00
s3. Sign. as b. Specimen. (De La Rue).	—	—	250.00

147 100 PISO
ND (1969). Purple on m/c unpt. M. Roxas at l. and as wmk. Central Bank Seal Type 2. Old Central Bank on back.

	VG	VF	UNC
a. Sign. 7.	4.00	10.00	30.00
b. Sign. 8.	3.00	7.50	25.00
p. Sign. as a. Proof.	—	—	475.00
s1. Sign. as a. Specimen.	—	—	50.00
s2. Sign. as a. Specimen. (De La Rue).	—	—	175.00
s3. Sign. as b. Specimen.	—	—	50.00
s4. Sign. as b. Specimen. (De La Rue).	—	—	200.00

1970's ND FIRST ISSUE

#148-151 Central Bank Seal Type 2. Heading at top in single outline, l. and r. ends completely filled in. Sign. 8. Replacement notes: Serial # prefix "+".

148 5 PISO
ND. Green on m/c unpt. Like #143 but A. Bonifacio in green.

	VG	VF	UNC
a. Issued note.	0.25	0.75	2.00
s. Specimen.	—	—	20.00

149 10 PISO
ND. Brown on m/c unpt. Like #144 but w/o white paper showing at sides on face or back.

	VG	VF	UNC
a. Issued note.	0.25	3.00	10.00
s. Specimen.	—	—	40.00

150 20 PISO
ND. Orange and blue on m/c unpt. Like #145 but M. L. Quezon in orange.

	VG	VF	UNC
a. Issued note.	0.25	1.00	3.00
s. Specimen.	—	—	75.00

151 50 PISO
ND. Red on m/c unpt. Similar to #146. Seal under denomination instead of over, sign. closer, *LIMAMPUNG PISO* in one line, and other modifications.

	VG	VF	UNC
a. Issued note.	1.00	5.00	15.00
s. Specimen.	—	—	70.00

1970's ND SECOND ISSUE

#152-158 Central Bank Seal Type 2. Ovpt: *ANG BAGONG LIPUNAN* (New Society) on wmk. area, 1974-85. Replacement notes: Serial # prefix "+".

#152-156, 158 sign. 8.

152 2 PISO
ND. Blue on m/c unpt. J. Rizal at l. and as wmk. Scene of Aguinaldo's Independence Declaration of June 12, 1898 on back.

	VG	VF	UNC
a. Issued note.	0.20	0.50	1.50
s1. Specimen.	—	—	12.00
s2. Specimen. (De La Rue).	—	—	225.00

153 5 PISO
ND. Green on m/c unpt. Like #148.

	VG	VF	UNC
a. Dark ovpt.	0.25	1.00	5.00
b. Light ovpt.	0.25	1.00	5.00
s1. Specimen.	—	—	20.00
s2. Specimen. (De La Rue).	—	—	225.00

154 10 PISO
ND. Brown on m/c unpt. Like #149.

	VG	VF	UNC
a. Issued note.	0.25	0.50	3.00
s1. Specimen.	—	—	25.00
s2. Specimen. (De La Rue).	—	—	225.00

Note: Varieties of light or dark overprints.

155 20 PISO
ND. Orange on m/c unpt. Like #150.

	VG	VF	UNC
a. Issued note.	0.25	1.50	5.00
s1. Specimen.	—	—	35.00
s2. Specimen. (De La Rue).	—	—	250.00

156	50 PISO		VG	VF	UNC
	ND. Red on m/c unpt. Like #151.				
	a. Brown sign. title.		1.00	4.00	7.50
	b. Red sign. title.		1.00	7.50	20.00
	s1. Sign. as b. Specimen.		—	—	40.00
	s2. Sign. as b. Specimen. (De La Rue).		—	—	250.00

157	100 PISO		VG	VF	UNC
	ND. Purple on m/c unpt. Like #147. Bank seal in purple at l.				
	a. Sign. 7.		2.50	20.00	55.00
	b. Sign. 8.		2.00	7.50	20.00
	s1. Sign. as a. Specimen.		—	—	200.00
	s2. Sign. as b. Specimen.		—	—	65.00

160	5 PISO		VG	VF	UNC
	ND. Green on m/c unpt. Like #153.				
	a. Sign. 8.		0.15	0.50	2.00
	b. Sign. 9. Black serial #.		0.15	1.00	3.00
	c. Sign. 9. Red serial #.		0.15	0.40	2.00
	d. Sign. 10.		0.15	0.40	2.00
	e. Sign. as b. Uncut sheet of 4.		—	—	30.00
	f. Sign. as d. Uncut sheet of 4.		—	—	30.00
	s1. Sign. as a. Specimen.		—	—	15.00
	s2. Sign. as b. Specimen.		—	—	20.00

158	100 PISO		VG	VF	UNC
	ND. Purple on m/c unpt. Face resembling #157 but heading at top solid letters, green bank seal at lower r., and denomination near upper r. Back similar to #157 but denomination at bottom.				
	a. Issued note.		10.00	30.00	75.00
	s. Specimen.		—	—	175.00

1978 ND Issue

#159-167 Central Bank Seal Type 4. Replacement notes: Serial # prefix "+".

161	10 PISO		VG	VF	UNC
	ND. Brown on m/c unpt. Like #154.				
	a. Sign. 8.		0.10	0.75	3.00
	b. Sign. 9.		0.10	1.00	6.00
	c. Sign. 10. Black serial #.		0.10	0.50	2.00
	d. Sign. 10. Red serial #.		0.10	1.00	8.00
	e. Sign. as b. Uncut sheet of 4.		—	—	35.00
	f. Sign. as c. Uncut sheet of 4.		—	—	35.00
	s1. Sign. as a. Specimen.		—	—	15.00
	s2. Sign. as b. Specimen.		—	—	15.00

159	2 PISO		VG	VF	UNC
	ND. Blue on m/c unpt. Like #152.				
	a. Sign. 8.		0.10	0.30	1.50
	b. Sign. 9. Black serial #.		0.10	0.50	1.50
	c. Sign. 9. Red serial #.		0.10	0.30	1.50
	d. Sign. as b. Uncut sheet of 4.		—	—	15.00
	s1. Sign. as a. Specimen.		—	—	15.00
	s2. Sign. as b. Specimen.		—	—	15.00

162	20 PISO		VG	VF	UNC
	ND. Orange and blue on m/c unpt. Like #155.				
	a. Sign. 8.		0.25	1.00	5.00
	b. Sign. 9.		0.25	1.00	5.00
	c. Sign. 10.		0.25	1.00	3.00
	d. Sign. as b. Uncut sheet of 4.		—	—	40.00
	e. Sign. as d. Uncut sheet of 4.		—	—	40.00
	s1. Sign. as a. Specimen.		—	—	20.00
	s2. Sign. as b. Specimen.		—	—	30.00

163	50 PISO	VG	VF	UNC
	ND. Red on m/c unpt. Like #156.			
	a. Sign. 8.	0.50	2.00	7.50
	b. Sign. 9.	0.50	2.00	5.00
	c. Sign. 10.	0.50	1.50	5.00
	s1. Sign. as a. Specimen.	—	—	35.00
	s2. Sign. as b. Specimen.	—	—	35.00

164	100 PISO	VG	VF	UNC
	ND. Purple and deep olive-green on m/c unpt. Face like #158. New Central Bank complex w/ships behind on back.			
	a. Sign. 8.	2.00	10.00	27.50
	b. Sign. 9.	1.00	4.00	10.00
	c. Sign. 10. Black serial #.	0.75	3.00	10.00
	s1. Sign. as a. Specimen.	—	—	35.00
	s2. Sign. as b. Specimen.	—	—	40.00

1978 COMMEMORATIVE ISSUE

#165, Centennial - Birth of Pres. Osmeña, 1978

165	50 PISO	VG	VF	UNC
	1978. Black circular commemorative ovpt. at l. on #163a.	1.00	4.00	12.50

1981 COMMEMORATIVE ISSUES

#166, Papal Visit of John Paul II, 1981

166	2 PISO	VG	VF	UNC
	1981. Black commemorative ovpt. at ctr. r. on #159b.			
	a. Regular prefix letters before serial #.	0.10	0.25	2.50
	b. Special prefix letters *JP* and all zero numbers (presentation).	—	—	100.00

#167, Inauguration of Pres. Marcos, 1981

167	10 PISO	VG	VF	UNC
	1981. Black commemorative ovpt. at ctr. r. on #161b.			
	a. Regular prefix letters before serial #. Wide and narrow collar varieties.	0.25	0.50	2.50
	b. Special prefix letters *FM* and all zero numbers (presentation).	—	—	35.00
	s. As a. Specimen. Wide or narrow collar.	—	—	50.00

1985-91 ND ISSUE

#168-173 replacement notes: Serial # prefix "+".

168	5 PISO	VG	VF	UNC
	ND (1985-94). Deep green and brown on m/c unpt. Aguinaldo at l. ctr. and as wmk., plaque w/cannon at r. Aguinaldo's Independence Declaration of June 12, 1898 on back.			
	a. Sign. 10. Black serial #.	FV	FV	2.50
	b. Sign. 11. Black serial #.	FV	FV	1.50
	c. Sign. as b. Red serial # (1990).	FV	FV	1.25
	d. Sign. 12. Red serial #.	FV	FV	1.00
	e. Sign. 13. Red serial #.	FV	FV	1.00
	f. Sign. as b. Uncut sheet of 4.	—	—	30.00
	g. Sign. as d. Uncut sheet of 4.	—	—	30.00
	h. Sign. as e. Uncut sheet of 4.	—	—	15.00
	s1. Sign. as b. Specimen.	—	—	15.00
	s2. Sign. as c. Specimen.	—	—	15.00
	s3. Sign. as d. Specimen.	—	—	20.00

169	10 PISO	VG	VF	UNC
	ND (1985-94). Dk. brown, brown and blue-gray on m/c unpt. Mabini at l. ctr. and as wmk., handwritten scroll handwritten scroll at r. Barasoain church on back.			
	a. Sign. 10.	FV	0.50	4.00
	b. Sign. 11.	FV	FV	2.00
	c. Sign. 12. Black serial #.	FV	FV	1.50
	d. Sign. as c. Red serial #.	FV	0.50	5.00
	e. Sign. 13.	—	—	2.00
	f. Sign. as b. Uncut sheet of 4.	—	—	25.00
	g. Sign. as b. Uncut sheet of 32.	—	—	100.00
	s. Sign. as b. Specimen.	—	—	25.00

170	20 PISO	VG	VF	UNC
	ND (1986-94). Orange and blue on m/c unpt. Pres. M. Quezon at l. ctr. and as wmk., arms at r. Malakanyang Palace on back.			
	a. Sign. 10. Black serial #.	FV	1.00	7.50
	b. Sign. 11. Black serial #.	FV	FV	3.00
	c. Sign. 12. Black serial #.	FV	FV	3.00
	d. Sign. as c. Red serial #.	FV	25.00	50.00
	e. Sign. 13. Red serial #.	FV	1.00	6.00
	f. Sign. as e. Black serial #.	FV	FV	4.00
	g. Sign. as b. Uncut sheet of 4.	—	—	45.00
	s. Sign. as b. Specimen.	—	—	35.00

171	50 PISO	VG	VF	UNC
	ND (1987-94). Red and purple on m/c unpt. Pres. Sergio Osmeña at l. ctr. and as wmk., gavel at r. Legislative bldg. on back.			
	a. Sign. 11. Black serial #.	FV	1.00	6.00
	b. Sign. 12. Black serial #.	FV	FV	5.00
	c. Sign. 13. Black serial #.	FV	FV	4.00
	s1. Sign. as a. Specimen.	—	—	75.00
	s2. Sign. as b. Specimen.	—	—	60.00
	s3. Sign. as b. Uncut sheet of 4. Specimen.	—	—	30.00
	s4. Sign. as c. Specimen.	—	—	50.00

172	100 PISO	VG	VF	UNC
	ND (1987-94). Purple on m/c unpt. Pres. M. Roxas at l. ctr. and as wmk. USA and Philippine flags at r. New Central Bank complex at l. ctr. w/old bldg. facade above on back.			

172	100 PISO	VG	VF	UNC
	a. Sign. 11.	FV	FV	7.50
	b. Sign. 12. Black serial #.	FV	FV	12.50
	c. Sign. as b. Red serial #.	FV	FV	12.50
	d. Sign. 13. Red serial #.	FV	FV	10.00
	e. Sign. as d. Blue serial #.	FV	FV	10.00
	s1. Sign. as a. Specimen.	—	—	120.00
	s2. Sign. as b. Specimen.	—	—	100.00
	s3. Sign. as c. Specimen.	—	—	50.00
	s4. Sign. as d. Specimen.	—	—	50.00
	s5. Sign. as d. Specimen. Uncut sheet of 4.	—	—	25.00
	s6. Sign. as b. Specimen. Uncut sheet of 4.	—	—	75.00
	s7. Sign. as b. Specimen. Uncut sheet of 32.	—	—	200.00
	s8. Sign. as e. Specimen. Blue serial #.	—	—	75.00

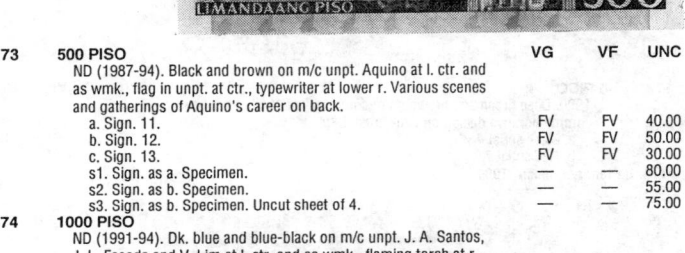

173	500 PISO	VG	VF	UNC
	ND (1987-94). Black and brown on m/c unpt. Aquino at l. ctr. and as wmk., flag in unpt. at ctr., typewriter at lower r. Various scenes and gatherings of Aquino's career on back.			
	a. Sign. 11.	FV	FV	40.00
	b. Sign. 12.	FV	FV	50.00
	c. Sign. 13.	FV	FV	30.00
	s1. Sign. as a. Specimen.	—	—	80.00
	s2. Sign. as b. Specimen.	—	—	55.00
	s3. Sign. as b. Specimen. Uncut sheet of 4.	—	—	75.00

174	1000 PISO			
	ND (1991-94). Dk. blue and blue-black on m/c unpt. J. A. Santos, J. L. Escoda and V. Lim at l. ctr. and as wmk., flaming torch at r. Banawe rice terraces at l. to ctr., local carving and hut at ctr. r. on back.			
	a. Sign. 12.	FV	FV	85.00
	b. Sign. 13.	FV	FV	60.00

1986-91 COMMEMORATIVE ISSUES

Commemorative ovpt. not listed were produced privately in the Philippines.

#175, Visit of Pres. Aquino to the United States

175	5 PISO	VG	VF	UNC
	1986. Deep green and brown on on m/c unpt. Like #168 but w/commemorative text, seal and visit dates on wmk. area. Prefix letters CA. Sign. 11.			
	a. Serial #1-20,000 in special folder.	FV	FV	12.50
	b. Serial # above 20,000.	FV	FV	1.50
	c. Uncut sheet of 4.	—	—	30.00

#176, Canonization of San Lorenzo Ruiz

176	5 PISO	VG	VF	UNC
	18.10.1987. Deep green and brown on m/c unpt. Like #168 but w/commemorative design, text and date on wmk. area. Sign. 11.			
	a. Issued note.	FV	FV	2.00
	b. Uncut sheet of 8 in special folder.	—	—	20.00

#177, 40th Anniversary of Central Bank

177	5 PISO	VG	VF	UNC
	1989. Deep green and brown on m/c unpt. Like #168 but w/red commemorative design, text and date on wmk. area. Sign. 11.			
	a. Issued note.	FV	FV	1.50
	b. Uncut sheet of 8 in special folder.	—	—	20.00

#178, Women's Rights, 1990

178	5 PISO	VG	VF	UNC
	1990. Deep green and brown on m/c unpt. Like #168 but w/black commemorative design on wmk. area. Sign. 11.			
	a. Black serial #.	FV	FV	1.50
	b. Red serial #.	FV	FV	4.00

#179, II Plenary Council, 1991

179	5 PISO	VG	VF	UNC
	1991. Deep green and brown on m/c unpt. Like #168 but w/black commemorative design and date on wmk. area. Red serial #. Sign. 12.	FV	FV	1.50

1995 ND; 1998-99 ISSUE

#180-186 like #168-174 but w/Central Bank Seal Type 5 w/date 1993 at r.

#180 and 181 sign. 14.

180	5 PISO	VG	VF	UNC
	ND (1995). Deep green and brown on m/c unpt. Like #168.	FV	FV	1.00
181	10 PISO			
	ND (1995-97). Dk. brown and blue-gray on m/c unpt. Like #169.			
	a. Red serial #.	FV	FV	1.50
	b. Sign. as a. Black serial #.	FV	FV	3.00

182	20 PISO	VG	VF	UNC
	ND (1997); 1998-. Orange and blue on m/c unpt. Like #170.			
	a. Sign. 14. Red serial #. ND.	FV	FV	2.00
	b. Sign. 14. Black serial #.	FV	FV	3.50
	c. Sign. 15. Black serial #. 1998; 1999.	FV	FV	2.50
	d. Sign. 15. Blue serial #. 1999.	FV	FV	6.50
	e. Sign. 16. Blue serial #. 2000.	FV	FV	5.00
	f. Sign. 16. Blue serial #. 2001.	FV	FV	6.00
	g. Sign. 17. Blue serial #. 2001.	FV	FV	5.00
	h. Sign. 17. Black serial #. 2001; 2002; 2003; 2004, 2005.	FV	FV	4.50
	i. Sign. 18. Black serial #. 2005.	FV	FV	3.50
	s1. As a. Specimen.	—	—	50.00
	s2. Uncut sheet of 4. Specimen.	—	—	100.00

183	50 PISO	VG	VF	UNC
	ND; 1998-2001. Red and purple on m/c unpt. Like #171.			
	a. Sign. 14. ND (1995).	FV	FV	4.00
	b. Sign. as a. Red serial #. 1998.	FV	FV	6.00
	c. Sign. 16. Red serial #. 1999; 2000; 2001.	FV	FV	4.50
	d. Sign. 16. Black serial #. 2001.	FV	FV	8.00

184	100 PISO	VG	VF	UNC
	ND; 1998-. Purple on m/c unpt. Like #172.			
	a. Sign. 14. ND.	FV	FV	12.50
	b. Sign. as a. 1998.	FV	FV	8.00
	c. Sign. 15. Red serial #. 1998.	FV	FV	5.00
	d. Sign. as c. Black serial #. 1998; 1999.	FV	FV	7.00
	e. Sign. 16. 1999; 2000.	FV	FV	6.00
	f. Sign. 16. 2001.	FV	FV	15.00
	s. Sign. as a. Specimen.	—	—	30.00

185	**500 PISO**	VG	VF	UNC
	ND; 1998-2000. Black on m/c unpt. Like #173.			
	a. Sign. 14. ND; 1998.	FV	FV	30.00
	b. Sign. 15. 1998; 1999.	FV	FV	25.00
	c. Sign. 16; 1999; 2000.	FV	FV	25.00
	s. As a. Specimen.	—	—	50.00

186	**1000 PISO**	VG	VF	UNC
	ND; 1998-. Dk. blue on m/c unpt. Like #174.			
	a. Sign. 14. ND; 1998.	FV	FV	45.00
	b. Sign. 15. 1998; 1999.	FV	FV	45.00
	c. Sign. 16. 1999; 2000.	FV	FV	45.00
	s1. Sign. as a. Specimen.	—	—	85.00
	s2. Sign. as c. Specimen. 1999.	—	—	50.00

1997 ISSUE

187	**10 PISO**	VG	VF	UNC
	1997-. Dk. brown and blue-gray on m/c unpt. A. Mabini and A. Bonifacio at l. ctr; flag, book, declaration and quill pen at r. Barasoain church at l., blood *Pacto de Sangre* meeting at lower r. on back. Wmk. varieties.			
	a. Sign. 14. Single figure wmk. 1997.	FV	FV	2.50
	b. Sign. 14. Single figure wmk. 1998.	FV	FV	2.50
	c. Sign. 14. Double figures as wmk. Black serial #. 1998.	FV	FV	4.00
	d. Sign. 14. Double figures as wmk. Red serial #.	FV	FV	20.00
	e. Sign. 15. Red serial #. 1999.	FV	FV	2.50
	f. Sign. 16. Red serial #. 1999; 2000; 2001.	FV	FV	3.00
	g. Sign. 16. Red serial #.	FV	FV	7.00
	h. Sign. 17. Red serial #. 2001.	FV	FV	3.00
	i. Sign. 17. Black serial #. 2001.	FV	FV	3.00

1998 COMMEMORATIVE ISSUE

#188-190, Centennial of First Republic, 1898-1998

188	**100 PISO**	VG	VF	UNC
	ND (1997); 1998. Purple on m/c unpt. Like #184 but w/centennial design and inscription in rectangular frame at l. on wmk. area. Sign. 14.			
	a. W/o date at upper l. (1997).	FV	FV	7.00
	b. 1998 under value at l.	FV	FV	12.00

189	**2000 PISO**	VG	VF	UNC
	1998. M/c. Pres. J. E. Estrada taking his oath of office on June 30, 1998 in the Barasoain Church at ctr. Re-enactment of the declaration of Philippine Independence at the Aguinaldo Shrine in Kawit, Cavite on June 12, 1998 by Pres. F. V. Ramos at ctr	—	—	125.00

190	**100,000 PISO**	VG	VF	UNC
	1998. Green, yellow and brown. Pres. F. V. Ramos being greeted by crowd, Bank seal at r. Pres. Ramos greeting crowd from inside enclosed porch. Sign. 14.	—	—	3500.00

Note: #190 only 1,000 pieces issued.

1999 COMMEMORATIVE ISSUE

#191, 50th Anniversary Bangko Sentral

191	50 PISO	VG	VF	UNC
	ND; 1999. Red and purple on m/c unpt. Ovpt. on #183.			
	a. W/o date at upper left. Sign. 14.	FV	FV	3.50
	b. 1999 at upper l. Sign. 15.	FV	FV	7.50

#192-194 held in reserve.

2001-02 ISSUE

#195-196 like #185-186 but w/iridescent denomination strip at l. ctr. and metallic segmented security strip at ctr. r.

193	50 PISO	VG	VF	UNC
	2001; 2002; 2003; 2004. Red and purple on m/c unpt. Like #183 but National Museum on back. Sign. 17.	FV	FV	4.50
194	100 PISO			
	2001; 2002; 2003; 2004. Purple on m/c unpt. Like #188. Black serial #. Sign. 16; 17; 18.	FV	FV	10.00
	a. 2001; 2002; 2003; 2004.	FV	FV	10.00
	b. 2005. Sign. 18.	FV	FV	7.50
	c. 2005. Sign. 18. Sign. spelled Arrovo.	FV	FV	20.00

195	200 PISO	VG	VF	UNC
	2002; 2003; 2004. Green and purple on m/c unpt. Diosdado Macapagal at l., Aguinaldo shrine at lower r. Scene of swearing in of Gloria Macapagal-Arroyo on back. Sign. 17.	FV	FV	12.50

196	500 PISO	VG	VF	UNC
	2001; 2002; 2003; 2004. Black on m/c unpt. Like #185. Sign. 17.	FV	FV	25.00

197	1000 PISO	VG	VF	UNC
	2001; 2002; 2003; 2004. Dk. blue on m/c unpt. Like #186. Sign. 17.	FV	FV	45.00

COLLECTOR SERIES

BANGKO SENTRAL NG PILIPINAS

1978 ND ISSUE

CS1	1978 ND 2-100 PISO	Issue Price	Mkt.	Value
	#159a-164a ovpt: SPECIMEN and w/serial # prefix Maltese cross.	14.00		50.00

POLAND

The Republic of Poland, formerly the Polish Peoples Republic, located in central Europe, has an area of 120,725 sq. mi. (312,677 sq. km.) and a population of 38.73 million. Capital: Warsaw. The economy is essentially agricultural, but industrial activity provides the products for foreign trade. Machinery, coal, coke, iron, steel and transport equipment are exported.

Poland, which began as a Slavic duchy in the 10th century and reached its peak of power between the 14th and 16th centuries, has had a turbulent history of invasion, occupation or partition by Mongols, Turkey, Hungary, Sweden, Austria, Prussia and Russia.

The first partition took place in 1772. Prussia took Polish Pomerania. Russia took part of the eastern provinces. Austria took Galicia, in which lay the fortress city of Krakow (Cracow). The second partition occurred in 1793 when Russia took another slice of the eastern provinces and Prussia took what remained of western Poland. The third partition, 1795, literally removed Poland from the map. Russia took what was left of the eastern provinces. Prussia seized most of central Poland, including Warsaw. Austria took what was left of the south. Napoleon restored to Poland much of the territory lost to Prussia and Austria, but after his defeat another partition returned the Duchy of Warsaw to Prussia, made Kracow into a tiny republic, and declared what remained to be the Kingdom of Poland under the czar and in permanent union with Russia.

Poland re-emerged as an independent state recognized by the Treaty of Versailles on June 28, 1919, and maintained its independence until 1939 when it was invaded by Germany, then partitioned between Germany and Russia. Poland's present boundaries were determined by the U.S.-British-Russian agreement of Aug. 16, 1945. The Government of National Unity was replaced when the Polish Communist-Socialist faction won a decisive victory at the polls in 1947 and established a "People's Democratic Republic" of the Soviet type. In Dec. 1989, Poland became a republic once again.

MONETARY SYSTEM:
1 Zloty = 100 Groszy, 1919-

PEOPLES REPUBLIC

NARODOWY BANK POLSKI

POLISH NATIONAL BANK

1962; 1965 ISSUE

		VG	VF	UNC
140A	**20 ZLOTYCH**			
	2.1.1965. M/c. Man at r., arms at upper l. ctr. (Not issued).	—	—	—

		VG	VF	UNC
141	**1000 ZLOTYCH**			
	1962; 1965. Orange, red and green on m/c unpt. Copernicus at ctr. r. and as wmk., arms at upper r. Zodiac signs in ornate sphere at l. on back.			
	a. 29.10.1965. Series S.	1.50	5.00	20.00
	b. 29.10.1965. Series X.	10.00	25.00	120.00
	s1. Specimen ovpt: *WZOR.* 24.5.1962. (Not issued).	—	—	200.00
	s2. Specimen ovpt: *WZOR* w/regular serial #. 29.10.1965.	—	—	30.00

1974-76 ISSUE

#142-146 eagle arms at lower ctr. or lower r. and as wmk. Sign. varieties.

		VG	VF	UNC
142	**50 ZLOTYCH**			
	1975-88. Olive-green on m/c unpt. K. Swierczewski at ctr. Order of Grunwald at l. on back.			
	a. 9.5.1975.	0.50	1.50	10.00
	b. 1.6.1979; 1.6.1982.	0.10	0.30	2.75
	c. 1.6.1986; 1.12.1988.	0.10	0.20	0.75
	s1. Specimen ovpt: *WZOR.* 1975; 1986; 1988.	—	—	8.00
	s2. Specimen ovpt: *WZOR.* 1979.	—	—	7.00
	s3. Specimen ovpt: *WZOR.* 1982.	—	—	10.00

		VG	VF	UNC
143	**100 ZLOTYCH**			
	1975-88. Brown on lilac and m/c unpt. L. Warynski at r. Old paper at l. on back.			
	a. 15.1.1975.	2.00	4.00	25.00
	b. 17.5.1976.	1.00	2.00	8.00
	c. 1.6.1979.	0.25	0.75	3.00
	d. 1.6.1982.	0.10	0.20	2.00
	e. 1.6.1986; 1.5.1988.	—	—	0.50
	s1. Specimen ovpt: *WZOR.* 1975; 1982.	—	—	8.00
	s2. Specimen ovpt: *WZOR.* 1976.	—	—	7.00
	s3. Specimen ovpt: *WZOR.* 1979.	—	—	10.00

		VG	VF	UNC
144	**200 ZLOTYCH**			
	1976-88. Purple on orange and m/c unpt. J. Dabrowski at r. standing woman at wall on back.			
	a. 25.5.1976.	1.00	4.00	20.00
	b. 1.6.1979; 1.6.1982.	0.10	0.30	4.50
	c. 1.6.1986; 1.12.1988.	0.10	0.25	1.00
	s1. Specimen ovpt: *WZOR.* 1976; 1986.	—	—	8.00
	s2. Specimen ovpt: *WZOR.* 1979.	—	—	7.00
	s3. Specimen ovpt: *WZOR.* 1982.	—	—	10.00

		VG	VF	UNC
145	**500 ZLOTYCH**			
	1974-82. Brown on tan and m/c unpt. T. Kosciuszko at ctr. Arms and flag at l. ctr. on back.			
	a. 16.12.1974.	2.00	7.00	30.00
	b. 15.6.1976.	1.00	3.00	10.00
	c. 1.6.1979.	0.20	0.75	7.00
	d. 1.6.1982.	0.10	0.25	1.00
	s1. Specimen ovpt: *WZOR.* 1974; 1976.	—	—	8.00
	s2. Specimen ovpt: *WZOR.* 1979.	—	—	7.00
	s3. Specimen ovpt: *WZOR.* 1982.	—	—	10.00

146	1000 ZLOTYCH	VG	VF	UNC
	1975-82. Blue on olive-green and m/c unpt. Copernicus at r. Atomic symbols on back.			
	a. 2.7.1975.	2.00	4.00	35.00
	b. 1.6.1979.	0.25	1.25	10.00
	c. 1.6.1982.	0.15	0.50	1.50
	s1. Specimen ovpt. *WZOR*. 1975; 1982.	—	—	10.00
	s2. Specimen ovpt. *WZOR*. 1979.	—	—	7.00

POLSKA RZECZPOSPOLITA LUDOWA

PEOPLES REPUBLIC OF POLAND

NARODOWY BANK POLSKI

POLISH NATIONAL BANK

1977 ISSUE

147	2000 ZLOTYCH	VG	VF	UNC
	1977-82. Dk. brown on m/c unpt. Mieszko I at r., arms at lower ctr. and as wmk. B. Chrobry on back.			
	a. 1.5.1977.	0.25	1.00	5.00
	b. 1.6.1979.	0.50	1.75	13.50
	c. 1.6.1982.	0.20	0.50	1.00
	s1. Specimen ovpt. *WZOR*. 1977.	—	—	10.00
	s2. Specimen ovpt. *WZOR*. 1979.	—	—	7.00
	s3. Specimen ovpt. *WZOR*. 1982.	—	—	15.00

1982 ISSUE

#148-150 wmk: Arms.

148	10 ZLOTYCH	VG	VF	UNC
	1.6.1982. Blue and green on m/c unpt. J. Bem at l. ctr., arms at lower r. Large value on back.			
	a. Issued note.	0.10	0.25	1.50
	s. Specimen ovpt. *WZOR*.	—	—	10.00

149	20 ZLOTYCH	VG	VF	UNC
	1.6.1982. Brown and purple on m/c unpt. R. Traugutt at l. ctr., arms at lower r. Large value on back.			
	a. Issued note.	0.10	0.25	0.75
	s. Specimen ovpt. *WZOR*.	—	—	10.00

150	5000 ZLOTYCH	VG	VF	UNC
	1982-88. Dk. green, purple and black on m/c unpt. F. Chopin at r., arms at lower ctr. *Polonaise* music score at ctr. on back.			
	a. 1.6.1982.	0.25	1.00	4.00
	b. 1.6.1986.	FV	2.00	7.00
	c. 1.12.1988.	FV	FV	2.50
	s. Specimen ovpt. *WZOR*.	—	—	12.50

1987-90 ISSUE

#151-158 arms at lower ctr. or lower r. and as wmk.

151	10,000 ZLOTYCH	VG	VF	UNC
	1.2.1987; 1.12.1988. Dk. blue and red on green and m/c unpt. S. Wyspianski at l. ctr. Trees and city scene on back.			
	a. 1.2.1987.	0.50	2.25	10.00
	b. 1.12.1988.	FV	0.50	3.00
	s. Specimen ovpt. *WZOR*.	—	—	10.00

		VG	VF	UNC
152	**20,000 ZLOTYCH**			
	1.2.1989. Dk. brown on tan and gold unpt. M. Curie at r. Scientific instrument on back.			
	a. Issued note.	FV	1.25	4.00
	s. Specimen ovpt. *WZOR*.	—	—	10.00

		VG	VF	UNC
153	**50,000 ZLOTYCH**			
	1.12.1989. Dk. brown and greenish black on m/c unpt. S. Staszic at l. ctr. Staszic Palace in Warsaw on back.			
	a. Issued note.	FV	5.00	10.00
	s. Specimen ovpt. *WZOR*.	—	—	10.00

		VG	VF	UNC
154	**100,000 ZLOTYCH**			
	1.2.1990. Black and grayish blue on m/c unpt. S. Moniuszko at r. Warsaw Theatre at l. on back.			
	a. Issued note.	FV	5.00	12.50
	s. Specimen ovpt. *WZOR*.	—	—	10.00

		VG	VF	UNC
155	**200,000 ZLOTYCH**			
	1.12.1989. Dk. purple on red, tan and m/c unpt. Coin of Sigismund III at lower ctr., arms at r. Back purple on brown unpt.; Warsaw shield at l., view of Warsaw. Wmk: Geometric design repeated.			
	a. Issued note.	FV	10.00	30.00
	s. Specimen ovpt. *WZOR*.	—	—	15.00

NOTICE

Readers with unlisted dates, signature varieties, etc.
are invited to submit photocopies of their notes to:
Standard Catalog of World Paper Money,
700 East State St. Iola, WI 54990-0001,
E-Mail: george.cuhaj@fwpubs.com.

RZECZPOSPOLITA POLSKA

REPUBLIC OF POLAND

NARODOWY BANK POLSKI

POLISH NATIONAL BANK

1990-92 ISSUE

		VG	VF	UNC
156	**500,000 ZLOTYCH**			
	20.4.1990. Dk. blue-green and black on m/c unpt. H. Sienkiewicz at l. ctr. Shield w/3 books, also 4 flags on back.			
	a. Issued note.	FV	25.00	65.00
	s. Specimen ovpt. *WZOR*.	—	—	37.50
157	**1,000,000 ZLOTYCH**			
	15.2.1991. Brown-violet, purple and red on m/c unpt. W. Reymont at r. Tree w/rural landscape in background on back.			
	a. Issued note.	FV	50.00	150.00
	s. Specimen ovpt. *WZOR*.	—	—	70.00

		VG	VF	UNC
158	**2,000,000 ZLOTYCH**			
	14.8.1992. Black and deep brown-violet on m/c unpt. I. Paderewski at l. ctr. Imperial eagle at l. on back.			
	a. Issued note, misspelling *KONSTYTUCYJY* on back. Series A.	—	—	250.00
	b. As a., but corrected spelling *KONSTYTUCYJNY* on back. Series B.	FV	90.00	200.00
	s. Specimen ovpt. *WZOR*.	—	—	100.00

1993 ISSUE

#159-163 similar to #153, 154, 156-158 but modified w/color in wmk. area, eagle w/crown at lower ctr. or ctr. r. Wmk: Eagle's head.

		VG	VF	UNC
159	**50,000 ZLOTYCH**			
	16.11.1993. Dk. blue-green and brown on m/c unpt. Similar to #153.			
	a. Issued note.	FV	3.00	7.00
	s. Specimen ovpt. *WZOR*.	—	—	8.50

160   100,000 ZLOTYCH
16.11.1993. Black and grayish blue on m/c unpt. Similar to #154.

	VG	VF	UNC
a. Issued note.	FV	5.00	10.00
s. Specimen ovpt: *WZOR*.	—		10.00

161   500,000 ZLOTYCH
16.11.1993. Dk. blue-green and black on m/c unpt. Similar to #156.

	VG	VF	UNC
a. Issued note.	FV	20.00	30.00
s. Specimen ovpt: *WZOR*.	—	—	37.50

162   1,000,000 ZLOTYCH
16.11.1993. Brown-violet, purple and red on m/c unpt. Similar to #157.

	VG	VF	UNC
a. Issued note.	FV	45.00	100.00
s. Specimen ovpt: *WZOR*.	—		70.00

163   2,000,000 ZLOTYCH
16.11.1993. Black and deep brown on m/c unpt. Similar to #158.

	VG	VF	UNC
a. Issued note.	FV	95.00	200.00
s. Specimen ovpt: *WZOR*.	—		100.00

1990 (1996) "CANCELLED" ISSUE

Currency Reform

1 "new" Zloty = 10,000 "old" Zlotych

#164-172 arms at l. and as wmk. These notes were printed in Germany (w/o imprint). Before their release, it was decided a more sophisticated issue of notes should be prepared and these notes were later ovpt: *NIEOBIEGOWY* (non-negotiable) in red and released to the collecting community. Specimens are also known.

164   1 ZLOTY
1.3.1990. Blue-gray and brown on m/c unpt. Bldg. in Gdynia at r. Sailing ship at l. on back.

	VG	VF	UNC
a. Cancelled note.	—	—	3.00
s. Specimen ovpt: *WZOR*.	—	—	25.00

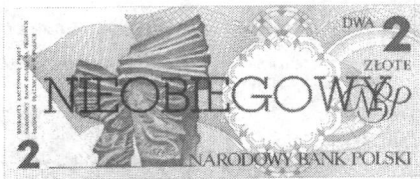

165   2 ZLOTE
1.3.1990. Dk. brown and brown on m/c unpt. Mining conveyor tower at Katowice at r. Battle of Upper Silesia (1921) monument at l. on back.

	VG	VF	UNC
a. Cancelled note.	—	—	3.00
s. Specimen ovpt: *WZOR*.	—	—	25.00

166   5 ZLOTYCH
1.3.1990. Deep green on m/c unpt. Bldg. in Zamosc at r. Order of Grunwald at l. on back.

	VG	VF	UNC
a. Cancelled note.	—	—	3.00
s. Specimen ovpt: *WZOR*.	—	—	25.00

167   10 ZLOTYCH
1.3.1990. Red and purple on m/c unpt. Bldg. in Warsaw at r. Statue of Warszawa at l. on back.

	VG	VF	UNC
a. Cancelled note.	—	—	3.00
s. Specimen ovpt: *WZOR*.	—	—	25.00

168   20 ZLOTYCH
1.3.1990. Brownish black and deep violet on m/c unpt. Grain storage facility in Gdansk at r. Male statue at l. on back.

	VG	VF	UNC
a. Cancelled note.	—	—	3.00
s. Specimen ovpt: *WZOR*.	—	—	25.00

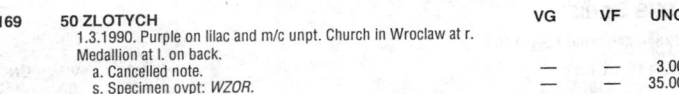

169 50 ZLOTYCH
1.3.1990. Purple on lilac and m/c unpt. Church in Wroclaw at r.
Medallion at l. on back.

	VG	VF	UNC
a. Cancelled note.	—	—	3.00
s. Specimen ovpt. *WZOR*.	—	—	35.00

170 100 ZLOTYCH
1.3.1990. Dk. brown and black on orange and m/c unpt. Bldg. in
Poznan at r. Medieval seal at l. on back.

	VG	VF	UNC
a. Cancelled note.	—	—	3.00
s. Specimen ovpt. *WZOR*.	—	—	35.00

171 200 ZLOTYCH
1.3.1990. Black and deep purple on m/c unpt. Bldgs. in Krakow at
r. Medieval coin at l. on back.

	VG	VF	UNC
a. Cancelled note.	—	—	3.00
s. Specimen ovpt. *WZOR*.	—	—	25.00

172 500 ZLOTYCH
1.3.1990. Black on green and m/c unpt. Church in Gniezno at r.
Medieval seal at l. on back.

	VG	VF	UNC
a. Cancelled note.	—	—	3.00
s. Specimen ovpt. *WZOR*.	—	—	25.00

1994 (1995) REGULAR ISSUE

#173-177 replacement notes: Serial # prefix *ZA*.

#173-175 arms at upper l. ctr.

---

173 10 ZLOTYCH
25.3.1994 (1995). Dk. brown, brown and olive-green on m/c unpt.
Prince Mieszko I at ctr. r. Medieval denar of Mieszko I at l. ctr. on
back.

	VG	VF	UNC
a. Issued note.	FV	FV	6.50
r. Replacement.	FV	FV	17.00
s. Specimen ovpt. *WZOR*.	—	—	7.50

174 20 ZLOTYCH
25.3.1994 (1995). Purple and deep blue on m/c unpt. Kg. Boleslaw
I Chrobry at ctr. r. Medieval denar of Boleslaw II at l. ctr. on back.

	VG	VF	UNC
a. Issued note.	FV	FV	10.00
r. Replacement.	FV	FV	27.00
s. Specimen ovpt. *WZOR*.	—	—	12.50

175 50 ZLOTYCH
25.3.1994 (1995). Blue-violet and deep blue and green on m/c
unpt. Kg. Kazimierz III Wielki at ctr. r. Eagle from seal, orb and
sceptre at l. ctr., town views of Cracow and Kazimierz on back.

	VG	VF	UNC
a. Issued note.	FV	FV	22.50
r. Replacement.	FV	FV	50.00
s. Specimen ovpt.: *WZOR*.	—	—	35.00

176 100 ZLOTYCH
25.3.1994 (1995). Olive-green on m/c unpt. Wladyslaw II Jagiello
at ctr. r. Arms and Teutonic Knights' castle in Malbork on back.

	VG	VF	UNC
a. Issued note.	FV	FV	45.00
r. Replacement.	FV	FV	100.00
s. Specimen ovpt. *WZOR*.	—	—	65.00

177   200 ZLOTYCH
25.3.1994. Brown on m/c unpt. Kg. Zygmunt I the old at ctr. r.
Arms and eagle in hexagon from the Zygmunt's chapel in the
Wawel Cathedral and Wawel's court on back.

	VG	VF	UNC
a. Issued note.	FV	FV	85.00
r. Replacement.	FV	FV	170.00
s. Specimen ovpt: *WZOR*.	—	—	100.00

FOREIGN EXCHANGE CERTIFICATES

PEKAO TRADING CO. (P.K.O.) / BANK POLSKA

BON TOWAROWY (TRADE VOUCHER)

1969 SERIES

#FX21-FX33 serial # prefix E; F; G.

FX21   1 CENT

	VG	VF	UNC
1969. Black and blue on pale blue unpt. Back brown on pale blue unpt.	1.25	3.00	5.00

FX22   2 CENTS

	VG	VF	UNC
1969. Black and green on orange and pink unpt. Back red on pink unpt.	1.25	3.00	5.00

FX23   5 CENTS

	VG	VF	UNC
1969. Black on orange unpt. Back brown on orange unpt.	1.50	4.50	7.50

FX24   10 CENTS

	VG	VF	UNC
1969. Blue and black on orange and yellow unpt. Back olive cn yellow unpt.	2.50	6.00	10.00
FX25 20 CENTS			
1969.	3.50	10.00	15.00
FX26 50 CENTS			
1969.	3.50	10.00	17.50
FX27 1 DOLLAR			
1969. Brown and green on lilac and violet unpt.	5.00	12.50	20.00

		VG	VF	UNC
FX28	**2 DOLLARS**			
	1969.	10.00	15.00	25.00
FX29	**5 DOLLARS**			
	1969.	10.00	25.00	—
FX30	**10 DOLLARS**			
	1969.	12.50	35.00	—
FX31	**20 DOLLARS**			
	1969.	17.50	45.00	—
FX32	**50 DOLLARS**			
	1969.	35.00	85.00	—
FX33	**100 DOLLARS**			
	1969.	100.00	175.00	—

1979 SERIES

#FX34-FX46 serial # prefix H; I.

		VG	VF	UNC
FX34	**1 CENT**			
	1979.	0.50	1.50	2.50

		VG	VF	UNC
FX35	**2 CENTS**			
	1979. Brown on pink and tan unpt.	0.75	1.75	3.00

		VG	VF	UNC
FX36	**5 CENTS**			
	1979. Brown-violet on pale green and yellow unpt. Back lilac on lt. green unpt.	1.00	2.50	4.00

		VG	VF	UNC
FX37	**10 CENTS**			
	1979. Deep green on pink and lilac unpt.	1.00	2.75	4.50

		VG	VF	UNC
FX38	**20 CENTS**			
	1979.	1.25	3.00	5.00

		VG	VF	UNC
FX39	**50 CENTS**			
	1979. Brown on orange and yellow unpt. Back red-brown on yellow unpt.	1.75	4.50	7.50
FX40	**1 DOLLAR**			
	1979. Olive-green on lt. blue and lilac unpt.	3.00	7.50	12.50
FX41	**2 DOLLARS**			
	1979.	5.00	12.00	20.00

		VG	VF	UNC
FX42	**5 DOLLARS**			
	1979.	5.00	15.00	35.00
FX43	**10 DOLLARS**			
	1979.	12.00	30.00	50.00
FX44	**20 DOLLARS**			
	1979.	17.50	45.00	80.00
FX45	**50 DOLLARS**			
	1979.	30.00	75.00	125.00
FX46	**100 DOLLARS**			
	1979.	50.00	125.00	200.00

MARYNARSKI BON TOWAROWY

SEAMEN'S TRADE VOUCHERS

1973 SERIES

#FX47-FX52 winged anchor w/knot at l.

		VG	VF	UNC
FX47	**1 CENT**			
	1.7.1973.	4.00	10.00	—
FX48	**2 CENTS**			
	1.7.1973.	5.00	12.50	—
FX49	**5 CENTS**			
	1.7.1973.	6.00	15.00	—
FX50	**10 CENTS**			
	1.7.1973.	7.00	17.50	—
FX51	**20 CENTS**			
	1.7.1973.	8.00	17.50	—
FX52	**50 CENTS**			
	1.7.1973. Blue and green on green unpt. Anchor at l. Back black on green unpt.	10.00	20.00	—
FX53	**1 DOLLAR**			
	1.7.1973.	15.00	25.00	—
FX54	**2 DOLLARS**			
	1.7.1973.	20.00	30.00	—
FX55	**5 DOLLARS**			
	1.7.1973.	25.00	40.00	—
FX56	**10 DOLLARS**			
	1.7.1973.	35.00	50.00	—

Note: Higher denominations may have been issued.

COLLECTOR SERIES

NARODOWY BANK POLSKI

ND (1948; 1965) ISSUE

		Issue Price	Mkt.	Value
CS1	**COLLECTOR SET**	—		75.00
	Deep red ovpt: *WZOR* on 1948-dated 20, 50, 100, 500 Zlotych #137, 138, 139 and on 1965-dated 1000 Zlotych #141a. All w/normal serial #.			

1967 ISSUE

		Issue Price	Mkt.	Value
CS2	**COLLECTOR SET**	—		50.00
	Red ovpt: *WYSTAWA PIENIEDZY RADZIECKICH - LISTOPAD 1967* and *50 LAT WIELKIEGO PAZDZIERNIKA.* w/*NBP* monogram at corners on faces of 1937 Russian 1, 3, 5, 10 Chervonetz #202-205. Made for the 50th anniversary of the Socialist revo.			

1974 ISSUE

		Issue Price	Mkt.	Value
CS3	**COLLECTOR SET**	12.50		20.00
	Reprints of 1944 Russian issue from 50 Groszy-500 Zlotych #104b-119b. Indicated as reprints of 1974 but w/o other ovpt. Made for the 30th anniversary of the Polish Peoples Republic.			

1978 ISSUE

		Issue Price	Mkt.	Value
CS4	**COLLECTOR SET**	—		25.00
	Dk. blue-black ovpt: *150 LAT BANKU POLSKIEGO 1828-1978* on faces of 1948-dated 20, 100 Zlotych #137, 139a. Made for 150th anniversary of Polish banknotes. Issued in a folder.			

1979 ISSUES

		Issue Price	Mkt.	Value
CS5	**COLLECTOR SET**	—		25.00
	Reprints of 1944 Soviet issue as #C3, but dated 1979 and w/red ovpt. on face: *XXXV - LECIE PRL 1944-1979.* Made for the 35th anniversary of the Polish Peoples Republic.			
CS6	**COLLECTOR SET**	—		15.00
	Reprint of 1919-dated 100 Marek w/red ovpt. on face: *60-LECIE POLSKIEGO BANKNOTU PO ODZY SANIU NIEPODLEGLOSCI 1919-1979.* Made for 60th anniversary of modern Polish bank notes. Released by National Bank of Poland in a folder.			
CS7	**COLLECTOR SET**	—		10.00
	Red ovpt: *WYSTAWA WSPOLCZESNE MONETY I BANKNOTY POLSKIE I OBCE NBP 1979* on 1948 dated 2 Zlote #134. Issued in a small leatherette folder by the National Bank of Poland for a numismatic exposition.			

1979-92 ISSUE

		Issue Price	Mkt.	Value
CS8	**COLLECTOR SET**	—		300.00
	#142-157a, 148a w/red ovpt: *WZOR* on face; all zero serial # and additional black specimen # w/star suffix. Red ovpt: *SPECIMEN* on back.			

Note: Originally #CS8 was sold in a special booklet by Pekao Trading Company at its New York City, NY, and Warsaw offices. Currently available only from the Polish Numismatic Society.

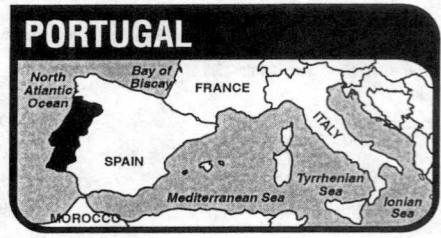

The Portuguese Republic, located in the western part of the Iberian Peninsula in southwestern Europe, has an area of 35,553 sq. mi. (91,905 sq. km.) and a population of 9.79 million. Capital: Lisbon. Portugal's economy is based on agriculture and a small but expanding industrial sector. Textiles, machinery, chemicals, wine and cork are exported.

After centuries of domination by Romans, Visigoths and Moors, Portugal emerged in the 12th century as an independent kingdom financially and philosophically prepared for the great period of exploration that would follow. Attuned to the inspiration of Prince Henry the Navigator (1394-1460), Portugal's daring explorers of the 14th and 15th centuries roamed the world's oceans from Brazil to Japan in an unprecedented burst of energy and endeavor that culminated in 1494 with Portugal laying claim to half the transoceanic world. Unfortunately for the fortunes of the tiny kingdom, the Portuguese proved to be inept colonizers. Less than a century after Portugal laid claim to half the world, English, French and Dutch trading companies had seized the lion's share of the world's colonies and commerce, and Portugal's place as an imperial power was lost forever. The monarchy was overthrown in 1910 and a republic established.

On April 25, 1974, the government of Portugal was seized by a military junta which reached agreements providing for independence for the Portuguese overseas provinces of Portuguese Guinea (Guinea-Bissau), Mozambique, Cape Verde Islands, Angola, and St. Thomas and Prince Islands (São Tomé e Príncipe).

MONETARY SYSTEM:
1 Escudo = 100 Centavos, 1910-2001
1 Euro = 100 Cents, 2002-

REPUBLIC

BANCO DE PORTUGAL

1960; 1961 ISSUE

163	20 ESCUDOS	VG	VF	UNC
	26.7.1960. Ch. 6A. Dk. green and purple on m/c unpt. Portr. Dom Antonio Luiz de Menezes at r. and as wmk. Back purple and m/c; bank seal at l. 8 sign. varieties. Printer: BWC (w/o imprint).	4.00	10.00	60.00

164	50 ESCUDOS	VG	VF	UNC
	24.6.1960. Ch. 7A. Blue on m/c unpt. Arms at upper ctr., Fontes Pereira de Mello at r. and as wmk. Back dk. green and m/c; bank seal at upper l., statue *The Thinker* at l. 8 sign. varieties. Printer: TDLR (w/o imprint).	10.00	30.00	100.00

165	100 ESCUDOS	VG	VF	UNC
	19.12.1961. Ch. 6A. Deep violet and purple on orange, green and m/c unpt. Pedro Nunes at r. and as wmk., arms at upper ctr. Fountain and arches at l., bank seal at ctr. on back. 7 sign. varieties. Printer: BWC (w/o imprint).	10.00	35.00	120.00

166	1000 ESCUDOS	VG	VF	UNC
	30.5.1961. Ch. 8A. Purple on m/c unpt. Qn. Filipa de Lancastre at r. and as wmk. Back blue. Printer: BWC (w/o imprint). 8 sign. varieties.	20.00	70.00	280.00

1964-66 ISSUE

167	20 ESCUDOS	VG	VF	UNC
	26.5.1964. Ch. 7. Olive-green and purple on m/c unpt. Santo Antonio of Padua at r. and as wmk. Church of Santo Antonio de Lisboa at l. on back. 7 sign. varieties.			
	a. Olive-brown unpt. at l. and r.	0.50	1.00	5.00
	b. Green unpt. at l. and r.	0.50	1.00	4.00
	ct. Color trial. Blue and purple on m/c unpt.	—	—	200.00

168   **50 ESCUDOS**

	VG	VF	UNC
28.2.1964. Ch. 8. Dk. brown on m/c unpt. Qn. Isabella at r. and as wmk. Old city Conimbria on back. 15 sign. varieties.	0.75	1.50	6.00

169   **100 ESCUDOS**

	VG	VF	UNC
1965; 1978. Ch. 7. Blue on lt. tan and m/c unpt. Camilo Castello Branco at r. and as wmk. City of Porto in 19th century at l. on back.			
a. 22 sign. varieties. 30.11.1965.	1.00	2.00	10.00
b. 6 sign. varieties. 20.9.1978.	1.00	1.75	8.50

170   **500 ESCUDOS**

	VG	VF	UNC
1966; 1979. Ch. 10. Brown on m/c unpt. Old map at ctr., João II at r. and as wmk. Compass-card or Rhumb-card and double statue on back. Printer: JEZ (w/o imprint).			
a. 7 sign. varieties. 25.1.1966.	5.00	10.00	40.00
b. 9 sign. varieties. 6.9.1979.	5.00	8.50	30.00

171   **1000 ESCUDOS**

	VG	VF	UNC
2.4.1965. Ch. 9. Gray-blue on red-brown and m/c unpt. Pillar at l., arms at upper ctr., Dom Diniz at r. and as wmk. Scene of founding of University of Lisbon in 1290 on back. Printer: JEZ (w/o imprint). 7 sign. varieties.	150.00	500.00	1500.00

1967 ISSUE

172   **1000 ESCUDOS**

	VG	VF	UNC
19.5.1967. Ch. 10. Blue, dk. brown and violet on m/c unpt. Flowers at l., Qn. Maria II at r. and as wmk. Her medallion portr. at l., Banco de Portugal in 1846 bldg. at lower r. on back. Printer: JEZ (w/o imprint). 24 sign. varieties.			
a. Sign. titles: *O GOVERNADOR* and *O ADMINISTRADOR.*	7.50	15.00	50.00
b. Sign. titles: *O VICE-GOVERNADOR* and *O ADMINISTRADOR.*	7.50	15.00	50.00

1968; 1971 ISSUE

173   **20 ESCUDOS**

	VG	VF	UNC
27.7.1971. Ch. 8. Green (shades) on m/c unpt. Garcia de Orta at r. and as wmk. 16th century market in Goa on back. 15 sign. varieties.	0.50	1.00	4.00

174   **50 ESCUDOS**

	VG	VF	UNC
1968; 1980. Ch. 9. Dk. brown on m/c unpt. Arms at l., Infante Dona Maria at r. and as wmk. Sintra in 1507 on back.			
a. 7 sign. varieties. 28.5.1968.	0.75	1.50	5.00
b. 9 sign. varieties. 1.2.1980.	0.75	1.50	4.00

175 1000 ESCUDOS

	VG	VF	UNC
1968-82. Ch. 11. Blue and black on m/c unpt. Dom Pedro V at ctr. and as wmk. Conjoined busts at l., ceremonial opening of the first railway at bottom ctr. and r. on back. Printer: BWC (w/o imprint).			
a. 24 sign. varieties. 28.5.1968.	7.50	12.50	25.00
b. 8 sign. varieties. 16.9.1980.	7.50	12.50	25.00
c. 9 sign. varieties. 3.12.1981.	7.50	12.50	25.00
ct. Color trial. Purple and green.	—	—	340.00
d. 9 sign. varieties. 21.9.1982.	15.00	25.00	80.00
e. 11 sign. varieties. 26.10.1982.	7.50	12.50	25.00

1978; 1979 ISSUE

176 20 ESCUDOS

	VG	VF	UNC
1978. Ch. 9. Green (shades) on m/c unpt. Admiral Gago Coutinho at r. and as wmk. Airplane on back. Lg. or sm. size numerals in serial #.			
a. 6 sign. varieties. 13.9.1978.	0.25	0.75	3.00
b. 6 sign. varieties. 4.10.1978.	0.25	0.75	3.00

177 500 ESCUDOS

	VG	VF	UNC
4.10.1979 (1982). Ch. 11. Brown on m/c unpt. Old street layout of part of Braga at ctr. Francisco Sanches at r. and as wmk. 17th century street scene in Braga on back. Printer: JEZ (w/o imprint). 9 sign. varieties.	3.50	8.00	25.00

1980-89 ISSUES

178 100 ESCUDOS

	VG	VF	UNC
1980-85. Ch. 8. Dk. blue on m/c unpt. Manuel M. B. du Bocage seated at r. and as wmk. Early 19th century scene of Rossio Square in Lisbon on back.			
a. 8 sign. varieties. Darker unpt. through ctr. 2.9.1980.	0.75	1.50	6.00
b. 8 sign. varieties. Light unpt. through ctr. 24.2.1981.	0.75	1.50	5.00
c. 7 sign. varieties. 31.1.1984.	0.75	1.50	5.00
ct. Color trial. Blue and green on m/c unpt.	—	—	185.00
d. 6 sign. varieties. 12.3.1985.	0.75	1.50	5.00
e. 6 sign. varieties. 4.6.1985.	0.75	1.50	5.00
s. Specimen.	—	—	135.00

179 100 ESCUDOS

	VG	VF	UNC
1986-88. Ch. 9. Blue (shades) on m/c unpt. Fernando Antonio Nogueira Pessoa at ctr. r. and as wmk. Rosebud on back.			
a. 5 sign. varieties. 16.10.1986.	0.75	1.50	5.00
b. 8 sign. varieties. 12.2.1987.	0.75	1.50	5.00
c. Prefix letters FIL. 12.2.1987.	—	—	75.00
d. 8 sign. varieties. 3.12.1987.	0.75	1.50	4.00
e. 6 sign. varieties. 26.5.1988.	0.75	1.50	4.00
f. 6 sign. varieties. 24.11.1988.	0.75	1.50	4.00

Note: #179c was issued in a special folder w/an adhesive postage stamp affixed on the upper r. corner of the folder commemorating the 300th Anniversary of Portuguese Paper Money.

180 500 ESCUDOS

	VG	VF	UNC
1987-94. Ch. 12. Brown and m/c. José Xavier Mouzinho da Silveira at ctr. r. and as wmk., arms at upper l. Sheaf on back.			
a. 8 sign. varieties. 20.11.1987.	3.50	7.50	15.00
b. 6 sign. varieties. 4.8.1988.	3.50	7.50	10.00
c. 6 sign. varieties. 4.10.1989.	3.50	7.50	10.00
d. 5 sign. varieties. 13.2.1992.	3.50	7.50	10.00
e. 7 sign. varieties. 18.3.1993.	3.50	7.50	10.00
f. 6 sign. varieties. 4.11.1993.	3.50	7.50	10.00
g. 5 sign. varieties. 29.9.1994.	3.50	6.00	8.50

184	5000 ESCUDOS	VG	VF	UNC
	1988-93. Ch. 2A. Olive-green and brown on m/c unpt. Like #183.			
	a. 6 sign. varieties. 28.10.1988.	30.00	40.00	70.00
	b. 6 sign. varieties. 6.7.1989.	30.00	40.00	80.00
	c. 6 sign. varieties. 19.10.1989.	30.00	40.00	70.00
	d. 5 sign. varieties. 31.10.1991.	30.00	40.00	70.00
	e. 7 sign. varieties. 18.3.1993.	30.00	40.00	70.00
	f. 7 sign. varieties. 2.9.1993.	30.00	40.00	70.00

181	1000 ESCUDOS	VG	VF	UNC
	1983-94. Ch. 12. Purple and dk. brown on m/c unpt. Teofilo Braga at ctr. r. and as wmk. Museum artifacts on back.			
	a. 9 sign. varieties. 2.8.1983.	7.50	10.00	17.50
	b. 5 sign. varieties. 12.6.1986.	7.50	10.00	20.00
	c. 8 sign. varieties. 26.2.1987.	7.50	10.00	20.00
	d. 8 sign. varieties. 3.9.1987.	7.50	10.00	20.00
	e. 6 sign. varieties. 22.12.1988.	7.50	10.00	20.00
	f. 6 sign. varieties. 9.11.1989.	7.50	10.00	17.50
	g. 5 sign. varieties. 26.7.1990.	7.50	10.00	17.50
	h. 5 sign. varieties. 20.12.1990.	7.50	10.00	17.50
	i. 5 sign. varieties. 6.2.1992.	7.50	10.00	17.50
	j. 6 sign. varieties. 17.6.1993.	7.50	10.00	17.50
	k. 6 sign. varieties. 3.3.1994.	7.50	10.00	17.50

185	10,000 ESCUDOS	VG	VF	UNC
	1989-91. Ch. 1. Orange, lt. brown and yellow. Dr. Antonio Gaetano de Abreu Preire Egas Moniz by human brain at ctr. and as wmk. Nobel Prize medal, snakes, tree at ctr. on back.			
	a. 6 sign. varieties. 12.1.1989.	70.00	100.00	150.00
	b. 6 sign. varieties. 14.12.1989.	70.00	100.00	125.00
	c. 5 sign. varieties. 16.5.1991.	70.00	100.00	125.00

1991 ISSUE

182	5000 ESCUDOS	VG	VF	UNC
	1980-86. Ch. 1. Brown and m/c. Antonio Sergio de Sousa at l. ctr. and as wmk. de Sousa walking at ctr. on back. Printer: TDLR (w/o imprint).			
	a. 8 sign. varieties. 10.9.1980.	35.00	50.00	100.00
	b. 8 sign. varieties. 27.1.1981.	35.00	50.00	90.00
	c. 10 sign. varieties. 24.5.1983.	35.00	50.00	90.00
	d. 6 sign. varieties. 4.6.1985.	35.00	50.00	80.00
	e. 6 sign. varieties. 7.1.1986.	35.00	50.00	80.00

183	5000 ESCUDOS			
	1987. Ch. 2. Olive-green and brown on m/c unpt. Antero de Quental at ctr. r. and as wmk. Six hands w/rope and chain at ctr. on back.			
	a. 8 sign. varieties. 12.2.1987.	30.00	40.00	75.00
	b. 8 sign. varieties. 3.12.1987.	30.00	40.00	75.00

186	2000 ESCUDOS	VG	VF	UNC
	1991-93. Ch. 1. Dk. brown and blue on m/c unpt. Bartholomeu Dias at l. and as wmk. astrolabe at ctr. Sailing ship at ctr., arms at r. on back.			
	a. 5 sign. varieties. 23.5.1991.	15.00	20.00	40.00
	b. 5 sign. varieties. 29.8.1991.	15.00	20.00	40.00
	c. 6 sign. varieties. 16.7.1992.	15.00	20.00	35.00
	d. 6 sign. varieties. 21.10.1993.	15.00	20.00	35.00

1995-97 ISSUE

Note: #187-191, Quincentenary of Portuguese Discoveries Series

187	500 ESCUDOS	VG	VF	UNC
	1997; 2000. Ch. 13. Violet and brown on m/c unpt. João de Barros at r. and as wmk., crowned shields on global view at upper ctr., angels below at l. and r. in unpt. Allegory of the Portuguese Discoveries at l. ctr., illustrations from the *Grammer*.			
	a. 6 sign. varieties. 17.4.1997.	FV	FV	8.50
	b. 6 sign. varieties. 11.9.1997.	FV	FV	7.50
	c. 7.11.2000.	FV	FV	7.50

188 1000 ESCUDOS
1996; 1998; 2000. Ch. 13. Purple and brown on m/c unpt. Pedro
Alvares Cabral wearing helmet at r. and as wmk., Brazilian arms at
ctr. Old sailing ship at ctr., birds and animals of Brazilian jungle in
unpt. on back. Sign. varieties.

	VG	VF	UNC
a. 6 sign. varieties. 18.4.1996.	FV	FV	15.00
b. 6 sign. varieties. 31.10.1996.	FV	FV	12.50
c. 6 sign. varieties. 12.3.1998; 21.5.1998.	FV	FV	12.50
d. 7.11.2000.	FV	FV	10.00

191 10,000 ESCUDOS
1996-98. Ch. 2. Violet and dk. brown on m/c unpt. Infante Dom
Henrique at r. and as wmk., arms at ctr. Old sailing ship at ctr. on
back. 6 sign. varieties.

	VG	VF	UNC
a. 2.5.1996.	FV	FV	90.00
b. 10.7.1997.	FV	FV	80.00
c. 12.2.1998; 12.7.1998.	FV	FV	80.00

Note: For later issues used in Portugal see European Union listings.

189 2000 ESCUDOS
1995-97. Ch. 2. Blue-violet and deep blue-green on m/c unpt.
Bartholomeu Dias at r. and as wmk., cruzado coin of Dom João II
at upper ctr., sailing instrument below. Old sailing ship at ctr. r.,
compass, map at l. ctr. on back.

	VG	VF	UNC
a. 5 sign. varieties. 21.9.1995.	FV	FV	25.00
b. 6 sign. varieties. 1.2.1996.	FV	FV	20.00
c. 31.7.1997; 11.9.1997.	FV	FV	20.00

190 5000 ESCUDOS
1995-98. Ch. 3. Deep olive-green and brown-violet on unpt. Vasco
da Gama at r. and as wmk., medallion at upper ctr. Old sailing ship
at ctr. r., da Gama w/authorities in Calcutta at l. on back.

	VG	VF	UNC
a. 5 sign. varieties. 5.1.1995.	FV	FV	60.00
b. 6 sign. varieties. 12.9.1996.	FV	FV	55.00
c. 6 sign. varieties. 20.2.1997.	FV	FV	55.00
d. 6 sign. varieties. 11.9.1997.	FV	FV	50.00
e. 2.7.1998.	FV	FV	50.00

PORTUGUESE GUINEA

Portuguese Guinea (now Guinea-Bissau), a former Portuguese province off the west coast of Africa bounded on the north by Senegal and on the east and southeast by Guinea, had an area of 13,948 sq. mi. (36,125 sq. km.). Capital: Bissau. The province exported peanuts, timber and beeswax.

Portuguese Guinea was discovered by Portuguese navigator Nuno Tristao in 1446. Trading rights in the area were granted to Cape Verde islanders but few prominent posts were established before 1851, and they were principally coastal installations. The chief export of this colony's early period was slaves for South America, a practice that adversely affected trade with the native people and retarded subjection of the interior. Territorial disputes with France delayed final demarcation of the colony's frontiers until 1905.

The African Party for the Independence of Guinea-Bissau was founded in 1956, and several years later began a guerrilla warfare that grew in effectiveness until 1974, when the rebels controlled most of the colony. Portugal's costly overseas wars in her African territories resulted in a military coup in Portugal in April 1974, that appreciably brightened the prospects for freedom for Guinea-Bissau. In August, 1974, the Lisbon government signed an agreement granting independence to Portuguese Guinea effective Sept. 10, 1974. The new republic took the name of Guinea-Bissau.

RULERS:
Portuguese to 1974

MONETARY SYSTEM:
1 Escudo = 100 Centavos, 1910-1975
Note: For later issues see Guinea-Bissau.

PORTUGUESE ADMINISTRATION

BANCO NACIONAL ULTRAMARINO, GUINÉ

DECRETOS - LEIS 39221 E 44891; 1964 ISSUE

#40-42 J. Texeira Pinto at l., bank ship seal at r. Woman sitting, ships through the ages in background at ctr. on back.

40	50 ESCUDOS	VG	VF	UNC
	30.6.1964. Dk. green on lilac and m/c unpt.			
	a. Issued note.	10.00	30.00	85.00
	s. Specimen, punch hole cancelled.	—	—	100.00

41	100 ESCUDOS	VG	VF	UNC
	30.6.1964. Blue-green on m/c unpt.			
	a. Issued note.	12.50	40.00	100.00
	s. Specimen, punch hole cancelled.	—	—	125.00
42	500 ESCUDOS			
	30.6.1964. Brown on m/c unpt.			
	a. Issued note.	35.00	100.00	350.00
	s. Specimen, punch hole cancelled.	—	—	150.00

43	1000 ESCUDOS	VG	VF	UNC
	30.4.1964. Red-orange on m/c unpt. Portr. H. Barreto at r., bank ship seal at upper ctr. Woman standing, ships through the ages in background at l. ctr. on back. Printer: BWC.			
	a. Issued note.	25.00	70.00	200.00
	ct. Color trial. Brown on m/c unpt.	—	—	250.00
	s. Specimen.	—	—	150.00

DECRETOS - LEIS 39221 E 44891; 1971 ISSUE

#44-46 Portuguese arms at upper ctr. Woman standing, ships through the ages in background at l. ctr., bank ship seal at lower l. on back.

44	50 ESCUDOS	VG	VF	UNC
	17.12.1971. Olive-green on m/c unpt. N. Tristao at r. and as wmk.			
	a. Issued note.	1.00	5.00	17.50
	ct. Color trial. Green on m/c unpt.	—	—	135.00

45 100 ESCUDOS
17.12.1971. Blue on m/c unpt. Portr. N. Tristao at r. and as wmk.

	VG	VF	UNC
a. Issued note.	1.00	5.00	17.50
ct. Color trial. Olive on m/c unpt.	—	—	135.00

46 500 ESCUDOS
27.7.1971. Purple on m/c unpt. Portr. H. Barreto at r.

	VG	VF	UNC
a. Issued note.	12.50	40.00	150.00
ct. Color trial. Brown on m/c unpt.	—	—	300.00

QATAR

The State of Qatar, an emirate in the Persian Gulf between Bahrain and the United Arab Emirates, has an an area 4,247 sq. mi. (11,437 sq. km.) and a population of 700,000. Capital: Doha. Oil is the chief industry and export.

Qatar was under Turkish control from 1872 until the beginning of World War I when the Ottoman Turks evacuated the Qatar Peninsula. In 1916 Sheikh Abdullah placed Qatar under the protection of Great Britain and gave Britain responsibility for its defense and foreign relations. Qatar joined with Dubai in a monetary union and issued coins and paper money in 1966 and 1969. When Britain announced in 1968 that it would end treaty relationships with the Persian Gulf sheikhdoms in 1971, this union was dissolved. Qatar joined Bahrain and the seven trucial sheikhdoms (the latter now called the United Arab Emirates) in an effort to form a union of Arab emirates. However, the nine sheikhdoms were unable to agree on terms of union, and Qatar declared its independence as the State of Qatar on Sept. 3, 1971.

Also see Qatar and Dubai.

MONETARY SYSTEM:
1 Riyal = 100 Dirhem

EMIRATE

QATAR MONETARY AGENCY
1973 ND ISSUE
#1-6 arms in circle at r. Wmk: Falcon's head.

1 1 RIYAL
ND (1973). Red on lilac and m/c unpt. Port of Doha at l. on back.

	VG	VF	UNC
a. Issued note.	0.75	3.00	15.00
s. Specimen.	—	—	35.00

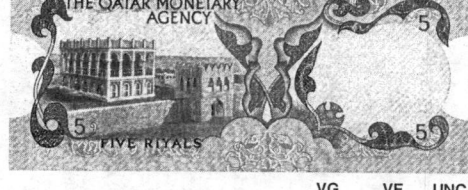

2 5 RIYALS
ND (1973). Dk. brown on lilac and m/c unpt. National Museum at l. on back.

	VG	VF	UNC
a. Issued note.	2.00	8.00	35.00
s. Specimen.	—	—	40.00

		VG	VF	UNC
6	**500 RIYALS** ND (1973). Blue-green on m/c unpt. Mosque of the Sheikhs and minaret at l. on back.			
	a. Issued note.	FV	600.00	1600.00
	s. Specimen.	—	—	700.00

1980's ND Issue

#7-13 arms at r. Wmk: Falcon's head.

		VG	VF	UNC
7	**1 RIYAL** ND. Brown on m/c unpt. City street scene in Doha at l. ctr. on back.	FV	0.75	4.00

		VG	VF	UNC
8	**5 RIYALS** ND. Dk. red and purple on m/c unpt. Back red-brown, green and brown; sheep and plants at l. ctr.			
	a. Wmk: Hawk, nostril visible, and top bill overlaps bottom.	FV	2.25	7.50
	b. Wmk: Hawk, w/o nostril, beak even.	FV	FV	6.00

		VG	VF	UNC
9	**10 RIYALS** ND. Green on blue and m/c unpt. National Museum at l. ctr. on back.	FV	4.00	12.00

		VG	VF	UNC
10	**50 RIYALS** ND (1989). Blue on m/c unpt. Furnace at a steel factory on back.	FV	20.00	40.00

		VG	VF	UNC
3	**10 RIYALS** ND (1973). Green on m/c unpt. Qatar Monetary Agency bldg. at l. on back.			
	a. Issued note.	3.50	7.50	32.50
	s. Specimen.	—	—	50.00

		VG	VF	UNC
4	**50 RIYALS** ND (1976). Blue on m/c unpt. Offshore oil drilling platform at l. on back.			
	a. Issued note.	70.00	275.00	1100.00
	s. Specimen.	—	—	500.00

		VG	VF	UNC
5	**100 RIYALS** ND (1973). Olive-green and orange-brown on m/c unpt. Ministry of Finance bldg. at l. on back.			
	a. Issued note.	FV	200.00	700.00
	s. Specimen.	—	—	225.00

11 100 RIYALS

	VG	VF	UNC
ND. Green on m/c unpt. Qatar Monetary Agency bldg. at l. ctr. on back.	FV	30.00	60.00

12 500 RIYALS

	VG	VF	UNC
ND. Blue and green on m/c unpt. Offshore oil drilling platform on vertical back.			
a. Issued note.	FV	150.00	275.00
s. Specimen.	—	—	—

1985 ND Issue

13 1 RIYAL

	VG	VF	UNC
ND (1985). Brown on m/c unpt. Face like #7. Back purple; boat beached at l., Ministry of Finance, Emir's Palace in background at ctr.			
a. Wmk: Hawk, nostril visible, and top bill overlaps bottom.	FV	FV	2.25
b. Wmk: Hawk, w/o nostril, beak even.	FV	FV	2.00

QATAR CENTRAL BANK

1996 ND Issue

#14-19 similar to #8-13 but w/two sign. Wmk: Falcon's head.

14 1 RIYAL

	VG	VF	UNC
ND (1996). Brown on m/c unpt. Similar to #13.			
a. Security thread reads: *QATAR MONETARY AGENCY.*	FV	FV	2.50
b. Security thread reads: *QATAR CENTRAL BANK.*	FV	FV	1.25

15 5 RIYALS

	VG	VF	UNC
ND (1996). Red and purple on m/c unpt. Similar to #8.			
a. Security thread reads: *QATAR MONETARY AGENCY.*	FV	FV	8.00
b. Security thread reads: *QATAR CENTRAL BANK.*	FV	FV	4.50

16 10 RIYALS

	VG	VF	UNC
ND (1996). Green and blue on m/c unpt. Similar to #9.			
a. Security thread reads: *QATAR MONETARY AGENCY.*	FV	FV	10.00
b. Security thread reads: *QATAR CENTRAL BANK.*	FV	FV	6.00

17 50 RIYALS

	VG	VF	UNC
ND (1996). Blue on m/c unpt. Similar to #10.	FV	FV	25.00

18   100 RIYALS
ND (1996). Green on m/c unpt. Similar to #11.

	VG	VF	UNC
	FV	FV	50.00

22   10 RIYALS
ND (2003). Oranbe-brown and tan on m/c unpt. Traditional Dhow and sand dunes Khor Al-Udeid at l. on back.

	VG	VF	UNC
	FV	FV	6.00

19   500 RIYALS
ND (1996). Blue on m/c unpt. Silver foil emblem at upper l. Similar to #12.

	VG	VF	UNC
	FV	FV	225.00

23   50 RIYALS
ND (2003). Rose on m/c unpt. Qatar Central Bank bldg. and Oyster and Pearl Monument at l. on back.

	VG	VF	UNC
	FV	FV	30.00

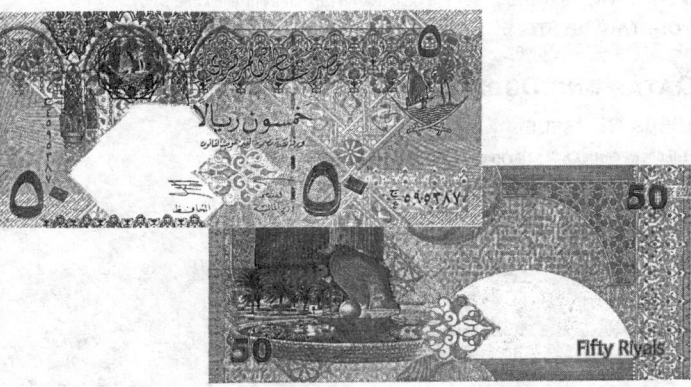

2003 ND Issue
#20-25 wmk: Falcon's head at l.

20   1 RIYAL
ND (2003). Purple and blue on m/c unpt. Three native birds - Crested Lark, Eurasian Bee Eater and Lesser Sand Plover at l. on back.

	VG	VF	UNC
	FV	FV	1.25

24   100 RIYALS
ND (2003). Green on m/c unpt. Mosque of the Sheikhs and Al-Shaqab Institute at l. on back.

	VG	VF	UNC
	FV	FV	45.00

21   5 RIYALS
ND (2003). Lt. and dk. green on m/c unpt. National Museum and native animals at l. on back.

	VG	VF	UNC
	FV	FV	4.00

25   500 RIYALS
ND (2003). Lt. and dk. blue on m/c unpt. Royal Palace, Al-Wajbah Fort and Falcon's head at l. on back.

	VG	VF	UNC
	FV	FV	185.00

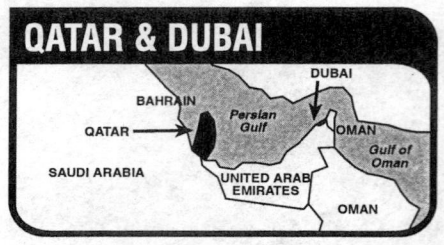

The State of Qatar, which occupies the Qatar Peninsula jutting into the Persian Gulf from eastern Saudi Arabia, has an area of 4,247 sq. mi. (11,000 sq. km.) and a population of 382,000. Capital: Doha. The traditional occupations of pearling, fishing and herding have been replaced in economics by petroleum-related industries. Crude oil, petroleum products, and tomatoes are exported.

Dubai is one of the seven sheikhdoms comprising the United Arab Emirates (formerly Trucial States) located along the southern shore of the Persian Gulf. It has a population of about 60,000. Qatar, which initiated protective treaty relations with Great Britain in 1820, achieved independence on Sept. 3, 1971, upon withdrawal of the British military presence from the Persian Gulf, and replaced its special treaty arrangement with Britain with a treaty of general friendship. Dubai attended independence on Dec. 1, 1971, upon termination of Britain's protective treaty with the trucial sheikhdoms, and on Dec. 2, 1971, entered into the union of the United Arab Emirates.

Despite the fact that the sultanate of Qatar and the sheikhdom of Dubai were merged under a monetary union, the two territories were governed independently from each other. Qatar now uses its own currency while Dubai uses the United Arab Emirates currency and coins.

MONETARY SYSTEM:
1 Riyal = 100 Dirhem

QATAR AND DUBAI CURRENCY BOARD

1960s ND ISSUE

#1-6 dhow, derrick and palm tree at l. Wmk: Falcon's head.

1	1 RIYAL	VG	VF	UNC
	ND. Dk. green on m/c unpt.			
	a. Issued note.	10.00	50.00	150.00
	s. Specimen, punch hole cancelled.	—	—	125.00

2	5 RIYALS	VG	VF	UNC
	ND. Purple on m/c unpt.			
	a. Issued note.	20.00	100.00	800.00
	s. Specimen, punch hole cancelled.	—	—	200.00

3	10 RIYALS	VG	VF	UNC
	ND. Gray-blue on m/c unpt.			
	a. Issued note.	40.00	175.00	1100.00
	s. Specimen, punch hole cancelled.	—	—	300.00

4	25 RIYALS	VG	VF	UNC
	ND. Blue on m/c unpt.			
	a. Issued note.	500.00	2000.00	5000.00
	s. Specimen, punch hole cancelled.	—	—	1500.00

5	50 RIYALS	VG	VF	UNC
	ND. Red on m/c unpt.			
	a. Issued note.	350.00	1500.00	4000.00
	s. Specimen, punch hole cancelled.	—	—	1300.00

6	100 RIYALS	VG	VF	UNC
	ND. Olive on m/c unpt.			
	a. Issued note.	250.00	1250.00	3000.00
	s. Specimen, punch hole cancelled.	—	—	1250.00

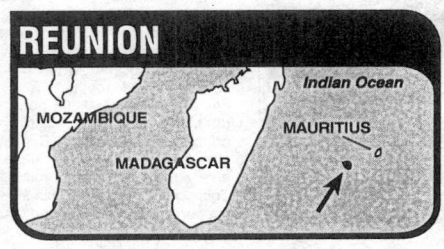

REUNION

The Department of Reunion, an overseas department of France located in the Indian Ocean 400 miles (640 km.) east of Madagascar, has an area of 969 sq. mi. (2,510 sq. km.) and a population of 556,000. Capital: Saint-Denis. The island's volcanic soil is extremely fertile. Sugar, vanilla, coffee and rum are exported.

Although first visited by Portuguese navigators in the 16th century, Reunion was uninhabited when claimed for France by Capt. Goubert in 1638. It was first colonized as Isle de Bourbon by the French in 1662 as a layover station for ships rounding the Cape of Good Hope to India. It was renamed Reunion in 1793. The island remained in French possession except for the period of 1810-15, when it was occupied by the British. Reunion became an overseas department of France in 1946, and in 1958 voted to continue that status within the new French Union. Banque de France notes were introduced 1.1.1973.

MONETARY SYSTEM:
    1 Franc = 100 Centimes
    1 Nouveau Franc = 50 Old Francs, 1960

INSTITUT D'EMISSION DES DÉPARTEMENTS D'OUTRE-MER, RÉPUBLIQUE FRANÇAISE

DEPARTMENT DE LA RÉUNION

1964; 1965 ND ISSUE

51	500 FRANCS	VG	VF	UNC
	ND (1964). M/c. 2 girls at r., sailboat at l. Farmers w/ox-carts on back.			
	a. Sign. A. Postel-Vinay and P. Calvet.	25.00	150.00	500.00
	b. Sign. A. Postel-Vinay and B. Clappier.	15.00	100.00	400.00
	s. Specimen.	—	—	175.00

52	1000 FRANCS	VG	VF	UNC
	ND (1964). M/c. 2 women (symbol of the "Union Française") at r. Sign. A. Postel-Vinay and P. Calvet.			
	a. Issued note.	20.00	125.00	600.00
	s. Specimen.	—	—	250.00

53	5000 FRANCS	VG	VF	UNC
	ND (1965). Brown on m/c unpt. Gen. Schoelcher at ctr. r. Sign. A. Postel-Vinay and P. Calvet.			
	a. Issued note.	50.00	250.00	1000.00
	s. Specimen.	—	—	450.00

1967 ND PROVISIONAL ISSUE

54	10 NOUVEAUX FRANCS ON 500 FRANCS	VG	VF	UNC
	ND (1967-71). M/c. Ovpt. on #51.			
	a. Sign. A. Postel-Vinay and P. Calvet. (1967).	12.50	50.00	300.00
	b. Sign. A. Postel-Vinay and B. Clappier. (1971).	10.00	35.00	275.00
55	20 NOUVEAUX FRANCS ON 1000 FRANCS	VG	VF	UNC
	ND (1967-71). M/c. Ovpt. on #52.			
	a. Sign. A. Postel-Vinay and P. Calvet. (1967).	12.50	75.00	375.00
	b. Sign. A. Postel-Vinay and B. Clappier. (1971).	10.00	50.00	350.00

56	100 NOUVEAUX FRANCS ON 5000 FRANCS	VG	VF	UNC
	ND (1967-71). M/c. Ovpt. on #53.			
	a. Sign. A. Postel-Vinay and P. Calvet. (1967).	25.00	200.00	800.00
	b. Sign. A. Postel-Vinay and B. Clappier. (1971).	22.50	150.00	675.00

RHODESIA

The "Republic of" Rhodesia (never recognized by the British government and was referred to as Southern Rhodesia, now Zimbabwe) located in the east-central part of southern Africa, has an area of 150,804 sq. mi. (390,580 sq. km.) and a population of 9.9 million. Capital: Harare. The economy is based on agriculture and mining. Tobacco, sugar, asbestos, copper and chrome ore and coal are exported.

The Rhodesian area, the habitat of paleolithic man, contains extensive evidence of earlier civilizations, notably the world-famous ruins of Zimbabwe, a gold-trading center that flourished about the 14th or 15th century AD. The Portuguese of the 16th century were the first Europeans to attempt to develop south-central Africa, but it remained for Cecil Rhodes and the British South Africa Co. to open the hinterlands. Rhodes obtained a concession for mineral rights from local chiefs in 1888 and administered his African empire (named Southern Rhodesia in 1895) through the British South Africa Co. until 1923, when the British government annexed the area after the white settlers voted for existence as a separate entity, rather than for incorporation into the Union of South Africa.

From Sept. of 1953 through 1963 Southern Rhodesia was joined with the British protectorates of Northern Rhodesia and Nyasaland into a multiracial federation. When the federation was dissolved at the end of 1963, Northern Rhodesia and Nyasaland became the independent states of Zambia and Malawi.

Britain was prepared to grant independence to Southern Rhodesia but declined to do so when the politically dominant white Rhodesians refused to give assurances of representative government. In November 1965, the white minority government of Southern Rhodesia unilaterally declared Southern Rhodesia an independent dominion. The United Nations and the British Parliament both proclaimed this unilateral declaration of independence null and void. Following a conference in London in December 1979, the opposition government conceded and it was agreed that the British government should resume control. In 1970, the government proclaimed a republic, but this too received no recognition. In 1979, the government purported to change the name of the Colony to Zimbabwe Rhodesia, but again this was never recognized. A British governor soon returned to Southern Rhodesia. One of his first acts was to affirm the nullification of the purported declaration of independence. On April 18, 1980, pursuant to an act of the British Parliament, the colony of Southern Rhodesia became independent within the commonwealth as the Republic of Zimbabwe.

RULERS:
British to 1970 (1980)

MONETARY SYSTEM:
1 Shilling = 12 Pence
1 Pound = 20 Shillings to 1970
1 Dollar = 100 Cents, 1970-80

REPLACEMENT NOTES:
#30-33 later dates, W/1, X/1, Y/1 and Z/1, respectively.

RESERVE BANK OF RHODESIA

1964 ISSUE

Pound System

#24-26 arms at upper ctr., Qn. Elizabeth II at r. Various date and sign. varieties. Wmk: C. Rhodes. Printer: BWC. Printed in England from engraved plates.

24	10 SHILLINGS	VG	VF	UNC
	30.9.1964-16.11.1964. Blue on m/c unpt. Blue portr. w/black serial			
	#. Tobacco field at l. ctr. on back.			
	a. Issued note.	20.00	80.00	425.00
	ct. Color trial. Brown on m/c unpt.	—	—	700.00

25 1 POUND
3.9.1964-16.11.1964. Red on m/c unpt. Red portr., black serial #.
Victoria Falls at l. ctr. on back.

	VG	VF	UNC
a. Issued note.	10.00	60.00	300.00
ct. Color trial. Green on m/c unpt.	—	—	600.00

26 5 POUNDS
10.11.1964; 12.11.1964; 16.11.1964. Blue-green on m/c unpt.
Blue portr., black serial #. Sable antelope at lower l. Zimbabwe
ruins at l. ctr. on back.

	VG	VF	UNC
a. Issued note.	15.00	65.00	275.00
ct. Color trial. Light blue on m/c unpt.	—	—	850.00

1966 ISSUE

#27-29 arms at upper ctr., Qn. Elizabeth II at r. Various date and sign. varieties. Wmk: C. Rhodes. Printed in Rhodesia (w/o imprint). Lithographed.

27 10 SHILLINGS
1.6.1966; 10.9.1968. Blue on m/c unpt. Similar to #24 but w/black portr. Red serial #.

	VG	VF	UNC
a. Issued note.	5.00	35.00	165.00
s. Specimen.			

28 1 POUND
15.6.1966-14.10.1968. Pale red on m/c unpt. Similar to #25 but brown portr. Red serial #.

	VG	VF	UNC
a. Issued note.	7.50	50.00	235.00
s. Specimen.			

29 5 POUNDS
1.7.1966. Blue-green on m/c unpt. Similar to #26 but purple portr. Red serial #.

	VG	VF	UNC
a. Issued note.	20.00	85.00	700.00
s. Specimen.			

Note: Before the issue of #26, 28 and 29, a series of Rhodesian banknotes was printed in Germany by Giesecke and Devrient, Munich. An injunction prevented delivery of this issue and it was never released. Subsequently it was destroyed.

REPUBLIC

RESERVE BANK OF RHODESIA

1970-72 ISSUE

Dollar System

#30-33 bank logo at upper ctr., arms at r. Replacement notes: Serial # prefixes W/1, X/1, Y/1, Z/1 respectively.

30 1 DOLLAR
1970-79. Blue on m/c unpt. Back like #27. 2 sign. varieties.

	VG	VF	UNC
a. Wmk: C. Rhodes. 17.2.1970-18.8.1971.	1.50	5.00	25.00
b. Wmk: as a. 14.2.1973-18.4.1978.	1.00	3.50	15.00
c. Wmk: Zimbabwe bird. 2.8.1979.	1.00	2.50	12.50
s. As b. Specimen.			

31 2 DOLLARS
1970-79. Red on m/c unpt. Back like #28. 2 sign. varieties.

	VG	VF	UNC
a. Wmk: C. Rhodes. 17.2.1970-4.1.1972.	2.00	10.00	35.00
b. Wmk: as a. 29.6.1973-5.8.1977.	1.50	5.00	25.00
c. Wmk: as a. 10.4.1979.	20.00	85.00	200.00
d. Wmk: Zimbabwe bird. 10.4.1979; 24.5.1979.	1.00	3.50	17.50
s. As b, d. Specimen.			

32 5 DOLLARS
1972-79. Brown on m/c unpt. Giraffe at lower l. 2 lions on back. 2 sign. varieties.

	VG	VF	UNC
a. Wmk: C. Rhodes. 16.10.1972.	3.00	10.00	35.00
b. Wmk: as a. 1.3.1976; 20.10.1978.	2.50	10.00	35.00
c. Wmk: Zimbabwe bird. 15.5.1979.	2.50	7.50	25.00
s. Specimen.			

Rhodesia and Nyasaland (now the Republics of Malawi, Zambia and Zimbabwe) was located in the east-central part of southern Africa, had an area of 487,133 sq. mi. (1,261,678 sq. km.). Capital: Salisbury. The area was the habitat of paleolithic man, contains extensive evidence of earlier civilizations, notably the world-famous ruins of Zimbabwe, a gold-trading center that flourished about the 14th or 15th century AD. The Portuguese of the 16th century were the first Europeans to attempt to develop south-central Africa, but it remained for Cecil Rhodes and the British South Africa Co. to open the hinterlands. Rhodes obtained a concession for mineral rights from local chiefs in 1888 and administered his African empire (named Southern Rhodesia in 1895) through the British South Africa Co. until 1923, when the British government annexed the area after the white settlers voted for existence as a separate entity, rather than for incorporation into the Union of South Africa. From Sept. of 1953 through 1963 Southern Rhodesia was joined with the British protectorates of Northern Rhodesia and Nyasaland into a multiracial federation. When the federation was dissolved at the end of 1963, Northern Rhodesia and Nyasaland became the independent states of Zambia and Malawi.

Britain was prepared to grant independence to Southern Rhodesia but declined to do so when the politically dominant white Rhodesians refused to give assurances of representative government. On May 11, 1965, following two years of unsuccessful negotiation with the British government, Prime Minister Ian Smith issued a unilateral declaration of independence. Britain responded with economic sanctions supported by the United Nations. After further futile attempts to effect an accommodation, the Rhodesian Parliament severed all ties with Britain, and on March 2, 1970, established the Republic of Rhodesia.

On March 3, 1978, Prime Minister Ian Smith and three moderate black nationalist leaders signed an agreement providing for black majority rule. The name of the country was changed to Zimbabwe Rhodesia.

After the election of March 3, 1980, the country again changed its name to the Republic of Zimbabwe. The Federation of Rhodesia and Nyasaland (or the Central African Federation), comprising the British protectorates of Northern Rhodesia and Nyasaland and the self-governing colony of Southern Rhodesia, was located in the east-central part of southern Africa. The multiracial federation had an area of about 487,000 sq. mi. (1,261,330 sq. km.) and a population of 6.8 million. Capital: Salisbury, in Southern Rhodesia. The geographical unity of the three British possessions suggested the desirability of political and economic union as early as 1924. Despite objections by the African constituency of Northern Rhodesia and Nyasaland, who feared the dominant influence of prosperious and self governing Southern Rhodesia, the Central African Federation was established in Sept. of 1953. As feared, the Federation was effectively and profitably dominated by the European consituency of Southern Rhodesia despite the fact that the three component countries retained their basic prefederation political structure. It was dissolved at the end of 1963, largely because of the effective opposition of the Nyasaland African Congress. Northern Rhodesia and Nyasaland became independent states of Zambia and Malawi in 1964. Southern Rhodesia unilaterally declared its independence as Rhodesia the following year; this act was not recognized by the British Government.

RULERS:
British to 1963

MONETARY SYSTEM:
1 Shilling = 12 Pence
1 Pound = 20 Shillings to 1963

BANK OF RHODESIA AND NYASALAND

1956 ISSUE

#20-23 portr. Qn. Elizabeth II at r. Various date and sign. varieties. Wmk: C. Rhodes. Printer: BWC.

	33	10 DOLLARS	VG	VF	UNC
		1970-79. Black on blue-green and m/c unpt. Sable antelope at lower l. Back like #29. 2 sign. varieties.			
		a. Wmk: C. Rhodes. 17.2.1970-8.5.1972.	20.00	65.00	160.00
		b. Wmk. as a. 20.11.1973-1.3.1976.	4.00	12.50	40.00
		c. Wmk: Zimbabwe bird. 2.1.1979.	3.50	12.50	35.00
		s. Specimen.	—	—	—

Note: For later issues see Zimbabwe.

	20	10 SHILLINGS	VG	VF	UNC
		1956-61. Reddish brown on m/c unpt. Fish eagle at lower l. River scene on back.			
		a. Sign. A. P. Grafftey-Smith. 3.4.1956-17.6.1960.	45.00	250.00	1000.00
		b. Sign. B. C. J. Richards. 30.12.1960-1.2.1961.	50.00	285.00	1100.00
		ct. Color trial. Green on pink unpt.	—	—	850.00
		s. As a. Specimen punched hole cancelled. 3.4.1956.	—	—	450.00

21 1 POUND

1956-61. Green on m/c unpt. Leopard at lower l. Zimbabwe ruins at ctr. on back.

	VG	VF	UNC
a. Sign. A. P. Grafftey-Smith. 3.4.1956-17.6.1960.	35.00	225.00	1100.00
b. Sign. B. C. J. Richards. 23.12.1960-1.2.1961.	40.00	235.00	1200.00
ct. Color trial. Blue on orange unpt.	—	—	850.00
s. As a. Specimen punched hole cancelled. 2.5.1956.	—	—	550.00

22 5 POUNDS

1956-61. Blue on m/c unpt. Sable antelope at lower l. Victoria Falls on back.

	VG	VF	UNC
a. Sign. A. P. Grafftey-Smith. 3.4.1956-17.6.1960.	85.00	375.00	1400.00
b. Sign. B. C. J. Richards. 23.1.1961-3.2.1961.	95.00	425.00	1750.00
ct. Color trial. Red-brown on blue unpt.	—	—	1350.00
s. As a. Specimen punched hole cancelled. 3.4.1956.	—	—	900.00

23 10 POUNDS

1956-61. Brown on m/c unpt. Back gray-green; elephants at ctr.

	VG	VF	UNC
a. Sign. A. P. Grafftey-Smith. 3.4.1956-17.6.1960.	350.00	1000.00	—
b. Sign. B. C. J. Richards. 1.2.1961; 3.1.1961.	400.00	1200.00	—
ct. Color trial. Green on m/c unpt.	—	—	2250.00
s. As a. Specimen punched hole cancelled. 3.4.1956.	—	—	1800.00

Note: For earlier issues refer to Southern Rhodesia in Volume 2. For later issues refer to Malawi, Zambia, Rhodesia and Zimbabwe in Volume 3.

ROMANIA

Romania, located in southeast Europe, has an area of 91,699 sq. mi. (237,500 sq. km.) and a population of 22.5 million. Capital: Bucharest. Machinery, foodstuffs, raw minerals and petroleum products are exported. The area of Romania, generally referred to as Dacia, was inhabited by Dacians or Getae, a people of Thracian stock. The kingdom of Dacia existed as early as 200 BC. After military campaigns in 105-106 AD the Roman Emperor Trajan conquered Dacia and converted it into a Roman province. During the third century AD, raids by the Goths became such a menace that the Roman legions were withdrawn across the Danube in 271AD. Successive waves of invaders, including Goths, Huns, Gepidae, Avars and Slavs, made the country a battleground although the Romanized population preserved a Latin speech and identity. Through gradual assimilation of the Slavonic tribes, these people developed into a distinct ethnic group called Wallachians (Valachs or Vlachs).

With defeat in 1526, Hungary came under Turkish rule. Transylvania became a separate principality under the protection of the Sultan (1541).

At the close of the sixteenth century, the three principalities were united (Transylvania in 1599 and Moldavia in 1600) by Prince Mihai Viteazul of Wallachia, who made continual war on the Turks in an attempt to gain and maintain independence. The Ottomans restored their control of the principalities after Michael's death. The last Turkish vassal was eliminated in 1699 and Austria obtained the possession of Transylvania by the Treaty of Karlowitz. Under Hapsburg's administration, the region was made into a grand principality in 1765.

Because of the decline of Turkish power during the eighteenth century, the Austrian and later Russian influence became preeminent in the area.

After 1821 Romanian rulers were reestablished. The principalities, although remaining under Sultan control, were more autonomous. In 1829, the Turkish monopoly of commerce was abolished. Important institutional reforms were adopted.

The results of the European insurrectionist movements of 1848 saw the Moldovaian and Wallachian provisional revolutionary governments put down by Russo-Turkish military intervention. In 1867, Transylvania was incorporated under Hungarian administration. The question of the union of Wallachia and Moldavia was resolved in 1859. The two assemblies elected a single prince, Alexandru Ioan Cuza, establishing the fruition of Romania. Prince Cuza was deposed in 1866. A provisional government then elected Prince Karl of Hohenzollern-Sigmaringen, who as Carol I was vested as hereditary prince. A rapid modernization of the country was perceived. Romania was successful in a war against Turkey (1877-78) and proclaimed itself to be independent. The Congress of Berlin (1878) recognized this fact. In 1881, Carol I became king. In 1888, Romania became a constitutional monarchy with a bicameral legislature.

A new constitution was adopted in 1923. During this time the government struggled with domestic problems, agrarian reform and economic reconstruction.

The government was reorganized along Fascist lines between September 14, 1940 - January 23, 1941. A military dictatorship followed. Marshal Ion Antonescu installed himself as chief of state. When the Germans invaded the Soviet Union, Romania also became involved in recovering the regions of Bessarabia and northern Bukovina annexed by Stalin in 1940.

On August 23, 1944, King Mihai I proclaimed an armistice with the Allied Forces. The Romanian army drove out the Germans and Hungarians in northern Transylvania, but the country was subsequently occupied by the Soviet army. That monarchy was abolished on December 30, 1947, and Romania became a "People's Republic" based on the Soviet regime. With the accession of N. Ceausescu to power, Romania began to exercise a considerable degree of independence, refusing to participate in the 1968 invasion of Czechoslovakia. In 1965, it was proclaimed a "Socialist Republic". After 1977, an oppressed and impoverished domestic scene worsened.

On December 17, 1989, an anti-Communist revolt began in Timisoara. On December 22, 1989 the Communist government was overthrown by organized freedom fighters in Bucharest. Ceausescu and his wife were arrested and later executed. The new government has established a republic.

MONETARY SYSTEM:
10,000 "old" Lei = 1 "new" Leu, 1.7.2005
1 Leu = 100 Bani

SOCIALIST REPUBLIC

BANCA NATIONALA A REPUBLICII SOCIALISTE ROMÂNIA

1966 ISSUE
#91-94 arms at ctr. Wmk: Rhombuses.

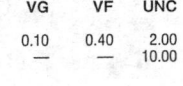

91 1 LEU

1966. Olive-brown and tan.

	VG	VF	UNC
a. Issued note.	0.10	0.40	2.00
s. Specimen.	—	—	10.00

92 3 LEI
1966. Blue on orange and m/c unpt.

	VG	VF	UNC
a. Issued note.	0.25	0.75	4.50
s. Specimen.	—	—	10.00

93 5 LEI
1966. Brown and dk. blue on m/c unpt. Cargo ships at dockside on back.

	VG	VF	UNC
a. Issued note.	0.20	0.50	3.00
s. Specimen.	—	—	10.00

94 10 LEI
1966. Purple on m/c unpt. Harvest scene on back.

	VG	VF	UNC
a. Issued note.	0.20	0.50	4.00
s. Specimen.	—	—	10.00

#95-97 arms at ctr. r. Wmk: Rhombuses.

95 25 LEI
1966. Dk. green on m/c unpt. Portr. Tudor Vladimirescu at l. Large refinery on back.

	VG	VF	UNC
a. Issued note.	0.25	0.75	5.00
s. Specimen.	—	—	15.00

96 50 LEI
1966. Dk. green on m/c unpt. Alexandru Ioan Cuza at l. Culture Palace in Iasi at ctr. r. on back.

	VG	VF	UNC
a. Issued note.	0.25	1.75	6.50
s. Specimen.	—	—	15.00

97 100 LEI
1966. Dk. blue and purple on m/c unpt. Portr. Nicolae Balcescu at l. The Athenaeum in Bucharest at ctr. r. on back.

	VG	VF	UNC
a. Issued note.	0.50	2.00	8.00
s. Specimen.	—	—	20.00

REPUBLIC

BANCA NATIONALA A ROMÂNIEI

1991 ISSUE

98 500 LEI
1991. Dk. brown on m/c unpt. Constantin Brâncusi at r. and as wmk. Brâncusi seated w/statue at l. ctr. on back. Sign. Isarescu.

	VG	VF	UNC
a. Jan. 1991.	0.75	5.00	15.00
b. April 1991.	0.25	1.50	6.00
x. As b, w/*APRILIED* (error).			

#99 renumbered to #101A.

1991-94 ISSUE

100 200 LEI
Dec. 1992. Dull deep brown and brown-violet on m/c unpt. Square-topped shield at l. ctr., steamboat *Tudor Vladimirescu* above grey heron and Sulina Lighthouse in unpt. at ctr., Grigore Antipa at at r. Herons, fish, and net on outline of Danube

	VG	VF	UNC
	0.10	0.60	3.00

104   5000 LEI
May 1993. Similar to #103 but square-topped shield at l. ctr.

	VG	VF	UNC
	0.50	1.00	4.25

101   500 LEI
Dec. 1992. Dull deep green, reddish brown and violet on m/c unpt.
Square topped shield at l. ctr., sculptures at ctr., Constantin
Brâncusi at r. Sculptures at l. ctr. on back. Wmk: Bust right.
  a. Wmk: Bust facing as #98.
  b. Wmk: Bust to r.

	VG	VF	UNC
a.	0.20	3.00	8.00
b.	0.10	0.60	2.50

105   10,000 LEI
Feb. 1994. Dull violet and reddish brown on m/c unpt. Nicolae Iorga
at r. and., as wmk., snake god Glycon at ctr. Statue of Fortuna at l.,
historical Museum in Bucharest at ctr. The Thinking Man of
Hamangia at lower ctr. r. on back.

	VG	VF	UNC
	0.50	2.00	6.50

1996-2000 PAPER ISSUE

#106-110 arms at top l., bank monogram at upper ctr. r. Bank monogram at top r. on back.

101A   1000 LEI
Sept. 1991. Red-brown, blue-green and brown-orange on m/c
unpt. Circular shield at l. ctr., sails of sailing ships at lower ctr.,
Mihai Eminescu at r. and as wmk. Putna monastery at l. ctr. on
back. Sign. Isarescu and Florescu.

	VG	VF	UNC
	1.00	3.00	11.00

102   1000 LEI
May 1993. Similar to #101A but square-topped shield of arms
at l. ctr.

	VG	VF	UNC
	0.20	1.00	3.25

106   1000 LEI
1998. Blue-violet, dk. green and olive-brown on m/c unpt. Mihai
Eminescu at r. and as wmk., lily flower and quill pen at ctr. Lime and
blue flowers at l. ctr., ruins of ancient fort of Histria at ctr. on back.

	VG	VF	UNC
	0.10	0.50	1.75

103   5000 LEI
March 1992. Pale purple on m/c unpt. Round seal at l. ctr., church
at ctr., Avram Iancu at r. and as wmk. Church at l., the gate of Alba
Iulia stronghold at l. ctr., seal at ctr. r. on back.

	VG	VF	UNC
	1.00	4.00	17.50

107   5000 LEI
1998. Violet, dk. brown and brown-orange on m/c unpt. Lucian
Blaga at r. and as wmk., daffodil at ctr. Vine leaf at l. ctr., roadside
crucifix at ctr. on back.

	VG	VF	UNC
	0.25	1.00	3.00

110	100,000 LEI	VG	VF	UNC
	1998. Dull red on olive-green and m/c unpt. Nicolae Grigorescu at r. and as wmk., mallow flowers and artist's brush at ctr. Peasant girl w/ewe at l., cottage at ctr. on back.	1.00	2.50	13.00

1999 COMMEMORATIVE ISSUE

#111, Total Solar Eclipse, August 11, 1999

111	2000 LEI	VG	VF	UNC
	1999. Blue on m/c unpt. Imaginative reproduction of the Solar System at r., with the mention of the event. The map of Romania having the colors of the national flag, (blue, yellow, red) marking the area where the phenomenon of the solar eclipse was t			
	a. Issued note.	0.25	0.50	2.00
	b. Serial # prefix 001A in folder. (One million pcs.)	—	—	8.00

2000-01 POLYMER ISSUE

108	10,000 LEI	VG	VF	UNC
	1999. Green-yellow and blue on m/c unpt. Nicolae Iorga at r. and as wmk., gentian flower at ctr. The church of Curtea de Arges monastery at ctr., Wallachian arms of Prince Constantin Brancoveanu (1686-1714) at l. on back.	0.50	1.25	4.50

109	50,000 LEI	VG	VF	UNC
	1996. Purple and red-violet on lilac and m/c unpt. George Enescu at r. and as wmk., floral ornament, musical notes at ctr., arms at upper l. Sphinx of Carpathian mountains at l. ctr., musical chord from *Oedip King* above on back.	0.50	3.00	17.50

112	10,000 LEI	VG	VF	UNC
	2000. Green and blue on m/c unpt. Similar to # 109. Sign. Ghizari; Nitu. Polymer plastic.			
	a. Issued note.	0.25	0.50	3.50
	b. Uncut sheet of 4 (5000 sheets) .	—	—	12.50

109A	50,000 LEI	VG	VF	UNC
	2000. Purple and red-violet on lilac and m/c unpt. Like #109 but violin shaped bronze area near portrait, and changed unpt design.	0.50	1.00	8.00

113	50,000 LEI	VG	VF	UNC
	2000. Purple and red-violet on lilac and m/c unpt. Like #109. Polymer plastic.			
	a. Issued note.	0.25	1.00	5.00
	b. Uncut sheet of 4 (500 sheets).	—	—	40.00

114	100,000 LEI	VG	VF	UNC
	2001. Dull red on olive-green and m/c unpt. Similar to #110. Sign. Isarescu; Nitu. Polymer plastic.	0.50	1.00	8.50

118	5 LEI	VG	VF	UNC
	2005.	FV	FV	3.00

119	10 LEI	VG	VF	UNC
	2005.	FV	FV	4.00

115	500,000 LEI	VG	VF	UNC
	2000. Brown on yellow and m/c unpt. Aurel Vlaicu at r., edelweiss flower at ctr. Imperial Eagle head at ctr. *Vlaicu II* plane and *Gnome* engine sketch at l. ctr. on back. Polymer plastic.			
	a. Issued note.	0.50	2.50	25.00
	b. Uncut sheet of 4 (2000 sheets) .	—	—	140.00
116	1,000,000 LEI			
	2003. Blue, green, violet and yellow. Luca Caragiale at r. Statue and building on back.	3.50	10.00	45.00

2005 REVALUATION ISSUE

120	50 LEI	VG	VF	UNC
	2005.	FV	FV	5.00
121	100 LEI			
	2005.	FV	FV	8.50

117	1 LEU	VG	VF	UNC
	2005.	FV	FV	2.00

122	500 LEI	VG	VF	UNC
	2005.	FV	FV	25.00

RUSSIA

Russia, (formerly the central power of the Union of Soviet Socialist Republics and now of the Commonwealth of Independent States) occupying the northern part of Asia and the far eastern part of Europe, has an area of 8,649,538 sq. mi. (17,075,450 sq. km.) and a population of 146.2 million. Capital: Moscow. Exports include machinery, iron and steel, oil, timber and nonferrous metals.

The first Russian dynasty was founded in Novgorod by the Viking, Rurik in 862 AD. Under Yaroslav the Wise (1019-54) the subsequent Kievan state (Kyiv's Rus') became one of the great commercial and cultural centers of Europe before falling to the Mongols in the 13th century, who ruled Russia until late in the 15th century when Ivan III threw off the Mongol yoke. The Russian Empire was enlarged and solidified during the reigns of Ivan the Terrible, Peter the Great and Catherine the Great, and by 1881 extended to the Pacific and into Central Asia.

Assignats, the first government paper money of the Russian Empire, were introduced in 1769, and gave way to State Credit Notes in 1843. Russia was put on the gold standard in 1897 and reformed its currency at that time.

All pre-1898 notes were destroyed as they were turned in to the Treasury, accounting for their uniform scarcity today.

The last Russian Czar, Nicholas II (1894-1917), was deposed by the provisional government under Prince Lvov and later Alexander Kerensky during the military defeat in World War I. This government rapidly lost ground to the Bolshevik wing of the Socialist Democratic Labor Party. During the Russian Civil War (1917-1922) many regional governments, national states and armies in the field were formed which issued their own paper money (see Vol. I).

After the victory of the Red armies, many of these areas became federal republics of the Russian Socialist Federal Soviet Republic (РСфСР), or autonomous soviet republics which united on Dec. 30, 1922, to form the Union of Soviet Socialist Republics (CCCP). Beginning with the downfall of the communist government in Poland (1989), other European countries occupied since WW II began democratic elections that spread into Russia itself, leaving the remaining states united in a newly founded Commonwealth of Independent States (C.I.S.). The USSR Supreme Soviet voted a formal end to the treaty of union signed in 1922 and dissolved itself.

MONETARY SYSTEM:
1 Ruble = 100 Kopeks, until 1997
1 Ruble = 1000 "old" Rubles, 1998-

А	а	*A*	*a*	A	С	с	*C*	*c*	S
Б	б	*Го*	*б*	B	Т	т	*T*	*m*	T
В	в	*B*	*в*	V	У	у	*У*	*у*	U
Г	г	*Г*	*г*	G	Ф	ф	*Ф*	*ф*	F
Д	д	*D*	*д*	D	Х	х	*X*	*х*	Kh
Е	е	*E*	*е*	ye	Ц	ц	*Ц*	*ц*	C
Ё	ё	*Ё*	*ё*	yo	Ч	ч	*Ч*	*ч*	ch
Ж	ж	*Ж*	*ж*	zh	Ш	ш	*Ш*	*ш*	sh
З	з	*З*	*з*	Z	Щ	щ	*Щ*	*щ*	shch
И	и	*И*	*и*	I	ъ *)	ъ *)	—	*ъ*	'
Й	й	*И*	*й*	J	Ы	ы	—	*ы*	i
К	к	*K*	*к.к*	K	Ь **)	ь **)	–	*ь*	b
Л	л	*Л*	*л*	L	Э	э	*Э*	*э*	E
М	м	*М*	*м*	M	Ю	ю	*Ю*	*ю*	yu
Н	н	*Н*	*н*	N	Я	я	*Я*	*я*	ya
О	о	*О*	*о*	O	I	I	*I*	*i*	I
П	п	*П*	*п*	P	ѣ	ѣ	*Ѣ*	*ѣ*	ye
Р	р	*Р*	*р*	R					

*) "hard", and **) "soft" signs; both soundless. I and Ѣ were dropped in 1918.

U.S.S.R. - Union of Soviet Socialist Republics

ГОСУДАРСТВЕННЫЙ КАЗНАЧЕЙСКИЙ БИЛЕТ

STATE TREASURY NOTE

1961 ISSUE

#222-224 arms at upper l. Wmk: Stars.

		VG	VF	UNC
222	**1 RUBLE**			
	1961. Brown on pale green unpt. Back red on m/c unpt.			
	a. Issued note.	0.05	0.10	0.50
	s. Specimen.	—	—	15.00

		VG	VF	UNC
223	**3 RUBLES**			
	1961. Dk. green on m/c unpt. View of Kremlin at ctr. Back lt. blue on green and m/c unpt.			
	a. Issued note.	0.05	0.10	1.00
	s. Specimen.	—	—	15.00

		VG	VF	UNC
224	**5 RUBLES**			
	1961. Blue on peach unpt. Kremlin Spasski tower at l. Back blue on m/c unpt.			
	a. Issued note.	0.05	0.15	1.50
	s. Specimen.	—	—	15.00

БИЛЕТ ГОСУДАРСТВЕННОГО БАНКА С.С.С.Р.

STATE BANK NOTE U.S.S.R.

1961 ISSUE

		VG	VF	UNC
233	**10 RUBLES**			
	1961. Red-brown on pale gold unpt. Arms at upper l., portr. V. I. Lenin at r. Wmk: Stars.			
	a. Issued note.	0.10	0.25	1.00
	s. Specimen.	—	—	15.00

#234-236 portr. V. I. Lenin at upper l., arms at upper ctr.

	VG	VF	UNC
238 3 RUBLES 1991. Green on blue and m/c unpt. Similar to #223.			
a. Issued note.	0.10	0.25	1.00
s. Specimen.	—	—	15.00

234 25 RUBLES	VG	VF	UNC
1961. Purple on pale lt. green unpt. Wmk: Stars.			
a. Lilac tinted paper. 124 x 61mm.	0.25	1.00	5.00
b. White paper. 121 x 62mm.	0.10	0.25	1.00
s. Specimen.	—	—	15.00

239 5 RUBLES	VG	VF	UNC
1991. Blue-gray on lt. blue, pale green and pink unpt. Similar to #224.	0.05	0.25	1.00
a. Issued note.			
s. Specimen.	—	—	15.00

235 50 RUBLES	VG	VF	UNC
1961. Dk. green and green on green and pink unpt. Kremlin at upper ctr. on back.			
a. Issued note.	0.25	1.00	8.00
s. Specimen.	—	—	15.00

240 10 RUBLES	VG	VF	UNC
1991. Red-brown and green on m/c unpt. Similar to #233.	0.15	0.25	1.25
a. Issued note.			
s. Specimen.	—	—	15.00

236 100 RUBLES	VG	VF	UNC
1961. Brown on lt. blue unpt. Kremlin tower at ctr. w/date on back. Wmk: Lenin.			
a. Issued note.	0.25	1.00	5.00
s. Specimen.	—	—	15.00

1991 Issue

#237-243 similar to #222-236.

#237-239 wmk: Star in circle repeated.

241 50 RUBLES	VG	VF	UNC
1991. Dk. brown, green and red on m/c unpt. Similar to #235.	0.20	1.00	6.00
a. Issued note.			
s. Specimen.	—	—	15.00

237 1 RUBLE	VG	VF	UNC
1991. Dk. green and red-brown on tan unpt. Similar to #222.			
a. Issued note.	0.05	0.10	0.50
s. Specimen.	—	—	15.00

242 **100 RUBLES**
1991. Deep red-brown and blue on m/c unpt. Similar to #236
w/date on face at r. Wmk: Lenin.

	VG	VF	UNC
a. Issued note.	0.25	0.75	4.00
s. Specimen.	—	—	15.00

243 **100 RUBLES**
1991. Like #242 but w/added pink and green guilloche at r. in wmk.
area, blue guilloche added at upper l. on back. Wmk: Stars.

	VG	VF	UNC
a. Issued note.	0.25	0.75	3.00
s. Specimen.	—	—	15.00

#244-246 portr. V. I. Lenin at upper l. and as wmk., arms at upper ctr. Different views of the Kremlin on back.

246 **1000 RUBLES**
1991. Brown and blue on green and m/c unpt.

VG	VF	UNC
1.50	5.50	20.00

RUSSIAN FEDERATION

РОССИЙСКАЯ ФЕДЕРАЦИЯ

RUSSIAN FEDERATION

1992 ISSUE

244 **200 RUBLES**
1991. Green and brown on m/c unpt.

VG	VF	UNC
0.50	3.00	10.00

247 **50 RUBLES**
1992. Brown and gray on green and m/c unpt. Similar to #241.
Wmk: Star in circle repeated.

	VG	VF	UNC
a. Issued note.	0.15	0.50	1.50
s. Specimen.	—	—	15.00

245 **500 RUBLES**
1991. Red and green on m/c unpt.

VG	VF	UNC
1.00	5.00	17.50

248 **200 RUBLES**
1992. Green and brown on m/c unpt. Similar to #244, but guilloche
added in wmk. area on back. Wmk. as #247.

	VG	VF	UNC
a. Issued note.	0.15	0.75	2.50
s. Specimen.	—	—	15.00

249	500 RUBLES		VG	VF	UNC
	1992. Red, violet and dk. green on m/c unpt. Similar to #245, but guilloche added in wmk. area on back. Wmk: Stars.				
	a. Issued note.		0.15	0.75	4.00
	s. Specimen.		—	—	15.00

250	1000 RUBLES		VG	VF	UNC
	1992. Dk. brown and deep green on m/c unpt. Similar to #246, but guilloche added in wmk. area on back. Wmk: Stars.				
	a. Issued note.		0.15	0.50	1.50
	s. Specimen.		—	—	15.00

1992 GOVERNMENT PRIVATIZATION CHECK ISSUE

251	10,000 RUBLES		VG	VF	UNC
	1992. Dk. brown on m/c unpt. Parliament White House in Moscow. Text indicating method of redemption into shares of govt.-owned property on back. Handstamp from bank added at bottom. Valid until Dec. 31, 1993.		7.50	15.00	35.00

Note: While not a regular banknote, #251 was easily negotiable and was widely distributed by the govt. It was to provide funds to allow citizens to "buy into" a business. Worth about $35. at time of issue (early 1992), inflation since then has cut its real value dramatically.

БАНК РОССИЙ

BANK OF RUSSIA

1992 ISSUE

252	5000 RUBLES		VG	VF	UNC
	1992. Blue and maroon on m/c unpt. St. Basil's Cathedral at l. Kremlin on back. Wmk: Stars. Sign. Georgui Matiukhin.				
	a. Issued note.		0.25	0.50	1.50
	s. Specimen.		—	—	15.00

253	10,000 RUBLES		VG	VF	UNC
	1992. Brown, black and red on m/c unpt. Kremlin w/new tricolor flag at l. ctr. and as wmk. Kremlin towers at ctr. r. on back.				
	a. Issued note.		0.25	0.75	2.00
	s. Specimen.		—	—	15.00

1993 ISSUE

#254-260 new tricolor flag over stylized Kremlin at l., monogram at upper r. or near ctr. on back.

#254-256 wmk: Stars within wavy lines repeated.

254	100 RUBLES	VG	VF	UNC
	1993. Blue-black on pink and lt. blue unpt. Kremlin, Spasski Tower at ctr. r. on back.	0.10	0.25	1.00

255   200 RUBLES
1993. Brown on pink and m/c unpt. Kremlin gate at ctr. on back.

VG	VF	UNC
0.10	0.25	1.00

256   500 RUBLES
1993. Green, blue and purple on m/c unpt. Kremlin at l. ctr. on back.

VG	VF	UNC
0.05	0.15	1.25

257   1000 RUBLES
1993. Green, olive-green and brown on m/c unpt. Kremlin at ctr. on back. Wmk: Stars.

VG	VF	UNC
0.10	0.50	2.00

#258-260 new flag over Kremlin at l. and as wmk. Kremlin at or near ctr. on back.

258   5000 RUBLES
1993; 1993//94. Blue, brown and violet on m/c unpt.
a. 1993.
b. 1993//94.

VG	VF	UNC
0.50	2.50	10.00
0.50	2.50	10.00

259   10,000 RUBLES
1993; 1993//94. Violet, greenish blue, brownish purple and m/c.
a. 1993.
b. 1993//94.

VG	VF	UNC
0.50	4.00	15.00
0.50	2.50	10.00

260   50,000 RUBLES
1993; 1993//94. Olive-green, black and reddish brown on m/c unpt.
a. 1993.
b. 1993//94.

VG	VF	UNC
1.00	5.00	30.00
1.00	5.00	30.00

1995 ISSUE

261   1000 RUBLES
1995. Dk. brown and brown on m/c unpt. Seaport of Vladivostok at l. ctr., memorial column at ctr. r. and as wmk. Entrance to Vladivostok Bay at ctr. on back. Wmk: *1000* and memorial column.

VG	VF	UNC
0.25	0.75	4.00

262   5000 RUBLES
1995. Deep blue-green and dk. olive-green on m/c unpt. Monument of the Russian Millennium in Novgorod at l. ctr. Cathedral of St. Sophia at ctr. and as wmk. Old towered city wall at upper l. ctr. on back.

VG	VF	UNC
0.25	1.00	4.00

263   10,000 RUBLES
1995. Dk. brown and dk. gray on m/c unpt. Arch bridge over Yenisei River in Krasnoyarsk at l. ctr., steeple at ctr. r. and as. wmk. Hydroelectric dam at ctr. on back.

VG	VF	UNC
0.25	2.00	6.00

264 50,000 RUBLES

	VG	VF	UNC
1995. Dk. brown, grayish purple and black on m/c unpt. Personification of river Neva on foot of Rostral Column, Peter and Paul Fortress in St. Petersburg. Rostral Column and Naval Museum at upper l. ctr. on back. Wmk: Bldg. w/steeple.	0.50	7.50	20.00

265 100,000 RUBLES

	VG	VF	UNC
1995. Purple and brown on m/c unpt. Apollo and chariot freize on Bolshoi (Great) Theatre in Moscow at ctr. Bolshoi Theatre on back. Wmk: Bldg. over value.	2.50	15.00	35.00

266 500,000 RUBLES

	VG	VF	UNC
1995 (1997). Brown-violet on m/c unpt. Statue of Peter the Great, sailing ship dockside in port of Arkhangelsk at ctr. Monastery in Solovetsky Island on back.	10.00	40.00	125.00

1997 (1998) "NEW RUBLE" ISSUE

1 Ruble = 1000 "old" Rubles

#267-271 like #262-266.

267 5 RUBLES

	VG	VF	UNC
1997 (1998). Deep blue-green and dk. olive-green on m/c unpt. Like #262.	0.10	0.25	2.00

268 10 RUBLES

	VG	VF	UNC
1997 (1998); 2001. Dk. brown and dk. gray on m/c unpt. Like #263.			
a. 1997.	0.25	0.35	2.50
b. 2001. Date in very small vertical text to l. of bridge.	0.25	0.35	2.50

269 50 RUBLES

	VG	VF	UNC
1997 (1998). Dk. brown, grayish purple and black on m/c unpt. Like #264.	0.50	1.75	4.00

270 100 RUBLES

	VG	VF	UNC
1997 (1998). Violet and brown on m/c unpt. Like #265.	1.00	4.00	7.50

271 500 RUBLES

	VG	VF	UNC
1997 (1998). Brown-violet on m/c unpt. Like #266.	5.00	16.00	35.00

272	1000 RUBLES	VG	VF	UNC
	1997 (2000). St. Basil Cathedral on back.	5.00	32.00	65.00

2004 AND 1997 DATED ISSUE

273	10 RUBLES	VG	VF	UNC
	2004. Dk. Brown and dk. gray on m/c unpt.	FV	FV	1.25

274	50 RUBLES	VG	VF	UNC
	2004. Dk. brown, grayish purple and black on m/c unpt.	FV	FV	4.00

275	100 RUBLES	VG	VF	UNC
	2004. Violet and brown on m/c unpt.	FV	FV	7.50

276	500 RUBLES	VG	VF	UNC
	2004. Brown-violet on m/c unpt.	FV	FV	35.00

277	1000 RUBLES	VG	VF	UNC
	2004. M/c.	FV	FV	65.00

FOREIGN EXCHANGE CERTIFICATES

HARD CURRENCY NOTES

1965-68 BLUE BAND ISSUE

FX10	1 KOPEK	VF	XF	UNC
	1965; 1966. Black on light orange unpt. in dark green frame. Back dark green.			
	a. 1965.	0.50	1.00	4.00
	b. 1966.	0.50	1.00	3.50
FX11	2 KOPEK			
	1965; 1966. Black on light orange unpt. in dark green frame. Back dark green.			
	a. 1965.	0.50	1.00	4.00
	b. 1966.	0.50	1.00	3.50

FX12	5 KOPEK	VF	XF	UNC
	1965; 1966. Black on light orange unpt. in dark green frame. Back dark green.			
	a. 1965.	0.75	2.00	5.00
	b. 1966.	0.75	2.00	5.00
	c. 1972.	1.00	3.00	7.00
FX13	10 KOPEK			
	1965; 1966. Black on light orange unpt. in dark green frame. Back dark green.			
	a. 1965.	1.00	2.50	8.00
	b. 1966.	1.00	2.50	8.00

		VF	XF	UNC
FX14	**25 KOPEK**			
	1965; 1966. Black on light orange unpt. in dark green frame. Back dark green.			
	a. 1965.	2.00	5.00	12.00
	b. 1966.	2.00	5.00	12.00
FX15	**50 KOPEK**			
	1965. Black on light orange unpt. in dark green frame. back dark green.	4.00	8.00	18.00

		VF	XF	UNC
FX16	**1 RUBLE**			
	1965; 1966. Black on gray-green unpt in red-brown frame. Back red-brown.			
	a. 1965.	6.00	10.00	25.00
	b. 1966.	6.00	10.00	25.00
FX17	**3 RUBLE**			
	1966; 1968. Black on gray-green unpt. in red-brown frame. Back red-brown.			
	a. 1966.	8.00	15.00	35.00
	b. 1968.	12.00	25.00	45.00
FX18	**5 RUBLE**			
	1965; 1968. Black on gray-green unpt. in red-brown frame. Back red-brown.			
	a. 1965.	10.00	20.00	40.00
	b. 1968.	15.00	28.00	50.00

		VF	XF	UNC
FX19	**10 RUBLES**			
	1967. Black on gray-green unpt. in 1967. red-brown frame. Back red-brown.	16.00	30.00	60.00
FX20	**20 RUBLES**			
	1965. Black on gray-green unpt. in red-brown frame. Back red-brown.	20.00	40.00	75.00

		VG	VF	UNC
FX21	**50 RUBLES**			
	1972.	—	—	—
FX22	**100 RUBLES**			
		Reported Not Confirmed		

1972 BLUE BAND ISSUE

FX25-FX28 like previous issue but for text added to back.

		VF	XF	UNC
FX25	**2 KOPEK**			
	1972. Black on light orange unpt. in dark green frame. Back dark green.	1.50	3.00	6.00
FX26	**5 KOPEK**			
	1972. Black on light orange unpt. in dark green frame. Back dark green.	1.00	3.00	7.00
FX27	**10 KOPEK**			
	1972. Black on light orange unpt. in dark green frame. Back dark green.	1.00	3.00	10.00
FX28	**3 RUBLE**			
	1972. Black on gray-green unpt. in red-brown frame. Back red-brown.	12.50	25.00	45.00

1965-67 YELLOW BAND ISSUE

		VF	XF	UNC
FX30	**1 KOPEK**			
	1965; 1966. Black on light orange unpt. in dark green frame. Back dark green.			
	a. 1965.	1.00	2.00	6.00
	b. 1966.	0.50	1.00	4.00

		VF	XF	UNC
FX31	**2 KOPEK**			
	1965; 1966. Black on light orange unpt. in dark green frame. Back dark green.			
	a. 1965.	1.00	2.00	6.00
	b. 1966.	0.75	1.50	5.00
FX32	**5 KOPEK**			
	1965; 1966. Black on light orange unpt. in dark green frame. Back dark green.			
	a. 1965.	1.50	3.00	7.00
	b. 1966.	1.00	2.00	6.00
FX33	**10 KOPEK**			
	1965; 1966. Black on light orange unpt. in dark green frame. Back dark green.			
	a. 1965.	2.00	4.00	8.00
	b. 1966.	1.75	3.50	7.50
FX34	**25 KOPEKS**			
	1965; 1966. Black on light orange unpt. in dark green frame. Back dark green.			
	a. 1965.	3.00	7.00	12.00
	b. 1966.	3.00	7.00	12.00
FX35	**50 KOPEKS**			
		Reported Not Confirmed		
FX36	**1 RUBLE**			
	1965; 1967. Black on gray-green unpt in red-brown frame. Back red-brown.			
	a. 1965.	8.00	16.00	30.00
	b. 1967.	8.00	16.00	30.00
FX37	**3 RUBLES**			
		Reported Not Confirmed		
FX38	**5 RUBLES**			
	1965. Black on gray-green unpt in red-brown frame. Back red-brown.	12.00	22.00	45.00
FX39	**10 RUBLES**			
		Reported Not Confirmed		
FX40	**20 RUBLES**			
		Reported Not Confirmed		
FX41	**50 RUBLES**			
		Reported Not Confirmed		
FX42	**100 RUBLES**			
		Reported Not Confirmed		

1965-66; 1972 NO BAND ISSUE

		VF	XF	UNC
FX45	**1 KOPEK**			
	1965; 1966. Black on light orange unpt. in dark green frame. Back dark green.			
	a. 1965.	0.75	1.50	4.50
	b. 1966.	0.50	1.00	4.00
FX46	**2 KOPEK**			
	1965; 1966. Black on light orange unpt. in dark green frame. Back dark green.			
	a. 1965.	0.75	1.50	4.50
	b. 1966.	0.50	1.00	4.00
FX47	**5 KOPEK**			
	1965; 1966; 1972. Black on light orange unpt. in dark green frame. Back dark green.			
	a. 1965.	1.00	2.00	5.00
	b. 1966.	0.75	1.50	4.50
	c. 1972.	1.25	2.50	6.50
FX48	**10 KOPEK**			
	1966; 1972. Black on light orange unpt. in dark green frame. Back dark green.			
	a. 1966.	2.00	4.00	8.00
	b. 1972.	2.50	5.00	10.00
FX49	**25 KOPEK**			
	1966. Black on light orange unpt. in dark green frame. Back dark green.	4.00	8.00	15.00
FX50	**50 KOPEK**			
	1965. Black on light orange unpt. in dark green frame. Back dark green.	5.00	10.00	20.00
FX51	**1 RUBLE**			
	1966. Black on gray-green unpt. in red-brown frame. Back red-brown.	8.00	16.00	28.00

		VF	XF	UNC
FX52	**3 RUBLE**			
	1966. Black on gray-green unpt. in red-brown frame. Back red-brown.	15.00	24.00	35.00
FX53	**5 RUBLE**			
	1968. Black on gray-green unpt. in red-brown frame. Back red-brown.	20.00	32.00	45.00
FX54	**10 RUBLES**			
		Reported Not Confirmed		
FX55	**20 RUBLES**			
		Reported Not Confirmed		

FX56	50 RUBLES		VF	XF	UNC
					Reported Not Confirmed
FX57	100 RUBLES				Reported Not Confirmed

1976 CIVILIAN ISSUE

FX60	1 KOPEK	VF	XF	UNC
	1976. Light orange, brown, blue. Back light brown, purple.	0.25	0.50	1.50
FX61	2 KOPEK			
	1976. Light orange, red-brown and blue. Back pink, dark green.	0.35	0.75	1.75
FX62	5 KOPEK			
	1976. Light orange, dark and light blue. Back light blue and dark red.	0.50	1.00	2.00
FX63	10 KOPEK			
	1976. Light orange, dark and light blue. Back blue and dark green.	0.75	1.50	3.00

FX64	25 KOPEK	VF	XF	UNC
	1976. Light orange, blue and purple. Back lilac and dark turquoise.	1.00	2.00	4.50
FX65	50 KOPEK			
	1976. Light orange, blue and green. Back green and brown.	2.00	4.00	8.00

FX66	1 RUBLE	VF	XF	UNC
	1976. Red-brown, green and m/c. Back brown and gray.	1.00	2.50	5.00
FX67	3 RUBLE			
	1976. Green, orange and m/c. Back blue and green.	2.50	5.00	10.00

FX68	5 RUBLE	VF	XF	UNC
	1976. Green, dark blue and m/c. Back turquoise and blue-gray.	3.50	7.00	15.00
FX69	10 RUBLES			
	1976. Light blue, red-brown and m/c. Back light brown, light red.	5.00	12.00	25.00
FX70	20 RUBLES			
	1976. Blue-green, dark red and m/c. Back dark green and gray-red.	10.00	18.00	35.00

FX71	50 RUBLES	VF	XF	UNC
	1976. Blue-green, green and red. Back brown-red and gray-green.	10.00	30.00	80.00
FX72	100 RUBLES			
	1976. Turquoise and brown. Back dark blue-green and brown.	25.00	50.00	160.00
FX73	250 RUBLES			
	1976. Pink, brown and m/c. Back olive and pink.	40.00	100.00	200.00

FX74	500 RUBLES	VF	XF	UNC
	1977.	75.00	150.00	300.00

GOSBANK (ГОСУДАРСТВЕННЫЙ ВАНК СССР)

1961 ISSUE

#FX80-FX85 issued in booklets. Used on ships to buy food.

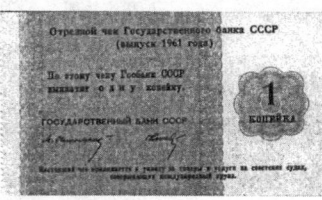

FX80	1 KOPEK	VF	XF	UNC
	1961. 2 sign. varieties.	1.00	2.00	4.00

FX81	2 KOPEK	VF	XF	UNC
	1961. 2 sign. varieties.	1.00	2.00	4.00
FX82	5 KOPEK			
	1961.	2.00	5.00	10.00
FX83	10 KOPEK			
	1961.			Reported Not Confirmed
FX84	50 KOPEK			
	1961.	7.50	15.00	30.00
FX85	1 RUBLE			
	1961.			Reported Not Confirmed

1967-74 SERIES

FX90	1 KOPEK	VF	XF	UNC
	1970; 1972; 1974.	1.00	2.00	4.00
FX91	2 KOPEK			
	1967; 1970.	1.00	2.00	4.00

FX92	5 KOPEK	VF	XF	UNC
	1967; 1970.	1.25	2.50	5.00
FX93	10 KOPEK			
	1970.	1.50	3.00	6.00

1970-76 ISSUE

FX95	1 KOPEK	VF	XF	UNC
	1970; 1974; 1976.	1.25	2.50	5.00
FX96	2 KOPEK			
	1970; 1976.	1.25	2.50	5.00
FX97	5 KOPEK			
	1976.			Reported Not Confirmed
FX98	10 KOPEK			
	1976.	1.50	3.00	6.00

NOTICE

Readers with unlisted dates, signature varieties, etc. are invited to submit photocopies of their notes to: Standard Catalog of World Paper Money, 700 East State St. Iola, WI 54990-0001, E-Mail: george.cuhaj@fwpubs.com.

VNESHTORGBANK (ВАНКА ДАЯВНЕШНЕЙ ТОРГОВАЙ ТОРГОВАЙ СССР)

1973 ISSUE

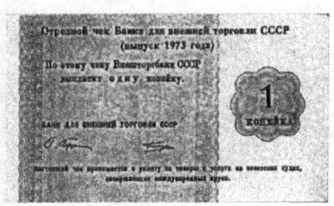

		VF	XF	UNC
FX100	1 KOPEK 1973.	1.00	3.00	6.00
FX101	2 KOPEK 1973.	—	—	—
FX102	5 KOPEK 1973.	—	—	—
FX103	10 KOPEK 1973.	—	—	—
FX104	50 KOPEK 1973.	—	—	—
FX105	1 RUBLE 1973.	—	—	—

1975 ISSUE

		VF	XF	UNC
FX110	1 KOPEK 1975.	1.00	3.00	6.00
FX111	2 KOPEK 1975.	1.50	3.50	7.00
FX112	5 KOPEK 1975.	2.00	4.00	8.00
FX113	10 KOPEK 1975.	2.50	4.50	9.00
FX114	50 KOPEK 1975.	—	—	—
FX115	1 RUBLE 1975.	—	—	—

1978 ISSUE

FX120-124 similar to FX95-98 but for new script on note.

		VF	XF	UNC
FX120	5 KOPEK 1978.	1.00	2.50	5.00
FX121	10 KOPEK 1978; 1980.	1.50	3.00	7.50

		VF	XF	UNC
FX122	50 KOPEK 1978.	2.00	5.00	9.00
FX123	1 RUBLE 1978.	3.00	8.00	14.00
FX124	5 RUBLE 1978.	5.00	10.00	20.00

BANK OF FOREIGN TRADE

1977; 1980 CRUISE SHIP SERIES

		VF	XF	UNC
FX135	1 KOPEK 1977; 1980.			
	a. 1977; 1980. W/o serial #.	0.15	0.50	1.00
	b. 1977. With serial #.	0.25	0.75	1.50

		VF	XF	UNC
FX136	2 KOPEK 1977; 1980.			
	a. 1977; 1980. W/o serial #.	0.15	0.50	1.00
	b. 1977. With serial #.	0.25	0.75	1.50

		VF	XF	UNC
FX137	5 KOPEK 1977; 1980.		Reported Not Confirmed	
	a. 1977; 1980. W/o serial #.	0.25	0.50	1.25
	b. 1977. With serial #.			

		VF	XF	UNC
FX138	10 KOPEK 1977; 1980.		Reported Not Confirmed	
	a. 1977; 1980. W/o serial #.			
	b. 1977. With serial #.	0.50	1.00	2.00
FX139	50 KOPEK 1977; 1980.			
	a. W/o serial #.	1.00	2.00	4.00
	b. With serial #.	1.00	2.00	4.00
FX140	1 RUBLE 1977; 1980.			
	a. W/o serial #.	2.00	4.00	8.00
	b. With serial #.	2.00	4.00	8.00

1985 CRUISE SHIP SERIES

This series has a white border around the printed area, the notes are larger than series 1977 and 1980.

		VF	XF	UNC
FX141	5 KOPEK 1985.	0.25	0.75	1.50

		VF	XF	UNC
FX142	10 KOPEK 1985.	0.50	1.00	1.75

		VF	XF	UNC
FX143	50 KOPEK 1985.	0.75	1.50	2.50
FX144	1 RUBLE 1985.	1.00	2.00	4.00

		VF	XF	UNC
FX145	5 RUBLE 1985.	1.25	2.50	5.00

1979; 1980 DIPLOMATIC SERIES

		VF	XF	UNC
FX146	1 KOPEK			
	1979; 1980.	0.10	0.35	0.75
FX147	2 KOPEK			
	1979; 1980.	0.15	0.40	0.85

		VF	XF	UNC
FX148	5 KOPEK			
	1979; 1980.	0.20	0.50	1.00

		VF	XF	UNC
FX149	10 KOPEK			
	1979; 1980.	0.20	0.50	1.00
FX150	20 KOPEK			
	1979; 1980.	0.50	1.00	2.00
FX151	50 KOPEK			
	1979; 1980.	0.50	1.00	2.00
FX152	1 RUBLE			
	1979; 1980.	1.00	2.00	4.00
FX153	2 RUBLE			
	1979; 1980.	1.00	2.50	5.00
FX154	5 RUBLE			
	1979; 1980.	1.50	3.00	6.00
FX155	10 RUBLES			
	1979; 1980.	—	Rare	—
FX156	25 RUBLES			
	1979; 1980.	—	Rare	—

BANK FOR FOREIGN ECONOMIC ACTIVITY

1989 SERIES

		VF	XF	UNC
FX157	5 KOPEK			
	1989.	0.25	0.75	1.50

		VF	XF	UNC
FX158	10 KOPEK			
	1989.	0.50	1.00	1.75
FX159	50 KOPEK	VF	XF	UNC
	1989.	0.75	1.50	2.50
FX160	1 RUBLE			
	1989.	1.00	2.00	4.00
FX161	5 RUBLE			
	1989.	1.25	2.50	5.00
FX162	10 RUBLES			
	1989.	—	Rare	—
FX163	25 RUBLES			
	1989.	—	Rare	—

HARD CURRENCY NOTES

1976 MILITARY ISSUE

		VF	XF	UNC
M10	1 KOPEK	7.50	16.00	35.00
	1976. Light orange, brown, blue. Back light brown, purple.			

		VG	VF	UNC
M11	2 KOPEK	8.00	17.50	40.00
	1976. Light orange, red-brown and blue. Back pink, dark green.			
M12	5 KOPEK	8.00	18.00	40.00
	1976. Light orange, dark and light blue. Back light blue and dark red.			
M13	10 KOPEK	10.00	20.00	45.00
	1976. Light orange, dark and light blue. Back blue and dark green.			
M14	25 KOPEK	Reported Not Confirmed		
	1976. Light orange, blue and purple. Back lilac and dark turquoise.			
M15	50 KOPEK	15.00	30.00	60.00
	1976. Light orange, blue and green. Back green and brown.			
M16	1 RUBLE	3.00	8.00	25.00
	1976. Red-brown, green and m/c. Back brown and gray.			
M17	3 RUBLE	5.00	10.00	30.00
	1976. Green, orange and m/c. Back blue and green.			
M18	5 RUBLE	5.00	10.00	30.00
	1976. Green, dark blue and m/c. Black turquoise and blue-gray.			
M19	10 RUBLES	7.50	15.00	40.00
	1976. Light blue, red-brown and m/c. Back light brown, light red.			
M20	20 RUBLES	VF	XF	UNC
	1976. Blue-green, dark red and m/c. Back dark green and gray-red.	15.00	50.00	150.00

		VG	VF	UNC
M21	50 RUBLES	—	—	—
	1976. Blue-green, green and red. Back brown-red and gray-green.			
M22	100 RUBLES	15.00	50.00	325.00
	1976. Turquoise and brown. Back dark blue-green and brown.			
M23	250 RUBLES	Reported Not Confirmed		
	1976. Pink, brown and m/c. Back olive and pink.			
M24	500 RUBLES	Reported Not Confirmed		
	1976.			

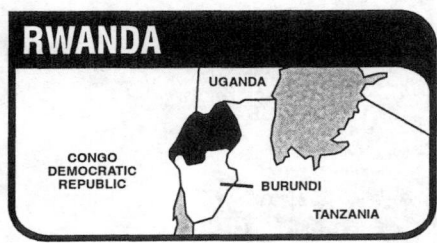

The Republic of Rwanda, located in central Africa between the Republic of the Congo and Tanzania, has an area of 10,169 sq. mi. (26,340 sq. km.) and a population of 7.67 million. Capital: Kigali. The economy is based on agriculture and mining. Coffee and tin are exported.

German lieutenant Count von Goetzen was the first European to visit Rwanda, 1894. Four years later the court of the Mwami (the Tutsi king of Rwanda) willingly permitted the kingdom to become a protectorate of Germany. In 1916, during the African campaigns of World War I, Belgian troops from the Congo occupied Rwanda. After the war it, together with Burundi, became a Belgian League of Nations mandate under the name of the Territory of Ruanda-Urundi. Following World War II, Ruanda-Urundi became a Belgian administered U.N. trust territory. The Tutsi monarchy was deposed by the U.N. supervised election of 1961, after which Belgium granted Rwanda internal autonomy. On July 1, 1962, the U.N. terminated the Belgian trusteeship and granted full independence to both Rwanda and Burundi. Banknotes were used in common with the Belgian Congo, and later with Burundi.

A coup in 1973 established a military government in the 1980's. There was increasing tension with refugees from neighboring Uganda, culminating in a 1990 Tutsi invasion. U.N. forces were posted in 1994-96 but civil strife continues.

Also see Belgian Congo, Rwanda-Burundi.

MONETARY SYSTEM:
1 Franc (Amafranga, Amafaranga) = 100 Centimes

REPLACEMENT NOTES:
#6e, 17:ZZ prefix. #12, VV prefix. Others probably exist.

REPUBLIC

BANQUE NATIONALE DU RWANDA

BANKI NASIYONALI Y'U RWANDA

1962 PROVISIONAL ISSUE

#1-5 ovpt: *BANQUE NATIONALE DU RWANDA* and sign. title: *LE GOUVERNEUR* on Banque d'Emission du Rwanda et du Burundi notes.

#1-3 stamped ovpt.

		Good	Fine	XF
1	**20 FRANCS** ND (1962 -old date 5.10.1960). Green on tan and pink unpt. Maroon or black ovpt. on Rwanda-Burundi #3.	70.00	190.00	475.00

		Good	Fine	XF
2	**50 FRANCS** ND (1962 -old dates 15.9.1960; 1.10.1960). Red on m/c unpt. Maroon ovpt. on Rwanda-Burundi #4.	75.00	250.00	600.00

		Good	Fine	XF
3	**100 FRANCS** ND (1962 -old dates 15.9.1960; 1.10.1960; 31.7.1962). Blue on lt. green and tan unpt. Ovpt. on Rwanda-Burundi #5. a. Black ovpt. b. Purple ovpt.	 75.00 75.00	 150.00 150.00	 375.00 375.00
4	**500 FRANCS** ND (1962 -old dates 15.9.1960; 15.9.1961). Lilac-brown on m/c unpt. Embossed ovpt. and blind embossed facsimile sign. on Rwanda-Burundi #6.	300.00	850.00	1300.00
5	**1000 FRANCS** ND (1962 -old dates 15.5.1961; 1.7.1962). Green on m/c unpt. Embossed ovpt. and blind facsimile sign. on Rwanda-Burundi #7.	250.00	800.00	1250.00

1964 ISSUE

#6-10 various date and sign. title varieties. Replacement notes: Serial # prefix *ZZ.*

		VG	VF	UNC
6	**20 FRANCS** 1964-76. Brown on m/c unpt. Flag of Rwanda at l. 4 young boys at l. ctr. w/pipeline in background at ctr. on back. a. Sign. titles: *VICE-GOUVERNEUR* and *GOUVERNEUR,* w/security thread. 1.7.1964; 31.3.1966; 15.3.1969. b. Sign. titles: *VICE GOUVERNEUR* and *ADMINISTRATEUR,* w/security thread. 1.7.1965. c. Sign. titles: *GOUVERNEUR* and *ADMINISTRATEUR,* w/security thread. 1.7.1971. d. Sign. titles: *ADMINISTRATEUR* and *ADMINISTRATEUR,* w/security thread. 30.10.1974. e. Sign. titles: *ADMINISTRATEUR* and *GOUVERNEUR,* w/o security thread. 1.1.1976. s1. As a. Specimen. 1.7.1964; 31.3.1966; 15.3.1969. s2. As b. Specimen. 1.7.1965. s3. As c. Specimen. 1.7.1971. s4. As d. Specimen. 30.10.1974.	 1.00 1.25 1.00 0.25 0.25 — — — —	 7.50 10.00 3.00 1.50 0.75 — — — —	 15.00 20.00 7.50 6.00 1.00 5.00 3.50 3.50 6.00

		VG	VF	UNC
7	**50 FRANCS** 1964-76. Blue on green unpt. Map of Rwanda at l. ctr. Miner at l. w/miners digging at ctr. a. Sign. titles: *VICE-GOUVERNEUR* and *GOUVERNEUR,* w/security thread. 1.7.1964; 31.1.1966; 1.9.1969. b. Sign. titles: *ADMINISTRATEUR* and *GOUVERNEUR,* w/security thread. 1.7.1971; 30.10.1974. c. Sign. titles: *ADMINISTRATEUR* and *GOUVERNEUR,* w/o security thread. 1.1.1976. s1. As a. Specimen. 1.7.1964; 31.1.1966; 1.9.1969. s2. As b. Specimen. 1.7.1971; 30.10.1974.	 1.00 0.50 0.25 — —	 10.00 2.00 1.00 — —	 20.00 7.00 2.50 4.00 4.00

8   **100 FRANCS**

	VG	VF	UNC
1964-76. Purple on m/c unpt. Map of Rwanda at l. Woman w/basket on head at l., banana trees at ctr. on back.			
a. Sign. titles: *VICE-GOUVERNEUR* and *GOUVERNEUR,* w/security thread. 1.7.1964; 31.3.1966; 31.10.1969.	1.00	3.50	10.00
b. Sign. titles: *VICE-GOUVERNEUR* and *ADMINISTRATEUR,* w/security thread. 1.7.1965.	2.50	8.00	20.00
c. Sign. titles: *ADMINISTRATEUR* and *GOUVERNEUR,* w/security thread. 1.7.1971; 30.10.1974.	1.00	3.50	8.50
d. Sign. titles: *ADMINISTRATEUR* and *GOUVERNEUR,* w/o security thread. 1.1.1976.	0.25	1.50	4.00
s1. As a. Specimen. 1.7.1964; 31.10.1969.	—	—	6.00
s2. As c. Specimen. 1.7.1971; 30.10.1974.	—	—	6.00

9   **500 FRANCS**

	VG	VF	UNC
1964-76. Dk. green and m/c. Arms of Rwanda at l. Man w/basket on head at l., rows of plants in background on back.			
a. Sign. titles: *VICE-GOUVERNEUR* and *GOUVERNEUR.* 1.7.1964; 31.3.1966; 31.10.1969.	3.50	10.00	42.50
b. Sign. titles: *ADMINISTRATEUR* and *GOUVERNEUR.* 1.7.1971; 30.10.1974; 1.1.1976.	2.50	7.50	25.00
s1. As a. Specimen. 1.7.1964; 31.3.1966.	—	—	12.50
s2. As b. Specimen. 1.7.1971; 30.10.1974	—	—	12.50

10   **1000 FRANCS**

	VG	VF	UNC
1964-76. Red and m/c. Arms of Rwanda at l. Man and terraced hills at ctr. on back.			
a. Sign. titles: *VICE-GOUVERNEUR* and *GOUVERNEUR.* 1.7.1964; 31.3.1966; 15.3.1969.	7.50	25.00	80.00
b. Sign. titles: *ADMINISTRATEUR>* and *GOUVERNEUR.* 1.7.1971; 30.10.1974.	7.50	20.00	45.00
c. Printed sign. titles like b. 1.1.1976.	5.00	15.00	30.00
s1. As a. Specimen. 31.3.1966; 15.3.1969.	—	—	17.50
s2. As b. Specimen. 1.7.1971.	—	—	17.50

1974 ISSUE

11   **500 FRANCS**

	VG	VF	UNC
19.4.1974. Green and m/c. Gen. Habyarimana at l. Back like #9.			
a. Issued note.	2.00	10.00	25.00
s. Specimen.	—	—	10.00

1978 ISSUE

12   **100 FRANCS**

	VG	VF	UNC
1.1.1978. Gray on lt. blue and m/c unpt. Zebras. Woman carrying child at l., mountains in background at ctr. r. on back.			
a. Issued note.	0.50	2.50	7.00
s. Specimen.	—	—	12.50

13   **500 FRANCS**

	VG	VF	UNC
1.1.1978. Brown, orange and m/c. Impalas. 8 drummers at l., strip mining at r. on back.			
a. Wmk: Impala's head.	1.00	7.50	15.00
b. W/o wmk.	20.00	60.00	150.00
s. As a. Specimen.	—	—	20.00

14 1000 FRANCS
1.1.1978. Green and m/c. Boys picking tea leaves at l. Tribal dancer at r. on back. Wmk: Impala's head.

	VG	VF	UNC
a. Issued note.	4.00	15.00	35.00
s. Specimen.	—	—	25.00

15 5000 FRANCS
1.1.1978. Green, blue and m/c. Female w/basket on her head at l., field workers at ctr. Lake and mountains on back. Wmk: Impala's head.

	VG	VF	UNC
a. Issued note.	40.00	65.00	150.00
s. Specimen.	—	—	100.00

1981 ISSUE

16 500 FRANCS
1.7.1981. Brown and m/c. Arms at l., 3 Impala at r. Men working in field at l. on back. Wmk: Crowned crane's head.

	VG	VF	UNC
a. Issued note.	2.00	7.50	22.50
s. Specimen.	—	—	20.00

17 1000 FRANCS
1.7.1981. Green, brown and m/c. 2 Watusi warriors at r. 2 Eastern Gorillas at l., canoe in lake at r. on back. Wmk: Crowned crane's head.

	VG	VF	UNC
a. Issued note.	4.00	12.00	30.00
s. Specimen.	—	—	32.50

1982 ISSUE

18 100 FRANCS
1.8.1982. Black on lilac and m/c unpt. Zebras at ctr. and r. Back purple and m/c; woman carrying baby at l., view of mountains at ctr. Wmk: Impala's head.

VG	VF	UNC
0.25	1.50	4.00

1988-89 ISSUE

#19, 21 and 22 similar to #18, #17 and #15, but new spelling *AMAFARANGA* on back. Slight color differences and new sign. titles: *2E VICE-GOUVERNEUR* and *GOUVERNEUR*.

19 100 FRANCS
24.4.1989. Similar to #18.

VG	VF	UNC
0.25	1.25	3.00

#20 *Not assigned.*

21 1000 FRANCS
1.1.1988; 24.4.1989. Similar to #17.

VG	VF	UNC
2.50	7.50	20.00

22	5000 FRANCS	VG	VF	UNC
	1.1.1988; 24.4.1989. Similar to #15.	7.50	30.00	60.00

1994 ISSUE

#23-25 mountainous landscape at ctr. r. Wmk: Impala's head. Printer: G&D (w/o imprint).

23	500 FRANCS	VG	VF	UNC
	1.12.1994. Blue-black, black and dk. blue-green on m/c unpt.	FV	FV	7.50
	Female Waterbuck at l. ctr. on back.			

24	1000 FRANCS	VG	VF	UNC
	1.12.1994. Purple, red-brown and dk. brown on m/c unpt.	FV	FV	15.00
	Vegetation at l., African Buffalo at ctr. on back.			

25	5000 FRANCS	VG	VF	UNC
	1.12.1994. Dk. brown, violet and purple on m/c unpt. Reclining lion	FV	FV	50.00
	at l. ctr. on back.			

1998 ISSUE

26	500 FRANCS	VG	VF	UNC
	1.12.1998. Blue and green on m/c unpt. Mountain gorillas at r.	FV	FV	7.00
	National Museum of Butare and schoolchildren on back.			

27	1000 FRANCS	VG	VF	UNC
	1.12.1998. Blue and brown on m/c unpt. Volcano range at r. Tea	FV	FV	15.00
	plantation and cattle on back.			

28	5000 FRANCS	VG	VF	UNC
	1.12.1998. Black, red and green on m/c unpt. *Intore* dancers at r.	FV	FV	50.00
	National Bank bldg. on back.			

2003 ISSUE

29	100 FRANCS	VG	VF	UNC
	1.5.2003. Green, brown and blue on yellow unpt. Oxen and farmer	FV	FV	2.00
	plowing at ctr. Mountain and lake on back.			

Rwanda-Burundi, a Belgian League of Nations mandate and United Nations trust territory comprising the provinces of Rwanda and Burundi of the former colony of German East Africa, was located in central Africa between the present Republic of the Congo, Uganda and mainland Tanzania. The mandate-trust territory had an area of 20,916 sq. mi. (54,272 sq. km.).

For specific statistics and history of Rwanda and Burundi see individual entries.

When Rwanda and Burundi were formed into a mandate for administration by Belgium, their names were changed to Ruanda and Urundi and they were organized as an integral part of the Belgian Congo, during which time they used a common banknote issue with the Belgian Congo. After the Belgian Congo acquired independence as the Republic of the Congo, the provinces of Ruanda and Urundi reverted to their former names of Rwanda and Burundi and issued notes with both names on them. In 1962, both Rwanda and Burundi became separate independent states.

Also see Belgian Congo, Burundi and Rwanda.

MONETARY SYSTEM:
1 Franc = 100 Centimes

BANQUE D'EMISSION DU RWANDA ET DU BURUNDI

1960 ISSUE

#1-7 various date and sign. varieties.

1	5 FRANCS	VG	VF	UNC
	1960-63. Lt. brown on green unpt. Impala at l.			
	a. 15.9.1960; 15.5.1961.	12.50	50.00	200.00
	b. 15.4.1963.	15.00	60.00	250.00

2	10 FRANCS	Good	Fine	XF
	15.9.1960; 5.10.1960. Dull gray on pale blue and pale orange unpt.	15.00	65.00	225.00
	Hippopotamus at l. Printer: TDLR.			

3	20 FRANCS	Good	Fine	XF
	15.9.1960; 5.10.1960. Green on tan and pink unpt. Crocodile at r.	20.00	85.00	325.00
	Printer: TDLR.			

30	500 FRANCS	VG	VF	UNC
	2004. M/c.	FV	FV	6.00

31	1000 FRANCS	VG	VF	UNC
	2004. M/c. Doggett's Guenon.	FV	FV	12.50

		Good	Fine	XF
4	**50 FRANCS** 15.9.1960; 1.10.1960. Red on m/c unpt. Lioness at ctr. r.	20.00	75.00	300.00

		Good	Fine	XF
5	**100 FRANCS** 15.9.1960; 1.10.1960; 31.7.1962. Blue on lt. green and tan unpt. Zebu at l.	15.00	60.00	175.00

		Good	Fine	XF
6	**500 FRANCS** 15.9.1960; 15.5.1961; 15.9.1961. Lilac-brown on m/c unpt. Black Rhinoceros at ctr. r.	185.00	800.00	1600.00

		VF	XF	UNC
7	**1000 FRANCS** 15.9.1960; 15.5.1961; 31.7.1962. Green on m/c unpt. Zebra at r. a. Issued note.	165.00	700.001 450.00	1450.00
	ct. Color trial in purple on m/c unpt.			1500.00

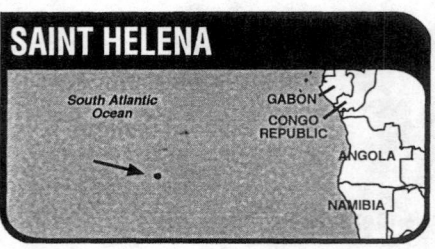

SAINT HELENA

The Colony of St. Helena, a British colony located about 1,150 miles (1,850 km.) from the west coast of Africa, has an area of 47 sq. mi. (122 sq. km.) and a population of 5,700. Capital: Jamestown. Flax, lace and rope are produced for export. Ascension and Tristan da Cunha are dependencies of St. Helena. The island was discovered and named by the Portuguese navigator João da Nova Castella in 1502. The Portuguese imported livestock, fruit trees and vegetables but established no permanent settlement. The Dutch occupied the island temporarily, 1645-1651. The original European settlement was founded by representatives of the British East India Company sent to annex the island after the departure of the Dutch. The Dutch returned and captured St. Helena from the British on New Year's Day, 1673, but were in turn ejected by a British force under Sir Richard Munden. Thereafter St. Helena was the undisputed possession of Great Britain. The island served as the place of exile for Napoleon, several Zulu chiefs, and and an ex-Sultan of Zanzibar.

St. Helena banknotes are also used on the islands of Assencion and Tristan de Cunia.

RULERS:
  British

MONETARY SYSTEM:
  1 Pound = 20 Shillings to 1971
  1 Pound = 100 New Pence, 1971-

SIGNATURE VARIETIES			
1			
2			
3			
4			
5			
6			

BRITISH ADMINISTRATION

GOVERNMENT OF ST. HELENA

1976; 1979 ND ISSUE

#5-8 views of the island at l., Qn. Elizabeth II at r.

#5-7 Royal arms w/motto at l., shield w/ship at ctr. r. on back.

		VG	VF	UNC
5	**50 PENCE** ND (1979). Purple on pink and pale yellow-green unpt. Correctly spelled *ANGLIAE* in motto. Sign. 2.			
	a. Issued note.	FV	3.00	27.50
	s. Specimen.	—	—	—

Note: #5 w/serial #170,001-200,000 are non-redeemable.

9	1 POUND		VG	VF	UNC
	ND (1981). Deep olive-green on pale orange and ochre unpt. Like #6 but corrected spelling *ANGLIAE* in motto. Reduced size, 147 x 66mm. Sign. 2.				
	a. Issued note.		FV	FV	9.00
	s. Specimen.		—	—	

Note: #9 w/serial #*A/1* 350,000 - *A/1* 400,000 are non-redeemable.

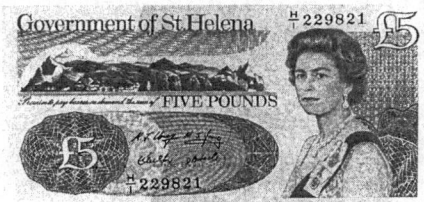

10	20 POUNDS		VG	VF	UNC
	ND (1986). Dk. brown on m/c unpt. Harbor view at l. ctr. Back lt. green; arms at ctr. 4 signs. in block form. Sign. 4. 164 x 85mm.				
	a. Issued note.		FV	FV	100.00
	s. Specimen.		—	—	

6	1 POUND		VG	VF	UNC
	ND (1976). Deep olive-green on pale orange and ochre unpt. Incorrect spelling *ANGLAE* in motto. 153 x 67mm.				
	a. Issued note.		FV	10.00	50.00
	s. Specimen.		—	—	

1998 ND Issue

11	5 POUNDS		VG	VF	UNC
	ND (1998). Similar to #7, but reduced size. 4 signs. in block form. Sign. 5. 135 x 71mm.				
	a. Issued note.		FV	FV	30.00
	s. Specimen.		—	—	85.00

2004 Issue

#12-13, Qn. Elizabeth II at r. Year on back. 135x71mm. Four sign. in block form.

7	5 POUNDS		VG	VF	UNC
	ND (1976). Blue on lt. brown unpt. 152x74mm.				
	a. Incorrect spelling *ANGLAE* in motto. Sign. 1. (1976).		FV	10.00	65.00
	b. Corrected spelling *ANGLIAE* in motto. Sign. 2. (1981).		FV	FV	37.50
	s. As a. Specimen.		—	—	150.00

12	10 POUNDS		VG	VF	UNC
	2004. Rose on m/c unpt. Historic harbor view at l. Arms at l. large 10 at r. on back.				
	a. Issued note.		FV	FV	50.00
	s. Specimen (300 issued).		—	—	100.00

8	10 POUNDS		VG	VF	UNC
	ND (1979). Pale red on m/c unpt. Arms on back, correctly spelled *ANGLIAE* in motto. 159x80mm.				
	a. Sign. 2. (1979).		FV	FV	110.00
	b. Sign. 3. (1985).		FV	FV	55.00
	c. As a. Uncut sheet of 3.		—	—	350.00
	r. Remainder w/o sign. or serial #.		—	—	180.00
	s. As a. Specimen.		—	—	→

1981; 1986 ND Issue

#9 and 10 Qn. Elizabeth II at r.

13	20 POUNDS		VG	VF	UNC
	2004. Brown on m/c unpt. Modern harbor view. Arms at l. large 20 at r. on back.				
	a. Issued note.		FV	FV	100.00
	s. Specimen (300 issued).		—	—	140.00

SAINT PIERRE & MIQUELON

CANADA (Quebec)

Newfoundland

Atlantic Ocean

The Territorial Collectivity of St. Pierre and Miquelon, a French overseas territory located 10 miles (16 km.) off the south coast of Newfoundland, has an area of 93 sq. mi. (242 sq. km.) and a population of about 6,000. Capital: St. Pierre. The economy of the barren archipelago is based on cod fishing and fur farming Fish and fish products, and mink and silver fox pelts are exported.

The islands, occupied by the French in 1604, were captured by the British in 1702 and held until 1763 when they were returned to the possession of France and employed as a fishing station. They passed between France and England on six more occasions between 1778 and 1814 when they were awarded permanently to France by the Treaty of Paris. The rugged, soil-poor granite islands, which will support only evergreen shrubs, are all that remain to France of her extensive colonies in North America. In 1958 St. Pierre and Miquelon voted in favor of the new constitution of the Fifth Republic of France, thereby choosing to remain within the French Community.

Notes of the Banque de France circulated 1937-1942; afterwards notes of the Caisse Centrale de la France Libre and the Caisse Centrale de la France d'Outre-Mer were in use.

RULERS:
　French

MONETARY SYSTEM:
　1 Franc = 100 Centimes
　1 Nouveau Franc = 100 "old" Francs, 1960-

CAISSE CENTRALE DE LA FRANCE D'OUTRE-MER

SAINT-PIERRE-ET-MIQUELON

1960 ND PROVISIONAL ISSUE

#30-35 ovpt: *SAINT-PIERRE-ET-MIQUELON* and new denomination.

30	1 NOUVEAU FRANC ON 50 FRANCS	VG	VF	UNC
	ND (1960). M/c. Ovpt. on Reunion #25.			
	a. Special series *A.1-Y.1* w/3 digit serial # and 5 digit control #.	10.00	40.00	200.00
	b. Normal series w/5 digit serial # and 9 digit control #.	6.00	20.00	75.00
	s. As a, b. Specimen.	—	—	—

1961; 1963 ND PROVISIONAL ISSUE

31	1 NOUVEAU FRANC ON 50 FRANCS	VG	VF	UNC
	ND (1961). M/c. B. d'Esnambuc at l., ship at r. Woman on back.	35.00	200.00	650.00

32	2 NOUVEAUX FRANCS ON 100 FRANCS	VG	VF	UNC
	ND (1963). M/c. La Bourdonnais at l., 2 women at r. Woman looking at mountains on back.	6.00	25.00	90.00

33	10 NOUVEAUX FRANCS ON 500 FRANCS	VG	VF	UNC
	ND (1964). M/c. Bldgs. and sailboat at l., 2 women at r. Ox-carts w/wood and plants on back.	15.00	60.00	275.00

34	20 NOUVEAUX FRANCS ON 1000 FRANCS	VG	VF	UNC
	ND (1964). M/c. 2 women at r. Women at r., 2 men in small boat on back.	35.00	110.00	375.00

35	100 NOUVEAUX FRANCS ON 5000 FRANCS	VG	VF	UNC
	ND (1961). M/c. Gen. Schoelcher at ctr. r. Family on back.	85.00	450.00	2000.00

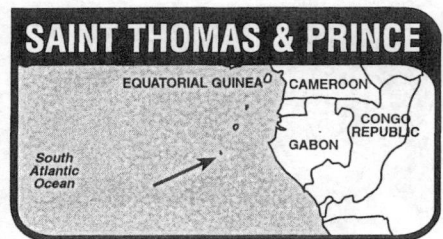

The Democratic Republic of Sao Tomé and Príncipe (formerly the Portuguese overseas province of St. Thomas and Prince Islands) is located in the Gulf of Guinea 150 miles (241 km.) off the West African coast. It has an area of 372 sq. mi. (960 sq. km.) and a population of 149,000. Capital: São Tomé. The economy of the islands is based on cocoa, copra and coffee.

St. Thomas and St. Prince were uninhabited when discovered by Portuguese navigators Joao de Santarem and Pedro de Escobar in 1470. After the failure of their initial settlement, 1485, the Portuguese successfully colonized St. Thomas with a colony of prisoners and exiled Jews, 1493. An initial prosperity based on the sugar trade gave way to a time of misfortune, 1567-1709, that saw the colony attacked and occupied or plundered by the French and Dutch; ravaged by the slave revolt of 1595; and finally rendered destitute by the transfer of the world sugar trade to Brazil. In the late 1800s, the colony turned from the production of sugar to cocoa, the basis of its present prosperity.

The islands were designated a Portuguese overseas province in 1951. On April 25, 1974, the government of Portugal was seized by a military junta which reached agreements providing for independence for the Portuguese overseas provinces of Portuguese Guinea (Guinea-Bissau), Mozambique, Cape Verde Islands, Angola, and St. Thomas and Prince Islands. The Democratic Republic of São Tomé and Príncipe was declared on July 12, 1975.

RULERS:
Portuguese to 1975

MONETARY SYSTEM:
1 Escudo = 100 Centavos, 1911-1976
1 Dobra = 100 Centimos, 1977-

PORTUGUESE ADMINISTRATION

BANCO NACIONAL ULTRAMARINO

S. TOMÉ E PRÍNCIPE

1956-64 ISSUE
#36-39 bank seal at l., Portuguese arms at lower ctr., D. Afonso V at lower r. Printer: BWC.

40	1000 ESCUDOS	VG	VF	UNC
	11.5.1964. Green on m/c unpt. J. de Santarem at r., bank arms at upper ctr. Woman, sailing ships at l. ctr., arms at upper r. on back.			
	a. Issued note.	25.00	95.00	250.00
	ct. Color trial. Purple on m/c unpt.	—	—	300.00
	s. Specimen, punch hole cancelled.	—	—	150.00

1974 CIRCULATING BEARER CHECK ISSUE

41	100 ESCUDOS	VG	VF	UNC
	31.3.1974.	—	—	—
42	500 ESCUDOS			
	28.4.1974.	—	—	—
43	500 ESCUDOS			
	31.12.1974.	45.00	85.00	160.00

43A	1000 ESCUDOS	VG	VF	UNC
	23.12.1974; 31.12.1974. Red.	45.00	85.00	160.00

DEMOCRATIC REPUBLIC

BANCO NACIONAL DE S. TOMÉ E PRÍNCIPE

1976 PROVISIONAL ISSUE
#44-48 new bank name ovpt. in red on both sides of Banco Nacional Ultramarino notes.
#44-46 bank seal at l., Portuguese arms at lower ctr., Kg. D. Afonso V at r. Printer: BWC.

44	20 ESCUDOS	VG	VF	UNC
	1.6.1976 (- old date 20.11.1958). Brown on m/c unpt. Ovpt. on #36.	3.00	10.00	25.00

45	50 ESCUDOS	VG	VF	UNC
	1.6.1976 (- old date 20.11.1958). Brown-violet on m/c unpt. Ovpt. on #37.	3.00	10.00	30.00

46	100 ESCUDOS	VG	VF	UNC
	1.6.1976 (- old date 20.11.1958). Purple on m/c unpt. Ovpt. on #38.	5.00	15.00	45.00

			VG	VF	UNC
47	500 ESCUDOS		15.00	40.00	150.00
	1.6.1976 (- old date 18.4.1956). Blue on m/c unpt. Ovpt. on #39.				
48	1000 ESCUDOS		15.00	40.00	120.00
	1.6.1976 (- old date 11.5.1964). Green on m/c unpt. Ovpt. on #40.				

#49 Deleted. See #43A.

1976 CIRCULATING BEARER CHECK ISSUE

			VG	VF	UNC
50	500 ESCUDOS		10.00	27.50	85.00
	21.6.1976. Black on pink and lt. aqua unpt. 167 x 75mm.				
51	1000 ESCUDOS		12.50	35.00	100.00
	21.6.1976. 167 x 75mm.				

DECRETO-LEI NO. 50/76; 1977 ISSUE

#52-55 Rei Amador at r. and as wmk., arms at lower l. Sign. titles: *O MINISTRO DA COORDENACÃO ECO-NOMICA* and *O GOVERNADOR*. Printer: BWC.

			VG	VF	UNC
52	50 DOBRAS				
	12.7.1977. Red and m/c. African grey parrot at ctr. in unpt. Scene w/2 fishermen in boats on back.				
	a. Issued note.		1.00	3.00	8.00
	s. Specimen.		—	—	125.00

			VG	VF	UNC
53	100 DOBRAS				
	12.7.1977. Green and m/c. Flower at ctr. in unpt. Group of people preparing food on back.				
	a. Issued note.		1.50	4.00	10.00
	s. Specimen.		—	—	125.00

			VG	VF	UNC
54	500 DOBRAS				
	12.7.1977. Purple and m/c. Sea Turtle at ctr. in unpt. Waterfall on back.				
	a. Issued note.		3.00	10.00	25.00
	s. Specimen.		—	—	150.00

			VG	VF	UNC
55	1000 DOBRAS				
	12.7.1977. Blue and m/c. Bananas at ctr. in unpt. Fruit gatherer on back.				
	a. Issued note.		9.00	35.00	90.00
	s. Specimen.		—	—	200.00

DECRETO-LEI NO. 6/82; 1982 ISSUE

#56-59 like #52-55 but w/sign. titles: *O MINISTRO DO PLANO* and *O GOVERNADOR*. Printer: BWC.

			VG	VF	UNC
56	50 DOBRAS		0.75	2.50	6.50
	30.9.1982. Like #52.				

			VG	VF	UNC
57	100 DOBRAS		1.00	3.50	9.00
	30.9.1982. Like #53.				
58	500 DOBRAS		2.50	9.00	22.50
	30.9.1982. Like #54.				

62	1000 DOBRAS	VG	VF	UNC
	4.1.1989. Blue, green and m/c unpt. Like #59.	2.00	7.00	17.50

BANCO CENTRAL DE S.TOMÉ E PRÍNCIPE

DECRETO LEI NO. 29/93; 1993 ISSUE

#63 and 64 like #61 and 62. Ascending size serial #. Printer: TDLR.

59	1000 DOBRAS	VG	VF	UNC
	30.9.1982. Like #55.	3.50	12.00	32.50

DECRETO-LEI NO. 1/88; 1989 ISSUE

#60-62 designs like #57-59 except sign. title at l.: *O MINISTRO DA ECONOMIA E FINANÇAS*. Printer: TDLR.

63	500 DOBRAS	VG	VF	UNC
	26.8.1993. Violet, red, orange and tan on blue and m/c unpt. Like #61 but arms at lower l. is blue. Green serial # at r.	FV	FV	4.00

60	100 DOBRAS	VG	VF	UNC
	4.1.1989. Green and m/c. Like #57.	0.75	2.50	6.00

64	1000 DOBRAS	VG	VF	UNC
	26.8.1993. Purple and deep blue and blue-green on m/c unpt. Similar to #62. Red serial # at r.	FV	FV	10.00

DECRETO LEI NO. 42/96; 1996 ISSUE

#65-68 Rei Amador at r. and as wmk., arms at upper ctr. r. Printer: TDLR. Replacement notes: Serial # prefix ZZ.

61	500 DOBRAS	VG	VF	UNC
	4.1.1989. Violet, red, orange and tan on m/c unpt. Like #58.	1.00	4.00	9.00

65	5000 DOBRAS	VG	VF	UNC
	22.10.1996. Purple, lilac and olive-green on m/c unpt. Papa Figo bird (Principe Glossy Starling) at l. ctr. Esplanade, modern bldg. at l. ctr. on back.			
	a. One security thread.	FV	FV	10.00
	b. Two security threads.	FV	FV	8.00
	s. Specimen.	FV	FV	75.00

66	10,000 DOBRAS	VG	VF	UNC
	22.10.1996. Dk. green, blue-violet and tan on m/c unpt. Emerald Cuckoo at l. ctr. Bridge over river at l. ctr. on back.			
	a. One security thread.	FV	FV	17.50
	b. Two security threads.	FV	FV	15.00
	s. Specimen.	—	—	75.00

67	20,000 DOBRAS	VG	VF	UNC
	22.10.1996. Red, olive-brown and blue-black on m/c unpt. Sao Tome Oriole at l. ctr. Beach scene at l. ctr. on back.			
	a. One security thread.	FV	FV	25.00
	b. Two security threads.	FV	FV	22.50
	s. Specimen.	—	—	75.00

68	50,000 DOBRAS	VG	VF	UNC
	22.10.1996. Brown, purple and red on m/c unpt. Black-winged Kingfisher at l. ctr. Central Bank bldg. at l. ctr. on back.			
	a. One security thread.	FV	FV	50.00
	b. Two security threads.	FV	FV	50.00
	s. Specimen ovpt: ESPECIME, 0's in serial #.	—	—	75.00

Listings for

Samoa, see Western Samoa

SAUDI ARABIA

The Kingdom of Saudi Arabia, an independent and absolute hereditary monarchy comprising the former sultanate of Nejd, the old kingdom of Hejaz, Asir and El Hasa, occupies four-fifths of the Arabian peninsula. The kingdom has an area of 830,000 sq. mi. (2,149,690 sq. km.) and a population of 21.66 million. Capital: Riyadh. The economy is based on oil, which provides 85 percent of Saudi Arabia's revenue.

Mohammed united the Arabs in the 7th century and his followers founded a great empire with its capital at Medina. The Turks established nominal rule over much of Arabia in the 16th and 17th centuries, and in the 18th century divided it into principalities.

The Kingdom of Saudi Arabia was created by King Ibn-Saud (1882-1953), a descendant of earlier Wahabi rulers of the Arabian peninsula. In 1901 he seized Riyadh, capital of the Sultanate of Nejd, and in 1905 established himself as Sultan. In 1913 he captured the Turkish province of Hasa; took the Hejaz in 1925 and by 1926 most of Asir. In 1932 he combined Nejd and Hejaz into the single kingdom of Saudi Arabia. Asir was incorporated into the kingdom a year later.

One of the principal cities, Mecca, is the Holy center of Islam and is the scene of an annual Pilgrimage from the entire Moslem world.

RULERS:
Sa'ud Ibn Abdul Aziz, AH1373-1383/1953-1964AD
Faisal, AH1383-1395/1964-1975AD
Khaled, AH1395-1402/1975-1982AD
Fahd, AH1402-/1982AD-

MONETARY SYSTEM:
1 Riyal = 20 Ghirsh

REPLACEMENT NOTES:
#1-4, serial number starting w/Arabic "O".

KINGDOM

SAUDI ARABIAN MONETARY AGENCY

SIGNATURE VARIETIES		
	GOVERNOR OF SAMA	MINISTER OF FINANCE
1	Anwar Ali	Tallal bin Abdul Aziz
2	Anwar Ali	Musa'id bin Abdul Rahman
3	Abdul Aziz al-Qurashi	Musa'id bin Abdul Rahman
4	Abdul Aziz al-Qurashi	Muhammad Ali Aba Al-Khail
5	Hamad Saud al-Sayyari	Muhammad Ali Aba Al-Khail
6	Hamad Saud al-Sayyari	Ibrahim bin Abdulaziz bin Abdullah al-Assaf

LAW OF 1.7. AH1379; 1961 ND ISSUE

#6-10 arms (palm tree and crossed swords) on back and as wmk. Embedded security thread.

6   1 RIYAL

	VG	VF	UNC
L. AH1379 (1961). Brown on lt. blue and green unpt. Hill of Light at ctr. Back violet-brown and green. Sign. #1.	2.00	10.00	45.00

7   5 RIYALS

	VG	VF	UNC
L. AH1379 (1961). Blue and green on m/c unpt. Fortress at ctr.			
a. Sign. #1.	12.00	75.00	325.00
b. Sign. #2.	20.00	100.00	400.00

8   10 RIYALS

	VG	VF	UNC
L. AH1379 (1961). Green on pink and m/c unpt. Dhows in Jedda harbor.			
a. Sign. #1.	15.00	75.00	325.00
b. Sign. #2.	20.00	100.00	400.00

9   50 RIYALS

	VG	VF	UNC
L. AH1379 (1961). Violet and olive-green on m/c unpt. Derrick at ctr. r.			
a. Sign. #1.	60.00	200.00	800.00
b. Sign. #2.	60.00	175.00	800.00

10   100 RIYALS

	VG	VF	UNC
L. AH1379 (1961). Red on m/c unpt. Bldg. at l., archway in background at ctr., bldg. at r.			
a. Sign. #1.	150.00	650.00	2000.00
b. Sign. #2.	125.00	550.00	1750.00

LAW OF 1.7. AH1379; 1968 ND ISSUE

#11-15 wmk: Arms. Embedded security thread.

11   1 RIYAL

	VG	VF	UNC
L. AH1379 (1968). Purple on m/c unpt. Goverment bldg. at ctr. r. Saudi arms on back.			
a. Sign. #2.	0.50	3.00	15.00
b. Sign. #3.	0.50	4.00	20.00
s. As a. Specimen.	—	—	—

12   5 RIYALS

	VG	VF	UNC
L. AH1379 (1968). Green on m/c unpt. Airport. Oil loading on ships at dockside on back.			
a. Sign. #2.	3.00	15.00	60.00
b. Sign. #3.	5.00	25.00	100.00

13   10 RIYALS
L. AH1379 (1968). Gray-blue on m/c unpt. Mosque. Al-Masa Wall
w/arches on back. Sign. #2.

	VG	VF	UNC
	2.50	15.00	60.00

14   50 RIYALS
L. AH1379 (1968). Brown on m/c unpt. Courtyard of mosque at r.
Saudi arms at l., row of palms at ctr. on back.

	VG	VF	UNC
a. Sign. #2.	20.00	80.00	275.00
b. Sign. #3.	17.50	70.00	250.00

Incorrect   Correct

17   5 RIYALS
L. AH1379 (1977). Green and brown on m/c unpt. Irrigation canal
at ctr. Dam at l. ctr. on back.

	VG	VF	UNC
a. Incorrect Khamsa (five) in lower ctr. panel of text.	1.50	5.00	15.00
b. Correct Khamsa (five) in lower ctr. panel of text.	1.00	2.00	7.50

15   100 RIYALS
L. AH1379 (1966). Red on m/c unpt. Gov't. bldg. at ctr. r. Derricks
at l. ctr. on back.

	VG	VF	UNC
a. Sign. #2.	30.00	100.00	350.00
b. Sign. #3.	25.00	90.00	300.00

LAW OF 1.7. AH1379; 1976; 1977 ND ISSUE

#16-19 portr. Kg. Faisal at r. and as wmk. Sign. 4.

18   10 RIYALS
L. AH1379 (1977). Lilac and brown on m/c unpt. Oil drilling
platform at ctr. Oil refinery on back.

	VG	VF	UNC
	FV	4.00	15.00

16   1 RIYAL
L. AH1379 (1977). Red-brown on m/c unpt. Hill of Light at ctr.
Airport at l. ctr. on back.

	VG	VF	UNC
	0.25	0.75	3.50

19   50 RIYALS
L. AH1379 (1976). Green, purple and brown on m/c unpt. Arches
of mosque at ctr. Courtyard of mosque at l. ctr. on back.

	VG	VF	UNC
	FV	20.00	60.00

20 100 RIYALS
L. AH1379 (1976). Blue and turquoise on m/c unpt. Mosque at ctr.,
Kg. 'Abd al-'Aziz Ibn Saud at r. Long bldg. w/arches on back.

	VG	VF	UNC
	FV	35.00	100.00

LAW OF 1.7. AH1379; 1983; 1984 ND ISSUE

#21-26 wmk: Kg. Fahd.

Lower l. serial # fluoresces gold under UV light. Non-visible portr. of King fluoresces yellow under UV light.

#21-24 upper l. panel also exists w/unnecessary upper accent mark in "Monetary." at ctr. r. in text.

Incorrect	Correct

21 1 RIYAL
L. AH1379 (1984). Dk. brown on m/c unpt. 7th century gold dinar
at l., Portr. Kg. Fahd at ctr. r. Flowers and landscape on back. 2
sign. varieties.

	VG	VF	UNC
a. Incorrect text. Sign. 5.	FV	1.00	2.00
b. Correct "Monetary." Sign. 5; 6.	FV	FV	1.25

22 5 RIYALS
L. AH1379 (1983). Purple, brown, and blue-green on m/c unpt.
Dhows at l., portr. Kg. Fahd at ctr. r. Oil refinery at ctr. r. on back.

	VG	VF	UNC
a. Incorrect text. Sign. 5.	FV	1.50	5.00
b. Correct "Monetary." Sign. 5.	FV	FV	4.00

23 10 RIYALS
L. AH1379 (1983). Black, brown and purple on m/c unpt. Fortress
at l., portr. Kg. Fahd at ctr. r. Palm trees at ctr. r. on back.

	VG	VF	UNC
a. Incorrect text. Sign. 5.	FV	4.00	10.00
b. Correct "Monetary." Sign. 5.	FV	FV	7.00

24 50 RIYALS
L. AH1379 (1983). Dk. green and dk. brown on m/c unpt. Mosque
of Omar (Dome of the Rock) in Jerusalem at l., portr. Kg. Fahd at
ctr. r. Mosque at ctr. on back.

	VG	VF	UNC
a. Incorrect text. Sign. 5.	FV	FV	35.00
b. Correct "Monetary." Sign. 5.	FV	FV	30.00

#25-26 Saudi arms in blind embossed latent image area at l. ctr.

Incorrect	Correct

25 100 RIYALS
L. AH1379 (1984). Brown-violet and olive-green on m/c unpt. Mosque
at l., portr. Kg. Fahd at ctr. r. Mosque at ctr. on back. Sign. 5; 6.

	VG	VF	UNC
	FV	FV	50.00

Incorrect	Correct

26 500 RIYALS
L. AH1379 (1983). Purple and green on m/c unpt. Courtyard at l.,
portr. Kg. 'Abd al-'Aziz Ibn Saud at ctr. r. Courtyard of Great
Mosque at ctr. on back.

	VG	VF	UNC
a. Incorrect "Five Hundred Riyals" in lower ctr. panel of text. Sign. 5.	FV	150.00	300.00
b. Correct "Five Hundred Riyals" in lower ctr. panel of text. Sign. 5.	FV	FV	185.00

2000 COMMEMORATIVE ISSUE
#27 and 28, Centennial of Kingdom

		VG	VF	UNC
27	**20 RIYALS**	FV	FV	10.00

AH1419, 1999. Brown, red, gray and blue on m/c unpt. Abdul Aziz at l. ctr. and as wmk. Annur Mouuntain at ctr., commemorative logo and text at l. Sign. 6.

		VG	VF	UNC
28	**200 RIYALS**	FV	FV	85.00

2000. Red, brown, gray and green on m/c unpt. Abdul Aziz at l. ctr. and as wmk. Al Mussmack Palace at lower r. and its gate on back. Commemorative logo and text at r. Sign. 6.

2003 ISSUE

		VG	VF	UNC
29	**100 RIYALS**	FV	FV	45.00

2003. Brown, violet and m/c. Hologram added at upper ctr.

		VG	VF	UNC
30	**500 RIYALS**	FV	FV	185.00

2003. Purple, green and peach on m/c unpt.

SCOTLAND

Scotland, a part of the United Kingdom of Great Britain and Northern Ireland, consists of the northern part of the island of Great Britain. It has an area of 30,414 sq. mi. (78,772 sq. km.). Capital: Edinburgh. Principal industries are agriculture, fishing, manufacturing and ship-building.

In the 5th century, Scotland consisted of four kingdoms; that of the Picts, the Scots, Strathclyde, and Northumbria. The Scottish kingdom was united by Malcolm II (1005-34), but its ruler was forced to payo homage to the English crown in 1174. Scotland won independence under Robert Bruce at Bannockburn in 1314 and was ruled by the house of Stuart from 1371 to 1688. The personal union of the kingdoms of England and Scotland was achieved in 1603 by the accession of King James VI of Scotland as James I of England. Scotland was united with England by Parliamentary act in 1707.

RULERS:
British

MONETARY SYSTEM:
1 Shilling = 12 Pence
1 Guinea = 21 Shillings
1 Pound = 20 Shillings to 1971
1 Pound = 100 New Pence, 1971-1981
1 Pound = 100 Pence, 1982-

REPLACEMENT NOTES:
#111, Z/1, Z/2 or Z/3 prefix; #112 ZA or ZB prefix; #113 ZB prefix.

BRITISH ADMINISTRATION

BANK OF SCOTLAND

1935; 1938 ISSUE

		VG	VF	UNC
91	**1 POUND**			

1937-43. Yellow-brown, dk. brown and gray-blue. Like #86 but arms of the bank at l.

	VG	VF	UNC
a. Sign. Lord Elphinstone and A. W. M. Beveridge. 15.1.1935-15.9.1937.	15.00	70.00	185.00
b. Sign. Lord Elphinstone and J. Macfarlane. 5.1.1939-7.5.1941.	15.00	60.00	150.00
c. Sign. Lord Elphinstone and J. B. Crawford. 2.6.1942; 16.10.1943.	15.00	75.00	175.00
s. As c. Specimen.	—	—	175.00

92	**5 POUNDS**	

1935-44. Like #86 but thistle motif at l.

	VG	VF	UNC
a. Sign. Lord Elphinstone and A. W. M. Beveridge. 17.1.1935-17.3.1938.	50.00	175.00	450.00
b. Sign. Lord Elphinstone and J. Macfarlane. Black value panels. 24.4.1939-16.10.1941.	50.00	175.00	450.00
c. Sign. Lord Elphinstone and J. B. Crawford. 5.6.1942-26.9.1944.	40.00	150.00	400.00
s. As c. Specimen.	—	—	175.00

93	**10 POUNDS**	

1938-63. Scottish arms in panel at l., medallion of Goddess of fortune below arms at r. Bank bldg. on back.

	VG	VF	UNC
a. Sign. Lord Elphinstone and A. W. M. Beveridge. 24.1.1935; 28.6.1938.	150.00	600.00	1500.00
b. Sign. Lord Elphinstone and J. B. Crawford. 16.7.1942; 15.10.1942.	125.00	500.00	1250.00
c. Sign. Lord Bilsland and Sir Wm. Watson. 26.9.1963; 27.9.1963.	100.00	350.00	900.00

94 **20 POUNDS**

	VG	VF	UNC
1935-65. Like #93.			
a. Sign. Lord Elphinstone and A. W. M. Beveridge. 11.1.1935-22.7.1938.	100.00	350.00	950.00
b. Sign. Lord Elphinstone and J. Macfarlane. 16.5.1939; 12.7.1939.	100.00	400.00	1000.00
c. Sign. Lord Elphinstone and J. B. Crawford. 5.6.1942-11.8.1952.	75.00	300.00	750.00
d. Sign. Lord Elphinstone and Sir Wm. Watson. 5.12.1952; 14.4.1953.	100.00	375.00	950.00
e. Sign. Sir J. Craig and Sir Wm. Watson. 6.4.1955-12.6.1956	60.00	250.00	700.00
f. Sign. Lord Bilsland and Sir Wm. Watson. 21.3.1958-3.10.1963.	60.00	250.00	650.00

95 **100 POUNDS**

	VG	VF	UNC
1935-62. Like #93.			
a. Sign. Lord Elphinstone and A. W. M. Beveridge. 8.1.1935-12.8.1937.	400.00	1350.00	3000.00
b. Sign. Lord Elphinstone and J. Macfarlane. 2.4.1940; 15.7.1940.	350.00	1100.00	2500.00
c. Sign. Lord Elphinestone and J. B. Crawford. 10.6.1942; 14.12.1951.	300.00	900.00	2250.00
d. Sign. John Craig and Sir Wm. Watson. 14.9.1956-3.12.1956.	300.00	850.00	2000.00
e. Sign. Lord Bilsland and Sir Wm. Watson. 24.3.1959-30.11.1962.	300.00	800.00	1850.00

1961 ISSUE

102 **1 POUND**

	VG	VF	UNC
1961-65. Lt. brown and pale blue. Medallion at ctr, date below. Ship at ctr. on back.			
a. Imprint ends: *LD.* Sign. Lord Bilsland and Sir Wm. Watson. 10.5.1961-13.2.1964.	4.00	17.50	60.00
b. Imprint ends: *LTD.* Sign. Lord Bilsland and Sir Wm. Watson. 4.5.1965; 11.5.1965.	4.00	17.50	60.00

103 **5 POUNDS**

	VG	VF	UNC
14.9.1961-22.9.1961. Lt. brown and pale blue. Medallion at ctr., date below. Arms at l., ship at r. on back. Reduced size. Sign. Lord Bilsland and Sir Wm. Watson.	20.00	40.00	125.00

#104 deleted, see #102.

1961; 1966 ISSUE

105 **1 POUND**

	VG	VF	UNC
1966; 1967. Lt. brown and pale blue. Similar to #102 but *EDINBURGH* and date at r. Sign. Lord Polwarth and J. Letham w/titles: *GOVERNOR* and *TREASURER & GENERAL MANAGER.* 2 wmk. varieties.			
a. W/o electronic sorting marks on back. 1.6.1966.	4.00	15.00	50.00
b. W/electronic sorting marks on back. 3.3.1967.	4.00	15.00	50.00
s. As b. Specimen.	—	—	—

106 **5 POUNDS**

	VG	VF	UNC
1961-67. Blue and lt. brown. Medallion of fortune at ctr., numerals of value filled in at base. Arms at l., ship at r. on back. Like #103.			
a. Sign. Lord Bilsland and Sir Wm. Watson w/titles: *GOVERNOR* and *TREASURER.* 25.9.1961-12.1.1965.	15.00	35.00	120.00
b. Sign. Lord Polwarth and Sir Wm. Watson. 7.3.1966-8.3.1966.	20.00	40.00	150.00
c. Lighter shades of printing. Sign. Lord Polwarth and J. Letham w/titles: *GOVERNOR* and *TREASURER & GENERAL MANAGER.* 1.2.1967; 2.2.1967.	15.00	35.00	120.00
d. Sign. titles as b. W/electronic sorting marks on back. 1.11.1967.	20.00	40.00	125.00

1968; 1969 ISSUE

109	1 POUND	VG	VF	UNC
	1968; 1969. Ochre on blue and m/c unpt. Arms at ctr. flanked by 2 women. Arms at upper l., shield at upper ctr., sailing ship at upper r. on back.			
	a. *EDINBURGH* 19mm in length. 17.7.1968.	5.00	20.00	55.00
	b. *EDINBURGH* 24mm in length. 18.8.1969.	5.00	20.00	55.00
	s. As b. Specimen.	—	—	—

110	5 POUNDS	VG	VF	UNC
	1968-69. Green on m/c unpt. Similar to #109.			
	a. *EDINBURGH* 19mm in length. 1.11.1968; 4.11.1968.	25.00	80.00	250.00
	b. *EDINBURGH* 24mm in length. 8.12.1969; 9.12.1969.	25.00	80.00	250.00

110A	20 POUNDS	VG	VF	UNC
	5.5.1969. Scottish arms in panel at l., medallion of Goddess of Fortune below arms at ctr. r. Sign.: Lord Polwarth and J. Letham. W/security thread. Wmk: Thistle.	60.00	150.00	375.00

Note: #110A was an emergency printing of 25,000 examples.

1970-74 ISSUE

#111-115 arms at ctr. flanked by 2 women. Sir W. Scott at r.

#111-113 replacement notes: #111 - Serial # prefix *Z/1, Z/2* or *Z/3*; #112 - Serial # prefix *ZA* or *ZB*; #113 - Serial # prefix *ZB*.

111	1 POUND	VG	VF	UNC
	1970-88. Green on m/c unpt. Sailing ship at l., arms at upper ctr., medallion of Pallas seated at r. on back.			
	a. Sign. Lord Polwarth and T. W. Walker. 10.8.1970; 31.8.1971.	5.00	15.00	50.00
	b. Sign. Lord Clydesmuir and T. W. Walker. 1.11.1972; 30.8.1973.	5.00	15.00	50.00
	c. Sign. Lord Clydesmuir and A. M. Russell. 28.10.1974-3.10.1978.	3.00	5.00	22.50
	d. Sign. Lord Clydesmuir and D. B. Pattullo. 15.10.1979; 4.11.1980.	3.00	5.00	15.00
	e. Sign. T. N. Risk and D. B. Pattullo. 30.7.1981.	4.00	7.00	18.00
	f. W/o sorting marks on back. Sign. like e. 7.10.1983; 9.11.1984; 12.12.1985; 18.11.1986.	2.00	4.00	14.00
	g. Sign. T. N. Risk and L. P. Burt. 19.8.1988.	2.00	3.00	8.00
	s. As a (1970); c (1974). Specimen.	—	—	125.00

112	5 POUNDS	VG	VF	UNC
	1970-88. Blue on m/c unpt. Back similar to #111.			
	a. Sign. Lord Polwarth and T. W. Walker. 10.8.1970; 2.9.1971.	20.00	50.00	150.00
	b. Sign. Lord Clydesmuir and T. W. Walker. 4.12.1972; 5.9.1973.	17.50	35.00	110.00
	c. Sign. Lord Clydesmuir and A. M. Russell. 4.11.1974; 1.12.1975; 21.11.1977; 19.10.1978.	15.00	30.00	90.00
	d. Sign. Lord Clydesmuir and D. B. Pattullo. 28.9.1979; 28.11.1980.	15.00	25.00	75.00
	e. Sign. T. N. Risk and D. B. Pattullo. 27.7.1981; 25.6.1982.	12.00	25.00	70.00
	f. W/o encoding marks. 13.10.1983; 3.12.1985; 29.2.1988.	12.00	20.00	55.00
	s. As a (1970); c (1974). Specimen.	—	—	150.00

113	10 POUNDS	VG	VF	UNC
	1974-90. Brown on m/c unpt. Medallions of sailing ship at lower l., Pallas seated at upper l. ctr., arms at r. on back.			
	a. Sign. Lord Clydesmuir and A. M. Russell. 1.5.1974-10.10.1979.	30.00	50.00	165.00
	b. Sign. Lord Clydesmuir and D. B. Pattullo. 5.2.1981.	30.00	50.00	150.00
	c. Sign. T. N. Risk and D. B. Pattullo. 22.7.1981; 16.6.1982; 14.10.1983; 17.9.1984; 20.10.1986; 6.8.1987.	20.00	30.00	75.00
	d. Sign. T. N. Risk and P. Burt. 1.9.1989; 31.10.1990.	20.00	30.00	65.00

		VG	**VF**	**UNC**
114	**20 POUNDS**			
	1970-87. Purple on m/c unpt. Arms at upper l. above sailing ship w/medallion of Pallas seated below, head office bldg. at ctr. on back.			
	a. Sign. Lord Polwarth and T. W. Walker. 1.10.1970.	55.00	120.00	350.00
	b. Sign. Lord Clydesmuir and T. W. Walker. 3.1.1973.	55.00	110.00	300.00
	c. Sign. Lord Clydesmuir and A. M. Russell. 8.11.1974; 14.1.1977.	50.00	90.00	265.00
	d. Sign. Lord Clydesmuir and D. B. Pattullo. 16.7.1979; 2.2.1981.	45.00	80.00	225.00
	e. Sign. T. N. Risk and D. B. Pattullo. 4.8.1981-15.12.1987.	40.00	55.00	175.00
	s. As a. Specimen. 1.10.1970.	—	—	250.00
115	**100 POUNDS**			
	1971-86. Red on m/c unpt. Arms at upper l., medallions of sailing ship at lower l., Pallas seated at lower r., head office bldg. at ctr. on back.			
	a. Sign. Lord Polwarth and T. W. Walker. 6.12.1971.	300.00	525.00	1250.00
	b. Sign. Lord Clydesmuir and T. W. Walker. 6.9.1973.	275.00	500.00	1200.00
	c. Sign. Lord Clydesmuir and A. M. Russell. 11.10.1978.	275.00	450.00	1000.00
	d. Sign. Lord Clydesmuir and D. B. Pattullo. 26.1.1981.	275.00	425.00	900.00
	e. Sign. T. N. Risk and D. B. Pattullo. 11.6.1982; 26.11.1986.	250.00	350.00	750.00
	s. As a. Specimen.	—	—	300.00

1990-92 STERLING ISSUE

#116-118 similar to previous issue but w/*STERLING* added below value. Smaller size notes.

		VG	**VF**	**UNC**
118	**20 POUNDS**			
	1.7.1991; 3.2.1992; 12.1.1993. Purple on m/c unpt. Similar to #114 but reduced size, 148 x 81mm. Sign. D. B. Pattullo and P. Burt.	FV	50.00	85.00

		VG	**VF**	**UNC**
118A	**100 POUNDS**			
	14.2.1990; 2.12.1992; 9.2.1994. Red on m/c unpt. Similar to #115 but in Sterling added to denomination. Sign. D. B. Pattullo and P. Burt.			
	a. 14.2.1990. Sign. T.N. Risk and Peter Burt.	200.00	285.00	550.00
	b. 22.1.1992; 2.12.1992; 9.2.1994. Sign. D.B. Pattullo and Peter Burt.	200.00	275.00	500.00

1995 COMMEMORATIVE ISSUE

#119-122, Tercentenary - Bank of Scotland

#119-123 Sir W. Scott at l. and as wmk., bank arms at ctr. Bank head office bldg. at lower l., medallion of Pallas seated, arms and medallion of sailing ships at r. on back. Printer: TDLR (W/o imprint).

		VG	**VF**	**UNC**
116	**5 POUNDS**			
	1990-94. Blue on m/c unpt. Similar to #112, but 135 x 70mm.			
	a. Sign. T. N. Risk and P. Burt. 20.6.1990.	FV	17.50	40.00
	b. Sign. D. B. Pattullo and P. Burt. 6.11.1991; 18.1.1993; 7.1.1994.	FV	15.00	35.00

		VG	**VF**	**UNC**
117	**10 POUNDS**			
	7.5.1992; 9.3.1993; 13.4.1994. Deep brown on m/c unpt. Similar to #113, but 142 x 75mm. Sign. D. B. Pattullo and P. Burt.	FV	25.00	50.00
119	**5 POUNDS**			
	1995-. Dk. blue and purple on m/c unpt. Oil well riggers working w/drill at ctr. on back.			
	a. Sign. D. Bruce Pattullo and Peter A. Burt. 4.1.1995. Sign. titles as: *GOVERNOR* and *TREASURER & CHIEF GENERAL MANAGER.*	FV	FV	22.00
	b. Sign. D. Bruce Pattullo and Gavin Masterton. 13.9.1996.	FV	FV	20.00
	c. Sign. Alistair Grant and Gavin Masterton. 5.8.1998.	FV	FV	18.50
	d. Sign. Peter Burt and George Mitchell. 25.6.2002. Sign. titles as: *GOVERNOR* and *TREASURER & MANAGING DIRECTOR.*	FV	FV	17.50

120   10 POUNDS

1995-. Dk. brown and deep olive-green on m/c unpt. Workers by distilling equipment at ctr. on back.

		VG	VF	UNC
a.	Sign. D. Bruce Pattullo and Peter A. Burt. 1.2.1995. Sign. titles as: GOVERNOR and TREASURER & CHIEF GENERAL MANAGER.	FV	FV	42.50
b.	Sign. Bruce Pattullo and Gavin Masterton. 5.8.1997.	FV	FV	37.50
c.	Sign. Alistair Grant and Gavin Masterton. 18.8.1998.	FV	FV	35.00
d.	Sign. John Shaw and George Mitchell. 18.6.2001. Sign. titles as: GOVERNOR and TREASURER & MANAGING DIRECTOR.	FV	FV	32.50
e.	Sign. George Mitchell. 26.11.2003. Sign. title as: GOVERNOR.	FV	FV	30.00

121   20 POUNDS

1995-. Violet and brown on m/c unpt. Woman researcher at laboratory station at ctr. on back.

		VG	VF	UNC
a.	Sign. D. Bruce Pattullo and Peter A. Burt. 1.5.1995. Sign. titles as: GOVERNOR and TREASURER & CHIEF GENERAL MANAGER.	FV	FV	80.00
b.	Sign. Bruce Pattullo and Gavin Masterton. 25.10.1996; 1.4.1998.	FV	FV	70.00
c.	Sign. Alistair Grant and Gavin Masterton. 22.3.1999. Sign. titles as: GOVERNOR and TREASURER & MANAGING DIRECTOR.	FV	FV	67.50
d.	Sign. John Shaw and George Mitchell. 18.6.2001.	FV	FV	65.00
e.	Sign. George Mitchell. 26.11.2003. Sign. title as: GOVERNOR.	FV	FV	65.00

122   50 POUNDS

1995; 1999. Dk. green and olive-brown on m/c unpt. Music director and violinists at ctr. on back.

		VG	VF	UNC
a.	Sign. D. Bruce Pattullo and Peter A. Burt. 1.5.1995. Sign. titles as: GOVERNOR and TREASURER & MANAGING DIRECTOR.	FV	110.00	225.00

122   50 POUNDS

		VG	VF 122
b.	Sign. Alistair Grant and Gavin Masterton. 15.4.1999. Sign. titles as: GOVERNOR and TREASURER & MANAGING DIRECTOR.	FV	FV 175.00
c.	Sign. George Mitchell. 29.1.2003. Sign. title as GOVERNOR.	FV	FV 150.00

123   100 POUNDS

1995-. Red-violet and red-orange on m/c unpt. Golf outing at ctr. on back.

		VG	VF	UNC
a.	Sign. D. Bruce Pattullo and Peter A. Burt. 17.7.1995. Sign. titles as: GOVERNOR and TREASURER & CHIEF GENERAL MANAGER.	FV	225.00	450.00
b.	Sign. D. Bruce Pattullo and Gavin Masterton. 18.8.1997.	FV	FV	400.00
c.	Sign. Alistair Grant and Gavin Masterton. 19.5.1999. Sign. titles as: GOVERNOR and TREASURER & MANAGING DIRECTOR.	FV	FV	350.00
d.	Sign. George Mitchell. 26.11.2003. Sign. title as: GOVERNOR.	FV	FV	300.00

BRITISH LINEN BANK

Note: Formerly the British Linen Company. See Vol. I. Merged with the Bank of Scotland in 1970.

1961; 1962 ISSUE

#162-170 sideview of seated Britannia in emblem at l., arms at upper r. Back blue. Printer: TDLR.

162   1 POUND

30.9.1961. Blue and red.

VG	VF	UNC
7.50	22.50	75.00

163	5 POUNDS		VG	VF	UNC
	2.1.1961; 3.2.1961. Blue and red.		25.00	100.00	300.00
164	20 POUNDS				
	14.2.1962; 5.3.1962; 4.4.1962. Blue and red.		75.00	275.00	600.00

165	100 POUNDS		VG	VF	UNC
	9.5.1962; 1.6.1962. Blue and red.		275.00	450.00	1250.00

1962 ISSUE

166	1 POUND		VG	VF	UNC
	1962-67. Blue and red. Similar to #162 but reduced size. 150 x 70mm.				
	a. Sign. A. P. Anderson. 31.3.1962.		7.00	22.50	60.00
	b. Test note w/lines for electronic sorting on back. 31.3.1962.		—	—	350.00
	c. Sign. T. W. Walker. 1.7.1963-13.6.1967.		5.00	17.50	50.00
	s. As a, c. Specimen.		—	—	150.00

167	5 POUNDS		VG	VF	UNC
	21.9.1962-18.8.1964. Blue and red. Sir Walter Scott at r. 140 x 85mm.				
	a. Sign. A. P. Anderson. 21.9.1962; 20.10.1962; 16.6.1962.		12.00	25.00	75.00
	b. Sign. T. W. Walker. 16.6.1964; 17.7.1964; 18.8.1964.		12.00	25.00	75.00
	c. As b. Test note w/lines for electronic sorting. 17.7.1964.		60.00	150.00	400.00

1967 ISSUE

168	1 POUND		VG	VF	UNC
	13.6.1967. Blue on m/c unpt. Similar to #166 but modified design and w/lines for electronic sorting on back.		4.00	20.00	55.00

1968 ISSUE

169	1 POUND		VG	VF	UNC
	1968-70. Blue on m/c unpt. Sir W. Scott at r., supported arms at top ctr.				
	a. 29.2.1968; 5.11.1969.		4.00	20.00	55.00
	b. 20.7.1970.		10.00	40.00	100.00

170	5 POUNDS		VG	VF	UNC
	22.3.1968; 23.4.1968; 24.5.1968. Blue and red. Similar to #167, but reduced size and many plate changes. 146 x 78 mm.		17.50	40.00	100.00

CLYDESDALE AND NORTH OF SCOTLAND BANK LTD.

Formerly, and later to become the Clydesdale Bank Ltd. again.

1950-51 ISSUE

191	1 POUND		VG	VF	UNC
	1950-60. Blue, red and orange. Ships at dockside at l., landscape (sheaves) at r. River scene w/trees on back.				
	a. 1.11.1950-1.11.1956.		10.00	45.00	150.00
	b. 1.5.1958-1.11.1960.		10.00	40.00	125.00
	s. As a. Specimen.		—	—	200.00

192	5 POUNDS	VG	VF	UNC
	2.5.1951-1.3.1960. Purple. King's College at Aberdeen at lower l., Glasgow Cathedral at lower r.			
	a. Sign. J. J. Campbell.	22.50	75.00	200.00
	b. Sign. R. D. Fairbairn.	22.50	75.00	200.00

193	20 POUNDS	VG	VF	UNC
	2.5.1951-1.8.1962. Green on m/c unpt. Like #192. 180 x 97mm.			
	a. Sign. J. J. Campbell.	45.00	80.00	325.00
	b. Sign. R. D. Fairbairn.	45.00	80.00	325.00
194	100 POUNDS			
	2.5.1951. Blue. Like #192. 180 x 97mm. Sign. J. J. Campbell.	350.00	750.00	1500.00

1961 ISSUE

#195 and 196 arms at r.

195	1 POUND	VG	VF	UNC
	1.3.1961; 2.5.1962; 1.2.1963. Green on m/c unpt. Ship and tug at ctr. on back.			
	a. Issued note.	6.50	30.00	90.00
	s. Specimen.	—	—	160.00

196	5 POUNDS	VG	VF	UNC
	20.9.1961; 1.6.1962; 1.2.1963. Dk. blue on m/c unpt. King's College at Aberdeen on back.	15.00	50.00	150.00

CLYDESDALE BANK LIMITED

Formerly the Clydesdale and North of Scotland Bank Ltd. Later became Clydesdale Bank PLC.

1963-64 ISSUE

197	1 POUND	VG	VF	UNC
	2.9.1963-3.4.1967. Green on m/c unpt. Like #195.	6.00	17.50	60.00
198	5 POUNDS			
	2.9.1963-1.9.1969. Blue and violet. Like #196.	15.00	50.00	150.00

199	10 POUNDS	VG	VF	UNC
	20.4.1964; 1.12.1967. Brown on m/c unpt. Arms at r., University of Glasgow on back.	50.00	200.00	600.00

203 5 POUNDS
1.5.1967; 1.11.1968; 1.9.1969. Blue and violet on m/c unpt. Like #198 but lines for electronic sorting on back.

	VG	VF	UNC
	15.00	50.00	150.00

1971-81 ISSUE

#204-210 wmk: Old sailing ships.

200 20 POUNDS
19.11.1964; 1.12.1967. Carmine on m/c unpt. Arms at r. George Square in Glasgow on back.

	VG	VF	UNC
	60.00	200.00	600.00

201 100 POUNDS
1.2.1965; 29.4.1965; 1.2.1968. Violet on m/c unpt. Multiple arch bridge across river at ctr. on back.

	VG	VF	UNC
	250.00	500.00	1500.00

1967 ISSUE

202 1 POUND
3.4.1967; 1.10.1968; 1.9.1969. Green on m/c unpt. Like #197 but lines for electronic sorting on back.

	VG	VF	UNC
	4.00	17.50	55.00

204 1 POUND
1971-81. Dk. olive-green on m/c unpt. Robert the Bruce at l. Scene of Battle of Bannockburn, 1314 on back.

	VG	VF	UNC
a. Sign. R. D. Fairbairn, w/title: *GENERAL MANAGER*. 1.3.1971.	4.00	10.00	40.00
b. Sign. A. R. Macmillan, w/title: *GENERAL MANAGER*. 1.5.1972; 1.8.1973.	4.00	10.00	45.00
c. Sign. A. R. Macmillan, w/title: *CHIEF GENERAL MANAGER*. 1.3.1974-27.2.1981.	3.00	8.00	30.00
s. As c. Specimen.	—	—	—

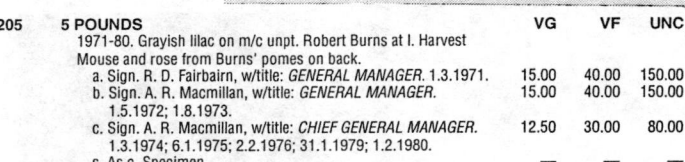

205 5 POUNDS
1971-80. Grayish lilac on m/c unpt. Robert Burns at l. Harvest Mouse and rose from Burns' pomes on back.

	VG	VF	UNC
a. Sign. R. D. Fairbairn, w/title: *GENERAL MANAGER*. 1.3.1971.	15.00	40.00	150.00
b. Sign. A. R. Macmillan, w/title: *GENERAL MANAGER*. 1.5.1972; 1.8.1973.	15.00	40.00	150.00
c. Sign. A. R. Macmillan, w/title: *CHIEF GENERAL MANAGER*. 1.3.1974; 6.1.1975; 2.2.1976; 31.1.1979; 1.2.1980.	12.50	30.00	80.00
s. As c. Specimen.	—	—	—

#206 *Deleted*. See #205.

207   10 POUNDS

		VG	VF	UNC
1972-81. Brown and pale purple on m/c unpt. David Livingstone at l. Dromedary Camel and African scene on back.				
a. Sign. A. R. MacMillan, w/title: *GENERAL MANAGER*. 1.3.1972; 1.8.1973.		30.00	100.00	400.00
b. Sign. A. R. MacMillan, w/title: *CHIEF GENERAL MANAGER*. 1.3.1974-27.2.1981.		27.50	75.00	350.00

208   20 POUNDS

	VG	VF	UNC
1972-81. Lilac on m/c unpt. Lord Kelvin at l. Kelvin's lecture room at Glasgow University on back.			
a. Sign. A. R. MacMillan, w/title: *GENERAL MANAGER*. 1.3.1972.	60.00	125.00	450.00
b. Sign. A. R. MacMillan, w/title: *CHIEF GENERAL MANAGER*. 2.2.1976; 27.2.1981.	60.00	125.00	400.00

209   50 POUNDS

	VG	VF	UNC
1.9.1981. Olive on m/c unpt. A. Smith at l. Sailing ships, blacksmith implements and farm on back.	125.00	210.00	550.00

210   100 POUNDS

	VG	VF	UNC
1972; 1976. Red on m/c unpt. Lord Kelvin at l. Kelvin's lecture room at Glasgow University on back.			
a. Sign. A. R. MacMillan, w/title: *GENERAL MANAGER*. 1.3.1972.	235.00	450.00	1150.00
b. Sign. A. R. MacMillan, w/title: *CHIEF GENERAL MANAGER*. 2.2.1976.	225.00	425.00	1050.00

CLYDESDALE BANK PLC

Formerly the Clydesdale Bank Limited.

1982-89 "STERLING" ISSUES

#211-217 wmk: Old sailing ship repeated vertically.

211   1 POUND

	VG	VF	UNC
1982-88. Dk. olive-green on m/c unpt. Like #204.			
a. W/sorting marks. Sign. A. R. Macmillan. 29.3.1982.	3.50	8.00	22.50
b. Like a. Sign. A. R. Cole Hamilton. 5.1.1983.	3.50	8.00	22.50
c. W/o sorting marks. Sign. A. R. Cole Hamilton. 8.4.1985; 25.11.1985.	3.00	6.00	20.00
d. Sign. title: *CHIEF EXECUTIVE*. 18.9.1987; 9.11.1988.	3.00	5.00	15.00

212   5 POUNDS

	VG	VF	UNC
1982-89. Blue on m/c unpt. Like #205.			
a. Sign. A. R. Macmillan. 29.3.1982.	15.00	30.00	100.00
b. Sign. A. R. Cole Hamilton. 5.1.1983.	12.50	25.00	85.00
c. W/o sorting marks. Sign. A. R. Cole Hamilton. 18.9.1986.	12.50	25.00	80.00
d. Sign. title: *CHIEF EXECUTIVE*. 18.9.1987; 2.8.1988; 28.6.1989.	10.00	20.00	60.00
s. As d. Specimen.	—	—	200.00

213   10 POUNDS

	VG	VF	UNC
1982-87. Brown and pale purple on m/c unpt. Like #207.			
a. Sign. A. R. Macmillan. 29.3.1982; 5.1.1983.	25.00	60.00	275.00
b. Sign. A. R. Cole Hamilton. 8.4.1985; 18.9.1986.	25.00	60.00	250.00
c. Sign. title: *CHIEF EXECUTIVE*. 18.9.1987.	22.50	55.00	225.00
s. As d. Specimen.	—	—	

214   10 POUNDS

	VG	VF	UNC
7.5.1988; 3.9.1989; 1.3.1990; 9.11.1990. Dk. brown on m/c unpt. D. Livingstone in front of map at l. Blantyre (Livingstone's birthplace) on back. Wmk: Sailing ships.	20.00	35.00	100.00

219 10 POUNDS

		VG	VF	UNC
1992-97. Deep brown and green on m/c unpt. Similar to #214 but with modified sailing ship outlines at r. 142 x 75mm.				
a. Sign. A. R. Cole Hamilton. 3.9.1992.		FV	32.50	70.00
b. Sign. Charles Love. 5.1.1993.		FV	30.00	65.00
c. Sign. F. Goodwin. 22.3.1996; 27.2.1997.		FV	30.00	60.00

215 20 POUNDS

	VG	VF	UNC
1982-90. Lilac on m/c unpt. Lord Kelvin at l. Lord Kelvin's lecture room at Glasgow University on back. Like #208.			
a. Sign. A. R. Macmillan. 29.3.1982.	50.00	125.00	400.00
b. Sign. A. R. Cole Hamilton. 5.1.1983; 8.4.1985.	50.00	110.00	375.00
c. Sign. title: *CHIEF EXECUTIVE*. 18.9.1987; 2.8.1990.	50.00	125.00	400.00

#216 Deleted. See #222.

220 20 POUNDS

	VG	VF	UNC
1990-93. Violet, purple, brown and brown-orange on m/c unpt. Robert the Bruce at l. His equestrian statue, Monymusk reliquary, Stirling Castle and Wallace Monument on back. 148 x 80mm.			
a. Sign. A. R. Cole Hamilton. 30.11.1990; 2.8.1991; 3.9.1992.	42.50	70.00	175.00
b. Sign. Charles Love. 5.1.1993.	42.50	70.00	150.00

217 100 POUNDS

	VG	VF	UNC
1985; 1991. Red on m/c unpt. Like #215. 163 x 90mm.			
a. Sign. title: *CHIEF GENERAL MANAGER*. 8.4.1985.	275.00	500.00	1000.00
b. Sign. title: *CHIEF EXECUTIVE*. 9.11.1991.	260.00	400.00	800.00

1989-96 "STERLING" ISSUE

#218-221 like #212-217 but reduced size notes. Wmk: Old sailing ship repeated vertically.

221 20 POUNDS

	VG	VF	UNC
1994-. Purple, dk. brown and deep orange on m/c unpt. Like #220. Ascending size serial # at upper l.			
a. Sign. F. Cicutto. 1.9.1994.	FV	50.00	95.00
b. Sign. F. Goodwin. 2.12.1996.	FV	40.00	80.00

218 5 POUNDS

	VG	VF	UNC
1990-. Black and gray on m/c unpt. Similar to #212, but 135 x 70mm.			
a. Sign. A. R. Cole Hamilton. 2.4.1990.	FV	15.00	30.00
b. Sign. F. Cicutto. 1.9.1994.	FV	12.50	25.00
c. Sign. F. Goodwin. 21.7.1996; 1.12.1997.	FV	FV	20.00
d. Sign. G. Savage. 19.6.2002.	FV	FV	20.00

222	50 POUNDS		VG	VF	UNC
	3.9.1989; 20.4.1992. Olive-green on m/c unpt. Similar to #209. Sign. A. R. Cole Hamilton.		FV	175.00	450.00
223	100 POUNDS				
	2.10.1996. Purple, red and violet on m/c unpt. Face similar to #217. Glasgow University on back. Sign. F. Goodwin. Vertical serial # at r.		FV	240.00	350.00

1996 COMMEMORATIVE ISSUE

#224, Poetry of Robert Burns

224	5 POUNDS		VG	VF	UNC
	21.7.1996. Black and gray on m/c unpt. Like #218 but w/lines of poetry. Wmk: Sailing ship.				
	a. "A man's a man for a'that - Then let us..."		FV	12.50	25.00
	b. "Tam O'Shanter - Now, wha this..."		FV	12.50	25.00
	c. "Ae Fond Kiss - But to see..."		FV	12.50	25.00
	d. "Scots wha hae - By oppressions woes..."		FV	12.50	25.00

Note: For sets w/matching serial # see Collector Series - CS1.

1996 REGULAR ISSUE

225	50 POUNDS		VG	VF	UNC
	22.3.1996. Olive-green on m/c unpt. Like #222 but reduced size. 157 x 85mm. Sign. F. Goodwin.		FV	125.00	200.00

NOTICE

Readers with unlisted dates, signature varieties, etc. are invited to submit photocopies of their notes to: Standard Catalog of World Paper Money, 700 East State St. Iola, WI 54990-0001, E-Mail: george.cuhaj@fwpubs.com.

1997 COMMEMORATIVE ISSUES

#226, Work of Mary Slessor

226	10 POUNDS		VG	VF	UNC
	1997-. Dk. brown and brown on m/c unpt. M. Slessor at l. and as wmk. Map of Calabar in Nigeria in wreath at ctr., sailing ship at upper l., Slessor seated below and w/children at r.				
	a. Sign. F. Goodwin. 1.5.1997.		FV	25.00	40.00
	b. Sign. J. Wright. 5.11.1998; 20.10.1999.		FV	25.00	40.00
	c. Sign. S. Targett. 26.1.2003.		FV	25.00	40.00
	d. Sign. Ross Pimney. 25.4.2003.		FV	FV	32.50
	e. Sign. David Thorburn as Chief Operating Officer. 21.11.2004.		FV	FV	32.50

Note: #226 exists w/serial # prefix NAB encapsulated in acrylic plastic w/text: 1987-1997 THE FIRST DECADE. Market value $150.

Non-encapsulated NAB market value in Unc. $70.

#227, Commonwealth heads of government meeting in Edinburgh, Oct. 1997

227	20 POUNDS		VG	VF	UNC
	30.9.1997. Purple, dk. brown and deep orange on m/c unpt. Face like #221. Edinburgh International Conference Centre at lower r., Clydesdale Bank plaza and Edinburgh Castle in background at ctr. on back. Sign. F. Goodwin.		FV	FV	75.00

Note: #227 was issued w/serial # prefix: CHG (Special Commemorative prefix). Market value $70.

1997 REGULAR ISSUE

228	20 POUNDS		VG	VF	UNC
	1.11.1997-. Purple, dk. brown and deep orange on m/c unpt. Like #221 but square design replaces £20 at lower l., segmented foil over security thread, bank logo added to value panel at lower ctr. r.				
	a. Sign. Fred Goodwin. 1.11.1997.		FV	FV	90.00
	b. Sign. John Wright. 12.10.1999.		FV	FV	70.00
	c. Sign. Grahm Savage. 19.6.2002.		FV	FV	85.00
	d. Sign. Steve Targett. 26.1.2003; 26.4.2003.		FV	FV	80.00
	e. Sign. Ross Pinney. 25.4.2003.		FV	FV	62.50
	f. Sign. David Thorburn as Chief Operating Officer. 21.11.2004.		FV	FV	62.50

1999 COMMEMORATIVE ISSUE

#229, Glasgow as UK City of Architecture and Design

		VG	VF	UNC
229	**20 POUNDS** 9.4.1999. Purple, brown and m/c. Alex "Greek" Thompson at l. Holmwood House on back. Special text at lower r. on both sides.	FV	FV	80.00

2000 COMMEMORATIVE ISSUES

#229A and 229B, special text: *COMMEMORATING THE YEAR 2000.*

		VG	VF	UNC
229A	**10 POUNDS** 1.1.2000. Brown and green on m/c unpt. Similar to #226 but commemorative text added at r.	FV	FV	35.00
229B	**20 POUNDS** 1.1.2000. Purple, dk. brown and deep orange on m/c unpt. Similar to #228 but commemorative text added at r.	FV	FV	65.00

#229C and 229D, Commemorating the 550th Anniversary of the University of Glasgow

		VG	VF	UNC
229C	**50 POUNDS** 6.1.2001. Olive-green on m/c unpt. Like #225 but w/commemorative emblem and l ext at r.	FV	FV	175.00

		VG	VF	UNC
229D	**100 POUNDS** 6.1.2001. Purple, red and violet on m/c unpt. Like #223 but w/commemorative emblem and text at r.	FV	FV	350.00

NATIONAL COMMERCIAL BANK OF SCOTLAND LIMITED

Formed by an amalgamation of The Commercial Bank of Scotland Ltd. and The National Bank of Scotland Ltd. in 1959. In 1969 it amalgamated with The Royal Bank of Scotland.

1961 ISSUE

		VG	VF	UNC
269	**1 POUND** 1.11.1961-4.1.1966. Green on m/c unpt. Forth Railway bridge. Arms at ctr. on back. Reduced size, 151 x 72mm. Printer: BWC.			
	a. Issued note.	4.00	17.50	55.00
	s. Specimen.	—	—	160.00

		VG	VF	UNC
270	**5 POUNDS** 3.1.1961. Green on m/c unpt. Arms at bottom ctr. r. Forth Railway bridge on back. Reduced size: 159 x 90mm. Printer: W&S.	25.00	60.00	225.00

1963-67 ISSUE

#271-273 printer: BWC.

		VG	VF	UNC
271	**1 POUND** 4.1.1967. Green on m/c unpt. Like #269, but lines for electronic sorting on back. 152 x 72mm.			
	a. Issue note.	6.00	20.00	65.00
	s. Specimen.	—	—	—

		VG	VF	UNC
272	**5 POUNDS** 2.1.1963; 1.8.1963; 1.10.1964; 4.1.1966; 1.8.1966. Blue on m/c unpt. Arms at lower ctr. Landscape w/Edinburgh Castle, National Gallery on back. 142 x 85mm.			
	a. Issued note.	15.00	32.50	100.00
	s. Specimen.	—	—	200.00
273	**10 POUNDS** 18.8.1966. Brown on m/c unpt. Arms at lower ctr. Forth Railway bridge on back. 151 x 94mm.	175.00	300.00	900.00

1967; 1968 ISSUE

#274 and 275 printer: BWC.

		VG	VF	UNC
274	**1 POUND** 4.1.1968. Green on m/c unpt. Similar to #271, but W/Forth Railway Bridge and road bridge on face. Reduced size. 136 x 67mm.			
	a. Issued note.	4.00	12.50	50.00
	s. Specimen.	—	—	160.00

		VG	VF	UNC
275	**5 POUNDS** 4.1.1968. Blue, red and green on m/c unpt. Like #272 but electronic sorting marks on back.			
	a. Issued note.	15.00	40.00	125.00
	s. Specimen.	—	—	225.00
275A	**20 POUNDS** 1.6.1967. Red on m/c unpt. Arms at lower r. Bridge on back. Printer: TDLR.			
	a. Issued note.	1500.00	4000.00	6000.00
	s. Specimen.	—	—	600.00
275B	**100 POUNDS** 1.6.1967. Purple on m/c unpt. Arms at lower r. Bridge on back. Printer: TDLR. Specimen.	—	—	1000.00

ROYAL BANK OF SCOTLAND
Later became the Royal Bank of Scotland Limited.

1875; 1887 ISSUE

		Good	Fine	XF
319	**20 POUNDS** 1877-1969. Blue and brown. Uniface.			
	a. Plate C. 1877-1911.	350.00	850.00	2500.00
	b. Plate D. Yellow unpt. Imprint: W. & A. K. Johnston 1931-47.	85.00	300.00	700.00
	c. Plates E; F; G; H. Unpt. w/o red. Imprint: W. & A. K. Johnston & G. W. Bacon Ltd. Both sign. printed 1947-66.	65.00	200.00	450.00
320	**100 POUNDS** 1877-1969. Blue and red. Uniface.			
	a. Plate C. 1877-1918.	1000.00	2250.00	—
	b. Plates D; E. Yellow unpt. 1918-60.	300.00	650.00	2000.00
	c. Plates F; G. Imprint: W. & A. K. Johnston & G. W. Bacon Ltd. Both sign. printed. 1960-69.	250.00	600.00	1800.00

1952 ISSUE

		VG	VF	UNC
323	**5 POUNDS** 1952-63. Blue and red on yellow unpt. Uniface. Like #317 but reduced size.			
	a. 2 sign. Imprint: W. & A.K. Johnston Ltd. 2.1.1952-1.7.1953.	30.00	85.00	250.00
	b. 3 sign. Imprint: W. & A. K. Johnston & G. W. Bacon Ltd. 1.7.1953-1.2.1954.	35.00	150.00	325.00
	c. 2 sign. Imprint: W. & A. K. Johnston & G. W. Bacon. 1.4.1955- 3.1.1963.	25.00	60.00	175.00

1955 ISSUE

		VG	VF	UNC
324	**1 POUND** 1955-64. Dk. blue on yellow and brown unpt. Sign. W. R. Ballantyne w/title: *General Manager.* 152 x 85mm.			
	a. W/o engraver's name on back. 1.4.1955-1.11.1955.	7.00	18.00	75.00
	b. W/engraver's name W. H. Egan upside down and in very small letters below the r. hand bank bldg. on back. 1.2.1956- 1.7.1964.	6.00	15.00	60.00
	s. As a. Specimen.	—	—	—

1964 ISSUE

			VG	VF	UNC
325	**1 POUND**				
	1964-67. Black and brown on yellow unpt. Like #324, but 150 x 71mm.				
	a. Sign. W. R. Ballantyne. 1.8.1964-1.6.1965.		5.00	15.00	55.00
	b. Sign. G. P. Robertson. 2.8.1965-1.11.1967.		4.00	12.50	50.00
	s. As a. Specimen.		—	—	150.00

			VG	VF	UNC
326	**5 POUNDS**				
	1964-65. Dk. blue, orange-brown and yellow. Uniface. Like #323, but 140 x 85mm.				
	a. 2.11.1964. Sign. W. R. Ballantyne & A. G. Campbell.		25.00	60.00	175.00
	b. 2.8.1965. Sign. G. P. Robertson & A. G. Campbell.		25.00	60.00	175.00
	s. As b. Specimen.		—	—	275.00

1966; 1967 ISSUE

#327 and 328 portr. D. Dale at l. and as wmk., bank arms at lower r. Bank head office bldg. at ctr. and upper r. on back.

			VG	VF	UNC
327	**1 POUND**				
	1.9.1967. Green on m/c unpt.				
	a. Issued note.		6.00	20.00	50.00
	s. Specimen.		—	—	125.00

			VG	VF	UNC
328	**5 POUNDS**				
	1.11.1966; 1.3.1967. Blue on m/c unpt.		25.00	55.00	160.00

ROYAL BANK OF SCOTLAND LIMITED

Formerly the Royal Bank of Scotland. Later became the Royal Bank of Scotland PLC.

1969 ISSUE

#329-333 wmk: D. Dale. Sign. G. P. Robertson and J. B. Burke. Printer: BWC.

			VG	VF	UNC
329	**1 POUND**				
	19.3.1969. Green on m/c unpt. Forth Road Bridge at l. ctr., old Forth Railway bridge in background. Arms at ctr. r. on back.				
	a. Issued note.		4.00	10.00	40.00
	s. Specimen.		—	—	125.00

			VG	VF	UNC
330	**5 POUNDS**				
	19.3.1969. Blue on m/c unpt. Arms at l. Edinburgh Castle on back.		20.00	45.00	140.00

			VG	VF	UNC
331	**10 POUNDS**				
	19.3.1969. Brown on m/c unpt. Arms at ctr. Tay road bridge on back.		35.00	100.00	350.00
332	**20 POUNDS**				
	19.3.1969. Purple on m/c unpt. Forth road bridge on back.		60.00	125.00	475.00

333	100 POUNDS	VG	VF	UNC
	19.3.1969. Red on m/c unpt. Similar to #332.			
	a. Issued note.	300.00	600.00	1250.00
	s. Specimen.	—	—	—

1970 ISSUE

#334 and 335 like #329 and 330 but w/only 1 sign, J. B. Burke.

334	1 POUND	VG	VF	UNC
	15.7.1970. Green on m/c unpt. Like #329.			
	a. Issued note.	4.00	12.50	40.00
	s. Specimen.	—	—	—

335	5 POUNDS	VG	VF	UNC
	15.7.1970. Blue on m/c unpt. Like #330.	20.00	50.00	150.00

1972 ISSUE

#336-340 arms at r. Wmk: A. Smith. Printer: BWC.

336	1 POUND	VG	VF	UNC
	5.1.1972-1.5.1981. Dk. green on m/c unpt. Edinburgh Castle at l. ctr. on back.			
	a. Issued note.	3.00	7.50	27.50
	s. Specimen.	—	—	100.00

337	5 POUNDS	VG	VF	UNC
	5.1.1972; 2.4.1973; 1.5.1975; 3.5.1976; 1.5.1979; 1.5.1980; 1.5.1981. Blue on m/c unpt. Culzean Castle at l. ctr. on back.			
	a. Issued note.	15.00	30.00	100.00
	s. Specimen.	—	—	175.00

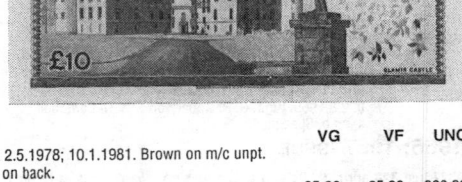

338	10 POUNDS	VG	VF	UNC
	5.1.1972; 15.12.1975; 2.5.1978; 10.1.1981. Brown on m/c unpt. Glamis Castle at l. ctr. on back.			
	a. Issued note.	25.00	65.00	200.00
	s. Specimen.	—	—	225.00
339	20 POUNDS			
	5.1.1972; 1.5.1981. Purple on m/c unpt. Brodick Castle on back.	55.00	120.00	300.00

340	100 POUNDS	VG	VF	UNC
	5.1.1972; 1.5.1981. Red on m/c unpt. Balmoral Castle on back.	250.00	500.00	1000.00

ROYAL BANK OF SCOTLAND PLC

Formerly the Royal Bank of Scotland Limited.

1982-86 ISSUES

REPLACEMENT NOTE #341-345 arms at r. Sign. title varieties.

#341, replacement note: Serial # prefix Y/1.

341 1 POUND
1982-85. Dk. green on m/c unpt. Like #336. Sign. C. Winter.
Printer: BWC.

	VG	VF	UNC
a. W/sorting marks. 3.5.1982.	4.50	12.50	40.00
b. W/o sorting marks. 1.10.1983; 4.1.1984; 3.1.1985.	2.00	6.00	20.00

341A 1 POUND
1986. Dk. green on m/c unpt. Like #341. Printer: TDLR.

	VG	VF	UNC
a. Sign. C. Winter. 1.5.1986.	2.00	4.50	15.00
b. Sign. R. M. Maiden. 17.12.1986.	2.50	5.00	17.50

342 5 POUNDS
1982-86. Blue on m/c unpt. Like #337. Printer: BWC.

	VG	VF	UNC
a. Sign. C. M. Winter. W/sorting marks. 3.5.1982; 5.1.1983.	12.00	30.00	105.00
b. W/o sorting marks. 4.1.1984.	12.00	30.00	100.00
c. Sign. C. M. Winter title larger size. 3.1.1985.	12.00	30.00	105.00
d. Sign. R. M. Maiden. 17.12.1986.	12.00	30.00	95.00

#342A *Deleted. See #342d.*

343 10 POUNDS
1982-86. Brown on m/c unpt. Like #338. Printer: BWC.

	VG	VF	UNC
a. Sign. C. M. Winter. 3.5.1982; 4.1.1984; 3.1.1985.	25.00	60.00	170.00
b. Sign. R. M. Maiden. 17.12.1986.	25.00	60.00	160.00

NOTICE
Readers with unlisted dates, signature varieties, etc. are invited to submit photocopies of their notes to: Standard Catalog of World Paper Money, 700 East State St. Iola, WI 54990-0001, E-Mail: george.cuhaj@fwpubs.com.

344 20 POUNDS
3.5.1982; 3.1.1985. Purple on m/c unpt. Like #339. Printer: BWC. 55.00 100.00 300.00

345 100 POUNDS
3.5.1982. Red on m/c unpt. Like #340. Printer: BWC. 225.00 375.00 850.00

1987 ISSUE

#346-350 Lord Ilay at r. and as wmk. Printer: TDLR. Replacement notes: Serial # prefix: *Z/1.*

346 1 POUND
25.3.1987. Dk. green and green on m/c unpt. Edinburgh Castle at l. ctr. on back.   FV 4.00 12.00

347 5 POUNDS
25.3.1987; 22.6.1988. Black and blue-black on m/c unpt. Culzean Castle at l. ctr. on back.   10.00 17.50 42.50

348 **10 POUNDS**
25.3.1987; 24.2.1988; 22.2.1989; 24.1.1990. Deep brown and brown on m/c unpt. Glamis Castle at l. ctr. on back. Sign. R. M. Maiden.

	VG	VF	UNC
	FV	25.00	65.00

349 **20 POUNDS**
25.3.1987; 24.1.1990. Black and purple on m/c unpt. Brodick Castle at l. ctr. on back. Sign. R. M. Maiden.

	VG	VF	UNC
	40.00	55.00	130.00

350 **100 POUNDS**
1987-. Red on m/c unpt. Balmoral Castle at l. ctr. on back.

	VG	VF	UNC
a. Sign. R. M. Maiden, w/title: *MANAGING DIRECTOR.* 25.3.1987; 24.1.1990.	FV	250.00	500.00
b. Sign. G. R. Mathewson, w/title: *CHIEF EXECUTIVE.* 28.1.1992; 23.3.1994; 24.1.1996; 26.3.1997; 30.9.1998.	FV	FV	400.00
c. Sign. G. R. Matthewson, w/title: *GROUP CHIEF EXECUTIVE.* 30.3.1999.	FV	FV	375.00
d. Sign. Fred Goodwin. 27.6.2000.	FV	FV	350.00

1988-92 ISSUE

#351-355 similar to #346-350, but reduced size. Replacement notes: Serial # prefix: *Z/1.*

#351-354 Lord Ilay at r. and as wmk.

351 **1 POUND**
1988-. Dk. green and green on m/c unpt. Similar to #346, but 127 x 65mm. Printer: TDLR.

	VG	VF	UNC
a. Sign. R. M. Maiden w/title: *MANAGING DIRECTOR.* 13.12.1988; 26.7.1989; 19.12.1990.	FV	3.00	9.00
b. Sign. C. Winter w/title: *CHIEF EXECUTIVE.* 24.7.1991.	FV	FV	6.00
c. Sign. G. R. Mathewson w/title: *CHIEF EXECUTIVE.* 24.3.1992; 24.2.1993; 24.2.1994; 24.1.1996; 1.10.1997.	FV	FV	4.50
d. Sign. G. R. Mathewson, w/title: *GROUP CHIEF EXECUTIVE.* 30.3.1999.	FV	FV	4.50
e. Sign. Fred Goodwin. 27.6.2000; 1.10.2001.	FV	FV	4.00

352 **5 POUNDS**
1988-. Black and blue-black on m/c unpt. Similar to #347, but 135 x 70mm.

	VG	VF	UNC
a. Sign. R. M. Maiden, w/title: *MANAGING DIRECTOR.* 13.12.1988; 24.1.1990.	FV	12.50	30.00
b. Sign. G. R. Mathewson w/title: *CHIEF EXECUTITIVE.* 23.3.1994; 24.1.1996; 26.3.1997; 29.4.1998.	FV	10.00	22.50
c. Sign. G. R. Matthewson, w/title: *GROUP CHIEF EXECUTIVE.* 30.3.1999.	FV	FV	20.00
d. Sign. Fred Goodwin. 27.6.2000.	FV	FV	17.50

353 **10 POUNDS**
1992- Deep brown and brown on m/c unpt. Similar to #348, but 142 x 75mm.

	VG	VF	UNC
a. Sign. G. R. Mathewson, w/title: *CHIEF EXECUTIVE.* 28.1.1992; 7.5.1992; 24.2.1993; 23.3.1994.	FV	FV	35.00
b. Sign. Fred Goodwin, w/title: *GROUP CHIEF EXECUTIVE.* 27.6.2000; 1.10.2001.	FV	FV	32.50

354 **20 POUNDS**
1991-. Black and purple on m/c unpt. Similiar to #349 but 150 x 81mm.

	VG	VF	UNC
a. Sign. C. Winter w/title: *CHIEF EXECUTIVE.* 27.3.1991.	FV	45.00	85.00
b. Sign. G. R. Mathewson. 28.1.1992; 24.2.1993; 26.3.1997; 29.4.1998.	FV	FV	65.00
c. Sign. G. R. Mathewson, w/title: *GROUP CHIEF EXECUTIVE.* 30.3.1999.	FV	45.00	85.00
d. Sign. Fred Goodwin. 27.6.2000.	FV	FV	62.50

#355 not assigned.

1992 COMMEMORATIVE ISSUE

#356, European Summit at Edinburgh, Dec. 1992

356 1 POUND   VG   VF   UNC
8.12.1992. Dk. green and green on m/c unpt. Like #351c but w/additional blue-violet ovpt. containing commemorative inscription at l. Serial # prefix: EC.
a. Issued note.   FV   FV   7.00
s. Specimen.   —   —   10—

1994 REGULAR ISSUE

Lord Ilay at r. Replacement note: Serial # prefix *Y/1*.

357 1 POUND   VG   VF   UNC
23.3.1994. Dk. green and green on m/c unpt. Like #351 but w/o wmk. Printer: BABN.   4.00   15.00   45.00

1994 COMMEMORATIVE ISSUE

#358, Centennial - Death of Robert Louis Stevenson

358 1 POUND   VG   VF   UNC
3.12.1994. Dk. green and green on m/c unpt. Commemorative ovpt. in wmk area on #351c. Portr. R. L. Stevenson and images of his life and works on back. Serial # prefix: RLS.
a. Issued note.   FV   3.00   7.50
s. Specimen.   —   —   100.00

1997 COMMEMORATIVE ISSUE

#359, 150th Anniversary - Birth of Alexander Graham Bell, 1847-1997

359 1 POUND   VG   VF   UNC
3.3.1997. Dk. green and green on m/c unpt. Ovpt. telephone, text and OVD on wmk. area of face like #351c. Portr. A. G. Bell and images of his life and work on back. Serial # prefix: AGB.   FV   FV   5.00

1999 COMMEMORATIVE ISSUE

#360, Opening of the Scottish Parliament

360 1 POUND   VG   VF   UNC
12.5.1999. Dk. green on m/c unpt. Ovpt. Scottish Parliament text at l. on wmk. area of face like #351c. Scottish Parliament bldg. on back. Serial # prefix: SP.   FV   FV   5.00

2000 COMMEMORATIVE ISSUE

#361, Birth centennial of the Queen Mother

361 20 POUNDS   VG   VF   UNC
4.8.2000. Black and purple on m/c unpt. Gold crown w/inscription beneath at l. Queen Mother on back. Serial # prefix: QETQM.   FV   FV   65.00
361A 100 POUNDS
4.8.2000. Black and purple on m/c unpt. Special presentation item for the Queen Mother.

2002 COMMEMORATIVE ISSUE

#362, Queen's Golden Jubilee. Printer: TDLR.

362 5 POUNDS   VG   VF   UNC
6.2.2002. Black and dk. blue on m/c unpt. Gold crown ovpt at l. Back dk. and lt. blue; 1952 and 2002 portraits of Queen Elizabeth II.   FV   FV   15.00

2004 COMMEMORATIVE ISSUE

#363 250th Anniversary of St. Andrews Royal & Ancient Golf Club.

			VG	VF	UNC
363	5 POUNDS		FV	FV	15.00
	14.5.2004. Black and blue-black on m/c unpt. Similar to #352 but shield and 1754 at I. Tom Morris and images of St. Andrews on back. Serial # prefix: *R&A*.				

Note: Also available in a presentation folder.

2005 COMMEMORATIVE ISSUES

500th Anniversary, College of Surgeons.

			VG	VF	UNC
364	5 POUNDS		FV	FV	15.00
	1.7.2005. Commemorative ovpt. at I.				

#365 Jack Nicholas retirement from Golf commemorative. RBS's sponsorship of the British Open at St. Andrew's.

			VG	VF	UNC
365	5 POUNDS		FV	FV	17.50
	14.7.2005. Commemorative ovpt. at I. Jack Nicolas on back.				

#366 New Bank Headquarters at Gogarburn.

366	50 POUNDS		FV	FV	150.00
	14.9.2005. New Bank headquarters at Gogarburn on back.				

2005 REGULAR ISSUE

			VG	VF	UNC
367	50 POUNDS		FV	FV	150.00
	14.9.2005. Inverness Castle on back.				

COLLECTOR SERIES

CLYDESDALE BANK PLC

1996 ISSUE

			Issue Price	Mkt.	Value
CS1	1996 5 POUNDS		60.00		90.00
	Matched serial # (prefix R/B 0 - R/B 3) set #224a-224d.				

Serbia, a former inland Balkan kingdom (now a federated republic with Montenegro) has an area of 34,116 sq. mi. (88,361 sq. km.) Capital: Belgrade.

Serbia emerged as a separate kingdom in the 12th century and attained its greatest expansion and political influence in the mid-14th century. After the Battle of Kosovo, 1389, Serbia became a vassal principality of Turkey and remained under Turkish suzerainty until it was re-established as an independent kingdom by the 1887 Treaty of Berlin. Following World War I, which was in part caused by the assassination of Austrian Archduke Francis Ferdinand by a Serbian nationalist, Serbia joined with the Croats and Slovenes to form the new kingdom of the South Slavs with Petar I of Serbia as king. The name of the kingdom was later changed to Yugoslavia. Invaded by Germany during World War II, Serbia emerged as a constituent republic of the Socialist Federal Republic of Yugoslavia.

With the breakup of Yugoslavia, a Federation of Serbia and Montenegro was formed, with each state using independent currencies.

MONETARY SYSTEM:
1 Dinara ДИНАРА = 100 Para ПАРА

Note: For additional issues refer to Bosnia-Herzegovina and Croatia-Knin in Volume 3, Modern Issues.

FEDERATION OF SERBIA AND MONTENEGRO

NARODNA BANKA SRBIJA

NATIONAL BANK OF SERBIA

2003 ISSUE

			VG	VF	UNC
40	50 DINARA				
	2005. Purple and tan on m/c unpt. Stevan Stojanovic Mokranjac at I. ctr., violin, keyboard and music score at ctr. Mokranjac standing, scores and linear art from Gospel of Miroslav illuminated manuscript.				
	a. Issued note.		FV	FV	2.00
	s. Specimen.		—	—	—

			VG	VF	UNC
41	100 DINARA				
	2003. Lt. and dk. blue on m/c unpt. Nikola Tesla at I. Detail from the Tesla electromagnetic induction engine. at ctr., Tesla at I. vertical format back.				
	a. Issued note.		—	—	4.00
	s. Specimen.		—	—	—

			VG	VF	UNC
42	200 DINARA				
	2005. Black and blue on tan unpt. Nadezda Petrovic at I. ctr., Petrovic sculpture and Gracanica monastery at ctr. Petrovic photo as WWI nurse, Gracanica monastery and painting detail.				
	a. Issued note.		FV	FV	8.50
	s. Specimen.		—	—	—

43   500 DINARA
2004. Green.

	VG	VF	UNC
a. Issued note.	FV	FV	17.50
s. Specimen.			—

44   1000 DINARA
2003. Red on m/c unpt. Dorde Vajfert at l. Vajfert seated, details of
National Bank's interior vertical format back.

	VG	VF	UNC
a. Sign. Mladjan Dinkic.	FV	FV	35.00
b. Sign. Kori Udovicki.	FV	FV	30.00
s. Specimen.			—

45   5000 DINARA
2003. Green on m/c unpt. Slibodan Jovanovic at l. Jovanovic and
Parliament bldg. views.

	VG	VF	UNC
a. Sign. Mladjan Dinkic	FV	FV	150.00
b. Sign. Kori Udovicki.			Expected New Issue
s. Specimen.			

The Republic of Seychelles, an archipelago of 85 granite and coral islands situated in the Indian Ocean 600 miles (965 km.) northeast of Madagascar, has an area of 156 sq. mi. (455 sq. km.) and a population of 82,400. Among these islands are the Aldabra Islands, the Farquhar Group, and Ile Desroches, which the United Kingdom ceded to the Seychelles upon its independence. Capital: Victoria, on Mahe. The economy is based on fishing, a plantation system of agriculture and tourism. Copra, cinnamon and vanilla are exported.

Although the Seychelles are marked on Portuguese charts of the early 16th century, the first recorded visit to the islands, by an English ship, occurred in 1609. The Seychelles were annexed to France by Captain Lazare Picault in 1743 and permanently settled in 1768, with the intention of establishing spice plantations to compete with the Dutch monopoly of the spice trade. British troops seized the islands in 1810, during the Napoleonic Wars; they were formally ceded to Britain by the Treaty of Paris, 1814. The Seychelles were a dependency of Mauritius until Aug. 31, 1903, when they became a separate British Crown Colony. The colony was granted limited internal self-government in 1970, and attained independence on June 28, 1976, becoming Britain's last African possession to do so. Seychelles is a member of the Commonwealth of Nations. The president is the Head of State and of Government.

RULERS:
British to 1976

MONETARY SYSTEM:
1 Rupee = 100 Cents

BRITISH ADMINISTRATION

GOVERNMENT OF SEYCHELLES

1954 ISSUE

#11-13 portr. Qn. Elizabeth II in profile at r. #12 and 13 portr. Qn. Elizabeth II in profile at r. Denominations on back. Various date and sign. varieties. Printer: TDLR.

11   5 RUPEES
1954; 1960. Lilac and green.

	VG	VF	UNC
a. 1.8.1954.	12.50	60.00	275.00
b. 1.8.1960.	7.50	50.00	265.00

12   10 RUPEES
1954-67. Green and red. Like #11.

	VG	VF	UNC
a. 1.8.1954.	12.50	85.00	850.00
b. 1.8.1960.	10.00	80.00	800.00
c. 1.5.1963.	10.00	75.00	750.00
d. 1.1.1967.	7.50	70.00	675.00

13 **50 RUPEES**
1954-67. Black. Like #11.

	VG	VF	UNC
a. 1.8.1954.	30.00	200.00	2000.00
b. 1.8.1960.	27.50	175.00	1750.00
c. 1.5.1963.	25.00	150.00	1700.00
d. 1.1.1967.	25.00	150.00	1600.00

1968 ISSUE

#14-18 Qn. Elizabeth II at r. Wmk: Black parrot's head. Various date and sign. varieties.

14 **5 RUPEES**
1.1.1968. Dk. brown on m/c unpt. Seychelles black parrot at l.

	VG	VF	UNC
a. Issued note.	3.00	20.00	100.00
ct. Color trial. Blue-green on m/c unpt.	—	—	350.00
s. Specimen.	—	—	—

15 **10 RUPEES**
1968; 1974. Lt. blue on m/c unpt. Sea tortoise at l. ctr. Letters *SCUM* discernible beneath tortoise's rear flipper at l.

	VG	VF	UNC
a. 1.1.1968.	7.50	75.00	350.00
b. 1.1.1974.	7.50	60.00	275.00
s. As a. Specimen.	—	—	—

16 **20 RUPEES**
1968-74. Purple on m/c unpt. Bridled tern at l. ctr.

	VG	VF	UNC
a. 1.1.1968.	15.00	125.00	550.00
b. 1.1.1971.	10.00	60.00	300.00
c. 1.1.1974.	10.00	75.00	375.00
s. As c. Specimen.	—	—	—

17 **50 RUPEES**
1968-73. Olive on m/c unpt. Sailing ship at l. Word *SEX* discernible in trees at r.

	VG	VF	UNC
a. 1.1.1968.	40.00	200.00	1250.00
b. 1.1.1969.	40.00	250.00	1500.00
c. 1.10.1970.	25.00	175.00	1200.00
ct. Color trial. Green on m/c unpt.	—	—	1600.00
d. 1.1.1972.	20.00	125.00	600.00
e. 1.8.1973.	25.00	150.00	700.00
s. As d. Specimen.	—	—	—

18 **100 RUPEES**
1968-75. Red on m/c unpt. Land turtles at l. ctr.

	VG	VF	UNC
a. 1.1.1968.	100.00	650.00	2800.00
b. 1.1.1969.	150.00	1000.00	3500.00
c. 1.1.1972.	80.00	600.00	2200.00
ct. Color trial. Blue on m/c unpt.	—	—	2750.00
d. 1.8.1973.	75.00	500.00	2100.00
e. 1.6.1975.	75.00	500.00	2000.00
s. Specimen.	—	—	—

REPUBLIC

REPUBLIC OF SEYCHELLES

1976; 1977 ND ISSUE

#19-22 Pres. J. R. Mancham at r. Wmk: Black parrot's head.

19 **10 RUPEES**
ND (1976). Dk. blue and blue on m/c unpt. Seashell at lower l. Hut w/boats and cliffs on back.

	VG	VF	UNC
a. Issued note.	1.50	5.00	17.50
s. Specimen.	—	—	175.00

		VG	VF	UNC
20	**20 RUPEES** ND (1977). Purple on m/c unpt. Sea tortoise at lower l. Sailboat at l. ctr. on back.			
	a. Issued note.	3.00	10.00	30.00
	s. Specimen.	—	—	125.00

		VG	VF	UNC
21	**50 RUPEES** ND (1977). Olive on m/c unpt. Fish at lower l. Fishermen at l. ctr. on back.			
	a. Issued note.	6.00	25.00	80.00
	s. Specimen.	—	—	165.00

		VG	VF	UNC
22	**100 RUPEES** ND (1977). Red and m/c. Fairy terns at lower l. Dock area and islands on back.			
	a. Issued note.	10.00	40.00	135.00
	s. Specimen.	—	—	235.00

NOTICE

Readers with unlisted dates, signature varieties, etc. are invited to submit photocopies of their notes to: Standard Catalog of World Paper Money, 700 East State St. Iola, WI 54990-0001, E-Mail: george.cuhaj@fwpubs.com.

SEYCHELLES MONETARY AUTHORITY

1979 ND Issue

#23-27 vertical format on back. Wmk: Black parrot's head.

		VG	VF	UNC
23	**10 RUPEES** ND (1979). Blue, green and lt. red on m/c unpt. Red-footed booby at ctr. Girl picking flowers on back.			
	a. Issued note.	FV	2.50	6.50
	s. Specimen.	—	—	125.00

		VG	VF	UNC
24	**25 RUPEES** ND (1979). Brown, purple and gold on m/c unpt. Coconuts at ctr. Man and basket on back.			
	a. Issued note.	FV	7.50	20.00
	s. Specimen.	—	—	125.00

		VG	VF	UNC
25	**50 RUPEES** ND (1979). Olive-green, brown and lilac on m/c unpt. Turtle at ctr. Bldgs. and palm trees on back.			
	a. Issued note.	FV	15.00	45.00
	s. Specimen.	—	—	150.00

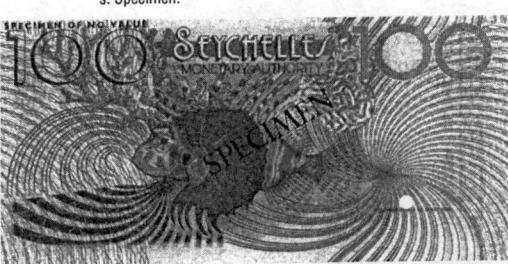

		VG	VF	UNC
26	**100 RUPEES** ND (1979). Red and lt. blue on m/c unpt. Tropical fish at ctr. Man w/tools, swordfish on back.			
	a. Issued note.	15.00	30.00	100.00
	s. Specimen.	—	—	250.00

Note: A shipment of #26 was lost at sea; only serial # A000,001 - A300,000 are valid numbers for exchange.

1980 ND ISSUE

27	100 RUPEES	VG	VF	UNC
	ND (1980). Brown and lt. blue on m/c unpt. Like #26.			
	a. Issued note.	FV	25.00	75.00
	s. Specimen, punch hole cancelled.	—	—	175.00

CENTRAL BANK OF SEYCHELLES

1983 ND ISSUE

#28-31 like previous issue except for new bank name and sign. title. Wmk: Black parrot's head.

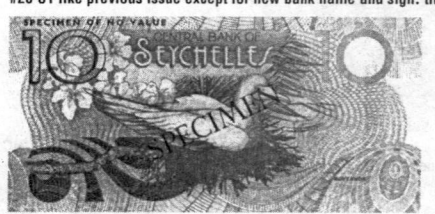

28	10 RUPEES	VG	VF	UNC
	ND (1983). Blue, green and lt. red on m/c unpt. Like #23.			
	a. Issued note.	FV	FV	6.00
	s. Specimen.	—	—	125.00

29	25 RUPEES	VG	VF	UNC
	ND (1983). Brown, purple and gold on m/c unpt. Like #24.			
	a. Issued note.	FV	FV	15.00
	s. Specimen.	—	—	125.00

30	50 RUPEES	VG	VF	UNC
	ND (1983). Olive-green, brown and lilac on m/c unpt. Like #25.			
	a. Issued note.	FV	FV	30.00
	s. Specimen.	—	—	150.00

31	100 RUPEES	VG	VF	UNC
	ND (1983). Brown and lt. blue on m/c unpt. Like #27.			
	a. Issued note.	FV	FV	55.00
	s. Specimen.	—	—	175.00

LABANK SANTRAL SESEL

CENTRAL BANK OF SEYCHELLES

1989 ND ISSUE

#32-35 bank at ctr., flying fish at l. and ctr. r. Wmk: Black parrot's head.

32	10 RUPEES	VG	VF	UNC
	ND (1989). Blue-black and deep blue-green on m/c unpt. Boy scouts at lower l., image of man w/flags and broken chain at r. Local people dancing to drummer at ctr. on back.	FV	FV	6.00

33	25 RUPEES	VG	VF	UNC
	ND (1989). Purple on m/c unpt. 2 men w/coconuts at lower l., boy near palms at upper r. Primitive ox-drawn farm equipment on back.	FV	FV	15.00

34	50 RUPEES	VG	VF	UNC
	ND (1989). Dk. green and brown on m/c unpt. 2 men in boat, Seychelles man at lower l., prow of boat in geometric outline at upper r. Lesser noddy at lower l., fishermen w/nets at ctr., modern cargo ships at r. on back.	FV	FV	27.50

35 **100 RUPEES**
ND (1989). Red and brown on m/c unpt. Men in ox-cart at lower l., girl w/shell at upper r. Bldg. at ctr. on back.

		VG	VF	UNC
		FV	FV	50.00

1998 ND Issue

#36-39 arms at upper l. Cowry shells at upper l. on back. Wmk: Sea tortoise. Ascending size serial #.

36 **10 RUPEES**
ND (1998). Deep blue, dk. green and green on m/c unpt. Coco-de-Mer palm at ctr., black-spotted trigger fish at lower l. Coco-de-Mer palm fruit at lower l., Fairy Terns at ctr., Hawksbill turtle at lower r. on back.

		VG	VF	UNC
		FV	FV	6.00

37 **25 RUPEES**
ND (1998). Purple, violet and blue-violet on m/c unpt. "Wrights gardenia" flower at ctr., Lion fish at lower l. "Bi-Centennary" monument at lower l., coconut crab at ctr., Seychelles blue pigeon at r. on back.

		VG	VF	UNC
		FV	FV	14.00

38 **50 RUPEES**
ND (1998). Dk. green, deep olive-green and brown on m/c unpt. *Paille en Que* orchids at ctr., Angel fish at lower l. Clock tower, autos at lower l., Yellow fin tuna at ctr., Flightless white throated rail or *Tiomitio* at r. on back.

		VG	VF	UNC
		FV	FV	25.00

39 **100 RUPEES**
ND (1998). Red, brown-orange and violet on m/c unpt. Pitcher plant at ctr., Vielle Babone Cecile fish at lower l. Shoreline at lower l., Bridled terns at ctr., giant land tortoise at lower r. on back.

		VG	VF	UNC
		FV	FV	47.50

40 **100 RUPEES**
ND (2001). Red, brown-orange and violet on m/c unpt. Similar to # 39, but w/gold foil impression of sailfish on face.

		VG	VF	UNC
		FV	FV	47.50

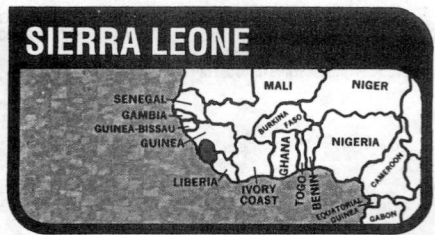

The Republic of Sierra Leone, a British Commonwealth nation located in western Africa between Guinea and Liberia, has an area of 27,699 sq. mi. (71,740 sq. km.) and a population of 4.87 million. Capital: Freetown. The economy is predominantly agricultural but mining contributes significantly to export revenues. Diamonds, iron ore, palm kernels, cocoa and coffee are exported.

The coast of Sierra Leone was first visited by Portuguese and British slavers in the 15th and 16th centuries. The first settlement at Freetown was established in 1787 as a refuge for freed slaves within the British Empire, runaway slaves from the United States and blacks discharged from the British armed forces. The first settlers were virtually wiped out by tribal attacks and disease. The colony was re-established under the auspices of the Sierra Leone Company and transferred to the British Crown in 1907. The interior region was secured and established as a protectorate in 1896. Sierra Leone became independent within the Commonwealth on April 27, 1961, and adopted a republican constitution ten years later. It is a member of the Commonwealth of Nations. The president is Chief of State and Head of Government.

RULERS:
British to 1971

MONETARY SYSTEM:
1 Leone = 100 Cents

REPUBLIC

BANK OF SIERRA LEONE

1964 ND ISSUE

#1-3 300-year-old cottonwood tree and court bldg. at I. on face. Sign. varieties. Wmk: Lion's head. Printer: TDLR.

1	1 LEONE	VG	VF	UNC
	ND (1964-70). Green on m/c unpt. Diamond mining on back.			
	a. ND (1964). Prefix A/1-A/6.	4.50	12.50	65.00
	b. ND (1969). Prefix A/7-A/8.	6.00	18.50	85.00
	c. ND (1970). Prefix A/9-A/12.	2.50	7.50	45.00
	s. As a. Specimen.	—	—	—

#2d replacement notes: Serial # prefix Z1.

2	2 LEONES	VG	VF	UNC
	ND (1964-70). Red on m/c unpt. Village scene on back.			
	a. ND (1964). Prefix B/1-B/21.	5.00	15.00	60.00
	b. ND (1967). Prefix B/22-B/25.	6.00	17.50	85.00
	c. ND (1969). Prefix B/26-B/30.	6.00	17.50	85.00
	d. ND (1970). Prefix B/31-B/41.	5.00	15.00	70.00
	s. As a. Specimen.	—	—	—

3	5 LEONES	VG	VF	UNC
	ND (1964). Purple on m/c unpt. Dockside at Freetown at ctr. r. w/boats in harbor on back. Prefix C/1.			
	a. Issued note.	20.00	75.00	450.00
	s. Specimen.	—	—	—

1974-80 ISSUE

#4-8 Pres. S. Stevens at I. Printer: TDLR. Replacement notes: Serial # prefix Z/1.

4	50 CENTS	VG	VF	UNC
	ND; 1979-84. Dk. brown on m/c unpt. Arms at upper l., flowers in unpt. at r. Central bank bldg. at ctr. on back.			
	a. ND (1972). Prefix D/1-D/2.	0.75	2.00	6.00
	b. ND (1974). Prefix D/3-D/5.	0.60	1.50	4.00
	c. Prefix D/6-D/8. 1.7.1979.	0.50	1.00	3.00
	d. Prefix D/9; D/10. 1.7.1981.	0.15	0.50	1.50
	e. 4.8.1984.	0.10	0.25	0.75
	s. As a. Specimen, w/o prefix.	—	—	—

#5-8 arms at upper r. on back. Wmk: Lion's head.

5	1 LEONE	VG	VF	UNC
	1974-84. Olive-green and dk. green on m/c unpt. Central bank bldg. at ctr. r. on back.			
	a. Prefix A/1-A/7. 19.4.1974.	0.75	2.25	7.50
	b. Prefix A/8-A/12. 1.1.1978.	1.00	4.00	10.00
	c. Prefix A/13-A/17. 1.3.1980.	0.25	1.00	4.00
	d. Prefix A/18-A/26. 1.7.1981.	0.25	0.50	2.00
	e. 4.8.1984.	0.25	0.50	1.00

6   2 LEONES

	VG	VF	UNC
1974-85. Red, deep red-orange and dk. brown on m/c unpt. Central bank bldg. at ctr. r. on back.			
a. Prefix B/1-B/20. 19.4.1974.	1.25	3.50	10.00
b. Prefix B/21-B/22. 1.1.1978.	6.00	15.00	65.00
c. Prefix B/23-B/27. 1.7.1978.	1.00	4.00	12.50
d. Prefix B/28-B/31. 1.7.1979.	0.75	2.00	7.50
e. Prefix B/32-B/37. 1.5.1980.	0.75	2.00	7.00
f. 1.7.1983.	0.25	0.75	3.00
g. 4.8.1984.	0.20	0.45	1.25
h. 4.8.1985.	0.20	0.45	1.25

7   5 LEONES

	VG	VF	UNC
1975-85. Purple and blue-black on m/c unpt. Plant leaves at ctr. Parliament bldg. at ctr. r. on back.			
a. Prefix C/1. 4.8.1975.	3.00	10.00	35.00
b. Prefix C/2. 1.7.1978.	2.00	7.00	25.00
c. Prefix C/3. 1.3.1980.	1.00	4.00	12.50
d. Prefix C/4-C/6. 1.7.1981.	0.75	3.00	7.50
e. 19.4.1984.	0.50	1.00	3.50
f. 4.8.1984.	0.50	1.00	3.50
g. 4.8.1985.	0.50	1.00	3.25

8   10 LEONES

	VG	VF	UNC
1981; 1984. Blue-gray, black and blue-green on m/c unpt. Dredging operation at ctr. r. on back.			
a. Prefix E/1-E/4. 1.7.1981.	1.00	4.00	12.50
b. 19.4.1984.	0.40	1.00	3.00
c. 4.8.1984.	0.40	1.00	3.00

1980 COMMEMORATIVE ISSUE

#9-13, Commemorating The Organisation of African Unity Conference in Freetown

Note: #9-13 were prepared in special booklets (1800 sets).

9   50 CENTS

	VG	VF	UNC
1.7.1980. Dk. brown on m/c unpt. Red ovpt. in 4 lines at upper l. ctr. on #4.	1.00	4.00	15.00

#10-13 red ovpt. in circle around wmk. area at r., date below.

10   1 LEONE

	VG	VF	UNC
1.7.1980. Olive-green and dk. green on m/c unpt. Ovpt. on #5.	1.25	5.00	15.00

11   2 LEONES

	VG	VF	UNC
1.7.1980. Red, deep red-orange and dk. brown on m/c unpt. Ovpt. on #6.	1.50	7.50	20.00

12   5 LEONES

	VG	VF	UNC
1.7.1980. Purple and blue-black on m/c unpt. Ovpt. on #7.	2.25	7.50	22.50

13 **10 LEONES**

	VG	VF	UNC
1.7.1980. Blue-gray, black and blue-green on m/c unpt. Ovpt. on #8.	2.50	10.00	30.00

1982 ISSUE

14 **20 LEONES**

	VG	VF	UNC
1982; 1984. Brown, red and green on m/c unpt. Tree at ctr., Pres. S. Stevens at r. 2 youths pan mining (gold or diamonds) on back. Printer: BWC. Wmk: Lion's head.			
a. 24.8.1982.	1.00	2.50	10.00
b. 24.8.1984.	0.25	1.00	4.00
s. As a, b. Specimen.	—	—	100.00

1988-93 ISSUE

#15-21 arms at upper ctr. Wmk: Lion's head. Replacement notes: Serial # prefix *Z/1*.

#15-19 Pres. Dr. Joseph Saidu Momoh at r.

15 **10 LEONES**

	VG	VF	UNC
27.4.1988. Dk. green and purple on m/c unpt. Steer at l., farmer harvesting at ctr. on back.	FV	0.50	2.00

16 **20 LEONES**

	VG	VF	UNC
27.4.1988. Brown, red and green on m/c unpt. Like #14, but new president at r.	FV	0.75	2.50

17 **50 LEONES**

	VG	VF	UNC
1988-89. Purple, blue and black on m/c unpt. Sports stadium at ctr. Dancers at l. ctr. on back.			
a. W/o imprint. 27.4.1988.	FV	1.50	3.00
b. Printer: TDLR. 27.4.1989.	FV	0.75	2.00

18 **100 LEONES**

	VG	VF	UNC
1988-90. Blue and black on m/c unpt. Bldg. and ship at l. ctr. Local designs at l. and r., Central Bank bldg. at l. ctr. on back.			
a. W/o imprint. 27.4.1988.	FV	1.00	5.00
b. Printer: TDLR. 27.4.1989.	FV	0.75	2.00
c. 26.9.1990.	FV	FV	2.00

19 **500 LEONES**

	VG	VF	UNC
27.4.1991. Red-brown and dark green on m/c unpt. Modern bldg. below arms at l. ctr. 2 fishing boats at l. ctr., artistic carp at r. on back.	FV	1.00	3.75

20	**1000 LEONES**	VG	VF	UNC
	4.8.1993; 27.4.1996. Black, red and yellow on m/c unpt. Bai Bureh at	FV	1.50	5.00
	r., carving at lower ctr. Dish antenna at l. ctr. on back. Printer: TDLR.			

25	**2000 LEONES**	VG	VF	UNC
	1.1.2000. Brown and blue on m/c unpt. I. T. A. Wallace-Johnson at	FV	FV	9.00
	r., cargo ship and storage shed at ctr. Modern bldg. at l. ctr. on			
	back. Printer: TDLR.			

2002-2004 ISSUE

27	**2000 LEONES**	VG	VF	UNC
	1.2.2002; 1.3.2003. Brown and blue on m/c unpt. Like #25 but	FV	FV	9.00
	w/metallic printing. Printer: TDLR.			

21	**5000 LEONES**	VG	VF	UNC
	4.8.1993. Blue and violet on m/c unpt. Sengbe Pieh at r., bldg. at	FV	6.00	22.50
	lower ctr. Dam at l. ctr. on back. Printer: TDLR.			

1995-2000 ISSUES

#22 Not assigned.

28	**5000 LEONES**	VG	VF	UNC
	1.2.2002. M/c.	FV	FV	22.50

29	**10,000 LEONES**	VG	VF	UNC
	4.8.2004. Blue, green and m/c.	FV	FV	40.00

23	**500 LEONES**	VG	VF	UNC
	27.4.1995 (1996); 15.7.1998. Blue-green, brown and green on m/c	FV	FV	3.00
	unpt. K. Londo at r., arms at upper ctr., spearhead at l., bldg. at			
	lower ctr. Fishing boats at l. ctr., artistic carp at r. on back. Similar			
	to #19. Wmk: Lion's head. Printer: TDLR.			

COLLECTOR SERIES

BANK OF SIERRA LEONE

1972 ND ISSUE

#CS1, First Anniversary of Republic, 1972

CS1	ND (19.4.1972) - 50 CENTS	Issue Price	Mkt.	Value
	#4 laminated in plastic w/2 50 cent coins in special maroon case.	—		10.00

Note: #CS1 note has serial # all zeros but w/o specimen ovpt.

1979 ND ISSUE

24	**1000 LEONES**	VG	VF	UNC
	15.7.1998. M/c.	FV	FV	5.00

CS2	ND (1979) 50 CENTS - 5 LEONES	Issue Price	Mkt.	Value
	#4, 5b-7b w/ovpt: SPECIMEN and serial # prefix Maltese cross.	14.00		20.00

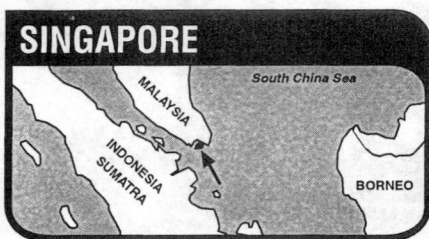

SINGAPORE

The Republic of Singapore, a British Commonwealth nation situated at the southern tip of the Malayan peninsula, has an area of 263 sq. mi. (682 sq. km.) and a population of 4.1 million. Capital: Singapore. The economy is based on electronics production, petrochemicals, pharmaceuticals and shipbuilding/repairs. It is a world financial, business E-commerce, oil refining and air services center, besides having the busiest port in terms of shipping tonnage and containers handled.

Singapore's modern. history - it was an important shipping center in the 14th century before the rise of Malacca and Penang - began in 1819 when Sir Thomas Stamford Raffles, an agent for the British East India Company, founded the town of Singapore. By 1825 its trade exceeded that of Malacca and Penang combined. The opening of the Suez Canal (1869) and the demand for rubber and tin created by the automobile and packaging industries combined to make Singapore one of the major ports of the world. In 1826 Singapore, Penang and Malacca were combined to form the Straits Settlements, which was made a Crown Colony in 1867. Singapore became a separate Crown Colony in 1946 when the Straits Settlements was dissolved. It joined in the formation of Malaysia in 1963, but broke away on Aug. 9, 1965, to become an independent republic. Continued economic prosperity has made Singapore an influential member of the Asian economic community. Singapore is a member of the Commonwealth of Nations. The president is Chief of State. The prime minister is Head of Government.

MONETARY SYSTEM:
1 Dollar = 100 Cents

REPUBLIC

BOARD OF COMMISSIONERS OF CURRENCY

SIGNATURE SEAL VARIETIES

Type I: Dragon, seal script, lion	Type II: Seal script w/symbol

1967-73 ND ISSUE

#1 and 2 wmk: Lion's head. Arms at r. Sign. varieties. Printer: BWC.

1 **1 DOLLAR**

	VG	VF	UNC
ND (1967-72) Blue on m/c unpt. Lt. red flowers (Janet Kaneali Orchid) at ctr., arms at r. Apartment bldgs. on back.			
a. W/o red seal. Sign. Lim Kim San (1967).	4.00	7.50	17.50
b. Red sign. seal Type I at center. Sign. Dr. Goh Keng Swee (1970).	8.00	17.50	35.00
c. W/o red seal. Sign. Hon Sui Sen (1971).	4.00	8.00	19.00
d. Red sign. seal Type II at ctr. Sign. Hon Sui Sen (1972).	2.00	5.00	12.50

2 **5 DOLLARS**

	VG	VF	UNC
ND (1967-73). Green on m/c unpt. Lt. orange flowers (T. M. A. Orchid) at ctr., arms at upper r. Busy scene on the Singapore River on back.			
a. W/o red seal. Sign. Lim Kim San (1967).	15.00	35.00	90.00
b. Red sign. seal Type I at ctr. Sign. Dr. Goh Keng Swee (1970).	80.00	200.00	400.00
c. W/o red seal. Sign. Hon Sui Sen (1972).	30.00	60.00	150.00
d. Red sign. seal Type II at ctr. Sign. Hon Sui Sen (1973).	10.00	22.50	80.00

#3-5 wmk: Lion's head. Printer: TDLR.

3 **10 DOLLARS**

	VG	VF	UNC
ND (1967-73). Red on m/c unpt. Lilac flowers (Dendrobium Marjorie Orchid) at ctr., arms at lower r. 4 hands clasping wrists over map of Singapore at l. ctr. on back.			
a. W/o red seal. Sign. Lim Kim San (1967).	17.50	40.00	100.00
b. Red sign. seal Type I at ctr. Sign. Dr. Goh Keng Swee (1970).	50.00	125.00	300.00
c. W/o red seal. Sign. Hon Sui Sen (1972).	20.00	40.00	100.00
d. Red sign. seal Type II at ctr. Sign. Hon Sui Sen (1973).	15.00	25.00	75.00
s. As d. Specimen.	—	—	250.00

4 **25 DOLLARS**

	VG	VF	UNC
ND (1972). Dk. brown on m/c unpt. Yellow flowers (Renanthopsis Aurora Orchid) at ctr., arms at upper r. Supreme Court bldg. on back.	60.00	100.00	180.00

5 **50 DOLLARS**

	VG	VF	UNC
ND (1967-73). Blue on m/c unpt. Violet flowers (Vanda Rothschildiana Orchid) at ctr., arms at lower r. Singapore seafront and Clifford Pier on back.			
a. W/o red seal. Sign. Lim Kim San (1967).	70.00	125.00	250.00
b. Red sign. seal Type I at ctr. Sign. Dr. Goh Keng Swee (1970).	90.00	225.00	350.00
c. W/o red seal. Sign. Hon Sui Se Sen (1972).	45.00	85.00	200.00
d. Red sign. seal Type II at ctr. Sign. Hon Sui Sen (1973).	35.00	75.00	175.00
s. As d. Specimen.	—	—	375.00

6   100 DOLLARS

		VG	VF	UNC
	ND (1967-73). Blue and violet on m/c unpt. Red flowers (Cattleya Orchid) at ctr., arms at r. Sailing vessels along Singapore waterfront on back. Wmk: Lion's head. Printer: BWC.			
a.	W/o red seal. Sign. Lim Kim San (1967).	90.00	150.00	350.00
b.	Red sign. seal Type I at ctr. Sign. Dr. Goh Keng Swee (1970).	125.00	500.00	825.00
c.	W/o red seal. Sign. Hon Sui Sen (1972).	90.00	175.00	375.00
d.	Red sign. seal Type II at ctr. Sign. Hon Sui Sen (1973).	80.00	150.00	325.00
s.	Specimen.	—	—	500.00

#7-8A wmk: Lion's head. Printer: TDLR.

7   500 DOLLARS

	VG	VF	UNC
ND (1972). Dk. green, lilac on m/c unpt. Pink flowers (Dendrobium Shangri-la) at ctr. Government offices at St. Andrew's road on back.	600.00	1000.00	1500.00

8   1000 DOLLARS

		VG	VF	UNC
	ND (1967-75). Purple on m/c unpt. Lilac-brown colored flowers (Dendrobium Kimiyo Kondo) at ctr., arms at r. Victoria Theatre and Empress Palace on back.			
a.	W/o red seal. Sign. Lim Kim San (1967).	750.00	1200.00	1800.00
b.	Red sign. seal Type I at ctr. Sign. Dr. Goh Keng Swee (1970).	800.00	1500.00	2200.00
c.	W/o red seal. Sign. Hon Sui Sen (1973).	700.00	1300.00	2000.00
d.	Red sign. seal Type II at ctr. Sign. Hon Sui Sen (1975).	650.00	900.00	1600.00

8A   10,000 DOLLARS

	VG	VF	UNC
ND (1973). Green on m/c unpt. Orchids (Aranda Majulah) at ctr., arms at at r. The Istana (Presidential residence) at l. ctr. on back. Sign. Hon Sui Sen.	FV	8000.00	12500.00

1976-80 ND ISSUE

#9-17 city skyline along bottom, arms at upper r. Wmk: Lion's head.

#9 and 10 printer: BWC.

9   1 DOLLAR

	VG	VF	UNC
ND (1976). Blue-black on m/c unpt. Black-naped tern at l. National Day parade passing lg. bldg. at ctr. r. on back.	FV	FV	4.00

10   5 DOLLARS

	VG	VF	UNC
ND (1976). Green and brown on m/c unpt. Red-whiskered bulbul at l. Ariel tram cars and view of harbor on back.	FV	FV	12.50

11   10 DOLLARS

		VG	VF	UNC
	ND (1976). Red and dk. blue on m/c unpt. White collared kingfisher at l. Garden City wiht high rise public housing in background on back. Printer: TDLR.			
a.	W/security thread (1979).	FV	20.00	60.00
b.	W/segmented foil over security thread (1980).	FV	15.00	30.00

12   20 DOLLARS

	VG	VF	UNC
ND (1979). Brown, yellow and blue on m/c unpt. Yellow-breasted Sunbird at l. Back brown; dancer at l., Concorde over Changi International airport ctr. r. Printer: BWC.	20.00	40.00	55.00

13 50 DOLLARS

	VG	VF	UNC
ND (1976). Dk. blue on m/c unpt. White-rumped shama at l. School band on parade on back. Printer: TDLR.			
a. W/security thread.	FV	40.00	100.00
b. W/segmented foil over security thread.	FV	35.00	85.00

14 100 DOLLARS

	VG	VF	UNC
ND (1977). Blue on m/c unpt. Blue-throated Bee eater at l. Various ethnic dancers on back. Printer: BWC.	FV	100.00	200.00

15 500 DOLLARS

	VG	VF	UNC
ND (1977). Green and m/c. Black-naped oriole at l. Back green; view of island and oil refinery at ctr. Printer: TDLR.			
a. Issued note.	FV	450.00	750.00
s. Specimen.	—	—	

16 1000 DOLLARS

	VG	VF	UNC
ND (1978). Violet and brown on m/c unpt. Brahminy Kite bird at l. Container ship terminal on back. Printer: TDLR.	FV	750.00	1250.00

17 10,000 DOLLARS

	VG	VF	UNC
ND (1980). Green on m/c unpt. White-bellied Sea Eagle at l. 19th century Singapore River scene above, modern view below on back. Printer: TDLR.			
a. Issued note.	FV	8000.00	10,000.
s. Specimen, punched hole cancelled.	—	—	1200.00

1984-89 ND Issue

#18-25 arms at upper l. Wmk: Lion's head. Printer: TDLR. Replacement notes: Serial # prefix *Z/1, Z/2,* etc.

18 1 DOLLAR

	VG	VF	UNC
ND (1987). Deep blue and green. Sailing ship *Sha Chuan* at l. Chinese Crasse and carp at lower r. Orchids and satellite tracking station at ctr., on back.			
a. Sign. Goh Keng Swee.	FV	FV	3.00
b. Sign. Hu Tsu Tau.	FV	FV	2.75

19 5 DOLLARS

	VG	VF	UNC
ND (1989). Green and red-violet on m/c unpt. Chinese lion w/ball and Commerson's Anchovy at r. *Twkow* boats at l., View of the PSA container terminal at r. on back.	FV	FV	7.50

25	1000 DOLLARS	VG	VF	UNC
	ND (1984). Purple and red on m/c unpt. Container ship *Neptune Garnet* at l. ctr., Phoenix and Polka-dot grouper at lower r. Shipyard on back.			
	a. Sign. Dr. Goh Keng Swee.	FV	FV	900.00
	b. Sign. Dr. Hu Tsu Tau.	FV	FV	850.00
	s. As a. Specimen.	—	—	—
26	10,000 DOLLARS			
	ND (1987). Red and purple on m/c unpt. General bulk carrier *Neptune Canopus* at l., Chinese dragon at ctr. r. 1987 National Day parade on back.	FV	7000.00	8000.00

20	10 DOLLARS	VG	VF	UNC
	ND (1988). Red-orange and violet on m/c unpt. Trader vessel *Palari* at l., Phoenix and round scad at lower r. Stylized map at ctr., public housing at r. on back.	FV	FV	10.00

#21 Not assigned.

22	50 DOLLARS	VG	VF	UNC
	ND (1987). Blue on m/c unpt. Coastal vessel *Perak* at l. Mountain ducks and six-banded grouper at lower r. 2 raised areas in circles at lower r. Benjamin Shears Bridge and city view on back.			
	a. W/security thread.	FV	FV	65.00
	b. W/segmented foil over security thread.	FV	FV	60.00

1990 ND ISSUE

#27 and 28 printer: TDLR. Replacement notes: Serial prefix *ZZ.*

23	100 DOLLARS	VG	VF	UNC
	ND (1985; 1995). Dk. brown, violet and orange-brown on m/c unpt. Passenger liner *Chusan* at l. ctr. Slender shad and 3 raised areas in circles at lower r. Airplane above w/Changi air terminal at ctr. r. on back.			
	a. W/security thread. Sign. Dr. Goh Keng Swee. (1985).	FV	FV	125.00
	b. W/segmented foil over "clear text" security thread w/$100 *SINGAPORE* in 4 languages. (1995).	FV	FV	110.00
	c. As b. Sign. Hu Tsu Tau.	FV	FV	125.00

27	2 DOLLARS	VG	VF	UNC
	ND (ca.1990). Orange and red on yellow-green unpt. Arms at upper l., *Tongkang* boat and two smaller boats at ctr. Chingay procession on back. Wmk: Lion's head. Printer: TDLR.	FV	FV	3.50

28	2 DOLLARS	VG	VF	UNC
	ND (1992). Deep purple and brown-violet on m/c unpt. Like #27, but w/ascending size serial #.	FV	FV	3.00

Note: #28 also issued in various uncut sheets from 2 to 40 subjects.

1992 COMMEMORATIVE ISSUES

#29, 25th Anniversary - Board of Commissioners of Currency

24	500 DOLLARS	VG	VF	UNC
	ND (1988). Green on m/c unpt. Cargo vessel *Neptune Sardonyx* at l. Members of the three Armed Forces and the Civil Defence Force w/outline map of Singapore on back.	FV	FV	450.00

29	2 DOLLARS	VG	VF	UNC
	ND(1992). Deep purple and brown-violet on m/c unpt. Ovpt: *25 YEARS OF CURRENCY 1967-1992*... on #28. (5000).			
	a. Issued note.	—	—	250.00
	x. W/ovpt. text: *COMMISSONERS* (error).	—	—	300.00

#30 and 31, 25th Anniversary of Independence

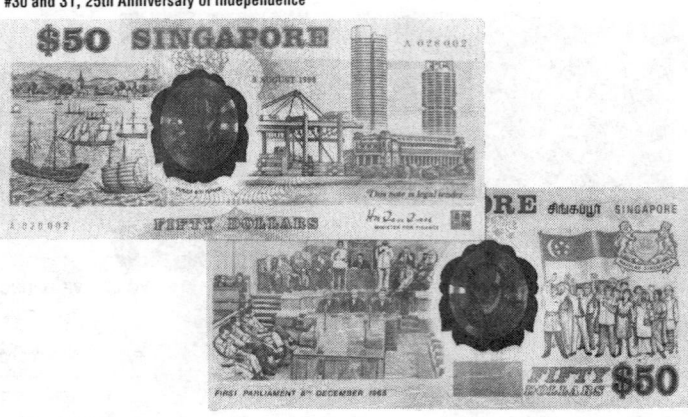

30	50 DOLLARS	VG	VF	UNC
	9.8.1990. Red and purple on m/c unpt. Silver hologram of Yusof bin Ishak at ctr. Old harbor scene at l., modern bldgs. at r. First parliament at l., group of people below flag and arms at r. on back. Plastic.	FV	FV	60.00

Note: #30 was issued in a special commemorative folder.

31	50 DOLLARS			
	ND (1990). Red and purple on m/c unpt. Like #30 but w/o date.	FV	FV	75.00

1994 ND COMMEMORATIVE ISSUE

#31A, 25th Anniversary - Board of Commissioners of Currency

31A	2 DOLLARS	VG	VF	UNC
	ND (1994). Red ovpt. logo of the Board at l. beneath arms on #28.	—	—	100.00

Note: #31A was issued in the book *Prudence at the Helm, 1967-1992.*

1994 REGULAR ISSUE

32	50 DOLLARS	VG	VF	UNC
	ND (1994). Deep blue-black and red on m/c unpt. Like #22. W/segmented foil over security thread. Printer: TDLR.	FV	FV	55.00

1996 COMMEMORATIVE ISSUE

#33, 25th Anniversary of Monetary Authority, 1971-1996

33	25 DOLLARS	VG	VF	UNC
	1.1.1996. Red-brown and green on m/c unpt. Arms at upper l., Monetary Authority bldg. at ctr. Optical variable device at l. ctr. in addition to many other security features. Financial sector skyline on back. Wmk: Lion's head. Sign. Hu Tsu Tau.	FV	FV	55.00

Note: #33 was offered in 2 varieties of special booklets, wide, narrow and uncut sheets of 20 subjects.

1997 ND REGULAR ISSUE

#34 and 35 wmk: Lion's head. Printer: H&S.

34	2 DOLLARS	VG	VF	UNC
	ND (1997). Deep purple and brown-violet on m/c unpt. Like #28.	FV	FV	2.50

35	5 DOLLARS	VG	VF	UNC
	ND (1997). Green and red-violet on m/c unpt. Like #19.	FV	FV	6.00
36	50 DOLLARS			
	ND (1997). Slate gray and red on m/c unpt. Like #32. W/segmented foil over "Cleartext" security thread. W/$50 *SINGAPORE* in 4 languages. Wmk: Lion's head.	FV	FV	45.00

1998 ND ISSUE

37	2 DOLLARS	VG	VF	UNC
	ND(1998). Deep purple and brown-violet on m/c unpt. Like #34. Wmk: Lion's head. Printer: BABN.	FV	FV	2.50

1999 ND ISSUE

#38-45 Pres. Encik Yusof bin Ishak at r. and as wmk. Each back w/different theme.

38	2 DOLLARS	VG	VF	UNC
	ND (1999). Purple, brown and unpt. Education - Victoria Bridge School, Raffles Institue, College of Medicine views with children on back.	FV	FV	2.50

39	5 DOLLARS		VG	VF	UNC
	ND (1999). Green, red and m/c. Garden City - trees and flowers, skyline in background on back.		FV	FV	6.00

40	10 DOLLARS		VG	VF	UNC
	ND (1999). Red, brown and m/c. Sports - swimming, tennis, soccer, sailing, running on back.		FV	FV	12.00

41	50 DOLLARS		VG	VF	UNC
	ND (1999). Slate blue and m/c. Arts - music, graphics on back.		FV	55.00	65.00

42	100 DOLLARS		VG	VF	UNC
	ND (1999). Orange, brown and m/c. Youth - Members of the Singapore Red Cross, St. John's Ambulance Brigade, National Police Cadet Corps, Scouts w/pioneering project, National Service officer w/cereminial sword, Safti Military Institute tower on back.		FV	FV	100.00

43	1000 DOLLARS		VG	VF	UNC
	ND (1999). Purple, lilac and m/c. Parlament House at l., Istana (Presidential residence) at ctr., Supreme Court at r. on back.		FV	FV	800.00
44	10,000 DOLLARS				
	ND (1999). Lt. brown and m/c. Technology - computer chip research lab on back.				
	a. Issued note.		FV	FV	7500.00
	s. Specimen.		—	—	300.00

2000 ISSUE

#45, Red ovpt. added to #38.

45	2 DOLLARS		VG	VF	UNC
	2000. Purple, brown and m/c. #38 with 2000 ovpt. in red at upper r. and lower l.		2.00	3.00	4.00

MONETARY AUTHORITY OF SINAPORE

2005 ISSUE

46	2 DOLLARS		VG	VF	UNC
	ND (2005). Like #38.		FV	FV	2.50
47	5 DOLLARS				
	ND (2005). Like #39.		FV	FV	5.00

48	10 DOLLARS		VG	VF	UNC
	ND (2005). Like #40 but polymer plastic.		FV	FV	10.00
49	50 DOLLARS				Expected New Issue
50	100 DOLLARS				Expected New Issue
51	1000 DOLLARS				Expected New Issue
52	10,000 DOLLARS				Expected New Issue

COLLECTOR SERIES

SINGAPORE

1989 ND ISSUES

		Issue Price	Mkt.	Value
CS1	ND (1989). 1 DOLLAR - 100 DOLLARS			
	#1a-3a, 5a and 6a ovpt: *SPECIMEN.* (77 sets).	—		1850.00
CS2	ND (1989). 1 DOLLAR - 100 DOLLARS			
	#1c-3c, 5c and 6c ovpt: *SPECIMEN.* (89 sets).	—		2250.00
CS3	ND (1989). 1 DOLLAR - 100 DOLLARS			
	#1d-3d, 4, 5d and 6d ovpt: *SPECIMEN.* (82 sets).	—		2400.00
CS4	ND (1989). 1-100 DOLLARS			
	#9-11, 13 and 14 ovpt: *SPECIMEN.* (311 sets).	—		1250.00

2000 ISSUE

		Issue Price	Mkt.	Value
CS5	2 DOLLARS	—		15.00
	Twin sets of albums, each w/3 Two Dollar notes that bear identical serial #s for the last 6 digits. Albums titled: *The Twin Collection of the Millennium Dragon Circa 2000 Singapore.*			

Slovakia as a republic has an area of 18,923 sq. mi. (49,011 sq. km.) and a population of 5.37 million. Capital: Bratislava. Textiles, steel, and wood products are exported.

Slovakia was settled by Slavic Slovaks in the 6th or 7th century and was incorporated into Greater Moravia in the 9th century. After the Moravian state was destroyed early in the 10th century, Slovakia was conquered by the Magyars and remained a land of the Hungarian crown until 1918, when it joined the Czechs in forming Czechoslovakia. In 1938, the Slovaks declared themselves an autonomous state within a federal Czecho-Slovak state. After the German occupation, Slovakia became nominally independent under the protection of Germany, March 16, 1939. Father Jozef Tiso was appointed President. Slovakia was liberated from German control in Oct. 1944, but in May 1945 ceased to be an independent Slovak state. In 1968 it became a constituent state of Czechoslovakia as Slovak Socialist Republic. In January 1991 the Czech and Slovak Federal Republic was formed, and after June 1992 elections, it was decided to split the federation into the Czech Republic and Slovakia on 1 January, 1993.

MONETARY SYSTEM:
1 Korun = 100 Halierov

REPUBLIC

SLOVENSKA REPUBLIKA

REPUBLIC OF SLOVAKIA

1993 ND PROVISIONAL ISSUE

#15-19 Czechoslovakian issue w/affixed adhesive stamps w/*SLOVENSKA / arms / REPUBLIKA.*

			VG	VF	UNC
15	20 KORUN	ND (1993- old date 1988). Black and lt. blue adhesive stamp on Czechoslovakia #95.	1.00	2.50	4.00

			VG	VF	UNC
16	50 KORUN	ND (1993- old date 1987). Black and yellow adhesive stamp on Czechoslovakia #96. Serial # prefixes: *F* and *I.*	2.25	3.50	8.00

			VG	VF	UNC
17	100 KORUN	ND (1993- old date 1961). Black and orange adhesive stamp on Czechoslovakia #91b. Series G37-.	4.00	5.00	9.00
18	500 KORUN	ND (1993- old date 1973). Adhesive stamp on Czechoslovakia #93. Serial # prefixes: *Z, V* and *W.*	17.50	25.00	50.00
19	1000 KORUN	ND (1993- old date 1985). Adhesive stamp on Czechoslovakia #98.	35.00	45.00	90.00

NÁRODNÁ BANKA SLOVENSKA

SLOVAK NATIONAL BANK

1993 ISSUE

#20-24 shield of arms at lower ctr. r. on back. Sign. varieties.

			VG	VF	UNC
20	20 KORUN	1993; 1995; 1997; 1999; 2001. Black and green on m/c unpt. Prince Pribina at r. and as wmk. Nitra Castle at l. on back. Printer: BABN.			
		a. Pale green unpt. 1.9.1993.	FV	FV	3.00
		b. As a. but w/green unpt. at r. Security thread closer at ctr. 1.6.1995.	FV	FV	2.50
		c. As b. 31.10.1997; 1.7.1999; 31.8.2001.	FV	FV	2.00
		d. As a. Serial # prefix A. Uncut sheet of 60 (6000 sheets).	—	—	60.00

			VG	VF	UNC
21	50 KORUN	1993; 1995; 1999; 2002. Black, blue and aqua on m/c unpt. St. Cyril and St. Method at r. and as wmk. Medieval church at Drazovce and first 7 letters of Slavic alphabet on back. Printer: BABN.			
		a. 1.8.1993.	FV	FV	5.00
		b. Security thread closer to ctr. 1.6.1995; 1.7.1999; 2.5.2002.	FV	FV	5.00
		c. As a. Serial # prefix A. Uncut sheet of 45 (4000 sheets).	—	—	100.00

			VG	VF	UNC
22	100 KORUN	1.9.1993. Red and black on orange and m/c unpt. Madonna (by master woodcarver Pavol) from the altar of the Birth in St. Jacob's Church in Levoca at r. Levoca town view on back. Printer: TDLR.			
		a. 1.9.1993. 6Serial # prefix D.	FV	FV	9.00
		b. Serial # prefix A. Uncut sheet of 35 (4000 sheets).	—	—	165.00

23 500 KORUN
1.10.1993. Dk. gray and brown on m/c unpt. Ludovit Stúr at r. and
as wmk. Bratislava Castle and St. Michael's Church at l. on back.
Printer: TDLR.

	VG	VF	UNC
a. Serial # prefix E; F.	FV	FV	30.00
b. Serial # prefix A. Uncut sheet of 28 (2500 sheets).	—	—	525.00
s. Specimen. Perforated; *SPECIMEN*.	—	—	—

24 1000 KORUN
1993; 1995; 1997. Dk. gray and purple on red-violet and m/c unpt.
Andrej Hlinka at r. and as wmk. Madonna of the Church of Liptovké
Sliace near Ruzomberok and Church of St. Andrew in Ruzomberok
at l. ctr. on back. Printer: TDLR.

	VG	VF	UNC
a. 1.10.1993.	FV	FV	55.00
b. Security thread closer to ctr. 1.6.1995.	FV	FV	52.50
c. Prefix B; G. 1.7.1997; 1.8.1997.	FV	FV	52.50
d. As a. Serial # prefix A. Uncut sheet of 28 (1500 sheets).	—	—	1050.00
s. Specimen. Perforated: *SPECIMEN*.	—	—	—

1995; 1996 ISSUE

#25-29 shield of arms at lower ctr. r. on back.

25 100 KORUN
1996-97; 1999; 2001. Like #22 but red-orange replaces dull orange
in corners on back.

	VG	VF	UNC
a. Printer as: *TDLR*. 31.10.1996.	FV	FV	7.00
b. Serial # prefix: *D, L.* 1.10.1997.	FV	FV	7.00
c. Printer as: *DLR.* 1.7.1999; 10.10.2001.	FV	FV	6.00
s. Specimen. Perforated: *SPECIMEN*.	—	—	—

26 200 KORUN
1.8.1995. Dk. gray and blue-green on m/c unpt. Anton Bernolák at
r. and as wmk. Trnava town view at l. ctr. on back. Printer: G&D.

	VG	VF	UNC
a. Issued note.	FV	FV	10.00
s. Specimen. Perforated: *SPECIMEN*.	—	—	—

27 500 KORUN
31.10.1996. Like #23 but blue unpt. at l. ctr. and in corners on face,
also in upper l. ctr. and in corners on back. Dk. brown at ctr. on
back.

	VG	VF	UNC
a. Issued note.	FV	FV	25.00
s. Specimen. Perforated: *SPECIMEN*.	—	—	—

#28 not assigned.

29 5000 KORUN
3.4.1995. Brown-violet and pale yellow-brown on m/c unpt. Milan
Rastislav Stefánik at r., sun and moon at ctr. Stefánik's grave at
Bradlo Hill, part of *Ursa Major* constellation, and a pasque flower at
l. ctr. on back. Printer: G&D.

	VG	VF	UNC
a. Issued note.	FV	FV	175.00
s. Specimen. Perforated: *SPECIMEN*.	—	—	—

1999-2000 ISSUE

Optical variable ink and dots added in wmk. areas. Printer: G&D.

30 200 KORUN
31.5.1999. Dk. gray and blue-green on m/c unpt. Like #26 but
w/optical variable ink in wmk. area.

VG	VF	UNC
FV	FV	7.50

31 500 KORUN
30.10.2000. Dk. gray and brown on m/c unpt. Like #27 but
w/optical variable device in wmk. area.

VG	VF	UNC
FV	FV	17.50

32 1000 KORUN
1.10.1999. Dk. gray and purple on red-violet and m/c unpt. Like
#24 but w/optical variable device in wmk. area.

VG	VF	UNC
FV	FV	30.00

33	5000 KORUN	VG	VF	UNC
	11.5.1999. Orange-brown and olive on m/c unpt. Like #29 but w/optical variable device in wmk. area and addition of a Kinegram l. ctr.	FV	FV	150.00

2000 COMMEMORATIVE ISSUE

Previously Series *A* notes were available only as uncut sheets. These overprints caused problems with bank counting machines and were not in circulation for an extended period of time.

34	20 KORUN	VG	VF	UNC
	1.9.1993. Silver ovpt. on #20. 330,000 pcs.	FV	FV	1.75
35	50 KORUN	VG	VF	UNC
	1.8.1993. Silver ovpt. on #21. 168,750 pcs.	FV	FV	2.50
36	100 KORUN	VG	VF	UNC
	1.9.1993. Silver ovpt. on #22. 133,000 pcs.	FV	FV	4.50

37	200 KORUN	VG	VF	UNC
	1.8.1995. Silver ovpt. on #26. 108,000 pcs.	FV	FV	7.50
38	500 KORUN	VG	VF	UNC
	1.10.1993. Silver ovpt. on #23. 67,200 pcs.	FV	FV	20.00
39	1000 KORUN	VG	VF	UNC
	1.10.1993. Silver ovpt on #24a. 40,600 pcs.	FV	FV	35.00

40	5000 KORUN	VG	VF	UNC
	3.4.1995. Gold ovpt. on #29. 10,800 pcs.	FV	FV	175.00

2002 ISSUE

41	200 KORUN	VG	VF	UNC
	30.8.2002. Dk. gray and blue-green on m/c unpt. Like #30 but with additional security features. Printer: FCO.	FV	FV	7.50
42	1000 KORUN	FV	FV	30.00
	10.6.2002. Dk. gray and purple on red-violet and m/c unpt. Similar to #32 but with additional security features. Printer: (T)DLR.			
43	5000 KORUN	FV	FV	150.00
	17.11.2003. Orange-brown and olive on m/c unpt. Like #33 but with additional security features.			

SLOVENIA

The Republic of Slovenia is bounded in the north by Austria, northeast by Hungary, southeast by Croatia and to the west by Italy. It has an area of 5,246 sq. mi. (20,251 sq. km.) and a population of 1.99 million. Capital: Ljubljana. The economy is based on electricity, minerals, forestry, agriculture and fishing. Small industries are being developed during privatization.

The lands originally settled by Slovenes in the 6th century were steadily encroached upon by Germans. Slovenia developed as part of Austro-Hungarian Empire after the defeat of the latter in World War I it became part of the Kingdom of the Serbs, Croats and Slovenes (Yugoslavia) established on December 1, 1918. A legal opposition group, the Slovene League of Social Democrats, was formed in Jan. 1989. In Oct. 1989 the Slovene Assembly voted a constitutional amendment giving it the right to secede from Yugoslavia. On July 2, 1990 the Assembly adopted a 'declaration of sovereignty' and in Sept. proclaimed its control over the territorial defense force on its soil. A referendum on Dec. 23 resulted in a majority vote for independence, which was formally declared on Dec. 26. In Feb. 1991 parliament ruled that henceforth Slovenian law took precedence over federal. On June 25, Slovenia declared independence, but agreed to suspend this for 3 months at peace talks sponsored by the EC. The moratorium having expired, Slovenia (and Croatia) declared their complete independence of the Yugoslav federation on Oct. 8, 1991.

MONETARY SYSTEM:
1 (Tolar) = 1 Yugoslavian Dinar
1 Tolar = 100 Stotinas

REPLACEMENT NOTES:
#11-19, ZA prefix.

REPUBLIC

BANKA SLOVENIJE (FIRST)

1989 ISSUE

A1	1 LIPA	VG	VF	UNC
	29.11.1989 (1990). Green. Plants at l., Dr. France Preseren at r. Slovenian Parliament on back.			
	a. Issued note.	3.00	8.00	20.00
	s. Specimen.	—	—	20.00

Note: reportedly 25,000 notes issued, of which more than 10,000 were distributed.

REPUBLIKA SLOVENIJA

1990-92 ISSUE

#1-10 pedimented behive at lower l., denomination numeral in guilloche over a representation of the dance of the Catrniolan bee on an underprint of honeycomb at ctr. r. Date given as first 2 numerals of serial #. Mountain ridge of Triglav at l. ctr. on back. Wmk: Symmetrical designs repeated.

Note: About 500 sets of Specimens #1s-10s were released to the general collecting public. Specimens exist with normal serial #'s and with 0's as serial #'s. Zero serial #'s are valued up to $20.00 each.

B1	50 (TOLARJEV)	VG	VF	UNC
	(19)90. Not issued.	—	—	50.00

Note: #B1 was not released in 1990, but sold to collectors with #9A about twelve years later.

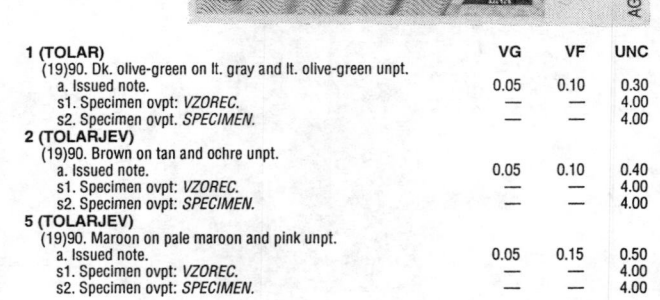

1	1 (TOLAR)	VG	VF	UNC
	(19)90. Dk. olive-green on lt. gray and lt. olive-green unpt.			
	a. Issued note.	0.05	0.10	0.30
	s1. Specimen ovpt: *VZOREC.*	—	—	4.00
	s2. Specimen ovpt: *SPECIMEN.*	—	—	4.00
2	2 (TOLARJEV)			
	(19)90. Brown on tan and ochre unpt.			
	a. Issued note.	0.05	0.10	0.40
	s1. Specimen ovpt: *VZOREC.*	—	—	4.00
	s2. Specimen ovpt: *SPECIMEN.*	—	—	4.00
3	5 (TOLARJEV)			
	(19)90. Maroon on pale maroon and pink unpt.			
	a. Issued note.	0.05	0.15	0.50
	s1. Specimen ovpt: *VZOREC.*	—	—	4.00
	s2. Specimen ovpt: *SPECIMEN.*	—	—	4.00

4	10 (TOLARJEV)	VG	VF	UNC
	(19)90. Dk. blue-green and grayish purple on lt. blue-green unpt.			
	a. Issued note.	FV	FV	3.00
	s1. Specimen ovpt: *VZOREC.*	—	—	4.00
	s2. Specimen ovpt: *SPECIMEN.*	—	—	4.00
5	50 (TOLARJEV)			
	(19)90. Dk. gray on tan and lt. gray unpt.			
	a. Issued note.	FV	FV	5.00
	s1. Specimen ovpt: *VZOREC.*	—	—	3.50
	s2. Specimen ovpt: *SPECIMEN.*	—	—	4.00

6	100 (TOLARJEV)	VG	VF	UNC
	(19)90. Reddish brown and violet on orange and lt. violet unpt.			
	a. Issued note.	FV	FV	8.00
	s1. Specimen ovpt: *VZOREC.*	—	—	3.50
	s2. Specimen ovpt: *SPECIMEN.*	—	—	4.00
7	200 (TOLARJEV)			
	(19)90. Greenish black and dk. brown on lt. gray and lt. green unpt.			
	a. Issued note.	FV	FV	25.00
	s. Specimen ovpt: *SPECIMEN.*	—	—	4.00

8	500 (TOLARJEV)	VG	VF	UNC
	(19)90; (19)92. Deep lilac and red on pink and pale blue unpt.			
	a. 1990.	FV	FV	25.00
	b. 1992.	FV	FV	40.00
	s1. Specimen ovpt: *VZOREC.*	—	—	3.50
	s2. Specimen ovpt: *SPECIMEN.*	—	—	4.00

9	1000 (TOLARJEV)	VG	VF	UNC
	(19)91; (19)92. Dk. blue-gray and gray on lt. gray and pale blue unpt.			
	a. 1991.	FV	FV	35.00
	b. 1992.	FV	FV	45.00
	s1. Specimen ovpt: *VZOREC.* Wmk: Column pedestal.	—	—	7.50
	s2. Specimen ovpt: *SPECIMEN.* Wmk: Column pedestal.	—	—	7.50
	s3. Specimen ovpt: *SPECIMEN.* Wmk: Snowflake (error).	—	—	150.00

9A	2000 (TOLARJEV)	VG	VF	UNC
	(19)91. M/c. (Not issued).	—	—	60.00

Note: #9A was not released into circulation, but sold along with #B1 to collectors about twelve years later.

10	5000 (TOLARJEV)	VG	VF	UNC
	(19)92. Purple and lilac on pink unpt.			
	a. Issued note.	FV	FV	130.00
	s1. Specimen ovpt: *VZOREC.*	—	—	20.00
	s2. Specimen ovpt: *SPECIMEN.*	—	—	10.00

BANKA SLOVENIJE

1992-93 ISSUE

#11-20 replacement notes: Serial # prefix *AZ* and possibly others.

		VG	VF	UNC
11	**10 TOLARJEV** 15.1.1992. Black, brown-violet and brown-orange on m/c unpt. P. Trubar at r. and as wmk. Quill pen at l. ctr. Ursuline church in Ljubljana at ctr. on back.			
	a. Issued note.	FV	FV	0.50
	s. Specimen ovpt: *VZOREC*.	—	—	8.50

		VG	VF	UNC
12	**20 TOLARJEV** 15.1.1992. Brownish black, deep brown and brown-orange on m/c unpt. J. Vajkard Valvasor at r. and as wmk., compass at l. Topographical outlines at l. ctr., cherub arms at r. on back.			
	a. Issued note.	FV	FV	0.75
	s. Specimen ovpt: *VZOREC*.	—	—	10.00

		VG	VF	UNC
13	**50 TOLARJEV** 15.1.1992. Black, purple and brown-orange on m/c unpt. J. Vega at r. and as wmk., geometric design and calculations at l. ctr. Academy at upper l., planets and geometric design at ctr. on back.			
	a. Issued note.	FV	FV	1.50
	s. Specimen ovpt: *VZOREC*.	—	—	12.50

		VG	VF	UNC
14	**100 TOLARJEV** 15.1.1992. Black, blue-black and brown-orange on m/c unpt. R. Jakopic at r. and as wmk. Outline of the Jakopicev Pavilion at ctr. r. on back.			
	a. Issued note.	FV	FV	2.75
	s. Specimen ovpt: *SPECIMEN* and *VZOREC*.	—	—	15.00

		VG	VF	UNC
15	**200 TOLARJEV** 1992; 1997; 2001. Black, violet-brown and brown-orange on m/c unpt. I. Gallus at r. and as wmk., musical façade at l. Drawing of Slovenia's Philharmonic bldg. at upper l., 5 lines of medieval music at upper ctr. on back.			
	a. 15.1.1992.	FV	FV	20.00
	b. 8.10.1997.	FV	FV	3.25
	c. 15.1.2001.	FV	FV	3.00
	s. Specimen ovpt: *SPECIMEN* and *VZOREC*.	—	—	17.50

		VG	VF	UNC
16	**500 TOLARJEV** 1992; 2001. Black, red and brown-orange on m/c unpt. J. Plecnik at r. and as wmk. Drawing of the National and University Library of Ljubljana at l. ctr. on back.			
	a. 15.1.1992.	FV	FV	9.00
	b. 15.1.2001.	FV	FV	8.00
	s. Specimen ovpt: *SPECIMEN* and *VZOREC*.	—	—	20.00

		VG	VF	UNC
17	**1000 TOLARJEV** 15.1.1992. Brownish black, deep green and brown-orange on m/c unpt. F. Preseren at r. and as wmk. The poem "Drinking Toast" at ctr. on back.			
	a. Issued note.	FV	FV	22.50
	s. Specimen ovpt: *SPECIMEN* and *VZOREC*.	—	—	25.00

		VG	VF	UNC
18	**1000 TOLARJEV** 1.6.1993. Black, deep blue-green and brown-orange on m/c unpt. Like #17 but modified portrait and other incidental changes including color.			
	a. W/o *1000* in UV ink on back.	FV	FV	15.00
	b. W/*1000* in UV ink on back.	FV	FV	15.00
	s. Specimen ovpt: *SPECIMEN* and *VZOREC*.	—	—	25.00

19	5000 TOLARJEV	VG	VF	UNC
	1.6.1993. Brownish black, dk. brown and brown-orange on m/c unpt. l. Kobilika at r. and as wmk. National Gallery in Ljubljana at upper l. on back.			
	a. Issued note.	FV	FV	80.00
	s. Specimen ovpt: *SPECIMEN* and *VZOREC*.	—	—	30.00

20	10,000 TOLARJEV	VG	VF	UNC
	28.6.1994. Black, purple and brown-orange on m/c unpt. l. Cankar at r. and as wmk. Chrysanthemum blossom at l. on back.			
	a. Issued note.	FV	FV	110.00
	s. Specimen ovpt: *SPECIMEN* and *VZOREC*.	—	—	35.00

1997 ISSUE

21	5000 TOLARJEV	VG	VF	UNC
	8.10.1997. Brownish black, dk. brown and brown-orange on m/c unpt. Like #19 but w/scalloped kinegram w/cameo portr.//value.			
	a. Kinegram 5000 vertical.	FV	FV	50.00
	b. Kinegram 5000 horizontal.	FV	FV	50.00
	s. Specimen ovpt: *SPECIMEN* and *VZOREC*.	—	—	25.00

2000 ISSUE

22	1000 TOLARJEV	VG	VF	UNC
	15.1.2000. Black, green and yellow. Similar to #18. Specimen ovpt. *SPECIMEN* and *VZOREC*.			
	a. Issued note.	FV	FV	10.00
	s. Specimen ovpt: *SPECIMEN* and *VZOREC*.			

23	5000 TOLARJEV	VG	VF	UNC
	15.1.2000. Black, green, red and orange. Similar to # 21a.			
	a. Issued note.	FV	FV	45.00
	s. Specimen ovpt: *SPECIMEN* and *VZOREC*.	—	—	—

24	10,000 TOLARJEV	VG	VF	UNC
	15.1.2000. Brown-black, purple and red. Similar to #20 but w/holographic band at r. edge.			
	a. Issued note.	FV	FV	80.00
	s. Specimen ovpt: *SPECIMEN* and *VZOREC*.	—	—	—

2000 COMMEMORATIVE ISSUE

#25-27, 10th Anniversary of Bank Slovenije

25	100 TOLARJEV		VG	VF	UNC
	2001. Like #14 but w/special text ovpt. (10,000 pieces).		FV	FV	3.00

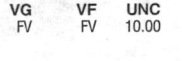

26	1000 TOLARJEV		VG	VF	UNC
	2001. Like #22 but w/special text ovpt. (5,000 pieces)		FV	FV	10.00

27	10,000 TOLARJEV		VG	VF	UNC
	2001. Like #24 but w/special text ovpt. (1,000 pieces).		FV	FV	80.00

2004 COMMEMORATIVE ISSUE

#28-30 EU entry on May 1, 2004.

28	100 TOLARJEV		VG	VF	UNC
	2003. M/c. Like #14 but w/special ovpt. (10,000 pieces).		FV	FV	7.50

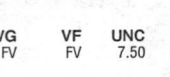

29	1000 TOLARJEV		VG	VF	UNC
	2003. M/c. Like #22 but w/special ovpt. (5,000 pieces).		FV	FV	25.00

30	10,000 TOLARJEV		VG	VF	UNC
	2003. M/c. Like #24 but w/special ovpt. (1,000 pieces).		FV	FV	125.00

2003 ISSUE

31	100 TOLARJEV		VG	VF	UNC
	15.1.2003. Black and blue on m/c unpt.				
	a. Issued note.		FV	FV	2.75
	s. Specimen ovpt: *SPECIMEN* and *VZOREC*.		—	—	—

32	1000 TOLARJEV		VG	VF	UNC
	15.1.2003. Black and green on m/c unpt.				
	a. Issued note.		FV	FV	10.00
	s. Specimen ovpt: *SPECIMEN* and *VZOREC*.		—	—	—

33 **5000 TOLARJEV**   VG   VF   UNC
15.1.2002. Black, green, red and orange. Similar to #23.
   a. Issued note.   FV   FV   45.00
   s. Specimen.

34 **10,000 TOLARJEV**   VG   VF   UNC
15.1.2003. Black and purple on m/c unpt. Iridescent ink added onto chrysanthemum on back.
   a. Issued note.   FV   FV   80.00
   s. Specimen ovpt: *SPECIMEN* and *VZOREC*.

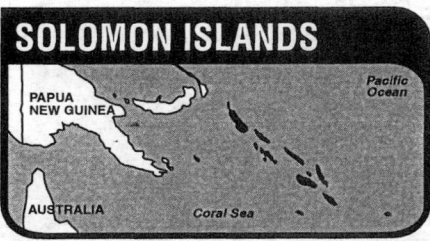

The Solomon Islands, located in the Southwest Pacific east of Papua New Guinea, has an area of 10,983 sq. mi. (28,450 sq. km.) and an estimated population of 444,000. Capital: Honiara. The most important islands of the Solomon chain are Guadalcanal (scene of some of the fiercest fighting of World War II), Malaitia, New Georgia, Florida, Vella Lavella, Choiseul, Rendova, San Cristobal, the Lord Howe group, the Santa Cruz islands, and the Duff group. Copra is the only important cash crop but it is hoped that timber will become an economic factor.

The Solomon Islands were discovered by Spanish navigator Alvaro de Mendana in 1567, and in 1569 he made an unsuccessful attempt to colonize them. European knowledge of the group would not be completed until the end of the 18th century. Germany declared a protectorate over the northern Solomons in 1885. The British protectorate over the southern Solomons was established in 1893. In 1899 Germany transferred its claim to all Solomon Islands except Buka and Bougainville to Great Britain in exchange for recognition of German claims in western Samoa. Australia occupied the two German held islands in 1914, and administered them after 1920.

The Japanese invaded the Solomons during 1942-43, but were driven out by an American counteroffensive after a series of bloody clashes.

Following World War II the islands returned to the status of a British protectorate. In 1976 the protectorate was abolished and the Solomons became a self-governing dependency. Full independence was achieved on July 7, 1978. Solomon Islands is a member of the Commonwealth of Nations. Elizabeth II is Head of State as Queen of the Solomon Islands.

RULERS:
   British

MONETARY SYSTEM:
   1 Shilling = 12 Pence
   1 Pound = 20 Shillings to 1966
   1 Dollar = 100 Cents, 1966-

SIGNATURE VARIETIES						
	CHAIRMAN	**MEMBER**			**GOVERNOR**	**DIRECTOR**
1			4			
2			5			
3			6			
	GOVERNOR	**SEC. OF FINANCE**			**GOVERNOR**	**SEC. OF FINANCE**
7		George Kiriau	8		Rick N. Houenipwela	

BRITISH ADMINISTRATION

SOLOMON ISLANDS MONETARY AUTHORITY

1977; 1981 ND ISSUE
Dollar System
#5-8 Qn. Elizabeth II at r. Wmk: Falcon. Printer: TDLR (w/o imprint). Replacement notes: Serial # prefix: *Z/1*.

5 **2 DOLLARS**   VG   VF   UNC
ND (1977). Dk. green on pink and pale green unpt. Fishermen on back. Sign. 1.
   a. Issued note.   1.00   2.00   10.00
   s. Specimen.   —   —   30.00

6	5 DOLLARS	VG	VF	UNC
	ND (1977). Dk. blue on m/c unpt. Long boats and hut on back.			
	a. Sign. 1.	2.25	4.00	22.50
	b. Sign. 2.	2.25	5.00	25.00
	s. As a. Specimen.	—	—	30.00

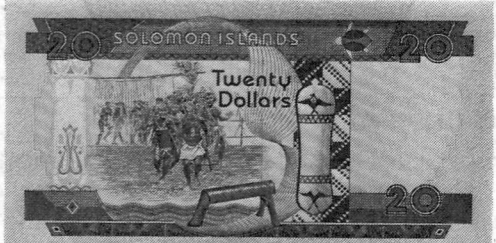

7	10 DOLLARS	VG	VF	UNC
	ND (1977). Purple and violet on m/c unpt. Weaver on back.			
	a. Sign. 1.	4.00	7.50	30.00
	b. Sign. 2.	4.00	8.00	37.50
	s. As a. Specimen.	—	—	30.00

8	20 DOLLARS	VG	VF	UNC
	ND (1981). Brown and deep orange on m/c unpt. Line of people on back. Sign. 3.	7.00	15.00	55.00

CENTRAL BANK OF SOLOMON ISLANDS
1984 ND ISSUE

#11 and 12 like #7 and 8 except for new bank name. Wmk: Falcon. Sign. 4. Replacement notes: Serial # prefix *Z/1*.

11	10 DOLLARS	VG	VF	UNC
	ND (1984). Purple and violet on m/c unpt.	FV	7.50	22.50

12	20 DOLLARS	VG	VF	UNC
	ND (1984). Brown and dk. orange on m/c unpt.	FV	12.50	45.00

1986 ND ISSUE
#13-17 arms at r. Wmk: Falcon. Sign. 5. Replacement notes: Replacement notes: Serial # prefix *Y/1*.
#13-16 backs like #5-8.

13	2 DOLLARS	VG	VF	UNC
	ND (1986). Green on m/c unpt.			
	a. Issued note.	FV	FV	2.25
	s. Specimen.	—	—	25.00

14	5 DOLLARS	VG	VF	UNC
	ND (1986). Dk. blue, deep purple and violet on m/c unpt.			
	a. Issued note.	FV	FV	5.00
	s. Specimen.	—	—	25.00

15	10 DOLLARS	VG	VF	UNC
	ND (1986). Purple and violet on m/c unpt.			
	a. Issued note.	FV	FV	10.00
	s. Specimen.	—	—	10.00

16	20 DOLLARS	VG	VF	UNC
	ND (1986). Brown and deep orange on m/c unpt.			
	a. Issued note.	FV	FV	20.00
	s. Specimen.	—	—	25.00

17	50 DOLLARS	VG	VF	UNC
	ND (1986). Blue-green and purple on m/c unpt. Butterflies and reptiles on back.			
	a. Issued note.	FV	FV	45.00
	s. Specimen.	—	—	30.00

1996; 1997 ND ISSUE

#18-22 similar to #13-17 but w/added security devices. Printing in wmk. area on back. Ascending size serial #. W/security thread. Wmk: Falcon. Replacement notes: Serial # prefix X/1.

18	2 DOLLARS	VG	VF	UNC
	ND (1997). Greenish black and olive-green on m/c unpt.	FV	FV	2.00

19	5 DOLLARS	VG	VF	UNC
	ND (1997). Dk. blue, deep purple and violet on m/c unpt.	FV	FV	4.00

20	10 DOLLARS	VG	VF	UNC
	ND (1996). Purple and red-violet on m/c unpt.	FV	FV	7.00

21	20 DOLLARS	VG	VF	UNC
	ND (1996). Brown and brown-orange on m/c unpt.	FV	FV	12.50

22	50 DOLLARS	VG	VF	UNC
	ND (1996). Green, Blue-gray and purple on m/c unpt.	FV	FV	30.00

2001 COMMEMORATIVE ISSUE

#23, 25th Anniversary Central Bank of Solomon Islands

23	2 DOLLARS	VG	VF	UNC
	(20)01. Dk. and lt. green on m/c unpt. Similar to #18 but w/ornate window design. Silver imprint *CBSI Silver Jubilee* on face, and *COMMEMORATING CBSI SILVER JUBILEE* on back. Polymer plastic.	FV	FV	2.00

2001 ND ISSUE

24	50 DOLLARS	VG	VF	UNC
	ND (2001). Green, blue-gray and purple on m/c unpt. Similar to #22 but flag added at l. ctr., segmented silver security strip at ctr. r., and vertical serial # at r. Smaller size in width.	FV	FV	30.00

COLLECTOR SERIES

SOLOMON ISLANDS MONETARY AUTHORITY

1979 ND ISSUE

		Issue Price	Mkt.	Value
CS1	ND (1979) 2-10 DOLLARS	14.00		25.00
	#5, 6b, 7b w/ovpt: *SPECIMEN* and serial # prefix Maltese cross.			

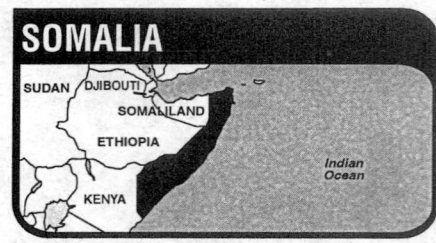

Somalia, the Somali Democratic Republic, comprising the former Italian Somaliland, is located on the coast of the eastern projection of the African continent commonly referred to as the *Horn*. It has an area of 178,201 sq. mi. (461,657 sq. km.) and a population of 11.53 million. Capitol Mogadishu. The economy is pastoral and agricultural. Livestock, bananas and hides are exported. The area of the British Somaliland Protectorate was known to the Egyptians at least 1,500 years B.C., and was occupied by the Arabs and Portuguese before British sea captains obtained trading and anchorage rights in 1827. The land of sandy clay and sporadic rainfall acquired a strategic importance with the opening of the Suez Canal in 1869. After negotiating treaties with the tribes, Britain declared the area a protectorate in 1888. Italy acquired Italian Somaliland in 1895 by purchase from the sultan of Zanzibar. Britain occupied Italian Somaliland in 1941 and administered it until April 1, 1950, when it was returned to Italy as a U.N. trusteeship. The British Somaliland protectorate became independent on June 26, 1960. Five days later it joined with Italian Somaliland to form the Somali Republic. The country was under a revolutionary military regime installed Oct. 21, 1969. After 11 years of civil war rebel forces fought their way into the capital. A. M. Muhammad became president in Aug. 1991 but interfactional fighting continued. A UN-sponsored truce was signed in March 1992 and a peace plan and pact was signed Jan. 15, 1993. The northern Somali National Movements (SNM) declared a secession of the northwestern Somaliland Republic on May 17, 1991 which is not recognized by the Somali Democratic Republic.

MONETARY SYSTEM:
    1 Scellino = 1 Shilling = 100 Centesimi
    1 Shilin = 1 Shilling = 100 Centi

REPUBLIC

BANCA NAZIONALE SOMALA

1962 ISSUE

#1-4 sign. title: *IL PRESIDENTE* at l. Wmk: Leopard's head. Printer OCV.

1	5 SCELLINI = 5 SHILLINGS	VG	VF	UNC
	1962. Red on green and orange unpt. Antelope at l. Back orange-brown; dhow at ctr.			
	a. Issued note.	15.00	35.00	200.00
	s. Specimen.	—	—	110.00

2	10 SCELLINI = 10 SHILLINGS	VG	VF	UNC
	1962. Green on red-brown and green unpt. Flower at l. Back brown and green; river scene at ctr. r.			
	a. Issued note.	20.00	55.00	325.00
	s. Specimen.	—	—	185.00

3	20 SCELLINI = 20 SHILLINGS	VG	VF	UNC
	1962. Brown on blue and gold unpt. Banana plant at l. Back brown and blue; bank bldg. at ctr. r.			
	a. Issued note.	25.00	75.00	600.00
	s. Specimen.	—	—	750.00

4	100 SCELLINI = 100 SHILLINGS	VG	VF	UNC
	1962. Blue on green and orange unpt. Artcraft at l. Back blue and red; bldg.			
	a. Issued note.	35.00	125.00	750.00
	s. Specimen.	—	—	400.00

1966 ISSUE

#5-8 slight changes in colors and design elements (w/o imprint). Wmk: Leopard's head.

5	5 SCELLINI = 5 SHILLINGS	VG	VF	UNC
	1966. Similar to #1 but different guilloche in unpt. Back w/blue unpt.			
	a. Issued note.	10.00	30.00	175.00
	s. Specimen perforated: *ANNULLATO*.	—	—	100.00
6	10 SCELLINI = 10 SHILLINGS	VG	VF	UNC
	1966. Similar to #2 but different guilloche in unpt. Back green w/lt. tan unpt.			
	a. Issued note.	15.00	50.00	325.00
	s. Specimen perforated: *ANNULLATO*.	—	—	225.00
7	20 SCELLINI = 20 SHILLINGS	VG	VF	UNC
	1966. Similar to #3 but unpt. is pink, blue and green. Brown bank bldg. on back.			
	a. Issued note.	25.00	65.00	450.00
	s. Specimen perforated: *ANNULLATO*.	—	—	325.00
8	100 SCELLINI = 100 SHILLINGS	VG	VF	UNC
	1966. Similar to #4 but unpt. is green, purple and tan.			
	a. Issued note.	35.00	120.00	600.00
	s. Specimen perforated: *ANNULLATO*.	—	—	435.00

1968 ISSUE

#9-12 Wmk: Leopard's head. Sign. title *IL GOVERNATORE* at l.

9	5 SCELLINI = 5 SHILLINGS	VG	VF	UNC
	1968. Red on green and orange unpt. Like #5.	15.00	40.00	250.00
10	10 SCELLINI = 10 SHILLINGS			
	1968. Green on red-brown and green unpt. Like #6.	20.00	55.00	450.00
11	20 SCELLINI = 20 SHILLINGS			
	1968. Brown on blue and gold unpt. Like #7.	25.00	85.00	575.00
12	100 SCELLINI = 100 SHILLINGS			
	1968. Blue on green and orange unpt. Like #8.	37.50	125.00	850.00

DEMOCRATIC REPUBLIC

BANCA NAZIONALE SOMALA

1971 ISSUE

#13-16 like #9-12. Wmk: Leopard's head. Sign. title: *IL GOVERNATORE* and *IL CASSIERE* at r.

13   5 SCELLINI = 5 SHILLINGS

	VG	VF	UNC
1971. Purple-brown on blue, green and gold unpt. Like #9.			
a. Issued note.	8.00	25.00	200.00
s. Specimen.	—	—	110.00

14   10 SCELLINI = 10 SHILLINGS

	VG	VF	UNC
1971. Green on red-brown and green unpt. Like #10.			
a. Issued note.	10.00	30.00	325.00
s. Specimen.	—	—	175.00

15   20 SCELLINI = 20 SHILLINGS

	VG	VF	UNC
1971. Brown on blue and gold unpt. Like #11.			
a. Issued note.	15.00	70.00	500.00
s. Specimen.	—	—	275.00

16   100 SCELLINI = 100 SHILLINGS

	VG	VF	UNC
1971. Blue on green and orange unpt. Like #12.			
a. Issued note.	20.00	85.00	650.00
s. Specimen.	—	—	375.00

BANKIGA QARANKA SOOMAALIYEED
SOMALI NATIONAL BANK
LAW OF 11.12.1974
#17-20 arms at l. Wmk: Sayyid Mohammed Aabdullah Hassan.

17   5 SHILIN = 5 SHILLINGS

	VG	VF	UNC
1975. Purple on gold and m/c unpt. Gnus and zebras at bottom ctr. Banana harvesting at ctr. r. on back.			
a. Issued note.	1.50	5.00	20.00
s. Specimen.	—	—	

18   10 SHILIN = 10 SHILLINGS

	VG	VF	UNC
1975. Dk. green on pink and m/c unpt. Minaret at l. ctr. Shipbuilders at work at ctr. r. on back.	2.00	7.50	37.50

19   20 SHILIN = 20 SHILLINGS

	VG	VF	UNC
1975. Brown on m/c unpt. Bank bldg. at ctr. Cattle on back.	3.00	10.00	100.00

20	100 SHILIN = 100 SHILLINGS	VG	VF	UNC
	1975. Blue on gold and m/c unpt. Woman w/baby, rifle and farm tools at l. ctr. Dagathur Monument at ctr. r. Workers in factory on back.	7.00	20.00	125.00

BANKIGA DHEXE EE SOOMAALIYA

CENTRAL BANK OF SOMALIA
LAW OF 6.12.1977
#20A-24 arms at l. Black series and serial #. Wmk: Sayyid Mohammed Abdullah Hassan.

24	100 SHILIN = 100 SHILLINGS	VG	VF	UNC
	1978. Blue on gold and m/c unpt. Like #20.			
	a. Issued note.	3.00	10.00	70.00
	s. Specimen.	—	—	25.00

LAW OF 5.4.1980
#26-28 arms at l. Red series and serial #. Different sign. title at l. Wmk: Sayyid Mohammed Abdullah Hassan. Replacement ntoes: Serial # prefix Z001.

#25 *Deleted.*

20A	5 SHILIN = 5 SHILLINGS	VG	VF	UNC
	1978. Purple on gold and m/c unpt. Like #17.			
	a. Issued note.	4.00	12.50	45.00
	s. Specimen.	—	—	25.00

26	10 SHILIN = 10 SHILLINGS	VG	VF	UNC
	1980. Dk. green on pink and m/c unpt. Like #22.	0.50	2.50	10.00

21	5 SHILIN = 5 SHILLINGS	VG	VF	UNC
	1978. Purple on gold and m/c unpt. Similar to #20A but Cape Buffalo herd at bottom l. ctr.	0.50	2.00	12.50

22	10 SHILIN = 10 SHILLINGS	VG	VF	UNC
	1978. Dk. green on pink and m/c unpt. Like #18.			
	a. Issued note.	1.00	4.00	25.00
	s. Specimen.	—	—	25.00

27	20 SHILIN = 20 SHILLINGS	VG	VF	UNC
	1980. Brown on m/c unpt. Like #23.	1.00	5.00	27.50

23	20 SHILIN = 20 SHILLINGS	VG	VF	UNC
	1978. Brown on m/c unpt. Like #19.			
	a. Issued note.	2.00	7.50	40.00
	s. Specimen.	—	—	40.00

28	100 SHILIN = 100 SHILLINGS	VG	VF	UNC
	1980. Blue on gold and m/c unpt. Like #24.	2.00	7.50	30.00

LAW OF 9.12.1981

#29-30 wmk: Sayyid Mohammed Abdullah Hassan. Replacement notes: Serial # prefix *ZZ001*.

		VG	VF	UNC
29	20 SHILIN = 20 SHILLINGS 1981. Brown on m/c unpt. Like #27.	2.00	10.00	37.50

		VG	VF	UNC
30	100 SHILIN = 100 SHILLINGS 1981. Blue on gold and m/c unpt. Like #28.	2.00	7.50	30.00

LAW OF 30.12.1982; 1983 ISSUE

#31-35 arms at top l. ctr., star at or near lower ctr. Reduced size notes. Replacement notes: Serial # prefix *Z001*.

		VG	VF	UNC
31	5 SHILIN = 5 SHILLINGS 1983-87. Brown-violet. Cape Buffalo herd at l. ctr. Harvesting bananas on back.			
	a. 1983.	0.10	0.50	2.50
	b. 1986.	0.10	0.40	2.00
	c. 1987.	0.10	0.25	1.00

#32-35 wmk: S. M. A. Hassan.

		VG	VF	UNC
32	10 SHILIN = 10 SHILLINGS 1983-87. Green and m/c. Lighthouse at l. Shipbuilders at ctr. r. on back.			
	a. 1983.	0.25	0.75	3.00
	b. 1986.	0.20	0.50	2.00
	c. 1987.	0.15	0.50	1.75
33	20 SHILIN = 20 SHILLINGS 1983-89. Brown and m/c. Bank at l. Back similar to #19.			
	a. 1983.	0.25	1.50	5.00
	b. 1986.	0.25	1.00	4.00
	c. 1987.	0.20	0.75	3.00
	d. 1989.	0.15	0.50	2.00

		VG	VF	UNC
34	50 SHILIN = 50 SHILLINGS 1983-89. Red-brown and m/c unpt. Walled city at l. and ctr. Watering animals at ctr. r. on back.			
	a. 1983.	0.50	1.50	6.00
	b. 1986; 1987. 2 sign. varieties for 1987.	0.15	0.40	4.00
	c. 1988.	0.15	0.50	2.50
	d. 1989.	0.10	0.40	2.00

		VG	VF	UNC
35	100 SHILIN = 100 SHILLINGS 1983-89. Blue-black, dk. blue and dk. green on m/c unpt. Similar to #20.			
	a. 1983.	0.50	2.50	7.50
	b. 1986; 1987. 2 sign. varieties for 1987.	0.30	1.00	4.00
	c. 1988.	0.15	0.50	2.50
	d. 1989.	0.15	0.40	2.00

LAW OF 1.1.1989

#36 and 37 arms at top l. ctr. Wmk: Sayyid Mohammed Abdullah Hassan.

		VG	VF	UNC
36	500 SHILIN = 500 SHILLINGS 1989; 1990; 1996. Green and aqua on m/c unpt. Fishermen mending net at l. ctr. Mosque at l. ctr. on back. 2 sign. varieties.			
	a. 1989.	FV	FV	6.00
	b. 1990.	FV	FV	5.50
	c. 1996.	FV	FV	5.00

LAW OF 1.1.1990; 1990 ISSUE

37	1000 SHILIN = 1000 SHILLINGS	VG	VF	UNC
	1990; 1996. Violet and orange on m/c unpt. Women seated weaving baskets at l. ctr.; arms above. City view at bottom, Port of Mogadishu at upper ctr. r. on back.			
	a. 1990.	FV	FV	2.50
	b. 1996.	FV	FV	3.50

REGIONAL

MOGADISHU NORTH FORCES

In Mogadishu-North, forces loyal to warlord Ali Mahdi Mohammed have issued currency valued in N Shilin. The notes have have originally been part of a plan to replace older currency.

1991 ISSUE

#R1 and R2 arms at top l. ctr. Wmk: Sayyid Mohammed Abdullah Hassan.

R1	20 N SHILIN = 20 N SHILLINGS	VG	VF	UNC
	1991. Purple, red-brown, brown-orange and olive-green on m/c unpt. Trader leading camel in unpt. at l. ctr. Picking cotton at ctr. r. on back.	0.50	1.50	7.00

R2	50 N SHILIN = 50 N SHILLINGS	VG	VF	UNC
	1991. Brown, green and black on m/c unpt. Man working loom. Young person leading a donkey w/3 children on back.	1.75	5.00	15.00

PUNTLAND REGION

2000 (1999) ISSUE

R10	1000 SHILIN = 1000 SHILLINGS	VG	VF	UNC
	1990 (2000). Purple and orange on m/c unpt. Lithographed copy of #37a.	0.50	1.00	5.00

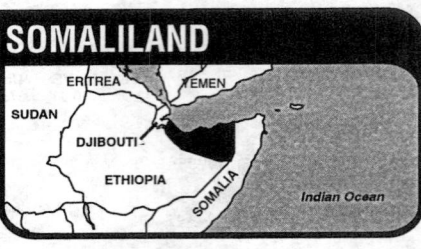

The Somaliland Republic, comprising the former British Somaliland Protectorate, is located on the coast of the northeastern projection of the African continent commonly referred to as the "Horn" on the southwestern end of the Gulf of Aden.

Bordered by Eritrea to the west, Ethiopia to west and south and Somalia to the east, it has an area of 68,000* sq. mi. (176,000* sq. km). Capital: Hargeysa. It is mostly arid and mounainous except for the gulf shoreline.

The Protectorate of British Somaliland was established in 1888 and from 1905 the territory was administered by a commissioner under the British Colonial Office. Italian Somaliland was administered as a colony from 1893 to 1941, when the territory was occupied by British forces. In 1950 the United Nations allowed Italy to resume control of Italian Somaliland under a trusteeship. In 1960 British and Italian Somaliland were united as Somalia, an independent republic outside the Commonwealth.

Civil War erupted in the late 1970's and continued until the capital of Somalia was taken in 1990. The United Nations provided aid and peacekeepers. A UN sponsored truce was signed in March 1992 and a peace plan and pact was signed Jan. 15, 1993. The northern Somali National Movement (SMN) declared a secession of the Somaliland Republic on May 17, 1991 which is not recognized by the Somali Democratic Republic.

The currency issued by the East African Currency Board was used in British Somaliland from 1945 to 1961. Somali currency was then used until 1995.

MONETARY SYSTEM:
   1 Somaliland Shilling = 1 Shilin

SIGNATURE VARIETIES					
1	Guddoomiyaha	Lacaghayaha	**2**	Lacaghayaha	Guddoomiyaha

REPUBLIC

BAANKA SOMALILAND

1994 ISSUE

#1-4 bldg. at ctr. Greater Kudu at r. Traders w/camels on back.

	5 SHILLINGS = 5 SHILIN	VG	VF	UNC
	1994. Bright green, olive-green and red-brown on m/c unpt.			
	a. Issued note.	FV	FV	1.00
	s. Specimen.	—	—	100.00

2	10 SHILLINGS = 10 SHILIN	VG	VF	UNC
	1994-96. Violet, purple and red-brown on m/c unpt.			
	a. 1994.	FV	FV	1.25
	b. 1996.	FV	FV	1.00
	s. Specimen.	—	—	100.00

3	20 SHILLINGS = 20 SHILIN	VG	VF	UNC
	1994-96. Brown and red-brown on m/c unpt.			
	a. 1994.	FV	FV	2.25
	b. 1996.	FV	FV	2.00
	s. Specimen.	—	—	110.00

4   50 SHILLINGS = 50 SHILIN

		VG	VF	UNC
1994-96. Blue-violet, blue-gray and red-brown on m/c unpt.				
a. 1994.		FV	FV	4.00
b. 1996.		FV	FV	3.50
s. Specimen.		—	—	110.00

#5 and 6 bldg. at ctr. Ship dockside in background, herdsmen w/sheep at front ctr. on back.

5   100 SHILLINGS = 100 SHILIN

		VG	VF	UNC
1994-99. Brownish black and red-violet on m/c unpt.				
a. 1994.		FV	FV	6.50
b. 1996.		FV	FV	5.00
c. Sign. 3. 1999.		FV	FV	5.00
s. Specimen.		—	—	110.00

6   500 SHILLINGS = 500 SHILIN

		VG	VF	UNC
1994-96. Purple, blue-black and blue-green on m/c unpt.				
a. 1994.		FV	FV	15.00
b. 1996.		FV	FV	10.00
s. Specimen.		—	—	125.00

1996 ISSUE

7   50 SHILLINGS = 50 SHILIN

		VG	VF	UNC
1996, 1999. Blue-violet, blue-gray and violet on m/c unpt. Like #4 but increased size. 130 x 58mm.				
a. Sign. 1.		FV	FV	2.50
b. Sign. 2.		FV	FV	2.25
c. Sign. 3. 1999.		FV	FV	2.25
s. Specimen.		—	—	125.00

1996 "BRONZE" COMMEMORATIVE ISSUE

#8-13, 5th Anniversary of Independence

#8-13 bronze ovpt. on face: *5th Anniversary of Independence 18 May 1996 - Sanad Gurada 5ee Gobanimadda 18 May 1996*

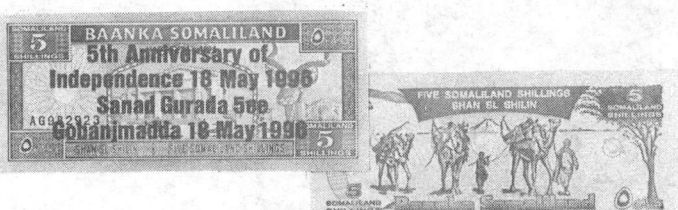

8	5 SHILLINGS = 5 SHILIN	VG	VF	UNC
	18.5.1996 (- old date 1994). Ovpt. on #1.	FV	FV	1.75

9	10 SHILLINGS = 10 SHILIN	VG	VF	UNC
	18.5.1996 (- old date 1994). Ovpt. on #2a.	FV	FV	2.00

10	20 SHILLINGS = 20 SHILIN	VG	VF	UNC
	18.5.1996 (- old date 1994). Ovpt. on #3a.	FV	FV	3.00

11	50 SHILLINGS = 50 SHILIN	VG	VF	UNC
	18.5.1996.			
	a. Ovpt. on #4a. (- old date 1994).	FV	FV	4.25
	b. Ovpt. on #4b. 1996.	FV	FV	3.00

11A	50 SHILLINGS = 50 SHILIN	VG	VF	UNC
	18.5.1996. Blue-violet, blue-gray and violet on m/c unpt. Bronze ovpt. on #7a.	FV	FV	3.50

12	100 SHILLINGS = 100 SHILIN	VG	VF	UNC
	18.5.1996 (- old date 1994). Ovpt. on #5a.	FV	FV	7.50

13	500 SHILLINGS = 500 SHILIN	VG	VF	UNC
	18.5.1996 (- old date 1994). Ovpt. on #6a.	FV	FV	25.00

1996 "SILVER" COMMEMORATIVE ISSUE

#14-19, 5th Anniversary of Independence

#14-19 silver ovpt. on face: *Sanad Gurada 5ee Gobanimadda 18 May 1996*

		VG	VF	UNC
14	5 SHILLINGS = 5 SHILIN	FV	FV	1.75
	18.5.1996 (- old date 1994). Ovpt. on #1.			

		VG	VF	UNC
15	10 SHILLINGS = 10 SHILIN	FV	FV	2.00
	18.5.1996 (- old date 1994). Ovpt. on #2a.			

		VG	VF	UNC
16	20 SHILLINGS = 20 SHILIN	FV	FV	3.00
	18.5.1996 (- old date 1994). Ovpt. on #3a.			

		VG	VF	UNC
17	50 SHILLINGS = 50 SHILIN			
	18.5.1996.			
	a. Ovpt. on #4a. (- old date 1994).	FV	FV	4.25
	b. Ovpt. on #4b. 1996.	FV	FV	3.00

		VG	VF	UNC
17A	50 SHILLINGS = 50 SHILIN	FV	FV	3.50
	1996. Blue-violet, blue-gray and violet on m/c unpt. Ovpt. on #7b.			

		VG	VF	UNC
18	100 SHILLINGS = 100 SHILIN	FV	FV	7.50
	18.5.1996 (- old date 1994). Ovpt. on #5a.			

		VG	VF	UNC
19	500 SHILLINGS = 500 SHILIN	FV	FV	25.00
	18.5.1996 (- old date 1994). Ovpt. on #6a.			

SOUTH AFRICA

The Republic of South Africa, located at the southern tip of Africa, has an area, including the enclave of Walvis Bay, of 472,359 sq. mi. (1,221,040 sq. km.) and a population of 46.26 million. Capital: Administrative, Pretoria; Legislative, Cape Town; Judicial, Bloemfontein. Manufacturing, mining and agriculture are the principal industries. Exports include wool, diamonds, gold and metallic ores. Portuguese navigator Bartholomeu Diaz became the first European to sight the region of South Africa when he rounded the Cape of Good Hope in 1488, but throughout the 16th century the only white men to come ashore were the survivors of ships wrecked while attempting the stormy Cape passage. The first permanent settlement was established by Jan van Riebeeck of the Dutch East India Company in 1652. In subsequent decades additional Dutch, Germans and Huguenot refugees from France settled in the Cape area to form the Afrikaner segment of today's population.

Great Britain captured the Cape colony in 1795, and again in 1806, receiving permanent title in 1814. To escape British political rule and cultural dominance, many Afrikaner farmers (Boers) migrated northward (the Great Trek) beginning in 1836, and established the independent Boer republics of the Transvaal (the South African Republic, Zuid-Afrikaansche Republiek) in 1852, and the Orange Free State in 1854. British political intrigues against the two republics, coupled with the discovery of diamonds and gold in the Boer-settled regions, led to the bitter Boer Wars (1880-1881, 1899-1902) and the incorporation of the Boer republics into the British Empire.

On May 31, 1910, the two former Boer republics (Transvaal and Orange Free State) were joined with the British colonies of Cape of Good Hope and Natal to form the Union of South Africa, a dominion of the British Empire. In 1934 the Union achieved status as a sovereign state within the British Empire. Political integration of the various colonies did not still the conflict between the Afrikaners and the English-speaking groups, which continued to have a significant impact on political developments. A resurgence of Afrikaner nationalism in the 1940s and 1950s led to a referendum in the white community authorizing the relinquishment of dominion status and the establishment of a republic. The decision took effect on May 31, 1961. The Republic of South Africa withdrew from the British Commonwealth in Oct., 1961. The apartheid era ended on April 27, 1994 with the first democratic election for all people of South Africa. Nelson Mandela was inaugurated as president on May 10, 1994. South Africa was readmitted to the Commonwealth of Nations.

South African currency carries inscriptions in both Afrikaans and English.

RULERS:

British to 1961

MONETARY SYSTEM:

1 Rand = 100 Cents (= 10 Shillings), 1961-

SIGNATURE VARIETIES			
3	M. H. de Kock, 1.7.1945-30.6.1962	4	G. Rissik, 1.7.1962-30.6.1967
5	T. W. de Jongh, 1.7.1967-31.12.1980	6	G. P. C. de Kock, 1.1.1981-7.8.1989
7	C. L. Stals, 8.8.1989-7.8.1999	8	T. T. Mboweni, 8.8.1999-

REPUBLIC OF SOUTH AFRICA

SOUTH AFRICAN RESERVE BANK

1961 ND ISSUE

#102-108A portr. Jan van Riebeeck at l. and as wmk.

#102-105 replacement notes: Serial # prefix Z/1; Y/1; X/1; W/1 respectively.

102   1 RAND
ND (1961-65). Rust brown on m/c unpt. First line of bank name and value in English. 135 x 77mm.

	VG	VF	UNC
a. Sign. 3. (1961).	6.50	22.50	65.00
b. Sign. 4. (1962-65).	3.25	11.00	28.00
s. As a. Specimen.	—	—	550.00

106   10 RAND
ND (1961-65). Green and brown on m/c unpt. First line of bank name and value in English. Sailing ship on back. 170 x 97mm.

	VG	VF	UNC
a. Sign. 3. (1961).	9.00	25.00	65.00
b. Sign. 4. (1962-65).	5.00	17.50	37.50

103   1 RAND
ND (1961-65). Rust brown on m/c unpt. Like #102 but first line of bank name and value in Afrikaans. 137 x 78mm.

	VG	VF	UNC
a. Sign. 3. (1961).	6.50	22.50	65.00
b. Sign. 4. (1962-65).	3.25	11.00	27.50

104   2 RAND
ND (1961-65). Blue on m/c unpt. First line of bank name and value in English. 150 x 85mm.

	VG	VF	UNC
a. Sign. 3. (1961).	3.75	12.50	36.00
b. Sign. 4. (1962-65).	2.50	6.50	20.00

107   10 RAND
ND (1961-65). Green and brown on m/c unpt. Like #106 but first line of bank name and value in Afrikaans. 170 x 97mm.

	VG	VF	UNC
a. Sign. 3. (1961).	9.00	25.00	65.00
b. Sign. 4. (1962-65).	5.00	17.50	37.50
s. Specimen.	—	—	550.00

105   2 RAND
ND (1961-65). Like #104 but first line of bank name and value in Afrikaans. 150 x 85mm.

	VG	VF	UNC
a. Sign. 3. (1961).	3.75	12.50	36.00
b. Sign. 4. (1962-65).	2.50	6.50	20.00
s. As a. Specimen.	—	—	550.00

108 **20 RAND**
ND (1961). Brown-violet. First line of bank name and value in
English. Machinery on back. Sign. 3.

	VG	VF	UNC
a. Issued note.	16.00	50.00	160.00
s. Specimen.	—	—	550.00

108A **20 RAND**
ND (1962-65). Like #108 but first line of bank name in Afrikaans.
Sign. 4.

	VG	VF	UNC
	15.00	50.00	160.00

1966 ND Issue

#109-114 J. van Riebeeck at l. Replacement notes: Serial # prefix Z/1; Y/1; X/1; W/1 respectively.

109 **1 RAND**
ND (1966-72). Dk. reddish brown on m/c unpt. First lines of bank
name and value in English. Rams in field on back. 126 x 64mm.
Wmk: Springbok.

	VG	VF	UNC
a. Sign. 4. (1966).	1.00	2.50	13.50
b. Sign. 5. (1967).	0.60	1.50	8.00
s1. As a. Specimen.	—	—	35.00
s2. As b. Specimen.	—	—	35.00

110 **1 RAND**
ND (1966-72). Dk. reddish brown on m/c unpt. Like #109 but first
lines of bank name and value in Afrikaans. 126 x 64mm. Wmk:
Springbok.

	VG	VF	UNC
a. Sign. 4. (1966).	1.00	2.50	13.50
b. Sign. 5. (1967).	0.60	1.50	8.00
s1. As a. Specimen.	—	—	35.00
s2. As b. Specimen.	—	—	35.00

111 **5 RAND**
ND (1966-76). Purple on m/c unpt. Covered wagons on trail at r.
corner. First lines of bank name and value in English. Factory
w/train on back. 133 x 70mm.

	VG	VF	UNC
a. Sign. 4. Wmk: Springbok (1966).	4.00	15.00	90.00
b. Sign. 5. Wmk: Springbok (1967-74).	2.00	6.00	17.50
c. Sign. 5. Wmk: J. van Riebeeck (1975).	2.25	6.50	20.00
s1. As a. Specimen.	—	—	35.00
s2. As b. Specimen.	—	—	35.00

112 **5 RAND**
ND (1966-76). Purple on m/c unpt. Like #111 but first lines of bank
name and value in Afrikaans.

	VG	VF	UNC
a. Sign. 4. Wmk: Springbok (1966).	4.00	15.00	90.00
b. Sign. 5. Wmk: Springbok (1967-74).	2.00	6.00	17.50
c. Sign. 5. Wmk: J. van Riebeeck (1975).	2.25	6.50	20.00
s1. As a. Specimen.	—	—	35.00
s2. As b. Specimen.	—	—	35.00

113 **10 RAND**
ND (1966-76). Dk. green and brown on m/c unpt. Capital bldg. at
ctr. First lines of bank name and value in English. Old sailing ships
on back. 140 x 76mm.

	VG	VF	UNC
a. Sign. 4. Wmk: Springbok (1966).	2.50	10.00	35.00
b. Sign. 5. Wmk: Springbok (1967-74).	2.00	5.00	16.50
c. Sign. 5. Wmk: J. van Riebeeck (1975).	2.00	5.00	16.50
s1. As a. Specimen.	—	—	50.00
s2. As b. Specimen.	—	—	50.00

114 **10 RAND**
ND (1966-76). Dk. green and brown on m/c unpt. Like #113 but
first lines of bank name and value in Afrikaans. 140 x 76mm.

	VG	VF	UNC
a. Sign. 4. Wmk: Springbok (1966).	2.50	10.00	35.00
b. Sign. 5. Wmk: Springbok (1967-74).	2.00	5.00	16.50
c. Sign. 5. Wmk: J. van Riebeeck (1975).	2.00	5.00	16.50
s1. As a. Specimen.	—	—	50.00
s2. As b. Specimen.	—	—	50.00

1973-84 ND Issue

#115-122 J. van Riebeeck at l.

115	1 RAND	VG	VF	UNC
	ND (1973-75). Dk. reddish brown on m/c unpt. Like #109 but 120 x 57mm. Sign. 5.			
	a. Wmk: Springbok (1973).	0.50	1.75	5.00
	b. Wmk: J. van Riebeeck (1975).	0.75	2.00	6.00

119	5 RAND	VG	VF	UNC
	ND (1978-94). Purple on m/c unpt. First lines of bank name and value in English. Diamond at ctr. Grain storage at l. ctr. on back. 127 x 63mm.			
	a. Sign. 5. (1978-81).	1.00	2.50	13.50
	b. Sign. 6. Fractional numbering system. W/o security thread (1981).	12.50	40.00	165.00
	c. As b. W/security thread. (1981-89).	FV	1.50	14.00
	d. As c. Alpha-numeric system. (1989-90).	FV	2.50	12.00
	e. Sign. 7. (1990-94).	FV	2.50	12.50

116	1 RAND	VG	VF	UNC
	ND (1973-75). Dk. reddish brown on m/c unpt. Like #110 but 120 x 57mm. Sign. 5.			
	a. Wmk: Springbok (1973).	0.50	1.75	5.00
	b. Wmk: J. van Riebeeck (1975).	0.65	2.00	6.00

120	10 RAND	VG	VF	UNC
	ND (1978-93). Green on m/c unpt. Flower at ctr. Bull and ram at l. ctr. on back. 134 x 70mm.			
	a. Sign. 5. (1978-81).	1.50	4.50	17.00
	b. Sign. 6. Fractional numbering system. W/o security thread (1981).	2.50	12.50	55.00
	c. As b. w/security thread. (1982-85).	FV	3.25	16.50
	d. As c. Alpha-numeric system. (1985-90).	FV	3.00	20.00
	e. Sign. 7. (1990-93).	FV	2.00	12.50

117	2 RAND	VG	VF	UNC
	ND (1974-76). Blue on m/c unpt. First lines of bank name and value in Afrikaans. Hydroelectric dam on back. 127 x 62mm. Sign. 5.			
	a. Wmk: Springbok (1974).	0.50	3.00	15.00
	b. Wmk: J. van Riebeeck (1976).	0.50	4.50	16.00

#118-122 wmk: J. van Riebeek.

118	2 RAND	VG	VF	UNC
	ND (1978-90). Blue on m/c unpt. Electrical tower at ctr. Refinery at l. ctr. on back. 120 x 57mm.			
	a. Sign. 5. (1978-81).	0.25	1.00	6.50
	b. Sign. 6. Fractional numbering system. W/o security thread (1981).	0.50	3.00	20.00
	c. As b. but w/security thread. (1981-83).	0.25	1.00	4.50
	d. As c. Alpha-numeric system. (1983-90).	0.25	0.50	3.50
	e. Sign. 7. (1990).	0.50	2.00	6.50

121	20 RAND	VG	VF	UNC
	ND (1984-93). Brown on m/c unpt. Bldg. in unpt. at ctr. 3 sailing ships at l. ctr. w/arms at r. on back. 144 x 77mm.			
	a. Sign. 5. (1978-81).	3.00	7.00	27.50
	b. Sign. 6. Fractional numbering system. W/o security thread (1981).	5.00	22.50	80.00
	c. As b. w/security thread. (1982-85).	FV	5.00	25.00
	d. As c. Alpha-numeric system. (1985-90).	FV	10.00	50.00
	e. Sign. 7. (1990-93).	FV	6.00	16.50

Note: #118b exists w/serial # w/sm. fractional letters and lg. numerals or larger letters w/sm. numerals.

122   50 RAND

		VG	VF	UNC
ND (1984-90). Red on m/c unpt. Lion in unpt. at ctr. Local animals at lower l., mountains at ctr., plants at r. on back. 147 x 83mm.				
	a. Sign. 6. (1984).	7.50	15.00	40.00
	b. Sign. 7. (1990).	10.00	22.50	50.00

1992-94 ISSUE

123   10 RAND

		VG	VF	UNC
ND (1993; 1999). Dk. green and dk. blue on brown and m/c unpt. White rhinoceros at ctr., lg. white rhino at r. and as wmk. Ram's head over sheep at l. on back.				
	a. Sign. 7. (1993).	FV	FV	10.00
	b. Sign. 8. (1999).	FV	2.50	4.50

124   20 RAND

		VG	VF	UNC
ND (1993; 1999). Deep brown and red-brown on m/c unpt. Elephants at ctr., lg. elephant head at r. and as wmk. Open pit mining at l. ctr. on back.				
	a. Sign. 7 (1993).	FV	FV	10.00
	b. Sign. 8 (1999).	FV	FV	7.50

125   50 RAND

		VG	VF	UNC
ND (1992; 1999). Maroon, brown and deep blue-green on m/c unpt. Lions w/cub drinking water at ctr., male lion head at r. and as wmk. Sasol oil refinery at lower l. ctr. on back.				
	a. Sign. 7 (1992). Reddish lion drinking water (serial # prefix lower than AL).	FV	25.00	85.00
	b. Sign. 7. (1992). Brownish blue lion drinking water. (serial # prefix greater than AL).	FV	FV	25.00
	c. Sign. 8 (1999).	FV	FV	17.50
	x. Like a. Wmk. on wrong side. Serial # prefix: *BP*.	FV	22.50	50.00

126   100 RAND

		VG	VF	UNC
ND (1994; 1999). Blue-violet and dk. gray on m/c unpt. Cape buffalo at ctr. and lg. water buffalo head at r. and as wmk. Zebras along bottom from l. to ctr. on back.				
	a. Sign. 7 (1994).	FV	FV	72.50
	b. Sign. 8 (1999).	FV	FV	30.00

127   200 RAND

		VG	VF	UNC
ND (1994; 1999). Orange on m/c unpt. Leopard at ctr., lg. leopard's head at r. Dish antenna at upper l., modern bridge at lower l. on back.				
	a. Sign. 7 (1994).	FV	FV	85.00
	b. Sign. 8 (1999).	FV	FV	60.00

2005 ISSUE

#128-132 silimar to #123-127 but with increased security features. Coat of arms at top left, various geometric shapes at lower portion of notes.

128 10 RAND
2005. Green on m/c unpt. Rhino head at r.

	VG	VF	UNC
	FV	FV	4.00

129 20 RAND
2005. Brown on tan unpt. Elephant head at r.

	VG	VF	UNC
	FV	FV	7.00

130 50 RAND
2005. Red on m/c unpt. Lion head at r.

	VG	VF	UNC
	FV	FV	13.00

131 100 RAND
2005. Blue on m/c unpt. Buffalo head at r.

	VG	VF	UNC
	FV	FV	30.00

132 200 RAND
2005. Brown on green and m/c unpt. Leopard head at r.

	VG	VF	UNC
	FV	FV	60.00

The Spanish State, forming the greater part of the Iberian Peninsula of southwest Europe, has an area of 194,884 sq. mi. (504,750 sq. km.) and a population of 40.5 million including the Balearic and the Canary Islands. Capital: Madrid. The economy is based on agriculture, industry and tourism. Machinery, fruit, vegetables and chemicals are exported.

It is not known when man first came to the Iberian Peninsula - the Altamira caves off the Cantabrian coast approximately 50 miles west of Santander were fashioned in Paleolithic times. Spain was a battleground for centuries before it became a united nation, fought for by Phoenicians, Carthaginians, Greeks, Celts, Romans, Vandals, Visigoths and Moors. Ferdinand and Isabella destroyed the last Moorish stronghold in 1492, freeing the national energy and resources for the era of discovery and colonization that would make Spain the most powerful country in Europe during the 16th century. After the destruction of the Spanish Armada, 1588, Spain never again played a major role in European politics. Napoleonic France ruled Spain between 1808 and 1814. The monarchy was restored in 1814 and continued, interrupted by the short-lived republic of 1873-74, until the exile of Alfonso XIII in 1931, when the Second Republic was established. A bloody civil war ensued in 1936, and Francisco Franco established himself as ruler of fascist Spain after his forces, aided by the Italians and especially the Germans, defeated the Republican forces.

The monarchy was reconstituted in 1947 under the regency of General Francisco Franco, the king designate to be crowned after Franco's death. Franco died on Nov. 30, 1975. Two days after his passing, Juan Carlos de Borbón, the grandson of Alfonso XIII, was proclaimed King of Spain.

RULERS:
Francisco Franco, regent, 1937-1975
Juan Carlos I, 1975-

MONETARY SYSTEM:
1 Peseta = 100 Centimos 1874-2001
1 Euro = 100 Cents, 2002-

REPLACEMENT NOTES:
#150 and later, 9A, 9B, 9C type prefix.

REPUBLIC

BANCO DE ESPAÑA

1965 (1970; 1971) ISSUE
#150-151 printer: FNMT.

150 100 PESETAS
19.11.1965 (1970). Brown on m/c unpt. Gustavo Adolfo Bécquer at ctr. r., couple near fountain at lower l. Woman w/parasol at ctr., Cathedral of Sevilla at l. on back. Wmk: Woman's head.

	VG	VF	UNC
	1.00	4.50	9.00

151   1000 PESETAS

	VG	VF	UNC
19.11.1965 (1971). Green on m/c unpt. San Isidoro at l. and as wmk. Imaginary figure w/basilica behind on back.	8.50	25.00	60.00

1970-71 ISSUE

152 and 153 printer: FNMT.

152   100 PESETAS

	VG	VF	UNC
17.11.1970 (1974). Brown on pale orange and m/c unpt. Manuel de Falla at r. and as wmk. The summer residence of the Moorish kings in Granada at l. ctr. on back.			
a. Issued note.	1.00	2.00	5.00
s. Specimen.	—	—	—

153   500 PESETAS

	VG	VF	UNC
23.7.1971 (1973). Blue-gray and black on m/c unpt. Jacinto Verdaguer at r. and as wmk. View of Mt. Canigó w/village of Vignolas d'Oris on back.			
a. Issued note.	4.00	18.00	40.00
s. Specimen.	—	—	—

1974 COMMEMORATIVE ISSUE

#154, Centennial of the Banco de España's becoming the sole issuing bank, 1874-1974

154   1000 PESETAS

	VG	VF	UNC
17.9.1971 (1974). Green and black on m/c unpt. José Echegaray at r. and as wmk. Bank of Spain in Madrid and commemorative legend on back. Printer: FNMT.	FV	17.50	40.00

1976 ISSUE

155   5000 PESETAS

	VG	VF	UNC
6.2.1976 (1978). Purple and brown on m/c unpt. Kg. Carlos III at r. and as wmk. Museum of Prado in Madrid at l. ctr. on back.	FV	55.00	120.00

1982-87 ISSUE

#156-161 printer: FNMT.

156   200 PESETAS

	VG	VF	UNC
16.9.1980 (1984). Brown and orange on m/c unpt. Leopoldo Garcí de las Alas, known as *Clarín* at r. and as wmk., cross at lower ctr. Tree at l., cross at ctr. on back.	FV	5.00	15.00

157 **500 PESETAS**
23.10.1979 (1983). Dk. blue and black on m/c unpt. Rosalia de
Castro at r. and as wmk. Villa at l. ctr. on back.

VG	VF	UNC
FV	6.00	17.50

158 **1000 PESETAS**
23.10.1979 (1982). Gray-blue and green on m/c unpt. Tree at ctr.
Benito Pérez Galdos at r. and as wmk. Rock formations, mountains
and map of Canary Islands on back.

VG	VF	UNC
FV	10.00	27.50

161 **10,000 PESETAS**
24.9.1985 (1987). Gray-black on m/c unpt. Arms at ctr., Kg. Juan
Carlos I at r. and as wmk. Back blue-gray on m/c unpt. Felipe,
Prince of Asturias at l., view of the Escorial at ctr.

VG	VF	UNC
FV	85.00	140.00

1992 ISSUE

159 **2000 PESETAS**
22.7.1980 (1983). Deep red and orange on m/c unpt. Rose at ctr.,
Juan Ramón Jiménez at r. and as wmk. Villa de la Rosa at l. ctr.
on back.

VG	VF	UNC
FV	17.50	45.00

162 **2000 PESETAS**
24.4.1992. Red-violet and orange on m/c unpt. José Celistino
Mutis observing flower at r. and as wmk. Royal Botanical Garden
and title page of Mutis' work on vertical format back. 2 serial #.

VG	VF	UNC
FV	15.00	40.00

1992 (1996) ISSUE

#163-166 w/blurred *BANCO DE ESPAÑA* at r. margin.

Note: Issued for the 5th Centennial of the Discovery of America by Spain.

160 **5000 PESETAS**
23.10.1979 (1982). Brown and purple on m/c unpt. Fleur-de-lis at
ctr., Kg. Juan Carlos I at r. and as wmk. Royal Palace in Madrid at
l. ctr. on back.

VG	VF	UNC
FV	37.50	80.00

163 **1000 PESETAS**
12.10.1992 (1996). Dk. green, purple and red-brown on m/c
Hernán Cortes at r. Francisco Pizarro on vertical format back and
as wmk.

VG	VF	UNC
FV	8.00	17.50

164   2000 PESETAS

24.4.1992 (1996). Red-violet and orange on m/c unpt. Like #162 but w/modified portr. 1 serial #.

	VG	VF	UNC
	FV	16.00	30.00

165   5000 PESETAS

12.10.1992 (1996). Violet-brown, brown and red-brown on m/c unpt. Christopher Columbus at r. and as wmk. Astrolabe at lower ctr. on vertical format back.

	VG	VF	UNC
	FV	37.50	75.00

166   10,000 PESETAS

12.10.1992 (1996). Slate blue on m/c unpt. Kg. Juan Carlos I at r. and as wmk. *Casa de América* in Madrid at lower ctr. de Ulloa y de Jorge Juan above astronomical navigation diagram on vertical format back.

	VG	VF	UNC
	FV	80.00	130.00

Note: For later issues used in Spain, see European Union listings.

SRI (SHRI) LANKA

The Democratic Socialist Republic of Sri (Shri) Lanka (formerly Ceylon), situated in the Indian Ocean 18 miles (29 km.) southeast of India, has an area of 25,332 sq. mi. (65,610 sq. km.) and a population of 18.7 million. Capital: Colombo. The economy is chiefly agricultural. Tea, coconut products and rubber are exported.

The earliest known inhabitants of Ceylon, the Veddahs, were subjugated by the Sinhalese from northern India in the 6th century BC. Sinhalese rule was maintained until 1505 when the costal areas came under Portuguese control which was maintained for 150 years. The Portuguese were supplanted by the Dutch in 1658, who were in turn supplanted by the British who seized the Dutch colonies in 1796, and made them into Crown Colony in 1802. In 1815, the British conquered the independent Kingdom of Kandy in the central part of the island. Constitutional changes in 1931 and 1946 granted the Ceylonese a measure of autonomy and a parliamentary form of government. Ceylon became a self-governing dominion of the British Commonwealth on February 4, 1948. On May 22, 1972, the Ceylonese adopted a new constitution which declared Ceylon to be the Republic of Sri Lanka - 'Resplendent Island'. Sri Lanka is a member of the Commonwealth of Nations. The president is Chief of State. The prime minister is Head of Government.

See also Ceylon for earlier listings.

RULERS:
British, 1796-1972

MONETARY SYSTEM:
1 Rupee = 100 Cents, ca. 1830-

REPUBLIC

CENTRAL BANK OF CEYLON

1977 ISSUE

#81 and 82 Sri Lanka arms at r. Wmk: Chinze. Printer: BWC.

81   50 RUPEES

26.8.1977. Purple and green on m/c unpt. Terraced hillside on back.

	VG	VF	UNC
	4.00	10.00	35.00

82   100 RUPEES

26.8.1977. Purple and brown on m/c unpt. Shrine at l. ctr. on back.

	VG	VF	UNC
a. Issued note.	5.00	12.50	65.00
s. Specimen.	—	—	150.00

1979 ISSUE

#83-88 backs vertical format. Wmk: Chinze. Replacement notes: Serial # prefix Z/1.

83	2 RUPEES	VG	VF	UNC
	26.3.1979. Red on m/c unpt. Fish at r. Butterfly and lizard on back.			
	a. Issued note.	0.50	1.00	3.50
	s. Specimen.	—	—	100.00

84	5 RUPEES	VG	VF	UNC
	26.3.1979. Gray on m/c unpt. Butterfly and lizard at r. Flying squirrel and White-faced Starling on back.			
	a. Issued note.	0.75	1.75	6.50
	s. Specimen.	—	—	100.00

85	10 RUPEES	VG	VF	UNC
	26.3.1979. Green, brown and black on m/c unpt. Sri Lanka Grey Hornbill in tree at ctr. Flowers and Yellow-eared Bulbul on back.			
	a. Issued note.	1.25	2.00	12.50
	s. Specimen.	—	—	125.00

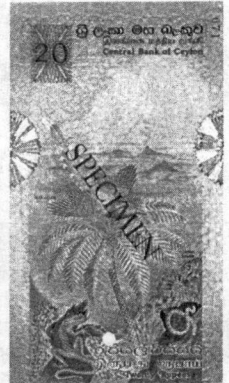

86	20 RUPEES	VG	VF	UNC
	26.3.1979. Brown and green on m/c unpt. Ceylon Wood Pigeon at ctr. monkey at r. Bird, tree and animals on back.			
	a. Issued note.	1.50	5.00	25.00
	s. Specimen.	—	—	150.00

87	50 RUPEES	VG	VF	UNC
	26.3.1979. Blue and brown on m/c unpt. Butterfly at ctr., Red-faced Malcoha at r. Lizard and Ceylon Spurfowl on back.			
	a. Issued note.	3.00	12.50	90.00
	s. Specimen.	—	—	220.00

88	100 RUPEES	VG	VF	UNC
	26.3.1979. Gold, green and black on m/c unpt. Snakes and tree at ctr., Sri Lanka Myna at r. Yellow-fronted Barbet in tree, butterfly below on back.			
	a. Issued note.	5.00	20.00	150.00
	s. Specimen.	—	—	325.00

1981 ISSUE

#89 and 90 backs vertical format. Wmk: Chinze.

89   500 RUPEES
1.1.1981; 1.1.1985. Brown and purple on m/c unpt. Elephant w/rider
at r. Abhayagiri Stupa, Anuradhapura temple on hill on back.

VG	VF	UNC
20.00	50.00	125.00

90   1000 RUPEES
1.1.1981. Green on m/c unpt. Dam at r. Peacock and mountains
on back.
a. Issued note.
s. Specimen.

VG	VF	UNC
30.00	75.00	250.00
—	—	—

1982 ISSUE

#91-95 backs vertical format. Wmk: Chinze. Printer: BWC.

93   20 RUPEES
1.1.1982; 1.1.1985. Purple and red on m/c unpt. Moonstone at r.
Dagoba Shrine on back.
a. Issued note.
s. Specimen.

VG	VF	UNC
0.50	1.00	6.00
—	—	110.00

94   50 RUPEES
1.1.1982. Dk. blue and dk. brown on m/c unpt. Bldg. in Kelaniya at
r. Ruins of temple at Polonnaruwa at ctr. on back.
a. Issued note.
s. Specimen.

VG	VF	UNC
1.00	3.00	12.50
—	—	125.00

91   5 RUPEES
1.1.1982. Lt. red on m/c unpt. Ruins at r. Stone carving of deity and
child on back.
a. Issued note.
s. Specimen.

VG	VF	UNC
FV	0.25	2.75
—	—	100.00

95   100 RUPEES
1.1.1982. Orange and brown on m/c unpt. Stone carving of lion at
lower r. Parliament bldg. on back.
a. Issued note.
s. Specimen.

VG	VF	UNC
2.00	4.00	25.00
—	—	160.00

92   10 RUPEES
1.1.1982; 1.1.1985. Olive-green on m/c unpt. Temple of the Tooth
in Kandy at r. Shrine on back.
a. Issued note.
s. Specimen.

VG	VF	UNC
0.25	0.50	4.50
—	—	100.00

Srí Lanká Maha Bänkuva
Central Bank of Sri Lanka

1987-89 Issue

#96-101 wmk: Chinze.

#96-100 similar to #89 and 92-95 but w/bank name changed in English from *CEYLON* to *Sri Lanka*. Printer: BWC.

		VG	VF	UNC
96	**10 RUPEES** 1.1.1987; 21.11.1988; 21.2.1989; 5.4.1990. Green on m/c unpt. Similar to #92.	FV	0.40	2.50

		VG	VF	UNC
101	**1000 RUPEES** 1.1.1987; 21.2.1989; 5.4.1990. Deep green and purple on m/c unpt. Victoria Dam at r. Peacock and University of Ruhuna on back. Printer: BWC.	FV	25.00	90.00

1991 Issue

#102-107 backs vertical format. Wmk: Chinze. Printer: TDLR. Replacement notes: Serial # prefix *Z/1*.

		VG	VF	UNC
97	**20 RUPEES** 1988-90. Purple and red on m/c unpt. Similar to #93.			
	a. 21.11.1988.	1.00	3.00	17.50
	b. 21.2.1989; 5.4.1990.	FV	0.75	3.75

		VG	VF	UNC
102	**10 RUPEES** 1.1.1991; 1.7.1992; 19.8.1994. Deep brown and green on m/c unpt. Sinhalese Chinze at r. Painted stork at top l., Presidential Secretariat bldg. in Colombo, flowers in lower foreground on back.	FV	0.25	1.25

		VG	VF	UNC
98	**50 RUPEES** 21.2.1989; 5.4.1990. Blue and brown on m/c unpt. Similar to #94.	FV	1.50	7.00
99	**100 RUPEES** 1.1.1987; 1.2.1988; 21.2.1989; 5.4.1990. Orange and brown on m/c unpt. Similar to #95.	FV	3.00	15.00
100	**500 RUPEES** 1.1.1987; 21.11.1988; 21.2.1989; 5.4.1990. Brown and purple on m/c unpt. Similar to #89 but w/larger wmk. area, vertical silver segmented security strip, bird and borders deeper red brown. Hill and temple in purple on back.	7.50	12.50	60.00

		VG	VF	UNC
103	**20 RUPEES** 1.1.1991; 1.7.1992; 19.8.1994. Purple and red on m/c unpt. Native bird mask at r. Two youths fishing, sea shells on back.	FV	0.50	2.50

NOTICE

Readers with unlisted dates, signature varieties, etc. are invited to submit photocopies of their notes to: Standard Catalog of World Paper Money, 700 East State St. Iola, WI 54990-0001, E-Mail: george.cuhaj@fwpubs.com.

104   50 RUPEES

		VG	VF	UNC
		FV	0.50	4.00

1.1.1991; 1.7.1992; 19.8.1994. Brown-violet, deep blue and blue-green on m/c unpt. Male dancer w/local headdress at r. Butterflies above temple ruins, w/shield and ornamental sword hilt in lower foreground on back.

107   1000 RUPEES

		VG	VF	UNC
		FV	FV	65.00

1.1.1991; 1.7.1992. Brown, dk. green and purple on m/c unpt. Chinze at lower l., 2-headed bird at bottom ctr., elephant w/trainer at r. Peacocks on palace lawn; lotus flowers above and Octagon of Temple of the Tooth in Kandy on back.

1995 ISSUE

#108-113 backs have a vertical format. Enhanced latent image security feature at lower ctr. on face. Printer: TDLR.

			VG	VF	UNC
108	**10 RUPEES**		FV	FV	1.00
	15.11.1995. Like #102 but w/additional security feature.				
109	**20 RUPEES**		FV	FV	2.00
	15.11.1995. Like #103 but w/additional security feature.				
110	**50 RUPEES**		FV	FV	4.00
	15.11.1995. Like #104 but w/additional security feature.				

105   100 RUPEES

	VG	VF	UNC
1991. Orange and dk. brown on m/c unpt. Decorative urn at r. Tea leaf pickers, two Rose-ringed Parakeets at bottom on back.			
a. W/o dot on value in Tamil at l. 1.1.1991.	FV	FV	35.00
b. W/dot on value in Tamil at l. 1.1.1991.	FV	FV	8.00

105A   100 RUPEES

	VG	VF	UNC
1.7.1992. Like #105a but back orange on m/c unpt.	FV	FV	6.00

			VG	VF	UNC
111	**100 RUPEES**		FV	FV	5.00
	15.11.1995. Dk. brown and orange on m/c unpt. Like #105A but w/additional security feature.				
112	**500 RUPEES**		FV	FV	32.50
	15.11.1995. Like #106 but w/additional security feature.				
113	**1000 RUPEES**		FV	FV	50.00
	15.11.1995. Like #107 but w/additional security feature.				

1998 COMMEMORATIVE ISSUE

#114, 50th Anniversary of Independence, 1948-1998

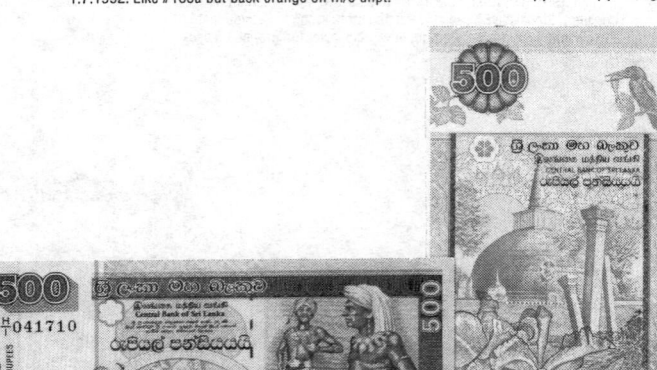

106   500 RUPEES

	VG	VF	UNC
1991-92. Dk. brown, purple and brown-orange on m/c unpt. Musicians at r., dancer at l. ctr. Stork-billed Kingfisher above temple and orchids on back.			
a. 1.1.1991.	FV	FV	35.00
b. 1.7.1992.	FV	10.00	50.00

114	200 RUPEES	VG	VF	UNC

4.2.1998. Greenish black on blue, orange and m/c unpt. Temple at upper ctr. r. above a collage of modern scenes across lower l. to r. Palace at upper l. ctr. above collage of medieval scenes of British landing across lower l. to r. on back. Polymer p

		VG	VF	UNC
	a. Red serial # in folder.	FV	FV	15.00
	b. Black serial #.	FV	FV	10.00

2001 ISSUE

115	10 RUPEES	VG	VF	UNC
	2001; 2004. Like #108.			
	a. 12.12.2001.	FV	FV	0.75
	b. 10.4.2004.	FV	FV	0.50
116	20 RUPEES			
	2001; 2004. Like #109.			
	a. 12.12.2001.	FV	FV	1.50
	b. 10.4.2004.	FV	FV	0.75
117	50 RUPEES			
	2001; 2004 Like #110.			
	a. 12.12.2001.	FV	FV	2.50
	b. 10.4.2004.	FV	FV	1.50
118	100 RUPEES			
	2001; 2004. Like #111.			
	a. 12.12.2001.	FV	FV	4.00
	b. 10.4.2004.	FV	FV	
119	500 RUPEES			
	2001; 2004. Like #112.			
	a. 12.12.2001.	FV	FV	17.50
	b. 10.4.2004.	FV	FV	15.00
120	1000 RUPEES			
	2001; 2004. Like #113.			
	a. 12.12.2001.	FV	FV	35.00
	b. 10.4.2004.	FV	FV	30.00

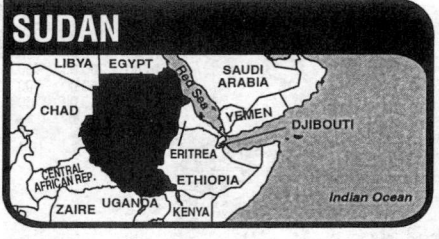

The Democratic Republic of the Sudan, located in northeast Africa on the Red Sea between Egypt and Ethiopia, has an area of 967,500 sq. mi. (2,505,810 sq. km.) and a population of 29.82 million. Capital: Khartoum. Agriculture and livestock raising are the chief occupations. Cotton, gum arabic and peanuts are exported.

The Sudan, site of the powerful Nubian kingdom of Roman times, was a collection of small independent states from the 14th century until 1820-22 when it was conquered and united by Mohammed Ali, Pasha of Egypt. Egyptian forces were driven from the area during the Mahdist revolt, 1881-98, but the Sudan was retaken by Anglo-Egyptian expeditions, 1896-98, and established as an Anglo-Egyptian condominium in 1899. Britain supplied the administrative apparatus and personnel, but the appearance of joint Anglo-Egyptian administration was continued until Jan. 9, 1954, when the first Sudanese self-government parliament was inaugurated.

The Sudan achieved independence on Jan. 1, 1956 with the consent of the British and Egyptian governments. On June 30, 1989 Gen. Omar Hassan Ahmad al-Bashir overthrew the civilian government in a military coup. The rebel guerrilla PLA forces are active in the south. Notes of Egypt were in use before 1956.

RULERS:
British, 1899-1954

MONETARY SYSTEM:
1 Ghirsh (Piastre) = 10 Millim (Milliemes)
1 Sudanese Pound = 100 Piastres to 1992
1 Dinar = 10 Old Sudanese Pounds, 1992

REPUBLIC

BANK OF SUDAN

1961-64 ISSUE

#6-10 various date and sign. varieties. Arms (desert camel rider) on back.

6	25 PIASTRES	VG	VF	UNC
	1964-68. Red on m/c unpt. Soldiers in formation at l.			
	a. 6.3.1964; 20.1.1966.	6.00	25.00	200.00
	b. 25.1.1967.	5.00	15.00	180.00
	c. W/o Arabic text al-Khartoum. 7.2.1968.	4.00	12.50	175.00

7	50 PIASTRES	VG	VF	UNC
	1964-68. Green on m/c unpt. Elephants at l.			
	a. 6.3.1964.	15.00	95.00	650.00
	b. 25.1.1967.	12.50	85.00	625.00
	c. W/o Arabic text al-Khartoum. 7.2.1968.	12.50	85.00	625.00

8	1 POUND	VG	VF	UNC
	1961-68. Blue on yellow and m/c unpt. Dam at l.			
	a. 8.4.1961.	7.50	35.00	300.00
	b. 2.3.1965.	7.50	35.00	300.00
	c. 20.1.1966.	6.00	17.50	250.00
	d. 25.1.1967.	6.00	17.50	250.00
	e. W/o Arabic text al-Khartoum. 7.2.1968.	5.00	15.00	225.00

9   **5 POUNDS**

1962-68. Lilac-brown on m/c unpt. Dhow at l.

	VG	VF	UNC
a. 1.7.1962.	20.00	100.00	900.00
b. 2.3.1965.	12.50	65.00	725.00
c. 20.1.1966.	10.00	60.00	700.00
d. 25.1.1967.	10.00	60.00	700.00
e. W/o Arabic text *al-Khartoum*. 7.2.1968.	8.00	60.00	750.00

10   **10 POUNDS**

1964-68. Gray-black on m/c unpt. Bank of Sudan bldg. at l.

	VG	VF	UNC
a. 6.3.1964.	10.00	75.00	800.00
b. 20.1.1966.	10.00	65.00	850.00
c. 25.1.1967.	10.00	65.00	800.00
d. W/o Arabic text *al-Khartoum*. 7.2.1968.	8.00	60.00	800.00

1970 ISSUE

#11-15 Bank of Sudan at l. on face. Various date and sign. varieties. Printer: TDLR.

11   **25 PIASTRES**

1970-80. Red on m/c unpt. Textile industry on back.

	VG	VF	UNC
a. Jan. 1970; Jan. 1971; Jan. 1972.	1.00	7.50	50.00
b. 1.4.1973-28.5.1978.	0.75	2.50	10.00
c. 2.1.1980.	0.50	1.00	6.00

12   **50 PIASTRES**

1970-80. Green on m/c unpt. University of Khartoum on back.

	VG	VF	UNC
a. Jan. 1970; Jan. 1971; Jan. 1972.	1.50	12.50	75.00
b. 1.4.1973-28.5.1978.	1.00	2.50	12.50
c. 2.1.1980.	1.00	3.50	15.00

13   **1 POUND**

1970-80. Blue on m/c unpt. Ancient temple on back.

	VG	VF	UNC
a. Wmk: Rhinoceros head. Jan. 1970; Jan. 1971.	5.00	25.00	100.00
b. Wmk: Arms (secretary bird). Jan. 1972-28.5.1978.	1.00	3.00	30.00
c. 2.1.1980.	1.00	4.00	35.00

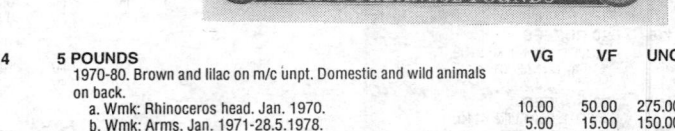

14   **5 POUNDS**

1970-80. Brown and lilac on m/c unpt. Domestic and wild animals on back.

	VG	VF	UNC
a. Wmk: Rhinoceros head. Jan. 1970.	10.00	50.00	275.00
b. Wmk: Arms. Jan. 1971-28.5.1978.	5.00	15.00	150.00
c. 2.1.1980.	5.00	17.50	165.00

15   **10 POUNDS**

1970-80. Purple and green on m/c unpt. Transportation elements (ship, plane, etc.) on back.

	VG	VF	UNC
a. Wmk: Rhinoceros head. Jan. 1970.	27.50	150.00	600.00
b. Wmk: Arms. Jan. 1971-28.5.1978.	7.50	20.00	95.00
c. 2.1.1980.	5.00	15.00	35.00

Note: A large horad of #15 has recently come onto the market, resulting in a collapse in the value.

1981 ISSUE

#16-21 Pres. J. Nimeiri wearing national headdress at l., arms at ctr.

#18-21 wmk: Arms.

16   **25 PIASTRES**

1.1.1981. Brown on m/c unpt. Kosti bridge on back.

	VG	VF	UNC
	0.25	1.00	2.50

17	50 PIASTRES	VG	VF	UNC
	1.1.1981. Purple on brown unpt. Bank of Sudan on back.	0.50	1.25	4.50

22	20 POUNDS	VG	VF	UNC
	1.1.1981. Green on m/c unpt. Pres. J. Nimeiri w/native headdress at l., map at ctr., commemorative legend in circle at r. around wmk., monument at r. Unity Monument at l., People's Palace at ctr. r. on back.	7.50	22.50	90.00

1983-84 Issue

#23-29 like previous issue but some in different colors.

23	25 PIASTRES	VG	VF	UNC
	1.1.1983. Red-orange on pale yellow unpt. Like #16.	0.25	0.50	1.50
24	50 PIASTRES			
	1.1.1983. Purple on brown unpt. Like #17.	0.50	1.25	2.00
25	1 POUND			
	1.1.1983. Blue on m/c unpt. Like #18 but bldg. on back is blue only.	0.50	1.25	2.50

18	1 POUND	VG	VF	UNC
	1.1.1981. Blue on m/c unpt. People's Assembly on back.	1.00	3.50	15.00

19	5 POUNDS	VG	VF	UNC
	1.1.1981. Green and brown on m/c unpt. Back green; Islamic Centre Mosque in Khartoum at r.	2.00	6.00	30.00

26	5 POUNDS	VG	VF	UNC
	1.1.1983. Green. Like #19.	1.00	2.50	15.00
27	10 POUNDS			
	1.1.1983. Purple and red-brown on m/c unpt. Like #20.	2.50	7.50	40.00
28	20 POUNDS			
	1.1.1983. Green on m/c unpt. Like #21.	5.00	10.00	60.00

20	10 POUNDS	VG	VF	UNC
	1.1.1981. Blue and brown on m/c unpt. Kenana sugar factory on back.	5.00	15.00	75.00
21	20 POUNDS			
	1.1.1981. Green on m/c unpt. Like #22 but w/o commemorative text.	7.50	30.00	120.00

1981 Commemorative Issue

#22, 25th Anniversary of Independence

29	50 POUNDS	VG	VF	UNC
	25.5.1984. Brown-orange, blue and olive-brown on m/c unpt. Pres. Nimeiri at l. Back blue on m/c unpt.; sailing ship at ctr., modern oil tanker at r. Wmk: Arms.	5.00	20.00	90.00

Law of 30.6.1985/AH1405

#30-36 outline map of Sudan at ctr. Bank of Sudan at ctr. r. on back. Wmk: Arms. Sign. title w/2 lines of Arabic text (Acting Governor).

Replacement notes: Serial # prefix Z/1; Z/11; Z/21; Z/31; Z/41; Z/51; Z/61; Z/71.

30	25 PIASTRES	VG	VF	UNC
	L.1985. Purple on m/c unpt. Camels at l.	0.10	0.40	1.50

31	50 PIASTRES	VG	VF	UNC
	L.1985. Red on lilac and peach unpt. Lyre and drum at l., peanut plant at r.	0.15	0.50	2.50

#32-36 wmk: Arms.

32	1 POUND	VG	VF	UNC
	L.1985. Green and blue on m/c unpt. Cotton boll at l. Back blue on m/c unpt.	0.20	0.75	3.00

33	5 POUNDS	VG	VF	UNC
	L.1985. Olive and brown on m/c unpt. Cattle at l.	0.50	4.00	25.00

34	10 POUNDS	VG	VF	UNC
	L.1985. Brown on m/c unpt. City gateway at l.	2.00	6.00	40.00

35	20 POUNDS	VG	VF	UNC
	L.1985. Green and purple on m/c unpt. Feluka at l.	5.00	20.00	225.00

36	50 POUNDS	VG	VF	UNC
	L.1985. Brown, purple and red-orange on m/c unpt. Columns along pool below National Museum at l., spear at r. Back red.	5.00	25.00	225.00

1987-90 ISSUE

#37-43 sign. title in 1 line of Arabic text (Governor).

37	25 PIASTRES	VG	VF	UNC
	1987. Purple on m/c unpt. Like #30.	0.05	0.15	0.50

38	50 PIASTRES	VG	VF	UNC
	1987. Red on lilac and peach unpt. Like #31.	0.05	0.25	0.75

39	1 POUND	VG	VF	UNC
	1987. Green and blue on m/c unpt. Like #32.	0.10	0.25	1.00

#40-44 wmk: Arms.

40	5 POUNDS	VG	VF	UNC
	1987-90. Olive and brown on m/c unpt. Like #33.			
	a. 1987.	0.25	0.75	7.50
	b. 1989.	2.00	12.50	32.50
	c. 1990.	0.50	3.00	20.00

41	10 POUNDS	VG	VF	UNC
	1987-90. Brown on m/c unpt. Like #34.			
	a. 1987.	0.50	1.50	22.50
	b. 1989.	0.75	3.00	27.50
	c. 1990.	0.75	3.00	27.50

42	20 POUNDS	VG	VF	UNC
	1987-90. Green and purple on m/c unpt. Like #35.			
	a. 1987.	0.50	2.00	17.50
	b. 1989.	0.50	2.00	15.00
	c. 1990.	0.50	3.00	30.00

43	50 POUNDS	VG	VF	UNC
	1987; 1989; 1990. Brown, purple and red-orange on m/c unpt. Like #36.			
	a. 1987.	1.00	4.00	17.50
	b. 1989.	1.00	3.00	12.50
	c. 1990.	4.00	8.00	12.50

44	100 POUNDS	VG	VF	UNC
	1988-90. Brown, purple and deep green on m/c unpt. Shield, University of Khartoum bldg. at l., open book at lower r. Bank of Sudan and shiny coin design on back.			
	a. 1988.	1.50	3.00	25.00
	b. 1989; 1990.	0.50	1.00	3.50

1991 ISSUE

#45-50 like #40-44. Wmk: Arms.

45	5 POUNDS	VG	VF	UNC
	1991/AH1411. Red, orange and violet on m/c unpt. Like #40. Back red-orange on m/c unpt.	0.20	0.50	1.75

46	10 POUNDS	VG	VF	UNC
	1991/AH1411. Black and deep green on m/c unpt. Like #41. Back black on m/c unpt.	0.20	0.75	2.00

47	20 POUNDS	VG	VF	UNC
	1991/AH1411. Purple and violet on m/c unpt. Like #42. Back violet on m/c unpt.	0.25	0.75	2.50

48   50 POUNDS

	VG	VF	UNC
1991/AH1411. Yellow-orange, brownish black and dk. brown on m/c unpt. Like #43. Back dk. brown on m/c unpt.	0.50	1.00	3.50

49   100 POUNDS

	VG	VF	UNC
1991/AH1411. Ultramarine and blue-green on m/c unpt. Like #44. Ultramarine shield at l., lt. blue-green map image at ctr. Shiny lt. green coin design at r. on back (partially engraved).	1.00	2.50	22.50

50   100 POUNDS

	VG	VF	UNC
1991/AH1411; 1992/AH1412. Similar to #49 but colors rearranged. Blue-green shield at l., darker details on bldg. and ultramarine map image at ctr. Pink coin design at r. on back. (litho).	0.50	1.00	3.00

1992-98 ISSUE

#51-55 People's Palace at ctr. or lower r. Wmk: Domed bldg. w/tower.

Note: First issues w/fractional serial # prefix (Type I) replaced w/local printings w/double letter serial # prefix (Type II).

51   5 DINARS

	VG	VF	UNC
1993/AH1413. Dk. brown and red-orange on m/c unpt. Plants including sunflowers at ctr. on back. Serial # Type II. Replacement note: *GZ*.			
a. Issued note.	FV	FV	3.00
s. Specimen.	—	—	85.00

52   10 DINARS

	VG	VF	UNC
1993/AH1413. Deep red and dk. brown on m/c unpt. Domed bldg. w/tower at l. ctr. on back. Serial # Type II. Replacement note: *HZ*.			
a. Issued note.	FV	FV	3.50
s. Specimen.	—	—	85.00

53   25 DINARS

	VG	VF	UNC
1992/AH1412. Brownish black and green on m/c unpt. Circular design at l. on back.			
a. W/artist's name *DOSOUGI* at lower r. Serial # Type I.	FV	FV	10.00
b. W/o artist's name. Serial # Type I. Replacement note: *IZ*.	FV	FV	5.00
c. As b. Serial # Type II.	FV	FV	2.00

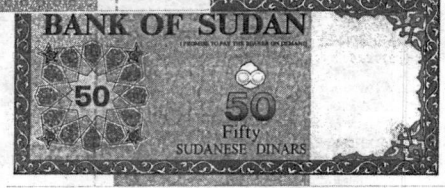

54   50 DINARS

	VG	VF	UNC
1992/AH1412. Dk. blue-green, black and purple on m/c unpt.			
a. W/artist's name *DOSOUGI* at lower r. below palace. Serial # Type I.	FV	FV	20.00
b. W/o artist's name. 2 sign. varieties. Serial # Type I.	FV	FV	4.50
c. As b. Serial # Type II. Replacement note: *JZ*.	FV	FV	5.50
d. As c. Segmented security thread.	FV	FV	3.50

55   100 DINARS

	VG	VF	UNC
1994/AH1414. Black and deep brown-violet on m/c unpt. Double doorway at ctr. Bldg. at l. ctr. on back. Serial # Type I. Replacement note: *KZ*.	FV	FV	7.50

		VG	VF	UNC
56	**100 DINARS** 1994/AH1414. Black and deep brown-violet on m/c unpt. Like #55 but w/segmented foil over security thread. Serial # Type II. Replacement note: *LZ*.	FV	FV	5.00

		VG	VF	UNC
60	**200 DINARS** 2002/AH1424.	FV	FV	12.50

		VG	VF	UNC
57	**200 DINARS** 1998/AH1419. Green and black on m/c unpt. Peoples Palace at r., crop line art at ctr. Bldg. at upper ctr., line art at lower ctr on back.	FV	FV	8.00

		VG	VF	UNC
61	**500 DINARS**	FV	FV	7.50
62	**1000 DINARS**			Expected New Issue
63	**2000 DINARS** 2002/AH1421. Tan, blue, maroon and black on m/c unpt. Dam, oil rig and Bank of Sudan bldg. on back.	FV	FV	25.00

		VG	VF	UNC
58	**500 DINARS** 1998/AH1419. Red, black and green on m/c unpt. Oil well and bldg. on back. Serial # Type II.	FV	FV	10.00

		VG	VF	UNC
59	**1000 DINARS** 1996/AH1416. Green, yellow-brown and purple. Seal at l. ctr., bldg. in background at ctr. Bldg. on back. Serial # Type II. Replacement note: *MZ*.	FV	FV	17.50

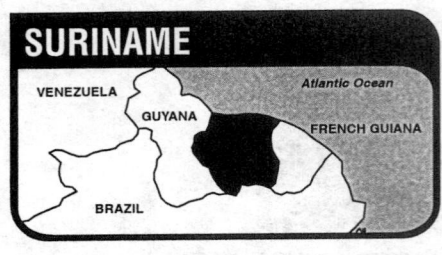

The Republic of Surinam, formerly known as Dutch Guiana, located on the north central coast of South America between Guyana and French Guiana, has an area of 63,037 sq. mi. (163,270 sq. km.) and a population of 452,000. Capital: Paramaribo. The country is rich in minerals and forests, and self-sufficient in rice, the staple food crop. The mining, processing and exporting of bauxite is the principal economic activity.

Lieutenants of Amerigo Vespucci sighted the Guiana coast in 1499. Spanish explorers of the 16th century, disappointed at finding no gold, departed leaving the area to be settled by the British in 1652. The colony prospered and the Netherlands acquired it in 1667 in exchange for the Dutch rights in Nieuw Nederland (state of New York). During the European wars of the 18th and 19th centuries, which were fought in part in the New World, Surinam was occupied by the British from 1799-1814. Surinam became an autonomous part of the Kingdom of the Netherlands on Dec. 15, 1954. Full independence was achieved on Nov. 25, 1975.

RULERS:
Dutch to 1975

MONETARY SYSTEM:
1 Gulden = 1 Florin = 100 Cents, to 2004
1 Dollar = 1000 "old" Gulden, 2004-

DUTCH ADMINISTRATION

MUNTBILJET

LAW 8.4.1960

#23-24 various date and sign. varieties. Printer: JEZ. Replacement notes: 6-digit serial number beginning with "1".

116	1 GULDEN	VG	VF	UNC
	1961-86. Dk. green w/black text on pale olive-green and brown unpt. Bldg. w/tower and flag at l. Back brown and green.			
	a. Sign. title: *De Minister van Financien* w/printed sign. but w/o name. 1.8.1961-1.4.1969.	0.75	2.00	10.00
	b. Sign. in facsimile w/printed name below. 1.4.1971.	0.50	2.00	7.00
	c. Similar to b., but printed name of signer at r. 1.11.1974.	0.50	2.00	5.50
	d. Like c. W/o printed name at r. 1.11.1974.	0.50	2.00	5.50
	e. Similar to a., but shorter text, and sign. title centered. 1.11.1974; 25.6.1979.	0.40	1.50	7.00
	f. Similar to d., but sign. title: *De Minister van Financien en Planning.* 1.9.1982.	0.15	0.50	2.50
	g. 2.1.1984.	0.15	0.50	2.25
	h. 1.12.1984.	0.15	0.50	2.25
	i. 1.10.1986.	0.15	0.50	2.00

117	2 1/2 GULDEN	VG	VF	UNC
	1961; 1967. Red-brown. Girl wearing hat at l. Back red-brown and brown.			
	a. 2.1.1961.	0.75	3.00	12.50
	b. 2.7.1967.	0.75	2.25	7.50

118	2 1/2 GULDEN	VG	VF	UNC
	1973; 1978. Red-brown, lt. blue and m/c. Blue-gray Tanager on branch at l. 3 lines of text above sign. title at ctr. Lizard and Afobaka Dam on back. Printer: BWC.			
	a. Sign. title: *De Minister van Financien.* Printed name below sign. 1.9.1973.	0.50	2.25	9.00
	b. W/o printed name below sign. 1.8.1978.	0.20	0.75	4.50

119	2 1/2 GULDEN	VG	VF	UNC
	1.11.1985. Like #24A but 4 lines of text above sign. W/sign. title: *De Minister van Financien en Planning* .	0.20	0.75	3.50

CENTRALE BANK VAN SURINAME

1963 ISSUE

#30-34 different arms than 1957 issue on back. Wmk: Toucan's head. Printer: JEZ. Replacement notes: Serial # prefix *ZZ*.

120	5 GULDEN	VG	VF	UNC
	1.9.1963. Blue on m/c unpt. 2 serial # varieties.			
	a. Small size serial #.	0.10	0.25	0.75
	b. Large size serial #.	0.10	0.25	0.75

121	10 GULDEN	VG	VF	UNC
	1.9.1963. Orange on m/c unpt.	0.10	0.25	1.00

122	25 GULDEN	VG	VF	UNC
	1.9.1963. Green on m/c unpt.	0.50	3.00	10.00

123	100 GULDEN	VG	VF	UNC
	1.9.1963. Purple on m/c unpt.	1.00	5.00	12.50

124	1000 GULDEN	VG	VF	UNC
	1.9.1963. Brown on m/c unpt.	1.00	5.00	12.50

Note: #34 was sold in quantity by the Central Bank to the numismatic community.

REPUBLIC
CENTRALE BANK VAN SURINAME
1982 ISSUE
#35-39 soldiers and woman at r. Bldg. w/flag on back. Wmk: Toucan's head. Printer: JEZ.

125	5 GULDEN	VG	VF	UNC
	1.4.1982. Blue on m/c unpt.	0.15	0.50	1.00
126	10 GULDEN			
	1.4.1982. Red on m/c unpt.	0.15	0.40	1.25

127	25 GULDEN	VG	VF	UNC
	1982; 1985. Green on m/c unpt.			
	a. 1.4.1982.	1.00	2.50	5.00
	b. 1.11.1985.	0.10	0.25	0.75

128	100 GULDEN	VG	VF	UNC
	1982; 1985. Purple on m/c unpt.			
	a. 1.4.1982.	5.00	10.00	20.00
	b. 1.11.1985.	0.25	1.25	3.50

129	500 GULDEN	VG	VF	UNC
	1.4.1982. Brown on m/c unpt.	0.25	1.00	7.50

Note: 1000 new notes of #39 were sold by the Central Bank to the numismatic community for USA $2.00 each.

1986-88 ISSUE
#40-44 Anton DeKom at l., militia at r., row of bldgs. across bottom. Toucan at l., speaker w/people at r. on back. Wmk: Toucan. Printer: TDLR.

130	5 GULDEN		VG	VF	UNC
	1986; 1988. Blue on m/c unpt.				
	a. 1.7.1986.		FV	0.75	3.00
	b. 9.1.1988.		FV	FV	2.00

131	10 GULDEN		VG	VF	UNC
	1986; 1988. Orange and red on m/c unpt.				
	a. 1.7.1986.		FV	1.25	4.00
	b. 9.1.1988.		FV	FV	2.00

132	25 GULDEN		VG	VF	UNC
	1986; 1988. Green on m/c unpt.				
	a. 1.7.1986.		FV	2.00	8.00
	b. 9.1.1988.		FV	FV	3.50

133	100 GULDEN		VG	VF	UNC
	1986; 1988. Purple on m/c unpt. 2 serial # varieties.				
	a. 1.7.1986.		FV	7.50	20.00
	b. 9.1.1988.		FV	FV	2.50

134	250 GULDEN		VG	VF	UNC
	9.1.1988. Blue-gray on m/c unpt.		FV	2.00	8.00

135	500 GULDEN		VG	VF	UNC
	1.7.1986; 9.1.1988. Brown and orange on m/c unpt.				
	a. 1.7.1986.		FV	15.00	50.00
	b. 9.1.1988.		FV	3.50	12.50

1991-97 ISSUE

#46-54 Central Bank bldg., Paramaribo at ctr. Toucan at l. ctr. and as wmk., arms at upper r. on back. Printer: TDLR.

136	5 GULDEN		VG	VF	UNC
	1991; 1995-96; 1998. Deep blue and green on m/c unpt. Log trucks at upper l. Logging at ctr. r. on back.				
	a. 9.7.1991.		FV	FV	1.50
	b. 1.6.1995; 1.12.1996; 12.2.1998.		FV	FV	0.25

137	10 GULDEN		VG	VF	UNC
	1991; 1995; 1998. Red and dk. green on m/c unpt. Bananas at upper l. Banana harvesting at ctr. r. on back.				
	a. 9.7.1991.		FV	FV	3.00
	b. 1.6.1995; 1.12.1996; 10.2.1998.		FV	FV	0.25

138	25 GULDEN		VG	VF	UNC
	1991; 1995; 1996; 1998. Green and brown-orange on m/c unpt. Track participants at upper l. Competition swimmer (Olympian Anthony Neste) in butterfly stroke at ctr. r. on back.				
	a. 9.7.1991.		FV	FV	4.00
	b. 1.6.1995.		FV	FV	3.50
	c. 1.12.1996.		FV	FV	2.50
	d. 10.2.1998.		FV	FV	2.50

139 100 GULDEN
9.7.1991. Violet and purple on m/c unpt. Factory at upper l. Strip mining at ctr. r. on back.

	VG	VF	UNC
	FV	FV	6.50

140 500 GULDEN
9.7.1991. Brown and red-orange on m/c unpt. Crude oil pump at upper l. Drilling for crude oil at ctr. r. on back.

	VG	VF	UNC
	FV	FV	10.00

141 1000 GULDEN
1993; 1995. Black and red on m/c unpt. Combine at upper l. Combining grain at ctr. r. on back.

		VG	VF	UNC
a. 1.7.1993.		FV	FV	10.00
b. 1.3.1995.		FV	FV	5.00

142 2000 GULDEN
1.6.1995. Purple and green on m/c unpt. Back like #46.

	VG	VF	UNC
	FV	FV	10.00

143 5000 GULDEN
5.10.1997; 1.2.1999. Purple on m/c unpt. Long Billed Gnatwren, banana bunches on back.

	VG	VF	UNC
	FV	FV	20.00

144 10,000 GULDEN
5.10.1997. Green, red and m/c. Silver segmented security thread. Bird, industrial complex on back.

	VG	VF	UNC
	FV	FV	37.50

145 10,000 GULDEN
5.10.1997. Green, red and m/c. Like #54 but purple segmented security thread. More red used on bldgs at ctr. and arms at l. ctr. on back than with #54.

	VG	VF	UNC
	FV	FV	37.50

2000 ISSUE

#56-64 arms at upper ctr. r. Ascending size serial #. Printer: TDLR.

146 5 GULDEN
1.1.2000. Blue and m/c. Red-necked Woodpecker at l. ctr. Flower on back.

	VG	VF	UNC
	FV	FV	1.00

147 10 GULDEN
1.1.2000. Green, purple, brown on m/c unpt. Black-throated Mango at l. ctr. Flower on back

	VG	VF	UNC
	FV	FV	1.25

148   25 GULDEN
    1.1.2000. Blue and black on m/c unpt. at l. ctr. Flower on back.
    Red-billed Toucan

	VG	VF	UNC
	FV	FV	1.50

149   100 GULDEN
    1.1.2000. Rose on m/c unpt. Long-tailed Hermit at l. ctr. Flower on
    back.

	VG	VF	UNC
	FV	FV	2.00

150   500 GULDEN
    1.1.2000. Orange and green on m/c unpt. Guianan Cock-of-the-
    Rock at l. ctr. Flower on back.

	VG	VF	UNC
	FV	FV	2.50

151   1000 GULDEN
    1.1.2000. Green and red on m/c unpt. Royal Flycatcher at l. ctr.
    Flower on back.

	VG	VF	UNC
	FV	FV	4.00

152   5000 GULDEN
    1.1.2000. Green, yellow, blue and orange on m/c unpt. Sun
    Parakeet at l. ctr. Flowers on back.

	VG	VF	UNC
	FV	FV	12.50

153   10,000 GULDEN
    1.1.2000. Brown, black and red on m/c unpt. Ornate Hawk-eagle at
    l. ctr. Flower on back.

	VG	VF	UNC
	FV	FV	20.00

154   25,000 GULDEN
    1.1.2000. Brown and green on m/c unpt. Specktacled Owl at l. ctr.
    Flower and long leaves on back.

	VG	VF	UNC
	FV	FV	40.00

SURINAME WETTIG BETAALMIDDEL

2004 ISSUE

155   1 DOLLAR
    2004.

	VG	VF	UNC
	FV	FV	1.00

156   2 1/2 DOLLARS
    2004.

	VG	VF	UNC
	FV	FV	2.00

CENTRALE BANK VAN SURINAME

2004 ISSUE

157	5 DOLLARS		VG	VF	UNC
	2004.		FV	FV	2.00

158	10 DOLLARS		VG	VF	UNC
	2004.		FV	FV	2.50

159	20 DOLLARS		VG	VF	UNC
	2004.		FV	FV	10.00

160	50 DOLLARS		VG	VF	UNC
	2004.		FV	FV	20.00

161	100 DOLLARS		VG	VF	UNC
	2004.		FV	FV	40.00

The Kingdom of Swaziland, located in southeastern Africa, has an area of 6,704 sq. mi. (17,360 sq. km.) and a population of 984,000. Capital: Mbabane (administrative); Lobamba (legislative). The diversified economy includes mining, agriculture and light industry. Asbestos, iron ore, wood pulp and sugar are exported.

The people of the present Swazi nation established themselves in an area including what is now Swaziland in the early 1800s. The first Swazi contact with the British came early in the reign of the extremely able Swazi leader King Mswati II when he asked the British for aid against Zulu raids into Swaziland. The British and Transvaal responded by guaranteeing the independence of Swaziland, 1881. South Africa assumed the power of protection and administration in 1894 and Swaziland continued under this administration until the conquest of the Transvaal during the Anglo-Boer War, when administration was transferred to the British government. After World War II, Britain began to prepare Swaziland for independence, which was achieved on Sept. 6, 1968 under the leadership of King Sobhuza II whose reign was of 61 years. His son, Prince Makhosetive was crowned King Mswati III on Apr. 25, 1986 at the age of 18 years. The kingdom is a member of the Commonwealth of Nations. The king of Swaziland is Chief of State. The prime minister is Head of Government.

RULERS:
British to 1968
Sobhuza II, 1968-82
Queen Ntombi, as regent, 1982-86
King Mswati III, 1986-

MONETARY SYSTEM:
1 Lilangeni = 100 Cents
(plural: Emalangeni)

	SIGNATURE VARIETIES	
	MINISTER FOR FINANCE	**GOVERNOR**
1	R. P. Stephens 1.6.1972 - 11.1.1979	E. A. Z. Maylsela 1.4.1974 - 31.10.1976
	J. L. F. Simelane 12.1.1979 - 20.11.1983	Deputy Governor H. B. B. Oliver 1.11.1976 - 30.6.1978 Acting Governor: A. D. Ockenden 1.6.1978 - 30.6.1981
2	J. L. F. Simelane 12.1.1979 - 20.11.1983	H. B. B. Oliver 1.7.1981 - 30.6.1992
3	Dr. S. S. Nxumalo 21.11.1983 - 8.6.1984	H. B. B. Oliver 1.7.1981 - 30.6.1992
4	B. S. Dlamini 27.8.1984 - 5.11.1993	H. B. B. Oliver 1.7.1981 - 30.6.1992
5	B. S. Dlamini 27.8.1984 - 5.11.1993	J. Nxumalo 1.7.1992 - 30.6.1997
6	I. S. Shabangu 10.11.1993 - 3.3.1995	J. Nxumalo 1.7.1992 - 30.6.1997
7A	Dr. D. von Wissell 3.3.1995 - 12.11.1996	J. Nxumalo 1.7.1992 - 30.6.1997
7B	Dr. D. von Wissell 3.3.1995 - 12.11.1996	J. Nxumalo 1.7.1992 - 30.6.1997

SIGNATURE VARIETIES

	MINISTER FOR FINANCE	GOVERNOR
8	*T. Masuku* T. Masuku 12.11.1996 - 19.11.1998	*J. Nxumalo* J. Nxumalo 1.7.1992 - 30.6.1997
9A	*Themba N. Masuku* T. Masuku 12.11.1996 - 19.11.1998	*Martin G Dlamini* M. G. Dlamini 1.7.1997 →
9B	*Themba N. Masuku* T. Masuku 12.11.1996 - 19.11.1998	*Martin G Dlamini* M. G. Dlamini 1.7.1997 →
	J. Charmichael 20.11.1998 - 14.2.2001	M. G. Dlamini 21.7.1997 →
10A	*Majozi V. Sithole* Majozi V. Sithole 15.2.2001 →	*Martin G Dlamini* M. G. Dlamini 1.7.1997 →
10B	*Majozi V. Sithole* Majozi V. Sithole 15.2.2001 →	*Martin G Dlamini* M. G. Dlamini 1.7.1997 →
11	*Majozi V. Sithole* Majozi V. Sithole	*Martin G Dlamini* M. G. Dlamini

KINGDOM

MONETARY AUTHORITY OF SWAZILAND

1974-78 ND ISSUE

#1-5 Kg. Sobhuza II at l., Parliament House at bottom ctr. r. Sign. 1. Wmk: Shield and spears. Printer: TDLR. Replacement notes: Serial # prefix Z.

1   **1 LILANGENI**

		VG	VF	UNC
ND (1974). Red-brown on m/c unpt. Princesses taking part in the *Ncwala* (kingship ceremony).				
	a. Issued note.	0.50	0.75	6.00
	s. Specimen. Serial # prefix *A; G.*	—	—	65.00

2   **2 EMALANGENI**

		VG	VF	UNC
ND (1974). Dk. brown on pink and m/c unpt. Sugar mill on back.				
	a. Issued note.	0.60	1.75	12.00
	s. Specimen. Serial # prefix *A; C.*	—	—	65.00

3   **5 EMALANGENI**

		VG	VF	UNC
ND (1974). Dk. green on yellow-green and m/c unpt. Mantenga Falls and landscape on back.				
	a. Issued note.	1.50	5.00	37.50
	s. Specimen. Serial # prefix *A; B.*	—	—	65.00

4   **10 EMALANGENI**

		VG	VF	UNC
ND (1974). Blue-black on blue and m/c unpt. Asbestos mine on back.				
	a. Issued note.	4.00	10.00	80.00
	s. Specimen. Serial # prefix *A; B.*	—	—	65.00

5   **20 EMALANGENI**

		VG	VF	UNC
ND (1978). Purple and green on m/c unpt. Agricultural products and cows on back.				
	a. Issued note.	12.50	35.00	185.00
	s. Specimen. Serial # prefix *A.*	—	—	65.00

CENTRAL BANK OF SWAZILAND

1981 COMMEMORATIVE ISSUE

#6 and 7, Diamond Jubilee of Kg. Sobhuza II
#6 and 7 printer: TDLR.

6 **10 EMALANGENI**
1981. Blue-black on blue and m/c unpt. Black commemorative text
on wmk. area. Back like #4. Wmk: Shield and spears. Sign. 2.

	VG	VF	UNC
a. Issued note.	25.00	85.00	300.00
s. Specimen. Serial # prefix K.	—	—	185.00

10 **10 EMALANGENI**
ND (1982-86). Blue-black on blue and m/c unpt. Like #6 but w/o
commemorative inscription on face.

	VG	VF	UNC
a. Sign. 2. (1982).	7.50	25.00	135.00
b. Sign. 3. (1984).	6.50	22.50	120.00
c. Sign. 4. (1985).	1.25	4.00	16.50
s1. As a. Specimen. Serial # prefix Q.	—	—	65.00
s2. As b. Specimen. Serial # prefix U.	—	—	65.00
s3. As c. Specimen. Serial # prefix W.	—	—	65.00

7 **20 EMALANGENI**
1981. Purple and green on m/c unpt. Like #8. Back like #5. Wmk:
Shield and spears. Sign. 2.

	VG	VF	UNC
a. Issued note.	25.00	100.00	335.00
s. Specimen. Serial # prefix C.	—	—	185.00

1982; 1983 ND ISSUE

#8-11 wmk: Shield and spears. Printer: TDLR. Replacement notes: Serial # prefix Z.

11 **20 EMALANGENI**
ND (1984-86). Purple and green on m/c unpt. Like #7 but w/o
commemorative inscription on face.

	VG	VF	UNC
a. Sign. 3. (1984).	12.00	45.00	200.00
b. Sign. 4. (1985).	FV	8.00	38.50
s1. As a. Specimen. Serial # prefix E.	—	—	65.00
s2. As b. Specimen. Serial # prefix F.	—	—	65.00

1986 ND ISSUE

8 **2 EMALANGENI**
ND (1983-86). Dk. brown on pink and m/c unpt. Like #2 but new
issuer's name at top.

	VG	VF	UNC
a. Sign. 2. (1983).	1.25	3.75	22.50
b. Sign. 4. (1984).	0.50	1.50	6.00
s1. As a. Specimen. Serial # prefix F.	—	—	65.00
s2. As b. Specimen. Serial # prefix G, J.	—	—	65.00

12 **20 EMALANGENI**
ND (1986). Purple and green on m/c unpt. Kg. Mswati III at l.,
otherwise like #11. Printer: TDLR. Sign. 4.

	VG	VF	UNC
a. Issued note.	3.00	6.50	30.00
s. Specimen. Serial # prefix A.	—	—	110.00

1986; 1987 ND ISSUES

#13-16 Facing portr. of young Kg. Mswati III at l., arms at lower ctr. Wmk: Shield and spears. Sign. 4.
Printer: TDLR. Replacement notes: Serial # prefix Z.

9 **5 EMALANGENI**
ND (1982-86). Dk. green on yellow-green and m/c unpt. Like #3 but
new issuer's name at top.

	VG	VF	UNC
a. Sign. 2. (1982).	1.50	5.00	37.50
b. Sign. 4. (1984).	1.00	2.00	11.00
s1. As a. Specimen. Serial # prefix D; E.	—	—	65.00
s2. As b. Specimen. Serial # prefix F.	—	—	65.00

13 **2 EMALANGENI**
ND (1987). Dk. brown and orange on m/c unpt. Grey lourie, blue
crane, hippos and other wildlife on back.

	VG	VF	UNC
a. Issued note.	0.50	1.50	7.00
s. Specimen. Serial # prefix A.	—	—	110.00

14	5 EMALANGENI	VG	VF	UNC
	ND (1987). Dk. green, dk. brown and bright green on m/c unpt. Warriors on back.			
	a. Issued note.	1.00	2.50	12.50
	s. Specimen. Serial # prefix A.	—	—	110.00

19	5 EMALANGENI	VG	VF	UNC
	ND (1990-95). Dk. green, dk. brown and bright green on m/c unpt. Like #14.			
	a. Sign. 4. (1990).	0.75	2.50	8.50
	b. Sign. 6. (1994).	2.00	7.50	37.50
	s1. As a. Specimen. Serial # prefix D.	—	—	100.00
	s2. As b. Specimen. Serial # prefix J.	—	—	90.00

15	10 EMALANGENI	VG	VF	UNC
	ND (1986). Dk. blue and black on m/c unpt. Hydroelectric plant at Luphohlo and bird on back.			
	a. Issued note.	FV	3.50	20.00
	s. Specimen. Serial # prefix A; F.	—	—	110.00

16	20 EMALANGENI			
	ND (1986). Violet, brown and purple on m/c unpt. Cattle and truck on back.			
	a. Issued note.	6.00	32.50	160.00
	s. Specimen. Serial # prefix A.	—	—	110.00

20	10 EMALANGENI	VG	VF	UNC
	ND (1990-95). Dk. blue and black on m/c unpt. Like #15.			
	a. Sign. 4. (1990).	1.25	4.50	22.50
	b. Sign. 5. (1992).	1.50	5.00	25.00
	s1. As a. Specimen. Serial # prefix J.	—	—	100.00
	s2. As b. Specimen. Serial # prefix N.	—	—	100.00

1989 COMMEMORATIVE ISSUE

#17, 21st Birthday of Kg. Mswati III

17	20 EMALANGENI	VG	VF	UNC
	19.4.1989. Like #16, w/silver commemorative text and dates ovpt. on wmk. area. Sign. 4.			
	a. Issued note.	2.50	7.50	27.50
	s. Specimen. Serial # prefix A.	—	—	100.00

1990; 1992 ND ISSUE

#18-22 printer: TDLR.

#18-21 similar to #13-16 but w/older portr. of Kg. Mswati III at l. facing half r. Backs like #13-16. Wmk: Shield and spears. Replacement notes: Serial # prefix Z.

21	20 EMALANGENI	VG	VF	UNC
	ND (1990-95). Violet, brown and purple on m/c unpt. Like #16.			
	a. Sign. 4. (1990).	FV	9.00	37.50
	b. Sign. 5. (1992).	FV	8.00	35.00
	s1. As a. Specimen. Serial # prefix D.	—	—	100.00
	s2. As b. Specimen. Serial # prefix G.	—	—	100.00

18	2 EMALANGENI	VG	VF	UNC
	ND (1992-95). Dk. brown on m/c unpt. Like #13.			
	a. Sign. 4. (1992).	FV	1.50	5.00
	b. Sign. 6. (1994).	1.00	4.00	15.00
	s1. As a. Specimen. Serial # prefix M.	—	—	100.00
	s2. As b. Specimen. Serial # prefix S.	—	—	100.00

22 50 EMALANGENI
ND (1990-95). Dull red-brown, orange and dk. green on m/c unpt.
Kg. Mswati III at l. Central Bank seal at l. ctr., head office bldg. at r.
on back.

	VG	VF	UNC
a. Sign. 4. (1990).	FV	20.00	80.00
b. Sign. 6. (1995).	20.00	60.00	240.00
s1. As a. Specimen. Serial # prefix A.	—	—	90.00
s2. As b. Specimen. Serial # prefix C.	—	—	85.00

1995 ND; 1995-98 ISSUE

#23-25 w/segmented foil over security thread.

23 5 EMALANGENI
ND (1995). Dk. green, dk. brown and bright green on m/c unpt. Like
#19 but warriors on back in dk. brown. Ascending size serial #.
Sign. 7a. Printer: H&S.

	VG	VF	UNC
a. Issued note.	FV	2.00	7.00
s. Specimen. Serial # prefix AA.	—	—	85.00

#24 and 25 printer: F-CO.

24 10 EMALANGENI
ND (1995); 1997; 1998. Dk. blue and black on m/c unpt. Like #20.

	VG	VF	UNC
a. Sign. 7a. ND.	FV	13.00	32.50
b. Sign. 8. 8.4.1997.	FV	4.50	18.50
c. Sign. 9a. 1.4.1998.	FV	1.75	5.00
s1. As a. Specimen. Serial # prefix AA.	—	—	85.00
s2. As b. Specimen. Serial # prefix AG.	—	—	85.00
s3. As c. Specimen. Serial # prefix AK, AL, AN.	—	—	85.00

25 20 EMALANGENI
ND (1995); 1997; 1998. Violet, brown and purple on m/c unpt.
Like #21.

	VG	VF	UNC
a. Sign. 7a. ND.	FV	5.00	22.50
b. Sign. 8. 8.4.1997.	FV	8.25	32.50
c. Sign. 9a. 1.4.1998.	FV	FV	8.50
s1. As a. Specimen. Serial # prefix AA.	—	—	85.00
s2. As b. Specimen. Serial # prefix AF; AG.	—	—	85.00
s3. As c. Specimen. Serial # prefix AK, AL.	—	—	85.00

#26 and 27 OVD strip at r. w/C B of S repeated. Printer: G&D.

26 50 EMALANGENI
1995; 1998. Dull red-brown and dk. green on m/c unpt. Like #22.

	VG	VF	UNC
a. Sign. 7b. 1.4.1995.	FV	12.00	50.00
b. Sign. 9b. 1.4.1998.	FV	FV	24.00
s1. As a. Specimen. Serial # prefix AA.	—	—	85.00
s2. As b. Specimen. Serial # prefix AA.	—	—	85.00

27 100 EMALANGENI
6.9.1996. Dk. brown on m/c unpt. Central Bank seal at upper l. ctr.,
rock formation at ctr. on back. Sign. 7b.

	VG	VF	UNC
a. Issued note.	FV	FV	40.00
s. Specimen. Serial # prefix AA.	—	—	85.00

1998 COMMEMORATIVE ISSUE

#28, 30th Anniversary of Independence

28 200 EMALANGENI
6.9.1998. Dk. green and green on m/c unpt. Face like #27.
Commemorative text vertically at l. and r. Swazi villagers by
thatched circular domed and fenced huts at ctr. on back. Printer:
G&D. Sign. 9b.

	VG	VF	UNC
a. Issued note.	FV	FV	65.00
s. Specimen. Serial # prefix AA.	—	—	85.00

2001 ISSUE

#29-32 like #24-27 but with motto GOD IS OUR SOURCE added to back. Sign. 10.
#29-30 printer: F-CO.

29	10 EMALANGENI		VG	VF	UNC
	1.4.2001. Dk. Blue and black on m/c unpt. Like #24.				
	a. Sign. 10a.		FV	FV	3.75
	b. Sign. 11.		FV	FV	3.75
	s. Specimen.		—	—	80.00
30	20 EMALANGENI				
	1.4.2001. Violet, brown and purple on m/c unpt. Like #25.				
	a. Sign. 10a.		FV	FV	6.50
	b. Sign. 11.		FV	FV	6.50
	s. Specimen.		—	—	80.00

#31-32 printer: G&D.

31	50 EMALANGENI		VG	VF	UNC
	1.4.2001. Dull red-brown and dk. green on m/c unpt. Like #26.				
	a. Sign. 10b.		FV	FV	17.00
	b. Sign. 11.		0.00VF	FV	17.00
	s. Specimen.		—	—	80.00
32	100 EMALANGENI				
	1.4.2001. Dk. brown on m/c unpt. Like #27.				
	a. Sign. 10b.		FV	FV	45.00
	b. Sign. 11.		FV	FV	45.00
	s. Specimen.		—	—	80.00

2004 COMMEMORATIVE ISSUE

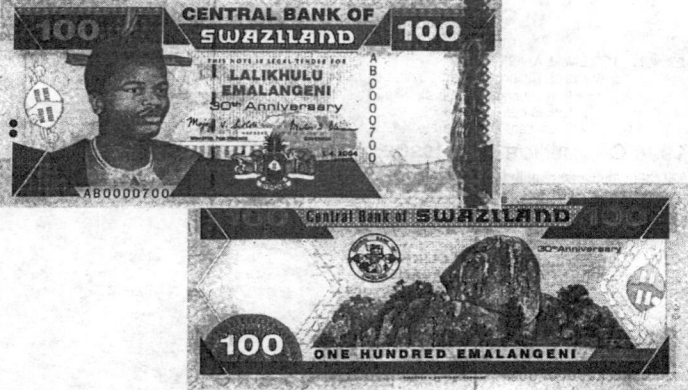

33	100 EMALANGENI		VG	VF	UNC
	2004. Like #32 but with commemorative ovpt. in ctr. Sign. 11.		FV	FV	35.00

COLLECTOR SERIES

MONETARY AUTHORITY OF SWAZILAND

1974 ISSUE

CS1	ND (1974). 1-20 EMALANGENI	Issue Price	Mkt.	Value
	#1-5 w/ovpt: SPECIMEN and serial # prefix Maltese cross.	14.00		80.00

SWEDEN

The Kingdom of Sweden, a limited constitutional monarchy located in northern Europe between Norway and Finland, has an area of 173,732 sq. mi. (449,964 sq. km.) and a population of 8.9 million. Capital: Stockholm. Mining, lumbering and a specialized machine industry dominate the economy. Machinery, paper, iron and steel, motor vehicles and wood pulp are exported.

Sweden was founded as a Christian stronghold by Olaf Skottkonung late in the 10th century. After conquering Finland late in the 13th century, Sweden, together with Norway, came under the rule of Denmark, 1397-1523, in an association known as the Union of Kalmar. Modern Sweden had its beginning in 1523 when Gustavus Vasa drove the Danes out of Sweden and was himself chosen king. Under Gustavus Adolphus II and Carl XII, Sweden was one of the great powers of 17th century Europe - until Carl invaded Russia, 1708, and was defeated at the Battle of Pultowa in June 1709. Early in the 18th century, a coalition of Russia, Poland and Denmark took away Sweden's Baltic empire and in 1809 Sweden was forced to cede Finland to Russia. Norway was ceded to Sweden by the Treaty of Kiel in January 1814. The Norwegians resisted for a time but later signed the Act of Union at the Convention of Moss in August 1814. The Union was dissolved in 1905 and Norway became independent.

A new constitution which took effect on Jan. 1, 1975, restricts the function of the king to a ceremonial role.

RULERS:
Gustaf VI Adolf, 1950-1973
Carl XVI Gustaf, 1973-

MONETARY SYSTEM:
1 Krona = 100 Öre

REPLACEMENT NOTES:
Issues since 1956 with asterisk following serial number. Asterisk following the serial number for note issued since 1956.

KINGDOM

SVERIGES RIKSBANK

1952-55 ISSUE

#42-43 replacement notes: Serial # suffix star.

42	5 KRONOR	VG	VF	UNC
	1954-61. Dk. brown on red and blue unpt. Beige paper w/ red safety fibers. Portr. Kg. Gustaf VI Adolf at r. ctr. and as wmk. Svea standing w/shield at l. ctr. on back.			
	a. 1954.	0.75	2.00	5.00
	b. 1955.	0.75	2.00	5.00
	c. 1956.	0.75	2.00	5.00
	d. 1959.	0.75	2.00	7.50
	e. 1960.	0.75	2.00	5.50
	f. 1961.	0.75	2.00	4.00
	r1. Replacement, w/star. 1956.	2.00	15.00	100.00
	r2. Replacement, w/star. 1959.	2.00	10.00	75.00
	r3. Replacement, w/star. 1960.	2.00	10.00	100.00
	r4. Replacement, w/star. 1961.	2.00	10.00	75.00

43	10 KRONOR	VG	VF	UNC
	1953-62. Gray-blue on m/c unpt. Like #40. Portr. Kg. Gustav Vasa at l. and as wmk. Arms at ctr. on back. Blue date and serial #.			

43	10 KRONOR	VG	VF	UNC
	a. 1953.	FV	1.50	5.50
	b. 1954.	FV	1.50	5.50
	c. 1955.	FV	1.50	5.50
	d. 1956.	FV	1.50	4.50
	e. 1957.	FV	1.50	4.50
	f. 1958.	FV	1.50	4.50
	g. 1959.	FV	1.50	4.50
	h. 1960.	FV	1.50	8.00
	i. 1962.	FV	1.50	4.50
	r1. Replacement, w/star. 1956.	2.00	20.00	120.00
	r2. Replacement, w/star. 1957.	2.00	10.00	70.00
	r3. Replacement, w/star. 1958.	2.00	10.00	70.00
	r4. Replacement, w/star. 1959.	2.00	10.00	75.00
	r5. Replacement, w/star. 1960.	2.00	15.00	100.00
	r6. Replacement, w/star. 1962.	2.00	40.00	70.00

46	1000 KRONOR	VG	VF	UNC
	1952-73. Brown and m/c. Svea standing. Kg. Gustaf V on back and as wmk.			
	a. Blue and red safety fibers. 1952.	FV	110.00	500.00
	b. 1957.	FV	110.00	500.00
	c. 1962.	FV	100.00	450.00
	d. 1965.	FV	100.00	450.00
	e. W/security thread. 1971.	FV	90.00	400.00
	f. 1973.	FV	90.00	350.00

1958; 1959 ISSUE

#47 and 48 seated Svea at lower r. Kg. Gustaf Vasa at ctr. on back. Replacement notes: Serial # star suffix.

47	50 KRONOR	VG	VF	UNC
	1959-62. Second sign. at l. Sm. date and serial #.			
	a. 1959.	FV	12.50	35.00
	b. 1960.	FV	12.50	35.00
	c. 1961.	FV	12.50	30.00
	d. 1962.	FV	12.50	30.00
	r1. Replacement, w/star. 1959.	12.50	20.00	120.00
	r2. Replacement, w/star. 1960.	12.50	20.00	100.00
	r3. Replacement, w/star. 1961.	12.50	20.00	100.00
	r4. Replacement, w/star. 1962.	FV	15.00	70.00
48	100 KRONOR			
	1959-63. Second sign. at l. Sm. date and serial #.			
	a. 1959.	FV	15.00	45.00
	b. 1960.	FV	15.00	45.00
	c. 1961.	FV	15.00	40.00
	d. 1962.	FV	15.00	35.00
	e. 1963.	FV	15.00	35.00
	r1. Remainder, w/star. 1959.	15.00	25.00	120.00
	r2. Remainder, w/star. 1960.	15.00	20.00	100.00
	r3. Remainder, w/star. 1961.	15.00	20.00	90.00
	r4. Remainder, w/star. 1962.	15.00	20.00	90.00
	r5. Remainder, w/star. 1963.	10.00	15.00	100.00

49	10,000 KRONOR	VG	VF	UNC
	1958. Green and m/c. King Gustaf VI Adolf at r. and as wmk. Svea standing w/shield at crt. on back.	1200.00	1750.00	3000.00

1962 ISSUE

#50 replacement notes: Star as serial # suffix.

50	5 KRONOR	VG	VF	UNC
	1962-63. Dk. brown on red and blue unpt. Like #42. Portr. Kg. Gustaf VI Adolf at ctr. Svea standing w/shield on back. Wmk: Esaias Tegnér (repeated). W/security thread.			
	a. 1962.	0.50	2.00	6.00
	b. 1963.	0.50	1.50	3.00
	r1. Replacement, w/star. 1962.	1.50	5.00	50.00
	r2. Replacement, w/star. 1963.	—	—	15.00

1963-76 ISSUE

#51-55 replacement notes: Serial # suffix star.

51	5 KRONOR	VG	VF	UNC
	1965-81. Purple, green and orange. Kg. Gustav Vasa at r. Back blue and reddish brown; abstract design of rooster crowing at l. Beige paper. Wmk: Square w/5 repeated.			
	a. W/year in dk. red letter press. 1965-69.	0.75	1.50	3.50
	b. W/year in deep red offset. 1970.	0.50	1.00	2.50
	c. As a. 1972-74; 1976-77.	0.50	1.00	2.00
	d. W/year in pale red offset. 1977-79; 1981.	0.50	1.00	2.00

52	10 KRONOR		VG	VF	UNC
	1963-90. Dk. green, w/red and blue guilloche at ctr. Kg. Gustaf VI Adolf at r., arms at ctr. Northern lights and snowflakes at l. ctr. on back. Pale blue paper. Wmk: August Strindberg (repeated).				
	a. W/year in dk. red letter press. 1963.		1.00	2.50	4.50
	b. As a. 1966; 1968.		1.00	1.50	3.50
	c. As a. 1971; 1972; 1975.		1.00	1.50	3.00
	d. W/year in pale red offset. Engraved sign. 1976-77; 1979; 1983; 1985.		1.00	1.00	3.00
	e. As d. but w/offset sign. 1980-81; 1983-84; 1987-90.		0.50	1.00	2.50

55	1000 KRONOR		VG	VF	UNC
	1976-88. Red-brown on green and violet unpt. Kg. Carl XIV Johan at r. Bessemer steel process on back. Wmk: Jacob Berzelius.				
	a. 1976-78.		100.00	150.00	300.00
	b. 1980; 1981; 1983-86; 1988.		100.00	125.00	235.00

1968 COMMEMORATIVE ISSUE
#56, 300th Anniversary Sveriges Riksbank, 1668-1968

56	10 KRONOR		VG	VF	UNC
	1968. Deep blue on m/c unpt. Svea standing w/ornaments at r. Back violet-brown; old Riksbank bldg. at l. ctr. Wmk: Crowned monogram Kg. Charles XI.				
	a. Issued note.		1.00	2.00	6.00
	b. In printed banquet program folder w/bank name, date and seal.		—	—	50.00

1985-89 REGULAR ISSUES
#57-65 the last digit of the year is first digit of the serial #. All notes have 2 sign. but only the right one is mentioned. Replacement notes: Serial # suffix star.

53	50 KRONOR		VG	VF	UNC
	1965-90. Blue on green and brown unpt. Beige paper. Kg. Gustaf III at r. Carl von Linné (Linnaeus) at ctr. on back. Wmk: Anna Maria Lenngren (repeated).				
	a. Sm. wmk. 1965; 1967; 1970.		5.00	7.50	20.00
	b. Lg. wmk. w/year in dk. red letter press. 1974; 1976.		5.00	7.50	17.50
	c. Lg. wmk. as b. w/year in red-brown offset. 1978; 1979; 1981.		5.00	7.50	15.00
	d. As c. Black serial #. 1982; 1984; 1986; 1989; 1990.		5.00	7.50	15.00

57	100 KRONOR		VG	VF	UNC
	(198)6-(200)0. Blue-green and brown-violet on m/c unpt. Carl von Linné (Linnaeus) at r. and as wmk., bldg. in background. Plants at l. ctr. Bee pollinating flowers at ctr. on back.				
	a. Wmk: Lg. portrait. Sign. Bengt Dennis. (198)6; 7; 8; (199)2.		FV	FV	22.50
	b. Wmk: Sm. portrait repeated vertically. Sign. Urban Bäckström. (199)6; 8; 9; (200)0.		FV	FV	20.00

54	100 KRONOR		VG	VF	UNC
	1965-85. Red-brown, blue and gray on lt. blue paper. King Gustav II Adolf at r. Figure head at l., Admiral ship *Vasa* of 1628 in ctr. on back. Wmk: Axel Oxenstierna.				
	a. Sm. wmk. 22mm. 1965; 1968; 1970.		10.00	15.00	30.00
	b. Lg. wmk. 27mm. w/year in dk. blue letter press. 1971; 1972; 1974; 1976.		10.00	15.00	25.00
	c. Lg. wmk. as b. w/year in blue-green offset. 1978; 1980-83; 1985.		10.00	15.00	20.00

58 500 KRONOR

			VG	VF	UNC
(198)5-(198)6. Gray-blue and red-brown. Kg. Carl XI at r. and as wmk. Christopher Polhem seated at l. ctr. on back.					
a. (198)5.			60.00	85.00	150.00
b. (198)6.			60.00	85.00	150.00

59 500 KRONOR

			VG	VF	UNC
(198)9-(200)0. Red and m/c unpt. Similar to #58 but w/o white margin on face, also other slight changes.					
a. Sign. Bengt Dennis. (198)9; (199)1; 2.			FV	FV	120.00
b. Sign. Urban Bäckström. (199)4; 5; 7; 8; 9; (200)0.			FV	FV	120.00

60 1000 KRONOR

			VG	VF	UNC
(198)9-(199)2. Brownish black on m/c unpt. Kg Gustav Vasa at r. and as wmk. Medieval harvest and threshing scene at l. ctr. on back.			FV	FV	175.00

1991; 1996 ISSUE

61 20 KRONOR

			VG	VF	UNC
(199)1-5. Dk. blue on m/c unpt. Horse-drawn carriage at lower ctr., Selma Lagerlöf at r. and as wmk. Story scene w/boy riding a snow goose in flight at l. ctr. on back. 130 x 72mm.					
a. Sign. Bengt Dennis. (199)1; 2.			FV	FV	7.50
b. Sign. Urban Bäckström. (199)4; 5.			FV	FV	5.00

62 50 KRONOR

			VG	VF	UNC
(199)6-(200)3. Deep olive-brown on m/c unpt. Jenny Lind at ctr. and as wmk. (repeated), music lines at l., stage at r. Violin, treble clef w/line of notes, abstract musical design on back.					
a. Sign. Urban Bäckström. (199)6; 7; 9; (200)0; 2.			FV	FV	10.00
b. Sign. Lars Heikensten. (200)3.			FV	FV	8.50

1997 ISSUE

63 20 KRONOR

			VG	VF	UNC
(199)7-(200)3. Purple on m/c unpt. Like #61 but reduced size, 120 x 67mm.					
a. Sign. Urban Bäckström. (199)7; 8; 9; (200)1; 2.			FV	FV	4.00
b. Sign. Lars Heikensten. (200)3.			FV	FV	3.50

2001 ISSUE

#64-65 w/enhanced security features.

64 100 KRONOR

			VG	VF	UNC
(200)1-(200)3. Blue-green and brown-violet on m/c unpt. Like #57 but w/foil hologram.					
a. Sign. Urban Bäckström. (200)1; 2.			FV	FV	20.00
b. Sign. Lars Heikensten. (200)3.			FV	FV	17.50

65 500 KRONOR

			VG	VF	UNC
(200)1-(200)3. Red on m/c unpt. Like #59 but w/foil hologram.					
a. Sign. Urban Bäckström. (200)1; 2.			FV	FV	80.00
b. Sign. Lars Heikensten. (200)3.			FV	FV	80.00

2005 COMMEMORATIVE ISSUE

#66 250th anniversary of the Tumba Paper Mill.

66 100 KRONOR

			VG	VF	UNC
2005. Green on m/c unpt. Seated Svea. Paper production and old map on back. Issued in a folder.			—	—	45.00

2006 ISSUE

		VG	VF	UNC
67	**50 KRONOR**			
	2006.			Expected New Issue
68	**100 KRONOR**			
	2006.			Expected New Issue

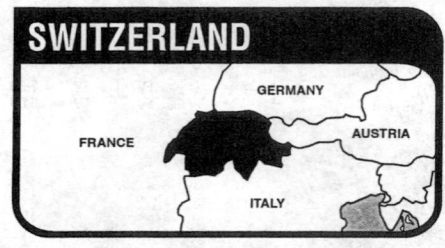

The Swiss Confederation, located in central Europe north of Italy and south of Germany, has an area of 15,941 sq. mi. (41,290 sq. km.) and a population of 7.41 million. Capital: Berne. The economy centers about a well developed manufacturing industry, however the most important economic factor is services (banks and insurance).

Switzerland, the habitat of lake dwellers in prehistoric times, was peopled by the Celtic Helvetians when Julius Caesar made it a part of the Roman Empire in 58 BC. After the decline of Rome, Switzerland was invaded by Teutonic tribes who established small temporal holdings which, in the Middle Ages, became a federation of fiefs of the Holy Roman Empire. As a nation, Switzerland originated in 1291 when the districts of Nidwalden, Schwyz and Uri united to defeat Austria and attain independence as the Swiss Confederation. After acquiring new cantons in the 14th century, Switzerland was made independent from the Holy Roman Empire by the 1648 Treaty of Westphalia. The revolutionary armies of Napoleonic France occupied Switzerland and set up the Helvetian Republic, 1798-1803. After the fall of Napoleon, the Congress of Vienna, 1815, recognized the independence of Switzerland and guaranteed its neutrality. The Swiss Constitutions of 1848, 1874, and 1999 established a union modeled upon that of the United States.

MONETARY SYSTEM:
1 Franc (Franken) = 10 Batzen = 100 Centimes (Rappen)
Plural: Francs, Franchi or Franken.

SIGNATURE VARIETIES

	PRESIDENT, BANK COUNCIL	DIRECTOR	CASHIER
39	Dr. Brenno Galli 1959-78	Dr. Walter Schwegler	Otto Kunz 1954-66
40	Dr. Brenno Galli	Dr. Riccardo Motta 1955-66	Otto Kunz
41	Dr. Brenno Galli	Dr. Max Iklé 1956-68	Otto Kunz
42	Dr. Brenno Galli 1959-78	Dr. Edwin Stopper 1966-74	Rudolf Aebersold 1954-66
43	Dr. Brenno Galli	Alexandre Hay 1966-75	Rudolf Aebersold
44	Dr. Brenno Galli	Max Iklé	Rudolf Aebersold
45	Dr. Brenno Galli	Dr. Fritz Leutwiler 1968-84	Rudolf Aebersold
46	Dr. Brenno Galli	Dr. Leo Schürmann 1974-80	Rudolf Aebersold
47	Dr. Brenno Galli	Dr. Pierre Languetin 1976-88	Rudolf Aebersold

NOTE: From #180 onward w/o the Chief Cashier's signature.

SIGNATURE VARIETIES

	PRESIDENT, BANK COUNCIL	DIRECTOR
48	Dr. Brenno Galli	Dr. Leo Schürmann
49	Dr. Brenno Galli	Alexandre Hay
50	Dr. Brenno Galli	Dr. Fritz Leutwiler
51	Dr. Brenno Galli	Dr. Pierre Languetin
52	Dr. Edmund Wyss 1978-86	Dr. Leo Schürmann
53	Dr. Edmund Wyss	Dr. Pierre Languetin
54	Dr. Edmund Wyss	Dr. Fritz Leutwiler
55	Dr. Edmund Wyss	Dr. Markus Lusser 1981-96
56	Dr. Edmund Wyss	Dr. Hans Meyer, 1985-2000
57	Dr. Francois Schaller 1986-89	Dr. Markus Lusser
58	Dr. Francois Schaller	Dr. Pierre Languetin
59	Dr. Francois Schaller	Dr. Hans Meyer
60	Dr. Francois Schaller	Jean Zwahlen (18mm)
61	Peter Gerber 1989-93	Dr. Markus Lusser

SIGNATURE VARIETIES

	PRESIDENT, BANK COUNCIL	DIRECTOR
62	*Peter Gerber*	*Jean Zwahlen (18mm)*
63	*Peter Gerber*	*Jean Zwahlen (15mm)*
64	*Peter Gerber*	*Dr. Hans Meyer*
65	*Dr. Jakob Schönenberger 1993-99*	*Dr. Markus Lusser*
66	*Dr. Jakob Schönenberger*	*Dr. Hans Meyer*
67	*Dr. Jakob Schönenberger*	*Jean Zwahlen (12mm)*
68	*Dr. Jakob Schönenberger*	*Dr. Jean-Pierre Roth 1996-*
69	*Dr. Jakob Schönenberger*	*Dr. Bruno Gehrig, 1996-2003*
70	*Eduard Belser, 1999-2002*	*Dr. Hans Meyer*
71	*Eduard Belser*	*Dr. Jean-Pierre Roth*
72	*Eduard Belser*	*Dr. Bruno Gehrig*
73	*Eduard Belser*	*Dr. Niklaus Blattner, 2001-*
74	*Dr. Hansueli Raggenbass*	*Dr. Jean-Pierre Roth*
75	*Dr. Hansueli Raggenbass*	*Dr. Bruno Gehrig*
76	*Dr. Hansueli Raggenbass*	*Dr. Niklaus Blattner*
77	*Dr. Hansueli Raggenbass*	*Dr. Phillipp Hildebrand, 2003-*

SCHWEIZERISCHE NATIONALBANK

SWISS NATIONAL BANK

1954-61 ISSUE

#45-46 printer: OFZ.

Note: Sign. varieties listed after date.

45	10 FRANKEN	VG	VF	UNC
	1955-77. Purple on red-brown unpt. Gottfried Keller at r. Carnation flower at l. ctr. on back. Printer: OFZ.			
	a. 25.8.1955 (34, 36, 37).	6.50	15.00	50.00
	b1. 20.10.1955 (34, 36, 37).	6.50	15.00	50.00
	c. 29.11.1956. (34, 37, 38).	6.50	15.00	45.00
	d. 18.12.1958 (34, 37, 38).	12.50	30.00	130.00
	e. 23.12.1959 (34, 37, 38).	1.50	3.50	30.00
	f. 22.12.1960 (39, 40, 41).	1.50	3.50	30.00
	g. 26.10.1961 (39, 40, 41).	1.50	3.50	30.00
	h. 28.3.1963 (39, 40, 41).	1.50	3.50	30.00
	i. 2.4.1964 (39, 40, 41).	1.50	3.50	25.00
	j. 21.1.1965 (39, 40, 41).	1.50	3.50	25.00
	k. 23.12.1965 (39, 40, 41).	1.50	3.50	25.00
	l. 1.1.1967 (42, 43, 44).	6.00	15.00	60.00
	m. 30.6.1967 (42, 43, 44).	1.50	3.50	20.00
	n. 15.5.1968 (42, 43, 45).	1.50	3.50	20.00
	o. 15.1.1969 (42, 43, 45).	1.50	3.50	20.00
	p. 5.1.1970 (42, 43, 45).	1.50	3.50	20.00
	q. 10.2.1971 (42, 43, 45).	1.50	3.50	15.00
	r. 24.1.1972 (42, 43, 45).	1.50	3.50	15.00
	s. 7.3.1973 (42, 43, 45).	1.50	3.50	12.50
	s1. As a. Specimen.	—		50.00
	t. 7.2.1974 (42, 43, 45).	1.50	3.50	12.50
	u. 6.1.1977 (45, 46, 47).	1.25	3.00	12.50

46	20 FRANKEN	VG	VF	UNC
	1954-76. Blue on m/c unpt. Gen. Guillaume-Henri Dufour at r. Silver thistle at l. ctr. on back. Printer: OFZ.			
	a. 1.7.1954 (34, 35, 36).	14.00	25.00	90.00
	b. 7.7.1955 (34, 36, 37).	14.00	25.00	90.00
	c. 20.10.1955 (34, 36, 37).	14.00	25.00	90.00
	d. 5.7.1956 (34, 37, 38).	14.00	25.00	90.00
	e. 4.10.1957 (34, 37, 38).	15.00	30.00	100.00
	f. 18.12.1958 (34, 37, 38).	25.00	45.00	120.00
	g. 23.12.1959 (39, 40, 41).	3.00	8.00	35.00
	h. 22.12.1960 (39, 40, 41).	3.00	8.00	37.50
	i. 26.10.1961 (39, 40, 41).	3.00	8.00	27.50
	j. 28.3.1963 (39, 40, 41).	3.00	8.00	26.00
	k. 2.4.1964 (39, 40, 41).	3.00	8.00	26.00
	l. 21.1.1965 (39, 40, 41).	3.00	8.00	26.00
	m. 23.12.1965 (39, 40, 41).	3.00	8.00	26.00
	n. 1.1.1967 (42, 43, 44).	3.00	10.00	32.50
	o. 30.6.1967 (42, 43, 44).	2.75	8.00	28.00
	p. 15.5.1968 (42, 43, 45).	2.75	8.00	28.00
	q. 15.1.1969 (42, 43, 45).	2.75	8.00	28.00

46	20 FRANKEN	VG	VF	UNC
	r. 5.1.1970 (42, 43, 45).	2.75	8.00	28.00
	s. 10.2.1971 (42, 43, 45).	2.75	8.00	28.00
	s1. As a. Specimen.	—	—	50.00
	t. 24.1.1972 (42, 43, 45).	2.75	8.00	28.00
	u. 7.3.1973 (42, 43, 45).	2.75	8.00	28.00
	v. 7.2.1974 (42, 43, 45).	2.75	8.00	28.00
	w. 9.4.1976 (45, 46, 47).	2.50	7.50	25.00

47	50 FRANKEN	VG	VF	UNC
	1955-58. Green and red-brown on yellow-green unpt. Girl at upper r. Apple harvesting scene on back (symbolizing fertility). Printer: W&S.			
	a. 7.7.1955 (34, 36, 37).	25.00	42.50	200.00
	b. 4.10.1957 (34, 37, 38).	20.00	37.50	125.00
	c. 18.12.1958 (34, 37, 38).	125.00	275.00	700.00

49	100 FRANKEN	VG	VF	UNC
	1956-73. Dk. blue and brown-olive on m/c unpt. Boy's head at upper r w/lamb. St. Martin cutting his cape (to share) at ctr. r. on back. Printer: TDLR.			
	a. 25.10.1956 (34, 37, 38).	30.00	60.00	200.00
	b. 4.10.1957 (34, 37, 38).	30.00	55.00	170.00
	c. 18.12.1958 (34, 37, 38).	32.50	60.00	320.00
	d. 21.12.1961 (39, 40, 41);	15.00	30.00	135.00
	e. 28.3.1963 (39, 40, 41).	15.00	30.00	135.00
	f. 2.4.1964 (39, 40, 41).	15.00	30.00	135.00
	g. 21.1.1965 (39, 40, 41).	15.00	32.50	135.00
	h. 23.12.1965 (39, 40, 41).	16.00	35.00	180.00
	i. 1.1.1967 (42, 43, 44).	16.00	35.00	170.00
	j. 30.6.1967 (42, 43, 44).	14.00	27.50	125.00
	k. 15.1.1969 (42, 43, 45).	14.00	25.00	125.00
	l. 5.1.1970 (42, 43, 45).	16.00	35.00	130.00
	m. 10.2.1971 (42, 43, 45).	12.00	25.00	120.00
	n. 24.1.1972 (42, 43, 45).	12.00	25.00	120.00
	o. 7.3.1973 (42, 43, 45).	12.00	25.00	120.00
	s. As a. Specimen.	—	—	100.00

50	500 FRANKEN	VG	VF	UNC
	1957-58. Red-brown and olive on m/c unpt. Woman looking in mirror at r. Elders w/4 girls bathing at ctr. r. on back (Fountain of Youth). Printer: W&S.			
	a. 31.1.1957 (34, 37, 38).	250.00	400.00	900.00
	b. 4.10.1957 (34, 37, 38).	200.00	350.00	800.00
	c. 18.12.1958 (34, 37, 38).	300.00	500.00	1000.00

48	50 FRANKEN	VG	VF	UNC
	1961-74. Green and red on m/c unpt. Like #47.			
	a. 4.5.1961 (39, 40, 41).	25.00	60.00	200.00
	b. 21.12.1961 (39, 40, 41).	12.50	30.00	75.00
	c. 28.3.1963 (39, 40, 41).	30.00	85.00	220.00
	d. 2.4.1964 (39, 40, 41).	35.00	90.00	225.00
	e. 21.1.1965 (39, 40, 41).	12.50	30.00	80.00
	f. 23.12.1965 (39, 40, 41).	12.50	30.00	80.00
	g. 30.6.1967 (42, 43, 44).	12.50	30.00	80.00
	h. 15.5.1968 (42, 43, 45).	12.50	30.00	80.00
	i. 15.1.1969 (42, 43, 45).	12.50	30.00	75.00
	j. 5.1.1970 (42, 43, 45).	12.50	30.00	75.00
	k. 10.2.1971 (42, 43, 45).	12.50	30.00	75.00
	l. 24.1.1972 (42, 43, 45).	12.50	30.00	75.00
	m. 7.3.1973 (42, 43, 45).	12.50	30.00	75.00
	n. 7.2.1974 (42, 43, 45).	12.50	30.00	75.00
	s. As a. Specimen.	—	—	50.00

51	500 FRANKEN	VG	VF	UNC
	1961-74. Brown-orange and olive on m/c unpt. Like #50.			
	a. 21.12.1961 (39, 40, 41).	150.00	275.00	750.00
	b. 28.3.1963 (39, 40, 41).	130.00	240.00	750.00
	c. 2.4.1964 (39, 40, 41).	140.00	250.00	750.00
	d. 21.1.1965 (39, 40, 41).	140.00	250.00	750.00
	e. 1.1.1967 (42, 43, 44).	140.00	250.00	700.00
	f. 15.5.1968 (42, 43, 45).	140.00	250.00	700.00
	g. 15.1.1969 (42, 43, 45).	140.00	250.00	700.00
	h. 5.1.1970 (42, 43, 45).	110.00	235.00	675.00
	i. 10.2.1971 (42, 43, 45).	110.00	235.00	675.00
	j. 24.1.1972 (42, 43, 45).	110.00	235.00	675.00
	k. 7.3.1973 (42, 43, 45).	100.00	230.00	675.00
	l. 7.2.1974 (42, 43, 45).	90.00	200.00	650.00
	s. As a. Specimen.	—	—	500.00

52	1000 FRANKEN	VG	VF	UNC
	1954-74. Red-violet and turquoise on green and lt. violet unpt. Female head at upper r. allegorical scene *Dance Macabre* on back. Printer: TDLR.			
	a. 30.9.1954 (34, 35, 36).	250.00	500.00	1900.00
	b. 4.10.1957 (34, 37, 38).	250.00	425.00	1650.00
	c. 18.12.1958 (34, 37, 38).	325.00	650.00	2000.00
	d. 22.12.1960 (39, 40, 41).	175.00	350.00	1550.00
	e. 21.12.1961 (39, 40, 41).	175.00	350.00	1550.00
	f. 28.3.1963 (39, 40, 41).	175.00	350.00	1400.00
	g. 21.1.1965 (39, 40, 41).	175.00	350.00	1300.00
	h. 1.1.1967 (42, 43, 44).	175.00	350.00	1300.00
	i. 5.1.1970 (42, 43, 45).	175.00	350.00	1300.00
	j. 10.2.1971 (42, 43, 45).	150.00	350.00	1175.00
	k. 24.1.1972 (42, 43, 45).	150.00	300.00	1175.00
	l. 1.10.1973 (42, 43, 45).	140.00	275.00	1175.00
	m. 7.2.1974 (42, 43, 45).	125.00	250.00	1150.00
	s. As a. Specimen.	—	—	1200.00

1976-79 ISSUE; 6TH SERIES

#53-59 series of notes printed in 4 languages - the traditional German, French and Italian plus Romansch; (Rhaeto - Romanic), the language of the mountainous areas of Graubünden Canton. Wmk. as portr. The first 2 numerals before the serial # prefix letter are date (year) indicators. Printer: OFZ.

Note: Sign. varieties listed after date.

53	10 FRANKEN	VG	VF	UNC
	(19)79-92. Orange-brown and m/c. Leonhard Euler at r. Water turbine, light rays through lenses and Solar System in vertical format on back.			
	a. 1979 (52, 53, 54).	FV	FV	15.00
	b. 1980 (52, 53, 54).	FV	FV	13.00
	c. 1981 (53, 54, 55).	FV	FV	12.00
	d. 1982 (53, 54, 55).	FV	FV	12.00
	e. 1983 (53, 54, 55).	FV	FV	12.00
	f. 1986 (53, 55, 56).	FV	FV	11.00
	g. 1987 (57, 58, 59).	FV	FV	11.00
	h. 1990 (61, 62, 63, 64). #62 is valued at $150 in Unc.	50.00	75.00FV	150.00
	i. 1991 (61, 63, 64).	FV	FV	10.00
	j. 1992 (61, 62, 64).	FV	FV	10.00

54	20 FRANKEN			
	1978 (52, 53, 54). Light blue on m/c unpt. Horace-Bénédict de Saussure at r., hygrometer at l. Fossel and early mountain expedition team hiking in the Alps on back. Unpt. on face ends 2mm before the margin, only plain blue unpt visible within the 2mm	FV	FV	35.00

55	20 FRANKEN	VG	VF	UNC
	(19)78-92. Blue and m/c. Similar to #54, but unpt. at upper margin on face goes to the margin.			
	a. 1978 (52, 53, 54).	FV	FV	42.50
	b. 1980 (52, 53, 54).	FV	FV	30.00
	c. 1981 (53, 54, 55).	FV	FV	27.50
	d. 1982 (53, 54, 55).	FV	FV	27.50
	e. 1983 (53, 54, 55).	FV	FV	32.50
	f. 1986 (57, 58, 59).	FV	FV	32.50
	g. 1987 (57, 58, 59).	FV	FV	25.00
	h. 1989 (61, 62, 64).	FV	FV	25.00
	i. 1990 (61, 63, 64).	FV	FV	22.50
	j. 1992 (61, 63, 64).	FV	FV	20.00
	s. Perforated: *SPECIMEN*.	—	—	250.00

56	50 FRANKEN	VG	VF	UNC
	(19)78-88. Green and m/c. Konrad Gessner at r. Eagle owl, *Primula auricu-la* plant and stars on vertical format back.			
	a. 1978 (48, 50, 51).	FV	FV	62.50
	b. 1979 (52, 53, 54).	FV	FV	57.50
	c. 1980 (52, 53, 54).	FV	FV	57.50
	d. 1981 (53, 54, 55).	FV	FV	55.00
	e. 1983 (53, 54, 55).	FV	FV	52.50
	f. 1985 (53, 55, 56).	FV	FV	52.50
	g. 1986 (57, 58, 59).	FV	FV	50.00
	h. 1988 (57, 59, 60).	FV	FV	50.00
	s. Perforated: *SPECIMEN*.	—	—	350.00

57 100 FRANKEN

	VG	VF	UNC
(19)75-93. Blue and m/c. Francesco Borromini at r. Baroque architectural drawing and view of S. Ivo alla Sapienza on vertical format back.			
a. 1975 (48, 49, 50).	FV	FV	140.00
b. 1977 (48, 50, 51).	FV	FV	140.00
c. 1980 (52, 53, 54).	FV	FV	140.00
d. 1981 (53, 54, 55).	FV	FV	120.00
e. 1982 (53, 54, 55).	FV	FV	120.00
f. 1983 (53, 54, 55).	FV	FV	120.00
g. 1984 (53, 54, 55).	FV	FV	130.00
h. 1986 (57, 58, 59).	FV	FV	120.00
i. 1988 (57, 59, 60).	FV	FV	135.00
j. 1989 (57, 59, 60).	FV	FV	120.00
k. 1991 (61, 63, 64).	FV	FV	105.00
l. 1992 (61, 63, 64).	FV	FV	100.00
m. 1993 (61, 63, 64).	FV	FV	105.00
s. Perforated: SPECIMEN.	—	—	400.00

58 500 FRANKEN

	VG	VF	UNC
(19)76-92. Brown and m/c. Albrecht von Haller at r. Mountains (Gemmi Pass) at l. Anatomical muscles of the back, schematic blood circulation and a purple orchid flower on vertical format back.			
a. 1976 (48, 50, 51).	FV	FV	625.00
b. 1986 (57, 58, 59).	FV	FV	600.00
c. 1992 (61, 63, 64).	FV	FV	550.00
s. Perforated: SPECIMEN.	—	—	500.00

59 1000 FRANKEN

	VG	VF	UNC
(19)77-93. Purple on m/c unpt. Auguste Forel at r.. diagrams through a brain and a nerve cell at l. Ants and ant-hill schematic on vertical format back.			
a. 1977 (48, 50, 51).	FV	FV	1150.00
b. 1980 (52, 53, 54).	FV	FV	1100.00
c. 1984 (53, 54, 55).	FV	FV	1075.00
d. 1987 (57, 58, 59).	FV	FV	1050.00
e. 1988 (57, 59, 60).	FV	FV	1050.00
f. 1993 (61, 63, 64).	FV	FV	1000.00
s. Perforated: SPECIMEN.	—	—	1000.00

1983-85 RESERVE ISSUE

		VG	VF	UNC
60	**10 FRANKEN**			
	1983. Orange-brown and m/c. Leonhard Euler at r. Polyhedron in ctr., calculations, table for calculation of numbers and solar system diagram on back.	—	—	—
61	**20 FRANKEN**			
	1985. Blue on m/c unpt. Horace-Bénédict de Saussure at r., crystal in ctr. Hair hygrometer, mountains and mountain team hiking on back.	—	—	—
62	**50 FRANKEN**			
	1985. Olive-green and m/c. Konrad Gessner at r. Cherry tree branch, eagle, animals on back.	—	—	—
63	**100 FRANKEN**			
	1985. Violet-blue and m/c. Francesco Borromini at r., architectural motif at ctr. Drawing and tower of S. Ivo on back.	—	—	—
64	**500 FRANKEN**			
	1985. Brown and m/c. Albrecht von Haller at r. hexagonal structure of a cell in ctr. Anatomy plate and X-ray of a human thorax on back.	—	—	—
65	**1000 FRANKEN**			
	1985. Violet and m/c. Louis Agassiz at r., structure of the surface of a shellfish. Perch in three parts: head, skeleton and fossil, fishscales and ammonite on back.	—	—	—

1994-98 ISSUE; 8TH SERIES

#66-71 vertical format, reduced size. First two numerals before serial # prefix letter indicates the year of printing. Many sophisticated security features added.

66 10 FRANKEN

	VG	VF	UNC
(19)95; (19)96 (1997). Brown-orange, dk. brown and blue on m/c unpt. Architect Le Corbusier (Charles Édouard Jeanneret-Gris) at upper l. and bottom ctr. and as wmk. "Modular" measuring system and bldgs. in Chandigarh designed by Le Corbusier on back.			
a. 1995. (65, 66, 67).	FV	FV	10.00
b. 1996. (65, 66, 67).	FV	FV	9.50

67 10 FRANKEN

	VG	VF	UNC
Brown-orange, dk. brown and blue on m/c unpt. Like #66 but with microperforation.			
a. 2000. (71, 72, 73).	FV	FV	9.50

68 20 FRANKEN

	VG	VF	UNC
(19)94; (19)95. Red-violet and green on m/c unpt. Composer Arthur Honegger at upper l. and bottom ctr. and as wmk. Trumpet valves at top, steam locomotive wheel at ctr., musical score and piano keys at bottom on back.			
a. 1994. (65, 66, 67).	FV	FV	21.00
b. 1995. (65, 66, 67).	FV	FV	20.00

69 20 FRANKEN

	VG	VF	UNC
(20)00; (20)03; (20)24. Red-violet and green on m/c unpt. Like #67 but with microperforated denomination.			
a. 2000. (71, 72, 73).	FV	FV	19.00
b. 2003. (74, 75, 76).	FV	FV	18.50
c. 2004. (74, 76, 77).	FV	FV	18.50

70 **50 FRANKEN**

(19)94 (1995). Deep olive-green and purple on m/c unpt. Artist Sophie Taeuber-Arp at upper l., bottom and as wmk. Examples of her abstract art works on back. (65, 66, 67).

	VG	VF	UNC
	FV	FV	50.00

71 **50 FRANKEN**

2002 (2003). Deep olive-green and purple on m/c unpt. Like #68 but with microperforation added. (71, 72, 73).

	VG	VF	UNC
a. 2002 (71, 72, 73).	FV	FV	47.50

72 **100 FRANKEN**

(19)96-99. Dk. blue, purple and brown-orange on m/c unpt. Alberto Giacometti (artist) at upper l., bottom and as wmk. Bronze bust *Lotar II* at top, sculpture *Homme Qui Marche I* repeated at ctr., time-space relationship scheme at lower ct

	VG	VF	UNC
a. 1996. (66, 68, 69).	FV	FV	100.00
b. 1997. (66, 68, 69).	FV	FV	95.00
c. 1998. (66, 68, 69).	FV	FV	90.00
d. 1999. (66, 68, 69).	FV	FV	90.00
e. 2000. (71, 72, 73).	FV	FV	90.00

73 **200 FRANKEN**

(19)96; (20)00. Brown and purple on m/c unpt. Author Charles-Ferdinand Ramuz at upper l. and at bottom ctr. and as wmk. Diablerets massif at top, Lavaux area by Lake Geneva repeated at ctr. to bottom w/partial manuscript overlay on back. (66, 69, 69).

	VG	VF	UNC
a. 1996 (66, 68, 69).	FV	FV	190.00
b. 2002 (71, 72, 73).	FV	FV	180.00

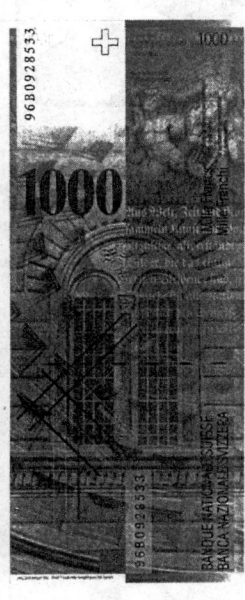

74 **1000 FRANKEN**

(19)96 (1998); (19)99. Purple and violet on m/c unpt. Jacob Burckhardt (art historian) at upper l., bottom and as wmk. Window and the Pergamon Altar at top, the Rotunda of the Pantheon in Rome and a section of the Façade of Palazzo Strozzi in Florenc

	VG	VF	UNC
a. 1996 (1998). (66; 67, 68).	FV	FV	950.00
b. 1999. (66, 68, 69).	FV	FV	925.00

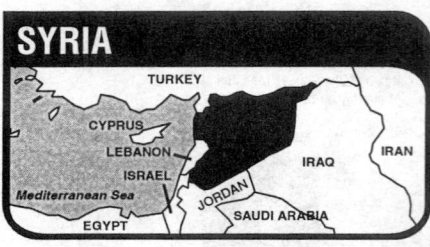

The Syrian Arab Republic, located in the Near East at the eastern end of the Mediterranean Sea, has an area of 71,498 sq. mi. (185,180 sq. km.) and a population of 16.13 million. Capital: Damascus. Agriculture and animal breeding are the chief industries. Cotton, crude oil and livestock are exported.

Ancient Syria, a land bridge connecting Europe, Africa and Asia, has spent much of its history in thrall to the conqueror's whim. Its subjection by Egypt about 1500 BC was followed by successive conquests by the Hebrews, Phoenicians, Babylonians, Assyrians, Persians, Macedonians, Romans, Byzantines and finally, in 636 AD, by the Moslems. The Arabs made Damascus, one of the oldest continuously inhabited cities of the world, the trade center and capital of an empire stretching from India to Spain. In 1517, following the total destruction of Damascus by the Mongols of Tamerlane, Syria fell to the Ottoman Turks and remained a Turkish province until World War I. The League of Nations gave France a mandate to the Levant states of Syria and Lebanon in 1920. In 1930, following a series of uprisings, France recognized Syria as an independent republic, but still subject to the mandate. Lebanon became fully independent on Nov. 22, 1943, and Syria on Jan. 1, 1944.

On Feb. 1, 1958, Egypt and Syria formed the United Arab Republic. Yemen joined on March 8 in an association known as the United Arab States. Syria withdrew from the United Arab Republic on Sept. 29, 1961, and on Dec. 26 Egypt dissolved its ties with Yemen in the United Arab States. Between 1961 and 1970 five coups brought in Lieut. Gen. Hafez el Assad as Prime Minister and in 1973 a new constitution was approved.

MONETARY SYSTEM:
1 Pound (Livre) = 100 Piastres

BANQUE CENTRALE DE SYRIE CENTRAL BANK OF SYRIA

1958 ISSUE

#86-92 bank name in English on back. Wmk: Arabian horse's head.

#86-88 printer: The Pakistan Security Printing Corporation Ltd., Karachi (w/o imprint).

		VG	VF	UNC
86	**1 POUND**			
	1958/AH1377. Brown on m/c unpt. Worker at r. Water wheel of Hama on back.			
	a. Issued note.	1.50	3.00	25.00
	s. Specimen.	—	—	25.00
87	**5 POUNDS**			
	1958/AH1377. Green on m/c unpt. Face similar to #86. Citadel of Aleppo on back.			
	a. Issued note.	5.00	15.00	85.00
	s. Specimen.	—	—	45.00

		VG	VF	UNC
88	**10 POUNDS**			
	1958/AH1377. Purple on m/c unpt. Face similar to #86. Courtyard of Omayad Mosque on back.			
	a. Issued note.	7.50	22.50	125.00
	s. Specimen.	—	—	90.00

#89-92 printer: JEZ.

		VG	VF	UNC
89	**25 POUNDS**			
	1958/AH1377. Blue on m/c unpt. Girl w/basket at r. Interior view of Azem Palace in Damascus on back.			
	a. Issued note.	8.00	30.00	120.00
	s. Specimen.	—	—	150.00
90	**50 POUNDS**			
	1958/AH1377. Red and brown on m/c unpt. Face similar to #89. Mosque of Sultan Selim on back.			
	a. Issued note.	8.00	30.00	120.00
	s. Specimen.	—	—	175.00

		VG	VF	UNC
91	**100 POUNDS**			
	1958;1962. Olive-green on m/c unpt. Face similar to #89. Old ruins of Palmyra on back.			
	a. 1958.	15.00	65.00	225.00
	b. 1962.	12.50	50.00	200.00
	s. Specimen.	—	—	200.00

		VG	VF	UNC
92	**500 POUNDS**			
	1958/AH1377. Brown and purple on m/c unpt. Motifs from ruins of Kingdom of Ugarit, head at r. Ancient religious wheel and cuneiform clay tablet on back.			
	a. Issued note.	35.00	150.00	400.00
	s. Specimen.	—	—	400.00

1963-66 ISSUE

#93-98 wmk: Arabian horse's head. W/o imprint.

#93-95 worker at r.

		VG	VF	UNC
93	**1 POUND**			
	1963-82/AH1383-1402. Brown on m/c unpt. Water wheel of Hama on back. Like #86.			
	a. W/o security thread. 1963/AH1383.	1.00	3.00	10.00
	b. 1967/AH1387.	0.75	2.50	8.00
	c. 1973/AH1393.	0.50	1.50	5.00
	d. Security thread w/*Central Bank of Syria* in sm. letters. 1978/AH1398.	0.30	1.00	4.00
	e. 1982/AH1402.	0.25	0.75	3.00
	s. As a. Specimen.	—	—	85.00

		VG	VF	UNC
94	**5 POUNDS**			
	1963-73/AH1383-93. Green on m/c unpt. Citadel of Aleppo on back. Like #87.			
	a. 1963/AH1383.	2.50	10.00	40.00
	b. 1967/AH1387.	1.75	6.00	35.00
	c. 1970.	1.00	4.00	25.00
	d. 1973/AH1393.	1.00	4.00	20.00

1976-77 ISSUE

#99-105 wmk: Arabian horse's head. Shades vary between early and late printings.

95	10 POUNDS	VG	VF	UNC
	1965-73/AH138x-93. Purple on m/c unpt. Courtyard of Omayad Mosque on back. Like #88.			
	a. 1965.	3.00	8.50	50.00
	b. 1968.	2.00	6.00	40.00
	c. 1973/AH1393.	1.50	5.00	25.00

96	25 POUNDS	VG	VF	UNC
	1966-73/AH1386-93. Blue and brown on m/c unpt. Worker at the loom at l. Bosra theater at ctr. r. on back.			
	a. 1966/AH1386.	4.00	22.50	125.00
	b. 1970.	4.00	20.00	120.00
	c. 1973/AH1393.	3.00	15.00	80.00

99	1 POUND	VG	VF	UNC
	1977/AH1397. Orange and brown on m/c unpt. Omayyad Mosque at ctr., craftsman at r. Back red-brown; combine at ctr.			
	a. Issued note.	1.00	3.00	12.50
	s. Specimen.	—	—	—

97	50 POUNDS	VG	VF	UNC
	1966-73/AH1386-93. Brown and olive-green on m/c unpt. Arab driving combine at l. Fortress on back.			
	a. 1966/AH1386; 1970.	10.00	30.00	175.00
	b. 1973/AH1393.	5.00	30.00	80.00

100	5 POUNDS	VG	VF	UNC
	1977-91/AH1397-1412. Dk. green on m/c unpt. Bosra theater and statue of female warrior at r. Cotton picking and spinning frame on back.			
	a. Security thread. 1977/AH1397.	0.75	2.50	7.50
	b. Security thread. W/*Central Bank of Syria* in sm. letters. 1978/AH1398.	FV	FV	4.00
	c. 1982/AH1402.	FV	FV	3.00
	d. 1988/AH1408.	FV	FV	2.00
	e. 1991/AH1412.	FV	FV	1.50
	s. As a. Specimen.	—	—	—

98	100 POUNDS	VG	VF	UNC
	1966-74/AH1386-139x. Green and blue on m/c unpt. Port installation at l. Back purple; dam at ctr.			
	a. 1966/AH1386.	12.50	40.00	110.00
	b. 1968.	15.00	50.00	130.00
	c. 1971/AH1391.	12.50	40.00	110.00
	d. 1974.	10.00	30.00	90.00

101	10 POUNDS	VG	VF	UNC
	1977-91/AH1397-1412. Purple and violet on m/c unpt. Al-Azem Palace in Damascus at ctr., dancing woman at r. Water treatment plant on back.			
	a. Like #100a. 1977/AH1397.	1.50	4.00	10.00
	b. Like #100b. 1978/AH1398.	FV	FV	3.50
	c. 1982/AH1402.	FV	FV	3.00
	d. 1988/AH1408.	FV	FV	1.50
	e. 1991/AH1412.	FV	FV	1.50

102 **25 POUNDS**
1977-91/AH1397-1412. Dk. blue and dk. green on m/c unpt. Krak
des Chevaliers castle at ctr., Saladdin at r. Central Bank bldg. on
back.

	VG	VF	UNC
a. Like #100a. 1977/AH1397.	3.00	8.00	20.00
b. Like #100b. 1978/AH1398.	FV	1.00	8.00
c. 1982/AH1402.	FV	FV	6.00
d. 1988/AH1408.	FV	FV	4.00
e. 1991/AH1412.	FV	FV	3.00

105 **500 POUNDS**
1976-90/AH1396-1411. Dk. violet-brown and brown on m/c unpt.
Like #92.

	VG	VF	UNC
a. 1976/AH1396.	FV	15.00	60.00
b. 1979.	15.00	40.00	180.00
c. 1982/AH1402.	FV	20.00	65.00
d. 1986.	FV	20.00	55.00
e. 1990/AH1411.	FV	FV	40.00
f. 1992/AH1413.	FV	FV	30.00

#106 not assigned.

1997-98 Issue

#107-109 wmk: Arabian horse's head.

103 **50 POUNDS**
1977-91/AH1397-1412. Brown, black and green on m/c unpt. Dam
at ctr., ancient statue at r. Citadel of Aleppo on back.

	VG	VF	UNC
a. Like #100a. 1977/AH1397.	4.50	10.00	25.00
b. Like #100b. 1978/AH1398.	FV	3.00	14.00
c. 1982/AH1402.	FV	3.00	10.00
d. 1988/AH1408.	FV	3.00	6.00
e. 1991/AH1412.	FV	FV	5.00

107 **50 POUNDS**
1998/AH1419. Dk. and lt. brown, green and lilac on m/c unpt.
Aleppo Citadel at ctr., water wheel of Hama at r. Al-Assad library,
Abbyssian stadium and students on back.

	VG	VF	UNC
	FV	FV	3.00

104 **100 POUNDS**
1977-90/AH1397-1411. Dk. blue, dk. green and dk. brown on m/c
unpt. Ancient Palmyra ruins at ctr., Qn. Zenobia bust at r. Grain
silos at Lattakia on back.

	VG	VF	UNC
a. Like #100a. 1977/AH1397.	5.00	15.00	50.00
b. Like #100b. 1978/AH1398.	FV	8.00	25.00
c. 1982/AH1402.	FV	FV	15.00
d. 1990/AH1411.	FV	FV	7.00

108 **100 POUNDS**
1998/AH1419. Lt. blue, red-brown and purple on m/c unpt. Bosra
theater at ctr., ancient bust of Philip at r. Hajaz railway locomotive;
Damascus station and road on back.

	VG	VF	UNC
	FV	FV	5.00

109 **200 POUNDS**
1997/AH1418. Red-orange, purple and lt. brown on m/c unpt.
Monument to the Unknown soldier at ctr., Islamic coin at lower
ctr. r., Statue of Saladdin at r. Cotton weaving and energy plant
on back.

	VG	VF	UNC
	FV	FV	8.00

110 **500 POUNDS**
1998/AH1419 (2000). Gray and bluish-green on m/c unpt. Qn.
Zenobia at r. Palmyra theater at ctr. Eufrate dam, irrigation and
agricultural products on back.

	VG	VF	UNC
	FV	FV	24.00

111 **1000 POUNDS**
1997/AH1418. Green, blue and lt. brown on m/c unpt. Omayyad
Mosque main entrance at ctr., Islamic dinar coin and clay tablet at
lower ctr., H. Assad at r. and as wmk. Oil industry workers at l.,
harvesting machinery and fishing boat on back. 2 slig

	VG	VF	UNC
	FV	FV	40.00

TAHITI

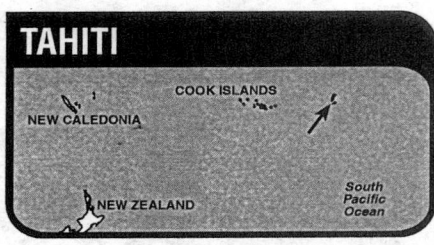

Tahiti, the largest island of the central South Pacific French overseas territory of French Polynesia, has an area of 402 sq. mi. (1,042 sq. km.) and a population of 79,024. Papeete on the northwest coast is the capital and administrative center of French Polynesia. Copra, sugar cane, vanilla and coffee are exported. Tourism is an important industry.

Capt. Samuel Wallis of the British Navy discovered Tahiti in 1768 and named it King George III Island. Louis-Antoine de Bougainville arrived the following year and claimed it for France. Subsequent English visits were by James Cook in 1769 and William Bligh in the HMS "Bounty" in 1788.

Members of the Protestant London Missionary Society established the first European settlement in 1797, and with the aid of the local Pomare family gained control of the entire island and established a "missionary kingdom" with a scriptural code of law. Nevertheless, Tahiti was subsequently declared a French protectorate (1842) and a colony (1880), and since 1958 is part of the overseas territory of French Polynesia.

RULERS:
French

MONETARY SYSTEM:
1 Franc = 100 Centimes

	SIGNATURE VARIETIES	
	DIRECTEUR GÉNÉRAL	**PREÉSIDENT DU CONSEIL DE SURVEILLANCE**
1	André Postel-Vinay, 1967-1972	Bernard Clappier, 1966-1972
2	Claude Panouillot, 1972-1973	André de Lattre, 1973
3	Claude Panouillot, 1974-1978	Marcel Theron, 1974-1979
4	Yves Roland-Billecart, 1979-1984	Gabriel Lefort, 1980-1984
5	Yves Roland-Billecart, 1985-	Jacques Waitzenegger, 1985-

BANQUE DE L'INDOCHINE

PAPEETE

1939-40 ND ISSUE

14 **100 FRANCS**
ND (1939-65). Brown and m/c. Woman wearing wreath and
holding sm. figure of Athena at ctr. Angkor statue on back.

		Good	Fine	XF
a. Sign. M. Borduge and P. Baudouin w/titles: *LE PRÉSIDENT* and *LE ADMINISTRATEUR DIRECTEUR GÉNÉRAL*.		6.00	20.00	70.00
b. Sign. titles: *LE PRÉSIDENT* and *LE ADMINISTRATEUR DIRECTEUR GÉNÉRAL*.		5.00	17.50	60.00
c. Sign. titles: *LE PRÉSIDENT* and *LE VICE-PRÉSIDENT DIRECTEUR GÉNÉRAL*.		4.00	15.00	40.00
d. Sign. titles: *LE PRÉSIDENT* and *LE DIRECTEUR GÉNÉRAL*.		3.00	12.50	30.00

1951 ND ISSUE

21 **20 FRANCS**
ND (1951-63). M/c. Youth at l., flute player at r. Fruit at l., woman
at r. on back. Wmk: Man w/hat.

		VG	VF	UNC
a. Sign. titles: *LE PRÉSIDENT* and *LE DIRECTEUR GAL*. (1951).		3.50	10.00	35.00
b. Sign. titles: *LE PRÉSIDENT* and *LE VICE-PRÉSIDENT DIRECTEUR GÉNÉRAL* (1954-1958).		1.50	6.00	20.00
c. Sign. titles: *LE PRÉSIDENT* and *LE DIRECTEUR GÉNÉRAL*. (1963).		1.50	5.00	15.00

INSTITUT D'EMISSION D'OUTRE-MER

PAPEETE

1969-71 ND ISSUES

23 **100 FRANCS**
ND (1969). Brown and m/c. Girl wearing wreath holding guitar at
r., w/o *REPUBLIQUE FRANCAISE* near bottom ctr. Girl at l., town
scene at ctr. on back. Sign. 1. Printed from engraved copper plates.

VG	VF	UNC
3.00	10.00	75.00

24 **100 FRANCS**
ND. (1971; 1973). M/c. Like #23 but w/ovpt: *REPUBLIQUE
FRANCAISE* at bottom ctr. Sign. 1.

	VG	VF	UNC
a. Printed from engraved copper plates. (1971).	1.00	4.00	32.50
b. Offset printing. (1973).	1.00	4.00	25.00

25 **500 FRANCS**
ND (1970-85). Blue and m/c. Harbor view w/boat in background at
ctr., fisherman at lower r. Man at l., objects at r. on back.

	VG	VF	UNC
a. Sign. 1. (1970).	FV	7.00	32.50
b1. Sign. 3. (1977).	FV	7.00	27.50
b2. Sign. 3A.	FV	7.00	30.00
c. Sign. 4. (1983).	FV	7.00	22.50
d. Sign. 5. (1985).	FV	5.00	15.00

26 **1000 FRANCS**
ND (1969). Dk. brown on red and m/c unpt. Hut under palms at l.,
girl at r. W/o *REPUBLIQUE FRANCAISE* ovpt. at bottom ctr. Kagu,
deer, bldgs., native carvings on back. Wmk: Marianne. Sign. 1.

VG	VF	UNC
12.00	35.00	165.00

27	1000 FRANCS		VG	VF	UNC
	ND (1971-85). Dk. brown on m/c unpt. Like #26 but w/ovpt: *REPUBLIQUE FRANCAISE* at lower l.				
	a. Sign. 1. (1971).		FV	12.50	32.50
	b. Sign. 3. (1977).		FV	12.50	27.50
	c. Sign. 4. (1983).		FV	12.50	27.50
	d. Sign. 5. (1985).		FV	FV	22.50

28	5000 FRANCS		VG	VF	UNC
	ND (1971-85). Brown w/black text on olive-green and m/c unpt. Bougainville at l., sailing ships at ctr. Admiral Febvrier-Despointes at r., sailboat at ctr. r. on back.				
	a. Sign. 1. (1971).		FV	65.00	165.00
	b. Sign. 2. (1975).		FV	60.00	135.00
	c. Sign. 4. (1982; 1984).		FV	60.00	120.00
	d. Sign. 5. (1985).		FV	60.00	100.00

The Republic of Tajikistan, was formed from those regions of Bukhara and Turkestan where the population consisted mainly of Tajiks. It is bordered in the north and west by Uzbekistan and Kyrgyzstan, in the east by China and in the south by Afghanistan. It has an area of 55,240 sq. miles (143,100 sq. km.) and a population of 6.4 million. It includes 2 provinces of Khudzand and Khatlon together with the Gorno-Badakhshan Autonomous Region with a population of 5,092,603. Capital: Dushanbe. Tajikistan was admitted as a constituent republic of the Soviet Union on December 5, 1929. In Aug. 1990 the Tajik Supreme Soviet adopted a declaration of republican sovereignty, and in December 1991 the republic became a member of the Commonwealth of Independent States.

MONETARY SYSTEM:
1 Ruble = 100 Tanga, to 2000
1 Somoni = 1,000 Rubles
1 Somoni = 100 Diram

БОНКИ МИЛЛИИ ЧУМХУРИИ

NATIONAL BANK OF THE REPUBLIC OF TAJIKISTAN
1994 ISSUE

#1-8 arms at upper l. or l. *Majlisi Olii* (Parliament) on back. Wmk: Multiple stars. Printer: Goznak, Moscow, w/o imprint.

1	1 RUBLE	VG	VF	UNC
	1994. Brown on m/c unpt.			
	a. Issued note.	0.05	0.15	1.00
	s. Specimen.	—	—	—

2	5 RUBLES	VG	VF	UNC
	1994. Deep blue on m/c unpt.			
	a. Issued note.	0.05	0.15	1.00
	s. Specimen.	—	—	—

3	10 RUBLES	VG	VF	UNC
	1994. Deep red on m/c unpt.			
	a. Issued note.	0.05	0.15	1.00
	s. Specimen.	—	—	1.00

4	20 RUBLES	VG	VF	UNC
	1994. Purple on m/c unpt.			
	a. Issued note.	0.05	0.15	1.00
	s. Specimen.	—	—	—

5   **50 RULES**

	VG	VF	UNC
1994. Dk. olive-green on m/c unpt.			
a. Issued note.	0.05	0.15	1.00
s. Specimen.	—		

6   **100 RUBLES**

	VG	VF	UNC
1994. Blue-black and brown on m/c unpt.			
a. Issued note.	0.10	0.20	1.00
s. Specimen.	—		

7   **200 RUBLES**

	VG	VF	UNC
1994. Deep olive-green and pale violet on m/c unpt.			
a. Issued note.	0.15	0.30	1.50
s. Specimen.	—		

8   **500 RUBLES**

	VG	VF	UNC
1994. Brown-violet on m/c unpt.			
a. Issued note.	0.25	0.50	2.00
s. Specimen.	—		

9   **1000 RUBLES**

	VG	VF	UNC
1994 (1999). Brown and purple on m/c unpt.			
a. Issued note.	0.25	0.50	2.50
s. Specimen.	—		

9A   **5000 RUBLES**

	VG	VF	UNC
1994. Dk. green and blue on m/c unpt. Coat of Arms at l. Parliament bldg. w/flag on back. (Not issued).	—	—	35.00

9B   **10,000 RUBLES**

	VG	VF	UNC
1994. Pink and brown on m/c unpt. Coat of Arms at ctr. parliament bldg. w/flag on back.	—	—	35.00

БОНКИ МИЛЛИИ ТОЧИКИСТОН

NATIONAL BANK OF TAJIKISTAN

1999 ISSUE

#10-19 Printed in Germany.

#10-13 wmk: two mountains over rectangle.

10   **1 DIRAM**

	VG	VF	UNC
1999 (2000). Brown on tan and red unpt. Sadriddin Ayni Theatre and Opera house at ctr. Pamir mountains on back.			
a. Issued note.	0.05	0.15	0.50
s. Specimen.	—		1.00

11   **5 DIRAM**

	VG	VF	UNC
1999 (2000). Blue on tan unpt. Arbob Culture Palace at ctr. Shrine of Mirzo Tursunzoda on back.			
a. Issued note.	0.05	0.15	0.50
s. Specimen.	—		1.00

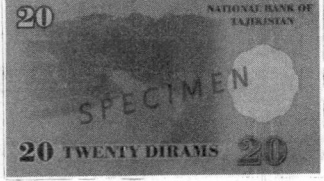

12   **20 DIRAM**

	VG	VF	UNC
1999 (2000). Green on tan unpt. *Majlisi Olii* (Tajik Parliament) interior. Road pass in the mountains on back.			
a. Issued note.	0.05	0.25	0.75
s. Specimen.	—		1.50

13	50 DIRAM	VG	VF	UNC
	1999 (2000). Purple on tan unpt. Statue of Ismoili Somoni at ctr. Road in a valley on back.			
	a. Issued note.	0.05	0.35	1.50
	s. Specimen.	—	—	2.50

#14-19 wmk: as portrait.

14	1 SOMONI	VG	VF	UNC
	1999 (2000). Green and blue on m/c unpt. Mirzo Tursunzoda (poet) at r. National Bank of Tajikistan bldg. on back.			
	a. Issued note.	0.05	0.50	2.50
	s. Specimen.	—	—	5.00

15	5 SOMONI	VG	VF	UNC
	1999 (2000). Blue and green on m/c unpt. Sadriddin Ayni at r. Shrine of Abuabdullo Rudaki on back.			
	a. Issued note.	FV	1.50	6.00
	s. Specimen.	—	—	10.00

16	10 SOMONI	VG	VF	UNC
	1999 (2000). Purple and orange red. Mir Saiid Alii Hamadoni at r. Historical medieval monument on back.			
	a. Issued note.	0.10	2.00	10.00
	s. Specimen.	—	—	17.50

#17-19 w/holographic strip at r.

17	20 SOMONI	VG	VF	UNC
	1999 (2000). Brown and blue on m/c unpt. Abuali Ibn Sino at r. Hissor fortress near Dushanbe on back.			
	a. Issued note.	0.50	3.00	15.00
	s. Specimen.	—	—	22.50

18	50 SOMONI	VG	VF	UNC
	1999 (2000). Dk. blue and black on m/c unpt. Bobojon Gafurov at r. *Choikhanai Sina*, a tea house in Dushanbe, on back.			
	a. Issued note.	1.00	3.00	15.00
	s. Specimen.	—	—	25.00

19	100 SOMONI	VG	VF	UNC
	1999 (2000). Brown and blue on m/c unpt. Ismoili Somoni at r. Presidential Palace in Dushanbe on back.			
	a. Issued note.	1.00	3.00	25.00
	s. Specimen.	—	—	35.00

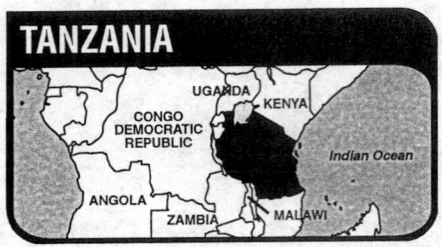

TANZANIA

The United Republic of Tanzania, located on the east coast of Africa between Kenya and Mozambique, consists of Tanganyika and the islands of Zanzibar and Pemba. It has an area of 364,900 sq. mi. (945,090 sq. km.) and a population of 33.69 million. Capital: Dodoma. The chief exports are cotton, coffee, diamonds, sisal, cloves, petroleum products and cashew nuts.

German East Africa (Tanganyika), located on the coast of east-central Africa between British East Africa (now Kenya) and Portuguese East Africa (now Mozambique), had an area of 362,284 sq. mi. (938,216 sq. km.) and a population of about 6 million. Capital: Dar es Salaam. Chief products prior to German control were ivory and slaves; after German control, sisal, coffee and rubber. Germany acquired control of the area by treaties with coastal chiefs in 1884, established it as a protectorate in 1891, and proclaimed it the Colony of German East Africa in 1897. After World War I, Tanganyika was entrusted to Great Britain as a League of Nations mandate, and after World War II as a United Nations trust territory. Tanganyika became an independent nation within the British Commonwealth on Dec. 9, 1961.

The British Protectorate of Zanzibar and Pemba, and adjacent small islands, located in the Indian Ocean 22 miles (35 km.) off the coast of Tanganyika, comprised a portion of British East Africa. Zanzibar was also the name of a sultanate which included the Zanzibar and Kenya protectorates. Zanzibar has an area of 637 sq. mi. (1,651 sq. km.). Chief city: Zanzibar. Pemba has an area of 380 sq. mi. (984 sq. km.). Chief city: Chake Chake. The islands are noted for their cloves, of which Zanzibar is the world's foremost producer.

Zanzibar and Pemba share a common history. Zanzibar came under Portuguese control in 1503, was conquered by the Omani Arabs in 1698, became independent of Oman in 1860, and (with Pemba) came under British control in 1890. Britain granted the protectorate self-government in 1961, and independence within the British Commonwealth on Dec. 19, 1963. On April 26, 1964, Tanganyika and Zanzibar (with Pemba) united to form the United Republic of Tanganyika and Zanzibar. The name of the country was changed to Tanzania on Oct. 29, 1964. The president is Chief of State.

Also see East Africa and Zanzibar, (Vol. 2).

MONETARY SYSTEM:
1 Shilingi (Shilling) = 100 Senti

BANK OF TANZANIA

	SIGNATURE VARIETIES				
	MINISTER FOR FINANCE	GOVERNOR		MINISTER FOR FINANCE	GOVERNOR
1			2		
3			4		
5			6	WAZIRI WA FEDHA	GAVANA
7	WAZIRI WA FEDHA	GAVANA	7A		
8			9		
10			11		
12			13		
14					

1966 ND ISSUE

Note: Sign. 3-5 w/English titles on #2 and 3, changed to Swahili titles for later issues.

#1-5 arms at ctr., Pres. J. Nyerere at r. Wmk: Giraffe's head. Replacement notes: Serial # prefix ZZ; ZY.

1	5 SHILLINGS	VG	VF	UNC
	ND (1966). Brown on m/c unpt. Sign. 1. Mountain view on back.			
	a. Issued note.	1.00	3.00	12.50
	s. Specimen.	—	—	25.00

2	10 SHILLINGS	VG	VF	UNC
	ND (1966). Green on m/c unpt. Sisal drying on back.			
	a. Sign. 1.	1.50	3.00	9.00
	b. Sign. 2.	2.00	4.00	10.00
	c. Sign. 3.	7.50	30.00	225.00
	d. Sign. 4.	1.00	2.00	7.50
	e. Sign. 5.	1.00	2.00	6.00
	s. As a. Specimen.	—	—	25.00

3	20 SHILLINGS	VG	VF	UNC
	ND (1966). Blue on m/c unpt. Work bldgs. on back.			
	a. Sign. 1.	2.00	5.00	12.50
	b. Sign. 2.	2.00	5.00	12.50
	c. Sign. 3.	3.00	7.00	20.00
	d. Sign. 4.	2.00	5.00	15.00
	e. Sign. 5.	1.50	3.00	9.00
	s. As a. Specimen.	—	—	25.00

7	20 SHILINGI		VG	VF	UNC
	ND (1978). Blue on m/c unpt. Cotton knitting machine on back.				
	a. Sign. 5.		0.50	2.25	7.50
	b. Sign. 6.		0.50	2.25	4.50
	c. Sign. 3. Sign. titles: *WAZIRI WA FEDHA* and *GAVANA*.		0.50	2.25	5.00

4	100 SHILLINGS		VG	VF	UNC
	ND (1966). Red on m/c unpt. Masai herdsman w/animals on back.				
	Sign. 1.				
	a. Issued note.		17.50	60.00	375.00
	s. Specimen.		—	—	85.00

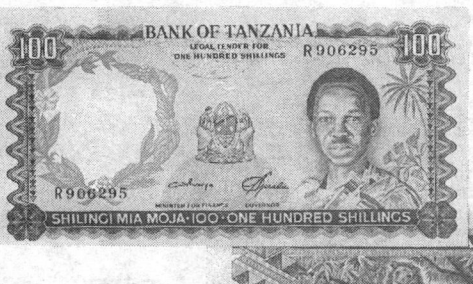

8	100 SHILINGI		VG	VF	UNC
	ND (1977). Purple on m/c unpt. Teacher and students at l., farmers at ctr. on back.				
	a. Sign. 4.		2.00	6.00	27.50
	b. Sign. 5.		1.50	5.00	25.00
	c. Sign. 6.		1.00	4.00	17.50
	d. Sign. 3. Sign. titles: *WAZIRI WA FEDHA* and *GAVANA*.		1.00	4.50	20.00

1985 ND Issue

#9-11 portr. of an older Pres. J. Nyerere at r., torch at l., arms at ctr. Islands of Mafia, Pemba and Zanzibar are omitted from map on back. Sign. 3. Wmk: Giraffe's head. Replacement notes: Serial # prefix *ZZ; ZY.*

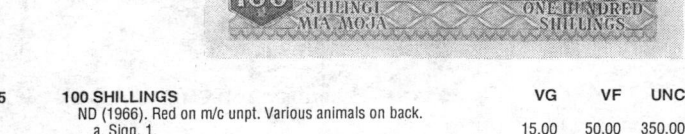

5	100 SHILLINGS		VG	VF	UNC
	ND (1966). Red on m/c unpt. Various animals on back.				
	a. Sign. 1.		15.00	50.00	350.00
	b. Sign. 3.		12.50	40.00	275.00

Benki Kuu Ya Tanzania

1977-78 ND Issue

#6-8 arms at top ctr., Pres. J. Nyerere at r. Wmk: Giraffe's head. Replacement notes: Serial # prefix *ZZ; ZY.*

Note: For #6-8, sign. are shown in chronological order of appearance. It seems sign. 3 was used again following several later combinations.

9	20 SHILINGI		VG	VF	UNC
	ND (1985). Purple, brown on m/c unpt. Tire factory scene on back.		0.15	0.50	2.50

6	10 SHILINGI		VG	VF	UNC
	ND (1978). Green on m/c unpt. Monument and mountain at ctr. on back.				
	a. Sign. 5.		0.25	1.50	5.50
	b. Sign. 6.		0.25	1.00	3.00
	c. Sign. 3. Sign. titles: *WAZIRI WA FEDHA* and *GAVANA*.		0.25	0.75	2.50

10	50 SHILINGI		VG	VF	UNC
	ND (1985). Red-orange, lt. brown on m/c unpt. Brick making on back.		0.25	1.50	5.00

11	100 SHILINGI		VG	VF	UNC
	ND (1985). Blue, purple on m/c unpt. Graduation procession on back.		0.50	3.00	8.50

1986 ND ISSUE

#12-14 like #9-11 but w/islands of Mafia, Pemba and Zanzibar now included in map on back. Replacement notes: Serial # prefix *ZZ; ZY.*

12	**20 SHILINGI**	VG	VF	UNC
	ND (1986). Like #9 but w/islands in map on back. Sign. 3. Sign. titles: *WAZIRI WA FEDHA* and *GAVANA.*	0.15	0.50	2.00

16	**50 SHILINGI**	VG	VF	UNC
	ND (1986). Red-orange, lt. brown on m/c unpt. Back like #13.			
	a. Sign. 3 but w/titles: *WAZIRI WA FEDHA* and *GAVANA.*	0.25	1.00	4.00
	b. Sign. 7.	0.20	0.75	3.00

13	**50 SHILINGI**	VG	VF	UNC
	ND (1986). Like #10 but w/islands in map on back. Sign. 3. Sign. titles: *WAZIRI WA FEDHA* and *GAVANA.*	0.25	1.00	3.50

18	**200 SHILINGI**	VG	VF	UNC
	ND (1986). Black, orange and ochre on m/c unpt. 2 fishermen on back.			
	a. Sign. 3 but w/titles: *WAZIRI WA FEDHA* and *GAVANA.*	0.50	2.00	7.50
	b. Sign. 7.	1.00	4.00	15.00

1989-92 ND ISSUE

#19-22 similar to #16 and #18 but w/modified portr. Wmk: Giraffe's head. Replacement notes: Serial # prefix *ZZ; ZY.*

14	**100 SHILINGI**	VG	VF	UNC
	ND (1986). Like #11 but w/islands in map on back.			
	a. Sign. 3 w/titles: *WAZIRI WA FEDHA* and *GAVANA.*	0.50	1.50	5.00
	b. Sign. 8.	0.25	1.00	4.00

1986-90 ND ISSUE

#15-18 arms at ctr., Pres. Mwinyi at r. Wmk: Giraffe's head. Replacement notes: Serial # prefix *ZZ; ZY.*

19	**50 SHILINGI**	VG	VF	UNC
	ND (1992). Red-orange and lt. brown on m/c unpt. Sign. 8.	0.10	0.50	1.75

15	**20 SHILINGI**	VG	VF	UNC
	ND (1987). Purple, red-brown on m/c unpt. Back like #12. Sign. 3 but w/titles: *WAZIRI WA FEDHA* and *GAVANA.*	0.10	0.25	2.00

20	200 SHILINGI	VG	VF	UNC
	ND (1992). Black, orange and ochre on m/c unpt. Sign. 8.	0.50	1.50	6.00

21	500 SHILINGI	VG	VF	UNC
	ND (1989). Dk. blue on m/c unpt. Zebra at lower l. Harvesting on back.			
	a. Sign. 3 but w/titles: *WAZIRI WA FEDHA* and *GAVANA*.	2.50	10.00	35.00
	b. Sign. 7.	1.50	5.00	22.50
	c. Sign. 8.	1.00	3.00	17.50

22	1000 SHILINGI	VG	VF	UNC
	ND (1990). Green and brown on m/c unpt. Elephants at lower l. Kiwira Coal Mine at l. ctr., door to the Peoples Bank of Zanzibar at lower r. on back. Sign. 8.	1.50	5.00	22.50

1993; 1995 ND ISSUE

#23, 25-27 arms at ctr., Pres. Mwinyi at r. Wmk: Giraffe's head. Reduced size. Replacement notes: Serial # prefix *ZZ; ZY*.

23	50 SHILINGI	VG	VF	UNC
	ND (1993). Red-orange and brown on m/c unpt. Wildebeest grazing at l. Men making bricks on back. Sign. 9.	FV	FV	1.00

24	100 SHILINGI	VG	VF	UNC
	ND (1993). Blue and aqua on m/c unpt. Kudu at l., arms at ctr., J. Nyerere at r. Graduation procession on back. Sign. 9.	FV	FV	2.00

Note: #24 honors the 70th birthday of Julius Nyerere.

25	200 SHILINGI	VG	VF	UNC
	ND (1993). Black and orange on m/c unpt. Leopards at l. Back similar to #18.			
	a. Sign. 9.	FV	FV	3.50
	b. Sign. 11.	FV	FV	3.00

26	500 SHILINGI	VG	VF	UNC
	ND (1993). Purple, blue-green and violet on m/c unpt. Zebra at lower l. Back similar to #21 w/arms at lower r.			
	a. Sign. 9.	FV	FV	8.00
	b. Sign. 10.	FV	FV	5.00
	c. Sign. 11.	FV	FV	4.50

27	1000 SHILINGI	VG	VF	UNC
	ND (1993). Dk. green, brown and orange-brown on m/c unpt. Similar to #22.			
	a. Sign. 9.	FV	FV	12.50
	b. Sign. 10.	FV	FV	10.00
	c. Sign. 11.	FV	FV	7.50

28   5000 SHILINGI

	VG	VF	UNC
	FV	FV	27.50

ND (1995). Brown on m/c unpt. Giraffes w/Mt. Kilimanjaro in background on back. Sign. 10.

29   10,000 SHILINGI

	VG	VF	UNC
	FV	FV	50.00

ND (1995). M/c. Lion at lower l. Sign. 10.

1997 ND ISSUE

#30-33 arms at upper ctr., giraffe's head at r. and as wmk. Sign. 12.

30   500 SHILINGI

	VG	VF	UNC
	FV	FV	2.50

ND (1997). Blue-black and dk. green on m/c unpt. Zebra at lower l. Woman harvesting cloves at l. ctr. on back.

31   1000 SHILINGI

	VG	VF	UNC
	FV	FV	5.00

ND (1997). Deep olive-green, red-orange and dk. brown on m/c unpt. Elephants at lower l. Industrial bldgs. at l. ctr., door to the Peoples Bank of Zanzibar at lower r. on back.

32   5000 SHILINGI

	VG	VF	UNC
	FV	FV	16.00

ND (1997). Dk. brown and purple on m/c unpt. Rhinoceros at lower l. Giraffes w/Mt. Kilimanjaro in background on back. Segmented foil over security thread.

33   10,000 SHILINGI

	VG	VF	UNC
	FV	FV	32.00

ND (1997). Blue-black and dk. gray on m/c unpt. Lion at lower l. Vertical foil strip at r. Bank of Tanzania Head Office bldg. at l. ctr., Zanzibar House of Wonder at lower r. on back.

2000 ND ISSUE

34   1000 SHILINGI

	VG	VF	UNC
	FV	FV	4.50

ND (2000). Brown and green on m/c unpt. Elephants at lower l., Julius Nyerere at r. Back like #31. Sign. 13.

2003 ND ISSUE

#35-39 sign. 14. Printer: G&D.

35   500 SHILINGI

	VG	VF	UNC
	FV	FV	2.50

ND (2003). Green and blue on m/c unpt. Cape Buffalo at ctr. r. Hospital at ctr, boats in background on back.

36   1000 SHILINGI

		VG	VF	UNC
	ND (2003). Blue and slate blue on m/c unpt. Julius Nyerere at ctr. r. Palace on back.	FV	FV	5.00

37   2000 SHILINGI

		VG	VF	UNC
	ND (2003). Brown, tan and green on m/c unpt. Lion and Mt. Kilimanjaro at ctr. Fort on back.	FV	FV	7.50

38   5000 SHILINGI

		VG	VF	UNC
	ND (2003). Purple on m/c unpt. Black Rhinoceros at ctr. l. Mining and House of Wonder on back.	FV	FV	15.00

39   10,000 SHILINGI

		VG	VF	UNC
	ND (2003). Rose and green on m/c unpt. Elephant at ctr. l. Central Bank bldg. on back.	FV	FV	30.00

TATARSTAN

Tatarstan, an autonomous republic in the Russian Federation, is situated between the middle of the Volga River and its tributary Kama, extends east to the Ural mountains, covering 26,500 sq. mi. (68,000 sq. km.) and as of the 1970 census has a population of 3,743,600. Captial: Kazan. Tatarstan's economy combines its ancient traditions in the craftsmanship of wood, leather, cloth and ceramics with modern engineering, chemical, and food industries.

Colonized by the Bulgars in the 5th century, the territory of the Volga-Kama Bulgar State was inhabited by Turks. In the 13th century, Ghengis Khan conquered the area and established control until the 15th century when residual Mongol influence left Tatarstan as the Tatar Khanate, seat of the Kazar (Tatar) Khans. In 1552, under Ivan IV (the Terrible), Russia conquered, absorbed and controlled Tatarstan until the dissolution of the U.S.S.R.

Constituted as an autonomous republic on May 27, 1990, and as a sovereign state equal with Russia in April, 1992, Tatarstan, signed a treaty in February, 1994, defining it as a state united with the Commonwealth of Independent States.

MONETARY SYSTEM:
1 Ruble = 100 Kopeks

TREASURY

1992 ND КУРОН - RUBLE CONTROL COUPON ISSUES

#1-3 red and green stripes w/black TATARSKAW repeated on back.

		VG	VF	UNC
1	**50 RUBLES**			
	ND (1992). Black text on green unpt. w/month: WNVAR_ (January).			
	a. Issued full sheet.	4.50	10.00	15.00
	b. Remainder full sheet.	2.50	6.00	10.00
	c. Coupon.	0.05	0.20	0.50
2	**50 RUBLES**	**VG**	**VF**	**UNC**
	ND (1992). Black text on pink unpt. w/month: FHVWAL_ (February).			
	a. Issued full sheet.	3.00	7.50	15.00
	b. Remainder full sheet.	2.00	5.00	9.00
	c. Coupon.	0.05	0.20	0.50
3	**50 RUBLES**	**VG**	**VF**	**UNC**
	ND (1992). Black text on blue unpt. w/month: MART (March).			
	a. Issued full sheet.	3.00	7.50	15.00
	b. Remainder full sheet.	1.50	4.00	8.00
	c. Coupon.	0.05	0.20	0.50

GOVERNMENT

1993 PRIVATIZATION CHECK ISSUE

4A **30,000 RUBLES**
1993. Black text on green unpt. Arms w/number. Back black text on white. Printer: USBN.

		VG	VF	UNC
a. Issued note. W/registration and w/o privatization book.		—	25.00	40.00
b. Issued note. W/registration and w/privatization book.		—	40.00	80.00
c. Not issued. All w/coupons and w/o registration.		—	—	50.00

4B **40,000 RUBLES**
1993. Black text on green. Arms w/number. Back black text on white. Printer: USBN.

		VG	VF	UNC
a. Issued note. W/registration and w/o privatization book.		—	17.50	30.00
b. Issued note. W/registration and w/privatization book.		—	30.00	50.00
c. Not issued. All w/coupons and w/o registration.		—	—	50.00

4C **60,000 RUBLES**
1993. Black text on green unpt. Arms w/number. Back black text on white. Printer: USBN (w/o imprint).

		VG	VF	UNC
a. Issued note. W/registration and w/o privatization book.		—	20.00	35.00
b. Issued note. W/registration and w/privatization book.		—	35.00	60.00
c. Not issued. All w/coupons and w/o registration.		—	—	50.00

4D **80,000 RUBLES**
1993. Black text on green. Arms w/number. Back black text on white. Printer: USBN.

		VG	VF	UNC
a. Issued note. W/registration and w/o privatization book.		—	25.00	40.00
b. Issued note. W/registration and w/privatization book.		—	40.00	75.00
c. Not issued. All w/coupons and w/o registration.		—	—	50.00

4E **90,000 RUBLES**
1993. Black text on green. Arms w/number. Black text on white. Printer: USBN.

		VG	VF	UNC
a. Issued note. W/registration and w/o privatization book.		—	30.00	50.00
b. Issued note. W/registration and w/privatization book.		—	40.00	80.00
c. Not issued. All w/coupons and w/o registration.		—	—	50.00

4F **100,000 RUBLES**
1993. Black text on green. Arms w/number. Black text on white. Printer: USBN.

		VG	VF	UNC
a. Issued note. W/registration and w/o privatization book.		—	35.00	60.00
b. Issued note. W/registration and w/privatization book.		—	45.00	85.00
c. Not issued. All w/coupons and w/o registration.		—	—	50.00

1991; 1993 ND FIRST CURRENCY CHECK ISSUE

#5 and 6 state flag inside circle at l., stylized image of old castle Suumbeky in Kazan (ca. 16th century) in ornate frame at r. Uniface.

5 **(100 RUBLES)**
ND (1991-92). Blue-gray. 138 x 66mm. Wmk: Lozenges.

		VG	VF	UNC
a. Gray unpt.		—	3.00	15.00
b. Red unpt.		—	10.00	25.00
c. Yellow unpt.		—	12.50	25.00
d. Orange unpt.		—	12.50	25.00

Note: Issued statewide. Checks probably printed in 1991, as coat of arms was accepted later than flag, but issued to circulation in 1992.

6 **(100 RUBLES)**
ND (1993). Red and pink. Red and green arms at l., stylized image of old castle Suumbeky in ornate frame at r. Wmk: Lozenges. Uniface.

		VG	VF	UNC
a. Gray unpt.		—	8.00	15.00
b. Violet on pink unpt.		—	8.00	15.00
c. Dk. blue on pale blue unpt.		—	8.00	15.00
d. Brown unpt.		—	6.00	12.50
e. Olive-green unpt.		—	8.00	15.00

Note: Issued for circulation in Kazan.

1994 ND SECOND CURRENCY CHECK ISSUE

7 **(200 RUBLES)**
ND (1994). Medical emblem inside oval at r., stylized image of old castle Suumbeky in Kazan (ca. 16th century) at l. 105 x 53mm. Wmk: Lozenges. Uniface.

		VG	VF	UNC
a. Blue-black and pale blue on m/c unpt.		1.50	7.50	10.00
b. Deep olive-green and green on tan and pale green unpt.		1.50	7.50	10.00

Note: Circulated in the republic from 3.10.1994 to 1.7.1995.

1993-95 ND THIRD CURRENCY CHECK ISSUE

#8-12 arms at top ctr., Kazan Kremlin (ca. 16th century) at lower l., Arabic *Tatar* at r.

#8-11 wmk.: Mosaic.

8 **(500 RUBLES)**
ND (1993). Red-brown on m/c unpt. Woman feeding geese on olive-green back. 105 x 53mm.

		VG	VF	UNC
		1.00	5.00	9.00

9 **(500 RUBLES)**
ND (1993). Green on m/c unpt. Horses galloping at ctr. on olive green back. 105 x 53mm.

		VG	VF	UNC
		1.00	5.00	9.00

10 **(1000 RUBLES)**
ND (1994). Pink on m/c unpt. Gulls flying over raging waves on back. 105 x 53mm.

		VG	VF	UNC
		1.00	5.00	9.00

11 **(1000 RUBLES)**
ND (1995). Blue on m/c unpt. Deer at watering hole on back. 105 x 53mm.

		VG	VF	UNC
		1.00	5.00	9.00

Note: Checks #8-11 found in circulation before Aug. 1996.

1996 ND FOURTH CURRENCY CHECK ISSUE

12 **(50 SHAMIL = 5000 RUBLES)**
ND (1996). Kazan Kremlin (ca. 16th century) w/English and Russian text "Tatarstan" in frame below. Women from national epic on back. 135 x 65mm. Wmk: Lt. lines.

		VG	VF	UNC
a. Dk. blue on pale blue-gray unpt.		1.00	4.00	12.50
b. Deep green on pale green unpt.		1.00	4.00	12.50

Note: Check #12 found in circulation from Aug. 1996 to date.

THAILAND

The Kingdom of Thailand, a constitutional monarchy located in the center of mainland southeast Asia between Burma and Lao, has an area of 198,457 sq. mi. (514,000 sq. km.) and a population of 60.49 million. Capital: Bangkok. The economy is based on agriculture and mining. Rubber, rice, teakwood, tin and tungsten are exported.

The history of Thailand, the only country in south and southeast Asia that was never colonized by an European power, dates from the 6th century AD when tribes of the Thai stock migrated into the area from the Asiatic continent, a process that accelerated with the Mongol invasion of China in the 13th century. After 400 years of sporadic warfare with the neighboring Burmese, King Taksin won the last battle in 1767. He founded a new capital, Dhonburi, on the west bank of Chao Praya River. King Rama I moved the capital to Bangkok in 1782.

The Thai were introduced to the Western world by the Portuguese, who were followed by the Dutch, British and French. Rama III of the present ruling dynasty negotiated a treaty of friendship and commerce with Britain in 1826, and in 1896 the independence of the kingdom was guaranteed by an Anglo-French accord. The absolute monarchy was changed into a constitutional monarchy in 1932. This was maintained when the name of the country was changed to Thailand in 1939.

On December 8, 1941, after five hours of fighting, Thailand agreed to permit Japanese troops passage through the country to invade northern British Malaya. This eventually led to increased Japanese intervention and finally occupation of the country. On January 25, 1942, Thailand declared war on Great Britain and the United States. A free Thai guerrilla movement was soon organized to counteract the Japanese. In July 1943, Japan transferred the four northern Malay States back to Thailand. These were returned to Great Britain after peace treaties were signed in 1946.

RULERS:
Rama IX (Bhumiphol Adulyadej), 1946-

MONETARY SYSTEM:
1 Baht (Tical) = 100 Satang

SIGNATURE VARIETIES

	MINISTER OF FINANCE	GOVERNOR OF THE BANK OF THAILAND
34		
35		
36		
37		
38		
39	Chote Kvnakasem - no error -	Chote Kvnakasem
40		
41	S. Vinichchaikul	Puey Ungpakorn
42	S. Vinichchaikul	Bisudhi Nimmanhaemin
43	Boonma Wongesesawan	Bisudhi Nimmanhaemin

SIGNATURE VARIETIES

	MINISTER OF FINANCE	GOVERNOR OF THE BANK OF THAILAND
44	Sommai Hoontrakul	Bisudhi Nimmanhaemin
45	Sawet Piempongsarn	Bisudhi Nimmanhaemin
46	Boonchu Rojanasathien	Bisudhi Nimmanhaemin
47	Boonchu Rojanasathien	Sanoh Unakul
48	Sawet Piempongsarn	Sanoh Unakul
	MINISTER OF FINANCE รัฐมนตรีว่าการกระทรวงการคลัง	GOVERNOR OF THE BANK OF THAILAND ผู้ว่าการธนาคารแห่งประเทศไทย
49	Suphat Suthatham	Sanoh Unakul
50	Gen. K. Chomanan	Sanoh Unakul
51	Gen. K. Chomanan	Nukul Prachuabmoh
52	Amnuey Virawan	Nukul Prachuabmoh
53	Sommai Hoontrakul	Nukul Prachuabmoh
54	Sommai Hoontrakul	Kamchorn Sathirakul
55	Suthee Singsaneh	Kamchorn Sathirakul
56	Pramual Sabhavasu	Kamchorn Sathirakul
57	Pramual Sabhavasu	Chavalit Thanachanan
57a	Virabongsa Ramangkul	Chavalit Thanachanan
58	Virabongsa Ramangkul	Vigit Supinit

SIGNATURE VARIETIES		
59	Baham Silpa-acha	Vigit Supinit
60	Suthee Singsaneh	Vigit Supinit
61		Vigit Supinit
62	Pedro Malan, 1999-	Vigit Supinit
63	Tharin Nimanhaemin	Vigit Supinit
64	Sukariart Satirathai	Vigit Supinit
65	Bhodi Joonanord	Vigit Supinit
66	Bhodi Joonanord	Rerngchai Marakanond
67	Amnuey Virawan	Rerngchai Marakanond
68	Thanon Pithaya	Rerngchai Marakanond
69	Thanon Pithaya	Chaiwat Viboon
70	Kasit Pampiern	Chaiwat Viboon
71	Tharin Nimahaemin	Chaiwat Viboon

GOVERNMENT OF THAILAND

1953-56 ND ISSUE

#74-78 slightly modified portr. Kg. in Field Marshal's uniform w/collar insignia and 3 decorations. Black serial #. Printer: TDLR.

Small letters in 2-line text on back.

Large letters in 2-line text on back.

74	1 BAHT	VG	VF	UNC
	ND (1955). Blue on m/c unpt. Like #69.			
	a. Wmk: Constitution. Red and blue security threads. Sign. 34.	0.20	1.00	5.00
	b. Wmk: Constitution. Metal security strip. Sign. 34; 35 (lg. size).	0.20	1.00	4.50
	c. Wmk: Kg. profile. Sm. letters in 2-line text on back. Sign. 35.	0.10	0.75	4.00
	d. Wmk: Kg. profile. Larger letters in 2-line text on back. Sign. 36; 37; 38; 39; 40; 4l.	0.10	0.75	3.50
	s. As a; d. Specimen.	—	—	250.00

75	5 BAHT	VG	VF	UNC
	ND (1956). Purple on m/c unpt. Like #70.			
	a. Wmk: Constitution. Red and blue security threads. Sign. 34.	0.50	3.00	6.00
	b. Wmk: Constitution. Metal security strip. Sign. 34; 35 (lg. size).	0.50	2.50	5.50
	c. Wmk: Kg. profile. Sm. letters in 2-line text on back. Sign. 35; 36.	0.50	2.00	5.00
	d. Wmk: Kg. profile. Larger letters in 2-line text on back. Sign. 38; 39; 40; 41.	0.50	1.50	4.50
	s. As a. Specimen.	—	—	250.00

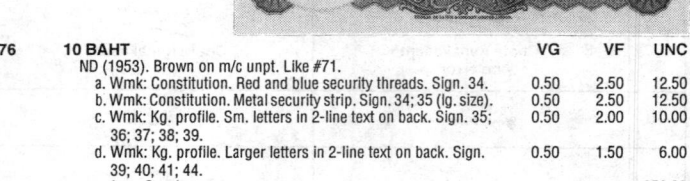

76	10 BAHT	VG	VF	UNC
	ND (1953). Brown on m/c unpt. Like #71.			
	a. Wmk: Constitution. Red and blue security threads. Sign. 34.	0.50	2.50	12.50
	b. Wmk: Constitution. Metal security strip. Sign. 34; 35 (lg. size).	0.50	2.50	12.50
	c. Wmk: Kg. profile. Sm. letters in 2-line text on back. Sign. 35; 36; 37; 38; 39.	0.50	2.00	10.00
	d. Wmk: Kg. profile. Larger letters in 2-line text on back. Sign. 39; 40; 41; 44.	0.50	1.50	6.00
	s. As a. Specimen.	—	—	250.00

77	**20 BAHT**	VG	VF	UNC
	ND (1953). Olive-green on m/c unpt. Like #72.			
	a. Wmk: Constitution. Red and blue security threads. Sign. 34.	1.00	3.50	12.50
	b. Wmk: Constitution. Metal security strip. Sign. 34; 35 (lg. size).	1.00	3.00	10.00
	c. Wmk: Kg. profile. Sm. letters in 2-line text on back. Sign. 35; 37; 38.	0.50	2.00	8.50
	d. Wmk: Kg. profile. Larger letters in 2-line text on back. Sign. 38; 39; 40; 41; 44.	0.50	2.00	10.00
	s. As a. Specimen.	—	—	250.00
78	**100 BAHT**			
	ND (1955). Red on m/c unpt. Like #73.			
	a. Wmk: Constitution. Red and blue security threads. Sign. 34.	4.00	12.50	25.00
	b. Wmk: Constitution. Metal security strip. Sign. 34; 35; 37; 38.	4.00	12.50	17.50
	c. Wmk: Kg. profile. Sm. letters in 2-line text on back. Sign. 38.	2.00	7.50	15.00
	d. Wmk: Kg. profile. Larger letters in 2-line text on back. Sign. 38-41.	2.00	6.00	12.50
	s. As a; c. Specimen.	—	—	250.00

BANK OF THAILAND

1968 ISSUE; SERIES 10

79	**100 BAHT**	VG	VF	UNC
	ND (1968). Red, blue and m/c. Rama IX in uniform at r. and as wmk. Royal barge on back. Sign. 41; 42. Printer: TDLR.			
	a. Issued note.	3.50	7.50	17.50
	s. Specimen.	—	—	—

1969 COMMEMORATIVE ISSUE

SERIES 11

Printed in Thailand by the Thai Banknote Printing Works. Officially described as "Series Eleven". Kg. Rama IX wearing traditional robes at r., sign. of Finance Minister (above) and Governor of the Bank of Thailand (below) at ctr. Wmk: Rama IX. Reportedly 6,000 or 7,000 sets issued.

#80 and 81 text at bottom: *opening of the Thai Banknote Printing Works 24 June 2512* (1969).

80	**5 BAHT**	VG	VF	UNC
	24.6.1969. Purple and m/c. Aphonphimok Prasat Pavilion on back. Serial # prefix 00A. Sign. 41.	—	—	150.00

81	**10 BAHT**	VG	VF	UNC
	24.6.1969. Brown on m/c unpt. Wat Benchamabophitr temple on back. Serial # and sign. like #80.	—	—	175.00

1969-75 ND ISSUE; SERIES 11

#82-86 replacement notes: Serial # prefix *S-(W)*.

82	**5 BAHT**	VG	VF	UNC
	ND (1969). Purple and m/c unpt. Like #80 but w/o commemorative line at bottom. Sign. 41; 42.			
	a. Issued note.	0.25	0.50	2.50
	s. Specimen.	—	—	—

83	**10 BAHT**	VG	VF	UNC
	ND (1969-78). Brown and m/c. Like #81 but w/o commemorative line at bottom. Sign. 41; 42; 43; 44; 45; 46; 47; 48; 49; 50; 51; 52; 53.			
	a. Issued note.	0.25	0.50	3.00
	s. Specimen.	—	—	—

84	**20 BAHT**	VG	VF	UNC
	ND (1971-81). Dk. green, olive-green and m/c. Royal barge at l. ctr. on back. Sign. 41; 42; 43; 44; 45; 46; 47; 48; 49; 50; 51; 52; 53.			
	a. Issued note.	0.50	1.00	4.00
	s. Specimen.			

85 100 BAHT

	VG	VF	UNC
ND (1969-78). Red-brown and m/c. Emerald Buddha section of Grand Palace on back.			
a. W/o black Thai ovpt. on face. Sign. 42; 43; 44; 45; 46; 47; 48; 49.	2.00	4.50	12.50
b. Black Thai ovpt. line just below upper sign. for change of title. Sign. 43.	10.00	17.50	40.00
s. As a. Specimen.	—	—	25.00

86 500 BAHT

	VG	VF	UNC
ND (1975-88). Purple and m/c. Pra Prang Sam Yod Lopburi (3 towers) on back. Sign. 47; 49; 50; 51; 52; 53; 54; 55.			
a. Issued note.	8.00	15.00	35.00
s. Specimen.	—	—	—

1978-81 ND ISSUE; SERIES 12

#87-89 Kg. Rama IX wearing dk. Field Marshal's uniform at r. and as wmk. Sign. of Finance Minister (upper) and Governor of the Bank of Thailand (lower) at ctr. Replacement notes: Serial # prefix *S-(W)*.

87 10 BAHT

	VG	VF	UNC
BE2523 (1980). Dk. brown on m/c unpt. Mounted statue of Kg. Chulalongkorn on back. Sign. 51; 52; 53; 54; 55; 56; 57; 58; 59; 60; 61; 63; 66.	FV	0.50	1.50

88 20 BAHT

	VG	VF	UNC
BE2524 (1981). Dk. green on m/c unpt. Kg. Taksin's statue at Chantaburi w/3 armed men on back. Sign. 53; 54; 55; 56; 57; 58; 59; 60; 61; 63; 64; 66; 67; 72; 73; 74.	FV	0.75	3.00

89 100 BAHT

	VG	VF	UNC
ND (1978). Violet, red and orange on m/c unpt. Kg. Narasuan the Great atop elephant on back. Sign. 49-63.	FV	2.00	8.00

1985-92 ND ISSUE; SERIES 13

#90-92 replacement notes: Serial # prefix *S-(W)*.

90 50 BAHT

	VG	VF	UNC
ND (1985-96). Dk. blue and purple on m/c unpt. Kg. Rama IX facing at r., wearing traditional robe and as wmk. Palace at l., statue of Kg. Rama VII at ctr., his arms and sign. at upper l. on back.			
a. Kg. w/pointed eartips. Sign. 54.	FV	2.00	7.50
b. Darker blue color obscuring pointed eartips. Sign. 54-60; 63.	FV	2.00	5.00

91 500 BAHT

	VG	VF	UNC
ND (1988-96). Purple and violet on m/c unpt. Kg. Rama IX at r. in Field Marshal's uniform and as wmk. Statue at ctr. r., palace in background in unpt. at l. ctr. on back. Sign. 55-61; 63.	FV	10.00	25.00

92 **1000 BAHT**
BE2535 (1992). Gray, brown, orange and m/c. Kg. at ctr. r. and as wmk. Kg. Rama IX and Qn. Sirikit greeting children at l. ctr. in unpt., viewing map at ctr. r. on back. Sign. 62-64; 66-67; 69; 71-72.

	VG	VF	UNC
	FV	20.00	45.00

1987 COMMEMORATIVE ISSUE

#93, King's 60th Birthday

93 **60 BAHT**
BE2530 (5.12.1987). Dk. brown on m/c unpt. Kg. Rama IX seated on throne at ctr., Victory crown at l., Royal regalia at r. Royal family seated w/subjects on back. Sign. 55.

	VG	VF	UNC
a. Issued note.	—	—	7.00
s. Specimen in blue folder.	—	—	100.00

Note: A 40 Baht surcharge was added to issue price of #93, for charity work and the expense of the special envelope which came with each issued note.

1992 COMMEMORATIVE ISSUE

#94 and 95, 90th Birthday of Princess Mother

94 **50 BAHT**
ND (1992). Blue on m/c unpt. Similar to #90. 2 lines of text added under Princess Mother's wmk. on face. Sign. 57.

	VG	VF	UNC
	FV	FV	8.00

95 **500 BAHT**
ND (1992). Purple and m/c. Similar to #91. 2 lines of text added under Princess Mother's wmk. on face. Sign. 57.

	VG	VF	UNC
	FV	FV	35.00

#96, Qn. Sirikit's 60th Birthday

96 **1000 BAHT**
ND (1992). Black, deep olive-green and yellow-brown on m/c unpt. Like #92 but w/commemorative text in 3 lines under Qn. Sirikit's wmk. on face and back. Sign. 61.

	VG	VF	UNC
	FV	FV	60.00

1994 ND ISSUE

97 **100 BAHT**
BE2537 (1994). Violet, red and brown-orange on m/c unpt. Kg. Rama IX at r. Statue of Kg. Rama V and Rama VI with children; Royal initial emblem in ctr. on back. 63, 64, 65, 67, 68, 69, 70, 71, 72, 73, 74; 75.

	VG	VF	UNC
	FV	FV	7.50

1995 COMMEMORATIVE ISSUE

Text at lower margin:

๑๒๐ ปี กระทรวงการคลัง วันที่ ๑๔ เมษายน พุทธศักราช ๒๕๓๘

#98, 120th Anniversary Ministry of Finance

98 10 BAHT   VG VF UNC
ND (1995). Dk. brown on m/c unpt. Like #87 but   — — 5.00
w/commemorative text in lower margin. Sign. 63.

1996 COMMEMORATIVE ISSUE

#99 and 101, 50th Anniversary of Reign

99 50 BAHT   VG VF UNC
ND (1996). Purple on lt. blue and m/c unpt. Kg. Rama IX wearing   FV FV 6.00
Field Marshal's uniform at r. and as a shadow design in clear area
at l., royal seal of kingdom at upper r. Back like #90. Polymer
plastic. Sign. 66, 67. Printer: NPA (w/o imprint).

100 500 BAHT   VG VF UNC
ND (1996). Purple and red-violet on m/c unpt. Similar to #103 but   FV FV 40.00
w/Crowned Royal seal w/*50* at ctr. r., arms above dancers at r.
replacing crowned radiant Chakra at l. ctr. Temple of the Emerald
Buddha at l., King Rama I and Rama II at l. ctr.

101 500 BAHT   VG VF UNC
ND (1996). M/c. Kg. Rama IX seated in royal attire at ctr. r.,   — — 60.00
hologram of Kg. at upper r. Kg. holding map at ctr., waterfalls at l.,
farmers in terraced landscape at r. on back. Polymer plastic. Sign.
64; 65; 66. Printer: NPA (w/o imprint).
Note: #101 was also issued in a box with booklet about the king. Issue price was $60.00.

1996-97 ND REGULAR ISSUE

102 50 BAHT   VG VF UNC
BE2540. (1997). Black on lt. blue and m/c unpt. Kg. Rama IX in   FV FV 4.00
Field Marshal's uniform at ctr. r., arms at upper l. Kg. Rama VI
seated at table at ctr. r., royal arms at upper l. ctr., medieval ship's
prow at lower r. on back. Sign. 67, 71; 72; 74. P

103 500 BAHT   VG VF UNC
BE2539 (1996). Purple and red-violet on m/c unpt. Kg. Rama IX at   FV FV 35.00
r. and as wmk. Arms at upper l., radiant crowned Chakra seal on
platform at l. ctr. Back similar to #100. Sign. 64; 66; 67; 69; 72.

1999 COMMEMORATIVE ISSUE

#104, 72nd Birthday of King

104 1000 BAHT   VG VF UNC
BE2542. 1999. Brown, orange and yellow on m/c unpt. Kg.   FV FV 55.00
Bhumibol at r. ctr., green seal has scroll below. King with camera
at r., Pa Sak Jolasid Dam at l. on back. Sign. 72.

2000 COMMEMORATIVE ISSUE

#105, 106 Golden Wedding Anniversary

	VG	VF	UNC
105 **50 BAHT**	—	—	25.00
ND (2000). Brown and tan on m/c unpt. Portr. of King and Queen. Views of their family life on back. 126 x 205mm. Issued in special folder. Sign. 72.			
106 **500,000 BAHT**			
ND (2000). As #105 but for value. (1998 pieces printed).	—	—	17,000.

2000-01 ND ISSUE

	VG	VF	UNC
107 **500 BAHT**	FV	FV	25.00
ND (2001). Blue and rose on m/c unpt. Portr. Kg. Bhumibol at r. Statue and palace on back. Sign. 74.			
108 **1000 BAHT**	FV	FV	40.00
ND (2000). Brown, orange and yellow on m/c unpt. Like #104 but ctr. green seal set on an octagonal base. Sign. 72; 73; 74.			

2002 COMMEMORATIVE ISSUE

	VG	VF	UNC
109 **20 BAHT**	FV	FV	2.00
ND (2003). Green on green and tan m/c unpt. King Rama IX wearing Field Marshal's uniform at ctr. r. Procession w/King in military uniform and new bridge on back. Sign. 74.			

	VG	VF	UNC
110 **100 BAHT**	—	—	8.00
ND (2002). Brown and slate blue on green and m/c unpt. King Rama V and King Rama IX at r. Back slate blue on green unpt. Facsimile print of #12a. Sign. 74; 75.			

2004 COMMEMORATIVE ISSUE

#111, Queen's 72nd Birthday. Issued in a folder.

	VG	VF	UNC
111 **100 BAHT**	—	—	7.50
Multicolor			

2004 ND ISSUE

			VG	VF	UNC
112	**50 BAHT** ND (2004). Slate black on lt. blue and m/c. Like #102 but paper.		FV	FV	4.00
113	**100 BAHT** (2004) Brown. Holographic strip at l. Like #97.		FV	FV	5.00
114	**100 BAHT** 21.10.2005. Red. Kg. Chulalongkorn in navy uniform and in scene ready to abolish slavery on back.		FV	FV	8.00
115	**1000 BAHT** ND. Like #108 but w/enhanced security features.		FV	FV	40.00

COLLECTOR SERIES

1991 COMMEMORATIVE ISSUE

#CS1, World Bank Group/IMF Annual Meetings

		Issue Price	Mkt.	Value
CS1	**1991 10, 20, 50, 100, 500 BAHT** #87-91 w/ovpt: 1991 World Bank Group/IMF Annual Meetings in English and Thai. Specimen. (Issued in blue hanging folder).	—		600.00

MILITARY - VIETNAM WAR

AUXILIARY MILITARY PAYMENT CERTIFICATE COUPONS

Issued to Thai troops in Vietnam to facilitate their use of United States MPC. These coupons could not be used as currency by themselves.

FIRST SERIES

#M1-M8 issued probably from January to April or May, 1970. Larger shield at ctr. on face and back. Words *Coupon* below shield or at r., *Non Negotiable* at r. Small Thai symbol only at upper l. corner; denomination at 3 corners. Black print on check-type security paper.

		Good	Fine	XF
M1	**5 CENTS** ND (1970). Yellow paper. Seahorse shield design.	100.00	250.00	—
M2	**10 CENTS** ND (1970). Lt. gray paper. Shield w/leaping panther and *RTAVF.* *Non Negotiable* under shield; *Coupon* deleted.	100.00	250.00	—
M3	**25 CENTS** ND (1970). Pink paper. Shield w/*Victory Vietnam. Coupon* at r.	160.00	400.00	—
M4	**50 CENTS** ND (1970). Lt. blue paper. Circle w/shaking hands and *Royal Thai* *Forces Vietnam.*	160.00	400.00	—
M5	**1 DOLLAR** ND (1970). Yellow paper. Inscription *Victory Vietnam. Coupon* at r.	160.00	400.00	—
M6	**5 DOLLARS** ND (1970). Lt. gray paper. Seahorse in shield.	200.00	500.00	—
M7	**10 DOLLARS** ND (1970). Yellow paper. Shield w/leaping panther.	225.00	550.00	—
M8	**20 DOLLARS** ND (1970). Lt. green paper. Circle w/hands shaking.	225.00	550.00	—

SECOND SERIES

#M9-M16 issued April or May, 1970 to possibly Oct. 7, 1970. Shield designs similar to previous issue, but paper colors are different. Larger shield outline around each shield at l. ctr. *Coupon* in margin at lower ctr., denomination at all 4 corners.

		Good	Fine	XF
M9	**5 CENTS** ND (1970). Yellow paper. Shield similar to #M1.	40.00	100.00	—
M10	**10 CENTS** ND (1970). Lt. green paper. Shield similar to #M2.	50.00	125.00	—
M11	**25 CENTS** ND (1970). Yellow paper. Shield similar to #M3.	60.00	150.00	—
M12	**50 CENTS** ND (1970). Lt. gray paper. Shield similar to #M4.	60.00	150.00	—
M13	**1 DOLLAR** ND (1970). Pink paper. Shield similar to #M5.	60.00	150.00	—
M14	**5 DOLLARS** ND (1970). Lt. green paper. Shield similar to #M6.	160.00	400.00	—
M15	**10 DOLLARS** ND (1970). Pale yellow paper. Shield similar to #M7.	160.00	400.00	—

		Good	Fine	XF
M16	**20 DOLLARS** ND (1970). Lt. green paper. Shield similar to #M8.	180.00	450.00	—

THIRD SERIES

#M17-M23 date of issue not known (Oct., 1970?). All notes w/hands shaking in shield at lower r. on face. Different shield designs at upper l. on back. More elaborate design across face and back.

		VG	VF	UNC
M17	**5 CENTS** ND. Lt. gray, maroon and green.	22.50	75.00	300.00

		VG	VF	UNC
M18	**10 CENTS** ND. Lt. yellow and green.	22.50	75.00	300.00

		VG	VF	UNC
M19	**25 CENTS** ND. Green, pink and maroon.	40.00	125.00	350.00

M20 50 CENTS
ND. Yellow, green, blue and red.

	VG	VF	UNC
	40.00	125.00	350.00

M21 1 DOLLAR
ND. Pink, blue and green.
a. Issued note.
r. Remainder w/o serial #.

	VG	VF	UNC
a.	125.00	225.00	—
r.	—	—	300.00

M22 5 DOLLARS
ND. Yellow, green, blue and red.
a. Issued note.
r. Remainder w/o serial #.

	VG	VF	UNC
a.	600.00	950.00	—
r.	—	—	375.00

M23 10 DOLLARS
ND. Green, maroon and dk. red.
a. Issued note.
r. Remainder w/o serial #.

	VG	VF	UNC
a.	125.00	225.00	—
r.	—	—	350.00

TIMOR

Timor, is an island between the Savu and Timor Seas, has an area, including the former colony of Portuguese Timor, of 11,883 sq. mi. (30,775 sq. km.) and a population of 1.5 million. Western Timor is administered as part of Nusa Tenggara Timur (East Nusa Tenggara) province. Capital: Kupang. The eastern half of the island, the former Portuguese colony, forms a single province, Timor Timur (East Timor). Originally the Portuguese colony also included the area around Ocussi-Ambeno and the small island of Atauro (Pulau Kambing) located north of Dili. Capital: Dili. Timor exports sandalwood, coffee, tea, hides, rubber and copra.

Portuguese traders reached Timor about 1520, and moved to the north and east when the Dutch established themselves in Kupang, a sheltered bay at the southwestern tip, in 1613. Treaties effective in 1860 and 1914 established the boundaries between the two colonies. Japan occupied the entire island during World War II. The former Dutch colony in the western part of the island became part of Indonesia in 1950.

At the end of Nov., 1975, the Portuguese Province of Timor attained independence as the People's Democratic Republic of East Timur. In Dec., 1975 or early in 1976 the government of the People's Democratic Republic was seized by a guerilla faction sympathetic to the Indonesian territorial claim to East Timur which ousted the constitutional government and replaced it with the Provisional Government of East Timur. On July 17, 1976, the Provisional Government enacted a law which dissolved the free republic and made East Timur the 24th province of Indonesia.

In 1999 a revolution suceeded, and it is once again an independent country. Note: For later issues see Indonesia.

MONETARY SYSTEM:
1 Escudo = 100 Centavos, 1958-1975

SIGNATURE VARIETIES		
1		
2		
3		
4		
5		
6		
7		
8		

PORTUGUESE ADMINISTRATION

BANCO NACIONAL ULTRAMARINO

DECRETOS - LEI 39221E 44891; 1963-68 ISSUE

#26-30 portr. R. D. Aleixo at r. Bank ship seal at l., crowned arms at ctr. on back. Printer: BWC.

1969 ND PROVISIONAL ISSUE

		VG	VF	UNC
26	**20 ESCUDOS** 24.10.1967. Olive-brown on m/c unpt. Sign. 3-7.			
	a. Issued note.	0.25	1.50	4.50
	s. Specimen.	—	—	—

		VG	VF	UNC
27	**50 ESCUDOS** 24.10.1967. Blue on m/c unpt. Sign. 2; 5; 6; 8.			
	a. Issued note.	0.25	3.00	8.50
	s. Specimen.	—	—	160.00

		VG	VF	UNC
31	**20 ESCUDOS** ND. Green on m/c unpt. Régulo Jose Nunes at l. Bank seal at ctr., local huts on pilings at r. on back. Specimen.	—	—	—
32	**500 ESCUDOS** ND (1969 - old date 22.3.1967). Brown and violet on m/c unpt. Ovpt: *PAGAVEL EM TIMOR* on Mozambique #110, face and back.	150.00	350.00	750.00

		VG	VF	UNC
28	**100 ESCUDOS** 25.4.1963. Brown on m/c unpt. Sign. 1-3; 8.			
	a. Issued note.	0.50	3.50	7.50
	s. Specimen. Punched hole cancelled.	—	—	160.00

		VG	VF	UNC
29	**500 ESCUDOS** 25.4.1963. Dk. brown on m/c unpt. Sign. 1-3; 8; 9.			
	a. Issued note.	3.00	10.00	20.00
	s. Specimen.	—	—	175.00

		VG	VF	UNC
30	**1000 ESCUDOS** 21.3.1968. Green on m/c unpt. Sign. 2-8.			
	a. Issued note.	4.00	17.50	40.00
	s. Specimen.	—	—	185.00

TONGA

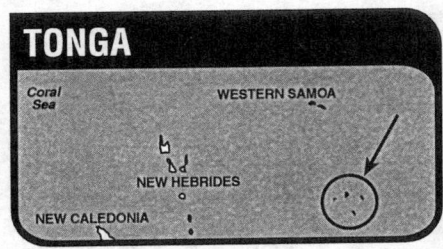

The Kingdom of Tonga (or Friendly Islands), a member of the British Commonwealth, is an archipelago situated in the southern Pacific Ocean south of Western Samoa and east of Fiji comprising 150 islands. Tonga has an area of 270 sq. mi. (748 sq. km.) and a population of 110,000. Capital: Nuku'alofa. Primarily agricultural, the kingdom exports bananas and copra.

Dutch navigators Willem Schouten and Jacob Lemaire were the first Europeans to visit Tonga in 1616. They were followed by the noted Dutch explorer Abel Tasman who visited the Tongatapu group in 1643. No further European contact was made until 1773 when British navigator Capt. James Cook arrived and, impressed by the peaceful deportment of the natives, named the islands the Friendly Islands. Within a few years of Cook's visit, Tonga was embroiled in a civil war that lasted until the great chief Taufa'ahau, who reigned as George Tupou I (1845-93), was converted to Christianity and brought unity and peace to the islands. Tonga became a self-governing protectorate of Great Britain in 1900 and a fully independent state on June 4, 1970. The monarchy is a member of the Commonwealth of Nations. The monarch is Chief of State and Head of Government.

RULERS:
Queen Salote III, 1918-1965
King Taufa'ahau IV, 1967-

MONETARY SYSTEM:
1 Shilling = 12 Pence
1 Pound = 20 Shillings to 1967
1 Pa'anga = 100 Seniti, 1967-

REPLACEMENT NOTES:
#18-24, Z/1 prefix.

GOVERNMENT OF TONGA

1939-42 ISSUE

#9-12 w/denomination spelled out on both sides of arms at ctr. Printer: TDLR.

		VG	VF	UNC
9	**4 SHILLINGS**			
	1941-66. Brown on m/c unpt. *FOUR SHILLINGS* at l. and r.			
	a. 1.12.1941-8.9.1947. 3 sign.	20.00	100.00	400.00
	b. 7.2.1949; 15.2.1951; 20.7.1951; 6.9.1954.	20.00	100.00	350.00
	c. 19.9.1955-30.11.1959.	7.50	25.00	100.00
	d. 24.10.1960-27.9.1966.	7.00	25.00	75.00
	e. 3.11.1966. 2 sign.	5.00	20.00	50.00
10	**10 SHILLINGS**			
	1939-66. Green on m/c unpt. *TEN SHILLINGS* at l. and r.			
	a. 3.5.1940; 17.10.1941-28.11.1944. 3 sign.	35.00	225.00	—
	b. 9.7.1949-1955.	30.00	150.00	400.00
	c. 2.5.1956; 22.7.1957; 10.12.1958; 13.10.1959.	7.50	35.00	250.00
	d. 24.10.1960; 28.11.1962; 29.7.1964; 22.6.1965.	7.00	30.00	100.00
	e. 3.11.1966. 2 sign.	5.00	22.50	65.00

		VG	VF	UNC
11	**1 POUND**			
	1940-66. Red on m/c unpt. *ONE POUND* at l. and r.			
	a. 3.5.1940-7.11.1944. 3 sign.	40.00	250.00	—
	b. 15.6.1951; 11.9.1951; 19.9.1955.	30.00	175.00	450.00
	c. 2.5.1956; 10.12.1958; 30.11.1959; 12.12.1961.	20.00	70.00	300.00
	d. 28.11.1962; 30.10.1964; 2.11.1965; 3.11.1966.	8.00	40.00	110.00
	e. 2.12.1966. 2 sign.	4.00	15.00	70.00
12	**5 POUNDS**			
	1942-66. Dk. blue on m/c unpt. *FIVE POUNDS* at l. and r.			
	a. 11.3.1942-1945. 3 sign.	550.00	1750.00	—
	b. 15.6.1951; 5.7.1955; 11.9.1956; 26.6.1958.	300.00	1250.00	—
	c. 30.11.1959; 2.11.1965.	175.00	500.00	1000.00
	d. 2.12.1966. 2 sign.	15.00	60.00	110.00

PULE' ANGA 'O TONGA

GOVERNMENT OF TONGA

1967 ISSUE

#13-17 arms at lower l., Qn. Salote III at r. Various date and sign. varieties.

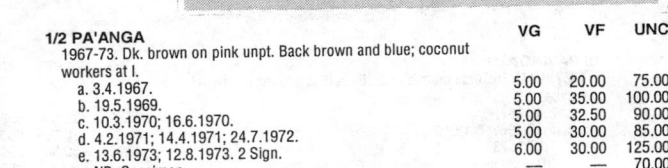

		VG	VF	UNC
13	**1/2 PA'ANGA**			
	1967-73. Dk. brown on pink unpt. Back brown and blue; coconut workers at l.			
	a. 3.4.1967.	5.00	20.00	75.00
	b. 19.5.1969.	5.00	35.00	100.00
	c. 10.3.1970; 16.6.1970.	5.00	32.50	90.00
	d. 4.2.1971; 14.4.1971; 24.7.1972.	5.00	30.00	85.00
	e. 13.6.1973; 12.8.1973. 2 Sign.	6.00	30.00	125.00
	s. ND. Specimen.	—	—	70.00

		VG	VF	UNC
14	**1 PA'ANGA**			
	1967; 1970-71. Olive-green on m/c unpt. Back olive and blue; river scene, palm trees.			
	a. 3.4.1967.	6.00	17.50	90.00
	b. 12.4.1967; 2.10.1967; 8.12.1967.	6.50	40.00	120.00
	c. 10.3.1970; 16.6.1970.	7.00	45.00	130.00
	d. 4.2.1971; 19.10.1971.	9.00	60.00	150.00
	s. ND. Specimen.	—	—	70.00

15   **2 PA'ANGA**

		VG	VF	UNC
1967-73. Red on m/c unpt. Back red and brown; women making Tapa cloth.				
	a. 3.4.1967.	7.00	35.00	140.00
	b. 2.10.1967; 8.12.1967.	7.00	50.00	170.00
	c. 19.5.1969; 10.3.1970; 19.10.1971.	8.00	60.00	160.00
	d. 24.7.1972; 10.11.1972; 2.8.1973.	7.50	60.00	175.00
	e. 12.11.1973. 2 sign.	10.00	80.00	275.00
	s. ND. Specimen.	—	—	70.00

19   **1 PA'ANGA**

		VG	VF	UNC
1974-89. Olive-green on m/c unpt. Back like #14.				
	a. 6.12.1973.	7.50	25.00	75.00
	b. 2 sign. 31.7.1974; 19.6.1975; 21.8.1975; 5.8.1976; 21.1.1981; 18.5.1983.	1.25	3.50	12.50
	c. 3 sign. 5.8.1976-11.6.1980; 31.7.1981-28.10.1982; 27.7.1983-30.6.1989.	FV	2.00	6.00
	s. As a. Specimen.	—	—	—

16   **5 PA'ANGA**

		VG	VF	UNC
1967; 1973. Purple on m/c unpt. Back purple and olive-green; Ha'amonga stone gateway.				
	a. 3.4.1967.	12.00	80.00	250.00
	b. 13.6.1973.	15.00	90.00	325.00
	c. 4.9.1973; 6.12.1973. 2 sign.	17.50	110.00	375.00
	s. ND. Specimen.	—	—	100.00

20   **2 PA'ANGA**

		VG	VF	UNC
1974-89. Red on m/c unpt. Back like #15.				
	a. 2 sign. 2.10.1974; 19.6.1975; 21.8.1975; 21.1.1981.	1.50	3.50	12.50
	b. 3 sign. 12.1.1977-27.8.1980.	2.50	4.00	15.00
	c. 3 sign. 31.7.1981-30.6.1989.	1.50	2.75	9.00
	s. As a. Specimen.	—	—	—

17   **10 PA'ANGA**

		VG	VF	UNC
1967; 1973. Dk. blue on m/c unpt. Back blue and purple; Royal Palace.				
	a. 3.4.1967.	25.00	125.00	550.00
	b. 2.10.1967; 8.12.1967.	25.00	175.00	600.00
	c. 16.7.1973.	30.00	150.00	750.00
	s. ND. Specimen.	—	—	150.00

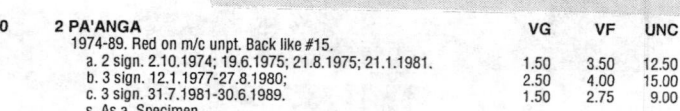

1974; 1985 ISSUE

#18-22 arms at lower l., Portr. Kg. Taufa'ahau at r. Various date and sign. varieties. Replacement notes: Serial # prefix Z/1.

21   **5 PA'ANGA**

		VG	VF	UNC
1974-89. Purple on m/c unpt. Back like #16.				
	a. 2 sign. 2.10.1974; 19.6.1975; 21.1.1981.	FV	6.00	30.00
	b. 3 sign. 21.12.1976-28.11.1980.	FV	5.00	20.00
	c. 3 sign. 27.5.1981-30.6.1989.	FV	3.00	15.00
	s. As a. Specimen.	—	—	—

22   **10 PA'ANGA**

		VG	VF	UNC
1974-89. Dk. blue on m/c unpt. Back like #17.				
	a. 2 sign. 31.7.1974; 3.9.1974; 19.6.1975; 21.1.1981.	FV	8.00	45.00
	b. 3 sign. 12.12.1976-28.11.1980.	FV	6.50	32.50
	c. 3 Sign. 27.5.1981-30.6.1989.	FV	6.00	25.00
	s. As a. Specimen.	—	—	—

18   **1/2 PA'ANGA**

		VG	VF	UNC
1974-83. Dk. brown on pink unpt. Back like #13.				
	a. 2 sign. 2.10.1974; 19.6.1975.	3.00	6.00	12.50
	b. 3 sign. 12.1.1977; 17.5.1977; 10.9.1979.	1.00	3.00	12.50
	c. As b. 28.11.1979; 27.8.1980; 31.7.1981; 17.8.1982; 29.7.1983.	0.75	2.00	8.00
	s. As a. Specimen.	—	—	—

23   **20 PA'ANGA**

		VG	VF	UNC
1985-89. Orange on green and m/c unpt. Kg. in new design at ctr. r. and as wmk., arms at r. Tonga Development Bank on back.				
	a. 4.7.1985.	FV	35.00	130.00
	b. 18.7.1985; 3.10.1985; 8.1.1986; 27.2.1987; 28.9.1987.	FV	27.50	45.00
	c. 20.5.1988; 14.12.1988; 23.1.1989; 30.6.1989.	FV	25.00	40.00

Note: #23a was made in limited quantities in celebration of the king's birthday.

KINGDOM OF TONGA

1988 ISSUE

		VG	VF	UNC
24	**50 PA'ANGA** 1988-89. Brown and green on m/c unpt. Kg. in new design at ctr. r. and as wmk., arms at r. Vava'u Harbour on back.			
	a. 4.7.1988.	FV	60.00	175.00
	b. 14.12.1988; 30.6.1989.	FV	55.00	100.00

Note: #24a was made in limited quantities in celebration of the king's birthday. (5,000 pcs.).

NATIONAL RESERVE BANK OF TONGA

1992 ND ISSUE

#25-29 designs like #19-23. 2 sign. w/Tongan titles beneath.

		VG	VF	UNC
25	**1 PA'ANGA** ND (1992-95). Olive-green on m/c unpt. Like #19.	FV	FV	3.50

		VG	VF	UNC
26	**2 PA'ANGA** ND (1992-95). Red on m/c unpt. Like #20.	FV	FV	6.00

		VG	VF	UNC
27	**5 PA'ANGA** ND (1992-95). Purple on m/c unpt. Like #21.	FV	FV	15.00
28	**10 PA'ANGA** ND (1992-95). Dk. blue on m/c unpt. Like #22.	FV	FV	25.00
29	**20 PA'ANGA** ND (1992-95). Orange and green on m/c unpt. Like #23.	FV	FV	45.00

1989 COMMEMORATIVE ISSUE

#30, Inauguration of National Reserve Bank of Tonga

		VG	VF	UNC
30	**20 PA'ANGA** 1.7.1989. Orange on green and m/c unpt. Similar to #24, but w/commemorative text in circle on wmk. area on face and back.	FV	20.00	60.00

1995 ND ISSUE

#31-34 Kg. Taufa'ahau at upper ctr. r. and as wmk., sign. varieties, arms at r. Printer: TDLR.

		VG	VF	UNC
31	**1 PA'ANGA** ND (1995). Olive-green and green on m/c unpt. River scene, palm trees on back.			
	a. Sign. N-D.	FV	2.00	6.00
	b. Sign. U-F.	FV	FV	3.00

		VG	VF	UNC
32	**2 PA'ANGA** ND (1995). Red and reddish-brown on m/c unpt. Women making Tapa cloth on back.			
	a. Sign. N-D.	FV	3.00	7.50
	b. Sign. U-F.	FV	FV	4.50

			VG	VF	UNC
33	**5 PA'ANGA** ND (1995). Purple and violet on m/c unpt. Ha'amonga stone gateway on back.				
	a. Sign. N-F.		FV	FV	10.00
	b. Sign. U-U.		FV	FV	8.00
34	**10 PA'ANGA** ND (1995). Dk. blue on m/c unpt. Royal Palace on back.				
	a. Sign. N-D.		FV	20.00	35.00
	b. Sign. U-F.		FV	FV	22.50
	c. Sign. U-U.		FV	FV	17.50
35	**20 PA'ANGA** ND. Orange and m/c. Similar to #29.				
	a. Sign. N-D.		FV	40.00	35.00
	b. Sign. N-F.		FV	FV	40.00
	c. Sign. U-U.		FV	FV	30.00
36	**50 PA'ANGA** ND. Brown and green on m/c unpt. Sign. U-U.		FV	FV	85.00

COLLECTOR SERIES

GOVERNMENT OF TONGA

1978 ISSUE

		Issue Price	Mkt.	Value
CS1	**1978 1-10 PA'ANGA** #19b-22b ovpt: *SPECIMEN* and prefix serial # Maltese cross.	14.00		70.00

TRANSNISTRIA

The Transnistria Moldavian Republic was formed in 1990, even before the separation of Moldavia from Russia. It has an area of 11,544 sq. mi. (29,900 sq. km). and a population of 700,000. Capital: Tiraspol.

The area was conquered from the Turks in the last half of the 18th Century, and in 1792 the capital city of Tiraspol was founded. After 1812, the area called Bessarabia (present Moldova and part of the Ukraine) became part of the Russian Empire. During the Russian Revolution, in 1918, the area was taken by Romanian troops, and in 1924 the Moldavian Autonomous SSR was formed on the left bank of the Dniester River. A Romanian occupation area between the Dniester and Bug Rivers called *Transnistria* was established in October 1941. Its center was the port of Odessa. A special issue of notes for use in Transnistria was made by the Romanian government. In 1944 the Russians recaptured Transnistria.

Once the Moldavian SSR declared independence in August 1991. Transnistria did not want to be a part of Moldavia. In 1992, Moldova tried to solve the issue militarily.

Transnistria has a president, parliament, army and police forces, but as yet is lacking international recognition.

MONETARY SYSTEM:
  1 Ruble = 1,000 old Rubles (August 1994)
  1 Ruble = 1,000,000 old Rubles (January 2001)

REPUBLIC

GOVERNMENT

1994 ND PROVISIONAL ISSUES

#1-15 issued 24.1.1994, invalidated on 1.12.1994.

The Bank purchased used Russian notes and placed stickers on them. Most collectors feel that "uncirculated" notes currently available were made after 1994.

		VG	VF	UNC
1	**10 RUBLEI** ND (1994- old date 1961). Green on pink tint adhesive stamp on Russia #233.	0.10	0.50	2.00

		VG	VF	UNC
2	**10 RUBLEI** ND (1994- old date 1991). Green on pink tint adhesive stamp on Russia #240.	0.10	0.50	2.00

		VG	VF	UNC
3	**25 RUBLEI** ND (1994- old date 1961). Red-violet on buff tint adhesive stamp on Russia #234.	0.10	0.50	2.50

NOTICE
Readers with unlisted dates, signature varieties, etc. are invited to submit photocopies of their notes to: Standard Catalog of World Paper Money, 700 East State St. Iola, WI 54990-0001, E-Mail: george.cuhaj@fwpubs.com.

			VG	VF	UNC
4	**50 RUBLEI**		0.20	1.00	7.00
	ND (1994- old date 1991). Red on pale green tint adhesive stamp on Russia #241.				
5	**50 RUBLEI**		0.15	0.75	4.00
	ND (1994- old date 1992). Red on pale green tint adhesive stamp on Russia #247.				

			VG	VF	UNC
6	**100 RUBLEI**		0.25	2.00	7.50
	ND (1994- old date 1991). Black on pale blue tint adhesive stamp on Russia #242.				
7	**100 RUBLEI**		0.15	0.75	4.50
	ND (1994- old date 1991). Black on pale blue tint adhesive stamp on Russia #243.				

			VG	VF	UNC
8	**200 RUBLEI**		0.50	4.00	17.50
	ND (1994- old date 1991). Green on yellow tint adhesive stamp on Russia #244.				
9	**200 RUBLEI**		0.10	0.50	3.50
	ND (1994- old date 1992). Green on yellow tint adhesive stamp on Russia #248.				

			VG	VF	UNC
10	**500 RUBLEI**		0.50	4.00	22.50
	ND (1994- old date 1991). Blue adhesive stamp on Russia #245.				
11	**500 RUBLEI**		0.05	0.25	3.50
	ND (1994- old date 1992). Blue adhesive stamp on Russia #249.				

			VG	VF	UNC
12	**1000 RUBLEI**		0.50	4.00	20.00
	ND (1994- old date 1991). Violet on yellow tint adhesive stamp on Russia #246.				
13	**1000 RUBLEI**		0.05	0.25	3.00
	ND (1994- old date 1992). Violet on yellow tint adhesive stamp on Russia #250.				

			VG	VF	UNC
14	**5000 RUBLEI**		0.15	0.75	3.50
	ND (1994- old date 1992). Dk. brown on pale blue-gray tint adhesive stamp on Russia #252.				

			VG	VF	UNC
14A	**5000 RUBLEI**		0.10	0.50	2.00
	ND (1994 -old date 1961). Adhesive stamp on Russia 5 Rubles #224.				
14B	**5000 RUBLEI**		0.10	0.50	3.50
	ND (1994 -old date 1991). Adhesive stamp on Russia 5 Rubles #239.				
15	**10,000 RUBLEI**		0.20	0.75	4.00
	ND (1994- old date 1992). Purple on yellow tint adhesive stamp on Russia #253.				

БАНКА НИСТРЯНЭ

BANKA NISTRIANA

1993; 1994 КУПОН KUPON ISSUE

#16-18 Alexander Vassilievitch Suvurov at r. Parliament bldg. at ctr. on back. Wmk: Block design.
Note: Postal adhesive stamps have been seen affixed to #16-18 to imitate revalidated notes.

			VG	VF	UNC
16	**1 RUBLE**		FV	0.10	0.30
	1994. Dk. green on m/c unpt.				
17	**5 RUBLEI**		FV	0.10	0.40
	1994. Blue on m/c unpt.				
18	**10 RUBLEI**		FV	0.10	0.50
	1994. Red-violet on m/c unpt.				

#19-24 equestrian statue of A. V. Suvorov at r. Parliament bldg. on back. Wmk: Block design.

			VG	VF	UNC
19	**50 RUBLEI**		FV	0.15	1.00
	1993 (1994). Green on m/c unpt.				
20	**100 RUBLEI**		FV	0.20	1.00
	1993 (1994). Dk. brown on m/c unpt.				
21	**200 RUBLEI**		FV	0.25	2.00
	1993 (1994). Red-violet on m/c unpt.				
22	**500 RUBLEI**		FV	0.25	2.50
	1993 (1994). Blue on m/c unpt.				
23	**1000 RUBLEI**		FV	0.50	2.00
	1993 (1994). Purple and red-violet on m/c unpt.				
24	**5000 RUBLEI**		FV	0.75	3.50
	1993 (1995). Black on deep olive-green and m/c unpt.				

#25 Not assigned.

1994 (1995) ISSUE

Currency Reform
1 Ruble = 1000 "Old" Rublei

26	1000 RUBLEI = 100,000 RUBLEI	VG	VF	UNC
	1994 (1995). Blue-violet and purple. V. Suvorov at r. Parliament bldg. on back. Printed in Germany.	FV	0.75	3.50

1995; ND (1996) PROVISIONAL ISSUE

31	100,000 RUBLEI ON 10 RUBLEI	VG	VF	UNC
	ND (1996 - old date 1994). Red-violet on m/c unpt. Ovpt. on face and back of #18.	FV	0.25	2.00

1997; 1999 ISSUE

32	10,000 RUBLES	VG	VF	UNC
	1999. M/c.	FV	1.00	3.00

27	50,000 RUBLEI ON 5 RUBLEI	VG	VF	UNC
	ND (1996 - old date 1994). Blue on m/c unpt. Hologram w/50,000 at upper l. on #17.	FV	0.75	2.00

28	50,000 RUBLEI = 500,000 RUBLEI	VG	VF	UNC
	1995 (1996). Brown-violet and brown on m/c unpt. Bogdan Khmelnitsky at r. Drama and comedy theatre on back. Sign. Vyacheslav Zagryatsky. Printed in Germany.	FV	0.75	5.00

33	500,000 RUBLEI	VG	VF	UNC
	1997. Purple and violet on m/c unpt. Like #24.	FV	1.00	3.00

2000 ISSUE

#34-37, Gen. Alexander Vassilievitch Suvorov at l.

1996 ND PROVISIONAL ISSUE

#29-31, Gen. Alexander Vassilievitch Suvorov at l.

29	10,000 RUBLEI ON 1 RUBLE	VG	VF	UNC
	ND (1996 - old date 1994). Dk. green on m/c unpt. Ovpt. on face and back of #16.	FV	0.50	1.25

34	1 RUBLE	VG	VF	UNC
	2000. Orange-brown on m/c unpt. Gen. Alexander V. Suvorov at l. Kitskansky Bridgehead Memorial complex on back.			
	a. Issued note.	FV	0.50	1.00
	s. Specimen.			

29A	10,000 RUBLEI ON 1 RUBLE	VG	VF	UNC
	1998. Green and tan on m/c unpt. Ovpt. only on face of #16.	FV	FV	1.00

35	5 RUBLEI	VG	VF	UNC
	2000. Blue on m/c unpt. Gen. Alexander V. Suvorov at l. Kvint destillery administrative bldg. on back.			
	a. Issued note.	FV	1.00	2.50
	s. Specimen. OBRAZH-.	—		

30	50,000 RUBLEI ON 5 RUBLEI	VG	VF	UNC
	ND (1996 - old date 1994). Blue on m/c unpt. Ovpt. on face and back of #17.	FV	0.25	1.50

36	10 RUBLEI	VG	VF	UNC
	2000. Brown on m/c unpt. Novo Nyametsky Monastery in Kitzkansk on back.			
	a. Issued note.	FV	FV	4.50
	s. Specimen.	—		

37	25 RUBLEI	VG	VF	UNC
	2000. Rose on m/c unpt. Bendery fortress and a Russian soldiers' Memorial on back.			
	a. Issued note.	FV	FV	9.00
	s. Specimen.	—		

38	50 RUBLEI	VG	VF	UNC
	2000. Deep green on m/c unpt. Taras Shevchenko (poet) at l. Transnistria Parliament bldg. on back.			
	a. Issued note.	FV	FV	15.00
	s. Specimen.	—		

39	100 RUBLEI	VG	VF	UNC
	2000. Purple on m/c unpt. Prince Dimitrie Cantemir at l. The Christmas Church on back.			
	a. Issued note.	FV	FV	30.00
	s. Specimen.	—		

40	200 RUBLEI	VG	VF	UNC
	2004. Brown. Bust at l. 1757 Battle scene on back.	FV	FV	45.00

41	500 RUBLEI	VG	VF	UNC
	2004. Green. Catherine II at l. Fort on back.	FV	FV	100.00

TRINIDAD & TOBAGO

The Republic of Trinidad and Tobago, a member of the British Commonwealth situated 7 miles (11 km.) off the coast of Venezuela, has an area of 1,981 sq. mi. (5,130 sq. km.) and a population of 1.34 million. Capital: Port-of-Spain. The Island of Trinidad contains the world's largest natural asphalt bog. Birds of Paradise live on little Tobago, the only place outside of their native New Guinea where they can be found in a wild state. Petroleum and petroleum products are the mainstay of the economy. Petroleum products, crude oil and sugar are exported.

Trinidad and Tobago were discovered by Columbus in 1498. Trinidad remained under Spanish rule from the time of its settlement in 1592 until its capture by the British in 1797. It was ceded to the British in 1802. Tobago was occupied at various times by the French, Dutch and British before being ceded to Britain in 1814. Trinidad and Tobago were merged into a single colony in 1888. The colony was part of the Federation of the West Indies until Aug. 31, 1962, when it became an independent member of the Commonwealth of Nations. A new constitution establishing a republican form of government was adopted on Aug. 1, 1976. The president is Chief of State. The prime minister is Head of Government.

Notes of the British Caribbean Territories circulated between 1950-1964.

RULERS:
British to 1976

MONETARY SYSTEM:
1 Dollar = 100 Cents
5 Dollars = 1 Pound 10 Pence

SIGNATURE VARIETIES			
1	J.F. Pierce	2	A.N. McLeod
3	J.E.Bruce	4	Linn OHB
5	W. Demas	6	N. Hareward
7	M. Duberan	8	

REPUBLIC

CENTRAL BANK OF TRINIDAD AND TOBAGO

1964 CENTRAL BANK ACT

#26-29 arms at l., portr. Qn. Elizabeth II at ctr. Central Bank bldg. at ctr. r. on back. Wmk: Bird of Paradise.

26	1 DOLLAR	VG	VF	UNC
	L.1964. Red on m/c unpt. Oil rig in water at upper r. on back.			
	a. Sign. 1.	1.50	5.00	30.00
	b. Sign. 2. Serial # single letter or fractional letters prefix.	2.00	5.50	45.00
	c. Sign. 3.	1.00	4.00	25.00
	s. As a, c. Specimen.	—	—	125.00

27	5 DOLLARS	VG	VF	UNC
	L.1964. Green on m/c unpt. Crane loading sugar cane at upper r. on back.			
	a. Sign. 1.	7.50	30.00	250.00
	b. Sign. 2.	5.00	20.00	200.00
	c. Sign. 3.	2.00	15.00	75.00
	s. As a, c. Specimen.	—	—	200.00

28	10 DOLLARS	VG	VF	UNC
	L.1964. Dk. brown on m/c unpt. Factory at upper r. on back.			
	a. Sign. 1.	10.00	75.00	1000.00
	b. Sign. 2.	10.00	50.00	800.00
	c. Sign. 3.	10.00	35.00	350.00
	s. As a, c. Specimen.	—	—	350.00

29	20 DOLLARS	VG	VF	UNC
	L.1964. Purple on m/c unpt. Cocoa pods at upper r. on back.			
	a. Sign. 1.	15.00	75.00	900.00
	b. Sign. 2.	12.50	60.00	750.00
	c. Sign. 3.	10.00	37.50	325.00
	s. As a, c. Specimen.	—	—	400.00

1977 ND Issue

#30-35 authorization date 1964. Arms at ctr. Back like #26-29. Wmk: Bird of Paradise. Replacement notes: Serial # prefix *XX*.

30	1 DOLLAR	VG	VF	UNC
	L.1964 (1977). Red on m/c unpt. Two scarlet ibis at l. Back like #26.			
	a. Sign. 3.	FV	0.50	2.50
	b. Sign. 4.	FV	1.00	4.00
	s. As a. Specimen.	—	—	150.00

31	5 DOLLARS	VG	VF	UNC
	L.1964 (1977). Dk. green on m/c unpt. Branches and leaves at l. Back like #27.			
	a. Sign. 3.	FV	1.00	6.00
	b. Sign. 4.	FV	3.00	17.50
	s. As a. Specimen.			

32	10 DOLLARS	VG	VF	UNC
	L.1964 (1977). Dk. brown on m/c unpt. Piping guan on branch at l. Sign. 3. Back like #28.			
	a. Issued note.	FV	2.50	12.50
	s. Specimen.			

33	20 DOLLARS	VG	VF	UNC
	L.1964 (1977). Purple on m/c unpt. Flowers at l. Sign. 3. Back like #29.			
	a. Issued note.	FV	5.00	25.00
	s. Specimen, punch hole cancelled.			

34	50 DOLLARS	VG	VF	UNC
	L.1964 (1977). Dk. brown on m/c unpt. Long-billed starthroat at l. Net fishing at upper r. on back. Sign. 3.			
	a. 1963 (error date in authorization).	20.00	45.00	250.00
	b. 1964 (corrected authorization date).	30.00	85.00	500.00
	s. As b. Specimen.			

35	100 DOLLARS	VG	VF	UNC
	L.1964 (1977). Deep blue on m/c unpt. Branch w/leaves and berries at l. Huts and palm trees at upper r. on back.			
	a. Sign. 3.	FV	30.00	125.00
	b. Sign. 4.	FV	35.00	150.00
	s. As a. Specimen.			

Central Bank Act Chap. 79.02; 1985 ND Issue

#36-40 arms at ctr. Twin towered modern bank bldg. at ctr. on back. Wmk: Bird of Paradise. Replacement notes: Serial # prefix *XX*.

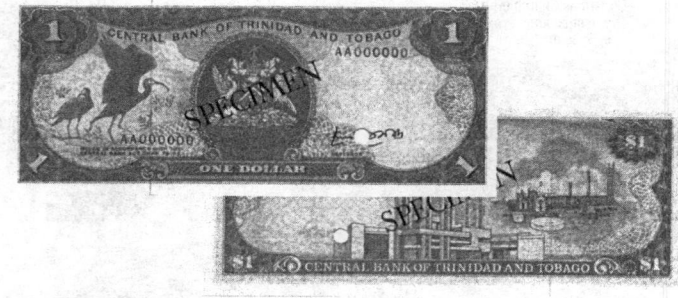

36	1 DOLLAR	VG	VF	UNC
	ND (1985). Red-orange and purple on m/c unpt. Scarlet Ibis at l. Oil refinery at r. on back.			
	a. Sign. 4.	FV	FV	1.50
	b. Sign. 5.	FV	FV	1.50
	c. Sign. 6.	FV	FV	1.00
	d. Sign. 7.	FV	FV	1.00
	s. Specimen.	—	—	150.00

37	5 DOLLARS	VG	VF	UNC
	ND (1985). Dk. green and blue on m/c unpt. Blue crowned motmot at l. Woman at roadside produce stand at r. on back.			
37	5 DOLLARS			
	a. Sign. 4.	FV	FV	5.00
	b. Sign. 5.	FV	FV	3.00
	c. Sign. 6.	FV	FV	2.00
	d. Sign. 7.	FV	FV	2.00
	s. Specimen.	—	—	150.00

38	10 DOLLARS	VG	VF	UNC
	ND (1985). Dk. green and brown on m/c unpt. Piping guan on branch at l. Cargo ship dockside at r. on back.			
	a. Sign. 4.	FV	FV	7.50
	b. Sign. 5.	FV	FV	6.00
	c. Sign. 6.	FV	FV	4.00
	d. Sign. 7.	FV	FV	4.00
	s. Specimen.	—	—	175.00

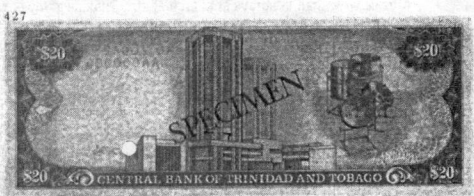

39	20 DOLLARS	VG	VF	UNC
	ND (1985). Purple and green on m/c unpt. White-tailed Saberwing in flowers at l. Steel drums at r. on back.			
	a. Sign. 4.	FV	FV	12.50
	b. Sign. 5.	FV	FV	7.50
	c. Sign. 6.	FV	FV	6.00
	s. Specimen.	—	—	175.00

40	100 DOLLARS	VG	VF	UNC
	ND (1985). Deep blue on m/c unpt. Greater Bird of Paradise at l. Oil rig at r. on back.			
	a. Sign. 4.	FV	FV	50.00
	b. Sign. 5.	FV	FV	37.50
	c. Sign. 6.	FV	FV	30.00
	d. Sign. 7.	FV	FV	30.00
	s. Specimen.	—	—	225.00

2002 ISSUE

#41-45 arms at ctr. Twin towered modern bank bldg. at ctr. on back. Wmk: Bird of Paradise. Segmented security thread.

41	1 DOLLAR	VG	VF	UNC
	2002. Red on m/c unpt. Scarlet Ibis at l. Oil refinery at r. on back.	FV	FV	1.00

42	5 DOLLARS	VG	VF	UNC
	2002. Green and blue on m/c unpt. Blue crowned motmot at l. Woman at roadside produce stand at r. on back.	FV	FV	2.00

43	10 DOLLARS	VG	VF	UNC
	2002. Dk. green on m/c unpt. Piping guan on branch at l. Cargo ship dockside at r. on back.	FV	FV	4.00

44	20 DOLLARS	VG	VF	UNC
	2002. Purple on m/c unpt. White-tailed Saberwing in flowers at l. Steel drums at r. on back.	FV	FV	6.00

45	100 DOLLARS	VG	VF	UNC
	2002. Deep blue on m/c unpt. Greater Bird of Paradise at l. Oil rig at r. on back.	FV	FV	30.00

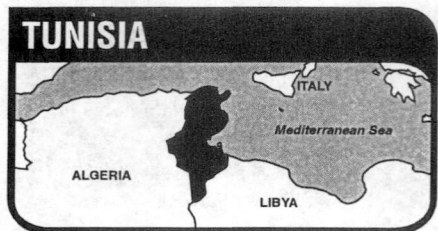

The Republic of Tunisia, located on the northern coast of Africa between Algeria and Libya, has an area of 63,170 sq. mi. (163,610 sq. km.) and a population of 9.84 million. Capital: Tunis. Agriculture is the backbone of the economy. Crude oil, phosphates, olive oil, and wine are exported.

Tunisia, settled by the Phoenicians in the 12th century BC, was the center of the seafaring Carthaginian empire. After the total destruction of Carthage, Tunisia became part of Rome's African province. It remained a part of of the Roman Empire (except for the 439-533 interval Vandal conquest) until taken by the Arabs, 648, who administered it until the Turkish invasion of 1570. Under Turkish control, the public revenue was heavily dependent upon the piracy of Mediterranean shipping, an endeavor that wasn't abandoned until 1819 when a coalition of powers threatened appropriate reprisal. Deprived of its major source of income, Tunisia underwent a financial regression that ended in bankruptcy, enabling France to establish a protectorate over the country in 1881. National agitation and guerrilla fighting forced France to grant Tunisia internal autonomy in 1955 and to recognize Tunisian independence on March 20, 1956. Tunisia abolished the monarchy and established a republic on July 25, 1957.

In 1975 the constitution was changed to make Bourguiba president for life. A two party system was started in 1981, but in the 1986 elections, all but the *Frout Nationals* boycotted. Bourguiba was ousted in 1987. His successor, Zine el Abidine Ben Ali introduced some democratic reforms, but a struggle with Islamic Fundamentalists lead to sporadic violence for some time.

RULERS:
French, 1881-1956

MONETARY SYSTEM:
1 Franc = 100 Centimes to 1960
1 Dinar = 1000 Millimes, 1960-

REPLACEMENT NOTES:
#61-89 with second prefix letter *R* added after regular letter.

REPUBLIC

BANQUE CENTRALE DE TUNISIE

1962 ISSUE

61	5 DINARS	VG	VF	UNC
	20.3.1962. Blue on m/c unpt. Habib Bourguiba at r., bridge at l. Archways on back. Wmk: Arms.	6.00	50.00	300.00

1965-69 ISSUE

62	1/2 DINAR	VG	VF	UNC
	1.6.1965. Blue on m/c unpt. Habib Bourguiba at l. and as wmk., mosque at r. Mosaic from Monastir on back.			
	a. Issued note.	3.00	25.00	135.00
	s. Specimen.	—	—	100.00

#63-65 Habib Bourguiba at r. and as wmk.

63	1 DINAR	VG	VF	UNC
	1.6.1965. Blue on purple and m/c unpt. Factory at l. Mosaic on back.			
	a. Issued note.	3.00	25.00	100.00
	s. Specimen.	—	—	100.00

64	5 DINARS	VG	VF	UNC
	1.6.1965. Lilac-brown and green on m/c unpt. Sadiki College at l. Mosaic w/woman in sprays at l., arch at ctr., Sunface at lower r. on back.			
	a. Issued note.	7.50	35.00	150.00
	s. Specimen.	—	—	100.00

65	10 DINARS	VG	VF	UNC
	1.6.1969. M/c. Refinery at l. Palm trees in field on back.			
	a. Issued note.	7.50	25.00	100.00
	s. Specimen.	—	—	100.00

1972 ISSUE

#66-68 Habib Bourguiba at r. and as wmk. Printer: (T)DLR.

66	1/2 DINAR	VG	VF	UNC
	3.8.1972. Brown on m/c unpt. City w/river at l. View of Tunis on back.			
	a. Issued note.	1.00	2.50	12.50
	s. Specimen.	—	—	40.00

67 1 DINAR
3.8.1972. Purple on m/c unpt. Old fort at l. Minaret at l., girl at ctr.
on back.

	VG	VF	UNC
a. Issued note.	1.50	5.00	22.50
s. Specimen.	—	—	40.00

68 5 DINARS
3.8.1972. Green on m/c unpt. Modern bldg. at l. Amphitheater at El-
Djem on back.

	VG	VF	UNC
a. Issued note.	5.00	15.00	50.00
s. Specimen.	—	—	40.00

1973 ISSUE

#69-72 H. Bourguiba at l. ctr. and as wmk.

69 1/2 DINAR

	VG	VF	UNC
15.10.1973. Green on m/c unpt. Man w/camel and trees at l. Landscape w/sheep and assorted produce on back.	1.00	2.50	7.50

70 1 DINAR

	VG	VF	UNC
15.10.1973. Blue and green on m/c unpt. Bldg. at r. Industrial scenes on back.	1.00	3.00	10.00

71 5 DINARS

	VG	VF	UNC
15.10.1973. Dk. brown on m/c unpt. City view at l. Montage of old and new on back.	2.00	7.50	35.00

72 10 DINARS

	VG	VF	UNC
15.10.1973. Purple and brown on m/c unpt. Refinery in background at ctr. Montage w/students, column, train and drummers on back.	3.50	15.00	60.00

#73 *not assigned.*

1980 ISSUE

#74, 75 and 77 Habib Bourguiba at r. and as wmk.

74 1 DINAR

	VG	VF	UNC
15.10.1980. Red-brown and brown on red and m/c unpt. Amphitheater at ctr. Village of Korbous in the "Cap Bon" on back.	0.50	2.00	7.50

75 5 DINARS

	VG	VF	UNC
15.10.1980. Brown, red-brown and olive-green on m/c unpt. Bldgs. at ctr. Ruins and hills at l. on back.	1.50	5.00	30.00

76 10 DINARS

	VG	VF	UNC
15.10.1980. Blue-green on bistre and m/c unpt. Habib Bourguiba at l., bldg. at ctr. Reservoir at ctr. on back.	3.00	15.00	85.00

77 **20 DINARS**
15.10.1980. Dk. blue-green and brown on m/c unpt. Amphitheater at ctr. Harbor of Sousse on back.

	VG	VF	UNC
	FV	20.00	75.00

1983 ISSUE

#79-81 Habib Bourguiba on face and as wmk.

79 **5 DINARS**
3.11.1983. Red-brown and purple on lilac unpt. Habib Bourguiba at l., desert scene at bottom ctr. Hydroelectric dam at ctr. r. on back.

	VG	VF	UNC
	FV	5.00	15.00

80 **10 DINARS**
3.11.1983. Blue and lilac on m/c unpt. Workers at lower l. ctr., Habib Bourguiba at ctr., offshore oil rig at r. Modern bldg. at ctr., old city gateways at r. on back.

	VG	VF	UNC
	FV	10.00	35.00

81 **20 DINARS**
3.11.1983. Lt. blue and dk. blue on green and m/c unpt. Habib Bourguiba at l., bldg. at bottom ctr. Bldg. at lower l., aerial view of harbor at r. on back.

	VG	VF	UNC
	FV	20.00	60.00

1986 ISSUE

#82 and 83 Held in reserve.

84 **10 DINARS**
20.3.1986. Yellow-brown on green unpt. Habib Bourguiba at l. ctr. and as wmk., agricultural scene at bottom ctr. Offshore oil rig at l. ctr. on back.

	VG	VF	UNC
	FV	10.00	30.00

#85 Held in reserve.

1992-97 ISSUE

#86-89 replacement notes: *R* in denomination of lower r. serial #.

86 **5 DINARS**
7.11.1993. Green, olive-brown and black. Head of Hannibal at l. ctr. and as wmk., Carthage harbor fortress at r. "Nov. 7, 1987" collage at l. ctr. on back.

	VG	VF	UNC
	FV	FV	12.50

Note: #86 issued on the 6th anniversary of the overthrow of the Bourguiba Government.

87 **10 DINARS**
7.11.1994. Purple, blue-green and red-brown on m/c unpt. ibn Khaldoun at ctr. and as wmk. Open book of "7 Novembre 1987" at l. ctr. on back.

	VG	VF	UNC
	FV	FV	20.00

Note: #87 issued on the 7th anniversary of the overthrow of the Bourguiba Government.

87A **10 DINARS**
7.11.1994 (2005). Brown on m/c unpt. ibn Khaldoun at ctr. and as wmk. Open book of '7 Novembre 1987' at l. ctr. on back.

	VG	VF	UNC
	FV	FV	15.00

88   20 DINARS
  7.11.1992. Deep purple, blue-black and red-brown on m/c unpt. K.
  Et-tounsi on horseback at l. ctr., his head as wmk., bldgs. in
  background. Montage of city view; a "7" w/1987 date over flag on
  stylized dove at ctr. on back.

	VG	VF	UNC
	FV	FV	30.00

Note: #88 issued on the 5th anniversary of the overthrow of the Bourguiba Government.

89   30 DINARS
  7.11.1997. Green and yellow on m/c unpt. Aboul El Kacem Chebbi
  at r. and as wmk. Schoolgirls, sheep and weaver on back.

	VG	VF	UNC
	FV	FV	45.00

TURKEY

The Republic of Turkey, a parliamentary democracy of the Near East located partially in Europe and partially in Asia between the Black and the Mediterranean seas, has an area of 301,382 sq. mi. (780,580 sq. km.) and a population of 65.73 million. Capital: Ankara. Turkey exports cotton, hazelnuts and tobacco, and enjoys a virtual monopoly in meerschaum.

The Ottoman Turks, a tribe from Central Asia, first appeared in the early 13th century, and by the 17th century had established the Ottoman Empire which stretched from the Persian Gulf to the southern frontier of Poland, and from the Caspian Sea to the Algerian plateau. The defeat of the Turkish navy by the Holy League in 1571, and of the Turkish forces besieging Vienna in 1683, began the steady decline of the Ottoman Empire which, accelerated by the rise of nationalism, contracted its European border, and by the end of World War I deprived it of its Arab lands. The present Turkish boundaries were largely fixed by the Treaty of Lausanne in 1923. The sultanate and caliphate, the political and spiritual ruling institutions of the old empire, were separated and the sultanate abolished in 1922 by Mustafa Kemal Atatürk. On Oct. 29, 1923, Turkey formally became a republic and Atatürk was selected as the first president.

MONETARY SYSTEM:
  1 Lira (Livre, Pound) = 100 Piastres

REPUBLIC

TÜRKIYE CÜMHURIYET MERKEZ BANKASI

CENTRAL BANK OF TURKEY

LAW 11 HAZIRAN 1930; 1961-65 ND ISSUE

#173-178 portr. Pres. K. Atatürk at r. and as wmk. Printer: DBM-A (w/o imprint).

173   5 LIRA
  L.1930 (25.10.1961). Blue w/orange, blue and m/c guilloche. Back
  blue; 3 women w/baskets of hazelnuts at ctr.

	VG	VF	UNC
a. Issue note.	3.00	10.00	60.00
s. Specimen.	—	—	200.00

174   5 LIRA
  L.1930 (4.1.1965). Blue-green. Back blue-gray, like #173.

	VG	VF	UNC
a. Issued note.	2.00	6.00	45.00
s. Specimen.	—	—	200.00

175	50 LIRA	VG	VF	UNC
	L.1930 (1.6.1964). Brown on m/c unpt. 3 sign. Soldier holding rifle figure from the Victory statue at Ulus Square in Ankara at ctr. on back.			
	a. Issued note.	5.00	20.00	75.00
	s. Specimen.	—	—	250.00

176	100 LIRA	VG	VF	UNC
	L.1930 (15.3.1962). Olive on orange and m/c guilloche. Youth Park w/bridge in Ankara on back.			
	a. Issued note.	12.50	50.00	125.00
	s. Specimen.	—	—	350.00

177	100 LIRA	VG	VF	UNC
	L.1930 (1.10.1964). Like #176, but guilloche blue, lilac and m/c. Different sign.			
	a. Issued note.	8.50	35.00	100.00
	s. Specimen.	—	—	350.00

178	500 LIRA	VG	VF	UNC
	L.1930 (1.12.1962). Purple and brown on m/c unpt. Sultan Ahmet Mosque, the Obelisc and the Hippodrome in Istanbul on back.			
	a. Issued note.	50.00	150.00	400.00
	s. Specimen.	—	—	500.00

Law 11 Haziran 1930; 1966-69 ND Issue

#179-183 Pres. Atatürk at r. and as wmk. 3 sign. Printer: DBM-A (w/o imprint).

179	5 LIRA	VG	VF	UNC
	L.1930 (8.1.1968). Grayish purple on m/c unpt. Manavgat waterfall in Antalya at l. ctr. on back.	0.25	1.00	4.00

180	10 LIRA	VG	VF	UNC
	L.1930 (4.7.1966). Green on m/c unpt. Maiden's Tower on the Bosphorus in Istanbul at ctr. on back.	0.50	2.00	7.00

181	20 LIRA	VG	VF	UNC
	L.1930 (15.6.1966). Orange-brown on m/c unpt. Back dull brown on pale green unpt., mausoleum of of Atatürk in Ankara at ctr. on back.			
	a. 7-digit serial #.	4.00	7.50	25.00
	b. 8-digit serial #.	1.50	2.50	15.00

182	100 LIRA	VG	VF	UNC
	L.1930 (17.3.1969). Like #176 but modified guilloche in pinkish red, blue and m/c unpt. Different sign.	10.00	30.00	90.00

183	500 LIRA	VG	VF	UNC
	L.1930 (3.6.1968). Purple, brown and m/c. Like #178.	25.00	75.00	225.00

#184 Not assigned.

Law Ocak 14 (Jan. 26), 1970; 1971-82 ND Issues

#185-191 Pres. Atatürk at r. and as wmk. 2 sign.
#185, 188, 190 and 191 replacement notes: Serial # prefix Z91-Z95.

185	5 LIRA	VG	VF	UNC
	L.1970 (1976). Like #179.	0.15	0.50	2.00

186	10 LIRA	VG	VF	UNC
	L.1970 (1975). Like #180.	0.25	1.00	4.00

187	20 LIRA	VG	VF	UNC
	L.1970 (1974). Like #181.			
	a. Black sign. 2 varieties.	0.25	1.00	4.50
	b. Brown sign.	0.25	0.50	1.00

187A 50 LIRA
L.1970 (2.8.1971). Brown on m/c unpt. Like #175 except for different inscription at ctr., Pres. Atatürk at r. Soldier figure from Statue of Victory at Ulus Square in Ankara on back. 2 sign. Series O-Y. Printer: Devlet Banknot Matbaasi (w/o imp

	VG	VF	UNC
a. Issued note.	1.50	4.00	15.00
s. Specimen.	—	—	—

188 50 LIRA
L.1970 (1976). Dk. brown on m/c unpt. New portr. at r. Marble Fountain in Topkapi Palace in Istanbul on back. 2 sign. varieties.

	VG	VF	UNC
	0.25	0.50	1.75

189 100 LIRA
L.1970 (15.5.1972). Blue-green on m/c unpt. Face similar to #188. Back brown; Mt. Ararat at ctr. 3 sign. varieties.

	VG	VF	UNC
a. Issued note.	0.25	1.00	2.00
s. Specimen.	—	—	—

190 500 LIRA
L.1970 (1.9.1971). Dk. blue and dk. green on m/c unpt. Main Gate of Istanbul University on back. 2 sign. varieties.

	VG	VF	UNC
	2.00	7.50	15.00

191 1000 LIRA
L.1970. Deep purple and brown-violet on m/c unpt. Bosphorus River w/boat and suspension bridge on back. 3 sign. varieties.

	VG	VF	UNC
	1.00	3.00	10.00

LAW OCAK 14 (JAN. 26), 1970; 1984-97 ND ISSUES

#192-204 Pres. Atatürk at r. and as wmk.
Some sign. varieties.

192 10 LIRA
L.1970 (1979). Dull gray-green on m/c unpt. Young boy and girl in medallion in unpt. at ctr. Children presenting flowers to Atatürk on back.

	VG	VF	UNC
	0.10	0.20	0.50

193 10 LIRA
L.1970 (1982). Black on m/c unpt. Like #192.

	VG	VF	UNC
	0.10	0.20	0.50

194 100 LIRA
L.1970 (1984). Violet and brown on m/c unpt. Fort of Ankara, Mehmet Akif Ersoy, his home and document on back.

	VG	VF	UNC
a. Wmk.: Head sm., bust facing r., dotted security thread.	0.15	0.30	1.25
b. Wmk.: Head lg., bust facing 3/4 r.	0.10	0.25	1.00

195 500 LIRA
L.1970 (1983). Blue on m/c unpt. Clock Tower in Izmir at l. ctr. on back. Wmk. varieties. 2 sign. varieties.

	VG	VF	UNC
	0.25	0.50	1.50

196 1000 LIRA
L.1970 (1986). Purple and blue on m/c unpt. One dot for blind at lower l. Istanbul coastline at l., Fathi Sultan Mehmet at ctr. r. on back. 2 sign. varieties.

	VG	VF	UNC
	0.25	0.75	1.75

196A 5000 LIRA
L.1970 (1981). Dk. brown and olive-green on m/c unpt. Mevlana Museum in Konya and figure of Mevlana at r., on back.

	VG	VF	UNC
	2.50	7.50	25.00

197 5000 LIRA
L.1970 (1985). Dk. brown, red-brown and blue on m/c unpt. Seated
Mevlana at l. ctr., Mevlana Museum at ctr. on back. 2 sign. varieties.

	VG	VF	UNC
	0.75	2.50	7.50

198 5000 LIRA
L.1970 (1990). Deep brown and deep green on m/c unpt. Afsin-
Elbistan thermal power plant at l. ctr. on back.

	VG	VF	UNC
	0.25	1.25	4.00

199 10,000 LIRA
L.1970 (1982). Purple and deep green on m/c unpt. 3 dots for blind
at lower l. Back darker green and m/c; Selimiye Mosque in Edirne,
Mimar Sinan (architect) at ctr.

	VG	VF	UNC
	FV	1.75	5.00

200 10,000 LIRA
L.1970 (1989). Like #199 but back pale green.

	VG	VF	UNC
	FV	0.50	2.25

201 20,000 LIRA
L.1970 (1988). Red-brown and purple on m/c unpt. New Central
Bank bldg. in Ankara at l. ctr. on back.

	VG	VF	UNC
	FV	FV	7.00

202 20,000 LIRA
L.1970 (1995). Like #201 but w/lighter unpt. at ctr. Red. sign.
Lithographed back in lighter shade. Series G-.

	VG	VF	UNC
	FV	FV	2.75

203 50,000 LIRA
L.1970 (1989). Blue-green and dk. green on m/c unpt. National
Parliament House in Ankara at l. ctr. on back.

	VG	VF	UNC
a. Issued note.	FV	FV	7.50
b. Issued note. Serial # prefix H01-H03.	20.00	50.00	300.00

204 50,000 LIRA
L.1970 (1995). Like #203 but w/value in gray on back. Series K-.

	VG	VF	UNC
	FV	FV	2.50

#205-211 Pres. Atatürk facing at ctr. r. and as wmk. Sign. varieties.

205 100,000 LIRA
L.1970 (1991). Reddish brown, dk. brown and dk. green on m/c
unpt. Equestrian statue of Atatürk at lower l. ctr. Children
presenting flowers to Atatürk at l. ctr. on back.

	VG	VF	UNC
	FV	FV	6.00

206 100,000 LIRA
L.1970 (1997). M/c. Like #205 but w/o security device at upper r.
Back lithographed; lighter brown color.

	VG	VF	UNC
	FV	FV	2.00

207 250,000 LIRA
L.1970 (1992). Blue-gray, dk. green and violet on m/c unpt.
Triangular security device at upper r. Kizilkale Fortress at Alunya at
ctr. on back.

	VG	VF	UNC
	FV	FV	5.00

208 500,000 LIRA
L.1970 (1993). Purple, blue-black and violet on m/c unpt. Square
security device at upper r. Aerial view of Canakkale Martyrs
Monument on back.

	VG	VF	UNC
	FV	FV	7.50

209 1,000,000 LIRA
L.1970 (1995). Claret red and blue-gray on m/c unpt. Atatürk dam
in Sanliurfa on back.

	VG	VF	UNC
	FV	FV	12.50

210 **5,000,000 LIRA** VG VF UNC
L.1970 Ocak (January) 1997 (at bottom left). Dk. brown and red-brown on m/c unpt. Gold oval seal w/AH1329 date at r. Anitkabir bldg. complex (mausoleum of Ataturk) in Ankara at l. ctr. on back.   FV FV 17.50

LAW OCAK 14 (JAN. 26), 1970; 1998-2002 ND ISSUE

211 **250,000 LIRA** VG VF UNC
L.1970 (1998). Blue-gray and violet on m/c unpt. Like #207 but triangular security device at upper r. printed in solid ink. Back blue litho.   FV FV 2.00

212 **500,000 LIRA** VG VF UNC
L.1970 (1998). Purple, blue-black and violet on m/c unpt. Like #208 but w/o square security device at upper r. Black pale purple. Litho.   FV FV 3.50

213 **1,000,000 LIRA** VG VF UNC
L.1970 (2002). Face same as #209. Back pale color, Litho. Name of dame changed to Sanliurfa-Adiyaman.   FV FV 6.00

214 **10,000,000 LIRA** VG VF UNC
L.1970 (1999). Red and purple on m/c unpt. Ataturk at l. ctr. Square security device in gold at r. World map of 1513 by Piri Reis on back.   FV FV 22.50

215 **20,000,000 LIRA** VG VF UNC
L.1970 (2000). Green and red. Atatük at ctr. globe and olive branch behind. Efes ancient city on back.   FV FV 37.50

2005 NEW LIRA ISSUE

#216-221 Atatürk at ctr. or r. and as wmk.

Monetary reform: 100,000 "old" lira = 1 "new" lira

216 **1 NEW LIRA** VG VF UNC
2005. Claret red and blue. Atatürk Dam in Sanliurfa-Adiyaman on back.   FV FV 3.00

217 **5 NEW LIRA** VG VF UNC
2005. Greenish brown. Mausolem of Atatürk on back.   FV FV 11.00

218 **10 NEW LIRA** VG VF UNC
2005. Greenish brown. View of Antkabir, The Mausoleum of Atatürk in Ankara.   FV FV 20.00

219　20 NEW LIRA
2005. Green. Ancient city of Ephesus on back.

	VG	VF	UNC
	FV	FV	40.00

220　50 NEW LIRA
2005. Orange. Goreme National Park, Capadoccia, on back.

	VG	VF	UNC
	FV	FV	75.00

221　100 NEW LIRA
2005. Blue. Ishak Pasha Palace, Dogu Bayazit, on back.

	VG	VF	UNC
	FV	FV	135.00

The Turkmenistan Republic covers the territory of the Trans-Caspian Region of Turkestan, the Charjiui Vilayet of Bukhara and the part of Khiva located on the right bank of the Oxus. Bordered on the north by the Autonomous Kara-Kalpak Republic (a constituent of Uzbekistan), by Iran and Afghanistan on the south, by the Uzbek Republic on the east and the Caspian Sea on the west. It has an area of 186,400 sq. mi. (488,100 sq. km.) and a population of 4.48 million. Capital: Ashgabat (formerly Poltoratsk). Main occupation is agricultural products including cotton and maize. It is rich in minerals, oil, coal, sulphur and salt,and is also famous for it's carpets, Turkoman horses and Karakul sheep.

The Turkomans arrived in Transcaspia as nomadic Seluk Turks in the 11th century. They often became subjected to one of the neighboring states. Late in the 19th century the Russians invaded with their first victory in 1877, arriving in Ashkhabad in 1882 resulting in submission of the Turkmen tribes. By 1884, the Transcaspian province of Russian Turkestan was formed. During WW I the Russian government tried to conscript the Turkmen; this led to a revolt in Oct. 1916 under the leadership of Aziz Chapykov. In 1918 the Turks captured Baku from the Red army and the British sent a contingent to Merv to prevent a German-Turkish offensive toward Afghanistan and India. In mid-1919 the Bureau of Turkistan Moslem Communist Organizations was formed in Moscow hoping to develop one large republic including all surrounding Turkic areas within a Soviet federation. A Turkistan Autonomous Soviet Socialist Republic was formed and was partitioned into five republics according to the principle of nationalities. On Oct. 27, 1924, Turkmenistan became a Soviet Socialist Republic and was accepted as a member of the U.S.S.R. on Jan. 29, 1925. In Aug. 1990 the Turkmen Supreme Soviet adopted a declaration of sovereignty followed by a declaration of independence in Oct. 1991. It joined the Commonwealth of Independent States in December. A new constitution was adopted in 1992 providing for an executive presidency.

REPUBLIC

TÜRKMENISTANYÑ MERKEZI DÖWLET BANKY

CENTRAL BANK OF TURKMENISTAN

1993 ND; 1995-98 ISSUE

#1-9 arms at l. on back. Wmk: Rearing Arabian horse. Sign. Khudaiberdy Orazov. Replacement notes: Serial # prefix ZZ.

1　1 MANAT
ND (1993). Brown and tan on orange and m/c unpt. Ylymlar Academy at ctr., native craft at r. Shield at l., Temple at ctr. on back.

	VG	VF	UNC
	FV	0.15	0.75

2　5 MANAT
ND (1993). Blue and green on m/c unpt. Bldg. at ctr. Bldg. at ctr. on back.

	VG	VF	UNC
	—	0.25	1.00

#3-10 Pres. S. Niazov at r.

3　10 MANAT
ND (1993). Brown and pale orange on m/c unpt. Govt. bldg. at ctr. Back red-violet; Govt. bldg. at ctr.

	VG	VF	UNC
	—	0.25	1.50

4   20 MANAT
ND (1993); 1995. Blue-gray and blue on m/c unpt. National library
at ctr. Lg. bldg. at ctr. on back.

	VG	VF	UNC
a. ND (1993).	0.15	0.25	3.00
b. 1995.	—	0.15	1.50

5   50 MANAT
ND (1993); 1995. Brown and green on m/c unpt. Monument at ctr.
Mosque ruins on back.

	VG	VF	UNC
a. ND (1993).	0.15	0.25	3.00
b. 1995.	0.15	0.25	1.75

6   100 MANAT
ND (1993); 1995. Dk. blue and dk. gray on m/c unpt. Presidential
Palace at ctr. Sultan Sanjaryn mausoleum on back.

	VG	VF	UNC
a. ND (1993).	0.50	1.00	5.00
b. 1995.	—	0.25	1.75

7   500 MANAT
ND (1993); 1995. Violet, dk. brown and orange on m/c unpt.
National theatre at ctr. Hanymyn mausoleum on back.

	VG	VF	UNC
a. ND (1993).	0.25	1.25	7.50
b. 1995.	0.15	1.00	5.00

8   1000 MANAT
1995. Green on m/c unpt. Bldg. at ctr. Arms at ctr. on back. FV 1.00 7.50

9   5000 MANAT
1996. Violet, purple and red on m/c unpt. Bldg. at ctr. Arms on back. FV 1.00 8.50

10   10,000 MANAT
1996. Dk. brown on m/c unpt. Presidential palace at ctr. Arms on back. FV 2.00 10.00

11   10,000 MANAT

	VG	VF	UNC
1998. Lt. blue, lt. brown, and red on m/c unpt. Palace of Turkmenbashy. Back lt. blue, violet, and purple on m/c unpt., Mosque of Saparmurat at ctr.	FV	2.00	10.00

1999-2000 ISSUE

12   5000 MANAT
1999; 2000. Violet, purple and red on m/c unpt. Like #9.

	VG	VF	UNC
a. 1999. Sign. Khudaiberdy Orazov.	FV	1.00	7.50
b. 2000. Sign. S. Kandymov.	FV	1.00	7.50

13   10,000 MANAT

	VG	VF	UNC
1999. Lt. blue and lt. brown on m/c unpt. Pres. Niyazov with medals at r. Palace of Turkmenbashy at ctr. Mosque of Saparmurat on back. Like #11. Sign. Khudaiberdy Orazov.	FV	1.50	10.00

14   10,000 MANAT

	VG	VF	UNC
2000. Face like #13 but stars and crescent at upper l. Circular design at upper r. on back. Sign. S. Kandymov.	FV	FV	10.00

15   10,000 MANAT

	VG	VF	UNC
2003. Like #14 but arms at upper l.	FV	FV	10.00

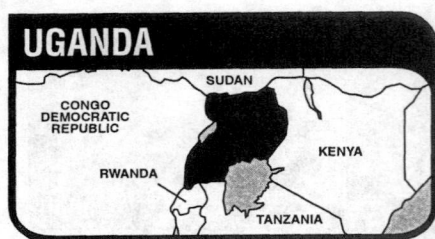

The Republic of Uganda, a former British protectorate located astride the equator in east-central Africa, has an area of 91,134 sq. mi. (236,036 sq. km.) and a population of 15.25 million. Capital: Kampala. Agriculture, including livestock, is the basis of the economy; there is some mining of copper, tin, gold and lead. Coffee, cotton, copper and tea are exported.

Uganda was first visited by Arab slavers in the 1830s. They were followed in the 1860s by British explorers searching for the headwaters of the Nile. The explorers, and the missionaries who followed them into the Lake Victoria region of south-central Africa in 1877-1879, found well developed African kingdoms dating back several centuries. In 1894 the local native Kingdom of Buganda was established as a British protectorate that was extended in 1896 to encompass an area substantially the same as the present Republic of Uganda. The protectorate was given a ministerial form of government in 1955, full internal self-government on March 1, 1962, and complete independence on Oct. 9, 1962. Uganda is a member of the Commonwealth of Nations. The president is Chief of State and Head of Government.

Notes of East African Currency Board circulated before Bank of Uganda notes were available. Also see East Africa.

MONETARY SYSTEM:
1 Shilling = 100 Cents

Caution: Several years ago the Bank of Uganda sold quantities of demonetized notes, most of which were made available for only $1.00 per note. Condition of notes thus sold is not reported. A listing of some pieces NOT available from the bank includes #4, 6a, 7a, 8a and b, 9a and b, 13a, 14a, 21, 23, and 24a and b.

BANK OF UGANDA

1966 ND ISSUE

#1-5 sign. titles: *GOVERNOR* and *SECRETARY*. Wmk: Hand. Replacement notes: Serial # prefix Z/1 (5/ and 10/); Y/1; X/1; W/1 respectively.

	5 SHILLINGS	VG	VF	UNC
1	ND (1966). Dk. blue on m/c unpt. Arms at r. River and waterfall on back.			
	a. Issued note.	0.25	1.50	5.00
	ct. Color trial.	—	—	75.00
	s. Specimen.	—	—	25.00
2	10 SHILLINGS			
	ND (1966). Brown on m/c unpt. Arms at ctr. Workers picking cotton on back.			
	a. Issued note.	0.50	2.50	5.00
	ct. Color trial.	—	—	125.00
	s. Specimen.	—	—	25.00

	20 SHILLINGS	VG	VF	UNC
3	ND (1966). Purple on m/c unpt. Marabou stork, Green Monkey, Lion, Elephants, Zebra and Impala on back.			
	a. Issued note.	0.50	2.00	6.00
	ct. Color trial.	—	—	250.00
	s. Specimen.	—	—	25.00

	100 SHILLINGS	VG	VF	UNC
4	ND (1966). Green on m/c unpt. Crowned crane at l., w/o *FOR BANK OF UGANDA* just below value at ctr. Bldg. at r. on back.			
	a. Issued note.	15.00	75.00	700.00
	ct. Color trial.	—	—	500.00
	s. Specimen.	—	—	125.00

	100 SHILLINGS	VG	VF	UNC
5	ND (1966). Green on m/c unpt. Like #4 but w/text: *FOR BANK OF UGANDA* under value.			
	a. Issued note.	0.25	1.50	6.00
	s. Specimen.	—	—	25.00

1973-77 ND ISSUE

SIGNATURE VARIETIES			
1	GOVERNOR / SECRETARY	2	GOVERNOR / SECRETARY

#5A-9 Pres. Idi Amin at l., arms at lower r. Wmk: Crested crane. Replacement notes: Serial # prefix Z/1 (5/ and 10/); Y/1; X/1; W/1 respectively.

	5 SHILLINGS	VG	VF	UNC
5A	ND (1977). Blue on m/c unpt. Woman picking coffee beans on back.	0.25	0.50	2.50

		VG	VF	UNC
6	**10 SHILLINGS**			
	ND (1973). Brown on m/c unpt. Elephants, antelope and hippopotamus on back.			
	a. Sign. titles: *GOVERNOR* and *DIRECTOR*.	7.50	40.00	285.00
	b. Sign. titles: *GOVERNOR* and *SECRETARY*. Sign. 1.	1.00	2.50	12.50
	c. Sign. titles as b. Sign. 2.	0.25	1.00	5.00
	s. As a. Specimen.	—	—	80.00

		VG	VF	UNC
7	**20 SHILLINGS**			
	ND (1973). Purple and brown on m/c unpt. Lg. bldg. on back.			
	a. Sign. titles: *GOVERNOR* and *DIRECTOR*.	7.50	40.00	275.00
	b. Sign. titles: *GOVERNOR* and *SECRETARY*. Sign. 1.	2.00	8.00	65.00
	c. Sign. titles as b. Sign. 2.	0.50	2.00	6.50
	s. As a. Specimen.	—	—	90.00

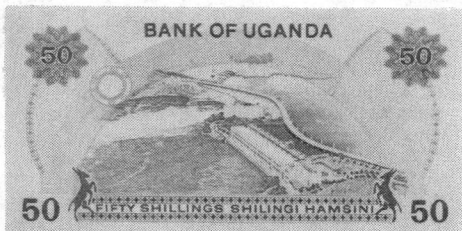

		VG	VF	UNC
8	**50 SHILLINGS**			
	ND (1973). Blue (shade) on m/c unpt. Hydroelectric dam on back.			
	a. Sign. titles: *GOVERNOR* and *DIRECTOR*.	7.50	40.00	275.00
	b. Sign. titles: *GOVERNOR* and *SECRETARY*. Sign. 1.	2.50	8.00	85.00
	c. Sign. titles as b. Sign. 2.	0.50	2.00	6.00
	s. As a. Specimen.	—	—	135.00

		VG	VF	UNC
9	**100 SHILLINGS**			
	ND (1973). Green (shades) on m/c unpt. Scene of lake and hills on back.			
	a. Sign. titles: *GOVERNOR* and *DIRECTOR*.	7.50	30.00	150.00
	b. Sign. titles: *GOVERNOR* and *SECRETARY*. Sign. 1.	3.00	12.50	85.00
	c. Sign. titles as b. Sign. 2.	0.75	2.00	8.50
	s. As a. Specimen.	—	—	110.00

1979 ISSUE

#10-14 Bank of Uganda at l. Sign. titles: *GOVERNOR* and *DIRECTOR*. Wmk: Crested crane's head. Replacement notes: Serial # prefix *Z/1* (5/ and 10/); *Y/1; X/1; W/1* respectively.

		VG	VF	UNC
10	**5 SHILLINGS**			
	ND (1979). Blue on m/c unpt. Back like #5A.	0.05	0.20	1.00

		VG	VF	UNC
11	**10 SHILLINGS**			
	ND (1979). Brown on m/c unpt. Back like #6.			
	a. Lt. printing on bank.	0.25	1.50	5.00
	b. Dk. printing on bank.	0.25	0.50	2.00

		VG	VF	UNC
12	**20 SHILLINGS**			
	ND (1979). Purple and brown on m/c unpt. Back like #7.			
	a. Lt. printing on bank.	0.50	2.00	7.50
	b. Dk. printing on bank.	0.25	0.50	2.50

		VG	VF	UNC
13	**50 SHILLINGS**			
	ND (1979). Dk. blue and purple on m/c unpt. Back like #8.			
	a. Lt. printing on bank.	5.00	17.50	100.00
	b. Dk. printing on bank.	0.25	1.00	4.50

		VG	VF	UNC
14	**100 SHILLINGS**			
	ND (1979). Green (shades) on m/c unpt. Back like #9.			
	a. Lt. printing on bank.	1.50	3.00	12.00
	b. Dk. printing on bank.	1.00	2.50	8.50

1982 ISSUE

#15-19 arms at l. Sign. titles: *GOVERNOR* and *SECRETARY*. Wmk: Crested crane's head. Replacement notes: Serial # prefix *Z/1* (5/ and 10/); *Y/1; X/1; W/1* respectively.

		VG	VF	UNC
15	**5 SHILLINGS**			
	ND (1982). Olive-green on m/c unpt. Back like #5A.	0.10	0.25	1.00

			VG	VF	UNC
16	**10 SHILLINGS**				
	ND (1982). Purple on m/c unpt. Back like #6.		0.10	0.25	2.00

			VG	VF	UNC
17	**20 SHILLINGS**				
	ND (1982). Green, dk. red and m/c. Back like #7.		0.25	1.00	5.00

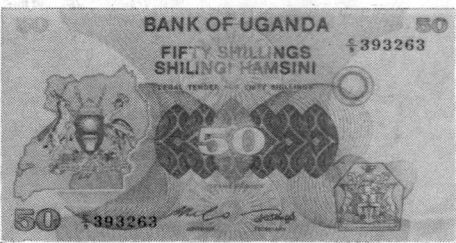

			VG	VF	UNC
18	**50 SHILLINGS**				
	ND (1982). Brown, orange and m/c. Back like #8.				
	a. Sign. titles: *GOVERNOR* and *SECRETARY*.		0.25	0.75	3.00
	b. Sign. titles: *GOVERNOR* and *DEPUTY GOVERNOR*.		0.25	1.00	10.00

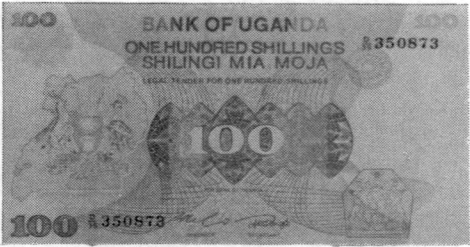

			VG	VF	UNC
19	**100 SHILLINGS**				
	ND (1982). Red-violet, orange and m/c. Back like #9.				
	a. Sign. titles: *GOVERNOR* and *SECRETARY*.		0.25	1.00	3.50
	b. Sign. titles: *GOVERNOR* and *DEPUTY GOVERNOR*. Sm. or lg. prefix letter and # before serial #.		0.25	1.00	3.50

1983-85 ISSUE

#20-23 Pres. Milton Obote at l. on face. Sign. titles: *GOVERNOR* and *DEPUTY GOVERNOR*. Wmk: Hand.
Replacement notes: Serial # prefix *X/1; W/1; U/1; T/1; S/1* respectively.

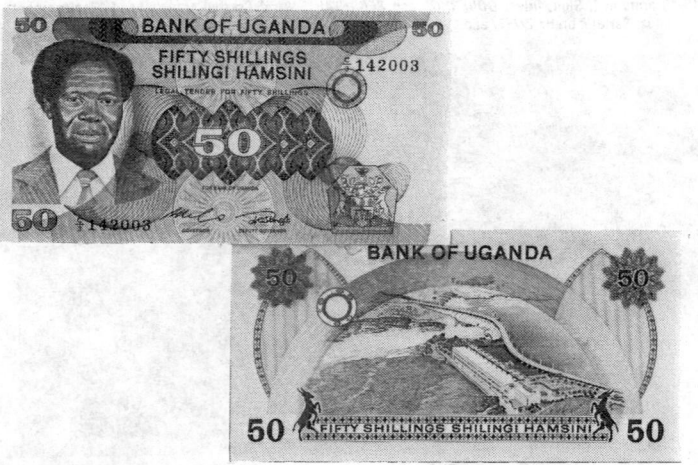

			VG	VF	UNC
20	**50 SHILLINGS**				
	ND (1985). Brown and orange on m/c unpt. Back like #8.		0.25	1.00	3.00

			VG	VF	UNC
21	**100 SHILLINGS**				
	ND (1985). Red-violet and orange on m/c unpt. Back like #9.		0.50	3.00	17.50

			VG	VF	UNC
22	**500 SHILLINGS**				
	ND (1983). Blue, purple and m/c. Cattle and harvesting on back. Serial # prefix varieties as #19b.				
	a. Issued note.		0.25	1.00	5.00
	s. Specimen.		—	—	10.00

			VG	VF	UNC
23	**1000 SHILLINGS**				
	ND (1983). Red and m/c. Bldg. on back. Serial # prefix varieties as #19b.				
	a. Issued note.		0.50	3.00	20.00
	s. Specimen.		—	—	12.50

			VG	VF	UNC
24	**5000 SHILLINGS**				
	1985-86. Purple and m/c. Arms at l. Bldg. w/clock tower at ctr. r. on back.				
	a. Wmk: Hand. 1985.		2.50	5.00	27.50
	b. Wmk: Crested crane. 1986.		0.50	1.50	5.00

1985-86 Issue

#25 and 26 face similar to #24. Wmk: Crested crane's head. Replacement notes: Serial # prefix *U/1; T/1* respectively.

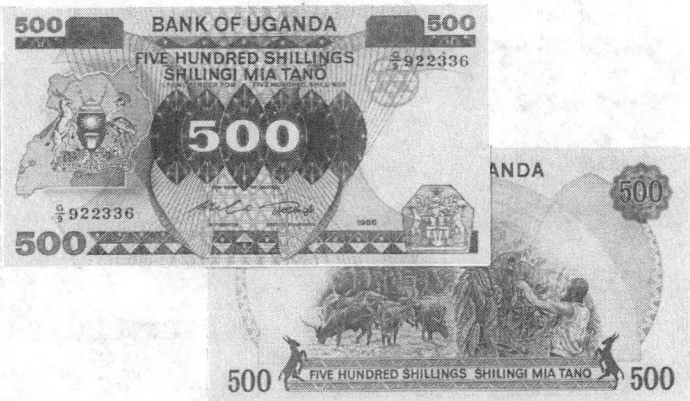

		VG	VF	UNC
25	**500 SHILLINGS**			
	1986. Blue, purple and m/c. Back like #22.	0.25	0.75	2.00

		VG	VF	UNC
26	**1000 SHILLINGS**			
	1986. Red and m/c. Back like #23.	0.25	1.00	3.00

1987 Issue

#27-34 replacement notes: Serial # prefix *ZZ.*

#27-32 arms at upper l., map at ctr. Printer: TDLR.

		VG	VF	UNC
27	**5 SHILLINGS**			
	1987. Brown on m/c unpt. Arms at r. also. Crowned crane, hippo, elephant and waterbuck on back.	0.10	0.25	1.00

		VG	VF	UNC
28	**10 SHILLINGS**			
	1987. Green on m/c unpt. Arms at r. also. 2 antelope grazing, 2 men fishing in canoe at ctr. on back.	0.10	0.25	1.00

#29-34 wmk: Crested crane's head.

		VG	VF	UNC
29	**20 SHILLINGS**			
	1987-88. Purple, blue-black and violet on m/c unpt. Modern bldgs. at ctr. r. on back.			
	a. Imprint on back. 1987.	0.10	0.50	2.50
	b. W/o imprint. 1988.	0.10	0.25	1.50

		VG	VF	UNC
30	**50 SHILLINGS**			
	1987-98. Red, orange and dk. brown on m/c unpt. Parliament bldg. at ctr. r. on back.			
	a. Imprint on back. 1987.	0.15	0.50	2.50
	b. W/o imprint. 1988; 1989.	0.15	0.50	2.00
	c. 1994; 1996; 1997; 1998.	0.10	0.25	1.00

		VG	VF	UNC
31	**100 SHILLINGS**			
	1987-98. Deep blue-violet, black and aqua on m/c unpt. High Court bldg. w/clock tower at ctr. r. on back.			
	a. Sign. titles: *GOVERNOR* and *SECRETARY, TREASURY.* Imprint on back. 1987.	0.25	1.00	3.00
	b. As a. but w/o imprint on back. 1988.	0.15	0.75	1.50
	c. As b. but w/sign. titles: *GOVERNOR* and *SECRETARY.* 1994; 1996; 1997; 1998.	0.10	0.25	1.00

		VG	VF	UNC
32	**200 SHILLINGS**			
	1987-98. Brown, orange and olive-brown on m/c unpt. Worker in textile factory at ctr. r. on back.			
	a. 1987.	0.15	0.50	3.00
	b. 1991; 1994; 1996; 1998.	0.15	0.50	1.50

1991 Issue

33   500 SHILLINGS

		VG	VF	UNC
1991. Dk. brown and deep purple on m/c unpt. Elephant at l., arms at upper ctr. and lower r. Uganda Independence Monument at l., municipal bldg. w/clock tower at ctr. on back.				
a. Sign. titles: *GOVERNOR* and *SECRETARY, TREASURY.*		FV	0.75	3.00
b. Sign. titles: *GOVERNOR* and *SECRETARY.*		FV	1.00	3.50
s. As a. Specimen.		—	—	25.00

34   1000 SHILLINGS

		VG	VF	UNC
1991. Black, deep brown-violet and dk. green on m/c unpt. Farmers at l., arms at upper ctr. and lower r. Grain storage facility at ctr. on back.				
a. Sign. titles: *GOVERNOR* and *SECRETARY, TREASURY.*		FV	2.50	5.00
b. Sign. titles: *GOVERNOR* and *SECRETARY.*		FV	1.25	4.00

1993-95 ISSUE

#35-38 arms at upper ctr. Ascending size serial # vertically at l. Wmk: Crested crane's head. Replacement notes: Serial # prefix ZZ.

35   500 SHILLINGS

		VG	VF	UNC
1994; 1996-98. Like #33. Segmented foil over security thread. Ascending size serial # at l.				
a. 1994; 1996.		FV	FV	3.00
b. 1997; 1998.		FV	2.50	5.00

36   1000 SHILLINGS

		VG	VF	UNC
1994; 1996; 1998. Like #34. Segmented foil over security thread. Ascending size serial # at l.		FV	1.25	3.50

37   5000 SHILLINGS

		VG	VF	UNC
1993; 1998. Red-violet, deep purple and dk. green on m/c unpt. Lake Bunyonyi, terraces at l. Railroad cars being loaded onto Kaawa Ferry at ctr., plant at lower r. on back.				
a. 1993.		FV	5.00	12.50
b. 1998.		FV	FV	9.50

38   10,000 SHILLINGS

		VG	VF	UNC
1995; 1998. Green and red on m/c unpt. Musical instruments at l. Owen Falls dam, kudu on back.				
a. 1995.		FV	10.00	25.00
b. 1998.		FV	FV	17.50

1999-2002 ISSUE

#39-41 like #36-38 but color variances and w/added security devices.

39   1000 SHILLINGS

		VG	VF	UNC
2000; 2002; 2003. Like #36 but arms at upper ctr. in brown and green. Numerals of value at lower r. all in dk. brown.		FV	FV	3.00

39A   1000 SHILLINGS

		VG	VF	UNC
2001. Like #39 but different security devices.		FV	FV	3.00

40   5000 SHILLINGS

		VG	VF	UNC
2000; 2002. Like #37 but w/silver leaf overlay at upper l. ctr. and security V symbol at lower r.		FV	FV	10.00

45	10,000 SHILLINGS	VG	VF	UNC
	2004.	FV	FV	15.00

41	10,000 SHILLINGS	VG	VF	UNC
	2001; 2003. Red, green, brown and m/c. Like #38 but w/changes in security devices.	FV	FV	17.50

46	20,000 SHILLINGS	VG	VF	UNC
	2004. Like #42 but different devices.	FV	FV	20.00

41A	5000 SHILLINGS	VG	VF	UNC
	2002. Like #40 but different devices added.	FV	FV	10.00

47	50,000 SHILLINGS	VG	VF	UNC
	2003. Brown. Monument at l. Cotton harvest on back.	FV	FV	50.00

42	20,000 SHILLINGS	VG	VF	UNC
	1999; 2002. Green on m/c unpt. Crested crane at l., arms at upper ctr. Silver vertical OVD strip w/repeated value at r. Modern bldg. on back. Wmk: Arms. 2 sign. varieties.	FV	FV	30.00

2003-04 ISSUE

43	1000 SHILLINGS	VG	VF	UNC
	2005. M/c. Silver OVD strip at r.	FV	FV	3.00

44	5000 SHILLINGS	VG	VF	UNC
	2004.	FV	FV	7.50

Ukraine is bordered by Russia to the east, Russia and Belarus to the north, Poland, Slovakia and Hungary to the west, Romania and Moldova to the southwest and in the south by the Black Sea and the Sea of Azov. It has an area of 233,088 sq. mi. (603,700 sq. km.) and a population of 50.8 million. Capital: Kyiv (Kiev). Coal, grain, vegetables and heavy industrial machinery are major exports.

The territory of Ukraine has been inhabited for over 30,000 years. As the result of its location, Ukraine has served as the gateway to Europe for millennia and its early history has been recorded by Arabic, Greek, Roman, as well as Ukrainian historians.

Ukraine, which was known as Rus' until the sixteenth century (and from which the name Russia was derived in the 17th century), became the major political and cultural center of Eastern Europe in the 9th century. The Rus' Kingdom, under a dynasty of Varangian origin, because of its position on the intersection of the north-south Scandinavia to Byzantium and the east-west Orient to Europe trade routes, became a focal point of world trade. At its apex Rus' stretched from the Baltic to the Black Sea and from the upper Volga River in the east, almost to the Vistula River in the west. In 988 the Rus' adopted Christianity from Byzantium. The Mongol invasion in 1240 brought an end to the might of the Rus' Kingdom.

In the seventeenth century, after almost four hundred years of Mongol, Lithuanian, Polish, and Turkish domination, the Cossack State regained Ukrainian independence. The Hetman State lasted until the mid-eighteenth century and was followed by a period of foreign rule: Eastern Ukraine was controlled by Russia; Western Ukraine came under relatively benign Austro-Hungarian rule.

With the disintegration of the Russian and Austro-Hungarian Empires in 1917 and 1918, Eastern Ukraine declared its full independence on January 22, 1918 and Western Ukraine followed suit on November 1 of that year. On January 22, 1919 both parts united into one state that had to defend itself on three fronts: from the "Red" Bolsheviks and their puppet Ukrainian Soviet Republic formed in Kharkiv, from the "White" czarist Russian forces, and from Poland. Ukraine lost the war. In 1920, Eastern Ukraine was occupied by the Bolsheviks and in 1922 was incorporated into the Soviet Union. There followed a brief resurgence of Ukrainian language and culture until it was suppressed in 1928. Western Ukraine was partitioned between Poland, Romania, Hungary and Czechoslovakia.

On August 24, 1991 Ukraine once again declared its independence. On December 5, 1991 the Ukrainian Parliament abrogated the 1922 treaty which incorporated Ukraine into the Soviet Union.

During the changeover from the Ruble currency of the Soviet Union to the Karbovanets of Ukraine, as a transition measure and to restrict unlicensed export of scarce goods, coupon cards (202 x 82mm), similar to ration cards, were issued in various denominations. They were valid for one month and were given to employees in amounts equal to their pay. Each card contained multiples of 1, 3, 5, 10, 25 and sometimes 50 Karbovanets valued coupons, to be cut apart. They were supposed to be used for purchases together with ruble notes. In January 1992 Ukraine began issuing individual coupons in Karbovanets denominations from 1 krb to 100 krb (printed in France and dated 1991). They were replaced by the Hryvnia.

Ukraine is a charter member of the United Nations.

MONETARY SYSTEM:
1 Karvovanets (Karbovantsiv) КАРБОВАНЕЦЬ, КАРБОВАНЦІВ = 1 Russian Ruble, 1991-96
1 Hryvnia (Hryvni, Hryven) ГРИВНЯ (ГРИВНІ, ГРИВЕНЬ) = 100,000 Karbovantsiv, 1996-

УКРАЇНСЬКА Р.С.Р.

TREASURY

1990 ND КУПОН RUBLE CONTROL COUPON ISSUE

#68 various authorization handstamps in registry. Uniface.

		VG	VF	UNC
68	**KARBOVANTSIV - VARIOUS AMOUNTS**			
	ND (1990). Sheet of 28 coupons and registry. Jovthn6.	—	—	4.00

#69-74 not assigned.

1991 КУПОН RUBLE CONTROL COUPON ISSUE

Consumer cards (coupons) were not legal tender but without them the U.S.S.R. rubles could not perform functions of money within Ukraine's territory.

#75 various authorization handstamps in registry. Uniface.

COMPANION CATALOGS
Volume 1 - Specialized Issues
Volume 2 - General Issues, 1368-1960

The Companion Catalogs in the Standard Catalog of World Paper Money series include a volume on Specialized Issues of the World - listed are those banknotes which were issued on a limited circulation basis rather than the central monetary authority note issues detailed in this work. The Specialized volume is currently in its 10th edition, and it is updated periodically. The General Issues volume lists national notes dated and issued, before 1960. The 11th edition is due out in Fall 2006. Inquiries about the availability of both these volumes are invited to contact Book Department, Krause Publications, 700 East State Street, Iola, WI 54990-0001 or you may call 1-800-258-0929 or www.fwpubs.com.

		VG	VF	UNC
75	**KARBOVANTSIV - VARIOUS AMOUNTS**			
	1991. Sheet of 28 coupons and registry.	—	—	4.00

#76-80 not assigned.

НАЦІОНАЛЬНИЙ БАНК УКРАЇНИ

UKRAINIAN NATIONAL BANK

1991 КУПОН CONTROL COUPON ISSUE

Karbovanets System

Originally issued at par and temporarily to be used jointly with Russian rubles in commodity purchases as a means of currency control (similar to Ruble Control Coupons above). They soon became more popular while the ruble slowly depreciated in exchange value. This did not last very long and the karbovanets has since suffered a higher inflation rate than the Russian ruble.

#81-87 Lybid, Viking sister of the founding brothers, at l. Cathedral of St. Sophia in Kiev at l. ctr. on back. All notes w/o serial #. Wmk. paper. All denominations had the value, i.e. *3 KRB*, printed sideways with fluorescent ink at l. Printer: ISPB (France) (Imprimerie Spéciale de Banque (France))

		VG	VF	UNC
81	**1 KARBOVANETS**			
	1991. Dull brown and pale orange on yellow unpt.			
	a. Issued note.	0.05	0.10	0.25
	s. Specimen.	—	—	45.00

		VG	VF	UNC
82	**3 KARBOVANTSI**			
	1991. Greenish gray and pale orange on yellow unpt.			
	a. Issued note.	0.05	0.10	0.25
	b. Issued note w/ imprint *3 Kpe* at l.	0.05	0.10	0.50
	s. As a. Specimen.	—	—	45.00

		VG	VF	UNC
83	**5 KARBOVANTSIV**			
	1991. Dull blue-violet and pale orange on yellow unpt.			
	a. Issued note.	0.05	0.20	0.50
	s. Specimen.	—	—	45.00
84	**10 KARBOVANTSIV**			
	1991. Pink and pale orange on yellow unpt.			
	a. Issued note.	0.05	0.20	1.00
	s. Specimen.	—	—	45.00
85	**25 KARBOVANTSIV**			
	1991. Purple and pale orange on yellow unpt.			
	a. Issued note.	0.15	0.50	4.00
	s. Specimen.	—	—	45.00
86	**50 KARBOVANTSIV**			
	1991. Blue-green and pale orange on yellow unpt.			
	a. Issued note.	0.10	0.35	1.50
	b. Issued note w/ 50 Kps at l.	0.20	0.70	0.30
	s. As a. Specimen.	—	—	45.00
87	**100 KARBOVANTSIV**			
	1991. Brown-violet and pale orange on yellow unpt.			
	a. Issued note.	0.50	1.50	4.50
	s. Specimen.	—	—	45.00
87A	**250 KARBOVANTSIV**			
	1991. Blue and red. (Not Issued). Specimen.	—	—	—
87B	**500 KARBOVANTSIV**	—	—	—

1992 ISSUE

#88-91 founding Viking brothers Kyi, Shchek and Khoryv w/sister Libyd in bow of boat at l. Backs like #81-87. All notes w/serial #. Wmk. paper. Replacement notes: Serial # prefix .../99 in denominator. Printer: TDLR (w/o imprint).

		VG	VF	UNC
88	**100 KARBOVANTSIV**			
	1992. Orange on lilac and ochre unpt.			
	a. Issued note.	0.10	0.50	1.75
	r. Replacement note.	0.50	2.50	6.00
	s. Specimen.	—	—	10.00
89	**200 KARBOVANTSIV**			
	1992. Dull brown and silver on lilac and ochre unpt.			
	a. Issued note.	0.25	1.25	5.00
	r. Replacement note.	0.50	2.50	7.00
	s. Specimen.	—	—	10.00
90	**500 KARBOVANTSIV**			
	1992. Blue-green and silver on lilac and ochre unpt.			
	a. Issued note.	0.25	1.00	4.00
	r. Replacement note.	0.50	2.50	6.00
	s. Specimen.	—	—	25.00
91	**1000 KARBOVANTSIV**			
	1992. Red-violet and lt. green on lilac and ochre unpt.			
	a. Issued note.	0.25	0.75	2.00
	r. Replacement note.	0.50	2.50	6.00
	s. Specimen.	—	—	25.00

GOVERNMENT

TREASURY

1992 СЕРТИФІКАТ - COMPENSATION CERTIFICATE ISSUE

#91A and 91B church at l., small arms at upper r. Text on back. The exact use of these notes has come into question.

		VG	VF	UNC
91A	**1,000,000 KARBOVANTSIV**	0.75	2.00	5.00
	1992. Dull blue-green, orange and gray on pale orange and pale green unpt.			

		VG	VF	UNC
91B	**2,000,000 KARBOVANTSIV**	1.00	3.00	8.00
	1992. Green, orange and pink w/black text on lt. blue, pink and m/c unpt.			

НАЦІОНАЛЬНИЙ БАНК УКРАЇНИ

UKRAINIAN NATIONAL BANK

1993 ISSUE

#92 and 93 similar to #88-91, but trident symbol added at l. on face; at r. on back. Replacement notes: Serial # prefix 001/92-001/99; 001/99 for notes dated 1993. Printer: TDLR (w/o imprint).

		VG	VF	UNC
92	**2000 KARBOVANTSIV**			
	1993. Blue and olive-green on aqua and gold unpt.			
	a. Issued note.	0.25	0.75	2.50
	s. Specimen.	—	—	10.00
93	**5000 KARBOVANTSIV**			
	1993; 1995. Red-orange and olive-brown on pale blue and ochre unpt.			
	a. 1993.	0.10	0.25	1.25
	b. 1995.	0.50	2.50	5.00
	r. Replacement note. 1993.	1.00	3.00	6.00
	s1. Specimen. 1993; 1995.	—	—	25.00
	s2. As b. Specimen.	—	—	15.00

#94-97 statue of St. Volodymyr standing w/long cross at l. Bldg. facade at l. on back. Trident at l. on face, at r. on back. Wmk: Ornamental shield repeated vertically. Replacement notes: Serial # prefix 001/92-001/99; 001/99 for notes dated 1993. Printer: TDLR (Serial # as a fraction) or Banknote Printing and Minting works of the National Bank of Ukraine, Kyiv (BPMW) (serial # prefix is 2 letters) (Both w/o imprint).

		VG	VF	UNC
94	**10,000 KARBOVANTSIV**			
	1993-96. Apple green and tan on pale blue and ochre unpt.			
	a. 1993.	0.10	0.25	2.00
	b. 1995.	0.05	0.20	0.50
	c. 1996. Wmk: Zig-zag of 4 bars. (parquet-paper).	0.10	0.25	1.50
	s1. Specimen. 1993.	—	—	25.00
	s2. Specimen. 1995; 1996.	—	—	15.00
95	**20,000 KARBOVANTSIV**			
	1993-96. Lilac and tan on blue and yellow unpt.			
	a. 1993.	0.10	0.50	2.00
	b. 1994; 1995.	0.10	0.25	1.00
	c. 1996. Wmk: Zig-zag of 4 bars. (parquet-paper).	0.10	0.50	2.00
	s1. Specimen. 1993.	—	—	25.00
	s2. Specimen. 1994; 1996.	—	—	15.00
96	**50,000 KARBOVANTSIV**			
	1993-95. Dull orange and blue on m/c unpt.			
	a. 1993.	0.15	0.50	4.00
	b. 1994; 1995.	0.20	0.75	2.50
	s1. Specimen. 1993.	—	—	25.00
	s2. Specimen. 1994.	—	—	15.00
97	**100,000 KARBOVANTSIV**			
	1993; 1994. Gray-green and ochre on m/c unpt. Wmk: Trident shield repeated.			
	a. Prefix fraction before serial #. 1993.	0.50	1.25	6.00
	b. Prefix letters w/serial #. 1994.	0.25	0.75	3.00
	s1. Specimen. 1993.	—	—	30.00
	s2. Specimen. 1994.	—	—	17.50

#98 and 99 statue of St. Volodymyr standing w/long cross at r. Opera house at l. ctr. on back. Wmk: Trident shield repeated. Replacement notes: Serial # prefix *001/92-001/99; 001-99* for notes dated 1994.

98	**200,000 KARBOVANTSIV**	VG	VF	UNC
	1994. Dull red-brown and lt. blue on aqua and gray unpt. Back m/c.			
	a. Prefix fraction before serial #. 1994.	0.75	2.50	10.00
	b. Prefix letters w/serial #. 1994.	0.50	1.50	5.00
	s1. Specimen. 1994. Serial # prefix as a fraction.	—	—	30.00
	s2. Specimen. 1994.	—	—	17.50
99	**500,000 KARBOVANTSIV**			
	1994. Lt. blue and lilac on yellow and gray unpt.			
	a. Issued note.	1.00	3.00	12.50
	s. Specimen.	—	—	30.00

1995 ISSUE

100	**1,000,000 KARBOVANTSIV**	VG	VF	UNC
	1995. Dk. brown on pale orange, lt. blue and m/c unpt. Statue of T. G. Shevchenko at r., arms at lower l. Kiev State University at l. ctr., arms at lower r. on back.			
	a. Issued note.	1.50	4.50	17.50
	s. Specimen.	—	—	30.00

1995 PRIVATIZATION CERTIFICATE ISSUE

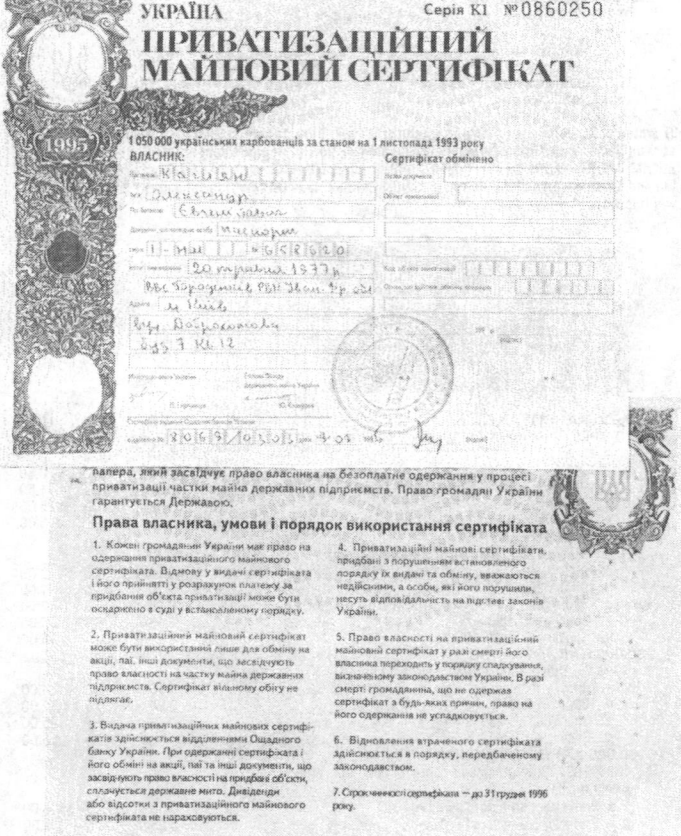

101	**1,050,000 KARBOVANTSIV**	VG	VF	UNC
	1995. Dk. gray on lt. gray and ochre unpt. Arms at upper l. Text on back.	2.00	7.50	25.00

#102 not assigned.

1992 (1996) REGULAR ISSUE

	SIGNATURE VARIETIES		
1	Getman	2	Matvienko
3	Yuschenko	3A	Yuschenko
4	Stelmah	5	Tigipko

#103-107 wmk: Trident repeated. Printer: CBNC (w/o imprint). Replacement notes: First digit of serial # is *9*.

103	**1 HRYVNIA**	VG	VF	UNC
	1992 (1996). Olive-brown on m/c unpt. Ruins of Kherson at ctr. St. Volodymr at ctr. on back.			
	a. Sign. 1.	—	0.25	1.00
	b. Sign. 2.	—	0.25	1.00
	c. Sign. 3.	—	0.25	1.00
	s. As a. Specimen.	—	—	25.00

104	**2 HRYVNI**	VG	VF	UNC
	1992 (1996). Brown on m/c unpt. Cathedral of St. Sophia at ctr. Prince Yaroslav at ctr. on back.			
	a. Sign. 1.	—	FV	1.50
	b. Sign. 2.	—	FV	3.00
	c. Sign. 3.	—	FV	1.50
	s. As a. Specimen.	—	—	25.00

105	**5 HRYVEN**	VG	VF	UNC
	1992 (1996). Blue-gray on m/c unpt. Illinska Church in Subotiv at ctr. B. Khmelnytsky at ctr. on back.			
	a. Sign. 1.	—	FV	3.00
	b. Sign. 2.	—	FV	4.00
	c. Sign. 3.	—	FV	2.50
	s. As a. Specimen.	—	—	25.00

106 10 HRYVEN

	VG	VF	UNC
1992 (1996). Purple on m/c unpt. Kyiv-Pecherska Monastery at ctr. I Mazepa at ctr. on back.			
a. Sign. 1.	FV	FV	5.00
b. Sign. 3.	FV	FV	4.50

110 5 HRYVEN

	VG	VF	UNC
1994; 1997; 2001. M/c. Bohdan Khmelnytsky at ctr. r. Illinska Church in Subotiv at ctr. Printer: TDLR (w/o imprint).			
a. 1994 (1997).	FV	FV	2.50
b. 1997 (1998).	FV	FV.	2.50
c. 2001.	FV	FV	2.50
s. As a. Specimen.	—	—	30.00

107 20 HRYVEN

	VG	VF	UNC
1992 (1996). Brown on m/c unpt. Lviv Opera House at ctr. Ivan Franko at ctr. on back.			
a. Sign. 1.	FV	5.00	8.50
b. Sign. 3.	FV	5.00	8.50

107A 50 HRYVEN

	VG	VF	UNC
1992. Man at ctr. (Not issued). Printer: CBNC.	—	—	—

107B 100 HRYVEN

	VG	VF	UNC
1992. Man at ctr. (Not issued). Printer: CBNC.	—	—	—

111 10 HRYVEN

	VG	VF	UNC
1994; 2000. M/c. L. Mazepa at ctr. r. and as wmk. Kyiv-Pecherska Monastery at ctr. on back.			
a. 1994 (1997). Printer: TDLR.	FV	FV	4.50
b. 2000. Ukranian printer.	FV	FV	4.50
s. As a. Specimen.	—	—	30.00

1994-98 ND AND DATED ISSUE

108 1 HRYVNIA

	VG	VF	UNC
1994; 1995. Grayish brown and green on m/c unpt. St. Volodymyr at ctr. r. and as wmk. City of Khersonnes at ctr. on back. Sign. 3.			
a. 1994 (1996).	FV	FV	1.00
b. 1995 (1997).	FV	FV	1.00
s. Specimen. 1994.	—	—	35.00

112 20 HRYVEN

	VG	VF	UNC
1995; 2000. M/c. Ivan Franko at r. and as wmk. Opera House in Lviv on back.			
a. 1995. W/segmented security thread.	FV	FV	7.50
b. 2000.	FV	FV	7.50
s. As a. Specimen.	—	—	30.00

113 50 HRYVEN

	VG	VF	UNC
ND (1996). Purple and dk. blue-gray on m/c unpt. M. Hrushevsky at r. and as wmk. Parliament bldg. at ctr. on back.			
a. Sign. 1.	FV	FV	20.00
b. Sign. 3.	FV	FV	20.00
s. Specimen.	—	—	150.00
x. Wmk. T. Shevchenko (error).	—	Rare	—

109 2 HRYVNI

	VG	VF	UNC
1995; 2001. M/c. Prince Yaroslav at ctr. r. and as wmk. Cathedral of St. Sophia in Kyiv on back.			
a. 1995 (1997).	FV	FV	1.75
b. 2001.	FV	FV	2.00
s. As a. Specimen.	—	—	30.00

114	**100 HRYVEN**	**VG**	**VF**	**UNC**
	ND (1996). Brown and dk. green on m/c unpt. T. Shevchenko at r. and as wmk. Cathedral of St. Sophia in Kyiv at ctr., statue of St. Volodymyr standing at l. on back.			
	a. Sign. 1.	FV	FV	35.00
	b. Sign. 3.	FV	FV	35.00
	s. Specimen.	—	—	175.00

115	**200 HRYVEN**	**VG**	**VF**	**UNC**
	ND (2001).Black and blue on m/c unpt. Lesia Ukrainka (L. P. Kosach) at r. and as wmk. Castle gate on back. Sign. 1.	FV	FV	65.00

#116 formerly listed has been changed to 110b.

2003 ISSUE

116	**1 HRYVNIA**	**VG**	**VF**	**UNC**
		FV	FV	1.00
117	**2 HRYVEN**			
	2004.	FV	FV	2.00
118	**5 HRYVEN**			
	2004.	FV	FV	2.50

119	**10 HRYVEN**	**VG**	**VF**	**UNC**
	2003.	FV	FV	4.50

120	**20 HRYVEN**	**VG**	**VF**	**UNC**
	2003.	FV	FV	7.50

121	**50 HRYVEN**	**VG**	**VF**	**UNC**
	2004.	FV	FV	20.00

COLLECTOR SERIES

НАЦІОНАЛЬНИЙ БАНК УКРАЇНИ

UKRAINIAN NATIONAL BANK

1996 ISSUE

CS1	**1 HRYVNIA**	**Issue Price**	**Mkt.**	**Value**
	#103 and 2 Karbovantsiv 1996 Independence coins in a folder.	—		

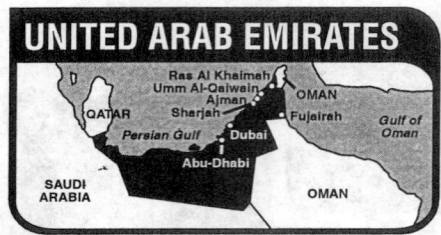

The seven United Arab Emirates (formerly known as the Trucial Sheikhdoms or States), located along the southern shore of the Persian Gulf, are comprised of the Sheikhdoms of Abu Dhabi, Dubai, Sharjah, Ajman, Umm al Qaiwain, Ras al-Khaimah and Fujairah. They have a combined area of about 32,000 sq. mi. (83,600 sq. km.) and a population of 2.44 million. Capital: Abu Dhabi. Since the oil strikes of 1958-60, the economy has centered on petroleum.

The Trucial States came under direct British influence in 1892 when the maritime truce treaty, enacted after the suppression of pirate activity along the Trucial Coast, was enlarged to enjoin the states from disposing of any territory, or entering into any foreign agreements, without British consent in return for British protection from external aggression. In March of 1971 Britain reaffirmed its decision to terminate its treaty relationships with the Trucial Sheikhdoms, whereupon the seven states joined with Bahrain and Qatar in an effort to form a union of Arab emirates under British protection. When the prospective members failed to agree on terms of union, Bahrain and Qatar declared their respective independence in Aug. and Sept. 1971. Six of the Sheikhdoms united to form the United Arab Emirates on Dec. 2, 1971. Ras al-Khaimah joined a few weeks later.

MONETARY SYSTEM:
1 Dirham = 1000 Fils

SHEIKHDOMS

UNITED ARAB EMIRATES CURRENCY BOARD

1973; 1976 ND ISSUE

#1-6 dhow, camel caravan, palm tree and oil derrick at l. Wmk: Arabian horse's head. Printer: (T)DLR.

1	**1 DIRHAM**	**VG**	**VF**	**UNC**
	ND (1973). Green on m/c unpt. Police station at ctr. r. on back.			
	a. Issued note.	1.00	5.00	25.00
	s. Specimen.	—	—	75.00

2	**5 DIRHAMS**	**VG**	**VF**	**UNC**
	ND (1973). Purple on m/c unpt. Fortress Fujairah at ctr. r. on back.			
	a. Issued note.	3.50	12.50	50.00
	s. Specimen.	—	—	75.00

3	**10 DIRHAMS**	**VG**	**VF**	**UNC**
	ND (1973). Gray-blue on m/c unpt. Aerial view of Umm al-Qaiwan at ctr. r. on back.			
	a. Issued note.	3.00	10.00	50.00
	s. Specimen.	—	—	100.00

4 **50 DIRHAMS** VG VF UNC
ND (1973). Red on m/c unpt. Sheikh's Palace of Ajman at ctr. r. on
back.
   a. Issued note.   10.00   45.00   250.00
   s. Specimen.   —   —   225.00

5 **100 DIRHAMS** VG VF UNC
ND (1973). Olive-green on m/c unpt. Ras al-Khaimah city at ctr. r.
on back.
   a. Issued note.   15.00   65.00   325.00
   s. Specimen.   —   —   325.00

6 **1000 DIRHAMS** VG VF UNC
ND (1976). Blue on m/c unpt. Fortress at ctr. r. on back.
   a. Issued note.   125.00   750.00   2500.00
   s. Specimen.   —   —   750.00

UNITED ARAB EMIRATES CENTRAL BANK

1982; 1983 ND ISSUE

#7-11 arms at upper ctr., sparrowhawk at l. on back. Wmk: Sparrowhawk's head.

7 **5 DIRHAMS** VG VF UNC
ND (1982). Brown on m/c unpt. Sharjah Market at r. Seacoast cove
w/tower on back.
   a. Issued note.   FV   3.50   10.00
   s. Specimen.   —   —   50.00

8 **10 DIRHAMS** VG VF UNC
ND (1982). Green on m/c unpt. Arab dagger at r. Ideal farm w/trees
at l. ctr. on back.
   a. Issued note.   FV   5.50   20.00
   s. Specimen.   —   —   50.00

9 **50 DIRHAMS** VG VF UNC
ND (1982). Purple, dk. brown and olive on m/c unpt. Oryx at r. Al
Jahilie Fort at l. ctr. on back.
   a. Issued note.   25.00   45.00   80.00
   s. Specimen.   —   —   95.00

10 **100 DIRHAMS** VG VF UNC
ND (1982). Red, violet and black on m/c unpt. Al Fahidie Fort at r.
Dubai Trade Ctr. at l. ctr. on back.
   a. Issued note.   FV   50.00   95.00
   s. Specimen.   —   —   100.00

11 **500 DIRHAMS** VG VF UNC
ND (1983). Dk. blue, purple and brown on m/c unpt. Sparrowhawk
at r. Mosque in Dubai at l. ctr. on back.
   a. Issued note.   FV   175.00   325.00
   s. Specimen.   —   —   350.00

1989-96 ISSUES

#12-15 and 17 similar to #7-11 w/condensed Arabic text in titles, modified designs and slight color varia-
tions. Large value outline type in wmk. area. Silver arms at upper ctr. Arabic serial # in red at l.,
electronic sorting style in black at r. Wmk: Sparrowhawk's head.

12 **5 DIRHAMS** VG VF UNC
1993-/AH1414-1995-/AH1416. Dk. brown, red-orange and violet
on m/c unpt. Similar to #7.
   a. 1993/AH1414.   FV   5.00   8.00
   b. 1995/AH1416.   FV   FV   7.50

13 **10 DIRHAMS** VG VF UNC
1993-/AH1414-199/AH1416. Green and pale olive-green on m/c
unpt. Similar to #8.
   a. 1993/AH1414.   FV   7.50   14.00
   b. 1995/AH1416.   FV   5.00   10.00

14 **50 DIRHAMS**
1995-/AH1415-1996/AH1417. Purple, black and violet on m/c
unpt. W/segmented foil over security thread. Similar to #9.
   a. 1995/AH1415.   FV   FV   45.00
   b. 1996/AH1417.   FV   FV   40.00

15 **100 DIRHAMS** VG VF UNC
1993-/AH1414-1995/AH1416. Red, red-violet and black on m/c
unpt. Fortress at l. ctr. on back. W/segmented foil over security
thread. Similar to #10.
   a. 1993/AH1414.   FV   FV   75.00
   b. 1995/AH1416.   FV   FV   65.00

16 **200 DIRHAMS**
1989/AH 1410. Brown, green and m/c. Sharia Court bldg. and   FV   FV   110.00
Zayed Sports City on face. Central Bank bldg. at l. ctr. on back.
W/segmented foil over security thread.

17 **500 DIRHAMS**
1993/AH1414. Dk. blue, black, purple and silver on m/c unpt.   FV   FV   300.00
W/segmented foil over security thread. Similar to #11.

18 **500 DIRHAMS**
1996/AH1416. Dk. blue, black, purple and silver on m/c unpt. Like   FV   FV   275.00
#17 but w/kinegram added at lower l.

1997-2000 ISSUE

#19-25 similar to #12-19 but wmk. area shaded.

		VG	VF	UNC
19	**5 DIRHAMS**			
	2000-04. Brown and orange. Similar to #12 but w/color and minor design variations.			
	a. 2000/AH1420.	FV	FV	6.00
	b. 2001/AH1422.	FV	FV	5.00
	c. 2004/AH1425.	FV	FV	5.00

		VG	VF	UNC
20	**10 DIRHAMS**			
	1998-2004. Similar to #13.			
	a. 1998/AH1419.	FV	FV	9.00
	b. 2001/AH1422.	FV	FV	8.00
	c. 2004/AH1425.	FV	FV	8.00

		VG	VF	UNC
21	**20 DIRHAMS**			
	1997/AH1418; 2000/AH1421. Green, blue and m/c. Dubai Creek Golf and Yacht Club at r. Dhow on back.			
	a. 1997/AH1419.	FV	FV	18.00
	b. 2000/AH/1420.	FV	FV	16.00

		VG	VF	UNC
22	**50 DIRHAMS**			
	1998/AH1419. Similar to #14.	FV	FV	35.00

		VG	VF	UNC
23	**100 DIRHAMS**			
	1998/AH1419. Similar to #15 but w/o value over wmk. area on face.			
	a. 1998/AH1419.	FV	FV	60.00

		VG	VF	UNC
24	**500 DIRHAMS**			
	1998/AH1419; 2000/AH1420. Similar to #18 but w/wide silver foil at r., silver seal at l.			
	a. 1998/AH1419.	FV	FV	260.00
	b. 2000/AH1420.	FV	FV	250.00

		VG	VF	UNC
25	**1000 DIRHAMS**			
	1998/AH1419; 2000/AH1421. Brown, green and m/c. Palace corner tower at r. Holographic strip vertically at r. City view on back.			
	a. 1998/AH1419.	FV	FV	425.00
	b. 2000/AH1420.	FV	FV	375.00

2003 ISSUE

#26-28 Dallah (coffee pot) added to wmk. area.

		VG	VF	UNC
26	**50 DIRHAMS**			
	2004/AH1424. Similar to #22.	FV	FV	27.50

		VG	VF	UNC
27	**100 DIRHAMS**			
	2003/AH1423; 2004/AH1425. Similar to #23 but w/silver overprint of tower at upper r.	FV	FV	45.00
28	**500 DIRHAMS**			
	2004/AH1424. Blue on m/c unpt.	FV	FV	200.00

UNITED STATES OF AMERICA

The area of the North American continent currently controlled by the United States of America was originally inhabited by numerous groups of Indian tribes. Some of these groups settled in particular areas, creating permanent settlements, while others were nomadic, traveling great distances and living off the land.

English explorers John and Sebastian Cabot reached Nova Scotia in what is today Canada in 1497; in 1534 the French gained a foothold with the explorations of Jacques Cartier. In 1541 the Spanish explorer Coronado traversed the south central portion of the country in what was to become the states of New Mexico, Texas, Nebraska and Oklahoma. In 1542 another Spaniard, Juan Cabrillo navigated north from Mexico along the Pacific coastline to California. The Spanish set up the first permanent settlement of Europeans in North America at St. Augustine, Florida in 1565. In 1607 the English settled in Jamestown, Virginia, and in 1620 at Plymouth, Massachusetts. This was followed closely by Dutch settlements in Albany and New York in 1624, and in 1638 the Swedes arrived in Delaware. From their foothold in Canada, French explorers pushed inland through the Great Lakes. Jean Nicolet explored what was to become Wisconsin in 1634, and in 1673 explorers Marquette and Joliet reached Iowa. In the 1650s the Dutch won the Swedish lands, and in 1664 the English gained control of the Dutch lands, thus giving the English control all along the Atlantic Coast. The resulting thirteen British colonies; New Hampshire, Vermont, Massachusetts, Rhode Island, Connecticut, New York, Pennsylvania, Delaware, Maryland, Virginia, North Carolina, South Carolina and Georgia formed the nucleus of what would become the United States of America.

From this point on tensions grew between the English, who could not expand westward from their settlements along the Atlantic Coast, and the French who had settled inland into the Ohio river valley. This dispute ended in 1763 after a war with the French loosing control of lands east of the Mississippi river. Manufacturing, textiles and other industry was developing at this time, and by 1775 about one-seventh of the world's production of raw iron came from the colonies. From 1771-1783 the war for American Independence was fought by the colonists against the English, and settled by the Peace of Paris in 1783. Americans gained control of lands south of the St. Lawrence and Great Lakes, and east of the Mississippi, with the exception of Florida which would remain under Spanish control until 1821. At the close of the war, the population was about 3 million, many of whom lived on self-sufficient family farms. Fishing, lumbering and the production of grains for export were becoming major economic endeavors. The newly independent states formed a loose confederation, but in 1787 approved the Constitution of the United States which is the framework for the goverment today. In 1789 it's first president, George Washington was elected, and the capitol was set up in New York City. In 1800 the capitol was moved to a planned city, Washington, D.C. where it remains.

Westward expansion was an inevitability as population grew. French territory west of the Mississippi, stretching to the northern Pacific was purchased in 1804 under the presidency of Thomas Jefferson, who then sent out Lewis and Clark on expedition of discovery. Spain granted independence to Mexico in 1821, which included lands which would become the states of California, New Mexico, Arizona and Texas. From 1836-1845 Texas was an independent republic, not joining the United States until 1845. Upon losing a war with the United States, Mexico ceded California (including most of Arizona and New Mexico) to the United States in 1848. Gold was discovered in California that year, and western migration took off on overland wagon trains or around-the-horn sail and steam ships. Hawaii came under U.S. protection in 1851. As the country developed in the 19th century, the northern states increased in commerce and industry while the southern states developed a vast agricultural base through the use of slave labor. Northern political and social threats to slavery lead twelve southern states to secede from the Union in 1860 forming the Confederate States of America. The ensuing Civil War lasted until 1865, at which time slavery was abolished and the States reunited.

In 1867 Alaska was purchased from Russia. The transcontinental railroad was completed in 1869. The central region of the country west of the Mississippi River and east of the Rocky Mountains was the last to be developed, beginning after the Civil War, with the establishment of cattle ranches and farms. Between 1870 and 1891 the nomadic Native American population clashed with settlers and federal troops. By 1891 the Native Americans were confined to reservations.

At the close of the 19th century the United States embarked on a colonial mission of its own, with advances into Cuba, Puerto Rico, Panama, Nicaragua and the Philippines. This resulted in the Spanish-American War which was quickly decided, ending Spanish colonial dominance, and signaling the rise of the United States as a world power. Slow to enter both World Wars of the 20th century, it was a major contributor to the conclusion of both, making it one of the major nations of the 20th century.

MONETARY SYSTEM:
1 Dollar = 100 Cents

SIGNATURE VARIETIES

SERIES	TREASURER	SECRETARY
1963	Kathryn O'Hay Granahan	C. Douglas Dillon
1963A	Kathryn O'Hay Granahan	Henry H. Fowler
1963B	Kathryn O'Hay Granahan	Joseph W. Barr
1969	Dorothy Andrews Elston	David M. Kennedy
1969A	Dorothy Andrews Kabis	David M. Kennedy
1969B	Dorothy Andrews Kabis	John B. Connally
1969C	Romana Acosta Banuelos	John B. Connally
1969D	Romana Acosta Banuelos	George P. Schultz
1974	Francine I. Neff	William E. Simon
1977	Azie Taylor Morton	W. Michael Blumenthal
1977A	Azie Taylor Morton	J. William Miller
1981	Angela M. Buchanan	Donald T. Regan
1981A	Katherine Davalos Ortega	Donald T. Regan
1985	Katherine Davalos Ortega	John A. Baker III
1988	Katherine Davalos Ortega	Nicholas F. Brady
1988A-1990	Catalina Vasquez Villalpando	Nicholas F. Brady
1993	Mary Ellen Withrow	Lloyd Bentson
1995, 1996	Mary Ellen Withrow	Robert E. Rubin
1999	Mary Ellen Withrow	Lawrence Summers
2001	Rosario Marin	Paul H. O'Neill
2003, 2004	Rosario Marin	John Snow

BANKNOTE DESIGNS

1 DOLLAR	Portr. George Washington. Great Seal flanking ONE on back.
2 DOLLAR	Portr. Thomas Jefferson. Monticello on back to 1963, signing of the Declaration of Independence, 1976; 1995 series.
5 DOLLAR	Portr. Abraham Lincoln. Lincoln Memorial on back.
10 DOLLAR	Portr. Alexander Hamilton. U. S. Treasury bldg. on back.
20 DOLLAR	Portr. Andrew Jackson. White House on back.
50 DOLLAR	Portr. Ulysses S. Grant. U. S. Capitol bldg. on back.
100 DOLLAR	Portr. Benjamin Franklin. Independence Hall on back.

REPLACEMENT NOTES:
All issues since about 1916 have a star either before or after the serial number, depending on type of note.
All government notes of the United States, since issue of the Demand Notes of 1861, are still valid as legal tender.
The different types of currency are treated in a number of specialized catalogs such as the following:
   Friedberg, Robert; *Paper Money of the United States.*
   Hickman, John and Oakes, Dean; *Standard Catalog of* National Bank Notes.
   Krause, Chester L. and Lemke, Robert F.; *Standard* Catalog of United States Paper Money.
Detailed information, as given in these catalogs, is not repeated here. The following listing is limited to the individual types and their principal varieties.

REPUBLIC

UNITED STATES NOTES - SMALL SIZE
Red Treasury seal.

SERIES OF 1963
Replacement Notes: Serial # suffix is an *.

382	2 DOLLARS		VG	VF	UNC
	1963				
	a.	1963.	FV	FV	10.00
	b.	1963A.	FV	FV	13.00
383	5 DOLLARS		VG	VF	UNC
	1963		FV	9.00	20.00

SERIES OF 1966

384	100 DOLLARS		VG	VF	UNC
	1966.				
	a.	1966.	FV	125.00	550.00
	b.	1966A.	FV	250.00	1250.00

FEDERAL RESERVE NOTES - SMALL SIZE

Green Treasury seal. Replacement notes: Serial # suffix is an *. Imprinted #, letter and name (in seal at l.) of 1 of the 12 Federal Reserve Banks: A-1: BostonE-5: RichmondI-9: Minneapolis B-2: New YorkF-6: AtlantaJ-10: Kansas City C-3: PhiladelphiaG-7: ChicagoK-11: Dallas D-4: ClevelandH-8: St. LouisL-12: San Francisco

1963 SERIES

443	1 DOLLAR		VG	VF	UNC
	1963.				
	a.	1963. (A-L).	FV	FV	4.00
	b.	1963A. (A-L).	FV	FV	4.00
	c.	1963B. (B; E; G; J; L).	FV	FV	5.00

444	5 DOLLARS		VG	VF	UNC
	1963.				
	a.	1963. (A-D; F-H; J-L).	FV	FV	20.00
	b.	1963A. (A-L).	FV	FV	15.00

445	10 DOLLARS		VG	VF	UNC
	1963.				
	a.	1963. (A-H; J-L).	FV	FV	50.00
	b.	1963A. (A-L).	FV	FV	37.50

446	20 DOLLARS		VG	VF	UNC
	1963.				
	a.	1963. (A-B; D-H; J-L).	FV	FV	75.00
	b.	1963A. (A-L).	FV	FV	60.00

447	50 DOLLARS		VG	VF	UNC
	1963A. (A-L).		FV	FV	150.00

448	100 DOLLARS		VG	VF	UNC
	1963A. (A-L).		FV	FV	275.00

1969 SERIES

449	1 DOLLAR		VG	VF	UNC
	1969.				
	a.	1969. (A-L).	FV	FV	4.00
	b.	1969A. (A-L).	FV	FV	4.00
	c.	1969B. (A-L).	FV	FV	4.00
	d.	1969C. (B; D-L).	FV	FV	5.00
	e.	1969D. (A-L).	FV	FV	5.00
450	5 DOLLARS				
	1969.				
	a.	1969. (A-L).	FV	FV	15.00
	b.	1969A. (A-L).	FV	FV	20.00
	c.	1969B. (A-L).	FV	FV	50.00
	d.	1969C. (A-L).	FV	FV	20.00
451	10 DOLLARS				
	1969.				
	a.	1969. (A-L).	FV	FV	35.00
	b.	1969A. (A-L).	FV	FV	35.00
	c.	1969B. (A-L).	FV	FV	100.00
	d.	1969C. (A-L).	FV	FV	40.00
452	20 DOLLARS				
	1969.				
	a.	1969. (A-L).	FV	FV	60.00
	b.	1969A. (A-L).	FV	FV	75.00
	c.	1969B. (B; D-L).	FV	FV	150.00
	d.	1969C. (A-L).	FV	FV	50.00

		VG	VF	UNC
453	**50 DOLLARS** 1969.	FV	FV	200.00
	a. 1969. (A-L).	FV	FV	200.00
	b. 1969A. (A-L).	FV	FV	200.00
	c. 1969B. (A-B; E-G; K).	FV	FV	1200.00
	d. 1969C. (A-L).	FV	FV	150.00
454	**100 DOLLARS** 1969.			
	a. 1969. (A-L).	FV	FV	225.00
	b. 1969A. (A-L).	FV	FV	225.00
	c. 1969C. (A-L).	FV	FV	225.00

1974 SERIES

		VG	VF	UNC
455	**1 DOLLAR** 1974. (A-L).	FV	FV	4.00
456	**5 DOLLARS** 1974. (A-L).	FV	FV	15.00
457	**10 DOLLARS** 1974. (A-L).	FV	FV	35.00
458	**20 DOLLARS** 1974. (A-L).	FV	FV	60.00
459	**50 DOLLARS** 1974. (A-L).	FV	FV	200.00
460	**100 DOLLARS** 1974. (A-L).	FV	FV	200.00

1976 SERIES

#461, U.S. Bicentennial - Trumbull's painting *Signing of the Declaration of Independence*

		VG	VF	UNC
461	**2 DOLLARS** 1976. (A-L).	FV	FV	6.00

Note: #461 is also available in uncut sheets of 4, 16 and 32 notes.

1977 SERIES

		VG	VF	UNC
462	**1 DOLLAR** 1977.			
	a. 1977. (A-L).	FV	FV	4.00
	b. 1977A. (A-L).	FV	FV	4.00
463	**5 DOLLARS** 1977.			
	a. 1977. (A-L).	FV	FV	10.00
	b. 1977A. (A-L).	FV	FV	18.00
464	**10 DOLLARS** 1977.			
	a. 1977. (A-L).	FV	FV	40.00
	b. 1977A. (A-L).	FV	FV	35.00
465	**20 DOLLARS** 1977. (A-L).	FV	FV	60.00
466	**50 DOLLARS** 1977. (A-L).	FV	FV	175.00

		VG	VF	UNC
467	**100 DOLLARS** 1977. (A-L).	FV	FV	225.00

1981 SERIES

Note: Since Oct. 1981 the Bureau of Engraving and Printing has made available to collectors uncut sheets of 4, 16, and 32 notes of the $1.00 and $2.00 denominations.

		VG	VF	UNC
468	**1 DOLLAR** 1981.			
	a. 1981. (A-L).	FV	FV	4.00
	b. 1981A. (A-L).	FV	FV	4.00
469	**5 DOLLARS** 1981.			
	a. 1981. (A-L).	FV	FV	20.00
	b. 1981A. (A-L).	FV	FV	20.00
470	**10 DOLLARS** 1981.			
	a. 1981. (A-L).	FV	FV	40.00
	b. 1981A. (A-L).	FV	FV	40.00
471	**20 DOLLARS** 1981.			
	a. 1981. (A-L).	FV	FV	75.00
	b. 1981A. (A-L).	FV	FV	60.00

		VG	VF	UNC
472	**50 DOLLARS** 1981.			
	a. 1981. (A-L).	FV	FV	200.00
	b. 1981A. (A-L).	FV	FV	225.00
473	**100 DOLLARS** 1981.			
	a. 1981. (A-L).	FV	FV	275.00
	b. 1981A. (A-L).	FV	FV	275.00

1985 SERIES

		VG	VF	UNC
474	**1 DOLLAR** 1985. (A-L).	FV	FV	4.00
475	**5 DOLLARS** 1985. (A-L).	FV	FV	15.00
476	**10 DOLLARS** 1985. (A-L).	FV	FV	35.00
477	**20 DOLLARS** 1985. (A-L).	FV	FV	50.00
478	**50 DOLLARS** 1985. (A-L).	FV	FV	120.00
479	**100 DOLLARS** 1985. (A-L).	FV	FV	175.00

1988 SERIES

		VG	VF	UNC
480	**1 DOLLAR** 1988.			
	a. 1988. (A-L).	FV	FV	4.00
	b. 1988A. (A-L).	FV	FV	4.00
	c. 1988A Web Press. (A-C; E-G).	FV	8.00	40.00
481	**5 DOLLARS** 1988.			
	a. 1988. (A-L).	FV	FV	15.00
	b. 1988A. (A-L).	FV	FV	15.00
482	**10 DOLLARS** 1988A (A-L).	FV	FV	35.00
483	**20 DOLLARS** 1988A (A-L).	FV	FV	50.00
484	**50 DOLLARS** 1988 (A-L).	FV	FV	150.00
485	**100 DOLLARS** 1988 (A-L).	FV	FV	200.00

1990 SERIES

#486-489 w/additional row of micro-printing: *THE UNITED STATES OF AMERICA* repeated around portr. Filament w/value and *U.S.A.* repeated inversely at l.

		VG	VF	UNC
486	**10 DOLLARS** 1990. (A-L).	FV	FV	20.00
487	**20 DOLLARS** 1990. (A-L).	FV	FV	30.00
488	**50 DOLLARS** 1990. (A-L).	FV	FV	100.00
489	**100 DOLLARS** 1990. (A-L).	FV	FV	150.00

1993 SERIES

		VG	VF	UNC
490	**1 DOLLAR** 1993.			
	a. 1993. (A-G; L).	FV	FV	2.00
	b. 1993. Web Press. (G-I; K; L).	FV	4.00	15.00
491	**5 DOLLARS** 1993 (A-C; E-L).		FV	15.00
492	**10 DOLLARS** 1993 (A-D, F-H, J, L).		FV	20.00
493	**20 DOLLARS** 1993. (A-L).		FV	40.00
494	**50 DOLLARS** 1993 (A, B, D, E, G, H, J, K).		FV	135.00
495	**100 DOLLARS** 1993. (A-L).		FV	150.00

1995 SERIES

		VG	VF	UNC
496	**1 DOLLAR** 1995.			
	a. 1995. (A-L).	FV	FV	2.00
	b. 1995. Web Press. (A; B; D; F).	FV	4.00	17.50
497	**2 DOLLARS** 1995. (F).	FV	FV	4.00
498	**5 DOLLARS** 1995 (A-L).	FV	FV	10.00
499	**10 DOLLARS** 1995 (A-L).	FV	FV	25.00
500	**20 DOLLARS** 1995 (B-L).	FV	FV	40.00

Federal Reserve Bank codes below serial # at upper l. for notes starting in 1996.

A-1: (Boston)	E-5: (Richmond)	I-9: (Minneapolis)
B-2: (New York)	F-6: (Atlanta)	J-10: (Kansas City)
C-3: (Philadelphia)	G-7: (Chicago)	K-11: (Dallas)
D-4: (Cleveland)	H-8: (St. Louis)	L-12: (San Francisco)

1996 SERIES

#501-503 redesigned and enlarged portr. on face at l. ctr. and as wmk. Green value at lower r. Security thread at l. Backs similar to #493-495.

501	20 DOLLARS	VG	VF	UNC
	1996. (A1-L12).	FV	FV	30.00

502	50 DOLLARS	VG	VF	UNC
	1996 (A1-L12).	FV	FV	60.00

503	100 DOLLARS	VG	VF	UNC
	1996 (A1-L12).	FV	FV	115.00

1999 SERIES

#505-507 redesigned and enlarged portr. on face at l. ctr. and as wmk.

504	1 DOLLAR	VG	VF	UNC
	1999 (A-L).	FV	FV	2.00

505	5 DOLLARS	VG	VF	UNC
	1999 (A1-L12).	FV	FV	10.00
506	10 DOLLARS			
	1999 (A1-L12).	FV	FV	15.00
507	20 DOLLARS			
	1999 (A1-L12).	FV	FV	30.00
508	100 DOLLARS			
	1999(A1-L12).	FV	FV	115.00

2001 SERIES

509	1 DOLLAR	VG	VF	UNC
	2001 (A-L).	FV	FV	2.00
510	5 DOLLARS			
	2001 (A1-L12).	FV	FV	10.00
511	10 DOLLARS			
	2001 (A1-L12).	FV	FV	20.00
512	20 DOLLARS			
	2001 (A1-L12).	FV	FV	30.00
513	50 DOLLARS			
	2001 (A1-L12).	FV	FV	60.00

514	100 DOLLARS	VG	VF	UNC
	2001 (A1-L12).	FV	FV	115.00

2003 SERIES

515	1 DOLLAR	VG	VF	UNC
	2003.	FV	FV	2.00
	a. 2003 (A-L).	FV	FV	2.00
	b. 2003A (A-L).	FV	FV	2.00
516	2 DOLLARS			
	2003 (A1-L12).	FV	FV	10.00
517	5 DOLLARS			
	2003 (A1-L12).	FV	FV	10.00
518	10 DOLLARS			
	2003 (A1-L12).	FV	FV	17.50
519	100 DOLLARS			
	2003.			
	a. 2003.	FV	FV	120.00
	b. 2003A.	FV	FV	120.00

2004 SERIES

#519-520 redesigned face and back, color underprint.

520	10 DOLLARS	VG	VF	UNC
	2004A (A1-L12).	FVFV		15.00

521	20 DOLLARS			
	2004. Black on lt. green, blue and tan unpt. Jackson at l. ctr. Back green. White House at ctr. on back.			
	a. 2004 (A1-L12).	FV	FV	27.50
	b. 2004A (A1-L12).	FV	FV	27.50

522	50 DOLLARS	VG	VF	UNC
	2004.			
	a. 2004 (A1-L12).	FV	FV	60.00
	b. 2004A (A1-L12).	FV	FV	60.00

MILITARY PAYMENT CERTIFICATES

Replacement Notes: Can be identified by serial # which will have a prefix letter but no suffix letter. All replacement notes are much scarcer than regular issues which have prefix and suffix letters.

Replacement Notes:

Can be identified by serial # which will have a prefix letter but no suffix letter. All replacement notes are much scarcer than regular issues which have prefix and suffix letters.

SERIES 591

26.5.1961 to 6.1.1964.

#M43-M46 Head of Statue of Liberty at r.

M43	5 CENTS	VF	XF	UNC
	ND (1961). Lilac on green and yellow unpt.	3.50	12.50	55.00

M44	10 CENTS	VF	XF	UNC
	ND (1961). Blue on lilac unpt.	4.00	15.00	65.00
M45	25 CENTS			
	ND (1961). Green on purple unpt.	17.50	55.00	140.00
M46	50 CENTS			
	ND (1961). Brown on aqua unpt.	35.00	85.00	240.00
M47	1 DOLLAR			
	ND (1961). Red on purple and m/c unpt. Portr. woman facing l. at r.	25.00	90.00	275.00
M48	5 DOLLARS			
	ND (1961). Blue on m/c unpt. Woman at l.	550.00	1750.00	4500.00

M49	10 DOLLARS	VF	XF	UNC
	ND (1961). Green on m/c unpt. Portr. woman 3/4 facing l. at r.	200.00	350.00	2000.00

SERIES 611

6.1.1964 to 28.4.1969.

#M50-M53 Liberty head profile facing r. at l.

M50	5 CENTS	VF	XF	UNC
	ND (1964). Blue on m/c unpt.	5.00	20.00	40.00
M51	10 CENTS			
	ND (1964). Green on m/c unpt.	5.00	20.00	45.00
M52	25 CENTS			
	ND (1964). Brown on m/c unpt.	30.00	110.00	275.00
M53	50 CENTS			
	ND (1964). Lilac on m/c unpt.	30.00	100.00	275.00

M54	1 DOLLAR	VF	XF	UNC
	ND (1964). Green on m/c unpt. Portr. woman w/tiara facing at l.	5.00	27.50	100.00
M55	5 DOLLARS			
	ND (1964). Red on m/c unpt. Woman facing at ctr.	125.00	375.00	2000.00
M56	10 DOLLARS			
	ND (1964). Blue on violet and m/c unpt. Portr. woman facing l. at ctr.	130.00	375.00	1400.00

SERIES 641

31.8.1965 to 21.10.1968.

#M57-M60 woman at l. Eagle with outstretched wings clasping fasces at ctr. on back.

M57	5 CENTS	VF	XF	UNC
	ND (1965). Purple on blue unpt.	1.00	3.50	13.50
M58	10 CENTS			
	ND (1965). Green on dk. red unpt.	1.00	4.00	18.50
M59	25 CENTS			
	ND (1965). Red on blue-green unpt.	2.50	10.00	24.00
M60	50 CENTS			
	ND (1965). Orange on m/c unpt.	3.50	15.00	35.00
M61	1 DOLLAR			
	ND (1965). Lt. red on m/c unpt. Woman at r.	4.00	17.50	45.00
M62	5 DOLLARS			
	ND (1965). Green on m/c unpt. Woman w/wreath of flowers at ctr. Woman facing r. at ctr. on back.	17.50	70.00	250.00

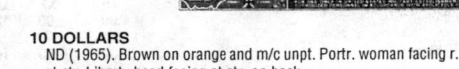

M63	10 DOLLARS	VF	XF	UNC
	ND (1965). Brown on orange and m/c unpt. Portr. woman facing r. at ctr. Liberty head facing at ctr. on back.	10.00	30.00	250.00

SERIES 661

21.10.1968 to 11.8.1969.

#M64-M67 woman wearing scarf at l.

M64	5 CENTS	VF	XF	UNC
	ND (1968). Lt. green and lilac on m/c unpt.	0.50	3.00	10.00
M65	10 CENTS			
	ND (1968). Blue and violet on m/c unpt.	0.50	3.00	10.00
M66	25 CENTS			
	ND (1968). Brown and orange on m/c unpt.	2.00	12.50	27.50
M67	50 CENTS			
	ND (1968). Red and green on m/c unpt.	2.00	10.00	22.50

M68	1 DOLLAR	VF	XF	UNC
	ND (1968). Blue on m/c unpt. Portr. woman 3/4 facing l. at r. Mountain scene on back.	5.00	12.50	24.00

M69	5 DOLLARS	VF	XF	UNC
	ND (1968). Dk. brown on red and m/c unpt. Woman holding flowers at ctr. Girl's head at ctr. on back.	5.00	15.00	30.00
M70	10 DOLLARS			
	ND (1968). Red and orange on m/c unpt. Woman holding fasces at l. Woman facing l. at ctr. r. on back.	200.00	750.00	1850.00
M71	20 DOLLARS			
	ND (1968). Black, brown and blue on m/c unpt. Woman at ctr. Standing woman at l. on back.	125.00	350.00	1450.00

SERIES 651

28.4.1969 to 19.11.1973.

#M72A-M74 similar to Series 641 except for colors and the addition of a "Minuteman statue" at l.

M72A	5 CENTS	VF	XF	UNC
	ND (1969). Dk. blue on m/c unpt.	—	—	700.00
M72B	10 CENTS			
	ND (1969). Red-violet on m/c unpt.	—	—	700.00
M72C	25 CENTS			
	ND (1969). Aqua blue on m/c unpt.	—	—	700.00
M72D	50 CENTS			
	ND (1969). Dk. brown on m/c unpt.	—	—	275.00
M72E	1 DOLLAR			
	ND (1969). Green on violet and m/c unpt. Portr. woman facing l. at r.	6.00	25.00	45.00

M73	5 DOLLARS	VF	XF	UNC
	ND (1969). Brown on green and m/c unpt. Portr. woman facing w/wreath of flowers at ctr.	50.00	150.00	275.00
M74	10 DOLLARS			
	ND (1969). Violet on m/c unpt. Woman at ctr.	50.00	150.00	275.00

SERIES 681

11.8.1969 to 7.10.1970.

#M75-M78 submarine at r. Astronaut in spacewalk at ctr. on back.

M75	5 CENTS	VF	XF	UNC
	ND (1969). Green and blue.	1.00	5.00	12.50
M76	10 CENTS			
	ND (1969). Violet and blue.	1.00	5.00	16.00
M77	25 CENTS			
	ND (1969). Red and blue.	2.00	10.00	27.50
M78	50 CENTS			
	ND (1969). Brown and blue.	3.00	15.00	25.00
M79	1 DOLLAR			
	ND (1969). Violet on m/c unpt. Air Force pilot at r. Four Thunderbirds in formation at ctr. on back.	3.00	15.00	25.00
M80	5 DOLLARS			
	ND (1969). Purple and green. Sailor at ctr. Eagle at ctr. on back.	10.00	50.00	125.00
M81	10 DOLLARS			
	ND (1969). Blue-green and black. Infantryman (Green Beret) at ctr. Tank at ctr. on back.	30.00	125.00	300.00
M82	20 DOLLARS			
	ND (1969). Brown, pink and blue. Portr. soldier facing wearing helmet at ctr. B-52 bomber at ctr. on back.	30.00	100.00	1100.00

SERIES 691

#M83-M85 not assigned.

M87	1 DOLLAR	VF	XF	UNC
	ND (1969). Slate gray on lt. blue unpt. Woman's port. ctr. Allegorical female seated at ctr. on back.	—	—	250.00

M88	5 DOLLARS	VF	XF	UNC
	ND (1969). Brown on lt. blue unpt. Woman's hd. at l. looking r. Woman's head at ctr.	—	—	1000.00

M89	10 DOLLARS	VF	XF	UNC
	ND (1969). Turquoise on lt. blue and red unpt. Bust of woman at ctr. Young girl's hd. at ctr. on back.	—	—	1000.00

M90	20 DOLLARS	VF	XF	UNC
	ND (1969). Purple on blue and lt. blue unpt. Veiled woman's hd. at ctr. Eagle perched on rock at ctr. on back.	—	—	300.00

SERIES 692

7.10.1970 to 15.3.1973.

#M83-M86 sculpture of seated Roman warrior at l. (National Archives, Washington DC façade). Eagle at ctr. on back.

M91	5 CENTS	VF	XF	UNC
	ND (1970). Red-brown and lilac on m/c unpt.	1.00	7.50	16.50
M92	10 CENTS			
	ND (1970). Green and blue on m/c unpt.	1.00	7.50	17.50
M93	25 CENTS			
	ND (1970). Dk. blue on yellow and m/c unpt.	3.00	15.00	30.00
M94	50 CENTS			
	ND (1970). Purple on yellow and m/c unpt.	4.00	17.50	40.00

M95	1 DOLLAR	VF	XF	UNC
	ND (1970). Blue-green on m/c unpt. Portr. woman facing r. at l., flowers at bottom ctr. Buffalo at ctr. on back.	8.00	35.00	95.00
M96	5 DOLLARS			
	ND (1970). Brown on orange and m/c unpt. Girl and flowers at ctr. Elk family at l. ctr. on back.	50.00	200.00	1000.00
M97	10 DOLLARS			
	ND (1970). Blue on pink and m/c unpt. Indian Chief Hollow Horn Bear at ctr. Eagle at l. ctr. on back.	75.00	275.00	1150.00
M98	20 DOLLARS			
	ND (1970). Violet on orange and m/c unpt. Indian Chief Ouray at ctr. Dam on back.	30.00	200.00	1200.00

SERIES 701

#M99-M102 not assigned.

		VF	XF	UNC
M103	**1 DOLLAR** ND (1970). Lt. green on brown and orange unpt. Washington Irving and open books. Hay harvesting on back.	—	—	750.00

		VF	XF	UNC
M104	**5 DOLLARS** ND (1970). Purple on green unpt. Thomas Edison at r, light bulb at ctr., Benjamin Franklin and kite/key at l. Rocky Mountain vista on back at l. ctr.	—	—	750.00

		VF	XF	UNC
M105	**10 DOLLARS** ND (1970). Red-brown on tan unpt. Mt. Vernon at ctr., George Washington at r. Mountain vista at l. on back.	—	—	750.00

		VF	XF	UNC
M106	**20 DOLLARS** ND (1970). Brown on lt. blue-green unpt. Steamboat *Clermont* at l., Robert Fulton at r. Coastline vista at ctr. r. on back.	—	—	750.00

AAFES (ARMY AND AIR FORCE EXCHANGE SERVICE)

These AAFES issues are full color 1.516" diameter "pogs" made from 23mil styrene. They are used at U.S. Military bases active in Operation Iraqi Freedom and Operation Enduring Freedom as a substitute for coins. These bases are located in Afghanistan, Kuwait and Iraq among others. They are now accepted at stateside military BX/PX stores, but are not redistributed. These issues are printed in Texas, then packed and shipped to a U.S. base in Germany, from which they are distributed as needed to bases in country. The number in ( ) after the descriptions are the catalog numbers from the website www.aafespogs.com. Used with permission.

FIRST ISSUE

		VG	VF	UNC
M121	**5 CENTS** Large value in red on both sides. (1A51).	FV	FV	0.25
M122	**10 CENTS** Large vlaue in blue on both sides. (1A101).	FV	FV	0.50
M123	**25 CENTS** Large value in white on both sides. (1A251).	FV	FV	0.75

SECOND ISSUE

		VG	VF	UNC
M124	**5 CENTS** A-10 Thunderbolt II. (2A51).	FV	FV	0.25
M125	**5 CENTS** B-2 Spirit. (2B51).	FV	FV	0.25
M126	**5 CENTS** Patriot missile truck. (2C51).	FV	FV	0.25
M127	**5 CENTS** Paratroopers skyjumping. (2D51).	FV	FV	0.25
M128	**5 CENTS** B-52 Stratoforress. (2E51).	FV	FV	0.25
M129	**5 CENTS** A-7 Corsair II. (2F51).	FV	FV	0.25

		FV	FV	
M130	**5 CENTS** AH-64 Apache helicopter. (2G51).	FV	FV	0.25
M131	**5 CENTS** Operation Iraqi Freedom legend in clouds from a Patriot missle launching. (2H51).	FV	FV	0.25
M132	**5 CENTS** Two F-15 Eagles, sun in background. (2J51).	FV	FV	0.25
M133	**5 CENTS** Two F-15 Eagles, one banking. (2K51).	FV	FV	0.25
M134	**5 CENTS** Dolphin jumping upwards. (2L51).	FV	FV	0.25
M135	**5 CENTS** CH-47 Chinook helicopter transporting tank. (2M51).	FV	FV	0.25
M136	**10 CENTS** AC-130 Spectre front view. (2A101).	FV	FV	0.50
M137	**10 CENTS** Two F-16 Fighting Falcons. (2B101).	FV	FV	0.50
M138	**10 CENTS** Two H-60 Black Hawk helicopters and a CH-47 Chinook helicopter. (2C101).	FV	FV	0.50
M139	**10 CENTS** Operation Iraqi Freedom legend, surface-to-air missile launcher. (2D101).	FV	FV	0.50
M140	**10 CENTS** F-15 Eagle in banking turn. (2E101).	FV	FV	0.50
M141	**10 CENTS** Warheads on bombs. (2F101).	FV	FV	0.50
M142	**10 CENTS** Two soldiers wearing gas masks. (2G101).	FV	FV	0.50
M143	**10 CENTS** Troops around anti-aircraft gun. (2H101).	FV	FV	0.50
M144	**10 CENTS** Battleship firing. (2J101).	FV	FV	0.50
M145	**10 CENTS** Four pilots being assisted into four F-15 Eagles. (2K101).	FV	FV	0.50
M146	**10 CENTS** Soldier aiming a gun. (2L101).	FV	FV	0.50
M147	**10 CENTS** Tank advancing right. (2M101).	FV	FV	0.50
M148	**25 CENTS** CH-46 Sea Knight helicopter. (2A251).	FV	FV	0.75
M149	**25 CENTS** F-16 Fighting Falcon diving. (2B251).	FV	FV	0.75
M150	**25 CENTS** Close-up of soldier wearing gas mask. (2C251).	FV	FV	0.75
M151	**25 CENTS** Two UH-1 Iroquois helicopters advancing forward. (2D251).	FV	FV	0.75
M152	**25 CENTS** E-3 Sentry AWACS. (2E251).	FV	FV	0.75
M153	**25 CENTS** Pilot in cockpit of F-16 Fighting Falcon as seen from above. (2F251).	FV	FV	0.75
M154	**25 CENTS** Operation Iraqi Freedom legend, top of tank. (2G251).	FV	FV	0.75
M155	**25 CENTS** Radar installation. (2H251).	FV	FV	0.75
M156	**25 CENTS** F/A-18 Hornet in a banking turn. (2J251).	FV	FV	0.75
M157	**25 CENTS** Mother of all Bombs MOAB, in flight. (2K251).	FV	FV	0.75
M158	**25 CENTS** H-60 helicopter with soldier on ladder. (2L251).	FV	FV	0.75
M159	**25 CENTS** Jeep. (2M251).	FV	FV	0.75

THIRD ISSUE

		VG	VF	UNC
M160	**5 CENTS** 2003. Soldier inspecting mouth of child. (3A51).	FV	FV	0.25
M161	**5 CENTS** 2003. Soldier seated in vehicle, flag in background. (3B51).	FV	FV	0.25
M162	**5 CENTS** 2003. Soldier standing by flag. (3C51).	FV	FV	0.25
M163	**5 CENTS** 2003. Child on shoulders of soldier. (3D51).	FV	FV	0.25
M164	**5 CENTS** 2003. Soldier wearing protective MOPP gear. (3E51).	FV	FV	0.25
M165	**5 CENTS** 2003. *Operation Iraqi Freedom* legend. H-3 Sea King helicopter and soldier. (3F51).	FV	FV	0.25
M166	**5 CENTS** 2003. SWIFT hight speed vessel, HSV 2. Wave piercing catamaran. (3G51).	FV	FV	0.25
M167	**5 CENTS** 2003. Statue of Liberty and HH-65 Dolphin helicopter. (3H51).	FV	FV	0.25
M168	**5 CENTS** 2003. Soldier at BX/PX store. *We go where you go* legend. (3J51).	FV	FV	0.25
M169	**5 CENTS** 2003. *Proudly serving those who serve* legend, flag background. (3K51).	FV	FV	0.25
M170	**5 CENTS** 2003. KC-Extender refueling F/A-22 Raptor. (3L51).	FV	FV	0.25
M171	**5 CENTS** 2003. F/A-18 Hornet. (3M51).	FV	FV	0.25
M172	**10 CENTS** 2003. AH-640 Apache-Longbow helicopter. (3A101).	FV	FV	0.50
M173	**10 CENTS** 2003. Child's face and flag. (3B101).	FV	FV	0.50

		VG	VF	UNC
M174	**10 CENTS**	FV	FV	0.50
	2003. Soldier and flag. (3C101).			
M175	**10 CENTS**	FV	FV	0.50
	2003. *Operation Iraqi Freedom* legend. Flight deck crewmember in red/white helmet. (3D101).			
M176	**10 CENTS**	FV	FV	0.50
	F-16 Fighting Falcon, view over pilot's shoulder. (3E101).			
M177	**10 CENTS**	FV	FV	0.50
	2003. Soldier left, rock pile in background. (3F101).			
M178	**10 CENTS**	FV	FV	0.50
	2003. Flair of a rocket. (3G101).			
M179	**10 CENTS**	FV	FV	0.50
	2003. Seated soldier with shoulder missile launcher. (3H101).			
M180	**10 CENTS**	FV	FV	0.50
	2003. Soldier looking over barrel of weapon. (3J101).			
M181	**10 CENTS**	FV	FV	0.50
	2003. Soldier with machine gun on H-60 Black Hawk helicopter. (3K101).			
M182	**10 CENTS**	FV	FV	0.50
	2003. Amphibious tank. (3L101).			
M183	**10 CENTS**	FV	FV	0.50
	2003. C-130 Hercules dumping red liquid during flight. (3M101).			
M184	**25 CENTS**	FV	FV	0.75
	2003. Silhouette of soldier with machine gun facing right. (3A251).			
M185	**25 CENTS**	FV	FV	0.75
	2003. Silhouette of soldier with mounted machine gun facing left. (3B251).			
M186	**25 CENTS**	FV	FV	0.75
	2003. *Operation Iraqi Freedom* legend. Soldier saluting flag. (3C251).			
M187	**25 CENTS**	FV	FV	0.75
	2003. Two AV-8B Harrier jets on approach. (3D251).			
M188	**25 CENTS**	FV	FV	0.75
	2003. Silhouette of soldier on vehicle. (3E251).			
M189	**25 CENTS**	FV	FV	0.75
	2003. V-22 Osprey lifting off from carrier deck. (3F251).			
M190	**25 CENTS**	FV	FV	0.75
	2003. Soldier inspecting child's ear. (3G251).			
M191	**25 CENTS**	FV	FV	0.75
	2003. Lineup of C-130 Hercules cargo planes on runway. (3H251).			
M192	**25 CENTS**	FV	FV	0.75
	2003. U.S. Coast Guard Barque *Eagle*, the Academy's training vessel based in New London, Conn. (3J251).			
M193	**25 CENTS**	FV	FV	0.75
	2003. *Operation Enduring Freedom* legend. Soldier at console. (3K251).			
M194	**25 CENTS**	FV	FV	0.75
	2003. American flag on deck of an Aircraft carrier. (3L251).			
M195	**25 CENTS**	FV	FV	0.75
	2003. Three Marines in dress uniform. (3M251).			

FOURTH ISSUE

		VG	VF	UNC
M196	**5 CENTS**	FV	FV	0.25
	2004. F-35 flying right. (4A51).			
M197	**5 CENTS**	FV	FV	0.25
	2004. Sailor holding child. (4B51).			
M198	**5 CENTS**	FV	FV	0.25
	2004. Soldier and child. (4C51).			
M199	**5 CENTS**	FV	FV	0.25
	2004. CH-47 Chinook helicopter transporting cargo in net. (4D51).			
M200	**5 CENTS**	FV	FV	0.25
	2004. Patrial view, B-17 Flying Fortress. (4E51).			
M201	**5 CENTS**	FV	FV	0.25
	2004. *Operation Iraqi Freedom* legend. Soldier with full gear. (4F51).			
M202	**5 CENTS**	FV	FV	0.25
	2004. Sailor walking away, toward row of flags. (4G51).			
M203	**5 CENTS**	FV	FV	0.25
	2004. Female soldier facing, looking thru gun. (4H51).			
M204	**5 CENTS**	FV	FV	0.25
	2004. *We go where you go* legned. Female soldier. (4J51).			
M205	**5 CENTS**	FV	FV	0.25
	2004. *Proudly serving those who serve* legend. Three soldiers. (4K51).			
M206	**5 CENTS**	FV	FV	0.25
	2004. WWII Troops landing off of an amphibious craft. (4L51).			
M207	**5 CENTS**	FV	FV	0.25
	2004. Lookout tower silhouette. (4M51).			
M208	**10 CENTS**	FV	FV	0.50
	2004. Soldier standing left, holding machine gun. (4A101).			
M209	**10 CENTS**	FV	FV	0.50
	2004. WWII era female working on plane. (4B101).			
M210	**10 CENTS**	FV	FV	0.50
	2004. Soldier pointing. (4B101).			
M211	**10 CENTS**	FV	FV	0.50
	2004. *Operation Iraqi Freedom* legend. Two soldiers in desert. (4D101).			
M212	**10 CENTS**	FV	FV	0.50
	2004. Navy ship #3 superstructure and flag. (4E101).			
M213	**10 CENTS**	FV	FV	0.50
	2004. H-60 Black Hawk helicopter approaching. (4F101).			
M214	**10 CENTS**	FV	FV	0.50
	2004. *Operation Enduring Freedom* legend. Oil well smoke. (4G101).			
M215	**10 CENTS**	FV	FV	0.50
	2004. Tank profile left. (4H101).			

		VG	VF	UNC
M216	**10 CENTS**	FV	FV	0.50
	2004. Eight WWII crewmembers by plane. (4J101).			
M217	**10 CENTS**		FV	
	2004. Two soldiers near burning item. (4K101).			
M218	**10 CENTS**		FV	
	2004. B-1B Lancer cockpit. (4L101).			
M219	**10 CENTS**		FV	
	2004. H-60 Black Hawk helicopter on aircraft carrier. (4M101).			
M220	**25 CENTS**		FV	0.75
	2004. Two sailors helping third into deep-sea diving suit. (4A251).			
M221	**25 CENTS**		FV	0.75
	2004. U.S. Coast Guard craft with men standing under deck canopy. (4B251).			
M222	**25 CENTS**		FV	0.75
	2004. Soldier seated with sandbags. (4C251).			
M223	**25 CENTS**		FV	0.75
	2004. Child with small flag. (4D251).			
M224	**25 CENTS**		FV	0.75
	2004. Five WWII era pilots. (4E251).			
M225	**25 CENTS**		FV	0.75
	2004. WWII era submarine officer looking thru periscope. (4F251).			
M226	**25 CENTS**		FV	0.75
	2004. AV-BB Harrier rifting off from carrier deck. (4G251).			
M227	**25 CENTS**		FV	0.75
	2004. Plane #63. (4H251).			
M228	**25 CENTS**		FV	0.75
	2004. Machine gunner atop Humvee. (4J251).			
M229	**25 CENTS**		FV	0.75
	2004. *Operation Enduring Freedom* legend. C-130 Hercules cargo plane. (4K251).			
M230	**25 CENTS**		FV	0.75
	2004. *Operation Iraqi Freedom* legend. Soldier with machine gun. (4L251).			
M231	**25 CENTS**		FV	0.75
	2004. H-60 Black Hawk helicopter above soldier in the desert. (4M251).			

FIFTH ISSUE

		VG	VF	UNC
M232	**5 CENTS**	FV	FV	0.25
	2004. *Proudly serving those who serve* legend. Burger King ad on truck being unloaded from plane. (5A51).			
M233	**5 CENTS**		FV	0.25
	2004. Soldiers lined up at a BX/PX grand opening. (5B51).			
M234	**5 CENTS**		FV	0.25
	2004. BX/PX sign, soldiers around. (5C51).			
M235	**5 CENTS**		FV	0.25
	2004. Flight deck officer sending off P-51 Mustang. (5D51).			
M236	**5 CENTS**		FV	0.25
	2004. HH-53 Jolly Green Giant helicopter in flight. (5E51).			
M237	**5 CENTS**		FV	0.25
	2004. F-86 Sabre accending skyward. (5F51).			
M238	**5 CENTS**		FV	0.25
	2004. Soldier with Iraqi blue topped building in background. (5G51).			
M239	**5 CENTS**			
	2004. H-60 Black Hawk helicopter and sunset. (5H51).			
	a. With legend: *Operation Iraqi Freedom.*	FV	FV	0.40
	b. Without legend.	FV	FV	0.40
M240	**5 CENTS**		FV	0.25
	2004. Six TBM Avenger bombers in formation. (5J51).			
M241	**5 CENTS**		FV	0.25
	2004. Five jets comprised of: F-15E Strike Eagles, F-15 Eagle and F-16 Fighting Falcon in formation. Burning oil wells in distance. (5K51).			
M242	**5 CENTS**		FV	0.25
	2004. Goast Guard vessel. (5L51).			
M243	**5 CENTS**		FV	0.25
	2004. Capt. Charles "Chuck" Yeager with Bell XS-1. (5M51).			
M244	**10 CENTS**		FV	0.50
	2004. Six crewmembers of the B-29 Super Fortress *Enola Gay*. (5A101).			
M245	**10 CENTS**		FV	0.50
	2004. Soldier with infant, wife, flag behind. (5B101).			
M246	**10 CENTS**		FV	0.50
	2004. *Operation Enduring Freedom* legend. F-14 Tomcat and crew member on flight deck. (5C101).			
M247	**10 CENTS**		FV	0.50
	2004. Guard tower and razor wire. (5D101).			
M248	**10 CENTS**		FV	0.50
	2004. Humvee approaching. (5E101).			
M249	**10 CENTS**		FV	0.50
	2004. Soldier silhouette with night vision scope. (5F101).			
M250	**10 CENTS**		FV	0.50
	2004. 4B-24 Liberator in flight. (5G101).			
M251	**10 CENTS**		FV	0.50
	2004. Soldiers boarding rear of C-130 Hercules cargo transport. (5H101).			
M252	**10 CENTS**		FV	0.50
	2004. Pilot standing before F-4 Phantom II. (5J101).			
M253	**10 CENTS**		FV	0.50
	2004. Soldier with goggles and chains. (5K101).			
M254	**10 CENTS**		FV	0.50
	2004. Sailor greeting young daughter. (5L101).			
M255	**10 CENTS**		FV	0.50
	2004. Soldier seated with rifle in field. (5M101).			
M256	**25 CENTS**		FV	0.75
	2004. KC-B5 Stratotanker refueling F-16 Fighting Falcon. (5A251).			
M257	**25 CENTS**		FV	0.75
	2004. (5B251). B-1B Lancer flying away.			

M258	25 CENTS	VG	VF	UNC
	2004. Soldier standing next to flag. (5C251).	FV	FV	0.75
M259	25 CENTS			
	2004. Six F-16 Falcons, USAF *Thunderbirds* in formation. (5D251).	FV	FV	0.75
M260	25 CENTS			
	2004. Four airmen under wing. WWII Tuskeegee airmen. (5E251).	FV	FV	0.75
M261	25 CENTS			
	2004. F/A Hornet crossing the sound barrier. (5F251).	FV	FV	0.75
M262	25 CENTS			
	2004. Humvee in rearview mirror. (5G251).			
	a. With legend: *Operation Enduring Freedom.*	FV	FV	1.00
	b. Without legend.	FV	FV	1.00
M263	25 CENTS			
	2004. WACS in front of B-17 Flying Fortress. (5H251).	FV	FV	0.75
M264	25 CENTS			
	2004. Flag raising on Iwo Jima. (5J251).	FV	FV	0.75
M265	25 CENTS			
	2004. *Operation Iraqi Freedom* legend. Man and german shepard. (5K251).	FV	FV	0.75
M266	25 CENTS			
	2004. B-17 Flying fortress and crew. (5L251).	FV	FV	0.75
M267	25 CENTS			
	2004. *Operation Iraqi Freedom* legend. Crew member inspecting plane nose. (5M251).	FV	FV	0.75

SIXTH ISSUE

Due to the use of selected Elvis Presley images, this issue was limited to 50,000 pieces of each design.

M268	5 CENTS	VG	VF	UNC
	2005. P-51 Mustang. (6A51).	FV	FV	0.75
M269	5 CENTS			
	2005. Two soldiers; one seated and one standing. (6B51).	FV	FV	0.75
M270	5 CENTS			
	2005. B-17 Flying Fortress *Our Mom* and crew. (6C51).	FV	FV	0.75
M271	5 CENTS			
	2005. A-10 Thunderbolt II in the sky, seen from below. (6D51).	FV	FV	0.75
M272	5 CENTS			
	2005. Soldier looking in hillside cave. (6E51).	FV	FV	0.75
M273	5 CENTS			
	2005. Air Force One, VC-25 in flight. (6F51).	FV	FV	0.75
M274	5 CENTS			
	2005. OH-58 Kiowa Warrior helicopter, sun behind. (6G51).	FV	FV	0.75
M275	5 CENTS			
	2005. *Operation Iraqi Freedom* legend. Soldier kneeling with gun. (6H51).	FV	FV	0.75
M276	5 CENTS			
	2005. *Operation Enduring Freedom* legend. Two soldiers walking, white domed building in background. (6J51).	FV	FV	0.75
M277	5 CENTS			
	2005. CH-46 Sea Knight helicopter, soldiers jumping out back. (6K51).	FV	FV	0.75
M278	5 CENTS			
	2005. Two soldiers launching mortar. (6L51).	FV	FV	0.75
M279	5 CENTS			
	2005. Elvis Presley in fatigues leaning against barrack wall. (6M51).	FV	FV	3.00
M280	10 CENTS			
	2005. CH-47 Chinook helicopter in desert, soldier with gun. (6A101).	FV	FV	1.00
M281	10 CENTS			
	2005. Six soldiers outside large tent, rainbow in background. (6B101).	FV	FV	1.00
M282	10 CENTS			
	2005. HH-60 Dolphin helicopter in flight. (6C101).	FV	FV	1.00
M283	10 CENTS			
	2005. Elvis Presley in dress uniform standing on river bridge. (6D101).	FV	FV	3.00
M284	10 CENTS			
	2005. Elvis Presley advancing between vertical opening. (6E101).	FV	FV	3.00
M285	10 CENTS			
	2005. Elvis Presley leaning against building wall. (6F101).	FV	FV	3.00
M286	10 CENTS			
	2005. Navy football player - Midshipman. (6G101).	FV	FV	1.00
M287	10 CENTS			
	2005. Air Force football player - Falcons. (6H101).	FV	FV	1.00
M288	10 CENTS			
	2005. Army football player - Black Knights. (6J101).	FV	FV	1.00
M289	10 CENTS			
	2005. Soldier sitting with child. (6K101).	FV	FV	1.00
M290	10 CENTS			
	2005. Soldier walking amongst confiscated weapons. (6L101).	FV	FV	1.00
M291	10 CENTS			
	2005. Three shoulders advancing with weapons pointed. (6M101).			
	a. With legend: *Operation Enduring Freedom.*	FV	FV	1.50
	b. Without legend.	FV	FV	1.50
M292	25 CENTS			
	2005. Female sailor and young child. (6A251).	FV	FV	1.50
M293	25 CENTS			
	2005. Soldier profile clutching rifle. Image from MPC #M81. (6B251).	FV	FV	1.50
M294	25 CENTS			
	2005. Submarine conning tower. (6C251).	FV	FV	1.50
M295	25 CENTS			
	2005. Oil wells buring. (6D251).	FV	FV	1.50
M296	25 CENTS			
	2005. B-1B Lancer flying before pyramids. (6E251).	FV	FV	1.50

M297	25 CENTS	VG	VF	UNC
	2005. *Operation Iraqi Freedom* legend. Red Cross H-60 Black Hawk helicopter. (6F251).	FV	FV	1.50
M298	25 CENTS			
	2005. Soldier standing before Humvee. (6G251).			
	a. With legend: *Operation Enduring Freedom.*	FV	FV	2.00
	b. Without legend.	FV	FV	2.00
M299	25 CENTS			
	2005. SR-71 Black Bird as seen from above. (6H251).	FV	FV	1.50
M300	25 CENTS			
	2005. Army NASCAR. (6J251).	FV	FV	1.50
M301	25 CENTS			
	2005. F/A-18 Hornet takeoff from aircraft carrier. (6K251).	FV	FV	1.50
M302	25 CENTS			
	2005. Flag montage of the Allies: United States, Australia and Great Britain. (6L251).	FV	FV	1.50
M303	25 CENTS			
	2005. *Proudly serving those who serve* legend. Soldiers with banner. (6M251).	FV	FV	1.50

SEVENTH ISSUE

M304	5 CENTS	VG	VF	UNC
	2005. General Eisenhower talking to 101st Airborne troops before the Normandy invasion. (7A51).	FV	FV	0.25
M305	5 CENTS			
	2005. Five soldiers before AAFES store. (7B51).	FV	FV	0.25
M306	5 CENTS			
	2005. Soldier and Medal of Honor. (7C51).	FV	FV	0.25
M307	5 CENTS			
	2005. Pilot close-up. (7D51).	FV	FV	0.25
M308	5 CENTS			
	2005. Ronald Reagan in tie close-up. (7E51).	FV	FV	0.25
M309	5 CENTS			
	2005. Two soldiers with guns beside jeep. (7F51).	FV	FV	0.25
M310	5 CENTS			
	2005. Soldier giving kid candy in street. (7G51).	FV	FV	0.25
M311	5 CENTS			
	2005. *Operation Iraqi Freedom*, plane in fligth right. (7H51).	FV	FV	0.25
M312	5 CENTS			
	2005. Four WWII planes above aircraft carrier. (7J51).	FV	FV	0.25
M313	5 CENTS			
	2005. Soldier holding Purple Heart. (7K51).	FV	FV	0.25
M314	5 CENTS			
	2005. *Operation Enduring Freedom* legend. Tank. (7L51).	FV	FV	0.25
M315	5 CENTS			
	2005. Four soldiers around anti-aircraft gun. (7M51).	FV	FV	0.25
M316	10 CENTS			
	2005. Mom holding child, soldier inspecting child's mouth. (7A101).			
	a. With legend: *Operation Enduring Freedom.*	FV	FV	0.75
	b. Without legend.	FV	FV	0.75
M317	10 CENTS			
	2005. John F. Kennedy, sirtless in PT boat. (7B101).	FV	FV	0.50
M318	10 CENTS			
	2005. George H. W. Bush close-up portrait as WWII pilot. (7C101).	FV	FV	0.50
M319	10 CENTS			
	2005. Gerald Ford in uniform wearing necktie. (7D101).	FV	FV	0.50
M320	10 CENTS			
	2005. Soldier holding silver star. (7D101).	FV	FV	0.50
M321	10 CENTS			
	2005. Two soldiers with guns behind sandbag line. (7E101).	FV	FV	0.50
M322	10 CENTS			
	2005. *Operation Iraqi Freedom* legend. Amphibious tank. (7G101).	FV	FV	0.50
M323	10 CENTS			
	2005. Air Force NASCAR #21. (7H101).	FV	FV	0.50
M324	10 CENTS			
	2005. Coast Guard NASCAR #44. (7J101).	FV	FV	0.50
M325	10 CENTS			
	2005. Marines NASCAR. (7K101).	FV	FV	0.50
M326	10 CENTS			
	2005. Navy NASCAR #14. (7L101).	FV	FV	0.50
M327	10 CENTS			
	2005. National Guard NASCAR #16. (7M101).	FV	FV	0.50
M328	25 CENTS			
	2005. Jet from the front and above. (7A251).	FV	FV	0.75
M329	25 CENTS			
	2005. George H. W. Bush standing before WWII plane. (7B251).	FV	FV	0.75
M330	25 CENTS			
	2005. Soldier standing with gun. (7C251).	FV	FV	0.75
M331	25 CENTS			
	2005. Three soldiers standing in line advancing forward. (7D251).	FV	FV	0.75
M332	25 CENTS			
	2005. Two soldiers atop tank. (7E251).	FV	FV	0.75
M333	25 CENTS			
	2005. Two soldiers by BX/PX sign superimposed on Iraq Campaign Medal. (7F251).	FV	FV	0.75
M334	25 CENTS			
	2005. Soldier directing excavator. (7G251).	FV	FV	0.75
M335	25 CENTS			
	2005. Soldier standing with British and American Flags atop vehicle. (7H251).	FV	FV	0.75
M336	25 CENTS			
	2005. Soldier playing bagpipes, flanked by flags. (7J251).	FV	FV	0.75
M337	25 CENTS			
	2005. Helicopter superimpsed on Afghanistan Campaign medal design. (7K251).	FV	FV	0.75
M338	25 CENTS			
	2005. Two soldiers walking in street with machine guns. (7L251).			

		VG	VF	UNC
M338	**25 CENTS**			
	a. With legend: *Operation Enduring Freedom*.	FV	FV	1.00
	b. Without legend.	FV	FV	1.00
M339	**25 CENTS**			
	2005. U.S. Army NHRA dragster. (7M251).	FV	FV	0.75

EIGHTH ISSUE

		VG	VF	UNC
M340	**10 CENTS**			
	2006. *Operation Enduring Freedom* legend. Soldier walking with German shepard. (8A101).	FV	FV	0.50
M341	**10 CENTS**			
	2006. Richard M. Nixon as Naval officer. (8B101).	FV	FV	0.50
M342	**10 CENTS**			
	2006. James E. Carter as Naval officer. (8C101).	FV	FV	0.50
M343	**10 CENTS**			
	2006. City convoy. (8D101).	FV	FV	0.50
M344	**10 CENTS**			
	2006. Female soldier helping child lying down. (8E101).	FV	FV	0.50
M345	**10 CENTS**			
	2006. Refuling helicopter. (8F101).	FV	FV	0.50
M346	**10 CENTS**			
	2006. Soldier boxing. (8G101).	FV	FV	0.50
M347	**10 CENTS**			
	2006. U.S. Army Motocyclye racer. (8H101).	FV	FV	0.50
M348	**10 CENTS**			
	2006. Rodeo. (8H101).	FV	FV	0.50
M349	**10 CENTS**			
	2006. Soldier firing shoulder rocket. (8K101).	FV	FV	0.50
M350	**10 CENTS**			
	2006. *Operation Iraqi Freedom* legend. Soldier loading bomb. (8L101).	FV	FV	0.50
M351	**10 CENTS**			
	2006. Iraqi placing paper ballot in box. (8M101).	FV	FV	0.50
M352	**25 CENTS**			
	2006. Soldier with machine gun in sand bag enclosure. (8A251).	FV	FV	0.75
M353	**25 CENTS**			
	2006. American flag flying above compound. (8B251).	FV	FV	0.75
M354	**25 CENTS**			
	2006. Tank firing left. (8C251).	FV	FV	0.75
M356	**25 CENTS**			
	2006. Roof mounted gun on Humvee. (8E251).	FV	FV	0.75
M357	**25 CENTS**			
	2006. Sailor portrait from MPC #M80. (8F251).	FV	FV	0.75
M358	**25 CENTS**			
	2006. Two soldiers in prone position firing guns. (8F251).	FV	FV	0.75
M359	**25 CENTS**			
	2006. Soldier with full pack advancing left. (8H251).	FV	FV	0.75
M360	**25 CENTS**			
	2006. Soldier with head set holding child. (8J251).	FV	FV	0.75
M361	**25 CENTS**			
	2006. Soldier kneeling shaking hand of child. (8K251).	FV	FV	0.75
M362	**25 CENTS**			
	2006. *Operation Enduring Freedom* legend. Solder on helicopter with machine gun. (8L251).	FV	FV	0.75
M363	**25 CENTS**			
	2006. Group of purple fingers after vote. (8M251).	FV	FV	0.75

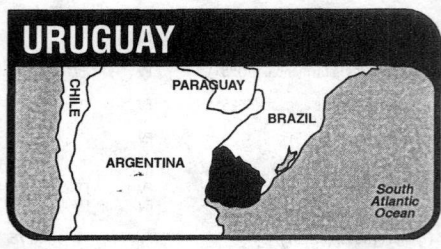

URUGUAY

The Oriental Republic of Uruguay (so called because of its location on the east bank of the Uruguay River) is situated on the Atlantic coast of South America between Argentina and Brazil. This most advanced of South American countries has an area of 68,536 sq. mi. (176,220 sq. km.) and a population of 3.27 million. Capital: Montevideo. Uruguay's chief economic asset is its rich, rolling grassy plains. Meat, wool, hides and skins are exported.

Uruguay was discovered in 1516 by Juan Diaz de Solis, a Spaniard, but settled by the Portuguese who founded Colonia in 1680. Spain contested Portuguese possession and, after a long struggle, gained control of the country in 1778. During the general South American struggle for independence, Uruguay's first attempt was led by gaucho soldier José Gervasio Artigas leading the Banda Oriental which was quelled by Spanish and Portuguese forces in 1811. The armistice was soon broken and Argentine forces from Buenos Aires cast off the Spanish bond in the Plata region in 1814, only to be reconquered by the Portuguese from Brazil in the struggle of 1816-20. Revolt flared anew in 1825 and independence was reasserted in 1828 with the help of Argentina. The Uruguayan Republic was established in 1830.

In 1919, a new constitution established a plural executive, but this was abolished in 1933. A presidential government existed from 1933 to 1951 at which time a collective form of leadership was formed through 1966. Strikes and riots in the 1960's brought the military to power until 1985 when Julio Maria Sanguinetti established a government of national unity.

MONETARY SYSTEM:
1 Peso = 100 Centésimos, 1860-1975
1 Doblon = 10 Pesos, 1860-1875
1 Nuevo Peso = 1000 Old Pesos, 1975-1993
1 Peso Uruguayo = 1000 Nuevos Pesos, 1993-

BANCO CENTRAL DEL URUGUAY

Office Titles:
1-Gerente General, Secretario General, Presidente
2-Co-Gerente General, Secretario General, Presidente
3-p.Gerente General, Secretario General, Presidente
4-Gerente General, Secretario General, Vicepresidente
5-Gerente General, Secretario General, 2o Vicepresidente
6-p.Gerente General, Secretario General, Vicepresidente
7-Secretario General, Presidente

1967 ND PROVISIONAL ISSUE

#42-45 Banco Central was organized in 1967 and used notes of previous issuing authority w/Banco Central sign. title ovpt. Series D. Printer: TDLR.

		VG	VF	UNC
42	**10 PESOS**			
	L.1939 (1967). Purple on m/c unpt. J. G. Artigas at lower ctr., arms at upper l. Farmer w/3-team ox-cart on back. Like #37. Sign. title: 1.			
	a. Bank name below title: *Banco Central de la República*.	1.00	3.00	10.00
	b. Bank name below title: *Banco Central del Uruguay*.	0.50	2.50	7.50
42A	**50 PESOS**			
	L.1939 (1967). Blue and brown on m/c unpt. Warrior wearing helmet at r., arms at upper l. Group of people w/flag on back. Like #38.			
	a. Bank name below all 3 sign. Sign. title: 1.	1.00	3.00	7.50
	b. Bank name below 2 sign. at r. Sign. title: 3.	1.00	3.00	10.00

43	100 PESOS	VG	VF	UNC
	L.1939 (1967). Red and brown. "Constitution" at r., arms at ctr. People in town square on back. Like #39.			
	a. Bank name below 3 sign. *Banco Central del Uruguay.* Sign. title: 1, 3; *PRESIDENTE* at r.	1.50	3.50	12.00
	b. Bank name below 2 sign. at l.: *Banco Central del Uruguay.* Sign. title: 4; 6 *VICE PRESIDENTE* at r.	1.00	3.50	12.00
	c. Bank name below 2 sign. at r. Sign. title: 3.	1.50	3.50	12.00
44	500 PESOS			
	L.1939. Green and blue. "Industry" at r., arms at upper l. People w/symbols of agriculture on back. Like #40.			
	a. Sign. Like #42a.	1.50	6.00	17.50
	b. Sign. like #42b.	1.50	6.00	17.50

45	1000 PESOS	VG	VF	UNC
	L.1939. Purple and black on pale yellow unpt. Jose Gervasio Artigas at r., arms at upper l. Man on horseback at ctr. on back. Like #41. Sign. like #42a.	4.00	8.00	25.00

1967 ND Issue

#46-51 Jose Gervasio Artigas at ctr. Sign. and sign. title varieties. Printer: TDLR.

46	50 PESOS	VG	VF	UNC
	ND (1967). Deep blue on lt. green and lilac unpt. Arms at l. Group of 33 men w/flag on back. Series A. Sign. titles: 1, 2, 4.			
	a. Issued note.	0.10	0.25	1.75
	s. Specimen.	—	—	55.00

47	100 PESOS	VG	VF	UNC
	ND (1967). Red on lilac and lt. gold unpt. Arms at l. Man presiding at independence meeting on back. Sign. titles: 1, 2, 3.			
	a. Issued note.	0.10	0.25	1.75
	s. Specimen.	—	—	55.00

#48-51 wmk: Arms.

48	500 PESOS	VG	VF	UNC
	ND (1967). Green and blue on orange and lt. green unpt. Dam on back. Sign. titles 1, 2.			
	a. Issued note.	0.50	1.25	7.00
	s. Specimen.	—	—	55.00

49	1000 PESOS	VG	VF	UNC
	ND (1967). Purple and black on blue and yellow unpt. Lg. bldg. on back. Sign. titles: 1, 2, 3, 4.			
	a. Issued note.	0.50	1.25	6.00
	s. Specimen.	—	—	60.00

50	5000 PESOS	VG	VF	UNC
	ND (1967). Brown and blue-green on lilac and lt. blue unpt. Bank on back.			
	a. Series A; B. Sign. titles: 1, 4, 5, 6.	2.00	5.00	25.00
	b. Series C. Sign. title: 2.	0.25	1.00	4.50
	s. Specimen.	—	—	60.00

51	10,000 PESOS	VG	VF	UNC
	ND (1967). Dk. green and black on yellow and lt. orange unpt. Bldg. on back.			
	a. Series A. Sign. title: 1.	5.00	12.50	35.00
	b. Series A. Sign. title: 6.	6.00	15.00	40.00
	c. Series B. Sign. titles: 2, 3, 4.	5.00	12.50	30.00
	s. Specimen.	—	—	65.00

1974 ND Issue

#52 and 53 sign. varieties. Wmk: Artigas.
#52 replacement notes: Serial # prefix *R.*

52	1000 PESOS	VG	VF	UNC
	ND (1974). Violet and dk. green on m/c unpt. Arms at upper l. ctr., Artigas at r. Bldg. on back. Printer: CdeM-A. Sign. title: 2.	0.25	1.00	3.00

#53 replacement notes: First digit of 8 digit serial # is *9.*

53	**10,000 PESOS**	VG	VF	UNC
	ND (1974). Orange on m/c unpt. arms at upper l. ctr., J. G. Artigas at r. Palace Esteze at l. ctr. on back. Printer: TDLR.			
	a. Series A. Sign. titles: 2.	1.00	3.00	10.00
	b. Series B. Sign. titles: 2.	0.75	2.50	7.00
	c. Series C. Sign. titles: 1.	0.50	2.00	6.00

1975 ND PROVISIONAL ISSUE

#54-58 new value ovpt. in black on wmk. area on face only.

54	**0.50 NUEVO PESO ON 500 PESOS**	VG	VF	UNC
	ND (1975). Ovpt. on #48. Sign. titles: 1.	0.10	0.25	1.50

55	**1 NUEVO PESO ON 1000 PESOS**	VG	VF	UNC
	ND (1975). Ovpt. on #49. Sign. titles: 1.	0.25	1.00	3.50

#56 and 57 replacement notes: 8 digit serial # prefix *R*.

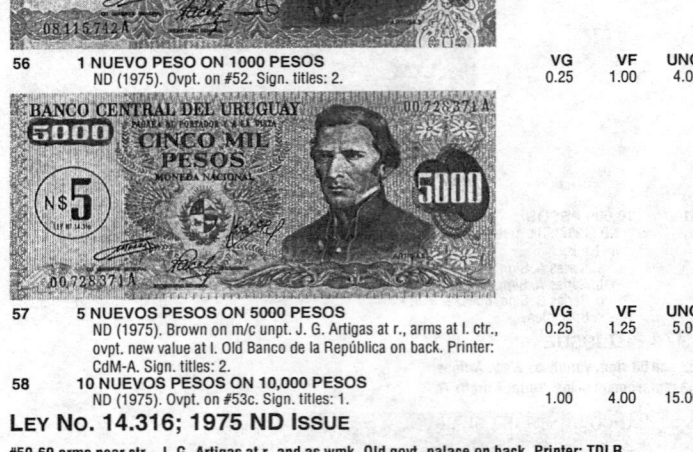

56	**1 NUEVO PESO ON 1000 PESOS**	VG	VF	UNC
	ND (1975). Ovpt. on #52. Sign. titles: 2.	0.25	1.00	4.00

57	**5 NUEVOS PESOS ON 5000 PESOS**	VG	VF	UNC
	ND (1975). Brown on m/c unpt. J. G. Artigas at r., arms at l. ctr., ovpt. new value at l. Old Banco de la República on back. Printer: CdM-A. Sign. titles: 2.	0.25	1.25	5.00
58	**10 NUEVOS PESOS ON 10,000 PESOS**			
	ND (1975). Ovpt. on #53c. Sign. titles: 1.	1.00	4.00	15.00

LEY NO. 14.316; 1975 ND ISSUE

#59-60 arms near ctr., J. G. Artigas at r. and as wmk. Old govt. palace on back. Printer: TDLR.

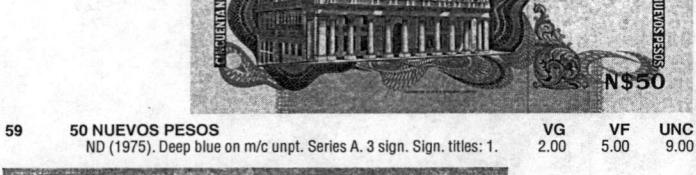

59	**50 NUEVOS PESOS**	VG	VF	UNC
	ND (1975). Deep blue on m/c unpt. Series A. 3 sign. Sign. titles: 1.	2.00	5.00	9.00

60	**100 NUEVOS PESOS**	VG	VF	UNC
	ND (1975). Olive-green on m/c unpt. Series A. 3 sign. Sign. titles: 1.	2.50	6.00	15.00

LEY NO. 14.316; 1978-88 ND ISSUES

#61-64A similar to previous issue but w/o text: *PAGARA .... A LA VISTA* at ctr. Printer: TDLR.
Replacement notes: 8 digit serial # starting w/9.

61	**50 NUEVOS PESOS**	VG	VF	UNC
	ND (1978-87). Similar to #59.			
	a. 2 sign. Series B (1978). Sign. titles: 7.	0.25	1.50	6.00
	b. 3 sign. Series C (1980). Sign. titles: 1.	0.25	1.00	5.00
	c. 2 sign. Series D (1981). Sign. titles: 7.	0.10	0.75	3.00
	d. 3 sign. Series E (1987). Sign. titles: 1.	0.10	0.50	2.00

61A	**50 NUEVOS PESOS**	VG	VF	UNC
	ND (1988-89). Like #61 but J. G. Artigas portr. printed in wmk. area. Series F (1988); Series G (1989). Sign. titles: 1.	0.05	0.20	0.75
62	**100 NUEVOS PESOS**			
	ND (1978-86). Similar to #60.			
	a. 2 sign. Series B (1978). Sign. titles: 7.	0.50	2.50	7.50
	b. 3 sign. Series C (1980); Series D (1981).	0.15	0.50	3.00
	c. Series E (1985); Series F (1986). Sign. titles: 1.	0.05	0.25	1.00

62A	**100 NUEVOS PESOS**	VG	VF	UNC
	ND (1987). Olive-green on m/c unpt. Like #62 but J. G. Artigas portr. printed in wmk. area. Series G (1987). Sign. titles: 1.	0.05	0.50	2.00

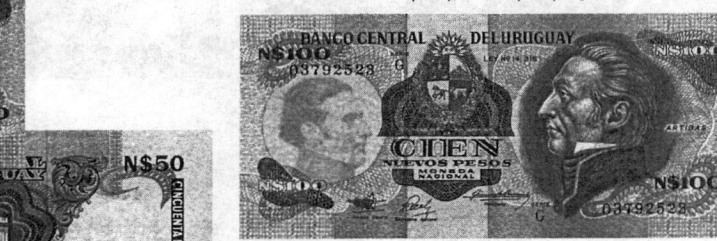

63	**500 NUEVOS PESOS**	VG	VF	UNC
	ND (1978-85). Red on m/c unpt.			
	a. 2 sign. Series A (1978). Sign. titles: 7.	1.00	4.00	12.50
	b. 3 sign. Series B (1978); Series C (1985). Sign. titles: 1.	0.25	0.75	3.50

63A	500 NUEVOS PESOS	VG	VF	UNC
	ND (1991). Red on m/c unpt. Like #63 but J. G. Artigas portr. printed in wmk. area. Series D (1991). Sign. titles: 1.	0.20	0.50	1.50

64	1000 NUEVOS PESOS	VG	VF	UNC
	ND(1978-81). Purple on m/c unpt.			
	a. 2 sign. Series A (1978). Sign. titles: 7.	2.00	4.50	12.50
	b. 3 sign. Series B (1981). Sign. titles: 1.	0.50	1.50	5.00

64A	1000 NUEVOS PESOS	VG	VF	UNC
	ND (1991-92). Purple on m/c unpt. Like #64 but Jose Gervasio Artigas portr. printed in wmk. area.			
	a. Series C (1991). Sign. titles: 1.	0.25	1.00	3.50
	b. Series D (1992). Sign. titles: 1.	0.20	0.50	2.50

65	5000 NUEVOS PESOS	VG	VF	UNC
	ND (1983). Deep brown, orange-brown and blue on m/c unpt. Arms at top l. ctr., Brig. Gen. Juan Antonio Lavalleja at r. Back m/c; 1830 scene of pledging allegiance at ctr. Series A; B; C. Printer: TDLR. Sign. titles: 1.	0.50	1.50	5.00

LEY NO. 14.316; 1986; 1987 ND ISSUE

#66 replacement notes: Series A-R. Wmk: J. G. Artigas.

66	200 NUEVOS PESOS	VG	VF	UNC
	1986. Dk. and lt. green on brown and m/c unpt. Quill and scroll at l., arms at ctr., J. E. Rodo at r. Rodo Monument at ctr., statuary at l. and ctr. on back. Series A. Printer: C. Ciccone S.A. Sign. titles: 1.	0.10	0.25	1.50
67	10,000 NUEVOS PESOS			
	ND (1987). Purple, dk. blue, dk. olive-green and violet on m/c unpt. Plaza of Democracy w/flag at l. ctr. 19 departmental arms on back. Printer: ABNC. Sign. titles: 1.			
	a. Ovpt. gold gilt bars on description and law designation. Series A.	7.50	25.00	75.00
	b. No ovpt. bars on new inscription at l., *DECRETO-LEY NO. 14.316* at upper. r. Series B; C.	0.75	2.00	7.50
	s. Entire note as printed and w/o ovpt. Series A. Specimen.	—	—	—

Note: On #67 the description *Plaza de la Nacionalidad Oriental/Monumento a la bandera* and *LEY 14.316* ovpt. was being blocked out because of a change of government from military to elected civil administration before the notes were released. The new government took the prepared notes, ovpt. the legend relating to the old government and issued them (Series A). Only Specimen notes are known w/o the ovpt.

1989-92 ISSUE

#68-73 arms at upper l., latent image (silver oval #69-73) at upper r. w/letters B/CU. Wmk: J. G. Artigas. Sign. titles: 1. Printer: TDLR.

67A	1000 NUEVOS PESOS	VG	VF	UNC
	1989. Brown and orange on m/c unpt. Pedro Figari at r. Allegory of Music on back. Ovpt: *NO EMITIDO*. Specimen. (Not issued.)	—	—	35.00

68	2000 NUEVOS PESOS	VG	VF	UNC
	1989. Dk. brown and orange on m/c unpt. J. M. Blanes at ctr. r. Altar of the Homeland (allegory of the Republic) on back. Series A.	0.25	0.50	2.00

68A	5000 NUEVOS PESOS	VG	VF	UNC
	1989. Brown and orange on m/c unpt. Pedro Figari at r. *Baile Antiguo* (old dance) on back. Ovpt: *NO EMITIDO*. Specimen. (Not issued.)	—	—	35.00

68B **10,000 NUEVOS PESOS**

	VG	VF	UNC
1989. Brown and orange on m/c unpt. Alfredo Vasquez Acevedo at r. University of the Republic. Ovpt: *NO EMITIDO*. Specimen. (Not issued.)	—	—	35.00

69 **20,000 NUEVOS PESOS**

	VG	VF	UNC
1989; 1991. Dk. green and violet on m/c unpt. Dr. J. Zorrilla de San Martin at ctr. r. Manuscript and allegory of the legend of the homeland (Victory w/wings) on back. Series A.	0.50	3.50	8.00

70 **50,000 NUEVOS PESOS**

	VG	VF	UNC
1989; 1991. Black, violet and red on m/c unpt. José Pedro Varela at ctr. r. Varela Monument at l. on back. Series A.	1.50	7.50	17.50

71 **100,000 NUEVOS PESOS**

	VG	VF	UNC
1991. Purple and dk. brown on m/c unpt. Eduardo Fabini at r. ctr. Musical allegory on back. Series A.	3.00	15.00	32.50

72 **200,000 NUEVOS PESOS**

	VG	VF	UNC
1992. Dk. brown and violet and orange on m/c unpt. Pedro Figari at ctr. r. Old dance at l. on back. Series A.	5.00	27.50	65.00

73 **500,000 NUEVOS PESOS**

	VG	VF	UNC
1992. Blue-gray, violet and pale red on m/c unpt. Alfredo Vaquez Acevedo at ctr. r. University of Montevideo at l. on back. Series A.	10.00	65.00	125.00

1994-97 Issue

Currency Reform

1 Peso Uruguayo = 1000 Nuevos Pesos, 1993-

73A **5 PESOS URUGUAYOS**

	VG	VF	UNC
ND (1997). Dk. brown, red-brown and blue on m/c unpt. Like 5000 Nuevos Pesos #65. Series A.	FV	FV	2.00

73B **10 PESOS URUGUAYOS**

	VG	VF	UNC
ND (1995). Purple, dk. blue, dk. olive-green and violet on m/c unpt. Like 10,000 Nuevos Pesos #67. Printer: G&D.			
a. W/Decreto-Ley No.14.316 (error). Series A.	FV	FV	4.00
b. W/o Ley. Series B.	FV	FV	3.50

#74-77 like #69-73 but w/new denominations. Arms at upper l. Series A. Wmk: J. G. Artigas. Printer: TDLR.

74 **20 PESOS URUGUAYOS**

	VG	VF	UNC
1994. Dk. green and violet on m/c unpt. Like #69.	FV	FV	4.50

75   50 PESOS URUGUAYOS
1994. Black, red and violet on m/c unpt. Like #70. Series A, B.

	VG	VF	UNC
	FV	FV	10.00

76   100 PESOS URUGUAYOS
1994; 1997. Purple and dk. brown on m/c unpt. Like #71. Series A; B; C.

	VG	VF	UNC
	FV	FV	17.50

77   200 PESOS URUGUAYOS
1995; 2000. Dk. brown-violet on m/c unpt. Like #72. Series A, B.

	VG	VF	UNC
	FV	FV	35.00

78   500 PESOS URUGUAYOS
1994, 1999. Blue-gray, violet and pale red on m/c unpt. Like #73.

	VG	VF	UNC
	FV	FV	75.00

79   1000 PESOS URUGUAYOS
1995. Brown and olive-green on m/c unpt. Juana de Ibarbourou at r. Palm tree in Ibarbourou Square at l., books on back.

	VG	VF	UNC
	FV	FV	140.00

Note: #79 issued in celebration of the 100th birthday of Juana de Ibarbourou.

1998 ISSUE

#80-81 printer: (T)DLR.

80   5 PESOS URUGUAYOS
1998. Brown and orange-brown on blue and m/c unpt. Joaquín Torres García at r. ctr. García's painting at l. on back. Series A.

	VG	VF	UNC
	FV	FV	2.00

81   10 PESOS URUGUAYOS
1998. Slate black and lt. rose on m/c unpt. Eduardo Acevedo Vásquez at r. Agronomy bldg. at l. on back. Series A.

	VG	VF	UNC
	FV	FV	3.00

1999 ISSUE

82   500 PESOS URUGUAYOS
1999. Blue on m/c unpt. Like #78, but printer: FC-O. Series B.

	VG	VF	UNC
	FV	FV	75.00

2000 ISSUE

83   20 PESOS URUGUAYOS
2000; 2003. Like # 74 but Series C; D.

	VG	VF	UNC
	FV	FV	4.50

84   50 PESOS URUGUAYOS
2000; 2003. Like # 75 but Series B, C.

	VG	VF	UNC
	FV	FV	10.00

85   100 PESOS URUGUAYOS
2000; 2003. Like #76 but Series C, D.

	VG	VF	UNC
	FV	FV	35.00

2003 ISSUE

86   2000 PESOS URUGUAYOS
2003. Gray and lt. olive-green. Dámaso Antonio Larrañaga at r. National Library on back. Series A.

	VG	VF	UNC
	FV	FV	250.00

UZBEKISTAN

The Republic of Uzbekistan (formerly the Uzbek S.S.R.), is bordered on the north by Kazakhstan, to the east by Kirghizia and Tajikistan, on the south by Afghanistan and on the west by Turkmenistan. It has an area of 172,741 sq. mi. (447,400 sq. km.) and a population of 23.5 million. Capital: Tashkent. Crude oil, natural gas, coal, copper and gold deposits make up the chief resources, while intensive farming, based on artificial irrigation, provides an abundance of cotton.

The original population was believed to be Iranian towards the north while the southern part hosted the satrapies of Sogdiana and Bactria, members of the Persian empire and once part of the empire of Alexander of Macedon. The Mongol invasion of Jenghiz Khan in 1219-20 brought destruction and great ethnic changes among the population. The khanate of Khiva, in 1688, became a vassal of Persia, but recovered its independence in 1747. While the Uzbek emirs and khans ruled central Turkestan, in the north were the Kazakhs, in the west lived the nomadic Turkmens, in the east dwelled the Kirghiz, and in the southeast was the homeland of the Persian-speaking Tajiks. In 1714-17 Peter the Great sent a military expedition against Khiva which ended in a disaster. In 1853 Ak-Mechet ("White Mosque," renamed Perovsk, later Kzyl Orda), was conquered by the Russians, and the following year the fortress of Vernoye (later Alma-Ata) was established. On July 29, 1867, Gen. C. P. Kaufmann was appointed governor general of Turkestan with headquarters in Tashkent. On July 5 Mozaffar ed-Din, emir of Bukhara, signed a treaty making his country a Russian vassal state with much-reduced territory. Khiva was conquered by Gen. N. N. Golovachev, and on Aug. The czarist government did not attempt to Russify the indigenous Turkic or Tajik populations, preferring to keep them backward and illiterate. The revolution of March 1917 created a confused situation in the area. On Sept. 18, 1924, the Uzbek and Turkmen peoples were authorized to form S.S.R.'s of their own, and the Kazakhs, Kirghiz and Tajiks to form autonomous S.S.R.'s. On Oct. 27, 1924, the Uzbek and Turkmen S.S.R. were officially constituted and the former was formally accepted on Jan. 15, 1925, as a member of the U.S.S.R. Tajikistan was an autonomous soviet republic within Uzbekistan until Dec. 5, 1929, when it became a S.S.R. On Dec. 5, 1936, Uzbekistan was territorially increased by incorporating into it the Kara-Kalpak A.S.S.R., which had belonged to Kazakhstan until 1930 and afterward had come under direct control of the R.S.F.S.R.

On June 20, 1990 the Uzbek Supreme Soviet adopted a declaration of sovereignty, and in Aug. 1991, following an unsuccessful coup, it declared itself independent as the 'Republic of Uzbekistan', which was confirmed by referendum in December. That same month Uzbekistan became a member of the CIS.

Monetary System:
1 Sum (Ruble) = 100 Kopeks, 1991
1 Sum = 1,000 Sum Coupon, 1994
1 СуМ (Sum) = 100 ТИЙИН (Tiyin)

REPUBLIC

GOVERNMENT

КУПОНГА КАРТОЧКА - 1993 RUBLE CONTROL COUPONS

#43-52 and 58 uniface.

		VG	VF	UNC
43	**10 AND 25 COUPONS**			
	ND (1993). Black on pale blue unpt.			
	a. Full sheet of 35 coupons w/2 registries.	—	—	3.00
	b. Top half sheet of 10 coupons w/registry.	—	—	2.00
	c. Bottom half sheet of 25 coupons w/registry.	—	—	2.00
	d. Coupon.	—	—	0.10
44	**10 AND 25 COUPONS**			
	ND (1993). Black on orange unpt.			
	a. Full sheet of 35 coupons w/2 registries.	—	—	3.00
	b. Top half sheet of 10 coupons w/registry.	—	—	2.00
	c. Bottom half sheet of 25 coupons w/registry.	—	—	2.00
	d. Coupon.	—	—	0.10
45	**10 AND 25 COUPONS**			
	ND (1993). Black on pink unpt.			
	a. Full sheet of 35 coupons w/2 registries.	—	—	5.00
	b. Top half sheet of 10 coupons w/registry.	—	—	2.00
	c. Bottom half sheet of 25 coupons w/registry.	—	—	2.00
	d. Coupon.	—	—	0.10
46	**50 COUPONS**			
	ND (1993). Black on pale ochre unpt.			
	a. Full sheet of 28 coupons w/registry.	—	—	3.00
	b. Coupon.	—	—	0.10
47	**100 COUPONS**			
	ND (1993). Black on violet unpt.			
	a. Full sheet of 100 coupons w/registry.	—	—	3.00
	b. Coupon.	—	—	0.10
48	**100 COUPONS**			
	ND (1993). Black on tan unpt.			
	a. Full sheet of 100 coupons w/registry.	—	—	3.00
	b. Coupon.	—	—	0.10
49	**100 COUPONS**			
	ND (1993). Black on lt. blue unpt.			
	a. Full sheet of 100 coupons w/registry.	—	—	3.00
	b. Coupon	—	—	0.10
50	**150 COUPONS**			
	ND (1993). Red on pale gray unpt.			
	a. Full sheet of 150 coupons w/registry.	—	—	3.00
	b. Coupon.	—	—	0.10

		VG	VF	UNC
51	**200 COUPONS**			
	ND (1993). Black on pink unpt.			
	a. Full sheet of 200 coupons w/registry.	—	—	3.00
	b. Coupon.	—	—	0.10
52	**200 COUPONS**			
	ND (1993). Black on tan unpt.			
	a. Full sheet of 200 coupons w/registry.	—	—	0.10
	b. Coupon.	—	—	0.10

#53-57 not assigned.

		VG	VF	UNC
58	**2000 COUPONS**			
	ND (1993). Blue on pink unpt. Uniface.			
	a. Full sheet of 28 coupons w/registry.	—	—	4.00
	b. Coupon.	—	—	0.10

#59 and 60 not assigned.

УЗБЕКИСТОН ДАВЛАТ БАНКИ

BANK OF UZBEKISTAN

1992 (1993) ISSUE

#61-72 arms at l. Mosque at ctr. on back. Printer: H&S (w/o imprint).

#61-65 wmk: Flower pattern repeated.

		VG	VF	UNC
61	**1 SUM**			
	1992 (1993). Blue-gray on lt. blue and gold unpt.			
	a. Issued note.	0.05	0.10	0.25
	s. Specimen.	—	—	25.00

		VG	VF	UNC
62	**3 SUM**			
	1992 (1993). Green on lt. blue and gold unpt.			
	a. Issued note.	0.05	0.10	0.50
	s. Specimen.	—	—	25.00
63	**5 SUM**			
	1992 (1993). Purple on lt. blue and gold unpt.			
	a. Issued note.	0.05	0.10	1.00
	s. Specimen.	—	—	25.00
64	**10 SUM**			
	1992 (1993). Red on lt. blue and gold unpt.			
	a. Issued note.	0.05	0.10	1.00
	s. Specimen.	—	—	25.00
65	**25 SUM**			
	1992 (1993). Blue-green on lt. blue and gold unpt. Back green.			
	a. Issued note.	—	0.20	1.00
	s. Specimen.	—	—	25.00

#66-72 wmk: Lg. detailed cotton flower.

		VG	VF	UNC
66	**50 SUM**			
	1992 (1993). Rose on lt. blue and gold unpt.			
	a. Issued note.	0.10	0.25	3.00
	s. Specimen.	—	—	25.00

			VG	VF	UNC
74	**3 SUM**		FV	FV	2.50
	1994. Violet and red-violet on m/c unpt. Arms at l. Mosque of				
	Çaçma Ayub Mazar in Bukhara on back.				

#75-79 arms at upper ctr. and as wmk.

		VG	VF	UNC
67	**100 SUM**			
	1992 (1993). Dk. brown on lt. blue and gold unpt. Back blue.			
	a. Issued note.	0.10	0.50	4.00
	s. Specimen.	—	—	25.00
68	**200 SUM**			
	1992 (1993). Violet on lt. blue and gold unpt.			
	a. Issued note.	0.15	0.75	4.50
	s. Specimen.	—	—	25.00
69	**500 SUM**			
	1992 (1993). Orange on lt. blue and gold unpt. Back lt. tan.			
	a. Larger and italicized serial #.	0.10	0.50	2.00
	b. Smaller and regular serial #.	0.25	1.50	5.00
	s. Specimen.	—	—	25.00
70	**1000 SUM**			
	1992 (1993). Brown on lilac and pale green unpt.			
	a. Prefix letters same size as the numbers.	0.15	0.75	3.00
	b. Serial # prefix letters taller than the numbers.	0.15	0.75	4.00
	s. Specimen.	—	—	30.00

			VG	VF	UNC
75	**5 SUM**		FV	FV	2.00
	1994. Dk. blue and red-violet on m/c unpt. Ali Shir Nawai				
	Monument in Tashkent at ctr. r. on back.				

			VG	VF	UNC
76	**10 SUM**		FV	FV	2.00
	1994. Purple and blue-gray on m/c unpt. Tomb of Tamerlane in				
	Samarkand at ctr. r. on back.				

		VG	VF	UNC
71	**5000 SUM**			
	1992 (1993). Blue-gray on lilac and pale green unpt.			
	a. Issued note.	0.50	2.50	12.50
	s. Specimen.	—	—	25.00
72	**10,000 SUM**			
	1992 (1993). Red-orange on lilac and pale green unpt.			
	a. Issued note. Serial # height of 3 or 3.5mm.	0.25	2.00	10.00
	s. Specimen.	—	—	30.00

			VG	VF	UNC
77	**25 SUM**		FV	FV	2.00
	1994. Dk. blue and brown on m/c unpt. Mausoleum Kazi Zadé Rumi				
	in the necropolis Shakhi-Zinda in Samarkand at ctr. r. on back.				

УЗБЕКИСТОН РЕСПУБЛИКАСИ МАРКАЗИЙ БАНКИ

CENTRAL BANK OF UZBEKISTAN REPUBLIC

1994; 1997 ISSUE

#73-80 wmk. paper. Replacement notes: serial # prefix *ZZ*.

			VG	VF	UNC
73	**1 SUM**		FV	FV	1.50
	1994. Dk. green on m/c unpt. Arms at l. Bldg., fountain at ctr. r.				
	on back.				

			VG	VF	UNC
78	**50 SUM**		FV	FV	2.50
	1994. Dk. brown, olive-brown and dull brown-orange on m/c unpt.				
	Esplanade in Reghistan and the 2 Medersas in Samarkand at ctr. r.				
	on back.				

79 100 SUM
1994. Purple and blue on m/c unpt. Stylized facing peacocks at l. *Drubja Narodov* palace in Tashkent at ctr. r. on back.

	VG	VF	UNC
	FV	FV	3.00

80 200 SUM
1997. Dk. blue, black, deep purple on green and m/c unpt. Arms at l. and as wmk. Sunface over mythological tiger at ctr. on back.

	VG	VF	UNC
	FV	FV	4.00

81 500 SUM
1999. Red, blue and green on m/c unpt. Arms at l. and as wmk. Equestrian statue at ctr. r. on back.

	VG	VF	UNC
	FV	FV	5.00

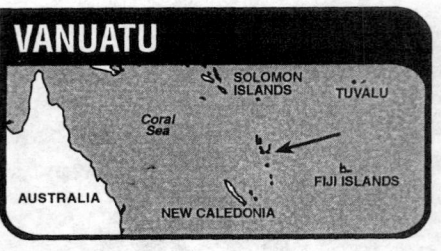

(1000 SUM note image)

82 1000 SUM
2001. Brown & purple. Arms at l. and as wmk. Amir Temur Museum on back.

	VG	VF	UNC
	FV	FV	7.50

VANUATU

Vanuatu (formerly the New Hebrides Condominium), a group of islands located in the South Pacific 500 miles (800 km.) west of Fiji, were under the joint sovereignty of Great Britain and France. The islands have an area of 5,700 sq. mi. (14,763 sq. km.) and a population of *181,350, mainly Melanesians of mixed blood. Capital: Vila. The volcanic and coral islands, while malarial and subject to frequent earthquakes, are extremely fertile, and produce copra, coffee, tropical fruits and timber for export.

The New Hebrides were discovered by Portuguese navigator Pedro de Quiros in 1606, visited by French explorer Bougainville in 1768, and named by British navigator Capt. James Cook in 1774. Ships of all nations converged on the islands to trade for sandalwood prompting France and Britain to relinquish their individual claims and declare the islands a neutral zone in 1878. The New Hebrides were placed under the control of a mixed Anglo-French commission of naval officers during the native uprisings of 1887, and established as a condominium under the joint sovereignty of France and Great Britain in 1906. Independence for the area was attained in 1982 under the new name of Vanuatu.

RULERS:
British and French to 1982

MONETARY SYSTEM:
100 Vatu = 100 Francs

SIGNATURE VARIETIES			
1	President — General Manager	2	Governor — Minister of Finance
3	President — General Manager	4	Governor — Minister of Finance

INDEPENDENT

BANQUE CENTRALE DE VANUATU

CENTRAL BANK OF VANUATU CENTRAL BANK BLONG VANUATU

1982; 1989 ND ISSUE
#1-4 arms w/Melanesian chief standing w/spear at ctr. r. Wmk: Melanesian male head. Printer: BWC.

1 100 VATU
ND (1982). Dk. green on m/c unpt. Cattle among palm trees at l. ctr. on back. Sign. 1.

	VG	VF	UNC
a. Issued note.	1.00	2.50	15.00
s. Specimen.	—	—	160.00

2 500 VATU
ND (1982). Lt. red on m/c unpt. 3 carvings at l., 2 men beating upright hollow log drums at l. ctr. on back. Sign. 1.

	VG	VF	UNC
a. Issued note.	FV	5.00	20.00
s. Specimen.	—	—	180.00

3   1000 VATU

	VG	VF	UNC
ND (1982). Black on lt. orange, green and m/c unpt. 3 carvings at lower l., 3 men in outrigger sailboat at ctr. on back. Sign. 1.			
a. Issued note.	FV	12.50	35.00
s. Specimen.	—	—	225.00

4   5000 VATU

	VG	VF	UNC
ND (1989). Brown and lilac on m/c unpt. Man watching another *Gol* diving from log tower at ctr. on back. Sign. 2.	FV	50.00	95.00

BANQUE DE RESERVE DE VANUATU

RESERVE BANK OF VANUATU/RESERVE BANK BLONG VANUATU

1993 ND ISSUE

#5-7 like #2-4 but w/new bank name. Sign. 3. Wmk: Melanesian male head.

5   500 VATU

	VG	VF	UNC
ND (1993). Lt. red on m/c unpt. Like #2.	FV	FV	12.50

6   1000 VATU

	VG	VF	UNC
ND (1993). Black on lt. orange, green and m/c unpt. Like #3.	FV	FV	22.50

7   5000 VATU
ND.   Expected New Issue

1995 ND ISSUE

8   200 VATU

	VG	VF	UNC
ND (1995). Purple and violet on m/c unpt. Arms w/Melanesian chief standing w/spear at ctr. r. Statue of family life, "Traditional parliament in session" and flag on back. Wmk: Melanesian male head. Sign. 4. Printer: TDLR.	FV	FV	7.50

1995 COMMEMORATIVE ISSUE

#9, 15th Anniversary of Independence

9   200 VATU

	VG	VF	UNC
ND (1995). Purple and violet on m/c unpt. Commemorative text ovpt. in wmk. area at l. on #8.	FV	FV	7.50

2002 ND ISSUE

10   1000 VATU

	VG	VF	UNC
ND (2002). Black and green on orange unpt. Printer: (T)DLR.	FV	FV	22.50

The Republic of Venezuela, located on the northern coast of South America between Colombia and Guyana, has an area of 352,145 sq. mi. (912,050 sq. km.) and a population of 24.17 million. Capital: Caracas. Petroleum and mining provide 90 percent of Venezuela's exports although they employ less than 2 percent of the work force. Coffee, grown on 60,000 plantations, is the chief crop.

Columbus discovered Venezuela on his third voyage in 1498. Initial exploration did not reveal Venezuela to be a land of great wealth. An active pearl trade operated on the off-shore islands and slavers raided the interior in search of Indians to be sold into slavery, but no significant mainland settlements were made before 1567 when Caracas was founded. Venezuela, the home of Bolívar, was among the first South American colonies to revolt against Spain in 1810. Independence was attained in 1821 but not recognized by Spain until 1845. Together with Ecuador, Panama and Colombia, Venezuela was part of "Gran Colombia" until 1830 when it became a sovereign and independent state.

MONETARY SYSTEM:
1 Bolívar = 100 Centimos, 1879-

BANCO CENTRAL DE VENEZUELA

Established in 1940. Sign. and date varieties. Note: Many specimen notes entered the market about 1982. Up to 200 of each are known for many of the types.

1940-45 ISSUES

#31-37 Simon Bolívar on front. Arms on back. Printer: ABNC. (Series I, W not used).

		VG	VF	UNC
31	**10 BOLÍVARES**			
	19.7.1945-11.3.1960. Purple on m/c unpt. Portr. Simon Bolívar at l., Antonio Jose de Sucre at r. Arms at r. on back.			
	a. 19.7.1945-17.5.1951.	5.00	40.00	125.00
	b. 31.7.1952. Serial # prefix F-G.	15.00	50.00	100.00
	c. 14.1.1954-17.4.1958.	5.00	30.00	60.00
	d. 18.6.1959-11.3.1960.	5.00	20.00	45.00
	s. As a. Specimen. W/o sign. Punched hole cancelled.	—	—	175.00
32	**20 BOLÍVARES**			
	15.2.1941-18.6.1959. Dk. green on m/c unpt. Portr. Simon Bolívar at r. Arms at l. on back.			
	a. 15.2.1941-17.1.1952.	15.00	60.00	125.00
	b. 21.8.1952. Serial # prefix G-H.	20.00	50.00	100.00
	c. 23.7.1953-18.6.1959.	5.00	30.00	75.00
	s. As a. Specimen. W/o sign. Punched hole cancelled.	—	—	75.00
33	**50 BOLÍVARES**			
	12.12.1940-11.3.1960. Black on m/c unpt. Portr. Simon Bolívar at l. Back orange; arms at r.			
	a. 12.12.1940-17.1.1952.	25.00	100.00	250.00
	b. 23.7.1953. Serial # prefix C.	25.00	125.00	225.00
	c. 22.4.1954-11.3.1960.	15.00	65.00	125.00
	s. As a. Specimen. W/o sign. Punched hole cancelled.	—	—	125.00
34	**100 BOLÍVARES**			
	11.12.1940-3.7.1962. Brown on m/c unpt. Portr. Simon Bolívar at ctr. Arms at ctr. on back.			
	a. 11.12.1940-30.10.1952.	30.00	125.00	300.00
	b. 23.7.1953. Serial # prefix D.	35.00	150.00	300.00
	c. 22.4.1954-29.5.1958.	20.00	75.00	175.00
	d. 24.9.1959-3.7.1962.	15.00	50.00	150.00
	s. As a. Specimen. W/o sign. Punched hole cancelled.	—	—	175.00
35	**500 BOLÍVARES**			
	10.12.1940-21.12.1940. Blue on m/c unpt. Portr. Simon Bolívar at r. Arms at l. on back.	175.00	500.00	—
36	**500 BOLÍVARES**			
	21.1.1943-29.11.1946. Red on m/c unpt. Like #35.	150.00	425.00	—

1947 ISSUE

		VG	VF	UNC
37	**500 BOLÍVARES**			
	1947-71. Orange on m/c unpt. Like #35.			
	a. 14.8.1947-21.8.1952.	75.00	250.00	—
	b. 23.7.1953-29.5.1958.	30.00	125.00	300.00
	c. 11.3.1960-17.8.1971.	17.50	80.00	200.00
	s. As b. Specimen. W/o sign. Punched hole cancelled.	—	—	135.00

1952-53 ISSUE

#38-41 cruder and differently engraved portr. of Simon Bolívar and Antonio Jose de Sucre. Monument at ctr. on back. Printer: TDLR.

		VG	VF	UNC
38	**10 BOLÍVARES**			
	31.7.1952-23.7.1953. Purple on m/c unpt. Similar to #31. Arms at r. on back. Series E, F, G. 6 or 7 digit serial #.	30.00	125.00	350.00
39	**20 BOLÍVARES**			
	21.8.1952. Similar to #43. Arms at l. on back. Series G. 7 digit serial #.	35.00	175.00	450.00

		VG	VF	UNC
40	**50 BOLÍVARES**			
	26.2.1953; 23.7.1953. Simon Bolívar at l., CINCUENTA BOLÍVARES at r. Arms at r. on back. Series C. 7 digit serial #.	50.00	135.00	450.00
41	**100 BOLÍVARES**			
	23.7.1953. Portr. Simon Bolívar at r. Arms at l. on back. Series C, D. 7 digit serial #.	25.00	125.00	425.00

1960-61 ISSUE

#42-44 printer: TDLR.

		VG	VF	UNC
42	**10 BOLÍVARES**			
	6.6.1961. Purple on m/c unpt. Portr. Simon Bolívar at l. Antonio Jose de Sucre at r. Arms at r., monument to Battle of Carabobo at ctr. on back. Face similar to #31, back like #38. Series E-J. 7 digit serial #.			
	a. Issued note.	2.50	15.00	35.00
	s. Specimen w/black ovpt: SPECIMEN. Serial # prefix E.	—	—	12.50

		VG	VF	UNC
43	**20 BOLÍVARES**			
	1960-66. Dk. green on m/c unpt. Face similar to #32. Portr. Simon Bolívar at r., bank name in 1 line. Arms at l., monument at ctr. on back. 7 digit serial #.			
	a. 11.3.1960. Serial # prefix U-X.	4.00	20.00	50.00
	b. 6.6.1961. Serial # prefix X-Z.	4.00	15.00	40.00
	c. 7.5.1963. Serial # prefix A-B.	4.00		40.00
	d. 2.6.1964. Serial # prefix C-D.	4.00	15.00	40.00
	e. 10.5.1966. Serial # preifx E-G.	4.00	15.00	40.00
	s1. Specimen w/red ovpt: SPECIMEN. Paper w/colored planchettes. Serial # prefix X.	—	—	15.00
	s2. Specimen w/red ovpt: ESPECIMEN SIN VALOR. Paper w/security thread. Punched hole cancelled.	—	—	15.00
	s3. Specimen w/black ovpt: SPECIMEN. Serial # prefix U.	—	—	15.00

		VG	VF	UNC
44	**50 BOLÍVARES**			
	6.6.1961; 7.5.1963. Black on m/c unpt. Modified portr. of Simon Bolívar at l., value CINCUENTA BOLÍVARES at r. Back orange; monument at ctr., arms at r. on back. 7 digit serial #. Serial # prefix H-J; J-K.			
	a. Issued note.	8.00	50.00	125.00
	s. Specimen w/red ovpt: SPECIMEN SIN VALOR. Punched hole cancelled.	—	—	17.50

1963-67 ISSUE

#45-48 monument to Battle of Carabobo on back similar to #42-44. Printer: TDLR.

45

10 BOLÍVARES

1963-70. Purple on m/c unpt. Similar to #42 but much different portr. of Antonio Jose de Sucre at r. 7-digit serial #.

	VG	VF	UNC
a. 7.5.1963. Serial # prefix K-N.	1.00	2.50	15.00
b. 2.6.1964. Serial # prefix P-T.	1.00	2.50	12.50
c. 10.5.1966. Serial # prefix T-V; X-Z.	1.00	2.50	12.50
d. 8.8.1967. Serial # prefix A-D.	1.00	2.50	10.00
e. 5.3.1968. Serial # prefix G-H; J-K.	1.00	2.50	10.00
f. 19.11.1968. Serial # prefix E-F.	1.00	2.50	7.50
g. 27.1.1970. Serial # prefix L-N; P-U.	1.00	2.50	7.50
s. Specimen w/red ovpt: ESPECIMEN SIN VALOR. ND. Punched hole cancelled.	—	—	30.00

49

5 BOLÍVARES

10.5.1966. Blue on green and yellow unpt. Scene of the founding and commemorative text at ctr. and l., portr. Simon Bolívar at r. Back blue; city arms at l., early map (1578) of the city at ctr., national arms at r. Printer: ABNC. Serial # prefix

VG	VF	UNC
FV	3.00	22.50

46

20 BOLÍVARES

1967-74. Green on orange and blue unpt. Portr. Simon Bolívar at r. and as wmk., bank name in 3 lines. Arms w/o circle at l. on back.

	VG	VF	UNC
a. 8.8.1967. Serial # prefix H-J.	1.00	4.00	20.00
b. 5.3.1968. Serial # prefix L-M.	1.00	3.50	17.50
c. 30.9.1969. Serial # prefix K.	1.00	3.50	17.50
d. 27.1.1970. Serial # prefix N; P-R.	1.00	3.00	15.00
e. 29.1.1974. Serial # prefix Y-Z (7 digits); A-C (7 or 8 digits).	1.00	3.00	15.00
s1. Specimen w/red ovpt: ESPECIMEN SIN VALOR. ND. Punched hole cancelled.	—	—	15.00
s2. Specimen w/red ovpt as S1. 27.1.1970.	—	—	15.00

47

50 BOLÍVARES

1964-72. Black on orange and green unpt. Portr. Simon Bolívar at l. CINCUENTA BOLÍVARES above 50 at ctr. Back orange; like #44.

	VG	VF	UNC
a. 2.6.1964. Serial # prefix K-L.	2.00	6.00	40.00
b. 27.7.1965. Serial # preifx L-M.	2.00	6.00	30.00
c. 10.5.1966. Serial # prefix M-N.	2.00	6.00	30.00
d. 8.8.1967. Serial # prefix P.	2.00	6.00	30.00
e. 18.3.1969. Serial # prefix P-Q.	2.00	6.00	30.00
f. 7.4.1970. Serial # prefix Q-S.	2.00	6.00	30.00
g. 22.2.1972. Serial # prefix T-U.	2.00	6.00	30.00
s. Specimen w/red ovpt: ESPECIMEN SIN VALOR. ND.	—	—	37.50

50

5 BOLÍVARES

1968-74. Red on m/c unpt. Simon Bolívar at l., Francisco de Miranda at r. Arms at l., National Pantheon at ctr. on back. Printer: TDLR.

	VG	VF	UNC
a. 24.9.1968. Serial # prefix E; F.	0.75	2.25	10.00
b. 29.4.1969. Serial # prefix H-J.	0.50	2.00	10.00
c. 30.9.1969. Serial # prefix G; H.	0.50	2.00	10.00
d. 27.1.1970. Serial # prefix J-M.	0.50	1.50	8.50
e. 22.6.1971. Serial # prefix M-P.	0.25	1.50	6.00
f. 11.4.1972. Serial # prefix P; R.	0.25	1.50	6.00
g. 13.3.1973. Serial # prefix S; T.	0.25	1.00	5.00
h. 29.1.1974. Serial # prefix U-Z (7 digits); A-E (7 or 8 digits).	0.25	1.00	5.00
r. Remainder w/o date, sign. or serial #.	—	—	8.00
s. Specimen.	—	—	10.00

48

100 BOLÍVARES

1963-73. Brown on m/c unpt. Portr. Simon Bolívar at r. and as wmk. Arms at l. on back.

	VG	VF	UNC
a. 7.5.1963. Serial # prefix M-N.	2.00	5.00	40.00
b. 2.6.1964. Serial # prefix P-Q.	2.00	5.00	40.00
c. 27.7.1965. Serial # prefix Q.	2.00	5.00	40.00
d. 10.5.1966. Serial # prefix Q-R.	2.00	5.00	40.00
e. 8.8.1967. Serial # prefix S-T.	2.00	5.00	40.00
f. 18.3.1969. Serial # prefix U-V.	2.00	5.00	40.00
g. 26.5.1970. Serial # prefix X-Y.	2.00	5.00	40.00
h. 17.8.1971. Serial # prefix Z; A-B.	2.00	5.00	40.00
i. 24.10.1972. Serial # prefix C-D.	2.00	5.00	40.00
j. 6.2.1973. Serial # prefix E-F.	2.00	5.00	40.00
s1. Specimen w/red ovpt: ESPECIMEN SIN VALOR. ND.	—	—	20.00
s2. Specimen w/red ovpt: SPECIMEN and TDLR oval stampings. ND. Punched hole cancelled.	—	—	95.00

51

10 BOLÍVARES

1971-79. Purple on green and lilac unpt. Similar to #45. Printer: ABNC.

	VG	VF	UNC
a. 22.6.1971. Dk. blue serial # w/prefix U-A.	0.75	2.50	12.50
b. 11.4.1972. Serial # prefix A-H.	0.75	2.00	10.00
c. 13.3.1973. Serial # prefix H-R.	0.50	1.50	9.00
d. 29.1.1974. Serial # prefix R-Z; A-H.	0.50	1.50	9.00
e. 27.1.1976. Serial # prefix J-Y.	0.50	1.50	8.00
f. 7.6.1977. Serial # prefix Y-C.	0.50	1.50	7.00
g. 18.9.1979. Black serial # w/prefix C; D.	0.50	1.50	7.50
s1. Specimen w/red ovpt: MUESTRA. Punched hole cancelled. 11.4.1972.	—	—	12.50
s2. Specimen w/red ovpt: MUESTRA. Punched hole cancelled. 27.1.1976.	—	—	12.50
s3. Specimen w/red ovpt: MUESTRA. Punched hole cancelled. 7.6.1977.	—	—	12.50
s4. Specimen w/red ovpt: MUESTRA. Punched hole cancelled. 18.9.1979.	—	—	12.50

52 20 BOLÍVARES
1971; 1972. Dk. green on m/c unpt. Similar to #46. Printer: ABNC.

	VG	VF	UNC
a. 22.6.1971. Serial # prefix *S-T.*	0.75	2.00	12.50
b. 11.4.1972. Serial # prefix *U-V; X-Y.*	0.75	2.00	12.50
s. Specimen w/red ovpt: *MUESTRA.* Punched hole cancelled. 11.4.1972.	—	—	12.50

1971-74 Issue

53 20 BOLÍVARES
1974-79. Dk. green on m/c unpt. Jose Antonio Paez at r. and as wmk. Arms at l., monument to Battle of Carabobo at ctr. on back. Printer: ABNC. 7 or 8 digit serial #.

	VG	VF	UNC
a. 23.4.1974. Serial # prefix *A-H; J.*	0.50	1.50	9.00
b. 7.6.1977. Serial # prefix *J-N; P-T.*	0.50	1.50	8.00
c. 18.9.1979. Serial # prefix *T-V; X-Z; A-D.* 7 or 8-digit serial #.	0.50	1.50	9.00
s1. Specimen w/red ovpt: *ESPECIMEN SIN VALOR.* 23.4.1974.	—	—	10.00
s2. Specimen w/red ovpt: *MUESTRA.* Punched hole cancelled. 7.6.1977.	—	—	10.00
s3. Specimen w/red ovpt: *MUESTRA.* Punched hole cancelled. 18.9.1979.	—	—	10.00

54 50 BOLÍVARES
1972-77. Purple, orange and m/c. Academic bldg. at ctr., Andres Bello at r. and as wmk. Back orange; arms at l., bank at ctr. Printer: TDLR.

	VG	VF	UNC
a. 21.11.1972. Serial # prefix *A-B.*	1.00	4.00	15.00
b. 29.1.1974. Serial # prefix *B-D.*	1.00	4.00	14.50
c. 27.1.1976. Serial # prefix *D-F.*	1.00	4.00	15.00
d. 7.6.1977. Serial # prefix *F-H; J-N.*	0.75	3.00	12.50
s. Specimen w/red ovpt: *ESPECIMEN SIN VALOR.* 21.11.1972.	—	—	17.50

55 100 BOLÍVARES
1972-81. Dk. brown and brown-violet on m/c unpt. Simon Bolivar at r. and as wmk. National Capitol at l., arms at r. on back. Printer: BDDK.

	VG	VF	UNC
a. Red serial #. 21.11.1972. Serial # prefix *A-D.*	4.00	12.50	65.00
b. Wmk: Bolívar. 5.3.1974. Serial # prefix *D-H; J.*	3.00	10.00	45.00
c. Blue serial #. *B-C* added to wmk. Serial # prefix *J-N; P-Q.* 27.1.1976.	1.50	5.00	27.50
d. 23.11.1976. Serial # prefix *Q-V; X-Z; A* (8 digit serial #.)	1.50	5.00	27.50
e. 12.12.1978. Serial # prefix *A-H; J-M.*	1.00	5.00	25.00
f. 18.9.1979. Serial # prefix *N; P-V; X-Z; A-F.*	1.00	5.00	25.00
g. 1.9.1981. Serial # prefix *F-H; J-N; P-R.*	1.00	4.50	20.00
s1. Specimen w/red ovpt: *ESPECIMEN SIN VALOR.* 21.11.1972.	—	—	15.00
s2. Specimen. 27.1.1976.	—	—	15.00

56 500 BOLÍVARES
1971-72. Brown and blue on m/c unpt. Simon Bolívar at l. and as wmk., horsemen w/rifles riding at ctr. Back brown; dam at ctr., arms at r. Serial # prefix *A.* Printer: TDLR.

	VG	VF	UNC
a. 9.11.1971.	4.00	15.00	50.00
b. 11.1.1972.	2.00	8.50	45.00
s. Specimen w/red ovpt: *ESPECIMEN SIN VALOR.* ND.	—	—	22.50

1980 Issue

57 10 BOLÍVARES
29.1.1980. Purple on m/c unpt. Antonio Jose de Sucre at r. Arms at l., officers on horseback at ctr. r. on back. Serial # prefix *A.* 7 or 8 digit serial #. Printer: ABNC.

	VG	VF	UNC
a. Issued note.	0.25	1.00	3.00
p. Uniface Proofs, face and back. 29.1.1980.	—	—	150.00
s. Specimen w/red ovpt: *MUESTRA.* Punched hole cancelled.	—	—	10.00

1980-81 Commemorative Issues

#58, Bicentennial Birth of Andres Bello, 1781-1981

58 50 BOLÍVARES
27.1.1981. Dk. brown and green on m/c unpt. Andres Bello at r. and as wmk. Arms at l., scene showing Bello teaching young Bolívar on back. Serial # prefix *A.* Printer: TDLR.

	VG	VF	UNC
a. Issued note.	0.50	3.00	12.50
s. Specimen.	—	—	

#59, 150th Anniversary Death of Simon Bolívar, 1830-1980

59   100 BOLÍVARES

	VG	VF	UNC
29.1.1980. Red, purple and black on m/c unpt. Simon Bolívar at r. and as wmk., his tomb at ctr. r. Arms at l., scene of hand to hand combat aboard ship on back. Serial # prefix *A*. Printer: TDLR.			
a. Issued note.	2.00	5.00	27.50
s. Specimen w/red ovpt: *ESPECIMEN SIN VALOR*.	—	—	15.00

1981-88 ISSUES

#60-67 w/o imprint.

60   10 BOLÍVARES

	VG	VF	UNC
6.10.1981. Purple on lt. blue and m/c unpt. Similar to #57 but unpt. is different, and there are many significant plate changes. Printer: CdM-B (w/o imprint).			
a. 7 or 8 digit serial #. Serial # prefix: *B-D*.	FV	0.50	3.50
s. Specimen w/red ovpt: *MUESTRA*.	—	—	12.50

61   10 BOLÍVARES

	VG	VF	UNC
1986-95. Purple on lt. green and lilac unpt. Like #51, but *CARACAS* removed from upper ctr. beneath bank title. Printer: ABNC (w/o imprint).			
a. 18.3.1986. Serial # prefix: *D-F*.	FV	FV	2.00
b. 31.5.1990. Serial # prefix: *G-H, J-L*.	FV	FV	1.00
c. 8.12.1992. Serial # prefix: *L-N, P*.	FV	FV	1.00
d. 5.6.1995. Serial # prefix: *P-U*.	FV	FV	1.00
s. Specimen. Ovpt: *MUESTRA SIN VALOR*.	—	—	—

62   10 BOLÍVARES

	VG	VF	UNC
3.11.1988. Purple on ochre unpt. Like #45, but *CARACAS* removed from upper ctr. beneath bank title. Serial # prefix *F-G*. Printer: TDLR (w/o imprint).	FV	FV	1.00

63   20 BOLÍVARES

	VG	VF	UNC
1981-95. Dk. green on m/c unpt. Similar to #53 but *CARACAS* deleted under bank title. Title 82mm, horizontal central design in l. ctr. guilloche. Printer: TDLR (w/o imprint).			
a. 6.10.1981. Serial # prefix: *D-H, J*.	FV	FV	3.00
b. 7.9.1989. Serial # prefix: *X-Z, A-H, J*.	FV	FV	2.50
c. 8.12.1992. Short design in guilloche. Serial # prefix: *D-H, J-N, P-Z, A*.	FV	FV	2.00
d. 5.6.1995. Serial # prefix: *A-E*.	FV	FV	1.00
e. 10.2.1998. Serial # prefix: *E-F*.	FV	FV	1.00
s. Specimen.	—	—	10.00

Note: Central design in l.h. guilloche: ➤■●■◀ or ➤●◀

64   20 BOLÍVARES

	VG	VF	UNC
25.9.1984. Dk. green on m/c unpt. Like #63, but title 84mm and w/o central design in l. ctr. guilloche, also other minor plate differences. Latent image *BCV* in guilloches easily seen. Serial # prefix *J* (8 digits); *K-N; P-S* (7 or	FV	FV	3.00

64A   20 BOLÍVARES

	VG	VF	UNC
7.7.1987. Dk. green on m/c unpt. Like #63 but printer: ABNC (w/o imprint). Serial # prefix *T-X*. 7 or 8 digit serial #.	FV	FV	2.50

65   50 BOLÍVARES

	VG	VF	UNC
1985-98. Purple, black and orange on m/c unpt. Like #54, but *CARACAS* removed under bank name. Printer: BDDK (w/o imprint).			
a. 10.12.1985. Serial # prefix: *N, P-S*.	FV	FV	4.00
b. 3.11.1988. Serial # prefix: *S-V, X-Z, A*.	FV	FV	4.00
c. 31.5.1990. Serial # prefix: *A-H, J-K*.	FV	FV	3.00
d. 8.12.1992. Serial # prefix: *K, L-N, P-V, X-Z*. 7 or 8 digit serial #.	FV	FV	2.50
e. 5.6.1995. Serial # prefix: *Q-U*.	FV	FV	2.00
f. 5.2.1998. Serial # prefix: *U-V*.	FV	FV	1.50
g. 13.10.1998. Serial # prefix: *V-Z*.	FV	FV	1.50
s. Specimen. 10.12.1985. Serial # prefix *N*.	—	—	20.00

66   100 BOLÍVARES

	VF	VF	UNC
1987-98. Dk. brown and brown-violet on m/c unpt. Like #55 but w/o imprint. Printer: BDDK (w/o imprint).	—	—	2.00

66   100 BOLÍVARES

a. 3.2.1987. Serial # prefix: *R-V, X-Z, A-H, J-K*.	FV	FV	5.00
b. 16.3.1989. Serial # prefix: *K-N, P-V, X-Z, A-G*.	FV	FV	3.50
c. 31.5.1990. Serial # prefix: *G-H, J-N, P-V, X-Y*.	FV	FV	3.50
d. 12.5.1992. Serial # prefix: *Y-Z, A-E*.	FV	FV	2.00
e. 8.12.1992. Serial # prefix: *E-H, K-N*.	FV	FV	2.00
f. 5.2.1998. Serial # prefix: *E-G*.	FV	FV	2.00

67 **500 BOLÍVARES**

1981-98. Purple and black on m/c unpt. Simon Bolívar at r. and as wmk. Back green and m/c; arms at l., orchids at ctr. Printer: BDDK (w/o imprint).

	VG	VF	UNC
a. 25.9.1981. Serial # prefix: A.	FV	5.00	30.00
b. 3.2.1987. Serial # prefix: B-C.	FV	FV	15.00
c. 16.3.1989. Serial # prefix: C-F.	FV	FV	15.00
d. 31.5.1990. Serial # prefix: F-H, J-N, P-V, X-Z, A-C.	FV	FV	5.00
e. 5.6.1995. Serial # prefix: C-H, J-N, P-Q.	FV	FV	5.00
f. 5.2.1998. Serial # prefix: Q-Z.	FV	FV	2.50

1989 Issue

#68 and 69 replacement notes: Serial # prefix *X XX* and *W*.

68 **1 BOLÍVAR**

5.10.1989. Purple on blue and green unpt. Lg. *1* at l., coin w/Simon Bolívar at r. Arms at l., rosette at r. on back. Wmk. paper. Printer: BDDK (w/o imprint). Serial # prefix: *A-D; X*.

VG	VF	UNC
FV	FV	0.25

69 **2 BOLÍVARES**

5.10.1989. Blue and brownish gray on lt. blue unpt. Coin head of Simon Bolívar at r. Lg. *2* at l., arms at r. on back. Printer: USBNC (w/o imprint). Serial # prefix: *AA-AH, AJ-AM, AW-AZ, BA, BJ, BL, BN, BP, BU-BW, XX*.

VG	VF	UNC
FV	FV	0.50

70 **5 BOLÍVARES**

21.9.1989. Red on m/c unpt. Like #50, but *CARACAS* removed from upper ctr. beneath bank title on face and back. Lithographed. Printer: TDLR (w/o imprint).

	VG	VF	UNC
a. 7 digit serial #. Serial # prefix: F-Z (no I or O.)	FV	FV	1.00
b. 8 digit serial #. Serial # prefix: A-E, W.	FV	FV	0.50

1989 Commemorative Issue

#71, Bicentennial Birth of General Rafael Urdaneta, 1789-1989

71 **20 BOLÍVARES**

20.10.1987 (1989). Deep green and black on m/c unpt. General Rafael Urdaneta at r. and as wmk. Battle of Lake Maracaibo at l. ctr. on back. Serial # prefix A-C.

VG	VF	UNC
FV	FV	2.00

1990-94 Issue

#72 and 73 w/o imprint.

72 **50 BOLÍVARES**

31.5.1990. Purple, black and orange on m/c unpt. Similar to #65 but modified plate design, ornaments in "50's". Back deeper orange. Serial # prefix A-H; J-K.

VG	VF	UNC
FV	FV	2.50

#73-75 arms at upper r. on back.

73 **1000 BOLÍVARES**

1991-92. Red-violet on m/c unpt. Part of independence text at far l., Simon Bolívar at l. and as wmk. Signing of the Declaration of Independence at ctr. r. on back.

	VG	VF	UNC
a. Dot instead of accent above *i* (error) in *Bolívares* on face and back. 8.8.1991. Serial # prefix: A.	3.00	10.00	45.00
b. Accent above *i* in *Bolívares* on face and back. 30.7.1992. Serial # prefix: A.	FV	FV	25.00
c. As a. 8.12.1992. Serial # prefix: A (8-digits); B (8 or 9-digits).	FV	FV	4.00
s1. As a. Specimen.	—	—	40.00
s2. As b. Specimen.	—	—	40.00

74 **2000 BOLÍVARES**

1994; 1995. Dk. green and black on m/c unpt. Antonio Jose de Sucre at r. and as wmk. Value at lower l. in green. Scene of Battle of Ayacucho at l. ctr. on back.

	VG	VF	UNC
a. 12.5.1994. Serial # prefix: A.	FV	FV	7.50
b. 21.12.1995. Large serial #. Serial # prefix: A-B.	FV	FV	6.00
b. 21.12.1995. Large serial #. Serial # prefix: A-B.	FV	FV	6.00

75 **5000 BOLÍVARES**

1994; 1996. Dk. brown and brown-violet on m/c unpt. Simon Bolívar at r. and as wmk. Gathering at palace for Declaration of Independence at ctr. on back.

	VG	VF	UNC
a. 12.5.1994. Serial # prefix A.	FV	FV	15.00
b. 14.3.1996. Serial # prefix A-B.	FV	FV	15.00

1994 Issue

76 **1000 BOLÍVARES**

1994-98. Red-violet on m/c unpt. Like #73 but w/green OVD *1000* at lower r.

VG	VF	UNC

		FV	FV	3.00
a. 17.3.1994. Serial # prefix: *C-E*. (8 or 9-digits).		FV	FV	3.00
b. 5.6.1995. Serial # prefix: *E-H, J, W*. (9 digits).		FV	FV	3.00
c. 5.2.1998. Serial # prefix: *J-M, Z*. (8 or 9 digits).		FV	FV	2.50
d. 6.8.1998. Serial # prefix: *M-Q, Z*. (8 or 9 digits)		FV	FV	2.50
e. 10.9.1998.		FV	FV	2.50

1997 ISSUE

			VG	VF	UNC
77	**2000 BOLÍVARES**				
	1997; 1998. Dk. green, brown and black on m/c unpt. Like #74 but w/*2000* at lower l. in black.				
	a. 16.6.1997. Serial # prefix *B-C*.		FV	FV	9.00
	b. 10.2.1998 Serial # prefix *C-D*.		FV	FV	9.00
	c. 6.8.1998. Serial # prefix: D-F.		FV	FV	9.00
78	**5000 BOLÍVARES**				
	1997-98 Brown and red-brown on m/c unpt. Simon Bolivar at l. ctr. Back like #75.				
	a. 16.6.1997. Serial # prefix: *B-C*.		FV	0.00VF	17.50
	b. 10.2.1998. Serial # prefix: *C-D*.		FV	FV	15.00
	c. 6.8.1998. Serial # prefix: *D-F*.		FV	FV	15.00

1998 ISSUE

Replacement notes are indicated by a *Z* serial # prefix for all notes dated 1998 but for the 5.6.1998 1000 Bolívares which uses a *W*.

			VG	VF	UNC
79	**1000 BOLÍVARES**				
	10.9.1998. Violet on m/c unpt. Simon Bolívar at r. Panteon Nacional at r. ctr. on back. Serial # prefix: A.		FV	FV	2.50
80	**2000 BOLÍVARES**				
	29.10.1998. Olive green and gray. Andrea Bello at r. Pico Bolívar mountain range at r. ctr. Serial # prefix: A.		FV	FV	5.00
81	**10,000 BOLÍVARES**				
	10.2.1998. Black, red and olive-brown on m/c unpt. Simon Bolívar at r. and as wmk. Teresa Carreño Theatre at l. ctr., arms at top ctr. r. on back. Serial # prefix: Z, A-B.		FV	FV	27.50
82	**20,000 BOLÍVARES**				
	24.8.1998. Green on m/c unpt. Simon Rodriguez at r. Arms at l., parrot at l. ctr., Angel Falls at ctr. r. on back. Serial # prefix: Z, A-B.		FV	FV	45.00
83	**50,000 BOLÍVARES**				
	24.8.1998. Orange and m/c. Dr. Jose Maria Vargas at ctr. Central University at ctr., araguaney flower at l. on back. Printer: CMV. Serial # prefix: A.		FV	FV	50.00

REPÚBLICA BOLIVARIANA DE VENEZUELA

2000-01 ISSUE

#91-93 printer: CMV.

			VG	VF	UNC
91	**5000 BOLÍVARES**				
	25.5.2000; 13.8.2002. Blue and m/c. Francisco de Miranda at r. and as wmk. Represat de Gury at ctr. on back.		FV	FV	7.50

			VG	VF	UNC
92	**10,000 BOLÍVARES**				
	25.5.2000; 13.8.2002; 15.8.2001. Black on brown and m/c unpt. Antonio J. Sucre at ctr. r. Supreme Court bldg. at ctr. on back. Serial # prefix: A.		FV	FV	20.00
93	**20,000 BOLÍVARES**				
	16.8.2001. Green on m/c unpt. Simon Rodriguez at r. Like #80.		FV	FV	30.00

VIET NAM

[map illustration]

The Socialist Republic of Viet Nam, located in Southeast Asia west of the South China Sea, has an area of 127,300 sq. mi. (329,560 sq. km.) and a population of 80.55 million. Capital: Hanoi. Agricultural products, saltwater fish, shellfish, coal, mineral ores and electronic products are exported.

The Viet Namese originated in North China, from where they were driven southward by the Han Chinese. They settled in the Red River Delta in northern Viet Nam. By 208 BC, much of present-day southern China and northern Viet Nam was incorporated into the independent kingdom of Nam Viet. China annexed Nam Viet in 111 BC and ruled it until 939, when independence was reestablished. The new state then expanded until it included much of Cambodia and southern Viet Nam. Viet Nam was reconquered by the Chinese in 1407; and although they were driven out, the country was divided into two, not to be reunited until 1802.

During the latter half of the 19th century, the French gradually overran Viet Nam. Cochin-China, fell to the French in 1862-67. In 1884, France established protectorates over Annam, the central region of Viet Nam and Tonkin in the north. Cambodia, Cochin-China, Annam and Tonkin were incorporated into the Indo-Chinese Union in 1887.

At the start of World War II, many nationalists, communist and non-communist alike, fled to China and joined the League for the Independence of Viet Nam ("Viet Minh") to free Viet Nam from French rule. The Japanese occupied Viet Nam during World War II. As the end of the war drew near, the Vichy French administration had granted Viet Nam independence under a government headed by Bao Dai, emperor of Annam. The Bao Dai government collapsed at the end of the war, and on September 2, 1945, the Viet Minh proclaimed the existence of an independent Viet Nam consisting of Cochin-China, Annam and Tonkin, and set up a provisional Communist government of the Democratic Republic of Viet Nam. France recognized the new government as a free state, but later reneged and in 1949 reinstalled Bao Dai as ruler of Viet Nam and extended the regime within the French Union. The first Indochina War, against the state that raged on to the disastrous defeat of the French by the Viet Minh on May 7, 1954.

An agreement of July 21, 1954, provided for a temporary division of Viet Nam at the 17th parallel of latitude, with the Democratic Republic of Viet Nam (North Viet Nam) to the north, and the Republic of Viet Nam (South Viet Nam) to the south. In October 1955, South Viet Nam held a referendum and authorized the establishment of a republic. This Republic of Viet Nam was proclaimed on October 26, 1955, and was recognized immediately by the Western powers.

The Democratic Republic of Viet Nam, working through Viet Cong guerrillas, instigated subversion in South Viet Nam which led to the second Indochina War. This war, from the viewpoint of the North was merely a continuation of the first (anti-French) war, which came to a brief halt in 1973 but did not end until April 30, 1975 when South Viet Nam surrendered. The National Liberation Front for South Viet Nam, the political arm of the Viet Cong, assumed governmental power in the south. On July 2, 1976, North and South Viet Nam were united as the Socialist Republic of Viet Nam with Hanoi as the capital.

MONETARY SYSTEM:
1 Hao = 10 Xu
1 Dông = 100 Xu
1 Dông = 100 "Old" Dong, 1951
Note: HCM = Ho Chi Minh

DEMOCRATIC REPUBLIC

NGÂN HÀNG NHÀ NU'Ó'C VIÊT NAM

STATE BANK OF VIET NAM

1964 ND; 1972; 1975 ISSUE

		VG	VF	UNC
74A	**20 Dông**			
	1969. Olive on dk. green unpt. HCM at l. Coat of arms at r. Tractor on back. (Not issued).	—	—	400.00
75	**2 XU**			
	ND (1964). Purple on green unpt. Arms at ctr.			
	a. Issued note.	4.00	15.00	75.00
	s. Specimen.	—	—	200.00

		VG	VF	UNC
76	**5 XU**			
	1975 (date in lt. brown above *VIET* at lower l. ctr.). Purple on brown unpt. Arms at upper r.			
	a. Wmk: 15mm stars.	1.00	3.00	10.00
	b. Wmk: 30mm radiant star.	1.00	3.00	10.00
	s. Specimen w/o wmk.	—	—	15.00

77 1 HAO
1972. Violet on m/c unpt. Arms at ctr. Woman feeding pigs on back. 103 x 57mm.

	VG	VF	UNC
a. Wmk: 15mm stars. Series KG-?.	1.00	3.00	10.00
b. Wmk: 32mm encircled stars. Series MK-?.	1.00	3.00	10.00
c. W/o wmk. Series ML.	1.00	3.00	10.00
s. Specimen w/o wmk.	—	—	15.00

77A 1 HAO
1972. Violet on m/c unpt. Like #77 but reduced size, 96 x 48mm.
Specimen.

	VG	VF	UNC
	—	—	20.00

78 2 HAO
1975. Brownish gray on green and peach unpt. Arms at ctr. 2 men spraying rice field on back.

	VG	VF	UNC
a. Issued note.	1.00	3.00	10.00
s. Specimen.	—	—	15.00

82 10 Dông
1976. Purple and brown on m/c unpt. Elephants logging at ctr. on back. (Counterfeits known.)

	VG	VF	UNC
a. Issued note.	0.25	1.00	5.00
s. Specimen.	—	—	25.00

SOCIALIST REPUBLIC

The country was united under the name of Socialist Republic of Viet Nam on July 2, 1976 after the Democratic Republic of (North) Viet Nam and the southern Peoples Revolutionary Government with assistance from China, Eastern Europe and the Soviet Union, won their long war against the Republic of (South) Viet Nam.

NGÂN HÀNG NHÀ NU'Ó'C VIÊT NAM

STATE BANK OF VIET NAM

1976 DATED ISSUE

Northern 1958 and Southern 1966-dated notes were exchanged in 1978 for 1976-dated notes to unify the currency of North and South Viet Nam. All of the old northern and southern Xu and Hao notes continued as legal tender, but the old Dong notes were overstamped with *Da Thu*, **marked with an *X*, and/or destroyed.**

83 20 Dông
1976. Blue on pink and green unpt. HCM at r., arms at l. Tractors and dam on back.

	VG	VF	UNC
a. Issued note.	0.25	1.25	10.00
s. Specimen.	—	—	25.00

84 50 Dông
1976. Red-brown on pink and green unpt. HCM at r., arms at l. Hong Gay open pit mining scene on back. 2 serial # varieties.

	VG	VF	UNC
a. Issued note.	0.25	1.25	7.00
s. Specimen.	—	—	25.00

79 5 HAO
1976. Purple on m/c unpt. Coconut palms amd river scene on back.

	VG	VF	UNC
a. Issued note.	0.25	1.00	3.00
s. Specimen.	—	—	100.00

SOCIALIST REPUBLIC OF VIET NAM

NGÂN HÀNG NHÀ NU'Ó'C VIÊT NAM

STATE BANK OF VIET NAM

1980; 1981 ISSUE

80 1 Dông
1976. Brown on m/c unpt. Arms at ctr. Factory on back.

	VG	VF	UNC
a. Issued note.	0.25	1.00	3.00
s. Specimen.	—	—	20.00

85 2 Dông
1980 (1981). Brown on m/c unpt. Arms at ctr. River scene on back.

	VG	VF	UNC
a. Issued note.	0.25	0.75	2.00
s. Specimen.	—	—	15.00

81 5 Dông
1976. Blue-gray and green on pink unpt. Back green on yellow unpt.; 2 women w/fish in foreground, boats in harbor in background.

	VG	VF	UNC
a. Issued note. Wmk: Flower. Block letter at l., serial # at r.	0.25	1.00	4.00
b. Block letter and serial # together. W/o wmk.	0.25	1.00	3.00
s. Specimen.	—	—	20.00

86 10 Dông
1980 (1981). Brown on m/c unpt. Arms at r. House and trees on back.

	VG	VF	UNC
a. Issued note.	0.25	0.75	4.00
s. Specimen.	—	—	15.00

87 30 Dông
1981 (1982). Purple, brown and m/c. Arms at l. ctr., HCM at r. Harbor scene on back. Large and small serial # varieties.

	VG	VF	UNC
a. Issued note.	0.50	1.50	8.00
s1. Specimen ovpt. *SPECIMEN.*	—	—	25.00
s2. Specimen ovpt. *GIAY MÂU.*	—	—	35.00

88 100 Dông
1980 (1981). Brown, dk. blue and m/c. Portr. HCM at r. and as wmk., arms at ctr. Back blue, purple and brown; boats and rock formations in sea cove. Lg. or sm. digits in serial #.

	VG	VF	UNC
a. Issued note.	0.25	1.00	8.00
s. Specimen.	—	—	30.00

1985 ISSUE

#89-93 tower at l. ctr., arms at r. on face.

89 5 HAO
1985. Red-violet on lt. blue unpt. Large 5 at ctr. on back.

	VG	VF	UNC
a. Issued note.	0.25	2.00	4.00
s. Specimen.	—	—	15.00

90 1 Dông
1985. Blue-green on m/c unpt. Sampans along rocky coastline on back.

	VG	VF	UNC
a. Issued note.	0.15	0.50	2.00
s. Specimen.	—	—	15.00

91 2 Dông
1985. Purple on m/c unpt. Sampans anchored along coastline on back.

	VG	VF	UNC
a. Issued note.	0.20	0.75	2.00
s. Specimen.	—	—	15.00

92 5 Dông
1985. Green on m/c unpt. Sampans anchored in river on back.

	VG	VF	UNC
a. Issued note.	0.15	0.50	2.00
s. Specimen.	—	—	15.00

93 10 Dông
1985. Brown-violet on m/c unpt. Village along stream at ctr. on back.

	VG	VF	UNC
a. Issued note.	0.25	0.75	3.00
s. Specimen.	—	—	15.00

#94-99 HCM at r.

94 20 Dông
1985 (1986). Brown, dk. purple and m/c. Arms at ctr. r. One pillar pagoda in Hanoi on back.

	VG	VF	UNC
a. Issued note.	0.25	0.75	2.00
s. Specimen.	—	—	15.00

95 30 Dông
1985 (1986). Blue and m/c. Arms at l. Lg. bldg. w/clock tower at ctr. on back.

	VG	VF	UNC
a. Issued note.	0.50	1.25	5.00
s. Specimen.	—	—	15.00

96 50 Dông
1985. Green, brown and m/c. Arms at l. ctr. Reservoir and electric power station on back.

	VG	VF	UNC
a. Issued note.	0.50	1.50	7.00
s. Specimen.	—	—	15.00

97 50 Dông
1985 (1987). Blue-gray on orange and m/c unpt. Arms at ctr. Bridge at ctr. on back.

	VG	VF	UNC
a. Issued note.	0.25	0.75	3.00
s. Specimen.	—	—	15.00

98	100 Dông	VG	VF	UNC
	1985. Brown, green, yellow and m/c. Arms at l. ctr. Planting rice on back. Wmk: HCM.			
	a. Issued note.	0.25	2.50	15.00
	s. Specimen.	—	—	15.00

99	500 Dông	VG	VF	UNC
	1985. Red on blue and m/c unpt. Arms at upper ctr. Factory at l. ctr. on back. Wmk: HCM.			
	a. Issued note.	1.00	3.00	12.50
	s. Specimen.	—	—	20.00

1987; 1988 ISSUE

#100-104 HCM at r., arms at l. or l. ctr.

100	200 Dông	VG	VF	UNC
	1987. Red-brown and tan on m/c unpt. Field workers at l. and tractor at ctr. r. on back. Lg. or sm. digits in serial #.			
	a. Issued note.	0.10	0.50	1.00
	s. Specimen.	—	—	15.00

101	500 Dông	VG	VF	UNC
	1988 (1989). Red-brown and red on m/c unpt. Dockside view on back. Lg. or sm. digits in serial #.			
	a. Issued note.	0.25	0.50	2.00
	s. Specimen.	—	—	15.00

#102-104 wmk: HCM.

102	1000 Dông	VG	VF	UNC
	1987 (1988). Dk. brown and deep olive-green on m/c unpt. Open pit mining equipment at l. ctr. on back.			
	a. Issued note.	0.50	1.50	12.00
	s. Specimen.	—	—	15.00

103	2000 Dông	VG	VF	UNC
	1987 (1988). Dk. and lt. brown on green and m/c unpt. Back dk. purple; industrial plant at l. ctr.			
	a. Issued note.	0.75	3.00	20.00
	s. Specimen.	—	—	15.00

104	5000 Dông	VG	VF	UNC
	1987 (1989). Deep blue, purple, brown and green on m/c unpt. Offshore oil rigs at l. ctr. on back.			
	a. Issued note.	0.25	1.25	8.00
	s. Specimen.	—	—	15.00

1988-91 ISSUE

#106-111 HCM at r., arms at l. or l. ctr.

105	100 Dông	VG	VF	UNC
	1991 (1992). Lt. brown on m/c unpt. Temple and pagoda at l. ctr. on back. Lg. or sm. digits in serial #.			
	a. Issued note.	0.05	0.15	0.50
	s1. Specimen w/ovpt: TIEN MÂU.	—	—	20.00
	s2. Specimen w/ovpt: SPECIMEN.	—	—	40.00

106	1000 Dông	VG	VF	UNC
	1988 (1989). Purple on gold and m/c unpt. Elephant logging at ctr. on back. Lg. or sm. digits in serial #.			
	a. Issued note.	0.10	0.25	1.50
	s. Specimen.	—	—	15.00

107	2000 Dông	VG	VF	UNC
	1988 (1989). Brownish purple on lilac and m/c unpt. Women workers in textile factory on back. Lg. or sm. digits in serial #.			
	a. Issued note.	0.15	0.50	2.00
	s. Specimen.	—	—	15.00

115	10,000 Đồng	VG	VF	UNC
	1993. Red and red-violet on m/c unpt. Like #109 but w/optical registry device at lower l., modified unpt. color around arms. Back brown-violet on m/c unpt.			
	a. Issued note.	FV	FV	4.00
	s. Specimen.	—	—	20.00

108	5000 Đồng	VG	VF	UNC
	1991 (1993). Dk. blue on m/c unpt. Electric lines on back.			
	a. Issued note.	0.25	0.75	3.00
	s. Specimen.	—	—	15.00

#109-111 wmk: HCM.

109	10,000 Đồng	VG	VF	UNC
	1990 (1992). Red and red-violet on m/c unpt. Junks along coastline at ctr. on back.			
	a. Issued note.	1.25	1.50	10.00
	s. Specimen.	—	—	15.00

116	50,000 Đồng	VG	VF	UNC
	1994. Dk. olive-green and black on m/c unpt. Like #111 but w/date under HCM.			
	a. Issued note.	FV	FV	8.00
	s. Specimen.	—	—	20.00
117	100,000 Đồng			
	1994 (2000). Brown and lt. green on m/c unpt. HCM at r. HCM's house on back.			
	a. Issued note.	FV	FV	20.00
	s. Specimen.	—	—	20.00

2001 COMMEMORATIVE ISSUE

#118, 50th Anniversary National Bank of Viet Nam
Released in a special folder. Face value is minimal.

110	20,000 Đồng	VG	VF	UNC
	1991 (1993). Blue-green on m/c unpt. Arms at ctr. Packing factory on back.			
	a. Issued note.	1.00	1.25	8.00
	s. Specimen.	—	—	20.00
111	50,000 Đồng			
	1990 (1993). Dk. olive-green and black on m/c unpt. Arms at upper l. ctr. Date at lower r. Dockside view on back.			
	a. Issued note.	1.75	3.50	20.00
	s. Specimen.	—	—	30.00

1992 BANK CHEQUE ISSUE

#112-114A Negotiable Bank Cheques/Certificates with expiration dates used for high value merchandise and large transactions. Specimens are valued a 2x the Unc. price.

112	100,000 Đồng	VG	VF	UNC
	1992-94.	20.00	50.00	200.00
113	500,000 Đồng			
	1992-2000.	25.00	75.00	150.00
114	1,000,000 Đồng			
	1992-2001.	50.00	100.00	250.00
114A	5,000,000 Đồng			
	1992-2001.	100.00	300.00	600.00

1993; 1994 REGULAR ISSUE

118	50 Đồng	VG	VF	UNC
	2001. Rose on m/c unpt. HCM at r. ctr. Bldg. on back. Commemorative text in clear area at upper l. on face, and upper r. on back. Polymer plastic.	—	—	30.00

2003 ISSUE

#119-121 HCM at r. Polymer plastic. Printed originally at NPA, later printings done at the State Printing Works in Viet Nam.

119	50,000 Đồng	VG	VF	UNC
	(20)03; (20)04; (20)05; (20)06. Rose on m/c unpt. Buildings in Hua on back. Polymer plastic. Issued in official folder.	FV	FV	8.00
120	100,000 Đồng			
	(20)04; (20)05; (20)06. Green on m/c unpt. Van Mieu Quoc Tu Giam (National University) on back. Ploymer plastic.	FV	FV	15.00
121	500,000 Đồng			
	(20)03; (20)04; (20)05; (20)06. Blue and pink on m/c unpt. HCM's birthplace in Kim Lien, Nghean Province on back. Polymer plastic.	FV	FV	70.00

FOREIGN EXCHANGE CERTIFICATES

NGÂN HANG NGOAI THUONG VIET NAM

BANK FOR FOREIGN TRADE

1987 ND DÔNG B ISSUE

#FX1-FX5 green on pale blue and yellow unpt. Back pale blue.

		VG	VF	UNC
FX1	**10 Dông B**			
	ND (1987).			
	a. Series AA; AB (not issued).	—	—	5.00
	s. Specimen. Series EE.	—	—	10.00
FX2	**50 Dông B**			
	ND (1987).			
	a. Series AD (not issued).	—	—	5.00
	s. Specimen. Series EE.	—	—	10.00
FX3	**100 Dông B**			
	ND (1987).			
	a. Series AC (not issued).	—	—	5.00
	s. Specimen. Series EE.	—	—	10.00
FX4	**200 Dông B**			
	ND (1987).			
	a. Series AD (not issued).	—	—	5.00
	s. Specimen. Series EE.	—	—	10.00
FX5	**500 Dông B**			
	ND (1987).			
	a. Series AC (not issued).	—	—	5.00
	s. Specimen. Series EE.	—	—	10.00

		VG	VF	UNC
FX6	**1000 Dông B**			
	ND (1987). Red-violet on pink and pale orange unpt. Back pink.			
	a. Issued note. Series AE.	—	—	5.00
	s. Specimen. Series EE.	—	—	10.00
FX7	**5000 Dông B**			
	ND (1987). Brown on ochre unpt. Back ochre.			
	a. Issued note. Series AA; AB; AE.	—	—	5.00
	s. Specimen. Series EE.	—	—	10.00

PHIÊU' THAY NGOAI TÊ

1981 US DOLLAR A ISSUE

		VG	VF	UNC
FX8	**1 DOLLAR**			
	1981-84. Green on peach and lt. blue unpt. Series AD.			
	a. Issued note with validation ovpt.	200.00	700.00	—
	b. Unissued note w/o validation ovpt.	—	—	1000.00

		VG	VF	UNC
FX9	**5 DOLLARS**			
	1981-84. Purple on peach and lt. blue unpt. Series AF.			
	a. Issued note with validation ovpt.	200.00	700.00	—
	b. Unissued note w/o validation ovpt.	—	—	1000.00

South Viet Nam (the former Republic of Viet Nam), located in Southeast Asia, bounded by North Viet Nam on the north, Laos and Cambodia on the west, and the South China Sea on the east and south, had an area of 66,280 sq. mi. (171,665 sq. km.) and a population of 20 million. Capital: Saigon. The economy of the area is predominantly agricultural.

South Viet Nam, the direct successor to the French-dominated regime (also known as the State of Viet Nam), was created after the first Indochina War (between the French and the Viet-Minh) by the Geneva agreement of 1954 which divided Viet Nam at the 17th parallel of latitude. Elections which would have reunified North and South Viet Nam in 1956 never took place, and the North continued the war for unification of Viet Nam under the the Democratic Republic of (North) Viet Nam. The Republic of Viet Nam surrendered unconditionally on April 30, 1975. There followed a short period of coexistence of the two Viet Namese states, but the South was governed by the North through the Peoples Revolutionary Government (PRG). On July 2, 1976, South and North Viet Nam joined to form the Socialist Republic of Viet Nam.

Also see Viet Nam.

MONETARY SYSTEM
1 Dông = 100 Xu

VIET NAM - SOUTH

NGÂN-HÀNG QUÔ'C-GIA VIÊT-NAM

NATIONAL BANK OF VIET NAM

1962 ND ISSUE

#5-6 printer: SBNC.

		VG	VF	UNC
5	**10 Dông**			
	ND (1962). Red. Young farm couple at l. Ornate arch on back.			
	Shade varieties.			
	a. Issued note.	0.50	2.00	8.00
	p. Uniface face or back proof.	—	—	150.00
	s. Specimen. *GIAY MAU.*	—	—	150.00

		VG	VF	UNC
6	**20 Dông**			
	ND (1962). Brown. Ox cart at l. Woman digging on back.			
	a. Issued note.	2.00	6.00	30.00
	p. Uniface face or back proof.	—	—	150.00
	s. Specimen. *GIAY MAU.*	—	—	175.00
	x. Counterfeit.	—	—	—

6A 500 Dông
ND (1962). Green-blue on gold and pinkish unpt. Dragon at l.,
palace-like bldg. at l. ctr. Farmer w/2 water buffalos at r. on back.
Wmk: Ngo Dinh Diem.

	VG	VF	UNC
a. Issued note.	100.00	200.00	700.00
s1. Specimen. *GIAY MAU.*	—	—	1000.00
s2. Specimen. TDLR oval.			

1964; 1966 ND ISSUES

15 1 Dông
ND (1964). Lt. and dk. brown on orange and lt. blue unpt. Back red-
brown; farm tractor at r. Wmk: Plant.

	VG	VF	UNC
a. Issued note.	1.00	3.00	5.00
s1. Specimen. *GIAY MAU.*	—	—	1200.00
s2. Specimen. TDLR oval.			

16 20 Dông
ND (1964). Green on m/c unpt. Stylized fish at ctr. on back. Wmk:
Dragon's head.

	VG	VF	UNC
a. Issued note.	0.25	0.75	9.00
s. Specimen. *GIAY MAU.*	—	—	300.00

Note: Three different #16 specimens have been reported This indicates that more varieties of issued notes
may exist. Please report all new varieties to the editors.

17 50 Dông
ND (1966). Purple on m/c unpt. Leaf tendrils at r.

	VG	VF	UNC
a. Issued note.	1.00	5.00	25.00
s. Specimen. *GIAY MAU.*	—	—	300.00

18 100 Dông
ND (1966). Lt. and dk. brown on lt. blue unpt. Bldg. w/domed roof
at r. Quarry and hills on back. Wmk: Plant.

	VG	VF	UNC
a. Issued note.	1.00	5.00	35.00
s1. Specimen. Red ovpt. *GIAY MAU.*	—	—	300.00
s2. Specimen. Black ovpt.	—	—	300.00

19 100 Dông
ND (1966). Red on m/c unpt. Le Van Duyet in national costume at
l. Bldg. and ornate gateway at ctr. r. on back.

	VG	VF	UNC
a. Wmk: Demon's head.	1.00	10.00	40.00
b. Wmk: Le Van Duyet's head.	0.25	3.00	15.00
s1. As a. Specimen.	—	—	500.00
s2. As b. Specimen.	—	—	500.00

20 200 Dông
ND (1966). Dk. brown on m/c unpt. Nguyen-Hue, warrior, at l.
Warrior on horseback leading soldiers on back.

	VG	VF	UNC
a. Wmk: Demon's head.	1.00	10.00	45.00
b. Wmk: Nguyen Hue's head.	0.25	3.00	25.00
s1. As a. Specimen.	—	—	500.00
s2. As b. Specimen.	—	—	500.00

#21 *Deleted.* See #6A.

22 500 Dông
ND (1964). Brown on m/c unpt. Museum in Saigon at ctr. Stylized
creatures at ctr. on back. Wmk: Demon's head.

	VG	VF	UNC
a. Issued note.	3.00	12.50	50.00
s1. Specimen.	—	—	300.00
s2. Specimen. TDLR oval.			

23 500 Dông
ND (1966). Blue on m/c unpt. Trâ'n-Hu'ng-Dao, warrior, at l. and
as wmk. Sailboat and rocks in water at ctr. r. on back.

	VG	VF	UNC
a. Issued note.	1.00	5.00	25.00
s. Specimen. TDLR oval.	—	—	500.00
x. Counterfeit. Series S; U; X.	—	—	15.00

1969-71 ND ISSUE

#24-29 bank bldg. at r. Lathework on all backs. Wmk. as #23.

942 VIET NAM (SOUTH)

24 20 Dong ND (1969). Red on m/c unpt. a. Issued note 0.25 0.50 5.00 s. Specimen. GIAY MAU — — 175.00

942 VIET NAM (SOUTH)

24 20 Dông
ND (1969). Red on m/c unpt.

	VG	VF	UNC
a. Issued note.	0.25	0.50	5.00
s. Specimen. *GIAY MAU.*	—	—	175.00

25 50 Dông
ND (1969). Blue-green on m/c unpt.

	VG	VF	UNC
a. Issued note.	0.25	0.50	5.00
s. Specimen. *GIAY MAU.*	—	—	175.00

26 100 Dông
ND (1970). Dk. green on m/c unpt.

	VG	VF	UNC
a. Issued note.	0.25	0.75	5.00
s. Specimen. *GIAY MAU.*	—	—	175.00

27 200 Dông
ND (1970). Purple on m/c unpt.

	VG	VF	UNC
a. Issued note.	0.50	1.25	25.00
s. Specimen.	—	—	300.00

28 500 Dông
ND (1970). Orange and dk. brown on m/c unpt. Back orange and pale olive-green on m/c unpt.

	VG	VF	UNC
a. Issued note.	0.25	0.75	5.00
s. Specimen.	—	—	200.00

#28A *Deleted.* See #28.

Note: The brown and black variety previously listed as #28A is believed to be the result of oxidation.

29 1000 Dông
ND (1971). Turquoise on m/c unpt.

	VG	VF	UNC
a. Issued note.	1.00	5.00	15.00
s. Specimen. *GIAY MAU.*	—	—	250.00

1972; 1975 ND Issue

#30-36 Palace of Independence at r. Wmk: Young woman's head in profile.

30 50 Dông
ND (1972). Blue-gray on m/c unpt. 3 horses at l. ctr. on back.

	VG	VF	UNC
a. Issued note.	0.25	0.50	4.00
s. Specimen.	—	—	400.00

31 100 Dông
ND (1972). Green on m/c unpt. Farmer w/2 water buffalos at l. ctr. on back.

	VG	VF	UNC
a. Issued note.	0.25	0.75	5.00
s. Specimen.	—	—	400.00

32 200 Dông
ND (1972). Wine red on m/c unpt. 3 deer at l. ctr. on back.

	VG	VF	UNC
a. Issued note.	1.00	2.50	15.00
s. Specimen. TDLR oval.	—	—	500.00

33 500 Dông
ND (1972). Orange and olive-brown on m/c unpt. Tiger at l. ctr. on back.

	VG	VF	UNC
a. Issued note.	0.50	1.25	6.00
s. Specimen.	—	—	500.00

Note: The brown and olive-brown variety previously listed as #33A is believed to be the result of oxidation by leading authorities.

#33A *Deleted.* See #33.

34 1000 Dông
ND (1972). Blue on m/c unpt. 3 elephants carrying loads at l. ctr.
on back.

	VG	VF	UNC
a. Issued note.	0.50	1.25	5.00
s. Specimen.	—	—	500.00

34A 1000 Dông
ND (1975). Green and m/c. Stylized fish at l., Truong Cong Dinh at
r. Dinh's tomb at upper l., stylized fish at r. on back. Specimen. (Not
issued).

	VG	VF	UNC
	—	—	4000.00

#35 and 36 printer: TDLR.

35 5000 Dông
ND (1975). Brown, blue and m/c. Leopard at l. ctr. on back. (Not
issued).

	VG	VF	UNC
a. Normal serial #.	30.00	80.00	500.00
s. Specimen.	—	—	600.00

36 10,000 Dông
ND (1975). Violet and m/c. Water buffalo at l. ctr. on back. (Not
issued).

	VG	VF	UNC
a. Normal serial #.	50.00	80.00	500.00
s. Specimen. GIAY MAU.	—	—	600.00

Ngân Hàng Việt Nam

1966 Dated (1975) Transitional Issue

#37-44 constitute a transitional issue of the Peoples Revolutionary Government that took over on April 30,
1975. The notes are dated 1966 but were not issued until 1975. They were used until the South's economic system was merged with that of the Democratic Republic of Viet Nam in 1978.

37 10 XU
1966 (1975). Brown on m/c unpt. Drying salt at ctr. Unloading
boats on back.

	VG	VF	UNC
a. Issued note.	0.50	1.25	3.00
s. Specimen.	—	—	15.00

38 20 XU
1966 (1975). Blue on m/c unpt. Workers on rubber plantation at
ctr. Soldiers greeting farmers w/oxen on back.

	VG	VF	UNC
a. Issued note.	0.50	1.25	3.00
s. Specimen.	—	—	15.00

39 50 XU
1966 (1975). Brownish purple on m/c unpt. Harvesting cane at ctr.
Women weaving rugs on back.

	VG	VF	UNC
a. Issued note.	0.50	2.50	8.00
s. Specimen.	—	—	20.00

40 1 Dông
1966 (1975). Red-orange on m/c unpt. Boats on canal at ctr.
Workers in field on back.

	VG	VF	UNC
a. Issued note.	1.00	3.00	10.00
s. Specimen.	—	—	20.00

41 2 Dông
1966 (1975). Blue and green on m/c unpt. Houseboats under a
bridge at ctr. Soldiers and workers on back.

	VG	VF	UNC
a. Issued note.	1.50	5.00	15.00
s. Specimen.	—	—	20.00

42 5 Dông
1966 (1975). Purple on m/c unpt. 4 women in textile factory at ctr.
Armed soldiers w/downed helicopters on back.

	VG	VF	UNC
a. Issued note.	2.00	6.00	20.00
s. Specimen.	—	—	25.00

43 10 Dông
1966 (1975). Red on m/c unpt. 3 women and train at ctr. Soldiers
and people w/flag on back.

	VG	VF	UNC
a. Issued note.	4.00	20.00	40.00
s. Specimen.	—	—	25.00

44 50 Dông
1966 (1975). Green and blue on m/c unpt. Workers in factory at ctr.
Combine harvester on back.

	VG	VF	UNC
a. Issued note.	12.00	75.00	200.00
s. Specimen.	—	—	50.00

REGIONAL
ÚY BAN TRUNG U'O'NG
CENTRAL COMMITTEE OF THE NATIO NAL FRONT
FOR THE LIBERATIO N OF SOUTH VIETNAM
1963 ND ISSUE

#R1-R8 were printed in China for use in territories under control of the National Liberation Front. They were never issued, but many were captured during a joint US/South Viet Nam military operation into Cambodia. Except for #R2, relatively few survived in uncirculated condition.

			VG	VF	UNC
R1	10 XU		0.25	1.00	3.00
	ND (1963). Purple and m/c. Star at ctr.				
R2	20 XU		0.25	1.00	5.00
	ND (1963). Red-brown on aqua and m/c unpt. Star at ctr.				
R3	50 XU		0.50	2.00	8.00
	ND (1963). Green and m/c. Star at ctr.				

		VG	VF	UNC
R4	1 Dông	1.00	3.00	8.00
	ND (1963). Lt. brown on m/c unpt. Harvesting at ctr. Schoolroom on back.			

		VG	VF	UNC
R5	2 Dông	1.00	5.00	25.00
	ND (1963). Blue on m/c unpt. Women in convoy at ctr. Fishermen w/boats on back.			
R6	5 Dông	1.50	6.00	50.00
	ND (1963). Lilac on m/c unpt. Women harvesting at ctr. Women militia patrol on back.			
R7	10 Dông	7.50	40.00	125.00
	ND (1963). Green on m/c unpt. Harvesting scene at ctr. War scene on back.			

		VG	VF	UNC
R8	50 Dông	12.50	75.00	175.00
	ND (1963). Orange on m/c unpt. Truck convoy at ctr. Soldiers shooting down helicopters on back.			

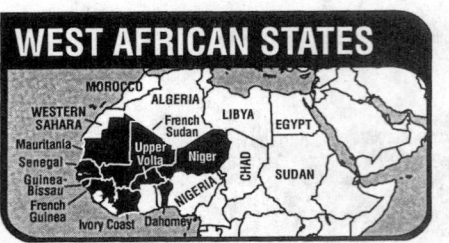

WEST AFRICAN STATES

The West African States, a former federation of eight French colonial territories on the northwest coast of Africa, had an area of 1,813,079 sq. mi. (4,742,495 sq. km.) and a population of about 60 million. Capital: Dakar. The constituent territories were Mauritania, Senegal, Dahomey, French Sudan, Ivory Coast, Upper Volta, Niger and French Guinea.

The members of the federation were overseas territories within the French Union until Sept. of 1958 when all but French Guinea approved the constitution of the Fifth French Republic, thereby electing to become autonomous members of the new French Community. French Guinea voted to become the fully independent Republic of Guinea. The other seven attained independence in 1960. The French West Africa territories were provided with a common currency, a practice which was continued as the monetary union of the West African States which provides a common currency to the autonomous republics of Dahomey (now Benin), Mali, Senegal, Upper Volta (now Burkina Faso) Ivory Coast, Togo, Niger, and Guinea-Bissau.

MONETARY SYSTEM:
1 Franc = 100 Centimes

DATING:
The year of issue on the current notes appear in the first 2 digits of the serial number, i.e. (19)91, (19)92, etc.

	SIGNATURE VARIETIES		
	LE PRÉSIDENT	**LE DIRECTEUR GÉNÉRAL**	**DATE**
1	*R. Yganin-Xhell*	*R. Julienne*	Various dates - 1959 20.3.1961
2	*Kugid*	*R. Julienne*	20.3.1961
3	*Pierangelady*	*R. Julienne*	20.12.1964
4	*Jf*	*R. Julienne*	2.3.1965; ND
5	*M*	*R. Julienne*	ND
6	*Tguny*	*R. Julienne*	ND
7	*cdant*	*R. Julienne*	ND
8	*Soy*	*R. Julienne*	ND
9	*Edllyj*	*R. Julienne*	ND
	LE PRÉSIDENT DU CONSEIL DES MINISTRES	**LE GOUVERNEUR**	**DATE**
10	*Edllyj*	*dfading*	ND
11	*unsering*	*dfading*	ND (1977); 1977
12	*Bf*	*dfading*	ND (1978); 1978; 1979
13	*Araf*	*dfading*	ND (1980); 1980

SIGNATURE VARIETIES

14		*d'arding*	ND (1977); 1977; 1988; 1989
15		*d'arding*	ND (1981); 1981; 1982
16		*d'arding*	ND (1983); 1983
17		*d'arding*	1981; 1983; 1984
18		*d'arding*	ND (1984); 1984
19		*d'arding*	1984; 1985
20		*d'arding*	1986; 1987
21		*Alasane*	1989
22		*Alasane*	1991
23		*Alasane*	1992
24		*Alasane*	1992
25		*Alasane*	1993
26		*B*	1994
27		*B*	1994; 1995
28		*B*	1996; 1997
29		*B*	1999
30		*B*	2000; 2001
31		*B*	2002; 2003
32		*B*	2003

NOTICE
Readers with unlisted dates, signature varieties, etc. are invited to submit photocopies of their notes to: Standard Catalog of World Paper Money, 700 East State St. Iola, WI 54990-0001, E-Mail: george.cuhaj@fwpubs.com.

WEST AFRICAN STATES

Note: Beginning with signature #21 the signature positions have been reversed on the 500 Francs.

BANQUE CENTRALE DES ETATS DE L'AFRIQUE DE L'OUEST

Notes of this bank were issued both w/and w/o code letters in the upper r. and lower l. corners. The code letter follows the control number and indicates which member country the note was issued for. Those w/o code letters are general issues. The code letters are as follows: A for Cote d' IvoireD for MaliK for Senegal B for Benin (Dahomey)E for MauritaniaS for Guinea-Bissau C for Burkina Faso (Upper Volta)H for NigerT for Togo

A FOR COTE D'IVOIRE (IVORY CO AST)

1959-65; ND ISSUE

		VG	VF	UNC
101A	**100 FRANCS**			
	1961-65; ND. Dk. brown, orange and m/c. Design like #201B.			
	a. Engraved. Sign. 1. 20.3.1961.	8.00	20.00	65.00
	b. Sign. 2. 20.3.1961.	8.00	20.00	65.00
	c. Litho. Sign. 2. 20.3.1961.	10.00	25.00	70.00
	d. Sign. 3. 2.12.1964.	10.00	25.00	70.00
	e. Sign. 4. 2.3.1965.	8.00	20.00	65.00
	f. Sign. 4. ND.	5.00	15.00	45.00
	g. Sign. 5. ND.	5.00	15.00	45.00
102A	**500 FRANCS**			
	1959-64; ND. Brown, green and m/c. Field workers at l., mask carving at r. Woman at l., farmer on tractor at r. on back. Wmk: Woman's head:			
	a. Engraved. Sign. 1. 15.4.1959.	25.00	55.00	150.00
	b. Sign. 1. 20.3.1961.	12.00	35.00	90.00
	c. Sign. 2. 20.3.1961.	12.00	35.00	90.00
	d. Sign. 3. 2.12.1964.	25.00	55.00	150.00
	e. Sign. 5. ND.	12.00	35.00	90.00
	f. Sign. 6. ND.	10.00	30.00	75.00
	g. Litho. Sign. 6. ND.	13.00	40.00	100.00
	h. Sign. 7. ND.	12.00	35.00	90.00
	i. Sign. 8. ND.	20.00	50.00	120.00
	j. Sign. 9. ND.	8.00	25.00	60.00
	k. Sign. 10. ND.	5.00	15.00	45.00
	l. Sign. 11. ND.	5.00	15.00	40.00
	m. Sign. 12. ND.	7.50	25.00	90.00
103A	**1000 FRANCS**			
	1959-65; ND. Brown, blue and m/c. Man and woman at ctr. Man w/rope suspension bridge in background and pineapples on back. Wmk: Man's head.			
	a. Engraved. Sign. 1. 17.9.1959.	50.00	150.00	—
	b. Sign. 1. 20.3.1961.	15.00	45.00	110.00
	c. Sign. 2. 20.3.1961.	15.00	45.00	110.00
	d. Sign. 4. 2.3.1965.	30.00	80.00	—
	e. Sign. 5. ND.	8.00	25.00	60.00
	f. Sign. 6. ND.	8.00	25.00	60.00
	g. Litho. Sign. 6. ND.	8.00	25.00	60.00
	h. Sign. 7. ND.	10.00	30.00	70.00
	i. Sign. 8. ND.	12.00	40.00	90.00
	j. Sign. 9. ND.	8.00	25.00	60.00
	k. Sign. 10. ND.	5.00	15.00	40.00
	l. Sign. 11. ND.	5.00	15.00	35.00
	m. Sign. 12. ND.	5.00	15.00	35.00
	n. Sign. 13. ND.	5.00	15.00	35.00

		VG	VF	UNC
104A	**5000 FRANCS**			
	1961-65; ND. Blue, brown and m/c. Bearded man at l., bldg. at ctr. Woman, corn grinders and huts on back.			
	a. Sign. 1. 20.3.1961.	35.00	100.00	300.00
	b. Sign. 2. 20.3.1961.	25.00	75.00	200.00

104A	5000 FRANCS	VG		104A
	c. Sign. 3. 2.12.1964.	25.00	75.00	200.00
	d. Sign. 4. 2.3.1965.	35.00	100.00	
	e. Sign. 6. ND.	25.00	50.00	175.00
	f. Sign. 7. ND.	25.00	50.00	175.00
	g. Sign. 8. ND.	35.00	100.00	
	h. Sign. 9. ND.	20.00	45.00	160.00
	i. Sign. 10. ND.	20.00	40.00	150.00
	j. Sign. 11. ND.	20.00	40.00	150.00

1977-81; ND ISSUE

#105A-109A smaller size notes.

105A	500 FRANCS	VG	VF	UNC
	1979-80. Lilac, lt. olive-green and m/c. Artwork at l., long horn animals at ctr., man wearing hat at r. Cultivated palm at l., aerial view at ctr., mask at r. on back. Wmk: Woman in profile.			
	a. Sign. 12. 1979.	3.00	10.00	25.00
	b. Sign. 13. 1980.	3.00	7.50	20.00

106A	500 FRANCS	VG	VF	UNC
	1981-90. Pale olive-green and m/c. Design like #105A.			
	a. Sign. 14. 1988.	0.50	1.00	6.00
	b. Sign. 15. 1981. (BF).	5.00	15.00	35.00
	c. Sign. 15. 1981. (F-CO).	0.50	3.00	7.00
	d. Sign. 15. 1982. (BF).	6.00	20.00	50.00
	e. Sign. 17. 1981. (F-CO).	6.00	20.00	50.00
	f. Sign. 17. 1983.	0.50	3.00	7.00
	g. Sign. 18. 1984.	0.50	3.00	7.00
	h. Sign. 19. 1984.	0.50	3.00	7.00
	i. Sign. 19. 1985.	0.50	3.00	7.00
	j. Sign. 20. 1986.	0.50	1.00	6.00
	k. Sign. 20. 1987.	0.50	3.00	10.00
	l. Sign. 21 (reversed order). 1989.	0.50	1.00	5.00
	m. Sign. 22. 1990.	0.50	1.00	5.00

Note: #106A w/10-digit small serial # were printed by Banque de France (BF) while those w/9-digit large serial # were printed by F-CO.

107A	1000 FRANCS	VG	VF	UNC
	1981-90. Brown on m/c unpt. Artwork at l., open pit mine at ctr., woman at r. and as wmk. Wood carver w/finished works on back.			
	a. Sign. 14. 1988.	1.00	2.00	10.00
	b. Sign. 15. 1981.	1.00	4.00	12.00
	c. Sign. 17. 1981.	1.00	4.00	12.00
	d. Sign. 18. 1984.	1.00	4.00	12.00
	e. Sign. 19. 1984.	1.00	12.00	30.00
	f. Sign. 19. 1985.	1.00	4.00	12.00
	g. Sign. 20. 1986.	1.00	2.00	10.00
	h. Sign. 20. 1987.	1.00	2.00	10.00
	i. Sign. 21. 1989.	1.00	2.00	9.00
	j. Sign. 22. 1990.	1.00	2.00	9.00

108A	5000 FRANCS	VG	VF	UNC
	1977-91. Black and red on m/c unpt. Woman at l., fish and boats on shore at ctr., carving at r. Carvings, fishing boats and mask on back.			
	a. Sign. 11. 1977.	15.00	25.00	60.00
	b. Sign. 12. 1978.	15.00	25.00	60.00

108A	5000 FRANCS	VG	VF	UNC
	c. Sign. 12. 1979.	25.00	45.00	100.00
	d. Sign. 13. 1980.	25.00	50.00	110.00
	e. Sign. 14. 1977.	20.00	35.00	80.00
	f. Sign. 14. 1988.	5.00	10.00	35.00
	g. Sign. 14. 1989.	5.00	10.00	35.00
	h. Sign. 15. 1981.	7.00	20.00	50.00
	i. Sign. 15. 1982.	7.00	20.00	50.00
	j. Sign. 16. 1983.	35.00	60.00	
	k. Sign. 17. 1983.	20.00	35.00	80.00
	l. Sign. 18. 1984.	15.00	25.00	60.00
	m. Sign. 19. 1984.	7.00	20.00	50.00
	n. Sign. 19. 1985.	7.00	20.00	50.00
	o. Sign. 20. 1986.	20.00	35.00	80.00
	p. Sign. 20. 1987.	5.00	10.00	35.00
	q. Sign. 21. 1990.	5.00	10.00	35.00
	r. Sign. 22. 1991.	5.00	10.00	40.00

109A	10,000 FRANCS			
	ND (1977-92). Red-brown on m/c unpt. 2 men seated operating primitive spinning apparatus, woman w/headwear at r. and as wmk. Figurine and girl at l., modern textile spinning machine at ctr. on back.			
	a. Sign. 11. ND.	20.00	35.00	85.00
	b. Sign. 12. ND.	20.00	35.00	95.00
	c. Sign. 13. ND.	20.00	35.00	95.00
	d. Sign. 14. ND.	20.00	35.00	85.00
	e. Sign. 15. ND.	10.00	20.00	60.00
	f. Sign. 18. ND.	20.00	35.00	85.00
	g. Sign. 19. ND.	25.00	40.00	100.00
	h. Sign. 20. ND.	10.00	20.00	60.00
	i. Sign. 21. ND.	10.00	20.00	55.00
	j. Sign. 22. ND.	10.00	20.00	55.00
	k. Sign. 23. ND.	10.00	20.00	55.00

1991-92 ISSUE

#113A and 114A were first issued on 19.9.1994.

110A	500 FRANCS	VG	VF	UNC
	(19)91-(20)02. Dk. brown and dk. green on m/c unpt. Man at r. and as wmk., flood control dam at ctr. Farmer riding spray rig behind garden tractor at ctr., native art at l. on back.			
	a. Sign. 22. (19)91.	0.25	1.00	4.00
	b. Sign. 23. (19)92.	1.00	4.00	10.00
	c. Sign. 25. (19)93.	0.25	1.00	4.00
	d. Sign. 26. (19)94.	0.25	1.00	4.00
	e. Sign. 27. (19)95.	0.25	1.00	3.00
	f. Sign. 28. (19)96.	0.25	1.00	3.00
	g. Sign. 28. (19)97.	0.25	1.00	3.00
	h. Sign. 28. (19)98.	0.25	1.00	3.00
	i. Sign. 28. (19)99.	0.25	1.00	3.00
	j. Sign. 29. (19)99.	0.25	1.00	3.00
	k. Sign. 30. (20)01.	0.25	1.00	3.00
	l. Sign. 31. (20)02.	0.25	1.00	3.00

111A	1000 FRANCS	VG	VF	UNC
	(19)91-(20)03. Dk. brown-violet on tan, yellow and m/c unpt. Workmen hauling peanuts to storage at ctr., woman's head at r. and as wmk. Twin statues and mask at l., 2 women w/baskets, elevated riverside storage bins in background at ctr. on back.			
	a. Sign. 22. (19)91.	0.50	1.00	7.00
	b. Sign. 23. (19)92.	0.50	1.00	7.00
	c. Sign. 25. (19)93.	0.50	1.00	7.00
	d. Sign. 26. (19)94.	0.50	1.00	7.00
	e. Sign. 27. (19)95.	0.50	1.00	6.00
	f. Sign. 28. (19)96.	0.50	1.00	6.00
	g. Sign. 28. (19)97.	0.50	1.00	6.00
	h. Sign. 28. (19)98.	0.50	1.00	6.00
	i. Sign. 29. (19)99.	0.50	1.00	6.00
	j. Sign. 30. (20)01.	0.50	1.00	5.00
	k. Sign. 31. (20)02.	0.50	1.00	5.00
	l. Sign. 31. (20)03.	0.50	1.00	5.00

112A	2500 FRANCS	VG	VF	UNC
	(19)92-(19)94. Deep purple and dk. brown on lilac and m/c unpt. Dam at ctr., young woman's head at r. and as wmk. Statue at l., harvesting and spraying of fruit at l. ctr. on back.			
	a. Sign. 23. (19)92.	1.00	4.00	20.00
	b. Sign. 25. (19)93.	1.00	4.00	20.00
	c. Sign. 27. (19)94.	1.00	4.00	20.00

113A	5000 FRANCS	VG	VF	UNC
	(19)92-(20)03. Dk. brown and deep blue on m/c unpt. Woman wearing headdress adorned w/cowrie shells at r. and as wmk., smelting plant at ctr. Women w/children and various pottery at l. ctr. on back.			
	a. Sign. 23. (19)92.	1.00	4.00	27.50
	b. Sign. 25. (19)93.	1.00	4.00	27.50
	c. Sign. 27. (19)94.	1.00	4.00	27.50
	d. Sign. 27. (19)95.	1.00	4.00	25.00
	e. Sign. 28. (19)96.	1.00	4.00	25.00
	f. Sign. 28. (19)97.	1.00	4.00	25.00
	g. Sign. 28. (19)98.	1.00	4.00	25.00
	h. Sign. 29. (19)98.	1.00	4.00	25.00
	i. Sign. 29. (19)99.	1.00	4.00	25.00
	j. Sign. 30. (20)00.	1.00	4.00	25.00
	k. Sign. 30. (20)01.	1.00	4.00	25.00
	l. Sign. 31. (20)02.	1.00	4.00	25.00
	m. Sign. 31. (20)03.	1.00	4.00	25.00

114A	10,000 FRANCS	VG	VF	UNC
	(19)92-(20)01. Dk. brown on m/c unpt. Headman w/scepter at r. and as wmk., skyscraper at ctr. Native art at l., woman crossing vine bridge over river at ctr. on back.			
	a. Sign. 25. (19)92.	1.00	7.00	50.00
	b. Sign. 27. (19)94.	1.00	7.00	50.00
	c. Sign. 27. (19)95.	1.00	7.00	45.00
	d. Sign. 28. (19)96.	1.00	7.00	45.00
	e. Sign. 28. (19)97.	1.00	7.00	45.00
	f. Sign. 28. (19)98.	1.00	7.00	45.00
	g. Sign. 29. (19)98.	1.00	7.00	45.00
	h. Sign. 29. (19)99.	1.00	7.00	45.00
	i. Sign. 30. (20)00.	1.00	7.00	45.00
	j. Sign. 30. (20)01.	1.00	7.00	45.00

2003 ISSUE

115A	1000 FRANCS	VG	VF	UNC
	(20)03-. Red-brown on red and m/c unpt.			
	a. Sign. 32. (20)03.	FV	FV	6.00
	b. Sign. 32. (20)04.	FV	FV	6.00

116A	2000 FRANCS	VG	VF	UNC
	(20)03-. Blue on lt. blue and m/c unpt.			
	a. Sign. 32. (20)03.	FV	FV	10.00
	b. Sign. 32. (20)04.	FV	FV	8.00

117A	5000 FRANCS	VG	VF	UNC
	(20)03-. M/c.			
	a. Sign. 32. (20)03.	FV	FV	25.00
	b. Sign. 32. (20)04.	FV	FV	17.50

118A	10,000 FRANCS	VG	VF	UNC
	(20)03-. M/c.			
	a. Sign. 32. (20)03.	FV	FV	40.00
	b. Sign. 32. (20)04.	FV	FV	30.00

1959-65; ND ISSUE

201B	100 FRANCS	VG	VF	UNC
	1961-65; ND. Like #101A.			
	a. Engraved. Sign. 1. 20.3.1961.	12.00	40.00	120.00
	b. Sign. 2. 20.3.1961.	10.00	35.00	100.00
	c. Litho. Sign. 2. 20.3.1961.	10.00	35.00	100.00
	d. Sign. 3. 2.12.1964.	12.00	40.00	120.00
	e. Sign. 4. 2.3.1965.	7.50	20.00	65.00
	f. Sign. 4. ND.	5.00	15.00	45.00

202B	500 FRANCS	VG	VF	UNC
	1961-64; ND. Like #102A.			
	a. Sign. 1. 20.3.1961.	50.00	—	—
	b. Engraved Sign. 2. 20.3.1961.	25.00	65.00	150.00
	d. Sign. 3. 2.12.1964.	—	—	—
	e. Sign. 4. 2.3.1965.	50.00	—	—
	f. Sign. 5. ND.	20.00	55.00	130.00
	g. Sign. 6. ND.	10.00	30.00	80.00
	h. Litho. Sign. 7. ND.	12.00	35.00	90.00
	i. Sign. 8. ND.	50.00	125.00	—
	j. Sign. 9. ND.	8.00	25.00	75.00
	k. Sign. 10. ND.	5.00	20.00	60.00
	l. Sign. 11. ND.	4.00	15.00	45.00

203B	1000 FRANCS	VG	VF	UNC
	1961-65; ND. Like #103A.			
	a. Engraved. Sign. 1. 17.9.1959.	35.00	90.00	—
	b. Sign. 1. 20.3.1961.	35.00	90.00	—
	c. Sign. 2. 20.3.1961.	35.00	90.00	—
	d. Sign. 4. 2.3.1965.	25.00	60.00	140.00
	g. Sign. 6. ND.	8.00	30.00	70.00
	h. Litho. Sign. 6. ND.	7.00	25.00	60.00
	i. Sign. 7. ND.	25.00	60.00	150.00
	j. Sign. 8. ND.	10.00	35.00	100.00
	k. Sign. 9. ND.	10.00	35.00	100.00
	l. Sign. 10. ND.	5.00	15.00	50.00
	m. Sign. 11. ND.	5.00	15.00	45.00
	n. Sign. 12. ND.	5.00	15.00	50.00

204B	5000 FRANCS	VG	VF	UNC
	1961; ND. Like #104A.			
	a. Sign. 1. 20.3.1961.	50.00	150.00	—
	b. Sign. 2. 20.3.1961.	50.00	150.00	—
	h. Sign. 6. ND.	25.00	75.00	200.00
	j. Sign. 7. ND.	25.00	75.00	200.00
	k. Sign. 9. ND.	20.00	50.00	175.00
	l. Sign. 10. ND.	20.00	50.00	175.00

1977-81; ND ISSUE

#205B-209B smaller size notes.

205B	500 FRANCS	VG	VF	UNC
	1979-80. Like #105A.			
	a. Sign. 12. 1979.	6.00	20.00	50.00
	b. Sign. 13. 1980.	3.00	10.00	25.00

206B	500 FRANCS	VG	VF	UNC
	1981-90. Like #106A.			
	a. Sign. 14. 1988.	4.00	12.00	—
	b. Sign. 15. 1981. (BF).	0.50	3.00	10.00
	c. Sign. 15. 1981. (F-CO).	0.50	3.00	10.00
	d. Sign. 15. 1982. (BF).	6.00	25.00	50.00
	e. Sign. 17. 1981. (F-CO).	6.00	25.00	—
	f. Sign. 17. 1983. (BF).	6.00	25.00	—
	g. Sign. 18. 1984.	0.50	3.00	10.00
	h. Sign. 19. 1984.	0.50	3.00	10.00
	i. Sign. 19. 1985.	2.00	8.00	20.00
	j. Sign. 20. 1986.	1.00	2.00	6.00
	k. Sign. 20. 1987.	2.00	8.00	20.00
	l. Sign. 21. 1989.	2.00	8.00	20.00
	m. Sign. 22. 1990.	1.00	2.00	6.00

Note: #206B w/10-digit small serial # were printed by Banque de France (BF) while those w/9-digit large serial # were printed by F-CO.

207B	1000 FRANCS	VG	VF	UNC
	1981-90. Like #107A.			
	a. Sign. 14. 1988.	1.00	3.00	12.00
	b. Sign. 15. 1981.	1.00	5.00	20.00
	c. Sign. 18. 1984.	1.00	4.00	15.00

207B 1000 FRANCS

	VG	VF	UNC
d. Sign. 19. 1984.	10.00	40.00	—
e. Sign. 19. 1985.	1.00	4.00	15.00
f. Sign. 20. 1986.	1.00	3.00	12.00
g. Sign. 20. 1987.	1.00	3.00	12.00
h. Sign. 21. 1989.	5.00	25.00	—
i. Sign. 22. 1990.	1.00	3.00	10.00

208B 5000 FRANCS
1977-92. Like #108A.

	VG	VF	UNC
a. Sign. 12. 1979.	20.00	35.00	75.00
b. Sign. 14. 1977.	20.00	35.00	80.00
c. Sign. 14. 1988.	35.00	75.00	—
d. Sign. 14. 1989.	5.00	10.00	35.00
e. Sign. 15. 1981.	7.00	25.00	65.00
f. Sign. 15. 1982.	7.00	20.00	55.00
g. Sign. 17. 1983.	35.00	75.00	—
h. Sign. 18. 1984.	35.00	75.00	—
i. Sign. 19. 1985.	35.00	75.00	—
j. Sign. 20. 1986.	35.00	75.00	—
k. Sign. 20. 1987.	7.00	20.00	55.00
l. Sign. 21. 1990.	5.00	10.00	35.00
m. Sign. 22. 1991.	5.00	10.00	55.00
n. Sign. 22. 1992.	5.00	10.00	30.00
o. Sign. 23. 1992.	5.00	10.00	30.00
p. Sign. 24. 1992.	20.00	40.00	—

209B 10,000 FRANCS
ND (1977-92). Like #109A.

	VG	VF	UNC
a. Sign. 11. ND.	40.00	75.00	175.00
b. Sign. 12. ND.	40.00	75.00	—
c. Sign. 14. ND.	15.00	40.00	100.00
d. Sign. 15. ND.	15.00	35.00	90.00
e. Sign. 16. ND.	40.00	75.00	—
f. Sign. 18. ND.	40.00	75.00	—
g. Sign. 19. ND.	10.00	35.00	90.00
h. Sign. 20. ND.	35.00	60.00	—
i. Sign. 21. ND.	10.00	20.00	60.00
j. Sign. 22. ND.	10.00	20.00	60.00
k. Sign. 23. ND.	10.00	20.00	60.00

1991-92 ISSUE

210B 500 FRANCS
(19)91-(20)02. Like #110A.

	VG	VF	UNC
a. Sign. 22. (19)91.	0.25	1.00	5.00
b. Sign. 22. (19)92.	1.00	5.00	15.00
c. Sign. 23. (19)92.	1.00	5.00	15.00
d. Sign. 25. (19)93.	0.25	1.00	5.00
e. Sign. 26. (19)94.	0.25	1.00	5.00
f. Sign. 27. (19)95.	0.25	1.00	4.00
g. Sign. 28. (19)96.	0.25	1.00	4.00
h. Sign. 28. (19)97.	0.25	1.00	4.00
i. Sign. 28. (19)98.	0.25	1.00	4.00
j. Sign. 29. (19)99.	0.25	1.00	4.00
k. Sign. 30. (20)00.	0.25	1.00	4.00
l. Sign. 30. (20)01.	0.25	1.00	4.00
m. Sign. 31. (20)02.	0.25	1.00	4.00

211B 1000 FRANCS
(19)91-(20)02. Like #111A.

	VG	VF	UNC
a. Sign. 22. (19)91.	0.50	2.00	8.00
b. Sign. 22. (19)92.	2.00	10.00	25.00
c. Sign. 23. (19)92.	2.00	10.00	25.00
d. Sign. 25. (19)93.	2.00	10.00	25.00
e. Sign. 26. (19)94.	0.50	1.50	8.00
f. Sign. 27. (19)95.	0.50	1.50	7.00
g. Sign. 28. (19)96.	0.50	1.50	7.00
h. Sign. 28. (19)97.	0.50	1.50	6.00
i. Sign. 28. (19)98.	0.50	1.50	6.00
j. Sign. 29. (19)99.	0.50	1.50	7.00
k. Sign. 30. (20)00.	0.50	1.50	6.00
l. Sign. 30. (20)01.	0.50	1.50	6.00
m. Sign. 31. (20)02.	0.50	1.50	6.00
n. Sign. 31. (20)03.	0.50	1.50	6.00

212B 2500 FRANCS
(19)92-(19)94. Like #112A.

	VG	VF	UNC
a. Sign. 23. (19)92.	1.00	4.00	20.00
b. Sign. 25. (19)93.	1.00	4.00	20.00
c. Sign. 27. (19)94.	1.00	4.00	20.00

213B 5000 FRANCS
(19)92-(20)02. Like #113A.

	VG	VF	UNC
a. Sign. 23. (19)92.	1.00	5.00	27.50
b. Sign. 25. (19)93.	1.00	5.00	27.50
c. Sign. 27. (19)94.	1.00	5.00	27.50
d. Sign. 27. (19)95.	1.00	5.00	27.50
e. Sign. 28. (19)96.	1.00	5.00	27.50
f. Sign. 28. (19)97.	1.00	5.00	27.50

213B 5000 FRANCS

	VG	VF	UNC
g. Sign. 28 (19)98.	1.00	5.00	28.00
h. Sign. 29. (19)98.	1.00	5.00	28.00
i. Sign. 29. (19)99.	1.00	5.00	25.00
j. Sign. 30. (20)00.	1.00	5.00	25.00
k. Sign. 30. (20)01.	1.00	5.00	25.00
l. Sign. 31. (20)02.	1.00	5.00	25.00
m. Sign. 31. (20)03.	1.00	5.00	25.00

214B 10,000 FRANCS
(19)92-(20)01. Like #114A.

	VG	VF	UNC
a. Sign. 25. (19)92.	2.00	8.00	50.00
b. Sign. 27. (19)94.	2.00	8.00	50.00
c. Sign. 27. (19)95.	2.00	8.00	45.00
d. Sign. 28. (19)96.	2.00	8.00	45.00
e. Sign. 28. (19)97.	2.00	8.00	45.00
f. Sign. 28. (19)98.	2.00	8.00	45.00
g. Sign. 29. (19)98.	2.00	8.00	45.00
h. Sign. 29. (19)99.	2.00	8.00	45.00
i. Sign. 30. (20)00.	2.00	8.00	45.00
j. Sign. 30. (20)01.	2.00	8.00	45.00

2003 ISSUE

215B 1000 FRANCS
(20)03-. Red-brown on red and m/c unpt.

	VG	VF	UNC
a. Sign. 32. (20)03.	FV	FV	6.00
b. Sign. 32. (20)04.	FV	FV	6.00

216B 2000 FRANCS
(20)03-. Blue on lt. blue and m/c unpt.

	VG	VF	UNC
a. Sign. 32. (20)03.	FV	FV	10.00
b. Sign. 32. (20)04.	FV	FV	8.00

217B 5000 FRANCS
(20)03-. M/c.

	VG	VF	UNC
a. Sign. 32. (20)03.	FV	FV	25.00
b. Sign. 32. (20)04.	FV	FV	17.50

218B 10,000 FRANCS
(20)03-. M/c.

	VG	VF	UNC
a. Sign. 32. (20)03.	FV	FV	40.00
b. Sign. 32. (20)04.	FV	FV	30.00

1961; ND ISSUE

301C 100 FRANCS
1961-65; ND. Like #101A.

	VG	VF	UNC
a. Engraved. Sign. 1. 20.3.1961.	15.00	45.00	140.00
b. Sign. 2. 20.3.1961.	12.00	40.00	120.00
c. Litho. Sign. 2. 20.3.1961.	30.00	60.00	—
d. Sign. 3. 2.12.1964.	—	—	—
e. Sign. 4. 2.3.1965.	7.50	25.00	75.00
f. Sign. 4. ND.	7.50	17.50	55.00

302C 500 FRANCS
1961-65; ND. Like #102A.

	VG	VF	UNC
a. Sign. 1. 15.4.1959.	50.00	100.00	—
b. Sign. 1. 20.3.1961.	50.00	100.00	—
c. Engraved. Sign. 2. 20.3.1961.	25.00	75.00	160.00
d. Sign. 4. 20.3.1961.	20.00	65.00	—
e. Sign. 4. 2.3.1965.	25.00	75.00	—
f. Sign. 5. ND.	25.00	75.00	—
g. Sign. 6. ND.	15.00	40.00	110.00
h. Litho. Sign. 6. ND.	10.00	30.00	100.00
i. Sign. 7. ND.	20.00	60.00	140.00
k. Sign. 8. ND.	15.00	40.00	90.00
l. Sign. 9. ND.	7.50	25.00	75.00
m. Sign. 11. ND.	5.00	15.00	45.00
n. Sign. 12. ND.	5.00	15.00	50.00

303C 1000 FRANCS
1961; ND. Like #103A.

	VG	VF	UNC
a. Sign. 1. 17.9.1959.	65.00	175.00	0.00 -
b. Sign. 1. 20.3.1961.	75.00	—	—
d. Sign. 2. 20.3.1961.	30.00	90.00	—
e. Sign. 4. 2.3.1965.	65.00	175.00	—
f. Sign. 5. ND.	65.00	175.00	—
g. Sign. 6. ND.	25.00	60.00	140.00
h. Sign. 6. ND. Litho.	35.00	100.00	—
i. Sign. 7. ND.	20.00	45.00	120.00
j. Sign. 8. ND.	25.00	60.00	150.00
k. Sign. 9. ND.	10.00	30.00	80.00
l. Sign. 10. ND.	5.00	15.00	50.00
m. Sign. 11. ND	5.00	15.00	45.00
n. Sign. 12. ND.	5.00	15.00	50.00
o. Sign. 13. ND.	8.00	20.00	55.00

304C 5000 FRANCS
1961; ND. Like #104A.

	VG	VF	UNC
a. Sign. 1. 20.3.1961.	35.00	90.00	300.00
b. Sign. 2. 20.3.1961.	100.00	—	—
d. Sign. 4. 2.3.1965.	100.00	—	—
h. Sign. 6. ND.	25.00	75.00	—
i. Sign. 7. ND.	25.00	75.00	—
k. Sign. 9. ND.	20.00	60.00	190.00
l. Sign. 11. ND.	20.00	50.00	175.00

1977-81; ND ISSUES

#305C-309C smaller size notes.

305C	500 FRANCS	VG	VF	UNC
	1979-80. Like #105A.			
	a. Sign. 12. 1979.	3.00	10.00	25.00
	b. Sign. 13. 1980.	2.50	8.00	20.00

306C	500 FRANCS	VG	VF	UNC
	1981-90. Like #106A.			
	a. Sign. 14. 1988.	0.60	3.00	7.00
	b. Sign. 15. 1981. (BF).	0.50	3.00	10.00
	c. Sign. 15. 1981. (F-CO).	0.50	3.00	8.00
	d. Sign. 15. 1982. (BF).	6.00	15.00	40.00
	e. Sign. 17. 1981. (F-CO).	6.00	15.00	—
	f. Sign. 17. 1983. (BF).	6.00	15.00	—
	g. Sign. 18. 1984.	0.50	3.00	8.00
	h. Sign. 19. 1984.	0.50	3.00	8.00
	i. Sign. 19. 1985.	0.50	3.00	8.00
	j. Sign. 20. 1986.	0.50	3.00	8.00
	k. Sign. 20. 1987.	3.00	10.00	25.00
	l. Sign. 21. 1989.	3.00	10.00	25.00
	m. Sign. 22. 1990.	0.50	2.00	7.00

Note: #306C w/10-digit small serial # were printed by Banque de France (BF) while those w/9-digit large serial # were printed by F-CO.

307C	1000 FRANCS	VG	VF	UNC
	1981-90. Like #107A.			
	a. Sign. 14. 1988.	1.00	3.00	10.00
	b. Sign. 15. 1981.	1.00	4.00	15.00
	c. Sign. 17. 1981.	5.00	25.00	—
	d. Sign. 18. 1984.	5.00	25.00	—
	e. Sign. 19. 1984.	5.00	25.00	—
	f. Sign. 19. 1985.	5.00	25.00	—
	g. Sign. 20. 1986.	1.00	4.00	15.00
	h. Sign. 20. 1987.	1.00	3.00	10.00
	i. Sign. 21. 1989.	1.00	4.00	15.00
	j. Sign. 22. 1990.	1.00	3.00	10.00

308C	5000 FRANCS	VG	VF	UNC
	1977-92. Like #108A.			
	a. Sign. 12. 1978.	20.00	35.00	80.00
	b. Sign. 12. 1979.	20.00	35.00	80.00
	c. Sign. 14. 1977.	20.00	35.00	80.00
	d. Sign. 14. 1988.	5.00	10.00	35.00
	e. Sign. 14. 1989.	5.00	10.00	40.00
	f. Sign. 15. 1981.	5.00	20.00	60.00
	g. Sign. 15. 1982.	5.00	20.00	55.00
	h. Sign. 17. 1983.	5.00	20.00	55.00
	i. Sign. 18. 1984.	20.00	35.00	80.00
	k. Sign. 19. 1985.	5.00	20.00	60.00
	l. Sign. 20. 1986.	5.00	25.00	75.00
	m. Sign. 20. 1987.	5.00	25.00	70.00
	n. Sign. 21. 1990.	5.00	10.00	35.00
	o. Sign. 22. 1991.	5.00	10.00	35.00
	p. Sign. 22. 1992.	5.00	10.00	35.00
	q. Sign. 23. 1992.	5.00	10.00	35.00
	r. Sign. 24. 1992.	20.00	40.00	—

309C	10,000 FRANCS	VG	VF	UNC
	ND (1977-92). Like #109A.			
	a. Sign. 11. ND.	40.00	75.00	175.00
	b. Sign. 12. ND.	25.00	50.00	100.00
	c. Sign. 13. ND.	25.00	50.00	100.00
	d. Sign. 14. ND.	30.00	65.00	150.00
	e. Sign. 15. ND.	25.00	55.00	120.00
	f. Sign. 20. ND.	10.00	30.00	80.00
	g. Sign. 21. ND.	8.00	15.00	55.00
	h. Sign. 22. ND.	8.00	15.00	55.00
	i. Sign. 23. ND.	8.00	15.00	55.00

1991 ISSUE

310C	500 FRANCS	VG	VF	UNC
	(19)91-(20)02. Like #110A.			
	a. Sign. 22. (19)91.	0.25	1.00	5.00
	b. Sign. 23. (19)92.	1.00	5.00	15.00
	c. Sign. 25. (19)93.	0.25	1.00	7.00
	d. Sign. 26. (19)94.	0.25	1.00	5.00
	e. Sign. 27. (19)95.	0.25	1.00	4.00
	f. Sign. 28. (19)96.	0.25	1.00	3.00
	g. Sign. 28. (19)97.	0.25	1.00	3.00
	h. Sign. 28. (19)98.	0.25	1.00	3.00
	i. Sign. 29. (19)99.	0.25	1.00	3.00
	j. Sign. 30. (20)00.	0.25	1.00	3.00
	k. Sign. 30. (20)01.	0.25	1.00	3.00
	l. Sign. 31. (20)02.	0.25	1.00	3.00

311C	1000 FRANCS	VG	VF	UNC
	(19)91-(20)02. Like #111A.			
	a. Sign. 22. (19)91.	0.50	1.50	8.00
	b. Sign. 22. (19)92.	3.00	8.00	25.00
	c. Sign. 23. (19)92.	3.00	8.00	25.00
	d. Sign. 25. (19)93.	0.50	1.50	8.00
	e. Sign. 26. (19)94.	0.50	1.50	7.00
	f. Sign. 27. (19)95.	0.50	1.50	6.00
	g. Sign. 28. (19)96.	0.50	1.50	6.00
	h. Sign. 28. (19)97.	0.50	1.50	6.00
	i. Sign. 28. (19)98.	0.50	1.50	6.00
	j. Sign. 29. (19)99.	0.50	1.50	6.00
	k. Sign. 30. (20)00.	0.50	1.50	6.00
	l. Sign. 30. (20)01.	0.50	1.50	6.00
	m. Sign. 31. (20)02.	0.50	1.50	6.00
	n. Sign. 31. (20)03.	0.50	1.50	6.00

312C	2500 FRANCS	VG	VF	UNC
	(19)92-(19)94. Like #112A.			
	a. Sign. 23. (19)92.	1.00	4.00	20.00
	b. Sign. 25. (19)93.	1.00	4.00	25.00
	c. Sign. 27. (19)94.	1.00	4.00	20.00

313C	5000 FRANCS	VG	VF	UNC
	(19)92-(20)02. Like #113A.			
	a. Sign. 23. (19)92.	1.00	5.00	27.50
	b. Sign. 25. (19)93.	1.00	5.00	27.50
	c. Sign. 27. (19)94.	1.00	5.00	27.50
	d. Sign. 27. (19)95.	1.00	5.00	25.00
	e. Sign. 28. (19)96.	1.00	5.00	25.00
	f. Sign. 28. (19)97.	1.00	5.00	25.00
	g. Sign. 28. (19)98.	1.00	5.00	25.00
	h. Sign. 29. (19)98.	1.00	5.00	25.00
	i. Sign. 29. (19)99.	1.00	5.00	26.00
	j. Sign. 30. (20)00.	1.00	5.00	26.00
	k. Sign. 30. (20)01.	1.00	5.00	26.00
	l. Sign. 31. (20)02.	1.00	5.00	26.00
	m. Sign. 31. (20)03.	1.00	5.00	25.00

314C	10,000 FRANCS	VG	VF	UNC
	(19)92-(20)01. Like #114A.			
	a. Sign. 25. (19)92.	2.00	8.00	50.00
	b. Sign. 27. (19)94.	2.00	8.00	50.00
	c. Sign. 27. (19)95.	2.00	8.00	45.00
	d. Sign. 28. (19)96.	2.00	8.00	45.00
	e. Sign. 28. (19)97.	2.00	8.00	45.00
	f. Sign. 28. (19)98.	2.00	8.00	45.00
	g. Sign. 29. (19)98.	2.00	8.00	45.00
	h. Sign. 29. (19)99.	2.00	8.00	45.00
	i. Sign. 30. (20)00.	2.00	8.00	45.00
	j. Sign. 30. (20)01.	2.00	8.00	45.00

2003 ISSUE

315C	1000 FRANCS	VG	VF	UNC
	(20)03-. Red-brown on red and m/c unpt.			
	a. Sign. 32. (20)03.	FV	FV	6.00
	b. Sign. 32. (20)04.	FV	FV	6.00

316C	2000 FRANCS			
	(20)03-. Blue on lt. blue and m/c unpt.			
	a. Sign. 32. (20)03.	FV	FV	10.00
	b. Sign. 32. (20)04.	FV	FV	8.00

317C	5000 FRANCS			
	(20)03-. M/c.			
	a. Sign. 32. (20)03.	FV	FV	25.00
	b. Sign. 32. (20)04.	FV	FV	17.50

318C	10,000 FRANCS	VG	VF	UNC
	(20)03-. M/c.			
	a. Sign. 32. (20)03.	FV	FV	40.00
	b. Sign. 32. (20)04.	FV	FV	30.00

1959-61; ND ISSUE

401D	100 FRANCS	Good	Fine	XF
	20.3.1961. Like #101A. Sign. I.	65.00	175.00	—
402D	500 FRANCS			
	1959; 1961. Like #102A.			
	a. Sign. I. 15.4.1959.	100.00	300.00	—
	b. Sign. I. 20.3.1961.	—	—	—
403D	1000 FRANCS			
	1959; 1961. Like #103A.			
	a. Sign. I. 17.9.1959.	85.00	250.00	500.00
	b. Sign. I. 20.3.1961.	85.00	250.00	500.00
404D	5000 FRANCS			
	20.3.1961. Like #104A. Sign. I.	150.00	350.00	650.00

1981; ND ISSUE

#405D-408D smaller size notes.

405D	500 FRANCS	VG	VF	UNC
	1981-90. Like #106A.			
	a. Sign. 14. 1988.	0.50	2.00	7.00
	b. Sign. 15. 1981. (BF).	0.50	3.00	9.00
	c. Sign. 17. 1981. (F-CO).	0.50	3.00	9.00
	e. Sign. 19. 1985.	0.50	2.00	8.00
	f. Sign. 20. 1986.	1.00	5.00	12.50
	g. Sign. 20. 1987.	1.00	5.00	12.50
	h. Sign. 21. 1989.	1.00	5.00	12.50
	i. Sign. 22. 1990.	0.50	2.00	5.00

Note: #405D w/10-digit small serial # were printed by Banque de France (BF) while those w/9-digit large serial # were printed by F-CO.

406D	1000 FRANCS	VG	VF	UNC
	1981-90. Like #107A.			
	a. Sign. 14. 1988.	1.00	2.00	10.00
	b. Sign. 15. 1981.	1.00	4.00	12.00
	c. Sign. 17. 1981.	4.00	10.00	30.00
	f. Sign. 19. 1985.	4.00	10.00	30.00
	g. Sign. 20. 1986.	4.00	10.00	30.00
	h. Sign. 20. 1987.	4.00	10.00	30.00
	i. Sign. 21. 1989.	1.00	2.00	9.00
	j. Sign. 22. 1990.	1.00	2.00	10.00
407D	5000 FRANCS			
	1981-92. Like #108A.			
	a. Sign. 14. 1988.	7.00	10.00	50.00
	b. Sign. 14. 1989.	20.00	35.00	75.00
	c. Sign. 15. 1981.	7.00	20.00	50.00
	d. Sign. 17. 1984.	7.00	20.00	50.00
	e. Sign. 18. 1984.	25.00	45.00	80.00
	f. Sign. 19. 1985.	7.00	20.00	50.00
	g. Sign. 20. 1986.	7.00	20.00	50.00
	h. Sign. 20. 1987.	7.00	20.00	50.00
	i. Sign. 21. 1990.	5.00	10.00	40.00
	j. Sign. 22. 1991.	5.00	10.00	35.00
	k. Sign. 23. 1992.	5.00	10.00	40.00
	l. Sign. 24. 1992.	7.00	20.00	50.00
408D	10,000 FRANCS			
	ND (1981-92). Like #109A.			
	a. Sign. 14. ND.	10.00	25.00	80.00
	b. Sign. 15. ND.	10.00	25.00	80.00
	c. Sign. 18. ND.	25.00	55.00	120.00
	d. Sign. 19. ND.	25.00	55.00	120.00
	e. Sign. 20. ND.	10.00	20.00	70.00
	f. Sign. 21. ND.	10.00	20.00	55.00
	g. Sign. 22. ND.	10.00	20.00	55.00

1991-92 ISSUE

410D	500 FRANCS	VG	VF	UNC
	(19)91-(20)02. Like #110A.			
	a. Sign. 22. (19)91.	0.25	1.00	4.00
	b. Sign. 23. (19)92.	3.00	6.00	15.00
	c. Sign. 25. (19)93.	0.25	1.00	4.00
	d. Sign. 26. (19)94.	0.25	1.00	4.00
	e. Sign. 27. (19)95.	0.25	1.00	3.00
	f. Sign. 28. (19)96.	0.25	1.00	3.00
	g. Sign. 28. (19)97.	0.25	1.00	3.00
	h. Sign. 28. (19)98.	0.25	1.00	3.00
	i. Sign. 29. (19)99.	0.25	1.00	3.00
	j. Sign. 30. (20)00.	0.25	1.00	3.00
	k. Sign. 30. (20)01.	0.25	1.00	3.00
	l. Sign. 31. (20)02.	0.25	1.00	3.00
	m. Sign. 31. (20)03.	0.25	1.00	4.00

411D	1000 FRANCS	VG	VF	UNC
	(19)91-(20)02. Like #111A.			
	a. Sign. 22. (19)91.	0.50	1.50	7.00
	b. Sign. 23. (19)92.	1.50	10.00	25.00
	c. Sign. 25. (19)93.	0.50	1.50	7.00
	d. Sign. 26. (19)94.	0.50	1.50	7.00
	e. Sign. 27. (19)95.	0.50	1.50	6.00
	f. Sign. 28. (19)96.	0.50	1.50	6.00
	g. Sign. 28. (19)97.	0.50	1.50	6.00
	h. Sign. 28. (19)98.	0.50	1.50	6.00
	i. Sign. 29. (19)99.	0.50	1.50	6.00
	j. Sign. 30. (20)00.	0.50	1.50	6.00
	k. Sign. 30. (20)01.	0.50	1.50	6.00
	l. Sign. 31. (20)02.	0.50	1.50	6.00
	m. Sign. 31. (20)03.	0.50	1.50	6.00
412D	2500 FRANCS			
	(19)92-(19)94. Like #112A.			
	a. Sign. 23. (19)92.	1.00	4.00	20.00
	b. Sign. 25. (19)93.	1.00	4.00	30.00
	c. Sign. 27. (19)94.	1.00	4.00	20.00
413D	5000 FRANCS			
	(19)92-(20)02. Like #113A.			
	a. Sign. 23. (19)92.	1.00	5.00	27.50
	b. Sign. 27. (19)94.	1.00	5.00	27.50
	c. Sign. 27. (19)95.	1.00	5.00	27.50
	d. Sign. 28. (19)96.	1.00	5.00	25.00
	e. Sign. 28. (19)97.	1.00	5.00	25.00
	f. Sign. 28. (19)98.	1.00	5.00	25.00
	g. Sign. 29. (19)98.	1.00	5.00	26.00
	h. Sign. 29. (19)99.	1.00	5.00	25.00
	i. Sign. 30. (20)00.	1.00	5.00	25.00
	j. Sign. 30. (20)01.	1.00	5.00	25.00
	k. Sign. 31. (20)02.	1.00	5.00	25.00
	l. Sign. 32. (20)03.	1.00	5.00	25.00
414D	10,000 FRANCS			
	(19)92-(20)02. Like #114A.			
	a. Sign. 25. (19)92.	2.00	8.00	50.00
	b. Sign. 27. (19)94.	2.00	8.00	50.00
	c. Sign. 27. (19)95.	2.00	8.00	45.00
	d. Sign. 28. (19)96.	2.00	8.00	45.00
	e. Sign. 28. (19)97.	2.00	8.00	45.00
	f. Sign. 28. (19)98.	2.00	8.00	45.00
	g. Sign. 29. (19)98.	2.00	8.00	45.00
	h. Sign. 29. (19)99.	2.00	8.00	45.00
	i. Sign. 30. (20)00.	2.00	8.00	45.00
	j. Sign. 30. (20)01.	2.00		45.00

2003 ISSUE

415D	1000 FRANCS	VG	VF	UNC
	(20)03-. Red on lt. red and m/c unpt.			
	a. Sign. 32. (20)03.	FV	FV	6.00
	b. Sign. 32. (20)04.	FV	FV	6.00
416D	2000 FRANCS			
	(20)03-. Red-brown on red and m/c unpt.			
	a. Sign. 32. (20)03.	FV	FV	10.00
	b. Sign. 32. (20)04.	FV	FV	8.00
417D	5000 FRANCS			
	(20)03-. M/c.			
	a. Sign. 32. (20)03.	FV	FV	25.00
	b. Sign. 32. (20)04.	FV	FV	17.50
	c. Sign. 33. (20)05.	FV	FV	17.50
418D	10,000 FRANCS			
	(20)03-. M/c.			
	a. Sign. 32. (20)03.	FV	FV	40.00
	b. Sign. 32. (20)04.	FV	FV	30.00

1959-64; ND ISSUE

501E	100 FRANCS	Good	Fine	XF
	1961-65; ND. Like #101A.			
	b. Sign. 1. 20.3.1961.	30.00	90.00	250.00
	c. Sign. 3. 2.12.1964.	30.00	90.00	250.00
	e. Sign. 4. 2.3.1965.	25.00	85.00	225.00
	f. Sign. 4. ND.	25.00	85.00	225.00
502E	500 FRANCS			
	1959-64; ND. Like #102A.			
	a. Engraved. Sign. 1. 15.4.1959.	55.00	120.00	400.00
	b. Sign. 1. 20.3.1961.	45.00	100.00	350.00
	c. Sign. 2. 20.3.1961.	45.00	100.00	350.00
	e. Sign. 4. 2.3.1965.	45.00	100.00	350.00
	f. Sign. 5. ND.	45.00	100.00	350.00
	g. Sign. 6. ND.	45.00	100.00	350.00
	h. Litho. Sign. 6. ND.	45.00	100.00	350.00
	i. Sign. 7. ND.	45.00	100.00	350.00
503E	1000 FRANCS			
	1961-65; ND. Like #103A.			
	a. Sign. 1. 17.9.1959.	100.00	—	—
	b. Engraved. Sign. 1. 20.3.1961.	55.00	130.00	400.00
	e. Sign. 4. 2.3.1965.	45.00	130.00	350.00
	g. Sign. 6. ND.	45.00	120.00	350.00
	h. Litho. Sign. 6. ND.	45.00	120.00	350.00
504E	5000 FRANCS			
	1961-65; ND. Like #104A.			
	a. Sign. 1. 20.3.1961.	65.00	150.00	450.00
	b. Sign. 2. 20.3.1961.	65.00	150.00	450.00
	c. Sign. 4. 2.3.1965.	65.00	150.00	450.00
	d. Sign. 6. ND.	60.00	130.00	400.00
	e. Sign. 7. ND.	60.00	130.00	400.00
601H	100 FRANCS			
	1961-65; ND. Like #101A.			
	a. Engraved. Sign. 1. 20.3.1961.	15.00	45.00	140.00
	b. Sign. 2. 20.3.1961.	12.00	40.00	120.00
	c. Litho. Sign. 2. 20.3.1961.	12.00	40.00	120.00
	d. Sign. 3. 2.12.1964.	20.00	55.00	160.00
	e. Sign. 4. 2.3.1965.	8.00	25.00	75.00
	f. Sign. 4. ND.	7.00	17.50	55.00
602H	500 FRANCS			
	1959-65; ND. Like #102A.			
	a. Engraved. Sign. 1. 15.4.1959.	50.00	125.00	

602H	500 FRANCS	Good	Fine	XF
	c. Sign. 2. 20.3.1961.	50.00	125.00	
	d. Sign. 3. 2.12.1964.	25.00	75.00	175.00
	e. Sign. 4. 2.3.1965.	25.00	75.00	175.00
	f. Sign. 5. ND.	45.00	100.00	—
	g. Sign. 6. ND.	10.00	30.00	100.00
	h. Litho. Sign. 6. ND.	10.00	30.00	100.00
	i. Sign. 7. ND.	20.00	65.00	150.00
	j. Sign. 8. ND.	10.00	30.00	100.00
	k. Sign. 9. ND.	8.00	25.00	80.00
	l. Sign. 10. ND.	75.00		
	m. Sign. 11. ND.	5.00	15.00	55.00

603H	1000 FRANCS	VG	VF	UNC
	1959-65; ND. Like #103A.			
	a. Sign. 1. 17.9.1959.	—	—	—
	b. Sign. 1. 20.3.1961.	30.00	65.00	175.00
	c. Sign. 2. 20.3.1961.	75.00		
	e. Sign. 4. 2.3.1965.	30.00	65.00	175.00
	f. Sign. 5. ND.	30.00	65.00	175.00
	g. Sign. 6. ND.	10.00	35.00	90.00
	h. Litho. Sign. 6. ND.	20.00	45.00	125.00
	i. Sign. 7. ND.	10.00	35.00	100.00
	j. Sign. 8. ND.	30.00	65.00	—
	k. Sign. 9. ND	8.00	30.00	70.00
	l. Sign. 10. ND.	5.00	15.00	50.00
	m. Sign. 11. ND.	5.00	15.00	45.00
	n. Sign. 12. ND.	5.00	15.00	50.00
	o. Sign. 13. ND.	5.00	20.00	60.00

604H	5000 FRANCS			
	1961; 1965; ND. Like #104A.			
	a. Sign. 1. 20.3.1961.	100.00	—	—
	b. Sign. 2. 20.3.1961.	40.00	150.00	—
	d. Sign. 4. 2.3.1965.	40.00	150.00	—
	e. Sign. 6. ND.	40.00	150.00	—
	i. Sign. 7. ND.	40.00	150.00	—
	k. Sign. 9. ND.	20.00	60.00	190.00
	l. Sign. 10. ND.	20.00	60.00	190.00
	m. Sign. 11. ND.	20.00	50.00	175.00

1977-81; ND Issue

#605H-608H smaller size notes.

605H	500 FRANCS	VG	VF	UNC
	1979-80. Like #105A.			
	a. Sign. 12. 1979.	6.00	17.50	40.00
	b. Sign. 13. 1980.	3.00	7.50	20.00

606H	500 FRANCS			
	1981-90. Like #106A.			
	a. Sign. 14. 1988.	0.50	2.00	7.00
	b. Sign. 15. 1981. (BF).	6.00	15.00	35.00
	c. Sign. 15. 1981. (F-CO).	0.50	3.00	8.00
	d. Sign. 15. 1982. (BF).	10.00	—	—
	e. Sign. 17. 1981. (F-CO).	0.50	3.00	8.00
	f. Sign. 18. 1984.	10.00	45.00	—
	g. Sign. 19. 1984.	10.00		—
	h. Sign. 19. 1985.	8.00	—	—
	i. Sign. 20. 1986.	0.50	2.00	7.00
	j. Sign. 20. 1987.	0.50	3.00	8.00
	k. Sign. 21. 1989.	0.50	2.00	6.00
	l. Sign. 22. 1990.	0.50	2.00	6.00

607H	1000 FRANCS	VG	VF	UNC
	1981-90. Like #107A.			
	a. Sign. 14. 1988.	1.00	2.00	10.00
	b. Sign. 15. 1981.	1.00	4.00	15.00
	c. Sign. 17. 1981.	10.00	—	—
	d. Sign. 18. 1984.	5.00	15.00	40.00
	e. Sign. 19. 1984.	5.00	20.00	50.00
	f. Sign. 19. 1985.	1.00	4.00	15.00
	g. Sign. 20. 1986.	1.00	2.00	10.00
	h. Sign. 20. 1987.	1.00	2.00	10.00
	i. Sign. 21. 1989.	1.00	2.00	10.00
	j. Sign. 22. 1990.	1.00	2.00	10.00

608H	5000 FRANCS	VG	VF	UNC
	1977-90. Like #108A.			
	a. Sign. 12. 1978.	20.00	35.00	80.00
	b. Sign. 12. 1979.	20.00	35.00	80.00
	c. Sign. 13. 1980.	30.00	50.00	110.00
	d. Sign. 14. 1977.	20.00	35.00	80.00
	e. Sign. 14. 1989.	7.00	10.00	35.00
	f. Sign. 15. 1981.	7.00	20.00	60.00
	g. Sign. 15. 1982.	7.00	20.00	55.00
	h. Sign. 17. 1983.	7.00	20.00	55.00
	i. Sign. 18. 1984.	20.00	35.00	80.00
	j. Sign. 19. 1985.	7.00	20.00	55.00
	k. Sign. 20. 1986.	7.00	20.00	55.00
	l. Sign. 20. 1987.	5.00	10.00	35.00
	m. Sign. 21. 1990.	5.00	10.00	35.00
	n. Sign. 27. 1995.	5.00	10.00	35.00

609H	10,000 FRANCS			
	ND (1977). Like #109A.			
	a. Sign. 11. ND.	30.00	55.00	130.00
	b. Sign. 12. ND.	50.00	—	—
	c. Sign. 13. ND.	50.00	—	—
	d. Sign. 14. ND.	10.00	20.00	65.00
	e. Sign. 15. ND.	15.00	35.00	90.00
	f. Sign. 18. ND.	30.00	55.00	130.00
	g. Sign. 19. ND.	30.00	55.00	130.00
	h. Sign. 20. ND.	10.00	20.00	65.00
	i. Sign. 21. ND.	10.00	20.00	60.00
	j. Sign. 22. ND.	10.00	20.00	50.00

1991-92 Issue

610H	500 FRANCS	VG	VF	UNC
	(19)91-(20)02. Like #110A.			
	a. Sign. 22. (19)91.	0.25	1.00	4.00
	b. Sign. 23. (19)92.	1.00	5.00	15.00
	c. Sign. 25. (19)93.	0.25	1.00	5.00
	d. Sign. 26. (19)94.	0.25	1.00	4.00
	e. Sign. 27. (19)95.	0.25	1.00	3.00
	f. Sign. 28. (19)96.	0.25	1.00	3.00
	g. Sign. 28. (19)97.	0.25	1.00	3.00
	h. Sign. 28. (19)98.	0.25	1.00	3.00
	i. Sign. 29. (19)99.	0.25	1.00	3.00
	j. Sign. 30. (20)00.	0.25	1.00	3.00
	k. Sign. 30. (20)01.	0.25	1.00	3.00
	l. Sign. 31. (20)02.	0.25	1.00	3.00

611H	1000 FRANCS			
	(19)91-(20)02. Like #111A.			
	a. Sign. 22. (19)91.	0.50	1.50	8.00
	b. Sign. 23. (19)92.	0.50	1.50	8.00
	c. Sign. 25. (19)93.	0.50	1.50	8.00
	d. Sign. 26. (19)94.	0.50	1.50	7.00
	e. Sign. 27. (19)95.	0.50	1.50	6.00
	f. Sign. 28. (19)96.	0.50	1.50	6.00
	g. Sign. 28. (19)97.	0.50	1.50	6.00
	h. Sign. 28. (19)98.	0.50	1.50	6.00
	i. Sign. 29. (19)99.	0.50	1.50	6.00
	j. Sign. 30. (20)00.	0.50	1.50	6.00
	k. Sign. 30. (20)02.	0.50	1.50	6.00
	l. Sign. 31. (20)03.	0.50	1.50	6.00

612H	2500 FRANCS			
	(19)92-(19)94. Like #112A.			
	a. Sign. 23. (19)92.	1.00	4.00	20.00
	b. Sign. 25. (19)93.	1.00	4.00	20.00
	c. Sign. 27. (19)94.	1.00	4.00	20.00

613H	5000 FRANCS			
	(19)92-(20)02. Like #113A.			
	a. Sign. 23. (19)92.	1.00	5.00	27.50
	b. Sign. 27. (19)94.	1.00	5.00	27.50
	c. Sign. 27. (19)95.	1.00	5.00	27.50
	d. Sign. 28. (19)96.	1.00	5.00	27.50
	e. Sign. 28. (19)97.	1.00	5.00	27.50
	f. Sign. 28. (19)98.	1.00	5.00	25.00
	g. Sign. 29. (19)98.	1.00	5.00	25.00
	h. Sign. 29. (19)99.	1.00	5.00	25.00
	i. Sign. 30. (20)00.	1.00	5.00	25.00
	j. Sign. 30. (20)01.	1.00	5.00	25.00
	k. Sign. 31. (20)02.	1.00	5.00	25.00
	l. Sign. 31. (20)03.	1.00	5.00	25.00

614H	10,000 FRANCS			
	(19)92-(20)01. Like #114A.			
	a. Sign. 25. (19)92.	2.00	8.00	50.00
	b. Sign. 27. (19)94.	2.00	8.00	50.00
	c. Sign. 27. (19)95.	2.00	8.00	45.00
	d. Sign. 28. (19)96.	2.00	8.00	45.00
	e. Sign. 28. (19)97.	2.00	8.00	45.00
	f. Sign. 28. (19)98.	2.00	8.00	45.00
	g. Sign. 29. (19)98.	2.00	8.00	45.00
	h. Sign. 29. (19)99.	2.00	8.00	45.00
	i. Sign. 30. (20)00.	2.00	8.00	45.00
	j. Sign. 30. (20)01.	2.00	8.00	45.00

2003 Issue

615H	1000 FRANCS	VG	VF	UNC
	(20)03-. Red-brown on red and m/c unpt.			
	a. Sign. 32. (20)03.	FV	FV	6.00
	b. Sign. 32. (20)04.	FV	FV	6.00

616H	2000 FRANCS			
	(20)03-. Blue on lt. blue and m/c unpt.			
	a. Sign. 32. (20)03.	FV	FV	10.00
	b. Sign. 32. (20)04.	FV	FV	8.00

617H	5000 FRANCS			
	(20)03-. M/c.			
	a. Sign. 32. (20)03.	FV	FV	25.00
	b. Sign. 32. (20)04.	FV	FV	17.50

618H	10,000 FRANCS			
	(20)03-. M/c.			
	a. Sign. 32. (20)03.	FV	FV	40.00
	b. Sign. 32. (20)04.	FV	FV	30.00

1959-65; ND ISSUE

701K   100 FRANCS
1961-65; ND. Like #101A.

	VG	VF	UNC
a. Engraved. Sign. 1. 20.3.1961.	15.00	35.00	100.00
b. Sign. 2. 20.3.1961.	10.00	25.00	70.00
c. Litho. Sign. 2. 20.3.1961.	10.00	25.00	70.00
d. Sign. 3. 2.12.1964.	10.00	25.00	80.00
e. Sign. 4. 2.3.1965.	8.00	20.00	65.00
f. Sign. 4. ND.	5.00	15.00	45.00
g. Sign. 5. ND.	15.00	35.00	100.00

702K   500 FRANCS
1959-65; ND. Like #102A.

	VG	VF	UNC
a. Engraved. Sign. 1. 15.4.1959.	25.00	55.00	150.00
b. Sign. 1. 20.3.1961.	15.00	45.00	120.00
c. Sign. 2. 20.3.1961.	15.00	45.00	120.00
d. Sign. 3. 2.12.1964.	15.00	45.00	120.00
e. Sign. 4. 2.3.1965.	12.00	40.00	100.00
f. Sign. 5. ND.	18.00	50.00	130.00
g. Sign. 6. ND.	8.00	25.00	75.00
h. Litho. Sign. 6. ND.	8.00	25.00	75.00
i. Sign. 7. ND.	12.00	40.00	100.00
j. Sign. 8. ND.	12.00	40.00	100.00
k. Sign. 9. ND.	5.00	20.00	60.00
l. Sign. 10. ND.	4.00	15.00	50.00
m. Sign. 11. ND.	4.00	12.00	40.00
n. Sign. 12. ND.	4.00	15.00	45.00

703K   1000 FRANCS
1959-65; ND. Like #103A.

	VG	VF	UNC
a. Engraved. Sign. 1. 17.9.1959.	20.00	60.00	150.00
b. Sign. 1. 20.3.1961.	20.00	60.00	150.00
c. Sign. 2. 20.3.1961.	12.00	45.00	110.00
e. Sign. 4. 2.3.1965.	12.00	45.00	110.00
f. Sign. 5. ND.	35.00	90.00	—
g. Sign. 6. ND.	35.00	90.00	—
h. Litho. Sign. 6. ND.	5.00	15.00	50.00
i. Sign. 7. ND.	8.00	20.00	60.00
j. Sign. 8. ND.	8.00	20.00	60.00
k. Sign. 9. ND.	5.00	15.00	50.00
l. Sign. 10. ND.	4.00	12.00	40.00
m. Sign. 11. ND.	4.00	10.00	35.00
n. Sign. 12. ND.	4.00	12.00	40.00
o. Sign. 13. ND.	4.00	12.00	40.00

704K   5000 FRANCS
1961-65; ND. Like #104A.

	VG	VF	UNC
b. Sign. 1. 20.3.1961.	30.00	80.00	225.00
c. Sign. 2. 20.3.1961.	30.00	80.00	225.00
d. Sign. 3. 2.12.1964.	30.00	80.00	225.00
e. Sign. 4. 2.3.1965.	25.00	65.00	180.00
h. Sign. 6. ND.	20.00	45.00	150.00
i. Sign. 7. ND.	25.00	65.00	180.00
j. Sign. 8. ND.	75.00	—	—
k. Sign. 9. ND.	20.00	65.00	180.00
l. Sign. 10. ND.	20.00	45.00	160.00
m. Sign. 11. ND.	20.00	40.00	140.00

1977-81; ND ISSUE

#705K-709K smaller size notes.

705K   500 FRANCS
1979-80. Like #105A.

	VG	VF	UNC
a. Sign. 12. 1979.	3.00	10.00	25.00
b. Sign. 13. 1980.	2.50	8.00	20.00

706K   500 FRANCS
1981-90. Like #106A.

	VG	VF	UNC
a. Sign. 14. 1988.	0.50	1.00	6.00
b. Sign. 15. 1981 (BF).	5.00	15.00	35.00
c. Sign. 15. 1981. (F-CO).	0.50	3.00	7.00
d. Sign. 15. 1982. (BF).	1.00	4.00	9.00
e. Sign. 17. 1981. (F-CO).	0.50	3.00	7.00
f. Sign. 17. 1983. (BF).	1.00	4.00	9.00
g. Sign. 18. 1984.	0.50	3.00	7.00
h. Sign. 19. 1985.	0.50	3.00	7.00
i. Sign. 20. 1986.	0.50	1.00	6.00
j. Sign. 20. 1987.	0.50	1.00	6.00
k. Sign. 21. (reversed order). 1989.	0.50	1.00	5.00
l. Sign. 22. 1990.	0.50	1.00	5.00

Note: #706K w/10-digit small serial # were printed by Banque de France (BF) while those w/9-digit large serial # were printed by F-CO.

707K   1000 FRANCS
1981-90. Like #107A.

	VG	VF	UNC
a. Sign. 14. 1988.	1.00	2.00	10.00
b. Sign. 15. 1981.	1.00	4.00	12.00
c. Sign. 17. 1981.	1.00	4.00	12.00
d. Sign. 18. 1984.	1.00	4.00	12.00
e. Sign. 19. 1984.	5.00	20.00	—
f. Sign. 19. 1985.	1.00	4.00	12.00
g. Sign. 20. 1986.	1.00	2.00	10.00
h. Sign. 20. 1987.	1.00	2.00	10.00
i. Sign. 21. 1989.	1.00	2.00	9.00
j. Sign. 22. 1990.	1.00	2.00	9.00

708K   5000 FRANCS
1977-92. Like #108A.

	VG	VF	UNC
a. Sign. 12. 1978.	15.00	25.00	60.00
b. Sign. 12. 1979.	20.00	35.00	90.00
c. Sign. 13. 1980.	25.00	45.00	110.00
d. Sign. 14. 1977.	15.00	25.00	60.00
e. Sign. 14. 1989.	7.00	15.00	50.00
f. Sign. 15. 1982.	25.00	45.00	110.00
g. Sign. 16. 1983.	30.00	50.00	130.00
h. Sign. 17. 1983.	15.00	25.00	60.00
i. Sign. 18. 1984.	17.50	25.00	60.00
j. Sign. 19. 1985.	20.00	50.00	—
k. Sign. 20. 1986.	20.00	50.00	—
l. Sign. 20. 1987.	5.00	10.00	35.00
m. Sign. 21. 1990.	5.00	10.00	35.00
n. Sign. 22. 1991.	5.00	10.00	35.00
o. Sign. 22. 1992.	5.00	10.00	35.00
p. Sign. 23. 1992.	5.00	10.00	35.00
q. Sign. 24. 1992.	5.00	10.00	35.00

709K   10,000 FRANCS
ND. (1977-92). Like #109A.

	VG	VF	UNC
a. Sign. 11. ND.	20.00	35.00	95.00
b. Sign. 12. ND.	20.00	35.00	95.00
c. Sign. 13. ND.	20.00	40.00	100.00
d. Sign. 14. ND.	10.00	20.00	60.00
e. Sign. 15. ND.	10.00	20.00	65.00
f. Sign. 16. ND.	20.00	45.00	110.00
h. Sign. 18. ND.	10.00	25.00	75.00
i. Sign. 19. ND.	20.00	35.00	100.00
j. Sign. 20. ND.	10.00	20.00	60.00
k. Sign. 21. ND.	10.00	20.00	55.00
l. Sign. 22. ND.	10.00	20.00	55.00
m. Sign. 23. ND.	10.00	20.00	55.00

1991-92 ISSUE

710K   500 FRANCS
(19)91-(20)02. Like #110A.

	VG	VF	UNC
a. Sign. 22. (19)91.	0.25	1.00	4.00
b. Sign. 23. (19)92.	0.25	1.00	4.00
c. Sign. 25. (19)93.	0.25	1.00	4.00
d. Sign. 26. (19)94.	0.25	1.00	4.00
e. Sign. 27. (19)95.	0.25	1.00	3.00

710K   500 FRANCS

	VG	VF	UNC
f. Sign. 28. (19)96.	0.25	1.00	3.00
g. Sign. 28. (19)97.	0.25	1.00	3.00
h. Sign. 28. (19)98.	0.25	1.00	3.00
i. Sign. 29. (19)99.	0.25	1.00	3.00
j. Sign. 30. (20)00.	0.25	1.00	3.00
k. Sign. 30. (20)01.	0.25	1.00	3.00
l. Sign. 31. (20)02.	0.25	1.00	3.00

711K   1000 FRANCS
(19)91-(20)02. Like #111A.

	VG	VF	UNC
a. Sign. 22. (19)91.	0.50	1.00	7.00
b. Sign. 23. (19)92.	0.50	1.00	7.00
c. Sign. 25. (19)93.	0.50	1.00	7.00
d. Sign. 26. (19)94.	0.50	1.00	10.00
e. Sign. 27. (19)95.	0.50	1.00	6.00
f. Sign. 28. (19)96.	0.50	1.00	6.00
g. Sign. 28. (19)97.	0.50	1.00	6.00
h. Sign. 28. (19)98.	0.50	1.00	6.00
i. Sign. 29. (19)99.	0.50	1.00	6.00
j. Sign. 30. (20)00.	0.50	1.00	6.00
k. Sign. 30. (20)01.	0.50	1.00	6.00
l. Sign. 31. (20)02.	0.50	1.00	6.00
m. Sign. 31. (20)03.	0.50	1.00	6.00

712K	2500 FRANCS	VG	VF	UNC
	(19)92-(19)94. Like #112A.			
	a. Sign. 23. (19)92.	1.00	4.00	20.00
	b. Sign. 25. (19)93.	1.00	4.00	20.00
	c. Sign. 27. (19)94.	1.00	4.00	20.00
713K	5000 FRANCS			
	(19)92-(20)02. Like #113A.			
	a. Sign. 23. (19)92.	1.00	4.00	27.00
	b. Sign. 25. (19)93.	1.00	4.00	27.00
	c. Sign. 27. (19)94.	1.00	4.00	27.00
	d. Sign. 27. (19)95.	1.00	4.00	27.00
	e. Sign. 28. (19)96.	1.00	4.00	27.00
	f. Sign. 28. (19)97.	1.00	4.00	25.00
	g. Sign. 28. (19)98.	1.00	4.00	25.00
	h. Sign. 29. (19)98.	1.00	4.00	25.00
	i. Sign. 29. (19)99.	1.00	4.00	25.00
	j. Sign. 30. (20)00.	1.00	4.00	25.00
	k. Sign. 30. (20)01.	1.00	4.00	25.00
	l. Sign. 31. (20)02.	1.00	4.00	25.00
	m. Sign. 31. (20)03.	1.00	4.00	25.00
714K	10,000 FRANCS			
	(19)92-(20)01. Like #114A.			
	a. Sign. 25. (19)92.	1.50	7.00	50.00
	b. Sign. 27. (19)94.	1.50	7.00	50.00
	c. Sign. 27. (19)95.	1.50	7.00	45.00
	d. Sign. 28. (19)96.	1.50	7.00	45.00
	e. Sign. 28. (19)97.	1.50	7.00	45.00
	f. Sign. 28. (19)98.	1.50	7.00	45.00
	g. Sign. 29. (19)98.	1.50	7.00	45.00
	h. Sign. 29. (19)99.	1.50	7.00	45.00
	i. Sign. 30. (20)00.	1.50	7.00	45.00
	j. Sign. 30. (20)01.	1.50	7.00	45.00

2003 Issue

715K	1000 FRANCS	VG	VF	UNC
	(20)03-. Red-brown on red and m/c unpt.			
	a. Sign. 32. (20)03.	FV	FV	6.00
	b. Sign. 32. (20)04.	FV	FV	6.00

716K	2000 FRANCS	VG	VF	UNC
	(20)03-. Blue on lt. blue and m/c unpt.			
	a. Sign. 32. (20)03.	FV	FV	10.00
	b. Sign. 32. (20)04.	FV	FV	8.00
717K	5000 FRANCS			
	(20)03-. M/c.			
	a. Sign. 32. (20)03.	FV	FV	25.00
	b. Sign. 32. (20)04.	FV	FV	17.50
718K	10,000 FRANCS			
	(20)03-. M/c.			
	a. Sign. 32. (20)03.	FV	FV	40.00
	b. Sign. 32. (20)04.	FV	FV	30.00

1959-65; ND Issue

801T	100 FRANCS	VG	VF	UNC
	1961-65; ND. Like #101A.			
	a. Engraved. Sign. 1. 20.3.1961.	15.00	35.00	100.00
	b. Sign. 2. 20.3.1961.	10.00	25.00	70.00
	c. Litho. Sign. 2. 20.3.1961.	10.00	25.00	70.00
	d. Sign. 3. 2.12.1964.	11.00	28.00	80.00
	e. Sign. 4. 2.3.1965.	8.00	20.00	60.00
	f. Sign. 4. ND.	5.00	15.00	45.00
	g. Sign. 5. ND.	11.00	28.00	80.00

802T	500 FRANCS	VG	VF	UNC
	1959-61; ND. Like #102A.			
	a. Engraved. Sign. 1. 15.4.1959.	25.00	55.00	150.00
	b. Sign. 1. 20.3.1961.	35.00	100.00	—
	c. Sign. 2. 20.3.1961.	35.00	100.00	—
	f. Sign. 5. ND.	25.00	55.00	150.00
	g. Sign. 6. ND.	8.00	25.00	75.00
	i. Litho. Sign. 7. ND.	20.00	50.00	130.00
	j. Sign. 8. ND.	20.00	50.00	130.00
	k. Sign. 9. ND.	5.00	20.00	60.00
	l. Sign. 10. ND.	10.00	30.00	90.00
	m. Sign. 11. ND.	1.00	5.00	30.00
803T	1000 FRANCS			
	1959-65; ND. Like #103A.			
	a. Engraved. Sign. 1. 17.9.1959.	75.00	—	—
	b. Sign. 1. 20.3.1961.	20.00	60.00	150.00
	c. Sign. 2. 20.3.1961.	35.00	90.00	—
	e. Sign. 4. 2.3.1965.	20.00	60.00	140.00
	f. Sign. 5. ND.	20.00	60.00	150.00
	g. Sign. 6. ND.	10.00	30.00	70.00
	h. Litho. Sign. 6. ND.	25.00	70.00	—
	i. Sign. 7. ND.	10.00	30.00	70.00
	j. Sign. 8. ND.	35.00	90.00	—
	k. Sign. 9. ND.	5.00	20.00	50.00
	l. Sign. 10. ND.	5.00	15.00	40.00
	m. Sign. 11. ND.	4.00	10.00	35.00
	n. Sign. 12. ND.	5.00	15.00	40.00
	o. Sign. 13. ND.	5.00	15.00	40.00
804T	5000 FRANCS			
	1961; ND. Like #104A.			
	b. Sign. 1. 20.3.1961.	35.00	90.00	250.00
	h. Sign. 6. ND.	25.00	75.00	200.00
	i. Sign. 7. ND.	50.00	150.00	—
	j. Sign. 8. ND.	50.00	150.00	—
	k. Sign. 9. ND.	25.00	65.00	175.00
	m. Sign. 11. ND.	20.00	40.00	140.00

1977-81; ND Issue

#805T-809T smaller size notes.

805T	500 FRANCS	VG	VF	UNC
	1979. Like #105A. Sign. 12.	3.00	8.00	20.00
806T	500 FRANCS			
	1981-90. Like #106A.			
	a. Sign. 14. 1988.	6.00	15.00	—
	b. Sign. 15. 1981. (BF).	1.00	3.00	7.00
	c. Sign. 15. 1981. (F-CO).	1.00	3.00	7.00
	d. Sign. 15. 1982. (BF).	1.50	5.00	20.00
	e. Sign. 17. 1981. (F-CO).	1.50	5.00	20.00
	f. Sign. 18. 1984.	6.00	15.00	40.00
	g. Sign. 19. 1984.	1.00	5.00	10.00
	h. Sign. 19. 1985.	0.50	3.00	7.00
	i. Sign. 20. 1986.	0.50	1.00	6.00
	j. Sign. 20. 1987.	0.50	1.00	6.00
	k. Sign. 21. 1989.	0.50	1.00	5.00
	l. Sign. 22. 1990.	0.50	1.00	5.00

Note: #806T w/10-digit small serial # were printed by Banque de France (BF) while those w/9-digit large serial # were printed by F-CO.

807T	1000 FRANCS	VG	VF	UNC
	1981-90. Like #107A.			
	a. Sign. 14. 1988.	1.00	2.00	10.00
807T	1000 FRANCS			
	b. Sign. 15. 1981.	1.00	4.00	12.00
	c. Sign. 17. 1981.	2.00	6.00	25.00
	d. Sign. 18. 1984.	2.00	6.00	25.00
	e. Sign. 19. 1984.	5.00	15.00	—
	f. Sign. 19. 1985.	1.00	4.00	12.00
	g. Sign. 20. 1986.	5.00	15.00	—
	h. Sign. 20. 1987.	1.00	2.00	10.00
	i. Sign. 21. 1989.	1.00	2.00	9.00
	j. Sign. 22. 1990.	1.00	2.00	9.00
808T	5000 FRANCS			
	1977-92. Like #108A.			
	a. Sign. 12. 1978.	20.00	35.00	90.00
	b. Sign. 12. 1979.	20.00	35.00	90.00
	c. Sign. 14. 1977.	15.00	25.00	60.00
	d. Sign. 14. 1989.	5.00	10.00	35.00
	e. Sign. 15. 1981.	25.00	45.00	—
	f. Sign. 15. 1982.	25.00	45.00	—
	g. Sign. 17. 1983.	40.00	—	—
	h. Sign. 18. 1984.	15.00	25.00	60.00
	i. Sign. 20. 1987.	5.00	10.00	35.00
	j. Sign. 21. 1990.	5.00	10.00	35.00
	k. Sign. 22. 1991.	5.00	10.00	35.00
	l. Sign. 22. 1992.	5.00	10.00	35.00
	m. Sign. 23. 1992.	5.00	10.00	35.00
	n. Sign. 24. 1992.	5.00	10.00	35.00

809T	10,000 FRANCS	VG	VF	UNC
	ND. (1977-92). Like #109A.			
	a. Sign. 11. ND.	20.00	40.00	95.00

809T	10,000 FRANCS	VG	VF	UNC
	b. Sign. 12. ND.	35.00	90.00	—
	c. Sign. 13. ND.	35.00	90.00	—
	d. Sign. 14. ND.	35.00	90.00	—
	e. Sign. 15. ND.	10.00	20.00	65.00
	f. Sign. 16. ND.	20.00	45.00	110.00
	h. Sign. 18. ND.	10.00	20.00	65.00
	k. Sign. 22. ND.	10.00	20.00	55.00
	l. Sign. 23. ND.	10.00	20.00	55.00

1991-92 ISSUE

810T	500 FRANCS	VG	VF	UNC
	(19)91-(20)02. Like #110A.			
	a. Sign. 22. (19)91.	0.25	1.00	4.00
	b. Sign. 23. (19)92.	1.00	5.00	15.00
	c. Sign. 25. (19)93.	0.25	1.00	4.00
	d. Sign. 26. (19)94.	0.25	1.00	4.00
	e. Sign. 27. (19)95.	0.25	1.00	3.00
	f. Sign. 28. (19)96.	0.25	1.00	3.00
	g. Sign. 28. (19)97.	0.25	1.00	3.00
	h. Sign. 28. (19)98.	0.25	1.00	3.00
	i. Sign. 29. (19)99.	0.25	1.00	3.00
	j. Sign. 30. (20)00.	0.25	1.00	3.00
	k. Sign. 30. (20)01.	0.25	1.00	3.00
	l. Sign. 31. (20)02.	0.25	1.00	3.00

811T	1000 FRANCS	VG	VF	UNC
	(19)91-(20)02. Like #111A.			
	a. Sign. 22. (19)91.	0.50	1.50	7.00
	b. Sign. 23. (19)92.	0.50	1.50	7.00
	c. Sign. 25. (19)93.	0.50	1.50	7.00
	d. Sign. 26. (19)94.	0.50	1.50	7.00
	e. Sign. 27. (19)95.	0.50	1.50	6.00
	f. Sign. 28. (19)96.	0.50	1.50	6.00
	g. Sign. 28. (19)97.	0.50	1.50	6.00
811T	**1000 FRANCS**			
	h. Sign. 28. (19)98.	0.50	1.50	6.00
	i. Sign. 29. (19)99.	0.50	1.50	6.00
	j. Sign. 30. (20)00.	0.50	1.50	6.00
	k. Sign. 30. (20)01.	0.50	1.50	6.00
	l. Sign. 31. (20)02.	0.50	1.50	6.00
	m. Sign. 31. (20)03.	0.50	1.50	6.00
812T	**2500 FRANCS**			
	(19)92-(19)94. Like #112A.			
	a. Sign. 23. (19)92.	1.00	4.00	20.00
	b. Sign. 25. (19)93.	1.00	4.00	20.00
	c. Sign. 27. (19)94.	1.00	4.00	20.00
813T	**5000 FRANCS**			
	(19)92-(20)02. Like #113A.			
	a. Sign. 23. (19)92.	1.00	5.00	27.50
	b. Sign. 25. (19)93.	1.00	5.00	27.50
	c. Sign. 27. (19)94.	1.00	5.00	27.50
	d. Sign. 27. (19)95.	1.00	5.00	25.00
	e. Sign. 28. (19)97.	1.00	5.00	25.00
	f. Sign. 28. (19)98.	1.00	5.00	25.00
	g. Sign. 29. (19)98.	1.00	5.00	25.00
	h. Sign. 29. (19)99.	1.00	5.00	25.00
	i. Sign. 30. (20)00.	1.00	5.00	25.00
	j. Sign. 30. (20)01.	1.00	5.00	25.00
	k. Sign. 31. (20)02.	1.00	5.00	25.00
	l. Sign. 31. (20)03.	1.00	5.00	25.00
814T	**10,000 FRANCS**			
	(19)92-(20)01. Like #114A.			
	a. Sign. 25. (19)92.	1.50	8.00	50.00
	b. Sign. 27. (19)94.	1.50	8.00	50.00
	c. Sign. 27. (19)95.	1.50	8.00	45.00
	d. Sign. 28. (19)96.	1.50	8.00	45.00
	e. Sign. 28. (19)97.	1.50	8.00	45.00
	f. Sign. 29. (19)99.	1.50	8.00	45.00
	g. Sign. 30. (20)00.	1.50	8.00	45.00
	h. Sign. 30. (20)01.	1.50	8.00	45.00

2003 ISSUE

815T	1000 FRANCS	VG	VF	UNC
	(20)03-. Red-brown on red and m/c unpt.			
	a. Sign. 32. (20)03.	FV	FV	6.00
	b. Sign. 32. (20)04.	FV	FV	6.00
816T	**2000 FRANCS**			
	(20)03-. Blue on lt. blue and m/c unpt.			
	a. Sign. 32. (20)03.	FV	FV	10.00
	b. Sign. 32. (20)04.	FV	FV	8.00

817T	5000 FRANCS	VG	VF	UNC
	(20)03-. M/c.			
	a. Sign. 32. (20)03.	FV	FV	25.00
	b. Sign. 32. (20)04.	FV	FV	17.50
818T	**10,000 FRANCS**			
	(20)03-. M/c.			
	a. Sign. 32. (20)03.	FV	FV	40.00
	b. Sign. 32. (20)04.	FV	FV	30.00

1997 ISSUE

910S	500 FRANCS	VG	VF	UNC
	(19)97-(19)99. Like #110A.			
	a. Sign. 28. (19)97.	0.25	1.00	5.00
	b. Sign. 28. (19)98.	0.25	1.00	3.00
	c. Sign. 29. (19)99.	0.25	1.00	3.00
	d. Sign. 30. (20)00.	0.25	1.00	3.00
	f. Sign. 31. (20)02.	0.25	1.00	3.00
911S	**1000 FRANCS**			
	(19)97-(19)99. Like #111A.			
	a. Sign. 28. (19)97.	0.50	2.00	8.00
	b. Sign. 28. (19)98.	0.50	2.00	6.00
	c. Sign. 29. (19)99.	0.50	2.00	6.00
	e. Sign. 30. (20)01.	0.50	2.00	6.00
	f. Sign. 31. (20)02.	0.50	2.00	6.00

913S	5000 FRANCS	VG	VF	UNC
	(19)97-(20)00. Like #113A.			
	a. Sign. 28. (19)97.	1.50	6.00	32.50
	b. Sign. 28. (19)98.	1.50	6.00	25.00
	c. Sign. 29. (19)98.	1.50	6.00	26.00
	d. Sign. 29. (19)99.	1.50	6.00	26.00
	e. Sign. 30. (20)00.	1.50	6.00	26.00
	g. Sign. 31. (20)02.	1.50	6.00	25.00
	h. Sign. 31. (20)03.	1.50	6.00	25.00
914S	**10,000 FRANCS**			
	(19)97-(19)98. Like #114A.			
	a. Sign. 28. (19)97.	2.50	15.00	55.00
	b. Sign. 28. (19)98.	2.50	15.00	50.00
	d. Sign. 29. (19)99.	2.50	15.00	45.00
	e. Sign. 30. (20)00.	2.50	15.00	45.00

2003 ISSUE

915S	1000 FRANCS	VG	VF	UNC
	(20)03-. Red-brown on red and m/c unpt.			
	a. Sign. 32. (20)03.	FV	FV	6.00
	b. Sign. 32. (20)04.	FV	FV	6.00
916S	**2000 FRANCS**			
	(20)03-. Blue on lt. blue and m/c unpt.			
	a. Sign. 32. (20)03.	FV	FV	10.00
	b. Sign. 32. (20)04.	FV	FV	8.00
917S	**5000 FRANCS**			
	(20)03-. M/c.			
	a. Sign. 32. (20)03.			
	b. Sign. 32. (20)04.	FV	FV	17.50
918S	**10,000 FRANCS**			
	(20)03-. M/c.			
	a. Sign. 32. (20)03.	FV	FV	40.00
	b. Sign. 32. (20)04.	FV	FV	30.00

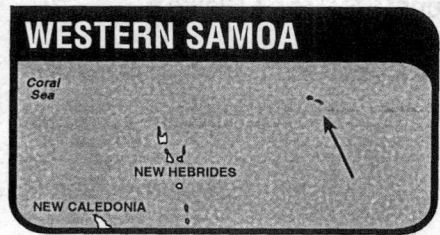

WESTERN SAMOA

The Independent State of Western Samoa (formerly German Samoa), located in the Pacific Ocean 1,600 miles (2,574 km.) northeast of New Zealand, has an area of 1,097 sq. mi. (2,860 sq. km.) and a population of 157,000. Capital: Apia. The economy is based on agriculture, fishing and tourism. Copra, cocoa and bananas are exported.

The Samoan group of islands was discovered by Dutch navigator Jacob Roggeveen in 1772. Great Britain, the United States and Germany established consular representation at Apia in 1847, 1853 and 1861 respectively. The conflicting interests of the three powers produced the Berlin agreement of 1889 which declared Samoa neutral and had the effect of establishing a tripartite protectorate over the islands. A further agreement, 1899, recognized the rights of the United States in those islands east of 171 deg. west longitude (American Samoa) and of Germany in the other islands (Western Samoa). New Zealand occupied Western Samoa at the start of World War I and administered it as a League of Nations mandate and U.N. trusteeship until Jan. 1, 1962, when it became an independent state.

Western Samoa is a member of the Commonwealth of Nations. The Chief Executive is Chief of State. The prime minister is the Head of Government. The present Head of State, Malietoa Tanumafili II, holds his position for life. Future Heads of State will be elected by the Legislature Assembly for five-year terms.

RULERS:
British, 1914-1962
Malietoa Tanumafili II, 1962-

MONETARY SYSTEM:
1 Shilling = 12 Pence
1 Pound = 20 Shillings to 1967
1 Tala = 100 Sene, 1967-

NEW ZEALAND ADMINISTRATION

TERRITORY OF WESTERN SAMOA
1920-22 TREASURY NOTE ISSUE
By Authority of New Zealand Government

#7-9 various date and sign. varieties. Printer: BWC.

Note: Some of these notes may appear to be ND, probably through error or washed out, faded or worn off hand-stamped dates.

		Good	Fine	XF
7	**10 SHILLINGS** 1922-59. Black on brown and green unpt. Palm trees along beach at ctr. a. 3.3.1922.	—	—	—
	b. Sign. title: *MINISTER OF EXTERNAL AFFAIRS FOR NEW ZEALAND* at l. 13.4.1938-21.11.1949.	50.00	175.00	500.00
	c. Sign. title: *MINISTER OF ISLAND TERRITORIES FOR NEW ZEALAND* at l. 24.5.1951-27.5.1958; 29.10.1959.	75.00	250.00	700.00
	d. Sign. title: *HIGH COMMISSIONER* at l. 20.3.1957-22.12.1959.	35.00	150.00	500.00
8A	**1 POUND** 1948-61. Purple on m/c unpt. Like #8 but *STERLING* omitted from ctr. a. Sign. title: *MINISTER OF ISLAND TERRITORIES FOR NEW ZEALAND* at l. 6.8.1948-7.8.1958.	100.00	400.00	1250.00
	b. Sign. title: *HIGH COMMISSIONER* at l. 20.4.1959; 10.12.1959; 1.5.1961.	65.00	225.00	1000.00

BANK OF WESTERN SAMOA
1960-61 PROVISIONAL ISSUE
#10-12 red ovpt: *Bank of Western Samoa, Legal Tender in Western Samoa by virtue of the Bank of Western Samoa Ordinance 1959* on older notes. Various date and sign. varieties.

		VG	VF	UNC
10	**10 SHILLINGS** 1960-61; ND. Ovpt. on #7. a. Sign. title: *HIGH COMMISSIONER* blocked out at lower l., w/*MINISTER OF FINANCE* below. 8.12.1960; 1.5.1961.	35.00	150.00	550.00
	b. ND. Sign. title: *MINISTER OF FINANCE* in plate w/o ovpt., at lower l.	35.00	150.00	550.00
11	**1 POUND** 1960-61. Ovpt. on #8. a. Sign. title: *HIGH COMMISSIONER* blocked out at lower l., w/*MINISTER OF FINANCE* below. 8.11.1960; 1.5.1961.	65.00	300.00	1150.00
	b. Sign. title: *MINISTER OF FINANCE* in plate w/o ovpt., at lower l. 1.5.1961.	65.00	275.00	1100.00
12	**5 POUNDS** 1.5.1961. Ovpt. on #9A.	500.00	1750.00	4500.00

STATE

FALE TUPE O SAMOA I SISIFO
BANK OF WESTERN SAMOA
1963 ND ISSUE

		VG	VF	UNC
13	**10 SHILLINGS** ND (1963). Dk. green on m/c unpt. Arms at l., boat at r. Hut and 2 palms at ctr. on back. a. Issued note.	2.50	10.00	65.00
	s. Specimen.	—	—	50.00

		VG	VF	UNC
14	**1 POUND** ND (1963). Blue on m/c unpt. Palms and rising sun at l. and r., arms at ctr. Sm. bldg. and lagoon at ctr. on back. 159 x 83mm. a. Issued note.	5.00	20.00	100.00
	s. Specimen.	—	—	50.00

1980-84 ND ISSUE

#19-23 national flag at l. ctr. on face and ctr. r. on back. Arms at lower ctr. r. on back. Wmk: M. Tanumafili II.

		VG	VF	UNC
15	**5 POUNDS**			
	ND (1963). Brown on m/c unpt. Rava bowl at l., red and blue flag over arms at r. Shoreline w/trees, sea and islands on back. 166 x 89mm.			
	a. Issued note.	20.00	50.00	200.00
	s. Specimen.	—	—	200.00

1967 ND ISSUE

Tala System

SIGNATURE VARIETIES			
1	*[signature]* MANAGER	2	*[signature]* MANAGER
3	*[signature]* MANAGER	4	*[signature]* SENIOR MANAGER

		VG	VF	UNC
16	**1 TALA**			
	ND (1967). Dk. green on m/c unpt. Like #13.			
	a. Sign. 1.	1.50	8.00	55.00
	b. Sign. 2.	1.00	7.00	45.00
	c. Sign. 3.	1.00	7.00	35.00
	d. Sign. 4.	1.50	8.00	40.00
	s. Sign. as a, b, d. Specimen.	—	—	40.00
17	**2 TALA**			
	ND (1967). Blue on m/c unpt. Like #14, but 144 x 77mm.			
	a. Sign. 1.	3.00	7.50	45.00
	b. Sign. 3.	2.50	5.00	40.00
	c. Sign. 4.	4.00	8.00	50.00
	s. Sign. as a, c. Specimen.	—	—	50.00

		VG	VF	UNC
18	**10 TALA**			
	ND (1967). Brown on m/c unpt. Like #15, but 150 x 76mm.			
	a. Sign. 1.	15.00	75.00	300.00
	b. Sign. 2.	15.00	90.00	350.00
	c. Sign. 3.	12.00	30.00	150.00
	d. Sign. 4.	12.00	35.00	165.00
	s. Sign. as a, b, d. Specimen.	—	—	60.00

		VG	VF	UNC
19	**1 TALA**			
	ND (1980). Dk. green on m/c unpt. 2 weavers at r. 2 fishermen in canoe at l. ctr. on back.	0.75	2.00	10.00

		VG	VF	UNC
20	**2 TALA**			
	ND (1980). Deep blue-violet on m/c unpt. Woodcarver at r. Hut w/palms on sm. island at l. ctr. on back.	1.50	3.00	15.00

		VG	VF	UNC
21	**5 TALA**			
	ND (1980). Red on m/c unpt. Child writing at r. Sm. port city at l. ctr. on back.	3.50	7.00	27.50

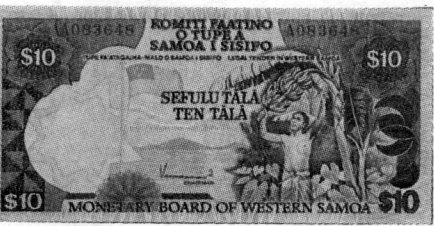

		VG	VF	UNC
22	**10 TALA**			
	ND (1980). Dk. brown and purple on m/c unpt. Man picking bananas at r. Shoreline landscape on back.	7.50	30.00	135.00

23   **20 TALA**
ND (1984). Brown and orange-brown on m/c unpt. Fisherman w/net at r. Round bldg. at l. on back.   30.00   90.00   350.00

#24 not assigned.

FALETUPE TUTOTONU O SAMOA

CENTRAL BANK OF SAMOA

1985 ND ISSUE

#25-30 like #20-23 but w/new issuer's name. Wmk: M. Tanumafili II.

			VG	VF	UNC
25	**2 TALA**	ND (1985). Deep blue-violet on m/c unpt. Like #20.	FV	FV	4.00
26	**5 TALA**	ND (1985). Red on m/c unpt. Like #21.	FV	FV	6.50
27	**10 TALA**	ND (1985). Dk. brown and purple on m/c unpt. Like #22.	FV	FV	10.00
28	**20 TALA**	ND (1985). Brown and orange-brown on m/c unpt. Like #23.	FV	FV	20.00

#29-30 M. Tanumafili II at r.

29	**50 TALA**	ND (ca.1990). Green on m/c unpt. Former home of R. L. Stevenson, current residence of Head of State at ctr. Man performing traditional knife dance on back.	FV	FV	40.00
30	**100 TALA**	ND (ca.1990). Violet and lt. brown on m/c unpt. Flag and Parliament bldg. at ctr. Harvest scene on back.	FV	FV	65.00

1990 COMMEMORATIVE ISSUE

#31, Golden Jubilee of Service of the Head of State, Susuga Malietoa Tanumafili II, 1990

			VG	VF	UNC
31	**2 TALA**	ND (1990). Brown, blue and purple on m/c unpt. Samoan village at ctr., M. Tanumafili II at r. Clear area at lower r. containing a Rava bowl visible from both sides. Family scene at ctr., arms at upper r. on back. Polymer plastic. Printer: NPA (w/o im			
		a. Text on face partly engraved. Serial # prefix *AAA*.	FV	FV	6.50
		b. Printing as a. Uncut sheet of 4 subjects. Serial # prefix *AAB*.	—	—	25.00
		c. Face completely lithographed, deeper blue, purple and dull brown. Serial # prefix *AAC*.	FV	FV	3.50
		d. Serial # prefix: *AAD*.	FV	FV	3.50
		e. Serial # prefix: *AAE*.	FV	FV	3.50

Note: #31a was also issued in a special folder.

2002 ND ISSUE

			VG	VF	UNC
32	**2 TALA**	ND (2003). Brown, blue and purple on m/c unpt.		Expected New Issue	

			VG	VF	UNC
33	**5 TALA**	ND (2002). Red on m/c unpt. Like #26.	FV	FV	6.50

			VG	VF	UNC
34	**10 TALA**	ND (2002). Dk. brown and purple on m/c unpt. Like #27.	FV	FV	10.00
35	**20 TALA**	ND (2002). Brown and orange-brown on m/c unpt. Like #28	FV	FV	20.00

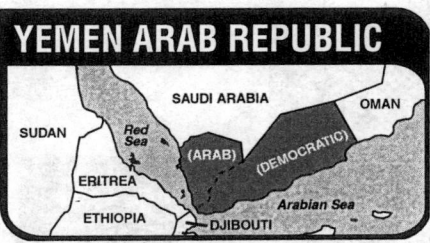

The Yemen Arab Republic, located in the southwestern corner of the Arabian Peninsula, has an area of 75,290 sq. mi. (195,000 sq. km.) and a population of 18.12 million. Capital: San'a. The industries of Yemen, one of the world's poorest countries, are agriculture and local handicrafts. Qat (a mildly narcotic leaf), coffee, cotton and rock salt are exported.

One of the oldest centers of civilization in the Near East, Yemen was once part of the Minaean Kingdom and of the ancient Kingdom of Sheba, after which it was captured successively by Egyptians, Ethiopians and Romans. It was converted to the Moslem religion in 628 AD and administered as a caliphate until 1538, when it came under Turkish occupation which was maintained until 1918 when autonomy was achieved through revolution.

On Feb. 1, 1958, Egypt and Syria formed the United Arab Republic. Yemen joined on March 8 in an association known as the United Arab States. Syria withdrew from the United Arab Republic on Sept. 29, 1961, and on Dec. 26 Egypt dissolved its ties with Yemen in the United Arab States.

Provoked by the harsh rule of Imam Mohammed al-Badr, last ruler of the Kingdom of Mutawwakkilite, the National Liberation Front seized control of the government on Sept. 27, 1962. Badr fled to Saudi Arabia.

An agreement for a constitution for a unified state was reached in Dec. 1989 uniting the Yemen Arab Republic with the People's Democratic Republic of Yemen into the Republic of Yemen on May 22, 1990. Both currencies circulated for a number of years, but the PDR dinar lost legal tender status on June 11, 1996.

RULERS:
Imam Ahmad, AH1367-1382/1948-1962AD
Imam al-Badr, AH1382-1388/1962-1968AD

MONETARY SYSTEM:
1 Rial = 40 Buqshas
1 Rial = 100 Fils (from April 1, 1995).

SIGNATURE VARIETIES			
1	Minister of the Treasury Abdul Ghani Ali, 1964	**2**	Minister of the Treasury and Economy Abdul Ghani Ali, 1967
3	Minister of the Treasury Ahmad al-Ruhumi, 1966 (actually inverted)	**4**	Minister of the Treasury Ahmad Abdu Said, 1968
5	Governor & Chairman, CBY Abdul Aziz Abdul Ghani, 1971-85	**6**	Governor & Chairman, CBY Abdulla Mohamed al-Sanabani, 1978-85
7	Governor & Chairman, CBY Abdulla Mohamed al-Sanabani, 1978-85	**8**	Governor, CBY Muhammad Ahmad Gunaid, 1985-94
9	Governor, CBY Aluwi Salih al-Salami, 1994	**10**	Governor, CBY Ahmed Abdul Rahman al-Samani, 1997-

ARAB REPUBLIC

YEMEN CURRENCY BOARD

1964 ND ISSUE

#1-3 wmk: Arms.

			VG	VF	UNC
1	**1 RIAL**	ND (1964; 1967). Green on m/c unpt. Arms at l. Houses in Sana'a w/minaret at ctr. on back.			
		a. Sign. 1. (1964).	2.50	15.00	100.00
		b. Sign. 2. (1967).	3.50	20.00	125.00
		s. As a. Specimen.	—	—	225.00

2 **5 RIALS**
ND (1964; 1967). Red on m/c unpt. Arms at l. Lion of Timna
sculpture at r. on back.

	VG	VF	UNC
a. Sign. 1. (1964).	7.00	65.00	275.00
b. Sign. 2. (1967).	8.00	75.00	300.00
s. As a. Specimen.	—	—	300.00

3 **10 RIALS**
ND (1964; 1967). Blue-green on m/c unpt. Arms at l. Dam at r. on
back.

	VG	VF	UNC
a. Sign. 1. (1964).	15.00	75.00	350.00
b. Sign. 2. (1967).	15.00	75.00	350.00
s. As a. Specimen.	—	—	300.00

1966-71 ND ISSUE

#4-10 wmk: Arms.

4 **10 BUQSHAS**
ND (1966). Brown on m/c unpt. Lion of Timna sculpture at l. Ancient
dedication stone from a temple at Ma'rib at r. on back. Sign. 3.

VG	VF	UNC
1.25	4.00	17.50

5 **20 BUQSHAS**
ND (1966). Green on m/c unpt. Tall alabaster head at l. Back olive-
green; ruins of the Bara'an temple at r. Sign. 3.

VG	VF	UNC
1.00	6.00	35.00

#6-8 backs like #1-3.

6 **1 RIAL**
ND (1969). Green on m/c unpt. Alabaster head at l. House in Sana'a
w/minaret on back. Sign. 4.

	VG	VF	UNC
a. Issued note.	2.00	15.00	75.00
s. Specimen.	—	—	175.00

7 **5 RIALS**
ND (1969). Red on m/c unpt. Bronze lion's head sculpture at l. Lion
of Timna sculpture at r. on back. Sign. 4.

	VG	VF	UNC
a. Issued note.	7.50	45.00	200.00
s. Specimen.	—	—	250.00

8 **10 RIALS**
ND (1969). Blue-green on m/c unpt. Shadhili Mosque at l. Dam at
r. on back. Sign. 4.

	VG	VF	UNC
a. Issued note.	6.00	35.00	175.00
s. Specimen.	—	—	250.00

9 **20 RIALS**
ND (1971). Purple and blue-green on m/c unpt. Palace on the rock
at Wadi Dahr. Back purple and gold; city view of Sana'a. Sign. 4.

	VG	VF	UNC
a. Issued note.	8.00	30.00	150.00
s. Specimen.			

10 **50 RIALS**
ND (1971). Dk. olive-green on m/c unpt. Crossed *jambiyas*
(daggers) at l. Coffee branch and tree, mountains in background at
ctr. r. on back. Sign. 4.

VG	VF	UNC
7.50	35.00	175.00

CENTRAL BANK OF YEMEN

1973-77 ND ISSUES

#11-16 wmk: Arms.

11   1 RIAL

	VG	VF	UNC
ND (1973). Green on m/c unpt. al Baqiliyah Mosque at l. Coffee plants w/mountains in background at ctr. on back.			
a. Sign. 5.	0.10	0.50	2.50
b. Sign. 7.	0.50	2.50	7.50
ct. Color trial.	—	—	—
s. Specimen.	—	—	—

12   5 RIALS

	VG	VF	UNC
ND (1973). Red on m/c unpt. Bldgs. in Wadi Du'an at l. Beit al Midie on high rock hill at ctr. on back. Sign. 5.			
a. Issued note.	0.50	2.50	10.00
s. Specimen.	—	—	—

13   10 RIALS

	VG	VF	UNC
ND (1973). Blue-green on m/c unpt. Bronze head of Kg. Dhamer Ali at l. Republican Palace in Sana'a at ctr. on back.			
a. Sign. 5.	1.00	3.50	15.00
b. Sign. 7.	0.50	2.50	12.50
ct. Color trial.	—	—	—
s. Specimen.	—	—	—

14   20 RIALS

	VG	VF	UNC
ND (1973). Purple on m/c unpt. Marble sculpture of seated figure w/grapes at l. Back purple and brown; terraced slopes along mountain at ctr. r. Sign. 5.			
a. Issued note.	1.00	3.00	15.00
ct. Color trial.	—	—	—

15   50 RIALS

	VG	VF	UNC
ND (1973). Dk. olive-green on m/c unpt. Bronze statue of Ma'adkarib at l. Bab al Yemen (main gate of Sana'a) on back.			
a. Sign. 5.	1.00	5.00	35.00
b. Sign. 7.	0.50	2.00	10.00
s. Specimen.	—	—	—

16   100 RIALS

	VG	VF	UNC
ND (1976). Red-violet on m/c unpt. Marble sculpture of cherub and griffin at l. View of Ta'izz on back. Sign. 5.			
a. Issued note.	10.00	40.00	200.00
s. Specimen.	—	—	—

1979-85 ND ISSUES

#16B-21A wmk: Arms.

16B   1 RIAL

	VG	VF	UNC
ND (1983). Like #11, but darker green and smaller serial #. Clearer unpt. design over wmk. area at r. Sign. 7.	0.10	0.25	1.00

17   5 RIALS

	VG	VF	UNC
ND (1981). Red on orange and m/c unpt. Dhahr al Dahab at l. Fortress Qal'at al Qahira overlooking Ta'izz at ctr. r. on back.			
a. Sign. 5. (1981).	0.25	1.00	5.00
b. Sign. 7. (1983).	0.15	0.75	5.00
c. Sign. 8. (1991).	0.10	0.40	2.00

18   10 RIALS

	VG	VF	UNC
ND (1981). Blue on green and m/c unpt. Village of Thulla at l. Al Baqiliyah Mosque on back.			
a. Sign. 5. (1981).	0.50	2.00	12.50
b. Sign. 7. (1983).	0.25	2.00	7.50

19   20 RIALS

	VG	VF	UNC
ND (1985). Purple on m/c unpt. Face like #14. View of San'a on back.			
a. Bank title on tan unpt. on back. Sign. 7. (1983). 4mm serial #.	1.00	7.50	35.00
b. As a. Sign. 8. 3mm serial #.	0.50	3.00	15.00
c. Bank title on lt. brown unpt. of vertical lines on back. Sign. 8.	0.50	2.00	10.00
s. Specimen.	—	—	—

#20 Deleted. See #26.

21   100 RIALS

	VG	VF	UNC
ND (1979). Red-violet on m/c unpt. Al Ashrafiya Mosque and Ta'izz city view at l. View of San'a w/mountains on back. Sign. 6.	1.00	5.00	25.00

21A 100 RIALS

		VG	VF	UNC
ND (1984). Red-violet on m/c unpt. Face like #16 but different sign. Central Bank of Yemen bldg. at ctr. r. on back. Sign. 7.				
a. Issued note.		0.75	2.50	10.00
s. Specimen.				

1990-97 ND Issues

#23-31 wmk: Arms.

23 10 RIALS

	VG	VF	UNC
ND (1990-). Blue and black on m/c unpt. al Baqilyah Mosque at l. Back blue and brown; Ma'rib Dam at ctr. r., 10 at upper corners. 2 wmk. varieties. Sign. 8.	FV	FV	3.00

24 10 RIALS

	VG	VF	UNC
ND (ca.1992). Face like #23. Back like #23, but w/10 at upper l. and lower r. 10 w/Arabic text: *Sadd Marib* near lower r. Sign. 8.	FV	FV	3.00

25 20 RIALS

	VG	VF	UNC
ND (1995). Dk. brown on m/c unpt. Arch ends straight border across upper ctr. Marble sculpture of cupid w/grapes at l. Coastal view of Aden, dhow on back. Sign. 8.	FV	FV	5.00

26 20 RIALS

		VG	VF	UNC
ND (1990). Dk. brown on m/c unpt. Face like #25. Different city view of San'a w/o minarets or dhow at ctr. r. on back. Sign. 8.				
a. W/o shading around title of the bank.		FV	3.00	10.00
b. W/shading around title of the bank.		FV	2.00	5.00

27 50 RIALS

	VG	VF	UNC
ND (1993). Black and deep olive-brown on m/c unpt. Face like #15. Shibam city view at ctr. r. w/o Arabic title at lower l. on back. Sign. 8.	FV	FV	4.50

27A 50 RIALS

	VG	VF	UNC
ND (199?). Black and deep olive-brown on m/c unpt. Like #27 but w/Arabic title *Shibam Hadramaut* at lower l. on back. Sign. 8, 9.	FV	FV	4.50

28 100 RIALS

	VG	VF	UNC
ND (1993). Violet, purple and black on m/c unpt. Ancient culvert in Aden at l. City view of Sana'a on back. Sign. 8, 9.	FV	FV	3.00

29 200 RIALS

	VG	VF	UNC
ND (1996). Deep blue-green on m/c unpt. Alabaster sculpture of a man at l. Harbor view of Mukalla at ctr. r. on back. Sign. 9.	FV	FV	7.50

30 500 RIALS

	VG	VF	UNC
ND (1997). Blue-violet and red-brown on m/c unpt. Central Bank of Yemen bldg. at l. Bara'an temple ruins in brown at r. on back. Sign. 9.	FV	FV	12.00

1998-2001 ND Issues

#31-32 holographic strip w/arms repeated at l. Sign. 10.

31 500 RIALS
AH1422/2001. Light blue and gray on beige and m/c unpt. Palace on the Rock at I. Al Muhdar mosque in Tarim, Hadramaut at ctr. on back.

	VG	VF	UNC
	FV	FV	12.00

32 1000 RIALS
ND (1998). Dk. brown and dk. green on m/c unpt. Sultan's palace in Seiyun, Hadramaut at ctr. Bab al-Yemen and old city of Sana'a on back.

	VG	VF	UNC
	FV	FV	20.00

33 1000 RIALS
2004/AH1424. Dk. brown and dk. green on m/c unpt. Similar to #15 but with color changes and date on front at lower right.

	VG	VF	UNC
	FV	FV	20.00

The People's Democratic Republic of Yemen, (formerly the Peoples Republic of Southern Yemen) was located on the southern coast of the Arabian Peninsula. It had an area of 128,560 sq. mi. (332,968 sq. km.). Capital: Aden. It consisted of the port city of Aden, 17 states of the former South Arabian Federation, 3 small sheikhdoms, 3 large sultanates, Quaiti, Kathiri and Mahri, which made up the Eastern Aden Protectorate, and Socotra, the largest island in the Arabian Sea. The port of Aden is the area's most valuable natural resource. Cotton, fish, coffee and hides are exported.

Between 1200 BC and the 6th century AD, what is now the People's Democratic Republic of Yemen was part of the Minaean kingdom. In subsequent years it was controlled by Persians, Egyptians and Turks. Aden, one of the cities mentioned in the Bible, had been a port for trade between the East and West for 2,000 years. British rule began in 1839 when the British East India Co. seized control to put an end to the piracy threatening trade with India. To protect their foothold in Aden, the British found it necessary to extend their control into the area known historically as the Hadramaut, and to sign protection treaties with the sheikhs of the hinterland. Eventually, 15 of the 16 Western Protectorate states, the Wahidi state of the Eastern Protectorate, and Aden Colony joined to form the Federation of South Arabia. In 1959, Britain agreed to prepare South Arabia for full independence, which was achieved on Nov. 30, 1967, at which time South Arabia, including Aden, changed its name to the People's Republic of Southern Yemen. On Dec. 1, 1970, following the overthrowing of the new government by the National Liberation Front, Southern Yemen changed its name to the People's Democratic Republic of Yemen. On May 22, 1990 the People's Democratic Republic merged with the Yemen Arab Republic into a unified Republic of Yemen. The YDR currency ceased to circulate on June 11, 1996.

MONETARY SYSTEM:
1 Dinar = 1000 Fils

FEDERATED STATE

SIGNATURE VARIETIES			
1		2	
3		4	

SOUTH ARABIAN CURRENCY AUTHORITY
1965 ND ISSUE
#1-5 Aden harbor, dhow at ctr. Wmk: Camel's head. Printer: TDLR.

1 250 FILS
ND (1965). Brown on m/c unpt. Date palm at ctr. on back.

	VG	VF	UNC
a. Sign. 1.	2.50	7.50	35.00
b. Sign. 2.	0.50	3.00	12.50
s. As a. Specimen.	—	—	35.00

2 500 FILS
ND (1965). Green on m/c unpt. Date palm at ctr., heads of wheat at lower l. on back.

	VG	VF	UNC
a. Sign. 1.	3.50	15.00	70.00
b. Sign. 2.	2.00	6.00	30.00
s. As a. Specimen.	—	—	50.00

3   1 DINAR
ND (1965). Dk blue on m/c unpt. Date palm at ctr., branch of a
cotton plant at l. on back.

		VG	VF	UNC
a. Sign. 1.		7.50	25.00	150.00
b. Sign. 2.		3.50	15.00	45.00
s. As a. Specimen.		—		75.00

4   5 DINARS
ND (1965). Red on m/c unpt. Date palm at ctr., cotton plant branch
and millet flanking on back.

		VG	VF	UNC
a. Sign. 1.		17.50	75.00	350.00
b. Sign. 2.		12.50	35.00	175.00
s. As a. Specimen.		—		100.00

5   10 DINARS
ND (1967). Deep olive-green on m/c unpt. Date palm at ctr;, cotton
branch, corn cobs and heads of wheat around on back. Sign. 2.

VG	VF	UNC
22.50	90.00	350.00

PEOPLES DEMOCRATIC REPUBLIC

BANK OF YEMEN

1984 ND ISSUE

#6-9 similar to #1-5 but w/o English on face and w/new bank name on back. Capital: *ADEN* added to bottom
r. on back. Wmk: Camel's head.

6   500 FILS
ND (1984). Green on m/c unpt. Similar to #2.

VG	VF	UNC
0.50	2.00	12.50

7   1 DINAR
ND (1984). Dk. blue on m/c unpt. Similar to #3.

VG	VF	UNC
1.00	5.00	20.00

8   5 DINARS
ND (1984). Red on m/c unpt. Similar to #4.

	VG	VF	UNC
a. Sign. 3.	5.00	20.00	100.00
b. Sign. 4.	3.00	10.00	32.50

9   10 DINARS
ND (1984). Deep olive-green on m/c unpt. Similar to #5.

	VG	VF	UNC
a. Sign. 3.	7.50	22.50	110.00
b. Sign. 4.	5.00	20.00	55.00

YUGOSLAVIA

The Federal Republic of Yugoslavia is a Balkan country located on the east shore of the Adriatic Sea bordering Bosnia-Herzegovina and Croatia to the west, Hungary and Romania to the north, Bulgaria to the east, and Albania and Macedonia to the south. It has an area of 39,449 sq. mi. (102,173 sq. km.) and a population of 10.5 million. Capital: Belgrade. The chief industries are agriculture, mining, manufacturing and tourism. Machinery, nonferrous metals, meat and fabrics are exported.

The first South-Slavian State - Yugoslavia - was proclaimed on Dec. 1, 1918, after the union of the Kingdom of Serbia, Montenegro and the South Slav territories of Austria-Hungary; it then changed its official name from the Kingdom of the Serbs, Croats, and Slovenes to the Kingdom of Yugoslavia on Oct. 3, 1929. The Royal government of Yugoslavia attempted to remain neutral in World War II but, yielding to German pressure, aligned itself with the Axis powers in March of 1941; a few days later it was overthrown by a military-led coup and its neutrality reasserted. The Nazis occupied the country on April 17, and throughout the remaining years were resisted by a number of guerrilla armies, notably that of Marshal Josip Broz known as Tito. After the defeat of the Axis powers, a leftist coalition headed by Tito abolished the monarchy and, on Jan. 31, 1946, established a "People's Republic". Tito's rival General Draza Mihajlovic, who led the Chetniks against the Germans and Tito's forces, was arrested on March 13, 1946 and executed the following day after having been convicted by a partisan court.

The Federal Republic of Yugoslavia was composed of six autonomous republics: Serbia, Croatia, Slovenia, Bosnia-Herzegovina, Macedonia and Montenegro with two autonomous provinces within Serbia: Kosovo-Metohija and Vojvodina. The collapse of the Socialist Federal Republic of Yugoslavia during 1991-92 has resulted in the autonomous republics of Croatia, Slovenia, Bosnia-Herzegovina and Macedonia declaring their respective independence.

The Federal Republic of Yugoslavia was proclaimed in 1992; it consists of the former Republics of Serbia and Montenegro.

RULERS:
Peter I, 1918-1921
Alexander I, 1921-1934

MONETARY SYSTEM:
1 Dinar = 100 Para
1 Dinar = 100 *Old* Dinara, 1965
1 Dinar = 10,000 *Old* Dinara, 1990-91
1 Dinar = 10 *Old* Dinara, 1992
1 Dinar = 1 Million *Old* Dinara, 1.10.1993
1 Dinar = 1 Milliard *Old* Dinara, 1.1.1994
1 Novi Dinar = 1 German Mark = 12,000,000 Dinara, 1.24.94

SIGNATURE VARIETIES

	VICE GOVERNOR	GOVERNOR
5	Isak Sion	Nikola Maljanich
6	Borivoje Jelich	Nikola Maljanich
7	Branislav Colanovich	Nikola Maljanich
8	Branislav Colanovich	Ivo Perishin
9	Joshko Shtrukelj	Branislav Colanovich
10	Ilija Marjanovich	Ksente Bogoev
11	Miodrag Veljkovich	Radovan Makich
12	Dr. Slobodan Stanojevich	Radovan Makich

SIGNATURE VARIETIES

13	Dr. Slobodan Stanojevich	Dushan Vlatkovitch
14	Mitja Gaspari	Dushan Vlatkovitch
15		Dushan Vlatkovitch
16		Vuk Ognjanovich
17		Borivoje Atanockovich
18		
19	Bozidar Gazivoda	
20	Bozidar Gazivoda	Dragoslav Avramovich

SOCIALIST FEDERAL REPUBLIC

НАРОДНА БАНКА ЈУГОСЛАВИЈЕ

NARODNA BANKA JUGOSLAVIJE

NATIONAL BANK OF YUGOSLAVIA

1963 ISSUE

#73-76 sign. 5. Replacement notes: Serial # prefix *ZA*.

73	100 DINARA	VG	VF	UNC
	1.5.1963. Dk. red on m/c unpt. Woman wearing national costume at l. View of Dubrovnik at ctr. on back.			
	a. Issued note.	0.10	0.25	2.00
	s. Specimen.	—	—	40.00

74	500 DINARA	VG	VF	UNC
	1.5.1963. Dk. green on m/c unpt. Farm woman w/sickle at l. 2 combine harvesters at ctr. on back.			
	a. Issued note.	0.50	1.00	4.00
	s. Specimen.	0.00 -	0.00 -	50.00

75	1000 DINARA	VG	VF	UNC
	1.5.1963. Dk. brown on m/c unpt. Male steelworker at l. Factory complex at ctr. on back.			
	a. Issued note.	0.50	1.00	4.00
	s. Specimen.	—	—	30.00
76	5000 DINARA			
	1.5.1963. Dk. blue on m/c unpt. Relief of Mestrovic at l. Parliament bldg. in Belgrade at ctr. on back.			
	a. Issued note.	10.00	30.00	150.00
	s. Specimen.	—	—	30.00
	x. Error. W/o serial #.	60.00	125.00	225.00

1965 ISSUE

#77-80 sign. 6. Replacement notes: Serial # prefix *ZA*.

77	5 DINARA	VG	VF	UNC
	1.8.1965. Dk. green on m/c unpt. Like #74. 134 x 64mm.			
	a. Sm. numerals in serial #.	0.50	3.00	25.00
	b. Lg. numerals in serial #.	0.50	1.50	15.00
	s. Specimen.	—	—	40.00
78	10 DINARA			
	1.8.1965. Dk. brown on m/c unpt. Like #75. 143 x 66mm.			
	a. Serial # like #77a.	0.50	1.50	15.00
	b. Serial # like #77b.	1.00	5.00	25.00
	s. Specimen.	—	—	40.00
79	50 DINARA			
	1.8.1965. Dk. blue on m/c unpt. Like #76. 151 x 72mm.			
	a. Serial # like #77a.	1.00	5.00	40.00
	b. Serial # like #77b.	1.00	5.00	50.00
	s. Specimen.	—	—	40.00

80	100 DINARA	VG	VF	UNC
	1.8.1965. Red on m/c unpt. Equestrian statue "Peace" of Augustincic in garden of United Nations, New York at l.			
	a. Serial # like #77a.	0.75	4.00	20.00
	b. Serial # like #77b, but w/o security thread.	0.50	2.00	10.00
	c. Serial # like #77b, but w/security thread. 7 digit serial #.	0.25	0.75	5.00
	s. Specimen.	—	—	40.00

1968-70 ISSUE

#81-84 lg. numerals of value at l. ctr. on back. Sign. 7 or 8. Replacement notes: Serial # prefix *ZA*.

81	5 DINARA	VG	VF	UNC
	1.5.1968. Dk. green on m/c unpt. Face like #77. 123 x 59mm.			
	a. Serial # like #77a.	0.05	0.20	1.00
	b. Serial # like #77b.	0.05	0.20	1.00
	s. Specimen.	—	—	30.00

82	10 DINARA	VG	VF	UNC
	1.5.1968. Dk. brown on m/c unpt. Face like #78. 131 x 63mm.			
	a. Serial # like #77a.	0.25	1.00	20.00
	b. Serial # like #80b.	0.50	3.00	25.00
	c. Serial # like #80c.	0.05	0.15	0.50
	s. Specimen.	—	—	30.00

83	50 DINARA	VG	VF	UNC
	1.5.1968. Dk. blue on m/c unpt. Face like #79. 139 x 66mm.			
	a. Serial # like #77a.	0.50	1.50	20.00
	b. Serial # like #80b.	0.20	0.50	4.00
	c. Serial # like #80c.	0.10	0.25	1.00
	s. Specimen.	—	—	45.00
84	500 DINARA			
	1.8.1970. Dk. olive-green on m/c unpt. Statue of N. Tesla seated w/open book at l.			
	a. W/o security thread. Sign. 8.	0.15	0.50	2.50
	b. W/security thread.	0.50	1.50	6.00

1974 ISSUE

#85 and 86 sign. 9. Replacement notes: Serial # prefix *ZA*.

85	20 DINARA	VG	VF	UNC
	19.12.1974. Purple on m/c unpt. Ship dockside at l. Two prefix letters plus 6 or 7-digit serial #.	0.10	0.25	1.50
86	1000 DINARA			
	19.12.1974. Blue-black on m/c unpt. Woman w/fruit at l.	0.25	1.00	4.50

1978 ISSUE

#87-92 long, 2-line sign. title at l. and different sign. Replacement notes: Serial # prefix *ZA; ZB; ZC*.

87	10 DINARA	VG	VF	UNC
	1978; 1981. Dk. brown on m/c unpt. Like #82.			
	a. Sign. 10. 12.8.1978.	0.10	0.20	0.75
	b. Sign. 11. 4.11.1981.	0.10	0.20	0.75
88	20 DINARA			
	1978; 1981. Purple on m/c unpt. Like #85.			
	a. Sign. 10. 12.8.1978.	0.05	0.15	0.75
	b. Sign. 11. 4.11.1981.	0.10	0.25	2.00
89	50 DINARA			
	1978; 1981. Dk. blue on m/c unpt. Like #83.			
	a. Sign. 10. 12.8.1978.	0.05	0.20	1.00
	b. Sign. 11. 4.11.1981.	0.05	0.20	1.00

90 100 DINARA

		VG	VF	UNC
	1978. Red on m/c unpt. Like #80.			
	a. Sign. 10. 12.8.1978.	0.10	0.25	1.25
	b. Sign. 11. 4.11.1981.	0.10	0.25	1.25
	c. Sign. 13. 16.5.1986.	0.10	0.20	1.00

91 500 DINARA

		VG	VF	UNC
	1978; 1981; 1986. Dk. olive-green on m/c unpt. Like #84.			
	a. Sign. 10. 12.8.1978.	0.15	0.50	2.00
	b. Sign. 11. 4.11.1981.	0.10	0.50	1.00
	c. Sign. 13. 16.5.1986.	0.15	0.50	2.00

92 1000 DINARA

		VG	VF	UNC
	1978; 1981. Blue-black on m/c unpt. Like #86.			
	a. Sign. 10 w/title at r.: *GUVERNE* in Latin w/o final letter *R* (engraving error). Series AF. 12.8.1978.	0.25	1.00	7.50
	b. As a. Series AR.	1.00	3.00	15.00
	c. Corrected sign. title.	0.15	0.50	3.00
	d. Sign. 11. 4.11.1981.	0.05	0.25	1.00

1985-89 Issue

93 5000 DINARA

		VG	VF	UNC
	1.5.1985. Deep blue on m/c unpt. Josip Broz Tito at l. and as wmk., arms at ctr. Jajce in Bosnia at ctr. on back. Sign. 12.			
	a. Corrected year of Tito's death - *1980*.	0.10	0.50	3.50
	x. Error: Tito's death date as *1930* instead of *1980*.	2.00	10.00	65.00

#94 not assigned.

95 20,000 DINARA

		VG	VF	UNC
	1.5.1987. Brown on m/c unpt. Miner at l. and as wmk., arms at ctr. Mining equipment at ctr. on back. Sign. 13.	0.05	0.25	1.50

96 50,000 DINARA

		VG	VF	UNC
	1.5.1988. Green and blue on m/c unpt. Girl at l. and as wmk., arms at ctr. City of Dubrovnik at ctr. on back. Sign. 13.	0.50	1.00	3.50

#97-100 sign. 14.

97 100,000 DINARA

		VG	VF	UNC
	1.5.1989. Violet and red on m/c unpt. Young girl at l. and as wmk., arms at ctr. Abstract design w/letters and numbers at ctr. r. on back.	0.20	0.75	3.50

98 500,000 DINARA

		VG	VF	UNC
	Aug. 1989. Deep purple and blue on lilac unpt. Arms at l., Partisan monument "Kozara" at r. Partisan monument "Sutjeska" at ctr. on back.			
	a. Issued note.	0.25	1.50	7.00
	s. Specimen.	—	—	50.00

99 1,000,000 DINARA

		VG	VF	UNC
	1.11.1989. Lt. olive-green on orange and gold unpt. Young woman at l. and as wmk., arms at ctr. Stylized stalk of wheat on back.	0.25	1.50	10.00

100 2,000,000 DINARA

		VG	VF	UNC
	Aug. 1989. Pale olive-green and brown on lt. orange unpt. Face like #98. Partisan "V3" monument at Kragujevac at ctr. on back.			
	a. Issued note.	2.00	12.50	65.00
	s. Specimen.	—	—	50.00

1990 First Issue

#101 and 102 sign. 14. Replacement notes: Serial # prefix ZA.

101 50 DINARA

		VG	VF	UNC
	1.1.1990. Deep purple and blue on lilac unpt. Similar to #98.			
	a. Issued note.	0.50	3.00	25.00
	s. Specimen.	—	—	50.00

		VG	VF	UNC
106	**500 DINARA**			
	1.3.1990. Blue and purple. Young man at l. and as wmk. Mountain scene on back.	0.20	0.50	7.00

		VG	VF	UNC
101A	**100 DINARA**			
	ND (1990). Black and dk. olive-green on pink and yellow-green unpt. Marshal Tito at r., flags in unpt. at ctr., arms at upper l. Partisan monument "Sutjeska" at ctr. on back. (Not issued).	—	—	1000.00

		VG	VF	UNC
106A	**500 DINARA**			
	Brown and orange. Like #106. (Not issued).	—	—	225.00

		VG	VF	UNC
102	**200 DINARA**			
	1.1.1990. Pale olive-green and brown on lt. orange unpt. Similar to #100.			
	a. Issued note.	1.00	4.00	25.00
	s. Specimen.	—	—	50.00

		VG	VF	UNC
107	**1000 DINARA**			
	26.11.1990. Brown and orange. N. Tesla at l. and as wmk. High frequency transformer on back.	0.25	1.00	12.50

1990 SECOND ISSUE

#103-107 arms at ctr. Sign. 14. Replacement notes: Serial # prefix *ZA*.

1991 ISSUE

#107A-111 year date only. Sign. 15. Replacement notes: Serial # prefix *ZA*.

		VG	VF	UNC
103	**10 DINARA**			
	1.9.1990. Violet and red on m/c unpt. Similar to #97.	0.05	0.20	1.50

		VG	VF	UNC
107A	**10 DINARA**			
	1991. Purple, black and lilac. Like #103. (Not issued).	—	—	175.00
107B	**50 DINARA**			
	1991. Orange and red. Like #104. (Not issued).	—	—	175.00
108	**100 DINARA**			
	1991. Black and olive-brown on yellow unpt. Similar to #105.	0.10	0.50	1.50
109	**500 DINARA**			
	1991. Brown, dk. brown and orange on tan unpt. Similar to #106.	0.25	0.50	2.50
110	**1000 DINARA**			
	1991. Blue and purple. Similar to #107.	0.20	0.50	7.00
111	**5000 DINARA**			
	1991. Purple, red-orange and blue-gray on gray unpt. Ivo Andric at l. and as wmk. Multiple arch stone bridge on the Drina River at Visegrad at ctr. on back.	0.50	1.50	7.50

		VG	VF	UNC
104	**50 DINARA**			
	1.6.1990. Purple. Young boy at l. and as wmk. Roses at ctr. r. on back.	0.05	0.25	1.50
105	**100 DINARA**			
	1.3.1990. Lt. olive-green on orange and gold unpt. Similar to #99.	0.20	0.50	7.00

1992 ISSUE

#112-117 National Bank monogram arms at ctr. Similar to previous issues. Replacement notes: Serial # prefix *ZA.*

#112-115 sign. 15.

			VG	VF	UNC
112	**100 DINARA**				
	1992. Pale blue and purple. Similar to #105.		0.20	0.40	1.00
113	**500 DINARA**				
	1992. Pale purple and lilac. Similar to #106.		0.15	0.50	4.00
114	**1000 DINARA**				
	1992. Red, orange and purple on lilac unpt. Similar to #107.		0.25	0.50	7.50
115	**5000 DINARA**				
	1992. Deep blue-green, purple and deep olive-brown on gray unpt. Similar to #111.		0.25	1.50	6.00
116	**10,000 DINARA**				
	1992. Varied shades of brown and salmon on tan unpt. Similar to #103. Sign. 16.				
	a. W/dot after date.		0.10	0.20	2.00
	b. W/o dot after date.		0.10	0.20	2.00
117	**50,000 DINARA**		**VG**	**VF**	**UNC**
	1992. Purple, olive-green and deep blue-green. Similar to #104. Sign. 16.		0.25	0.75	4.50

1993 ISSUE

#118-127 replacement notes: Serial # prefix *ZA.*

#118-123 sign. 16.

			VG	VF	UNC
118	**100,000 DINARA**				
	1993. Olive-green on orange and gold unpt. Face like #112. Sunflowers at ctr. r. on back.		0.15	0.50	3.50

			VG	VF	UNC
119	**500,000 DINARA**				
	1993. Blue-violet and orange on m/c unpt. Face like #113. Koponik Sky Center on back.		0.50	2.50	20.00
120	**1,000,000 DINARA**				
	1993. Purple on blue, orange and m/c unpt. Face like #117. Iris flowers at ctr. r. on back.		0.50	4.00	20.00

			VG	VF	UNC
121	**5,000,000 DINARA**				
	1993. Violet, lilac, turquoise and m/c. Face like #114. Vertical rendition of high frequency transformer at ctr., hydroelectric dam at r. on back.		0.15	0.50	3.00

			VG	VF	UNC
122	**10,000,000 DINARA**				
	1993. Slate blue, lt. and dk. brown. Face like #115. National library at ctr. r. on back.		0.20	0.50	3.00
123	**50,000,000 DINARA**				
	1993. Black and orange. Face like #116. Belgrade University on back.		0.25	0.75	5.00

#124-127 sign. 17.

			VG	VF	UNC
124	**100,000,000 DINARA**				
	1993. Grayish purple and blue. Face like #113. Academy of Science at ctr. r. on back.		0.20	0.50	3.00
125	**500,000,000 DINARA**				
	1993. Black and lilac. Face like #118. Dept. of Agriculture bldg. on back.		0.25	1.00	6.00

			VG	VF	UNC
126	**1,000,000,000 DINARA**				
	1993. Red and purple on orange and blue-gray unpt. Face like #123. Parliament bldg. (National Assembly) at ctr. on back.		0.25	2.50	12.50

127	10,000,000,000 DINARA	VG	VF	UNC
	1993. Black, purple and red. Like #114.	0.25	1.50	10.00

1993 REFORM ISSUE

#128-137 replacement notes: Serial # prefix *ZA*.

#128-130 sign. 17.

128	5000 DINARA	VG	VF	UNC
	1993. Pale reddish brown, pale olive-green and orange. Face like #114. Tesla Museum at ctr. r. on back.	0.25	1.00	6.00

129	10,000 DINARA	VG	VF	UNC
	1993. Gray and green on orange and olive-green unpt. Vuk. Stefanovic Karadzic at l. Orthodox church, house on back.	0.25	0.75	5.00

130	50,000 DINARA	VG	VF	UNC
	1993. Dk. blue on pink and aqua unpt. Petar II Petrovic Niegos Prince-Bishop of Montenegro, at l. Monastery in Cetinje at r. on back.	0.10	0.50	2.00

#131-137 sign. 18.

131	500,000 DINARA	VG	VF	UNC
	1993. Dk. green on blue-green and yellow-orange unpt. Dositej Obradovic at l. Monastery Hopovo at ctr. r. on back.	0.25	0.50	2.00

132	5,000,000 DINARA	VG	VF	UNC
	1993. Dk. brown on orange, blue-green and pale olive-brown unpt. Karadjordj Petrovich, Prince of Serbia, at l. Orthodox church at ctr. r. on back.	0.20	0.50	2.00

133	50,000,000 DINARA	VG	VF	UNC
	1993. Red and purple on orange and lilac unpt. Michajlo Pupin at l. Telephone Exchange bldg. at ctr. r. on back.	0.10	0.25	2.00

134	500,000,000 DINARA	VG	VF	UNC
	1993. Purple on aqua, brown-orange and dull pink unpt. Jovan Cvijich at l. University at ctr. r. on back.	0.20	0.50	3.00

135	5,000,000,000 DINARA	VG	VF	UNC
	1993. Olive-brown on lt. green, ochre and orange unpt. D. Jaksich at l. Monastery in Vrazcevsnitza at ctr. r. on back.			
	a. Issued note.	0.20	0.50	3.00
	s. Specimen w/red ovpt.	—	—	60.00

136	50,000,000,000 DINARA	VG	VF	UNC
	1993. Dk. brown on blue-violet, orange, red-violet and gray unpt. Serbian Prince Milan Obrenovich at l. Villa of Obrenovich at ctr. r. on back.	0.25	0.75	5.00

137	500,000,000,000 DINARA	VG	VF	UNC
	1993. Red-violet on orange, pale blue-gray and olive-brown unpt. Poet J. Zmaj at l. National Library at ctr. r. on back.			
	a. Issued note.	0.50	1.50	10.00
	s. Specimen w/red ovpt.	—	—	70.00

1994 ISSUE

#138-143 wmk. paper. Sign. 18.

138	10 DINARA	VG	VF	UNC
	1994. Chocolate brown on brown and gray-green unpt. Joseph Panchic at l. Back aqua; mountain view, pine trees at ctr. r. W/o serial #.			
	a. Issued note w/o serial #.	0.10	0.50	1.00
	b. W/serial #, serial # prefix *AR*.	—	—	—
	s. Specimen w/red ovpt.	—	—	40.00

Note: Violet or orange specimen ovpts. are forgeries. Notes w/serial #s were privately added.

139 100 DINARA

	VG	VF	UNC
1994. Grayish purple on pink and pale blue unpt. Similar to #128.			
a. Issued note w/o serial #.	0.10	0.25	1.00
s. Specimen w/red ovpt.	—	—	40.00

Note: examples are know with serial #s privately added.

140 1000 DINARA

	VG	VF	UNC
1994. Dk. olive-gray on red-orange, olive-brown and lilac unpt. Similar to #130.			
a. Issued note.	0.20	0.50	2.00
s. Specimen w/red ovpt.	—	—	40.00

141 5000 DINARA

	VG	VF	UNC
1994. Dk. blue on lilac, orange and aqua unpt. Similar to #131.			
a. Issued note.	0.20	0.50	2.00
s. Specimen w/red ovpt.	—	—	40.00

142 50,000 DINARA

	VG	VF	UNC
1994. Dull red and lilac on orange unpt. Similar to #132.			
a. Issued note.	0.20	0.75	3.00
s. Specimen w/red ovpt.	—	—	40.00

142A 100,000 DINARA

	VG	VF	UNC
1994. Red-brown on ochre and pale olive-green unpt. Like #133. Michajlo Pupin at l. Telephone Exchange bldg. on back. W/o serial #. (Not issued).	—	—	350.00

143 500,000 DINARA

	VG	VF	UNC
1994. Dull olive-green and orange on yellow unpt. Similar to #134.			
a. Issued note.	0.10	0.40	1.50
s. Specimen w/red ovpt.	—	—	40.00

1994 PROVISIONAL ISSUE

144 10,000,000 DINARA

	VG	VF	UNC
1994 (-old date 1993). Red ovpt: 1994 on face and back w/new silver ovpt. sign. 18 and sign. title on back on #122.			
a. Issued note.	0.20	1.00	5.00
s. Specimen w/red ovpt.	—	—	50.00

1994 REFORM ISSUES

#145-147 wmk: Diamond grid. Sign. 19.

Note: #145-147 withdrawn from circulation on 1.1.1995.

145 1 NOVI DINAR

	VG	VF	UNC
1.1.1994. Blue-gray and brown on pale olive-green and tan unpt. Similar to #138.	0.25	1.00	4.00

146 5 NOVIH DINARA

	VG	VF	UNC
1.1.1994. Red-brown and pink on ochre and pale orange unpt. Similar to #139.	0.50	2.50	15.00

147 10 NOVIH DINARA

	VG	VF	UNC
1.1.1994. Purple and pink on aqua and olive-green unpt. Similar to #140.	0.50	2.50	15.00

1994; 1996 ISSUE

#148-152 arms w/double-headed eagle at upper ctr. Wmk: Symmetrical design repeated.

#148-150 sign. 20. Replacement notes: Serial # prefix *3A*.

		VG	VF	UNC
148	**5 NOVIH DINARA**			
	3.3.1994. Black, deep purple and violet. Nicola Tesla at l. Back like #146.	FV	0.25	2.00

		VG	VF	UNC
149	**10 NOVIH DINARA**			
	3.3.1994. Purple, violet and brown. Like #147.	FV	0.50	3.75

		VG	VF	UNC
150	**20 NOVIH DINARA**			
	3.3.1994. Dk. green, brown-orange and brown. Similar to #135.	FV	0.75	6.00

#151 and 152 sign. 19. Replacement notes: Serial # prefix *ZA*.

		VG	VF	UNC
151	**50 NOVIH DINARA**			
	June 1996. Black and blue. Similar to #136.	FV	1.50	12.50

		VG	VF	UNC
152	**100 NOVIH DINARA**			
	Oct. 1996. Black on olive-brown and grayish green unpt. Similar to #141.	FV	2.50	25.00

2000-01 ISSUE

#153-157 Portr. as wmk. Arms at upper l. on vertical backs.

153 **10 DINARA**
2000. Brown on ochre-yellow and green unpt. Stefanovich Karadzic at l. Karadzic and alphabet on back.

	VG	VF	UNC
a. Sign. Dusan Vlatkovic (not issued).	—	—	150.00
b. Sign. Mladjan Dinkich.	FV	FV	1.25

		VG	VF	UNC
154	**20 DINARA**	FV	FV	1.75
	2000 (2001). Green and black on tan unpt. Petar II Petrovic Njegos, Prince-Bishop of Montenegro at l. Statue from Njegos' mausoleum, mosaic and mountains on back.			

		VG	VF	UNC
155	**50 DINARA**	FV	FV	3.50
	2000. Light and dark violet on tan unpt. Stevan Stojanovic Mokranjac at l., piano keyboard at lower ctr. Full-length photo and musical bars on back.			

$$T t \frac{Wb}{m^2}$$

		VG	VF	UNC
156	**100 DINARA**	FV	FV	5.50
	2000. Blue on green and tan unpt. Nikola Tesla at l., motor at lower ctr. Tesla photo, schematic of electro-magnetic induction engine, dove on back.			

		VG	VF	UNC
157	**200 DINARA**	FV	FV	12.50
	2001. Black and blue on tan unpt. Nadezda Petrovic at l. Figure of the artist and Gracanica monastery on back.			

		VG	VF	UNC
158	**1000 DINARA**	FV	FV	40.00
	2001. Red on blue and tan unpt. Dorde Vajfert at l. Vajfert portrait and Central Bank interior on back.			

		VG	FV	UNC
159	**5000 DINARA**	FV		175.00
	2002. Green, violet and gray on m/c unpt. Slobodan Jovanovic at l. Details of the federal parliament.			

ZAÏRE

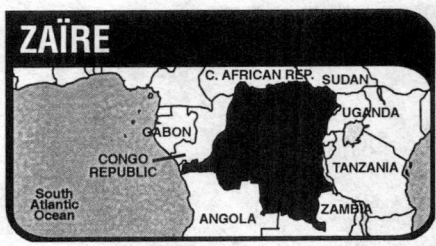

The Republic of Zaïre (formerly the Congo Democratic Republic) located in the south-central part of Africa, has an area of 905,568 sq. mi. (2,345,409 sq. km.) and a population of 43.81 million. Capital: Kinshasa. The mineral-rich country produces copper, tin, diamonds, gold, zinc, cobalt and uranium.

In ancient times the territory comprising Zaïre was occupied by Negrito peoples (Pygmies) pushed into the mountains by Bantu and Nilotic invaders. The interior was first explored by the American correspondent Henry Stanley, who was subsequently commissioned by King Leopold II of Belgium to conclude development treaties with the local chiefs. The Berlin conference of 1885 awarded the area to Leopold, who administered and exploited it as his private property until it was annexed to Belgium in 1908. Following the eruption of bloody independence riots in 1959, Belgium granted the Belgian Congo independence as the Republic of the Congo on June 30, 1960. The Belgian Congo attained independence with the distinction of being the most ill-prepared country to ever undertake self-government. Without a single doctor, lawyer or engineer, with no organized unit capable of maintaining law and order, independence disintegrated into an orgy of anarchy. Provinces seceded. Intertribal warfare erupted. Belgian troops intervened to protect Belgian citizens from retributive massacre. By 1961, four groups were fighting for political dominance. The most serious threat to the viability of the country was posed by the secession of mineral-rich Katanga province on July 11, 1960.

After two and one-half years of sporadic warfare with a U.N. military force, Katanga's leaders capitulated, Jan. 14, 1963 and the rebellious province was partioned into three provinces. The nation officially changed its name to Zaïre on Oct. 27, 1971. In May 1997, the dictator was overthrown after a three-year rebellion. The country changed its name to the Democratic Republic of the Congo.

See also Rwanda, Rwanda-Burundi or Congo Democratic Republic.

MONETARY SYSTEM:
1 Franc = 100 Centimes to 1967
1 Zaïre = 100 Makuta, 1967-1993
1 Nouveau Zaïre = 100 N Makuta = 3 million "old"

Banque du Zaïre			
	GOVERNOR		GOVERNOR
3	J. Sambwa Mbagui	4	Bofossa W. Amba
5	EmonyJ	6	Sambwa Mbagui
7	Pay Pay wa Syakassighe	8	Nyembo Shabanga
9	B. Mushaba	10	Ndiang Kabul
11	L. O. Djamboleka		

REPUBLIC

BANQUE DU ZAÏRE

1971-80 ISSUES

#16-25 Mobutu at l. and as wmk., leopard at lower r. facing r. Various date and sign. varieties. Printer: G&D. Replacement notes: Serial # suffix Z.

16	50 MAKUTA	VG	VF	UNC
	1973-78. Red, dk. brown and m/c. Man and structure in water on back. Intaglio.			
	a. Red guilloche at l. ctr. on back. Sign. 3. 30.6.1973; 4.10.1974; 4.10.1975.	1.00	6.00	30.00
	b. Red and purple guilloche at l. ctr. on back. Sign. 3. 24.6.1976; 24.6.1977.	1.50	7.00	35.00
	c. Guilloche as b. Sign 4. 20.5.1978.	1.00	5.00	24.00

17	50 MAKUTA	VG	VF	UNC
	1979; 1980. Like #16 but slight color differences and lithographed.			
	a. Sign. 5. 24.11.1979.	0.40	1.25	7.00
	b. Sign. 3. 14.10.1980.	0.40	1.25	6.00

18	1 ZAÏRE	VG	VF	UNC
	1972-77. Brown and m/c. Factory, pyramid, flora and elephant tusks at ctr. r. on back. Intaglio.			
	a. Sign. 3 w/title: *LE GOUVERNEUR* placed below line. 15.3.1972; 27.10.1974; 20.5.1975; 27.10.1975; 27.10.1976.	1.00	2.25	14.00
	b. Sign. 4 w/title: *LE GOUVERNEUR* placed above line. 27.10.1977.	0.75	2.00	10.00

19	1 ZAÏRE	VG	VF	UNC
	1979-81. Like #18 but slight color differences and lithographed.			
	a. Sign. 5. 22.10.1979.	0.40	1.25	5.25
	b. Sign. 3. 27.10.1980; 20.5.1981.	0.25	1.00	4.50

25	50 ZAÏRES	VG	VF	UNC
	1980. Red, violet, brown and m/c. Face similar to #21. Arms at l. ctr. on back.			
	a. Sign. 5. 4.2.1980.	5.00	12.50	47.50
	b. Sign. 3. 24.11.1980.	5.00	20.00	70.00
	s. Specimen. 4.2.1980.	—	—	100.00

1982-85 ISSUES

#26-31 replacement notes: Serial # suffix Z. #26-29 leopard at lower l. facing l. Mobutu in civilian dress at ctr. r. and as wmk. Sign. varieties.

20	5 ZAÏRES	VG	VF	UNC
	24.11.1972. Green, black, brown and m/c. Carving at l., hydroelectric dam at ctr. r. on back. Like Congo #14. Sign. 3.	15.00	50.00	200.00

26	5 ZAÏRES	VG	VF	UNC
	17.11.1982. Blue, black and m/c. Hydroelectric dam at ctr. r. on back. Printer: G&D. Sign. 6.			
	a. Issued note.	0.25	1.00	5.00
	s. Specimen.	—	—	85.00
26A	5 ZAÏRES			
	24.11.1985. Like #26, but printer: HdMZ. Sign. 7.	0.20	0.50	1.75

21	5 ZAÏRES	VG	VF	UNC
	1974-77. Green, black, brown and m/c. Similar to #20 but Mobutu w/cap.			
	a. Sign. 3. 30.11.1974; 30.6.1975; 24.11.1975; 24.11.1976.	2.50	7.50	30.00
	b. Sign. 4. 24.11.1977.	1.00	3.00	14.00
	s. As a. Specimen.	—	—	75.00
22	5 ZAÏRES			
	1979; 1980. Blue, brown, violet and m/c. Like #21.			
	a. Sign. 5. 20.5.1979.	0.50	2.00	9.50
	b. Sign. 3. 27.10.1980.	0.75	3.00	17.50
	s. Specimen. 20.5.1979.	—	—	65.00

27	10 ZAÏRES	VG	VF	UNC
	27.10.1982. Green, black and m/c. Arms w/hand holding torch on back. Printer: G&D. Sign. 6.			
	a. Issued note.	0.50	1.00	5.50
	s. Specimen.	—	—	50.00
27A	10 ZAÏRES			
	27.10.1985. Like #27, but printer: HdMZ. Sign. 7.	0.20	0.50	1.75

#28 and 29 printer: G&D.

23	10 ZAÏRES	VG	VF	UNC
	1972-77. Dk. brown and blue on m/c unpt. Similar to Congo #15 but arms w/hand holding torch at l. ctr. on back.			
	a. Sign. 3. 30.6.1972; 22.6.1974; 30.6.1975; 30.6.1976; 27.10.1976.	4.00	12.00	65.00
	b. Sign. 4. 27.10.1977.	1.00	3.00	15.00
	s. As a. Specimen w/o serial #.	—	—	85.00

24	10 ZAÏRES	VG	VF	UNC
	1979; 1981. Green, brown and m/c. Like #23.			
	a. Sign. 5. 24.6.1979.	1.00	4.00	17.50
	b. Sign. 3. 4.1.1981.	1.00	3.00	15.00
	s. Specimen. 24.6.1979.	—	—	85.00

28	50 ZAÏRES	VG	VF	UNC
	1982; 1985. Purple, blue and m/c. Back blue and m/c; men fishing w/stick nets at ctr.			
	a. Sign. 6. 24.11.1982.	0.75	2.50	15.00
	b. Sign. 7. 24.6.1985.	0.50	1.50	9.00
	s. Specimen.	—	—	50.00

29 **100 ZAÏRES**
1983; 1985. Dk. brown, orange and m/c. Bank of Zaïre at ctr. r. on back.

	VG	VF	UNC
a. Sign. 6. 30.6.1983.	0.75	3.00	16.50
b. Sign. 7. 30.6.1985.	0.25	1.00	7.50
s. Specimen.	—	—	50.00

#30 and 31 leopard at lower l. facing l., Mobutu in military dress at ctr. r. and as wmk., arms at lower r. Printer: G&D.

30 **500 ZAÏRES**
1984; 1985. Gray, purple and m/c. Suspension bridge over river at ctr. r. on back.

	VG	VF	UNC
a. Sign. 6. 14.10.1984.	3.00	15.00	70.00
b. Sign. 7. 14.10.1985.	1.25	6.00	30.00
s. Specimen.	—	75.00	100.00

31 **1000 ZAÏRES**
24.11.1985. Blue-black and green on m/c unpt. Civic bldg., water fountain at ctr. r. on back. Sign. 7.

	VG	VF	UNC
a. Issued note.	2.00	6.00	15.00
s. Specimen.	—	85.00	125.00

1988-92 ISSUES

#32-46 Mobutu in military dress at r. and as wmk., leopard at lower l. ctr. facing l., arms at lower r. Reduced size notes. Replacement notes: serial # suffix Z.

#32-36 printer: HdMZ.

32 **50 ZAÏRES**
30.6.1988. Green and m/c. Men fishing w/stick nets at l. on back. Similar to #28. Sign. 7.

	VG	VF	UNC
a. Issued note.	0.10	0.50	1.50
s. Specimen.	—	45.00	55.00

33 **100 ZAÏRES**
14.10.1988. Blue and m/c. Bank of Zaïre at l. ctr. on back. Similar to #29. Sign. 7.

	VG	VF	UNC
a. Issued note.	0.15	0.75	3.00
s. Specimen.	—	45.00	55.00

34 **500 ZAÏRES**
24.6.1989. Brown, orange and m/c. Suspension bridge over river at l. ctr. on back. Similar to #30. Sign. 7.

	VG	VF	UNC
a. Issued note.	0.25	1.25	6.00
s. Specimen.	—	50.00	65.00

35 **1000 ZAÏRES**
24.11.1989. Purple, brown and m/c. Civic bldg and fountain at l. ctr. on back. Similar to #31. Sign. 7.

	VG	VF	UNC
a. Issued note.	0.50	4.00	21.00
s. Specimen.	—	60.00	75.00

36 **2000 ZAÏRES**
1.10.1991. Purple and peach on m/c unpt. Men fishing w/stick nets at l., carved figure at ctr. r. on back. (Smaller size than #35.) Sign. 8.

	VG	VF	UNC
a. Issued note.	0.25	0.75	2.50
s. Specimen.	—	55.00	65.00

#37 and 38 printer: G&D. Replacement notes: Serial # suffix Z.

37 5000 ZAÏRES
20.5.1988. Blue, green and m/c. Factory at l., elephant tusks and plants at ctr. on back. Sign. 7.

	VG	VF	UNC
a. Brown triangle at lower r.	6.00	30.00	150.00
b. Green triangle at lower r.	0.25	1.25	6.00

38 10,000 ZAÏRES
24.11.1989. Purple, brown-orange and red on m/c unpt. Govt. bldg. complex at l. ctr. on back. Sign. 7.

	VG	VF	UNC
a. Issued note.	0.25	1.25	5.50
s. Specimen.	—	50.00	65.00

39 20,000 ZAÏRES
1.7.1991. Black on m/c unpt. Bank of Zaïre at l., other bldgs. across ctr. on back. Similar to #29. Printer: HdMZ. Sign. 8.

	VG	VF	UNC
a. Issued note.	0.25	0.50	3.50
s. Specimen.	—	60.00	70.00

#40 and 41 printer: G&D. Replacement notes: Serial # suffix *Z*.

40 50,000 ZAÏRES
24.4.1991. Wine and blue-black on m/c unpt. Family of Western Gorillas on back. Sign. 7.

	VG	VF	UNC
a. Issued note.	0.75	2.50	8.00
s. Specimen.	—	60.00	70.00

41 100,000 ZAÏRES
4.1.1992. Black and deep olive-green on m/c unpt. Domed bldg. at l. ctr. on back. Sign. 8.

	VG	VF	UNC
a. Issued note.	0.50	1.25	6.00
s. Specimen.	—	50.00	65.00

42 200,000 ZAÏRES
1.3.1992. Deep purple and deep blue on m/c unpt. Back similar to #31; civic bldg. and fountain at l. ctr. Printer: HdMZ. Sign. 8.

42 200,000 ZAÏRES

	VG	VF	UNC
a. Issued note.	0.25	1.00	5.50
s. Specimen.	—	50.00	65.00

#43 and 44 printer: G&D.

43 500,000 ZAÏRES
15.3.1992. Brown and orange on m/c unpt. Hydroelectric dam at l. ctr. on back. Sign. 8.

	VG	VF	UNC
a. Issued note.	0.50	1.50	7.75
s. Specimen.	—	50.00	65.00

44 1,000,000 ZAÏRES
31.7.1992. Red-violet and deep red on m/c unpt. Suspension bridge at l. ctr. on back. Sign. 8.

	VG	VF	UNC
	0.50	3.00	12.00

45 1,000,000 ZAÏRES
1993. Like #44. Printer: HdMZ.

	VG	VF	UNC
a. Sign. 8. 15.3.1993.	0.75	2.50	13.00
b. Sign. 9. 17.5.1993; 30.6.1993.	0.50	1.25	7.00
s. Specimen.	—	60.00	85.00

46 5,000,000 ZAÏRES
1.10.1992. Deep brown and brown on m/c unpt. Factory, pyramids at ctr., flora and elephant tusks at l. on back. Printer: H&S. Sign. 8.

	VG	VF	UNC
a. Issued note.	0.50	2.00	8.25
s. Specimen.	—	60.00	75.00

1993 ISSUE

#47-58 leopard at lower l., Mobutu in military dress at r., arms at lower r. Replacement notes: serial # suffix *Z*.
#47 and 48 Independence Monument at l. on back. W/o wmk. Printer: G&D.
#49-58 wmk: Mobutu.

47 1 NOUVEAU MIKUTA
24.6.1993. Lt. brown on pink and m/c unpt. Sign. 9.

	VG	VF	UNC
	0.05	0.20	0.75

48	5 NOUVEAUX MAKUTA	VG	VF	UNC
	24.6.1993. Black on pale violet and blue-green unpt. Sign. 9.	0.05	0.20	1.00

#49 and 51 printer: HdMZ (CdM-A).

54	10 NOUVEAUX ZAÏRES	VG	VF	UNC
	24.6.1993. Dk. gray and dk. blue-green on m/c unpt. Back like #31. Sign. 9.	0.25	0.75	3.00
55	10 NOUVEAUX ZAÏRES			
	24.6.1993. Dk. gray and dk. blue-green on m/c unpt. Back like #31. Printer: HdMZ (CdM-A). Sign. 9.	0.15	0.50	1.75

#56 and 57 printer: HdMZ (CdM-A).

56	20 NOUVEAUX ZAÏRES			
	24.6.1993. Brown and blue on pale green and lilac unpt. Back similar to #42. Sign. 9.	0.20	0.75	3.50

49	10 NOUVEAUX MAKUTA	VG	VF	UNC
	24.6.1993. Green on m/c unpt. Factory, pyramids at ctr., flora and elephant tusks at l. on back. Sign. 9.	0.10	0.50	1.75

#50 *Not assigned.*

57	50 NOUVEAUX ZAÏRES	VG	VF	UNC
	24.6.1993. Brown and deep red on m/c unpt. Back like #43. Sign. 9.	0.20	0.75	4.00

51	50 NOUVEAUX MAKUTA	VG	VF	UNC
	24.6.1993. Brown-orange on lt. green and m/c unpt. Chieftain at l., men fishing w/stick nets at ctr. on back. Sign. 9.	0.10	0.30	1.25

#52-54 printer: G&D.

58	100 NOUVEAUX ZAÏRES	VG	VF	UNC
	1993-94. Grayish purple and blue-violet on aqua and ochre unpt. Back like #44. Printer: G&D.			
	a. Sign. 9. 24.6.1993.	0.50	1.00	4.75
	b. Sign. 10. 15.2.1994.	0.50	1.25	5.50
58A	100 NOUVEAUX ZAÏRES			
	1993. Grayish purple and blue-violet on aqua and ochre unpt. Like #58a. Printer: HdMZ.	0.50	1.00	4.75

1994-96 ISSUES

#59-77 a leopard at lower l. ctr., Mobutu in military dress at r. and as wmk., arms at lower r.
Replacement notes: serial # suffix Z.
#59-61 printer: HdMZ.

59	50 NOUVEAUX ZAÏRES	VG	VF	UNC
	15.2.1994. Dull red-violet and red on m/c unpt. Like #57. Sign. 10.	0.50	2.00	8.25
60	100 NOUVEAUX ZAÏRES			
	15.2.1994. Grayish purple and blue-violet on aqua and ochre unpt. Like #58. Sign. 10.	0.25	1.00	4.75
61	200 NOUVEAUX ZAÏRES			
	15.2.1994. Deep olive-brown on orange and m/c unpt. Men fishing w/stick nets at l. ctr. on back. Sign. 10.	0.05	0.25	3.00
62	200 NOUVEAUX ZAÏRES			
	15.2.1994. Deep olive-brown on orange and m/c unpt. Like #61. Printer: G&D.	0.10	0.50	3.00

52	1 NOUVEAU ZAÏRE	VG	VF	UNC
	24.6.1993. Violet and purple on m/c unpt. Banque du Zaïre at l. ctr. on back. Sign. 9.	0.10	0.30	1.75

53	5 NOUVEAUX ZAÏRES	VG	VF	UNC
	24.6.1993. Brown on m/c unpt. Back like #41.			
	a. Sign. 9.	0.20	0.50	1.75
	b. Sign. 10.	0.50	1.50	4.00

63 500 NOUVEAUX ZAÏRES
15.2.1994. Gray and deep olive-green on m/c unpt. Banque du Zaïre at l. ctr. on back. Printer: HdMZ.

	VG	VF	UNC
	0.10	0.50	1.75

64 500 NOUVEAUX ZAÏRES
15.2.1994. Gray and deep olive-green on m/c unpt. Like #63. Printer: G&D.

	VG	VF	UNC
	0.10	0.50	4.00

64A 500 NOUVEAUX ZAÏRES
15.2.1994. Like #63. Serial # prefix X. Printed in Argentina.

	VG	VF	UNC
	0.20	1.00	4.75

65 500 NOUVEAUX ZAÏRES
30.1.1995. Blue on m/c unpt. Lg. value on back. Sign. 11.

	VG	VF	UNC
	0.10	0.50	1.75

66 1000 NOUVEAUX ZAÏRES
30.1.1995. Olive-green and olive-gray on m/c unpt. Printer: G&D. Sign. 11.

	VG	VF	UNC
	0.20	1.00	4.75

67 1000 NOUVEAUX ZAÏRES
30.1.1995. Like #66. Printer: HdMZ. Sign. 11.

	VG	VF	UNC
	0.10	0.75	4.00

68 5000 NOUVEAUX ZAÏRES
30.1.1995. Brown-violet and red-violet on m/c unpt. Printer: G&D. Sign. 11.

	VG	VF	UNC
	0.50	2.00	9.50

69 5000 NOUVEAUX ZAÏRES
31.1.1995. Brown-violet and red-violet on m/c unpt. Like #68. Printer: HdMZ. Sign. 11.

	VG	VF	UNC
	0.25	1.25	7.00

#70-77 w/OVD vertical band at l.

70 10,000 NOUVEAUX ZAÏRES
30.1.1995. Blue-violet on m/c unpt. Printer: G&D. Sign. 11.

	VG	VF	UNC
	0.30	1.50	7.50

71 10,000 NOUVEAUX ZAÏRES
30.1.1995. Blue-violet on m/c unpt. Like #70. Printer: HdMZ. Sign. 11.

	VG	VF	UNC
	0.25	1.25	6.00

72 20,000 NOUVEAUX ZAÏRES
30.1.1996. Brown on m/c unpt. Printer: G&D. Sign. 11.

	VG	VF	UNC
	0.40	1.50	7.00

73 20,000 NOUVEAUX ZAÏRES
30.1.1996. Brown on m/c unpt. Like #72. Printer: HdMZ. Sign. 11.

	VG	VF	UNC
	0.40	1.50	7.00

74 50,000 NOUVEAUX ZAÏRES
30.1.1996. Violet and pale blue on m/c unpt. Printer: G&D. Sign. 11.

	VG	VF	UNC
	0.75	3.00	12.00

75 50,000 NOUVEAUX ZAÏRES
30.1.1996. Violet and pale blue on m/c unpt. Like #74. Printer: HdMZ. Sign. 11.

	VG	VF	UNC
	0.75	3.00	12.00

76 100,000 NOUVEAUX ZAÏRES
30.6.1996. Dull orange on green and m/c unpt. Printer: G&D. Sign. 11.

	VG	VF	UNC
	0.50	2.00	9.50

77 100,000 NOUVEAUX ZAÏRES
30.6.1996. Dull orange on green and m/c unpt. Like #76. Printer: HdMZ. Sign. 11.

	VG	VF	UNC
	0.50	2.00	9.50

77A 100,000 NOUVEAUX ZAÏRES
30.6.1996. Gray and blue-green on m/c unpt. Like #76 and 77. Printer: HdMZ.

	VG	VF	UNC
	1.00	4.50	20.00

#78 and 79 Mobutu at r. and as wmk. Printer: G&D. Sign. 11.

78 500,000 NOUVEAUX ZAÏRES
25.10.1996. Green and yellow-green on m/c unpt. Map of Zaïre, family in canoe on back.

	VG	VF	UNC
a. Issued note.	0.75	3.00	12.00
s. Specimen.	—	—	40.00

79 1,000,000 NOUVEAUX ZAÏRES
25.10.1996. Lt. violet and red on m/c unpt. Diamonds at lower l. ctr. Map of Zaïre, mining facility on back.

	VG	VF	UNC
a. Issued note.	1.00	4.00	17.50
s. Specimen.	—	—	75.00

REGIONAL

Validation Ovpt.
  Type I: Circular handstamp: *REPUBLIQUE DU ZAÏRE-REGION DU BAS-ZAÏRE; GARAGE - STA/BANANA* around arms.

BANQUE DU ZAÏRE BRANCHES

Note: #R3 and R4 are just 2 examples of handstamps applied to notes being turned in for exchange for a new issue. It appears that is some locations (i.e. Bas Fleuve, Bas Zaïre and Shaba Sons) there were not enough of the new notes to trade for the older ones. In such cases, an ovpt. was applied to the older piece indicating its validity and acceptability for future redemption into new currency. A number of different ovpt. are known, and more information is needed.

1980's ND PROVISIONAL ISSUE

R3 5 ZAÏRES
1980's ND (- old date 1972-77). Handstamp on #21b.

	Good	Fine	XF
a. 1972.	5.00	15.00	60.00
b. 1974-76.	3.00	7.00	30.00
c. 1977.	1.00	3.00	7.50

R4 10 ZAÏRES
1980's ND (-old date various). Handstamp on #23b.

a. 1975-76.	4.00	7.00	30.00
b. 1977.	1.00	3.00	10.00

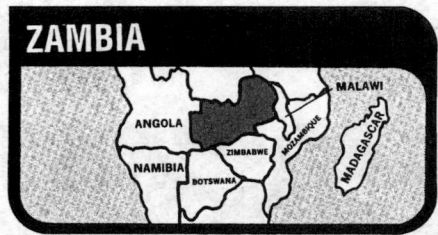

ZAMBIA

The Republic of Zambia (formerly Northern Rhodesia), a landlocked country in south-central Africa, has an area of 290,586 sq. mi. (752,614 sq. km.) and a population of nearly 9.87 million. Capital: Lusaka. The economy is based principally on copper, of which Zambia is the world's third largest producer. Copper, zinc, lead, cobalt and tobacco are exported.

The area that is now Zambia was brought within the British sphere of influence in 1888 by empire builder Cecil Rhodes, who obtained mining concessions in south-central Africa from indigenous chiefs. The territory was ruled by the British South Africa Company, which Rhodes established, until 1924 when its administration was transferred to the British government as a protectorate. In 1953, Northern Rhodesia was joined with Nyasaland and the colony of Southern Rhodesia to form the Federation of Rhodesia and Nyasaland. Northern Rhodesia seceded from the Federation on Oct. 24, 1964, and became the independent Republic of Zambia. It is a member of the Commonwealth of Nations. The president is Chief of State.

Zambia adopted a decimal currency system on Jan. 16, 1969.

Also see Rhodesia and Malawi.

RULERS:
British to 1964

MONETARY SYSTEM:
1 Shilling = 12 Pence
1 Pound = 20 Shillings to 1968
1 Kwacha = 100 Ngwee, 1968-

SIGNATURE VARIETIES			
1	R. C. Hallet, 1964-67	2	Dr. J. B. Zulu, 1967-70
3	V. S. Musakanya, 1970-72	4	B. R. Kuwani, 1972-76, 1982-84
5	L. J. Mwananshiku, 1976-81	6	D. A. R. Phiri, 1984-8
7	Dr. L. S. Chivuno, 1986-88	8	F. Nkhoma, 1988-9
9	J. A. Bussiere, 1991- (ca.1993)	10	D. Mulaisho, 1993-95
11	Dr. J. Mwanza, 1995-2002	12	K. Fundanga 2002 -

REPUBLIC

BANK OF ZAMBIA
1963 ND Issue

A1 1 POUND
1963. Blue on lilac unpt. Fisherman w/net and boat at ctr., portr. Qn. Elizabeth II at r. Back purple; Ross's Turaco at l. ctr. Imprint: H&S (Not issued).

	VG	VF	UNC
	—	—	2750.00

Note: #A1 exists in a number of different color varieties.

1964 ND Issue
#1-3 sign. 1. Arms at upper ctr. Wmk: Wildebeest's head. Printer: TDLR .

1 10 SHILLINGS
ND (1964). Brown on m/c unpt. Chaplins Barbet bird at r. Farmers plowing w/tractor and oxen on back.

	VG	VF	UNC
a. Issued note.	70.00	150.00	400.00
s. Specimen.	—	—	300.00

2 1 POUND
ND (1964). Green on m/c unpt. Black-cheeked Lovebird at r. Mining tower and conveyors at l. ctr. on back.

	VG	VF	UNC
a. Issued note.	100.00	200.00	900.00
s. Specimen.	—	—	300.00

3 5 POUNDS
ND (1964). Blue on m/c unpt. Wildebeest at r. Victoria Falls of Zambezi at l. ctr. on back.

	VG	VF	UNC
a. Issued note.	175.00	450.00	2250.00
s. Specimen.	—	—	400.00

1968 ND Issue
#4-8 Pres. K. Kaunda at r. Dot between letter and value. Sign. 2. Printer: TDLR. Replacement notes: Serial # prefix 1/Z; 1/Y; 1/X; 1/W; 1/V respectively.

	50 NGWEE		VG	VF	UNC
4	50 NGWEE				
	ND (1968). Red-violet on m/c unpt. Arms at l. 2 antelope on back. W/o wmk.				
	a. Issued note.		10.00	27.50	80.00
	s. Specimen.		—	—	75.00

#5-8 arms at upper ctr. Wmk: Kaunda.

5	1 KWACHA				
	ND (1968). Dk. brown on m/c unpt. Farmers plowing w/tractor and oxen on back.				
	a. Issued note.		11.50	40.00	95.00
	s. Specimen.		—	—	80.00
6	2 KWACHA				
	ND (1968). Green on m/c unpt. Back like #2; mining tower and conveyors at l. ctr.				
	a. Issued note.		12.50	50.00	140.00
	s. Specimen.		—	—	120.00
7	10 KWACHA				
	ND (1968). Blue on m/c unpt. Back like #3; waterfalls at ctr.				
	a. Issued note.		35.00	90.00	600.00
	s. Specimen.		—	—	170.00
8	20 KWACHA				
	ND (1968). Purple on m/c unpt. National Assembly on back.				
	a. Issued note.		50.00	150.00	800.00
	s. Specimen.		—	—	220.00

1969 ND Issue

#9-13 Pres. K. Kaunda at r., w/o dot between letter and value. Backs and wmks. like #4-8. Replacement notes: Serial # prefix *1/Z; 1/Y; 1/X; 1/W; 1/V* respectively.

9	50 NGWEE		VG	VF	UNC
	ND (1969). Red-violet on m/c unpt. Like #4.				
	a. Sign. 3.		4.00	20.00	75.00
	b. Sign. 4.		2.50	9.00	40.00
	s. As c. Specimen.		—	—	50.00
10	1 KWACHA		VG	VF	UNC
	ND (1969). Dk. brown on m/c unpt. Like #5.				
	a. Sign. 2.		4.00	20.00	75.00
	b. Sign. 3.		2.50	9.00	40.00
	s. Specimen.		—	—	50.00
11	2 KWACHA				
	ND (1969). Green on m/c unpt. Like #6.				
	a. Sign. 2.		7.00	40.00	200.00
	b. Sign. 3.		6.00	30.00	200.00
	c. Sign. 4.		5.00	22.50	160.00
	s. As s. Specimen.		—	—	90.00

12	10 KWACHA	VG	VF	UNC
	ND (1969). Blue on m/c unpt. Like #7.			
	a. Sign. 2.	20.00	60.00	325.00
	b. Sign. 3.	25.00	90.00	550.00
	c. Sign. 4.	18.00	60.00	300.00
	s. Specimen.	—	—	90.00

13	20 KWACHA	VG	VF	UNC
	ND (1969). Purple on m/c unpt. Like #8.			
	a. Sign. 2.	25.00	75.00	450.00
	b. Sign. 3.	50.00	130.00	600.00
	c. Sign. 4.	20.00	40.00	100.00
	s. Specimen.	—	—	120.00

1973 ND Issue

#14 and 15 Pres. K. Kaunda at r. and as wmk., arms at upper ctr. Replacement notes: Serial # prefix *1/Z; 1/U* respectively.

14	50 NGWEE	VG	VF	UNC
	ND (1973). Black on lilac and m/c unpt. Miners on back. W/o wmk. Printer: TDLR. Sign. 4.			
	a. Issued note.	1.75	7.00	15.00
	s. Specimen.	—	—	40.00
15	5 KWACHA			
	ND (1973). Red-violet on m/c unpt. Children by school on back. Sign. 4.			
	a. Issued note.	25.00	150.00	450.00
	s. Specimen.	—	—	200.00

1973 ND Commemorative Issue

#16, Birth of the Second Republic, December 13, 1972

16	1 KWACHA	VG	VF	UNC
	ND (1973). Red-orange and brown on m/c unpt. Pres. K. Kaunda at r. and as wmk. Document signing, commemorative text and crowd on back. Printer: TDLR. Sign. 4.			
	a. Issued note.	4.00	12.50	40.00
	s. Specimen.	—	—	40.00

1974 ND Issue

#17 and 18 Pres. K. Kaunda at r. and as wmk., arms at upper ctr. Sign. 4. Printer: BWC. Replacement notes: Serial # prefix *1/W; 1/V* respectively.

1980; 1986 ND Issue

#23-28 Pres. K. Kaunda at r. and as wmk., African fish eagle at l. ctr. Printer: TDLR. Replacement notes: Serial # prefix Z/1.

		VG	VF	UNC
23	**1 KWACHA**			
	ND (1980-88). Dk. brown on m/c unpt. Workers picking cotton at l. ctr. on back.			
	a. Sign. 5.	0.40	1.00	4.00
	b. Sign. 7.	0.25	0.75	3.00
	s. Specimen.	—	—	40.00

		VG	VF	UNC
17	**10 KWACHA**			
	ND (1974). Blue on m/c unpt. Waterfalls at l. ctr. on back.			
	a. Issued note.	20.00	75.00	325.00
	s. Specimen.	—	—	175.00
18	**20 KWACHA**			
	ND (1974). Purple and red on m/c unpt. National Assembly on back.			
	a. Issued note.	17.50	65.00	260.00
	s. Specimen.	—	—	220.00

1974-76 ND Issue

#19-22A earlier frame design, arms at upper ctr. Older Pres. K. Kaunda at r. but same wmk. as previous issues. Printer: TDLR. Replacement notes: Serial # prefix 1/Y; 1/X; 1/U; 1/W respectively.

		VG	VF	UNC
24	**2 KWACHA**			
	ND (1980-88). Olive-green on m/c unpt. Teacher w/student at l., school bldg. at ctr. on back.			
	a. Sign. 5.	0.50	1.25	6.50
	b. Sign. 6.	0.50	1.00	4.00
	c. Sign. 7.	0.25	0.75	3.25
	s. Specimen.	—	—	40.00

		VG	VF	UNC
19	**1 KWACHA**			
	ND (1976). Brown on m/c unpt. Back like #5. Sign. 5.			
	a. Issued note.	1.50	6.00	12.50
	s. Specimen.	—	—	30.00
20	**2 KWACHA**			
	ND (1974). Green on m/c unpt. Back like #6. Sign. 4.			
	a. Issued note.	1.50	7.00	22.50
	s. Specimen.	—	—	30.00
21	**5 KWACHA**			
	ND (1976). Brown and violet on m/c unpt. Back like #16. Sign. 5.			
	a. Issued note.	3.00	10.00	35.00
	s. Specimen.	—	—	55.00
22	**10 KWACHA**			
	ND (1976). Blue on m/c unpt. Back like #17. Sign. 5.			
	a. Issued note.	3.50	20.00	50.00
	s. Specimen.	—	—	75.00

		VG	VF	UNC
25	**5 KWACHA**			
	ND (1980-88). Brown on m/c unpt. Hydroelectric dam at l. ctr. on back.			
	a. Sign. 5.	0.50	1.75	7.50
	b. Sign. 4.	1.00	5.00	32.50
	c. Sign. 6.	0.25	0.50	3.50
	d. Sign. 7.	0.25	0.50	1.60
	s. Specimen.	—	—	40.00

		VG	VF	UNC
26	**10 KWACHA**			
	ND (1980-88). Blue, green and black on m/c unpt. Bank at l. ctr. on back.			
	a. Sign. 5.	2.00	8.00	42.50
	b. Sign. 4 in black.	3.00	15.00	75.00
	c. Sign. 4 in blue.	2.50	10.00	55.00
	d. Sign. 6.	2.00	5.00	12.50
	e. Sign. 7.	1.50	4.00	10.00
	s. Specimen.	—	—	40.00

		VG	VF	UNC
22A	**20 KWACHA**			
	ND. Purple, red and m/c. Back like #13. (Not issued.)	—	—	—

27   20 KWACHA

	VG	VF	UNC
ND (1980-88). Green and olive-brown on m/c unpt. Woman w/basket on head at ctr. r. on back.			
a. Sign. 5.	3.00	12.00	50.00
b. Sign. 4 in black.	4.00	15.00	100.00
c. Sign. 4 in dk. green.	2.50	8.00	55.00
d. Sign. 6.	2.00	7.00	15.00
e. Sign. 7.	2.00	7.00	12.00
s. Specimen.	—	—	60.00

28   50 KWACHA

	VG	VF	UNC
ND (1986-88). Purple, violet and m/c. "Chainbreaker" statue at l., modern bldg. at l. ctr. on back. Sign. 7.			
a. Issued note.	3.00	8.00	22.50
s. Specimen.	—	—	60.00

1989 ND ISSUE

#29-33 Pres. K. Kaunda at r. and as wmk., fish eagle at lower l., butterfly over arms at ctr. "Chainbreaker" statue at l. on back.

29   2 KWACHA

	VG	VF	UNC
ND (1989). Olive-brown on m/c unpt. Rhinoceros head at lower l. facing l., cornfield at ctr., tool at r. on back. Sign. 8.			
a. Issued note.	0.25	0.50	1.75
s. Specimen.	—	—	40.00

30   5 KWACHA

	VG	VF	UNC
ND (1989). Brown and red-orange on m/c unpt. Back brown; lion cub head facing at lower l., bldg. at ctr., jar at r. Sign. 8.			
a. Issued note.	0.30	0.70	2.50
s. Specimen.	—	—	40.00

31   10 KWACHA

	VG	VF	UNC
ND (1989-91). Black, dk. blue and red-violet on m/c unpt. Back dk. blue; giraffe head at lower l. facing l., bldg. at ctr., carving of man's head at r.			
a. Sign. 8.	0.40	1.00	5.00
b. Sign. 9.	0.30	0.90	3.00
s. Specimen.	—	—	40.00

32   20 KWACHA

	VG	VF	UNC
ND (1989-91). Dk. olive-green, brown and blue on m/c unpt. Back dk. green; Dama gazelle head at lower l. facing 3/4 l., bldg. at ctr., carving of man's head at r.			
a. Sign. 8.	0.50	1.00	5.00
b. Sign. 9.	0.30	1.00	5.00
s. Specimen.	—	—	60.00

33   50 KWACHA

	VG	VF	UNC
ND (1989-91). Red-violet and purple on m/c unpt. Zebra head at lower l. facing l., manufacturing at ctr., carving of woman's bust at r. on back.			
a. Sign. 8.	0.75	5.50	30.00
b. Sign. 9.	0.50	3.50	10.00
s. Specimen.	—	—	60.00

1991 ND ISSUE

#34-35 older Pres. K. Kaunda at r. and as wmk., fish eagle at l., tree over arms at ctr. "Chainbreaker" statue at l. on back. Sign. 9.

34   100 KWACHA

	VG	VF	UNC
ND (1991). Purple, red and blue on m/c unpt. Water buffalo head at l. facing, Victoria Falls of Zambezi w/rainbow through ctr. on back.			
a. Issued note.	3.00	10.00	15.00
s. Specimen.	—	—	50.00

35   500 KWACHA

	VG	VF	UNC
ND (1991). Brown on m/c unpt. Elephant at l., workers picking cotton at ctr. on back.			
a. Issued note.	5.00	15.00	25.00
s. Specimen.	—	—	60.00

1992; 1996 ND ISSUE

#36-42 seal of arms w/date at lower l., fish eagle at r. Wmk: Fish eagle's head. "Chainbreaker" statue at lower ctr. r. on back. Printer: TDLR. Replacement notes: Serial # prefix 1/X.

36   20 KWACHA

	VG	VF	UNC
1992. Green on m/c unpt. Fig tree at ctr., Kudu at l., 3/4 facing l., State House at Lusaka at ctr. on back.			
a. Sign. 10.	0.10	0.50	3.00
b. Sign. 11.	0.10	0.50	2.50
s. Specimen.	—	—	40.00

37 50 KWACHA
1992; 2001; 2003. Red on m/c unpt. Sausage tree at ctr., Zebra at l. facing, Copper refining at Nkana Mine at ctr. on back.

	VG	VF	UNC
a. 1992. Sign. 10.	0.20	0.60	3.25
b. 1992. Sign. 11.	0.20	0.60	3.00
c. 2001. Sign. 11.	FV	0.50	2.75
d. 2003. Sign. 12.	FV	0.50	2.50
s. Specimen.	—	—	40.00

38 100 KWACHA
1992; 2001; 2003. Deep purple on m/c unpt. Palm tree at ctr. Water buffalo head facing at l., Victoria falls at ctr. on back. Serial # varieties.

	VG	VF	UNC
a. 1992. Sign. 10.	FV	0.60	3.00
b. 1992. Sign. 11.	FV	0.60	3.00
c. 2001. Sign. 11.	FV	0.60	2.50
d. 2003. Sign. 12.	FV	FV	2.00
e. 2005. Sign. 12.	FV	FV	2.00
s. Specimen.	—	—	40.00

39 500 KWACHA
1992; 2003. Brown on m/c unpt. Baobab tree. Elephant head at l., workers picking cotton at ctr. on back.

	VG	VF	UNC
a. 1992. Sign. 10.	FV	1.75	6.00
b. 1992. Sign. 11.	FV	1.00	5.00
c. 2001. Sign. 11.	FV	FV	3.00
d. 2003. Sign. 12.	VF	FV	3.00
s. Specimen.	—	—	40.00

40 1000 KWACHA
1992 (1996); 2001; 2003. Red-violet, deep orange and dk. olive-green on m/c unpt. Jacaranda tree. Aardvark at l., Sorghum farmer on tractor at ctr. on back.

	VG	VF	UNC
a. 1992 (1996). Sign. 11.	FV	1.25	5.50
b. 2001. Sign. 11.	FV	0.75	4.50
c. 2003. Sign. 12.	FV	FV	3.00
s. Specimen.	—	—	40.00

41 5000 KWACHA
1992 (1996); 2001. Purple, dk. brown and deep red on m/c unpt. Murera / Acacia / Mopani tree at ctr. Lion facing at l., root cassava plant at ctr. on back.

	VG	VF	UNC
a. 1992 (1996). Sign. 11.	FV	2.50	10.00
b. 2001. Sign. 11.	FV	1.75	5.50
s. Specimen.	—	—	40.00

42 10,000 KWACHA
1992 (1996). Aqua, brown-violet and yellow-brown on m/c unpt. Musuku tree at ctr. Porcupine at l., harvesting rice paddy at ctr. on back. Sign. 11.

	VG	VF	UNC
a. Issued note.	FV	5.00	17.50
s. Specimen.	—	—	50.00

2001 ISSUE

43 10,000 KWACHA
2001. Aqua, brown-violet and yellow-brown on m/c unpt. Like #42 but w/foil fish eagle head at lower l.

	VG	VF	UNC
a. 2001. Sign. 11.	FV	FV	7.00

2003 ISSUE

44 500 KWACHA
2003-5. M/c. Polymer plastic.

	VG	VF	UNC
a. 2003. Serial # wears off.	—	—	15.00
b. 2003. Second printing.	FV	FV	1.00
c. 2004.	FV	FV	1.00
d. 2005.	FV	FV	1.00

45 1000 KWACHA
2003-5. M/c. Polymer plastic.

	VG	VF	UNC
a. 2003. Serial # wears off.	—	—	20.00
b. 2003. Second Printing.	FV	FV	3.00
c. 2004.	FV	FV	3.00
d. 2005.	FV	FV	3.00

46 5000 KWACHA
2003; 2005. FV FV 4.00

47 10,000 KWACHA
2003; 2005. Sign. 12. FV FV 6.00

48 20,000 KWACHA
2003. M/c. FV FV 10.00

49 50,000 KWACHA
2003. M/c. FV FV 25.00

ZIMBABWE

The Republic of Zimbabwe (formerly Rhodesia or Southern Rhodesia), located in the east-central part of southern Africa, has an area of 150,820 sq. mi. (390,580 sq. km.) and a population of 12.39 million. Capital: Harare (formerly Salisbury). The economy is based on agriculture and mining. Tobacco, sugar, asbestos, copper and chrome ore and coal are exported.

The Rhodesian area, the habitat of paleolithic man, contains extensive evidence of earlier civilizations, notably the world-famous ruins of Zimbabwe, a gold-trading center that flourished about the 14th or 15th century AD. The Portuguese of the 16th century were the first Europeans to attempt to develop south-central Africa, but it remained for Cecil Rhodes and the British South Africa Co. to open the hinterlands. Rhodes obtained a concession for mineral rights from local chiefs in 1888 and administered his African empire (named Southern Rhodesia in 1895) through the British South Africa Co. until 1923, when the British government annexed the area after the white settlers voted for existence as a separate entity, rather than for incorporation into the Union of South Africa. From Sept. of 1953 through 1963 Southern Rhodesia was joined with the British protectorates of Northern Rhodesia and Nyasaland into a multiracial federation. When the federation was dissolved at the end of 1963, Northern Rhodesia and Nyasaland became the independent states of Zambia and Malawi.

Britain was prepared to grant independence to Southern Rhodesia but declined to do so when the politically dominant white Rhodesians refused to give assurances of representative government. In November 1965, the white minority government of Southern Rhodesia unilaterally declared Southern Rhodesia an independent dominion. The United Nations and the British Parliament both proclaimed this unilateral declaration of independence null and void. In 1970, the government proclaimed a republic, but this too received no recognition. In 1979, the government purported to change the name of the colony to Zimbabwe Rhodesia, but this was never recognized. Following a conference in London in December 1979, the opposition government conceded and it was agreed that the British government should resume control. A British governor soon returned to Southern Rhodesia. One of his first acts was to affirm the nullification of the purported declaration of independence. On April 18, 1980, pursuant to an act of the British Parliament, the Colony of Southern Rhodesia became independent within the Commonwealth as the Republic of Zimbabwe.

For earlier issues see Rhodesia.

MONETARY SYSTEM:
1 Dollar = 100 Cents

SIGNATURE/TITLE VARIETIES

	GOVERNOR		GOVERNOR
1	Dr. D. C. Krogh	2	K. Moyana
3	L. Tsumba	4	Dr. D. C. Krogh
5	Dr. K. J. Moyana	6	Dr. L. L. Tsumba
7	C. Chikaura	8	Dr. G. Gono
	FINANCE DIRECTOR		OPERATIONS DIRECTOR
A	Priscilla P. Mutembwa		Stephen J. Newton-Howes

ZIMBABWEAN BIRD WATERMARK VARIETIES

Type A	Type B	Type C
Profile short neck	3/4 view medium neck	3/4 view long neck

RESERVE BANK OF ZIMBABWE

1980 ISSUE

#1-4 Chiremba balancing rock formation, Epworth (Harare) at ctr. r. Sign. varieties. Wmk: Zimbabwe bird.
Replacement notes: Serial # prefix: *AW; BW; CW; DW* respectively.

1   2 DOLLARS
1980 (1981); 1983; 1994. Blue and m/c. Water buffalo at l. Tigerfish at ctr., Kariba Dam and reservoir at r. on back.

		VG	VF	UNC
a.	Sign. 1. Salisbury. 1980.	0.50	2.25	10.00
b.	Sign. 2. Harare. 1983.	0.25	1.25	5.00
c.	Sign. 3. Wmk: Type A. 1994.	0.20	0.75	3.75
d.	Sign. 3. Wmk: Type B. 1994.	4.75	22.50	95.00

2   5 DOLLARS
1980 (1981); 1982-83; 1994. Green and m/c. Zebra at l. Village scene w/2 workers on back.

		VG	VF	UNC
a.	Sign. 1. Salisbury. 1980.	1.75	5.50	24.00
b.	Sign. 1. Harare. 1982.	1.00	4.75	20.00
c.	Sign. 2. 1983.	0.25	1.50	6.50
d.	Sign. 3. 1994. Wmk: Type A.	0.75	2.75	11.00
e.	Sign. 3. 1994. Wmk: Type B.	3.00	12.50	50.00

3	**10 DOLLARS**	VG	VF	UNC
	1980 (1981); 1982-83; 1994. Red and m/c. Sable antelope at l. View of Harare and Freedom Flame monument on back.			
	a. Sign. 1. Salisbury. 1980.	2.25	10.00	50.00
	b. Sign. 1. Salisbury. 1982 (error).	5.00	20.00	100.00
	c. Sign. 1. Harare. 1982.	4.50	17.50	75.00
	d. Sign. 2. 1983.	0.75	2.75	11.00
	e. Sign. 3. 1994.	0.25	1.50	6.50

4	**20 DOLLARS**	VG	VF	UNC
	1980 (1982); 1982-83; 1994. Blue, black and dk. green on m/c unpt. Giraffe at l. Elephant and Victoria Falls on back.			
	a. Sign. 1. Salisbury. 1980.	4.25	17.50	70.00
	b. Sign. 1. Harare. 1982.	15.00	65.00	275.00
	c. Sign. 2. 1983.	1.25	5.00	15.00
	d. Sign. 3. 1994.	0.75	3.50	14.00

1994; 1997; 2001 ISSUES

#5-6 Chiremba balancing rock formation, Epworth (Harare) at ctr. r. Wmk: Zimbabwe bird, Type C. Sign. 3.
Replacement notes: Serial # prefix *AA; AB; AC; AD; AE;* and *AF* respectively.

5	**5 DOLLARS**	VG	VF	UNC
	1997. Brown, red-orange and purple on m/c unpt. Terraced hills at ctr. r. on back.			
	a. Light brown back (litho).	0.15	0.75	3.00
	b. Darker brown back (intaglio).	0.05	0.20	1.00

6	**10 DOLLARS**	VG	VF	UNC
	1997. Red-brown, deep green and blue-black on m/c unpt. Chilolo Cliffs at ctr. r. on back.	FV	FV	0.35

7	**20 DOLLARS**	VG	VF	UNC
	1997. Deep blue, purple and gray-green on m/c unpt. Victoria Falls at ctr. r.	FV	FV	0.40

8	**50 DOLLARS**	VG	VF	UNC
	1994. Dk. brown, olive-brown and red-orange on m/c unpt. Great Zimbabwe ruins on back.	FV	FV	0.50

9	**100 DOLLARS**	VG	VF	UNC
	1995. Brownish black and purple on m/c unpt. Aerial view of Kariba Dam and reservoir at ctr. r. on back.	FV	FV	0.60

10	**500 DOLLARS**	VG	VF	UNC
	2001. Dark brown and red on m/c unpt. Hwange power station on back. Hologram silver foil at l., *500* added to bird wmk.	FV	FV	4.00
11	**500 DOLLARS**			
	2001. Dk. brown on tan and m/c unpt. Like #10, without foil at l.	FV	FV	1.00
12	**1000 DOLLARS**			
	2003. Brown, purple and green on m/c unpt. Elephants on back.	FV	FV	1.00

2003 EMERGENCY CARGILL BEARER CHECKS

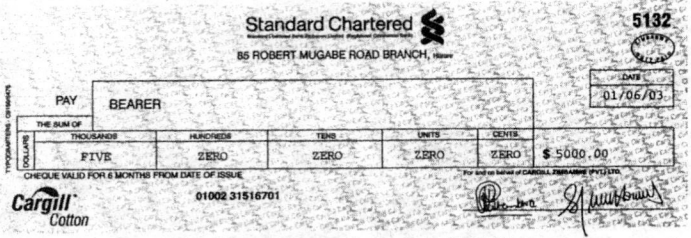

13	**5000 DOLLARS**	VG	VF	UNC
	2003. Green. Wmk: Cotton plant. Printer: Typocrafters.			
	a. 1.6.2003.	3.00	12.00	50.00
	b. 1.9.2003.	2.50	10.00	40.00
14	**10,000 DOLLARS**			
	2003. Blue. Wmk: Cotton plant. Printer: Typocrafters.			
	a. 1.5.2003.	10.00	45.00	175.00
	b. 1.5.2003.	6.50		100.00

2003 EMERGENCY TRAVELLERS' CHECKS

#13-18 Reserve bank of Zimbabwe logo. Wave pattern on back. Pink and green unpt. Wmk: Zimbabwe bird, Type 1. Sign. 4.

15	**1000 DOLLARS**	VG	VF	UNC
	2003. Gray.	FV	FV	3.00
16	**5000 DOLLARS**			
	2003. Red.	FV	FV	15.00

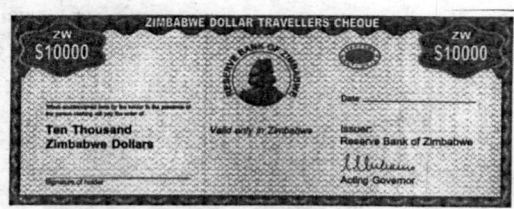

			VG	VF	UNC
17	**10,000 DOLLARS**				
	2003. Light blue.	FV	FV	25.00
18	**20,000 DOLLARS**				
	2003. Olive green.		FV	FV	35.00
19	**50,000 DOLLARS**				
	2003. Dark blue.		FV	FV	75.00
20	**100,000 DOLLARS**				
	2003. Brown.		FV	FV	150.00

2003 EMERGENCY BEARER CHECKS

#19-21 Rezerve Bank of Zimbabwe logo. Printed on paper stock from #8, $50.00. Wmk: Zimbabwe bird, Type 3.

			VG	VF	UNC
21	**5000 DOLLARS**				
	2003. Blue.				
	a. Sign. 4. Redemption date: 31.1.2004. No RZB in wmk. Serial # prefix: A.	FV	5.00	20.00
	b. Sign. 4. Redemption date: 30.6.2004. No RBZ in wmk. Serial # prefix: B-C.	FV	2.00	8.00
	c. Sign.5. Redemption date: 31.12.2004. With RZB in wmk. Serial # prefix: AA.	FV	2.50	10.00
	d. Sign. 5. Redemption date: 31.12.2004. *GOVERNOR / DR. G. GONO.*	FV	1.25	5.00

			VG	VF	UNC
22	**10,000 DOLLARS**				
	2003. Red.				
	a. Sign. 4. Redemption date: 31.1.2004. W/o RZB in wmk. Serial # prefix: E.	FV	10.00	45.00
	b. Sign. 4. Redemption date: 30.6.2004. W/o RZB in wmk. Serial # prefix: F-G.	FV	3.75	30.00
	c. Sign. 5. Redemption date: 31.12.2004. W/RZB in wmk. Serial # prefix: BA.	FV	4.50	25.00
	d. Sign. 5. Redemption date: 12.31.2001. W/RZB in wmk. *GOVERNOR / DR. G. GONO.*	FV	FV	10.00
23	**20,000 DOLLARS**				
	2003. Brown.				
	a. Sign. 4. Redemption date: 31.1.2004. W/o RZB in wmk. Serial # prefix: J.	FV	12.50	85.00
	b. Sign. 4. Redemption date: 30.6.2004. W/o RZB in wmk. Serial # prefix: K-L.	FV	6.25	50.00
	c. Sign. 5. Redemption date: 31.12.2004. W/o RZB in wmk. Serial # prefix: AA.	FV	55.00	225.00
	d. Sign. 5. Redemption date: 12.31.2004. *GOVERNOR* with RZB in wmk. Serial # prefix AA.	FV	7.50	50.00
	e. Sign. 5. Redemption date: 12.31.2004. *GOVERNOR / DR. G. GONO.* W/RZB in wmk.	FV	FV	35.00

2004 EMERGENCY CARGILL BEARERChecks

			VG	VF	UNC
24	**10,000 DOLLARS**				
	1.4.2004. Blue.		2.00	9.00	35.00
25	**20,000 DOLLARS**				
	1.4.2004. Green.		4.00	15.00	60.00
26	**50,000 DOLLARS**				
	1.4.2004. Orange.		6.25	25.00	100.00

			VG	VF	UNC
27	**100,000 DOLLARS**				
	1.4.2004. Red.		8.00	32.50	130.00